S0-BCM-971

Supplements

to

Novum Testamentum

VOLUME 116

Perspectives on New Testament Textual Criticism

Collected Essays, 1962–2004

By

Eldon Jay Epp

BRILL
LEIDEN • BOSTON

This book is printed on acid-free paper.

Library of Congress Cataloging-in-Publication data

Epp, Eldon Jay.
Perspectives on New Testament textual criticism : collected essays, 1962–2004/by Eldon Jay Epp.
p. cm.—(Supplements to Novum Testamentum, ISSN 0167-9732; v. 116)
Includes bibliographical references (p. 00) and indexes.
ISBN 90-04-14246-0
1. Bible. N.T.—Criticism, Textual. I. Title. II. Series.

BS2325.E65 2005
225.4'86—dc22

2004065467

ISSN 0167-9732
ISBN 90 04 14246 0

PRINTED IN THE NETHERLANDS

Dedicated, with deep affection, to
ElDoris B. Epp, Ph.D.,
interlocutor extraordinaire,

and to our son,
Gregory Thomas Epp, Ph.D.,

and to our daughter,
Jennifer E. Merrell, M.D.

CONTENTS

LOCATION OF ORIGINAL PUBLICATIONS

1. The "Ignorance Motif" in Acts and Anti-Judaic Tendencies in Codex Bezae
   Harvard Theological Review 55 (1962) 51–62.
2. Coptic Manuscript G67 and the Rôle of Codex Bezae as a Western Witness in Acts
   Journal of Biblical Literature 85 (1966) 197–212.
3. The Claremont Profile Method for Grouping New Testament Minuscule Manuscripts
   Studies in the History and Text of the New Testament in Honor of Kenneth Willis Clark, Ph.D. (eds. Boyd L. Daniels and M. Jack Suggs; Studies and Documents, 29; Salt Lake City: University of Utah Press, 1967) 27–38. [Reprinted in Eldon Jay Epp and Gordon D. Fee, *Studies in the Theory and Method of New Testament Textual Criticism* (Studies and Documents, 45. Grand Rapids: Eerdmans, 1993) 211–20.]
4. The Twentieth Century Interlude in New Testament Textual Criticism
   Journal of Biblical Literature 93 (1974) 386–414. [Reprinted in Epp and Fee, *Studies*, 83–108.]
5. Toward the Clarification of the Term "Textual Variant"
   Studies in New Testament Language and Text: Essays in Honour of George D. Kilpatrick on the Occasion of his Sixty-Fifth Birthday (ed. J. K. Elliott; Supplements to Novum Testamentum, 44; Leiden: Brill, 1976) 153–73. [Reprinted in Epp and Fee, *Studies*, 47–61.]
6. The Eclectic Method in New Testament Textual Criticism: Solution or Symptom?
   Harvard Theological Review 69 (1976) 211–57. [Reprinted in Epp and Fee, *Studies*, 141–73.]
7. New Testament Textual Criticism in America: Requiem for a Discipline
   Journal of Biblical Literature 98 (1979) 94–98.
8. A Continuing Interlude in New Testament Textual Criticism?
   Harvard Theological Review 73 (1980) 131–51. [Reprinted in Epp and Fee, *Studies*, 109–23.]

9. The Ascension in the Textual Tradition of Luke–Acts
New Testament Textual Criticism: Its Significance for Exegesis: Essays in Honour of Bruce M. Metzger (eds. E. J. Epp and Gordon D. Fee; Oxford: Clarendon Press, 1981) 131–45.
10. Decision Points in Past, Present, and Future New Testament Textual Criticism
Originally "Textual Criticism," in *The New Testament and Its Modern Interpreters* (eds. E. J. Epp and †G. W. MacRae, S.J.; Philadelphia: Fortress Press; Atlanta: Scholars Press, 1989) 75–126. [Reprinted in Epp and Fee, *Studies*, 17–44.]
11. New Testament Textual Criticism Past, Present, and Future: Reflections on the Alands' *Text of the New Testament*
Harvard Theological Review 82 (1989) 213–29.
12. The New Testament Papyrus Manuscripts in Historical Perspective
To Touch the Text: Studies in Honor of Joseph A. Fitzmyer, S.J. (eds. M. P. Horgan and P. J. Kobelski; New York: Crossroad, 1989) 261–88.
13. The Significance of the Papyri for Determining the Nature of the New Testament Text in the Second Century: A Dynamic View of Textual Transmission
Gospel Traditions in the Second Century (ed. William L. Petersen; Studies in Christianity and Judaism in Antiquity, 3; Notre Dame, IN: University of Notre Dame Press, 1989) 71–103. [Reprinted in Epp and Fee, *Studies*, 274–97.]
14. New Testament Papyrus Manuscripts and Letter Carrying in Greco-Roman Times
The Future of Early Christianity: Essays in Honor of Helmut Koester (ed. B. A. Pearson, in collaboration with A. T. Kraabel, G. W. E. Nickelsburg, and N. R. Petersen; Minneapolis, MN: Fortress, 1991) 35–56.
15. The Papyrus Manuscripts of the New Testament
The Text of the New Testament in Contemporary Research: Essays on the Status Quaestionis (eds. B. D. Ehrman and M. W. Holmes; Studies and Documents, 46; Grand Rapids, MI: Eerdmans, 1995) 3–21.
16. The International Greek New Testament Project: Motivation and History
Novum Testamentum 39 (1997) 1–20.
17. Textual Criticism in the Exegesis of the New Testament
Originally ". . . with an Excursus on Canon," *Handbook to Exegesis*

of the New Testament (ed. Stanley E. Porter; New Testament Tools and Studies, 25; Leiden: Brill, 1997) 45–97.

18. The New Testament Papyri at Oxyrhynchus in Their Social and Intellectual Context
    Sayings of Jesus: Canonical and Non-Canonical. Essays in Honour of Tjitze Baarda (eds. W. L. Petersen, J. S. Vos, and H. J. de Jonge; Supplements to Novum Testamentum, 89; Leiden: Brill, 1997) 47–68.
19. The Codex and Literacy in Early Christianity and at Oxyrhynchus: Issues Raised by Harry Y. Gamble's *Books and Readers in the Early Church*
    Critical Review of Books in Religion 11 (1998) 15–37.
20. The Multivalence of the Term "Original Text" in New Testament Textual Criticism
    Harvard Theological Review 92 (1999) 245–81.
21. Issues in the Interrelation of New Testament Textual Criticism and Canon
    The Canon Debate: On the Origins and Formation of the Bible (eds. Lee M. McDonald and James A. Sanders; Peabody, MA: Hendrickson, 2002) 485–515.
22. Issues in New Testament Textual Criticism: Moving from the Nineteenth Century to the Twenty-First Century
    Rethinking New Testament Textual Criticism (ed. David Alan Black; Grand Rapids, MI: Baker Academic, 2002) 17–76.
23. Anti-Judaic Tendencies in the D-Text of Acts: Forty Years of Conversation
    The Book of Acts as Church History: Text, Textual Traditions and Ancient Interpretations/Apostelgeschichte als Kirchengeschichte: Text, Texttraditionen und antike Auslegungen (eds. Tobias Nicklas and Michael Tilly; BZNW 120; Berlin/New York: de Gruyter, 2003) 111–46.
    Introduction to the "Presidential Address"
    Journal of Biblical Literature 123 (2004) 3–4.
24. The Oxyrhynchus New Testament Papyri: "Not without honor except in their hometown"?
    Journal of Biblical Literature 123 (2004) 5–55. [Presidential Address, Society of Biblical Literature, 2003.]

PREFACE

The twenty-four articles that follow range widely over the discipline of New Testament textual criticism, treating many of the critical issues. Fifteen are papers first read in the Textual Criticism Section at national meetings of the Society of Biblical Literature, one is a Plenary Address given at the 1973 Annual Meeting, and the last essay in the volume constituted the Presidential Address before the Society in 2003. Another was presented at the Pacific Coast Section of the Society of Biblical Literature, and two others originated as conference presentations. All were revised and most were expanded for publication. The remaining four essays were written first for direct publication. My debt to the Society of Biblical Literature for the opportunities to air my research will be obvious.

This volume would have been very brief indeed were it not for the myriad textual critics and other scholars worldwide, whose works I have utilized, built upon, and at times employed as foils in my attempts to explain or advance the discipline to which my career largely has been devoted. The extensive footnotes in the articles that follow are ample evidence of the vast debt owed to those whose scholarship preceded my own.

At least one additional article logically should have been included, "Text-Critical, Exegetical, and Socio-Cultural Factors Affecting the Junia/Junias Variation in Romans 16,7" (2002), but its length requires that it be published as a separate monograph, and it should appear shortly in that format. Also omitted from the present volume are encyclopedia articles, notably the extensive entry on "Textual Criticism (NT)" in the *Anchor Bible Dictionary* (1992), an earlier one in the *Interpreter's Dictionary of the Bible, Supplementary Volume* (1976), and one recently in the *New Interpreter's Bible* (1995). Two critiques of the English paraphrase, *The Living Bible* ("Jews and Judaism in The Living New Testament" [1978], and "Should 'The Book' Be Panned?" [1986]), have been left out, along with a few other very brief essays relevant to textual criticism. [See the author's bibliography at the end of the volume.]

It should be noted that readers will encounter some repetition of material across these two dozen essays. I have not attempted to eliminate such duplication, but have left each article basically intact in the form in which it was written and as appropriate to the situation for which it was prepared.

Finally, this volume would not have appeared except for the unsolicited invitation from the Executive Editors of Supplements to Novum Testamentum, Professors Margaret M. Mitchell and David P. Moessner. I am grateful also to the members of the Editorial Board, with special thanks to Professor Abraham J. Malherbe. The staff members of Brill, particularly Wilma de Weert have performed helpfully, patiently, and competently through a long and, at times, complex process of production, and I am most grateful.

Lexington, Massachusetts E. J. E.

ACKNOWLEDGMENTS

I wish to express my gratitude to the various editors and publishers who have granted permission to republish the essays in this volume. Full bibliographic information may be found above, under "Location of Original Publications":

The President and Fellows of Harvard College, for chapters 1, 6, 8, 11, and 20, published in the *Harvard Theological Review*, © 1962, 1976, 1980, 1989, and 1999, respectively.

The Society of Biblical Literature for chapters 2, 4, 7, and 24, published in the *Journal of Biblical Literature*, © 1966, 1974, 1979, and 2004, respectively; and for chapter 10, published in *The New Testament and Its Modern Interpreters*, © 1989; and for chapter 19, first in the *Critical Review of Books in Religion*, © 1998.

The University of Utah Press, for chapter 3, published in *Studies in the History and Text of the New Testament*, © 1967.

E. J. Brill, Academic Publishers, for chapter 5, in *Studies in New Testament Language and Text*, © 1976; chapter 16, in *Novum Testamentum*, © 1997; chapter 17, published in *Handbook to Exegesis of the New Testament*, © 1997; and chapter 18, in *Sayings of Jesus: Canonical and Non-Canonical*, © 1997.

The Clarendon Press of Oxford University Press, for chapter 9, published in *New Testament Textual Criticism: Its Significance for Exegesis*, © 1981.

The Crossroad Publishing Company, for chapter 12, published in *To Touch the Text: Studies in Honor of Joseph A. Fitzmyer, S.J.*, © 1989.

The University of Notre Dame Press, for chapter 13, published in *Gospel Traditions in the Second Century*, © 1989.

Fortress Press, a division of Augsburg Fortress Publishers, for chapter 14, published in *The Future of Early Christianity: Essays in Honor of Helmut Koester*, © 1991.

Wm. B. Eerdmans Publishing Co., for chapter 15, published in *The Text of the New Testament in Contemporary Research*, © 1995; and for reprinting again chapters 3, 4, 5, 6, 8, 10, and 13, which appeared in *Studies in the Theory and Method of New Testament Textual Criticism*, © 1993.

Hendrickson Publishers, for chapter 21, in *The Canon Debate: On the Origins and Formation of the Bible*, © 2002.
Baker Academic, a division of Baker Publishing Group, for chapter 22, in *Rethinking New Testament Textual Criticism*, © 2002.
Walter de Gruyter, Inc., for chapter 23, in *The Book of Acts as Church History/Apostelgeschichte als Kirchengeschichte*, © 2003.

I am grateful to the following institutions for research grants supporting various publications over the years:
The John Simon Guggenheim Memorial Foundation, 1974–1975.
The National Endowment for the Humanities, 1988.
The Ohio Board of Regents, Research Initiation Grant, 1991–1992.
Case Western Reserve University, various research grants and sabbatical leave support, 1968–1998.

ABBREVIATIONS

Abbreviations follow *The SBL Handbook of Style for Ancient Near Eastern, Biblical, and Early Christian Studies* (ed. Patrick H. Alexander et al.; Peabody, MA: Hendrickson, 1999), and, for additional journals and series, Siegfried M. Schwertner, *IATG²: Internationales Abkürzungsverzeichnis für Theologie und Grenzgebiete* (2nd ed.; Berlin/New York: de Gruyter, 1992).

Abbreviations for papyri follow the *Checklist of Editions of Greek, Latin, Demotic and Coptic Papyri, Ostraca and Tablets* (eds. John F. Oates, Roger Bagnall, et al.; 5th ed.; BASP Supplements, 9; Oakville, CT: David Brown for the American Society of Papyrologists, 2001).

ABD	*Anchor Bible Dictionary*
ABR	*Australian Biblical Review*
Aeg	*Aegyptus*
AJP	*American Journal of Philology*
ALBO	Analecta lovaniensia biblica et orientalia
AnBib	Analecta biblica
ANRW	*Aufstieg und Niedergang der römischen Welt: Geschichte und Kultur Roms im Spiegel der neueren Forschung* (ed. H. Temporini and W. Haase; Berlin, 1972–)
ANTF	Arbeiten zur neutestamentlichen Textforschung
APF	*Archiv für Papyrusforschung*
ASP	American Studies in Papyrology
ATG	*Archivo teológico Granadino*
AThR	*Anglican Theological Review*
Aug	*Augustinianum*
AUSS	*Andrews University Seminary Studies*
BASP	*Bulletin of the American Society of Papyrologists*
BBB	Bonner biblische Beiträge
BBR	*Bulletin for Biblical Research*
BDAG	*Greek-English Lexicon of the New Testament and Other Early Christian Literature* (ed. W. Bauer, F. W. Arndt, and F. W. Gingrich; 3rd ed., 2000)
BETL	Bibliotheca ephemeridum theologicarum Lovaniensium
BEvT	Beiträge zur evangelischen Theologie
Bib	*Biblica*
BibOr	Biblica et orientalia

Bijdr *Bijdragen: Tijdschrift voor filosofie en theologie*
BJRL *Bulletin of the John Rylands Library* (Manchester)
BSac *Bibliotheca sacra*
BT *The Bible Translator*
BZ *Biblische Zeitschrift*
BZNW Beihefte zur Zeitschrift für die neutestamentliche Wissenschaft
CBET Contributions to Biblical Exegesis and Theology
CBM Chester Beatty Monographs
CBQ *Catholic Biblical Quarterly*
CBQMS Catholic Biblical Quarterly Monograph Series
CClCr *Civilità classica e cristiana*
ChrEg *Chronique d'Egypte*
ChrTo *Christianity Today*
CP *Classical Philology*
CPJ *Corpus Papyrorum Judaicarum*
CQ *Classical Quarterly*
CRBR *Critical Review of Books in Religion* [succeeded by the *Review of Biblical Literature*]
CSCO Corpus scriptorum christianorum orientalium
CTM *Concordia Theological Monthly*
DRev *Downside Review*
EBib Études bibliques
EFN Estudios de Filología Neotestamentaria (Cordoba)
EvQ *Evangelical Quarterly*
ET English translation
ETR *Etudes théologiques et religieuses*
ETL *Ephemerides theologicae lovanienses*
ExpT *Expository Times*
FF Foundations and Facets
FilolNT *Filologia Neotestamentaria*
GBS Guides to Biblical Scholarship
GCS Die griechische christliche Schriftsteller der ersten drei Jahrhunderte
Gn *Gnomon*
GRBS *Greek, Roman, and Byzantine Studies*
HeyJ *Heythrop Journal*
HSCP *Harvard Studies in Classical Philology*
HTB Histoire du texte bibliques (Lausanne)
HTR *Harvard Theological Review*

ICC	International Critical Commentary
IDB	*Interpreter's Dictionary of the Bible* (4 vols., 1962))
IDBSup	*Interpreter's Dictionary of the Bible: Supplementary Volume* (1976)
IGNTP	International Greek New Testament Project
Int	*Interpretation*
JAC	Jahrbuch für Antike und Christentum
JBL	*Journal of Biblical Literature*
JBR	*Journal of Bible and Religion*
JEA	*Journal of Egyptian Archaeology*
JHS	*Journal of Hellenic Studies*
JJP	*Journal of Juristic Papyrology*
JNSL	*Journal of Northwest Semitic Languages*
JR	*Journal of Religion*
JSNT	*Journal for the Study of the New Testament*
JSNTSup	Journal for the Study of the New Testament: Supplement Series
JTS	*Journal of Theological Studies*
LCL	Loeb Classical Library
LD	Lectio divina
LEC	Library of Early Christianity
LQHR	*London Quarterly and Holborn Review*
LXX	Septuagint
MH	*Museum helveticum*
MThSt	Marburger theologische Studien
N-A *or* NA *or* Nestle-Aland	Nestle-Aland, *Novum Testamentum Graece*
Neot	*Neotestamentica*
NewDocs	*New Documents Illustrating Early Christianity*
NHMS	Nag Hammidi and Manichaean Studies
NHS	Nag Hammadi Studies
NICNT	New International Commentary on the New Testament
NovT	*Novum Testamentum*
NovTSup	Supplements to Novum Testamentum
NRSV	New Revised Standard Version
NTOA	Novum Testamentum et Orbis Antiquus
NTS	*New Testament Studies*
NTTS	New Testament Tools and Studies
OBO	Orbis biblicus et orientalis

OCD	*Oxford Classical Dictionary* (2nd ed., 1970; 3rd ed., 1996)
OCP	*Orientalia christiana periodica*
OTP	*Old Testament Pseudepigrapha* (2 vols.; ed. J. H. Charlesworth, 1983–1985)
OTS	*Old Testament Studies*
Pap.Lugd, Bat.	Papyrologica Lugduno-Batava
PBA	*Proceedings of the British Academy*
PG	Patrologia graeca (ed. J.-P. Migne, 1857–1886)
PO	Patrologia orientalis
PTA	Papyrologische Texte und Abhandlungen
PTMS	Pittsburgh Theological Monograph Series
PTS	Patristische Texte und Studien
RB	*Revue biblique*
RCT	*Revista catalana de teologia*
REG	*Revue des études grecques*
ResQ	*Restoration Quarterly*
RevExp	*Review and Expositor*
RevThom	*Revue thomiste*
RSV	Revised Standard Version
SAC	Studies in Antiquity and Christianity
SBL	Society of Biblical Literature
SBLBMI	Society of Biblical Literature, The Bible and Its Modern Interpreters
SBLDS	Society of Biblical Literature, Dissertation Series
SBLSP	*Society of Biblical Literature Seminar Papers*
SBLTCS	Society of Biblical Literature, Text-Critical Studies
SBLNTGF	Society of Biblical Literature, The New Testament in the Greek Fathers
SD	Studies and Documents
SE	*Studia evangelica* (= various volumes of TU)
SJT	*Scottish Journal of Theology*
SNTS	Society for New Testament Studies/Studiorum novi testamenti societas
SNTSMS	Society for New Testament Studies Monograph Series
SO	Symbolae osloenses
SPAW	Sitzungsberichte der preussischen Akademie der Wissenschaften
StPatr	*Studia patristica*
TEV	Today's English Version (= Good News Bible)

TextsS	= TS: Texts and Studies
Theol	*Theology* (London)
TLZ	*Theologische Lituraturzeitung*
TS	*Theological Studies*
TS	Texts and Studies
TSAJ	Texte und Studien zum antiken Judentum
TSK	*Theologische Studien und Kritiken*
TU	Texte und Untersuchungen
TynBul	*Tyndale Bulletin*
TZ	*Theologische Zeitschrift*
UBS*GNT* *or* UBS	United Bible Societies' *Greek New Testament*
VC	*Vigiliae christianae*
VCSup	Supplements to Vigiliae Christianae
VD	*Verbum domini*
VF	*Verkündigung und Forschung*
VL	Vetus Latina: Die Reste der altlateinischen Bibel (Beuron)
VLAGLB	Vetus Latina: Aus der Geschichte der lateinischen Bibel
VT	*Vetus Testamentum*
WTJ	*Westminster Theological Journal*
WUNT	Wissenschaftliche Untersuchungen zum Neuen Testament
YCS	*Yale Classical Studies*
ZNW	*Zeitschrift für die neutestamentliche Wissenschaft und die Kunde der älteren Kirche*
ZPE	*Zeitschrift für Papyrologie und Epigraphik*

Note: Chapter 23 retains the style of its publisher (Walter de Gruyter, Berlin). Hence:

AncBD = *ABD*
AthR = *AThR*
BEThL = BETL
BEvTh = BEvT
ET = *ExpT*
EThR = *ETR*
EThL = *ETL*
FS = *Festschrift*
HThR = *HTR*

JSNT.S = JSNTSup
JThS = *JTS*
NT = *NovT*
NT.S = NovTSup
PCB = *Peake's Commentary on the Bible* (1962)
RCatT = *RCT*
SchwL = Schweich Lectures
VigChr = *VC*

NOTES TO READERS

Original page numbers: Pagination in the original publication of each essay is indicated in the present volume by bracketed numbers placed in the outside margins of each page. To avoid confusion, citations in footnotes and references to other essays in the volume are to the original pages–not to the pagination in the present volume.

Cross-references. These essays covers vast aspects of the New Testament text-critical discipline. To avoid even more extensive footnotes, the reader often is pointed to my earlier writings for detailed discussions with full documentation. Apologies are due, therefore, to researchers whose works are bypassed here, though fully acknowledged in those earlier publications. This practice tends, temporarily, to obscure the enormous debt that I owe to past and current generations of scholars, but the sections referenced make that obligation abundantly clear.

Added notes: Updated and additional material–bibliography and comments–have been placed in brackets in footnotes. More general or extended comments will be found in the "Added Notes, 2004" at the end of each essay. The essays have been reprinted in their original published form, except for corrections, occasional minor changes, and alterations for stylistic and format consistency.

On the term "original text." In view of the complex issues involved in the term "original," I now would place that term in quotation marks consistently, as I have for some years. [Occasionally the quotation marks were removed by editors.] See my essay in this volume, "The Multivalence of the Term 'Original Text' in New Testament Textual Criticism."

On the terms "Western" and "Neutral" texts. The well-entrenched though misleading terms, "Western text" and "Neutral text" (championed by Westcott and Hort) are used at times for convenience, though I prefer "D-text" and "B-text," respectively, which lack the prejudgments inherent in the terms they replace, namely, that "Western" denotes geographical location (which it does not) and that "Neutral" means pure or uncontaminated (which cannot be substantiated). Normally I place the terms in quotation marks, though editors sometimes have removed them. The term "D-text" also has its ambiguous aspect: though I use it to refer to the larger (and earlier) type of text, now best exemplified in Codex Bezae (Codex D), some scholars use it for or understand it to refer only to the text of Codex Bezae.

INTRODUCTION: A HALF-CENTURY ADVENTURE WITH NEW TESTAMENT TEXTUAL CRITICISM

Developing Perspective

A Greek course around 1950 provided my first encounter with textual criticism through an assignment to decipher portions of the critical apparatus in the Nestle Greek New Testament. The notion of variants in a multitude of manuscripts and versions raised a host of questions about how the text of the New Testament had reached us and how scholars had decided on the text printed above the apparatus. At the time, rumor had it that the United States Army in Germany, about 1946, had confiscated the sixteenth edition of Erwin Nestle's *Greek New Testament* (1936), permitting the American Bible Society to reprint it—and for me to purchase a copy in 1948 for $1.35. The volume carries no date, nor have I been able to follow up on the rumor, but the fact remains that a critical edition of the New Testament in Greek (without the German, Latin, and Norwegian introductions) became available in North America just after World War II. That was the beginning of my fascination with and more than forty years of active participation in a discipline replete with problems of long standing, but problems that turned into opportunities for creative exploration.

I found such an opportunity at Harvard University, where, during my first year, Krister Stendahl asked me to review for the graduate seminar Erich Fascher's recent book on *Textgeschichte als hermeneutische Problem.*[1] Fascher argued persuasively that, already in the first generations of Christianity, scribes "on the basis of their own reflection, improved, elucidated, or made the text more understandable,"[2] thereby forcing their interpretations on later readers. Subsequently, my doctoral committee (Professors Stendahl, Helmut Koester, Amos Niven

[1] Halle (Saale): Max Niemeyer, 1953.

[2] Ibid., 12; for Fascher's more complete statement, see my volume on *The Theological Tendency of Codex Bezae Cantabrigiensis in Acts* (SNTSMS 3; Cambridge: Cambridge University Press, 1966) 20. [unchanged reprint: Eugene, OR: Wipf and Stock, 2001]).

Wilder, and Arthur Darby Nock, as well as an outside member, Henry M. Shires of the Episcopal Theological School) encouraged me to pursue a text-critical dissertation moving in that same direction. That dissertation, in a revised and expanded version, appeared in 1966 as *The Theological Tendency of Codex Bezae Cantabrigiensis in Acts*,[3] and its thrust differed distinctly from my earlier experiences with textual criticism, when the focus had been on the nature of the critical apparatus of the Greek New Testament, but especially on the quest for the "original" text—a term that many of us currently use with great caution, if at all.[4]

To be sure, during the early 1950s European textual critics like Erich Fascher and Philippe H. Menoud, and—in North America, in more radical terms—members of the "Chicago School" of textual criticism had elevated textual variants to a position of high significance by emphasizing that they represent historically contextual theological interpretations.[5] Merrill M. Parvis, for example, pushed the claim that there are no "spurious readings"—a common phrase in those days—for "all are part of the tradition; all contribute to our knowledge of the history of Christian thought" and "they are interpretations . . . highly enough thought of in some places and at some time to be incorporated into the Scripture itself."[6] Did these variants arise because—as is often claimed—there was yet no authoritative New Testament Scripture? Ernest C. Colwell, affirming that "the majority of the variant readings were created for theological or dogmatic

[3] *Theological Tendency* [see preceding note].

[4] See my essay, below, on "The Multivalence of the Term 'Original Text' in New Testament Textual Criticism," *HTR* 92 (1999) 245–81. On a related issue, in my *Theological Tendency* [see note 2, above], I made no attempt to determine the "original" text of Acts—whether the B-text or the D-text. Rather, given the difficulty (then and now) in deciding on the priority of the B-text or D-text, I remained neutral on the issue and focused on the differing nuances of each text-type: see below, "Anti-Judaic Tendencies in the D-Text of Acts: Forty Years of Conversation," *The Book of Acts as Church History: Text, Textual Traditions and Ancient Interpretations—Apostelgeschichte als Kirchengeschichte: Text, Texttraditionen und antike Auslegungen* (ed. T. Nicklas and M. Tilly; BZNW 120; Berlin/New York: de Gruyter, 2003) 123–31.

[5] See a summary of these various views in my *Theological Tendency*, 12–22; also, below, "Multivalence of the Term 'Original Text,'" 271–74; and "Issues in New Testament Textual Criticism: Moving from the Nineteenth Century to the Twenty-First Century," *Rethinking New Testament Textual Criticism* (ed. D. A. Black; Grand Rapids, MI: Baker Academic, 2002) 54–55.

[6] M. M. Parvis, "The Nature and Tasks of New Testament Textual Criticism: An Appraisal," *JR* 32 (1952) 172.

reasons," claimed the opposite: the writings of the New Testament were changed "*because* they were the religious treasure of the church":[7]

> The paradox is that the variations came into existence because they were religious books, sacred books, canonical books. The devout scribe felt compelled to correct misstatements which he found in the manuscripts he was copying.[8]

At the time, however these views did not attract a significant following. One reason why this new interest in the church-historical context of variants failed to gain support may have been its tendency to de-emphasize the "original" text, for attention now was directed not only to variants accredited for the New Testament text, but also to motivations behind those variants that had been relegated to the apparatus. Whatever the cause, the discipline of New Testament textual criticism failed to move in clear, fresh directions in the middle decades of the twentieth century. Though my 1966 volume received some fifty reviews and was cited rather widely for its general theme, as well as in discussions of individual variants,[9] at the time it too failed to foster a groundswell of fresh studies in the same mode,[10] and I published only one further study on this approach

---

[7] E. C. Colwell, *What Is the Best New Testament?* (Chicago: University of Chicago Press, 1952) 52–53 [emphasis added].

[8] Ibid., 52. I would have put quotation marks around "correct," as indeed Colwell does in his explanation on the next page: "The importance of the Book in their religious life led them to 'correct' the mistakes. Unfortunately, they thought they knew more than they actually did, and thus, with the best intentions in the world, they corrupted the text of the New Testament."

[9] See now, below, my "Anti-Judaic Tendencies in the D-Text of Acts," which I was invited to write and which brings full circle a lengthy engagement with this topic.

[10] Except for two of my students: see Howard Eshbaugh, "Textual Variants and Theology: A Study of the Galatians Text of Papyrus 46," *JSNT* 3 (1979) 60–72; and George E. Rice, "Luke 3:22–38 in Codex Bezae: The Messianic King," *AUSS* 17 (1979) 203–8; idem, "The Anti-Judaic Bias of the Western Text in the Gospel of Luke," *AUSS* 18 (1980) 51–57; idem, "Some Further Examples of Anti-Judaic Bias in the Western Text of the Gospel of Luke," *AUSS* 18 (1980) 149–56; idem, "The Role of the Populace in the Passion Narrative of Luke in Codex Bezae," *AUSS* 19 (1981) 147–53; idem, "Western Non-Interpolations: A Defense of the Apostolate," *Luke-Acts: New Perspectives from the Society of Biblical Literature Seminar* (ed. C. H. Talbert; New York: Crossroad, 1984) 1–16; and idem, "Is Bezae a Homogeneous Codex?" *Perspectives on the New Testament: Essays in Honor of Frank Stagg* (ed. C. H. Talbert; Macon, GA: Mercer University Press, 1985) 39–54.

Note also Michael W. Holmes, "Early Editorial Activity and the Text of Codex Bezae in Matthew" (Ph.D. dissertation, Princeton Theological Seminary, 1984).

to theological tendency.[11] Indeed, only some thirty years later was *Theological Tendency* acknowledged to have provided a stimulus for views that carried the method forward in impressive new directions.[12]

Beginning in the late1960s—and continuing for some thirty years—I directed my attention rather to several mainline issues—various methodologies for identifying the "earliest attainable" New Testament text (as opposed to a search for a simplistic "original" text). I realize now that I was following the same path that several "Chicago School" scholars had taken when their foray into the theology of variants—which was certainly insightful and significant—appeared to be abortive. Colwell, Parvis, and also Kenneth W. Clark of Duke University (a Chicago "product")[13] pursued manuscript studies relevant to the International Greek New Testament Project (IGNTP),[14] in which all held positions of leadership and whose object was to construct a full apparatus of the Greek New Testament. Colwell, author of several magisterial methodological studies, chaired the American Executive Committee of the IGNTP, to which I was appointed in 1968. During the preceding two years I had served as consultant to this Project while the Claremont Profile Method[15] was under development, and in a real sense Colwell became my mentor and model[16] for New Testament text-critical scholarship. He and

[11] "The Ascension in the Textual Tradition of Luke-Acts," *New Testament Textual Criticism: Its Significance for Exegesis: Essays in Honour of Bruce M. Metzger* (ed. E. J. Epp and G. D. Fee; Oxford: Clarendon Press, 1981) 131–45.

[12] See Bart D. Ehrman, "The Text as Window: New Testament Manuscripts and the Social History of Early Christianity," *The Text of the New Testament in Contemporary Research: Essays on the* Status Quaestionis (ed. B. D. Ehrman and M. W. Holmes; SD 46; Grand Rapids, MI: Eerdmans, 1995) 364; cf. 367; cf. idem, *The Orthodox Corruption of Scripture: The Effect of Early Christological Controversies on the Text of the New Testament* (New York/Oxford: Oxford University Press, 1993) 42, n. 94.

[13] See K. W. Clark, "Textual Criticism and Doctrine," *Studia Paulina in honorem Johannis De Zwaan septuagenarii* (ed. J. N. Sevenster and W. C. van Unnik; Haarlem: Bohn, 1953) 52–65; idem, "The Theological Relevance of Textual Variation in Current Criticism of the Greek New Testament," *JBL* 85 (1966)1–16.

[14] See my essay, below, on "The International Greek New Testament Project: Motivation and History," *NovT* 39 (1997) 1–20.

[15] See my article, below, on "The Claremont Profile Method for Grouping New Testament Minuscule Manuscripts," *Studies in the History and Text of the New Testament in Honor of Kenneth Willis Clark, Ph.D.* (ed. B. L. Daniels and M. J. Suggs; SD 29; Salt Lake City: University of Utah Press, 1967) 27–38.

[16] Ernest C. Colwell (1901–1974) served as Dean of the Divinity School at the University of Chicago (1938–1943), then Dean of Faculties (1943–1945) and Vice President (1944), finally succeeding Robert Hutchins as President of the University

his colleagues had been an inspiration for detecting doctrinal viewpoints inherent in variants, and now for providing the methods and the critical apparatus for constructing a well-founded and early Greek text of the New Testament. It was clear, of course, that any text created from this more complete apparatus still would be only a hypothetical text made up largely of randomly preserved variants from among the surviving manuscripts and hammered out by selecting the earliest likely variant within each variation unit at a given point in the text. Hence, it would be a text that undoubtedly never had existed in any given manuscript. Even as a compromise, however, such a baseline text was essential for biblical scholarship, and the methods for selecting its component parts required clarification and refinement—matters left unresolved in many cases, in spite of a century of sophisticated scholarship.[17]

Indeed, some fourteen of the articles in the present volume relate directly to an approach I termed the "historical-documentary" method—so named because it emphasizes history and documents in concert.[18] More specifically, I meant a method that would attempt to trace out for us a history (I probably meant *the* history) of the text by emphasizing the earliest documents (i.e., manuscripts) or the earliest text that might be extracted from those documents. This approach, to be sure, included a strong measure of idealism, for it

(1945–1951). Subsequently he was Vice President of Emory University (1951–1957) and completed his administrative career as President of the newly reorganized School of Theology at Claremont (1957–1968), where he appointed me a post-doctoral fellow and "expert consultant" to the IGNTP (1966–1968), while I was an Associate Professor of Religion and also of Classics at the University of Southern California. I considered him my mentor in textual criticism and have characterized him as the "Dean of New Testament Textual Criticism" on the grounds of his incisive critiques and his creative insights in the field. Moreover, I took him as a model, for he maintained a leading role in his scholarly field while involved at high levels of university administration—something I tried to emulate during my near decade as Dean of Humanities and Social Sciences (1976–1985) at Case Western Reserve University. From Colwell I learned much and to him I owe a large debt personally and also to his scholarship—as numerous references throughout my publications attest.

[17] See below my articles on "The Eclectic Method in New Testament Textual Criticism: Solution or Symptom?" *HTR* 69 (1976) 211–57; and "Decision Points in Past, Present, and Future New Testament Textual Criticism" [originally "Textual Criticism"], *The New Testament and Its Modern Interpreters* (ed. E. J. Epp and G. W. MacRae, S.J.; Philadelphia: Fortress; Atlanta, GA: Scholars Press, 1989) 75–126.

[18] For a succinct description, see E. J. Epp, "Textual Criticism (NT)," *ABD* 6.412–35, and also, "Eclectic Method," 248–50.

presumed that by properly defining "textual variants,"[19] by skillfully applying the "criteria for the priority of readings,"[20] and by isolating the early "text-types,"[21] textual critics could write such a history and construct an early text. More specifically, the method involved, on the one hand, evaluating each variation-unit so as to distinguish the most likely earliest variant, and, on the other hand, assessing the textual character of the manuscripts so as to place each in one of the early (or later) text-types. As a result of this admittedly highly complex process, material would be in hand for constructing a very early form of the New Testament text. Yet the method was by no means entirely idealistic, for the first half-dozen decades of the twentieth century yielded numerous new manuscripts of great importance, including, for example, the Chester Beatty papyri in the 1930s and the Bodmer papyri in the mid-1950s. In addition, the 1960s and 1970s were periods of refinement in the procedures for determining the priority of readings and in the precision by which manuscript relationships were measured quantitatively. These positive developments contributed directly to my "historical-documentary" agenda for establishing an early text, and I was encouraged to think that significant progress could be made. It would come, I was sure, as the discipline refined and eventually moved away from its compromising yet almost universally employed "eclectic method."[22] And I was confident that the shift would be toward a theory more solid (I probably meant *objective*) because it would comprise an emphasis on the history of the text (how variants developed from others, and how text-types evolved) and on freshly discovered documents that were increasingly numerous and early.

The Society of Biblical Literature provided avenues for a small

---

[19] See my essay, below, "Toward the Clarification of the Term 'Textual Variant,'" *Studies in New Testament Language and Text: Essays in Honour of George D. Kilpatrick on the Occasion of his Sixty-Fifth Birthday* (ed. J. K. Elliott; NovTSup 44; Leiden: Brill, 1976) 153–73.

[20] See "Eclectic Method" and "Issues in New Testament Textual Criticism."

[21] See my essays, below, on "The Twentieth Century Interlude in New Testament Textual Criticism," *JBL* 93 (1974) 390–399; "The Significance of the Papyri for Determining the Nature of the New Testament Text in the Second Century: A Dynamic View of Textual Transmission," *Gospel Traditions in the Second Century* (ed. W. L. Petersen; Studies in Christianity and Judaism in Antiquity, 3; Notre Dame, IN: University of Notre Dame Press, 1989) 92–103; and "Issues in New Testament Textual Criticism," 34–44.

[22] See "Eclectic Method."

group of us to participate in and undoubtedly to shape New Testament textual criticism in North America and beyond. During fourteen years as chair of the Textual Criticism Section (1971–1984) I had the privilege—and responsibility—of arranging thematic programs to explore several basic issues: quantitative methods (1971 and 1972), textual criticism as science (1973), the definition of "textual variant" (1974), the eclectic method (1975), the current status of manuscripts, versions, and patristic quotations (1980), the significance of Lachmann and Westcott-Hort (1981–150 and 100 years, respectively, after their editions of the Greek New Testament), and textual criticism and Bible translations (1984). In these and other sessions we reexamined current processes and reconsidered fundamental assumptions operative in the field. All along we raised questions, sought clear definitions, heard opposing viewpoints, engaged in productive conversation, sought at many points to reconceptualize New Testament textual criticism for a new generation, and published our results. Audacious perhaps, but successful in a fair measure, for North American scholarship went on to achieve prominence for its contributions in these traditional aspects, but also later for its innovation in New Testament textual criticism.

Textual criticism, for me, had to take a back seat for nearly a decade while I served as Dean of Humanities and Social Sciences at my university (1976–1985). Then, in the late 1980s through the mid-1990s, the New Testament papyri emerged as my major interest.[23] Again, however, this fresh emphasis was prompted by my conviction that these earliest witnesses to the New Testament text could move us forward to a historical-documentary solution to the textual problems we faced. Certainly my thirty years' pursuit of several complex and largely unresolved issues enhanced the discussion of some items, and, I trust, moved others toward resolution, including how

[23] See "Decision Points in New Testament Textual Criticism"; and my essays on "The New Testament Papyrus Manuscripts in Historical Perspective," *To Touch the Text: Studies in Honor of Joseph A. Fitzmyer, S.J.* (ed. M. P. Horgan and P. J. Kobelski; New York: Crossroad, 1989) 261–88; "Significance of the Papyri"; "New Testament Papyrus Manuscripts and Letter Carrying in Greco-Roman Times," *The Future of Early Christianity: Essays in Honor of Helmut Koester* (ed. B. A. Pearson, et al.; Minneapolis, MN: Fortress, 1991) 35–56; and "The Papyrus Manuscripts of the New Testament," *The Text of the New Testament in Contemporary Research: Essays on the* Status Quaestionis (ed. B. D. Ehrman and M. W. Holmes; SD 46; Grand Rapids, MI: Eerdmans, 1995) 3–21.

the priority of readings might be determined by balancing internal and external criteria; how text-types might be isolated; how the papyri might contribute to text-critical theory, and, overall, how all of this aids in the construction of the earliest attainable text of the New Testament. For many scholars, this is the entire task and the single goal of textual criticism. For me, it was not enough.

My early adventure in assessing the theological tendency in the so-called "Western" text of Acts retained its fascination, though not as something to which I might add, but rather on which to build. Hence, in the late 1990s and the early years of the twenty-first century, three new emphases developed, and the first was an assessment of the New Testament papyri in their larger contexts, especially at Oxyrhynchus—where forty-seven percent of our New Testament papyri were found.[24] In a real sense this was a return to the early interest in "theological tendency," encouraged in part by a climate now more congenial to its acceptance, but primarily because the study of manuscripts in their socio-cultural and intellectual contexts is another dimension of grasping any tendencies they might possess, while more generally enlightening us about the Christian communities out of which they stem and/or in which they were used.

The second new interest was the largely unexamined meaning and the implications of the term "original text,"[25] while the third (closely related to the second), concerned the relationship of textual criticism to canon.[26] All three emphases were in some ways new directions, not only for me, but also for the discipline itself, and not the least because "original" text and issues of canon, at least as I believe they must be understood, now must be viewed in new, globally diverse contexts quite unlike any that had existed previously.

---

[24] See my articles, below, on "The New Testament Papyri at Oxyrhynchus in Their Social and Intellectual Context," *Sayings of Jesus: Canonical and Non-Canonical. Essays in Honour of Tjitze Baarda* (ed. W. L. Petersen, J. S. Vos, and H. J. de Jonge; NovTSup 89; Leiden: Brill, 1997) 47–68; "The Codex and Literacy in Early Christianity and at Oxyrhynchus: Issues Raised by Harry Y. Gamble's *Books and Readers in the Early Church*," *CRBR* 11 (1997) 15–37; and "The Oxyrhynchus New Testament Papyri: 'Not without honor except in their hometown'?" *JBL* 123 (2004) 5–55.

[25] See "The Multivalence of the Term 'Original Text.'"

[26] See below the essay on "Issues in the Interrelation of New Testament Textual Criticism and Canon," *The Canon Debate: On the Origins and Formation of the Bible* (ed. L. M. McDonald and J. A. Sanders; Peabody, MA: Hendrickson, 2002) 485–515.

So, what has changed? In simple terms, our world has changed, and not least the world of scholarship. It is clear to me that we in our diverse intellectual world—if at times pulled and dragged—have moved beyond the "certainties" of historicism and even beyond the comforts of modernism to a recognition that the notion of "multiple truths" is more than a novel fad or a passing fancy. I believe that we now must acknowledge that claims to a single interpretation are increasingly difficult to justify in our multicultural and pluralist world—both secular and religious. I have come to recognize that multiple interpretations by an array of fellow human beings across the globe are, in numerous instances, each defensible and credible when seen within their varying intellectual and socio-cultural frameworks. Acknowledged or not, this is the environment in which all of us now work, and in some way we all must come to terms with this new world. In New Testament textual criticism this emergent reality places at risk not only "*the* original text" but even the concept of "original text"[27] as commonly understood, and it also jeopardizes not only "a single original reading"[28] in a variation unit, but also the notion of a single "correct" interpretation of a variant.

Contextual Perspectives

Several years ago I offered a formal definition of New Testament textual criticism in the following terms:

> The science and art of assessing the transmission of the New Testament text by (1) evaluating its variations, alterations, and distortions, and then attempting its restoration—its earliest recoverable forms—and (2) seeking to place variants within the history and culture of the early church, both to determine the age, meaning, and likely motivation of variants and also to extract from them some knowledge of the development and character of early Christian theology, ecclesiology, and culture.[29]

---

[27] See "The Multivalence of the Term 'Original Text.'"

[28] Kurt Aland and Barbara Aland, *The Text of the New Testament: An Introduction to the Critical Editions and to the Theory and Practice of Modern Textual Criticism* (trans. E. F. Rhodes; 2nd ed.; Grand Rapids, MI: Eerdmans; Leiden: Brill, 1989) 280, set down as the first of twelve basic principles in text-critical praxis that "only *one* reading can be original, however many variant readings there may be" [their emphasis].

[29] "Issues in New Testament Textual Criticism," 24–25; cf. 31–32. The word "restoration" may imply more than is possible, but it is properly clarified by "its

At that time I had in mind a two-fold task for textual criticism (as numbered above), but now I would see the task much more as singular, integrated, and unitary. Naturally, we need a baseline—the earliest attainable text—to show the intersections where meaningful variants emerge, but then these variants immediately will—and must—be seen to have their own distinct contexts, and, of course, they reveal themselves to be interpretations. Textual variation, therefore, confronts us with differing voices and with varying narratives that arise from the text. Currently, the text in the Nestle-Aland and the United Bible Societies' Greek New Testaments represents such a baseline text, though scholars and exegetes will each fine-tune the text in accordance with differing judgments in selecting the earliest or "best" reading at each point.

Of course, the process of constructing a baseline text is not linear, as if it were a mechanical fabrication of a relatively languid, lifeless string of words[30] (and which some might view as fixed and authoritative)—a text that speaks, to be sure, but only with a muffled voice. Rather, the text-critical process is the on-going discovery of a vibrant, living text, a text that is alive in each meaningful variant and illuminates the lived-experiences of early Christians and the challenges they faced in worship and thought, in ethical dilemmas, and in doctrinal controversies. The establishment of the baseline text, then, while important and essential, is not the primary goal, much less the *only* goal (as often has been asserted). What a base text does, actually, is facilitate the fuller and richer insights that arise from locating all the variants in their church-historical contexts. *Thus, the search for the baseline text enlivens the variations it discloses, while the variants, in turn, bring the base text to life as well.* Once this process has been launched and as variants spring forth like new members of a family tree, the New Testament text can never again be read as if it were long settled and fixed, an unchanged and unchanging artifact of the past. Rather, every reading will be informed by the array of accompanying variants as the latter reveal the variety of interpreta-

earliest recoverable forms" (though "earliest attainable" might be better). I have added "likely" before "motivation," since intentions in most cases can only be surmised.

[30] As noted earlier, every critical text of the New Testament, as a whole and in its parts, is a construct—an artificial, compromised text that without doubt never existed in that form in an actual manuscript.

tions that have arisen from the many readers and copyists of the New Testament throughout the early centuries of the church. The text becomes a virtual museum, with its variation units comprising exhibits of narratives and interpretations located, whenever possible, contextually in time and place.

To take some obvious examples, how can I read the Gospel of Mark with its variant endings (after Mark 16:8) and not wonder how I, as a scribe, might have finished out this apparently unfinished narrative? Or, who can read the Gospel of John and not ponder the origin or be grasped by the message of the story of the adulterous woman (John 7:53–8:11), despite its variant locations in John and Luke? Who can read the Book of Acts, with its extensive alternate tradition of the D-text, and not be amazed that two early versions of Acts exist with differing conceptions of numerous events? Or, at the micro-level, what would have prompted someone to add or to subtract the poignant prayer of Jesus from the cross (Luke 23:34), "Father, forgive them, for they do not know what they are doing"? Or, how was it decided that the Lord's Prayer needed the additional petition (in Luke 11:2), "Let your Holy Spirit come upon us and cleanse us," or that the prayer should conclude (at Matthew 6:13) with the grandeur of "For yours is the kingdom and the power and the glory forever. Amen"?

Even if we follow what textual critics generally have done and refuse to place any of these particular variants—or the D-text version of Acts—in the baseline text, the baseline nonetheless is enriched for having spawned or attracted to itself this array of interpretive readings. What is revealed in this phenomenon of variation is the dynamism of the Christian community and the wealth of interpretive possibilities and creative impulses that Christians sensed were inherent in the text. Naturally, most of the estimated one-third of a million variant readings among the New Testament manuscripts are unintended changes—scribal errors—yet the meaningful and presumably intentional alterations are legion, witnessing to the hermeneutical ferment in the life of the church.

Indeed, my 1966 volume on the theological tendency of the "Western" text of Acts occasioned my recognition that textual variants are more than mere competitors for a place in the established text of a writing, only to be relegated to an apparatus at the foot of the page if they fail to be accredited for the baseline text. It became obvious to me that variants have been chosen—but often created—to make a point, to give the writing a certain ideological thrust that was not present in the text being copied or used. Hence, it is an integral part of the task of textual criticism, not only to consider all meaningful variants for a possible place in the baseline text, but actively and fully to explore the individual interpretations that they provide by locating variants—and explaining them—both within their immediate textual contexts and also within their likely contexts in the life and history of the church. When the emphasis fell exclusively on establishing the most likely "original" text, rejected readings fell—as it were—on the cutting room floor, only to be scrapped, but now we realize that the discarded snippets must be carefully gathered up and reintroduced into the narrative as subplots or, on occasion, even as the main event.

Such placement of individual variant readings—and also manuscripts—in their church-historical, socio-cultural, and intellectual contexts often will disclose how textual variants were influenced by the church, its theology, worship, and practice, and by the surrounding culture, but also—at the same time—may reveal how the developing text and its variant readings shaped the church. This exercise requires acquaintance with the people, the theology, the practices, and the broader culture of the church of the first several centuries. Moreover, it is worth reemphasizing that nothing like a perfunctory approach is in view here, but an effort to grasp the real-life experiences and exigencies of a church that was expanding rapidly into diverse regions and cultures, was engaging in increasingly sophisticated theological dialogue, and of necessity was coping with varying moral convictions and religious practices.

If formulating a baseline text may be described as focusing more on discrete and circumscribed aspects of the discipline—where criteria, rules, and principles are employed, where quantitative measurements of manuscript relationships are applied, where formulas exist for determining members of a text-type, and where manuscripts are placed into a set of differing categories—then it could be said that this procedure appears to be the more objective, quantifying, and "scientific" side, implying that its results are securely based, definitive, and invariable. While such descriptors might have been appropriate for much of the period through World War II, they would hardly fit the succeeding fifty years, because I believe that across all of New Testament textual criticism we have moved, as it were, farther away from "science" and more closely toward "art."

This means that if some of the rules, some of the older, unrefined measures, and even the venerated term, "original text," once were viewed as "objective," a "reality check" today shows them to be more flexible in definition and more ambiguous in application. That is, not only is the term "original text" multivalent, with several dimensions of meaning, but terms such as "textual variant," and "singular reading" abound in ambiguities; quantitative measures of manuscript relationships now require a measure of qualitative evaluation; and particularly the so-called "criteria" for the priority of readings are not so much "criteria" as they are arguments, often conflicting with one another and possessing greater or less cogency in given situations.[31] Some "science," to be sure, but increasing elements of "art."

Most clearly an "art" is placing our manuscripts and their readings in their ancient, nuanced contexts. The phenomenon that long ago I called theological tendency in scribal alterations recently has been designated "narrative textual criticism," recognizing that textual variants have a story to tell.[32] This approach, currently renewed, has been exemplified in the last decade or so in the works of Bart D. Ehrman and David C. Parker—and in a striking fashion.[33] To be sure, the view that variants disclose considerable influence on the text by scribes and copyists had roots in Europe (as noted earlier), but it is fair to say, I think, that North America and the United Kingdom have been fertile ground for its unfolding and maturity. This situating of textual variants in the theological controversies of the first centuries of Christianity and recognizing that multiple variants at a single point in the text reveal multifaceted viewpoints in the lived experiences of the church constitute bold moves forward in allowing the voices of many early Christians—theologians and ordinary people—to be heard anew in our day. These approaches also demonstrate the complementarity of textual criticism and exegesis. Moreover, the complaint of some that textual criticism has failed to develop connections to church history[34] has been answered

[31] See "Issues in New Testament Textual Criticism," 24–25.

[32] D. C. Parker, [review of Ehrman, *Orthodox Corruption*], in *JTS* 45 (1994) 704; cf. my "Oxyrhynchus New Testament Papyri: 'Not without honor,'" 9 and n. 16.

[33] I have highlighted Ehrman's and Parker's works [see note 12, above, and note 37, below] in a few of my recent articles: "Multivalence of the Term 'Original Text,'" 258–60; 264–66; "Issues in New Testament Textual Criticism," 55–61; and "Oxyrhynchus New Testament Papyri: 'Not without honor,'" 6–9.

[34] For example, Aland and Aland, *Text of the New Testament*, 49: "New Testament

thoughtfully and effectively. Finally, the use of the literary and everyday papyri of a city like Oxyrhynchus to expose the real-life context of the fifty-nine New Testament papyri and parchments discovered there is another way of accessing and displaying the socio-cultural environment of and influences upon our textual resources.[35]

These new directions taken by New Testament textual criticism surely will thrive in the years to come, if only because of their poignancy in bringing us face to face with real people and with their genuine concerns in the period when the New Testament text was evolving as it was being transmitted to us, manuscript by manuscript, scribe by scribe—and variant by variant. Though we cannot always or easily grasp the motivations of copyists, we can be reasonably sure that most of the time they are conveying to us—in their meaningful alterations of the text—views of their church or monastery, their community, or their region, though perhaps at times very individualized, independent judgments as well. After all, meaningful variants introduced into manuscripts arise from experience and conviction, though, I would venture, most often out of community or communal contexts. To quote Bart Ehrman, as I have several times recently, scribes make the texts they copy "*say* what they were already known to *mean*,"[36] and, in a memorable word from David Parker, "Luke is not, in these early centuries, a closed book. It is open, and successive generations write on its pages."[37] Through its variation units, the "living text" of the New Testament could not be otherwise, for thoughts, convictions, controversies, ethical dilemmas, and worship expressions burst out of life and onto the pages of the evolving New Testament, and even today we feel their impact. Textual criticism no longer can be written off as perfunctory or mechanical or as arcane or irrelevant—it is, on its cutting edge, primarily art, primarily a humanistic discipline that reveals to us, not a lifeless text, but an exciting, dynamic world of people and ideas in action.

---

textual criticism has traditionally neglected the findings of early Church history, but only to its own injury. . . ."

[35] See note 24, above.

[36] Bart D. Ehrman, *Orthodox Corruption*, xii (emphasis in original).

[37] David C. Parker, *The Living Text of the Gospels* (Cambridge: Cambridge University Press, 1997) 174.

CHAPTER ONE

THE "IGNORANCE MOTIF" IN ACTS AND ANTI-JUDAIC TENDENCIES IN CODEX BEZAE

The striking text that Codex Bezae presents, aside from evoking 51
much controversy and several novel theories,[1] has long been at the center of the yet unsolved mystery of the so-called "Western" text, which is itself one of the most urgent and yet most enigmatic areas of New Testament textual criticism. B. H. Streeter did not exaggerate when he said that many a scholar ". . . has met his Waterloo in the attempt to account for, or explain away, the existence of the Bezan text."[2]

What might be called a theological approach to textual criticism does, however, offer a fresh environment for the investigation of Codex Bezae. This approach accepts the fact that textual variants may conceal, and therefore can reveal, not only historical situations, but even dogmatic bias or some other tendentious viewpoint from which they arose. In other words, textual variants become a source for the study of the history of the church,[3] and they do so apart from any *primary* concern for the elusive "original text" of the New Testament. Of course, this approach is not new; it was employed some sixty years ago by J. Rendel Harris[4] and Kirsopp Lake,[5] chiefly

---

[1] For example, Blass's theory of two editions by Luke himself; Harris's theory of Latinization; Chase's theory of Syriac origin; Torrey's of Aramaic; and A. C. Clark's theory that the D-text was abbreviated to form the B-text.

[2] B. H. Streeter, "Codices 157, 1071, and the Caesarean Text," *Quantulacumque, Studies Presented to Kirsopp Lake* (London: Christophers, 1937) 150.

[3] See J. Rendel Harris, "New Points of View in Textual Criticism," *Expositor* VIII: 7 (1914) 319–20, cf. 322; D. W. Riddle, "Textual Criticism as a Historical Discipline," *AThR*, 18 (1936) 221.

[4] J. R. Harris, *Codex Bezae, A Study of the So-Called Western Text of the New Testament* (Texts and Studies, II.1; Cambridge: Cambridge University Press, 1891) 148–53; 228–34; idem, *Side-Lights on New Testament Research* (London: Kingsgate/James Clarke, 1908) 6; 29–35; 107–110; idem, *Expositor* VIII: 7 (1914) 316–34; idem, "Was the Diatessaron Anti-Judaic?" *HTR* 18 (1925) 103–5; idem, *Bulletin of the Bezan Club* 3 (1926) 4–7; 6 (1929) 2; 9 (1931) 8.

[5] K. Lake, *The Influence of Textual Criticism on the Exegesis of the New Testament* (Oxford: Parker, 1904) 8–23.

52 against Hort's view that, except for Marcion, there was no tampering with the text of the New Testament for dogmatic reasons.[6] More recently this theological approach has been vigorously advocated by D. W. Riddle,[7] Merrill M. Parvis,[8] K. W. Clark,[9] and Erich Fascher,[10] among others.

Although successive isolated suggestions as to various theological tendencies or other motivations revealed by the textual variants of Codex Bezae have been made,[11] no one apparently has undertaken a thorough investigation of these variants to see if some predominant and controlling tendency can be discerned, in which perhaps a great many of the variants might find their motivation. When, in fact, the variants of D in Acts are examined in this manner, a considerable body of evidence emerges indicating that a heightened anti-Judaism was a major preoccupation of the person or persons responsible for the text represented in this manuscript.[12]

---

[6] B. F. Westcott and F. J. A. Hort, *The New Testament in the Original Greek* (2 vols.; Cambridge: Macmillan, 1882) 2.282–83.

[7] Riddle, "Textual Criticism as a Historical Discipline," AThR 18 (1936) 220–33.

[8] Parvis, "The Nature and Tasks of New Testament Textual Criticism: An Appraisal," *JR* 32 (1952) 165–74.

[9] K. W. Clark, "Textual Criticism and Doctrine," *Studia Paulina in honorem Johannis de Zwaan septuagenarii* (Haarlem: Bohn, 1953) 52–65; idem, "The Effect of Recent Textual Criticism upon New Testament Studies," *The Background of the New Testament and Its Eschatology* (eds. W. D. Davies and D. Daube; Cambridge: Cambridge University Press, 1956) 44–46.

[10] E. Fascher, *Textgeschichte als hermeneutisches Problem* (Halle (Saale): Niemeyer, 1953).

[11] In addition to Harris (above, n. 4) and Fascher (above, n. 10), see, for example, the following: M.-J. Lagrange, *Critique textuelle, II, La critique rationnelle* (Paris: Gabalda, 1935) 388–94; 54–55; C. S. C. Williams, *Alterations to the Text of the Synoptic Gospels and Acts* (Oxford: Blackwell, 1951) passim; P. H. Menoud, "The Western Text and the Theology of Acts," *Studiorum Novi Testamenti Societas, Bulletin II* (1951) 19–32; J. Crehan, "Peter according to the D-Text of Acts," *TS* 18 (1957) 596–603.

[12] Detailed evidence for this view may be found in the writer's doctoral dissertation, of which this paper is a part: "Theological Tendency in the Textual Variants of Codex Bezae Cantabrigiensis: Anti-Judaic Tendencies in Acts" (Ph.D. dissertation, Harvard University, 1961) 251pp. [See the précis in *HTR* 54 (1961) 299.] [Revised and published as *The Theological Tendency of Codex Bezae Cantabrigiensis in Acts* (SNTSMS 3; Cambridge: Cambridge University Press, 1966); unchanged reprint: Eugene, OR: Wipf and Stock, 2001.]

In such an investigation, the interest is not, of course, in the viewpoint of the late fifth century manuscript D itself, but in the early "Western" text of perhaps the second century, of which D is the best Greek representative. D has textual strata more recent than this, but these can be avoided by not basing judgments on D-variants opposed by other "Western" witnesses, notably, for Acts, Old Latin Codex h, sy^{hmg}, sy$^{h\ cum\ *}$, Iren, Cypr, Aug, Ephr. Where none of these is available, D must be given its due weight as a "Western" witness. [Now cop^{G67} must be added as a primary "Western" witness: see "Added Notes, 2004" below.]

One interesting example of the many such tendentious readings 53
that might be discussed involves variations in the D-text of the passages that concern the "ignorance motif" in Acts.

Hans Conzelmann has emphasized the tendency of the Lucan writings to place all the blame for the crucifixion of Jesus on the Jews.[13] This tendency is clearer in the Gospel of Luke than in Acts, and, in fact, as Conzelmann admits, the book of Acts leaves room for the Jews to be excused on the grounds of ignorance. These contrasting views of Luke in Acts may be due, as Conzelmann suggested in his first two German editions (and in the English edition), to the fact that one, the guilt of the Jews, derives from Luke's source, while the other, that ignorance is a ground for excuse, is Luke's own interpretation.[14] In any event, Luke uses the theme of the guilt of the Jews in polemic against Judaism, while that of ignorance as a ground for excuse arises out of missionary needs.[15] Thus, Luke's emphasis on the guilt of the Jews for the crucifixion of Jesus stands in opposition to his report of the offered pardon, extended even to their rulers, because of ignorance.

A text-critical examination of the passages in Acts concerned with this "ignorance motif" discloses, however, that in Codex Bezae these two attitudes no longer stand in sharp conflict, for in D the element of excuse is virtually absent, while that of guilt finds more emphasis.

I

The passages in question all occur in speeches. The first of these, Acts 3:17, is found in Peter's speech in Solomon's Portico (Acts 3:12–26). Here, in both the B- and D-texts, the Jews are saddled with
the responsibility for delivering up Jesus, denying him before Pilate, 54
and finally killing him (3:13–15). There is for the Jews, however, an

[13] Hans Conzelmann, *Die Mitte der Zeit* (Tübingen: Siebeck-Mohr, 1960^{3}) 78–85; English trans., *The Theology of Saint Luke* (London: Faber and Faber, 1960) 85–93. (He confines himself to the B-text.)

[14] Ibid., German, 1957^{2}, 75; 77; 139–40; English trans., 90; 92; 162 n. 2. But, cf. Conzelmann's 2d German ed., 1957, 75, with his 3d German edition, 1960, 83, where he apparently is not so sure that these contrasting views are due to Luke's source and to Luke's own view, respectively. Nevertheless, these contrasting views in Luke remain.

[15] Ibid., 3d German ed., 84–85; 151; English trans., 92; 162 n. 2.

extenuating circumstance—they, as well as their rulers, "acted in ignorance" (3:17).

The D-version of the speech retains this exonerative feature, but its textual variants reveal a different underlying conception, placing the Jews in quite another light.

ACTS 3:17

B	D
καὶ νῦν, ἀδελφοί,	καὶ νῦν, ἄνδρες, ἀδελφοί,
οἶδα	ἐπιστάμεθα
ὅτι	ὅτι ὑμεῖς μὲν
κατὰ ἄγνοιαν	κατὰ ἄγνοιαν
ἐπράξατε,	ἐπράξατε πονηρόν,
ὥσπερ καὶ οἱ ἄρχοντες ὑμῶν·	ὥσπερ καὶ οἱ ἄρχοντες ὑμῶν·

ἄνδρες D d E e h p q w prov cop^{G67}
ἐπιστάμεθα D h cop^{G67} geo arm^{codd} Ephr$^{(p398)}$] om d (d^{2} scimus)] οἶδα sy^{h*} Ir$^{iii.12,3}$
ὑμεῖς μέν D d] μέν h (but Blass: [vos q]uidem h)
κατὰ ἄγνοιαν] [no]n quidem per scientiam h (but Blass: [vos q]uidem per <in>scientiam h)
πονηρόν D* (+ τό D^{c}) d gig h p q w cod.ard prov cop^{G67} sy^{hmg} Ir$^{iii.12,3}$ Aug^{q66} Ambst$^{86\ et\ 118}$] om Ephr$^{(p398)}$
(iniquitatem d; nequam h Ir; hoc malum gig p q w vg^{codd} prov cop Aug Ambst; scelus hoc cod.ard; "this evil" cop^{G67})
ὥσπερ . . . ὑμῶν] om Ir$^{iii.12,3}$

Notice, first of all, some minor variants that set the tone for what is to follow. The ἐπιστάμεθα of D (where B reads οἶδα)[16] changes the affirmation from "I, Peter, know . . ." to "We, the apostles, the μάρτυρες (3:15), know . . .," thereby emphasizing the contrast between the Christians and the Jews in the ensuing discussion. Whether the D-text's ὑμεῖς is emphatic, strengthening this contrast and pointing the finger more directly at the Jews and their rulers, or merely provides better balance in the Greek sentence, is difficult to say. The μέν, however, places this act of the Jews over against the action of God in the δέ-clause of the next verse (3:18).[17] The result so far in D may be paraphrased as follows:

[16] Matthew Black, *An Aramaic Approach to the Gospels and Acts* (2d ed.; Oxford: Clarendon Press, 1954) 179, cites these variants as examples of synonyms that could be viewed as different attempts at translation from an original Aramaic, but, he adds, they could also have arisen in Greek texts "in the process of διόρθωσις" at an early period.

[17] Th. Zahn, *Die Apostelgeschichte des Lucas* (3d ed.; Leipzig: Deichert, 1922), I.154

> *We*, the apostles of Christ, know that *you*, the Jews, *on the one hand*, acted in ignorance, as did also your rulers, but, *on the other hand*, God in this way fulfilled that which he foretold . . ., that his Christ should suffer.

In D, then, not only is the contrast sharpened between Jews and Christians, but also the disparity between what the Jews did and what God did is more clearly emphasized.[18]

The most significant variant, D's πονηρόν ("evil thing"), confirms all this. The presence of this word now leaves no doubt as to how Peter, according to the D-text, really viewed what the Jews did to Jesus; it may have been done κατὰ ἄγνοιαν ("out of ignorance"), but it was no less a culpable deed: ὑμεῖς ἐπράξατε πονηρόν ("you did an evil thing").[19] In D the responsibility for Jesus' death rests squarely on the Jews.[20]

These textual variants, like so many others in D, are small—there is, after all, a basic conservatism in all New Testament texts. These small variants, nevertheless, combine to reveal the calculated anti-Judaic sentiment from which they first sprang.

An interesting sideline is the occurrence of πονηρόν in the D-text of Luke 23:41. One of the criminals crucified with Jesus says concerning him: οὗτος δὲ οὐδὲν ἄτοπον ἔπραξεν (B-text)—"But he did nothing amiss," for which the D-text has οὗτος δὲ οὐδὲν πονηρὸν[21] ἔπραξεν—"But he did nothing evil." When this D-version of Luke
23:41 is compared with the D-version of Acts 3:17, the parallelism 56
seems too striking to be mere coincidence:

---

n. 62. Harnack, *TLZ* 32 (1907) 399, viewed μέν as secondary, since, he claimed, there was no contrast here. Once seen as an anti-Judaic passage, however, the contrast is both evident and meaningful.

[18] Harnack (ibid.) thought that the introduction to this speech in D went back to that in Acts 15:7 (B and D), ἄνδρες ἀδελφοί, ὑμεῖς ἐπίστασθε ὅτι. . . . The function of ὑμεῖς, however, is quite different; μέν is not accounted for, and, if 15:7 were the source, why did the D-text not simply take over ὑμεῖς ἐπίστασθε ὅτι . . ., which would have made perfect sense in 3:17 (and cf. 10:28; 19:25), or why not ἐπίσταμαι? The first person plural is not accounted for from 15:7.

[19] According to Harnack (ibid.) and B. Weiss, *Der Codex D in der Apostelgeschichte* (TU XVII.1; Leipzig, 1897) 61, πονηρόν is secondary because it is in conflict with κατὰ ἄγνοιαν. This, however, is just the point here—according to the D-text, the Jews cannot be guiltless because of their ignorance.

[20] Menoud, "Western Text," 28.

[21] Πονηρόν D lat Chr[2,480(but not 2,492)]. Cf. inicum = iniquum d; nihil mali it[p1]; nihil male q.

Acts: ὑμεῖς [i.e., the Jews] μὲν . . . ἐπράξατε πονηρόν.
Luke: οὗτος [i.e., Jesus] δὲ οὐδὲν πονηρὸν ἔπραξεν.

As far as the D-text is concerned, the Jews had done an evil thing to Jesus, who himself, in fact, had done nothing evil. The contrast is vivid and effective.[22]

It is noteworthy that the idea of the Jews acting in ignorance with reference to Jesus' death is peculiar to Luke. The obvious parallel to Acts 3:17 is Luke 23:34,[23] the words of Jesus from the cross: Πάτερ, ἄφες αὐτοῖς· οὐ γὰρ οἴδασιν τί ποιοῦσιν· Of significance here is the well-known but revealing fact that D in Luke lacks this prayer of forgiveness.[24] J. Rendel Harris, indeed, has argued vigorously that the prayer was excised from the text because of "an early and violent anti-Judaic polemic . . ., involving an actual abrenuntiation of all fellowship with the Jews."[25]

57 The variants in Acts 3:17, then, bring to focus the fact that, for the D-text, the Jews could not so easily be excused on the basis of ignorance.

---

[22] D, with d cop^{G67} sa, reads πονηρόν also in Acts 5:4, in Peter's question to Ananias: τί ὅτι ἔθου ἐν τῇ καρδίᾳ σου ποιῆσαι πονηρὸν τοῦτο; (B om ποιῆσαι and reads τὸ πρᾶγμα for πονηρόν), and in Lk. 5:22, in Jesus' reply to the scribes and Pharisees: τί διαλογίζεσθε ἐν ταῖς καρδίαις ὑμῶν πονηρά; (D it). The latter case is undoubtedly a harmonization with Matt 9:4, and the former is patterned after it, as is shown by the parallelism in Acts 5:4D and Luke 5:22D. No such relationship appears with reference to Acts 3:17 or Lk. 23:41, so that they remain separate cases. Whether these additional occurrences of πονηρόν in D are sufficient to indicate a preoccupation with this term by the D-text is not clear because of the evidence of harmonization. On the other hand, it is quite possible that the term was found or remembered in the parallels and used consciously according to a predilection for it.

[23] Menoud, "Western Text," 28 n. 32, says Luke 23:34 is the only parallel, rightly rejecting I Cor 2:8, which speaks of heavenly powers, not Jews. He has, however, overlooked Acts 13:27, which is discussed below. Note that Ephrem, for example, brings together the two passages (Acts 3:17 and Luke 23:34); quoting Acts 3:17, he says these are the very words which the Lord used, "They do not know what they do" (see J. H. Ropes, *The Text of Acts* [vol. 3 of *The Beginnings of Christianity. Part I. The Acts of the Apostles*; eds. F. J. Foakes Jackson and Kirsopp Lake; 5 vols.; London: Macmillan, 1920–33] 398).

[24] Lacking in D* (add D^{L}) d P^{75} $\aleph^{a}$ B W Θ pc a b sy^{s} sa bo^{codd} eth.

[25] Harris, *Expositor* VIII: 7 (1914) 333–34; cf. 324–25; 331 ff. See also Harnack, *Studien zur Geschichte des Neuen Testaments und der alten Kirche. I. Zur neutestamentlichen Textkritik* (Berlin: de Gruyter, 1931) 91–98, especially 96–98, who defends the originality of the prayer of forgiveness and its subsequent excision for dogmatic reasons—because of anti-Judaic feelings. See also B. H. Streeter, *The Four Gospels* (London: Macmillan, 1924) 138–39. (This view assumes that the αὐτοῖς refers to the Jews, not to the Romans.) The refusal of Hort to admit any dogmatic alterations in the New Testament has been noted earlier; observe his comment on this passage (*New Testament in the Original Greek*, "Notes on Selected Readings," 2.68):

II

The "ignorance motif" recurs in Acts 13:27, which relates part of Paul's speech at Pisidian Antioch.

ACTS 13:27

B	D
οἱ γὰρ κατοικοῦντες	οἱ γὰρ κατοικοῦντες
ἐν Ἱερουσαλὴμ	ἐν Ἱερουσαλὴμ
καὶ οἱ ἄρχοντες αὐτῶν	καὶ οἱ ἄρχοντες αὐτ [ῆ]ς
τοῦτον ἀγνοήσαντες	μ[ὴ συνιέν] τες
καὶ τὰς φωνὰς	τὰς γρ [αφ] ὰς
τῶν προφητῶν	τῶν προφητῶν
τὰς κατὰ πᾶν σάββατον ἀναγεινωσκομένας	τὰς κατὰ πᾶν σάββατον ἀναγεινωσκομένας
κρείναντες ἐπλήρωσαν, . . .	καὶ κρείναντες ἐπλήρωσαν, . . .

αὐτῆς D^{*vid} d gig t vg
τοῦτον ἀγνοήσαντες] hunc Christum ignorantes cod.ard; hunc Iesum ignor. cor.vat* cop^{G67}; hunc (om vg^{codS*}) ignor. Iesum vg^{coddSU}
μὴ συνιέντες τὰς γραφάς D^{*vid} [see note[26]] (D^{F}: τοῦτον ἀγνοήσαντες καί) (D^{H}: φωνάς); non intelligentes scripturas d (καὶ τὰς γραφάς E e sy^{p} [eth])
καί pro κρείναντες D d (cf. sy^{p} and Zahn's opinion[27])

Here it is not so clear whether the ignorance referred to (especially
in the B-text) provides an excuse or involves guilt. Conzelmann argues 58
that Luke here shares the view of Mark 12:24 that ignorance of the
scriptures incurs blame,[28] but this is hardly convincing when one

'Wilful excision, on account of the love and forgiveness shown to the Lord's own murderers, is absolutely incredible: no various reading in the New Testament gives evidence of having arisen from any such cause." This view, here and elsewhere, cannot bear the weight of evidence against it; thus Harnack, *Studien*, I. 98.

[26] See Frederick H. A. Scrivener, ed., *Bezae Codex Cantabrigiensis, Being an Exact Copy in Ordinary Type* (Cambridge: Deighton, Bell, 1864) 444, note to Fol. 468b; the editions of Friedrich Blass, *Acta Apostolorum sive Lucae ad Theophilum liber alter: Editio philologica* (Göttingen: Vandenhoeck & Ruprecht, 1895); Adolf Hilgenfeld, *Acta Apostolorum graece et latine secundum antiquissimos testes* (Berlin: Georg Reimer, 1899); Ropes [see note 23, above]; and Albert C. Clark, *The Acts of the Apostles: A Critical Edition with Introduction and Notes* (Oxford: Clarendon Press, 1933); Frederick H. Chase, *The Old Syriac Element in the Text of Codex Bezae* (London: Macmillan, 1893) 89–92; and Theolor Zahn, *Die Urausgabe der Apostelgeschichte des Lucas* (Leipzig: Deichert, 1916) ad loc., who says συνιέντες is assured through d.

[27] Zahn, *Urausgabe*, 283.

[28] Conzelmann, 3d German ed., 147 n. 4; cf. 83; English trans., 158 n. 4; cf. 90. Conzelmann's assumption here that τὰς φωνὰς τῶν προφητῶν is the object of ἀγνοήσαντες is also questionable. The choice is whether the καί of the B-text is copulative or epexegetic, and thus whether both τοῦτον and τὰς φωνάς are objects

compares the features of Acts 3:17 with those of Acts 13:27. There is in both, first, the element of ignorance (ἄγνοια, ἀγνοεῖν), namely a failure to recognize God's Χριστός.[29] Secondly, both passages specify the fulfillment of the scriptures, within the Divine Decree, by the unknowing act of the Jews (3:18; 13:27, 29, 32–33). (Already the fact that the death of Jesus conforms to the scriptures somewhat alleviates the severity of judgment on the Jews.)[30] Finally, both passages name the Jews, with their rulers, as the subjects of the action against Jesus. This close parallelism permits us to take these passages in the same way. Now in the B-text of 3:17, ignorance clearly provides an excuse, and there is no reason why 13:27, in the same text, should not be taken in the same way.[31]

59 Turning, then, to the text of D, it is at once apparent that D again has differently conceived the ignorance on the part of the Jews. The D-text reads μὴ συνιέντες τὰς γραφάς . . . ("not understanding the scriptures") for B's τοῦτον [i.e., Jesus] ἀγνοήσαντες καὶ τὰς φωνάς . . .

---

of ἀγνοήσαντες, or only τοῦτον, with τὰς φωνάς as the object of ἐπλήρωσαν. See E. Jacquier, *Les Actes des Apôtres* (EBib; 2d ed.; Paris: Gabalda, 1926) 400. Compelling reasons for one choice over the other are lacking. M. Dibelius, *Studies in the Acts of the Apostles* (London: SCM, 1956) 91 [*Aufsätze zur Apostelgeschichte* (FRLANT 60; Göttingen: Vandenhoeck & Ruprecht, 1951) 83], excises τοῦτον, making "the voices of the prophets" the only object of ἀγνοήσαντες. He apparently follows Ropes (*Text of Acts*, 262), but Ropes's view was based on his explanation of the D-text—that the "Western" reviser wished to clarify the simple reading ἀγνοήσαντες *sine* τοῦτον and substituted μὴ συνιέντες. The B-text, says Ropes, supplied a new object, τοῦτον. Unfortunately for this view, there is no evidence for the reading ἀγνοήσαντες *sine* τοῦτον except the reading of D d (i.e., μὴ συνιέντες *sine* τοῦτον), and the explanation about to be given for D's lack of τοῦτον and its reading of μὴ συνιέντες for ἀγνοήσαντες obviates the need for Ropes's elaborate explanation.

This is not, however, to gloss over the textual problem in 13:27–29. The texts of both B and D do offer difficulty. Reconstructions of the "Western" text, however, generally follow D (Hilgenfeld, Zahn, Clark, Ropes), though Ropes deletes καὶ κρείναντες in favor of the same word in the next line (verse 28) (Ropes, *Text of Acts*, 261–63). The text of D, then, can be accepted (with this possible exception) as the early "Western" reading.

[29] See Acts 3:13–18; note τοῦτον in 13:27 and the vg codices that read *hunc Christum/Iesum* here. This assumes the view that τοῦτον refers to the Ἰησοῦν of verse 23: ὁ θεὸς . . . ἤγαγεν τῷ Ἰσραὴλ σωτῆρα Ἰησοῦν [Lake and Cadbury, *The Beginnings of Christianity*, 4.153; Ernst Haenchen, *Die Apostelgeschichte* (12th ed.; Göttingen: Vandenhoeck & Ruprecht, 1959) 352], and not to ὁ λόγος τῆς σωτηρίας (verse 26). For the latter view, see Zahn, Apostelgeschichte (3/4 ed.) II. 439.

[30] Bo Reicke, *Glaube und Leben der Urgemeinde* (Zürich, 1957) 67.

[31] Nor does the fact that 13:27 is in a speech of Paul require that ἄγνοια be interpreted in a Pauline fashion, for two reasons: (1) Though in Paul ἄγνοια is regularly guilt-laden, Acts 3:17 and 13:27 alone in the New Testament use the term in quite another connection. Thus B. Gärtner, *The Areopagus Speech and Natural Revelation* (Acta Seminarii Neotestamentici Upsaliensis, 21; Uppsala, 1955) 234 n. 2; cf. 229–40; see also E. Fascher, "Gott und die Götter," *TLZ* 81 (1956), 298. (2) The paral-

ἐπλήρωσαν ("being ignorant of this one [Jesus]"). Here, as in 3:17, the tendency of the B-text to excuse the Jews by reason of ignorance for crucifying Jesus appears in a more subdued manner in D, which refuses to let the Jews off so lightly. The lack of τοῦτον and the reading of μὴ συνιέντες for ἀγνοήσαντες divest D of any thought that might suggest a relative pardon from guilt because of a disregard for or non-recognition of Jesus as Χριστός—the D-text has no room for such a formula of excuse. Indeed, the only exonerative factor left to the Jews here in D is a lack of understanding (συνιέναι) their scriptures, an excuse hardly complimentary or acceptable to the Jews.

III

The only two other occurrences of ἀγνοεῖν and ἄγνοια ("to be ignorant," "ignorance") in Acts [but see on 16:39D, below] are in Paul's Areopagus speech in chapter 17 (verses 23, 30). Notice verse 30:

ACTS 17:30

B	D
τοὺς μὲν οὖν χρόνους	τοὺς μὲν οὖν χρόνους
τῆς ἀγνοίας	τῆς ἀγνοίας ταύτης
ὑπεριδὼν ὁ θεὸς	παριδὼν ὁ θεὸς
τὰ νῦν ἀπαγγέλλει	τὰ νῦν παραγγέλλει
τοῖς ἀνθρώποις	τοῖς ἀνθρώποις
πάντας πανταχοῦ μετανοεῖν, . . .	ἵνα πάντες πανταχοῦ μετανοεῖν, . . .

ταύτης D d vg (cf. geo)] om cett Ir$^{\text{iii.12,9(11)}}$
παριδών D
παραγγέλλει D P^{41} P^{74} ℵ^{c} A E H L P S Ψ 614 383 1739 sa sy^{h} Ir^{lat} Ath Cyr$^{\text{abac 573}}$
ἵνα πάντες D sy^{p}; ut . . . paenitentiam agant d gig vg] πᾶσιν H L P S 614 383 sy^{h} Ir$^{\text{iii.12,9(11)}}$
μετανοεῖν] + εἰς αὐτόν Ir$^{\text{iii.12,9(11)}}$ (in ipsum)

Here, οἱ χρόνοι τῆς ἀγνοίας ("the times of ignorance") that God overlooked[32] refer back to the ἄγνωστος θεός ("unknown god") that the 60
Athenians worshiped ἀγνοοῦντες ("as unknown," verse 23).[33] The

lelism shown here between Acts 3:17 and 13:27 (not to mention other evidence) reveals the hand of Luke in each, rather than providing evidence for the unity of the preaching of Peter and Paul (Haenchen, *Apostelgeschichte*, 352).

[32] Dibelius, *Studies*, 56 n. 89, thinks ὑπεριδών is a stronger term than παριδών. However, Gärtner, *Areopagus Speech*, 230, thinks the two terms give the same sense—that God does not intervene to change the situation.

[33] Haenchen, *Apostelgeschichte*, 463.

"times of ignorance" have reference, here, only to heathen religion.

Why, then, does D read ταύτης in verse 30, "the times of *this* ignorance," unless it is to distinguish the ignorance in the present context ("this ignorance"), which has nothing to do with the Jews' treatment of Jesus,[34] from the D-text's other mention of ignorance in 3:17. Since the presence of πονηρόν, etc. in the latter passage in D already afforded the excuse of ignorance a much smaller place, the D-text wanted to be certain that no reader thought it was *that* ignorance which God had overlooked.[35] In other words, the D-text is saying that the times of ignorance spoken of here in Acts 17:30 refer to the Athenian worship, and God overlooks *this* ignorance. But, says the D-text, let no one think that God overlooks *that* ignorance, referred to in 3:17, through which the Jews crucified Jesus; God overlooks *this* ignorance of the Athenians, but not *that* ignorance of the Jews.

This variant of D in Acts 17:30 provides striking confirmation of the view taken here as to the meaning of the D-text's variants in Acts 3:17, along with those in 13:27.

Moreover, the textual variants of D in the immediate context of Acts 3:17 and 13:27 (especially 3:13–14 and 13:28–29) lend additional support, for they also emphasize the Jews' greater responsibility and their more direct and hostile action in the condemnation of Jesus.[36]

61 In summary, the rather minute textual variations discussed here stand in contrast to the larger and more elaborate readings usually singled out for study in Codex Bezae. Both the large and small variants, however, reveal this strain of anti-Judaic sentiment. The variants connected with the "ignorance motif" are of special interest because they show an instance where the D-text's viewpoint is carried through the text consistently.[37] Since texts may be corrected to

[34] Gärtner, *Areopagus Speech*, 234 n. 2, distinguishes carefully the use of ἄγνοια in 3:17 (to be taken with 13:27) from its meaning in 17:30, and in the epistles, LXX, Philo, pagan philosophy, etc. See his excellent discussion of the "ignorance" theme, 229–40.

[35] A passage closely related to 17:30 and one to which the "ignorance motif" might be applied is Acts 14:16, in the Lystra speech: (B and D) ὃς ἐν ταῖς παρῳχημέναις γενεαῖς εἴασεν πάντα τὰ ἔθνη πορεύεσθαι ταῖς ὁδοῖς αὐτῶν. The specific mention of ἔθνη, however, excludes any confusion as to Jewish or Gentile reference.

[36] These passages are discussed in "Theological Tendency in the Textual Variants of Codex-Bezae," 66–77 [see now Epp, *Theological Tendency*, 48–50].

[37] Another notable case of consistency in D is the lack of καὶ πνικτοῦ(-όν) or καὶ

and influenced by other texts, such consistency can neither always be found nor expected. Consequently, the consistency evident in this instance lends added significance to the results and demands further attention to the theological tendency that motivated such constructions in the "ignorance" passages. This case, of course, forms only one small piece in a rather complex puzzle. The difficulty lies not so much in fitting the pieces together, for the bias seems clear, but rather in fashioning the pieces themselves through the painstaking process of defining *theologically significant* variants within the welter of textual aberrations found in Codex Bezae Cantabrigiensis.

An additional occurrence in Acts of the verb ἀγνοεῖν is found within a longer variant reading of D in 16:39. The context of 16:39 tells of the release of Paul and Silas from prison at Philippi. The magistrates had just learned that the apostles were Romans and, hearing this, they were afraid. The B-text then reads (16:39):

> . . . καὶ ἐλθόντες παρεκάλεσαν αὐτούς, καὶ ἐξαγαγόντες ἠρώτων ἀπελθεῖν ἀπὸ τῆς πόλεως.
>
> ("So they came and tried to placate them. And they took them out and asked them to leave the city.")

The D-text, however, is much fuller:

> . . . καὶ παραγενόμενοι μετὰ φίλων πολλῶν εἰς τὴν φυλακὴν παρεκάλεσαν αὐτοὺς ἐξελθεῖν εἰπόντες· Ἠγνοήσαμεν τὰ καθ' ὑμᾶς ὅτι ἐστὲ ἄνδρες δίκαιοι. καὶ ἐξαγαγόντες παρεκάλεσαν αὐτοὺς λέγοντες· Ἐκ τῆς πόλεως ταύτης ἐξέλθατε μήποτε πάλιν συνστραφῶσιν ἡμεῖν ἐπικράζοντες καθ' ὑμῶν.
>
> ("And they came with many friends into the prison, and asked them to leave, saying, 'We were ignorant about you that you were upright men.' And when they led them out, they urged them to leave, saying, 'Leave this city so that those who cried out against you do not again assemble against us.'")

παραγενόμενοι D
μετὰ φίλων πολλῶν D d
εἰς τὴν φυλακήν D d 614 383 ro^{2} sy^{h}*
ἐξελθεῖν εἰπόντες D d 614 383 ro^{2} sy^{h}*
ἠγνοήσαμεν . . . δίκαιοι D d 614 383 ro^{2} sy^{h}* Ephr$^{(p432)\ et\ cat\ (p433)}$
καὶ ἐξαγ. . . . λέγοντες D d 62
ἐκ . . . ὑμῶν D d 614 383 sy^{h}* Ephr$^{(p432)\ et\ cat\ (p433)}$ [with minor variations in each]

πνικτῶν in 15:20; 15:29; and 21:25, and the additional negative "Golden Rule" in 15:20 and 29 (though not in 21:25).

Significant is the statement of the magistrates, Ἠγνοήσαμεν τὰ καθ' ὑμᾶς ὅτι ἐστὲ ἄνδρες δίκαιοι. The word ἠγνοήσαμεν ("we were ignorant") here is clearly in the context of excuse; the magistrates are excusing themselves for beating and imprisoning the apostles, and the basis of their excuse is ignorance—ignorance that Paul and Silas were, as they put it, "righteous men" (i.e., Roman citizens). What is interesting is that the D-text allows this excuse of ignorance in the case of the Roman officials.[38]

The word δίκαιοι ("just, upright") reminds one immediately of the words of the centurion at the cross (Luke 23:47): ὄντως ὁ ἄνθρωπος οὗτος δίκαιος ἦν (D has ὄντως δίκαιος ἦν ὁ ἄνθρωπος οὗτος).[39] The D-text's account here in Acts 16:39 parallels the experience of the apostles with that of Jesus:[40] A Roman centurion calls Jesus δίκαιος, and Roman magistrates call the apostles δίκαιοι; the Jews do not recognize Jesus for what he is (κατὰ ἄγνοιαν, Acts 3:17) but, nevertheless, are not excused by the D-text on these grounds, while the Roman magistrates, who acknowledge that they had been ignorant (ἠγνοήσαμεν) of the apostles' identity (allegedly as "righteous men") are allowed the excuse of ignorance in D. Once again the D-text is hard on the Jews.

Added Notes, 2004

This essay was first presented at the 1960 Annual Meeting of the Society of Biblical Literature and Exegesis (as SBL was then called) at Union Theological Seminary in New York City, with Professor Joseph A. Fitzmyer, S.J., presiding—the beginning of a long friendship, including six years as New Testament Book Review Editor of the *Journal of Biblical Literature* while he served as Editor.

The article, my first publication, was incorporated into *The Theological*

[38] Other instances of leniency or favor toward the Roman officials in the D-text of Acts appear in the context of 16:39 and elsewhere; see "Theological Tendency in the Textual Variants of Codex Bezae," 200–205 [See now Epp, *Theological Tendency*, 147–51].

[39] Δίκαιος is used of Jesus also in Matt 27:19; 24 (though not in B or D); Acts 3:14; 7:52; 22:14. Note also that in Acts 14:2D δίκαιοι is used of the Christians.

[40] Other cases of such paralleling by the D-text occur in Acts 4:13 and 4:21; see "Theological Tendency in the Textual Variants of Codex Bezae," 167–168; 171–172 [See now Epp, *Theological Tendency*, 121–26].

Tendency of Codex Bezae Cantabrigiensis in Acts (SNTSMS 3; Cambridge: Cambridge University Press, 1966 [unchanged reprint: Eugene, Oregon: Wipf and Stock, 2001]), 41–51, which develops fully the overriding theme of this essay. The latter appears now with some slight corrections and additions to the critical apparatus. Most important are the added references to the Codex Glazier (cop^{G67}), a fifth century manuscript of Acts 1:1–15:3 in Middle Egyptian that agrees with so-called "Western" readings with striking frequency. Its variants have been included in Nestle-Aland$^{26 \text{ and ff.}}$ with the designation "mae" and in the UBSGNT$^{3 \text{ and ff.}}$ as "meg."

For further discussion of manuscript G67, see the following essays in the present volume: "Coptic Manuscript G67 and the Role of Codex Bezae as a Western Witness in Acts" (1966); and "Anti-Judaic Tendencies in the D-Text of Acts: Forty Years of Conversation" (2003), § 2II.A on "Coptic G67 and Petersen's Work," and § II.B on "Schenke's Critical Edition of G67."

CHAPTER TWO

COPTIC MANUSCRIPT G67 AND THE RÔLE OF CODEX BEZAE AS A WESTERN WITNESS IN ACTS

Father T. C. Petersen's English translation of numerous passages in 197
the newly discovered Coptic manuscript of Acts,[1] containing Acts 1:1–15:3 and now designated as G67 in the Glazier Collection in the Pierpont Morgan Library,[2] will be appreciated by all who concern themselves with the textual tradition of Acts or with the so-called Western text of the New Testament in general. The late fourth- or early fifth-century date[3] of this manuscript makes it the earliest nonfragmentary Western manuscript of the text of Acts, and, since it antedates Codex Bezae by a century,[4] this new manuscript will have considerable significance, not only for the general question of the Western text in Acts, but also for such questions as the accuracy and individuality of the scribe of Codex Bezae (and perhaps of his immediately preceding ancestors), for the broader, related problem of recent textual strata in D, and for the question of the extent to which the Western element in D has been contaminated by conformation to other text-types. In short, the rôle of Codex Bezae as a Western witness can be re-evaluated and clarified in several ways with the aid of this new discovery.

In addition to its early date, the obvious affinity of the text of cop^{G67} with that of previously recognized leading Western witnesses

[1] T. C. Petersen, "An Early Coptic Manuscript of Acts: An Unrevised Version of the Ancient So-Called Western Text," *CBQ* 26 (1964) 225–41.

[2] This designation was communicated in a letter dated Nov. 9, 1964, from John H. Plummer, curator of mediaeval and renaissance manuscripts in the Pierpont Morgan Library, New York City. Other abbreviations used below which may be unfamiliar are: cod.ard = Codex Ardmachanus (vg^{D}); dutch = Mediaeval Dutch [Klijn, *NTS*, 1 (1954/55), pp. 51–56]; l = León Palimpsest (see below); *minn* = two or more minuscules; sy^{msK} = Christian-Palestinian fragment from Khirbet Mird (see below).

[3] See Petersen, "Early Coptic Manuscript of Acts," 225 and n. 3. [On a revised date for G67, see "Added Notes, 2004" below.]

[4] Unless H. J. Frede, *Altlateinische Paulus-Handschriften* (VLAGLB 4; Freiburg: Herder, 1964) 18 and n. 4, is correct that Codex Bezae should be dated in the fourth century! [On the current dating of Codex Bezae, see "Added Notes, 2004" below.]

gives assurance that this manuscript itself must now be numbered among those few leading or "pure" Western witnesses to the text of Acts. This preliminary judgment on the purity of its Western character will without doubt be more clearly and finally demonstrated when the manuscript is fully published (which Fr. Petersen hopes to do soon), but the nearly 140 passages—containing some 250 variation-
198 units—that he presents already indicate in a striking fashion the validity of this judgment. Moreover, a full assessment of cop^{G67} should shed at least some light on the long-standing question of homogeneity in the Western text.

Although this new manuscript contains only the first half of Acts, its nonfragmentary character is of special significance, for the study of the Western text has long been plagued by fragmentary witnesses, to say nothing of the problem of mixed witnesses. Of the best or pure Western witnesses in Acts, only Codex Bezae previously has offered a more or less continuous text of a substantially Western character, while the Old Latin Codex h in eight fragments contains parts of thirteen chapters, totaling about one-fifth of Acts; and Irenaeus, Cyprian, Augustine, Tertullian, Ephrem, and the marginal notes to and asterisked portions of the Harclean Syriac offer passages here and there, often with distinctly Western readings.

Now cop^{G67} is extant for some 520 verses of Acts (out of just over 1000),[5] and of these 520, D has all but 68 (8:29–10:14), but h contains only 142. In the same portion of Acts, sy^{hmg} and sy^{h*} together have noted some 138 variants (not verses), while some 120 verses are quoted by Irenaeus, some 37 by Augustine from a Cyprianic text, some 28 by Cyprian, and some 20 by Tertullian. These figures show at once the very great importance of the new Coptic manuscript for the study of the Western text of Acts 1:1–15:3. Add to this its relative purity as a Western witness (as the variants given below indicate) and it is justifiable to say that the discovery of cop^{G67} may well represent the most significant development of our century as far as the investigation of the Western text of Acts is concerned.

It has long been argued, and quite correctly, that Codex Bezae, the Old Latin, and the Old Syriac (especially where they agree)

[5] Petersen, "Early Coptic Manuscript of Acts," 226, n. 4, reports that in terms of lines of script, cop^{G67} stops at the exact middle of Acts.

represent the early Western text of the second century.[6] Yet the bulk of evidence for any given Western reading comes from a much later date. Of course, where the evidence of early fathers (e. g., Irenaeus, Cyprian, Tertullian) supports the later Western witnesses, there is more confidence that early—perhaps second century—Western readings are present, and in other cases, for example where the Old Syriac (as in Ephrem, sy^{hmg}, sy^{h*}) or Old Latin (as in non-Vulgate manuscripts) support Codex Bezae, there is less but still considerable confidence that these again are early Western readings. Even in these cases, however, the earliest manuscript evidence for these Western readings will date from the late fifth century (unless the readings occur in P^{38}, P^{48}, or P^{29}, though none of these is extant in Acts 1–15). Now the support of cop^{G67} will push back the actual manuscript date of this evidence by a full century, and the gain of a century in non- 199
fragmentary evidence is great gain indeed. Moreover, the evidence of cop^{G67} is earlier than the date of the manuscript itself (though it is difficult to say how much), for, as Petersen points out, this manuscript is not the working copy of the translator of this Coptic version, but is the work of a professional copyist working from an older manuscript.[7] Thus, until such a time as a Western manuscript of Acts comparable in date and scope to P^{66} and P^{75} appears, the evidence of cop^{G67} must be accorded the very great importance that it properly deserves.

I

The significance, then, of cop^{G67} for the long-standing question of scribal innovations and recent textual strata in Codex Bezae is obvious enough: readings hitherto found only in D, but that now find support in cop^{G67}, at the least cannot be due to the vagary of the scribe who produced Codex Bezae, nor can they represent a textual stratum which entered the Western tradition about the time of the origin of D. Petersen's translation discloses at least four and perhaps eight such instances in Acts where cop^{G67} now combines with D to offer the only known support for these readings:

[6] This complex question is treated in some detail by the present writer in the Introduction of *The Theological Tendency of Codex Bezae Cantabrigiensis in Acts* (SNTSMS 3; Cambridge: Cambridge University Press, 1966).

[7] Petersen, "Early Coptic Manuscript of Acts," 229, n. 12.

1) Acts 4:24. ἀκούσαντες]+καὶ ἐπιγνόντες τὴν τοῦ θεοῦ ἐνέργειαν D d. Codex Bezae is supported now by the very similar reading of cop^{G67}: "When they *understood that our strength was of God.*"

2) Acts 5:18. δημοσίᾳ]+καὶ ἐπορεύθη εἷς ἕκαστος εἰς τὰ ἴδια D d cop^{G67}: "And each one went to his own home."

3) Acts 11:2. The long Western variant here concludes, in D and d only, by referring to Peter "who also met them [the brethren] and reported to them the grace of God." The last part of this, καὶ ἀπήγγειλαν αὐτοῖς τὴν χάριν τοῦ θεοῦ, is now attested also by the very similar reading of cop^{G67}, "and spoke to them of the mercy of God." (The rest of the variant in 11:2, also found in cop^{G67}, is discussed below.)

4) Acts 13:44. According to D and d, at Antioch nearly the whole city gathered to hear *Paul, "and when he had made a long discourse about the Lord"* (πολύν τε λόγον ποιησαμένου περὶ τοῦ κυρίου), the Jews contradicted what he had said. Lake and Cadbury remarked[8] that unfortunately there was no other Western witness at this point, but now we have it in cop^{G67}: "But Paul spoke lengthily in the discourse concerning the Lord Jesus."

Possibly also the following variants:

5) Acts 13:29. Here the reading of D and d already has the partial support of sy^{hmg}, and the textual problem in this passage (which must
200 be studied along with vss. 27–28) is complex,[9] but it is clear at least that cop^{G67} ("they asked Pilate to crucify him, and they went again to him") attests the variant of D* and d: ᾐτοῦντο τὸν Πειλᾶτον τοῦτον μὲν σταυρῶσαι καὶ ἐπιτυχόντες πάλιν καί. . . .

[8] Kirsopp Lake and Henry J. Cadbury, *The Acts of the* Apostles (The Beginnings of Christianity, iv; London: Macmillan, 1933) 159.

[9] See further James Hardy Ropes, *The Text of Acts* (Beginnings of Christianity, 3; London: Macmillan, 1926) 261–63; Albert C. Clark, *The Acts of the Apostles: A Critical Edition with Introduction and Notes* (Oxford: Clarendon Press, 1933) 81; 356.

6) Acts 5:8. Peter's question to Sapphira begins with an imperative in the Neutral text (and in d): εἰπέ μοι εἰ . . . ("Tell me if . . ."), while D alone reads ἐπερωτήσω σε εἰ ἄρα. . . . ("I will ask you if indeed. . . .") Now cop^{G67} also has the first person: "*I asked you* about the sale."

7) Acts 7:31. Following κατανοῆσαι ("to look"), apparently D and d alone read ὁ κύριος εἶπεν αὐτῷ ("The Lord said to him"), which occurs also in cop^{G67}, though in a conflated form (but partially also in sy^{p}).

8) Acts 7:54. The Neutral text (except ℵ) reads, "Now when they heard *these things* (ταῦτα)," while D and d alone read, "Now when they heard *him* (αὐτοῦ)." The reading of cop^{G67} is conflate: "As they heard *these things from him*."

Admittedly, moving back a hundred years or so in manuscript evidence does not guarantee that these readings are now authentic early Western readings, but the earlier, added support makes this conclusion far more plausible than when they stood alone in Codex Bezae. It is doubtful, moreover, that anyone will argue that the Coptic translation represented in G67 was made from a direct ancestor of D—the two texts are not that much alike.

II

Another characteristic of Codex Bezae, long recognized, is that at some stage or stages in its history it has been conformed to the Neutral (Alexandrian) and Byzantine (Koine) types of text at numerous points.[10] One obvious example of almost total conformation of D to B occurs in Acts 14:5, where nothing of the distinctive Western text remains in D, though it is preserved in varying degrees in d h Ephr sy^{hmg} and now also by cop^{G67}. Such conformation in Codex Bezae is quite easily recognized when two or three other leading Western witnesses (such as Irenaeus, h, Ephrem, sy^{hmg}, and sy^{h*}) are available and stand in opposition to D. But when a reading of D is opposed by only one such pure Western witness, it is difficult to

[10] See, e.g., Ropes, *Text of Acts*, lxxx–lxxxiii. Sometimes this conformation comes by adjustment of the Greek to the Latin d.

decide whether D has suffered contamination and the other witness represents the early Western text, or whether the latter witness simply attests a unique and/or a recent innovation in the text.

Now cop^{G67}, in at least six instances, supports a reading attested,
201 against D, by only one pure Western witness, and this strengthens (though it does not prove)[11] the supposition that in these cases D has been conformed to a non-Western text-type:

1) Acts 4:13/14. The sentence describing how the Jewish rulers regarded Peter and John, "and they recognized that they had been with Jesus," is placed in vs. 13 by the Neutral text and also by D. Codex h, however, placed it at the end of vs. 14, after *contradicere* (ἀντειπεῖν). Lake and Cadbury,[12] as well as Ropes,[13] took h to represent the Western text at this point, but A. C. Clark[14] felt that h was "clearly wrong" in placing the clause here. Few Western witnesses are available for these verses, but now cop^{G67} follows h and strengthens the case that this order represents the Western text and that D at this point has been conformed to the Neutral type of text. (Notice that cop^{G67} also follows h and sy^{p} in reading *tunc* at the beginning of vs. 15. This is lacking in D, while B reads δέ.)

2) Acts 4:15. αὐτούς] *Petrum et Iohanem* h cop^{G67}.

3) Acts 5:39. In the speech of Gamaliel all witnesses read εἰ δὲ ἐκ θεοῦ ἐστίν, ("but if it is of God") except h which has *si autem haec potestas ex dei volun*[*tate est*], and cop^{G67} which is similar: "but if it is of the *power* of God."

4) Acts 6:1. D d h and cop^{G67} are unanimous in specifying that the daily distribution was handled by the Hebrews: ἐν τῇ διακονίᾳ Ἑβραίων ("in the ministration of the Hebrews") D d, similarly h cop^{G67}, but only h and cop^{G67} are just as explicit that it was the *Greek* widows who were neglected: *viduae Graecorum*.

[11] Naturally, neither D nor any other Western witness should be expected to contain or to have contained every Western reading.

[12] Lake and Cadbury, *Beginnings of Christianity*, 4.44.

[13] Ropes, *Text of Acts*, 38.

[14] Clark, *Acts of the Apostles*, 340; cf. 23.

5) Acts 10:30. ἀνήρ] ἄγγελος ("an angel") cop^{G67} sy^{hmg}.

6) Acts 14:20. Only h and now cop^{G67}, in the report that the disciples gathered around Paul after he was stoned and cast out of the city, state that he rose up *after the crowd had left*: h = *et* [*cum disce*]*ssisset populus*; cop^{G67} = "and the crowd left." (Incidentally, cop^{G67} demonstrates the correctness of this restoration of the broken text in h, as given by Fr. Blass in 1895.)[15] The additional *vespere* in h (similarly sa cop^{G67} Ephr and Ephr^{cat}), which follows *populus* and precedes *levavit se*, is quite clearly Western, and its absence in D strengthens the supposition that D has been conformed to the Neutral type text in this verse; the only possibly Western element remaining in D is the Λύστραν (d = *Lystram*; h = *Lystrum*). This instance, by the way, illustrates the significance of cop^{G67} for establishing many details of the Western text, for here at the same time it aids the restoration of a 202
mutilated manuscript (h), confirms the likely Western version of a passage, and brings to light an example in D of conformation to another text-type.

The following variants, which are supported by cop^{G67} but not by D, may also represent places where D has suffered by conformation, though here the readings are already more strongly attested by pure or mixed Western witnesses than are the six just considered. In each case the text of D closely follows that of the Neutral tradition:

1) Acts 5:29. *cui obaudire oportet, deo an hominibus?* h, similarly gig cop^{G67} Aug Lucif; +*at illi dixerunt: deo* cod.ard q w vg^{codd} prov cop^{G67}; cf. *ille autem ait: deo* h, similarly gig: "'Whom is it right to obey, God or man?' and he said, 'God.'"

2) Acts 5:33. ἀκούσαντες]+τὰ ῥήματα ταῦτα 614 *minn* h p cop^{G67} sy^{p} sy^{h*}.

3) Acts 7:3. συγγενείας σου]+καὶ ἐκ τοῦ οἴκου τοῦ πατρός σου ("and from the house of his father") (= LXX) E e *minn* cod.ard cop^{G67}

[15] Friedrich Blass, *Acta apostolorum . . . Editio philologica* (Göttingen: Vandenhoeck & Ruprecht, 1895) 162, and found also in Buchanan, Zahn, Ropes, and A. C. Clark; to the contrary, Wordsworth and White, and cf. Lake and Cadbury, *Beginnings of Christianity*, 4.167.

Aug. This variant incorporates the fuller text of Gen 12:1, which makes it difficult to say whether a distinctly Western reading is present, with D suffering conformation here, or whether these are independent expansions of the Old Testament quotation by several copyists. Cop^{G67} does, in fact, expand its Old Testament quotations on numerous occasions: 2:28 (Ps 15[16]:11) with no support; 3:22–24 (Deut 18:17–19 is quoted rather than 18:15, 19) with no support; 7:6 (a fuller and more direct citation of Gen 15:13) with no support; 7:7 (Gen 15:14) with no support; 7:24 (Exod 2:11) with Western support [though cop^{G67} does not have the expanded "he hid him in the sand" (Exod 2:12) of other Western witnesses]; 7:31–34 (much expanded, from Exod 3:4–10) with no support except in a few minor details; 7:35 (Exod 2:14) with Western support; 7:40 (Exod 32:1) with no support; 7:43 (Amos 5:27) with Western and mixed Western support; and 13:33 (Ps 2: 7–8) with Western support. There is no reason to assume that those expansions unique to cop^{G67} represent the Western text, but there is every reason to assume that the others, all of which have Western support (and are discussed below), are Western readings.

4) Acts 7:39. πατέρες ἡμῶν] πατέρες ὑμῶν ("your fathers") Ψ 81 *minn* sa^{ms} cop^{G67} geo Ir^{lat} (but not Ir^{arm}).

5) Acts 7:43. Βαβυλῶνος]+λέγει κύριος ὁ θεὸς ὁ παντοκράτωρ ὄνομα αὐτοῦ ("says the Lord God the Almighty is his name") (= LXX) *minn* cop^{G67} sy^{h} sy^{h*}; λέγει κύριος παντοκράτωρ 614 431 Filaster (in vs. 42).

6) Acts 7:46. οἴκῳ] θεῷ ℵ^{c} A C E e Ψ 33 81 614 1739 *minn* c cod.ard dem gig h p ph ro vg sa^{mss} bo cop^{G67} sy^{p} sy^{h} arm eth geo Chr *et al.*

7) Acts 8:21. τῷ λόγῳ τούτῳ] *hac fide* gig p r cop^{G67} sy^{p} arab Aug Ambr Const.Apost. Notice that Ropes, though not A. C. Clark, took τῇ πίστει ταύτῃ ("in this faith") to be the Western text.

203 8) Acts 10:39. ὃν]+*Judaei reppulerunt et* ("whom the *Jews rejected and* put to death") l t, similarly p* p^{2} cop^{G67} sy^{h*} sy^{p} sy^{msK}; *Judaei* p* p^{2} sy^{p}. It is of interest that the other two recently discovered Western witnesses of Acts, l (León Palimpsest)[16] and sy^{msK} (Christian-Palestinian

[16] Published by Bonifatius Fischer, "Ein neuer Zeuge zum westlichen Text der

fragment from Khirbet Mird),[17] agree in this reading with cop^{G67} and sy^{h*}, the latter previously the only leading Western witness supporting this variant. Ropes apparently did not consider it Western, nor did A. C. Clark, but the newly discovered evidence strongly supports such a view and points to another case of conformation in D.

9) Acts 11:1. θεοῦ]+*et glorificabant deum* ("and they glorified God") l gig, similarly p^{2} q w dem vg^{codd} prov tepl cop^{G67} sy^{h*} dutch. Again cop^{G67} and l confirm this as a Western reading, as Ropes took it, though A. C. Clark and (apparently) Lake and Cadbury did not include it in the Western text.

10) Acts 12:5. ἐτηρεῖτο]+*a cohorte regis* ("by the cohort of the king") p* ro cop^{G67} sy^{h*}.

11) Acts 12:25. Σαῦλος]+ ὃς ἐπεκλήθη Παύλος ("who was called Paul") 614 p* cop^{G67} sy^{h*}.

12) Acts 14:5. The variant specifying a *second* persecution of the apostles at Iconium (referred to above) is attested by cop^{G67} sy^{hmg} Ephr^{comm} $^{II\ Tim3}$2; cf. d h. Although these Western witnesses do not allow an easy reconstruction of the precise Western text here, it is clear at least that D, except for two very minor details, has been completely conformed to the B-text.

13) Acts 14:19. 'Αντιοχείας]+καὶ διαλεγομένων αὐτῶν παρρησίᾳ ἔπεισαν τοὺς ὄχλους ἀποστῆναι ἀπ' αὐτῶν λέγοντες ὅτι οὐδὲν ἀληθὲς λέγουσιν, ἀλλὰ πάντα ψεύδονται ("and as they were openly disputing, they persuaded the crowds to withdraw from them, saying that they were not telling the truth, but were liars in every respect") (C) 81 (1739) *minn* (h) cop^{G67} sy^{hmg} arm geo. That the ἐπισείσαντες of D which

Apostelgeschichte," *Biblical and Patristic Studies in Memory of Robert Pierce Casey* (eds. J. N. Birdsall and Robert W. Thomson; Freiburg: Herder, 1963) 33–63. The manuscript dates in the seventh century and contains Acts 8:27–11:13 and 14:21–17:25 in alternating Old Latin and vg sections. See the review by E. J. Epp, *JBL*, 84 (1965) 173.

[17] This manuscript, which we designate sy^{msK}, was published by Ch. Perrot, "Un fragment christo-palestinien découvert à Khirbet Mird (Actes des Apôtres, X, 28–29; 32–41)," *RB* 70 (1963) 506–55. The fragment dates from the sixth century.

follows is no mere corruption of the πείσαντες of the Neutral tradition is clear from the attestation of the former by D d h e gig sy^{p} sy^{hmg}. As Ropes argued,[18] it is a remnant in D of this larger Western reading that has otherwise disappeared from Codex Bezae. This, plus the evidence of cop^{G67} for the longer, preceding variant, again points to a case of conformation in D and leads to surer knowledge of the Western text in this verse.

There are two additional cases of conformation in D that are disclosed by cop^{G67}, though here the text of D only partly follows the Neutral tradition:

14) Acts 2:33. τοῦτο (om D* d)]+τὸ δῶρον ("the gift") E e c p r q t dem cod.ard cor.vat* vg^{codd} vg^{s} prov tepl sa sy^{p} sy^{h} arab^{e} Aug Hier
204 Ambr Didy Bede; *donationem hanc* Ir; *hanc gratiam* cop^{G67} Filaster. D and d alone in this passage have ὑμῖν ὅ for τοῦτο ὃ ὑμεῖς, indicating that D has suffered corruption that at some stage involved conformation to the Neutral text-type in the omission of τὸ δῶρον.

15) Acts 2:41. λόγον αὐτοῦ]+*et* (om *et* p r) *crediderunt et* ("those who received his word *and believed and* were baptized") p r (cod.ard) cop^{G67} sy^{p} sy^{hmg} Aug. D and d have this reading in place of ἀποδεξάμενοι rather than in addition to it, and this πιστεύσαντες of D is probably what remains of the original Western reading following a process of partial conformation. It could be argued, of course, that D represents the Western text and that the other Western witnesses have a conflated reading, but fullness is characteristic of the Western text, and it is easier to view the reading of Codex Bezae as the result of conformation and readjustment.

III

Where it is extant, cop^{G67} is of considerable significance also for determining the Western text of Acts at those points where Codex Bezae has suffered from mutilation and is now lacking, namely 8:29 to 10:14. Codex h is also lacking in this section up to 9:4 and after 9:24a, which further enhances the interest and importance of the Coptic manuscript. At least twenty-one readings of cop^{G67} may here

[18] *Ropes, Text of Acts*, 134.

represent the Western text, either in readings already established as Western or by supporting previously less well-established but quite probably Western variants. (Readings unique to cop^{G67} are not taken into consideration.) Noteworthy is the frequency with which l (León Palimpsest), a divided manuscript that is Old Latin rather than vg in the portion lacking in Codex Bezae, supports the variants of cop^{G67}:

1) Acts 8:37. The entire vs. 37 is clearly Western: E e 1739 *minn* c cod.ard dem gig l m p ph r ro t w tepl vg$^{s, cl}$ cop^{G67} sy^{h*} arm eth geo Aug Ambst Cypr Ir Bede Pacian Spec Tert Thphl^{b} *et al.*, and it is now supported by cop^{G67} and l.

2) Acts 8:39. a) πνεῦμα]+ἅγιον ἐπέπεσεν ἐπὶ τὸν εὐνοῦχον, ἄγγελος δέ . . . ("the *Holy* Spirit *fell on the Eunuch, and an angel* of the Lord caught up Philip") A^{1} 1739 *minn* l p q (w) cod.ard tepl cop^{G67} sy^{h*} arm geo Aug Cass Cyr^{hr} Didy Ephr Hier, *et al.* This, again, is a clearly Western reading, widely attested, and now supported by both cop^{G67} and l.

b) Φίλιππον]+*ab eo* p Aug cop^{G67} sy^{hmg}.

3) Acts 9:4. a) γῆν]+*cum magna mentis alienatione* p; *cum . . . consternatione* ("with great mental aversion/with confusion") t; [*in pa*]*vore* h; similarly cop^{G67} Ambr Ephr [l lacking].

b) διώκεις]+σκληρόν σοι πρὸς κέντρα λακτίζειν ("It hurts you to kick against the goads") E e 431 vg^{codd} cop^{G67} sy^{p} sy^{h*} arab^{e} geo Aug Petil Hil Ephr; similarly, but in vs. 6: h l c dem gig p r t w cod.ard vg^{codd} tepl (sy^{hmg}) eth arm arab^{p} slav dutch Ambr Lucif Thphyl. Again, cop^{G67} and l are in agreement.

4) Acts 9:5. a) εἶπεν δέ] *qui respondit, dicens* h cop^{G67} sy^{p} (geo). 205

b) ὁ δέ]+κύριος εἶπεν with variations E e H L P S (Ψ) 383 *minn* h l p t sa cop^{G67} sy^{p} sy^{hmg} Chr. Codex l and cop^{G67} again agree.

5) Acts 9:6. ἀλλά] *et ille tremens ac stupens* (+*in eo quod factum erat* vg^{codd}, similarly h t sy^{hmg} Hil Ephr) *ait domine quid me vis facere dominusque ad illum* ("And trembling and astonished he said, 'Lord, what would you have me do?' And the Lord [said] to him,") l t, similarly h c dem gig p cod.ard vg^{codd} vg$^{s, cl}$ tepl cop^{G67} sy^{h*} sy^{hmg} arm^{osc} eth arab^{p} dutch (Ambr) Aug Petil Hil Ephr Lcf Thphyl. Notice cop^{G67} and l in agreement.

6) Acts 9:7. θεωροῦντες]+*cum quo loqueretur* ("with whom he was speaking.") l gig, similarly h p q w tepl cop^{G67}; +*sed ait ad eos: levate me de terra. Et cum levassent illum*, ("And he said to them, 'Lift me from the ground.' And when they had lifted him,") h q p w vg^{codd} cop^{G67}. On the first variant, cop^{G67} and l again are in agreement.

7) Acts 9:17. τὰς χεῖρας] *manum* h r t sa cop^{G67} sy^{p}; +*in nomine domini* (om *domini* h) *Iesu Christi* ("in the name of the Lord Jesus Christ") h vg^{codd} cop^{G67} Chr.

8) Acts 9:19. ἡμέρας τινάς] ἡμέρας ἱκανάς ("for many days") P^{45} h cop^{G67}.

9) Acts 9:20. a) εὐθέως ἐν ταῖς συναγωγαῖς] *introibit in sinagogas Judaeorum, et* ("he entered the synagogues of the Jews") h, similarly m p w cop^{G67}, and in part c q cor.vat^{mg} prov sa sy^{p}.

b) Ἰησοῦν] praem *dominum* h m sa cop^{G67}; +Χριστόν H L P S 383 cop^{G67} eth arm^{codd} Chr; ὁ Χριστός post ἐστίν 441 h l m t sa Ir Ir$^{gk\ cat}$ Thphyl.

10) Acts 9:22. ἐνεδυναμοῦτο]+ἐν (om ἐν C 467) τῷ λόγῳ ("in the word") C E e 467 h l p cop^{G67}. Again cop^{G67} and l are in agreement.

11) Acts 9:32. πάντων] *civitates et regiones* ("cities and regions") l p q w cop^{G67} (sy^{p}) (cf. geo) [h defective]. Notice again the coincidence of l and cop^{G67}.

12) Acts 9:40. a) ἀνάστηθι]+*in nomine domini nostri Iesu Christi* ("in the name of our Lord Jesus Christ") gig l m p (cod.ard) vg^{codd} sa cop^{G67} sy^{h*} arm (geo) Ambr(Cass) (Cypr) (cf. Acta Joh.) Spec [h defective]. Here again cop^{G67} and l are in agreement.

b) ἡ δέ]+παραχρῆμα ("immediately") E e gig m p r sa cop^{G67} eth (geo) [h defective].

13) Acts 10:11. καὶ καταβαῖνον σκεῦός τι ὡς ὀθόνην μεγάλην τέσσαρσιν ἀρχαῖς] καὶ τέσσαρσιν ἀρχαῖς δεδεμένον σκεῦός τι ὡς ὀθόνην λαμπρὰν καί ("and a container like a large bright/transparent cloth tied at four corners and. . . .") (P$^{45\ vid}$ *minn*) Ψ 33 d l gig (sy^{p}) sa bo cop^{G67} arm Aug Cass Const.Apost Thphyl (Ambr) [D h defective]; δεδεμένον

is attested also by C^{vid} L P S 81 614 383 sa sy^{p} sy^{h} Chr Clem. Observe the agreement of cop^{G67} and l.

It is striking that eleven out of the twenty of these variants that occur in passages extant in l are now supported also by l. That cop^{G67} and l (in its Old Latin portions) agree so often in this section with the pure and mixed Western witnesses not only points to the distinctly Western character of these newly discovered witnesses to
the text of Acts, but also increases the likelihood that these common 206
readings are indeed early Western readings. Moreover, fourteen of these variants of cop^{G67} occur in passages where the very important Western witness h is extant, and in every case h agrees with cop^{G67}.

Readings unique to cop^{G67} have not been included in the lists above, but two are worthy of mention here, both from Acts 8 35:

a) "And now he [Philip] was in the spirit" cop^{G67}.
b) ". . . preached *the Lord* Jesus *Christ* to him" cop^{G67}.

Although none of the leading Western witnesses is extant here, l in an Old Latin section is, but it does not attest these readings. Both variants, however, are so characteristic of the Western text of Acts—emphasis on the Holy Spirit and on the full title of Jesus—that cop^{G67} is likely to represent the Western text here, especially when it is recognized that l, even in its Old Latin sections, is by no means so frequent in supporting already established Western readings as is cop^{G67}.

IV

A number of readings in Codex Bezae until now have had the support only of later, mixed Western witnesses and of no leading or pure witnesses. In such cases it is always difficult to decide with confidence whether the reading is to be taken as Western or not, but now, where it occurs, the supporting evidence of cop^{G67} confirms or at least greatly strengthens the assumption that these variants are to be accepted as early Western readings. Such evidence, moreover, removes the possibility of regarding these variants as having originated in or at the time of Codex Bezae; like the readings in section I above, these variants are not thereby guaranteed as second-century readings, but the earlier manuscript evidence plus the wider support tend toward that conclusion.

1) Acts 2:30. αὐτοῦ]+κατὰ σάρκα ἀναστῆσαι τὸν Χριστὸν καί ("according to the flesh to raise up the Christ, and . . .") D* d cop^{G67}; similarly P Ψ 33 181 614 383 Byz sy^{h} sy^{p} geo Or Chr Thret; cf. E e 1739 Bede.

2) Acts 2:47 (3:1). ἡμέραν]+ἐν τῇ ἐκκλησίᾳ ("in the church") D d (praem ἐπὶ τὸ αὐτό D d) E e P Ψ 33 181 614 383 1739 *minn* p r vg^{mss} cop^{G67} sy^{h} sy^{p} geo Chr Basil Bede (some without ἐν).

3) Acts 3:1. Πέτρος δέ] Ἐν δὲ ταῖς ἡμέραις ταύταις Πέτρος ("in those days") D d p r (vg$^{cod\Theta}$) cop^{G67} (cf. sy^{p}).

4) Acts 5:4. τὸ πρᾶγμα] ποιῆσαι πονηρόν[19] τοῦτο ("to do this evil thing") D d sa sy^{p} cop^{G67}.

5) Acts 5:12. πάντες]+ἐν τῷ ἱερῷ ("in the Temple") (ναῷ E) D d E e 42 sa cop^{G67} eth.

6) Acts 5:15. τινὶ αὐτῶν]+ἀπηλλάσσοντο γὰρ ἀπὸ πάσης ἀσθενείας ὡς εἶχεν ἕκαστος αὐτῶν ("for they were being freed from every sickness such as each of them had") D (d), similarly E e c dem gig p cod.ard
207 cor.vat* vg$^{s, cl}$ cop^{G67} dutch Lcf.

7) Acts 5:41. οὖν]+ἀπόστολοι D d 614 p cop^{G67} sy^{h} Ambst. [h is extant in this passage but has a lacuna for the first word of the sentence, though *illi* rather than *apostoli* is generally adopted by the editors.]

8) Acts 8:16. Ἰησοῦ]+Χριστοῦ D d H L P S 383 181 vg^{codd} cop^{G67} dutch Didy (cf. eth).

9) Acts 10:30. ἤμην]+νηστεύων καί (τε D) ("and fasting") D d P^{50} A^{2} E e H) (L) P Ψ 181 614 *minn* cod.ard l ph ro t cor.vat* sa cop^{G67} sy^{h} sy^{p} Chr Bede.

10) Acts 11:2. περιτομῆς]+ἀδελφοί D d l p ro w cop^{G67} sy^{h*} geo.

[19] That this is the reading of cop^{G67} was conveyed in a letter from Fr. Petersen.

11) Acts 11:27/28. 'Αντιόχειαν]+ ἦν δὲ πολλὴ ἀγαλλίασις ("and there was much rejoicing") D d p q w vg^{codd} prov tepl cop^{G67} Aug Proph. The additional συνεστραμμένων δὲ ἡμῶν of D (and the other witnesses above, plus Ado) is perhaps attested also by the "about *our* returning" of cop^{G67}.

12) Acts 12:10. ἐξελθόντες]+κατέβησαν τοὺς ζ̄ βαθμοὺς καί ("walked down the seven steps") D d p (om *septem*); "beyond the steps" cop^{G67}.

V

Finally, there are numerous well-established Western readings that now find added and early support in G67. These are variants supported by D and at least one, though often two, three, or more other leading Western witnesses and usually also by a number of mixed witnesses—witnesses with numerous Western readings, such as 614, 383, gig, l, p, t, cod.ard, sa, sy^{p}, sy^{h}, etc. These strongly attested Western readings that now find additional support in cop^{G67} serve to confirm the judgment that this newly found manuscript must be counted among those few pure or leading Western witnesses that provide the best attestation for early, genuine Western readings, notably D, Irenaeus, h, Cyprian, Augustine (where he uses a Cyprianic text), Tertullian, Ephrem, sy^{hmg}, and sy^{h*}:[20]

1) Acts 1: 2. ἐξελέξατο]+(καὶ ἐκέλευσε D d sy^{hmg} Aug Varimadum Ephr) κηρύσσειν τὸ εὐαγγέλιον D d gig t cod.ard sa cop^{G67} sy^{hmg} Aug Vigil Ephr (cf. EpBarn 5 9; Tert). [Not h or sy^{p}, as Petersen.]

2) Acts 1:5. ἡμέρας]+ἕως τῆς πεντηκοστῆς ("until Pentecost") D* d sa cop^{G67} Aug^{pt} Cass Ephr.

3) Acts 1:21. 'Ιησοῦς]+Χριστός D d cop^{G67} sy^{h} eth Aug.

4) Acts 2:37. ἀδελφοί;]+ὑποδείξατε ἡμῖν ("Show us") D d E e gig p q r t w cod.ard vg^{codd} prov tepl cop^{G67} sy^{hmg} Aug Bede Prom.

---

[20] See the detailed discussion in Epp, *Theological Tendency of Codex Bezae*, 27–34. The attestation given for the following variants is intended to supplement, and in some cases to correct, Petersen's minimal citation of authorities.

5) Acts 2:38. ὀνόματι]+τοῦ κυρίου D d E e 614 1739 *minn* c (p) r vg^{mss} sa cop^{G67} sy^{p} sy^{h} eth arm geo dutch Aug Ambr Bas Cypr Cyr Cyr^{hier} Lucif* Thdrt Epiph Vigil.

208 6) Acts 3:17. a) νῦν]+ἄνδρες D d E e h p q w prov cop^{G67}.
b) οἶδα] ἐπιστάμεθα D d^{2} h cop^{G67} arm^{codd} geo Ephr.
c) ἐπράξατε]+πονηρόν[21] D d gig h p q w cod.ard vg^{codd} prov cop^{G67} sy^{hmg} Ir Aug Ambst.

7) Acts 3:22. εἶπεν]+πρὸς τοὺς πατέρας ἡμῶν ("to our fathers") (ὑμῶν E e *minn* Bede: om P Ψ 614 383 181 1739 sy^{h} Chr Thphyl) D d (E e) 33^{vid} *minn* h gig p q vg^{codd} tepl prov sa cop^{G67} sy^{h} eth arm^{mss} geo Ir^{lat} Bede.

8) Acts 4:8. πρεσβύτεροι]+τοῦ Ἰσραήλ ("of Israel") D d E e P Ψ 33 181 614 383 1739 *minn* h gig p* (w) vg^{codd} cop^{G67} sy^{h} arm geo Ambr Cypr Ir^{lat} Bede; τοῦ οἴκου Ἰσραήλ p^{2} q w vg^{codd} prov tepl sy^{p}.

9) Acts 4:18. καὶ καλέσαντες] συνκατατιθεμένων δὲ αὐτῶν (+πάντων d gig cop^{G67} Lucif) τῇ γνώμῃ φωνήσαντες ("when they had all agreed to the decision, having called them. . . .") D d h (gig) (vg^{cod}) cop^{G67} sy^{hmg} (Lucif).

10) Acts 4:31. παρρησίας]+παντὶ τῷ θέλοντι πιστεύειν ("to every one who wished to believe") D d E e q r w cod.ard vg^{codd} cop^{G67} Ir Ir^{cat} Ephr Bede (cf. Aug).

11) Acts 5:29/30. ἀνθρώποις]+ ὁ δὲ Πέτρος εἶπεν πρὸς αὐτούς ("and Peter said to them/him") (*eum* h) D (d) h gig cod.ard vg$^{cod\Theta mg}$ cop^{G67}.

12) Acts 5:36. τινά]+μέγαν D d A^{2} E e 614 *minn* gig h cod.ard vg^{codd} cop^{G67} sy^{p} (eth) Orig Hier Cyr.

13) Acts 5:38. αὐτούς]+μὴ μιάναντες (μολύνοντες E Bede) τὰς χεῖρας ("without defiling your hands") D d E e 61 h cop^{G67} Bede.

14) Acts 5:39. αὐτούς]+οὔτε ὑμεῖς οὔτε βασιλεῖς οὔτε τύραννοι D d h cop^{G67} sy^{h*}, similarly E e gig w dem cod.ard sa Bede; +ἀπέχεσθε οὖν

[21] That this is the reading of cop^{G67} was conveyed in a letter from Fr. Petersen.

ἀπὸ τῶν ἀνθρώπων τούτων D d (614) *minn* h w dem cop^{G67} sy^{h*} ("neither you nor kings nor tyrants. Therefore, keep away from these men").

15) Acts 6:1. χῆραι αὐτῶν]+ἐν τῇ διακονίᾳ τῶν Ἑβραίων ("in the ministration of the Hebrews") D* d h cop^{G67}.

16) Acts 6:3. ἐπισκέψασθε δέ, ἀδελφοί] τί οὖν ἐστίν, ἀδελφοί; ἐπισκέψασθε ("What then is to be done, brothers? Pick out. . . .") D d h p cop^{G67}.

17) Acts 6:5. πλήθους]+τῶν μαθητῶν ("of the disciples") D d h cop^{G67}.

18) Acts 6:10/11. a) σοφίᾳ]+τῇ οὔσῃ ἐν αὐτῷ ("that was in him") D d E e h cop^{G67} Bede.

b) πνεύματι]+τῷ ἁγίῳ D d E e gig g$_2$ h p t cop^{G67} eth Ado Bede.

c) ἐλάλει]+διὰ τὸ ἐλέγχεσθαι αὐτοὺς ἐπ' αὐτοῦ μετὰ πάσης παρρησίας [6:11] μὴ δυνάμενοι οὖν ἀντοφθαλμεῖν τῇ ἀληθείᾳ ("because they were confuted by him with all boldness. Being unable therefore to confront the truth. . . .") D d, similarly E e h t w (cod.ard) vg^{codd} tepl bohem cop^{G67} sy^{hmg} Bede (cf. Ephr).

19) Acts 6:15. ἀγγέλου]+ἑστῶτος ἐν μέσῳ αὐτῶν ("standing in their midst") D d h t cop^{G67} Ephr^{cat}.

20) Acts 7:1. ἀρχιερεύς]+τῷ Στεφάνῳ ("to Stephen") D d E e gig g$_2$
h p q t w cod.ard vg^{codd} cop^{G67} sy^{p} Bede. 209

21) Acts 7:4. κατοικεῖτε]+καὶ οἱ πατέρες ἡμῶν ("and our fathers") (ὑμῶν E e cop^{G67} sy^{h*} Aug) (+οἱ πρὸ ἡμῶν D d; ὑμῶν sy^{h*}) D d E e (cop^{G67}) sy^{h*} Aug.

22) Acts 7:21. αὐτοῦ]+παρὰ (εἰς E e) τὸν ποταμόν ("into the river") D d E e cod.ard w vg^{codd} tepl cop^{G67} sy^{h*}.

23) Acts 7:24. ἀδικούμενον]+ἐκ τοῦ γένους αὐτοῦ ("of his race") (om αὐτοῦ D) D d E e gig vg^{cod} cop^{G67} sy^{p} sy^{h*} eth arab^{e}.

24) Acts 7:35. δικαστήν]+ἐφ' ἡμῶν (= LXX) ℵ C D d (E) e *minn* c dem gig p vg^{codd} sa bo cop^{G67} sy^{p} sy^{h*} eth arm geo dutch (Chr) Thphyl^{b}.

25) Acts 7:55. Ἰησοῦν]+τὸν κύριον D d 614 h p sa cop^{G67}.

26) Acts 8:1. ἀποστόλων]+οἳ ἔμειναν ἐν Ἰερουσαλήμ ("who remained in Jerusalem") D* d gig g2 h t prov^{mg} sa cop^{G67} eth Ephr Aug Bede.

27) Acts 8:24. εἰρήκατε]+ὃς πολλὰ κλαίων οὐ διελίμπανεν ("who did not stop weeping copiously") D* cop^{G67} sy^{hmg} Tert Ephr^{cat} (cf. Chr).

28) Acts 10:25. a) Πέτρον]+εἰς τὴν Καισαρίαν D d p q t w prov tepl cop^{G67} sy^{hmg}; + προδραμὼν εἷς τῶν δούλων διεσάφησεν παραγεγονέναι αὐτόν D d gig (cop^{G67}) sy^{hmg}.

b) Κορνήλιος]+ἐκπηδήσας καί D d sy^{hmg}; cf. *processit* l p t, and cop^{G67} = "came out before him and. . . ."

c) προσεκύνησεν]+αὐτόν D* d l^{vid} p t w dem cod.ard cor.vat* vg^{codd} tepl sa cop^{G67} geo.

("And as Peter was drawing near to Caesarea, one of the servants ran ahead and announced that he had arrived. And Cornelius jumped up and . . . worshiped him.")

29) Acts 10:26. εἰμί]+ὡς καὶ σύ ("even as you are") D* d (E e) gig l^{vid} p t w cod.ard cor.vat* vg^{codd} tepl cop^{G67} bo^{codd}.

30) Acts 10:33. σέ]+ παρακαλῶν ἐλθεῖν πρὸς ἡμᾶς ("asking you to come to us") D d p q prov sa^{cod} cop^{G67} sy^{h*} sy^{msK}.

31) Acts 11:2. The long Western version of vs. 2 as found in D and d is supported, in similar form, by p q w vg^{codd} prov tepl cop^{G67} sy^{h*}.

32) Acts 11:17. κωλῦσαι τὸν θεόν]+ τοῦ μὴ δοῦναι αὐτοῖς πνεῦμα ἅγιον D d p ph ro q w cod.ard vg^{codd} prov tepl bohem cop^{G67} sy^{h*} Aug; +πιστεύσασιν ἐπ' αὐτῷ D d, similarly q w cod.ard vg^{codd} prov tepl bohem sy^{h*} (Peter asks how he could withstand God "that he should not give to them the Holy Spirit after they had believed on him").

33) Acts 11:25. ἐξῆλθεν δὲ εἰς Ταρσόν] ἀκούσας δὲ ὅτι Σαῦλός ἐστιν εἰς Ταρσὸν ἐξῆλθεν ("having heard that Saul was at Tarsus, he went out. . . .") D d gig p (vg^{codR}) cop^{G67} sy^{hmg} Cass.

34) Acts 12:1. ἐκκλησίας]+ἐν τῇ Ἰουδαίᾳ D d 614 p q w vg^{cod} prov tepl sy^{h*}; "who are in Jerusalem" cop^{G67}. Since cop^{G67} has an additional "who are in Jerusalem" following "presbyters" in the preced-

ing verse (11:30), it is likely that its reading in 12:1 represents an original "in Judaea" which has been conformed by a scribe to the earlier expression. (The variant in 11:30 has no other attestation.)

[Note: Petersen misread "who are in Jerusalem" in cop^{G67}; it reads "who are in Judaea" (see "Added Notes, 2004" below).]

210

35) Acts 12:21/22. αὐτούς]+καταλλαγέντος δὲ αὐτοῦ τοῖς Τυρίοις ("and when he had been reconciled with the Tyrians/and the Sidonians") (+ καὶ Σιδωνίοις p^{2} q w vg^{codd} tepl) D d p^{2} q w vg^{codd} tepl cop^{G67} (sy^{h*}). [For Τυρίοις, sy^{h*} reads αὐτοῖς.]

36) Acts 12:23. Compare the reading of cop^{G67}, "and he went out upon the judgment seat," with the καὶ καταβὰς ἀπὸ τοῦ βήματος (post θεῷ) of D d Ephr^{bis}.

37) Acts 13:8. πίστεως]+ ἐπειδὴ ἥδιστα ἤκουεν αὐτῶν ("because he [the proconsul] was listening to them with the greatest pleasure") D* d sy^{h*}, similarly E e cop^{G67} Bede.

38) Acts 13:19. αὐτῶν] τῶν ἀλλοφύλων ("of the foreigners") D* d cop^{G67} sy^{h*}.

39) Acts 13:33. The quotation of Ps 2:7 is followed by the additional quotation of Ps 2:8 (= LXX) in D d cod.ard cop^{G67} sy^{hmg}.

40) Acts 13:38. καταγγέλλεται]+καὶ μετάνοια ("and repentance") D d, and in varying positions cop^{G67} sy^{h*} cod.ard.

41) Acts 13:41. ἐκδιηγῆται ὑμῖν]+καὶ ἐσίγησαν ("and they were/he was silent") D d; καὶ ἐσίγησεν 614 cop^{G67} sy^{h*}.

42) Acts 13:43. θεοῦ]+ἐγένετο δὲ καθ' ὅλης τῆς πόλεως διελθεῖν τὸν λόγον τοῦ θεοῦ ("and it happened that the word of God went throughout the whole city") D d, similarly E e p q w vg^{codd} prov tepl cop^{G67} sy^{hmg} Bede.

43) Acts 14:2. ἀδελφῶν]+ὁ δὲ κύριος ἔδωκεν ταχὺ εἰρήνην ("but the Lord soon gave peace") D d gig p q w dem vg^{codd} prov tepl cop^{G67} sy^{hmg} Cass, similarly E e cod.ard Bede.

44) Acts 14:4. ἀποστόλοις]+κολλώμενοι διὰ τὸν λόγον τοῦ θεοῦ ("cleaving to them on account of the word of God") D d sy^{hmg}, similarly cop^{G67}; cf. sy^{p}.

45) Acts 14:7. ἦσαν]+καὶ ἐκεινήθη ὅλον τὸ πλῆθος ἐπὶ τῇ διδαχῇ. ὁ δὲ Παῦλος καὶ Βαρνάβας διέτριβον ἐν Λύστροις ("and the whole multitude was moved by the teaching. And Paul and Barnabas stayed on in Lystra") D d (E) e h p q w vg^{cod} vg^{s} prov tepl cop^{G67} (Cass) Bede.

46) Acts 14:10. a) φωνῇ]+σοὶ λέγω ἐν τῷ ὀνόματι τοῦ κυρίου Ἰησοῦ Χριστοῦ ("I say to you in the name of the Lord Jesus Christ") D d C E e Ψ 614 383 1739 *minn* h p^{l} t w vg^{cod} prov sa bo^{pt} cop^{G67} sy^{p} sy^{hmg} arm geo Ambr (Ir^{lat}) Cass Bede Thphyl^{b}.
b) ὀρθός]+καὶ περιπάτει ("and he walked") D d h cop^{G67} sy^{hmg}.

47) Acts 14:15. εὐαγγελιζόμενοι ὑμᾶς] εὐαγγ. ὑμῖν τὸν θεόν ("proclaiming *God* to you") D d h^{vid} m cop^{G67} Ir^{lat} Aug Ephr.

48) Acts 14:19. a) ante ἐπῆλθαν] διατριβόντων δὲ (om δέ D d) αὐτῶν καὶ διδασκόντων ("But while they were staying there and teaching, . . .") D d C E e 33 1739 *minn* h cop^{G67} sy^{hmg} arm geo arab^{e} Cass Bede.
b) ἐπῆλθαν]+τινές D E e h vg cop^{G67} (sy^{p}) (sy^{hmg}) Cass Bede.

49) Acts 14:25. Ἀττάλειαν]+εὐαγγελιζόμενοι αὐτούς ("preaching the gospel to them") D d 614 383 *minn* cop^{G67} sy^{h*}.

50) Acts 15:2. Βαρναβᾷ πρὸς αὐτούς]+ἔλεγεν γὰρ ὁ Παῦλος μένειν οὕτως καθὼς ἐπίστευσαν ("for Paul spoke maintaining firmly that they should stay as they were when converted") D d gig ph q w vg^{codd} prov tepl cop^{G67} sy^{hmg} Ephr; +διισχυριζόμενος D (cop^{G67}) sy^{hmg} cf. Ephr; +οἱ δὲ ἐληλυθότες ἀπὸ Ἱερουσαλήμ D d sy^{hmg} Ephr^{cat}; cop^{G67} = "Then they who had come."

211

VI

It cannot be said, simply, that the new evidence of cop^{G67} *enhances* the quality of D as a witness to the Western text; certainly it does so at many points and in several ways, but it also discloses or confirms a number of cases where D has suffered conformation. Rather, then, this new evidence *clarifies* the rôle of Codex Bezae as a Western witness and indicates again that careful comparison of witnesses and detailed analysis of textual evidence are necessary before speaking of a reading or a text as Western. Certainly cop^{G67} places us in a vastly improved situation and will be a most valuable aid in establishing the Western text of Acts.

To a smaller degree, the two other recent discoveries, Codex 1 and sy^{msK} (referred to above), contribute also to this improved situation. The considerable agreement of cop^{G67} and 1 has been shown above, but the significance of all three new manuscripts is dramatically illustrated in Acts 10:39, where the phrase, "whom the Jews rejected," was not in D and was previously known only from t and sy^{h*}, with remnants in p* and p^{2}, and sy^{p}, but only sy^{h*} carried much weight in deciding whether it was Western. Moreover, Irenaeus, though quoting this verse, does not read the variant in question. Thus, neither Ropes (apparently), nor A. C. Clark, nor Hilgenfeld before them, considered it Western. Now suddenly three new witnesses appear, all with strong though varying Western qualities, and each of them contains this variant—one in Coptic, one in Syriac, and one in Latin, ranging from the fourth to the seventh centuries. The conclusion that this is an early Western reading can hardly be doubted.[22] Such coincidence of evidence will not often occur, but it symbolizes the remarkably improved circumstances for determining with considerable assurance the reading of the early Western text of Acts in vastly more places than was conceivable a mere two years ago.

The Syriac fragment from Khirbet Mird (sy^{msK}) calls for a further brief comment. This manuscript is extant for only two of the passages included in Petersen's list of readings from cop^{G67}, but in both cases the two manuscripts agree: in 10:39, as already noted, and in 10:33. Already this speaks clearly for the Western character of the

[22] This conclusion is the more significant to the present writer because of his view, set forth in his *Theological Tendency of Codex* Bezae, that the Western text of Acts reveals an anti-Judaic bias, and this Western variant in 10:39 is one of many that emphasize the rôle of the Jews in the crucifixion of Jesus, cf. E. J. Epp, "The 'Ignorance Motif' in Acts and Anti-Judaic Tendencies in Codex Bezae," *HTR* 55 (1962) 51–62.

tiny Syriac fragment, as Perrot noted in his edition.[23] A further analysis of the text of 10:33 shows that sy^{msK} agrees with D d p q sa^{cod}
cop$^{\text{G67}}$ sy$^{\text{h*}}$ prov in reading παρακαλῶν ἐλθεῖν πρὸς ἡμᾶς ("asking you
to come to us"); with D d in reading ἐν τάχει (a variant previously
known only from Codex Bezae); [sy^{msK} is defective for ἰδού]; it appar-
212 ently agrees with D* d c l p vg tepl sa eth arm^{osc} sy^{p} cop$^{\text{G67}}$ in reading ἐνώπιόν σου; it agrees with D* d gig sa sy^{p} in omitting πάρεσμεν
and with D* d gig l t sy^{p} in reading βουλόμενοι; it may support παρά
σου with D d gig (sy^{msK} is obscured); and, finally, sy^{msK} follows D d
P^{74} 383 p sa bo^{m} cop$^{\text{G67}}$ sy^{p} Chr *et al.* in reading θεοῦ. These constitute eight out of the nine variants between B and D in this verse,
and sy^{msK} is defective for one, possibly agrees with D and the Western
text in one, apparently agrees in another, and clearly agrees in the
remaining five.

In summary, these new manuscripts of Acts, and notably cop$^{\text{G67}}$, in a real sense open the way for a renewed and fresh investigation of the Western text of Acts and of many related questions. One of the more intriguing problems that perhaps now may be pursued with profit is that of the homogeneity of this Western text and whether or not it is the result of a process of revision. For example, of some 250 variation-units supplied by Petersen, about 40 to 50 are unique to G67 (excluding expansions of Old Testament quotations and references to Old Testament books or persons that are their sources—apparently a special tendency of the manuscript or its ancestor). How do these figures compare with other pure Western witnesses, and can a revision (or better, a recension) tolerate this ratio of unique readings and still be a recension? At the same time, it must be emphasized that a not inconsiderable number of unique readings in D, h, or other pure Western witnesses are now attested by cop$^{\text{G67}}$, and this is an indication at least that the question of homogeneity deserves further study now.

Any final answers to the various matters dealt with here must await the full publication of the Coptic manuscript, and should the other half of this Coptic Acts turn up, scholarship would be doubly enriched. Furthermore, if the similar Coptic manuscript of Matthew, which Petersen reports, should be as distinctly Western in character as that of Acts, we should have riches added to riches.

[23] Perrot, "Un fragment christo-palestinien," 535–42.

Added Notes, 2004

This paper was first presented at the invitation of the American Textual Criticism Seminar of the Society of Biblical Literature during its annual meeting at Vanderbilt University in 1965. The text-critical material from the essay was utilized as appropriate in my 1966 monograph, *The Theological Tendency of Codex Bezae Cantabrigiensis in Acts* (SNTMS 3; Cambridge: Cambridge University Press, 1966 [unchanged reprint: Eugene, Oregon: Wipf and Stock, 2001]).

English translation of D-text readings. The present reprint of "Coptic Manuscript G67," slightly corrects and supplements the textual attestation, and—to make the material more accessible—it provides additional English translations of Greek and Latin phrases and clauses. Often these are taken from Metzger's *Textual Commentary* ad loc. An English translation of Codex Bezae in Acts was published by J. M. Wilson, *The Acts of the Apostles Translated from the Codex Bezae with an Introduction on Its Lucan Origin and Importance* (London: SPCK, 1923), but Joseph A. Fitzmyer, S.J. (*The Acts of the Apostles: A New Translation with Introduction and Commentary* [AB 31; New York: Doubleday, 1998] has provided a more informed English translation of important words and phrases of the "Western" text (rather than only of Codex Bezae) in separate paragraphs (headed "WT") just beneath his section-by-section English translation of the Nestle-Aland^{27} Greek New Testament text of Acts. Fitzmyer's basis for the "Western" text is M.-E. Boismard and A. Lamouille, *Texte occidental des Actes des Apôtres: Reconstitution et réhabilitation* (2 vols.; Paris: Éditions Recherche sur les Civilisations, 1984) 1.123–226.

The text and current use of G67. The Codex Glazier (cop^{G67}), a fifth century manuscript of Acts 1:1–15:3 in Middle Egyptian, agrees with high frequency with distinctive and characteristic readings of the so-called "Western" text, so much so that it must be considered one of the primary witnesses to that text-form. G67's variants have been included in Nestle-Aland$^{26 \text{ and ff.}}$ under the symbol "mae" and in the UBS*GNT*$^{3 \text{ and ff.}}$ with the designation "meg" (*Mittelägyptische*/Middle Egyptian). Hans-Martin Schenke, though he acknowledges that I introduced the abbreviation, cop^{G67}, prefers "Codex Glazier," though B. M. Metzger uses cop^{G67} in A *Textual Commentary on the Greek New Testament* (2nd ed.; Stuttgart: Deutsche Bibelgesellschaft/United Bible Societies, 1994).

The text of G67, as noted in the preceding article, made its first appearance as a list of selected readings presented in English—about 140 passages containing some 250 variation-units, published in 1964 by T. C. Petersen (*CBQ* 26, 225–41). He died in 1966 without fulfilling his plan to publish an edition. His successor, Paulinus Bellet, appears to have completed an edition, but he died in 1987, and to date his work remains unpublished. Hence, it fell to Hans-Martin Schenke to bring an edition to light in 1991 (though he died in 2002): H.-M. Schenke (ed.), *Apostelgeschichte 1,1–15,3 im mittelägyptischen Dialekt des Koptischen (Codex Glazier)* (TU 137; Berlin: Akademie Verlag, 1991). It contains the Coptic text with a German translation. As Schenke explains, his edition emphasizes linguistic aspects of G67, while Bellet's will emphasize textual criticism—and the two editions are "meant to complement one another" (249).

The long twenty-seven year delay between Petersen's article and Schenke's edition had its controversy. Ernst Haenchen and Peter Weigandt in "The Original Text of Acts? (*NTS* 14 [1967–1968] 469–81) took Petersen's article and mine seriously to task for overstating the value of G67 as a very early "Western" (or better, D-Text) witness. Haenchen and Weigandt's concluding judgment was stated in "flowery" language:

> Thus only one conclusion seems possible to us: our manuscript is . . . a late and exotic flower in the tree of our text tradition, which soon withered and fell to the ground without bearing fruit (481).

But Schenke has had the last word, at least to date:

> While the Americans (Petersen, Epp) were inclined to stress—perhaps to exaggerate—the importance of the new witness, German scholarship (Haenchen, Weigandt, K. Aland, B. Aland) tends to minimize its relevance, for fear that this witness might be overestimated. No doubt there is some prepossession at work. And truth does not, in this case, lie in the middle, but very near to the American position. It is the conviction of the present editor . . . that the value of G67 as a witness to the western text can hardly be overrated and that its publication will change the textual basis considerably, thereby enabling a completely new approach of the whole issue of the western text of Acts (250–51).

For the larger context of the preceding discussion of G67, see the essay in the present volume on "Anti-Judaic Tendencies in the D-Text of Acts: Forty Years of Conversation" (2003), § II.A on "Coptic G67 and Petersen's Work," and § II.B on "Schenke's Critical Edition of G67."

Haenchen and Weigandt (481), however, correctly pointed to several misreadings in Petersen's study of G67, including one that I repeated in the present essay: Acts 12:1, where G67 reads "in Judaea" (along with other D-text witnesses) and not "in Jerusalem."

The dates of G67 and Codex Bezae. One more important matter requires revision: the dating of G67 and of Codex Bezae (D). Petersen and I were working with a late 4th (or early 5th) century date for G67; Schenke places it in the 5th (see Schenke, *Apostelgeschichte*, 5–6); and, at the same time, we were assuming a late 5th century date for D. That made G67 as much as a century earlier than D and accounted for the high excitement about G67 and for Petersen's claim that G67 might be the earliest "completely preserved and entirely unadulterated" witness to the "Western" text of Acts (Petersen, "Early Coptic Manuscript," 226). However, in the meantime, Codex Bezae's date has been revised to around 400 C.E., reversing the chronological relationship from what had been assumed in the mid-1960s. Though the date of the famous codex has been long debated, the meticulous volume by David C. Parker, *Codex Bezae: An Early Christian Manuscript and Its Text* (Cambridge: Cambridge University Press, 1992) 30; 281, comes down on "about the year 400" for its date of writing.

Two other similar discoveries. Coincidentally, as pointed out in the article but worthy of emphasis, two other manuscripts with strong D-text leanings appeared in the year before Petersen's essay on G67: Old Latin l (León, 7th century), published by Bonifatius Fischer, "Ein neuer Zeuge zum westlichen Text der Apostelgeschichte," *Biblical and Patristic Studies in Memory of Robert Pierce Casey* (ed. J. N. Birdsall and R. W. Thomson; Freiburg: Herder, 1963) 33–63; and a Syriac fragment from the 6th century: Ch. Perrot, "Un fragment christo-palestinien découvert à Khirbet Mird (Actes des Apôtres, X, 28–29; 32–41)", *RB* 70 (1963) 506–55. Their significance is discussed in the present essay, 203; 211–12. [See also my review of both in *JBL* 84 (1965) 172–75.]

CHAPTER THREE

THE CLAREMONT PROFILE METHOD FOR GROUPING NEW TESTAMENT MINUSCULE MANUSCRIPTS

New Testament textual critics have always welcomed with enthusi- 27
asm the discovery of a Codex Sinaiticus or of each new series of biblical papyri, such as the Chester Beatty or the Bodmer, and with each such discovery they welcome also the accompanying labors of analysis, the difficult reassessment of previously-known material, and the often painful revisions in method and theory that must be faced. In a similar way, textual critics invariably are delighted to find an early versional manuscript or that of a Church Father containing a portion of New Testament text, and they accept with pleasure the riches that are thereby added to the store of materials. But, I dare say, few indeed are the textual scholars who are elated by an additional Greek *minuscule* manuscript or who view the many hundreds of New Testament minuscules as comprising anything less than a formidable mass of vexing and insoluble problems.

Sheer quantity accounts for part of the problem. While there are presently eighty-one Greek papyri of the New Testament and 266 majuscule manuscripts, there are at last count 2754 Greek minuscules.[2] The difficulty of this minuscule problem may be indicated

---

[1] A paper first read before the Society of Biblical Literature, Pacific Coast Section, in May, 1967, with the kind permission of Messrs. Paul R. McReynolds and Frederic Wisse and the other members of the staff of the International Greek New Testament Project at Claremont, where the present writer served as Post-Doctoral Fellow and consultant during the academic year, 1966/1967. The writer's debt to these staff members and to President Ernest C. Colwell, Chairman of the American Executive Committee of the Project, will be obvious to all.

[2] These figures are the latest given by Kurt Aland, "Die Konsequenzen der neueren Handschriftenfunde für die neutestamentliche Textkritik," in K. Aland, *Studien zur Überlieferung des Neuen Testaments und seines Textes* (ANTF 2; Berlin: De Gruyter, 1967) 183. The figures below for the year 1909 are from Frederic G. Kenyon, *Handbook to the Textual Criticism of the New Testament* (London: Macmillan, 1912[1]) 57, 128–29 [1926[2]]. [For current figures, see K. Aland, *Kurzgefasste Liste der griechischen Handschriften des Neuen Testaments* (ed. Kurt Aland; ANTF 1; Berlin: De Gruyter, 1994[2]); for P100–P115, majuscules 0307–0309, minuscules 2857–2862, and lectionaries *ll* 2404–2412, see H. Kunst, *Bericht der Hermann Kunst-Stiftung zur Förderung der neutestamentliche Textforschung für die Jahre 1995 bis 1998* (ed. Hermann Kunst;

also in the following comparative figures: in 1909, only fourteen papyri were known, but these have increased in number nearly 600%, and the extensive energy devoted to their analysis in recent years is not surprising; likewise, majuscule manuscripts have increased by nearly 60%. This means that textual critics have for generations been confronted by this burdensome mass of manuscripts, and yet—with one notable exception—they have failed or been unable to prosecute a broad scale methodological effort directed toward the sorting and classification of this massive and intractable complex.[3]

The one exception, of course, was the work of Hermann von

Münster/W.: Hermann Kunst-Stiftung 1998) 14–18; for P116, majuscules 0310–0316; minuscules 2863–2877; and lectionaries *ll* 2413–2432, see *Bericht der Hermann Kunst-Stiftung zur Förderung der neutestamentliche Textforschung für die Jahre 1998 bis 2003* (Münster/W.: Hermann Kunst-Stiftung 2003) 74–79.]

[3] The current work on "1000 minuscules examined in 1000 passages" at the Münster Institut für neutestamentliche Textforschung can hardly qualify as classification of the minuscules, for its aim is to show which manuscripts belong to the Byzantine text so that they "may be henceforth neglected" in establishing the original text: see K. Aland, "The Significance of the Papyri for Progress in New Testament Research," *The Bible in Modern Scholarship: Papers Read at the 100th Meeting of the Society of Biblical Literature, December 28–30, 1964* (ed., J. Philip Hyatt; Nashville/New York: Abingdon, 1965) 342–44; K. Aland, "Konsequenzen der neueren Handschriftenfunde," 194–96. The publication of these data could aid a later process of classification, but it may be that the variants chosen will be unsuitable for the detailed analysis demanded.

[The preceding statement was, in retrospect, overly pessimistic. The Münster Institut, over the past thirty-five or more years has pursued the analysis of New Testament by the use of test passages, not only to exclude those manuscripts deemed "of no value for reconstructing the original text and its early history," but also to examine "the remaining manuscripts for their interrelationships, establishing families and groups among them where possible" (Kurt Aland and Barbara Aland, *The Text of the New Testament: An Introduction to the Critical Editions and to the Theory and Practice of Modern Textual Criticism* [tr. Erroll F. Rhodes; Grand Rapids: Eerdmans; Leiden: Brill, 1989^2] 318; see the description of their method, by B. Aland, ibid., 317–37). In the process, the Alands, through the Münster Institut für neutestamentliche Textforschung, have produced an enormous amount of valuable data: *Text und Textwert der griechischen Handschriften des Neuen Testaments* (ed. K. Aland; ANTF 9–11 [Catholic Epistles, 3 vols. in 4, 1987]; 16–19 [Pauline Epistles, 4 vols., 1991]; 20–21 [Acts, 2 vols., 1993]; 26–27 [Mark, 2 vols., 1998]; 28–29 [Matthew, 2 vols., 2003]; 30–31 [Luke, 2 vols., 2003]; Berlin/New York: de Gruyter, 1987–2003).

For assessment, see Bart D. Ehrman, "A Problem of Textual Circularity: The Alands on the Classification of New Testament Manuscripts," *Bib* 70 (1989) 381–88; W. Larry Richards, "Test Passages *or* Profiles: A Comparison of Two Text-critical Methods," *JBL* 115 (1996) 251–69; idem, "A Closer Look: *Text und Textwert der griechischen Handschriften des Neuen Testaments: Die Katholischen Briefe*," *AUSS* 34 (1996) 37–46; and idem, "An Analysis of Aland's *Teststellen* in 1 John," *NTS* 44 (1998) 26–44.]

Soden, which appeared between 1902 and 1910 as part of the voluminous prolegomena to his critical edition of the New Testament.[4] It is well known that von Soden classified all the textual witnesses under one of three recensions or text-forms, I, H, or K. Beyond this broad grouping, von Soden further subdivided the K and I forms 28
into such groups as K^1, K^i, K^x, and K^r; I^α, I^η (with further subgroups), I^ι (with subgroups), I^φ (with subgroups), I^β (with subgroups), I^o, I^π, I^σ, I^κ (with subgroups), and I^r. The details of these classifications and subclassifications for the Gospels may be found in some 500 large and closely-packed pages of volume two in the three-volume prolegomena,[5] and the enormity of von Soden's achievement can be grasped when it is recognized that he classified, under the K and I text-forms, more than 1260 minuscules of the Gospels out of the nearly 1350 known to him. A count of Gospel minuscules known as of 1963 comes to about 2000, which means that von Soden classified approximately sixty-three per cent of all the minuscules of the Gospels available to us now. Yet, as will appear presently, von Soden's specific classifications did not always have a sufficient basis, nor were they always determined by a uniform or consistent method. In spite of this qualification and regardless of what may be said of the details of von Soden's group-classifications, it is none the less abundantly clear that his work has, since his day, formed the basis for all classification of minuscule manuscripts, and his groupings and their symbols have, almost without exception, been employed whenever a new manuscript has been classified; moreover, it may also be stated that, in general terms, von Soden's groupings, wherever tested, have held up remarkably well in the face of analysis. This statement, as already intimated, needs to be qualified in precise terms later, and it is essential also to emphasize that this affirmation of the general validity of von Soden's judgments on *groups* should by no means be understood as approval of his broader textual theory involving the I-H-K text, or as approval of the symbols by which he designated the smaller groups, if these symbols are understood as he intended them—that is, within the context of and in accordance with his textual theory. In other words, what has stood the test of time is the

[4] H. von Soden, *Die Schriften des Neuen Testaments in ihrer ältesten erreichbaren Textgestalt hergestellt auf Grund ihrer Textgeschichte* (2 parts in 4 vols.; Göttingen: Vandenhoeck & Ruprecht, 1911^2–1913).

[5] Ibid., 712–893 = K; 1041–1358 = I.

general integrity of the individual, smaller groups, and only that; the identifications with certain text-forms or recensions, or the indications of intra- and inter-group relationships that the group designations convey, are open to serious question at many points, but the isolation, homogeneity, and independent existence of most of his small groups and often also of his subgroups as individual groups have become contributions of abiding value.

When this has been said, several questions immediately come to the forefront: What precisely is von Soden's system or method for arriving at groups? On the basis of von Soden's work, could suitable representatives of each group, and thus suitable representative minuscule manuscripts of the New Testament as a whole, be selected quickly and conveniently from the mass of manuscripts for use in a critical apparatus? Do his groupings readily lend themselves to testing at any desired point, and do they provide for the easy classification of newly-found and previously unclassified manuscripts?

The answer to the first question carries with it the answer to the other two: apparently von Soden began to investigate, in a systematic fashion, the text of the μοιχαλίς (= μ) or *pericope adulterae*, and he produced a *stemma* consisting of seven textual forms derived from the original of the pericope. This analysis may well have provided
29 the clue for his procedure in grouping manuscripts,[6] but only a very few groups that were arrived at on the basis of the μοιχαλίς also fall into the same groupings under his I or K text-forms[7] Apart from the μοιχαλίς, then, von Soden apparently had neither a systematic nor a consistent means for arriving at his groupings; certainly he did not have a *rigidly* consistent or a *rigidly* systematic method, or if he did it is no longer obvious in his work, for even a superficial examination of his data shows at once that manuscripts were collated in varying places and with various degrees of completeness. For instance, some manuscripts were collated word for word and completely; some only in one Gospel or two (and not always the same one or two); some only in one chapter of one or more Gospels, others in several chapters; some closely-related manuscripts were collated in entirely different passages; some groups were identified on the basis of a few

[6] Von Soden also used lectionary apparatus as an aid in classification.

[7] I^{β} is one example, though even here the weaker half of the group has variant forms of μ. See von Soden: 1159–60; cf. 504–5, 1152.

selected chapters in Mark (as was the I^{φ} group), but other groups on the basis of broader or different samplings; and, finally, some manuscripts were collated only "cursorily" in longer or shorter passages. Indeed, if there was any consistent system of collation and sampling in von Soden's study, it is perhaps now to be seen only in the fact that certain chapters of the Gospels appear frequently in the lists of collated passages, for example, Matthew 1, 5, 15, 21; Mark 10, 11, 12; Luke 7, 8; John 6, 7, and so forth.

Thus, while von Soden left us with a series of groups and with lists of manuscripts that were strong and pure or weak and mixed members of those various groups, he did not leave us with either clear-cut principles or precise means for understanding, describing, or identifying the distinctive characteristics of a given group, nor did he leave with us a ready and convenient method for classifying any given additional minuscule manuscript. (If it should be suggested that the critical apparatus of his text-volume provides such a means for identifying group-readings and then classifying further manuscripts, it is sufficient, in reply, merely to point to the incompleteness and inconsistency in the citation of manuscript evidence and to the extensive inaccuracy of his apparatus. Moreover, von Soden's apparatus in the Gospels contains the evidence of only about 100 minuscule manuscripts representing the numerous I groups, of merely five minuscules of the K^{1} group, and of no specific minuscules of the K^{i}, K^{x}, or K^{r} groups.)

A rigid consistency in choosing his sample passages for collation would have been a step in the right direction, but his lack of this consistency and the sheer mass of his data leave us frustrated, bewildered, and without an easily accessible stepping stone to further progress. Those, like E. C. Colwell, David Voss, Kirsopp and Silva Lake, Jacob Geerlings, and others,[8] who have tested the integrity of some of von Soden's groups or made further group identifications,

[8] See, e.g., Kirsopp Lake, Robert P. Blake, and Silva New [later, Silva Lake], "The Caesarean Text of the Gospel of Mark," *HTR* 21 (1928) 207–404; Silva New, "A Patmos Family of Gospel Manuscripts," *HTR* 25 (1932) 85–92; E. C. Colwell, *The Four Gospels of Karahissar* (2 vols.; Chicago: University of Chicago Press, 1936), vol. 1, on Fam 2327 and Fam 574; Silva Lake, *Family Π and the Codex Alexandrinus: The Text according to Mark* (SD 5; London: Christophers, 1937); David Voss, "Is von Soden's K^{r} a Distinct Type of Text?" *JBL* 57 (1936) 311–18; K. Lake and S. Lake, *Family 13 (The Ferrar Group): The Text according to Mark, with a Collation of Codex 28 of the Gospels* (SD 11; London: Christophers, 1941); Jacob Geerlings, *Family 13—The*

have done so only by taking von Soden's data as a mere starting point and working out a systematic and consistent testing procedure. But perhaps we are ungrateful if we expect von Soden to have given us more than the data for a starting point, for the provision of a base and a place to begin is itself a significant contribution.

30 Recently the IGNTP has also taken its starting point from von Soden, for one of the critical problems facing the Project—and one that confronts every *apparatus criticus*—is what to do with the mass of minuscule manuscripts. To cite them all *and* completely could be defended as an ideal, but there are also weighty theoretical considerations against such a procedure, to say nothing of the time-consuming task of accumulating hundreds and hundreds of full collations and the problems of editing and printing the volumes of additional data thereby produced. Clearly some other procedure must be adopted. To eliminate from the critical apparatus all of the estimated 2400 minuscules that represent the Byzantine text, as Professor Kurt Aland proposes for his edition (a more extreme measure than von Soden adopted), makes little if any contribution to the study of the history of the text in the Byzantine period.[9] No, the answer to the problem of the minuscule manuscripts in a critical apparatus must be *selection in the interest of providing appropriate representation.* Such appropriate representation could involve the use of several criteria, such as the age of manuscripts, place of origin and geographical distribution, and the inclusion of dated manuscripts, but the most obvious primary consideration should be adequate representation of all known groups of manuscripts as determined by their textual character. Certainly a collection of suitable examples of minuscule manuscripts

Ferrar Group: The Text according to Matthew (SD 19; Salt Lake City, UT: University of Utah Press, 1961); idem, *Family 13—The Ferrar Group: The Text according to Luke* (SD 20; Salt Lake City, UT: University of Utah Press, 1961); idem, *Family 13—The Ferrar Group: The Text according to John* (SD 21; Salt Lake City, UT: University of Utah Press, 1962); idem, *Family Π in Luke* (SD 22; Salt Lake City, UT: University of Utah Press, 1962); idem, *Family Π in John* (SD 23; Salt Lake City, UT: University of Utah Press, 1963); Russell Champlin, *Family Π in Matthew* (SD 24; Salt Lake City, UT: University of Utah Press, 1964); J. Geerlings, *Family E and Its Allies in Mark* (SD 31; Salt Lake City, UT: University of Utah Press, 1968); idem, *Family E and Its Allies in Luke* (SD 35; Salt Lake City, UT: University of Utah Press, 1968); Russell Champlin, *Family E and Its Allies in Matthew* (SD 28; Salt Lake City, UT: University of Utah Press, 1966).

[9] See n. 3, above [and the corrective update].

selected for their date, provenance, and textual complexion, each cited in full in the *apparatus criticus*, would constitute a gold mine of information for the historian of the Byzantine text and would also provide a reasoned, balanced, and adequate sampling of this wide-ranging late text of the Greek New Testament. (This selection of minuscules for the critical apparatus would, of course, be additional to the full citation of all Greek papyri and uncials, and additional to an adequate selection of lectionary,[10] patristic, and versional evidence, which together would constitute the full *apparatus criticus* proposed by the International Greek New Testament Project.)

The general history of the IGNTP is well known—alas! perhaps too well known—for the optimistic hopes expressed in 1945 before the Society of Biblical Literature, when the project was approved by that Society, indicated that an "exhaustive . . . critical apparatus to the four Gospels" was to be prepared and "ready for publication within the period of a decade."[11] Such prospects, renewed and updated from time to time, unfortunately have not been realized, nor is the first volume on Luke ready to be published now some twenty years after the formal launching of the Project.[12] Prospects of material support and enthusiastic cooperation by many scholars largely justified the early optimism. Subsequently, however, financial and other problems have seriously impeded progress, but I would venture to say that the failure to find a way to untie the Gordian knot of the minuscule complex of manuscripts has perhaps as much as any other single

[10] The Greek lectionaries, incidentally, may pose a problem similar in many ways to that of the minuscules, for there are now 2135 lectionaries of the New Testament [see n. 2 above], and these need to be sorted and classified. Indeed, this appears to be the next major task facing the staff of the Project, and such work is now under way. [See now Ernest C. Colwell, Irving Alan Sparks, Frederik Wisse, and Paul R. McReynolds, "The International Greek New Testament Project: A Status Report," *JBL* 87 (1968) 188–91; and American and British Committees of the International Greek New Testament Project, ed., *The New Testament in Greek: The Gospel according to St. Luke: Part One: Chapters 1–12. Part Two: Chapters 13–24* (Oxford: Clarendon Press, 1984–1987) 1.vi, xi.]

[11] "Proceedings, 1945" of the Society of Biblical Literature, *JBL* 65 (1946) ii.

[12] Others might date the Project from 1942 rather than 1945; others from 1948, when it was endorsed by the American Textual Criticism Seminar and (again) by the SBL; see "Proceedings, 1948," *JBL* 68 (1949) xxv; "Proceedings, 1949," 69 (1950) ii–iii; xxv–xxvi; and Merrill M. Parvis, "The International Project to Establish a New Critical Apparatus of the Greek New Testament," *Crozer Quarterly* 27 (1950) 302–3. [The two-volume critical apparatus of Luke finally was published in 1984–87 (see n. 10, above).]

factor—and surely more than any other *methodological* factor—prevented the desired progress in completing the new apparatus.

While the adjectives "exhaustive," "complete," and "comprehensive" in early descriptions of the proposed critical apparatus obviously were hyperbolic, by at least 1950 it was clear that, in addition
31 to the full citation of all papyri and all uncials, "enough minuscule manuscripts [would be cited] to give an adequate representation to every known text-type, family or subfamily, as well as to any such groups as may be discovered in the course of our work."[13] By the middle 1950s, two principles had been stated for the selection and inclusion of minuscule data: the apparatus would take account of (1) "the Greek manuscripts which belong to some already established family or subfamily"; and (2) "the Greek manuscripts which show relevant divergence from the late Byzantine text."[14] Following the lines of these earlier statements, three principles for the selection of minuscules were approved in the autumn of 1966 at a joint meeting of the British and American Committees of the Project: (1) all known groups should be adequately represented; (2) some manuscripts should be included that throw light on the history of the text in the Byzantine period; and (3) some minuscules should be selected that are akin to early witnesses.[15] It was subsequently estimated that 300 minuscules would be the highest number feasible for inclusion.

But how is it to be determined which minuscules best or adequately represent the known groups? What, indeed, is adequate representation of a group—are only the purest or strongest members to be included, or also some weak, peripheral, and mixed members? Are the so-called known groups in fact demonstrable as groups? How is it to be decided which manuscripts throw light on the history of the Byzantine text? And how, except by full collation, are minuscules that show kinship to early witnesses to be isolated? Questions such as these faced the staff of the Project in the autumn of 1966, and we found ourselves in a most difficult—indeed, an impossible—situation. We were expected, in order to produce an *apparatus criticus*, to answer in advance the very questions that the *apparatus criticus* was

[13] Parvis, "International Project," 307.

[14] M. M. Parvis, "Greek's Not Greek to Them," *Emory Alumnus* (December, 1955) 9.

[15] Minutes of the joint meeting held at Selwyn College, Cambridge, September 5–7, 1966.

designed to answer; we were required to determine *in advance* the very groupings from which appropriate and representative examples could be selected for an apparatus that was designed, in part, to provide a basis for such a determination of groupings; we were expected to delve into the history of the Byzantine text in order to provide materials suitable for the eventual understanding of its complex history. In short, we were preparing a critical apparatus that was designed to be a half-way house toward the solution of numerous textual questions, including the vexing minuscule problem, but we were being forced, by the impossibility of including all the data, to draw conclusions that could properly be drawn only from the material of our own completed project!

Nevertheless, the Claremont staff of the Project turned its attention to the various criteria for the selection of minuscule manuscripts, in the hope that, by happenstance, an adequate representation would emerge. Dated manuscripts were deemed important for unraveling the history of the Byzantine text, as were manuscripts that could be identified with specific localities or scriptoria, and certain wild, independent, mixed, or otherwise unusual manuscripts were considered for inclusion in the select list of perhaps 300 minuscule manuscripts for Luke. But more important and more difficult was the examination of von Soden's groups—and of the work of scholars building upon his classifications—in an effort to isolate the most appropriate representatives of each. The method here was basically that employed
by von Soden but much more clearly exemplified in the work of 32
the Lakes, of Voss, and others, namely the identification of distinctive group-readings for each suspected group and, on the basis of such an analysis, the isolation of the best representatives.

Early in November, 1966, when this work was substantially complete for most groups, President Colwell and Professor Clark reported, as they had been requested to do by the American and British Committees, on proposed criteria for the selection of minuscules *outside* of established groups and of minuscules that are akin to early witnesses. They suggested that a single criterion would be sufficient—a simple "quantitative measurement of the amount of variation from the *Textus Receptus*."[16] President Colwell had earlier published several

[16] Letter of President Colwell to Members of the Executive Committee of the Project, dated 7 November 1966.

methodological treatises on quantitative measurement (two with Ernest W. Tune),[17] and thus the Claremont staff prepared to test various manuscripts to determine their distance from the *textus receptus*.

Claremont's answer to the minuscule problem arose, it seems to me, out of the confluence of these two procedures: (1) the search for the best representatives of known groups, with the accompanying identification of group-readings, and (2) the quantitative measurement of minuscules in terms of their distance from the *textus receptus*. First, the three graduate students working with the Project investigated the various known groups under procedure one, with procedure two in the background. Paul McReynolds, a Graduate Assistant in the Project, had undertaken the study of the K groups of von Soden, and, by good fortune, was compiling information concurrently on all four K groups; since the collation-base for the Project is the *textus receptus* (Oxford, 1873 edition), McReynolds placed in juxtaposition the information for the four groups as they were related to the *textus receptus*, and this provided ready ground for the observation by Frederik Wisse, a graduate student who had volunteered a considerable amount of time to the Project, that the group-readings, as determined for von Soden's groups and subgroups, revealed distinctive patterns in terms of their relationship to or distance from the *textus receptus*. Wisse had himself worked extensively on several of the I groups, and he and McReynolds had observed that the older procedure of identifying distinctive readings for each group was helpful but, by itself, not adequate as a grouping methodology, for distinctive readings—where they existed at all—were generally few and far between for most groups, and any random sampling technique, even though the sample consisted of a long passage, was likely to

[17] E.g., Colwell, "The Significance of Grouping of New Testament Manuscripts," *NTS* 4 (1957/58) 73–92 [repr. as "Method in Grouping New Testament Manuscripts," in Colwell, *Studies in Methodology in Textual Criticism of the New Testament* (NTTS 9; Leiden: Brill, 1969) 1–25]; "Method in Locating a Newly-Discovered Manuscript within the Manuscript Tradition of the Greek New Testament," *SE* 1 (1959) 757–77 [repr. in Colwell, *Studies in Methodology*, 26–44]; Colwell and Tune, "The Quantitative Relationships between MS. Text-types," *Biblical and Patristic Studies in Memory of Robert Pierce Casey* (ed. J. N. Birdsall and R. W. Thomson; Freiburg/Basel/New York: Herder, 1963) 25–32 [repr. as "Method in Establishing Quantitative Relationships between Text-Types of New Testament Manuscripts," in Colwell, *Studies in Methodology*, 56–62]; Colwell and Tune, "Variant Readings: Classification and Use," *JBL* 83 (1964) 253–61 [repr. as "Method in Classifying and Evaluating Variant Readings," in Colwell, *Studies in Methodology*, 96–105].

be inconclusive. If, on the other hand, a group pattern of readings, not necessarily unique to but characteristic of each group, could now be determined from a selected sample passage consistently examined in numerous manuscripts, perhaps a usable method could be fashioned. Thus, they devised a series of test-readings in Luke, chapter 1, which took into account all of the variant readings of all of the majuscules and some 180 minuscule manuscripts of Luke. To qualify as a test-reading, a variant from the *textus receptus* had to have the support of a two-thirds majority of the members of some known group (i.e., some previously identified group, usually one of von Soden's). Admittedly, there is a certain arbitrariness in this method of selecting the test-readings; for one thing, the test-readings were taken from variants in perhaps only nine or ten percent of the total 33
number of minuscules of the Gospels. Is it not possible, then, that some variation-units that would be significant for such a testing have been overlooked because they do not happen to occur in this small portion of manuscripts?

In reply, two things can be said: (1) First, the previous assessment of the holdings of the Project in terms of adequate representatives of all known groups gave assurance that the Master File of the Project contained a satisfactorily representative selection, at least in so far as the earlier methods could ascertain. (2) Second, the Byzantine manuscripts together form, after all, a rather closely-knit group, and the variations in question within this entire large group are relatively minor in character. It is possible, of course, that some group-readings have been missed in the ten percent sampled; but the danger is nothing like that of selecting, say, ten percent of the papyri or of the majuscules and basing a methodology of grouping on these selected few, for in that case it is probable that manuscripts like P^{75}, ℵ, B, D, Θ, or W might one or even all be overlooked. The minuscules, however, stand in a different situation: if von Soden is generally correct in his isolation of groups (as we have affirmed earlier), then the vast majority of minuscules are of the K^x and K^r type (which stand nearest to the *textus receptus*), and the percentage of manuscripts in the I group and in the other K groups that are in the files of the Project is proportionately very, very much greater than for the vast K^x and K^r groups. This is added assurance that hardly any readings that stand at any considerable distance from the *textus receptus* are likely to have been overlooked in the selection of test-readings. Subsequently, in fact, the actual investigation of manuscripts not already in the Master File demonstrated that very few new readings were uncovered by adding full collations of new manuscripts.

A further aspect of arbitrariness could be found in the fact that von Soden's groupings provided the general limits for the selection of test-readings: only those readings were retained that were supported by at least two-thirds of the manuscripts in our files that belonged to some identifiable group, and these identifiable groups were usually von Soden's. Is it not possible, then, that additional or different groupings exist that will now be even further obscured? Again, it is possible but unlikely (in view of what has been said above) that such additional group-readings have been missed; nor does the use of previously identified groups as a base preclude the discovery, from these test-readings, of new groups or of new arrangements of groups, for the test-readings measure relative distance from the *textus receptus*.[18] Thus, from the data that the test-readings provide, it should be possible to arrive at any actually existing pattern of groupings, for broadly representative test-readings, even though derived from previous groupings, do not predetermine the groups themselves. Furthermore, unlike many sampling procedures, the density of test-readings per sentence or verse is very high—so high that it is inconceivable that a group as yet unknown could exist without eventually silhouetting itself in an identifiable pattern against these test-readings.

34 Finally, in defense of the test-readings, it should be emphasized that the method about to be described is itself to some considerable extent self-sharpening and self-corrective, especially with reference to determining primary and secondary readings for specific groups; that is to say that, as more and more manuscripts are examined, the ever-increasing data reveal that certain test-readings lose their status as primary readings for a given group and become secondary readings for that group (though remaining primary readings for other groups), or move from secondary readings to primary, or in another group may lose entirely their position as characteristic readings for that particular group.

[18] Any objection to the use of the *textus receptus* as a standard in this process will not be well founded, for the same relative patterns should emerge regardless of the standard, although the use of something like Codex Vaticanus would unduly complicate matters, for the standard in this case would be unnecessarily remote from the text whose characteristics are being examined.

McReynolds and Wisse found that in the first chapter of Luke, sixty-one variants qualified as test readings. The reading of each collated manuscript in the Project's files was then checked at these sixty-one places, and each agreement was recorded on a tally sheet by a simple "X" mark—and each disagreement, conversely, by the absence of a mark—producing for each manuscript a pattern of its agreement and disagreement with these test-readings, and soon it was possible to plot a configuration or profile of the readings characteristic of each of the various groups that emerged. Some fourteen distinct groups finally appeared, each with a distinctive profile of readings.

It is important to emphasize that the profile-method is based not on the determination of *distinctive* readings for each group, but upon the identification of *characteristic* readings for each group; that is, each group reveals a distinctive profile that is formed by the readings characteristic of but not necessarily distinctive to that group. Thus, some of the test-readings are shared by many or by nearly all groups, others by several or by two or three, and still others are found only in the manuscripts of a single group (and then are distinctive readings for that group), but it is the overall, distinctive *profile* or configuration emerging from the characteristic readings that is the genius of the method.

A method now had been born that appeared promising indeed, for if it could be validated it would mean that any given manuscript could be examined in a relatively small number of predetermined and systematically selected places, and its resulting textual profile—and therefore its textual character—could, in most cases, be almost instantly identified with that of an established group, or, if its profile did not match or show a close relationship to a known group, manageable data would be in hand for further group classification as the body of information expanded.

The developing method was carefully scrutinized by the full Claremont staff of the Project, namely, President Ernest C. Colwell, who is Chairman of the American Executive Committee of the Project, Mr. Alan Sparks, a graduate student and Administrative Assistant for the Claremont branch, Messrs. McReynolds and Wisse, and the present writer, as a member of the Committee on Straight-Text Greek Manuscripts and special consultant to the Project. It was the consensus of the group that not one chapter of Luke but three should be employed, so as to give the sampling procedure a broader base and also to allow to each manuscript a three-fold verification

of a group identification. In addition to Luke 1, chapters 10 and 20
35 were selected. Chapter 10 produced sixty-seven test-readings, while seventy-nine appeared in chapter 20, and profiles for each of the fourteen groups so far identified were constructed for each of the additional test chapters. It is sufficient here to say that the use of chapters 10 and 20 quite strikingly confirms the results reached on the basis of chapter 1; or, to put it differently, individual manuscripts, except where they contain block or "box-car" mixture, quite consistently receive the same group designation in each of the three test chapters, and the same manuscripts quite consistently fall together into the same groups in each of the three chapters. In those cases where a manuscript conforms to one group in one chapter, but to some extent moves away from that group in another, the third test area is available as a deciding factor. It should be noted also that while some fourteen groups have clearly and decisively emerged, there still are some manuscripts that defy classification at this time. When sufficient instances have come to light and can be analyzed, it is to be hoped that some further group classifications will be feasible.

It has not been my intention to expose the details of this rather sophisticated profile-method, for that privilege must be reserved for the two young scholars who developed the method, who did all the detailed and exacting work, and who endured the tedium of such an investigation. Rather, it has been my aim only to set down something of the broad background out of which the method arises, to place the method in its more immediate context of the IGNTP, to describe ever so briefly the instrument itself, and, finally now, to emphasize some facets of its immediate and practical usefulness as well as its more far-reaching significance.

First of all, it should be obvious enough that the Claremont profile-method has important implications for and applications to the Project's proposed *apparatus criticus*, for it should now be possible to examine, in the space of perhaps two hours, any manuscript or microfilm of a manuscript containing Luke (and later of other portions of the New Testament)[19] and to determine with relative ease and considerable certainty its group identity. Hundreds of manuscripts can now

[19] Appropriate series of test-readings will presumably be drawn up for Matthew, Mark, John, and eventually other sections of the New Testament as the Project moves to these areas. If the group designations resulting from the application of

be scanned, and the entire minuscule mass should become amenable to a long-overdue sorting process. As a result, much of the log jam of minuscules should break up, clearing the way not only for speedier completion of the proposed critical apparatus, but providing also a significantly less fortuitous selection of minuscules for that apparatus.

The method has other practical applications. For instance, the K^x and K^r types of manuscripts, which stand nearest to the *textus receptus*, are doubtless already represented adequately in the files of the Project, and the profile-method allows those who are searching for and microfilming additional manuscripts to use short-cuts in identifying these K^x and K^r manuscripts, which can then be passed by in favor of manuscripts that will be of greater immediate interest. Thus, it can be determined from the K^x and K^r profiles that if a manuscript has more than six of the test-readings in Luke 1, or more than ten in Luke 10, it is not K^x or K^r and should be microfilmed;
or, if a manuscript lacks a specified test-reading in Luke 1, it should 36
be microfilmed regardless of other readings, and so forth. On the other hand, if it should at any time be deemed a necessary or desirable task, the profile-method will readily allow for determining the "best" K^x or K^r manuscripts and lends itself also to determining further inner groupings or finer distinctions within these groups (or any other).

But what of the more far-reaching significance? For one thing, the profile-method has already called for certain adjustments, on solid grounds, in von Soden's classifications. The specific conclusions must await an official presentation of the method by its originators, but the following generalizations may be offered here: to date, two of von Soden's (minor) groups have been eliminated, since they reveal no distinctive pattern; also, one subgroup has disappeared because four-fifths of its members fall into other groups; the subgroups in another group were not sustained, for subgrouping was found to be superfluous within the closely-knit larger, original group; and a number of individual manuscripts have been reclassified. On the other hand, many of von Soden's groupings and classifications have been

---

the method in Luke are generally borne out in, say, one test chapter in John, then perhaps only a rather limited further testing—such as a single chapter in each Gospel—will be necessary for the Gospels. The implicit assumption is that in most cases the results in Luke will be valid at least for the Gospels in any minuscule, but this is an assumption whose correctness needs to be demonstrated.

strikingly confirmed, including designations of groups, subgroups, and individual manuscripts.

In broader terms, finally, it would appear that the Claremont profile-method for grouping New Testament minuscule manuscripts may well mark the turning point in the study of this class of Greek witnesses to the New Testament text, for it offers, as has nothing previously, a consistent and systematic method for classifying minuscules and, in addition, recognizes the all-important methodological principle that both agreements and disagreements between manuscripts, as well as between groups, must be fully taken into account and measured. If the optimism expressed here needs to be tempered with caution, it should be understood, naturally, that the profile-method requires further and final testing and possibly refinement, calls for detailed explication and defense, invites the provocation of every possible criticism, and in the end, of course, must stand the test of further scholarly judgment. Nevertheless, when the method's practical usefulness and immediate application are added to its wide-ranging and long-term methodological significance, any description other than "major breakthrough" would appear to be less than adequate.[20]

---

[20] [In the years following the completion of this journalistic report, Paul R. McReynolds and Frederik Wisse published brief reports: Wisse and McReynolds, "Family E and the Profile Method," *Bib* 51 (1970) 67–75; McReynolds, "The Value and Limitations of the Claremont Profile Method," *SBLSP* 1 (1972) 1–7; and "Establishing Text Families," *The Critical Study of the Sacred Texts* (ed. Wendy Doniger O'Flaherty; Berkeley, CA: Berkeley Religious Studies Series, 1979) 97–113; and Wisse published a full explication of the method: *The Profile Method for the Classification and Evaluation of Manuscript Evidence as Applied to the Continuous Greek Text of the Gospel of Luke* (SD 44; Grand Rapids, MI: Eerdmans, 1982).

Refinements and critiques of the "Claremont Profile Method" (now a well-established designation) include W. Larry Richards, *The Classification of the Greek Manuscripts of the Johannine Epistles* (SBLDS 35; Missoula, MT: Scholars Press, 1977) esp. 131–36; 207–9; idem, "A Critique of a New Testament Text-critical Methodology—the Claremont Profile Method," *JBL* 96 (1977) 555–66; idem, "Manuscript Grouping in Luke 10 by Quantitative Analysis," *JBL* 98 (1979) 379–91; idem, "An Examination of the Claremont Profile Method in the Gospel of Luke: A Study in Text-Critical Methodology," *NTS* 27 (1980/81) 52–63; idem, "Gregory 1175: Alexandrian or Byzantine in the Catholic Epistles?" *AUSS* 21 (1983) 155–68; idem, "Test Passages *or* Profiles: A Comparison of Two Text-Critical Methods," *JBL* 115 (1996) 251–69; idem, "An Analysis of Aland's *Textstellen* in 1 John[1]," *NTS* 44 (1998) 26–44; O. M. Kvalheim, D. Apollon, and R. H. Price, "A Data-Analytical Examination of the Claremont Profile Method for Classifying and Evaluating Manuscript Evidence," *SO* 63 (1988) 133–44; Bart D. Ehrman, "The Use of Group Profiles for the Classification of New Testament Documentary Evidence," *JBL* 106 (1987) 468–71; idem, "Methodological Developments in the Analysis and Classification of New

Added Notes, 2004

Recent developments. Facilitated by a mutual desire for cooperation after years of competition and by enhanced computer capabilities, the IGNTP and the Münster Institut für Neutestamentliche Textforschung signed a joint agreement in October 2000 to collaborate fully on the Editio Critica Maior of the Gospel of John. The two projects would maintain their separate identities, but the IGNTP would no longer insist that the apparatus be displayed under the *textus receptus*, and the Institut would agree to a joint comparison and assessment of both the Claremont Profile Method and their own use of Teststellen and the COLLATE computer program for grouping Johannine manuscripts. See further the essay, below, on "The International Greek New Testament Project: Motivation and History," *NovT* 39 (1997) 1–20.

Testament Documentary Evidence," *NovT* 29 (1987) 40–44; idem, "A Problem of Textual Circularity," 377–88, esp. 381–88; Thomas C. Geer, Jr., "Analyzing and Categorizing New Testament Greek Manuscripts: Colwell Revisited," *The Text of the New Testament in Contemporary Research: Essays on the* Status Quaestionis (SD 46; ed. B. D. Ehrman and M. W. Holmes; Grand Rapids, MI: Eerdmans, 1995) 253–67, esp. 257–58; and David C. Parker, "A Comparison between the *Text und Textwert* and the Claremont Profile Method Analyses of Manuscripts in the Gospel of Luke," *NTS* 49 (2003) 108–38.]

CHAPTER FOUR

THE TWENTIETH CENTURY INTERLUDE IN NEW TESTAMENT TEXTUAL CRITICISM

The W. H. P. Hatch Memorial Lecture, The Society of Biblical Literature, 11 November 1973, The Palmer House, Chicago, Illinois.

I. Introduction 386

At the time of his death, William Henry Paine Hatch (2 August 1875–11 November 1972) had been a member of the Society of Biblical Literature for sixty-seven years—longer than any other living person—and doubtless was the oldest current member of the Society. When he served as president of SBL in 1938, he already had been on the membership rolls for thirty-three years. Our purpose here, however, is not to recount or to assess the life and work of this distinguished American textual critic,[1] instructive as that approach might be, but Professor Hatch's long life coincides almost exactly with the period of New Testament textual criticism that I wish to examine, for he was born within a year of Tischendorf's death (which occurred 7 December 1874); in the same year as the death of S. P. Tregelles (1875); and at the time when Westcott and Hort were in the late stages of their nearly thirty-year project to produce the text of the New Testament "in the original Greek," which finally was published in 1881—when Hatch was just six years

[1] Nearly all of Hatch's published volumes dealt with manuscripts of the Greek New Testament or with Syriac manuscript studies, as did many of his articles. A bibliography of his writings appeared in the *Festschrift* for his 70th birthday, *Munera studiosa* (eds. M. H. Shepherd, Jr. and S. E. Johnson; Cambridge, MA: Episcopal Theological School, 1946) 179–82. Something of the significance of Hatch's work for New Testament textual criticism may be indicated by the index to B. M. Metzger's *The Text of the New Testament* (2d ed.; New York: Oxford University Press, 1992), for here Hatch is referred to 15 times [13 times, though it should be 14, in the 3d ed., 1992], while no other scholar, including the great figures of the field, is referred to more than 11 times.

old. As all will recognize, Tischendorf, Tregelles, and Westcott-Hort were among the foremost figures in the final overthrow of the tyrannical *textus receptus* in favor of older and better New Testament manuscripts (though, as a matter of fact, Karl Lachmann some fifty years earlier—in 1831—had effected the first clean break with the *textus receptus*). Simply stated, an old era had come to its end, the era of the *textus receptus*, and a whole new era of New Testament textual criticism had been fully established in the last decades of the nineteenth century, culminating in the work of Westcott-Hort; and the lifetime of our distinguished—and lamented—contemporary, W. H. P. Hatch, bridges that period between the self-confident, optimistic,
387 and resolute textual criticism of the late nineteenth and early twentieth centuries and the diffuse, indeterminate, and eclectic New Testament textual criticism of our own present and recent past. Indeed, I have ventured to call this latter period the twentieth century interlude in New Testament textual criticism, and I use the term "interlude," not in its everyday sense as a period of waiting between two events, often with the implication of merely marking time or of inactivity, but in its classical meaning in theater and music as a performance between the acts of a play or the parts of a composition.

To characterize twentieth century textual criticism as an interlude is, on the one hand, to suggest something negative: it affirms that the critical work of the period is not a main feature, but a subsidiary or a secondary and minor performance following a portion of the main event. On the other hand, there is a positive aspect, for interlude implies—if not demands—that another major act is to follow, and it is this to which the interlude leads and for which it prepares. It does not mean inactivity, but if it is a pause or an interval, it is a meaningful and preparatory pause.

Certainly for New Testament textual criticism the twentieth century has been anything but a period of inactivity. To attempt here a survey of this period in terms either of its rich yield of new manuscripts or manuscript studies or its extensive bibliographical contributions not only would be inappropriate but would be too easy a way out and would fail to strike at the central issues. Yet the productivity of the period is obvious from mere mention, e.g., of the Oxyrhynchus papyri (1896 ff.), the Chester Beatty papyri (1930–31), and the Bodmer papyri (1956 ff.), which together represent a 600% increase over the number of New Testament papyri known at the turn of the century. This productivity is evident also in the isolation of the lectionary text and the wide-ranging work on the versions, and by recalling the tedious labors expended for the production of new critical editions. All of this amounts to a sizable achievement, involving the tireless efforts of hundreds of scholars, not the least of whom were W. H. P. Hatch and other members of our own Society past and present. Clearly, it is not my intention to minimize or to denigrate these numerous and worthwhile accomplishments; yet the twentieth century, as far as we have lived and worked in it, has been an *interlude* between the grand achievement of Westcott-Hort and whatever significant second act is to follow. What that succeeding act might be or ought to be will occupy us presently, but that it has not occurred in the years since Westcott-Hort must be established first.

II. Evidences of the Interlude

A. *Lack of Progress in Popular Critical Editions*

The first and clearest indication that we have passed through and still find ourselves in an interlude is found in the critical hand-editions of the New Testament produced since Westcott-Hort. There have been many, but nine or ten stand out as the most widely known and used, and they are the following, listed in the chronological order of their first editions:

1. R. F. Weymouth, 1886. 388
2. B. Weiss, 1894–1900.
3. Eberhard Nestle, 1898–1912, lst to 9th eds.; Erwin Nestle, 1914–1952, 10th–21th eds.; Erwin Nestle and K. Aland, 1956–1963, 22nd–25th eds.
4. British and Foreign Bible Society, 1904 [= Nestle, 4th ed.]; 2nd ed. by G. D. Kilpatrick, 1958.
5. A. Souter, 1910; revised ed., 1947.

[6. Hermann von Soden, 1913—not a hand-edition, though a smaller edition of the text with a short apparatus appeared the same year.]

7. H. J. Vogels, 1920 (+ Vulgate 1922); 4th ed., 1955.
8. A. Merk, 1933; 9th ed., revised, 1965; 10th ed., 1984.
9. J. M. Bover, 1943; 5th ed., 1968.
10. United Bible Societies' *Greek New Testament*, 1966; 2d ed., 1968; 3d ed., 1975.

Most would agree that, besides the Westcott-Hort text, the various editions of Nestle (and Nestle-Aland) have received the greatest use in the past generation, though Souter has had wide usage in England and in Anglican circles, and the editions of Vogels, Merk, and Bover have served Catholic scholars; in our own day, Nestle-Aland and the recent UBS *Greek New Testament* are the leading critical hand-editions of the Greek New Testament.

When these most popular editions are analyzed and compared, the first surprise is that two of them, Vogels and Souter—even in their later editions—side with the *textus receptus* in textual character rather than with Westcott-Hort (or with Nestle-Aland) and belong, therefore, to the old era of the *textus receptus* rather than to the current period of textual criticism. This is shown, for example, by K. W. Clark's test of Mark 1–5, where Souter showed 191 differences from Westcott-Hort, of which 168 were *textus receptus* readings, and where Vogels showed 103 differences from Westcott-Hort, of which seventy-five were *textus receptus* readings. It is shown also by J. Harold Greenlee's comparison of five current critical texts with the *textus receptus* in eleven chapters from various sections of the New Testament; the differences from the *textus receptus* were as follows: Nestle-Aland = 233; Merk = 160; Bover = 111; Vogels = 67; and Souter = 47, showing Vogels and Souter strikingly close to the *textus receptus* when compared with Nestle-Aland.[2] Other tests show similar results.[3] Thus,

[2] K. W. Clark, "The Effect of Recent Textual Criticism upon New Testament Studies," *The Background of the New Testament and its Eschatology* (eds. W. D. Davies and D. Daube; Cambridge: Cambridge University Press, 1956) 31–33. Clark reports a more recent test, with similar results, in "Today's Problem with the Critical Text of the New Testament," *Transitions in Biblical Scholarship* (ed. J. C. Rylaarsdam; Chicago: University of Chicago, 1968) 158–60. Greenlee's study is reported by K. Aland, "The Present Position of New Testament Textual Criticism," *SE* I (1959) 719–20. (It should be noted that a simple counting of gross differences from the *textus receptus*, or any standard, is considered now a questionable procedure; rather, the variation-units common to two or more of all the members in the comparison must be determined and total agreement and disagreement taken into account—see below.)

[3] Aland ("The Present Position," 720–21) compares the Markan text in four current editions with Westcott-Hort, and—counting significant variants—the differences from Westcott-Hort are as follows: Vogels = 239; Bover = 160; Merk = 128; and Nestle-Aland = 65, implying that Vogels is significantly closer to the *textus receptus* than, e.g., Nestle-Aland (on the reasonable assumption that Westcott-Hort and the *textus receptus* are at opposite poles). Another comparison reported by Aland ("Der heutige Text des griechischen Neuen Testaments," in his *Studien zur Überlieferung des Neuen Testaments und seines Textes* [Berlin: de Gruyter, 1967] 59–61) shows that through-

we may safely disregard the texts (though not the apparatuses) of 389
Souter and Vogels, for they show insufficient signs of having participated in the Lachmann/Westcott-Hort overthrow of the *textus receptus*.

The Nestle-Aland, Merk, and Bover editions form a group fairly close to Westcott-Hort in textual character, and among them Nestle-Aland is the closest to Westcott-Hort. This is demonstrated, again by K. W. Clark, in a comparison throughout Mark of the 21st edition of Nestle (1952) with Westcott-Hort, which revealed only eighty-nine variants between the two texts; yet of these only thirty-two were "substantial" and only twelve involved a difference in meaning. He reports, curiously enough, that of the seventy-five changes made in the text of Mark through twenty-one editions of Nestle (1898 to 1952) thirty-five were restorations of Westcott-Hort readings. Clark's conclusion, on the basis of Mark, is that the 1952 Nestle "still rests heavily upon Westcott-Hort".[4] Kurt Aland made a similar comparison of Nestle-Aland^{25} with Westcott-Hort and with the latest editions of Merk and Bover, and he reached a similar result: when Nestle-Aland^{25} is compared with texts such as those of von Soden, Vogels, and even Tischendorf, the texts of Bover, Merk, and Westcott-Hort are markedly closer to Nestle-Aland^{25} than are the others, and of the group consisting of Bover, Merk, and Westcott-Hort, it is Westcott-Hort that is the nearest to Nestle-Aland^{25} in its textual character. The statistics show that throughout the New Testament von Soden is farthest from Nestle-Aland^{25}, with 2047 variants; then Vogels with 1996; then Tischendorf with 1262; then Bover with 1161; Merk with 770; and finally Westcott-Hort with only 558 variants from Nestle-Aland.[5] An earlier comparison of significant variants in the Markan text of Westcott-Hort with those of the Nestle-Aland^{25}/Merk/Bover cluster yielded the following results: Bover showed 160 differences from Westcott-Hort; Merk 128; but Nestle-Aland^{25} only sixty-five differences from Westcott-Hort [Vogels showed 239 variations and may serve as a control].[6] The conclusion is clear: These

---

out the New Testament Westcott-Hort has 558 variants from Nestle-Aland, while Vogels has 1996 variants from Nestle-Aland. (Bover shows 1161, and Merk 770 variants from Nestle-Aland.)

[4] Clark, "The Effect of Recent Textual Criticism," 34–35.

[5] Aland, "Der heutige Text," 59–61.

[6] Aland, "The Present Position," 721. The same cluster (Nestle-Aland/Merk/Bover)

three most widely used Greek New Testaments of the mid-twentieth century (Nestle-Aland, Merk, and Bover) "show little change from Westcott-Hort and only rarely present a significant variant".[7]

If one now considers the recent and increasingly widely used UBS
390 *Greek New Testament*, it will be observed at once that its editors began their work on the basis of Westcott-Hort[8] and that the text of the UBS edition is close to the text of Codex Vaticanus (B)[8]—Westcott-Hort's primary manuscript—and close, therefore, to Westcott-Hort's text.[9]

What all of this means is that none of the currently popular hand-editions of the Greek New Testament takes us beyond Westcott-Hort in any substantive way as far as textual character is concerned, for two of them stand—anachronistically—with the *textus receptus*, which was the Westcott-Hort opposition, and the others stand with Westcott-Hort. What progress, then, have we made if "even the modern editions which claim to break new ground still in general present the text of Westcott-Hort?".[10] We are compelled to face the simple but pointed question: Is it adequate to have as our best New Testament text one that, in essence, is more than ninety years old? Westcott-Hort's text was based (a) on no papyrus manuscripts, whereas more than eighty of these early witnesses now are available; (b) on perhaps forty-five uncials, whereas nearly 270 of these important documents now are known; (c) on about 150 minuscules [though more were known], whereas now the number is approaching 2800; and (d) on an unknown, but small, number of lectionaries, whereas more than 2100 have now been catalogued. Moreover, since Westcott-Hort's day, our knowledge of ancient versions and patristic quotations has been advanced significantly.

Some of us were startled at the one-hundredth meeting of the SBL in 1964 when Kurt Aland employed what seemed to be an overly dramatic conclusion to his paper on "The Significance of the

---

emerges when distance from the *textus receptus* is tested; see the statistics of Greenlee, cited above.

[7] Clark, "The Effect of Recent Textual Criticism," 36.

[8] Kurt Aland, Matthew Black, Bruce M. Metzger, and Allen Wikgren, eds., *The Greek New Testament* (Stuttgart: American Bible Society, British and Foreign Bible Society, National Bible Society of Scotland, Netherlands Bible Society, Würtemberg Bible Society, 1966[1]) v.

[9] I. A. Moir, "The Bible Societies' Greek New Testament," *NTS* 14 (1967–68) 136–43.

[10] Aland, "The Present Position," 721.

Papyri for Progress in New Testament Research." His final sentences were: "*None* of us would entrust himself to a ship of the year 1881 in order to cross the Atlantic, even if the ship were renovated or he was promised danger money. Why then do we still do so in NT textual criticism?"[11] The question, however, *was* appropriate then; unfortunately, now—nearly a decade later—it is still both a valid and an embarrassing question.

B. *Lack of Progress toward a Theory and History of the Earliest New Testament Text*

One response to the fact that our popular critical texts are still so close to that of Westcott-Hort might be that the kind of text arrived at by them and supported so widely by subsequent criticism is in fact and without question the best attainable New Testament text. Yet every textual critic knows that this similarity of text indicates, rather, that we have made little progress in textual *theory* since Westcott-Hort; that we simply do not know how to make a definitive determination as to what the best text is; that we do not have a 391
clear picture of the transmission and alteration of the text in the first few centuries; and, accordingly, that the Westcott-Hort kind of text has maintained its dominant position largely by default. Günther Zuntz enforces the point in a slightly different way when he says that "the agreement between our modern editions does not mean that we have recovered the original text. It is due to the simple fact that their editors . . . follow one narrow section of the evidence, namely, the non-Western Old Uncials".[12] This lack of progress toward a theory and history of the earliest New Testament text is a second strong indication that the twentieth century has been an interlude in New Testament textual criticism.

The quest for the early history of the text of the New Testament has its own and surprisingly inconclusive history. The process of

[11] *The Bible in Modern Scholarship* (ed. J. P. Hyatt; Nashville: Abingdon, 1965) 346; the article was updated in "Die Konsequenzen der neueren Handschriftenfunde für die neutestamentliche Textkritik," *NovT* 9 (1967) 81–106, repr. in Aland's *Studien zur Überlieferung des Neuen Testaments und seines Textes* (Berlin: de Gruyter, 1967) 180–201, though without this concluding illustration.

[12] G. Zuntz, *The Text of the Epistles: A Disquisition upon the* Corpus Paulinum. Schweich Lectures, 1946 (London: British Academy by Oxford University Press, 1953) 8.

sorting and grouping the thousands of manuscript witnesses to the New Testament text is fundamental to the discovery of its history and development, and such groupings have been attempted ever since J. A. Bengel in 1725 proposed a classification of the textual witnesses into "companies," "families," "tribes," and "nations" so that manuscripts could be "weighed" for their evidential value rather than merely counted. As new manuscript discoveries were made, particularly discoveries of early uncials, the grouping of manuscripts led to the separation of the relatively few early manuscripts from the mass of later ones, and eventually the process reached its climactic point of development and its classical statement in the work of Westcott and Hort (1881–1882), and particularly in their [actually Hort's] clear and firm view of the early history of the New Testament text. This clear picture was formed from Hort's isolation of essentially three [though he said four] basic textual groups or text-types. On the basis largely of Greek manuscript evidence from the middle of the fourth century and later and from the early versional and patristic evidence, two of these, the so-called Neutral and Western text-types, were regarded as competing texts from about the middle of the second century, while the third, now designated Byzantine, was a later, conflate and polished ecclesiastical text. The lateness of the Byzantine text-type was established from test passages in which the Byzantine variants represent a conflation of the Western and the Neutral [i.e., Alexandrian/Egyptian] variants and from the fact that the Greek and Latin Fathers up to the middle of the third century support one or another of the pre-Byzantine texts, but do not support the conflate Byzantine variants or any other distinctively Byzantine readings; the logical conclusion was that the Byzantine text had not yet been formed by the middle of the third century.[13] This left essen-

[13] B. F. Westcott and F. J. A. Hort, *The New Testament in the Original Greek* (Cambridge/London: Macmillan, 1881–82), 2.91–119. NOTE: The Westcott-Hort terms "Neutral" and "Western" are used throughout this paper for convenience, though in full recognition of their inadequacy. The most common alternative for "Neutral" is "Alexandrian," though "Beta" is preferred by some; the "D-text" and "Delta" have been proposed in place of "Western," but neither they nor any other terms have been successful in supplanting the only partially accurate "Western." [On terminology, see now E. J. Epp, "The Significance of the Papyri for Determining the Nature of the New Testament Text in the Second Century: A Dynamic View of Textual Transmission," *Gospel Traditions in the Second Century: Origins, Recensions, Text, and Transmission* (ed. W. L. Petersen; Christianity and Judaism in Antiquity, 3; Notre Dame, IN: University of Notre Dame Press, 1989) 84–88; 92–100.]

tially two basic text-types competing in the earliest traceable period 392
of textual transmission, the Western and the Neutral, but this historical reconstruction could not be carried farther so as to reveal—on historical grounds—which of the two was closer to and therefore more likely to represent the original New Testament text.

Actually, Hort made it quite clear that "the earliest readings which can be fixed chronologically" belong to the Western text and, moreover, that "the most widely spread text of Ante-Nicene times" was the Western.[14] Now, when he argues that the text-groups that can be documented as pre-Byzantine are closer to the original than is the Byzantine, his argument is convincing; however, it requires some elaborate gymnastics in argumentation to move then, as he does, to the contention that the earliest attested text, the Western, is *not* closer to the original than is the Neutral, whose documentation is in fact later. Anyone who looks again at Hort will observe that he presents his case in such a way as to prejudice his readers against the Western text (by describing it as given to paraphrase and as otherwise corrupt) well before he discusses the "pure" or Neutral text from the standpoint of its historical reconstruction. Hence, when Hort has worked back to a situation sometime in the second century when an early Western text was competing with an early Neutral text, and when historical reconstruction fails to yield a solution, subjective (or "internal") judgments enter to render a decision as to whether the Western or the Neutral is superior in the quality of its text and therefore closer to the original. The same test of "prevailing internal excellence"[15] that was used negatively to discredit the Western is now applied to the Neutral, with the result that "certain peculiar omissions excepted, the Western text is probably always corrupt as compared with the Non-Western text."[16] What we see, then, is that Westcott-Hort's text is (a) based partly on a clearly delineated view of the history of the New Testament text—two early texts competing in the second century church,[17] one corrupted by paraphrastic expansions and the other virtually untouched in its course of transmission

[14] Westcott-Hort, *New Testament in the Original Greek*, 2.120; cf. 126.

[15] Ibid., 2.193.

[16] Ibid., 2.194.

[17] See ibid., 2.112–13, 222–23, where the 2nd, and at times the early 2nd, century is in view.

from the original—and (b) based partly on subjective judgments about the respective quality of those earliest texts.

The pointed question for us is what methodological advance have we made over this scheme? Tedious and impressive labors have been expended since 1881 on the great Neutral uncials, B and ℵ; a small library has been produced on the Western centerpiece, Codex Bezae (D), and on its Old Latin and Old Syriac allies; vigorous and lengthy debates have focused on the originality of Neutral versus Western variants; and numerous new discoveries have been brought to bear on these several questions. Yet, nearly a century later we still affirm the general superiority of the Neutral text-type and the generally
393 secondary character of the Western, and we do so largely on the same grounds as did Hort: a similar picture of the early history of the text and a similar subjective judgment about the respective quality of the two early text-groups.

If these statements appear too sweeping and somewhat oversimplified, it should be added at once that even the discovery of P^{75}, so extraordinarily significant in several respects, does not—as many seem to think—solve this puzzle of Neutral versus Western, nor does it in this respect carry us beyond Westcott-Hort. P^{75} takes us back to about 200 C.E. and shows us a text—as much of it as we have—that is virtually identical with the mid-fourth century Codex B. To be sure, we have no extant Greek or versional manuscripts of this early date on the Western side, though we do have quotations from some of the Patristic writers of this period, which—with all their complications and without getting into the vexing complexities of the Old Syriac and Old Latin as witnesses to an early Western text—are perhaps evidence enough of a second century Western text. Even with P^{75}, then, we still can move no farther back with a historical reconstruction than Hort did. We can say with confidence, of course, that B faithfully represents a text extant, not only in 350, but already around 200, but P^{75} does not answer the question whether this B-type of text (now including P^{75}) does or does not represent a recension; twentieth century scholarship had viewed B as the product of a fourth century recension,[18] and P^{75} rules this out; yet the B-text may represent a late second century recension—or it may not. The

[18] See Clark, "The Effect of Recent Textual Criticism," 37.

question is pushed back, but not settled by P^{75}. We are still faced, as were Westcott-Hort, with two early, competing texts whose epicenters are represented in B (or now P^{75}) and in D.[19] How is this in any essential and substantive way an advance beyond Westcott-Hort?

Someone will remind us, however, that a fourth major text-type, the Caesarean, was isolated two generations after Westcott-Hort and will suggest, first, that this provides further material for reconstructing the early history of the New Testament text and, secondly, that its discovery represents significant progress not only in the history, but also in the theory, of the text. Certainly the studies in and around the Caesarean text have contributed immensely to our knowledge of individual manuscripts and of some families, but it is my contention that the Caesarean text affair is another and rather striking evidence that the twentieth century has been an interlude in New Testament textual criticism.

This was indicted already in 1945 by Bruce Metzger in his concise and incisive survey of the development and criticism of the Caesarean text when he concluded that "it must be acknowledged that at present the Caesarean text is disintegrating."[20] A major reason for such a conclusion was the growing recognition—encouraged
most notably by Ayuso's work—that what had been called the 394
Caesarean text by Streeter, the Lakes, and others must be divided into (1) a primitive, pre-Caesarean text and (2) a recensional, or properly Caesarean text, each of which shows cohesion and homogeneity within itself, as well as a close relationship with the other.[21] This, essentially, is where the matter has rested for the past thirty-five years. Most recently, however, a 1973 dissertation by Larry W. Hurtado appears to demonstrate that at least in Mark (where most of the work on the Caesarean text has been done) the validity of this earlier or pre-Caesarean text as a distinct text-type is seriously—and I think convincingly—called into question.[22] This, of course, is

---

[19] B. M. Metzger (*ExpT* 78 [1966–67] 374) remarks that "the general lineaments of the textual theory of Westcott and Hort have been confirmed rather than weakened by the discovery of P75."

[20] B. M. Metzger, "The Caesarean Text of the Gospels," *JBL* 64 (1945) 483; reprinted, with some updating to about 1960, in his *Chapters in the History of New Testament Textual Criticism* (NTTS 4; Leiden: Brill, 1963), see p. 67.

[21] I rely on Metzger (*Chapters*, 63–64, 124–26).

[22] L. W. Hurtado, "Codex Washingtonianus in the Gospel of Mark: Its Textual Relationships and Scribal Characteristics" (Cleveland: Ph.D. dissertation, Case Western

not a new view, for two decades ago C. S. C. Williams, for example, offered his opinion that "any hopes . . . that here [in the Caesarean manuscripts] we should find a pre-Byzantine textual type independent of and as valuable as the 'Western' and the Alexandrian [or Egyptian = Neutral] seem now very remote";[23] furthermore, a decade ago, before this very Society, Kurt Aland expressed his judgment that no Caesarean text-type existed.[24] Nevertheless, Hurtado's more cautious conclusion is based not only on the latest quantitative methods for determining manuscript relationships, but also on collations and analyses *throughout* Mark and not merely in sample chapters; therefore, the negative conclusions concerning the Caesarean text receive both a broader and firmer basis than previously possible. Hurtado's study focuses on the Washington Codex (W) in Mark, which traditionally has been classified as Caesarean in 5:31–16:20 and has been taken, along with P[45], fam. 1, and fam. 13, as a leading witness to the pre-Caesarean text. At the same time, Codex Koridethi (Θ) has been taken as the leading member of the later or Caesarean text proper. His thorough quantitative analysis shows that W and Θ, assessed chapter by chapter in Mark, have an average agreement in chapters 5 through 16 of 40%, far below the 70% established norm for significant intra-text-type relationship,[25] which means that if Θ is a good representative of the Caesarean text, then W cannot be a Caesarean witness. Furthermore, the element common to Θ and W is mainly Western in its character, with the result that both show considerable affinity with D, the leading Western witness: W and D show an average agreement through all the chapters in Mark of 40% (36% in chapters 5–16), while Θ and D show an average agreement of 48% (51% in chapters 5–16). This means that if W, with its 39% average agreement with Θ throughout Mark

Reserve University, 1973). [Published later as, *Text-Critical Methodology and the Pre-Caesarean Text: Codex W in the Gospel of Mark* (SD 43; Grand Rapids, MI: Eerdmans, 1981).]

[23] C. S. C. Williams in his revision of A. H. McNeile, *An Introduction to the Study of the New Testament* (2nd ed. revised; Oxford: Clarendon, 1953) 389.

[24] Aland, "The Significance of the Papyri," 337.

[25] Hurtado relies on the general quantitative method and criteria of Ernest C. Colwell (with Ernest W. Tune), "Method in Establishing Quantitative Relationships between Text-types of New Testament Manuscripts," in Colwell, *Studies in Methodology in Textual Criticism of the New Testament* (NTTS 9; Leiden: Brill, 1969) 56–61; and Colwell, "Hort Redivivus: A Plea and a Program," ibid., 163.

(and 40% in chapters 5–16), were to be classified as a Caesarean
witness, D would be a better Caesarean witness![26] Moreover, the 395
nearly 50% agreement between Θ and D might suggest that Θ should
be taken as a secondary witness to the Western text.[27]

Secondly, the quantitative relationships among W, P^{45}, and fam. 13 are such that, in 103 variation-units where P^{45} is extant in Mark 6–9, W and P^{45} show a 68% agreement; W and fam. 13 show a 60% agreement in these same variation-units, and for P^{45} and fam. 13 the figure is 59%; no other control manuscript shows more than 42% agreement with either W or P^{45} in this section of Mark. In chapters 5–16 of Mark, W and fam. 13 show a 55% agreement; but notice that fam. 13 also shows a 55% agreement with the *textus receptus*—56% over all of Mark; but only a 46% agreement with Θ; 33% with B; and 32% with D.

All these figures suggest that W and P^{45} are primary members of a text-group (since their agreement approaches the 70% norm), while fam. 13 is (at best) a loose third member.[28] These figures mean, furthermore, that W and P^{45} (and fam. 13) do not have a significantly close relationship with the so-called Caesarean text of Θ, that they represent "in no way an early stage of the text of Θ,"[29] and that the term "pre-Caesarean" is inappropriate and should be abandoned. In short, the so-called "pre-Caesarean" witnesses are neither pre-Caesarean nor Caesarean at all.[30] It has, of course, been argued by others that the Caesarean text was not Caesarean,[31] but our concern is not with the name or its geographical appropriateness; rather, Hurtado's point—and ours—is that the so-called "pre-Caesarean" witnesses are not related significantly to the so-called "later Caesarean" witnesses, with the result that the P^{45}-W line of text has no continuity with the

[26] Hurtado, "Codex Washingtonianus," 130–31. The percentages have been recalculated from his charts, 267–74. [See now, Hurtado, *Text-Critical Methodology and the Pre-Caesarean Text*, 24–45, esp. 43–45; 81–89.]

[27] Hurtado, "Codex Washingtonianus," 245; 249. [See now, Hurtado, *Text-Critical Methodology and the Pre-Caesarean Text*, 44–45; 86–87.]

[28] Hurtado, "Codex Washingtonianus," iii. [See now, Hurtado, *Text-Critical Methodology and the Pre-Caesarean Text*, 63; 65–66.] Hurtado does not treat fam. 1.

[29] Hurtado, "Codex Washingtonianus," 251; cf. 191–92; 248. [See now, Hurtado, *Text-Critical Methodology and the Pre-Caesarean Text*, 24; 43–45; 65.]

[30] Hurtado, "Codex Washingtonianus," 191–92; 251. [See now, Hurtado, *Text-Critical Methodology and the Pre-Caesarean Text*, 88–89.]

[31] Cf., e.g., E. C. Colwell, "Method in Establishing the Nature of Text-Types of New Testament Manuscripts," in Colwell, *Studies in Methodology*, 54.

Θ-line of text and, furthermore, that the P^{45}-W line stops with W and leads no farther.

If, however, these former Caesarean witnesses are not Caesarean, what are they? Codex Θ, as we have seen, drifts off toward the Western camp; fam. 13 drifts off distinctly toward the Byzantine text when compared with the leading Neutral and Western representatives; and W and P^{45} constitute a textual group with no close relationship (a) to the Neutral text (P^{45} and B have a 42% agreement; W and B show a 34% agreement in Mark 5–16, 32% overall), or (b) to the Western text (P^{45} and D have a 38% agreement; W and D 36% in Mark 5–16, 40% overall), or (c) to the Byzantine (P^{45} and the *textus receptus* have a 40% agreement; W and the *textus receptus* show a 38% agreement in Mark 5–16, 36% overall), though Hurtado thinks he can argue that the P^{45}-W kind of text is basically and was originally—that is, in its early stages of development—nearer to the Neutral, and that it later developed toward the Byzantine type (as
396 evidenced by fam. 13).[32] Regardless of this last point, the result in broad strokes reveals, first, a disintegrating Caesarean text, with its presumed components falling back into place among the other established text-groupings, and show us, secondly, an early kind of text (P^{45} with W) which is almost equidistant in its agreement from those textual types designated Neutral and Western. Every contemporary textual critic knows that to locate a manuscript or a text-type by describing it as "midway" between Neutral and Western is no way to determine a manuscript's relationships or to define a text-type; if any did not know this, Colwell made the point in a forceful manner fifteen years ago in his much-used article on "Locating a Newly-Discovered Manuscript"[33] Nevertheless, the quantitative demonstration of this midway position of P^{45}-W—a distinctive textual pair—does support in a rather striking way the 1961 proposition, also of Colwell, that the so-called "pre-Caesarean" text is "a proto-type, an early stage in the process which produced the mature Beta [= Neutral] and Delta [= Western] text-types."[34] This observation undoubtedly

[32] Hurtado, "Codex Washingtonianus," iii, 250. [See now, Hurtado, *Text-Critical Methodology and the Pre-Caesarean Text*, 88–89.]

[33] Colwell, "Method in Locating a Newly-Discovered Manuscript within the Manuscript Tradition of the Greek New Testament," *SE* I (1959) 757–77; reprinted in his *Studies in Methodology*, 26–44; see 36–37.

[34] Colwell, "Method in Establishing the Nature of Text-Types," 54.

is correct; the mistakenly designated pre-Caesarean witnesses attest one kind of text—a "midway" text—that existed in that early period when the Neutral and Western texts represented the competing extremes of a spectrum of texts whose intervening members in varying degrees shared the characteristics of each extreme.

What, then, is our picture of the earliest documented century or two of the New Testament text? Were there text-types or not? Kurt Aland denies that *any* text-types existed in that early period in Egypt, where virtually all the papyri were found, because he thinks that the New Testament papyri show that *numerous* distinctive texts existed side by side in the same area in the same period. Hence, Aland views P^{45}, P^{46}, P^{66}, P^{75}, and the other early papyri as representatives of these numerous individual texts—but not text-types—that were to be found in the second and third centuries.[35] Such a view would seem to take us beyond, or perhaps behind, Westcott-Hort in the sense that Hort's two early text-types have been replaced by many texts. But is Aland correct in this view, and does it really move us beyond Westcott-Hort, as Aland claims? As is so often the case, we are indebted once again to Ernest Colwell for pointing out that Hort, in his basic theory of the text and its history, allowed for a range of early texts by his insistence on an early ancestor for the Neutral text (something perhaps like our P^{75}), an archetype of an early revised form of the Neutral text (perhaps like our P^{66}?), and an early ancestor for the Western text (maybe something like our P^{45}?).[36] It seems
clear, then, that Aland's claim[37] that the discovery of early papyri 397
invalidates Westcott-Hort's whole scheme and places us in an entirely new situation is not well founded; rather, the papyri provide hard documents to replace, roughly speaking, a number of Hort's theoretical ones.

What picture emerges, then, of the first two centuries of New Testament textual transmission? It can be argued, I think, that text-types, as Hort conceived them, surely were in the process of development

[35] Aland, "The Significance of the Papyri," 334–37; cf. Colwell, "Method in Establishing the Nature of Text-Types," 55, who says that ". . . very few, if any, text-types were established by that time [200 C.E.]."

[36] Colwell, "Hort Redivivus," 156–57; Westcott-Hort, *New Testament in the Original Greek*, 2.122; 220–23.

[37] Aland, "The Significance of the Papyri," 336–37; contrast his earlier view ("The Present Position," 721–22, 730–31), implying that little if any progress had been made and that we stand within the Westcott-Hort era.

and did exist, for when we survey this period from 200 to 300 C.E. we find a series of papyri, notably P45, P46, P66, and P75, but also fragments of many others, to which should be added some early uncials, such as 0171, 0189, 0212, and 0220, all dated within the third century.[38] Actually, there are thirty-one papyri of the Gospels, Acts, or Epistles that quite certainly can be dated 300 or earlier, thirty-seven if those of the third/fourth century are included, and four uncial fragments from the second and third centuries.[39] It would be unwise to claim definitive identifications of textual character on the basis of a few variants in a dozen lines of text, which themselves are often incomplete, yet most of these papyri have been identified variously as Neutral (notably P75, but also the fragmentary P1, P4, P13, P15, P16, P20, P23, P28, P39, P40, P49, P52, P64, P65, and P67), or as Western (the fragmentary P5, P29, P37, P38, P48, and also 0171), or as midway between (notably P45, P46, and P66, and the fragmentary P22, P27, P30, P32, P53, P69, and P72) in terms of their textual character.[40]

Although we are told that text-types, subsequent to the discovery of these early witnesses, should no longer be classified according to the much later codices B and D, it is true none the less that our extant materials and our much enhanced hindsight reveal *only two clear textual streams or trajectories* through all of our material from the first four centuries or so of textual transmission, and these two trajectories are what we have long called the Neutral (or Alexandrian/Egyptian) and the Western text-types. The Neutral line is the clearest, plotted first from P75, then perhaps through P23, P20, 0220, P50,

[38] 0171 is now dated 300; in addition to the fragments containing Luke 21:45–47, 50–53; 22:44–56, 61–63, additional portions of this manuscript have been identified, containing several verses from Matthew 10; see K. Aland, "Die griechischen Handschriften des Neuen Testaments," *Materialen zur neutestamentliche Handschriftenfunde* I (ed. K. Aland; Berlin: de Gruyter, 1969) 8; the manuscript was published by K. Treu ("Neue neutestamentliche Fragmente der Berliner Papyrussammlung," *APF* 18 [1966] 25–28), who dates it ca. 300. Manuscript 0189 has been redated 2nd/3rd century by C. H. Roberts (see Aland, *Materialen*, 8).

[39] The dates are those accepted by Aland (*Studien zur Überlieferung*, 104–6). Papyri of the Apocalypse, of which two are from this early period, are not included, nor is the Apocalypse taken into account in any of our preceding discussions.

[40] I simply have taken over the classifications of Metzger (*Text of the New Testament*, 247–55), though I have held to H. A. Sanders's judgment ("An Early Papyrus Fragment of the Gospel of Matthew in the Michigan Collection," *HTR* 19 [1926] 223) that P37 is Western. [See now the caveats in the Added Notes to "The Significance of the Papyri for Determining the Nature of the New Testament Text in the Second Century," below.]

etc., to Codex B and thence on through the centuries, e.g., to Codex 398
L (eighth century), minuscules 33 (ninth century), 1739 (tenth century), and 579 (thirteenth century). The Western line takes us, e.g., from P^{48} and P^{69} through P^{38}, and 0171, then to codices D and D_p, and thence on through the centuries to F_p and G_p (ninth century) and minuscules 614 and 383 (thirteenth century). The other extensive and early papyri (P^{45}, P^{46}, P^{66}, and also the others in the "midway" category) stand between these extremes and, as far as we know, develop no "midway" trajectories of their own, except for P^{45}, which leads abortively to Codex W, though that line leads no farther (as we have seen). Rather, beginning perhaps in the general period of Codex W (ca. 400), the two extremes of the early spectrum, namely the Neutral and the Western, became confluent, producing a form of text represented in the gospel portion of Codex Alexandrinus (A, fifth century) and forming the Byzantine line that carries on through the centuries, e.g., in the uncials Ω, V, H_a, H, L_{ap}, S, and most of the minuscules. Naturally, this rough sketch should not be understood to mean that the manuscripts mentioned under each of the three categories above necessarily had any *direct* connections one with another; rather, they stand as randomly surviving members of these three broad streams of textual tradition. Moreover, this sketch does not include the versions or the patristic witnesses, which—as suggested earlier—could reasonably locate some additional early points, especially on the Western textual trajectory.

Now, to argue as we have in terms of recognizable textual streams or trajectories—which can be plotted from known points and also can point backwards from them—may not in any way *prove* that text-types (as we commonly define that term) existed in the period of 200 to 300 or so, but the perspective that is provided by these extended trajectories (and the lack of one in the "midway" category) is a valuable aid to sorting out the wide range of texts in the earliest documented period and in determining (albeit by hindsight) the extent to which these various early texts were utilized and the relative degree of influence that they brought to bear on the developing lines of New Testament textual transmission. Is it mere accident that our spectrum of the earliest texts, comprised of some forty papyri and uncials from around 300 C.E. and earlier, issues in *only two* distinct lines of development, each at one extreme of that spectrum? Some will say "Yes," but I would suggest, rather, that the sorting process, of which only a portion remains open to our view, functioned as though it were under some centrifugal force and resulted in the concentration and consolidation of textual masses at the outer—and opposite—edges of the textual spectrum. The reasons for this may be obscure, but the phenomenon itself is visible enough.

To be sure, the question of originality is not aided materially by this approach, for we cannot move easily behind the series of earliest papyri to the situation in the first century or so after the writing of the Gospels, Acts, and Epistles, although the citations in the sub-Apostolic church writers may be of some help in that direction. Hence, the question that faced Westcott-Hort remains for us: Is the original text something nearer to the Neutral or to the Western kind of text? And what about the development of these two competing
399 text-types? Did the range of early texts now available to us develop laterally, starting from something like P^{75}, then undergo changes toward texts like those in P^{45}, P^{46}, and P^{66}, and finally yield a Western text (through, e.g., P^{48}, P^{69}, P^{38}, and 0171) like that of Codex D? Or, was the original text at the Western extreme and did it then move laterally in the other direction toward something like P^{75}? Or, as a third model, was the original one of those "midway" texts something like P^{45} or P^{66}, and did it develop in two lateral directions—toward the Neutral on the one hand and toward the Western on the other? This is where we stand, and this is precisely where Westcott-Hort stood; Hort resolved the issue, not on the basis of the *history of the text*, but in terms of the presumed *inner quality* of the texts and on grounds of largely subjective judgments of that quality.

Actually, the extension of the trajectories backwards to include the earliest patristic writers available for any extensive New Testament textual evidence (Justin Martyr, Tatian [= Diatessaron], Marcion, Irenaeus, Clement of Alexandria, Tertullian, Origen, and Cyprian) would prompt us to say—as Westcott-Hort did—that the earliest text known to us is Western in its character and, furthermore, that most of these earliest patristic witnesses attest that Western kind of text. Again, we are left in the company of Westcott-Hort, and in this respect the extraordinary papyrus discoveries of the past three quarters of a century do not alter our basic dilemma as to whether Neutral or Western better represents the original New Testament text—at least they provide no new objective criteria to bear on the solution.

This approach in terms of developing streams or trajectories in the earliest period is quite a different approach and involves a different

conception from that of Kurt Aland, who has written so frequently of the significance that the papyri have for modern textual studies. It may not be entirely fair to Aland to say that he views the earliest documented period of textual transmission in somewhat *static* terms, yet this is the impression made, for example, when he says: "The simple fact that all these papyri, with their various distinctive characteristics, did exist side by side, in the same ecclesiastical province ... is the best argument against the existence of any text-types."[41] Aland does, in another passage, speak of the early papyri as evidence that "the NT Greek text had been circulating in many and divergent forms, proceeding in different directions, at about the same time, in the same ecclesiastical province";[42] hence, it might be more accurate to say that Aland sees the period of the early papyri as a slice of time largely isolated from the preceding and especially from the subsequent period, for he states that "it is impossible to fit the papyri, from the time prior to the fourth century, into these two text-types [i.e., the Egyptian (= Neutral) and the Byzantine], to say nothing of trying to fit them into other types."[43] The period of the early papyri, it seems, is viewed as an archipelagic phenomenon and one insulated from the period of the great uncials that followed, for Aland finds no continuity between those early papyri and the fourth
century and later textual developments. The term "static" still may 400
be appropriate, then, if one considers that the phenomenon of the early papyri is seen by him as failing to interact in and with the subsequent developments.

In contrast to this conception, my major concern is with the *dynamic* situation of the text in those first centuries, as it can be observed by looking at the papyri, not in isolation, but in their broad historical context and especially from the larger perspective provided by the manuscript situation in the succeeding century or so. In other words, the tracing of textual streams or trajectories shows us that something was happening between 200 and 300; the trajectory approach sets the constellations in motion, and the patterns of textual movement become visible to us. The feeling is akin to that of gazing at the projections of the stars and planets in a planetarium before the

[41] Aland, "The Significance of the Papyri," 336–37.
[42] Ibid., 334.
[43] Ibid., 336.

machinery is engaged, and then, when it is set in rapid motion, the regular paths, the orderly directions of movement, and the shaping of constellations are vividly portrayed. The vast spectrum of early but diverse papyri does present a formidable barrier to our understanding of New Testament textual history before 300 or 400, but look at the dynamic situation, set the machinery in motion, start moving the gears of historical development and the lenses of historical perspective, and perhaps there will be some chance of charting that early history of the New Testament text.

Professor Aland, furthermore, seems always to be emphasizing the *number* of early witnesses, especially papyri, that now are available in the quest for the earliest attainable New Testament text. He can point, for example, to seventeen papyri of the Fourth Gospel alone, and certainly the papyri discovered in our century represent a striking advance in the *quantity of papyri* as compared with the time of Westcott-Hort. Yet, most of the New Testament papyri are extremely fragmentary, and what net gain we have in actual *quantity* of text comes almost entirely from seven papyri (P^{45}, P^{46}, P^{47}, P^{66}, P^{72}, P^{74}, and P^{75}). It must be noted—as Aland correctly emphasizes—that our distinction between "papyri" and "uncials" is an artificial one, since both are uncials and differ only in the materials on which they are written; hence, papyri have an "automatic significance" only when they take us back behind the great uncials of the fourth century.[44] With this in mind, P^{74}, of the seventh century, would not be among the "automatically significant" papyri, and this leaves us with six papyri that are both early and extensive. As a group, these manuscripts contain a quantity of text perhaps equivalent to about one-third the amount of text in Codex B, and these early and extensive papyri provide almost complete coverage of the Fourth Gospel, about three-fourths of Luke, about one-half of Acts, much of the Epistles, and about one-third of the Apocalypse of John. (All of the papyri together contain perhaps half the amount of text in B and include some portion of every New Testament book except 1–2 Timothy.)

It is obvious, then, that in spite of the many lacunae, large and small, the textual gains from the papyri are impressive and highly
401 prized. But is it the *number* of early papyri or even the quantity of

[44] K. Aland, "Das Neue Testament auf Papyrus," in his *Studien zur Überlieferung*, 93.

their text that is significant? If so, the text-critic might well reach the point of saying—as I sometimes, perhaps unjustly, imagine Aland saying—(if we may paraphrase Ignatius, *Philadelphians* 8.2), "Unless I find it written in the *papyri*, I do not believe it in the gospel." Merely counting papyri when assessing variant readings may very well be as wrong-headed as counting witnesses was in the days of the *textus receptus*, for the crucial question for any textual witnesses, whether early or late, is—as Colwell states it: "Where do they fit into a plausible reconstruction of the history of the manuscript tradition?"[45] Certainly Colwell's question is precisely the correct one, and it is another way of stating that the text of the New Testament cannot be established on the basis of an array of early papyri, even if the entire New Testament should be contained in them; rather, the establishment of the New Testament text can be achieved only by a reconstruction of the history of that early text and by extracting the earliest text from manuscripts that have been clearly located in that reconstruction and found to be integral parts of a stream of tradition that flows continuously form the earliest points that can be documented (or that can be recognized or established on adequate and reasonable grounds). Obviously, doing this is harder than saying it, and for this reason we have suggested the trajectory approach as a way of seeing this early history in more dynamic terms than perhaps previously has been the case; naturally, the recent emphasis on text-types as process[46] plays into this, but we need to find ways of observing the entire early textual movement or flow and of drawing firm conclusions from such observation.

Yet, all of our past discoveries and also these present suggestions, as far as they concern the methodology and early history of the text, still leave us largely in the position of Westcott-Hort and within a twentieth century interlude in New Testament textual criticism, and, what is more, they leave us with the major and decisive tasks still ahead.

[45] Colwell, "Hort Redivivus," 156–57. Colwell speaks of Aland in a rather cutting fashion about the counting of papyri, though this is modified slightly a few paragraphs later; these remarks may not be fair, for I do not find statements in Aland that are explicit concerning his attitude toward and treatment of the papyri as textual evidence; cf., however, Aland, "Das Neue Testament auf Papyrus," 93.

[46] See Colwell, "Method in Grouping New Testament Manuscripts," in his *Studies in Methodology*, 15–20; idem, "Method in Establishing the Nature of Text-Types," 53.

C. *Lack of Progress in Major Critical Editions/Apparatuses*

We began by referring to the popular hand-editions of the Greek New Testament as one evidence that we had not moved beyond Westcott-Hort; the similarity between these popular texts and that of Westcott-Hort was seen as symptomatic of the lack of progress toward a theory and history of the text. Now we return—though in a different way—to the editions of the Greek New Testament to show how this lack of progress in textual theory has lead to an extended debate and a serious difference of opinion as to how a *major* critical edition or apparatus should be constructed. When it is observed that this debate about basic procedures goes back to post-World War I times, it will be clear again that the twentieth century has been an interlude.

402 It is disheartening to discover that nearly fifty years ago now, when a number of British and German scholars were considering the compilation of a new critical apparatus to the Greek New Testament, the German group withdrew when no agreement could be reached on the text to be used.[47] At that point the British carried on, but—ignoring the sound advice of B. H. Streeter to employ the Byzantine text as a base[48]—they used the Westcott-Hort text and produced the two volumes edited by S. C. E. Legg.[49] A similar impasse exists now between the so-called International Greek New Testament Project (IGNTP) and the Münster Institut für neutestamentliche Textforschung. These two projects and the collations produced for them have, in each case, a different base or standard text. On the one hand, the recognition of the inadequacy of Legg's volumes had resulted, for one thing, in compelling arguments for the adoption of some form of Byzantine text as a collation base in any

---

[47] M. M. Parvis, "The International Project to Establish a New Critical Apparatus of the Greek New Testament," *Crozer Quarterly* 27 (1950) 301; see O. Stählin, "Zur Vorbereitung des neuen Tischendorf," *ZNW* 25 (1926) 165–68; E. von Dobschütz, "Neutestamentlertagung zu Erlangen am 29. und 30. September 1925," *ZNW* 25 (1926) 171–72; 318.

[48] B. H. Streeter, *The Four Gospels: A Study of Origins* (London: Macmillan, 1924) 147.

[49] S. C. E. Legg, ed., *Nouum Testamentum graece secundum textum Westcotto-Hortianum: Euangelium secundum Marcum* (Oxford: Clarendon Press, 1935); idem, ed., *Nouum Testamentum graece secundum textum Westcotto-Hortianum: Euangelium secundum Matthaeum* (Oxford: Clarendon Press, 1940).

future apparatus,[50] and accordingly the Oxford 1873 edition of the *textus receptus* was selected by the IGNTP. The Münster Institut, however, has followed the views put forward by the German group earlier mentioned—views that found expression, e.g., in 1926 by Stählin and von Dobschütz—that the Nestle text should form the basis for a "new Tischendorf."[51] Thus, Münster is employing the Nestle-Aland text as a base and will display the resultant apparatus against the new critical text derived from the apparatus.[52] Both projects have persisted in their divergent ways, with the British and North American group presently involved in the final editing of the critical apparatus for the Gospel of Luke and the German group working, with the aid of computers, on the General Epistles.[53]

This is not the place to debate the merits of these different approaches; rather, we merely wish to point out that the selection of different collation bases by the two projects and the persistence in these judgments over a period of forty years implies far more than appears on the surface, for it veils two basic but differing attitudes concerning the status of text-critical theory. This is revealed most sharply perhaps in Kurt Aland's 1965 critique of the IGNTP's specimen page when he spoke of the use of the *textus receptus* for a base as, in view of our advanced knowledge, an "anachronism,"[54]
almost as if the printing of the *textus receptus* at the top of the page 403
implied that it represents a good critical text. It is not only curious but striking to discover that von Dobschütz in 1926 used precisely the same term—anachronism—in reference to Streeter's proposal that the *textus receptus* be used as a collation base at that time.[55] In 1967 Professor Aland remarked that, in the IGNTP's edition, the original text of the New Testament would have to be sought from

[50] See, e.g., the reviews of Legg by G. D. Kilpatrick (*JTS* 43 [1942] 33) and by T. W. Manson (*JTS* 43 [1942] 88–89); cf. G. Zuntz (*JTS* 43 [1942] 28–30).

[51] See n. 47, above.

[52] Aland, "Novi Testamenti graeci editio maior critica," *NTS* 16 (1969–70) 166; 172.

[53] See ibid., 163–77; cf. W. Ott, "Computer Applications in Textual Criticism," *Computer and Literary Studies* (eds. A. J. Aitken, R. W. Bailey, and N. Hamilton-Smith; Edinburgh: University Press, 1973) 199–223.

[54] Aland, "Bemerkungen zu Probeseiten einer grossen kritischen Ausgabe des Neuen Testaments," *NTS* 12 (1965–66) 184; repr. in his *Studien zur Überlieferung*, 89–90.

[55] von Dobschütz, "Neutestamentlertagung zu Erlangen," *ZNW* 24 (1926) 318.

the apparatus by subtraction from the printed *textus receptus*,[56] a statement suggesting that he now understood the purpose of the British/American project, for Professor Aland, even though he may not agree, knows well, of course, that the purpose of the IGNTP is to produce an *apparatus criticus* and not a new critical text of the New Testament; this purpose had been specified and emphasized in every printed description of the Project from its very beginning, and it had been made just as clear that this critical apparatus was understood to be only a halfway house to a much needed new critical text. The reason for stopping halfway rather than pushing immediately to the principal destination was simply that there existed no theory of the text that would allow for the establishment of a definitive critical text; the assumption, rather, was that both the theory and the text must be determined from an adequate display of textual evidence, and the IGNTP was modest enough to recognize that this could not be done in one sitting. It was not modesty alone, however, that brought the British and North American participants to this view, but the hard facts and the actual situation in which our text-critical discipline found—and still finds—itself: we simply do not have a theory of the text. What Kenneth W. Clark wrote in 1956 is as true today; he spoke of "a day like ours in which we know only that the traditional theory of the text is faulty but cannot yet see clearly to correct the fault."[57] Professor Aland and the Münster Institut prefer to move immediately and decisively to the construction of a critical text; certainly this aim, the boldness with which it is pursued, and the courage that lies behind it are all commendable, but the pointed question remains: On what theory and history of the text is it based? If no clear and adequate answer is forthcoming, then the more cautious and methodical approach of the IGNTP may be taken as justifiable and, indeed, as mandatory in the present circumstances.

The single, simple point that stands out and that is our interest here is this: the lack of progress toward a theory and history of the earliest New Testament text has seriously hindered and extensively delayed the production of those major critical editions that would

---

[56] Aland, "Die Konsequenzen der neueren Handschriftenfunde," 103–4 (repr., 198–99). This paragraph was not in Aland's English version ("The Significance of the Papyri" [1965]). [See now, E. J. Epp, "The International Greek New Testament Project: Motivation and History," *NovT* 39 (1997) 13–14.]

[57] K. W. Clark, "The Effect of Recent Textual Criticism," 37–38.

provide the detailed apparatuses required for the determination of that history and theory. We are caught in a vicious circle of long standing, and it constitutes another dimension of the twentieth century interlude in New Testament textual criticism in which we find ourselves.

D. *Lack of Progress in the Evaluation of Readings*

The lack of definitive theory and history of the early text and the 404
lack of progress in critical editions has caused, during the twentieth century, a chaotic situation in the evaluation of variant readings in the New Testament text. The result has been the almost universal employment of the "eclectic" method, and this is perhaps the most visible evidence that we are in an interlude. The "eclectic" method is, in fact, *the* twentieth century method of New Testament textual criticism, and anyone who criticizes it immediately becomes a self-critic, for we all use it, some of us with a certain measure of reluctance and restraint, others with complete abandon. Those in the latter category seem to assume that the eclectic method is, for all practical purposes, fully legitimated and acceptable and represents a final method, a permanent procedure, while others of us find K. W. Clark's 1956 judgment the only acceptable assessment of eclecticism:

> It is the only procedure available to us at this stage, but it is very important to recognize that it is a secondary and tentative method. It is not a new method nor a permanent one. The eclectic method cannot by itself create a text to displace Westcott-Hort and its offspring. It is suitable only for exploration and experimentation.... The eclectic method, by its very nature [and here we pick up the quotation referred to a moment ago], belongs to a day like ours in which we know only that the traditional theory of the text is faulty but cannot yet see clearly to correct the fault.[58]

Actually, those who employ the eclectic method with the greatest abandon seem to be the least eclectic, for they tend, usually, to emphasize not a selection of various principles and canons of textual criticism—as the term would imply—but only principles from one corner of criticism, particularly the internal criteria (what the author most likely wrote/what the scribe most likely wrote), with

[58] Ibid.; see his similar, but later statement in "Today's Problem with the Critical Text," 166.

heavy emphasis on harmony with the author's style or suitability to the context. In the process, they tend to de-emphasize, sometimes drastically, the historical factors in textual criticism, including the date and provenance of manuscripts, and they generally eschew the task of reconstructing the history of the text.[59] It probably is not unfair to say that when external evidence, including historical factors and judgments about the quality of given manuscripts and text-types, is disregarded, then the numerous variant readings become little more than detached pieces of a puzzle that must now be selected entirely on the basis of their shape and fitness for the space to be filled. This kind of "eclecticism" becomes the great leveler—all variants are equals and equally candidates for the original text, regardless of date, residence, lineage, or textual context. In this case, would it not be appropriate to suggest, further, that a few more conjectural readings be added to the available supply of variants on the assumption that they must have existed but have been lost at some point in the history of the textual transmission?

All this is not to say that even the "thoroughgoing" or "rigorous" eclectics, as they have been called,[60] have not made important con-
405 tributions to text-critical method. For instance, G. D. Kilpatrick's emphasis on the non-Atticizing reading as the more likely original reading yields a canon of criticism that may find a place among the older canons of Bengel and Griesbach, but—like those older canons—it too has limited applications and serious shortcomings.[61] Beyond this isolated example, the broad utilization of an eclectic methodology by numerous scholars throughout the twentieth century has helped us to sharpen our critical senses, to evaluate the traditional canons and principles of textual criticism, and to maintain a plau-

---

[59] See Colwell, "Hort Redivivus," 154–56.

[60] E.g., by G. D. Fee, who distinguishes "rigorous" eclecticism from "reasoned" eclecticism ("The Significance of Papyrus Bodmer II and Papyrus Bodmer XIV–XV for Methodology in New Testament Textual Criticism" [Ph.D. dissertation, University of Southern California, 1966] 4–6; 264–65). [See his subsequent article, "Rigorous or Reasoned Eclecticism—Which?" *Studies in New Testament Language and Text: Essays in Honour of George D. Kilpatrick on the Occasion of His Sixty-Fifth Birthday* (ed. J. K. Elliott; NovTSup 44; Leiden: Brill, 1976) 174–97.]

[61] For dangers and difficulties, see Metzger, *Text of the New Testament*, 177–78; and Colwell, "Hort Redivivus," 154–55. Kilpatrick's main treatment of this matter is "Atticism and the Text of the Greek New Testament," *Neutestamentliche Aufsätze: Festschrift für Prof. Josef Schmid zum 70. Geburtstag* (eds. J. Blinzler, O. Kuss, F. Mussner; Regensburg: Pustet, 1963), 125–37.

sible critical text for use in the exegetical and historical studies in the general New Testament field. In short, eclecticism is a holding action, a temporary and interim method with presumably equally temporary results. It is, however, what the twentieth century has produced and worked with, and, as a twentieth century emphasis, it evidences again our twentieth century pause in New Testament textual criticism.

E. *The Return of the* Textus Receptus

Perhaps the most curious and certainly the most ironic evidence that we stand in the situation of Westcott-Hort is the revival in our own generation of the view that the *textus receptus* represents the best New Testament text. In 1956 Edward F. Hills published a work entitled, *The King James Version Defended! A Christian View of the New Testament Manuscripts*,[62] and only months ago David Otis Fuller (1973) edited a volume called *True or False? The Westcott-Hort Textual Theory Examined*,[63] both of which defend the *textus receptus*.

I suspect that no one of us will or need take these books seriously, but that they could be written at all and published in our own day is, in a way, an indictment of our discipline. These works not only attack the theories of Westcott-Hort, but they attack us as representatives of Westcott-Hort's views, and in a striking way they return us to the days when Dean Burgon made his vehement, acrimonious, and abusive attacks upon Westcott and Hort and upon what he called their malicious intentions and corrupt manuscripts.[64] I am being facetious only to a limited extent when I ask, If the *textus receptus* can still be defended, albeit in what most of us would characterize as merely a pseudo-scholarly fashion, how much solid progress have we made in textual criticism in the twentieth century?

---

[62] Des Moines, IA: Christian Research, 1956.

[63] Grand Rapids, MI: Grand Rapids International [Kregel], 1973; see also the 3rd ed. of his earlier compilation, *Which Bible?* (Grand Rapids, MI: Grand Rapids International, 1973).

[64] J. W. Burgon, *The Revision Revised* (London: John Murray, 1883); *The Causes of the Corruption of the Traditional Text of the Holy Gospels* (London: G. Bell, 1896); and *The Traditional Text of the Holy Gospels Vindicated and Established* (London: G. Bell, 1896). The last two volumes were completed and edited by E. Miller.

406 III. The Post-Interlude Performance

We have described the first major performance or act of modern New Testament textual criticism as the destruction of the tyrannical *textus receptus* during the last half of the nineteenth century. The *textus receptus* and its precursor, the Byzantine ecclesiastical text, had maintained a position of dominance for as long as a millennium and a half when the mortal wound was inflicted by Westcott and Hort. A brief death struggle ensued in the 1880's and 1890's when Dean Burgon, to whom we have just referred, and his allies attacked the attackers in a desperate but unsuccessful attempt to reverse the issue. But the verdict held, and the twentieth century opened with the newly found optimism that, by excluding the mass of late manuscripts from the search, textual critics had extracted the original text of the New Testament from the best of the earliest uncials, or that at very least they were now in the immediate neighborhood of the original text. Challenges arising from the Westcott-Hort scheme were tackled quickly and enthusiastically within this same spirit of optimism. One of those challenges was to carry further the search for the history of the text, and the extraordinarily ambitious and well-provisioned project of Herman Freiherr von Soden faced that problem broadly and on all fronts. The first fascicle of his three-volume prolegomena appeared in 1902, and the last, after 2200 closely-packed pages of fine print, came out in 1910, followed by his critical edition of the text in 1913.[65] Something of the magnitude of labor involved can be grasped by noting that von Soden classified as to their textual character some 1260 minuscule manuscripts out of the 1350 known to him—an astounding 93%. Yet his great work, the scale of which has not been matched again in the twentieth century, was as deep a disappointment to the scholarly world as the expectations for it had been high. His comprehensive history of the text was only partially satisfactory; his classification of manuscript groupings had questionable—and largely unknown—methodological bases; his new system of manuscript sigla was complex and calamitous; and (as Kenyon says) "his resultant text was no advance on its

[65] H. von Soden, *Die Schriften des Neuen Testaments in ihrer ältesten erreichbaren Textgestalt hergestellt auf Grund ihrer Textgeschichte* (2 parts in 4 vols.; Göttingen: Vandenhoeck & Ruprecht, 1911[2]–1913).

predecessors."[66] I employ this reference to von Soden to show the magnificently grand fashion in which the twentieth century interlude in New Testament textual criticism was inaugurated!

For me to bring upon my own discipline so sweeping an indictment as I have is no pleasant undertaking. Surely some will dispute its necessity, and others its justification; and none will like it. I dislike it as much as anyone, but both the popular and major critical editions and the state of research in both the theory and history of the text stand as vivid evidence of its reality.

If we have been in an interlude, what are the prospects of moving from it into a new phase—a second major and significant act? On balance, and in view of some rather recent developments—some
of which I have already mentioned—the chances are considerably 407
better than they were a generation ago. Naturally, the papyrus discoveries have contributed to this hopeful situation, but I refer more directly to developments in method that will aid in the reconstruction of the early history of the text, for it is this task—as urged above—that is basic to progress in New Testament textual criticism.

A. *Quantitative Measurement of Manuscript Relationships*

The first reason for optimism is found in the methodological advances that have been made during the past decade in the quantitative measurement of manuscript relationships.

Throughout the twentieth century (and also earlier) analyses of manuscript relationships have been based, generally, on a comparison of the number of agreements that two or more manuscripts shared in their variation from an external standard, usually the *textus receptus*. For example, a given manuscript, let us call it x, in three sample chapters from Mark, would be collated against the *textus receptus*, showing fifteen variants; then these fifteen variants would be checked, e.g., against Codex B, showing that in ten of these fifteen variants manuscript x and Codex B were in agreement—in agreement, that is, against the *textus receptus*. More than likely a conclusion would be drawn that manuscript x was a Neutral witness. If, however, Codex B in these three chapters should show fifty additional

[66] F. G. Kenyon, *Recent Developments in the Textual Criticism of the Greek Bible* (Schweich Lectures, 1932; London: British Academy by Oxford University Press, 1933) 44.

variations from the *textus receptus* that manuscript x does not share, would manuscript x have any claim to be classified as Neutral when its ratio of agreement to disagreement with B against the *textus receptus* was 1 to 5? Hardly, but frequently, if not normally, this comparison of *total agreement and disagreement* was not taken into account. Suppose, using the same example, that manuscript x showed that in five of its variants from the *textus receptus* it agreed with Codex D, as compared with ten of the fifteen in which it agreed with B; it would, as before, be called Neutral, but what if D differed from the *textus receptus* in these sections of Mark a total of only two additional times, leaving manuscript x agreeing with D against the *textus receptus* five out seven times, or roughly 70% of the time; should it not then be classified as Western rather than Neutral? To extend the example, if manuscript y were found also to have fifteen variants from the *textus receptus* in the same sample chapters and ten of these were the same readings as ten of the fifteen variants in which manuscript x differed from the *textus receptus*, what conclusions would be drawn? Older methods would have claimed, perhaps, that manuscripts x and y are closely related, and perhaps they are. But how close a relationships is it? Suppose that the two manuscripts being compared, x and y, have between them a total of twenty variations from the *textus receptus*; that they agree in ten of these, but that they also fail to agree in the other ten, resulting in only 50% agreement with one another in their total variation from the external standard. That is quite different from the implication that they are closely related because they agree with one another 67% of the time against the *textus receptus*. Sometimes even more superficial comparisons and more careless conclusions were made. For example, two or three manuscripts might be shown to have a similar number of variants from the *textus receptus*, even though they are not the same variants;
408 therefore, the argument would go, the two or three manuscripts are related textually because of their supposedly similar distance from the common standard. There were other ways in which these longstanding methods were inadequate. For example, variants involving obvious scribal errors, nonsense readings, singular readings, and insignificant variations (such as orthographical changes) were not evaluated for their usefulness (or lack of it) in tracing manuscript relationships. The result, to put it mildly, was inexactness, inclusiveness, and miscalculation in the determination of manuscript relationships.

At least two developments that have achieved a certain measure of maturity only during the past decade have changed all of this, and shoddy, indecisive, and misleading methods for establishing manuscript relationships can no longer be tolerated. The first development stems from an eight-page article by Ernest C. Colwell and his collaborator, Ernest W. Tune, on "The Quantitative Relationships between MS Text-Types," which appeared in 1963.[67] Building on some earlier suggestions (by H. S. Murphy and B. M. Metzger),[68] they devised a quantitative method in which "the total amount of variation" is taken into account among all the manuscripts of a wide-ranging panel of manuscripts employed in the comparison, rather than merely tabulating agreements against an external norm. This means that each manuscript in the study must be measured against every other one in the study, including a carefully selected list of control manuscripts that represent the major points on the broad textual spectrum of the New Testament, and this measurement must be made in terms of the total number of variation-units that occur among all the manuscripts involved in the study—a variation-unit being defined as every point where two or more of the witnesses agree in a variation from the rest. Moreover, all variants are "classified as either genetically significant or not," with the result that scribal errors, alternative spellings, and especially singular [they use the term "unique"] readings are eliminated, since they "tell us nothing about manuscript relationships" and seriously distort the tabulations of other manuscript agreements. An important final suggestion is that "the quantitative definition of a text-type is a group of manuscripts that agree more than 70 per cent of the time and is separated by a gap of about 10 per cent from its neighbors."[69] It should be pointed out

---

[67] In *Biblical and Patristic Studies in Memory of Robert Pierce Casey* (eds. J. N. Birdsall and R. W. Thomson; Freiburg: Herder, 1963) 25–32; repr., with some revisions, as "Method in Establishing Quantitative Relationships between Text-Types of New Testament Manuscripts," in Colwell, *Studies in Methodology*, 56–62. References are to the latter.

[68] Harold S. Murphy, "Eusebius' NT Text in the *Demonstratio Evangelica*," *JBL* 73 (1954) 167; B. M. Metzger, "The Caesarean Text of the Gospels," *JBL* 64 (1945) 489, as cited by Colwell, "Method in Establishing Quantitative Relationships," 56 n. 4; 57 n. 1. To these might have been added the points made, mostly against K. Lake's methods, by E. F. Hills, "The Inter-Relationship of the Caesarean Manuscripts," *JBL* 68 (1949) 141–59, esp. p. 153; and the method employed by C. L. Porter, "A Textual Analysis of the Earliest Manuscripts of the Gospel of John" (Durham: Dissertation, Duke University, 1961).

[69] Colwell, "Method in Establishing Quantitative Relationships," 59. [See now

that, as Colwell and Tune conceived it, this method was still a *sampling* method; sound method, however, requires that total variation of numerous manuscripts throughout entire books of the New Testament be analyzed, though it should, at the same time, be done section by section or chapter by chapter. The fullest utilization and
409 the most thorough exposition of the method to date are by Gordon D. Fee, who has devised and employed some refinements as he investigated the text of the Fourth Gospel in P^{66}, P^{75}, ℵ, and in Origen and Cyril of Alexandria.[70] Hurtado, in the study referred to above, also applied the method in a thoroughgoing fashion to the Caesarean witnesses.[71] In addition to the original Colwell article, Fee's study of "Codex Sinaiticus in the Gospel of John: A Contribution to Methodology in Establishing Textual Relationships"[72] is essential for understanding the method and for some account of its history.

This quantitative method is not for the indolent; endless hours of tedious manuscript collation, of careful isolation of variation-units, and of meticulous tabulation of results are required over large areas of text, but the method yields those precise quantitative measures of manuscript relationships and textual character that are mandatory for reconstructing the textual history of the New Testament. Hence, there is vibrant new hope if scholars can be found and enlisted to carry out these procedures. Moreover, the computer program in use at the Münster Institut yields data for this kind of measurement [see below on "Computers in Textual Criticism"].

The second development in quantitative method is the so-called Claremont Profile Method for grouping New Testament minuscule manuscripts. This approach was developed by Frederik Wisse and Paul R. McReynolds for the IGNTP as a means of assuring that the Project's *apparatus criticus* would contain a selection of truly rep-

---

Klaus Wachtel, "Colwell Revisited: Grouping New Testament Manuscripts," *The New Testament Text in Early Christianity: Proceedings of the Lille Colloquium, July 2000* (eds. C.-B Amphoux and J. K. Elliott; HTB 6; Lausanne: Zèbre), 31–43, esp. 32–35.]

[70] Fee, *Papyrus Bodmer II (P66): Its Textual Relationships and Scribal Characteristics* (SD 34; Salt Lake City: University of Utah Press, 1968); "Codex Sinaiticus in the Gospel of John: A Contribution to Methodology in Establishing Textual Relationships," *NTS* 15 (1968–69) 23–44; and "The Text of John in Origen and Cyril of Alexandria: A Contribution to Methodology in the Recovery and Analysis of Patristic Citations," *Bib* 52 (1971) 357–94.

[71] See n. 22, above.

[72] *NTS* 15 (1968–69) 23–44, esp. pp. 25–31.

resentative minuscule manuscripts—representative, that is, of all the identifiable groups in terms of textual character. Since only about 150 out of more than 1700 minuscules of Luke could be included in the apparatus, and since the majority of these Lukan manuscripts had never been collated, a highly efficient yet sufficiently sophisticated means had to be devised to locate the desired 9% without unduly over- or under-representing any identifiable group.

It would not be practicable to describe this method in detail here; this has been done several times already, though the full exposition and justification has not yet appeared.[73] In short, a series of test readings in three chapters of Luke were isolated from collations of 550 manuscripts; when a manuscript was checked for its agreement or disagreement with these test readings, a certain pattern or profile
of its own readings in these variation-units results, and manuscripts 410
with the same or closely similar profiles fell into groups showing a similar configuration of characteristic readings. Hence, each group revealed a distinctive profile, and new manuscripts could quickly be checked in the test passages and fitted—according to its profile—into one of the groups established by the method. The Profile Method is applicable particularly to the location of Byzantine sub-groups, which previously were identified through "unique group readings," but such unique or distinctive group readings are rare in Byzantine groups. The Profile Method relies, rather, upon *characteristic* group readings that yield a distinctive group profile, and it replaces an older instrument with one of higher fidelity, encouraging correspondingly high hopes that some measure of order can be brought to the chaotic mass of New Testament minuscule manuscripts. Finally, it is important to note, however, that the Profile Method is still a sampling method, thereby sharing the general weaknesses of sampling methods, but it operates with rigid principles in the determination of its test readings, and it has perhaps as many safeguards

[73] Frederik Wisse and Paul R. McReynolds, *JBL* 87 (1968) 191–97; "Family E and the Profile Method," *Bib* 51 (1970) 67–75; P. R. McReynolds, "The Value and Limitations of the Claremont Profile Method," *SBLSP* (1972) 1.1–7; E. J. Epp, "The Claremont Profile Method for Grouping New Testament Minuscule Manuscripts," *Studies in the History and Text of the New Testament in Honor of Kenneth Willis Clark*, Ph.D. (SD 29; eds. B. L. Daniels and M. J. Suggs; Salt Lake City: University of Utah Press, 1967) 27–38. [See now F. Wisse, *The Profile Method for the Classification and Evaluation of Manuscript Evidence as Applied to the Continuous Greek Text of the Gospel of Luke* (SD 44; Grand Rapids, MI: Eerdmans, 1982).]

as can be worked into a sampling method. Furthermore, it will bring to the surface those relatively few manuscripts that deserve thorough and detailed study.

These two quantitative methods have come to us out of the twentieth century interlude, the latter taking its departure largely from von Soden's attempts to group the Byzantine manuscripts, and the former arising largely from the efforts to quantify the relationships among the Caesarean witnesses. Both, however, stem more immediately from Colwell's work on locating new manuscripts within the textual tradition; on grouping manuscripts; on determining text-types; and, of course, on his actual proposal for a quantitative method. Perhaps the coincident appearance of the extensive papyri, with their textual material of great intrinsic significance, gave the whole enterprise a measure of cogency and heightened the strategic import of quantitative analysis that now could offer such precise and confident results. In any event, it is these exact and assured results in determining manuscript relationships that hold rich promise for a movement out of the interlude into a new phase of New Testament text-critical achievement.[74]

B. *Homogeneity and Recension in Early New Testament Text-Types*

The twentieth century appears to have created and then destroyed the Caesarean text-type, returning us once again—as in the days of Westcott-Hort—to two major textual streams traceable from the earliest period. It is clear, however, that the witnesses that can be identified as on or in the vicinity of these two textual lines are of varying textual character, especially many of the fragmentary papyri. This means that two old, difficult, but important problems remain
411 for resolution: the problems of homogeneity and recension in the Neutral and Western traditions. Positions on these issues have come full circle since Westcott-Hort, and little progress has been made. Hort viewed neither text as the product of a recension, but took both, apparently, to be homogeneous in their textual character (though

[74] Reference may be made also to Vinton A. Dearing's method of "textual analysis": *A Manual of Textual Analysis* (Berkeley, CA: University of California Press, 1959); idem, "Some Notes on Genealogical Methods in Textual Criticism," *NovT* 9 (1967) 278–97, for which he has utilized the computer, and recently he has made further applications to New Testament texts.

the Western showed evidence, he said, of "homogeneously progressive change").[75] Subsequent scholarship, however, soon argued that both the Neutral (Bousset; von Soden; Kenyon)[76] and the Western (Blass; Ropes)[77] text-types were the products of systematic revision. More recent scholarship has often viewed the Western as "the uncontrolled, popular text of the second century,"[78] hence unrevised and lacking homogeneity, while the close relationship of P^{75} to B has suggested to some that any view of the Neutral text as the result of recension should now be reversed [see above].

These two questions, homogeneity and recension, may or may not be closely related: homogeneity may imply—but need not require—a recension; evidence of recension may lead to the expectation—but not automatically to the discovery—of homogeneity. Clearly, however, these questions press themselves most critically upon the Neutral and Western texts, if only because they represent the earliest of the recognized textual traditions and because, therefore, the further issue of the original text of the New Testament is encountered more immediately in these textual streams. As the history of scholarship shows, these are problems of extreme complexity and difficulty, but decisions about either homogeneity or recension in these texts would aid significantly in the required reconstruction of the history of the text.

Obviously, the newly developed and refined quantitative method provides a means for investigating these issues afresh and with precision. As for the Neutral text, its homogeneity and recensional nature have been touched anew by the discovery of P^{75}: Was there an early recension in Egypt of this Neutral text-type, which seems to bear the marks of a recension when compared with the more problematic and divergent Western witnesses, or does the striking agreement of P^{75} and B reflect accurate transmission of an early, smooth, but

[75] Westcott-Hort, *New Testament in the Original Greek*, 2.122.

[76] See, e.g., Wilhelm Bousset, *Textkritische Studien zum Neuen Testament: Die Recension des Hesychius* (TU 11/4; Leipzig: Hinrichs, 1894); von Soden, *Schriften des Neuen Testaments* (1911–13); Kenyon, *Recent Developments*, 67–69; 81–83; idem, "Hesychius and the Text of the New Testament," *Mémorial Lagrange* (Paris: Gabalda, 1940) 245–50.

[77] See E. J. Epp, *The Theological Tendency of Codex Bezae Cantabrigiensis in Acts* (SNTSMS 3; Cambridge: Cambridge University Press, 1966) 4–6.

[78] Colwell, "Method in Establishing the Nature of Text-Types," 53; idem, "Hort Redivivus," 166; cf. D. W. Riddle, "Textual Criticism as a Historical Discipline," *AThR* 18 (1936) 230.

unrevised text? The homogeneity of witnesses placed in the Neutral text-type has been tested rather widely, though only recently by adequate quantitative methods; still, one of its leading members, ℵ, continues to show interesting and puzzling deviations.[79]

It is in the Western text, however, that the questions of homo-
412 geneity and recension are the more problematic, for here one is faced with a relatively small number of witnesses (which is advantageous methodologically), but with an unusually fragmentary set of witnesses in several ancient languages (which is disadvantageous both for developing a methodology and for an easy solution). Whether or not the Western text of the Gospels and Acts has passed through a recensional process or has a homogeneous character are questions that have resisted resolution, primarily, perhaps, because of the lack of *extensive* Greek witnesses to this textual tradition; actually, there is only one such witness, Codex Bezae (D), though some may wish to add manuscripts 614 and 383 for Acts; the other important witnesses are the Old Latin and Old Syriac manuscripts, which not only are few (about thirty-two of the Gospels and twelve of Acts in Latin; only two of the Gospels and part of a single leaf for Acts in Syriac) and fragmentary (all of the above are mutilated), but date from the fourth through the thirteenth centuries, on the average quite far removed from the presumed origin of this textual tradition in the second century. Patristic quotations and commentaries and a few other manuscripts (including several fragmentary papyri) offer additional testimony with a Western flavor. When, however, all of the available witnesses are compared, for example in Acts, a number of variation-units emerge as points where two, three, or more of these witnesses can be compared. This is a hopeful sign for the use of quantitative methods to probe the issues of homogeneity and recension. On the other hand, it is not a little discouraging to discover, from preliminary checks, that not often are three or more of the "hard core" Western witnesses available for any given variation-unit; this may place a critical strain on methodology if extensive demonstration of uniform results is required.

[79] See Fee, "Codex Sinaiticus in the Gospel of John." Fee argues, on quantitative and other grounds, that the early P^{75}-B text-type is not a recension: "P75, P66, and Origen: The Myth of Early Textual Recension in Alexandria," *New Dimensions in New Testament Study* (ed. R. N. Longenecker and M. C. Tenney; Grand Rapids: Zondervan, 1974) 28; 32–33; 44–45.

The degree of success that can be expected in these investigations of homogeneity and recension is not yet clear, but during the past two decades the dual factors of (1) improved quantitative methods (which may prove applicable even to the more fragmentary witnesses) and (2) the discovery of strategically significant new witnesses for both of the earliest textual streams may tip the scales toward a successful resolution of these old and intractable problems.

C. *Computers in Textual Criticism*

The expectations from new technological developments and applications tend at times to be greatly underestimated and at other times to be vastly overrated. How computer applications to textual criticism should be evaluated is not entirely clear, for many assertions as to how it can or should be utilized differ markedly from more sober statements about it actual use and present limitations.

The latest, most extensive, and most direct application of computers to New Testament textual criticism is that utilized by the Münster Institut for its major critical edition of the Greek New Testament. Under the expert hand of Dr. Wilhelm Ott, information derived from its collations of manuscripts of the General Epistles—which must be done in the traditional way by hand[80]—is carefully coded and punched on tape. Ott makes very clear what can and 413
what cannot be done by the computer: it cannot make judgments on the truth or falsity of readings; it cannot restore the text or reconstruct the history of its transmission;[81] nor can manuscripts be collated by the computer, though presently this limitation is a technical and economic limitation rather than a theoretical one; and there are not now—nor will there be in the foreseeable future—optical scanning devices capable of reading the kind of manuscripts with which New Testament textual criticism works.[82] Accordingly, one recent estimate is that "to encode the available manuscripts by hand on

[80] B. Fischer, "The Use of Computers in New Testament Studies, with Special Reference to Textual Criticism," *JTS* 21 (1970) 307.

[81] W. Ott, "Computer Applications in Textual Criticism," 200.

[82] I rely on a letter from Mr. George Nagy of IBM (dated 17 March 1970), who said of several samples of New Testament minuscule manuscripts that their Greek text "is beyond the capabilities of any mechanical systems now in sight." Cf. R. S. Morgan, "Optical Readers: 1970," *Computers and the Humanities* 5 (1970–71) 75–78.

punched cards or tape would demand the resources of 200 man-years."[83] On the other hand, the computer *can* classify witnesses and define the relationships among them, and it can "guarantee consistent and error-free execution of the more mechanical part of the work," viz., the compilation of the *apparatus criticus* and the printing of the text and of the apparatus.[84]

These are significant gains that already can be demonstrated in a partial way through actual accomplishment and are not mere dreams of what might be done. Those who are working with these techniques—Ott, Fischer, Aland—are careful to emphasize, again, that this by no means implies that they have approached anything comparable to automatic textual editing or "automatic textual criticism." And there are other cautions here for the incurable dreamer whose confidence in modern technology knows no realistic bounds, for Ott points out that these new tools may mean that the costs for critical editions may be even higher than in the days when these tools were not available.[85] Much of this expense will be for the labor of providing the coded collation data to the computer, and—as one observer put it—scholars will still be "doing much drudgery, but a new kind"—hence, "it seems less accurate to say that they are freed from drudgery than to say that their drudgery can handle a much larger volume per human drudge-hour."[86]

Certainly even this realistic assessment of the computer in New Testament textual criticism is a hopeful sign, but it hardly has been touched by North American scholars.[87]

IV. Conclusion

The few areas broached here do not exhaust the hopeful signs for the post-interlude period. A further example, and one quite different from those presented earlier, is the recent development of more pre-

[83] Reported by H. Greeven to SNTS, 1970; see *NTS* 17 (1970–71) 478.
[84] Ott, "Computer Applications in Textual Criticism," 200; cf. Fischer, "The Use of Computers," 306.
[85] Ott, "Computer Applications in Textual Criticism," 201.
[86] J. Leed, *Computers and the Humanities* 1 (1966–67) 14.
[87] [See the "Added Notes" to my essay on "The International Greek New Testament Project: Motivation and History," below.]

cise methods for the radiocarbon dating of parchment manuscripts.[88]
Yet the items we have discussed may be harbingers of a movement 414
out of a long, though not inactive, pause in New Testament textual criticism and into a fresh and qualitatively different phase of our discipline. Unfortunately, however, any such hopes must be balanced, at least in North America, by a somber reflection. Any one of us who faces the present status of New Testament textual criticism with some reasonable measure of honesty and detachment will recognize that changes of a kind very much unlike any mentioned to this point have forced themselves upon us. In 1955, the very first volume of *New Testament Studies*, itself a symbol of a new era in international and ecumenical scholarship, carried a lecture by W. G. Kümmel on "New Testament Research and Teaching in Present Day Germany." There were five lines devoted to textual criticism, including the statement that:

> Textual criticism has virtually ceased to be a subject of active research in present day Germany, that is to say so far as the investigation of textual families, relationships between texts, etc. are concerned. This kind of research requires a great deal of time and money, so that it has almost entirely been transferred to America.[89]

If Kümmel's assessment, which came just ten years after World War II, was correct for the middle 1950s, quite the reverse is true today. Given the ironic twists of national economies, one now has to say—to change the wording slightly—that since textual criticism requires a great deal of manpower and money it has almost entirely been transferred to Germany. To cite only a few points of support for this dispiriting statement, the grand tradition of textual criticism at the University of Chicago from Goodspeed through Willoughby, Colwell, and Wikgren apparently has ended with the latter's recent retirement, and other text-critical centers, such as Emory and Duke, no longer seem to be active in graduate studies in the field. It is, in fact, difficult to name more than one or two recognized graduate institutions in North America where doctoral studies in the textual

[88] R. Berger, N. Evans, J. M. Abel, and M. A. Resnik, "Radiocarbon Dating of Parchment," *Nature* 235 (1973) 160–61. So far, however, "the best periods for dating . . . are the thirteenth and fifteenth centuries."
[89] W. G. Kümmel, "New Testament Research and Teaching in Present-Day Germany," *NTS* 1 (1954–55) 231.

criticism of the New Testament can be pursued under some established specialist. It is disheartening to say that I doubt whether the working and publishing New Testament textual critics in all of North America are equal in number to the post-doctoral researchers in the Münster Institut. To speak of the lack of personnel in the present is one thing; what is more worrisome is the dismal prospect for specialists in the future, particularly on this side of the Atlantic. In short, New Testament textual criticism is an area seriously affected by decreasing attention, diminishing graduate opportunities, and dwindling personnel. It is ironic that this state of affairs—a situation contrasting sharply with any during the long life of W. H. P. Hatch—obtains just at the time when methodological advances warrant a renewed optimism for the discipline and offer fresh challenges that, if met, would carry New Testament textual criticism beyond its twentieth century interlude to a new and distinctive period of achievement.[90]

Added Notes, 2004

This article, in large part, was translated into Japanese for serial publication in *Studia Textus Novi Testamenti* [Osaka, Japan] 103–109 (1975) 856–60; 866–68; 875–76; 890–92; 898–90; 907–8, by the editor, Toshio Hirunuma.

Broadly speaking, I stand by the views espoused in this essay, though, first, I agree with the critique of Professor Larry W. Hurtado (University of Edinburgh), my Ph.D. student, that the "interlude" in recent decades has been undercut by increased interest in the field, significantly larger numbers of participants, numerous text-critical projects and publications, and brighter prospects for the future: see his "Beyond the Interlude? Developments and Directions in New Testament Textual Criticism," *Studies in the Early Text of the Gospels and Acts: The Papers of the First Birmingham Colloquium on the Textual Criticism of the New Testament* (ed. D. G. K. Taylor; SBLTCS 1; Atlanta, GA: Society of Biblical Literature, 1999) 26–48.

Second, I would no longer defend the use of the *textus receptus* as

[90] [See now E. J. Epp, "New Testament Textual Criticism in America: Requiem for a Discipline," *JBL* 98 (1979) 94–98.]

a collation base for the International Greek New Testament Project: see the "Added Notes" below in the essay on "The International Greek New Testament Project: Motivation and History."

On terms: I would now—as I have for many years—place the text-type designations "Neutral," and "Western," as well as the term "original text" in parentheses, inasmuch as they all have lost their literal sense. "Egyptian," "Alexandrian," or "B-text" are to be preferred for "Neutral," and "D-text" for "Western." On the complex issues arising from the term "original," see my "The Multivalence of the Term 'Original Text' in New Testament Textual Criticism," *HTR* 92 (1999) 245–81.

On the evaluation of readings: See my essays below on "The Eclectic Method in New Testament Textual Criticism: Solution or Symptom?" *HTR* 69 (1976) 211–57; and "Issues in New Testament Textual Criticism: Moving from the Nineteenth Century to the Twenty-First Century," *Rethinking New Testament Textual Criticism* (ed. D. A. Black; Grand Rapids, MI: Baker Academic, 2002) 17–76, esp. 20–34. In the latter volume, see M. W. Holmes, "The Case for Reasoned Eclecticism," 77–100; and J. K. Elliott, "The Case for Thoroughgoing Eclecticism," 101–24.

On the return of the textus receptus: I mention only the following, where additional references to recent work can be found: G. D. Fee, "The Majority Text and the Original Text of the New Testament," E. J. Epp and G. D. Fee, *Studies in the Theory and Method of New Testament Textual Criticism* (SD 45; Grand Rapids, MI: Eerdmans, 1993) 183–208; Daniel B. Wallace, "The Majority Text Theory: History, Methods, and Critique," in *The Text of the New Testament in Contemporary Research: Essays on the* Statis Quaestionis (ed. B. D. Ehrman and M. W. Holmes; SD 46; Grand Rapids, MI: Eerdmans, 1995) 297–320; J. L. North, "The Oxford Debate on the Textual Criticism of the New Testament, Held at New College on May 6, 1897: An End, Not a Beginning, for the Textus Receptus," in Taylor (ed.), *Studies in the Early Text of the Gospels and Acts*, 1–25; Maurice A. Robinson, "The Case for Byzantine Priority," in Black (ed.), *Rethinking New Testament Textual Criticism*, 125–39.

On computers: My 1974 discussion, obviously, is entirely out of date; see the discussion below in "The International Greek New Testament Project: Motivation and History" and the "Added Notes"; but especially Robert A. Kraft, "The Use of Computers in New Testament Textual Criticism," in Ehrman and Holmes (eds.), *The Text of the*

New Testament in Contemporary Research, 268–82, with extensive bibliography; and David C. Parker, "The Principio Project: A Reconstruction of the Johannine Tradition," *Filologia Neotestamentaria* XIII (2000) 111–18; idem, "Manuscripts of the Gospels in the Electronic Age," *ResQ* 42 (2000) 221–31; idem, "A Comparison between the *Text und Textwert* and the Claremont Profile Method Analyses of Manuscripts in the Gospel of Luke," *NTS* 49 (2003) 108–38; idem, Through a Screen Darkly: Digital Texts and the New Testament," *JSNT* 25 (2003) 395–411.

CHAPTER FIVE

TOWARD THE CLARIFICATION OF THE TERM "TEXTUAL VARIANT"[1]

Professor George D. Kilpatrick's text-critical studies, spanning more 153
than thirty years and treating myriad New Testament passages and countless textual variations, have been particularly instructive and indeed provocative in their attention to the so-called internal criteria for deciding between or among variant readings in the New Testament manuscript tradition. By these contributions he has placed all of us much in his debt, and it would be in no way an overstatement to say that he has brought the whole question of text-critical criteria to the forefront of our current discussion. All textual critics, whether they pay more attention to internal evidence or to external, are concerned with textual variants—they are their stock in trade—and the careful definition of "textual variant" and its associated terms is not only important but fundamental to the entire discipline. This study attempts such definitions, for, surprising though it may seem, some of the basic terminology of New Testament textual criticism has been used much too loosely in the past.

The perspective and thrust of this essay admittedly are quite different from the major emphases of Kilpatrick's own text-critical work; whereas he has emphasized increasingly the stylistic, linguistic, and scribal factors in textual variation, the writer and his several American colleagues mentioned in this paper have emphasized the rôle of so-called external evidence, including the possible reconstruction of the earliest history of the New Testament text, the grouping of manuscripts and the quantitative measurement of their relationships, and the relative weight to be given to such groups and

[1] This paper received its first hearing on 25 October 1974 in the Textual Criticism Seminar of the Society of Biblical Literature, Washington, D.C., and it appears here with revisions that were prompted by the Seminar discussion. Publication of the paper in a *Festschrift* for George D. Kilpatrick accounts for the introductory remarks. [See now *The Principles and Practice of New Testament Textual Criticism: Collected Essays of G. D. Kilpatrick* (ed. J. K. Elliott; BETL 96; Leuven: Peters/Leuven University Press, 1990).]

to individual manuscripts in text-critical decisions. To those by whom variants are treated much more as independent entities, that is, as readings in isolation from any presumed text-type or any other particular textual tradition or history, some of the discussion that fol-
154 lows will appear to be inconsequential. In this respect, a number of differences with Kilpatrick doubtless can be anticipated, but the following treatise is presented with the direct aim and with the sincere hope both of clarifying the terminology used by all of us and of stimulating discussion on those crucial points where differences remain.

I. Introduction: The Problems

The clarification, definition, and delimitation of the term "textual variant" are vastly more complex and difficult matters than at first would appear. The common or surface assumption is that any textual reading that differs in any way from any other reading in the same unit of text is a "textual variant," but this simplistic definition will not suffice. Actually, in New Testament textual criticism the term "textual variant" really means—and must mean—"*significant*" or "*meaningful* textual variant," but immediately this raises the further question of the meaning of "significant" or "meaningful." For example, a clear scribal error is certainly a variant in the common sense of the term, but is it a significant variant? A nonsense reading clearly is a variation, but is it meaningful? A singular reading, particularly when it can be construed grammatically or gives a new denotation, is even more clearly a variant in the everyday sense, but is it significant?

Involved in these questions is a further one: significant for what? Here the complexities multiply. For instance, a *clear* scribal error is a textual variation, but it is not a significant textual variant for recovering the original text, nor is it significant for determining manuscript relationships—unless, of course, the error has been copied and reproduced in an uncorrected form by a later scribe, but even then coincidence in a commonly committed scribal error cannot easily or often be utilized as *proof* of a direct manuscript relationship. The scribal error, however, may be a "significant" variant reading for the study of scribal habits and characteristics even though it is not "significant" for broader text-critical tasks. Orthographic variations are similar in nature and pose similar problems. A further example

is the nonsense reading, that is, one that cannot be construed grammatically; it is a textual variant of the ordinary sense, but in almost no conceivable way is it a meaningful or significant variant. Singular readings are more complex than these other examples and raise the question of "significance" in even sharper ways. A distinction must be made, therefore, between "reading" and "variant"—where the 155
latter term means "significant variant," and it becomes clear that textual critics must raise the question of when a textual *reading* is also a textual *variant*.

There are other aspects to the problem of defining a textual reading or variant. One such issue is what are the limits of a textual variant? That is, what grammatical unit or other measure is to delimit a textual variation when two or more manuscripts differ? Another issue—a large and complicated one—concerns readings in ancient versions of the New Testament; how are they to be understood as "variants" to the Greek New Testament? And, by extension, how are patristic quotations, whether Greek, Latin, Syriac, Coptic, or other, to be treated in terms of variants?

Like most aspects of life and learning, the seemingly simple turns out, upon analysis, to be complex and to veil a multitude of uncertainties and ambiguities. In the present case, a fresh scrutiny of that irreducibly basic entity in New Testament textual criticism, the "textual variant," is essential, first, to alert those who use the term simplistically to the serious terminological and methodological issues involved and, in the second place, to push toward the clarification and definition of the term and of related expressions.

II. Colwell and Tune on the Classification of Insignificant Variants

The problems posed above by way of example must, today, be approached with reference first of all to the brief 1964 article of Ernest C. Colwell (1901–1974) and Ernest W. Tune on "Variant Readings: Classification and Use."[2] Like all of Colwell's articles, this is a terse presentation that offers a penetrating analysis of the problems

[2] E. C. Colwell and Ernest W. Tune, "Variant Readings: Classification and Use," *JBL* 83 (1964) 253–61; reprinted as "Method in Classifying and Evaluating Variant Readings," in Colwell, *Studies in Methodology in Textual Criticism of the New Testament* (NTTS 9; Leiden: Brill, 1969) 96–105. References that follow are to the latter.

and then moves rapidly, by a series of programmatic statements, toward the solution of those problems. Accordingly, the article was quickly and properly recognized as a methodological milestone, particularly on the path toward the successful quantitative measurement of manuscript relationships. Its weaknesses are its brevity and the consequent lack of detail and of attention to further implications of
156 the principles there established. It is evident, however, that Colwell and Tune's apposite term, "variation-unit," has become standard, referring to each and every section or "length of the text wherein our manuscripts present at least two variant forms."[3] The "length" or extent of a variation-unit, they said, is determined according to "those elements of expression in the Greek text which regularly exist together."[4] The two examples they give are clear enough: when an alteration of an initial conjunction in a sentence is accompanied regularly by a change in verbal form, the unit includes both the conjunction and the verbal form; when a transposition in word order affects the presence/absence of an article, all the words involved constitute a single unit. What is not so clear is whether this understanding of the limits of a variation-unit is formulated with adequate precision or what problems emerge in actual practice. For one thing, at times a multitude of readings will be clustered within a single grammatical or syntactical unit and, upon analysis, will group themselves into two or more sub-formations of variants, with the sub-formations bearing no relationship to one another. In such a case the delimitation of a variation-unit in terms of "elements of expression which regularly exist together" is not adequate to the complexities of the actual situation, and the question arises, are the various sub-formations of such a "variation-unit" to be understood as variation-units in themselves?

Colwell and Tune, however, have provided a simple but fundamental—and therefore important—clarification that a "variation-unit" is not the same as a "variant," for "a variant . . . is one of the possible alternative readings which are found in a variation-unit."[5] It is of considerable importance to note, furthermore, that Colwell and Tune actually—though much less directly—defined "variation-unit"

[3] Ibid., 97.
[4] Ibid., 99.
[5] Ibid., 99–100.

in more precise terms than found in the statements quoted above; for them a variation-unit, as is evident from the full discussion in the article, is that length of text (1) where our Greek New Testament manuscripts present at least two variant forms *and* (2) where each variant form is supported by at least two Greek manuscripts.[6] This further qualification arises out of and depends upon their analysis of "singular readings," a matter to be discussed at length presently. In
reality, however, a still further qualification would have to be added— 157
based on their assessment of other "insignificant" readings (also discussed below), so that the full definition of a variation-unit, according to Colwell and Tune, would be something like this: that length of the text (1) where our Greek New Testament manuscripts present at least two variant forms, and (2) where each variant form is supported by at least two Greek manuscripts, and (3) from which all "insignificant" readings have been excluded (viz., nonsense readings and clear scribal errors of the homoeoteleuton type). Somewhat simplified and arranged more suitably, the definition might read: *In New Testament textual criticism, a variation-unit is that segment of text where our Greek manuscripts present at least two variant forms and where, after insignificant readings have been excluded, each variant form has the support of at least two manuscripts.*[7] Several aspects of this conception of the variation-unit, as held by Colwell and Tune, will figure prominently in the discussion to follow.

These basic clarifications of the terms "variant" and "variation-unit"—at least in their broad strokes and leaving aside for the moment the details—may seem self-evident to us now, but they were timely and requisite; already they have aided considerably the refinement of quantitative measurements of manuscript relationships[8] and should allow for greater precision in text-critical work generally. For one thing, a New Testament textual reading or variant is no longer to be defined (as so often in the past) in terms of variation from a

[6] Ibid., 103–5.

[7] From Colwell's work in the International Greek New Testament Project (IGNTP), it is clear that he considered as "insignificant" also those readings that consist of orthographic difference, particularly itacisms and the presence of the nu-movable.

[8] See, e.g., Gordon D. Fee, *Papyrus Bodmer II (P^{66}): Its Textual Relationships and Scribal Characteristics* (SD 34; Salt Lake City, UT: University of Utah Press, 1968) iv–v ; idem, "Codex Sinaiticus in the Gospel of John: A Contribution to Methodology in Establishing Textual Relationships," *NTS* 15 (1968/69) 25–31.

printed text (such as the *textus receptus*, Westcott-Hort, or Nestle-Aland), but the term refers only and should be limited to variations among actual New Testament manuscripts.[9] Furthermore, Colwell's work
158 would imply that only a variation involving *Greek* New Testament manuscripts deserves the designation "textual variant," though this is an issue requiring further discussion below.

Colwell and Tune proceeded to classify readings that in their judgment were insignificant for purposes of isolating the original text, tracing the history of the text, or determining manuscript kinship and that—for this and other reasons—were to be excluded from the critical apparatus and, for the most part, excluded also from further text-critical tasks. These classes include, first, the *Nonsense Reading*, "that variant reading which does not make sense, and/or cannot be found in the lexicon, and/or is not Greek grammar." Why is it to be excluded both as the original reading and from the critical apparatus? Because, say Colwell and Tune, it is highly unlikely that either the author or scribe wrote nonsense, except as an error, and moreover, because it is more likely that a scribe would write nonsense than that the author would; also the nonsense reading is excluded from the apparatus because "agreement in error" has not commended itself as a method for establishing manuscript relationships; rather, "agreement in readings" has emerged as sound method.[10] This category, the nonsense reading, is clearly established, and the arguments for excluding such readings are sound; few will argue for their originality or even for their retention in the critical apparatus, though the grounds for this exclusion may be variously formulated.

[9] This limitation need not preclude the often useful comparison of manuscript variation with the text, e.g., of the *textus receptus*, which in such cases is used as the general representative of a vast number of late manuscripts, nor should it preclude the use of the *textus receptus* as a base or standard, as in the IGNTP, where it serves without prejudice as the collation base, or in a process like the Claremont Profile Method, where it serves as a fixed, neutral reflecting board. In both instances the *textus receptus* actually facilitates the comparison of manuscripts with one another, and in both cases true "variants" and "variation-units" as defined above are easily derived or formulated from the data provided. Yet, technically speaking, the readings of the *textus receptus* or any other constructed text are not "variants" as here so far defined; they only become variants when they are identified as readings of particular Greek manuscripts. Nor are the readings of a particular manuscript "variants" when they are isolated by comparison with the *textus receptus*; they also become variants only when the *textus receptus* readings in question are identified as actual manuscript readings.

[10] Colwell and Tune, "Method in Classifying," 101–2.

The second class of reading to be excluded is the *Dislocated Reading*, which is Colwell's term for the unintentional deletion of a passage (haplography) or the unintentional repetition of a passage (dittography) because of similar or identical words in a narrow context. Usually such an error is clear and demonstrable.[11] The brevity of this discussion in Colwell's work, as well as the tentative terminology that is employed, suggest that further analysis of the Dislocated 159
Reading category is warranted. For one thing, are not harmonizations—particularly within the Gospels, but also involving Old Testament quotations and epistolary material in Paul—really dislocated readings? Very often readings of this kind can be demonstrated to be harmonistic additions or conformations, and very often—though this is more difficult to document—they were unintentional, almost unconscious alterations, though inevitably they would yield sense, not nonsense. Should they be designated as insignificant, meaningless readings? One would be inclined to say "yes" if their secondary character were unambiguously demonstrable, though this is unlikely to be the case.

Furthermore, so-called errors of the ear, involving the alteration from one letter or word to a similar-sounding letter or word, might be included in the Dislocated Reading category, for such readings often can be identified as clear errors, though occasionally (especially in the case of the plural personal pronouns) it is difficult to determine the direction in which the alteration moved.[12] If such alterations produce nonsense, both the direction of the change and the certainty of an error will be clear; when the result makes sense, however, it will become much more risky to exclude it as a dislocated reading, for not always will it be an indisputably demonstrable error.

Finally, the transposition of letters within a word or changes in the sequence of words[13] might be called dislocated readings and thereby be excluded if nonsense is produced, but again, when sense is maintained in the variant reading, exclusion from the apparatus or from other text-critical tasks would be dangerous and unwarranted.

None of these further candidates for dislocated readings figures in

---

[11] Ibid., 102–3.

[12] See some examples in Bruce M. Metzger, *The Text of the New Testament: Its Transmission, Corruption, and Restoration* (2nd ed.; Oxford/New York: Oxford University Press, 1968) 190–92 [= 3rd ed., 1992].

[13] For examples, ibid., 193 [= 3rd ed., 1992].

Colwell and Tune's discussion, but it will be apparent, I think, that their Dislocated Readings and any extension of that category to other kinds of readings along the lines suggested above will isolate insignificant readings with a measure of certainty *only* when those readings produce nonsense or when the process of error can be clearly recognized; however, the category is plagued by considerable uncertainty when alleged dislocated readings yield sense, for then it is difficult to tell whether some form of haplography or dittography has occurred, whether without any doubt harmonization has taken place, whether
160 a hearing error was in fact the cause of a variation or which of two similar-sounding but construable words came first in the textual tradition, or whether or not the transposition of a letter or word resulted from error and, if so, which reading occasioned the other. These uncertainties suggest that perhaps this classification, the Dislocated Reading, should be abandoned and that those readings that constitute nonsense simply should be relegated to the first category, that of nonsense readings. If, however, there are some readings that make sense and yet *with certainty* can be traced to scribal error, they should be grouped under a new category discussed below (i.e., clear and demonstrable scribal errors).

The third kind of reading that Colwell and Tune suggested for exclusion from the critical apparatus is the *Singular Reading*, of which some will be nonsense or may be dislocations (to use their term), while others will make sense; all, however, stand alone in the (known) Greek manuscript tradition, for a singular reading is a variation of text within a variation-unit that is supported by one Greek manuscript but has no other (known) support in the Greek tradition. This category bristles with problems, some of which Colwell and Tune acknowledge (e.g., that future collations or discoveries may eliminate the "singular" status of a reading, or that singular readings may be of value in assessing scribal habits and thereby in evaluating the non-singular readings of a particular manuscript—calling in question their exclusion),[14] though other problems are not discussed (e.g., is a singular reading in the [known] Greek manuscript tradition still a "singular" reading when it has the support of manuscripts of the ancient versions? This is an issue of considerable importance in connection with a textual stream like that of the "Western," in which relatively

[14] Colwell and Tune, "Method in Classifying," 103–5.

little attestation is available in Greek, though relatively much more is available in certain ancient versional manuscripts).

Some researchers in recent attempts at the quantitative measurement of manuscript relationships have eliminated singular readings from their tabulations and tacitly, if not always explicitly, have defended this point in Colwell's methodology.[15] Naturally, Colwell and Tune themselves excluded singular readings (referred to, at that time, as "unique readings") from their tabulations in another programmatic and subsequently influential essay, "Method in Establishing Quantitative Relationships between Text-Types of New Testament 161
Manuscripts."[16] Other recent researchers in this area have included singular readings in their first assessment of manuscript variation, but—utilizing conscious and careful refinements of Colwell's method—have removed such readings from their final tabulations when these were designed to reveal manuscript relationships, thus supporting, essentially, Colwell's point. In these cases the singular readings have been employed for other, more restricted text-critical purposes,[17] following methods elaborated elsewhere by Colwell himself.[18] The usefulness of singular readings in discerning scribal patterns, purposes, and characteristics, both in recent and older studies, should caution us against the simple or premature exclusion of singular readings from all text-critical tasks other than, to use Colwell's phrase, "the

[15] See, e.g., Frederik Wisse and Paul R. McReynolds in E. C. Colwell, I. A. Sparks, F. Wisse, and P. R. McReynolds, "The International Greek New Testament Project: A Status Report," *JBL* 87 (1968) 193.

[16] E. C. Colwell and E. W. Tune, "The Quantitative Relationships between MS. Text-types," in J. N. Birdsall and R. W. Thomson, eds., *Biblical and Patristic Studies in Memory of Robert Pierce Casey* (Freiburg/Basel/New York: Herder, 1963) 25–32; reprinted as "Method in Establishing Quantitative Relationships between Text-Types of New Testament Manuscripts," in Colwell, *Studies in Methodology*, 56–62.

[17] See G. D. Fee, "Codex Sinaiticus in the Gospel of John: A Contribution to Methodology in Establishing Textual Relationships," *NTS* 15 (1968/69) 28–34; 42–43; Larry W. Hurtado, "Codex Washingtonianus in the Gospel of Mark: Its Textual Relationships and Scribal Characteristics" (Ph.D. dissertation, Case Western Reserve University, 1973) 50–54; 194–201; 231–39 [but see now L. W. Hurtado, *Text-critical Methodology and the Pre-Caesarean Text: Codex W in the Gospel of Mark* (SD 43; Grand Rapids, MI: Eerdmans, 1981) 67–84, 86–88].

[18] E. C. Colwell, "Scribal Habits in Early Papyri: A Study in the Corruption of the Text," *The Bible in Modern Scholarship: Papers Read at the 100th Meeting of the Society of Biblical Literature, December 28–30, 1964* (ed. J. Philip Hyatt; Nashville/New York: Abingdon, 1965) 370–89; reprinted as "Method in Evaluating Scribal Habits: A Study of P^{45}, P^{66}, P^{75}," in Colwell, *Studies in Methodology*, 106–24.

initial appraisal of the work of the scribe in a particular manuscript."[19] Colwell and Tune, however, appear to have made two valid points: (1) singular readings are not genetically or genealogically significant and should not be counted in quantitative measures of manuscript kinship, and (2) in a textual tradition as rich as that of the New Testament, the high probability is that no original reading has survived solely in a singular reading.[20] Not all readily will grant the validity of these points, especially the latter one, but they form two rules that may be affirmed generally, though—as with all rules—allowance will have to be made for noteworthy exceptions.

In addition, there are some terminological problems with respect to the designation, "singular reading." Gordon D. Fee, for example, speaks in one of his articles of "singular agreements" of א and D,[21] by which he means that א and D alone among the Greek manu-
162 scripts have a particular reading. It is quite clear what he means by this, but the juxtaposition of "singular agreements" with the term "singular readings" perhaps complicates unnecessarily an already confusing terminological situation; surely a term such as "dual agreements" or, better, "peculiar dual agreements" would relieve the ambiguities encouraged by the use of similar language when referring, on the one hand, to a reading with single and solitary support (a genuinely singular reading) and, on the other, to a reading with dual, but only dual, support.

Just as understandable perhaps, but more problematic are terms such as "nearly singular" and "subsingular."[22] The latter term apparently was introduced by Westcott-Hort, who defined subsingular readings as those having "only secondary support, namely, that of inferior Greek MSS, of Versions, or of Fathers, or of combinations of docu-

---

[19] Colwell and Tune, "Variant Readings,"104.

[20] Ibid.

[21] Fee, "Codex Sinaiticus in the Gospel of John," 38; 42–43; cf. 31–32.

[22] For the former, see, e.g., ibid., 34; 43; for the latter, see Brooke Foss Westcott and Fenton John Anthony Hort, *The New Testament in the Original Greek* (2 vols.; Cambridge/London: Macmillan, 1881–1882) 2.230; 238; 246–50; Wisse and McReynolds in Colwell et al., "International Greek New Testament Project," 193; and Fee in an unpublished paper presented to the Textual Criticism Seminar of the SBL, 1974: "Toward the Clarification of Textual Variation: Colwell and Tune Revisited" [published as "On the Types, Classification, and Presentation of Textual Variation," E. J. Epp and G. D. Fee, *Studies in the Theory and Method of New Testament Textual Criticism* (SD 45; Grand Rapids, MI: Eerdmans, 1993) 62–79].

mentary authorities of these kinds."[23] Obviously, for Westcott-Hort "subsingular" involved more of a qualitative judgment than a quantitative measure. Today in the quantitative measurement of manuscript relationships, the term "inferior" would not be applied to any Greek manuscript or to any other textual witnesses, for qualitative judgments (and especially pre-judgments) have no place in this phase of text-critical methodology. Subsingular, therefore, never should be employed in Westcott-Hort's sense of readings with relatively narrow support, for in such a loose use of the terms "nearly singular" and "subsingular" the singularity aspect is lacking completely. To be sure, in these cases the self-contradictory nature of the terms themselves could be overlooked, for language demands ways of expressing—if colloquially—"almost unique," hence "almost singular"; yet it is difficult to know where to draw the line on a spectrum that, at one end, has singular, singular-plus-one, singular-plus-two, etc., all of which still are referred to by using some form of the term "singular."

Gordon Fee has given a new and different sense to the term "subsingular reading"; he defines it as "a non-genetic, accidental agreement in variation between two MSS which are not otherwise closely 163
related,"[24] and here "related" refers to a tested quantitative relationship. The difficulty with this use of "subsingular," of course, is that at least plausible grounds must be established in each case for the *accidental* or *coincidental* nature of the agreement between two readings that are in reality two independent "singular" readings; not always will this be easy to do, though Fee's presumption is that the lack of relatedness as judged by quantitative tests is itself sufficient evidence of their independence. Thus, if the independence of the two readings is reasonably certain, the term "subsingular" in Fee's sense is an apt and useful term, for "singular" in the term actually is intended to specify *singular*, but the coincidence in the singularity of reading in the two manuscripts warrants the qualification *sub*singular—less than completely singular, nevertheless still within the category of singular.

Finally, even more complex is the use of the term "singular" for a reading of a Greek manuscript that is a reading unique in the

[23] Westcott-Hort, *New Testament in the Original Greek*, 2.230.

[24] Fee, "Toward Clarification," 10 [see now Fee, "On the Types . . . of Textual Variation," 67].

(known) Greek manuscript tradition, but that has some additional support from ancient versional manuscripts—a problem alluded to earlier. To cite an example again from Fee's indispensable treatise on quantitative method, he speaks at one point of Codex Bezae's "twenty-three singular readings in this chapter [John 8], nine of which have Old Latin and/or Old Syriac support."[25] All of these are, as far as we know, singular readings in the *Greek* manuscript tradition, and in Colwell's terms that is the proper framework and appropriate limitation for defining singular readings. But are the nine with Old Latin or Old Syriac support really singular readings in any final sense of that term? Logic would seem to require an answer in the negative, but such an answer, if acted upon, would multiply vastly the complexity of quantitative methods now so successfully employed for determining manuscript groupings, for not only would the versional evidence have to be fed into the process at *all* points (not only in cases of alleged singular readings), but this evidence would have to come from full collations of numerous versional manuscripts in several languages and, what is more problematic, would have to be stated in terms of its Greek equivalent at every variation-
164 unit.[26] Even a cursory acquaintance with the versional evidence will expose the difficulties, the uncertainties and ambiguities, and the inconveniences of such a procedure. Would the benefits that might flow from such added labors be commensurate with those efforts? A superficial guess would be that in a book like the Fourth Gospel, with its rich and extensive Greek attestation, the results would not repay the efforts; yet a procedure that would utilize a fuller range of versional evidence has interesting implications for the application of quantitative methods, for example, to the "Western" text of Acts, where often only one "clearly" "Western" witness in Greek is extant for a given variation-unit, but where several additional "Western" witnesses in Latin, Coptic, or Syriac offer the same or similar reading.

As a matter of fact, a major source of disquietude about the Colwell-Tune definition of a singular reading—singularity defined by

[25] Fee, "Codex Sinaiticus in the Gospel of John," 43.

[26] Critical apparatuses, unless they include *all* significant variants (however that is defined) in the manuscripts treated, cannot be used in such a process, for sound method demands that *total* agreement and disagreement among witnesses be measured.

taking into account only the Greek tradition—is Codex Bezae. As so often in New Testament textual criticism, this troublesome codex and the "Western" text in general have a way of ruining standard procedure and neat distinctions. The leading principles that Colwell and Tune enunciated with reference to the utility of singular readings are basically sound and acceptable: singular readings are not genetically or genealogically significant, and in a rich textual tradition like that of the New Testament an original reading is not likely to have been preserved only in a singular reading; hence, singular readings are "insignificant" for the text-critical tasks related to these two principles. Yet, the obvious importance of Codex Bezae in tracking the early history of the New Testament text and the early and widespread nature of the "Western" text in general should caution against any procedure that would rule out of court, almost without a hearing, a large body of early, interesting, and unmistakably important evidence. This indeed would be the fate of a great many of D's readings if singularity is to be defined with reference solely to the Greek manuscript tradition, for these numerous singular readings of D, particularly in Acts, then could play no rôle in questions of the original text of Acts when in reality the greater number of the "unique" D-readings have support—sometimes broad support—from manuscripts of one, two, or more of the most ancient versions of the New Testament. Presumably some accident of history stunted the preservation in Greek of this rich and colorful "Western" tradi- 165
tion and confined its transmission largely to Latin and Syriac (and the Coptic manuscript G67). Furthermore, the determination and measurement of textual relationships *within* the "Western" tradition of the Gospels and Acts is entirely excluded if quantitative methods are to be limited to nothing but Greek witnesses. Yet, the alternating claims to cohesiveness and to diversity in that "Western" tradition need to be tested by such methods, and this can be done only on the basis of a more restrictive criterion for the identification and subsequent exclusion of "singular readings"—that is, fewer singular readings must be allowed to succumb to exclusion if quantitative methods are to function in the sphere of the "Western" textual tradition.

Acts 3:17, with its four variation-units [though the term is used loosely here for the sake of illustration], represents a typical case in the "Western" text of Acts and serves to illustrate the problem:

Acts 3:17

Note: The reading on the top line is that of the entire manuscript tradition with the exception, of course, of the witnesses attesting the readings on the lower lines or lines.

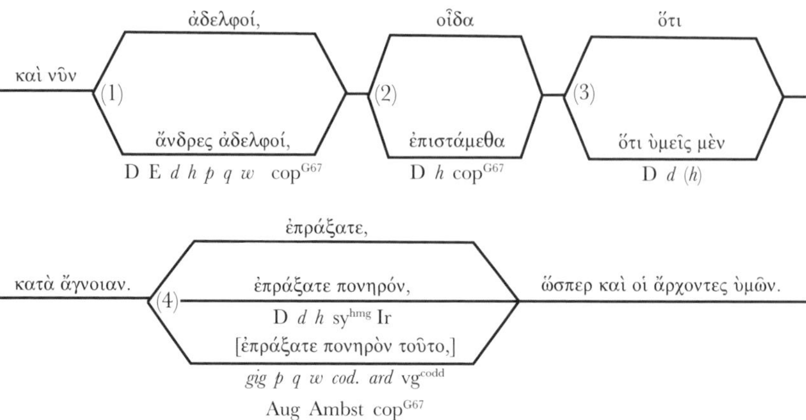

In this example, D and its versional and patristic allies have the support of a Greek manuscript only in variation-unit (1), in this case Codex E. Accordingly, the lower readings in variation-units (2), (3), and (4) would be singular readings if only the Greek tradition were taken into account. The D-reading in variation-unit (3), because of the uncertain reading in the text of *h*, may have to be taken as a singular reading in any event, since only Codex Bezae (D and d)
166 supports it; in variation-unit (2), D is supported by two of the rather primary "Western" witnesses to the text of Acts; and in variation-unit (4), containing the obviously most striking and important of the textual divergences in the passage, the D-reading would be a singular reading if only Greek witnesses were consulted, but it has strong support from *h*, sy^{hmg}, and cop^{G67}, three primary "Western" witnesses, plus the widespread support of mixed or secondary "Western" witnesses, though cop^{G67} and all the secondary witnesses add the demonstrative, "this," to form, in actuality, an additional reading not found in the Greek tradition (though all witnesses listed support the focal point of the variation-unit, the term πονηρόν, "evil thing").

The point is a simple one, though clear: on the Colwell-Tune definition the most interesting and widely-attested alternative reading in this passage fails to achieve the status of "variant," with all the rights and responsibilities attached thereto, for it—and two of the other three D-readings—are relegated to a kind of textual Sheol, a shadowy textual existence, by the failure of the term "singular" to mean singular.

Beyond the complexities already enumerated, any alteration of the category, "singular reading," by taking into account versional manuscript evidence opens up also the further vexing question of whether Greek and other *patristic evidence* should be accounted when verifying singular readings. The additional difficulties that accompany the use of this kind of testimony are well known, and the total, monumental task of coping with the masses of material—Greek, versional, patristic—and with the several sublevels of complexity that they entail staggers the imagination and surely will be a deterrent to what otherwise commends itself as a desirable goal, namely, the casting of the text-critical net as widely as possible in the sea of apposite witnesses to the New Testament text.

The ten-page article of Colwell and Tune has provided us, either directly or upon our further analysis, with several fundamental clarifications of basic terminology in textual criticism, such as "reading," "variant," "significant reading," "insignificant reading," "singular reading," and "variation-unit." Some of these clarifications are definitive just as Colwell and Tune formulated them; others challenge us to reach for definitive formulations that will add greater precision and self-confidence to our practice of New Testament textual criticism.

III. Recommended Definitions and Limitations

The preceding discussions quite clearly demand an attempt at formal and precise definitions of the major terms related to the phe- 167
nomenon of textual variation. If these proposed definitions and limitations serve only to alert us to the issues involved, they will have served one of their chief purposes; if, in addition, they should lead to or commend themselves as standard formulations, they will have fulfilled their further goal.

A. *Reading*

The term "reading" is a general term designating a textual difference or a varying text-formulation and refers to any divergence of text in a passage or segment of text in one manuscript as compared with the same segment of text in any other manuscript, or even by the comparison of two or more hands in the same manuscript. The term "reading," therefore, may designate any kind of textual disagreement, whether it is later to be classified as nonsense or meaningless error, as an orthographic difference, as a singular reading, as a correction, as a significant reading, or as falling into any other category. "Reading" is the broadest term for a dissimilarity disclosed by the comparison of two or more manuscripts or of different hands in the same manuscript. It may be used also to designate the text-formulation in any segment of a constructed text (e.g., such recognized texts as the *textus receptus* or Westcott-Hort) or of any critical edition of any part of the New Testament. Moreover, any textual divergence is always a "reading" before it is anything else, and the term should be distinguished from the narrower term "variant"; as we shall see, a "reading" may remain a "reading" permanently, or, depending upon its nature, may become a "variant." This leads to the remaining and more specific terms requiring definition.

B. *Significant and Insignificant Readings*

"Readings" fall into two large sub-divisions; they are either "significant" readings or "insignificant" readings, and in this context "significant" means meaningful or useful for the broad tasks of New Testament textual criticism, including the determination of a manuscript's relationship with all other manuscripts, the location of a manuscript within the textual history and transmission of the New Testament, and the ultimate goal of establishing the original text. By the same token, "insignificant" means inappropriate, inadequate, or inconclusive for those broad tasks of textual criticism, but it does not mean insignificant in any absolute and final sense. Both "significant" and
168 "insignificant" readings—that is, all readings—may be useful for understanding the nature and characteristics of an *individual manuscript* and of the scribe or scribes of that manuscript,[27] and for this reason it is essential that an edition of any manuscript isolate and analyze thoroughly all of its readings prior to separating the "insignificant" readings from the "significant." (This isolation of a

[27] See esp. Colwell, "Method in Evaluating Scribal Habits," 106–24.

manuscript's readings ideally must employ a quantitative measure, utilizing adequate representatives of all major groups of New Testament manuscripts). "Insignificant readings" may be subdivided into four classes, and any reading that is identified as belonging to one or another of these classes should be eliminated from the data employed for the broad tasks of New Testament textual criticism, as these have been described above. "Significant readings," on the other hand, are "textual variants" in the technical and restricted sense; they alone are accorded the designation "variants" and are treated separately below under the heading, "Significant Readings or Variants."

1. *Insignificant Readings*

Insignificant readings, as described in general terms above, may be subdivided adequately under four headings:

a. *Nonsense Readings*

The "nonsense reading" is a reading that fails to make sense because it cannot be construed grammatically, either in terms of grammatical/lexical form or in terms of grammatical structure, or because in some other way it lacks a recognizable meaning. Since authors and scribes do not produce nonsense intentionally, it is to be assumed (1) that nonsense readings resulted from errors in transmission, (2) that they, therefore, cannot represent either the original text or the intended text of any manuscript or alert scribe, and (3) that they do not aid in the process of discerning the relationships among manuscripts. The one exception would be the slavish, overly-scrupulous scribe who would reproduce an uncorrected error, but—as pointed out earlier—agreement in a *common* (that is, commonplace) scribal error certainly could not be taken as demonstrable proof of manuscript kinship, nor would the copying of an *uncommon* error be easily or certainly demonstrable as proof for such a relationship between manuscripts. The "nonsense reading," accordingly, is an "insignificant reading" and should never be called a "variant."

b. *Clear and Demonstrable Scribal Errors*

A second class of "insignificant readings" is comprised of readings 169
that can be construed grammatically and make sense but can be demonstrated with reasonable certainty to be scribal errors. (Any scribal errors that produce nonsense are placed in the preceding classification). Candidates for scribal errors that make sense would

be certain instances of haplography and dittography, cases of harmonization with similar contexts, hearing errors producing a similar-sounding word, and the transposition of letters or words with a resultant change in meaning. The snare in this category, naturally, is the phrase "clear and demonstrable," for no reading that makes sense should be consigned lightly to the "insignificant" category; on the other hand, if the process of error can be recognized and traced with reasonable certainty, there is no reason to retain the erroneous alteration among the "significant readings." A reasonably certain recognition of error may be possible in some instances of each type mentioned above, such as certain cases involving homoeoteleuton, but the use of this classification of "insignificant readings" will by its nature require caution lest some "significant" variant be cast aside prematurely.

c. *Orthographic Difference*

Mere orthographic differences, particularly itacisms and nu-movables (as well as abbreviations) are "insignificant" as here defined; they cannot be utilized in any decisive way for establishing manuscript relationships, and they are not substantive in the search for the original text. Again, the exception might be the work of a slavish scribe, whose scrupulousness might be considered useful in tracing manuscript descent, but the pervasive character of itacism, for example, over wide areas and time-spans precludes the "significance" of orthographic differences for this important text-critical task. Nor is "correct" spelling a material issue when establishing the original text, provided, of course, that no ambiguity in meaning results from the alternative spelling formulations. There is, however, a genuine area of exception, and that concerns the spelling of proper nouns; some classic text-critical and historical problems turn on the forms of names for persons or places, and both experience and prudence suggest that, other things being equal, these particular orthographic differences be preserved in the critical apparatus and as part of the "significant" data of textual criticism.

d. *Singular Readings*

A "singular reading" is a "reading" found in one New Testament manuscript but with the support of no other; it is a unique reading as far as our knowledge of New Testament manuscripts extends.
170 "Singular readings," more so than the other classes of "insignificant readings," may be especially useful in assessing the nature and char-

acteristics of an individual manuscript and its scribe, but "singular readings" are not genetically or genealogically significant, nor is an original reading to be expected among them. Hence, they are to be utilized in the study of individual manuscripts and scribal habits, but should be excluded from those procedures in textual criticism that attempt to determine manuscript kinship or to establish the text of the New Testament.

Singular readings are of two major kinds, "nonsense singular readings" and "singular readings that make sense."[28] Nonsense singular readings should be treated (and classified) as nonsense readings in general, for they will contribute almost nothing to text-critical study, except perhaps a general insight as to the carefulness/carelessness of a particular scribe. Singular readings that make sense, including certain orthographic differences, scribal corrections, harmonizations, and various alterations of a historical, descriptive, ideological, theological, or generally editorial nature, will aid in understanding the particular manuscript under consideration, both in terms of the habits of its scribe and in terms of any stylistic peculiarities or ideological biases.

Whether the term "singular reading" should be applied to a reading that stands alone when only the straight-text Greek manuscript tradition is taken into account (resulting in many singular readings) or should be further limited to a reading that stands alone when not only the Greek manuscripts, but also the ancient versional manuscripts and perhaps the early patristic quotations are taken into account (resulting in fewer singular readings) is a difficult but nonetheless urgent issue, as is evident from our earlier discussion. Exploration of this question is desirable, if not mandatory, in the near future, but for the present, if only for practical reasons, the former limitation—a reading in the Greek manuscript tradition that is found in one manuscript only—should govern the term "singular reading" (1) when quantitative methods are used to search out manuscript relationships and to locate a Greek manuscript within the New Testament textual tradition and (2) when the establishment of the original text is in view. However, for purposes of discerning, for example, the

[28] Colwell, ibid., employs the terms "Nonsense Singular Readings" and "Sensible Singular Readings."

ideological bias of a New Testament manuscript, it will be prudent, if not essential, to adopt the more restrictive view of "singular read-
171 ings," that they must be unique—without support—in the *entire* (known) textual tradition before they can be excluded from consideration. Under the latter principle many previously "singular readings" will lose that status by their support, for example, from Old Latin or Old Syriac manuscripts; particularly, for instance, this will be the case in the text of Acts, where Codex Bezae has numerous "singular" readings when judged solely in terms of the Greek manuscript tradition, but most of these have early versional or patristic support and no longer would be "singular readings" under a more severe policy for establishing singularity. Actually, such an assessment of ideological bias in a manuscript—to extend the example—falls within the scope of the study of an individual manuscript for which otherwise "insignificant readings" are employed anyway, and the suggestion made here, therefore, does not go beyond the basic Colwell-Tune principles for the use of singular readings. What is essential, however, is that the criteria for singularity be reassessed along the lines suggested earlier to determine whether the singular readings hitherto confined to the analysis of an individual manuscript might not be liberated by their versional support for use both in establishing manuscript kinship and in seeking the original text.

We are left, then, with the definition of a "singular reading" as a textual divergence within the Greek manuscript tradition that is attested by one Greek manuscript only, and we are left also with a challenge whether that definition ought to be restated so that the term "singular reading" applies only to a textual divergence without Greek or ancient versional support and without support in the patristic quotations of the New Testament.

2. *Significant Readings or Variants*

The term "variant" or "textual variant" should be reserved for those readings that are "significant" or "meaningful" in the broad tasks of New Testament textual criticism, as specified in B above. It is easier to define "variant" in this proper sense of "significant reading" by indicating what it is not than to specify what it is. To state the obvious, a "significant variant" is any reading that is not determined to be "insignificant," that is, a reading that is not a nonsense reading, not a demonstrable scribal error, not an inconsequential orthographic

difference, and not a singular reading. "Variants," then, will constitute a distillation from the "readings" of a manuscript, though "readings"—including "variants"—can emerge only by comparison with one or more other manuscripts. Normally, a wide range of manu- 172
scripts, that together represent adequately the major manuscript groupings in the New Testament textual tradition, must be employed in the comparison and distillation process so that the isolation and subtraction of the "insignificant readings" and the consequent determination of the "variants" of the manuscript in question can be achieved with a reasonable measure of confidence, thoroughness, and definitiveness. These "variants"—the distillate—then are utilized in text-critical tasks reaching beyond the study of a given manuscript itself, including, of course, that manuscript's relationship with all other manuscripts and ultimately the quest for the original text of the New Testament.

Subclassifications of "significant readings" or "variants" require exploration, for they will provide the means for describing and understanding "variants" from a more positive standpoint; this, however, is beyond the scope of the present discussion.[29]

C. *Variation-Unit*

A "variation-unit" is that determinate quantity or segment of text, constituting a normal and proper grammatical combination, where our manuscripts present at least two variant readings and where, after insignificant readings have been excluded, each variant reading has the support of at least two manuscripts. Of course, if the technical definition of "variant" (B.2 above) is clearly understood and carefully applied, the definition of a variation-unit can be stated much more succinctly as *that segment of text, constituting a normal and proper grammatical combination, where our manuscripts present at least two "variants."* Whether the word "Greek" should be specified and inserted before the word "manuscripts" in the definitions above involves those same issues explored in connection with singular readings. Again, for the present let us assume that "manuscripts" means "Greek manuscripts" in the definitions, but at the same time let us face the

[29] [Such classifications have been proposed by Fee, "On the Types . . . of Textual Variation."]

challenge of broadening the term "manuscripts" to include ancient versional witnesses and perhaps also early patristic quotations.

The attempt to define the limits or extent of a variation-unit by the phrase, "constituting a normal and proper grammatical combination," may lack precision when it comes to actual practice, for
173 what may appear to be a single variation-unit in the sense just described often will contain, in fact, more than one set of separate and genetically unrelated variants.[30] This complicates matters, for is such a "variation-unit" really more than one unit, or should such a variation-unit be said to consist of several inner sets of variants, each of which is tabulated separately in a quantitative analysis? Gordon D. Fee, who calls attention to this problem, suggests from extensive experience that "a count of agreements in variation-units alone will reveal clear patterns of relationships, while a count including sets of variants refines the details of agreements within major groups."[31] The delimitation of "variation-unit" as constituting a normal and proper grammatical unit lacks precision also in another respect, for there are larger and smaller "proper grammatical combinations"; a suggested refinement, which still will depend on the peculiarities of each situation, is that in every case where a variation-unit is being defined the *shortest* or *smallest possible* grammatical unit be selected, that is, the shortest grammatically-related segment of text that still will encompass all the variants from across the manuscript tradition that present themselves at that point.

IV. Conclusion

When is a "reading" a "variant"? When the reading is a "significant" reading by virtue of its fitness for genetic and genealogical tracking and by virtue of its appropriateness as a possibly original reading. And how is a variant thus fit and appropriate? By virtue of its character as a reading that makes sense, that is not an indisputably

[30] [See Fee, ibid., and the exhibits appended. This phenomenon is referred to as the "nesting" of variants by Vinton A. Dearing, "Determining Variations by Computer," *SBLSP* (1974) 22; see the entire essay for a somewhat different approach to the analysis and identification of textual variation.]

[31] [See Fee, "On the Types . . . of Textual Variation," 66.]

demonstrable scribal error, that is not a mere orthographic difference, and that is not a singular reading. And, because a "reading" in general and a "variant" in particular exist only over against another and divergent reading, a variant to be a variant must be a member of a "variation-unit," that entity that brings into direct confrontation two or more variants and thereby constitutes the basic and indispensable factor in the discipline of textual criticism.

Added Notes, 2004

In general. The essay above is complementary to a significant contribution by Gordon D. Fee, "On the Types, Classification, and Presentation of Textual Variation," E. J. Epp and G. D. Fee, *Studies in the Theory and Method of New Testament Textual Criticism* (SD 45; Grand Rapids, MI: Eerdmans, 1993) 62–79. His paper and mine, along with others by Vinton A. Dearing and James T. Clemons, comprised the program titled "Toward the Clarification and Definition of the Term 'Textual Variant'" for the New Testament Textual Criticism Seminar at the 1974 Society of Biblical Literature Annual meeting in Washington, D.C. Along with a discussion on defining variants, etc., Fee's paper provides extensive detail, with eleven full-page exemplary charts, on how to arrange and display the elements in a variation-unit.

On Singular Readings. Undoubtedly the most controversial matter discussed in the essay is the meaning and use of "singular readings." For example, see James R. Royse, "Scribal Habits in the Transmission of New Testament Texts," *The Critical Study of the Sacred Texts* (ed. Wendy Doniger O'Flaherty; Berkeley, CA: Berkeley Religious Studies Series, 1979) 154–55; idem, "Scribal Tendencies in the Transmission of the Text of the New Testament," *The Text of the New Testament in Contemporary Research: Essays on the* Status Quaestionis (eds. B. D. Ehrman and M. W. Holmes; SD 46; Grand Rapids, MI: Eerdmans, 1995) 239–52; idem, *Scribal Habits in Early New Testament Papyri* (SD 47; Grand Rapids, MI: Eerdmans, 2005), whose large volume offers massive data on early scribal habits based on singular readings. See also Moisés Silva, "The Text of Galatians: Evidence from the Earliest Greek Manuscripts," *Scribes and Scripture: New Testament Essays in Honor of J. Harold Greenlee* (ed. David Alan Black; Winona Lake, Ind.: Eisenbrauns, 1992) 18, who asserts that singular readings are "of great value . . . for determining scribal tendencies."; Eberhard Güting, "Der editorische Bericht zur Text," *Editio* 7 (1993) 107, who states that "readings that clarify the development of the early textual history should not . . . be excluded from the apparatus"; and Klaus Wachtel, "Colwell Revisited: Grouping New Testament Manuscripts," *The New Testament Text in Early Christianity: Proceedings of the Lille Colloquium, July 2000* (eds. C.-B. Amphoux and J. K. Elliott; HTB 6; Lausanne: Zèbre, 2003), 34–35, says that disregarding singular readings "cannot be methodologically sound and may even be regarded as a violation of logic." See also, E. J. Epp, "Issues in New Testament Textual Criticism: Moving from the Nineteenth Century to the Twenty-First Century," *Rethinking New Testament Textual Criticism* (ed. D. A. Black; Grand Rapids, MI.: Baker Academic, 2002) 29.

CHAPTER SIX

THE ECLECTIC METHOD IN NEW TESTAMENT TEXTUAL CRITICISM: SOLUTION OR SYMPTOM?[1]

I. Problem and Purpose 211

The "eclectic method" in New Testament textual criticism is one of several disguises for the broad and basic problem of the "canons of criticism" or of the "criteria for originality" as applied to the various readings in the New Testament textual tradition, and in a real sense eclectic methodology—in its several forms as currently practiced—is as much a *symptom* of basic problems in the discipline as it is a proposed and widely applied *solution* to those problems. By the same token, perhaps every methodological approach and even every discussion of methodology in New Testament textual criticism could be described as symptomatic of the problems. Yet the eclectic method seems in a particularly pointed way to veil the problems of the discipline, for by its very nature it tries in one way or another to utilize all available approaches to textual problems, and in a single
given case of seeking the original text it often wishes to apply to the 212
problem several established text-critical criteria, even if these criteria have the appearance of being mutually exclusive or contradictory. If indeed basic problems are disguised by the eclectic approach, perhaps they also can be disclosed by a careful scrutiny of the eclectic method.

The eclectic approach to the recovery of the most likely original text of the New Testament is, in its broadest definition, a method (1) that treats each text-critical problem (normally a single "variation-unit") separately and largely in isolation from other problems,

[1] A paper prepared originally for the Textual Criticism Group of the Society of Biblical Literature, Chicago, 30 October 1975, and printed in *SBLSP* 1975, 2.47–82; it appears here by permission and with revisions prompted by the seminar discussion.

This study was conducted while the author was a Fellow of the John Simon Guggenheim Memorial Foundation, 1974–75, and the support and generosity of the Foundation are gratefully acknowledged.

(2) that "chooses" or "selects" (ἐκλέγομαι) from among the available and recognized text-critical criteria those that presumably are appropriate to that particular text-critical situation, and (3) that then applies the selected criteria in such a way as to "pick" or "choose" (ἐκλέγομαι) a reading from one or another manuscript and thereby arrive at a text-critical decision for that particular variation-unit. (Incidentally, it is not clear whether the term "eclectic" refers primarily to the *selection of readings* from here and there or to the *choice of criteria* from among the many and various ones available. It is clear, however, that both kinds of choice are prominent in the eclectic approach.)

The term "eclectic," as applied to New Testament textual criticism, not only is comparatively recent in its use but also varied in its meaning and emphasis, as the succeeding pages show. Its earliest occurrence in this context may have been in L. Vaganay's text-critical manual of 1934, where he employed "eclectic" to describe an evenhanded method that took into account the analysis of error in textual transmission as well as the assessment of both documentary evidence and intrinsic quality of readings. A decade later the term "eclecticism" (with certain restrictive adjectives, such as "rigorous," "impartial," and "consistent") was used by G. D. Kilpatrick to refer to a decidedly one-sided approach, which emphasized stylistic rather than documentary considerations and which earlier had been designated "rational criticism" (*critique rationnelle*) by M.-J. Lagrange
213 in 1935.[2] "Eclecticism," then, has been applied not only to the proposal for a balanced text-critical method that would utilize critical principles drawn from both external and internal criticism, but also—strangely enough—to a method emphasizing only one of these, namely, internal criticism; still more recently, "eclecticism" has been used to designate a method that actually gives the deciding voice to external evidence. Whether a single term is appropriate for such a wide

[2] L. Vaganay, *An Introduction to the Textual Criticism of the New Testament* (London: Sands, 1937) 91–94; French original, Paris: Bloud & Gay, 1934. For Kilpatrick, see nn. 87 and 96 below. For Lagrange, see his *Critique textuelle: II. La critique rationnelle* (EBib; Paris: Gabalda, 1935), esp. 27–40; cf. A. F. J. Klijn, *A Survey of the Researches into the Western Text of the Gospels and Acts* (Utrecht: Kemink, 1949) 170–71. Further on the designation and use of "eclectic," see B. M. Metzger, *The Text of the New Testament: Its Transmission, Corruption, and Restoration* (2d ed.; New York/Oxford: Oxford University, 1968) 175–79; and the references to the works of Grant and Birdsall in the following note.

range of emphases is open to question, but that "eclectic" is used currently in these varied ways is a matter of fact.

The terms "eclectic" and "eclecticism" may have appeared only recently in New Testament textual criticism. Yet in a real sense the eclectic method, taken in its broadest meaning, is as old as the formulation and application of the traditional "canons of criticism," such as those promulgated by J. A. Bengel in 1725, by J. J. Griesbach in 1796, by K. Lachmann in 1842, and others, for if it is axiomatic that "the harder reading is to be preferred," and that "the ancient and weighty witnesses" are to be given priority, then one is forced to choose between or among conflicting criteria when the shorter reading is the easier or the harder reading is the longer, or the shorter or harder reading is attested only by late manuscripts. It is at this point that the delicate and ingenious phrase, "the balance of relative probabilities," comes into play, for when two or more conflicting criteria seem applicable to a given variation-unit, then both the choice of the most appropriate criterion (or criteria) and the textual decision itself become increasingly complex and problematic. In precisely such a situation (logically at least) the eclectic method was born, for at this juncture factors on the external, historical, and documentary side of the transmission of the text are thrown into the balance with factors on the internal, contextual, and stylistic side, and an eclecticism that takes into consideration all conceivably applicable criteria—though always within a "balance of relative probabilities" context—is applied to each case to isolate the most "suitable" criteria or criterion, which then becomes the basis for the selection of the one variant reading that is to be accredited as the most likely original.

Difficulties are multiplied, however, when different values are placed upon different sets of criteria (e.g., on the "external" criteria as opposed to the "internal") by different schools of thought. For instance, when the criterion of the "oldest and best manuscripts" is valued more highly than the criterion of "conformity to the author's style," then textual decisions will vary markedly from those made when
these relative valuations are reversed. Such differing valuations rep- 214
resent, in fact, not only a general problem faced by contemporary textual critics, but also a very special crux in text-critical methodology, for among practitioners of an eclectic approach there is a distinction to be drawn between what might be called *eclectic generalists*

(true eclectics), who in each case of textual variation try to employ the appropriate criteria without prejudice as to their relative weight or value [Do any such "true" eclectics exist?],[3] and *eclectic specialists* (biased eclectics), who tend to fall into two distinct subgroups, (1) those who quite obviously value external criteria above the internal and who utilize the latter mainly to clarify cases plagued by an ambiguous array of external evidence, and (2) those who forthrightly value internal criteria above the external and who rely almost exclusively on grammatical, stylistic, and contextual factors in their textual decisions. The issues underlying these distinctive eclectic approaches determine and constitute the subject matter of the discussion to follow.[4]

[3] Vaganay, *Introduction*. 91–95, would appear to qualify on the basis of his description of "proper" method; F. C. Grant's description of the procedures adopted by the RSV commission may fit this category ("The Greek Text of the New Testament," *An Introduction to the Revised Standard Version of the New Testament*, by members of the Revision Committee [L. A. Weigle, chm.; International Council of Religious Education, 1946] 38–41); also, the combination found in J. N. Birdsall's "The Text of the New Testament," The *Cambridge History of the Bible: Volume I: From the Beginnings to Jerome* (eds. P. R. Ackroyd and C. F. Evans; London/New York: Cambridge University, 1970) 308–77, esp. 316–18, 374–77, of an extensive treatment of the history of the New Testament text in its earliest period and of a strong emphasis on "rational criticism" to achieve, by this twofold approach, the goal of an "eclectic text" suggests that his method fits the category of "true" eclecticism.

[4] These broad classifications (eclectic generalists and specialists), it should be noted, encompass all contemporary New Testament textual critics with the exception of the genealogical scholars; the latter construct stemmata for New Testament textual transmission and thereby affirm the feasibility either of reconstructing the archetype or of isolating the earliest "state" of the New Testament text (or, better, of each major segment or transmissional unit of that text). The older, simplistic genealogical approach (stemmata and archetypes) has been abandoned almost entirely by New Testament textual critics (except in connection with small "families" of manuscripts) because it is both inapplicable to the massive and disparate New Testament data and ineffectual in tracing sure developmental lines through manuscripts with such complex mixture as those of the New Testament textual tradition: see Ernest C. Colwell, "Genealogical Method: Its Achievements and Its Limitations," *JBL* 66 (1947) 113–17; 130–32; reprinted in his *Studies in Methodology in Textual Criticism of the New Testament* (NTTS 9; Leiden: Brill, 1969) 66–70; 81–83; idem, "Hort Redivivus: A Plea and a Program," *Transitions in Biblical Scholarship* (ed. J. Coert Rylaarsdam; Essays in Divinity, 6; Chicago: University of Chicago Press, 1968) 147; reprinted in Colwell's *Studies in Methodology*, 164; Frederic G. Kenyon, *The Text of the Greek Bible* (3rd ed. rev. and augmented by A. W. Adams; London: Duckworth, 1975), 254. An approach known as "textual analysis," which (somewhat more modestly) determines the genealogical relationship between and among the various "states" of a text (though not the genealogy of the documents containing them) with a view

The problem of eclectic methodology, then, has at least two aspects. 215
First, integral to the eclectic method—in all its forms—are the criteria for originality of readings, and these need to be described with some care and assessed, for they are the stock in trade of eclecticism. In the second place, the various eclectic approaches need to be examined, not only to see whether what we have called the eclectic-generalist method is viable, but particularly to scrutinize the relative merits and usefulness of the two competing eclectic-specialist approaches. It has been said often before,[5] but bears repetition, that all of us—except the genealogists—employ an eclectic method, for it is *the* contemporary procedure both for handling separate cases of textual variation and also for formulating critical texts of the New Testament. Yet, recent handbooks and other technical literature of the discipline all too seldom engage in serious self-criticism of this central and basic matter of the methodology employed in isolating the most likely original New Testament text. Above all, our aim in this present discussion is the clear definition and description of the eclectic method and of attendant issues, and beyond that our purpose is the critical evaluation of the eclectic approaches currently in use. In fulfilling these goals it will be instructive, as is so often the case, to employ a historical approach, attempting to show whence and why current eclectic methods developed. Accordingly, a history of the criteria for originality of readings will form the first step in our analysis of the eclectic method and will provide the context for its evaluation.

II. Criteria for Originality of Readings 216

The traditional "canons of criticism" are in reality, of course, criteria for determining the originality of variant readings in a textual tradition, that is, they are principles devised to countervail the corrupting processes attendant to the manuscript transmission of ancient

to identifying the "state" from which all the others have descended (see Vinton A. Dearing, *Principles and Practice of Textual Analysis* [Berkeley/Los Angeles: University of California Press, 1974] 1–2) has not as yet been widely assessed—and certainly not definitively so—by New Testament textual critics in general.

[5] For a recent statement, see Eldon J. Epp, "The Twentieth Century Interlude in New Testament Textual Criticism," *JBL* 93 (1974) 403–5.

texts and are based both on knowledge of the documents transmitting the texts and on acquaintance with the scribal habits of those who copied them.

A. *Use of the Critical Canons in Antiquity*

Undoubtedly the first application—rudimentary and unsystematic as it was—of such canons of criticism to the New Testament text was made by Origen, who, for example, could characterize certain variant readings as found in "few," "many," or "most" manuscripts known to him,[6] an adumbration of the much more modern canon underlying the sixteenth-century phrase, *textus receptus* (TR) or "text received by all," a canon that in reality declares that the reading supported by the largest number of manuscripts is to be accounted original. Although Origen does not always follow the majority reading and at times even rejects a reading of the entire known manuscript tradition,[7] yet the canon of the majority reading is latent in his comments. Moreover, at other times Origen employs etymological and theological canons,[8] and he preferred readings that suited the immediate context (once he uses the phrase, "inner probability") and that were harmonious with parallel passages.[9] A century and a half later, Jerome evidences the use of the canons of age (old manuscripts are given more weight), of scribal quality (the care in writing and in correcting a manuscript affects its reliability), of a reading's suitability to its context, of a reading's grammatical appropriateness,[10]
217 and of harmonization from parallel passages.[11] Though it would be useful to pursue such early uses of critical canons down through the middle ages, in the final analysis it is their formulation and utilization in modern New Testament textual criticism that will be most instructive for us.

---

[6] B. M. Metzger, "Explicit References in the Works of Origen to Variant Readings in New Testament Manuscripts," *Biblical and Patristic Studies in Memory of Robert Pierce Casey* (eds. J. N. Birdsall and R. W. Thomson; Freiburg: Herder, 1963) 81.

[7] Ibid., 91–92.

[8] Ibid., 82, 85, 87.

[9] F. Pack, "Origen's Evaluation of Textual Variants in the Greek Bible," *ResQ* 4 (1960) 144–45.

[10] K. K. Hulley, "Principles of Textual Criticism Known to St. Jerome," *HSCP* 55 (1944) 87–109.

[11] M.-J. Lagrange, *Critique textuelle: II. La critique rationnelle* (EBib; Paris: Gabalda, 1935) 37.

B. *Use of Critical Canons in Modern Times*

It was only in modern times that canons were drawn up in formal fashion, ranging from the first such attempt by Gerhard von Mastricht in his 1711 edition of the Greek New Testament,[12] who lists forty-three canons and comments at length on most of them, to the terse *proclivi scriptioni praestat ardua* ("the harder reading is to be preferred") of Bengel, to Griesbach's fifteen canons and Lachmann's six, and to the various lists of critical principles found in manuals of New Testament textual criticism.[13]

It is instructive to peruse these lists of critical canons, especially those given and employed by various editors of the Greek New Testament down through the years. John Mill of Oxford listed no canons of criticism for his edition in 1707, but he appears to have relied primarily on two canons, that smooth and easy readings are
not necessarily genuine and that the united testimony of different 218
kinds of authorities carries more weight than mere numerical preponderance of authorities, though at the same time he does not regard as important the mere number of manuscripts attesting a

[12] ῾Η ΚΑΙΝΗ ΔΙΑΘΗΚΗ, *Novum Testamentum . . . ac tandem Crisis Perpetua. qua singulas Variantes earumque valorem aut originem ad XLIII. Canones examinat G. D. T. M. D.* [Gerhardus de Trajecto Mosae Doctor] (Amsterdam: ex officinia Wetsteniana, 1711) 11–16, 48–68.

[13] See, as examples, J. D. Michaelis, *Introduction to the New Testament* (tr. H. Marsh; 2nd ed.; London, 1802) I: 1.328–39, who lists about 20 canons; J. L. Hug, *Introduction to the New Testament* (tr. from 3rd German ed. by D. Fosdick, Jr., with notes by M. Stuart; Andover, 1836) 301–7; S. P. Tregelles in T. H. Horne, *An Introduction to the Critical Study and Knowledge of the Holy Scriptures* (4 vols.; 11th ed.; London, 1860) 4.343–45 (this same work, without the "Additions" and "Postscript," was issued earlier under the title, *An Introduction to the Textual Criticism of the New Testament* [London, 1856], with page numbers the same in both); C. E. Hammond, *Outlines of Textual Criticism Applied to the New Testament* (3rd ed., rev.; Oxford: Clarendon, 1880) 93–99; F. H. A. Scrivener, *A Plain Introduction to the Criticism of the New Testament* (4th ed. by E. Miller; 2 vols.; London: G. Bell, 1894) 2.247–56; Eb. Nestle, *Introduction to the Textual Criticism of the Greek New Testament* (London: Williams & Norgate, 1901) 239–41; P. Schaff, *A Companion to the Greek Testament and the English Version* (New York/London: Harper, 1903) 202–5; E. Jacquier, *Le Nouveau Testament dans l'église* chrétienne (2 vols.; Paris: Gabalda, 1911–13) 2.328–35; B. M. Metzger, *The Text of the New Testament: Its Transmission, Corruption, and Restoration* (2nd ed.; New York/Oxford: Oxford University Press, 1968) 209–10; idem, *A Textual Commentary on the Greek New Testament* (London/New York: United Bible Societies, 1971) xxiv–xxviii. Cf. also Lagrange, *Critique textuelle,* 17–40; several canon lists are reproduced in E. C. Colwell, *What Is the Best New Testament?* (Chicago: University of Chicago Press, 1952) 32–33; 73–75; 111–15.

reading. In addition, he considered patristic quotations decisive and highly valued the Latin versions, particularly the Old Latin, in textual decisions.[14] Mill's own formulations of Bengel's later canon concerning the "harder" reading are of interest: ". . . In proportion as a [reading] is more obscure, it is generally speaking more authentic, and among various readings that occur, those that seem clearer are justly suspected of falsification by having crept in from the margins of a MS in place of other more obscure ones." Or, "I consider this reading [in Rom 7:23] to be genuine, as also almost all that are somewhat hard and look absurd"; also, Mill at one point describes a variant as "clearer [*argutius*] rather than correct."[15]

The canons of GERHARD VON MASTRICHT,[16] referred to earlier, were designed to disparage the value of those variant readings that he had taken from the 1710 edition of Mill and Küster's Greek New Testament and had reprinted in his own 1711 edition. His forty-three canons are no longer important in themselves, though extolled by some at the time; they take on significance, however, when it is observed that both Wettstein (b. 1693) and Bengel (b. 1687), very soon after 1711, encountered these canons and the text that accompanied them and apparently were rather profoundly affected by them. Bengel became acquainted with the canons in Heidelberg about 1713, and he published three separate refutations, first in the *apparatus criticus* attached to his edition of 1734 and finally, with considerable detail, in his preface to *Gnomon Novi Testamenti* in 1742.[17]

Many of von Mastricht's canons are concerned with scribal habits
and the causes of variant readings, such as the "negligence, listless-
219 ness, haste, and . . . malice" of scribes (Canon I), the repetition of
words or sentences from the context (II, III), the substitution, addi-

[14] See S. P. Tregelles, *An Account of the Printed Text of the* Greek *New Testament* (London: Bagster, 1854) 44–45; A. Fox, *John Mill and Richard Bentley: A Study of the Textual Criticism of the New Testament* 1675–1729 (Oxford: Blackwell, 1954) 7–71.

[15] Adapted from Fox, *John Mill and Richard Bentley*, 147, where the pertinent Latin texts may be found.

[16] On the name, which has been the subject of controversy, see Ezra Abbot, "Gerhard von Mastricht," in his *The Authorship of the Fourth Gospel and Other Critical Essays* (Boston: Ellis, 1888) 184–88.

[17] I have used the 3rd ed., ed. by J. Steudel (Tübingen, 1855) xiv–xxi. The detailed refutation has been omitted from the English ed. of *Gnomon* (Philadelphia, 1864) and from its recent reprint, *New Testament Word Studies* (2 vols.; Grand Rapids: Kregel, 1971); cf. xx–xxi; xxxiv (= reprint, vol. 1).

tion, omission, or alteration of letters, syllables, words, and the like (V, VI, VII, XXVI, and XXVII), and the growth of variant readings from gospel parallels (XVI, XXIV); moreover, variations recognizable as due to the presumption or impudence of a copyist are not "variant readings" (XXVI, XXVII, cf. IX) and are to be rejected in favor of the "received readings" (cf. VIII), as also to be rejected are "absurd" readings (XXII). Moreover, copyists as well as manuscripts can be observed and described as prone, e.g., to add or to omit (XV, XXX, XXXI). More specifically, especially in cases involving omission, one codex does not make for a variant reading (IX), nor do two codices in agreement against a received reading that makes sense (X), nor do three or four codices produce a viable variant against twenty manuscripts (XI), for "a great number of manuscript codices, for instance twenty or more, establish and approve a received and common reading of good sense, above all in a case of a variant involving an omission" (XII), nor does a reading of three or four codices that does not alter the sense—whether consisting of addition, deletion, or change of construction—command attention, for "certainly no reason is compelling that will prefer a variant reading to a received reading" (VIII). Finally, Canon XXIV indicates that a variant reading commonly disappears when the origin of that variant reading is discovered.

Richard Bentley, in his 1720 pamphlet on *Proposals for Printing* a Greek and Latin New Testament[18] (which task, as is well known, was never completed), made it clear that the criterion of the antiquity of manuscripts (". . . the most ancient and venerable MSS, in Greek and Roman capital letters") was primary (Proposal I), with the corollary that readings chosen for the text must be confirmed by the use of "the old versions, Syriac, Coptic, Gothic, and Aethiopic, and of all the fathers, Greeks and Latins, within the first five centuries," adding that any reading intruding upon any copies since that time is "of no value or authority" (Proposal IV). Bentley's overriding concern appears to be with what are now called external criteria rather than with internal evidence.

J. A. Bengel, in a 1725 "Prodromus" to his proposed edition of

[18] See the text in Arthur A. Ellis, *Bentleii critica sacra: Notes on the Greek and Latin Text of the New Testament, Extracted from the Bentley MSS. in Trinity College Library.* (Cambridge: Deighton, Bell, 1862) xvii–xix.

the Greek New Testament (which appeared in 1734), stated his leading and classic canon, "the harder reading is to be preferred," a principle already utilized with some frequency by Mill in his lengthy prolegomenon. In this celebrated canon, Bengel was responding to his own urgent question as to which reading (in a given case) is
220 likely to have arisen out of the others,[19] and actually he was reducing all of von Mastricht's forty-three canons "to one comprehensive rule of four words":[20] *proclivi scriptioni praestat ardua*. Since Bengel's time, this canon often has been expressed as *difficilior lectio potior*. Akin to this canon are some others issued by Bengel and relating also to internal considerations: readings representing obvious scribal errors or scribal elaborations are inferior (cf. his numbers 13 and 14 below), as are readings showing alliteration, parallelism, or lectionary adjustments to the text (number 14):[21]

> 13. A reading which does not allure by too great facility, but shines by its native dignity, is always to be preferred to that which may fairly be supposed to owe its origin to either the carelessness or the injudicious care of copyists.
> 14. Thus, a corrupted text is often betrayed by *alliteration*, *parallelism*, a modification for the beginning or end of a church lesson. The recurrence of the same words suggests an *omission*; too great facility, a *gloss*. Where various readings are many, the *middle* reading is the best.

Though Bengel's "harder reading" canon is not in this list in so many words, it is presupposed (and actually contained) in both 13 and 14 where the word "facility" occurs.

For text-critical decisions, Bengel also valued highly, as did Mill and Bentley before him, the oldest Greek manuscripts and the Latin versions; this is clear from the preface to his *Gnomon* (1742), where he gives his list of twenty-seven "canons" (he calls them *monitis*—"admonitions,"[22] two of which we have quoted above and many of which range well beyond what normally would be designated as text-critical canons. Admonition 12 is by far the most telling of his rules:

---

[19] W. G. Kümmel, *The New Testament: The History of the Investigation of Its Problems* (Nashville/New York: Abingdon, 1972) 48; cf. 414 n. 45.

[20] Nestle, *Introduction to the Textual Criticism*, 16–17, 239.

[21] Bengel, *Gnomon Novi Testamenti* (3rd ed., ed. by J. Steudel; Tübingen, 1855) xiii; English ed. (see n. 17, above) 1.xviii.

[22] Ibid., Latin ed., xii–xiv; English ed., 1.xvi–xx.

> . . . More witnesses are to be preferred to fewer; and, which is *more important*, witnesses which *differ* in country, age, and language, [are to be preferred] to those which are closely connected with each other; and *most important of all, ancient* witnesses [are to be preferred] to modern ones. For, since the original autographs (which were in Greek) can alone claim to be the Fountain-head, the highest value belongs to those streams which are least removed from it; that is, to the most ancient codices, in Greek, Latin, &c.[23]

Two other canons are closely related to this one: number 9, which 221
refers to versions and patristic quotations as carrying little weight when they differ from Greek manuscripts of the New Testament, but "where Greek manuscripts vary, those have the greatest authority, with which versions and fathers agree"; and number 10, which commends the Latin Vulgate, when supported by Latin fathers, because of its singular "high antiquity."[24]

Just at this point it is essential to emphasize that no discussion of critical canons dare overlook Bengel's greatest contribution to this aspect of New Testament text-critical methodology, namely, his pioneering division of the extant manuscripts into classes or groups (syzygies, he called them), for a fundamental and far-reaching "canon" or principle emerges from (or perhaps underlies) this methodological procedure. For Bengel, all New Testament manuscripts fall either into the *African* "family," consisting of the most ancient Greek manuscripts and the most ancient versions (Codex A, the Greco-Latin codices, and the Ethiopic, Coptic, and Latin versions), or into the *Asiatic* family, made up of the more recent Greek manuscripts and versions. He then speaks of the readings of the African family as "always ancient" and states that those of the Asiatic family, "many as they are, have often but little weight. . . ."[25] Though there were adumbrations of these views, particularly in Mill—who recognized the greater importance of certain combinations of witnesses (such as A and the Latin versions) than of mere numbers of witnesses—and also in Bentley—who viewed the Greek manuscripts as transmitted from three areas (Egypt, Asia, and the West) and who gave preference to the more ancient readings—yet here in Bengel's classification

---

[23] Ibid., Latin ed., xiii; English ed., 1.xviii [italics in original].

[24] Ibid., Latin ed., xiii; English ed., 1.xvii.

[25] See Tregelles in Horne, *Introduction*, 4.69–70; he also gives Bengel's Latin text of these statements.

of known sources of the New Testament text was enunciated for the first time in a systematic formulation the significant and fundamental principle that *textual witnesses must be weighed and not merely counted.* It is noteworthy, too, that in Bengel's text-critical system the internal and external criteria are counterparts, though it is sufficiently clear nonetheless that for him the external considerations have both the first and the decisive voice. This is evident from his Admonition 12 (quoted above), but also by implication from the very phrasing of his summary statement on text-critical principles (Admonition 15):

> 222 There are, therefore, five principle means of judging the Text. The *Antiquity* of witnesses, the *Diversity* of their extraction, and their *Multitude*; in the next place, the *Origin of the corrupt* reading, and the *Native* appearance of the *genuine.*[26]

Obviously, the first three items here involve external criteria, the other two internal, and Bengel—significantly—separates the categories with a semicolon and *tum* ("then," "in the next place"). The last two items refer to Bengel's 13th and 14th Admonitions (see above), covering scribal errors, elaborations, and improvements. Since the first three items of Admonition 15 correspond to the three criteria in Admonition 12 (reversed in order of listing, though not in their order of importance, as the different phrasing will show), we know precisely how Bengel valued these criteria: antiquity of witnesses was most important, then their geographical, language, and age distribution, and last—though still significant—their number. When Bengel in his summary statement then lists, both in a separate category and as "in the next place," matters involving internal considerations, we may be sure that these are subsidiary to the external criteria first listed, and this indication of the superiority of external criteria is supported also by the system of classification that he applied to the textual witnesses.

Bengel, therefore, suggests that text-critical criteria are of two distinct and separable kinds, external and internal, and that external are superior to and more decisive than the internal. Bengel implies moreover, that an eclecticism becomes operative when the evidence or the canons are in conflict: he says of his five principles for judg-

[26] Bengel, *Gnomon.* Latin ed., xiii; English ed., 1.xviii. I have added "in the next place" (*tum*) from Bengel's Latin text, quoting otherwise the English ed.

ing the text, "Where these concur, none can doubt but a skeptic; when, however, it happens that some of these favor one reading, and some another, the critic may be drawn now in this, now in that direction; or, even should he decide, others may be slow to agree with him" (Admonitions 16 and 17).[27]

To what extent did Bengel's canons of criticism shape his text of the New Testament? Actually, his text was hardly affected when measured against the effects that would naturally have been expected to flow from his theories, for he chose to retain the *textus receptus* except when readings judged by him to be original had appeared already in some printed edition of the New Testament. He did, however, impose his judgment on the text in a more direct way by rating variant readings (placed under the text, without reference to
supporting witnesses) according to their closeness to the original and 223
according to their relative merits in comparison with the reading of his printed text. There were five categories, each indicated by a Greek letter: (α) the genuine reading, in Bengel's judgment; (β) a reading whose genuineness was not entirely certain, but which was preferable to the reading in the text; (γ) a reading equal in worth to that in the text, but the choice was unsure; (δ) a reading of less value than that in the text; and (ε) a spurious reading.[28]

Despite his failure to carry through consistently on his principles, Bengel effectively set in motion two processes, each of which was destined to have far-reaching effects upon the establishment of the New Testament text and upon New Testament textual criticism as a discipline. One of these processes would involve the increasing recognition that the oldest manuscripts, rather than the most numerous or smoothest, were the best manuscripts; the other process would involve the alternating cooperation and tension between external criteria and internal considerations in determining the most likely original New Testament text. These processes had only the dimmest beginnings in Mill and Bentley, but with Bengel came the basis for their swift development. The former process would lead, through

[27] Ibid., Latin ed., xiii; English ed., 1.xviii.

[28] Cf. the ratings in the *UBSGNT*, which "indicate the relative degree of certainty . . . for the reading adopted as the text": *The Greek New Testament* (ed. Kurt Aland, Matthew Black, Carlo M. Martini, Bruce M. Metzger, and Allen Wikgren; New York/London/Edinburgh/Amsterdam/Stuttgart: United Bible Societies, 1966^{1}; 1968^{2}) x–xi; (1975^{3}) xii–xiii [notice the changed language in 1983^{4}, 3*].

Griesbach and then Lachmann, more than a hundred years later, to the decisive overthrow of the *textus receptus* in favor of a New Testament text based solely on ancient witnesses; the latter process would lead through many editors of the New Testament text—and their editions—to the problematic juxtaposition of external and internal criteria and to the current ambivalence and ambiguity in their application. It would seem not too far from the truth, then, to say that the origins of eclecticism can be traced with some assuredness to Bengel's formulary intermingling or conjoining of external and internal canons and that, in terms of our earlier definitions, Bengel appears to be an eclectic specialist and one on the side of those who consider external evidence decisive but who employ internal criteria to settle matters for which the external evidence is conflicting or ambiguous.

J. J. Wettstein, whose two-volume *Novum Testamentum Graecum* appeared in 1751–52, took an interest in variant readings before he was twenty years old (in 1713), following the appearance of G. von Mastricht's Greek New Testament of 1711—published by Wettstein and Smith of Amsterdam, whose senior partner was Wettstein's relative. During the several years of direct preparation for his own
224 Greek New Testament and during the nearly twenty years of delay (due largely to theological issues—his Arian views), Wettstein's critical principles were altered from a generally high view of the oldest manuscripts to quite the opposite, a change based on his acceptance of the latinization theory—that all of the oldest Greek manuscripts had been corrupted by interpolation from Latin manuscripts. Consequently, he said, the textual critic must move several centuries beyond the oldest Greek manuscripts to more recent ones if a pure text is to be found. Yet, in his 1751–52 edition, Wettstein enunciates many of the critical canons that he had published separately in 1730, before his views on the oldest Greek manuscripts had changed, and the result is curious: his approved readings (over against the Elzevir text printed in Wettstein's edition) often stand in opposition to his stated principles or canons of criticism. Among those principles are the following: the reading in clearer or better Greek is not necessarily preferable; more often the contrary (item 7); among readings equally suitable to the context, that which employs an unusual expression is preferable (8); the fuller, more ample reading is not preferable to the shorter (9); the reading found in the same words elsewhere is not preferable to one that is not (10); a reading con-

formable in every respect to the style of the author is preferable (11); the more orthodox reading is not necessarily preferable (12); the Greek reading more in accord with the ancient versions is preferable (13); patristic testimony has much weight in attesting the true reading, and silence in the Fathers on readings of importance in the controversies of their times renders such readings suspect (14 and 15); the more ancient reading is preferable, other things being equal (17); and the reading of the majority of manuscripts, other things being equal, is preferable (18).[29]

Obviously, many standard—if sometimes mutually exclusive—criteria are to be found in this list. It is equally obvious, however, that Wettstein abandoned many of them in establishing his final textual theories and in printing his own preferred readings for the New
Testament text. Some of Wettstein's theories and canons and par- 225
ticularly the contradictions among them can be explained by his change of views between 1730 and 1751, especially his growing opposition to the views of Bengel, who (as noted earlier) held to a high view of the oldest Greek manuscripts and of the Latin versions, and whose views Wettstein combated by pushing farther than anyone else the theory of the latinization of the oldest Greek manuscripts of the New Testament. Wettstein's inconsistencies become obvious when, for his edition, he prefers later, presumably unlatinized, codices to the earlier ones—against his canon 17 that the more ancient reading normally is preferable—and when he can state in the same work that any division of readings into groups with more or less weight is useless (canon 6) but also can affirm that "codices are to be appraised by weight, not by number."[30]

Our interest here, however, is not in Wettstein's consistency or his lack of it, but only in the formulation of criteria for the recovery of the most likely original readings. His list of canons, whether

[29] Selected from nineteen items in chap. 16 of Wettstein's [anonymous] *Prolegomena* of 1730, which appear as eighteen items in the appendix to his 1751–52 edition of the NT: "*Animadversiones et cautiones ad examen variarum lectionum N. T. necessariae,*" 2.851–74. Cf. Tregelles, *Account of the Printed Text,* 80; C. L. Hulbert-Powell, *John James Wettstein 1693–1754* (London: SPCK, 1938) 114–21. If not otherwise available, the text of Wettstein's 1752 "*Animadversiones*" can be found in F. Wrangham, *Briani Waltoni . . . in biblia polyglotta prolegomena . . .* (Cambridge: 1828) 1.511–12.

[30] Metzger, *Text of the New Testament,* 114. Note that Wettstein, in his 1752 appendix, has dropped the original 18th canon—that the reading of the majority of manuscripts normally is preferable.

he followed them or not, represents a thoughtful approach at a time now judged by all to precede a genuinely scientific understanding of New Testament textual criticism; as such, they are as worthy of our attention as any other list of critical canons from this general period. Finally, for our purposes it is of interest to observe that the external and internal criteria are undifferentiated in Wettstein's canon list.

J. J. GRIESBACH published three editions of the Greek New Testament between 1775 and 1807, and the second edition of 1796–1806 contained his canons of criticism, fifteen in number. These canons are concerned with internal criteria for determining the originality of readings, and they include numerous points made earlier by Bengel and Wettstein. Griesbach's first canon,[31] judging both from its primary position in that list and from the detailed attention accorded it by Griesbach, must have been regarded by him both as first in importance and fundamental in nature. The canon states that "the shorter reading . . . is preferable to the more verbose"; this, says Griesbach—quite correctly—is based on the principle that scribes are far more prone to add to their texts than to omit.[32] He qualifies
226 the canon carefully and in several ways, noting, e.g., (1) that the canon applies only when the reading in question has some support from "the old and weighty witnesses"; and (2) that the originality of a shorter reading is more certain still (a) if it is also a harsher, more obscure, ambiguous, elliptical, Hebraizing, or ungrammatical reading, (b) if the same matter is expressed differently in various codices, (c) if the order of words is inconsistent and unstable, (d) if the reading stands first in a pericope (or church lesson) or (e) if the *fuller reading* shows evidence of a gloss or an interpretation, or is in accord with words in parallel passages, or appears to have been taken from a lectionary. He continues, however, that the shorter reading would

[31] The canon in its entirety may be seen conveniently in Metzger, *Text of the New Testament*, 120. The Latin text of all of Griesbach's canons—should the 2nd ed. of his Greek New Testament [see note 33] not be available—will be readily accessible to most in H. Alford, *The Greek Testament. . . .* (4 vols.; new ed.; Boston, 1883) 1.81–85.

[32] [Though this is a well-established and long-standing principle, see now the questions raised about its validity by James R. Royse, "Scribal Habits in the Transmission of New Testament Texts," *The Critical Study of the Sacred Texts* (ed. Wendy Doniger O'Flaherty; Berkeley, CA: Berkeley Religious Studies Series, 1979) 139–61; idem, *Scribal Habits in Early New Testament Papyri* (SD 47; Grand Rapids, MI: Eerdmans, 2005).]

not have a strong claim to originality (unless supported by *many notable* witnesses) (1) if the missing portion of the longer reading (a) can be attributed to homoeoteleuton, (b) would have appeared to scribes as obscure, rough, superfluous, unusual, paradoxical, an offense to piety, an error, or inconsistent with parallels, or (c) does not, by its omission, destroy the sense or the word structure, or (2) if the shorter reading (a) is less suitable to the author's character, style, or goal, (b) makes no sense at all, or (c) probably represents an intrusion from a parallel passage or a lectionary. In these qualifications and elaborations of his first canon, Griesbach has anticipated many of his succeeding canons, thereby providing an instructive illustration of how the various critical canons overlap and intertwine in actual practice.

Griesbach's fourteen other canons specify that:

2. "The more difficult and more obscure reading is preferable to that in which everything is so intelligible and cleared of difficulties that every scribe is easily able to understand it."
3. "The harsher [or rougher] reading is preferable to that which flows pleasantly and smoothly." "Harsher" refers to readings that are elliptical, Hebraizing, ungrammatical, contrary to normal Greek usage, or offensive to the ears.
4. "The more unusual reading is preferable to that which constitutes nothing unusual." "Unusual" includes rare words, words with rarely used meanings, and uncommon phrases and constructions. Scribes seized on the more customary expressions rather than the more exquisite, and for the latter they substitute glosses and explanations (especially if these are provided in the margin or from parallel passages).
5. "Expressions less emphatic [rhetorically], provided that the context and goal of the author do not demand emphasis, are closer to the genuine text than readings possessing, or appearing to possess, a greater vigor, for polished 227
scribes, like commentators, love and seek out [rhetorical] emphases."
6. "The reading, compared with others, that produces a meaning suited to the support of piety (especially monastic piety) is suspect."
7. "Preferable to others is the reading that conveys [at first

glance] an apparently false meaning, but which meaning, upon thorough examination, is found to be true."

8. "Among many readings in one place, that reading is rightly considered suspect that clearly suits the opinions of the orthodox better than the other readings," for it was impossible for a scribe who was a monk devoted to the church to overlook any reading that appeared strongly to confirm any catholic doctrine or to destroy a heresy.

9 and 10. These canons treat homoeoteleuton and related phenomena, and readings arising from this "symmetry" of language are of "no value" and are "rightly rejected."

11. "The reading is preferable, among many in the same place, that lies midway between the others, that is, the reading that, as it were, holds together the threads in such a way that, if this reading is admitted as original, it becomes obvious how or, better stated, by what origin in error all the other readings have arisen from it."

12. "Readings having the odor of a gloss or an interpretation may be rejected."

13. "Readings that have been introduced into the text from ancient commentaries or scholia of the Fathers are to be spurned."

14. "We reject readings appearing originally in lectionaries."

15. Finally, "readings introduced from the Latin versions into the Greek books are disapproved."

These internal criteria supplemented Griesbach's theory of the history of the text that was evident already in his first edition of the Greek New Testament in 1775–77. He divided the extant manuscripts of the gospels into three groups (following J. S. Semler's 1764 expansion of Bengel's two-family scheme): two ancient "recensions" or families (the Western and Alexandrian, dating to the beginning of the third century) and one more recent (the Constantinopolitan, dating to the late fourth century and following). One of Griesbach's critical principles, arising out of this understanding of the early history of the text, was that a reading had high claim to originality when supported by two of these three "recensions"; more particularly, (1) a reading was accounted genuine when supported by all three of these old "recensions" ("Prolegomena," sec. III, item e); (2)
228 a reading attested by the Western and Alexandrian against the
Constantinopolitan was the most ancient reading—and was, indeed,

to be regarded as genuine if at the same times its "internal excellence" shone forth (item g); (3) a reading supported by the Alexandrian and the Constantinopolitan "recensions" but not by the Western (or by the Western and the Constantinopolitan but not by the Alexandrian) was examined to see whether faults characteristic of the Alexandrian (or, in the other case, of the Western) "recension" were apparent; if so, the reading was suspect; accompanying the evaluative process in these cases, however, was the careful weighing of internal evidences (items h, i); and, finally, (4) when different readings were found in the "recensions," they had to be judged, not according to the greater number of supporting witnesses, but by weighing "internal criteria of excellence." Even then, however, any such "remarkably good reading" (on internal evidence) had to be attested first as a "primitive reading of an old recension" if it were to be esteemed (item k).[33]

It becomes clear, then, that Griesbach's *external* criteria for establishing the original New Testament readings, as these criteria arise out of his theory of the early history of the text, take precedence over the *internal* criteria in the entire text-critical task. That the internal criteria are subsidiary to the external appears already in the first dependent clause of his first canon, where he indicates that this most basic of the internal criteria does not even apply to a shorter reading should that reading lack the support of all "old and weighty witnesses." Notice, furthermore, that the "weight of internal evidence" comes into play when there are differing readings in the two oldest groups of manuscripts or when different readings occur in all his groups. In other words, when the external evidence is inconclusive, then the internal canons become decisive, but normally external evidence alone should be sufficient for a confident decision. This is not essentially different from Bengel's understanding of the interrelationship between external and internal criteria, but this relationship—including (1) the differentiation of the two categories, (2) the precedence of the external criteria and their superiority, and (3) the decisive role of the internal criteria *only* when the external criteria are ambiguous or in conflict—becomes more explicit in Griesbach. It is self-evident, of course, that Griesbach, like Bengel, relied on a basic rationale of weighing rather than counting witnesses, and this principle becomes well established with Griesbach's work, though by no means does it 229
yet become universal. Griesbach's contribution in this area was

[33] J. J. Griesbach, *Novum Testamentum Graece* (2nd ed.; Halle/London: 1796–1806) 1.lxxiii–lxxxi; reprinted in later eds. See also Tregelles in Horne, *Introduction*, 4.76.

considerably greater than may appear from the present summary, for when Griesbach began to formulate his views, particularly those on the great worth of the oldest manuscripts, Wettstein's denigration of all the older manuscripts (and his latinization theories) were highly influential and dominant. Griesbach's reestablishment of the principle put forward by Bengel was, therefore, neither a natural direction in which to move nor an easy task to accomplish.[34] This context of Griesbach's work also makes more understandable his failure to abandon the *textus receptus* to a greater extent than he does and to the extent that his text-critical theories would seem to require; the time for a decisive break with the *textus receptus* had arrived in theory, but the time for putting good theory into practice still lay in the future.

The foregoing discussions should alert us again to observe closely the pattern of interrelationship between the external criteria and the internal whenever text-critical methods and principles are under consideration, for the development of modern eclectic approaches is related to this interplay and to the incipient polarity between them, as pointed out earlier in connection with Bengel.

Karl Lachmann published a Greek New Testament in 1831, the fruit of five years of work, whose purpose was to present the text of the New Testament as it existed in the fourth century. The only statement in this edition giving Lachmann's principles for selecting the readings of his text was a paragraph of fewer than one hundred words,[35] indicating that he followed "nowhere his own judgment," but "the usage of the most ancient eastern churches" as a first principle of selection; when the evidence was not consistent, he preferred the reading established by the agreement of the "Italian and African" witnesses. When these principles did not lead to the resolution of a textual issue, Lachmann employed brackets in the text and alterna-
230 tive readings in the margin to indicate indecision and other possible readings. His entire work, however, gave no consideration to the "received readings" (i.e., the *textus receptus*), but sought, from the older

[34] See Tregelles, *Account of the Printed Text*, 91–92; witness also the views of J. M. A. Scholz, whose Greek New Testament text (1830–36) followed the Constantinopolitan "recension," and who relied on *numbers* of manuscripts (ibid., 92–97).

[35] The Latin text is given in C. R. Gregory, *Textkritik des Neuen Testament* (Leipzig: Hinrichs, 1909) 966–67, and in Tregelles, *Account of the Printed Text*, 98n. Lachmann also refers the reader of his first edition to his article of the preceding year, "Rechenschaft über seine Ausgabe des Neuen Testaments von Professor Lachmann in Berlin," *TSK* 3 (1830) 817–45, for the rationale and plan of the edition. This article, however, contains neither a list nor a discussion of critical canons.

manuscripts and by his stated principles, to establish the text of the fourth century.

Lachmann states his text-critical principles in a more systematic fashion, though still concisely, in the preface to his second edition of the Greek New Testament (1842–50) as follows:

1. Nothing is better attested than that on which all authorities agree.
2. If some of the authorities are silent or defective, the weight of evidence is somewhat lessened.
3. When the witnesses are of different regions, their agreement is of more importance than when those of some particular locality differ from the rest, either from negligence or from set purpose.
4. When witnesses of different widely separated regions disagree, the testimony must be considered to be doubtfully balanced.
5. When readings are in one form in one region and in another form in another region, with great uniformity, they are quite uncertain.
6. Lastly, readings are of weak authority when not even the same region presents a uniform testimony.[36]

These are all external criteria, for it was Lachmann's aim to reconstruct the *transmitted text* of the fourth century, and for this purpose external criteria seemed sufficient. The *transmitted text* of a certain period is, after all, recognizably different from the *most likely original text*, yet the transmitted text of the fourth century obviously was, for Lachmann, a step on the way toward the most likely original text (and a giant step of twelve hundred years away from the "received text" of the sixteenth century, which was accorded no authority by Lachmann, the first scholar to make such a clean break with the *textus receptus*), and accordingly we may assume with some justification that external criteria would have held the same dominant—though perhaps not exclusive—position whether Lachmann were seeking the fourth century transmitted text or the original text itself. This assumption is, in fact, confirmed to some extent in Lachmann's second volume (1850), which contains notes with occasional conjectures as

[36] Translation adapted from Tregelles in Horne, *Introduction,* 4.135–36, and in Tregelles, *Account of the Printed Text,* 103; the Latin text may be found in Gregory, *Textkritik,* 968, or in Gregory's *Prolegomena* to C. Tischendorf's *Novum Testamentum Graece* (8th major ed.; Leipzig: Hinrichs, 1869–94) 3.260.

231 to the original text, and here he uses "the traditive readings of the oldest documents as his basis of argument."[37] Clearly, then, with Lachmann the weight in text-critical decisions shifts heavily to the side of external criteria.

There is no need for a detailed description of the criteria used by the many succeeding editors of the Greek New Testament until the time of Westcott and Hort. Brief notice, however, should be given to the critical canons of such notable figures as Tischendorf and Tregelles.

Constantin von Tischendorf, in his second edition of the Greek New Testament in 1849, gave as his rationale for his text the basic principle, much like Lachmann's, that:

> The text should be sought solely from ancient witness, and chiefly from Greek codices, but by no means neglecting the testimonies of the versions and the fathers. Thus, the whole arrangement of the text is bound by necessity to arise from the witnesses themselves . . ., not from the edition of Elzevir, which is called "received"; however, to be placed first among disagreeing witnesses are those regarded as the oldest Greek codices, i.e., written from the fourth to about the ninth century. Again, among these, those that excel in antiquity prevail in authority, and this authority increases if testimonies of the versions or fathers are added, nor is this authority surmounted by the disagreement of most or even of all the recent codices, i.e., those written from the ninth to the sixteenth centuries.[38]

This fundamental external criterion is supplemented by Tischendorf's further canons, some external, some internal:

1. Readings wholly peculiar to one or another [ancient] witness are suspect, as are readings, in a class of documents, that appear to have originated from critical, scholarly correction.
2. Excluded are readings, no matter what their attestation, that clearly or very probably have originated from a copyist's error.
3. Witnesses with passages parallel to the Old Testament, the New Testament, and especially the synoptic gospels, when they attest disagreements, are preferable to witnesses that show agreement, for the ancients paid particular attention to parallels.

---

[37] Tregelles, *Account of the Printed Text*, 111.

[38] Quoted by Gregory in his *Prolegomena* to Tischendorf, *Novum Testamentum Graece (Prolegomena)*, 3.47–48; also in Tischendorf's 7th ed., 1859, xxvii–xviii.

4. More probable than others is the reading that appears to have occasioned the other readings or that still contains within itself elements of the other readings. Taken broadly, says Tischendorf, this is the foundation of all rules.
5. Readings should be studiously retained that are in accord with 232
the Greek language and style of the individual authors of the New Testament.

Both the basic principle and the five canons of Tischendorf are repeated in C. R. Gregory's *Prolegomena* to Tischendorf's eighth major edition of the Greek New Testament (1869–94)[39] and may be taken as those governing all of Tischendorf's efforts to establish the text of the Greek New Testament.

The combination in Tischendorf of a dominant external criterion—the oldest Greek manuscripts are the most authoritative—and of further, intermingled external and internal criteria means that the basic reliance on the oldest witnesses cannot be carried through consistently, for the further internal criteria force the modification of the basic principle at point after point and thwart its comprehensive application. The result is that at numerous points the "balance of probabilities" formula must be invoked. This is evident from the illustrative passages discussed by Tischendorf, where, as examples, he prefers a reading in Mark 2:22, attested by only two ancient witnesses, to another reading, better attested (on his principles), that shows evidence of harmonization to Matthew;[40] and in Matt 24:38 he prefers a shorter reading, rather sparsely attested, to longer forms that are better attested but that are due, according to Tischendorf, to scribal expansion and are explicable as occasioned by the shorter (original) reading.[41] Yet Tischendorf's basic approach to textual decisions is by way of an external criticism that in each case invokes any internal criteria especially appropriate to that particular situation.

---

[39] Tischendorf, *Novum Testamentum Graece (Prolegomena)*, 3.53–54; 63; see 47–68 for the entire discussion of Tischendorf's text-critical principles, with examples. Cf. Tregelles in Horne, *Introduction*, 4.138–39, and Tregelles, *Account of the Printed Text*, 119–29, for a full discussion of Tischendorf's rules. Tischendorf's view of two pairs of documentary groups, one pair comprised of the more ancient, the other of the more recent witnesses, does not affect his use of canons; see Tregelles, *Account of the Printed Text*, 126–28.

[40] Tischendorf, *Novum Testamentum Graece (Prolegomena)*, 3.54–55.

[41] Ibid., 3.63–64.

S. P. TREGELLES published his text-critical principles in 1854,[42] summarized them in his rewriting of the text-critical portion of T. H. Horne's *Introduction* in 1856,[43] and published his edition of the Greek New Testament between 1857 and 1872. Unaware of Lachmann's principles, Tregelles arrived at a similar view, i.e., "to
233 form a text on the authority of ancient copies without allowing the 'received text' any prescriptive rights."[44] This basic principle, consisting of an external criterion of reliance upon the oldest documents, was supplemented by a general statement on the decisive role of internal criteria whenever the old witnesses are in disagreement:

> In confining the examination to the ancient documents, all care must be taken rightly to understand their testimony, and to weigh it in all its particulars.
>
> Authorities cannot be followed mechanically; and thus, where there is a difference of reading amongst the more trustworthy witnesses, all that we know of the nature and origin of various readings, and of the kind of errors to which copyists were liable, must be employed. But, let it be observed, that discrimination of this kind is only required when the witnesses differ; for otherwise, we should fall into the error of determining by conjecture what the text *ought* to be, instead of accepting it as it is.[45]

When Tregelles is forced to move to internal considerations so that a decision may be made between or among readings with ancient attestation, factors such as the following determine which way his "balance of probabilities" turns: favor the reading that appears to have occasioned the others;[46] reject readings that clearly involve scribal errors, such as homoeoteleuton;[47] prefer the reading that at first glance is incongruous but that makes good sense upon further scrutiny;[48] reject harmonizations,[49] marginal intrusions into the text,[50]

---

[42] Tregelles, *Account of the Printed Text*, 174–226; cf. 151–74.

[43] See n. 13 above; the canons are found on pp. 342–45 in both the 1856 and 1860 editions of Tregelles's work.

[44] Tregelles, *Account of the Printed Text*, 152; cf. idem in Horne, *Introduction*, 4.140–41: "The ancient MSS. should be the authorities for every word"; "the ancient authorities should be allowed a primary place"; "the general principle in the formation of the text is that of following [external] evidence."

[45] Tregelles, *Account of the Printed Text*, 186; cf. idem in Horne, *Introduction*, 4.344 (item 6).

[46] Tregelles, *Account of the Printed Text*, 191–92; 222; 230.

[47] Ibid., 194–96; 205–6; 220–21.

[48] Ibid., 196–200.

[49] Ibid., 206–7; 220–21; 224–25.

[50] Ibid., 221; 245–46.

and dogmatic alterations;[51] prefer the reading that accords with the author's style;[52] and, more generally (since they encompass some of the above), prefer the harder reading,[53] and prefer the shorter reading.[54]

Tregelles thought it impossible to classify manuscripts in any definite 234
fashion, though he recognized that they fall into two large groups of documents, the Alexandrian or more ancient and the Constantinopolitan or more recent witnesses.[55] As in the case of Tischendorf, however, manuscript grouping does not affect Tregelles's text-critical principles in any material way, except, of course, to place together in a convenient category those early witnesses that form the basic materials for his recovery of the most likely original text.

Once again, like Bengel, Griesbach, Lachmann, and Tischendorf before him, Tregelles operates with a fundamental external criterion, supplemented when necessary by subsidiary criteria of an internal kind.

The twenty years of prodigious labor by B. F. Westcott and F. J. A. Hort in preparing their edition of *The New Testament in the Original Greek* of 1881–82 and the text-critical insight and theory that accompanied this influential critical text bring to a climax the entire development and interaction of external and internal "canons of criticism." Westcott and Hort do not give a list of canons in any traditional fashion, and they do not even like the term,[56] yet their "canons of criticism" are easily enough compiled from their direct statements or by inference from them; however, any abstraction of "rules" from their carefully drawn contexts or any formulation of simple principles by epitomizing Westcott and Hort's full discussions will invite both oversimplification and possible misrepresentation. Nevertheless, if Westcott and Hort's canons were to be formulated for such a list, it would include the following:

---

[51] Ibid., 222–23. Tregelles allows these as "occasional" occurrences, such as alterations in the interest and support of asceticism, but he says that it would be "an entire mistake to suppose that there was any evidence of doctrinal corruption of the sacred records. . . ." (223); cf. 224–25.

[52] Ibid., 256–57.

[53] Ibid., 201–2; 221–22.

[54] Ibid., 220–21.

[55] Tregelles in Horne, *Introduction*, 4.104–7.

[56] B. F. Westcott and F. J. A. Hort, *The New Testament in the Original Greek* (Cambridge/London: Macmillan, 1881–82) 2.23. All references are to vol. 2, *Introduction. Appendix.* which, as is well known, was authored by Hort, though both are fully responsible for the "principles, arguments, and conclusions set forth" (2.18).

1. Older readings, manuscripts, or groups are to be preferred. ("The shorter the interval between the time of the autograph and the end of the period of transmission in question, the stronger the presumption that earlier date implies greater purity of text.") (2.59; cf. 2.5–6; 31)[57]
2. Readings are approved or rejected by reason of the quality, and not the number, of their supporting witnesses. ("No available presumptions whatever as to text can be obtained from number alone, that is, from number not as yet interpreted by descent.") (2.44)

235 3. A reading combining two simple, alternative readings is later than the two readings comprising the conflation, and manuscripts rarely or never supporting conflate reading are texts antecedent to mixture and are of special value. (2.49–50)
4. The reading is to be preferred that makes the best sense, that is, that best conforms to the grammar and is most congruous with the purport of the rest of the sentence and of the larger context. (2.20)
5. The reading is to be preferred that best conforms to the usual style of the author and to that author's material in other passages. (2.20)
6. The reading is to be preferred that most fitly explains the existence of the others. (2.22–23)
7. The reading is less likely to be original that combines the appearance of an improvement in the sense with the absence of its reality; the scribal alteration will have an apparent excellence, while the original will have the highest real excellence. (2.27; 29)
8. The reading is less likely to be original that shows a disposition to smooth away difficulties (another way of stating that the harder reading is preferable). (2.28)
9. Readings are to be preferred that are found in a manuscript that habitually contains superior readings as determined by intrinsic and transcriptional probability. Certainty is increased if such a better manuscript is found also to be an older manuscript (2.32–33) and if such a manuscript habitually contains readings that prove themselves antecedent to mixture and independent of external contamination by other, inferior texts (2.150–51). The same principles apply to groups of manuscripts (2.260–61).

---

[57] References in this section will be given in the text and refer to Westcott-Hort, *New Testament in the Original Greek*, specifically to vol. 2 [see preceding note].

The extraction and tabulation of such canons do not, however, enlighten us as to the real significance of Westcott and Hort's treatment of text-critical principles. Rather, their contribution (and our major interest) rests in the fact, first, that they combined in a unique fashion the internal and external criteria as they had evolved and had been used over the years and, second, that they utilized the resulting combination in a new way—with far-reaching effects on New Testament text-critical theory and method.

Westcott and Hort had the highest regard for Griesbach—"a name 236
we venerate above that of every other textual critic of the New Testament"—with respect to his historical reconstruction of the "genealogical relations of the whole extant documentary evidence" (2.185–86), that is, Griesbach's scheme of two ancient and one more recent group of manuscripts. Westcott and Hort's own reconstruction followed this general pattern, though with well-known modifications. On the other hand, they complain that Griesbach's two great weaknesses were, first, his use of the *textus receptus* as a basis for correcting the New Testament text and, second and chiefly, his propensity "to give a dangerously disproportionate weight to internal evidence, and especially to transcriptional probability, on which indeed for its own sake he placed excessive reliance" (2.184). This criticism of Griesbach by Westcott and Hort will be perplexing to anyone who knows Westcott and Hort's own text-critical theory. Although they claim that genealogy is primary (2.63–64),[58] thereby leaving the impression that external evidence provides the solid foundation for their text-critical theory, yet a closer reading shows that Westcott and Hort employed genealogy only on a broad scale and in a generic and almost loose fashion to separate the pre-Syrian lines of text from the Syrian line and that they never worked out their genealogical method (at least as far as we know) in terms of specific stemmata of actual New Testament manuscripts.[59] Moreover, when the crucial question of deciding between the two earliest text-types (Neutral and Western) is broached, they admit that genealogical method cannot lead to a decision (2.41–42). At this point, the whole range of internal considerations comes into play, as Westcott and Hort elaborated

[58] Cf. 2.17 on the primacy of external evidence.

[59] Colwell, "Genealogical Method," 109–114; reprinted in his *Studies in Methodology*, 63–67; cf. the section on "Genealogical Evidence" in Westcott-Hort, *New Testament in the Original Greek*, 2.39–62; also 90–119; 178–79.

them (2.19–39; 60–66): (1) the Internal Evidence of Readings, that is, consideration of individual readings in terms of (a) Intrinsic Probability (what the author most likely wrote) and (b) Transcriptional Probability (what the scribe most likely wrote), yielding great certainty about the most probable reading when both methods certify the same reading, but with transcriptional probability decisive when the two methods are in conflict; (2) the Internal Evidence of Documents, that is, consideration of each single group of readings that consti-
237 tutes a manuscript so as to acquire "knowledge of documents," that is, knowledge of that manuscript's general quality and reliability, so that the weight of its readings can be assessed when the Internal Evidence of (individual) Readings is unclear; and (3) the Internal Evidence of Groups, or consideration of a single group of manuscripts to determine its overall character in relation to other groups as a bearer of generally reliable documents.

Westcott and Hort's *quantitative* use of internal considerations adds up, in the final analysis, to a *qualitative* judgment on internal evidence as superior to and more decisive than external (genealogical) evidence. In fact, for all practical purposes, it is internal evidence alone that is determinative for them in virtually all text-critical decisions once the early text-types have been separated from the later Syrian type, and, moreover, internal criteria are thereafter utilized to support this basic distinction between the early and the later types of text.

This qualitative judgment on the superiority of internal evidence is obvious from Westcott and Hort's descriptions of the basic text-types. Though the Syrian and pre-Syrian texts ostensibly were isolated and differentiated in the first instance by objective, genealogical procedures (2.90–117), it seems clear enough from Westcott and Hort's characterization, e.g., of the Syrian type (a text that is smooth, eminently readable, complete, and conflate, filled out by harmonization, assimilation, and appropriate connecting tissue [2.134–35]), that reliance on internal evidence alone would have yielded the same result—that the Syrian text is a relatively late derivative text, posterior to, built upon, and incorporating numerous elements of its antecedent texts (the Western, Neutral, and Alexandrian).

What actually develops for Westcott and Hort, then—to be more specific—is a theory that leads, first, to a division of manuscripts and groups of manuscripts into early and later text-types presumably by an external, genealogical method, and, second (though concurrently),

to an assessment of the relative quality or reliability of these various manuscripts and groups of manuscripts. The result is their well-known judgment (1) that the later Syrian (or Byzantine) manuscripts are conflate and therefore farthest removed both chronologically and qualitatively from the original text; (2) that manuscripts like C, L, and 33 (the Alexandrian text) are individually and as a group good
but refined and polished texts and thereby removed somewhat from 238
the original; (3) that manuscripts like D and D^{paul} (the Western text) and their group are ancient but corrupt texts and thereby removed in quality—though not so much in date—from the original text; and (4) that manuscripts B and ℵ are the "best" manuscripts and that their group (the Neutral text) is the "best" group because they are at once close in time and closest in quality to the original New Testament text.

It will be obvious that this distinctive textual theory and these confident judgments of Westcott and Hort were produced by a unique *synergism of external and internal evidence.* This coaction of the two kinds of criteria involved two separate but concurrent processes. On the one hand, the earliest and least mixed (and thereby presumably the purest) readings and also the groups of manuscript witnesses supporting such early, unmixed readings were isolated; this process utilized external data (the date or relative antiquity of the manuscript, the age of the reading as determined by patristic support, etc.) and employed genealogical-like methods (locating pre-Syrian readings and text by analysis—primarily—of conflate readings) to achieve its goal. Secondly, and concurrently, the anterior (in the sense of logical rather than temporal priority) and "best" readings and groups of witnesses (and thereby presumably the purest readings and groups) were isolated; this was accomplished by utilizing the Internal Evidence of Readings (both Intrinsic and Transcriptional Probabilities) to assess variation-units that included, again, conflate readings, thereby permitting the "superior" readings and texts to be separated from the "inferior" (2.90–119).

The first result of these processes was that Westcott and Hort's synergism of external and internal evidence separated the later Syrian (or Byzantine) text and its readings from the earlier texts and readings of the three other groups, the Western, Neutral, and Alexandrian. Furthermore, the Alexandrian text was shown, by the same cooperation of external and internal evidence, to be posterior (both in terms of time and logical sequence) to the Western and Neutral

groups because its readings were shown to have been derived from one of these two other pre-Syrian text-types (the Neutral) and could be dated externally to about the beginning of the third century (2.130–32). The further result of these processes was Westcott and
239 Hort's characterization of these groups or text-types: the Syrian text is a late, critically edited, and polished text, incorporating the bulk of available readings to form a full text; the Alexandrian is a somewhat earlier, inventively interpolated, and philologically refined text; and the two other, still earlier texts, the Western and the Neutral, are rather drastically different from each other in character, for the Western is judged, on internal grounds, to have "a love of paraphrase" and "a disposition to enrich the text at the cost of its purity," and a "fondness for assimilation" (2.122–26), while the Neutral text is "a relatively pure Non-Western text" (2.128; cf. 178). Hence, the Neutral text emerges as the "best" New Testament text.

From these conclusions, the synergism of external and internal evidence proceeds, in Westcott and Hort, to the identification, not only of the "best" (that is the purest) text or group of witnesses (the Neutral), but of the "best" (that is, the purest) manuscripts. Their well-known assertion is that Codex Vaticanus (B) "holds a unique position" since "its text is not only Pre-Syrian but substantially free from Western and Alexandrian adulteration" (2.150–51); moreover, "B very far exceeds all other documents in neutrality of text . . ., being in fact always or nearly always neutral" (2.171) and this conclusion is based both on genealogical or external evidence and on internal evidence (2.150–51; 170–71; 210–71; esp. 210). The corollary to this assessment of B is that Codex Sinaiticus (א) is next in purity among all other manuscripts (2.171; 210–13; 222–23), and Westcott and Hort can speak of "the preeminent excellence of the Vatican and Sinaitic MSS, which happen likewise to be the oldest extant Greek MSS of the New Testament" (2.212). Again, this judgment on א arises from the coaction of external and internal evidence.

As is common knowledge, Westcott and Hort go on from these settled points to make use of the Neutral text generally, but particularly of codices B and א, as the lodestar for locating and establishing the original New Testament text.

It is precisely at this point of determining the single best text, however, that the synergism of external and internal evidence in Westcott and Hort's scheme suddenly breaks down to reveal instead—and quite unexpectedly—a tension between the external and the

internal criteria. This tension turns out, upon examination, to be a 240
genuine *polarity of external and internal evidence* and it comes to light as these two methodological procedures and their resultant data are employed by Westcott and Hort in building their text-critical theory. It is the so-called Western text and its leading representative, Codex Bezae (D), that bring this polarity to view, in the following way: the combination of external and internal evidence had led Westcott and Hort to the "best" readings (the pre-Syrian); thence to the "best" text or group of manuscripts (the non-Western pre-Syrian Neutral text), since this "best" text consistently contained these "best" readings; thence, finally, to the "best" manuscripts (B, with א), since they are the "constant element" of those groups that are "found to have habitually the best readings" (2.212).[60]

This line of argumentation established, in effect, a new "objective" standard for originality, namely, the *criterion of the best manuscript* or *best manuscripts*, and this canon then could be invoked for a decision between or among readings in cases where the evidence was otherwise ambiguous or where other criteria were inconclusive. (Critics have called this Westcott and Hort approach "the cult of the best manuscript.")[61] That this new criterion was established by the coaction of external and internal evidence is not to be disputed, but an inconsistency is soon disclosed in Westcott and Hort's scheme when their treatment of D and the Western text is investigated, for Westcott and Hort's external evidence isolated *two* "earliest" texts or groups, the Neutral *and* the Western, and suddenly it becomes apparent that the criterion of the best manuscript(s), which focuses on B (with א), was not the exclusive fruit of Westcott and Hort's genealogical and

[60] Cf. Westcott-Hort, *New Testament in the Original Greek*, 2.210: "Every group containing both א and B is found, where Internal Evidence is tolerably unambiguous, to have an apparently more original text than every opposed group containing neither."

[61] J. K. Elliott, "Rational Criticism and the Text of the New Testament," *Theology* 75 (1972) 339–340; idem, "Can We Recover the Original New Testament?" *Theology* 77 (1974) 345–46; 349; cf. idem, "The United Bible Societies Greek New Testament: An Evaluation," *NovT* 15 (1973) 278–300, esp. 297; and idem, "Ho baptizōn and Mark I.4," *TZ* 31 (1975) 15. A view similar to Westcott and Hort's—the championing of a "best manuscript" as an almost "external" criterion but one based essentially on internal judgments—can be seen in the work of M.-J. Lagrange and would be worth exploring as another step on the way to the current chaos in New Testament text-critical method; cf. Colwell, "The Significance of Grouping of New Testament Manuscripts," *NTS* 4 (1957/58) 76–77; reprinted as "Method in Grouping New Testament Manuscripts," in his *Studies in Methodology*, 5–6; idem, "Genealogical Method," 129–30; reprinted in his *Studies in Methodology*, 80–81.

external considerations. Actually, and by their explicit admission, external evidence shows that the Western text, in fact, has the earliest documentation:

> 241 The earliest readings which can be fixed chronologically belong to it. As far as we can judge from extant evidence, it was the most widely spread text of Ante-Nicene times; and sooner or later every version directly or indirectly felt its influence. (2.120)

And of Codex Bezae they say:

> . . . When every allowance has been made for possible individual license, the text of D presents a truer image of the form in which the Gospels and Acts were most widely read in the third and probably a great part of the second century than any other extant Greek MS. (2.149)

On what grounds, then, do Westcott and Hort strain and apparently violate their presumably basic genealogical principle by an unequivocal preference for the Neutral text rather than the Western? On grounds of internal evidence, for "any prepossessions in [the Western text's] favour that might be created by this imposing early ascendancy are for the most part soon dissipated by continuous study of its internal character" (2.120). The harmonious synergism of external and internal evidence may have enthroned B as the best manuscript on both grounds (perhaps, in isolation, a reasonable conclusion), but the case made at the same time by Westcott and Hort for the dethronement of D cannot with consistency be based on the external evidence admitted by them for D and the Western text. In other words, to accept the readings of B in virtually all cases as practically identical with the original text and to utilize B as the standard of excellence because it represents the purest and an extremely ancient text, and at the same time to reject possibly even older readings (in terms of demonstrable evidence) simply because they are found in a manuscript like D, containing (according to Westcott and Hort) a "prodigious amount of error" (2.149), or in a "licentious" (2.178), "corrupt" (2.124, 127, 131), and "aberrant" text like the Western (when judged by internal evidence), not only violates their genealogical principle, thereby placing a strain on logic, but also is a clear capitulation to the primacy of internal evidence, and it effects a shift from a cooperative role between external and internal evidence to a situation of polarity. Now the rather clear external evidence concerning D and the Western text is pushed aside and stands in oppo-
242 sition to internal considerations, forcing upon critics a choice between

them; in fact, the two kinds of evidence have been separated to the extent that they assume a dualistic posture, breaking once and for all Westcott and Hort's harmonious synergism of external and internal evidence and highlighting the ambiguity of both the external testimony and the internal judgments. When there is conflict of evidence, as is so often the case, are basic text-critical decisions to be made (or able to be made) on the basis of historical-development and documentary (external) considerations or on the assessment of contextual, stylistic, and scribal (internal) factors? When the evidence fails to point to a single conclusion, one or the other—but never both—must assume the determinative role, and it will not immediately be clear to most textual critics whether it is the external evidence or the internal considerations that should play that decisive role. What is clear, however, is that the failure of Westcott and Hort's synergism of external-internal evidence precisely at the crucial point of the earliest demonstrable fork in the New Testament textual stream (the separation of the Western and Neutral traditions) has evoked, in large measure, the uncertainty, the bewilderment, and the virtual anarchy of recent and current New Testament textual criticism, and—to be more specific—has occasioned the entire eclectic movement as presently practiced in the textual criticism of the New Testament.[62]

This inordinately lengthy "survey" of the "canons of criticism" and the accompanying assessment of their formative role in text-critical theory and practice hardly would be complete without a summary list of canons that have survived the test of time and that are recognized generally as viable principles. These canons fall, of course, into the two major categories that have been discussed above, (1) criteria appealing to *external evidence*, that is, to documentary and historical-development factors in the textual transmission process, and (2) criteria appealing to *internal evidence*, that is, to factors relating to scribal habits, the contexts of passages, and the author's style, language, and thought.

In the following outline, which aims to be comprehensive but could never be exhaustive, *each criterion is phrased in such a way that, if it accurately describes a textual variant, there would be a presumption* (other things being equal) *to regard that variant as the most likely original reading:*

[62] These ideas, in compressed form, were first developed for my article "Textual Criticism, NT," *IDBSup*, 891–95.

Summary List of Generally Accepted Canons

243 A. Criteria related to external evidence.

1. A variant's support by the earliest manuscripts, or by manuscripts assuredly preserving the earliest texts.
2. A variant's support by the "best quality" manuscripts.
3. A variant's support by manuscripts with the widest geographical distribution.
4. A variant's support by one or more established groups of manuscripts of recognized antiquity, character, and perhaps location, that is, of recognized "best quality."

B. Criteria related to internal evidence.

1. A variant's status as the shorter or shortest reading.
2. A variant's status as the harder or hardest reading.
3. A variant's fitness to account for the origin, development, or presence of all other readings.
4. A variant's conformity to the author's style and vocabulary.
5. A variant's conformity to the author's theology or ideology.
6. A variant's conformity to Koine (rather than Attic) Greek.[63]
7. A variant's conformity to Semitic forms of expression.
8. A variant's lack of conformity to parallel passages or to extraneous items in its context generally.
9. A variant's lack of conformity to Old Testament passages.
10. A variant's lack of conformity to liturgical forms and usages.
11. A variant's lack of conformity to extrinsic doctrinal views.

244 This list does not include those further criteria for originality that must be applied to readings at an earlier stage in the text-critical process to determine whether readings are "significant" or "insignificant" for the establishment of the most likely original text. Hence,

[63] This canon is based on the suggestions of G. D. Kilpatrick, "Atticism and the Text of the Greek New Testament," *Neutestamentliche Aufsätze: Festschrift für Prof. Josef Schmid zum 70. Geburtstag* (eds. J. Blinzler, O. Kuss, and F. Mussner; Regensburg: Pustet, 1963) 125–37. Cf. now the compelling cautions and objections of C. M. Martini, "Eclecticism and Atticism in the Textual Criticism of the Greek New Testament," *On Language, Culture, and Religion in Honor of Eugene A. Nida* (eds. M. Black and W. A. Smalley; Approaches to Semiotics; The Hague/Paris: Mouton, 1974) 149–56; and of G. D. Fee, "Rigorous or Reasoned Eclecticism—Which?" *Studies in New Testament Language and Text: Essays in Honour of George D. Kilpatrick* (ed. J. K. Elliott; NovTSup 44; Leiden: Brill, 1976) 174–97. [See Kilpatrick's response to Martini in "Eclecticism and Atticism," *ETL* 53 (1977) 107–12.]

readings that obviously are (1) nonsense readings, (2) clear and demonstrable scribal errors, (3) mere orthographic variations, and (4) singular readings will be assumed to have been excluded from the process, for they are not "textual variants" in the proper, restricted sense of that term[64] and therefore, do not constitute appropriate raw material for the actual determination of the most likely original New Testament text.

C. *Use of Critical Canons in Current Eclecticism*

The categories earlier specified as including all contemporary New Testament textual critics (except the genealogical scholars), namely, *eclectic generalists* and *eclectic specialists*, will provide an appropriate framework for a brief assessment of text-critical methodology in the present, post-Westcott-Hort situation—a situation characterized by a polarity of external and internal evidence. That "all of us" employ an eclectic approach in New Testament textual criticism may stand as a fair generalization; it is also a fair generalization that eclecticism is of two distinct kinds, variously designated, on the one hand, as "moderate" or "reasoned" eclecticism, and, on the other hand, as "thoroughgoing" or "rigorous" eclecticism, though the more descriptively accurate and less question-begging terms used here, *eclectic generalists* and *eclectic specialists*, perhaps are preferable. As will appear presently, eclectics in both groups attempt to break down or neutralize the polarity between the external criteria for originality and the internal, some by ignoring it, and others by emphasizing one pole to the diminution or even the banishment of the other pole. All, however, stand within the dualistic situation created by the conflict of text-critical criteria that has issued from Westcott and Hort's failure to hold the external and internal canons together.

1. *Use of Critical Canons by Eclectic Generalists*

An *eclectic generalist* is a textual critic who recognizes that no single
criterion or constant combination of criteria will adjudicate all text- 245
critical cases and who tries, within this acknowledged limitation, to

[64] These not uncontroversial matters have been treated by the present writer in a paper presented to the Society of Biblical Literature's Textual Criticism Seminar, Washington, D.C., 1974, entitled "Toward the Clarification of the Term 'Textual Variant,'" *Studies in New Testament Language and Text: Essays in Honour of George D. Kilpatrick* (ed. J. K. Elliott; NovTSup 44; Leiden: Brill, 1976) 153–73.

apply with evenness and without prejudice any and all criteria appropriate to the given case and who attempts, further, to arrive at a reasonable solution based on the relative probabilities among those applicable criteria.

Eclectic generalists acknowledge the validity, for the appropriate situations and with other things being equal, of the various canons of criticism or criteria for originality that have emerged in the history of textual criticism and have demonstrated their worth, such as those in the formal list above, including both kinds—external and internal. Accordingly, the eclectic generalist would overcome the polarity of these external and internal criteria by ignoring that polarity or by attempting to ignore it. This is easily possible when, e.g., one variant reading among several is the hardest reading from the perspective of scribal habits; is also in accord with the author's ascertained vocabulary and style and with that author's theology as critically determined; and happens at the same time to be attested by "excellent" manuscripts and by ancient versions or early Fathers of wide geographical distribution. In such cases, where textual decisions are easy, the eclectic generalist (and every other textual critic!) will be oblivious both to the dualistic framework of two distinct classes of criteria for originality and also to the ambiguities so often attendant upon the application of those criteria. When, however, as is so frequently the case, several "strong" criteria do not favor a single reading but variously approve one or another reading, and when—also a frequent occurrence—there is a further bifurcation of evidence between the external and internal poles, then the critic finds himself or herself in a dilemma as he or she faces the difficult "crisis of criteria." If the reading that better suits the author's style is found only in later manuscripts, while the rival reading is found in codices B and ℵ (cf. Matt 6:33),[65] which is to be chosen? If one of five variant readings is attested by B and D, but two other similar readings more adequately account for the origin of all the others (cf. Matt 15:14),[66] which is to be selected? If a wide variety of textual types attest a reading that is clearly "easier" than its alternative (cf. Matt 15:38),[67] which should be preferred? If a variant that quite possibly
246 arose from a parallel passage is omitted by the "best" witnesses (cf.

[65] See Metzger, *Textual Commentary*, ad loc.
[66] Ibid., ad loc.
[67] Ibid., ad loc. [not in Metzger, 1994^{2}].

Matt 16:2–3),[68] should it be admitted into the text? If a longer reading that is almost certainly explicable as a scribal addition due to the influence of the immediate context is supported by B and ℵ (cf. Matt 16:21),[69] should it be approved? If the vast majority of manuscripts, including the "best" manuscripts, attest a shorter reading that could easily be explained as a doctrinal modification of an original longer reading (cf. Matt 27:16,17),[70] which is to be chosen? If the majority of witnesses support a reading that appears to be original on grounds of transcriptional probability, but a few of the earliest and "best" manuscripts have a shorter reading (cf. Acts 3:6),[71] which reading is to be approved?

Examples of this kind easily could be multiplied, but it will be obvious that textual problems involving the conflict of external and internal criteria are common. Of course, many textual problems are even more complex than these examples, for at the same time they may involve, on the one hand, evenly divided external evidence and, on the other hand, conflicting but evenly balanced internal factors. These situations not only demand considerably more refinement in all of the criteria and call for ways to weigh them against one another, but they also highlight the vexing ambiguities to be found in both the external and internal aspects of text-critical criteria.

Most contemporary New Testament textual critics, if asked to classify themselves, probably would affirm that they belong to this eclectic generalist class, for most textual critics today, recognizing the inconclusiveness of modern text-critical theory, would profess to have adopted this evenhanded employment of the available means for judging between and among textual variants, that is, a balanced and impartial application of the relevant external and internal criteria to each case of textual variation. To take an example, certainly this was the intention of the distinguished editors of the UBS^{3} *Greek New Testament*,[72] as evidenced by the careful delineation of the criteria in the report of their textual deliberations and decisions.[73] This intention comes to the fore time and again as the editors, e.g., go against 247

68 Ibid., ad loc.

69 Ibid., ad loc. [not in Metzger, 1994^{2}].

70 Ibid., ad loc.

71 Ibid., ad loc.

72 K. Aland, M. Black, C. M. Martini, B. M. Metzger, and A. Wikgren (3rd ed.; New York/London/Edinburgh/Amsterdam/Stuttgart: United Bible Societies, 1975).

73 Metzger, *Textual Commentary*, xxiv–xxviii [1994^{2} = 11*–14*].

a variant supported by Westcott and Hort's lodestar, Codex B (with ℵ), when other evidence—external or (perhaps more often) internal—suggests the originality of an alternative variant. It appears also in the scrupulous and judicious evaluations of relevant criteria in those numerous cases where the evidence is very closely divided. Yet, a perusal of *A Textual Commentary on the Greek New Testament* by Metzger for the editorial committee of the UBS[3] strongly suggests that the steady repetition of such phrases as "the preponderant weight of external attestation," "the overwhelming weight of manuscript evidence," and "superior manuscript support," along with such expressions as "the earliest and best witnesses," "the oldest and best attested reading," and "attested by inferior authorities," all signal a predilection for an external principle along the lines of "the readings of the oldest and best manuscripts are to be preferred," and most often this means B with ℵ and, where applicable, the early papyri, such as P^{75}, P^{66}, P^{45}, P^{72}, and others.[74] This assessment, based as it is on impressions from extended interaction with the *Textual Commentary*, just possibly could be an unfair generalization; more likely, however, it is a reasonable and fair judgment, and, if so, it signifies that the editors of the UBS[3] in the final analysis are not eclectic generalists after all, nor in fact are there many among contemporary New Testament textual critics who could be so classified, despite the good

[74] That B played this decisive role in the *UBSGNT* is confirmed by the statement in the *Textual Commentary*, 295: ". . . The possibility must be left open that occasionally the text of B represents a secondary development." The fact that this comment occurs in connection with an Acts passage makes it all the more significant, for Metzger reports (271–72) that the editors recognized that in the text of Acts "neither the Alexandrian nor the Western group of witnesses always preserves the original text, but that in order to attain the earliest text one must compare the two divergent traditions point by point and in each case select the reading which commends itself in the light of transcriptional and intrinsic probabilities," and that, therefore, the Editorial Committee "proceeded in an eclectic fashion." The clear implication is that, for the *UBSGNT* Committee, B was indeed the lodestar of the original text, for if in Acts—where there is the greatest uncertainty as to whether B and its group or its early rival, the Western text, represents the original—if here in Acts the *possibility* must be allowed that B *occasionally* represents the non-original text, then elsewhere B must surely stand as the most reliable guide. Incidentally, the statement from pp. 272–73 quoted above does not mean that in Acts the editors gave primacy to internal evidence, for what they sought, as stated explicitly, was "the earliest text"—an external criterion—though internal criteria were employed, as part of an overall eclectic process, to determine which of the two rival texts or which of the various alternative readings was in fact the earlier or earliest. [The quotations from Metzger (1971[1]) may be found in 1994[2] on the following pages, respectively: 255; 235.]

intentions of most of them to follow this balanced approach.[75] Rather, 248
contemporary textual critics for the most part are to be classed as eclectic specialists, whether on the right wing of that subdivision or on the left.

2. *Use of Critical Canons by Eclectic Specialists*

The *eclectic specialist* recognizes quite clearly the polarity between external and internal evidence, and he or she tries to overcome it by *specializing* in or by *emphasizing* one of the poles to the minimizing or even exclusion of the other. Whether one can escape the dualistic dilemma by this one-sidedness remains to be seen, but such a critic is aware that a *major* choice between text-critical criteria (in addition to and quite different in character from the innumerable minor choices) must be made in order to solve the textual problems that one faces, and the choice—when the chips are down—is between *final reliance* either on evidence from the historical-development and documentary side of textual history (external evidence) or from scribal, stylistic, contextual, and ideological factors in manuscript transmission (internal evidence).

At least two subgroups are to be found among the eclectic specialists. On the right hand are those textual critics who permit external evidence to cast the decisive vote in cases where there is equiponderance of evidence, but the utilization of historical-documentary evidence in this way requires that the critic first shall have accepted as valid a particular historical-development scheme for the earliest transmission of the New Testament text. Usually the scheme adopted will follow the general lines of Westcott and Hort's understanding of a twofold Syrian (or, better, Byzantine or Koine) and pre-Syrian textual history, including their further demarcation of a "Neutral" (or, better, Alexandrian or Egyptian) text-type and a "Western" text-type as the earliest (and competing) texts, but also the recognition of a third early text, the Caesarean type.[76] For critics

[75] Cf. n. 3 above.

[76] See Epp, "Twentieth Century Interlude," 393–96, for a statement on the status of the Caesarean text in current criticism. [The diminution and likely demise of the "Caesarean" text-type finds striking confirmation in a comparison of the "List of Witnesses according to Type of Text" in Metzger, *Textual Commentary*, 1st ed. of 1971 (xxix–xxx) under four headings: Alexandrian, Western, Caesarean, and Byzantine, with the same list in the 2nd ed. of 1994 (15*–16*), where there are only three: Alexandrian, Western, and Byzantine—the Caesarean has disappeared altogether!]

of this kind, normally a reading strongly attested by widely diversified witnesses from all of the early groups would be preferred, as would a reading very strongly attested by the Alexandrian (Westcott and Hort's Neutral) group. When the probabilities are more evenly balanced (such as divided support among the Alexandrian witnesses or among the early text-types), then other criteria will come into play, particularly internal considerations (hence, the designation, *eclectic* spe-
249 cialists), such as the search for the reading that best explains the origin of all the others, or any other applicable criteria. The complicating factors attending textual decisions can be severe and vexing, but the point is that in the final analysis an eclectic specialist, as one who emphasizes external criteria, *characteristically* will flee for refuge to any relevant historical-development and documentary considerations that will permit a resolution of the problem. This does not necessarily mean that this is done automatically or even consistently, but only *characteristically*, for there are times when the internal evidence will show unambiguously that a scribal error or some other transmissional phenomenon—whether intentional or unintentional—lies at the root of the reading in one's "best" manuscript or group. In that case, as an eclectic, he or she will choose another reading. Yet the textual critic of this type has a prevailing predilection—though hardly a whimsical or haphazard one—for the supremacy of external evidence and usually for external evidence of a particular brand. Obviously, not all such eclectic specialists will lean toward the Alexandrian text-type or its members as determinative; some few may prefer, for instance, the so-called Western witnesses.

The major difficulty with an eclectic approach that specializes in external evidence emerges precisely at this point, that is, with the uncertainty as to which historical-development scheme to adopt as normative. Is it to be the basic Westcott-Hort conception as modified by new developments and discoveries, or some other reconstruction of the earliest history of New Testament textual transmission? This inconclusiveness, of course, is no fault of the eclectic method, but is rather a weakness—perhaps *the* weakness—of modern New Testament textual theory in general.[77] As a matter of fact, far from being at fault in this circumstance, the eclectic method is merely a reflection or a symptom of this fundamental problem. If there were any reason-

[77] Cf. Epp, "Twentieth Century Interlude," 390–401.

able certainty about this very earliest history of the New Testament text and if reasonably confident assertions could be formulated as to precisely how our extant manuscripts are related to that history of transmission, these difficulties in the eclectic method would disappear—and perhaps also the eclectic method as we know it would itself disappear! Such basic solutions, however, appear not to be close at hand, though certainly some significant advances in methodology, coupled with the extraordinary discoveries of early papyri during the past generation or two, are a source of optimism.[78] In the meantime, most New Testament textual critics doubtless will follow some 250
form of this moderate or reasoned eclecticism that we have designated the eclectic-specialist approach.

(Observe that genealogists, while they are "specialists" who emphasize external evidence, are not *eclectic* specialists, for internal considerations play virtually no role in their establishment of a text.)

On the left wing of the eclectic-specialist class are those who rely largely, primarily, or even exclusively on internal criteria for resolving text-critical problems and for establishing the original New Testament text. Obviously, scholars of this persuasion overcome the external-internal polarity by granting to internal evidence the determinative role. This dominance of internal factors, notably the author's style and contextual considerations, was operative, for instance, in the work of Bernhard Weiss, whose editions of the Greek New Testament appeared between 1894 and 1905,[79] in C. H. Turner's "Notes" (consisting of 100 pages!) on "Marcan Usage,"[80] and in M.-J. Lagrange's "critique rationnelle."[81] Both Weiss and Lagrange in effect depart, however, from their proclaimed reliance on internal criticism and move instead to a practical dependence on a "best manuscript" criterion, and in both cases Codex B is employed as the touchstone of purity. Though customarily mentioned as the leading exponent of "rational criticism,"[82] it can be said of Lagrange that "in almost

[78] Cf. ibid., 387; 406–14.

[79] See Metzger, *Text of the New Testament*, 137–38, for a succinct description of Weiss's procedures, and 175–79 for a general summary of this kind of eclectic methodology.

[80] C. H. Turner, "Marcan Usage: Notes, Critical and Exegetical, on the Second Gospel," *JTS* 25 (1923–1924) 377–86; 26 (1924–1925) 12–20; 145–56; 225–40; 337–46; 27 (1925–1926) 58–62; 28 (1926–1927) 9–30; 349–62; 29 (1927–1928) 275–89; 346–61.

[81] Lagrange, *Critique textuelle*, esp. 17–40.

[82] E.g., A. F. J. Klijn, *A Survey of the Researches into the Western Text of the Gospels and Acts* (Utrecht: Kemink, 1949) 170.

Hortian terms he pleads for following Codex Vaticanus even where the evidence is not clear—on the grounds of its general excellence."[83]

C. H. Turner opened his series of studies on Marcan usage by altering Westcott and Hort's famous dictum, "Knowledge of documents should precede final judgement upon readings,"[84] to "Knowledge of an author's usage should precede final judgement,"[85] thereby indi-
251 cating in a striking fashion the need to take internal evidence most seriously, particularly stylistic and philological features, and that these are crucial if not conclusive in text-critical decisions.

Turner's description of grammatical usages in Mark bore fruit in the work of George D. Kilpatrick, whose views developed from their rather cautious beginnings in 1943 and 1944[86] until the present time, when they represent what justly may be called the far left of the eclectic-specialist emphasis on internal criteria. Kilpatrick's early views were expressed in statements such as, "We cannot accept or reject textual types or manuscripts as wholes," for each segment of text is only a collection of variants, "each of which is to be judged on its own merits," and by calling for scholars to apply a "rigorous eclecticism" in the Gospels and Acts and to "pursue an impartial eclecticism" also in the Epistles, but to do so in a consistent way everywhere.[87] By eclecticism he apparently meant, at this time, the serious application of text-critical criteria additional to those that tried to move "from the textual families and types to the original text,"[88] that is, criteria additional to external evidence. In other words, for the establishment of the original text, he was urging that all mechanical application of "best manuscript" and "best text-type" criteria cease and that in addition to the normal criteria arising from knowledge of manuscripts and palaeographic principles the textual critic should employ also—and with great seriousness—those criteria

[83] Colwell, "Significance of Grouping," 76–77, reprinted in his *Studies in Methodology*, 5–6; cf. n. 61 above.

[84] Westcott-Hort, *New Testament in the Original Greek*, 2.ix; 2.31.

[85] Turner, "Marcan Usage," *JTS* 25 (1923–24) 377.

[86] Kilpatrick, "Western Text and Original Text in the Gospels and Acts," *JTS* 44 (1943) 24–36; idem, "Western Text and Original Text in the Epistles," *JTS* 45 (1944) 60–65.

[87] Kilpatrick, "Western Text and Original Text in the Gospels and Acts," 33–34; 36; idem, "Western Text and Original Text in the Epistles," 65; see also idem, "Atticism," 136: "At each point the text must be decided impartially on the merits of the readings involved." Similar statements appear inevitably in his articles on the subject.

[88] Idem, "Western Text and Original Text in the Gospels and Acts," 36.

concerned with harmonization, style, language, theology, and a reading's fitness to account for all others (internal evidence), but with special emphasis on the assertion that in this eclectic method "the decision rests ultimately with the criteria as distinct from the manuscripts, and that our evaluation of the manuscripts must be determined by the criteria."[89] Kilpatrick claimed that his proposals entailed no disparagement of external evidence[90] (of none, that is, except claims for a normative "best text" or "best manuscript"), yet in a real sense external criteria were seriously undermined. Whereas he seemed to be asking only that external evidence be removed from
its seemingly exclusive position of supremacy in textual decisions, 252
that critics lay aside their predispositions in its favor, and that all criteria be allowed to stand on an equal plane, in actuality external criteria were negatively affected to a much greater extent than these statements would imply, for how can external criteria play a role when "each reading has to be judged on its merits and not on its supports"?[91] How, for example, can the date or geographical provenance of a reading be relevant when "the decision rests ultimately with the criteria *as distinct from the manuscripts*"? [italics added]. The effect of this presumed eclecticism of internal *and* external evidence is that the external evidence virtually is ruled out of court in advance, for this particular presiding judge will allow no evidence along the lines of "general opinions about the value of the manuscripts or textual types,"[92] nor any, presumably, about the date or provenance of a manuscript containing a given reading or its place in any reconstruction of the history of New Testament textual transmission. That leaves little if anything on the external side of the case.[93]

To be fair to Professor Kilpatrick, it must be added that his two earliest articles on this subject encompassed as possibly original only those readings from text-types and witnesses that were acknowledged to be early (notably the Alexandrian and Western texts and their witnesses).[94] Nevertheless, the principles established there by Kilpatrick

[89] Ibid., 25–26.
[90] Ibid., 36.
[91] Ibid., 33.
[92] Ibid., 26.
[93] Kilpatrick, ibid., does speak of assessing the "antiquity of the tradition in a certain manuscript" from its spelling, abbreviations, script, number of columns, and errors.
[94] Ibid., 36.

for evaluating these *early* readings were thereafter applied by him to *all* readings. This becomes explicit when in 1963 he repeated his conclusion that "no manuscript or type of text is uniformly right or wrong" and then affirmed that "this conclusion applies as much to the Byzantine text . . . as to the Western text and the old Uncials," adding that the "outright condemnation" of the Byzantine text was one of Westcott and Hort's greatest errors.[95] In 1965, Kilpatrick supported and illustrated this conviction from scores of variation-units where he felt that the Byzantine witnesses preserved the original text, and he concluded by saying:

> 253 We have to pursue a consistent eclecticism. Readings must be considered severally on their intrinsic character. Further, contrary to what Hort maintained, decisions about readings must precede decisions about the value or weight of manuscripts.[96]

It is, then, this assessment and judgment of individual readings, inevitably on internal grounds and in complete detachment from any value or weight that may be assigned to the manuscripts or groups that contain them, that is the heart of this form of the eclectic-specialist approach, though this characterization, as pointed out earlier, does not adequately convey the degree to which external evidence has been excluded by this method. In fact, for all practical purposes it has been eliminated from the text-critical decisions on the original text.

The accuracy of our estimation of the true character of this form of eclecticism is confirmed by the handling of the method in the work of J. K. Elliott, who calls for a "thoroughgoing eclecticism," in which "the cult of the best manuscripts gives way to the cult of the best reading" and which "devotes its main attention to the individual variants themselves and very little attention to external evidence."[97] The phrase, "very little attention to external evidence," is actually, however, an understatement, for nowhere in either of his brief but recent expositions of "thoroughgoing eclecticism" does Elliott

---

[95] Kilpatrick, "An Eclectic Study of the Text of Acts," *Biblical and Patristic Studies in Memory of Robert Pierce Casey* (eds. J. N. Birdsall and R. W. Thomson; Freiburg: Herder, 1963) 76.

[96] Kilpatrick, "The Greek New Testament Text of Today and the *Textus Receptus*," *The New Testament in Historical and Contemporary Perspective: Essays in Memory of G. H. C. Macgregor* (eds. H. Anderson and W. Barclay; Oxford: Blackwell, 1965) 189–206; the quotation is from 205–6.

[97] Elliott, "Rational Criticism," 340–41.

mention, much less approve, any external criterion among his extensive listing of critical canons; rather, external criteria are excluded, for his approach "is concerned with finding plausible explanations based on internal considerations to justify the choice of one reading as original and the others as secondary,"[98] or again, ". . . We are concerned with which reading is likely to represent what our original author wrote. We are not concerned with the age, prestige, or popularity of the manuscripts supporting the readings we would adopt as original."[99] In an earlier exposition of the method, a reference presumably to external evidence—stated in terms of palaeographic phenomena and manuscript characteristics—appears to refer only to aids in recovering scribal habits and peculiarities, in actuality internal evidence.[100] Elliott, furthermore, is quite explicit about the antithe- 254
sis between external and internal criteria, for which he often uses the designations (respectively) of "documentary" and "eclectic" methods, and he is equally explicit about his clear preference for the latter: ". . . It is reasonable to depart from a documentary study and to examine the N.T. text from a purely eclectic standpoint," and "The eclectic method, by using different criteria and by working from a different standpoint, tries to arrive at the true reading, untrammeled by discussion about the weight of MS support."[101]

One of the difficulties with the eclectic approach that specializes in internal criticism may be only a terminological inconsistency, but it should be obvious that those who insist most strongly on an "eclectic" approach actually are the least eclectic, for their partiality toward internal criteria virtually excludes the external. Moreover, since the critical principles of these eclectics are focused for the most part rather narrowly on the style of the author (including language and grammar, and how scribes are likely to have treated what the author wrote),[102] the term "eclectic" loses much of its appropriateness. It is

---

[98] Ibid., 340–43 (the quotation is from 341); idem, "Can We Recover the Original New Testament?" 349–53.

[99] Ibid., 352.

[100] Elliott, *The Greek Text of the Epistles to Timothy and Titus* (SD 36; Salt Lake City: University of Utah, 1968) 10. There are some ambiguous references to "weak" and "strong" support on 11.

[101] Ibid., 5–6; 11; cf. also 12: "Often such a study serves as further ammunition against the documentary method"; and his "Rational Criticism," 341: ". . . internal rather than on documentary criteria."

[102] Cf., e.g., Kilpatrick, "Eclectic Study of the Text of Acts," 77; Elliott, *Greek*

not clear either what the adjectives "rigorous," "impartial," or "thoroughgoing" signify when they modify "eclecticism," for the method's self-imposed limitation to internal criteria surely makes it less "impartial" and less "thorough" than an eclectic-generalist approach or than that of the specialist emphasizing external evidence, for these latter methods utilize both external and internal criteria. Moreover, the term "rigorous" is ambiguous here, for it is not evident whether it signifies "strict," "severe" in the sense of "narrow," "restricted" (an appropriate designation), or has the sense of "inflexible," that is, rigidly conforming to the eclectic principle (which this school seems not to do). Since the latter meaning is close to "thoroughgoing" and since Kilpatrick calls for a "consistent eclecticism,"[103] it would appear
255 that "rigorous" is meant to refer to thoroughness and consistency in being eclectic (traits that seem not to be the possession of this school).

This semantic problem could more likely be solved, however, by taking "eclectic" to specify the open choice, not of criteria, but of readings from any extant manuscripts; if so, this kind of eclecticism would be "impartial" in the sense that it shows no favoritism toward any particular manuscript and has no predilection for any specific text (which is true). And it would be "thoroughgoing" in the sense that is considers all readings candidates for the original reading until some internal test rules them out. And it would be "rigorous" and "consistent" in that it never swerves from this openness to every extant reading. The only difficulty here is that nearly all the contexts, in both Kilpatrick and Elliott, that characterize or describe "eclecticism" suggest that "eclectic" is concerned primarily with the open and wide choice of criteria and not of readings, though the latter also is certainly a prominent feature of this branch of eclecticism.

More substantive criticisms of this eclecticism of internal criteria arise from the side of the evolution and history of New Testament textual transmission—a tangled history, one must add. Yet there *was* such a history and there *is* such a history to be reconstructed, even though exactly how it is to be done is by no means clear. Eclectic specialists on the side of internal evidence, however, have pushed their partiality for internal criteria—and also their aversion to exter-

---

Text of . . . Timothy and Titus, 8, who calls conformity to the author's style and usage the eclectic method's "basic rule of thumb."

[103] Kilpatrick, "The Greek New Testament Text of Today," 205; cf. idem, "Western Text and Original Text in the Gospels and Acts," 34.

nal evidence—to such an extent that it is doubtful whether even a definitive reconstruction of the history of early New Testament transmission (if by some miracle it should appear) would occasion any alteration in their procedures for determining the original New Testament text. Everyone, I think, will recognize that to utilize history judiciously is always difficult, and most will acknowledge that to ignore history is always perilous. In the case of the New Testament text, to ignore its external history and the relevant historical factors of its transmission—with or without a definitive reconstruction—and to follow instead an exclusively internal eclecticism may be the surest path to what A. F. J. Klijn already has called the "complete chaos" attendant upon the application of the eclectic method to the recovery of the original New Testament text. This is not to deny, of 256
course, the very considerable and stimulating methodological contributions and the continuing new insights into textual criteria that flow from this eclecticism that is restricted to internal evidence, though the appropriateness of the particular limitation to one kind of criteria is called into question.

III. Conclusion

The extended, though not devious, path that has taken us all the way from the early "canons of criticism" to contemporary eclectic emphases on internal criteria alone, including the several broader forms of eclectic procedure along the way, provides an answer to the question posed at the outset in the title, "the eclectic method—solution or symptom?" Each exponent or practitioner of an eclectic method feels assured, naturally, that his or her method, given the present circumstances, is the best available solution to New Testament

---

[104] A. F. J. Klijn, "In Search of the Original Text of Acts," *Studies in Luke-Acts: Essays Presented in Honor of Paul Schubert* (eds. L. E. Keck and J. L. Martyn; Nashville/New York: Abingdon, 1966) 104; cf. 108. Klijn makes this highly critical judgment while affirming at the same time that "the eclectic method seems to be the only adequate method to regain the original text" (104). While Klijn's attribution of chaos to the eclectic method explicitly encompasses Kilpatrick's work, observe also that Klijn's own views on external evidence are radically different from Kilpatrick's, for Klijn, while approving the "rational criticism" of readings (mainly on grounds of intrinsic probability), states that textual criticism must attempt to render this approach superfluous, mainly by the grouping of manuscripts into families and texts (external evidence): Klijn, *Survey of the Researches into the Western Text*, 170.

text-critical problems. Only a very few, however, are willing to assert that eclecticism is anything like a final solution, and it is precisely the finality expressed by those few that is the most questionable of all. This widespread caution, if not always humility, among at least the majority of eclectics should indicate that every eclectic method is at best a temporary "solution" to our basic problems in New Testament textual criticism, and if such a method really is a solution at all, it is of the most tentative kind. It would appear, rather, that the eclectic method—regardless of type—is more certainly a highly visible symptom of those basic problems. After all, the most fundamental and longest-standing problem of the entire discipline and one that encompasses virtually all others (as this study has attempted to show) is the problem of the criteria for originality of readings. In the foregoing pages, the alternating history of cooperation and antithesis between the two classes of criteria, external and
257 internal, has been sketched in an effort to show (as this study's further purpose) not only how eclecticism has developed within and from this context but where the discipline of New Testament textual criticism stands today on this central issue. One result is that the eclectic method is seen most clearly as symptomatic of this severe and crucial problem. Yet, eclecticism is not more than this, for it is unable to find a conclusive way to overcome the "crisis of criteria." Indeed, the very name "eclectic" (if—as seems likely—it refers to the choice of appropriate criteria from among many) discloses the fact that the method does not have the solution. Yet, symptoms are extremely useful and important; no disease should be without them, lest there be no warning of trouble and no efforts toward remedy. Certainly the eclectic method provides us with detailed indications of the difficulties in New Testament textual theory and method, and thereby it assists us greatly both in clarifying those problems and in exploring appropriate solutions. We must, however, beware of treating symptoms rather than the disorder itself.

Added Notes, 2004

On eclectic methods. The present essay and a paper by Gordon Fee on "Rigorous or Reasoned Eclecticism—Which?" (later published in *Studies in New Testament Language and Text: Essays in Honour of George D. Kilpatrick* [ed. J. K. Elliott; NovTSup 44; Leiden: Brill, 1976]

174–97) comprised a program on "The Eclectic Method" at the 1975 Society of Biblical Literature "Textual Criticism Group," along with a response by Ernest W. Saunders. After both papers were published in 1976—with their rather blunt and harsh critiques of Kilpatrick's and Elliott's views, we were surprised—but also disappointed—that no rejoinders were immediately forthcoming, for the whole purpose of our SBL program and the publication of its results was to stimulate dialogue and discussion. Indeed, Professor Kilpatrick (who died in 1989) never did respond to our assessments of his influential views, though he did take on, point by point, the 1974 critique of his Atticism criterion by Carlo M. Martini (see n. 63, above). However, Keith Elliott, Kilpatrick's student and subsequent spokesperson for their shared views, did publish a number of further descriptions of "thoroughgoing eclecticism," with responses to critics, including "In Defence of Thoroughgoing Eclecticism in New Testament Textual Criticism," *ResQ* 21 (1978) 95–115; idem, "Can We Recover the Original Text of the New Testament? An Examination of the Rôle of Thoroughgoing Eclecticism," in his *Essays and Studies in New Testament Textual Criticism* (EFN 3; Cordoba: Ediciones el Almendro, 1992) 17–43, esp. 27–37; idem, "Thoroughgoing Eclecticism in New Testament Textual Criticism," *The Text of the New Testament in Contemporary Research: Essays on the* Status Quaestionis (eds. B. D. Ehrman and M. W. Holmes; SD 46; Grand Rapids, MI: Eerdmans, 1995) 321–335; idem, "The Case for Thoroughgoing Eclecticism," *Rethinking New Testament Textual Criticism* (ed. D. A. Black; Grand Rapids, MI: Baker Academic, 2002) 101–24.

Kilpatrick's cited essays have been reprinted in *The Principles and Practice of New Testament Textual Criticism: Collected Essays of G. D. Kilpatrick* (ed. J. K. Elliott; BETL 96; Leuven: University Press/Peeters, 1990).

Subsequent discussions of the eclectic methods include Michael W. Holmes, "Reasoned Eclecticism in New Testament Textual Criticism," in Ehrman and Holmes (eds.), *Text of the New Testament in Contemporary Research*, 336–360 [see his bibliography, 354–60]; idem, "The Case for Reasoned Eclecticism," in Black (ed.), *Rethinking New Testament Textual Criticism*, 77–100.

On the "criteria for priority of readings." Further discussions in the present volume include "Decision Points," 100–103; but especially "Issues in New Testament Textual Criticism," 20–34.

CHAPTER SEVEN

NEW TESTAMENT TEXTUAL CRITICISM IN AMERICA: REQUIEM FOR A DISCIPLINE*

In view of the rapid approach of the 100th anniversary of the Society 94
of Biblical Literature (1980), it is appropriate to consider the position held by New Testament textual criticism in American biblical scholarship during that century and especially the place that it holds today.

To speak of textual criticism in *America* may give pause to some. I, for one, have never considered even for a moment the long-term history of *American* New Testament textual criticism as an isolated phenomenon, or that of any other country for that matter, because textual criticism hardly can be thought of in terms of any distinct geographical area, nor can its development be separated along national lines. Rather, from its earliest period, New Testament textual criticism has been a genuinely international effort, with various discoveries, theories, breakthroughs, or even setbacks espoused now by a scholar of one nation and then by a scholar of another, and so on, so that scholars of all nations together have woven the fabric of our discipline, though with various yet intertwining threads. Witness, for example, the pivotal editions of the Greek New Testament, which generally were built one upon another, starting with Erasmus in Holland, to Stephanus in France (and Switzerland), to Th. Beza in Switzerland, then to John Fell, John Mill and Richard Bentley in England, then J. A. Bengel in Germany, J. J. Wettstein in Switzerland and Holland, then to J. J. Griesbach, Karl Lachmann, and Constantin von Tischendorf in Germany, and again to S. P. Tregelles and B. F. Westcott and F. J. A. Hort in England, to Bernhard Weiss in Germany, A. Souter in England, H. von Soden, H. J. Vogels, and Eberhard and Erwin Nestle in Germany, to A. Merk of Rome, J. M. Bover of Spain, and finally to the Nestle-Aland editions in Germany

* A paper presented in the New Testament Textual Criticism Section of the Society of Biblical Literature, San Francisco, 30 December 1977.

(edited by Kurt Aland after 1972) and the recent international edition of the United Bible Societies.

This zigzag course from nation to nation to nation could be traced as easily in a number of other spheres of New Testament textual criticism, for example, that which encompasses the history and theory of the New Testament text. Again, if the great names in this category were to be listed, many of those previously mentioned would be included, such as Bentley, Bengel, Wettstein, Griesbach, Lachmann, Tischendorf, Tregelles, Westcott and Hort, and von Soden, which brings the matter nearly to World War I, but with no Americans in that early group. From von Soden on, as is well known, text-critical scholarship concentrated on the great text-types that had been isolated, the so-called Neutral (or Alexandrian), the Western, and the Byzantine. Here the significant names are legion if one wishes to pursue the subject at some length, but selecting only the most obvious figures in each of several important subject-areas of textual theory and history will show again the national diversity and the presence or absence of American names. For example, in the study of the so-called *Western text*, one would have to mention J. Rendel Harris, F. H. Chase, and A. C. Clark of England, Friedrich Blass of Germany, and at least two Americans, J. H. Ropes and W. H. P. Hatch. On the isolation of the *Caesarean text*, B. H. Streeter of England and T. Ayuso of Spain are prominent, but also those who worked in America, Kirsopp and Silva (New) Lake and Robert P. Blake. If one turns to methodological issues, the names of Henri Quentin of Rome and our own Ernest C. Colwell should be mentioned in connection with *quantitative methods*, as well as a number of contemporary American scholars employing genealogical, "profile," or other quantitative methods for determining manuscript relationships. The *eclectic method*, with emphasis on internal considerations, gained ground through the work of Bernhard Weiss in Germany, C. H. Turner in England, and M.-J. Lagrange, a French scholar in Jerusalem, and is stressed currently in England by George D. Kilpatrick and J. Keith Elliott. Two other sub-specialties, however, have been dominated by Americans in recent times, first the study of the *lectionary text* of the New Testament by E. C. Colwell, D. W. Riddle, Allen P. Wikgren, Bruce M. Metzger, and their students; and, secondly, in very recent times the defense of the *textus receptus*, which—as a revival of the almost century-old
95 view of J. W. Burgon in England—is a curious and (for me) regret-

table retrogression emphasized by a few North American scholars of a conservative theological persuasion.

This hasty survey has shown that only occasionally have North American scholars figured prominently in the production of important critical editions of the Greek New Testament or in noteworthy theoretical or methodological developments, though after World War I American names become more prominent than in the earlier periods. Some further perspective might be gained, however, by taking what otherwise might be termed a myopic look at the discipline of textual criticism as it was pursued *in North America*, that is, by focusing on New Testament text-critical work only in that geographical area encompassed by the Society of Biblical Literature.

In this respect, the first issues of the *Journal of the Society of Biblical Literature and Exegesis*, which appeared in 1881 and following, contained several articles on New Testament textual criticism, including some of the last essays to come from the hand of one of the founders of SBL, Ezra Abbot of Harvard, who died early in 1884. Already in 1852, nearly thirty years before the founding of SBL, Abbot published a "Notice of Tischendorf's Greek Testament,"[1] and during his long career that followed, he produced many text-critical studies, among them contributions to Gregory's famed *Prolegomena* to Tischendorf's eighth major edition; Abbot's name, in fact, is listed with Gregory's on the title page of that monumental work. Certainly, New Testament textual criticism in America did not begin with Ezra Abbot, but just as certainly Ezra Abbot was the first great name of an American scholar working in that field. Abbot's articles were, of course, only the first in a stream of text-critical contributions to appear in *JBL*, to take only our own journal as a sample source for data; the list of authors is impressive indeed as one peruses the pages of *JBL* over the years, even if only selected scholars and only those who are no longer with us are mentioned here: Isaac H. Hall, Edgar J. Goodspeed, W. H. P. Hatch, Kirsopp and Silva Lake, James Hardy Ropes, Robert P. Casey, Henry A. Sanders, B. W. Bacon, H. R. Willoughby, D. W. Riddle, and Ernest C. Colwell. If scholars still active in the field were to be added to this list, the result would be a Who's Who of American textual criticism.

---

[1] E. Abbot, "Tischendorf's Greek Testament," *BSac* 9 (July, 1852) 623–28.

If one were to consider only this short list of *JBL* contributors and to survey some of their more extensive studies in New Testament textual criticism, one would begin to grasp the proportions of the worthy and inspiring text-critical legacy that has come to us from this side of the Atlantic. For example, E. J. Goodspeed, who authored fifty-four books and monographs, co-authored sixteen more, and published 118 articles, was "the first American to collect, decipher, and publish Greek papyri";[2] he published editions of numerous minuscule manuscripts of the New Testament, including the deluxe facsimile edition of the magnificent Rockefeller McCormick New Testament that he discovered in Paris in 1928. There may be a sense, however, in which Goodspeed's encouragement and inspiration of text-critical work in America—and particularly at the University of Chicago—may be more important than his own large volume of text-critical studies, for Goodspeed played a major role in the development of a significant New Testament manuscript collection at Chicago,[3] and this—along with his own influence and scholarly work—did much to make the University of Chicago the one great American center for New Testament textual criticism over a long and productive period. The records show some thirty theses and dissertations on text-critical subjects from Chicago through 1970, with more than half originating in the period of Goodspeed's tenure, and these included the works of such textual critics as E. C. Colwell, K. W. Clark, and A. P. Wikgren.[4]

96 W. H. P. Hatch, as a second example, published several volumes of facsimiles and descriptions of New Testament manuscripts in Greek and Syriac, as well as a spate of text-critical studies on the Greek and Syriac New Testament, extending from 1908 to 1958. Henry A. Sanders of the University of Michigan published the texts or collations of a number of New Testament manuscripts; Kirsopp and Silva Lake, separately or together, published the edition of Codex I (1902), studies of the Caesarean text (1928), of Families 13 (1941)

[2] James Harrel Cobb and Louis B. Jennings, *A Biography and Bibliography of Edgar Johnson Goodspeed* (Chicago: University of Chicago Press, 1948) 2.

[3] Merrill M. Parvis and Allen P. Wikgren (eds.), *New Testament Manuscript Studies* (Chicago: University of Chicago Press, 1950) ix.

[4] See *Criterion: A Publication of the Divinity School of the University of Chicago* 12 (1, Autumn, 1972), a special issue: "Dissertations in the Divinity School," 63 pp.

and Pi (1937), as well as their magisterial ten-volume album of *Dated Greek Minuscule Manuscripts to the Year 1200* (1934–39), and a host of shorter studies. James Hardy Ropes's *Text of Acts* in *The Beginnings of Christianity* (1926) has not been surpassed for its detail; and Colwell and Riddle's *Prolegomena to the Study of the Lectionary Text of the Gospels* (1933) opened up the whole area of the New Testament lectionary text.

This haphazard survey of a few figures from the recent and not so recent past indicates that American New Testament textual criticism may not have had a Tischendorf or a Hort, but it did have its Goodspeed, its Hatch, and its Kirsopp Lake, and the contributions made by these and scores of others on this side of the Atlantic stand as a fitting tribute to American scholarly industry and at times ingenuity in this demanding and complex discipline. If anyone should minimize the work of these giants or of those American scholars who have followed them, I would rise at once to their defense. Yet, at the same time, objectivity and honesty require the admission that American contributions to New Testament textual criticism from Ezra Abbot's day and through the century of SBL's existence have been, I dare say, more of a random and piecemeal nature than of a unified or epoch-making kind. This rather sweeping indictment is not made lightly, and certainly it demands not only explication, but justification. For one thing, as the survey above shows, it will be acknowledged readily that individual American scholars did not produce either the large-scale or the widely used critical editions of the Greek New Testament, as did Tregelles, Tischendorf, Westcott-Hort, Weiss, Nestle, von Soden, or the others referred to earlier. Several American scholars, to be sure, played very major—and others secondary—roles in the production of the recent international edition known as the United Bible Societies' Greek New Testament, and their contribution is well known and greatly appreciated. Yet, earlier team efforts—whether of a national or international kind—have not fared well. The massive project of von Soden, which had its patroness and utilized a cadre of assistants, was brought to completion in four large and fine-print volumes over a period of sixteen years, though the magnificent faults of this project are universally recognized and neither its critical text nor its theory of the text has found acceptance. The fact remains, however, that this extensive project actually was completed!—and in sixteen years. By contrast, a far better project—in terms of aim, conception, and quality

control—that began thirty-five years after von Soden's edition appeared and was conceived as a joint American and British effort, namely, the International Greek New Testament Project, has not been able—after an additional thirty years—to bring to completion the critical apparatus for even one gospel. It must be said, however, that the "fringe benefits" of the IGNTP were strikingly significant for American textual criticism over the first twenty years or so of the Project's history, providing for the discipline a positive thrust in at least four ways: First, beginning in 1948, it forged a core group of American textual critics who would play a crucial role in the discipline over the succeeding generation, as is evident from the roster of the first American Editorial Board, which included Robert P. Blake, Robert P. Casey, Kenneth W. Clark, Ernest C. Colwell, Jacob Geerlings, Edgar J. Goodspeed, W. H. P. Hatch, Silva Lake, Bruce M. Metzger, Merrill M. Parvis, Henry A. Sanders, Ernest W. Saunders, and Allen P. Wikgren. Secondly, and of great significance, the Project created a series of geographical centers for its work, first at the University of Chicago, then—from 1955—at Emory University, and concurrently from 1963 at Duke University, and finally at the Claremont Graduate School within the Institute for Antiquity and Christianity from 1966 on. Thirdly, the Project solicited the volunteer labors of scores of scholars (eventually more than two hundred) for the collation of New Testament manuscripts and thereby functioned, with respect to those collators, either as an agency for recruiting them into the text-critical discipline as productive scholars or as an instru-
97 mentality for impressing indelibly upon them—as exegetes or historians—the fundamental nature of textual criticism for the entire scholarly enterprise of New Testament studies. Fourthly, the Project, especially in the last decade, has opened its files freely for use by qualified researchers.

In spite of these beneficial side effects, however, it must be admitted now that the promise and bright hopes of the International Greek New Testament Project will find fulfillment perhaps only in a full critical apparatus for the Gospel of Luke, for virtually no one presently can foresee ways in which the Project can be carried on in any vigorous fashion in the future; more regrettable perhaps is the fact that the company of trained collators rapidly has disintegrated and that, unfortunately, each geographical center of text-critical work—as a place for graduate studies—successively has disappeared also. More distressing still is the distinct loss of visibility suffered by New Testament textual criticism as a concomitant of the other factors, for the result already has been and surely will continue to be a diminution of interest in and of competence to pursue text-critical assessments of the New Testament when its text is studied by biblical historians, exegetes, and theologians. This is not to say that the Project in any way has been the cause or even the occasion for this collapse of interest and capability—far from it! Yet the growing lack of concern and support for New Testament textual criticism in America is a reality, as is the dissolution of graduate programs in the discipline of New Testament textual criticism at all four of the university centers mentioned and, for that matter, at virtually every other such center in North America. This is a cause for grave concern, a concern that I have expressed previously and one that has been voiced by others. What is particularly discouraging, however, is that each occasion for this lament seems to be accompanied by a still broader and deeper basis for the lament. Four years ago it could be said that it was "difficult to name more than one or two recognized graduate institutions in North America where doctoral studies in the textual criticism of the New Testament can be pursued under some established specialist."[5] I think now that there may be none at all.

The reasons for this recent and rapid erosion of the field of New Testament textual criticism are elusive. Most of it has taken place in little more than a decade. Whether the disappearance of opportunities for graduate study in the field is a cause or a symptom of the erosion is not clear, though certainly the discipline would seem to have no bright future in America and little hope of survival here without such opportunities. The recent or near retirement of virtually every senior New Testament textual critic in North America is a fact to be reckoned with, and another—perhaps trivial—cause, but one nonetheless real, is that younger and middle range textual critics in America tend to drift into academic administration. This could be due to factors that drew them to textual criticism in the first place, such as a penchant for organizing discontinuous data, interest in large-scale, complex problems, and meticulous attention to details, or it could be sheer coincidence. Ernest Colwell was the

[5] E. J. Epp, "The Twentieth Century Interlude in New Testament Textual Criticism," *JBL* 93 (1974) 414.

example of the past generation, holding responsibilities of the highest order at Chicago, Emory, and Claremont, while at the same time and over a lengthy period maintaining a position also as the "dean" of New Testament textual criticism in America. Not all, however, can be expected to follow his worthy example of an effective combination of scholarship and administration. The current American Executive Committee of the International Greek New Testament Project, of which Colwell was the first chairman already in 1948, illustrates both factors—loss to retirement and to administration—for three members of the present Committee are in or are approaching retirement (K. W. Clark, A. P. Wikgren, B. M. Metzger) and four of the other five have moved recently into academic deanships (I. A. Sparks, M. J. Suggs, P. R. McReynolds, E. J. Epp-only G. D. Fee remains inviolable!).

One might reach farther afield for reasons that might account for the recent loss of interest in textual criticism, such as the general decline in the study of Greek (and Latin) in the past generation, or the sheer tediousness of the field and the complexity, difficulty, and seeming intractability of the problems that it entails. These latter
98 characteristics, however, have never deterred the spirit of free, critical inquiry in other areas, but seem rather to challenge the best efforts of the bright and imaginative student. Whatever the reasons, we are left with the reality itself—the rapid decline of New Testament text-critical studies and perhaps even its demise in America because of virtually no opportunities at the entrance level. Time and time again in the last few years my advice to would-be graduate students of New Testament textual criticism has had to be that they should seek admission to a major graduate school where New Testament studies are strong and then work toward a dissertation in an area of textual criticism (something, it might be interjected, that the present writer did two decades ago at Harvard). It will be obvious, however, that the distractions along such a path will be numerous and varied, and few if any such students are likely to complete their graduate programs with a text-critical specialty. Are there other avenues of remedy or better solutions for replenishing our American ranks? None seems ready to hand.

I may have pushed too far the figure of speech in the subtitle of this paper when I chose the expression, "*Requiem* for a Discipline." Yet, that ominous eventuality is all too likely should the clear trends of the recent past continue even into the near future.

Added Notes, 2004

The context of this rather strange publication may help to explain why it was presented to the New Testament Textual Criticism Section of the Society of Biblical Literature in 1977. I doubt that the essay makes any direct scholarly contribution, yet it has been cited far more often than its nature and length would seem to justify. In the printed abstract and in the introduction to the oral presentation, I described it as "a practical assessment of some recent developments and current factors militating against the viability of New Testament textual criticism as a continuing scholarly discipline in America," and indicated that its clear intention was "to prompt discussion of suitable ways to stimulate scholarly work in the field."

Basically, the brief paper arose out of frustration. In 1977, I was in the seventh year of a fourteen-year stint as Chair of the New Testament text-critical segment of the SBL Annual Meeting, and—while attendance at the sessions had been respectable [statistics are not available until the early 1980s]—those presenting papers from 1971 to 1977 numbered only sixteen different scholars, with half of them making presentations two to four times each over that period. As Chair, I felt compelled to broaden the field's appeal, and in examining the situation, I found future prospects much dimmer than I had imagined—hence the dire picture painted in the essay. Happily, during the next seven years, attendance increased somewhat, but, more significant, some twenty new presenters participated in the Annual Meeting programs, along with many of those from the earlier period. During the last two decades and currently, the sessions at the Annual Meetings more often than not have been overcrowded by some sixty to more than a hundred in attendance, with numerous new scholars joining the continuing group as presenters.

A second source of frustration led to the negative comments on the International Greek New Testament Project (IGNTP), on whose American Executive Committee I had served since 1968. As in the text-critical discipline as a whole, retirements and lack of personnel, as well as a lack of supporting funds, cast a dark shadow on that Project—not only on how and when the critical apparatus for the Gospel of Luke might be completed, but also on whether there was "life" for the Project after Luke. To be sure, significant progress had been made since 1968: the Claremont Profile Method had been developed and applied to numerous minuscule manuscripts, and a sorting of minuscules to be cited in the apparatus had been carried through (see the essay on "The Claremont Profile Method" in the present volume); in addition, the extensive materials for the Luke publication had been sent to England, where J. Neville Birdsall began his editing for the joint British and American Project in late 1971. He kept at this Herculean task full-time for three years and then as "caretaker editor" until 1978, but he was compelled for professional and personal reasons to step down, which brought another pause in the Project—now almost thirty years in process (on the whole matter, see "The International Greek New Testament Project: Motivation and History" in the present volume). In 1977, therefore, those responsible for the Project once again despaired of its completion, and no one "had the stomach" for thinking about the next phase of the Project—the Gospel of John. All of this was a matter of great concern for the SBL Textual Criticism group, for not only the leadership, but the collators, of the American side of the Project were active members, and a report on the Project had been a standard feature of its annual program. In 1978 J. Keith Elliott became editor and brought the two volumes of Lukan apparatus to publication in 1984 and 1987. Then in 1988 the SBL Textual Criticism Section created the current North American Executive Committee as a counterpart to the British committee, and work was launched on the Fourth Gospel—with concrete published results and bright prospects (in this computer age) to complete this second massive project in good time (see the IGNTP essay and the "Added Notes, 2004" there.)

I agree with the critique of my Ph.D. student, Professor Larry W. Hurtado (University of Edinburgh), that New Testament textual criticism in recent years has experienced increased interest and more numerous participants, has spawned a wider range of projects and publications, and has brighter prospects for the future: see his "Beyond the Interlude? Developments and Directions in New Testament Textual Criticism," *Studies in the Early Text of the Gospels and Acts: The Papers of the First Birmingham Colloquium on the Textual Criticism of the New Testament* (ed. D. G. K. Taylor; SBLTCS 1; Atlanta, GA: Society of Biblical Literature, 1999) 26–48.

CHAPTER EIGHT

A CONTINUING INTERLUDE IN NEW TESTAMENT TEXTUAL CRITICISM?[1]

The following reassessment of present-day New Testament textual 131
criticism requires, by its very nature, a brief statement of the circumstances that occasioned it. Seven years ago, in the W. H. P. Hatch Memorial Lecture at the 1973 Annual Meeting of the Society of Biblical Literature, I attempted in fifty minutes an adventuresome—if not audacious—assessment of the entire scope of New Testament textual criticism during the past century. Though this was an instructive exercise for me and one that others report as instructive also for them, it was inevitable that so bold an undertaking would elicit sharp criticism. The first hint of this came from Münster in 1976,[2] but more clearly within the past year or so in an invitation to subscribe to a *Festschrift* for Matthew Black containing an article by Kurt Aland of Münster with an announced title—appearing as it did in English—that had a highly familiar ring: "The Twentieth-Century Interlude in New Testament Textual Criticism." Obviously this was the title of the Hatch Lecture, which, following its presentation, had been published in the 1974 volume of *JBL*.[3] When the *Festschrift* itself appeared, it seemed obvious from Professor Aland's article[4] (which, except for its title, was written in German) that some
reassessment of the course and significance of twentieth century New 132
Testament textual criticism was in order. Late in September 1979,

---

[1] A paper presented originally in the New Testament Textual Criticism Section, Society of Biblical Literature, New York City, 17 November 1979, now considerably revised for publication.

[2] Barbara Aland, "Neutestamentliche Textkritik Heute," *VF* 21 (1976) 5.

[3] E. J. Epp, "The Twentieth Century Interlude in New Testament Textual Criticism," *JBL* 93 (1974) 386–414. A major portion was translated into Japanese and published in *Studia Textus Novi Testamenti* 103–109 (1975) 856–60; 866–68; 875–76; 890–92; 898–900; 907–8.

[4] Though the title is English ("The Twentieth-Century Interlude in New Testament Textual Criticism"), the article is in German in Ernest Best and R. McL. Wilson (eds.), *Text and Interpretation: Studies in the New Testament Presented to Matthew Black* (Cambridge/New York: Cambridge University Press, 1979) 1–14.

Aland's article was reprinted in the annual report of his Münster foundation for New Testament textual research, now under the title of "Die Rolle des 20. Jahrhunderts in der Geschichte der neutestamentlichen Textkritik."[5]

The introduction to this reprint claims that in the *JBL* article I "take the floor as spokesman for American textual criticism,"[6] a claim I would renounce emphatically. It indicates also that only occasionally has Professor Aland "let himself be lured out of his reserve" to reply to views that disparage the way the Münster Institut für neutestamentliche Textforschung has assembled the data of New Testament research or that go (as he phrases it) in an impossible direction. Thus, quite explicitly the *JBL* essay was seen as a challenge both to the views of Professor Aland himself and to the work and significance of the Münster Institut, for which he undeniably is the spokesman. Certainly his reply is negatively—and, in its intent, destructively—critical, sometimes harshly so, yet no one could welcome this response more than I, for the primary purpose of the Hatch Memorial Lecture was to evince responses that might help us all to see where we—as late twentieth century New Testament textual critics—stood. More particularly, its major thrust was to raise questions (as well as to offer some answers) as to where we stood *methodologically*, that is, where we found ourselves with reference to a *theory* of the New Testament text and with respect to an *understanding of the history* of the earliest New Testament text. In precisely these respects, I submit—perhaps with no less arrogance and audacity than in 1973—that little could have been more disappointing than the lengthy response from Aland, for his argumentation at point after point seems to confirm the selfsame conclusions at which the Hatch Lecture arrived and which he is attempting to refute. This observation is presented, not with any sense of self-satisfaction, but out of deep regret, for the response (while it does enlighten us as to Aland's own method of establishing the original New Testament text and does refer to methodological procedures employed in the important computer

[5] K. Aland, "Die Rolle des 20. Jahrhunderts in der Geschichte der neutestamentlichen Textkritik," *Bericht der Hermann Kunst-Stiftung zur Förderung der neutestamentlichen Textforschung für die Jahre 1977 bis 1979* (ed. Hermann Kunst; Münster/W.: Hermann Kunst-Stiftung, 1979) 28–42. The first two paragraphs and the last few lines of the original article were omitted in the reprint.

[6] Ibid., 28.

applications at the Münster Institut) tells us little that is either new
or constructive concerning the issues raised in the Hatch Lecture,
though it does strongly imply that discussion of many of those issues 133
is misguided. I, for one, regret also that this solitary negative response to the Hatch Lecture has been so long delayed, for even with its negative bent it earlier could have provided an appropriate stimulus for our discussion of the important issues upon which it touches. Presently I shall attempt to show, however, why I still persist in the views defended earlier and why I remain unrepentant in the face of Professor Aland's stinging and at times sarcastic criticism.

This lengthy introduction may suggest that what follows will be merely a personal defense on a point-by-point basis or a personalized polemic. Certainly Aland's response scored some "debating points" against the Hatch Lecture, and just as surely some could be scored against him. Such an approach, however, would be basically unproductive; rather, the focus here will be on the issues that are, I think, important for all of us—Professor Aland and his Münster colleagues included—and whose open discussion and clarification could provide significant stepping stones to progress in our knowledge of how the original text of the New Testament has been transmitted to us and of how it might be recovered.

A further prefatory word is appropriate and essential. Apparently the Hatch Lecture's repeated emphasis on "little progress," "no progress," and "little or no progress" has led to a misunderstanding, and that must be corrected. Let there be no mistake about this: the twentieth century has been an extraordinarily rich period for New Testament textual criticism; never have I suggested otherwise,[7] nor would anyone else find a defensible basis for claiming that nothing has been done or that little has been accomplished during the last eighty years. For example, if New Testament papyri are considered—an area of crucial interest to Aland and to every textual critic—all of the most important papyri have been brought to light during this remarkably productive period (the Oxyrhynchus, 1896ff.; the Chester Beatty, 1930–31; and the Bodmer, 1956ff.) and have been edited and published. Very recently the impressive Münster Fragment Identification Program has been developed, which employs

[7] See Epp, "Twentieth Century Interlude," 387.

a computer concordance to place independent papyrus fragments back into their proper places in larger papyrus manuscripts of the
134 New Testament;[8] and for some time the Münster Institut has been in the process of producing a study of "The New Testament on Papyrus" (announced at least as long ago as 1965),[9] a display of all the texts of the papyri with an apparatus indicating the results of full collations. Depending upon how one counts, the quantitative increase from the one papyrus (P^{11}) evaluated for an edition of the New Testament in the nineteenth century to the papyri presently available may be as much as 9000% (to use Aland's figures).[10] Furthermore, as a second example, known Greek manuscripts as a whole have increased significantly in the twentieth century, by 1000 in number or 25% in our generation (again to use Aland's figures).[11] As is well known, over the years the industrious Münster Institut has collected microfilms and photographs of about 5000 of the known 5300 Greek New Testament manuscripts and, in more recent years, has begun the computer collation of these manuscripts, first by comparing them in approximately 1000 test-passages selected throughout the New Testament, resulting to date in some two million items of information in computerized form, with more work proportionately being done on the Catholic and Pauline Epistles than in the four Gospels.[12] As a final instance of twentieth century accomplishment, the new "standard text" (as Aland is wont to call it), common to the 3rd edition of the UBS *Greek New Testament* (1975) and the NA^{26} (1979), has become a reality.

This list of attainments could go on at length, but let us simply recognize the prominent contributions made to these and other areas

---

[8] K. Aland, "Neutestamentliche Textforschung und elektronische Datenverarbeitung," in Kunst, *Bericht der Hermann Kunst-Stiftung . . . für die Jahre 1977 bis 1979*, 70–82.

[9] K. Aland, "Der gegenwärtige Stand der Arbeit an den Handschriften wie am Text des griechischen Neuen Testaments und das Institut für Neutestamentliche Textforschung in Münster (Westf.)," *Jahrbuch* 1965 of the Landesamts für Forschung des Landes Nordheim-Westfalen, 11ff.). Reprinted (and abbreviated) in his *Studien zur Überlieferung des Neuen Testaments und seines Textes* (ANTF 2; Berlin: De Gruyter, 1967), 213. [See now, W. Grunewald (ed.) with Klaus Junack, *Das Neue Testament auf Papyrus: I. Die Katholische Briefe* (ANTF 6; Berlin/New York: de Gruyter, 1986), followed by further volumes: ANTF 12 (1989); 22 (1994).]

[10] K. Aland, "Twentieth-Century Interlude," 3.

[11] Ibid., 2.

[12] K. Aland, "Neutestamentliche Textforschung und elektronische Datenverarbeitung," 74–75.

of achievement, not only by the Münster Institut, but also by the United Bible Societies, the Vetus Latina Institute at Beuron, the Centre d'Analyse et de Documentation Patristiques at Strasbourg, and many other groups and individuals in the twentieth century. Let us celebrate these accomplishments and give due credit to those whose names are prominently associated with them, including Kurt Aland as one prominent among the most prominent, and also to others who contribute to such projects but whose names may not be well known or remembered. Their labors have produced the "grist for our mills" and will continue to do so into the future. Without 135
these resources, our scholarship could not function productively or efficiently—if at all—for they furnish us the materials and data required for progress in New Testament textual criticism. What is more, these twentieth century projects at Münster and elsewhere—as Aland is so intent on pointing out—do themselves represent progress, something I have never denied. Yet, and here is the crucial point—indeed, the only point in this respect—that the Hatch Lecture was trying to make: all of these exemplary advances in our accumulated materials, in the tools of research, and in our control of the data have not yet resulted, it seems to me, in decisive progress in certain critical areas of New Testament textual criticism, namely in the textual character of the critical editions of the twentieth century; in the theory and history of the earliest New Testament text; or in the evaluation of readings.[13] These points need to be reexamined, if only briefly, to see whether Aland has—as he supposes—refuted the claim that the twentieth century has been an interlude in New Testament textual criticism, though only two matters can be treated here.

[13] The Hatch Lecture mentioned two other areas in which progress was not evident: (1) major critical editions/apparatuses of the Greek New Testament (in addition to popular critical editions), but these can be treated together since the major editions/apparatuses that have been announced have not appeared as yet; and (2) the return to the *textus receptus* as the best New Testament text by a few, but this requires no additional comment, though there are continuing attempts to provide a scholarly basis for that viewpoint. Treatment of the evaluation of readings has been incorporated into point 2, below, but see also Epp, "The Eclectic Method in New Testament Textual Criticism: Solution or Symptom?" *HTR* 69 (1976) 211–57.

I. Progress in Popular Critical Editions

The claim in the Hatch Lecture that little progress has been made in establishing the text or altering the textual character of the most popular hand-editions of the Greek New Testament, says Aland, "causes surprise to cease and astonishment to begin."[14] What chiefly causes astonishment, it seems, is the employment of the descriptive term "Westcott-Hort" in attempting to characterize the text presented in the NA edition (the 25th edition was referred to at the time) and insisting that substantial progress had not been made in this area in the twentieth century because the text of that 25th edition was closer to Westcott-Hort than was the text of any of the
136 other popular hand-editions. Yet, it is not so much that Aland disagrees with this characterization of the New Testament text, for—after all—his own analyses and statements had been used (apparently properly) in the Hatch Lecture to support the point.[15] Rather, it would appear that what is actually astonishing to him is the claim that the new "standard text" of the UBS^{3} and (now) NA^{26} represents no substantive progress over Westcott-Hort (or, as Aland prefers to call it, Westcott-Hort-Weiss),[16] for whom Codex B was the primary manuscript, in spite of the fact—as Aland sees it—(1) that the new "standard text" almost always departs from the B-text when only an ℵ versus B attestation is in question; (2) that the "standard text" has followed B only after a full external and internal criticism of B's text shows its reading to be "correct"; and (3) that the new Münster collations of the papyri and parchment fragments up to the third/fourth century provide "emphatic corroboration" that the "standard text" is correct because these early witnesses seldom deviated from it, and if they do, they do so "incorrectly,"[17] a somewhat curious statement!

[14] Aland, "Twentieth Century Interlude," 3.

[15] See Epp, "Twentieth Century Interlude," 388–90.

[16] Aland, "Twentieth Century Interlude," 3. The Weiss text, which highly valued Codex B, held the deciding vote for the older Nestle editions. [Note that the term "Standard Text" has been replaced by "new text" in Kurt Aland and Barbara Aland, *The Text of the New Testament: An Introduction to the Critical Editions and to the Theory and Practice of Modern Textual Criticism* (tr. Erroll F. Rhodes; Grand Rapids: Eerdmans; Leiden: Brill, 2nd ed., 1989) e.g., 24, 34–36, as compared with the first ed., 1987, 25, 34–35.]

[17] Aland, "Twentieth Century Interlude," 4.

Now, simply because the UBS[3] and the NA[26] text (i.e., the new "standard text") is still close to that of Westcott-Hort, that is, close to B, will lead no one—certainly not me—to suggest that nothing has happened in New Testament textual criticism since 1881. Quite the contrary; much has taken place, and yet the question remains—the only question that the Hatch Lecture raised at this point—as to what progress has been made in nearly a century if our standard critical texts today are so very close to those of a hundred years ago, in spite of the fact that our present critical texts have or could have utilized more than eighty papyri, more than 200 additional uncials, more than 2600 additional minuscules, and perhaps 2000 additional lectionaries that were unavailable to or were not utilized by Westcott-Hort. Furthermore, this close similarity between the text of our best hand-editions today and that of Westcott-Hort does not mean—as Aland wants to make the Hatch Lecture say—that Westcott-Hort "return with their theories, as if 100 years had not passed since the appearance of their edition,"[18] for the similarity of texts does not
validate Westcott-Hort's theories (as Aland misunderstands me to 137
advocate), nor should it be thought that to arrive at a critical text concurrent with that of Westcott-Hort is necessarily intrinsically undesirable—or that it is necessarily desirable. That is not the issue. What this textual resemblance does, however, is to raise the question of progress; this was and still is my argument: With all of our new manuscript materials and the many valuable research tools produced in the twentieth century, where is the *methodological* advance if our critical text still approximates that of the late nineteenth century or if we still cannot clearly trace its early history? This is a complicated but not unimportant question. Certainly the apparatuses of present-day editions, when compared with their predecessors, are laden with more abundant and more accurate information from earlier and more numerous Greek manuscripts and also contain improved data on the versions and Patristic writers, all of which represent a century's rich harvest, but if exegetes still use a text only moderately different from what they used a hundred years ago, what have our vastly increased manuscript discoveries and analyses done for us? Do they confirm the methods and theories that produced the text of a

[18] Ibid., 5.

hundred years ago? All of us would quickly answer "Certainly not!" Do they show that new methods and theories coincidentally yield a generally similar result? That would be a clear possibility and represents the answer that we would like to give, but it would be a possible answer only if we happened to possess distinctly new methods and theories. Or have we perchance arrived at a text roughly similar in character to that of the past by somehow circumventing the whole methodological question? I would venture the suggestion that it is more by default than by reason and design that our best critical text today bears the image of the best nineteenth century text, and in this connection it is not adequate to affirm, as Aland does, that "the New Testament can have possessed only *one* text" [a truism][19] and therefore hand-editions are not likely to deviate radically from one another, for each is likely to have a close relation to the *Vorlage* upon which its text is built.[20] That is too easy an avoidance of the methodological issue, and surely we should be able to offer a better explanation than that for the close concurrence of present and past texts of the New Testament. To recall again Aland's
138 1964 comparison of the New Testament text to a ship,[21] we seem still—whether we like it or not—to be crossing the Atlantic in an 1881 vessel, although its hull seems to have been strengthened with additional, recently discovered materials, its superstructure has been adorned with new furnishings, and therefore we launch out on it with a certain increased sense of confidence. Yet, if the ship has not been redesigned and reconstructed in accordance with new technological theories and engineering principles, which in turn utilize an advanced knowledge of the new and better materials, where is the progress? This point in the Hatch Lecture was as simple as that: Where is the substantive advance if the "standard" texts of the Greek New Testament then and now are so closely similar in character

---

[19] [I would now draw back from affirming that this is a truism; see my "The Multivalence of the Term 'Original Text' in New Testament Textual Criticism," *Harvard Theological Review* 92 (1999) 245–81.]

[20] Aland, "Twentieth Century Interlude," 4–5.

[21] K. Aland, "The Significance of the Papyri for Progress in New Testament Research," *The Bible in Modern Scholarship: Papers Read at the 100th Meeting of the Society of Biblical Literature, December 28–30, 1964* (J. Philip Hyatt, ed.; Nashville/New York: Abingdon, 1965), 346. The article was updated for publication, *but without this comparison*: "Die Konsequenzen der neueren Handschriftenfunde für die neutestamentliche Textkritik," in K. Aland, *Studien zur Überlieferung*, 180–201.

and if, at the same time, we possess no comprehensive and generally accepted theory to support and justify that form of the text? All of this, however, leads directly into the next area of concern.

II. Progress toward a Theory and History of the Earliest New Testament Text

Nearly forty per cent of the Hatch Memorial Lecture was devoted to the methodological issues just alluded to, issues that I considered (and still do) to be both among the most difficult and also the most crucial in New Testament textual criticism, namely, (1) the formulation of theories or hypotheses to explain both the striking diversities as well as the positive relationships between and among the New Testament manuscript witnesses and groups of witnesses, especially in the earliest period of their transmission, and then, if possible, (2) the reconstruction of the history of the earliest New Testament text. Aland in this general connection speaks of the "naïveté" and of the "fundamental error" of anyone who still hopes to find ways to trace back through our manuscript tradition in some kind of objective fashion and to recover the pathways of early textual transmission, hoping thereby to isolate the original text. Moreover, he says, to hope for the recovery of early exemplars or to envision "lodestar" manuscripts (like Westcott-Hort's B or Tischendorf's א, or even P^{75}) that would point the way directly to the original text is "to dream the impossible dream."[22] Above all, says Aland, textual theories and historical reconstructions such as those of Westcott-Hort must be laid 139
to rest, for "the age of Westcott-Hort and of Tischendorf is definitely over!".[23]

Now, as is well known, the genealogical method of classical philology, which established a stemma for the manuscript transmission of a literary work, has been almost entirely abandoned by New Testament textual critics, though its validity for establishing relationships within a smaller group (a "family") of manuscripts (though not in a "tribe"

---

[22] K. Aland, "Twentieth Century Interlude," 11; cf. Nestle-Aland^{26}, 43*. His phrase is "the unfulfillable dream," but I have taken the liberty of using the language of the popular song, "The Impossible Dream," from Dale Wasserman, *Man of La Mancha* (music by Mitch Leigh, lyrics by Joe Darion), which conveys, of course, the same meaning.

[23] Nestle-Aland^{26}, 43*.

or "text-type") has been generally recognized.[24] As is also well known, Westcott-Hort and others, such as von Soden and Streeter—to take some random examples—advocated various, often discrete theories to explain how the textual tradition developed as it did in its early history, and how it has left to us the manuscript remains that we possess, and—as is equally well known—we have rejected, in whole or in part, these particular theories. For example, we no longer think of Westcott-Hort's "Neutral" text as neutral; we no longer think of their "Western" text as western or as uniting the textual elements they selected; and, of course, we no longer think so simplistically or so confidently about recovering "the New Testament in the Original Greek."

The pertinent question raised seven years ago was what progress have we made in the twentieth century in this broad area of theory and history, for we seem to have been unable to formulate a theory of the New Testament text that would explain and justify the modern critical text, which, coincidentally or otherwise, still stands so close to that of the preceding century. In addition, we remain largely in the dark as to how we might reconstruct the textual history that has left in its wake—in the form of manuscripts and fragments—numerous pieces of a puzzle that we seem incapable of fitting together. Westcott-Hort, von Soden, and others had sweeping theories (which we have largely rejected) to undergird their critical texts, but we seem now to have no such theories and no plausible sketches of the early history of the text that are widely accepted. What
140 progress, then, have we made? Are we more advanced than our predecessors when, after showing their theories to be unacceptable, we offer no such theories at all to vindicate our accepted text? Hardly! As a matter of fact, our failure becomes all the more glaring in juxtaposition with the abundance of newly found textual materials and fresh knowledge.

In precisely this connection, however, Aland seems now to call into question the whole search for a theory and history of the New Testament text. He does so in two ways: first, by his recent, though

[24] E. C. Colwell, "Genealogical Method: Its Achievements and Its Limitations," *JBL* 66 (1947) 109–33, esp. 113–17; 130–32; reprinted in his *Studies in Methodology in Textual Criticism of the New Testament* (NTTS 9; Leiden: Brill, 1969) 63–83, esp. 66–70; 81–83.

very brief, statement of his own text-critical method, and second, by his long-standing but recently reemphasized position on the importance and role of the New Testament papyri. As to the first, in two places recently Aland has furnished a thumbnail sketch of his method—put forward as the only proper and only possible method—in New Testament textual criticism, and he has even ventured (though reluctantly) to give it a name: the "local-genealogical method." These descriptions are found in the "Introduction" to Nestle-Aland^{26} and in the article in the Matthew Black *Festschrift*;[25] elsewhere he is referred to already as the method's "champion."[26] He describes his method as follows, stating first, however, that:

> It is impossible to proceed from the assumption of a manuscript stemma, and on the basis of a full review and analysis of the relationships obtaining among the variety of interrelated branches in the manuscript tradition, to undertake a *recensio* of the data as one would do with other Greek texts.

He then goes on to say:

> Decisions must be made one by one, instance by instance. This method has been characterized as eclecticism, but wrongly so. After carefully establishing the variety of readings offered in a passage and the possibilities of their interpretation, it must always then be determined afresh on the basis of external and internal criteria which of these readings (and frequently they are quite numerous) is the original, from which the others may be regarded as derivative. From the perspective of our present knowledge, this local-genealogical method (if it must be given a name) is the only one which meets the requirements of the New Testament textual tradition.[27]

The designation, "local-genealogical," is more clearly explained elsewhere. Following the collection of the variants and their attestation in the Greek manuscripts, the versions, and the Patristic writers, the
method involves—just as in classical philology—the application of 141
the genealogical method, only with the distinction that the stemma drawn up is valid, not for the entire writing, but only for the places under discussion (and their surrounding text!).[28] Aland justifies this

[25] Nestle-Aland^{26}, 43*; K. Aland, "Twentieth Century Interlude," 10.
[26] K. Aland, "Die Rolle des 20. Jahrhunderts," 42.
[27] Nestle-Aland^{26}, 43*.
[28] K. Aland, "Twentieth Century Interlude," 10.

independent treatment of separate variation-units by saying that the "living" text of the New Testament—continually influenced as it was by various, strong forces—follows other laws than does the "dead" standard text of a classical author transmitted by scholars and schoolmasters; the result is that a New Testament manuscript "almost from place to place may have a different value."[29] In each locale, then, the genealogy of variants is constructed so as to isolate that variant reading from which all the others successively are to be explained, at the same time taking into full consideration all applicable internal criteria (such as the writing's style, vocabulary, and theology). This process, says Aland, "must yield the original text,"[30] and, as he emphasizes, it is the process that was employed by the editorial committee that produced the new "standard text" to be found in the UBS^{3} and Nestle-Aland^{26}.

Although the name is new, naturally this "local-genealogical" method is not itself new, but in the formulation that Aland gives it the method both affirms and rejects text-critical method as practiced in classical philology, for it accepts and applies the genealogical method to New Testament manuscripts, but in a most important way it also rejects it, for—as mentioned earlier—the stemma drawn up is valid, not for an entire literary work, but only for the particular variation-unit under discussion. One acknowledged result is that a given manuscript may have a varying value from reading to reading and, accordingly, may be expected to reflect a multifarious textual character or complexion. This application of the genealogical method means that Aland has amended the almost universal agreement among New Testament textual critics regarding the classical genealogical method—namely, that while it is not applicable at the level of "text-types," it may be useful at the level of textual "families"—for Aland now goes one step farther by claiming that the method is applicable only at the level of the individual variation-unit. Furthermore, although Aland in a very recent study speaks of the formation (by
142 computer) of manuscript groups and "large complexes" of manuscripts,[31] his "local-genealogical" approach really seems to represent

[29] Ibid.

[30] Ibid.

[31] K. Aland, "Neutestamentliche Textforschung und elektronische Datenverarbeitung," 80–82.

a rejection of the whole enterprise of grouping New Testament manuscript witnesses for the purpose of tracing the history of the text. Perhaps that is why he finds my pleading for a theory and history of the New Testament text to be "dreaming the impossible dream."[32]

It is curious that precisely in the context of explaining the "local-genealogical" method Aland interjects a striking statement that would seem to invalidate not only that method—which he is in the course of describing—but every objective method in New Testament textual criticism, a statement that might be said to leave us nearly speechless: in referring to the "expert practitioner," whom he describes (in a footnote) as one who stands "in contrast to 'amateurs,' who in general live on theory," he defines the "expert" textual critic not only as one who cares not for theory, but also as one:

> who himself has carried out countless collations and interacts constantly with the variants and the variation possibilities of the New Testament tradition, from which he gains judgment as to the value of the statements of individual manuscripts, [and who] at sight of the variants and their attestation at a given place generally will very soon be clear as to where the original text is to be sought.[33]

Now, while all of us recognize the strategic importance of practiced experience, this statement—appearing as it does in the very discussion of method—could be understood, on the one hand, as advocating something akin to what has been called "the cult of the best manuscript," for it suggests that the expert learns to look upon certain individual manuscripts as time and time again possessing a certain positive (or, conversely, negative) value. It is clear from this immediate context and elsewhere, however, that this is not what Aland means, for he consistently rejects any single manuscript as "a guideline we can normally depend on for determining the text."[34] On the other hand, his statement might more easily—though more shockingly—be understood as advocating textual criticism by *intuition*. Could he be suggesting that New Testament textual criticism is entirely art?—that the practiced expert knows almost instinctively where the original lies? To be sure, some have tried to make tex- 143
tual criticism entirely *science*, but certainly Metzger is correct when

[32] See n. 22, above.
[33] K. Aland, "Twentieth Century Interlude," 10.
[34] Nestle-Aland[26], 43*, where the "local-genealogical" method is also discussed.

he begins his standard manual by characterizing it as *both science and art*.[35] All things considered, however, it is doubtful that Aland really intends to advocate textual criticism by intuition, for in the immediate context he simultaneously affirms the "local-genealogical" method, thereby ruling out intuition; yet his statement remains an anomaly—and a somewhat disturbing one—to those many scholars who search for text-critical methods that are based in some way on knowledge of the broader history of New Testament textual transmission and who consciously affirm the value of theory (something Aland seems to denigrate) as the supporting foundation upon which the practiced expert might base his work.

It is worth probing another point arising from the discussion of the "local-genealogical" method, namely, Aland's suggestion that a New Testament manuscript may have a different worth virtually from variation-unit to variation-unit. From one perspective, this statement is, of course, not surprising, for we all recognize the extraordinary degree of "mixture" (if that is the proper term) to be found in New Testament manuscripts. From another perspective, however, the statement might be understood to mean that separate New Testament manuscripts do not possess or manifest a particular textual character or stamp. That view would, I think, fly in the face of much demonstrable evidence; for example, Codex Bezae possesses and evinces something that can only be called a "textual character" or "complexion," and it is evident, not merely at an occasional or isolated locale, but at point after point, at reading after reading. P^{38} in a striking fashion shares with Codex Bezae numerous textual features, revealing a distinctive textual "character." P^{66} has a textual "character," both in its text and in its corrections;[36] various profiling methods suggest that manuscripts (often in common) show distinctive textual "patterns"; and many Byzantine manuscripts show (and share) a "quality" of fullness. These are merely random and rather obvious examples. If, however, as Aland's statement implies, manuscripts may not be described in terms of something we are permitted to call their

[35] Bruce M. Metzger, *The Text of the New Testament: Its Transmission, Corruption, and Restoration* (2nd ed.; Oxford/New York: Oxford University Press, 1968) v. [Page numbers are generally the same in the 3rd ed., 1992.]

[36] Gordon D. Fee, *Papyrus Bodmer II (P^{66}): Its Textual Relationships and Scribal Characteristics* (SD 34; Salt Lake City, UT: University of Utah Press, 1968) esp. 76–83.

textual character, then the traditional way of grouping manuscripts 144
does become problematic, and that, in turn, would call into question any reconstruction of the history of the New Testament text that proceeds through identification of texts similar in character. I sincerely doubt that we have reached the point of abandoning the claim that textual character can be identified in and for entire manuscripts, though it must be emphasized again that the construction of a stemma is *not* what is envisioned in a reconstruction of the history of the New Testament text, but something considerably looser, for the New Testament was indeed a "living" text.

To summarize, Aland does seem to allow for a "theory" of the text and for a sketch of its "history" at the level of the individual variation-unit, but he states directly and in other ways implies that a broader theory of the New Testament text is neither necessary nor possible and that the search for a history of the text beyond that of the individual variation-unit has little validity and even less likelihood of success. The Hatch Lecture clearly acknowledged the immense difficulty of establishing such a theory and history of the New Testament text, but unambiguous responses from numerous New Testament textual critics in Great Britain, Europe, and North America suggest that few would support Aland's implication that the search for a broad theory and a comprehensive history of the text is invalid, unnecessary, or—in the final analysis—impossible. As suggested below, rightly understood and conceived, it is a difficult but not an impossible dream.

The second way in which Aland seems to call into question the search for a theory and history of the earliest New Testament text is through the prominence that he gives to the New Testament papyri. The Hatch Lecture devoted nearly three pages to his views on this matter,[37] which need not be covered again here, and Aland's otherwise hypercritical response contains no complaint that these particular views have been misunderstood or misrepresented, though he does take strong exception to what he sees in the Hatch Lecture as a severe undervaluing of the papyri. For example, he objects to fixing the increase in known papyri since the turn of the century at 600%; rather—using a different basis of comparison—he states that the increase in the use of the papyri in critical editions since then amounts

[37] Epp, "Twentieth Century Interlude," 399–401.

to 9000%, and he insists that *qualitatively* the increased significance of the papyri is a "multiple" of that very high figure.[38] This prime importance of the papyri is reinforced in the recent "Introduction"
145 to NA^{26}, where Aland claims that the forty earliest papyri and the four earliest (but fragmentary) uncials are "of automatic [*automatisch*] significance, because they were written before the third/fourth century, and therefore belong to the period before the rise of the major text types."[39] Among these, the most significant of all, he says, is P^{75}, followed closely by P^{45} and P^{66}. (These, of course, are the three early papyri with the greatest *quantity* of text [only P^{46} and P^{47} come close in amount of preserved content], but if a textual "character" can be observed in a fragment like P^{38}, who is to say that it is *qualitatively* less significant because an accident of history allowed only a dozen of its verses to survive?) Aland, then, views the papyri as having changed everything, for "the manuscript basis for Westcott-Hort's work dates from the IV century. . . . Today the early papyri provide a wide range of witness to the text of about 200 A.D., and these are Greek witnesses."[40] It comes as no surprise, therefore—as a response to a claim in the Hatch Lecture that, while papyri discoveries will contribute to positive text-critical developments in the future, recent methodological developments (such as certain quantitative methods) will more likely aid in the reconstruction of the early history of the text[41]—to find Aland exclaiming that "great astonishment strikes once again." Why? Because, he explains:

> . . . if this "early history of the text" is visible anywhere, it is directly and immediately [visible] only in the nearly forty papyri and uncials from the time up to the third/fourth century. Here it [the early history of the text] can be studied in the original [!]; all other efforts must remain reconstructed theories.[42]

In view of what is known about New Testament textual transmission, this is an extraordinary—an astonishing—statement of the importance of the papyri, though not inconsistent with Aland's previously expressed viewpoints on the subject. When seven years ago,

[38] K. Aland, "Twentieth Century Interlude," 3.
[39] Nestle-Aland^{26}, 12*; cf. 49*.
[40] Ibid., 43*.
[41] Epp, "Twentieth Century Interlude," 407.
[42] K. Aland, "Twentieth Century Interlude," 11.

with some admitted reservation, I applied to him the paraphrase of
a well known passage from Ignatius (*Philadelphians* 8), I thought that
I perhaps was going too far with what might well be seen as a
"smart alecky" remark, but it appears, after all, that Professor Aland
really does embrace the view, "Unless I find it written in the papyri, 146
I do not believe it in the gospel."[43]

The New Testament papyri *are* extraordinarily significant, and the earliest ones even more so; that we can all freely acknowledge, and it may be strictly correct to say that the early history of the text is *directly* and *immediately* visible *only* in these earliest papyri and uncials. Yet, can we really be satisfied with so limited a view of that early history? Can we really be content with Egypt as the almost exclusive locale for this glimpse into the earliest textual history? Was any New Testament book written there,[44] and does not Egypt therefore clearly represent only a secondary and derivative stage in textual history? Is the accident of circumstance—that papyrus survives almost exclusively in the hot climate and dry sands of Egypt—to dominate and determine how we ultimately write our textual history? Can we proceed with any assurance that these forty randomly surviving earliest manuscripts are in any real sense *representative* of the entire earliest history of the text? Actually, as a logical principle of proper procedure—as well as common sense—there must be a substantive and defensible basis if something is to have "automatic" significance. But if the only basis that can be established for even this select group of treasured papyri is their early age, it is doubtful that the phrase "of automatic significance" will or ought to be so readily accepted. Should we not seek to assure ourselves—if it can be done—that these most precious earliest monuments of the text constitute, not merely "a wide range of witness to the text of about 200 A.D." (as Aland characterizes them),[45] but a genuine representation of discrete forms of the text current in that earliest period—and not only in Egypt. If that cannot be done, nothing is lost and we still have numerous very early Egyptian witnesses that have significance for understand-

[43] Epp, "Twentieth Century Interlude," 401.

[44] Some scholars past and present have suggested that the Fourth Gospel may have been written in Alexandria, but the view has meager support; see the standard commentaries on John. No other New Testament writing has even a plausible claim to authorship in Egypt.

[45] Nestle-Aland[26], 43*.

ing that period of textual history in Egypt between 200 and 300 C.E., but we would have witnesses that—in spite of their age—are not necessarily of "automatic significance" for *the* original text of the New Testament. Yet even this limitation would in no way deny their very great importance. If, however, the earliest papyri can be shown
147 to be representative in a larger sense, much might be gained.[46] To carry the point a bit farther, is it appropriate to hold, as Aland seems to do, that the earliest text circulated in "many and divergent forms, proceeding in different directions, at about the same time, in the same ecclesiastical province"[47]—a quite acceptable statement—and yet to say (as he does) that these earliest papyri do not fit into the text-types identified from later manuscripts, suggesting thereby that there is no continuity between those early papyri and the fourth century and later textual developments? My question, earlier and now, is can we not do better than this? Can we not perhaps draw some connections between these earliest papyri and the later points of textual transmission as represented in the more extensive early uncials, the exceptional minuscules, the early Patristic writers, and the earliest versions as far as these can be isolated? Following that, can we not attempt to trace the history of the text and formulate some theory as to how the text developed? The earliest papyri and uncials can furnish the starting point for this process, which in turn can provide a substantive basis for describing their significance with respect to ascertaining the original text, though it is doubtful even

[46] [In subsequent years I pursued this topic and argued that the earliest group of papyri and uncials—those up to and around the turn of the third/fourth centuries—can be taken as representative:

> . . . It is not only theoretically possible, but quite probable, that the present array of text-types represented in the Egyptian New Testament papyri do, in fact, represent text-types from the *entire* Mediterranean region, and, furthermore, that they could very likely represent *all* of the existent text-types in that large region in the early period of New Testament textual transmission.

E. J. Epp, "New Testament Papyrus Manuscripts and Letter Carrying in Greco-Roman Times," *The Future of Early Christianity: Essays in Honor of Helmut Koester* (ed. B. A. Pearson in collaboration with A. T. Kraabel, G. W. E. Nickelsburg, and N. R. Petersen; Minneapolis, MN: Fortress, 1991) 56; cf. idem, "The Significance of the Papyri for Determining the Nature of the New Testament Text in the Second Century: A Dynamic View of Textual Transmission," *Gospel Traditions in the Second Century: Origins, Recensions, Text, and Transmission* (ed. W. L. Petersen; Christianity and Judaism in Antiquity 3; Notre Dame, IN: University of Notre Dame Press, 1989) 101.]

[47] K. Aland, "Significance of the Papyri for Progress," 334.

then that all of them equally will come to be described as "of automatic significance" for establishing the original New Testament text.

The "trajectory" model[48] that I earlier proposed, obviously with the tentativeness of a suggestion, was an attempt to draw the earliest papyri into some appropriate relationships with the later textual history and to show the continuity between the earliest witnesses and the massive tradition that followed. The model involved plotting a loose and tentative series of textual streams or trajectories, beginning with those forty earliest papyri and uncials and—based on an assessment of their textual "character" or "complexion"—drawing the appropriate connecting lines with later manuscripts of similar textual "complexion." The result was the disclosure of only two basic textual streams from that earliest period, one that emerges later as the B-text and one that coalesces later as the D-text.[49] It is this restriction to only two textual streams in the earliest period that leaves 148
Professor Aland, as he puts it, "finally speechless,"[50] implying that at best an incredible naïveté must lie behind such a simplistic and foolish view. I am inclined, however, to persist in this foolishness at least a little longer (as will many other New Testament textual critics), for with the increase of very early manuscript witnesses—and I fully agree with Aland that these have increased dramatically in the twentieth century—we are in a vastly improved situation for tracing these connections. Moreover, as we refine current methods and as we develop more sophisticated methods for assessing the textual "character" or "complexion" of manuscripts, we shall be able to make such assessments more confidently. Yet, even our *present* judgments as to the textual character of the earliest papyri and uncials (upon which Aland rightly focuses) permit us to trace textual trajectories *forward* from them to further points on the same line represented by major (and still early) uncials, such as codices B, D, A, and W, and still further to later uncial and minuscule codices. This results, to take some obvious examples, in a trajectory traced from

[48] Borrowing a term (but only that) from James M. Robinson and Helmut Koester, *Trajectories through Early Christianity* (Philadelphia: Fortress, 1971).

[49] Epp, "Twentieth Century Interlude," 397–400. The reader is directed to the Hatch Lecture for details, for they cannot be repeated here.

[50] K. Aland, "Twentieth Century Interlude," 6. Actually—and unfortunately—he quotes my *description* of Westcott-Hort as *my view*, but the point about two early textual streams is made later by me, though not in Westcott-Hort's terms.

P^{75} (third century) through Codex B (fourth century) to Codex L (eighth century), 33 (ninth century), 1739 (tenth century), and 579 (thirteenth century); or (in Acts) from P^{48} (third century) through P^{38} (ca. 300) to Codex D (fifth century)[51] to 614 and 383 (thirteenth century). With admitted caution, these lines of trajectory also may be extended *backwards* behind (i.e., earlier than) the earliest papyri and uncials to show presumed lines of development, though considerable speculation is involved in such an exercise. Merely connecting the *known* points—based on the identifiable textual character of the extant witnesses—can, however, be instructive for understanding the earlier history of the New Testament text and may constitute the basis for a broader theory of the text. That was the point that the Hatch Lecture was making, as well as pointing out (I think indisputably) that looking at the forty earliest papyri and uncials *in isolation* (as Aland seems intent upon doing) cannot enlighten us very much as to how the New Testament text developed in the early generations of Christianity. Rather, we need to draw the trajectories and mark the appropriate connections between these earliest witnesses and the
149 later witnesses of similar textual character so as to show thereby the direction and movement of the text in that early developmental period. It was for this reason that I referred in the Hatch Lecture—perhaps somewhat ungraciously—to Professor Aland's view of the early papyri in isolation from the later witnesses as a "somewhat *static*" view and attributed to him a portrayal of the period of the early papyri as "an archipelagic phenomenon and one insulated from the period of the great uncials that followed,"[52] yet that is the image that he continues to project. We can, on the contrary, show that there *is* continuity between the earliest papyri (or at least many of them) and the fourth century and later textual developments, and we can and ought to utilize these connections as the basis for formulating a theory and for tracing the history of the New Testament text in the earliest periods of its transmission. It would be uneconomical to repeat here the preliminary proposals—already alluded to—on textual trajectories (i.e., that only two distinctive *and continuing* streams of text—at opposite edges of a spectrum—emerge from

[51] [Codex Bezae is now dated about 400: see David C. Parker, *Codex Bezae: An Early Christian Manuscript and Its Text* (Cambridge: Cambridge University Press, 1992) 30; 280–81.]

[52] Epp, "Twentieth Century Interlude," 399.

our textual history, which we designate the B-text and D-text, with a third stream leading abortively to Codex W) or to rehearse the issues raised in this connection in the Hatch Lecture,[53] but this is an area that continues to impress me (and many of my colleagues) as both an obvious and a legitimate field of inquiry, as well as one with renewed possibilities in the wake of the unprecedented papyri discoveries of the twentieth century.

Finally, in connection with Aland's high valuation of the New Testament papyri, we are confronted with an additional claim from him that will astonish many. I refer to a forthcoming article on "Der neue 'Standard-Text' in seinem Verhältnis zu den frühen Papyri und Majuskeln," which—as its title indicates—raises the question of how the "early text" contained in the earliest manuscripts is related to the new "standard text" of UBS^{3} and Nestle-Aland^{26}, and in which Aland renders his judgment that:

> The new "standard text" has passed the test of the early papyri and uncials. It corresponds, in fact, to the text of the early time. . . . At no place and at no time do we find readings here [i.e., in the earliest papyri and uncials] that require a change in the "standard text." If
> the investigation conducted here in all its brevity and compactness 150
> could be presented fully, the detailed apparatus accompanying each variant would convince the last doubter. A hundred years after Westcott-Hort, the goal of an edition of the New Testament "in the original Greek" appears to have been reached. . . . In the framework of the present possibilities, the desired goal appears now to have been attained, to offer the writings of the New Testament in the form of the text that comes nearest to that which, from the hand of their authors or redactors, they set out on their journey in the church of the 1st and 2nd centuries.[54]

[53] Ibid., 390–401.

[54] K. Aland, "Der neue 'Standard Text' in seinem Verhältnis zu den frühen Papyri und Majuskeln," *New Testament Textual Criticism: Its Significance for Exegesis: Essays in Honour of Bruce M. Metzger* (eds. E. J. Epp and G. D. Fee; Oxford: Clarendon Press, 1981) 275. This (with some omissions) is the last paragraph of the essay. Aland gives in English the words "in the original Greek," quoting from the title of Westcott-Hort's edition. He does qualify his statement to the extent of acknowledging that it is not made with the "self-certainty of Westcott-Hort," for the "standard text" has an extensive apparatus that will alert scholars to numerous "thoughtful considerations" (whereas Westcott-Hort presented no apparatus to suggest that other options were viable—although vol. 1 has a ten-page list of rejected readings and vol. 2 has an "Appendix" containing 140 pages of "Notes on Select Readings").

With this striking announcement that in and through the new "standard text" found in UBS[3] and Nestle-Aland[26] "a hundred years after Westcott-Hort the goal of an edition of the New Testament 'in the original Greek' appears to have been reached," we seem to have come full circle. On the one hand, we are told in no uncertain terms that the Hatch Lecture was misguided even in invoking the Westcott-Hort categories in a discussion of the history and theory of the New Testament text and was näive in demanding that some broad text-critical theory ought to be sought to justify the form of the New Testament text that scholars and exegetes use, for "the age of Westcott-Hort . . . is definitely over!"[55] On the other hand, the same audacious claim that Westcott-Hort made in the title of their 1881 work—that their textual method had yielded "The New Testament in the Original Greek"—is made now for a text not greatly dissimilar from that of Westcott-Hort and one that disclaims any comprehensive textual theory as its basis and justification except a "local-genealogical" assessment of each variation-unit and the "automatic significance" of the earliest papyri and uncials.

Lest I be misunderstood again, emphasis must be placed on the fact that both the UBS[3] and the Nestle-Aland[26] editions are monumental achievements of twentieth century New Testament textual criticism, for both their common text and their differing but extensive apparatuses will well serve textual critics and exegetes for some time to come; and our gratitude to Professors Aland, Black, Martini,
151 Metzger, and Wikgren and to the United Bible Societies for the former volume (as well as the accompanying *Textual Commentary*) and to Professor Aland and Dr. Barbara Aland and to the Münster Institut for the latter can hardly be overemphasized—we are grateful beyond measure. Yet, an edition of the New Testament "in the original Greek" cannot, it seems to me, be made a reality by fiat or proclamation, nor can the validity of such a claim be so easily pontificated. Rather, textual critics at large will require a more comprehensive and convincing rationale for the text they accredit as the nearest possible approximation to the original—a rationale that reaches beyond the highly valuable but severely limited assessment of individual variation-units *in isolation* and a rationale that seeks and finds a broader historical base than the early and precious but narrowly

[55] Nestle-Aland[26], 43*.

restricted and clearly derivative manuscript witnesses of Egypt. Naturally, to state these *desiderata* is much easier than to fulfill them, but that difficulty does not relieve the scholar of his or her obligation to evaluate critically the methods employed by New Testament textual critics down through the years and the claims they make for the New Testament texts produced on the basis of their methods and principles of criticism. It is in that spirit that this evaluation is presented.

In conclusion, then, we may very well be able to live for the present on a "practitioner" approach to New Testament textual criticism, employing a "local-genealogical" method that includes the application of the appropriate external and internal criteria variation-unit by variation-unit, but in the long run we shall want—and I think need—to have something better, something that rests more firmly on the solid rock of historical reconstruction and less upon the shifting sands of a serviceable but tentative and sometimes slippery eclecticism[56] or a myopic variant-by-variant assessment, even though it is in the hands of an expert practitioner. It is to be freely confessed however, that thus far we have failed to reach down to that desired bedrock and that we also are not entirely sure of the procedures that will bring us to it. Nevertheless, I am confident that we should and must press on toward that goal. Perhaps we should dare even to "dream the impossible dream."

Added Notes, 2004

I was pleased when the editor of the *Harvard Theological Review*, Helmut Koester, offered to publish this paper in an issue "Dedicated to the Centennial of the Society of Biblical Literature." This special double-issue (vol. 73:1–2, January-April 1980) contained contributions by biblical faculty at Harvard Divinity School and by alumni of Harvard doctoral programs in biblical studies.

On context. The context of my essay will be clear from its first three or four pages, occasioned by my W. H. P. Hatch Memorial Lecture in a plenary session at the Society of Biblical Literature in 1973, which focused heavily on projects and views of Kurt Aland (1915–1994)

[56] See Epp, "The Eclectic Method," esp. 244–57.

and his Institut für neutestamentliche Textforschung at Münster, including the Nestle-Aland and United Bible Societies' editions of the Greek New Testament. When my address, which contained its share of blunt and harsh statements about Professor Aland's views, was published as "The Twentieth Century Interlude in New Testament Textual Criticism" (*JBL* 93 [1974] 386–414), it quite naturally evoked a response from him—with its own share of strong words. The present essay, then, was my rejoinder, reaffirming and defending positions taken in the Hatch Lecture, again with harsh words to counter harsh words.

The first comment I would want to make now is that the interchanges, in spite of their appearances, were not personal attacks, but were vigorous attempts to describe precisely and to justify logically the scholarly positions each of us held with great conviction. Indeed, I made repeated efforts in both of my papers to emphasize my deep respect for Professor Aland and his work—for certainly he was the premier New Testament textual critic of the second half of the twentieth century, as evidenced not only by his Herculean labors in that field but by his pervasive influence on the discipline. On the more personal level, early in my career Professor Aland had considered my volume on *The Theological Tendency of Codex Bezae Cantabrigiensis in Acts* for publication by de Gruyter—in, as I recall, his newly established series, Arbeiten zur Neutestamentlichen Textforschung, which at the time consisted of only one published volume. After negotiations over several months, Professor Aland wrote me in July 1963 that, "although it had appeared for a while that the publisher would consent to my wish [to publish the book], . . . just now [he] has communicated to me that the production costs for the book would be too high to justify its publication. . . . It makes me very sad that I must report this to you." Subsequently, I spent two hours in stimulating conversation with him at the 100th Meeting of the Society of Biblical Literature in New York City in 1964, though thereafter I met him only once or twice.

My book on Codex Bezae [but really on the "Western" text] in Acts appeared in 1966 as volume 3 of the new Studiorum Novi Testamenti Societas Monograph Series (Cambridge University Press), edited by Matthew Black. Imagine my surprise, then, when a *Festschrift* for Professor Black appeared in 1979, also under the imprint of Cambridge University Press, to discover that the titles of the first two essays had a very familiar ring: "The Twentieth Century Interlude in New Testament Textual Criticism," by Kurt Aland and "Is There a Theological Tendency in Codex Bezae?" by C. K. Barrett—one recalling the Hatch Lecture and the other my monograph—and both devoted entirely to my work and both critical of my conclusions. The day the Black *Festschrift* arrived was somewhat traumatic, but I had learned earlier that it is better to have one's work noticed critically than not at all. The present essay was my response to Aland, and, though many years later, an essay below on "Anti-Judaic Tendencies in the D-Text of Acts: Forty Years of Conversation" treats the assessment by Barrett—and many others—of *The Theological Tendency of Codex Bezae*.

CHAPTER NINE

THE ASCENSION IN THE TEXTUAL TRADITION OF LUKE—ACTS

I. Introduction: The Ascension in the New Testament

New Testament passages that offer a narrative description of the ascension of the risen Christ as "an observable incident,"[1] that is, as a physical, visible transfer from earth to heaven, are extremely few; those passages that refer to the ascension as a theological event, without specifying its temporal or physical aspects, are slightly more numerous; and those that assume the "heavenly abode" of the risen Christ without reference to an ascension at all are the most numerous. These data are well known[2] and hardly require documentation, though a brief summary will provide the necessary introduction for this study.

The exalted Christ. In the last category listed above are a number of passages that mention Christ's resurrection and then affirm his heavenly, exalted position at God's right hand, but with no reference to an ascension: Acts 2:33–34 (cf. 2:25); 5:31;[3] Rom 8:34; 10:6; Eph 1:20–1; 2:6; Col 3:1; 1 Thess 1:10; 4:14–16; cf. 2 Cor 4:14. A similar set of passages refers to the exalted Christ, with his death—but not the resurrection or ascension—mentioned in the context: Phil 2:8–9; Heb 1:3 and 13; 7:26; 10:12; 12:2. Finally, though still in this same category, are passages that refer merely to Christ's

---

[1] This is C. K. Barrett's apt phrase in *The Gospel according to St. John: An Introduction with Commentary and Notes on the Greek Text* (2d ed.; Philadelphia: Westminster, 1978), 566.

[2] The full range of New Testament references can be found in such treatments as those by P. Benoit, "The Ascension," in his *Jesus and the Gospel* (2 vols.; New York: Herder and Herder, 1973–74), 1.209–53, originally in *RB* 56 (1949), 161–303; or by B. M. Metzger, "The Ascension of Jesus Christ," in his *Historical and Literary Studies: Pagan, Jewish, and Christian* (NTTS 8; Grand Rapids: Eerdmans, 1968), 77–87.

[3] The "Western" text at Acts 5:31 reads τῇ δόξῃ ("for his glory") rather than τῇ δεξιᾷ ("on his right hand"); see B. M. Metzger, for the Editorial Committee, *A Textual Commentary on the Greek New Testament* (London/New York: United Bible Societies, 1971), 332.

132 present heavenly abode: Acts 7:55–56; Eph 6:9; Phil 3:20; 2 Thess 1:7; Heb 8:1; and Rev 3:21. None of these passages contains the language of ascension or describes the mode of ascension, nor does any one of them otherwise indicate how Christ attained his heavenly position at God's right hand (since the use of the word "exalted" [ὑψόω/ὑπερυψόω] at Acts 2:33; 5:31; and Phil 2:9 does not specify the mode of exaltation, and an ascension by "going up" (ἀναβαίνω) is only implied by the use of that term in Rom 10:6 and by the use of the opposite term, "going down" (καταβαίνω), in 1 Thess 4:16.

The language of ascension without a narrative of ascension. The second category of New Testament passages consists of those that employ direct language describing Jesus as "going up," "ascending," or being "taken up," but which still fall short of describing the ascension of Christ as an objectified historical and physical event, or which in some other way involve an ambiguity about the ascension in spite of the direct language of ascension. The few passages of this type are in the Fourth Gospel, the deutero-Pauline letters, and the Catholic Epistles. The Fourth Gospel contains three passages in which Jesus predicts that he will be "lifted up/exalted" (ὑψόω) from the earth: 3:14; 8:28; and 12:32–34; but in the third passage the author of the gospel explains that the term "lifted up" signifies Jesus' death. Thus, whereas in the previous category ὑψόω is used in Acts only of Christ's exaltation to God's right hand (2:33; 5:31), that is not its meaning in John—though the Fourth Gospel, as often with other terms, may very well have intended a double reference to death and exaltation. In any event, a reference to the ascension of Christ is ambiguous at best here in the Fourth Gospel, and certainly nothing of its mode is discernible from these passages. Two statements more specific in nature occur on the lips of Jesus as John portrays him. One is a question to his disciples, "What if you were to see the Son of Man ascending (ἀναβαίνω) where he was before?" (6:62; cf. 3:13), and the other is a post-resurrection saying in John 20:17, "I have not yet ascended (ἀναβαίνω) to the Father; but go to my brethren and say to them, 'I am ascending (ἀναβαίνω) to my Father and your Father, to my God and your God.'" Clearly the reference in both is to an ascension, and in the latter passage to an ascension subsequent both
133 to his resurrection and to the post-resurrection appearances, yet neither is a narrative of a specific, observable event.

Other passages in the Fourth Gospel might be adduced, such as those in which Jesus announces that he is "going (ὑπάγω) to the one who sent me" (7:33; 16:5–7), or "going (πορεύομαι, ὑπάγω, or ἔρχομαι) to the Father" (14:12, 28; 16:10, 17, 28; 17:11, 13; cf. 13:1; 14:2; 15:26), or "going (ὑπάγω) to God" (13:3), but—again—neither these passages nor any others in the Fourth Gospel narrate the ascension as a specific observable event in time and place.

Also in the second category are several passages from the epistles. First, Eph 4:8–10 quotes Ps 68:18 ("he ascended on high [ἀναβὰς εἰς ὕψος] . . . and gave gifts to men") and applies it to the exalted Christ as the one "who also ascended far above all the heavens" (ὁ ἀναβὰς ὑπεράνω πάντων τῶν οὐρανῶν). The ascension portion of this discussion, however, is entirely parenthetical to the writer's main point, which is spiritual gifts, and the ascension of Christ is only peripherally in the author's purview. Moreover, an ascension "far above all the heavens" would seem to have in view a suprahistorical event and not one with terrestrial ties. Secondly, 1 Tim 3:16 recites an early Christian hymn that refers to Christ as "manifested in the flesh . . ., preached among the nations, believed on in the world, taken up (ἀνελήμφθη) in glory." The inclusion of the ascension in this recital of a series of historical occurrences could suggest that a datable ascension is in view, though this is an implication at best, and the passage provides, of course, no specific historical description. Finally, Heb 9:24 says that Christ "entered (εἰσέρχομαι) . . . into heaven itself" (cf. 9:12; 6:20; and 4:14: Jesus "passed through [διέρχομαι] the heavens"), and 1 Pet 3:21–22 refers to the "resurrection of Jesus Christ, who is at the right hand of God, having gone (πορευθείς) into heaven," passages which—again—contain the language of a literal ascension but no narrative description. Incidentally, Luke 9:51 might be included here: "When the days drew near for him to be received up (ἀνάλημψις), he set his face to go to Jerusalem" (*RSV*), but the term quite clearly means "death," as in *Psalms of Solomon.* 4:18, Ps-Clem. *Hom.* 3.47, and elsewhere.[4]

The ascension narrated as an observable incident. The final category of 134
New Testament references includes those that portray the ascension more concretely and explicitly in objectifying terms as a local and temporal occurrence with attendant witnesses. Such references are limited to a single New Testament author and to a few passages in

[4] On this question, see P. A. van Stempvoort, "The Interpretation of the Ascension in Luke and Acts," *NTS* 5 (1958–59), 32–3.

Luke-Acts. If these Lucan texts are read in the so-called "Neutral" textual tradition, they convey a very specific literal and observable ascension to heaven of the resuscitated physical body of Jesus. The first passage comes at the conclusion of Luke's gospel, where it provides only a minimal description of the event: "As he was blessing them, he departed (διέστη) from them and was taken up (ἀνεφέρετο) into heaven" (Luke 24:51, *TEV*). Then, as Luke recapitulates the closing events of Jesus' career at the beginning of Acts (1:2), he refers to "... the day when he was taken up (ἀνελήμφθη) ...," and proceeds to a full narrative in 1:9–11:

> And when he had said this, as they were looking on, he was lifted up (ἐπήρθη), and a cloud took (ὑπέλαβεν) him out of their sight. And while they were gazing into heaven as he went (πορευομένου), behold, two men stood by them in white robes, and said, "Men of Galilee, why do you stand looking into heaven? This Jesus, who was taken up (ἀναλημφθείς) from you into heaven, will come in the same way as you saw him go (πορευόμενον) into heaven." (*RSV*)

Finally, Luke refers again (in 1:22) to "... the day when he was taken up (ἀνελήμφθη) from us. . . ."

Nowhere else in the New Testament is such a portrayal of the ascension to be found, though it should be noted, parenthetically for the moment, that the "longer ending" of Mark (16:9–20) has a statement of the ascension that, in the context, is similar to though less specific than Luke's: "So then the Lord Jesus, after he had spoken to them, was taken up (ἀνελήμφθη) into heaven, and sat down at the right hand of God" (16:19, *RSV*). If, however, we ignore for the moment this pseudo-Marcan account, the ascension described in objectifying terms is restricted, in reality, to four New Testament passages: Luke 24:51, Acts 1:2 and 1:22, and Acts 1:9–11, a rather meager harvest.

II. The Ascension in the 'Western' Textual Configuration

The narrowing of the data supporting an objectified ascension to
135 four Lucan passages provides a convenient focus for a thorough text-critical examination of the treatment of the ascension in the so-called "Western" textual tradition. Such an investigation will show that the "Western" variants present a most interesting—if not absolutely consistent—textual configuration. Some of the basic points were proffered

ninety years ago by F. Graefe[5] and again fifty years ago by Daniel Plooij in a less than easily accessible publication on "The Ascension in the 'Western' Textual Tradition,"[6] but the issue is worth reviving and presenting here, along with some additional points and considerable refinement.

Luke 24:51. The first observation to be made is that the "Western" text of Luke 24:51 lacks the clause, ". . . and was taken up into heaven":

Luke 24:51

Codex Vaticanus	Codex Bezae
καὶ ἐγένετο ἐν τῷ εὐλογεῖν αὐτὸν αὐτοὺς	καὶ ἐγένετο ἐν τῷ εὐλογεῖν αὐτὸν αὐτοὺς
διέστη ἀπ' αὐτῶν	ἀπέστη ἀπ' αὐτῶν.
καὶ ἀνεφέρετο εἰς τὸν οὐρανόν.	

διέστη (= recessit) ℵ* B *cett*] ἀπέστη (= discessit) D d a b c e l Augustine.
καὶ ἀνεφέρετο εἰς τὸν οὐρανόν P^{75} ℵ^{c} A B C L W Δ Θ Ψ *f*^{1} *f*^{13} Byz aur c f q (r^{1}) vg sy^{p,h,pal} cop^{sa,bo} arm geo^{2} eth Diatessaron Augustine$^{2/3}$ Cyril Cosmas Severian] *om* ℵ* D d a b e ff^{2} j l* geo^{1} Augustine$^{1/3}$ (Note: sy^{s} = 'lifted up from them').

The result, in the "Western" text, is that the risen Christ, as he was blessing his followers, "parted" or "went away from them," leaving now a highly unclear picture of what the author of the gospel intended to portray in the final paragraph of his first volume. Is it an ascension? One fact to be noted is that neither the διΐστημι of B nor the ἀφίστημι of D appears in any other New Testament reference to the ascension.[7]
Is the lack of the more concrete ascension-clause in the "Western" 136
text a casual slip or does it have greater significance? The answer surely lies in the treatment of the ascension in Acts by the same "Western" textual tradition.

[5] F. Graefe, "Der Schluss des Lukasevangeliums und der Anfang der Apostelgeschichte: Eine textkritische Studie, zugleich ein Beitrag zur Italaforschung," *TSK* 61 (1888), 522–41. He treats Luke 24:51 and Acts 1:2.

[6] *Mededeelingen der koninklijke Akademie van Wetenschappen, Afdeeling letterkunde*, 67: A.2 (Amsterdam, 1929), 39–58.

[7] There is no significant difference between the two Greek terms—at least for our purposes. D also uses ἀφίστημι (instead of ἀπέρχομαι) in Luke 1:38 of the angel "departing" from Mary. Actually, the term might be viewed as one favored by D for it occurs four times as a variant in D (Mark 7:6; Luke 1:38; 22:41; and 24:51), but never in place of the same term. Διΐστημι, in the New Testament, occurs only in Luke—Acts, and no other gospel uses ἀφίστημι.

Acts 1:2, 9–11, 22. Turning to Acts, it should be observed first that the "Western" text (though not Codex Bezae) lacks the word ἀνελήμφθη in Acts 1:2:

Acts 1:2

Codex Vaticanus	"Western" Text
ἄχρι ἧς ἡμέρας	ἐν ᾗ ἡμέρᾳ
ἐντειλάμενος τοῖς ἀποστόλοις	τοὺς ἀποστόλους
διά πνεύματος ἁγίου οὓς ἐξελέξατο	ἐξελέξατο διὰ πνεύματος ἁγίου
ἀνελήμφθη.	
	καὶ ἐκέλευσε κηρύσσειν τὸ εὐαγγέλιον.
	Augustine: In die quo apostolos elegit per spiritum sanctum et praecepit praedicare evangelium, . . .
	Codex Gigas (*gig*) and Liber comicus (*t*): In die, qua praecepit apostolis per spiritum sanctum praedicare evangelium quos elegerat, . . .

ἄχρι ἧς ἡμέρας D sy^{hmg} *cett*] ἐν ᾗ ἡμέρᾳ Augustine$^{2/3}$ Vigilius$^{2/2}$.
ἐντειλάμενος τοῖς ἀποστόλοις . . . οὓς ἐξελέξατο B D *cett*] τοὺς ἀποστόλους ἐξελέξατο διὰ πνεύματος ἁγίου Augustine$^{3/3}$ Vigilius$^{2/2}$.
ἀνελήμφθη] *ante* ἐντειλάμενος D d sy^{p,hmg} cop^{sa} | *om* gig t* Augustine$^{3/3}$ Vigilius$^{2/2}$ Ephraem.
καὶ ἐκέλευσε D d sy^{hmg} Augustine$^{3/3}$ Vigilius$^{1/2}$ Ephraem Varimadum.
κηρύσσειν τὸ εὐαγγέλιον D d ar gig t lux vg^{codd} sy^{hmg} cop^{sa,G67} Tertullian$^{apol\ 21[vid]}$ Augustine$^{3/3}$ Vigilius$^{2/2}$ Ephraem Varimadum [cf. Epistle of Barnabas v. 2].

The effect here is dramatic: the ascension is eliminated entirely from the passage, for the "Western" text reports that the author of Acts merely says, "I have dealt, O Theophilus, with all that Jesus began
137 to do and to teach on the day when he chose the apostles through the Holy Spirit and commanded [them] to preach the gospel."

Secondly, the absence of a clause, the use of a synonym, and the slight rearrangement of the passage in the "Western" text of Acts 1:9 produces a somewhat similar though less dramatic result:

Acts 1:9

Codex Vaticanus	'Western' Text
καὶ ταῦτα εἰπὼν	καὶ ταῦτα εἰπόντος αὐτοῦ
αὐτῶν βλεπόντων	
ἐπήρθη,	
καὶ νεφέλη ὑπέλαβεν αὐτὸν	νεφέλη ὑπέλαβεν αὐτὸν
ἀπὸ τῶν ὀφθαλμῶν αὐτῶν.	

καὶ ἀπήρθη
ἀπὸ ὀφθαλμῶν αὐτῶν.

αὐτῶν βλεπόντων] *om* D d cop^{sa} Augustine.
ἐπήρθη B *cett* (= levatus est)] ἀπήρθη (= sublatus est) cop^{sa} Augustine Promissionibus.
ἀπὸ (τῶν) ὀφθαλμῶν αὐτῶν] ἀπ' αὐτῶν cop^{sa} Cyprian Augustine | ἀπὸ τῶν μαθητῶν (a discentibus) Promissionibus.

The lack of the expression, "as they were looking on," reduces—if only slightly—the nature of the ascension as an observable incident, and the "Western" text goes on to say that Jesus was "taken away/removed" (ἀπαίρω; *sublatus est*) rather than "taken up/lifted up" (ἐπαίρω; *levatus est*),[8] again reducing—in a similar fashion—the explicit emphasis on a vertical, objectified ascension. Finally, the clause, "a cloud took him" (*RSV*) has a slightly different nuance in the "Western" text due to the rearrangement of the passage and the consequent change in the force of the verb ὑπολαμβάνω (whose meanings include "take up," "take away," 'remove', 'seize', 'come suddenly upon', 'receive and protect'):

Codex Vaticanus (*RSV*)	'Western' Text	
And when he had said this,	And when he had said this,	
as they were looking on,		
he was lifted up,		
and a cloud took him	a cloud suddenly came upon him,	138
	and he was removed	
out of their sight.[9]	from their sight.[10]	

Plooij, long ago, suggested that for the "Western reviser" "the 'ascension' was alright [*sic*!], but a bodily ascension was too much for him."[11] This, however, may be saying too much, for while the "Western" formulation certainly does not *demand* an ascension in the usual sense, it also cannot be said to *preclude* such an understanding. Yet the reduction of the objectifying features is noticeable and significant.

[8] The variant ὑπέβαλεν in D (for ὑπέλαβεν), though a construable form, does not easily make sense and must be viewed as an error.

[9] van Stempvoort, "Interpretation of the Ascension," 37–8, stresses the "verticality" in various terms in the usual text of Acts 1:9.

[10] The "Western" text may have lacked "from their eyes/sight" and read simply "from them," as in Augustine (*ab eis*).

[11] Plooij, "Ascension in the 'Western' Textual Tradition," 53.

As the reader of Acts continues through this context, however, the "Western" textual variations pertaining to the ascension suddenly—almost inexplicably—diminish, though they do not disappear, and the expected consistency in reducing the historical, observable aspects of the ascension is not carried through, leaving the scholar unsatisfied but not without some intriguing questions. In v. 10, both the "Neutral" and "Western" texts, without significant variation between or within the two traditions, describe the apostles as "gazing into heaven as he [Jesus] went" (*RSV*). Verse 11 continues with the statement of the "two men in white clothing" to the apostles: "Why do you stand looking into heaven? This Jesus, who was taken up from you into heaven, will come in the same way as you saw him go into heaven" (*RSV*). In this verse, only two traces of consistency with "Western" variants in the passages previously discussed remain: one is the lack of the second occurrence of the expression, "into heaven" (though not of the first or the third or the occurrence in v. 10).

Acts 1:11

	Codex Vaticanus	Codex Bezae
	Ἄνδρες Γαλιλαῖοι, τί ἑστήκατε	Ἄνδρες Γαλιλαῖοι, τί ἑστήκατε
	βλέποντες εἰς τὸν οὐρανόν;	ἐμβλέποντες εἰς τὸν οὐρανόν;
	οὗτος ὁ Ἰησοῦς	οὗτος ὁ Ἰησοῦς
	ὁ ἀναλημφθεὶς ἀφ᾽ ὑμῶν	ὁ ἀναλημφθεὶς ἀφ᾽ ὑμῶν
139	εἰς τὸν οὐρανὸν	
	οὕτως ἐλεύσεται ὃν τρόπον ἐθεάσασθε αὐτὸν	οὕτως ἐλεύσεται ὃν τρόπον ἐθεάσασθε αὐτὸν
	πορευόμενον εἰς τὸν οὐρανόν.	πορευόμενον εἰς τὸν οὐρανόν.
		Codex Gigas (*gig*) & Augustine, *sermon* 277: Viri Galilaei, quid statis aspicientes in caelum? Hic Jesus, qui receptus [acceptus (Aug)] est a vobis sic veniet, quemadmodum [quomodo (Aug)] vidistis eum euntem in caelum.
		Tertullian, *Adversus Praxeam* c. 30: Hic et venturus est rursus super nubes caeli, talis qualis et ascendit.

ἀναλημφθείς (= assumptus est) B D *cett*] receptus est e gig p; acceptus est Augustine$^{serm277(= ½)}$.

εἰς τὸν οὐρανόν (2nd) ℵ B *cett* ar e ph vg sy^{p,h} cop^{sa,bo} arm geo] *om* D d 33^{c} *minn* l^{60} gig t* vg^{ccdd} cop$^{bo\ mss}$ Augustine$^{serm\ 277(= ½)}$ Vigilius Promissionibus:

The absence of the phrase, "into heaven," only one out of four times cannot be marshaled as evidence that the "Western" text of vv. 10–11 lacked a narrative of the ascension as an observable phenomenon, yet the fact that it is the *second* occurrence of the phrase in v. 11 that is involved (and not one of the others) takes on added significance upon the further scrutiny of the "Western" textual evidence. Two of the Old Latin witnesses that lack this second "into heaven" (and two others that do not) also employ a different term for *assumptus est*, that is, for the Greek expression, ἀναλημφθείς or "taken up"; instead, they use *receptus est* or *acceptus est*, that is, "taken." The result—admittedly only for that single clause of v. 11 (though cf. below on 1:22)—is that the text of these witnesses, rather than reading "This Jesus who was taken up from you into heaven . . .," reads now "This Jesus who was taken from you. . . ." An ascension is neither explicit nor required in the latter formulation (though, of course, it remains in the other portions of vv. 10–11). It is of more than passing interest, moreover, that the same two witnesses, Augustine 140
(though not in the same writing) and Codex Gigas (*gig*), also drop the term ἀνελήμφθη, that is, *assumptus est* from Acts 1:2 (see above), suggesting a "Western" textual strain that was reluctant, in these two passages, to describe Jesus as "taken up (into heaven)." This formulation should be compared with the absence in the "Western" text at Luke 24:51 of the clause, "and was taken up into heaven" (see above), a further evidence of the same reluctance. Also, Acts 1:22, the final passage that treats the ascension as an observable event involving transfer from earth to heaven, fits into this discussion in a similar way. In the context of replacing Judas among the apostles, the verse specifies that the person chosen must be (v. 21) "one of the men who have accompanied us during all the time that the Lord Jesus went in and out among us, (v. 22) beginning from the baptism of John until the day when he was taken up from us . . ." (*RSV*). This passage, which yields no major variants in the textual tradition, envisions a historical, datable ascension, but it offers no further narrative description of the event. Yet, the same phenomenon observed above in certain Old Latin witnesses appears here as well and should not be viewed in isolation. Whereas the Greek textual tradition uniformly reads "until the day when he was taken up . . ." (ἕως [or ἄχρι] τῆς ἡμέρας ἧς ἀνελήμφθη ἀφ' ἡμῶν), once again the Old Latin witnesses *gig* and *p* have *receptus est* for ἀνελήμφθη (*assumptus est*), perfectly consistent with their reading of 1:11, so that

in both cases Jesus is merely "taken from them/us," rather than explicitly "taken up (into heaven)."

The remaining trace in Acts 1:11 of consistency with the "Western" tendencies regarding the ascension is minor but perhaps worth noting. Tertullian's reading of the clause in 11b, "This Jesus . . . will come in the same way as you saw him go into heaven," is as follows: "This [Jesus] also will come back again on a cloud, such as he went up" (*Hic et venturus est rursus super nubes caeli, talis qualis et ascendit*). The result is that here the disciples are not represented as having *seen* Jesus ascend, supporting (though in a somewhat different way) the deobjectifying tendency seen elsewhere in other "Western" witnesses to this passage.[12]

141 A comparison of the witnesses attesting these "Western" variants presently being discussed, namely, (1) the omission in Luke 24:51; (2) the omission of ἀνελήμφθη in Acts 1:2; (3) the use of *sublatus est* for *levatus est* in Acts 1:9; (4) the omission of 'into heaven' in 1:11; (5) the use of *receptus est* or *acceptus est* in 1:11 or (6) of *receptus est* in 1:22, shows that Augustine supports five of these six (though not consistently in citing a given passage); that Codex Gigas supports four of the five pertaining to Acts; and that Codex Bezae (D and *d*), *p*, *t**, *De promissionibus*, and Vigilius each support two of the six variations. (Not all, of course, are extant at all places.) This suggests—though certainly it cannot prove—that the "Western" text tended strongly to resist any description of Jesus as being "taken up into heaven" (and perhaps also as being *seen* going up into heaven), even though our extant witnesses to that "Western" textual tradition do not show that this tendency was carried through with rigid consistency.

Indeed, anyone who has worked extensively with the "Western" text knows that this aberrant textual tradition—like any other—is only imperfectly preserved for us in available Greek manuscripts, versions, and patristic quotations; that much effort must be expended to ascertain the likely original "Western" text; and also that significant clues about its character must be pursued not only with vigor but also with some reasoned imagination. (After all, the Greek "Western" tradition suffered over time by assimilation to its rival "Neutral" text, just as the "Western" Old Latin and Old Syriac witnesses were quite

---

[12] See J. Rendel Harris, *Four Lectures on the Western Text of the New Testament* (London: Clay, 1894), 56–7; Plooij, "The Ascension," 17.

thoroughly overshadowed by their respective vulgate editions.) In the present case—the ascension in Luke-Acts—there is enough consistency of viewpoint presented in the relevant "Western" variants to encourage that kind of further exploration and creative imagination. As demonstrated above, the relevant textual variations comprising the evidence serve—rather strikingly, though not with the consistency that might be desired—to diminish most effectively—though not completely—the entire New Testament's portrayal of the ascension as an objectified event. Indeed, to put it differently, had the "Western" text carried through its tendency here with full rigor, and were the "Western" text to be adjudged the original Lucan text, the ascension as an observable incident would all but disappear from the New Testament. Alternatively, were the standard (i.e. the "Neutral")
Lucan text to be taken as original—which seems more likely—an 142
argument could be made (with only some slightly rough edges) that the "Western" text assumed for itself the task of reducing if not eliminating the observable, objectifying aspects of the ascension from the gospels and Acts.

This view, however, has two difficulties that cannot be overcome easily or with complete satisfaction. The first—mentioned several times already—is the lack of complete consistency in the "Western" text at the pertinent points. The extent to which consistency actually is absent could be discerned, of course, if the original, presumably "pure" form of the "Western" text at Luke 24:51 and Acts 1:2, 9–11, and 22 were available to us. At best, however, that text has been preserved only incompletely, yet with extensive and provocative indications of what it might have been—indeed, what it must have been. Taking the clues provided by these known points, as we have observed them here and there among the "Western" witnesses, can we plot the trajectory that the "Western" textual tradition has followed with respect to the ascension? Can we trace its path backwards along these remaining observable points, and can we then break through boldly to what the uncontaminated, presumably early "Western" text must have been? The clues are clear enough: numerous variations in the "Western" witnesses that vitiate the observable aspects of the ascension. Hence, a tendency is adequately evident: a pattern of recurrent reduction of these objectifying features by the "Western" tradition. The only thing lacking is *rigorous* consistency. Accordingly, I would venture that, whereas the "Neutral" textual tradition yields a narrative description of the ascension as an observable transfer from earth to heaven, on the contrary the "Western" configuration of the ascension material in these same passages originally read as follows (with demonstrable support lacking at only a few points):

(Luke 24:50–3) Then he led them out as far as Bethany, and lifting up his hands he blessed them. While he was blessing them, he went away from them. And they returned to Jerusalem with great joy, and were continually in the temple praising God.[13]

(Acts 1:1–2) In the first book, O Theophilus, I have dealt with
all that Jesus began to do and to teach on the day
143 when he chose the apostles through the Holy Spirit
and commanded them to preach the gospel.

(Acts 1:6–7) So when they had come together . . . he said to them.

(Acts 1:8b–12a) ". . . And you shall be my witnesses in Jerusalem and in all Judea and Samaria and to the end of the earth." And when he had said this, a cloud suddenly came upon him, and he was removed from their sight. And while they were looking intently as he departed, behold, two men stood by them in white clothing and said, "Men of Galilee, why do you stand and stare? This Jesus, who was taken from you, will come back in the same way that you saw him depart." Then they returned to Jerusalem from the mount called Olivet. . . .

(Acts 1:15, 21–2) In those days Peter stood up among the disciples . . . and said, ". . . So one of the men who have accompanied us during all the time that the Lord Jesus Christ went in and out among us, beginning from the baptism of John until the day when he was taken from us—one of these men must become with us a witness to his resurrection." (*RSV* modified)

In this "Western" version, the ascension does not occur at all until at least Acts 1:9, or more probably not until 1:10 or 11, whereas

[13] The rationale for "joy" and "praise" admittedly is less clear in the "Western" text.

in the "Neutral" text it appears clearly at both Luke 24:51 and again at Acts 1:2 and 1:9. Furthermore, this carrying of the "Western" tendencies in Luke's treatment of the ascension to their logical conclusion leaves an account that describes the ascension only as a removal of the risen Christ from the presence of his disciples, with no descriptive narrative of the transfer from earth to heaven. All of the undocumented changes, incidentally, involve words or phrases that are elsewhere suppressed or modified in this same context in the 'Western' tradition, namely the phrase "into heaven" in Acts 1:10 and 11 (in accordance with its omission in v. 11), and the verb ἀναλημφθείς in Acts 1:11 and 22 as modified by Augustine and Codex Gigas in v. 11.

If the slight liberties taken here with respect to these few words can be tolerated, perhaps one more inconsistency in the "Western" tradition can be overlooked, for the second and remaining difficulty in the present study is one not mentioned earlier, the fact that Codex Bezae, along with numerous "Western" and other witnesses, contains the longer ending of Mark, which—in turn—contains a brief narrative description of the ascension in a historical context, as quoted earlier (16:19): "So then the Lord Jesus, after he had spoken to them,
was taken up (ἀνελήμφθη) into heaven, and sat down at the right 144
hand of God" (*RSV*). The answer to this anomaly of the preservation by the 'Western' text of an appended ascension story lies somewhere in that still mysterious history of New Testament textual transmission, and within the scope of this study it must remain unanswered.

III. Conclusion

Our familiarity with the great creeds of Christianity may have led us to assume that the ascension looms much larger in the New Testament than it actually does. That the risen Christ has been exalted and is at God's right hand is clear from Acts, the Pauline letters, Hebrews, and Revelation. And that the risen Christ "went up" or "ascended" (though without further description) is presupposed by the Fourth Gospel and is clear also from the deutero-Pauline and general epistles (though it well to note that—perhaps surprisingly—there is no mention of the ascension at all in the early credal formulation quoted by Paul in 1 Cor. 15:4). The passages that describe an objectified transfer of the risen Christ from earth to heaven are, however, strikingly few in number, rather restrained in their descriptive character, and severely restricted in location: Luke-Acts only. The early creeds of Christianity and their successors do, of course, depict an observable event: he was crucified, dead, buried, rose again, and "ascended into heaven" (or "into the heavens" [ἀνάβαντα εἰς τοὺς οὐρανούς] as the Old Roman Symbol has it), but the New Testament, as we have seen, keeps this kind of description to a minimum.

Our analysis of the text of the Lucan passages reveals a further limitation in the notion of an observable ascension in early Christianity, namely, that the "Western" tradition bears only fragmentary traces of such an objectified ascension. This situation leaves us with some searching questions about the process of textual transmission. First, since the primary remnant of an objectified ascension in the "Western" text of Luke-Acts consists of the phrase, "into heaven" (εἰς τὸν οὐρανόν), could it be that the presence of that phrase in the old creeds (though there it is in the plural) made it virtually impossible to keep the phrase completely out of the various witnesses to the "Western" text? Second, if the "Western" text *were* the original text of the gospels and Acts (or even Luke-Acts alone)—an issue quite beyond the scope
145 of this paper—could it then not be argued with considerable persuasion that the notion of the ascension of the risen Christ as a visible transfer from earth to heaven was only a secondary and later development in early Christian thought?

Quite apart from the answers to these questions, and even disregarding the slight liberties taken in this paper so as to make the "Western" text rigorously consistent with its obvious tendency, one conclusion is clear: the "Western" textual tradition restricts the narrative description of an objectified ascension virtually to a single passage in the New Testament: Acts 1:10–11, with an additional brief mention of it in 1:22—a total of about eight lines in the Greek New Testament!

Added Notes, 2004

This essay was first presented in the New Testament Textual Criticism Section at the 1978 Annual Meeting of the Society of Biblical Literature in New Orleans.

I have found no reason to modify the position taken in this essay. Text-critical discussions of Luke 24:51 and Acts 1:2, 11 may be found in Bruce M. Metzger, *A Textual Commentary on the Greek New Testament* (2nd ed.; Stuttgart: Deutsche Bibelgesellschaft/United Bible Societies, 1994) 162–63; 236–41; 245. See also Mikeal C. Parsons, *The Departure of Jesus in Luke-Acts: The Ascension Narratives in Context* (JSNTSup 21; Sheffield: JSOT Press, 1987), esp. 29–35; 124–35; idem, "The Text of Acts 1:2 Reconsidered," *CBQ* 50 (1988) 58–71.

On the terms "Western" and "Neutral" texts. See the "Notes to Readers" in the front matter of this volume.

CHAPTER TEN

DECISION POINTS IN PAST, PRESENT, AND FUTURE NEW TESTAMENT TEXTUAL CRITICISM[1]

New Testament textual criticism, like every other area of academic 75
inquiry, is always in process. Its history is a record of various discoveries, insights, methods, and distinctive achievements that provide the basis for further investigation, but with fewer definitive conclusions or final resolutions than might be expected. A periodic assessment of the "state of the discipline," or of one segment in its long history, can be enlightening both with respect to understanding those accomplishments of the past and in facing the tasks of the future. Though history is eminently instructive, obviously it is more urgent for us to understand the unfinished tasks and to seek ways to accomplish them. Any assessment of such decision points in current New Testament textual criticism, however, almost of necessity requires at least a brief review of decision points in past New Testament textual criticism. If the "past is prologue," such a review will provide, at the very least, the necessary perspective for understanding the current and future issues, and at best will contain the basis for their resolution. This chapter, therefore, includes those two aspects—past turning points in New Testament text-critical study and decision points in the current discipline of New Testament textual criticism—with an intervening section on specific developments since World War II that assists us in grasping those current issues that require our attention.

[1] This essay was published originally under the simple title, "Textual Criticism." It incorporates material presented in the two Kenneth Willis Clark Lectures at Duke University on 9 April 1986: "Papyrus Manuscripts of the New Testament: Treasure from the Past—Challenge for the Future." It draws also upon presentations at the Annual Meetings of the Society of Biblical Literature in 1980 and 1981 and of the Eastern Great Lakes Biblical Society in 1983, though with much revision, and some portions utilize material from the author's "A Continuing Interlude in New Testament Textual Criticism," *HTR* 73 (1980) 131–51.

I. Past Decision Points in New Testament Textual Criticism

It is a curious but intriguing fact that if the past is divided roughly into fifty-year periods, starting in 1980 and moving backward through time, many of the major landmarks or turning points in New Testament textual criticism appear or find their impetus at such fifty-year intervals—give or take a few years—and most of them are landmarks in text-critical methodology. This will provide a convenient framework
76 for our quick review of the major factors in the development of the discipline as we know it today.

One should begin at the beginning—some 1750 years ago—with Origen of Caesarea, who undoubtedly was the first to apply critical canons to the New Testament text. His *Commentary on John* was written in the few years before and after 230 CE, followed by commentaries on Matthew and Romans, and these works contain most of his references to variant readings in the New Testament that have the support of "few," "many," or "most" manuscripts accessible to him, as well as applications of such canons as suitability to context and harmony with parallel passages.[2] Origen's lack of sophistication and consistency in applying such "rules" hardly qualifies him as a model of text-critical method, but his use of these embryonic guidelines does suggest that he was the discipline's founder. One hundred and fifty years later, beginning with his *Commentary on Galatians* in the late 380s, Jerome noted variant readings and was employing canons such as an older manuscript carries more weight than a recent one and a reading is preferable that fits the grammar or context of its passage.[3]

---

[2] Bruce M. Metzger, "Explicit References in the Works of Origen to Variant Readings in New Testament Manuscripts," *Biblical and Patristic Studies in Memory of Robert Pierce Casey* (ed. J. Neville Birdsall and Robert W. Thomson; Freiburg/Basel/New York: Herder, 1963) 78–95 [repr. in Metzger, *Historical and Literary Studies: Pagan, Jewish, and Christian* (NTTS 8; Leiden: Brill, 1968) 88–103]; Frank Pack, "Origen's Evaluation of Textual Variants in the Greek Bible," *ResQ* 4 (1960) 144–45; cf. E. J. Epp, "The Eclectic Method in New Testament Textual Criticism: Solution or Symptom?" *HTR* 69 (1976) 216 [repr. in E. J. Epp and Gordon D. Fee, *Studies in the Theory and Method of New Testament Textual Criticism* (SD 45; Grand Rapids, MI: Eerdmans, 1993) 144].

[3] K. K. Hulley, "Principles of Textual Criticism Known to St. Jerome," *HSCP* 55 (1944) 91–93 *et passim*; Bruce M. Metzger, "St. Jerome's Explicit References to Variant Readings in Manuscripts of the New Testament," *Text and Interpretation:*

These first, rudimentary "landmarks" of text-critical method bore little fruit prior to modern times, though 1050 years later Lorenzo Valla, in his "Neopolitan period" (1435–1448) produced two editions of his *Collatio novi testamenti*, for which he collated several Greek manuscripts of the New Testament and in which he pointed out both involuntary and conscious scribal alterations, including variants due to homonyms and assimilation.[4] Though these early efforts were but adumbrations of modern critical approaches, the modern period does begin somewhere in the century between Valla's work on the New Testament text and Erasmus's final edition of his *Annotations* in 1535, which—in a much less developed form—had accompanied his 1516 *editio princeps* of the Greek New Testament and which rather fully explained the use of manuscripts and methods employed in his New Testament text. Of interest in this transition to modernity is the fact that Erasmus published Valla's second edition of the *Collatio* (which Erasmus called *Adnotationes*) in the very year (1505) that Erasmus himself began studying and collating New Testament manuscripts and observing thousands of variant readings in preparation for his own edition.[5] In the middle of this transitional century, that is, in 1481 (500 years ago), the first publication of any portion of the New Testament in Greek took place, the Magnificat and the Benedictus, printed in Milan and appended to a Greek Psalter[6]—not a methodological landmark, of course, but the very beginning point of a stream of editions of the New Testament in its original language.

As the development of the new discipline of textual criticism continued, a few other early milestones can be identified in that formative period before variant readings in New Testament manuscripts were systematically sought and published. One such event occurred 400
years ago, when around 1582 the Reformation theologian Theodore 77
Beza presented two important uncial manuscripts to Cambridge

Studies in the New Testament Presented to Matthew Black (ed. Ernest Best and R. McL. Wilson; Cambridge/New York: Cambridge University Press, 1979) 179–86 [repr. in Metzger, *New Testament Studies: Philological, Versional, and Patristic* (NTTS 10; Leiden: Brill, 1980) 199–208].

[4] Jerry H. Bentley, *Humanists and Holy Writ: New Testament Scholarship in the Renaissance* (Princeton, NJ: Princeton University Press, 1983) 34–46.

[5] Ibid., 35, 138.

[6] T. H. Darlow and H. F. Moule, *Historical Catalogue of the Printed Editions of Holy Scripture in the Library of the British and Foreign Bible Society* (2 vols. in 4; London: Bible House, 1903) 2.574.

University, Codex Bezae and Codex Claromontanus. Beza himself apparently made little, perhaps no, use of these in his own editions of the Greek New Testament, nor did other editors until Brian Walton some seventy-five years later, but Beza's gift meant that these important and early codices became part of the accessible sources for critical study.

Similarly, one could look back 350 years to a pair of more noteworthy landmarks in the period of the 1630s, the first of which also consisted of the placing of an important manuscript in the public domain, when the fifth-century Codex Alexandrinus was presented in 1627 to King Charles I by the patriarch of Constantinople. The variant readings of Alexandrinus first appeared at the foot of the pages of the Greek New Testament portion of Brian Walton's *Polyglot Bible* (1655–1657), and his was the first report of these variants; in addition, Walton was the first to use a capital letter as a siglum for a majuscule manuscript, employing "A" for Alexandrinus. More important, however, is the fact that the availability of the very ancient Codex Alexandrinus around 1630 and the recognition and use of this fifth century manuscript by Walton represented, as K. W. Clark described it, "the beginning of a fundamental critical process."[7] This was not the beginning of genuinely modern or scientific New Testament textual criticism, for that is more likely to be identified at our next fifty-year interval with John Mill, but it is of more than passing interest to note that Codex Alexandrinus figured prominently in Mill's work.

The second milestone of the 1630s is the occurrence in the second edition of Elzevir's Greek New Testament (1633) of the instantly famous phrase, *textus receptus*, in the declaration "You have the text, now received by all," a marker not particularly noteworthy in itself, but one that two centuries later was to have special significance in the pivotal work of Karl Lachmann and the great modern textual critics who followed. Indeed, without this arrogant—though not unrealistic—generalization, challenges to this sweeping claim might have been even slower in coming.

Looking back 300 years to the period around 1680 brings into view two important figures from the beginning of a very lengthy

[7] Kenneth W. Clark, "The Textual Criticism of the New Testament," *Peake's Commentary on the Bible* (ed. M. Black and H. H. Rowley; London/New York: Thomas Nelson, 1962) 666.

period during which textual critics collected variant readings and printed them in various editions of the *textus receptus*. The two figures are John Fell and John Mill. In 1675 Fell produced the first Greek New Testament printed at Oxford, an elegant octavo volume that presented variants (so he claimed) from more than one hundred manuscripts and versions and provided an important stimulus for seeking and assembling additional variants. Edward Miller[8] refers to Fell's small Greek New Testament as "the legitimate parent of one of the noblest works" of this type, John Mill's large Greek New Testament. It was Mill, our second figure, who began almost precisely at this time (1677) his thirty years of "labours nearly Herculean" (as Mill himself describes them)[9] that were to lead to the publication of his impressive Greek New Testament of 1707, which was important not for its text (since he printed the 1550 text of Stephanus) but for its 78
extensive apparatus (containing evidence on more than 21,000 variation-units and comprising more than 30,000 various readings)[10] and for its prolegomena, where some interesting principles of textual criticism were enunciated and where "a foreshadowing of the genealogical method in noting relationships between manuscripts" appears.[11] Mill, of course, was not without his opponents,[12] yet both his innovative, massive apparatus (which, by its very presence and its size, raised disturbing questions about the *textus receptus* and his rudimentary canons of criticism were to affect all succeeding work. As a matter of fact, M. R. Vincent, in his 1903 *History of the Textual Criticism of the New Testament*, asserts—not unjustly—that John Mill "marked the foundation of textual criticism,"[13] that is, of the genuinely modern discipline.

The next fifty-year stopping place, around the 1730s–250 years ago—brings to light an event that is more a curious and fortunate occurrence than a methodological marker, for in October 1731

[8] Edward Miller, ed., *A Plain Introduction to the Criticism of the New Testament*, by F. H. A. Scrivener (4th ed.; 2 vols.; New York: Bell, 1894) 2.200.

[9] See Adam Fox, *John Mill and Richard Bentley: A Study of the Textual Criticism of the New Testament 1675–1729* (Oxford: Blackwell, 1954) 60, cf. 61–64.

[10] Ibid., 64, 105.

[11] Marvin R. Vincent, *A History of the Textual Criticism of the New Testament* (New Testament Handbooks; New York: Macmillan, 1903) 68.

[12] See Fox, *John Mill and Richard Bentley*, 105–15; Merrill M. Parvis, *IDB* 4.604.

[13] Vincent, *History of the Textual Criticism*, 67.

Richard Bentley, at the age of sixty-nine, rescued the four-volume Codex Alexandrinus (so important in this period of textual criticism) from a fire in the Cottonian Library.[14] For much of twenty years prior to this event, Bentley had been planning and collecting materials for an edition of the Greek and Latin New Testament that would present the text of the time of Origen ("the true exemplar of Origen") and thereby supplant the *textus receptus*,[15] a project never brought to completion but one significant nonetheless for the very fact of its proposal and for the text-critical principles that were intended to form its basis.

Another event of 1730, however, was more properly a milestone, though it too had its curious aspect. In that year, one of Bentley's collators, J. J. Wettstein, published (anonymously) the *Prolegomena* for his proposed edition of the Greek New Testament, an edition that was to make its appearance only twenty-one years later in 1751–1752. Wettstein's *Prolegomena* listed nineteen principles of textual criticism, including such items as the more ample reading is not preferable to the shorter (no. 9), the Greek reading more in accord with the ancient versions is preferable (no. 13), and the more ancient reading is preferable (no. 17),[16] principles (especially the last two) closely akin to those of Bentley before him (which is not surprising) and to those of J. A. Bengel, who was shortly to follow. What is curious, however, is that Wettstein backed away from these canons in the interval before his edition appeared, and the text he printed was the *textus receptus* of Elzevir, rather than a text based on Codex Alexandrinus, as had been his original intention. Hence, neither did the methodological breakthrough that Bentley might have made come to fruition, nor did Wettstein put into practice his stated principles of 1730.

79 It is for these reasons that we take notice, next, of the genuine landmark of 250 years ago, the publication of J. A. Bengel's Greek New Testament in 1734. His printed text was still the *textus receptus*, but in at least three respects his work was to have far-reaching effects nonetheless. One was his pioneering division of the extant manu-

[14] Fox, *John Mill and Richard Bentley*, 125.

[15] Ibid., 118–19; Arthur A. Ellis, *Bentleii critica sacra: Notes on the Greek and Latin Text of the New Testament, Extracted from the Bentley MSS. in Trinity College Library* (Cambridge: Deighton, Bell, 1862) xvii.

[16] See Epp "Eclectic Method," 224 [repr. in Epp and Fee, *Studies in the Theory and Method*, 149–50].

scripts into groups; another was his system of signs in the text, showing how close or far from the original he judged variants to be; and the third involved the canons of criticism that he enunciated and practiced, including his insistence that textual witnesses must be weighed and not merely counted. In these and other ways Bengel greatly accelerated the notion that the oldest manuscripts—rather than the most numerous or smoothest—were the best manuscripts, and the negative impact of this principle upon the *textus receptus* would show itself increasingly as time passed.

These developments by Bentley,[17] Wettstein,[18] and Bengel[19] were to bear fruit roughly at the next fifty-year landmark, namely, J. J. Griesbach's Greek New Testament of 1775–1777, which—along with its subsequent editions and his influential canons of criticism—constituted the first daring though measured departure at numerous points from the *textus receptus*. Thus, it was with Griesbach that a decisive break with the *textus receptus* had arrived in theory—but only in theory—for by no means had it yet been achieved in clear and thorough practice. In fact, however, the preceding one hundred years (from Mill's work in 1677 until Griesbach in 1777) and the fifty years following Griesbach comprised that lengthy period of exploration and experimentation in text-critical method that effectually laid the foundation for the final overthrow of the *textus receptus*—which so long had dominated the field.

The decisive departure from the *textus receptus* in actual accomplishment and practice arrived with the next fifty-year landmark, now 150 years ago: Karl Lachmann's Greek New Testament of 1831. A classical scholar like many editors of the Greek New Testament before him, Lachmann made a proposal that actually was quite modest, for he sought only to establish the text as it had existed in Eastern Christianity just prior to 400 CE. Lachmann's method of achieving his goal, however, was anything but modest or reserved. Rather, it was both innovative and bold, for he relied for his New Testament text on no previous printed edition, but, laying aside the

---

[17] Fox, *John Mill and Richard Bentley*, 122–24.

[18] Epp "Eclectic Method," 223–25 [repr. in Epp and Fee, *Studies in the Theory and Method*, 149–150].

[19] Bruce M. Metzger, *The Text of the New Testament: Its Transmission, Corruption, and Restoration* (2nd ed.; Oxford/New York: Oxford University Press, 1968) 113.

whole established traditional text, he devised a text entirely from the most ancient witnesses known to him, including, of course, the oldest Greek majuscules (though no minuscules), but also the Old Latin and Vulgate versions and some early Fathers, such as Origen, Irenaeus, and Cyprian.[20] Lachmann's 1831 edition contained fewer than one hundred words describing his principles for selecting the readings of his text; his first principle of selection was that he followed "nowhere his own judgment," but "the usage of the most ancient eastern churches"; when this evidence was not consistent, he preferred the
80 reading on which the "Italian and African" witnesses agreed. Worth emphasis again is the fact that he gave no consideration to the "received readings," and in this respect Lachmann, the first scholar to make such a clean break with the *textus receptus*, had taken a giant step forward by backing away 1200 years from the "received text" of the sixteenth century and seeking to establish that of the fourth.

The period from Lachmann to Westcott-Hort, 1831–1881, undoubtedly constitutes the single most significant fifty-year period in the history of New Testament textual criticism, for important new materials appeared and significant new methodologies were implemented. Together these would bring us fully into the modern period. This fifty-year period opened with the beachhead by Lachmann against the *textus receptus*—a beachhead that was fiercely resisted, just as were the earlier assaults upon the *textus receptus* by Bentley and Bengel. But Lachmann represents more than a beachhead; his edition stands for the decisive battle—it was D-Day—and now it was only a matter of time until the territory hitherto held by the *textus receptus* would be fully occupied by the triumphant forces led by a vanguard of the earliest New Testament witnesses. If this military imagery can be tolerated a bit longer, one of the leading "generals," soon on the scene, was Constantin Tischendorf, whose eight editions of the Greek New Testament between 1841 and 1872 and whose nearly two dozen volumes publishing new manuscripts were major factors in the occupation of the newly won territory. Codex Sinaiticus was, of course, the most prominent of these discoveries.

Tischendorf's second edition in 1849 provided the rationale for his text—a basic principle similar to Lachmann's:

[20] See Frederic G. Kenyon, *Handbook to the Textual Criticism of the New Testament* (2nd ed.; London: Macmillan, 1926 [1st ed., 1912]) 286–88; Metzger, *Text of the New Testament*, 125–26.

> The text should be sought solely from ancient witnesses, and chiefly from Greek codices, but by no means neglecting the testimonies of the fathers and versions. Thus, the whole arrangement of the text is bound by necessity to arise from the witnesses themselves . . ., not from the edition of Elzevir, which is called "received"; however, to be placed first among disagreeing witnesses are those regarded as the oldest Greek codices, i.e., written from the fourth to about the ninth century. Again, among these those that excel in antiquity prevail in authority, and this authority increases if testimonies of the versions and fathers are added, nor is this authority surmounted by the disagreement of most or even of all the recent codices, i.e., those written from the ninth to the sixteenth centuries.[21]

Tischendorf's terse and quotable dictum, witnesses "that excel in antiquity prevail in authority," no longer required defense, for Lachmann had already firmly established the point.

Another "officer" in the campaign—perhaps a brigadier general—was S. P. Tregelles, who announced his text-critical principles in 1854, unaware of Lachmann's similar principles. Tregelles's aim was "to form a text on the authority of ancient copies without allowing the 'received text' any prescriptive rights."[22] The occupation of the ground formerly held by the *textus receptus* was occurring at an increas- 81
ing pace.

If D-Day belonged to Lachmann, V-Day—fifty years later at our next landmark—belonged to the undisputed "general of the army," F. J. A. Hort, and his "first officer," B. F. Westcott. The Westcott-Hort text (WH) of 1881—just about one hundred years ago—resulted from a skillful plan of attack and a sophisticated strategy for undermining the validity of the *textus receptus*. Hort, the strategic expert, outlined in the introductory volume to the edition certain guidelines that were crucial in the plan. Some of these were old, others new, such as:

1. Older readings, manuscripts, or groups are to be preferred.
2. Readings are approved or rejected by reason of the quality, and not the number of their supporting witnesses.

---

[21] Quoted in C. R. Gregory's *Prolegomena* to Tischendorf's 8th ed., 3.47–48: Constantin Tischendorf, *Novum Testamentum Graece* (8th major ed.; 3 vols.: 1–2 = text [Leipzig: Giesecke & Devrient, 1869–1872]; 3 = *Prolegomena*, [Leipzig: Hinrichs, 1894]).

[22] Samuel Prideaux Tregelles, *An Account of the Printed Text of the Greek New Testament* (London: Bagster, 1854) 152; see Epp, "Eclectic Method," 233 [repr. in Epp and Fee, *Studies in the Theory and Method*, 156.

3. A reading combining two simple, alternative readings is later than the two readings comprising the conflation, and manuscripts rarely or never supporting conflate readings are texts antecedent of mixture and are of special value.
4. The reading is to be preferred that most fitly explains the existence of the others.
5. The reading is less likely to be original that shows a disposition to smooth away difficulties.
6. Readings are to be preferred that are found in a manuscript that habitually contains superior readings as determined by intrinsic and transcriptional probability.[23]

The application of these (and other) principles effected a thorough and dramatic rout of the *textus receptus* (which Westcott-Hort called the "Syrian" text), for its chief witnesses could not withstand the charges concerning (1) their recent date, (2) their conflated readings and smoothening of difficulties, (3) the inability of their readings to explain the other readings, and (4) the fact that they kept company with numerous other manuscripts sharing these same characteristics. This strategy pushed to the forefront the oldest and "best" manuscripts and the "best" groups of manuscripts, those witnesses which—they said—had virtually escaped corruption and contamination, and which they called—understandably—the "Neutral" text. Accordingly, this Neutral text was acclaimed by Westcott-Hort and accepted by many others as "The New Testament in the Original Greek," as the title of their edition reads.

What was most surprising in this final campaign in the overthrow of the *textus receptus* was the last point, the audacious move by Westcott-Hort radically beyond the kind of modest proposal of Lachmann—to establish the text of the fourth century—to the unqualified claim to have established the text of the New Testament "in the original Greek." Would it not have been adequate for Westcott-Hort to have sought the text of the second century, for they were able with some assurance (based primarily on patristic quotations) to trace important portions of the text to that period? As it turned out, their final
82 daring thrust—to identify the Neutral text with the original—repre-

[23] Brooke Foss Westcott and Fenton John Anthony Hort, *The New Testament in the Original Greek* (2 vols.; Cambridge/London: Macmillan, 1881–1882 [1896[2]]) 2.55, 44, 49–50, 22–23, 28, 32–33, respectively.

sented an overkill (something not uncommon in a final military drive). It is the more understandable, then, that the strategy that had led to this result was itself quickly attacked at its vulnerable points. Some of these vulnerable points, as is well known, concern (1) Westcott-Hort's overly negative valuation of both the Byzantine text and the so-called Western text; (2) questions about their assessment of the components of the Western text and of what they termed the "Alexandrian" text; and, of course, (3) whether the Neutral text was really as pure and neutral and stood in so close and direct a relationship to the original as they claimed. The discussion of these and other questions was quick to be undertaken and ranged from the measured criticism of F. H. A. Scrivener and George Salmon[24] to the vehement attacks by J. W. Burgon.

What was far more significant than such immediate responses, however, was the fact that Westcott-Hort's edition and the hypotheses behind it provided an incentive for text-critical investigations that led directly to many of the major opportunities and problems that face us currently in the discipline. Such discussions occupied the succeeding fifty-year period until the next landmark was reached in the 1930s and when an unexpected development at that point infused new life and new directions into the older discussions and brought fresh issues into view. These developments will occupy our attention momentarily, but some of the investigations most obviously stimulated by Westcott-Hort deserve mention. For example, Hort's staunch defense of the three most prominent text-types of their theory (Syrian, Western, and Neutral) evoked two major branches of studies. One concerned the Syrian or Byzantine text, and investigations took at least two directions: efforts were made to redeem Byzantine readings (if not the entire text-type) from the low status accorded them by Westcott-Hort, and attempts—most notably by H. von Soden—were made to classify the massive body of Byzantine manuscripts into manageable groups and to assess their respective character. Another major branch of studies concerned the so-called Western text. Here Hort's judgment—that Western readings, though very ancient, evidenced extensive corruption—provided a challenge to defend their originality at many points and, for example, encouraged Friedrich Blass to develop fully the view that Luke wrote two

[24] See Metzger, *Text of the New Testament*, 137.

versions of his canonical books, one represented by the Neutral and the other by the Western text[25] (Such a view had been mentioned and rejected by Hort himself, but is now being revived—in the 1980s—by E. Delebecque.[26]) In addition, Hort's assignment to the Western text-type of witnesses soon recognized to be disparate and divergent rather than homogeneous converged with a series of new manuscript discoveries (such as codices Washingtonianus [W] and Koridethi [Θ] and the Sinaitic Syriac) to quicken studies that would lead to the identification of a separate text-type, the Caesarean. All
83 of these developments are well known to us, and numerous analyses of the Western, Byzantine, and Caesarean text-types occupied textual critics for fifty years and longer.

It was, as a matter of fact, just fifty years after the Westcott-Hort edition that the next landmark appeared, for in 1930–1931 Chester Beatty acquired the famous papyri that bear his name, notably—for our purposes—P^{45}, P^{46}, and P^{47}, and the London *Times* of 19 November 1931 carried the first public announcement of the discovery. These were the first early and extensive New Testament papyri to come to light, and a whole new era of New Testament textual criticism suddenly unfolded. This discovery is a landmark not because New Testament papyri had not been found before but because the Chester Beatty papyri effected not merely a *quantitative change in the materials* available, but a *qualitative change in the discipline*. The Oxyrhynchus papyri, of course, had been discovered and published already beginning in 1898, providing many fragments of New Testament text,

[25] Friedrich Wilhelm Blass, *Acta Apostolorum sive Lucae ad Theophilum liber alter. Editio philologica apparatu critico* . . . (Göttingen: Vandenhoeck & Ruprecht, 1895); idem, *Acta Apostolorum sive Lucae ad Theophilum liber alter, secundum formam quae videtur Romanam* (Leipzig: Teubner, 1896); idem, *Evangelium secundum Lucam sive Lucae ad Theophilum liber prior, secundum formam quae videtur Romanam* (Leipzig: Teubner, 1897); idem, *Philology of the Gospels* (London: Macmillan, 1898) 96–137.

[26] Edouard Delebecque, "Les deux prologues des Actes des Apôtres," *RevThom* 80 (1980) 628–34; idem, "Ascension et Pentecôte dans les Actes des Apôtres selon le codex Bezae," *RevThom* 82 (1982) 79–89; idem, "De Lystres à Philippes (Ac 16) avec le *codex Bezae*," *Bib* 63 (1982) 395–405; idem, "Paul à Thessalonique et à Bérée selon le text occidental des Actes (XVII, 4–15)," *RevThom* 82 (1982) 604–16; idem, "Les deux versions du voyage de saint Paul de Corinthe à Troas (Ac 20,3–6)," *Bib* 64 (1983) 556–64; idem, *Les deux Actes des Apôtres* (EBib ns 6; Paris: Gabalda, 1986); M.-E. Boismard and A. Lamouille, *Le texte occidental des Actes des Apôtres: Reconstitution et réhabilitation. Tome I: Introduction et textes. Tome II: Apparat critique, Index des caractéristiques stylistiques, Index des citations patristiques* (Synthèse 17; Paris: Editions Recherche sur le Civilisations, 1984).

and the Bodmer papyri from 1956 and following were in some significant ways to overshadow the Chester Beatty, yet the Chester Beatty papyri were so extensive and so early in date that they rightly demanded a restructuring of New Testament text-critical theory and practice. Such a restructuring, of course, did not actually take place; for example, when P^{45} in the Gospels was aligned with the Caesarean text, critics still called that text Caesarean rather than the P^{45} text or the Chester Beatty text (either of which would have been an appropriate and natural designation). Nevertheless, the ultimate effects of these papyri upon critical editions—both text and apparatus—and as stimuli to studies across the entire discipline were enormous and lasting, and the landmark quality of the discovery is indisputable. When the Bodmer papyri, most notably P^{66} and P^{75}, are recognized also as ingredients of the period since 1930, it is quite appropriate to refer to the fifty-year period from 1930 to 1980 as the "Period of the Papyri," for, given the high valuation placed upon these and the other papyri, we seem to have reached a new stage—perhaps "plateau" is the word—which provides a new and refreshing vantage point for viewing the New Testament text, but a plateau from which, for the moment at least, we have not been led to an obvious higher plane.

All of us share this high valuation of these extraordinarily early and significant New Testament witnesses that have rightly received such close attention during the fifty-year "Period of the Papyri," and perhaps our newest fifty-year landmark—that of the 1980s—has now made its appearance in the "Introduction" to the NA^{26} (1979), where the editors affirm that for this new "Standard Text" of the New Testament the forty earliest papyri (and the four earliest but fragmentary uncials) are "of automatic [*automatisch*] significance, because they were written before the III/IV century, and therefore belong to the period before the rise of major text types."[27] Whether this is a legitimate claim, or a plausible claim, or a claim much overdrawn is a highly complex question to which we shall return, yet—unless significant new papyrus discoveries are made—it seems clear that 84

[27] Kurt Aland *et al.*, eds., *Novum Testamentum Graece post Eberhard Nestle et Erwin Nestle, communiter ediderunt Kurt Aland, Matthew Black, Carlo M. Martini, Bruce M. Metzger, Allen Wikgren* (26th ed.; Stuttgart: Deutsche Bibelstiftung, 1979 [11th printing, 1987]) 12*, cf. 49*. See E. J. Epp, "A Continuing Interlude in New Testament Textual Criticism," *HTR* 73 (1980) 144–51 [repr. in Epp and Fee, *Studies in the Theory and Method*, 118–23].

the fifty-year "Period of the Papyri" from 1930 to 1980, that period of the discovery, analysis, and utilization of the earliest and most substantial papyri, may have to give way to a fresh period of the *re*assessment of the papyri and perhaps of their *re*application to the history and theory of the New Testament text. This, however, brings us up to date and leads directly to that part of our discussion concerned with current challenges in the discipline. Before joining these issues, the post-World War II period requires finer scrutiny.

II. The Post-World War II Setting

New Testament textual criticism was a quiet discipline as the scholarly community regrouped and reemerged following World War II. How text critics viewed themselves and their work can be garnered from any of the numerous "state-of-the-discipline" reports that appeared in the first decade of the period. An interesting contrast appears, however, when one takes a prewar status report from one of the most prominent textual critics and compares it with the postwar reports. Sir Frederic Kenyon, when asked in 1938 to contribute an article on "The Text of the Greek New Testament" for the *Expository Times* series "After Fifty Years," describes in glowing terms the astounding manuscript discoveries since 1888, refers to "much progress" in textual theory, and, with reference to the confidence of scholars in the Alexandrian text [Hort's Neutral, or the Egyptian], concludes with a statement, which—while cautious and modest on the surface—exudes that same high confidence in what has been achieved: "We shall," he said, "do well to recognize that complete certainty in details is not obtainable, and that there may be something yet to be learned from discoveries still to be made."[28] In contrast, Merrill Parvis, in *The Study of the Bible Today and Tomorrow*—a 1947 collaborative volume like the present one[29]—affirmed that "no great advance has been made in the method of textual study since the days of Westcott and Hort";[30] several years later K. W. Clark, in a 1956 status report,

[28] Frederic G. Kenyon, "The Text of the Greek New Testament," *ExpTim* 50 (1938/39) 68–71.

[29] Namely, *The New Testament and Its Modern Interpreters* (ed. E. J. Epp and †George W. MacRae; SBLBMI, 3; Philadelphia: Fortress Press; Atlanta: Scholars Press, 1989), in which the present essay first appeared.

[30] Merrill M. Parvis, "New Testament Criticism in the World-Wars Period," *The*

echoed the same sentiments in referring to "how little, and how tentatively, textual criticism since 1930—and much earlier—has altered the New Testament text we study" and in positing that "any substantial effort to improve the basic critical text must 'mark time' until the whole complex of textual studies reveals a new integrating pattern;"[31] and—as a third example—in 1962 H. H. Oliver's status report indicated that "so far, the twentieth century has been a period characterized by general pessimism about the possibility of recovering the original text by objective criteria. This pessimism has persisted despite the appearance of new materials."[32] The change in mood is of more than passing interest, for this same lack of progress—attributed to an even broader portion of the discipline—could be claimed by at least one person in the field as recently as 1973.[33] We shall return to these issues after a brief survey of post-World War 85
II efforts under three categories: critical editions, discoveries, and methods.

A. Critical Editions and Studies

1. *Editions of the Greek New Testament*

The critical apparatuses of Mark and Matthew produced by S. C. E. Legg[34] just prior to and during the war (1935 and 1940) were not highly acclaimed either for their conception, accuracy, or usefulness. One by one, however, the various hand-editions of the Greek New Testament reappeared after the war. That of H. J. Vogels first appeared in 1920 (then with the Vulgate in 1922), with a fourth

---

Study of the Bible Today and Tomorrow (ed. H. R. Willoughby; Chicago: University of Chicago Press, 1947) 58.

[31] Kenneth Willis Clark, "The Effect of Recent Textual Criticism upon New Testament Studies," *The Background of the New Testament and Its Eschatology* (ed. W. D. Davies and D. Daube; Cambridge: Cambridge University Press, 1956) 41–42. [Repr. in Clark, *The Gentile Bias and Other Essays* (selected by John L. Sharpe III; NovTSup 54; Leiden: Brill, 1980) 79–80].

[32] Harold H. Oliver, "Present Trends in the Textual Criticism of the New Testament," *JBR* 30 (1962) 308.

[33] E. J. Epp, "The Twentieth Century Interlude in New Testament Textual Criticism," *JBL* 93 (1974) *passim* [repr. in Epp and Fee, *Studies in the Theory and Method*].

[34] S. C. E. Legg, ed., *Nouum Testamentum graece secundum textum Westcotto-Hortianum: Euangelium secundum Marcum* (Oxford: Clarendon Press, 1935); idem, ed., *Nouum Testamentum graece secundum textum Westcotto-Hortianum: Euangelium secundum Matthaeum* (Oxford: Clarendon Press, 1940).

edition in 1955;[35] A. Merk's originated in 1933, with a third edition in 1938, followed by a postwar sixth edition completed in 1948, and a current ninth edition, 1964.[36] J. M. Bover's was a wartime product, appearing in 1943, with several postwar editions through the fifth of 1968,[37] and revised by J. O'Callaghan for inclusion in the 1977 *Nuevo Testamento Trilingüe*.[38] A. Souter's Greek New Testament (original, 1910) made a postwar appearance in a revised form in 1947.[39] G. D. Kilpatrick revised the 1904 *British and Foreign Bible Societies Greek New Testament* to produce its second edition in 1958.[40] In 1964 R. V. G. Tasker published "the actual Greek text, of which *The New English Bible* is a translation."[41] In the same year K. Aland issued his *Synopsis quattuor evangliorum*, with text and apparatus of the four gospels,[42] and in 1981 H. Greeven produced a new critical text of the four Gospels (with apparatus) for his *Synopsis*.[43] Finally, in 1982, Z. C. Hodges and A. L. Farstad edited a "majority text" New Testament, based on the Byzantine manuscripts.[44]

---

[35] Heinrich Joseph Vogels, *Novum Testamentum graece et latine* (Düsseldorf: Schwann, 1920[1]; 1922 with Vulgate; 1955[4]).

[36] Augustinus Merk, S.J., ed. *Novum Testamentum graece et latine* (Rome: Biblical Institute Press, 1933[1]; 1984[10]).

[37] Joseph M. Bover, S.J., ed., *Novi Testamenti biblia graeca et latina* (5th ed. Madrid: Consejo superior de investigaciones científicas, 1943[1]; 1968[5]).

[38] Joseph M. Bover and José O'Callaghan, eds., *Nuevo Testamento trilingüe* (BAC 400; Madrid: La editorial católica, 1977).

[39] Alexander Souter, ed., *Novvm Testmentvm Graece: Textvi a retractatoribvs anglis adhibito brevem adnotationem criticam svbiecit* (Oxford: Clarendon Press, 1910[1]; 1947[2]).

[40] George Dunbar Kilpatrick, ed., *Η ΚΑΙΝΗ ΔΙΑΘΗΚΗ*. (2nd ed., with revised critical apparatus; London: British and Foreign Bible Society, 1958).

[41] R. V. G. Tasker, ed., *The Greek New Testament, Being the Text Translated in the New English Bible* (London: Oxford University Press; Cambridge: Cambridge University Press, 1964) ix.

[42] Kurt Aland, ed., *Synopsis quattuor evangeliorum* (Stuttgart: Württembergische Bibelanstalt, 1964). Reissued as *Synopsis of the Four Gospels: Greek-English Edition of the Synopsis quattuor evangeliorum with the Text of the Revised Standard Version* (London: United Bible Societies, 1972).

[43] Heinrich Greeven, *Synopse der drei ersten Evangelien mit Beigabe der johanneischen Parallelstellen/Synopsis of the First Three Gospels with the Addition of the Johannine Parallels* (13th rev. ed. of Albert Huck, *Synopse der drei ersten Evangelien mit Beigabe der johanneischen Parallelstellen* [Tübingen: Mohr-Siebeck, 1981]).

[44] Zane C. Hodges and Arthur L. Farstad, ed., *The Greek New Testament according to the Majority Text* (Nashville/Camden/New York: Thomas Nelson, 1982). For earlier attempts to rehabilitate the *textus receptus*, see Edward F. Hills, *The King James Version Defended! A Christian View of the New Testament Manuscripts* (Des Moines, IA: Christian Research Press, 1956; 2nd ed. rev.: *The King James Version Defended! A Space-Age Defense of the Historic Christian Faith*, 1973); David Otis Fuller, ed., *Which Bible?* (Grand Rapids, MI: Grand Rapids International Publications, 1970; 3rd ed. rev. and enlarged,

But the most widely used hand-edition of the Greek New Testament, at least in Europe, was that of Eberhard Nestle,[45] which had passed through sixteen editions prior to the war (by 1936) and made its first reappearance after the war in a photographic reproduction by the American Bible Society in New York sometime prior to 1948 (when I purchased my copy), though it bears no publication date. The Nestle edition had been edited, beginning with the thirteenth edition of 1927, by Nestle's son, Erwin, but Kurt Aland appears as coeditor after the twenty-first edition of 1952, and later as sole editor until Barbara Aland became the second editor of the twenty-sixth edition of 1979.[45] The text of this latest edition is, by agreement, identical with that of the third edition of the United Bible Societies' *Greek New Testament* (*UBSGNT*) of 1975, and this Greek New Testament text (contained in these two hand-editions) has recently been designated the "Standard Text" by Kurt Aland.[46] As the most readily available and most widely used Greek New Testament text, it may justly be called the "Standard Text," though claims made for it as a text universally accepted as the "best" or "original" New Testament continue to be debated.[47]

1972); idem, ed., *True or False? The Westcott-Hort Textual Theory Examined* (Grand Rapids, MI: Grand Rapids International Publications, 1973); idem, ed., *Counterfeit or Genuine: Mark 16? John 8?* (Grand Rapids, Mi: Grand Rapids International Publications, 1975); Wilbur N. Pickering, *The Identity of the New Testament Text* (Nashville: Thomas Nelson, 1977 [see now *The Identity of the New Testament Text II* (Eugene, OR: Wipf and Stock, 2003)].

[45] Kurt Aland, Matthew Black, Carlo M. Martini, Bruce M. Metzger, Allen Wikgren, eds., *Novum Testamentum Graece post Eberhard Nestle et Erwin Nestle* (26th ed.; Stuttgart: Deutsche Bibelstiftung, 1979. [The 27th ed. was ed. by Barbara and Kurt Aland, Johannes Karavidopoulos, Carlo M. Martini, and Bruce M. Metzger (Stuttgart: Deutsche Bibelgesellschaft, 1993; 5th corrected ed., 1998; 8th corrected ed., with Papyri 99–116, 2001).]

[46] Kurt Aland, "Der neue 'Standard Text' in seinem Verhältnis zu den frühen Papyri und Majuskeln," E. J. Epp and Gordon D. Fee, eds., *New Testament Textual Criticism: Its Significance for Exegesis: Essays in Honour of Bruce M. Metzger* (Oxford: Clarendon Press, 1981) 257–75; K. Aland, "Die Grundurkunde des Glaubens: Ein Bericht über 40 Jahre Arbeit an ihrem Text," *Bericht der Hermann Kunst-Stiftung zur Förderung der neutestamentlichen Textforschung für die Jahre 1982 bis 1984* (ed. Hermann Kunst; Münster/W.: Hermann Kunst-Stiftung, 1985) 12–17. The term "Standard Text" has been replaced by "new text" in Kurt Aland and Barbara Aland, *The Text of the New Testament: An Introduction to the Critical Editions and to the Theory and Practice of Modern Textual Criticism* (tr. Erroll F. Rhodes; Grand Rapids: Eerdmans; Leiden: Brill, 2nd ed., 1989) e.g., 24, 34–36, as compared with the first ed., 1987, 25, 34–35.

[47] E.g., Ian A. Moir, "Can We Risk Another 'Textus Receptus'?" *JBL* 100 (1981) 614–18; J. Keith Elliott, [review of Aland and Aland, *Text of the New Testament*,

86 The Westcott-Hort text of 1881, some three or four generations in the past by the outbreak of the war, perhaps retained more status as a modern *textus receptus* than any other critical text, at least in English-speaking scholarship. The ground swell, however, for a new major critical edition or apparatus was beginning to form in the period between the wars, prompted more than anything else by the new manuscript discoveries of the twentieth century. A push for a "new Tischendorf" based on the Nestle text had emerged already in the mid-1920s in a British-German group, but the German group withdrew when no agreement could be reached on the textual base to be utilized; it was at this point that the British group carried on, producing the ill-fated Legg volumes. Recognition of their inadequacy led to a British-American undertaking, the so-called International Greek New Testament Project (IGNTP), whose goal was a new critical apparatus of the New Testament—that is, the provision of the *data* essential for a new critical text of the New Testament, though not proposing to create that *critical text* itself. This project was conceived on a large scale but began where Legg left off—with the Gospel of Luke—though envisioning a vastly enlarged manuscript coverage as compared with Legg. Its collation base was the *textus receptus*, employed on the correct assumption that the most economical way in which to display the variants in the apparatus was against this "fullest" of texts. The choice of the *textus receptus* was misunderstood and, indeed, ridiculed by Kurt Aland,[48] but the British-American project persisted through nearly forty years of cooperative efforts and

1982[German]], *TZ* 39 (1983) 247–49; Hans-Werner Bartsch, "Ein neuer Textus Receptus für das griechische Neue Testament?" *NTS* 27 (1980/81) 585–92; see Aland's reply, "Ein neuer Textus Receptus für das griechische Neue Testament?" *NTS* 28 (1982) 145–53.

[48] Kurt Aland, "Bemerkungen zu Probeseiten einer grossen kritischen Ausgabe des Neuen Testaments," *NTS* 12 (1965/66) 176–85 [repr. in K. Aland, *Studien zur Überlieferung des Neuen Testaments und seines Textes* (ANTF 2; Berlin: de Gruyter, 1967) 81–90]. See the replies by M. Jack Suggs in Jean Duplacy and M. Jack Suggs, "Les citations greques et la critique du texte du Nouveau Testament: Le passé, le présent et l'avenir," *La Bible et les Pères: Colloque de Strasbourg (1er–3 octobre 1969)* (ed., André Benoit and Pierre Prigent; Bibliothèque des centres d'études supérieurs spécialisés; Paris: Presses universitaires de France, 1971) 197–98; 204–6 [repr. in Jean Duplacy, *Etudes de critique textuelle du Nouveau Testament* (ed. Joël Delobel; BETL 78; Leuven: Leuven University Press/Peeters, 1987) 133–34; 141–42]; and E. J. Epp, "Twentieth Century Interlude," 402–3 [repr. in Epp and Fee, *Studies in the Theory and Method*, 97–98].

discouraging delays until the first—and perhaps only—results appeared in 1984 and 1987, an apparatus to the text of Luke's Gospel (*The New Testament in Greek: The Gospel according to St. Luke, Part One: Chapters 1–12* [1984]; *Part Two: Chapters 13–24* [1987]).[49] Users and critics will have to judge its usefulness, but the economical display of vast amounts of material seems to be a self-justification for the principles on which this critical apparatus of the Greek New Testament [it is not really an edition] was constructed.

The IGNTP's long history began in 1948 with a large British committee, chaired successively by R. H. Lightfoot, H. I. Bell, G. H. C. McGregor, and J. M. Plumley; J. N. Birdsall served as executive editor from 1968 to 1977 and was succeeded by J. K. Elliott. A somewhat smaller American committee was organized, chaired from 1949 to 1970 by E. C. Colwell, who was succeeded by B. M. Metzger. K. W. Clark served as executive editor of the materials prepared by the American committee.[50]

The current British committee (now a committee of the British Academy) consists of H. F. D. Sparks, G. D. Kilpatrick, J. M. Plumley (chm.), S. P. Brock, M. Black, T. S. Pattie, J. L. North, J. K. Elliott, and W. J. Elliott, and the present American committee consists of B. M. Metzger (chm.), A. P. Wikgren, M. J. Suggs, E. J. Epp, G. D.
Fee, I. A. Sparks, and P. R. McReynolds (American and British 87
Committees: 1.xiv–xv). Whether the IGNTP will carry forward its original plan to provide next a critical apparatus for the Fourth Gospel is unclear at this time.[51]

---

[49] American and British Committees of the International Greek New Testament Project, ed., *The New Testament in Greek: The Gospel according to St. Luke: Part One: Chapters 1–12. Part Two: Chapters 13–24* (Oxford: Clarendon Press, 1984–1987).

[50] Merrill M. Parvis, "The International Project to Establish a New Critical Apparatus of the Greek New Testament," *Crozer Quarterly* 27 (1950) 301–8; Ernest C. Colwell, Irving Alan Sparks, Frederik Wisse, and Paul R. McReynolds, "The International Greek New Testament Project: A Status Report," *JBL* 87 (1968) 187–97; James M. Robinson *et al.*, "The Institute for Antiquity and Christianity: International Greek New Testament Project," *NTS* 16 (1969/70) 180–82; J. Keith Elliott, "The International Project to Establish a Critical Apparatus to Luke's Gospel," *NTS* 29 (1983) 531–38. [See now E. J. Epp, "The International Greek New Testament Project: Motivation and History," *NovT* 39 (1997) 1–20.]

[51] A new phase of IGNTP was launched during 1987–1988, whose purpose is to produce an *apparatus criticus* of the Gospel of John. The British Committee is now composed of J. K. Elliott, W. J. Elliott, J. L. North, D. C. Parker, and T. S. Pattie [with G. D. Kilpatrick until his death in 1989]; and the North American Committee consists of J. Brooks, B. D. Ehrman, E. J. Epp, G. D. Fee, T. C. Geer,

The division of work provided that the British committee assemble most of the patristic and versional evidence, while the American committee was to oversee the collation of the Greek manuscripts and Greek lectionaries and obtain the textual evidence for most of the Greek Fathers and for the Armenian, Ethiopic, Georgian, Gothic, and Old Church Slavonic versions. Two hundred and eighty-three scholars, mostly from North America, participated in the collection of data from the Greek manuscripts and Greek Fathers, and many other scholars from Great Britain, America, and other countries assisted in collecting the versional evidence.[52]

Several methodological issues were faced in connection with the American assignments, resulting in the Claremont Profile Method for quickly assessing the character of minuscule manuscripts—permitting the selection of a relatively small number of manuscripts for inclusion in the apparatus that would adequately represent the various manuscript types in the minuscule mass,[53] and a considerable literature is developing around this Profile Method.[54] In addition, cri-

M. W. Holmes, P. R. McReynolds, C. D. Osburn, and W. L. Petersen. Brooks, Geer, and Osburn subsequently have resigned; B. Morrill and K. Haines-Eitzen have been added to the American Committee, which functions under the auspices of the Society of Biblical Literature. A further result of the revived IGNTP is *The New Testament in Greek IV: The Gospel according to St. John: Volume One: The Papyri* (ed. W. J. Elliott and D. C. Parker—for the American and British Committees of the IGNTP; NTTS 20; Leiden: Brill, 1995).

[52] American and British Committees of the International Greek New Testament Project, ed., *The New Testament in Greek: The Gospel according to St. Luke*, 1.v; xiv–xvi.

[53] Colwell *et al.*, "The International Greek New Testament Project," 191–97; E. J. Epp, "The Claremont Profile-Method for Grouping New Testament Minuscule Manuscripts," *Studies in the History and Text of the New Testament* (ed. Boyd L. Daniels and M. Jack Suggs; SD 29; Salt Lake City, UT: University of Utah Press, 1967) 27–38 [repr. in Epp and Fee, *Studies in the Theory and Method*, 211–20]; Frederik W. Wisse and Paul R. McReynolds, "Family E and the Profile Method," *Bib* 51 (1970) 67–75; P. R. McReynolds, "The Value and Limitations of the Claremont Profile Method," SBLSP 1 (1972) 1–7; "Establishing Text Families," *The Critical Study of the Sacred Texts* (ed. Wendy Doniger O'Flaherty; Berkeley, CA: Berkeley Religious Studies Series, 1979) 97–113; now esp. F. W. Wisse, *The Profile Method for the Classification and Evaluation of Manuscript Evidence as Applied to the Continuous Greek Text of the Gospel of Luke* (SD 44; Grand Rapids, MI: Eerdmans, 1982).

[54] E.g., William Larry Richards, *The Classification of the Greek Manuscripts of the Johannine Epistles* (SBLDS 35; Missoula, MT: Scholars Press, 1977); idem, "A Critique of a New Testament Text-critical Methodology—the Claremont Profile Method," *JBL* 96 (1977) 555–66; "Manuscript Grouping in Luke 10 by Quantitative Analysis," *JBL* 98 (1979) 379–91; "An Examination of the Claremont Profile Method in the Gospel of Luke: A Study in Text-Critical Methodology," *NTS* 27 (1980/81) 52–63.

teria were devised for choosing appropriate representatives of the complex lectionary text,[55] and, finally, precision was introduced into the process of differentiating patristic "citations," "allusions," and "adaptations."[56]

The Greek text that appears in NA^{26}, which seems to have replaced all the hand-editions and which (as indicated above) has been proclaimed recently as the "Standard Text" by Kurt Aland, was produced, beginning in 1955, by an international team working under the sponsorship of the United Bible Societies. Titled simply *The Greek New Testament*, it is referred to as the *UBSGNT*. Eugene A. Nida of the American Bible Society initiated and administered the project, and the editorial committee for the first edition was composed of K. Aland, M. Black, B. M. Metzger, A. Wikgren, and A. Vööbus; for the second and third editions, C. M. Martini replaced Vööbus. The first edition appeared in 1966, the second in 1968, and a third, more thorough revision in 1975 (UBS^{3}), which—by design—is identical in

[55] Colwell et al., "The International Greek New Testament Project," 188–91; cf. Jean Duplacy, "Les lectionnaires et l'édition du Nouveau Testament grec," *Mélanges bibliques en hommage au R. P. Béda Rigaux* (ed. A. Descamps and A. de Halleux; Gembloux: Duculot, 1970) 509–45 [repr. in Duplacy, *Etudes de critique textuelle du Nouveau Testament*, 81–117].

[56] Colwell et al., "The International Greek New Testament Project," 187–88; M. J. Suggs, "The Use of Patristic Evidence in the Search for a Primitive New Testament Text," *NTS* 4 (1957/58) 139–47; B. M. Metzger, "Patristic Evidence and the Textual Criticism of the New Testament," *NTS* 18 (1971/72) 379–400 [repr. in Metzger, *New Testament Studies: Philological, Versional, and Patristic*, 167–88]; but esp. Gordon D. Fee, "The Text of John in Origen and Cyril of Alexandria: A Contribution to Methodology in the Recovery and Analysis of Patristic Citations," *Bib* 52 (1971) 357–94 [repr. in Epp and Fee, *Studies in the Theory and Method*, 301–34]; idem, "The Text of John in *The Jerusalem Bible*: A Critique of the Use of Patristic Citations in New Testament Textual Criticism," *JBL* 90 (1971) 163–73 [repr. in Epp and Fee, *Studies in the Theory and Method*, 335–43]; idem, "The Use of Greek Patristic Citations in New Testament Textual Criticism: The State of the Question," *ANRW* II/26/1.246–65 [repr. in Epp and Fee, *Studies in the Theory and Method*, 344–59]; cf. Robert M. Grant, "The Citation of Patristic Evidence in an Apparatus Criticus," *New Testament Manuscript Studies: The Materials and the Making of a Critical Apparatus* (ed. Merrill M. Parvis and Allen P. Wikgren; Chicago: University of Chicago Press, 1950) 117–24; P. Prigent, "Les citations des Pères Grecs et la critique textuelle du Nouveau Testament," *Die alten Übersetzungen des Neuen Testaments, die Kirchenväterzitate und Lektionare: Der gegenwärtige Stand ihrer Erforschung und ihre Bedeutung für die griechische Textgeschichte* (ed. Kurt Aland; ANTF 5; Berlin/New York: de Gruyter, 1972) 436–54; Hermann Josef Frede, "Die Zitate des Neuen Testaments bei den lateinischen Kirchenvätern," ibid., 455–78.

text to that of NA[26]. A fourth edition is in preparation.[57] Assistance was provided all along by the Münster Institut für neutestamentliche Textforschung. An accompanying *Textual Commentary*,[58] written for the committee by Bruce M. Metzger and published in 1971, comments
88 on hundreds of variation-units in the New Testament and provides explanations for the choice of one reading over others. A torrent of reviews and assessments of both the *UBSGNT* and the companion *Commentary* have been published since these volumes appeared, and the flow has resumed as each new edition has been issued.

Finally, it was the leading critic of the IGNTP, Kurt Aland, who spearheaded several projects involving New Testament editions and other text-critical work at his Institut für neutestamentliche Textforschung (just mentioned above). The NA hand-edition and the cooperative *UBSGNT* have already been described. In addition, Aland and his Institut produced the monograph series, Arbeiten zur neutestamentlichen Textforschung. The first volume (1963) is the *Kurzgefasste Liste der griechischen Handschriften des Neuen Testaments*, which, with a supplement in volume 3 (1969:1–53), provides the official list of the Greek manuscripts of the New Testament,[59] covering the papyri, majuscules, minuscules, and lectionaries. The numerous essays in volumes 2, 3, and 5 are of great importance for the study and research of the New Testament text, with volume 5 devoted to New Testament versions, patristic citations, and lectionaries.[60] Volume 4 of the series

[57] *The Greek New Testament*, 4th revised ed., appeared in 1993, edited by Barbara Aland, Kurt Aland, Johannes Karavidopoulos, Carlo M. Martini, and B. M. Metzger (Stuttgart: Deutsche Bibelgesellschaft/United Bible Societies).

[58] *A Textual Commentary on the Greek New Testament: A Companion Volume to the United Bible Societies' Greek New Testament (Third Edition)* (London/New York: United Bible Societies, 1971). A 2nd ed., with numerous revisions, appeared in 1994: *A Textual Commentary on the Greek New Testament: A Companion Volume to the United Bible Societies' Greek New Testament (Fourth Revised Edition)* (Stuttgart: Deutsche Bibelgesellschaft/United Bible Societies).

[59] K. Aland, *Kurzgefasste Liste der griechischen Handschriften des Neuen Testaments: I: Gesamtübersicht* (ANTF 1; Berlin: de Gruyter, 1963). Continued in "Die griechischen Handschriften des Neuen Testaments: Ergänzungen zur 'Kurzgefasste Liste' (Fortsetzungsliste VII)," idem, ed., *Materialien zur neutestamentlichen Handschriftenkunde I* (ANTF 3; Berlin: de Gruyter, 1969) 1–53. See now K. Aland's updated 2nd ed. of the *Kurzgefasste Liste* (ANTF 1; Berlin/New York: de Gruyter, 1994).

[60] K. Aland, *Studien zur Überlieferung*; idem, ed., *Materialien*; and idem, ed., *Die alten Übersetzungen.*

is the now standard *Vollständige Konkordanz zum griechischen Neuen Testament*,[61] an indispensable tool for New Testament exegetes as well as textual critics. The Institut continues to work toward its *editio maior critica*—its major critical edition of the Greek New Testament—which began with the Catholic Epistles.[62] All of these projects are carried through with meticulous care and thoroughness, and the discipline owes much to Professor Aland and his Institut.[63]

2. *Critical Editions of Versions and Fathers*

Limitation of space permits reference only to post-World War II monographic works and not to periodical literature.

The study of the Latin New Testament has been greatly assisted by two projects. The first is *Itala*,[64] an edition of the Old Latin Gospels begun by A. Jülicher but later edited by W. Matzkow and K. Aland. The second is the *Vetus Latina*, a large-format edition of the Old Latin Bible with a detailed critical apparatus, carried out

---

[61] K. Aland, *Vollständige Konkordanz zum griechischen Neuen Testament: Unter Zugrundelegung aller modernen kritischen Textausgaben und des Textus Receptus* (ANTF 4; 2 vols. in 3; Berlin/New York: de Gruyter, 1975–1983). See the reviews, e.g., by Joseph A. Fitzmyer, *JBL* 95 (1976) 679–81; 97 (1978) 604–6; 100 (1981) 147–49; 102 (1983) 639–40; 104 (1985) 360–62; and E. J. Epp, *CBQ* 41 (1979) 148–51; 42 (1980) 258–61; 46 (1984) 778–80.

[62] See K. Aland, "Novi testamenti graeci editio maior critica: Der gegenwärtige Stand der Arbeit an einer neuen grossen kritischen Ausgabe des Neuen Testamentes," *NTS* 16 (1969/70) 163–77; idem, ed., in collaboration with Annette Benduhn-Mertz and Gerd Mink, *Text und Textwert der griechischen Handschriften des Neuen Testaments. I: Die Katholischen Briefe. Vol. 1: Das Material. Vol. 2.1: Die Auswertung (P^{23}–999); Vol. 2.2: Die Auswertung (1003–2805); Vol. 3: Die Einzelhandschriften* (ANTF 9; 10:1–2; 11; 3 vols. in 4; Berlin/New York: de Gruyter, 1987).

[The first fascicles of the edition itself have now appeared: The Institute for New Testament Textual Research (ed.), *Novum Testamentum Graecum, Editio Critica Maior: IV, Catholic Epistles, Installment 1: James* (ed. Barbara Aland, Kurt Aland†, Gerd Mink, and Klaus Wachtel; 2 parts; Stuttgart Deutsche Bibelgesellschaft, 1997); . . . *Installment 2: The Letters of Peter* (2 parts, 2000); . . . *Installment 3: The First Letter of John* (2 parts, 2003).]

[63] For reports on the status of various projects, see Hermann Kunst, ed., *Bericht der Hermann Kunst-Stiftung zur Förderung der neutestamentlichen Textforschung für die Jahre 1977 bis 1979* (Münster/W.: Hermann Kunst-Stiftung, 1979); subsequent issues: 1982–1984 (1985); 1985–1987 (1988) [and more recently: 1988–1991 (1992); 1992–1994 (1995); 1995–1998 (1998); and 1998–2003 (2003)].

[64] Adolf Jülicher, *Itala: Das Neue Testament in altlateinischer Überlieferung* (ed., Walter Matzkow and Kurt Aland; Berlin: de Gruyter, 1954–1972): *Matthäus-Evangelium* (2nd ed., 1972); *Markus-Evangelium* (2nd ed., 1970); *Lucas-Evangelium* (1954); *Johannes-Evangelium* (1963).

at the Beuron monastery under the supervision of Alban Dold until his death in 1960 and then directed by Bonifatius Fischer under the auspices of the Vetus Latina Institut. Currently Walter Thiele oversees the work, and, to date, the Catholic Epistles have been completed by him,[65] as well as Ephesians, Philippians, Colossians, and 1–2 Thessalonians, 1–2 Timothy, Titus, and Philemon by H. J. Frede.[66] In addition, an index of the Fathers has been compiled by
89 Frede,[67] and an accompanying monograph series provides specialized studies.[68]

The Old Georgian version of the Gospels has been edited for Mark and Matthew by Robert P. Blake,[69] for John by Blake and Maurice Brière,[70] and for Luke by Brière.[71] The Georgian version of Acts was edited by Gérard Garitte,[72] the Ethiopic of the

---

[65] Walter Thiele, ed. *Epistulae Catholicae* (VL 26; Freiburg: Herder, 1956–69).

[66] Hermann Josef Frede, ed., *Vol. 24. Epistula ad Ephesios; Epistulae ad Philippenses et ad Colossenses* (VL 24; Freiburg: Herder, 1962–1971); idem, ed., *Epistula ad Thessalonicenses, Timotheum, Titum, Philemonem, Hebraeos* (VL 25; Freiburg: Herder, 1975–1991).

[67] H. J. Frede, *Kirchenschriftsteller: Verzeichnis und Sigel* (VL 1/1; Freiburg: Herder, 1981^{3}, superseded by 1995^{4}); idem, *Kirchenschriftsteller: Verzeichnis und Sigel: Aktualisierungsheft* (VL 1/1A; Freiburg: Herder, 1984, superseded by VL 1/1C, 1999 ed., by Roger Gryson). [Gryson has also published *Altlateinische Handschriften, Manuscrits vieux latins: Répertoire descriptif: Première partie: Mss 1–275* (VL 1/2A; Freiburg: Herder, 1999).]

On both projects, see B. M. Metzger, *The Early Versions of the New Testament: Their Origin, Transmission, and Limitations* (Oxford: Clarendon Press, 1977) 320–22.

[It appears that B. Fischer directed the Vetus Latina Institut until 1972, followed by Ursmar Engelmann until his death in 1986 (though *apud* Metzger, above, W. Thiele was in charge *de facto*); H. J. Frede then became director and he was succeeded in 1998 by Roger Gryson as head of the Institut. B. Fischer died in 1997; H. J. Frede in 1998.]

[68] Vetus Latina: Aus der Geschichte der lateinischen Bibel (Freiburg: Herder) [36 vols. through 1999].

[69] Robert P. Blake, ed., *The Old Georgian Version of the Gospel of Mark from the Adysh Gospels with the Variants of the Opiza and Tbet' Gospels* (PO 20:3; Turnhout, Belgium: Brepols, 1974); idem, ed., *The Old Georgian Version of the Gospel of Matthew from the Adysh Gospels with the Variants of the Opiza and Tbet' Gospels* (PO 24:1; Turnhout, Belgium: Brepols, 1976).

[70] Robert P. Blake and Maurice Brière, ed., *The Old Georgian Version of the Gospel of John from the Adysh Gospels with the Variants of the Opiza and Tbet' Gospels* (PO 26:4; Paris: Firmin-Didot, 1950).

[71] Maurice Brière, ed., *La version géorgienne ancienne de l'Evangile de Luc d'après les Evangiles d'Adich avec les variantes des Evangiles d'Opiza et de Tbet'* (PO 28:3; Paris: Firmin-Didot, 1955).

[72] Gérard Garitte, ed., *L'ancienne version géorgienne des Actes des Apôtres d'après deux*

Apocalypse by Josef Hofmann,[73] and the Coptic of John by Rodolphe Kasser.[74]

Among numerous studies of the versions are the comprehensive manuals by Vööbus[75] and Metzger,[76] and the masterful survey edited by Aland,[77] which contains studies by B. Fischer and W. Thiele on the Latin versions, M. Black on the Syriac, G. Mink on the Coptic, L. Leloir on the Armenian, J. Molitor on the Georgian, J. Hofmann on the Ethiopic, E. Stutz on the Gothic, and C. Hannick on the Old Church Slavonic, as well as chapters on the New Testament citations in Greek Fathers by P. Prigent and in Latin Fathers by H. J. Frede. Lists of versional manuscripts are provided by Metzger,[78] by Clemons for the Syriac of the Epistles and the Apocalypse,[79] and by Rhodes for the Armenian.[80] Monographs on the Latin versions have been authored by Zimmermann, Tinnefeld, Frede, Nellessen, Thiele, and Fischer;[81] on the Old Syriac Gospels

manuscrits du Sinaï (Bibliothèque du Muséon, 38; Louvain: Publications Universitaires, 1955).

[73] Josef Hofmann, ed., *Die äthiopische Übersetzung der Johannes-Apokalypse* (CSCO 281–82, Scriptores Aethiopici 55–56; Louvain: CSCO, 1967); idem, ed., *Die äthiopische Johannes-Apokalypse kritisch untersucht* (CSCO 297, Subsidia 33; Louvain: CSCO 1969).

[74] Rodolphe Kasser, *L'Evangile selon Saint Jean et les Versions coptes de la Bible* (Bibliotheque théologique; Neuchâtel: Delachaux et Niestlé, 1966).

[75] Arthur Vööbus, *Early Versions of the New Testament: Manuscript Studies* (Papers of the Estonian Theological Society in Exile 6; Stockholm: n.p., 1954).

[76] Bruce M. Metzger, *The Early Versions of the New Testament: Their Origin, Transmission, and Limitations* (Oxford: Clarendon Press, 1977).

[77] Kurt Aland, ed., *Die alten Übersetzungen des Neuen Testaments, die Kirchenväterzitate und Lektionare: Der gegenwärtige Stand ihrer Erforschung und ihre Bedeutung für die griechische Textgeschichte* (ANTF 5; Berlin/New York: de Gruyter, 1972).

[78] Metzger, *Early Versions*, in the sections on the various versions.

[79] James T. Clemons, *An Index of Syriac Manuscripts Containing the Epistles and the Apocalypse* (SD 33; Salt Lake City, UT: University of Utah Press, 1968).

[80] Erroll F. Rhodes, *An Annotated List of Armenian New Testament Manuscripts* (Annual Report of Theology, Monograph Series 1; Tokyo: Rikkyo [St. Paul's] University, 1959).

[81] Heinrich Zimmermann, *Untersuchungen zur Geschichte der altlateinischen Überlieferung des zweiten Korintherbriefes* (BBB 16; Bonn: Hanstein, 1960); Franz Hermann Tinnefeld, *Untersuchungen zur altlateinischen Überlieferung des 1. Timotheusbriefes* (Klassisch-philologische Studien 26; Wiesbaden: Harrassowitz, 1963); Hermann Josef Frede, *Altlateinische Paulus-Handschriften* (VLAGLB 4; Freiburg: Herder, 1964); Ernst Nellessen, *Untersuchungen zur altlateinischen Überlieferung des ersten Thessalonicherbriefes* (BBB 22; Bonn: Hanstein, 1965); Walter Thiele, *Die lateinischen Texte des 1. Petrusbriefes* (VLAGLB 5; Freiburg: Herder, 1965); Bonifatius Fischer, *Lateinische Bibelhandschriften im frühen Mittelalter* (VLAGLB 11; Freiburg: Herder, 1985).

by Vööbus[82] and the Old Syriac Paul by Kerschensteiner;[83] on the Syriac of the Gospels by Vööbus and by Strothmann;[84] on the Harclean Syriac by Zuntz,[85] and on the Peshitta by Vööbus;[86] on the Diatessaron by Lyonnet, Messina, Leloir, Henss, Ortiz de Urbina, Quispel, and W. L. Petersen;[87] on the Coptic Acts by Joussen;[88] on the Ethiopic Gospels by Vööbus and the Apocalypse by Hofmann;[89] on the Armenian by Lyonnet and by Leloir;[90] on the Old Georgian

---

[82] Arthur Vööbus, *Neue Angaben über die textgeschichtlichen Zustände in Edessa in den Jahren ca 326–340: Ein Beitrag zur Geschichte des altsyrischen Tetraevangeliums* (Papers of the Estonian Theological Society in Exile 3; Stockholm: n.p., 1951).

[83] Josef Kerschensteiner, *Der altsyrische Paulustext* (CSCO 315, Subsidia 37; Louvain: CSCO, 1970).

[84] Arthur Vööbus, *Studies in the History of the Gospel Text in Syriac* (CSCO 128, Subsidia 3; Louvain: Durbecq, 1951); Werner Strothmann, *Das Wolfenbütteler tetraevangelium syriacum: Lesarten und Lesungen* (Göttinger Orientforschungen, 1st series: Syriaca 2; Wiesbaden: Harrassowitz, 1971).

[85] Gunther Zuntz, *The Ancestry of the Harklean New Testament* (British Academy Supplemental Papers, 7; London: Oxford University Press, 1945; see now Sebastian Brock, "The Resolution of the Philoxenian/Harclean Problem," in Epp and Fee, eds., *New Testament Textual Criticism: Its Significance for Exegesis*, 325–43.

[86] Arthur Vööbus, *Researches on the Circulation of the Peshitta in the Middle of the Fifth Century* (Contributions of Baltic University, 64; Pinneburg: Baltic University, 1948).

[87] Stanislas Lyonnet, S.J., *Les origines de la version arménienne et le Diatessaron* (BibOr 13; Rome: Biblical Institute Press, 1950); Giuseppe Messina, S.J., *Diatessaron Persiano* (BibOr 14; Rome: Biblical Institute Press, 1951); Louis Leloir, *Le Témoignage d'Ephrem sur le Diatessaron* (CSCO 227, Subsidia 19; Louvain: CSCO, 1962); Walter Henss, *Das Verhältnis zwischen Diatessaron, christlicher Gnosis und "Western Text."* (BZNW 33; Berlin: Töpelmann, 1967); Ignatius Ortiz de Urbina, S.J., ed., *Vetus Evangeliorum Syrorum et exinde excerptum Diatessaron Tatiani* (Biblia Polyglotta Matritensia, 6; Madrid: Consejo Superior de investigaciones científicas, 1967); Gilles Quispel, *Tatian and the Gospel of Thomas: Studies in the History of the Western Diatessaron* (Leiden: Brill, 1975); and William Lawrence Petersen, *The Diatessaron and Ephrem Syrus as Sources of Romanos the Melodist* (CSCO 475, Subsidia 74; Louvain: CSCO/Peeters, 1985; [see now idem, *Tatian's Diatessaron: Its Creation, Dissemination, Significance, and History in Scholarship* (VCSup 25; Leiden: Brill, 1994)].

[88] Anton Joussen, *Die Koptischen Versionen der Apostelgeschichte (Kritik und Wertung)* (BBB 34; Bonn: Hanstein, 1969).

[89] Arthur Vööbus, *Die Spuren eines älteren äthiopischen Evangelientextes im Lichte der literarischen Monumente* (Papers of the Estonian Theological Society in Exile, 2; Stockholm, n.p., 1951); Josef Hofmann, ed., *Die äthiopische Übersetzung der Johannes-Apokalypse* (CSCO 281–82, Scriptores Aethiopici 55–56; Louvain: CSCO, 1967); idem, ed., *Die äthiopische Johannes-Apokalypse kritisch untersucht* (CSCO 297, Subsidia 33; Louvain: CSCO, 1969).

[90] Stanislas Lyonnet, S.J., *Les origines de la version arménienne et le Diatessaron* (BibOr 13; Rome: Biblical Institute Press, 1950); Louis Leloir, *Citations du Nouveau Testament dans l'ancienne tradition arménienne* (2 vols.; CSCO 283–84, Subsidia 31–32; Louvain: CSCO, 1967).

Gospels by Vööbus and by Molitor;[91] and on the Gothic by Friedrichsen.[92]

Regarding patristic quotations of the New Testament text, the postwar period has provided us with a four-volume index of citations by Allenbach et al.[93] and with a number of studies: Muncey on Ambrose;[94] Baarda on Aphrahat;[95] Mees and also Zaphris on Clement of Alexandria;[96] Greenlee on Cyril of Jerusalem;[97] Ehrman on Didymus the Blind;[98] Leloir and also Petersen on Ephrem;[99] Eldridge on Epiphanius of Salamis;[100] Blackman on Marcion;[101] Frede and also

[91] Arthur Vööbus, *Zur Geschichte des altgeorgischen Evangelientextes* (Papers of the Estonian Theological Society in Exile, 4; Stockholm, n.p., 1953); Joseph Molitor, *Synopsis latina evangeliorum Ibericorum antiquissimorum secundum Matthaeum, Marcum, Lucam desumpta e codicibus Adysh, Opiza, Tbeth necnon e fragmentis biblicis et patristicis quae dicuntur Chanmeti et Haemeti* (CSCO 256, Subsidia 24; Louvain: CSCO, 1965).

[92] George W. S. Friedrichsen, *Gothic Studies* (Medium Aevum Monographs, 6; Oxford: Blackwell, 1961).

[93] J. Allenbach *et al.*, *Biblia Patristica: Index des citations et allusions bibliques dans la littérature patristique* (Centre d'analyse et de documentation patristiques; Paris: Centre National de la Recherche Scientifique, 1975–1987). [Vol. 5 (1991); vol. 6 (1996).]

[94] R. W. Muncey, *The New Testament Text of Saint Ambrose* (TextsS 4; Cambridge: Cambridge University Press, 1959), but see the warning in B. M. Metzger, "Patristic Evidence," *NTS* 18 (1971/1972) 384 [repr. in Metzger, *New Testament Studies: Philological, Versional, and Patristic*, 172].

[95] Tjitze Baarda, *The Gospel Quotations of Aphrahat the Persian Sage. I: Aphrahat's Text of the Fourth Gospel* (2 vols.; Akademisch Proefschrift, Free University; Amsterdam: Krips Repro B. V. Meppel, 1975).

[96] Michael Mees, *Die Zitate aus dem Neuen Testament bei Clemons von Alexandrien* (Quaderni di "Vetera Christianorum," 2; Bari: Istituto di Letteratura Cristiana Antica, 1970); Gérassime Zaphiris, *Le texte de l'Evangile selon saint Matthieu d'après les citations de Clément d'Alexandrie comparées aux citations des Pères et des Théologiens grecs du IIe au XVe siecle* (Gembloux: Duculot, 1970).

[97] J. Harold Greenlee, *The Gospel Text of Cyril of Jerusalem* (SD 17; Copenhagen: Munksgaard, 1955).

[98] Bart D. Ehrman, *Didymus the Blind and the Text of the Gospels* (SBLNTGF 1; Atlanta: Scholars Press, 1986).

[99] Louis Leloir, *Saint Ephrem: Commentaire de l'Evangile concordant, version arménienne* (2 vols.; CSCO 137, 145, Scriptores armeniaci 1–2; Louvain: CSCO, 1953–1954); idem, *L'Evangile d'Ephrem d'après les oeuvres éditées: Recueil des Textes* (CSCO 180, Subsidia 12; Louvain: CSCO, 1958); idem, *Le Témoignage d'Ephrem sur le Diatessaron* (CSCO 227, Subsidia 19; Louvain: CSCO, 1962); idem, *Saint Ephrem: Commentaire de l'Evangile concordant, texte syriaque (Manuscrit Chester Beatty 709)* (Chester Beatty Monographs, 8; Dublin: Hodges Figgis, 1963); cf. idem, *Citations du Nouveau Testament dans l'ancienne tradition arménienne* (2 vols.; CSCO 283–84, Subsidia 31–32; Louvain: CSCO, 1967). W. L. Petersen, *The Diatessaron and Ephrem Syrus as Sources of Romanos the Melodist* (CSCO 475, Subsidia 74; Louvain: CSCO/Peeters, 1985).

[100] Lawrence Allen Eldridge, *The Gospel Text of Epiphanius of Salamis* (SD 41; Salt Lake City, UT: University of Utah Press, 1969).

[101] Edwin Cyril Blackman, *Marcion and His Influence* (London: SPCK, 1948).

Borse on Pelagius;[102] D. J. Fox on Philoxenus;[103] Hammond Bammel on Rufinus;[104] Vogels on Rufinus and Ambrosiaster;[105] Quispel on Tatian;[106] and Lo Bue on Tyconius.[107]

B. *Discoveries*

New materials are the "grist" of the text-critical "mill," and the premier discoveries of the post-World War II period are the Bodmer
90 papyri, notably P^{66}, P^{72}, P^{74}, and P^{75}.[108] These discoveries brought the
Chester Beatty papyri into renewed discussion, and a large literature developed on the New Testament papyrus manuscripts. In addition to the three Bodmer papyri mentioned above, other New Testament papyri numbered from P^{55} through P^{88} came to light after World War II.[109] P^{58} was found to belong to P^{33}; P^{64} and P^{67} were

[102] Hermann Josef Frede, *Pelagius der irische Paulustext Sedulius Scottus* (VLAGLB 3; Freiburg: Herder, 1961); Udo Borse, "Der Kolosserbrieftext des Pelagius" (Inaugural dissertation, Bonn; Bonn, 1966).

[103] Douglas J. Fox, *The "Matthew-Luke Commentary" of Philoxenus: Text, Translation and Critical Analysis* (SBLDS 43; Missoula, MT: Scholars Press, 1979).

[104] Caroline P. Hammond Bammel, *Der Römerbrieftext des Rufin und seine Origenes-Übersetzung* (VLAGLB 10; Freiburg: Herder, 1985). [See her later works: *Der Römerbriefkommentar des Origenes: Kritische Ausgabe der Übersetzung Rufins, Buch 1–3* (VLAGLB 16; Freiburg: Herder, 1990); idem, . . . *Buch 4–6* (VLAGLB 33; 1997); idem, *Buch 7–10* (VLAGLB 34; 1998); idem, *Origeniana et Rufiniana* (VLAGLB 29; Freiburg: Herder, 1996).]

[105] Heinrich Joseph Vogels, *Untersuchungen zum Text paulinischer Briefe bei Rufin und Ambrosiaster* (BBB 9; Bonn: Hanstein, 1955); idem, *Das Corpus Paulinum des Ambrosiaster* (BBB 13; Bonn: Hanstein, 1957).

[106] Gilles Quispel, *Tatian and the Gospel of Thomas: Studies in the History of the Western Diatessaron* (Leiden: Brill, 1975).

[107] Francesco Lo Bue, ed., *The Turin Fragments of Tyconius' Commentary on Revelation* (TextsS ns. 7; Cambridge: Cambridge University Press, 1963).

[108] Victor Martin, ed., *Papyrus Bodmer II: Evangile de Jean chap. 1–14* (Cologny-Genève: Bibliotheca Bodmeriana, 1956); idem, ed., *Papyrus Bodmer II: Supplement: Evangile de Jean chaps. 14–21* (new ed. [with facsimiles]; Cologny-Genève: Bibliotheca Bodmeriana, 1962); Michel Testuz, ed., *Papyrus Bodmer VII–IX. VII: L'Epître de Jude, VIII: Les deux Epîtres de Pierre, IX: Les Psaumes 33 et 34* (Cologny-Genève: Bibliotheca Bodmeriana, 1959); Rodolphe Kasser, ed., *Papyrus Bodmer XVII: Actes des Apôtres, Epîtres de Jacques, Pierre, Jean et Jude* (Cologny-Genève: Bibliotheca Bodmeriana, 1961); and Victor Martin and Rodolphe Kasser, eds., *Papyrus Bodmer XIV: Evangile de Luc chaps. 3–24 (P^{75})* (Cologny-Genève: Bibliotheca Bodmeriana, 1961) and eidem, *Papyrus Bodmer XV: Evangile de Jean chaps. 1–15 (P^{75})* (Cologny-Genève: Bibliotheca Bodmeriana, 1961).

[109] For P55, P56, P57, see Peter Sanz, ed., *Griechische literarische Papyri christlichen Inhaltes I (Biblica, Väterschriften und Verwandtes)* (Mitteilungen aus der Papyrussammlung

parts of the same manuscript;[110] and P[73], P[83], P[84], and P[87] remain unedited.[111]

This is not the place to attempt a survey of other manuscript discoveries since World War II, but additional Greek manuscripts were published in monograph form, including the Greek portions (with parts of the Gospels) of Codex Climaci Rescriptus by Moir; and nine majuscules (all palimpsests) by Greenlee.[112] Latin texts were published by Vogels and by Frede;[113] Syriac by Vööbus;[114] Coptic by Browne, Hintze and Schenke, Husselman, Kasser, Orlandi, Quecke, and Schenke;[115] and an Arabic manuscript of Paul by

der Nationalbibliothek in Wien, ns 4; Baden bei Wien: Rohrer, 1946); for P59, P60, P61, see Lionel Casson and Ernest L. Hettich, eds., *Excavations at Nessana. Volume 2: Literary Papyri* (Colt Archaeological Institute; Princeton, NJ: Princeton University Press; London: Oxford University Press, 1950); and for P81, Sergio Daris, ed., *Un nuovo frammento della prima lettera di Pietro (1 Petr 2,20–3,12)* (Papyrologica Castroctaviana 2. Barcelona: Papyrologica Castroctaviana, 1967). See also K. Aland, "Neue Neutestamentliche Papyri," *NTS* 3 (1956/57): 261–86; 9 (1962/63): 303–16; 10 (1963/64): 62–79; 11 (1964/65): 1–21; 20 (1973/74): 357–81; 22 (1975/76): 375–96. Parts 1 and 2 repr. in K. Aland, *Studien zur Überlieferung*, 91–136; 137–54; and idem, ed. for the Patristischen Arbeitsstelle of Münster: *Repertorium der griechischen christlichen Papyri. I: Biblische Papyri: Altes Testament, Neues Testament, Varia, Apokryphen* (PTS 18; Berlin/New York: De Gruyter, 1976).

110 Ramon Roca-Puig, ed., *Un papiro griego del evangelo de san Mateo* (2nd ed., with a note by Colin Roberts; Barcelona: Gremio Sindical de Maestros Impresores, 1962).

111 Place of publication for New Testament papyri may be found in the handbooks by Metzger, *Text of the New Testament*, 247–56, and by Aland and Aland, *Text of the New Testament*, 96–102. [Especially now Aland, *Kurzgefasste Liste*, 1994², 3–16, on New Testament papyri through P99, including P73 and P87; for P100–P115, see Kunst, *Bericht der Hermann Kunst-Stiftung für die Jahre 1995 bis 1998* (1998) 14–15; *Bericht der Hermann Kunst-Stiftung für die Jahre 1998 bis 2003* (2003) 74–80, which includes P116.]

112 Ian A. Moir, *"Codex Climaci Rescriptus Graecus": A Study of Portions of the Greek New Testament Comprising the Underwriting of Part of a Palimpsest in the Library of Westminster College, Cambridge (Ms. Gregory 1561, L)* (TextsS ns. 2; Cambridge: Cambridge University Press, 1956); J. Harold Greenlee, *Nine Uncial Palimpsests of the Greek New Testament* (SD 39; Salt Lake City, UT: University of Utah Press, 1968).

113 Heinrich Joseph Vogels, *Evangelium Colbertinum: Codex Lat. 254 der Bibliothèque Nationale zu Paris* (BBB 4–5; 2 vols.; Bonn: Hanstein, 1953); Hermann Josef Frede, *Ein Neuer Paulustext und Kommentar* (2 vols.; VLAGLB 7; Freiburg: Herder, 1973).

114 Arthur Vööbus, *The Apocalypse in the Harklean Version: A Facsimile Edition of MS. Mardin Orth. 35, fols. 143r–159v, with an Introduction* (CSCO 400 Subsidia 56; Louvain: CSCO, 1978).

115 Gerald M. Browne, ed., *Michigan Coptic Texts* (Studia et textus 7; Barcelona: Papyrologica Castroctaviana, 1979); Fritz Hintze and Hans-Martin Schenke, eds., *Die Berliner Handschrift der Sahidischen Apostelgeschichte (P. 15 926)* (TU 109; Berlin: Akademie-Verlag, 1970); Elinor M. Husselman, ed., *The Gospel of John in Fayumic Coptic (P. Mich. Inv. 3521)* (University of Michigan, Kelsey Museum of Archaeology

Staal.[116] Publication of additional texts can be found in various other places,[117] including a new series inaugurated in 1981, *New Documents Illustrating Early Christianity*, edited by G. H. R. Horsley, which treats both papyri and inscriptions.[118]

Additional studies of Greek manuscripts were contributed by Fee on P66;[119] by Kubo on P72 and Vaticanus;[120] by Cavallo on Greek majuscules;[121] by M. Davies on several Pauline minuscules;[122] by

---

Studies, 2; Ann Arbor, MI: Kelsey Museum of Archaeology, 1962); Rodolphe Kasser, ed., *Papyrus Bodmer III: Evangile de Jean et Genèse I–IV,2 en Bohaïrique* (CSCO 177–78, Scriptores coptici 25–26; Louvain: CSCO, 1958); idem, ed., *Papyrus Bodmer XIX: Evangile de Matthieu XIV,28–XXVIII,20, Epître aux Romains I,1–II,3 en sahidique* (Cologny-Genève: Bibliotheca Bodmeriana, 1962); Tito Orlandi, ed., *Papiri della Università degli Studi di Milano (P. Mil. Copti). Volume Quinto: Lettere di San Paolo in Copto-Ossirinchita* (Milan: Istituto Editoriale Cisalpino-La Goliardica, 1974); Hans Quecke, ed., *Das Markusevangelium saïdisch: Text der Handschrift PPalau Rib. Inv.-Nr. 182 mit den Varianten der Handschrift M 569* (Studia et textus 4; Barcelona: Papyrologica Castroctaviana, 1972); idem, ed., *Das Lukasevangelium saïdisch: Text der Handschrift PPalau Rib. Inv.-Nr. 181 mit den Varianten der Handschrift M 569* (Studia et textus 6; Barcelona: Papyrologica Castroctaviana, 1977); idem, ed., *Das Johannesevangelium saïdisch: Text der Handschrift PPalau Rib. Inv.-Nr. 183 mit den Varianten der Handschrift M 813 und 814 der Chester Beatty Library und der Handschrift M 569* (Studia et textus 11; Barcelona: Papyrologica Castroctaviana, 1984); and Hans-Martin Schenke, ed., *Das Matthäus-Evangelium im mittelägyptischen Dialekt des Koptischen (Codex Scheide)* (TU 127; Berlin: Akademie-Verlag, 1981).

[116] Harvey Staal, *Codex Sinai Arabic 151: Pauline Epistles* (2 vols.; SD 40; Salt Lake City, UT: University of Utah Press, 1969).

[117] For instance, ten items by various editors in K. Aland, ed., *Materialien zur neutestamentlichen Handschriftenkunde I* (ANTF 3; Berlin: De Gruyter, 1969); J. Neville Birdsall and Robert W. Thomson, eds., *Biblical and Patristic Studies in Memory of Robert Pierce Casey* (Freiburg/Basel/New York: Herder, 1963) 33–63; three in J. Keith Elliott, ed., *Studies in New Testament Language and Text: Essays in Honour of George D. Kilpatrick on the Occasion of His Sixty-fifth Birthday* (NovTSup 44; Leiden: Brill, 1976) 235–38, 262–75, 301–12.

[118] *New Documents Illustrating Early Christianity: A Review of the Greek Inscriptions and Papyri Published in 1976* (ed. G. H. R. Horsley; North Ryde, Australia: Ancient History Documentary Research Centre, Macquarie University, 1981). [Vols. 1–5 (1985) ed. by Horsley; vol. 6 (1992)-9 (2002) by S. R. Llewelyn; vol. 8 (1998) ff. co-published by Eerdmans.]

[119] Gordon D. Fee, *Papyrus Bodmer II (P^{66}): Its Textual Relationships and Scribal Characteristics* (SD 34. Salt Lake City, UT: University of Utah Press, 1968).

[120] Sakae Kubo, *P^{72} and the Codex Vaticanus* (SD 27; Salt Lake City, UT: University of Utah Press, 1965).

[121] Guglielmo Cavallo, *Ricerche sulla maiuscola biblica* (2 vols.; Studi e testi di papirologia 2; Florence: Le Monnier, 1967). Note also the curious matter discussed by J. K. Elliott in *Codex Sinaiticus and the Simonides Affair: Examination of the Nineteenth Century Claim That the Codex Sinaiticus Was Not an Ancient Manuscript* (Analecta Vlatadon 33; Thessaloniki: Patriarchal Institute for Patristic Studies, 1982).

[122] Margaret Davies, *The Text of the Pauline Epistles in Manuscript 2344 and Its Relationship to the Text of Other Known Manuscripts, in Particular to 330, 436 and 462* (SD

Geerlings on *Family 13, Family Π,* and (also by Champlin) on *Family E.*[123] Studies of the Greek lectionary text were provided by Bray, Buck, and Harms[124] in the Chicago series on Studies in the Lectionary Text of the Greek New Testament; by Cocroft[125] in Studies and Documents; and in a virtual monograph by Junack.[126] Finally, Reuss issued three volumes on Greek catena;[127] Treu published a list of New Testament manuscripts in the U.S.S.R.;[128] and Voicu and D'Alisera furnished an index of facsimiles of Greek New Testament manuscripts.[129] Naturally, there was much more activity that cannot be encompassed in this brief survey.

38; Salt Lake City, UT: University of Utah Press, 1968). Note also the publication by William Henry Paine Hatch, *Facsimiles and Descriptions of Minuscule Manuscripts of the New Testament* (Cambridge, MA: Harvard University Press, 1951); and B. M. Metzger, *Manuscripts of the Greek Bible: An Introduction to Greek Palaeography* (New York/Oxford: Oxford University Press, 1981).

[123] Jacob Geerlings, *Family 13—The Ferrar Group: The Text according to Matthew* (SD 19; Salt Lake City, UT: University of Utah Press, 1961); idem, *Family 13—The Ferrar Group: The Text according to Luke* (SD 20; Salt Lake City, UT: University of Utah Press, 1961); idem, *Family 13—The Ferrar Group: The Text according to John* (SD 21; Salt Lake City, UT: University of Utah Press, 1962); idem, *Family Π in Luke* (SD 22; Salt Lake City, UT: University of Utah Press, 1962); idem, *Family Π in John* (SD 23; Salt Lake City, UT: University of Utah Press, 1963); idem, *Family Π in Matthew* (SD 24; Salt Lake City, UT: University of Utah Press, 1964); idem, *Family E and Its Allies in Mark* (SD 31; Salt Lake City, UT: University of Utah Press, 1968); idem, *Family E and Its Allies in Luke* (SD 35; Salt Lake City, UT: University of Utah Press, 1968); Russell Champlin, *Family E and Its Allies in Matthew* (SD 28; Salt Lake City, UT: University of Utah Press, 1966).

[124] William D. Bray, *The Weekday Lessons from Luke in the Greek Gospel Lectionary* (Studies in the Lectionary Text of the Greek New Testament 2:5; Chicago: University of Chicago Press, 1959); Harry Merwyn Buck, *The Johannine Lessons in the Greek Gospel Lectionary* (Studies in the Lectionary Text of the Greek New Testament 2:4; Chicago: University of Chicago Press, 1958); Ray Harms, *The Matthean Weekday Lessons in the Greek Gospel Lectionary* (Studies in the Lectionary Text of the Greek New Testament 2:6; Chicago: University of Chicago Press, 1966).

[125] Ronald E. Cocroft, *A Study of the Pauline Lessons in the Matthean Section of the Greek Lectionary* (SD 32; Salt Lake City, UT: University of Utah Press, 1968).

[126] Klaus Junack, "Zu den griechischen Lektionaren und ihrer Überlieferung der Katholischen Briefe," in K. Aland, ed., *Die alten Übersetzungen des Neuen Testaments,* 498–591; cf. B. M. Metzger, "Greek Lectionaries and a Critical Edition of the Greek New Testament," ibid., 479–97.

[127] Joseph Reuss, *Matthäus-Kommentare aus der grieschischen Kirche aus Katenenhandschriften* (TU 61; Berlin: Akademie-Verlag, 1957); idem, *Johannes-Kommentare aus der grieschischen Kirche aus Katenenhandschriften* (TU 89; Berlin: Akademie-Verlag, 1966); idem, *Lukas-Kommentare aus der grieschischen Kirche aus Katenenhandschriften* (TU 130; Berlin: Akademie-Verlag, 1984).

[128] Kurt Treu, *Die griechischen Handschriften des Neuen Testaments in der UdSSR* (TU 91; Berlin: Akademie-Verlag, 1966).

[129] Sever J. Voicu and Serenella D'Alisera, *I.MA.G.E.S.: Index in manuscriptorum graecorum edita specimina* (Rome: Borla, 1981).

Current lists of all majuscules and important minuscules can be found in Aland and Aland's *Text of the New Testament*[130] and in Kurt Aland's *Kurzgefasste Liste*.[131] Surveys of discoveries, not only of Greek manuscripts but also of versional materials, have been offered by Metzger in various articles.[132]

C. *Methods*

The postwar period was a rich one for text-critical methodology. This evaluation may be placed in context by recalling the basic (though not the only) task of New Testament textual criticism—recovery of the original text—and by reviewing the fundamental methods employed to accomplish that task. In view of our earlier survey of its history, New Testament textual criticism obviously is a
91 highly complex discipline, yet in conception it really is relatively simple. Actually, the same circumstance accounts for both descriptions—both its complexity and its simplicity—and that circumstance is the vast quantity of raw material available to us: For the New Testament—a rather small volume of writings—we possess some 5,355 Greek manuscripts alone (86 different papyri, 274 uncials, 2795 minuscules, and about 2,200 lectionaries),[133] plus thousands of versional documents and an untold number of patristic citations. The point is that we have so many manuscripts of the New Testament and that these manuscripts contain so many variant readings that surely the original reading in every case is somewhere present in our vast store of material. In theory, then, that should make the task of recovering the original text relatively simple. Incidentally, this vast number of

[130] Aland and Aland, *Text of the New Testament*, 103–38.

[131] K. Aland, *Kurzgefasste Liste* (1963^{1}), 37–202; for lectionaries, 205–318 [see now ibid., 1994^{2}, 19–215 (majuscules through 0306; minuscules through 2856); 219–370 (lectionaries through *l*2403). For 0307–0309; 2857–2862; *ll*2404–2412 see H. Kunst, *Bericht der Hermann Kunst-Stiftung . . . 1995 bis 1998* (1998) 16–18.]

[132] Metzger, "A Survey of Recent Research on the Ancient Versions of the New Testament," *NTS* 2 (1955/56) 1–16; idem, "Recent Discoveries and Investigations of New Testament Manuscripts," *JBL* 78 (1959) 13–20; idem, "Recent Contributions to the Study of the Ancient Versions of the New Testament," *The Bible in Modern Scholarship: Papers Read at the 100th Meeting of the Society of Biblical Literature, December 28–30, 1964* (ed. J. Philip Hyatt; Nashville/New York: Abingdon, 1965) 347–69.

[133] Aland and Aland, *Text of the New Testament*, 96–106, 128, 163. [See n. 131 above; in 1998 there were about 5,700 Greek manuscripts of the New Testament, and perhaps in excess of 5,300 *different* Greek manuscripts.]

manuscripts is the reason that conjectures—which play so large a role in the textual criticism of classical literature, and also in that of the Old Testament—are rare and almost nonexistent in New Testament textual studies.[134]

We have, therefore, a genuine embarrassment of riches in the quantity of manuscripts that we possess, and this accounts, on the one hand, for the optimism in the discipline and for the promise of solid results, but also, on the other hand, for the extreme complexity in the study of the New Testament text. The writings of no Greek classical author are preserved on this scale. Among the most popular ancient authors, Homer's *Iliad* is found in fewer than 700 Greek manuscripts, Euripides' tragedies in somewhat more than 300, but other ancient writings, such as the first six books of the Latin *Annals* of Tacitus, are preserved only in a single manuscript.[135]

The riches in New Testament manuscripts, however, are not only in their *quantity* but also in their *quality*. Here I refer primarily to age. As is well known, the interval between the author and the earliest extant manuscripts for most classical writings is commonly hundreds—sometimes many hundreds—of years, and a thousand-year interval is not uncommon. In the examples given a moment ago, that single manuscript of Tacitus dates from the ninth century, and most of Euripides' manuscripts are from the Byzantine period.[136] Of course, most of the New Testament manuscripts are also of late date, but what is striking is that so many others are early and that the interval between the New Testament authors' times and the transmission dates of a sizable number of extensive manuscripts is only a century, more or less. In at least one case, P^{52} of John's Gospel, the interval may be as brief as twenty-five years. In addition, we have two elegant parchment manuscripts from about the year 350, codices Vaticanus (B) and Sinaiticus (א). This aspect of quality stands in sharp contrast to much other ancient literature. By the way, for

[134] See, e.g., J. K. Elliott, "Can We Recover the Original New Testament?" *Theology* 77 (1974) 352; G. D. Kilpatrick, "Conjectural Emendation in the New Testament," in Epp and Fee, eds., *New Testament Textual Criticism: Its Significance for Exegesis*, 349–60; Erroll F. Rhodes, "Conjectural Emendations in Modern Translations," ibid., 361–74; but to the contrary, see, e.g., John Strugnell, "A Plea for Conjectural Emendation in the New Testament, with a Coda on 1 Cor 4:6," *CBQ* 36 (1971) 543–58.

[135] See Metzger, *Text of the New Testament*, 34–35.

[136] Ibid.

the most part the oldest manuscripts of the New Testament have been found most recently, for the Chester Beatty and Bodmer papyri turned up in the 1930s and 1950s, respectively.

92 We must not exaggerate the New Testament manuscript materials, however, for the vast majority of the early papyri are highly fragmentary, and among the earliest uncial manuscripts only Codex Sinaiticus (א) contains the entire New Testament—though about fifty later manuscripts also provide complete coverage. The Apocalypse of John is the least well preserved, being found in only 287 Greek manuscripts—still a rather lavish scale of preservation for a writing of modest size.[137] Far more numerous are the witnesses to the Gospel of Luke, for which the IGNTP's elaborate apparatus has recently been published.[138] The new apparatus presents the textual evidence from eight papyri that contain portions of Luke; from sixty-two uncial manuscripts (out of sixty-nine that contain Luke); from 128 minuscules (scientifically selected from the nearly 1700 extant minuscule manuscripts of Luke); and from 41 lectionary manuscripts (scientifically selected to represent the hundreds that contain Luke); as well as evidence from the Latin, Syriac, Coptic, Armenian, Georgian, Ethiopic, Gothic, and Old Church Slavonic versions, from the Arabic and Persian Diatessaron; and from all Greek and Latin Church Fathers up to 500 C.E., as well as evidence from selected Syriac Church Fathers. And that is just the Gospel of Luke as it has come down to us in the process of transmission!

These are some indications of the riches in manuscripts that we possess for determining the original text of the New Testament; the embarrassment is that we have not often been able to agree on solutions or, in fact, to find satisfactory solutions at all for some of our leading problems.

If, then, the original reading in virtually every case is somewhere present in our raw material, the only problem is how to find that original reading—and, by extension, how to find the original text of the Greek New Testament as a whole. There are essentially three ways to identify the most likely original reading:

---

[137] Aland and Aland, *Text of the New Testament*, 78–79.

[138] American and British Committees of the International Greek New Testament Project, ed., *The New Testament in Greek: The Gospel according to St. Luke* (2 vols.).

1. *Historical-documentary method*

A first method attempts to reconstruct the history of the New Testament text by tracing the lines of transmission back through our extant manuscripts to the very earliest stages and then choosing the reading that represents the earliest attainable level of the textual tradition.

It is not, of course, that simple, but the theory is that we should be able to organize all of our extant manuscripts into groups or clusters, each of which has a very similar type of text. Then, as a result of this process of reconstruction, we would or should be able to identify some clusters of manuscripts—or ideally one such cluster—that represent the earliest known group, and therefore to identify other groups that fall into an identifiable chronological succession—groups, that is, that are later. Further, this method attempts to reconstruct the streams of textual transmission that have brought our extant manuscripts to us, conceiving of each manuscript as a point on a 93
trajectory of textual transmission. If these clusters and streams can be reconstructed with any measure of certainty, then we shall have isolated the earliest stages of those streams or the earliest points on those trajectories, and we shall have isolated also the earliest clusters, that is, the earliest types of text in the transmission process. If this were to result in the identification of only one very early cluster, succeeded by one or more later clusters, then readings belonging to that earliest cluster might legitimately be identified as those closest to the original and as most plausibly the original readings.

Ideally, then, when faced with a variation-unit—that is, a New Testament passage in which the manuscript tradition presents two or more differing textual readings—the reading would be chosen that comes from the earliest cluster or stream of textual tradition. This is the traditional method of external or documentary textual criticism, so-called because it emphasizes external criteria—such as the age and provenance of a document or manuscript, as well as the general quality of its scribe and its text.[139] It might, therefore, be

[139] On scribal habits, see Colwell, "External Evidence and New Testament Criticism," in Daniels and Suggs, *Studies in the History and Text of the New Testament*, 9–11; idem, "Method in Evaluating Scribal Habits: A Study in the Corruption of the Text," in Hyatt, *Bible in Modern Scholarship* 370–89 [repr. as "Method in Evaluating Scribal Habits: A Study of the Text of P^{45}, P^{66}, P^{75}," in Colwell, *Studies in Methodology*

called the "historical-documentary" (or even the "historical-genealogical" method, though strict genealogical method has never been feasible in New Testament textual criticism, for there is too much textual mixture in the complex array of manuscripts.[140]

The earliest papyri, as well as the early majuscule manuscripts, play a significant role in this historical-documentary method. These early manuscripts have the highest possible value, which is even more greatly enhanced in proportion to their age, and the reason for this high value is just as obvious: the early papyri offer for the first time a realistic hope of reconstructing the history of the New Testament text in the 150- to 200-year period preceding the great parchment codices Vaticanus (B) and Sinaiticus (א) and the other great landmarks of textual history, such as codices Alexandrinus (A), Bezae (D), Washingtonianus (W), and a grand host of others. We shall explore these possibilities in Section III, below.

There are, of course, complications of enormous complexity in pursuing this historical-documentary model, some of which will be discussed later.[141] Yet many textual critics, particularly those in this country who were inspired by recent scholars like Kenneth Clark and Ernest Colwell,[142] are convinced that this is the path that must be followed and that the isolation of the earliest text-types must be

---

in *Textual Criticism of the New Testament* (NTTS 9; Leiden: Brill, 1969) 106–24]; Fee, *Papyrus Bodmer II (P^{66})*; James R. Royse, "Scribal Habits in the Transmission of New Testament Texts," in O'Flaherty, *Critical Study of the Sacred Texts*, 139–61 [see his forthcoming *Scribal Habits in Early Greek New Testament Papyri* (SD 47; Grand Rapids, MI: Eerdmans, 2005]; Klaus Junack, "Abschreibpraktiken und Schreibergewohnheiten in ihrer Auswirkung auf die Textüberlieferung," in Epp and Fee (eds.), *New Testament Textual Criticism: Its Significance for Exegesis*, 277–95.

[140] Colwell, "Genealogical Method: Its Achievements and Its Limitations," *JBL* 66 (1947) 109–33, esp. 114–16; 130–32 [repr. in Colwell, *Studies in Methodology in Textual Criticism*, 63–83, esp. 67–69; 81–83]; J. Neville Birdsall, "The New Testament Text," *The Cambridge History of the Bible: Volume 1: From the Beginnings to Jerome* (ed. P. R. Ackroyd and C. F. Evans; Cambridge: Cambridge University Press, 1970) 317; cf. Gunther Zuntz, *The Text of the Epistles: A Disquisition upon the Corpus Paulinum* (Schweich Lectures, 1946; London: British Academy, 1953) 8–9.

[141] See also Birdsall, "The New Testament Text," 309–17.

[142] See, e.g., Kenneth W. Clark, "The Effect of Recent Textual Criticism upon New Testament Studies," *The Background of the New Testament and Its Eschatology* (ed. W. D. Davies and D. Daube; Cambridge: Cambridge University Press, 1956) 27–50 [repr. 65–89 in Clark, *The Gentile Bias*, 65–89]; idem, "Today's Problem with the Critical Text of the New Testament," *Transitions in Biblical Scholarship* (ed. J. Coert Rylaarsdam; Essays in Divinity, 6; Chicago/London: University of Chicago Press, 1968) 157–69]; and Ernest Colwell, "External Evidence and New Testament Criticism," 1–12; idem, *Studies in Methodology in Textual Criticism*, esp. chaps. 1–8, 11.

our goal. We are convinced that only in this way can a solid foundation be laid for understanding the history of our New Testament text and that only in this way can we secure a large measure of confidence that we are genuinely in touch with the actual, historical origin of the New Testament writings. It was in this spirit and with these goals that the IGNTP was developed and that much postwar text-critical work was pursued, including the extensive studies 94
in quantitative measurements of manuscript relationships.

The development of quantitative measures to establish relationships between and among manuscripts by comparing the extent to which they share significant readings has an extended history, as demonstrated by Duplacy,[143] but E. C. Colwell, with E. W. Tune, provided (in 1963) the recent inspiration for the methods currently in use,[144] with important refinements provided by Gordon Fee, and others subsequently.[145]

[143] Jean Duplacy, "Classification des états d'un texte, mathématiques et informatique: Repères historiques et recherches méthodologiques," *Revue d'Histoire des Textes* 5 (1975) 249–309 [repr. in Duplacy, *Etudes de critique textuelle du Nouveau Testament* (ed. Joël Delobel; BETL 78; Leuven: Leuven University Press/Peeters, 1987) 193–257.

[144] Ernest C. Colwell and Ernst W. Tune, "The Quantitative Relationships between MS. Text-types," in Birdsall and Thomson, *Biblical and Patristic Studies*, 25–32 [repr. as "Method in Establishing Quantitative Relationships between Text-Types of New Testament Manuscripts," in Colwell, *Studies in Methodology in Textual Criticism*, 56–62.

[145] Fee, *Papyrus Bodmer II (P[66])*; idem, "Codex Sinaiticus in the Gospel of John: A Contribution to Methodology in Establishing Textual Relationships," *NTS* 15 (1968/69) 23–44; idem, "Text of John in Origen and Cyril of Alexandria"; idem, "P[75], P[66], and Origen: The Myth of Early Textual Recension in Alexandria," *New Dimensions in New Testament Study* (ed. Richard N. Longenecker, and Merrill C. Tenney; Grand Rapids, MI: Zondervan, 1974) 3–45 [preceding three articles repr. in Epp and Fee, *Studies in the Theory and Method*, 221–43; 301–34; 247–73 respectively]; see also Larry W. Hurtado, *Text-critical Methodology and the Pre-Caesarean Text: Codex W in the Gospel of Mark* (SD 43; Grand Rapids, MI: Eerdmans, 1981); Paul R. McReynolds, "Establishing Text Families"; John G. Griffith, "Numerical Taxonomy and Some Primary Manuscripts of the Gospels," *JTS* 20 (1969) 389–406; idem, "The Interrelations of Some Primary MSS of the Gospels in the Light of Numerical Analysis," *SE* 6 (1973) 221–38; idem, "A Three-Dimensional Model for Classifying Arrays of Manuscripts by Cluster-Analysis," *Studia Patristica* 15 1984) 79–83; Wisse, *The Profile Method* and the discussion above on the Claremont Profile Method; cf. Vinton A. Dearing, *A Manual Textual Analysis* (Berkeley/Los Angeles: University of California Press, 1959); idem, *Principles and Practice of Textual Analysis* (Berkeley/Los Angeles: University of California Press, 1974); idem, "Determining Variations by Computer," *SBLSP* (1974) 14–35. For surveys of such methods, see Wisse, *The Profile Method*, 19–32; Epp, "Twentieth Century Interlude," 407–10 [repr. in Epp and Fee, *Studies in the Theory and Method*, 101–4], but above all the comprehensive treatment of the entire history of quantitative methods by Duplacy (see n. 143, above).

Even the assessment of textual variation for theological motivation arose out of this approach, for the aim of the historical-documentary method has always been the better understanding of manuscripts (à la Hort). If theological or ideological bias could be identified in any manuscript, that would aid in placing it in its proper position in the textual streams or clusters—or identifying it as an aberrant member of a cluster. The postwar period witnessed much discussion and some controversy in this area, primarily related to the "Western" text.[146]

---

[146] See Philippe Henri Menoud, "The Western Text and the Theology of Acts," *Studiorum Novi Testamenti Societas, Bulletin* 2 (1951) 19–32 [repr. in *Bulletin of the Studiorum Novi Testamenti Societas I–III* (Cambridge: Cambridge University Press, 1963, and in Menoud, *Jesus Christ and the Faith: A Collection of Studies* (PTMS 18; Pittsburgh: Pickwick, 1978) 61–83]; Leon E. Wright, *Alterations of the Words of Jesus as Quoted in the Literature of the Second Century* (Harvard Historical Monographs 25; Cambridge, MA: Harvard University Press, 1952); Erich Fascher, *Textgeschichte als hermeneutisches Problem* (Halle [Salle]: Niemeyer, 1953); Epp, *The Theological Tendency of Codex Bezae Cantabrigiensis in Acts* (SNTSMS 3; Cambridge/New York: Cambridge University Press, 1966) [repr. Eugene, OR: Wipf and Scott, 2001]; idem, "The Ascension in the Textual Tradition of Luke-Acts," in Epp and Fee *New Testament Textual Criticism: Its Significance for Exegesis*, 131–45; Charles Kingsley Barrett, "Is There a Theological Tendency in Codex Bezae?" in Best and Wilson, *Text and Interpretation*, 15–27; Carlo M. Martini, *La parola di Dio alle origini della Chiesa* (AnBib 93; Rome: Biblical Institute Press, 1980) 103–13; 165–79; (181–88); George E. Rice, "The Anti-Judaic Bias of the Western Text in the Gospel of Luke," *AUSS* 18 (1980) 51–57; idem, "Some Further Examples of Anti-Judaic Bias in the Western Text of the Gospel of Luke," *AUSS* 18 (1980) 149–56; idem, "Western Non-interpolations: A Defense of the Apostolate," pp. 1–16 in *Luke-Acts: New Perspectives from the Society of Biblical Literature Seminar* (ed. C. H. Talbert; New York: Crossroad, 1984); idem, "Is Bezae a Homogeneous Codex?" pp. 39–54 in *Perspectives on the New Testament: Essays in Honor of Frank Stagg* (ed. C. H. Talbert; Macon, GA: Mercer University Press, 1985); Howard Eshbaugh, "Textual Variants and Theology: A Study of the Galatians Text of Papyrus 46," *JSNT* 3 (1979) 60–72; Alexander Globe, "Some Doctrinal Variants in Matthew 1 and Luke 2, and the Authority of the Neutral Text," *CBQ* 42 (1980) 52–72; Matthew Black, "Notes on the Longer and Shorter Text of Acts," *On Language, Culture, and Religion in Honor of Eugene A. Nida* (ed. M. Black and W. A. Smalley; The Hague/Paris: Mouton, 1974) 119–31; idem, "The Holy Spirit in the Western Text of Acts," in Epp and Fee, *New Testament Textual Criticism: Its Significance for Exegesis*, 159–70; Richard I. Pervo, "Social and Religious Aspects of the Western Text," *The Living Text: Essays in Honor of Ernest W. Saunders* (ed. D. E. Groh and R. Jewett; Lanham/New York/London: University Press of America, 1985) 229–41; Ben Witherington, "The Anti-Feminist Tendencies of the 'Western' Text of Acts," *JBL* 103 (1984) 82–84; Joël Delobel, "Luke 6,5 in Codex Bezae: The Man Who Worked on Sabbath," *A cause de l'évangile: Mélanges offerts à Dom Jacques Dupont* (LD 123; Paris: Cerf, 1985) 453–77; also C. S. C. Williams, *Alterations to the Text of the Synoptic Gospels and Acts* (Oxford: Blackwell, 1951); K. W. Clark, "Textual Criticism and Doctrine," *Studia Paulina in honorem Johannes de Zwaan septuagenari* (ed. J. N. Sevenster and W. C. Van Unnik; Haarlem: Bohn, 1953) 52–65 [repr. in Clark,

E. C. Colwell[147] referred to the working out of this external method of textual criticism as "the task of the next generation," and some of its leading problems and possible ways toward solutions will be explored in Section III, below.

2. *Rigorous eclectic method*

At the opposite extreme stands a second method, which examines all the variants available to us in a given variation unit and selects the reading that makes the best sense in terms of the internal criteria. That is, we select the variant reading that best suits the context of the passage, the author's style and vocabulary, or the author's theology, while taking into account such factors as scribal habits, including their tendency of conformity to Koine or Attic Greek style,[148] to Semitic forms of expression, to parallel passages, to Old Testament passages, or to liturgical forms and usage. This method, therefore, emphasizes internal evidence and is called "rigorous" or "thoroughgoing" eclecticism, and also "rational" or "impartial criticism" by its proponents.[149]

Actually, this is a method of recent vintage that is practiced primarily by two fine and persistent British scholars, George D. Kilpatrick [who died in 1989] and J. Keith Elliott. It stems largely, however, from C. H. Turner's famous "Notes" on Marcan usage published 95

The Gentile Bias, 90–103] idem, "The Theological Relevance of Textual Variation in Current Criticism of the Greek New Testament," *JBL* 85 (1966) 1–16 [repr. in Clark, *The Gentile Bias*, 104–19]. [For a review of issues on tendencies in the "Western" text of Acts, see now, E. J. Epp, "The Anti-Judaic Tendencies in the D-Text of Acts: Forty Years of Conversation," *The Book of Acts as Church History: Text, Textual Traditions and Ancient Interpretations/Apostelgeschichte als Kirchengeschichte: Text, Texttraditionen und antike Auslegungen* (ed. Tobias Nicklas and Michael Tilly; BZNW120; Berlin/New York: de Gruyter, 2003) 111–46.] See also James D. Yoder, *Concordance to the Distinctive Greek Text of Codex Bezae* (NTTS 2. Leiden: Brill, 1961).

147 Colwell, "External Evidence and New Testament Criticism," 5.

148 George D. Kilpatrick, "Atticism and the Text of the Greek New Testament," in *Neutestamentliche Aufsätze: Festschrift für Prof. Josef Schmid zum 70. Geburtstag* (ed. J. Blinzler, O. Kuss, and F. Mussner; Regensburg: Pustet, 1963) 125–37; see the caution by Martini, "Eclecticism and Atticism in the Textual Criticism of the Greek New Testament," *On Language, Culture, and Religion: In Honor of Eugene A. Nida* (ed. M. Black and W. A. Smalley; The Hague/Paris: Mouton, 1974) 145–52.

149 J. K. Elliott, "In Defense of Thoroughgoing Eclecticism in New Testament Textual Criticism," *ResQ* 21 (1978) 95; Epp, "Eclectic Method," 251–55; Fee, "Rigorous or Reasoned Eclecticism–Which?" in Elliott, *Studies in New Testament Language and Text*, 174–76.

during the 1920s, on the first page of which Turner altered Westcott-Hort's famous dictum "Knowledge of documents should precede final judgement upon readings" to "Knowledge of an author's usage should precede final judgement."[150] Kilpatrick's views appeared during World War II, beginning in 1943 and 1944, and a few phrases quoted from him and Elliott will clarify the method further. Kilpatrick says: "The decision rests ultimately with the criteria as distinct from the manuscripts, and . . . our evaluation of the manuscripts must be determined by the criteria";[151] or "Each reading has to be judged on its merits and not on its [manuscript] supports"; or "Readings must be considered severally on their intrinsic character. Further, contrary to what Hort maintained, decisions about readings must precede decisions about the value or weight of manuscripts."[152] Elliott says: "The cult of the best manuscripts gives way to the cult of the best reading"; and the method "devotes its main attention to the individual variants themselves and very little attention to external evidence,"[153] for "we are concerned with which reading is likely to represent what our original author wrote. We are not concerned with the age, prestige or popularity of the manuscripts supporting the readings we would adopt as original";[154] or "The thoroughgoing eclectic would accept the reading which best suited the context and would base his reasons on exclusively internal criteria";[155] or, finally, "It seems to be more constructive to discuss as a priority the worth of readings rather than the worth of manuscripts."[156]

From these quotations it is at once apparent that to these rigorous eclectics the New Testament manuscripts are repositories of raw material and have independent importance only to the extent that they may furnish textual variants or readings that may commend

---

[150] C. H. Turner, "Marcan Usage: Notes, Critical and Exegetical, on the Second Gospel," *JTS* 25 (1923/1924) 377; Westcott and Hort, *The New Testament in the Original Greek*, 2.ix; 31; see Epp, "Eclectic Method," 250–51.

[151] G. D. Kilpatrick, "Western Text and Original Text in the Gospels and Acts," *JTS* 44 (1943) 25–26.

[152] Idem, "The Greek New Testament Text of Today and the *Textus Receptus*," *The New Testament in Historical and Contemporary Perspective: Essays in Memory of G. H. C. MacGregor* (ed. H. Anderson and W. Barclay; Oxford: Blackwell, 1965) 205–6.

[153] J. K. Elliott, "Rational Criticism and the Text of the New Testament," *Theology* 75 (1972) 340).

[154] Idem, "Can We Recover the Original New Testament?" 352.

[155] Idem, "In Defense of Thoroughgoing Eclecticism, 99.

[156] Ibid., 115.

themselves as original by the application of internal criteria: Does a new reading conform to the author's style and vocabulary, to his theology, to the context? Can it explain the origin of the other readings? If so, it may well be judged the original reading. The fact that many of the papyri and the great fourth century uncials are extremely early does not, in this method, lend to them any special consideration or authority, nor does it account them as possessing any special character or value. It is well known that rigorous eclectics diligently search the late Byzantine manuscripts for readings that might be original and that they have accredited scores of such readings, for—as Kilpatrick put it—"the outright condemnation of the Byzantine text by Westcott and Hort was one of the main errors in practice of their work."[157] So, for "rigorous" eclectics, readings are readings are readings, whether early or late.

The challenge of this view is discussed in Section III below.

3. *Reasoned eclectic method*

A third approach combines these two procedures. It is essential to have this third method if—as is realistically the case—the criteria for making decisions on the basis of the first method (the historical-
documentary) are not obvious or clear, and if—as many textual crit- 96
ics think—the second method (rigorous eclecticism), though valuable for its numerous insights, is—in isolation—a one-sided and less than adequate method. On this third procedure, when faced with any variation-unit, we would choose the variant reading that appears to be in the earliest chronological group *and* that also makes the best sense when the internal criteria are applied. Moreover, if no one cluster or type of text can be identified unambiguously as the earliest, then we would choose the variant reading in any given case that is in *one* of the earliest clusters *and* that best fits the relevant internal considerations. This method, therefore, utilizes both external and internal criteria and is called "reasoned eclecticism" or "moderate" or "genuine" eclecticism, or simply the "eclectic" method,[158] for it utilizes the best available methods from across the methodological spectrum. In this method it is recognized that no single criterion or

[157] Kilpatrick, "Atticism and the Text of the Greek New Testament," 76.

[158] Fee, "Rigorous or Reasoned Eclecticism—Which?" 174–76; Epp, "The Eclectic Method," 212–14; 244–45.

invariable combination of criteria will resolve all cases of textual variation, and it attempts, therefore, to apply evenly and without prejudice any and all criteria—external and internal—appropriate to a given case, arriving at an answer based on the relative probabilities among those applicable criteria.[159] As Kenneth Clark said of the method in 1956:

> It is the only procedure available to us at this stage, but it is very important to recognize that it is a secondary and tentative method. It is not a new method nor a permanent one. The eclectic method cannot by itself create a text to displace Westcott-Hort and its offspring. It is suitable only for exploration and experimentation. . . . The eclectic method, by its very nature, belongs to an age like ours in which we know only that the traditional theory of the text is faulty but cannot yet see clearly to correct the fault.[160]

This is to say that if we had worked out the early history of the text, as prescribed under the first method, neither rigorous nor reasoned eclecticism would be necessary. Until that is accomplished, however, most textual critics will rely upon the latter—a genuinely eclectic method that pays careful attention both to the documentary evidence from the history of the manuscript tradition and also to the internal criteria of readings. Together they can help us with the urgent textual decisions that we must make until the time when the historical-documentary method has been fully worked out. And, if the reconstruction of the early textual history cannot be achieved, the eclectic method will continue to be the method of choice—and of necessity.

97 The text common to the NA[26] and UBS[3] was formed in accordance with this kind of eclectic method, though placing emphasis, wherever possible, on the reading that explains the other readings and treating that as the most likely original. This latter procedure is what Kurt Aland calls the "local-genealogical method,[161] which is discussed further in Section III below.

---

[159] Birdsall, in his masterly survey of New Testament textual criticism in *The Cambridge History of the Bible* ("The New Testament Text," 1.316–18) uses the original term "rational criticism," from M.-J. Lagrange, for this method, but the co-opting of this term by "rigorous eclectics" suggests that a more specific term, such as "reasoned eclecticism," is now preferable to the less precise, generic term "eclectic."

[160] Clark, "The Effect of Recent Textual Criticism," 37–38.

[161] Nestle-Aland, *Novum Testamentum graece*, 1979[26], 42*–43*. Cf. Epp, "Continuing Interlude," 140–42 [repr. in Epp and Fee, *Studies in the Theory and Method*, 115–16].

It will already be recognized from the very mention of these several optional methods that the situation in New Testament textual criticism is not ideal and that neither automatic formulas nor easy decisions are readily forthcoming. The challenges emerging from the postwar discussions of method will be treated in Section III below.

Regrettably, our survey of editions, discoveries, and methods cannot begin to cover the hundreds of contributions made by scholars worldwide to these important areas of research.

III. Current and Future Decision Points in New Testament Textual Criticism

The decision points in current and future New Testament textual criticism all arise out of this lengthy, productive, and yet largely inconclusive past history, and they present us with a degree of difficulty and with a measure of urgency that are disquieting. I wish to focus on three turning points or issues currently under investigation. Certainly there are others, but these seem to me the most critical. The three items have a common characteristic: each constitutes a distinct "battleground" in the discipline; that is, they represent disputed areas that recently have been or shortly will be contested not only with vigor but even with some vehemence. The three conflicts that face us are the following.

A. *The Struggle over the Text-Type*

Perhaps the word "struggle" is too strong, yet there is a continuing and genuine disagreement, if not contention, as to whether or not "text-types" existed in the earliest centuries of the transmission of the New Testament text. That question in itself may not seem to involve a significant issue, but the answer to it does affect rather directly the obviously important issue of whether or not—and if so, how—we can trace the history of the earliest New Testament text, which—in turn—is related directly to the ultimate goal of recovering the original text. The validity of these steps is, at any rate, the conviction of many of us, with the result that the question of early text-types deserves close attention.

When J. A. Bengel long ago placed manuscripts into classes or groups, the development of text-types was under way in the textual
critic's mind, reaching its classical formulation in the system of 98

Westcott-Hort, though the more elaborate classifications of von Soden were still to come. As new manuscripts were analyzed, they were placed into a Westcott-Hort or a von Soden framework; this was appropriate enough if the manuscripts in question were generally later in time than the cornerstone manuscripts of each text-type. When, however, much earlier manuscripts—primarily papyri—began to appear (particularly those well beyond the fragmentary stage), we began to recognize the anachronism of placing these earlier manuscripts into groups whose nature had been determined on the basis only of the complexion of later manuscripts.[162]

The identification of text-types and of the manuscripts comprising them was a controversial matter for two centuries from Bengel to the discussions about the Caesarean text (roughly 1735 to 1935), but it was the analysis of papyri like P^{45}, P^{46}, P^{66}, and P^{75} that brought a new dimension to the controversy, namely, whether the established text-type categories any longer made sense or were even useful for the earliest period, or—to push the question even farther—whether there were, in fact, any identifiable text-types at all in that period.

Discussions of papyri in relation to text-types during the 1950s and 1960s led to statements like that of E. C. Colwell in 1961 that "very few, if any, text-types were established" by 200 C.E.,[163] or the more radical statement of Kurt Aland in 1964 that one can speak of an Alexandrian [or Egyptian] and of an Antiochian [or Byzantine] text-type, but:

> These are, it seems to me, the only text-types which may be regarded as certain, and that only since the fourth century. Everything else is extremely doubtful. It is impossible to fit the papyri, from the time prior to the fourth century, into these two text-types, to say nothing

[162] See J. N. Birdsall, *The Bodmer Papyrus of the Gospel of John* (Tyndale New Testament Lecture, 1958; London: Tyndale, 1960) 8–9; 17; A. F. J. Klijn, *A Survey of the Researches into the Western Text of the Gospels and Acts: Part Two 1949–1969* (NovTSup 21; Leiden: Brill, 1969) 33–38; 50.

[163] Colwell, "The Origin of Texttypes of New Testament Manuscripts," in *Early Christian Origins: Studies in Honor of Harold R. Willoughby* (ed. A. Wikgren; Chicago: Quadrangle, 1961) 138 [repr. as "Method in Establishing Quantitative Relationships between Text-Types of New Testament Manuscripts," in Colwell, *Studies in Methodology*, 55].

> of trying to fit them into other types, as frequently happens. The simple fact that all these papyri . . . did exist side by side . . . in Egypt . . . is the best argument against the existence of any text-types, including the Alexandrian [Egyptian] and the Antiochian [Byzantine].[164]

P^{75} had been published when these statements were made, and perhaps its close affinity with Codex Vaticanus (B), pointed out in 1966 by (the now archbishop of Milan) Carlo Martini,[165] should have acted as a restraint on this all-too-rapidly developed view that there were no entities in the first centuries that can be called "text-types." Yet it is clear enough that the study of the early and extensive papyri constitutes the turning point from confidence to skepticism about early text-types.[166]

These varying skeptical opinions about early text-types were not, 99
however, the only judgments on the subject in the 1950s and 1960s. A. F. J. Klijn, for example, argued that two text-types existed side by side in Egypt, a Western text and a Neutral text (to use Hort's terms).[167] It seems to me, therefore, that we should not yet withdraw from this battlefield, as though the matter were settled or as though we ought to abandon hope that the early papyri can be classified according to varying textual complexions[168] or that they can be linked with later manuscripts that can be said to possess a similar textual character.[169]

I am reluctant to repeat suggestions that I have made over the past several years and which still await development, but it seems clear to me, first, that differing *textual complexions can be identified* in the various papyri, even in the fragmentary ones—and many textual critics assign them to textual categories, including Aland himself.

---

[164] K. Aland, "The Significance of the Papyri for Progress in New Testament Research," in Hyatt, *Bible in Modern Scholarship*, 336–37.

[165] C. M. Martini, *Il problema della recensionalità del codice B alla luca del papiro Bodmer XIV* (AnBib 26; Rome: Biblical Institute Press, 1966); see G. D. Fee, "P^{75}, P^{66}, and Origen," 24–28 [repr. in Epp and Fee, *Studies in the Theory and Method*, 251–56].

[166] It is one thing, of course, to say that the traditional text-types are not useful as pigeonholes into which the early papyri may be placed, which—as his context shows—is the force of Colwell's statement, and something quite different to affirm that no text-types existed in the earliest period, which seems clearly to be what Aland means.

[167] Klijn, *Survey of the Researches . . . Part Two*, 39–40.

[168] Colwell, "External Evidence and New Testament Criticism," 5: "individual manuscripts can be characterized."

[169] Ibid.: "manuscripts can still be grouped and the group characterized."

Second, if this is so, it seems clear to me that the *grouping of early witnesses is possible* (and such groups or clusters might very well be designated "text-types"). Third, it seems clear to me that *lines of connection or trajectories can be traced* from early to later witnesses of similar textual character or complexion. When such an exercise is carried out, we may find that a text-type labeled "P^{75}" appears for the Gospels in the earliest period (third century) and has later representatives in Codex B in the fourth century, in Codex L in the eighth century, in Codex 33 in the ninth century, in manuscript 1739 in the tenth, and so on. In addition, we may find that a less well-documented but still adequate trajectory can be traced for Acts from a type of text found in P^{29} and P^{48} in the third century, with later representatives in P^{38} around 300 CE, in Codex D of the fourth/fifth century, and in manuscripts 614 and 383 in the thirteenth century; or that another type of text of the Gospels (and Acts), to be named for P^{45}, appears in the third century and follows a line to Codex W in the fifth century, though it seems to stop there.[170]

Much more work, admittedly, is required in this area, but we should not so easily capitulate to those forces that contend that no text-types existed or can be identified in the pre-fourth century period of New Testament textual transmission. We need answers; we need them soon; and I think that—by diligent effort—they can be found for this important issue. As will be obvious, it is precisely the papyri that can lead the way, for they extend the textual streams or trajectories much farther back than was previously possible, and they assist us in identifying the earliest textual clusters.

Reference to a debate over the text-types, however, is only another way of saying that we face a crisis over *methodology* in New Testament textual criticism. Identifying early text-types is one means—or at least one aspect—of reconstructing the earliest history of the transmission
100 of the New Testament text. Such a history of the text—if indeed it could be written for the earliest period—would provide a rather firm methodological track back to a point very close to the original text. Thus, to the extent that all Greek manuscripts of the New Testament

[170] See Hurtado, *Text-critical Methodology and the Pre-Caesarean Text*, 63–66; Epp, "Twentieth Century Interlude," 395–98; on manuscript trajectories, 397–400 [repr. in Epp and Fee, *Studies in the Theory and Method*, 90–93; 92–95]; idem, "Continuing Interlude," 147–49 [repr. in Epp and Fee, 120–21].

can be classified according to types of text, or at least placed on a continuum in accordance with their differing textual complexion, and to the extent that a history of the text can be reconstructed, to that extent we can speak of having formulated a theory of the New Testament text (or at least a portion of such a theory). To state it differently, we need to devise a plausible and defensible hypothesis that explains how the original New Testament text issued in our thousands of extant manuscripts, with their varying textual complexions. We seem not to have such a theory, though most of the great figures of the past ventured to formulate one. Westcott-Hort surmised that two early text-types were in competition in the second-century church, one corrupted by paraphrastic expansions (the Western) and the other virtually untouched in its course of transmission from the original (the Neutral).[171] Von Soden and B. H. Streeter and a host of others announced and defended their theories of the New Testament text, but none has stood the tests of criticism or of time. Yet the task is not to be abandoned, for it is a correct and proper task if significant progress is to be made in New Testament textual criticism. Though a hundred years have passed, it is still prudent to keep in mind the two—and the only two—principles that Hort printed in large type in his chapter on method: "Knowledge of documents should precede final judgement upon readings" and "All trustworthy restoration of corrupted texts is founded on the study of their history"[172] So the decision point over text-types becomes a broader and more significant decision point about basic textual history and theory and about fundamental methodology in the discipline of New Testament textual criticism. To resolve the issue of early text-types, therefore, would have far-reaching theoretical implications. For one thing, it would fulfill the hope implied in K. W. Clark's 1956 statement that "we know only that the traditional theory of the text is faulty but cannot yet see clearly to correct the fault"[173]

[171] See Epp, "Twentieth Century Interlude," 392 [repr. in Epp and Fee, *Studies in the Theory and Method*, 88].

[172] Westcott and Hort, *The New Testament in the Original Greek*, 2.31; 40.

[173] Clark, "The Effect of Recent Textual Criticism," 37–38.

B. *The Crisis of Criteria*

The second area of conflict is the present crisis over the criteria for determining the originality of readings,[174] or the "canons of criticism," as they were known in earlier times. This is a significant decision point, for New Testament text-critical methodology—though more on the practical level now than the theoretical—in its essence and at its very heart is concerned with the criteria employed to choose the most likely original reading wherever the textual tradition presents two or more readings at a given point in the text. To be quite blunt—if also a bit cynical—it is this simple-sounding matter of how to choose the "right" or "best" reading that is not only the major interest, but (I fear) often the *only* interest that exegetes
101 have in textual criticism. Yet this attitude—whether widespread or not—is actually a compliment to textual criticism, for it points to the important practical application and utility that the discipline has, as well as to the high expectations that our colleagues hold for it and for us. They may care little for our theories and disputations, but they do care greatly about how they shall make those decisions between and among competing readings that exegesis so regularly demands.

These critical canons or criteria have been of concern to New Testament textual critics since Origen and Jerome in ancient times, since Gerhard von Mastricht's formal list—the first such attempt—in his Greek New Testament of 1711, and particularly since they were given prominence by such notables as J. A. Bengel, J. J. Wettstein, J. J. Griesbach, K. Lachmann, C. Tischendorf, S. P. Tregelles, and Westcott-Hort. Throughout this lengthy period, during which the criteria were evolving, the clash (as is well known) was between reliance on the numerous later manuscripts, or on the growing—

[174] On defining readings, see two papers from the SBL New Testament Textual Criticism Seminar, 1974: G. D. Fee, "On the Types, Classification, and Presentation of Textual Variation," in Epp and Fee, *Studies in the Theory and Method*, 62–79; E. J. Epp, "Toward the Clarification of the Term 'Textual Variant'," *Studies in New Testament Language and Text: Essays in Honour of George D. Kilpatrick on the Occasion of His Sixty-fifth Birthday* (NovTSup 44; Leiden: Brill, 1976) 153–73 [repr. in Epp and Fee, *Studies in the Theory and Method*, 47–61]. See the earlier assessment by E. C. Colwell and Ernest W. Tune, "Variant Readings: Classification and Use," *JBL* 83 (1964) 253–61 [repr. as "Method in Classifying and Evaluating Variant Readings," in Colwell, *Studies in Methodology*, 96–105].

but still relatively small—number of older manuscripts, or, to put it differently, the struggle was between *quantity* of the manuscripts and "weight" or *quality* of the manuscripts supporting a reading, culminating in the triumph of the few earlier manuscripts over the many that represented the *textus receptus*. Though this period concluded with bitter conflict, complete with the acrimonious language of J. W. Burgon, it is not this skirmish that interests us.[175] Rather, what does interest us is that, following Westcott-Hort but beginning particularly with C. H. Turner (1923 ff.), M.-J. Lagrange (1935), G. D. Kilpatrick (1943 ff.), and J. K. Elliott (1972 ff.)[176] a new crisis of the criteria became prominent and is very much with us today: a duel between external and internal criteria and the widespread uncertainty as to precisely what kind of compromise ought to or can be worked out between them. The temporary "cease-fire" that most—but certainly not all—textual critics have agreed upon is called "moderate" or

---

[175] In spite of the present-day revival of the *textus receptus* by some who take Burgon's side against the rest of us—e.g., the recent edition by Hodges and Farstad, *The Greek New Testament according to the Majority Text* (1982): see their Introduction, ix–xiii.

[176] C. H. Turner, "Marcan Usage: Notes, Critical and Exegetical on the Second Gospel," *JTS* 25 (1923/24) 377–86; 26 (1924/25) 12–20; 145–56; 225–40; 337–46; 27 (1925/26) 58–62; 28 (1926/27) 9–30; 349–62; 29 (1927/28) 275–89; 346–61; M.-J. Lagrange, *Critique textuelle. II: La critique rationnelle* (EBib; Paris: Gabalda, 1935); G. D. Kilpatrick, "Western Text and Original Text in the Gospels and Acts"; idem, "Western Text and Original Text in the Epistles," *JTS* 45 (1944) 60–65; idem, "An Eclectic Study of the Text of Acts," in Birdsall and Thomson, *Biblical and Patristic Studies*, 64–77; idem, "Atticism and the Text of the Greek New Testament"; idem, "The Greek New Testament Text of Today and the *Textus Receptus*," *The New Testament in Historical and Contemporary Perspective: Essays in Memory of G. H. C. MacGregor* (ed. H. Anderson and W. Barclay; Oxford: Blackwell, 1965) 189–208; idem, "Style and Text in the Greek New Testament," *Studies in the History and Text of the New Testament in Honor of Kenneth Willis Clark, Ph.D.* (ed. B. L. Daniels and M. Jack Suggs; SD 29; Salt Lake City, UT: University of Utah Press, 1967) 153–60; idem, "Some Problems in New Testament Text and Language," *Neotestamentica et Semitica: Studies in Honour of Matthew Black* (ed. E. E. Ellis and M. Wilcox; Edinburgh: T. & T. Clark, 1969) 198–208; idem, "Conjectural Emendation in the New Testament"; cf. now *The Principles and Practice of New Testament Textual Criticism: Collected Essays of G. D. Kilpatrick* (ed. J. K. Elliott; BETL 96; Leuven: Leuven University Press/Peeters, 1990); and J. K. Elliott, "Rational Criticism and the Text of the New Testament," *Theology* 75 (1972) 338–43; idem, "Can We Recover the Original New Testament?" *Theology* 77 (1974) 338–53; idem, "Plaidoyer pour un éclectisme intégral appliqué a la critique textuelle du Nouveau Testament," *RB* 84 (1977) 5–25; idem, "In Defense of Thoroughgoing Eclecticism in New Testament Textual Criticism," *ResQ* 21 (1978) 95–115; idem, "An Eclectic Textual Commentary on the Greek Text of Mark's Gospel," in Epp and Fee, eds., *New Testament Textual Criticism: Its Significance for Exegesis*, 47–60.

"reasoned" eclecticism,[177] or what I have designated the "eclectic generalist" approach,[178] in which it is recognized that no single criterion or invariable combination of criteria will resolve all cases of textual variation and which, therefore, attempts to apply evenly and without prejudice any and all criteria—external and internal—appropriate to a given case, arriving then at an answer based on the relative probabilities among those applicable criteria.[179] We are all familiar with this method, for we all—or nearly all—employ it, as did the committee who prepared the UBS^3, and abundant examples of the method at work can be observed in the pages of that edition's *Textual Commentary*. This "reasoned" eclecticism is not recognized as appropriate by those "eclectic specialists" who practice a "rigorous" or "thoroughgoing" eclecticism that emphasizes the inter-
102 nal criteria, notably (as described earlier) George D. Kilpatrick and J. Keith Elliott. Even a "reasoned" eclecticism is accorded only a temporary "victory" by many of us who feel strongly that it is indeed a method for our time but not the ultimate method. As J. Neville Birdsall put it already a quarter of a century ago:

> Although for the present we must utilize these diverse criteria and establish a text by an eclectic method, it is impossible to stifle the hope that, at some future time, we shall find our methods and our resultant text justified by manuscript discoveries and by the classical methods . . . which Hort exemplified so brilliantly in his work.[180]

Many of us share this hope that the eclectic method can be replaced by something more permanent—a confidently reconstructed history and a persuasive theory of the text—and we are working actively toward that goal. In the meantime, all of us need to recognize, first, that the crisis of the criteria is real; second, that the literature of the past two or three decades is replete with controversy over the eclectic method, or at least is abundant with evidence of the frustration that accompanies its use; and, third, that we must devote our best and most serious efforts to refining the eclectic method in any and

[177] For the terminology, see Fee, "Rigorous or Reasoned Eclecticism—Which?" 174–77, and the discussion above.

[178] Epp, "The Eclectic Method," 244–48.

[179] Ibid.

[180] J. N. Birdsall, "The Text of the Fourth Gospel: Some Current Questions," *EvQ* 29 (1957) 199.

all appropriate ways, for it is likely to be our only guide for some time to come.

How can we refine the eclectic method? An important first step (which will not be necessary for all) is to understand the criteria themselves, their history, development, and use; I attempted such an assessment in some fifty pages in the *Harvard Theological Review* for 1977[181] that proved to be instructive for me. Second, we need to analyze critically each of the fifteen or so external and internal criteria as to their validity and relative worth. Is it really incontrovertible that the shorter or harder reading is to be preferred? Does wide geographical distribution of a reading or its attestation by several established groups give it added weight? Does antiquity of documentary evidence outweigh everything else? Is fitness to the context or with the author's style or theology automatically decisive? As a matter of fact, can our various criteria be placed in some hierarchic order, so that some are consistently more decisive than others? These and many other questions require continued and conscientious attention, and they need to be addressed both at the theoretical level and at the level of practice. Naturally, the trial and error of the laboratory and the give-and-take of everyday application can lead to significant insights and subsequent refinements in method. In addition, we can learn much from those who elevate one category of criteria or even a single criterion to a dominant position, as have those, for example, who practice "rigorous" eclecticism. Very recently a new challenge of this kind has come from Kurt Aland through the published definition of his "local-genealogical" method, which appears to be a refinement or a very special form of eclecticism, though he vigorously denies that it can properly be called "eclec- 103
tic."[182] This method arrives at the most likely original text by selecting that variant that best explains all the other variants in the variation-unit, and in the process Aland employs the various criteria or canons of criticism as possible ways of explaining how each secondary reading might have arisen. Professor Aland will surprise some—perhaps many—by his forthright statement that "from the perspective of our recent knowledge, this local-genealogical method . . . is the only one which meets the requirements of the New Testament

[181] Epp, "Eclectic Method."
[182] Nestle-Aland[26], 43*; Aland and Aland, *Text of the New Testament*, 34.

textual tradition,"[183] and it is, he claims further, the method that produced the new "Standard Text" (as he calls it) in the UBS[3] and NA[26] editions.[184] Testing his claim that this local-genealogical procedure has exclusive validity can be a further avenue for refining the eclectic method—an urgent decision point for current New Testament textual criticism. All the while, however, many of us will continue to hope—but more than that, to work—toward those more objective methods (like the historical-documentary method), based on better knowledge of the history of the New Testament text and its transmission, which will enable us to surmount the "crisis of the criteria."

C. *The Approaching Battle over the Papyri*

I referred earlier to three fields of conflict, and the third is the approaching battle over the papyri. This represents our final, but doubtless most critical, decision point in current text-critical discussion. I emphasize the word "approaching" for good reason. Since the discovery of the early New Testament papyri, but particularly since the nonfragmentary P^{45}, P^{46}, P^{66}, P^{75}, and others have come to light, there has been hardly anything that one could call strife or conflict in this area, for each new papyrus, whether extensive or fragmentary, has been welcomed with rejoicing and analyzed in anticipation of positive and constructive results. When, for example, P^{75} was shown to possess a text virtually identical to that of Codex B,[185] yet two centuries or so earlier in date, the long-standing conviction of a fourth century recension of what had been called the B-text was freely given up—no struggle, no strife.

My suggestion of an *approaching battle* over the papyri refers to something else: it concerns primarily two issues. The first of these is the *worth* of the papyri as textual witnesses, though this—as all will recognize—is merely a question of *relative* worth, for it goes without

[183] Nestle-Aland[26], 43*.

[184] See also K. Aland, "The Twentieth-Century Interlude in New Testament Textual Criticism," in Best and Wilson, 10 [repr. as "Die Rolle des 20. Jahrhunderts in der Geschichte der neutestamentlichen Textkritik," in Kunst, *Bericht der Hermann Kunst-Stiftung . . . 1977 bis 1979* (1979), 38].

[185] Martini, *Il problema della recensionalità del codice B*; see Fee, "P^{75}, P^{66}, and Origen," 24–28 [repr. in Epp and Fee, *Studies in the Theory and Method*, 251–56].

saying that the New Testament papyri are of exceptionally high value and will be thus esteemed by all textual critics (with the possible exception of the few "rigorous eclectics," who tend to view even the earliest manuscripts—along with all others—merely as sources for potentially original readings). The question, rather, is whether these papyri, or at least the earliest ones—those dating up to about 300
C.E.—are to be accorded what might be characterized as a rightful 104
status one or two rungs above that of our great uncials of the fourth century, or are to be accorded a considerably or even vastly higher status than that, one that raises them in significance far above our other eminent witnesses and that elevates them to a position somewhat akin to that accorded the relics of the saints. I am alluding here, of course, to the extraordinary status afforded these earliest papyri by Kurt Aland, who not only affirms their "automatic significance" as textual witnesses,[186] but in a later article makes the astounding claim that in the forty papyri (and uncials) prior to about 300 CE the early history of the New Testament text "can be studied in the original," and that all other efforts to get a glimpse of the early text "must remain reconstructed theories."[187]

Such an exceptionally high valuation of the earliest papyri has its problems, and included among these is the second issue over which conflict is inevitable, namely, the question of how *representative* of the earliest history of the text these early papyri are? If his statement means what it seems to mean, Professor Aland is virtually identifying the text of the pre-fourth century papyri with the "original" text. If this seems incredible or unlikely, it may be added that, in a still more recent article on "the new 'Standard Text' in its relation to the early papyri and uncials," Aland employs these pre-fourth century papyri and uncials as the "touchstone" of originality, for he states that the common text of the NA^{26} and UBS^{3} "has passed the test of the early papyri and uncials. It corresponds, in fact, to the text of the early time," and he then goes on to a more startling conclusion: speaking of the text of NA^{26}, he asserts: "A hundred years after Westcott-Hort, the goal of an edition of the New Testament 'in the original Greek' seems to have been reached."[188] It is, of

[186] In his "Introduction" to the NA^{26}: 12*, 49*.
[187] K. Aland, "Twentieth-Century Interlude," 11.
[188] K. Aland, "Der neue 'Standard Text'," 274–75.

course, the unique value ascribed to the papyri that is the key to this remarkable claim.

It seems clear to me that a struggle over the papyri—about their relative worth as textual evidence and about their representative nature—has in fact begun, will increase in intensity, and is a crucial decision point requiring our serious attention. Can such high claims as Aland makes be sustained? I for one wish that they could be readily accepted and be as easily substantiated, for that would constitute a breakthrough in both method and practice that would be highly significant and warmly welcomed. Yet some disturbing questions arise and call for answers before we rush to embrace such claims about the papyri.

To begin with an obvious question—yet one too rarely discussed or even raised—how representative, really, of the earliest history of the New Testament text are these earliest papyri? What assurance do we have that these randomly surviving manuscripts represent in any real sense the entire earliest period of the text? Subsidiary questions appear: First, virtually all of these documents come from one
105 region, Egypt. Can we be satisfied with Egypt as the all-but-exclusive locale for viewing this earliest history of the text? Was Egypt in the third century C.E. representative of the New Testament text for *all* of Christianity at that period? Was any New Testament book written in Egypt? Probably not. Does not Egypt then represent at best a secondary and derivative stage in the history of the New Testament text? After all, is it not merely an accident of history (though a most fortunate one) that papyrus survives almost exclusively in the dry sands of Egypt?

If textual witnesses, then, are to have "automatic significance" (to use Aland's phrase), should there not be a basis for so significant a role that is more substantive than merely their early age? And, before we claim that in these papyri the history of the New Testament text "can be studied in the original" (again to use Aland's words), should we not assure ourselves either that these earliest witnesses present a unitary text (which, of course, they do not), or—lacking that assurance—should we not require a guarantee (or at least some persuasive evidence) that they are genuinely representative of the earliest history of the text, representative, that is, of the various textual complexions that existed in the earliest period? As a matter of fact, as suggested earlier, certain "types" of text or textual complexions do seem to be represented by the various early papyri, including (1) the

Alexandrian or Egyptian (Hort's Neutral) text, (2) the so-called "Western" text, and (3) a text somewhere in between (now usually designated pre-Caesarean).[189]

We are faced, then, with a puzzle, for there is one rather clear sense in which the early papyri seem *not* to be representative—and that is their restriction to virtually a single geographical segment of Christianity—and another sense in which they *may* be representative—and that is their presentation of textual complexions characteristic of what have previously been identified as the major early text-types. For these reasons, it seems that we have been thrust into a period of the *reassessment* of the papyri. Certainly it is more than mere curiosity or coincidence to find that fifty years ago, after his preliminary analysis of the Chester Beatty papyri, Sir Frederic Kenyon made the following provocative statement in his Schweich Lectures of the British Academy for 1932: "There remains what is perhaps the most perplexing problem of all, the problem of the Biblical text in Egypt"[190] And in 1949, before the Bodmer papyri came to light, A. F. J. Klijn said, "Egypt appears to be more and more important for the history of the text."[191] How much closer to solving that puzzle have the past fifty years brought us? Certainly we have more abundant materials for the task than Kenyon and Klijn had—notably the Bodmer papyri—and we may hope that we will not have to wait for another fifty-year landmark to see these questions about the significance of the papyri resolved. After all, there is virtually unanimous agreement that the New Testament papyri not only are textual
criticism's greatest treasure but also its best hope for "cracking" the 106
textual "code" and breaking through to the original text.

Despite confident claims to the contrary, however, we have not yet reached the point of readily and assuredly identifying any

[189] See Epp, "Twentieth Century Interlude," 393–96; cf. idem, "Continuing Interlude," 146–47; Hurtado, *Text-critical Methodology and the Pre-Caesarean Text*, 88–89. For new directions in pursuing the question of how representative of the entire New Testament text the papyri of Egypt might be, see now E. J. Epp, "New Testament Papyrus Manuscripts and Letter Carrying in Greco-Roman Times," *The Future of Early Christianity: Essays in Honor of Helmut Koester* (ed. B. A. Pearson et al.; Minneapolis, MN: Fortress, 1991) esp. 52–56.

[190] Frederic G. Kenyon, *Recent Developments in the Textual Criticism of the Greek Bible* (Schweich Lectures, 1932; London: British Academy, 1933) 80.

[191] A. F. J. Klijn, *A Survey of the Researches into the Western Text of the Gospels and Acts* (Utrecht: Kemink, 1949) 145.

manuscript, any group of manuscripts, or any critical text with that elusive "original," but the papyri most certainly will be the instruments that we shall use to settle the struggle over the text-type, to resolve the crisis of the criteria, and to push toward a "standard text" acknowledged by all. The difficult question that remains, of course, is exactly *how* we are to use them to achieve these urgent goals.

IV. Conclusion

New Testament textual criticism is a vigorous and stimulating discipline, in which—as history demonstrates—new discoveries are always possible (though not assured) and in which many theoretical decisions—fundamental to the discipline—remain to be made on the basis of the materials we have. Since World War II new discoveries have come to light and new methods have been devised (or old ones refined), and there has been much progress. On the other hand, as we have noted, major issues still require resolution. In these cases textual critics and not the discoveries or theories themselves will lead to further progress, and in this connection the words of Georg Luck, a prominent classical textual critic, are discomfiting but nonetheless true: "Part of the problem is that our critical texts are no better than our textual critics."[192] If competent textual critics can be rallied in New Testament studies, our new materials and refined methods can be utilized to solve the critical problems, and the discipline can move toward the ideal of a critical text that closely approximates the "original" New Testament text.

Added Notes, 2004

This lengthy article evolved over time (see n. 1, above) and appeared under the title, "Textual Criticism," as a chapter in *The New Testament and Its Modern Interpreters* (eds. Eldon Jay Epp and †George W. MacRae; Philadelphia: Fortress; Atlanta, GA: Scholars Press, 1989) 75–126. Its particular shape—sections 1 and 3, with an intervening survey

[192] Georg Luck, "Textual Criticism Today," *AJP* 102 (1981) 166.

of New Testament manuscript and text-critical publications since World War II—is due to the mission of this volume and its two companion volumes in the Society of Biblical Literature's The Bible and Its Modern Interpreters series, namely, to describe and to assess biblical scholarship from World War II until the early 1980s. This trilogy was commissioned by the Society's Centennial Publications Editorial Board as the centerpiece of its commemorative publication series—which eventually comprised some twenty-five volumes. This New Testament volume, like the other two on the Hebrew Bible and Early Judaism, has served students and scholars well, and continues to do so, though perhaps more now as a historical record since a generation has passed. My co-editor, George W. MacRae, S.J., the first permanent Stillman Professor of Roman Catholic Studies at Harvard Divinity School, participated fully in planning the volume, but he died suddenly in 1985 at age fifty-six, and it remained for me to see the volume through the press. He is no less missed now by all who were his students or colleagues.

My essay, therefore, assesses past New Testament textual criticism from its beginnings to the 1980s, with emphasis on methods and principles for establishing the New Testament text (section 1), and concludes (section 3) with an analysis of major challenges: the text-type, the criteria for priority of readings, and the worth and representative nature of the New Testament papyri. All of these topics are treated in various essays in this volume—for none can be said to have been settled with any finality.

On the terms "original text," "Neutral" text, "Western" text, etc., see "Notes to Readers," in the front matter.

CHAPTER ELEVEN

NEW TESTAMENT TEXTUAL CRITICISM PAST, PRESENT, AND FUTURE: REFLECTIONS ON THE ALANDS' *TEXT OF THE NEW TESTAMENT*

Introduction

History, theory, and practice are interwoven in most realms of human knowledge, yet students approaching a field often care little about its history. They are more concerned with its application and how the discipline is practiced. This may be illustrated from the physical and biological sciences, where it is common not only for novices but even experts to take an interest only very late—if at all—in the history of science, and more so among physicians, to whom the history of medicine is usually a curiosity at best. Students first grappling with New Testament textual criticism are not likely to be different—they want to know the "jargon," the "rules," and the basic methods that will permit them to practice the art and (as they are more likely to view it) the science of textual criticism. In this particular subfield of New Testament studies, however, the history and the practice of the discipline cannot easily be separated. After all, the canons of criticism—the so-called "rules" in textual criticism—are anything but objective standards that can be applied in a rigid, mechanical fashion. Rather—often as not—they are overlapping or competing guidelines, or they involve principles that depend on elusive historical information or reconstructions, or on theoretical judgments about developments largely lost to us in the remote past. This is the case both with respect to the so-called external canons (Is a reading in the earliest, or in the "best," or in geographically diffuse manuscripts, etc.?) and also the internal canons (Is a reading shorter, or "harder," or does it conform to the author's style or theology, etc.?). These canons have not appeared randomly, nor do they operate independently, but they issue from and interact with their own on-going history. It is doubtless for this reason that standard text-critical handbooks down through the years almost invariably have opened, not only with a description of the manuscript witnesses from which the New Testament text has been derived, but also with a

history of the printed Greek text and a history of evolving text-
214 critical theory. Then, at the end of the handbook, it has been customary to describe the praxis of textual criticism, including a statement of principles (the "canons") of criticism and numerous sample passages to illustrate the application of those principles.

To the expert in the field, therefore, it is virtually unthinkable to divorce practice from history, for the methodological principles operative in the art of New Testament textual criticism—which is only minimally a science—have been forged out of the heat of controversy and have evolved through trial and error over a long and instructive history of development. To be sure, a student can be taught merely the "rules" and can apply them to textual problems with a fair measure of success, for these "rules," after all, represent the consensus—and presumably the wisdom—of scholars over that long history. Yet, the thoroughly prepared student must be conversant with the history that lies behind and that has produced the principles, and must understand the extensive interconnections between the two.

Handbooks of New Testament textual criticism appear at the rate of only one or two in each generation, so the appearance of a new introduction to the discipline attracts the attention of all in the field, particularly if it is one written by two of the world's most influential New Testament textual critics. Kurt and Barbara Aland's *The Text of the New Testament*[1] appeared in German in 1982 and in English in 1987. The last standard work of this kind, by Bruce M. Metzger, was published in 1964, with an abiding (though now dated) second edition of 1968.[2] The Alands' volume—even though it claims to be for beginners—was received with the expected acclaim and accolades, both in its German dress and in English. One would expect, after all, that this would be the best of books, and in many ways it is.

Foremost among the praiseworthy features, in fact, are some that render the book clearly indispensable in the field. Above all, the

[1] Kurt Aland and Barbara Aland, *The Text of the New Testament: An Introduction to the Critical Editions and to the Theory and Practice of Modern Textual Criticism* (trans. Erroll F. Rhodes; Grand Rapids: Eerdmans; Leiden: Brill, 1987). Throughout the text of this article, numbers in parentheses refer to page numbers in this volume. [A 2d German ed. appeared in 1988 and in English in 1989. The page numbers in the English editions are not significantly different (see n. 5 below).]

[2] Bruce M. Metzger, *The Text of the New Testament: Its Transmission, Corruption, and Restoration* (2d ed.; New York/Oxford: Oxford University Press, 1968).

current and comprehensive lists of manuscripts of the Greek New Testament stand out as a major service to the discipline. This is covered in the longest chapter in the volume (chapter 3), which includes a number of informative charts and graphs showing the distribution of New Testament manuscripts by century and by content, thirty-six facsimiles of New Testament manuscripts, and authoritative discussions and complete lists of the eighty-eight papyri known at the time[3] and of the 274 uncials. In addition, about 150 minuscules are listed, and there are discussions of the lectionaries (but no list) and of the patristic citations (with a list of the Greek fathers cited in
Nestle-Aland[26]). Then follows a chapter on the early versions (chap- 215
ter 4), briefly describing the Latin, Syriac, Coptic, Armenian, Georgian, Ethiopic, Gothic, and Old Church Slavonic versions, noting editions of each and listing the Latin and Eastern fathers cited in Nestle-Aland[26]. This is a compact but serviceable summary of the state of scholarship in that complex area.[4] Finally, on the praxis side, two chapters show how to use modern editions of the Greek New Testament (chapter 5), and how to make text-critical decisions (chapter 7). The latter is a methodical treatment of the practice of textual criticism, with selected sample passages.

These several chapters,[5] containing this vital and useful material, will and must be consulted by novice and expert alike. The value of these portions of the volume, therefore, should not be underestimated,

---

[3] Though the text (p. 13) refers to ninety-three. [The official list of New Testament manuscripts is Kurt Aland (ed.), *Kurzgefasste Liste der griechischen Handschriften des Neuen Testaments* (ANTF 1; 2d ed., rev. and enl.; Berlin/New York: de Gruyter, 1994), which lists papyri through P99. Aland's list is continued, for P100–P115, majuscules 0307–0309, and minuscules 2857–2862, in *Bericht der Hermann Kunst-Stiftung zur Förderung der neutestamentlichen Textforschung für die Jahre 1995 bis 1998* (Münster/Westfalen, 1998) 14–16; and for P116, majuscules 0310–0316, and minuscules 2863–2877, in *Bericht der Hermann Kunst-Stiftung zur Förderung der neutestamentlichen Textforschung für die Jahre 1998 bis 2003* (Münster/Westfalen, 2003) 74–79].

[4] But see the criticism of this chapter in the review by J. Neville Birdsall, *BT* 39 (1988) 339.

[5] These chapters and their relative lengths are as follows: chapter 3, pp. 72–180; chapter 4, 181–217; chapter 5, 218–62; chapter 7, pp. 275–311. There is also a brief chapter 6 on "Resources" (pp. 263–74), though it may appear to be more of an advertisement for the various (and important) research tools produced by the editors than an essential part of a handbook on New Testament textual criticism. [Pages in the 2d English ed.: chapter 3 = 72–184; chapter 4 = 185–221; chapter 5 = 222–67; chapter 6 = 268–79; chapter 7 = 280–316. An important additional chapter 8 by Barbara Aland treats "Categories and Text Types, and the Textual Analysis of Manuscripts" (317–37).]

for the detailed information on the manuscripts and versions is clearly indispensable, eminently reliable, and readily available for reference, while the introduction to the use of the third edition of the United Bible Societies *Greek New Testament* and the twenty-sixth edition of the Nestle-Aland Greek New Testament is both meticulous and thorough in its explanations. As a matter of fact, these valuable portions constitute 78% of the volume's text (242 out of 311 pages). It is, however, the remaining 22% of the material, plus occasional sentences and paragraphs elsewhere, that make this a most puzzling book, and one that requires a careful analysis and evaluation of how it presents the history and theory of New Testament textual criticism. In this evaluative process, some light may be cast on the history and method of the discipline and certain aspects of it may be brought into proper perspective.

That puzzle begins in a small way in the volume's preface, which—in the course of announcing the book's primarily utilitarian purposes—places a surprisingly secondary evaluation upon the history of New Testament textual criticism:

> The present book gives the basic information necessary for using the Greek New Testament and for forming an independent judgment on the many kinds of variant readings characteristic of the New Testament textual tradition. Matters primarily of antiquarian interest (e.g., the early printed editions of the New Testament, which have often been discussed in detail elsewhere) have generally been restricted here to their bare essentials, while more concern has been given (within the compass permitted by the book) to forming an overall perspective . . ., to practical experience in dealing with complex problems, and to developing sound independent judgment (19).

This quotation raises an issue of considerable significance to New
216 Testament textual criticism, for it was, of course, during the preparation of printed editions over the years that text-critical principles were developed. This process of listing as prolegomena the canons of criticism employed in determining a critical text of the Greek New Testament began with the 1711 edition of Gerhard von Mastricht and was continued by J. A. Bengel in 1725, J. J. Wettstein in 1751–52, J. J. Griesbach in 1796–1806, Karl Lachmann in 1842–50, Constantin Tischendorf in 1849, and Westcott-Hort in 1881–82, among others.[6]

---

[6] For an extensive discussion of these and other canons—and their historical

The history of those "antiquarian matters," therefore, is not only highly informative but perhaps essential for an understanding of text-critical theory. The importance of these matters to the discipline is witnessed, in addition, by their presence in all previous handbooks of New Testament textual criticism. That the Alands consider this historical background largely dispensable is attested by their further suggestion in the preface that "readers wishing to begin immediately using a particular edition of the Greek New Testament . . . should begin with chapter V," that is, with the description of the UBS*GNT*[3] and Nestle-Aland[26], and then proceed to the chapter on text-critical practice with selected examples (20; cf. 19 [English translation only]). To be sure, the reader who follows this advice will find that these meticulous final chapters do provide extensive (although largely incidental) discussion of various canons of criticism; yet do these practical exercises—apart from an adequate history and theory of the text—easily lead to "sound independent judgments"? The same question arises when it is observed that the authors' recommendation to ignore the first four chapters means that beginners will miss the important chapters describing the available manuscripts and versions (though admittedly much of this information is too sophisticated and detailed for the novice). Yet, can "independent judgment" be developed without a basic knowledge of this primary material? That would appear to be an issue of more than passing interest.

It will now be apparent that the preface of the Alands' volume raises some fundamental questions about their approach—at least in this book—to textual criticism, and we need to move toward some further inquiries. These can be grouped under three topics, namely, the authors' portrayal of the past, present, and future of New Testament textual criticism.

New Testament Textual Criticism Past

The portrayal by the Alands of New Testament textual criticism's past deserves close examination. In fairness, it must be said at the outset that their volume does not claim to be a history of New Testament textual criticism, yet it does claim to be "An Introduction

development—see E. J. Epp, "The Eclectic Method in New Testament Textual Criticism: Solution or Symptom?" *HTR* 69 (1976) 217–42.

217 to the Critical Editions and to the Theory and Practice of Modern Textual Criticism." Since this subtitle refers to the *theory* of modern textual criticism, it is pertinent to ask what theories are exemplified.

The volume opens with a forty-seven page historical summary of "The Editions of the New Testament" and divides that history into three periods. The first, "From Erasmus to Griesbach," is succinctly but appropriately described in fewer than five pages of text. The second, "From Lachmann to Nestle," covers the editions of Lachmann, Tregelles, Tischendorf, Westcott-Hort, and Eberhard Nestle. This was the period that witnessed the decline and defeat of the *textus receptus* (the late text found in the majority of manuscripts) and most of us would have labeled the section "From Lachmann to Westcott-Hort," for the triumph over the *textus receptus* was achieved by those editions—and the ones in between—but not (as the Alands claim) by Nestle. This, in itself, is hardly a major issue, yet it is symptomatic of what is to follow in this volume. As everyone knows, Nestle's edition—from its beginning and for many years to follow—was based simply on a majority vote among the texts in the editions of Tischendorf, Westcott-Hort, and Weymouth or (later) Weiss, that is, Nestle chose among competing readings by selecting the one supported by two of these three editions. Nestle's edition put forth no other principles for determining the text and certainly offered no theory of the text—both of which are prominent features of editions like those of Tischendorf and Westcott-Hort. Furthermore, the Nestle edition paid "relatively little attention to manuscripts," as the Alands admit (19). It comes as a surprise, therefore, to discover that they call the Nestle edition a "breakthrough" that represents the "conclusive" "battle" against the *textus receptus* (18–19). Prior to this assertion, they do—to be sure—acknowledge the role of Tischendorf and Westcott-Hort in rendering the *textus receptus* "obsolete for the scholarly world," but this is followed immediately by a two-fold claim that the 1898 Nestle edition itself and the 1904 choice of its text by the British and Foreign Bible Society to replace the previously used *textus receptus* establish forever the Nestle edition's firm place in history (19).[7]

[7] Incidentally but curiously, the Alands criticize Westcott-Hort for not collating manuscripts and for basing their text entirely on previous critical editions, while at the same time they extol the Nestle edition for its "purely mechanical system of [selecting] a majority text" from the three specified editions (20). A small matter, but one curiosity among many others.

Although the Nestle edition holds and deserves a solid place in history and also was a prominent influence in the exclusion of the *textus receptus*, particularly in Europe, certainly its influence was only at the practical and not at the theoretical level. Just as certainly, on the other hand, the influence of Westcott-Hort's edition in dethroning the *textus receptus*, not only in Great Britain and North America, but elsewhere as well, was not merely on the practical level, but far more distinctively in the theoretical realm. That is clear from the history of the discipline itself and is reflected in virtually every handbook and encyclopedia article on New Testament textual criticism 218
since the time of Westcott-Hort. The reason is simple enough: in addition to the first volume, containing the Greek New Testament text, the second of Westcott-Hort's two volumes was a closely argued book (by Hort), extending to more than 500 pages, that presented a compelling case for the greater antiquity, accuracy, and authority of the text in the earlier manuscripts over against that in the later ones (the *textus receptus*).[8] That is, the text of Westcott-Hort was epoch-making because it was backed up by a meticulously argued history and theory of that text. Nestle's majority-vote text, on the other hand, was not reinforced in any such manner.

This is not to say that no one before Westcott-Hort had made a case against the *textus receptus* or that all of Hort's points are equally convincing, but it was the clear perception in the scholarly world—then and since—that Westcott-Hort had marshaled the forces earlier led by Lachmann, Tischendorf, and Tregelles and that with their text of 1881 the battle defending the *textus receptus* was "conclusively lost" (to use the phrase the Alands use when touting the 1898 Nestle edition as the victorious factor [19]). So it is Westcott-Hort's work that is termed "epoch-making," for example, by Oscar von Gebhardt and by Sir Frederic Kenyon, among others,[9] and Kenyon says elsewhere that the labors of Lachmann, Tischendorf, and Tregelles "were

[8] Brooke Foss Westcott and Fenton John Anthony Hort, *The New Testament in the Original Greek* (Cambridge/London: Macmillan, 1881–82 [2d ed., 1896]).

[9] On Gebhardt (and the same term used by Louis Duchesne), see Philip Schaff, *A Companion to the Greek New Testament and the English Version* (4th ed.; New York/London: Harper, 1903) 281–82; for Kenyon, see his *Handbook to the Textual Criticism of the New Testament* (2d ed.; London: Macmillan, 1926) 294. He says further: Westcott-Hort's work "has coloured all that has been written on the subject for the last thirty years, and supplies the basis of all work done in this field today" (ibid.).

brought to a head by Westcott and Hort."[10] Moreover, M.-J. Lagrange affirms that "the edition of Westcott-Hort marks the victory of critical method over the simple reproduction of the *textus receptus*," and he relegates the Nestle editions to a footnote.[11] H. J. Vogels, while devoting a full page to Westcott-Hort's work, does not mention the Nestle edition in his extended discussions of New Testament text-critical method and of the history of the printed editions—or apparently anywhere else in his 1955 handbook![12] Even Eberhard Nestle
219 himself—though not uncritical in this context—can say: "In his *Introduction*, Hort, in the most brilliant manner one must admit, has established the principle that the restoration of the text must be grounded on the study of its history, and no one has studied that history as carefully as Hort has done."[13]

Citation of authorities does not, of course, settle an issue, but any decision as to whether it was the edition of Westcott-Hort or that of Nestle that constituted a "breakthrough" or a "conclusive" triumph over the *textus receptus* is not likely to be made in favor of Nestle. In fact, as far as I can discover, only Caspar René Gregory, in his diffuse volume, supports the Alands in their claim. Though not uncritical of Nestle's method of deciding his text, Gregory is "deeply thankful to Nestle" for his "incredible" achievement in convincing the British and Foreign Bible Society to replace its *textus receptus* with his 1898 text, and adds: "It was desirable for the cause of the Bible, of the Church, and of science that the great apparatus of that Society should cease to deluge Europe with this imperfect text. Nestle has effected the change."[14] Yet, a page earlier,

---

[10] Frederic G. Kenyon, *Recent Developments in the Textual Criticism of the Greek Bible* (Schweich Lectures, 1932; London: Oxford University Press for the British Academy, 1933) 4.

[11] M.-J. Lagrange, *Critique textuelle: II. La critique rationelle* (ÉtBib; Paris: Gabalda, 1935) 7; on Nestle's 1st and 9th editions, see p. 8 n. 3.

[12] Heinrich J. Vogels, *Handbuch der Textkritik des Neuen Testaments* (2d ed.; Bonn: Hanstein, 1955) 152–220; on Westcott-Hort, see 202–3. Vogels refers to Nestle's *Einführung in das griechische Neue Testament* (3d ed.; Göttingen: Vandenhoeck & Ruprecht, 1909) about fifteen times, but not to his editions (though Vogels, 182, may contain such a reference, yet not unambiguously).

[13] Eberhard Nestle, *Introduction to the Textual Criticism of the Greek New Testament* (English trans. from 2d German ed. with additions; London: Williams & Norgate, 1901) 171.

[14] Caspar René Gregory, *Canon and Text of the New Testament* (International Theological Library; Edinburgh: T. & T. Clark, 1907) 464.

Gregory affirms that Westcott and Hort "did more than anyone else ever did to place the history of the text of the New Testament on a sound basis."[15] The conclusion seems obvious enough: we can give due credit to Nestle for effecting a practical—perhaps we should say political—triumph over the *textus receptus*, while acknowledging that it was Westcott-Hort (building upon their predecessors) who mark the definitive "breakthrough" in moving away from the late text "received by all."

Returning to the Alands' volume we face a puzzling question: Why the unexpected—and quite undeserved—heightening of the significance of the old Nestle edition? Why the emphasis on the 1898 Nestle edition as a breakthrough? The answer becomes clear as we turn to the Alands' third period in the history of the critical editions of the Greek New Testament, "From Nestle to the New 'Standard Text'" (20–36), which is accorded the longest discussion though it covers the shortest period of the three segments—only about forty years. The section begins by noting Erwin Nestle's editorship in succession to his father, Eberhard, and ends with a description of the Nestle-Aland edition as the new, so-called "Standard text." In the course of the discussion, other editions and other textual works are mentioned, though almost incidentally as a background for Erwin Nestle's text (and that of the later Nestle-Aland edition). For example, the editions of von Soden (1902–13) and Legg (1935, 1940) are described briefly, followed by a (disparaging) reference to the
International Greek New Testament Project, a mention of the Münster 220
Institute—much extolled throughout the volume—and a listing of hand-editions of the Greek New Testament, such as those of Vogels, Merk, Bover, as well as Souter, Tasker, Kilpatrick, and Greeven (in his *Synopsis*). At this point we are confronted by a striking statement: "Except for the three editions mentioned above [Vogels, Merk, and Bover], the last fifty years have produced nothing of note apart from the new 'Standard text'" (25).[16]

Suddenly, then, the Alands' schema becomes clear: after Tischendorf and Westcott-Hort, the turning point—the breakthrough—in the

[15] Ibid., 463.

[16] The English translator of the Alands' volume informs me that the second German edition (which will appear also as a second English edition) will drop the term "Standard text" throughout the volume (letter from Dr. Erroll F. Rhodes, 24 November 1988). [See "Added Notes, 2004" below.]

Alands' history is the first Nestle edition, which then moves, through its successive revisions, in a straight line of development to the final achievement: the twenty-sixth edition of Nestle-Aland, containing the "Standard text." Almost nothing in between is worthy of mention, for the Nestle accomplishment of 1898 issues directly—even if not immediately—in the ultimate achievement embodied in the Nestle-Aland text of 1979. To put it differently, in the history of the printed editions of the Greek New Testament, what is the immediate successor of the *textus receptus*? Their answer is the 1898 Nestle edition. Eighty years of New Testament text-critical work have been collapsed into a single line of development, and very little need be said about those eighty years of the discipline except to imply at several points in the volume that the final breakthrough to the "Standard text" was possible only because of the materials collected and collated by the Münster Institute. This portrayal, it would appear, can only be described as a revisionist history of New Testament textual criticism. Indeed, the entire volume virtually ignores four generations of non-German scholarship in the field, something that has not escaped the notice of reviewers of the Alands' book in Great Britain or North America.[17] In fact, if one largely ignores scholars who published New Testament manuscripts, editions, versions, or patristic citations (and who therefore are cited as editors in these various lists), references in this volume to British and American scholarship—that is, to historical and theoretical studies—are restricted to the following: on the British side, a reference to J. W. Burgon (19), several to Westcott and/or Hort, including one that is quite mistaken (18),[18] and two disparaging comments on G. D. Kilpatrick's *Greek-English*
221 *Diglot* (25, 32), though this is really an edition and could be excluded from our survey.[19] On the North American side, there are several

[17] See, e.g., the reviews by Michael Holmes in *JBL* 108 (1989) 139–44, and by J. Neville Birdsall (n. 4 above); cf. the reviews by Larry W. Hurtado in *CBQ* 50 (1988) 313–15, and by Moisés Silva in *WTJ* 50 (1988) 195–200 [and some additional reviews in "Added Notes, 2004" below].

[18] Other references include 14–15, 18, 20, 55, 182, 232; rare positive comments are on 11 n. 16, 273. The misleading item concerns their attribution of "highest quality" to Codex Bezae—see below.

[19] Also on the British side, there are positive assessments of commentaries by Westcott, Hort, J. B. Lightfoot, and E. G. Selwyn, which are said to be still "valuable today for textual criticism" (273), but these are not theoretical studies in the discipline.

references to Bruce Metzger's work—usually disparaging (e.g., 18 n. 38; 58–59, 163; cf. 34, 165, 185); two complimentary mentions of Ernest Colwell (24, 270), though with no indication that his work was consulted or with any suggestion as to its significance; three positive general remarks on Eugene Nida—on whose initiative the United Bible Societies' *Greek New Testament* was undertaken (31, 33, 34); a mention of Vinton Dearing's proposed edition (accompanied by an incorrect and disparaging remark about the International Greek New Testament Project (24); a negative comment on J. H. Greenlee's introduction (270); and curiously, four comments on the Farstad-Hodges *Majority Text* (vii, 19, 25, 292)[20]—almost as if to suggest that while American scholarship has produced little of significance, what it has presented lately is an anachronistic defense of the *textus receptus*. That is it for Great Britain and North America during the past four generations of text-critical scholarship!

This lack of recognition of Anglo-American work could be overlooked if nothing else were at stake, but other evidences of the revisionist character of the volume accompany these oversights—raising questions as to whether they are, in fact, merely inadvertent omissions. Notice how the authors, after discussing for nearly five pages the Nestle editions through the twenty-fifth, conclude that the data "show for Nestle a closer affinity to Westcott-Hort" than to any other edition (26; cf. 26–30).[21] Then follows a more general conclusion:
"This result is quite amazing, demonstrating a far greater agreement 222

[20] Farstad-Hodges and also Dearing are editors of editions and could be excluded from this survey, thus further diminishing representation in the volume of American scholars who are not editors of manuscripts, versions, or patristic works, though, of course, both the *Majority Text* version of Farstad-Hodges and Dearing's work on "states of the text" involve theoretical issues.

[21] This is a curious reversal of Kurt Aland's earlier position, one in which he took offense when the Nestle-Aland text was spoken of as being closer to that of Westcott-Hort, and which he understood to imply that no progress had been made in textual criticism since Westcott-Hort's time. Actually, the more careful statement of my 1974 conclusion (to which he took offense) was that "none of the currently popular hand-editions of the Greek New Testament takes us beyond Westcott-Hort in any substantive way as far as textual character is concerned" (*JBL* 93 [1974] 390), and the more specific point was that the text of Nestle-Aland^{25} was closer to Westcott-Hort than to any other critical text, using as evidence statistics that Kurt Aland had reported in 1959 and again in 1967 ("The Present Position of New Testament Textual Criticism," *StEv* 1 [1959] 720–21; idem, "Der heutige Text des griechischen Neuen Testaments" in his *Studien zur Überlieferung des Neuen Testaments und seines Textes* [ANTF 2; Berlin: de Gruyter, 1967] 59–61). His response, not with-

among the Greek texts of the New Testament during the past century than textual scholars would have suspected" (29).

The point here is to disclose how the Alands view the past of textual criticism, for they use this data on the closeness of the Nestle edition to that of Westcott-Hort in a curious way. Nestle, they say, "produced a text that not only lasted seventy years, but on the whole truly represents the modern state of knowledge," to which they add that during the last eighty years the Nestle text "has remained the same (apart from a few minor changes adopted by Erwin Nestle—no more than a dozen at most)" (20, 26).[22] Therefore, in summarizing "the textual scene of the past century," they see this long continuity in the Nestle text as a demonstration that "the Nestle text has been the dominant text for eighty of these one hundred years" (26).

It is therefore not an unfair observation to say that their entire survey of "The Editions of the New Testament" is designed to accredit the successive Nestle editions, beginning in 1898, then continuing through the twenty-first edition of 1952, when Kurt Aland's name first appears on the title page (as the present volume is quick to point out, p. 20), and finally the current twenty-sixth edition edited by both Kurt and Barbara Aland. That this is a proper interpretation is confirmed by their statement, "It is significant that in its 657 printed pages the early Nestle text differs from the modern 'Standard text' in merely seven hundred passages" (20). As indicated earlier, it

out some rather bitter sarcasm in the context, was that this judgment about the relation of the texts of Westcott-Hort and Nestle-Aland "causes surprise to cease and astonishment to begin" (Aland, "Twentieth Century Interlude," 3 [see below]). Now it is perhaps our turn for astonishment, for in the present volume—fifteen years later—the Alands, in nearly five pages, reprint and expand upon the very same statistics, and they conclude (as I had) that the data on the Nestle editions through the 25th "show for Nestle a closer affinity to Westcott-Hort" than to any other (Aland and Aland, *Text of the New Testament*, 26; cf. 26–30). So, it would appear that a "twentieth century interlude" in the progress of hand-editions, which Kurt Aland earlier had vigorously denied, is now essentially affirmed.

See the full interaction in E. J. Epp, "The Twentieth Century Interlude in New Testament Textual Criticism," *JBL* 93 (1974) 387–90; Kurt Aland, "The Twentieth Century Interlude in New Testament Textual Criticism," in E. Best and R. McL. Wilson, eds., *Text and Interpretation: Studies in the New Testament Presented to Matthew Black* (Cambridge/New York: Cambridge University Press, 1979) 3–5; and E. J. Epp, "A Continuing Interlude in New Testament Textual Criticism?" *HTR* 73 (1980) 135–38.

[22] The discrepancy between "seventy" and "eighty" years in these two passages may be due to the fact that a fair measure of the volume is made up of previously published materials—as pointed out, e.g., by J. Keith Elliott's review in *ThZ* 39 (1983) 247, and by Frans Neirynck, *ETL* 58 (1982) 389.

might be granted them that the Nestle text has been the dominant edition in terms of practical use down through the years, but it is difficult to see how it has been a major force at the theoretical level in our discipline, and to that extent their portrayal supports our characterization of their volume as a revisionist history of New Testament textual criticism.

If this rewriting of history is an error of commission, there is much more on the side of omission in the book. By and large, for example, editions of the New Testament are described in terms of the manuscript evidence known in their time and the utilization of that evidence by the editor, but only rarely do the theoretical principles that shaped an edition come into the discussion. Lachmann, for
example, receives three lines (11), and the page-and-a-half descrip- 223
tion of Tischendorf refers to the manuscripts he discovered and made use of and then explains the theoretical basis of his edition by saying only that Codex Sinaiticus "served as the critical standard for establishing the text" (14). Only the Westcott-Hort edition and that of Hermann von Soden receive any analysis of their theoretical principles and basis. The von Soden edition is given a balanced assessment in a few paragraphs, pointing out both its theoretical weaknesses and its lasting contributions (22–23), and Westcott-Hort is treated in two pages, a fair portion of which is used to debunk their distinctive term "neutral" (14–15, 18). The Alands also point out, somewhat polemically, that "Westcott and Hort had no direct witness to the New Testament text earlier than the fourth century" (14), and they emphasize (with apparent sarcasm) that Westcott-Hort's theories have influence "even today, especially in the English-speaking world" (18). The footnote here chastizes Bruce Metzger—unfairly—for what the Alands take to be an overestimation of Westcott-Hort's importance. It is actually the Alands, however, whose brief description of Westcott-Hort on the very same page presents a serious distortion. They assert that Westcott-Hort ascribe to Codex Bezae "the highest quality" (18). Nothing, however, could be farther from the truth: Hort may have claimed high antiquity for the D-text, but not high quality. Indeed, as is well known, Hort's entire theory turned on a quality judgment between the so-called Neutral and the so-called Western texts, and the latter came out as distinctly inferior in quality.[23]

[23] In part, the Alands are referring to the so-called "Western Non-Interpolations," whose significance they take every opportunity to deny (e.g., 15, 33, 232).

New Testament Textual Criticism Present

The portrayal of New Testament textual criticism in the present is more implicit than explicit in the volume by the Alands. They do, however, raise the question, "What of the present scene where the reader of the Greek New Testament now meets the new 'Standard text'?" (30);[24] and the brief section that follows is fully occupied with a description of the text found in Nestle-Aland^{26} and the UBS*GNT*^{3}, with a brief discussion of its history. We may recall the statement quoted earlier, that this "Standard text" is virtually the only noteworthy achievement of the past fifty years,[25] and we may add to that the authors' affirmation that the UBS*GNT*^{3} and Nestle-Aland^{26} "fully satisfy the high standards required by the academic and exegetical disciplines" (43), as well as their claim, not otherwise substantiated, that "the new 'Standard text' comes closer to the original text of the New Testament than did Tischendorf or Westcott and Hort" (24).

224 Something that is omitted in the Alands' volume—in addition to what has been said earlier—is an adequate statement of the theoretical base for this so-called "Standard text." In view of the many pages devoted to it in the volume, it is surprising to discover that the description of this text largely concerns procedural aspects of the committee's work, the story of how the text of the Nestle-Aland Greek New Testament and the UBS*GNT* came together, and the differing formats of the two editions. There is little on the theory of the text itself, except to say that the theories of Westcott-Hort were abandoned (33) and that a local-genealogical method is used (34). The latter is described as "applying to each passage individually the approach used by classical philology for a whole tradition," which may not help a beginning student very much; indeed, the local-genealogical method is neither carefully nor well defined anywhere in the volume, though tucked away twenty-five pages from the very end one might discover that it accredits as the original reading the reading that best explains the rise of the other readings.[26]

---

[24] The section treating this consists of pp. 30–36.

[25] See n. 16 above.

[26] Cf. 286, 289, which refer to their Rules 6 and 8 on 275–76; only on 286 is the method defined in any direct fashion. [I should have pointed out that the "local-genealogical method" had been described and named in the "Introduction" to Nestle-Aland^{26}, 43*; see my earlier discussion in "Continuing Interlude," 140–43.]

For the Alands, what replaces a history and theory of the text—which has occupied so much international scholarly attention over the years—are two new systems of categorizing or classifying New Testament manuscripts. One system uses the classification of "free text," "normal text," "strict text," and "D text." These classifications attempt to describe the degree of freedom or strictness with which a manuscript follows its exemplar: a "free text" treats its exemplar in "a relatively free manner" (59, 93–95); a "normal text" represents "a relatively faithful tradition that departs from its exemplar only occasionally"; a "strict text" transmits its exemplar's text "with meticulous care (e.g., P^{75})" and departs from it "only rarely" (they state that ten to twenty percent of the Greek manuscripts faithfully preserve their various exemplars [70]); and, finally, some transitional forms, including a "D text," which is a kind of text like that in Codex Bezae, though they emphasize that there are only a few representatives extant (64, 93–95; cf. 69). As a sample of how these classifications are applied, among the papyri, for example, the Alands classify eight as "free," nine as "strict," ten as "normal," and three as "D text" (94–95).

How is this classification system to be evaluated? First, Gordon Fee has convincingly demonstrated that both P^{75} and Codex B are relatively faithful preservations of a common exemplar,[27] but beyond such isolated cases it is not at all clear how it can so easily be determined that a manuscript has or has not strictly followed its exemplar or to what degree it has done so. Secondly, three of these categories (free text, normal text, strict text) involve scribal standards 225
of copying and gradations of faithfulness of a manuscript to its exemplar, but the fourth category, D-text, represents something entirely different—a particular textual stream or configuration. So, these categories lack coherence and symmetry. The novice, of course, will welcome such labels as this volume offers, and they will use them qualitatively and simplistically, but most experts are likely to feel that greater clarification as to the basis, the meaning, and the significance of this classification system is required before they will adopt it for themselves.

[27] Gordon D. Fee, "P^{75}, P^{66}, and Origen: The Myth of Early Textual Recension in Alexandria," in R. N. Longenecker and M. C. Tenney, eds., *New Dimensions in New Testament Study* (Grand Rapids: Zondervan, 1974) 33–40.

The other system of classification assigns each New Testament manuscript to one of five categories, as follows (95, 105–6; cf. 155–59):

Category I: "Manuscripts of a very special quality which should always be considered in establishing the original text (e.g., the Alexandrian text belongs here)."
Category II: "Manuscripts of a special quality," but with "alien influences (particularly of the Byzantine text), and yet of importance for establishing the original text (e.g., the Egyptian text belongs here)."
Category III: "Manuscripts of a distinctive character with an independent text, usually important for establishing the original text, but particularly important for the history of the text (e.g., f^1, f^{13})."
Category IV: "Manuscripts of the D text."
Category V: "Manuscripts with a purely or predominantly Byzantine text, or with a text too brief or too colorless to be of any real importance for establishing the original text."

The chart in their volume (155–59) places about 500 papyri, uncials, and minuscules into these various categories.

Much thought and extensive labor have been expended in formulating these classifications, but is it fair, nonetheless, to ask what they really do for us? It would appear that they establish three categories of New Testament manuscripts that range from (a) very important to (b) important to c) usually important for establishing the original text, and two categories (the D and Byzantine texts) that are not important for that purpose. If these categorizations prove or could be proved to be trustworthy, they would provide a valuable service, replacing in effect the need for a reliable history and theory of the New Testament text. But what is lacking, at least so far, is a convincing basis—or any substantial basis at all—for the placement of manuscripts into these various categories. We are told one criterion: age, for all papyri and uncials dating before the third/fourth century are automatically included in Category I, because they have "an inherent significance" (56). We are told a second criterion: quality of text, for P^{74}, though dating to the seventh century, is in Category I "because of its textual quality" (95). And we know a third criterion: manuscripts with the D text are automatically placed in Category IV, which is not important for the original text because the Alands

have concluded that the D text could not have existed prior to the
third/fourth century, though they admit that a few early papyri con- 226
tain this type of text (51, 64, 69). In addition, we know a fourth criterion: manuscripts with a Byzantine text are placed in Category V and are of no importance for establishing the original text—though that was already known from Westcott-Hort and others. Finally, two additional criteria involve measurements of a New Testament manuscript's agreements with the Byzantine text and its agreements with the "original text" (apparently they mean the text of Nestle-Aland^{26}) (106).

Once again, the novice will welcome these categories and—again—will use them qualitatively, as indeed is intended, but unfortunately they will also use them simplistically. Yet, this classification scheme also requires greater explanation, clearer definition, and a more substantive rationale before it will either be accepted or become meaningful to the expert. For one thing, there is a certain measure of question-begging or circularity of argument in this schema when, for example, a manuscript is placed into Category I on the basis of its "incidence of agreements with the original text" (see above) but when—at the same time— manuscripts in Category I constitute those that possess "a very special quality which should always be considered in establishing the original text." In addition, there is a fair measure of prejudgment or arbitrariness if, for example, numerous manuscripts are automatically included in Category I merely because of their age and another manuscript (P^{74}) is included in that same category despite its age. The issue becomes more complicated because, in this case, the inclusion of the manuscript (P^{74}) in the top category is due to its textual quality, which has been determined, presumably, on the basis of its affinity with the (predetermined) "original text." So we are back to circularity. And finally, does not the predilection for a certain group of manuscripts that have "an inherent significance" (all the third/fourth century papyri and uncials) come rather close—in principle at least—to what the Alands call the "extreme" of Westcott-Hort "with their partiality to [Codex] B"?[28] Is it not a small step from the "cult of the best manuscript" (of

[28] See 20; cf. 14–20, where Westcott-Hort's claims for the "Neutral" text (primarily Codex B) receive much criticism.

which Westcott-Hort have frequently been accused)[29] to the "cult of the best manuscripts"? Reliance on the "best" manuscripts is, of course, one legitimate canon of criticism (among others), but the crucial issue is the procedure by which it is determined that they indeed are the "best" manuscripts.

A further aspect of the present scene in New Testament textual criticism concerns text types, a subject to which—proportionately—the Alands' volume devotes a good deal of space in the first two chapters. This is a highly complex and controversial subject and yet
227 one that is of great importance for present-day textual criticism.[30] Space limitations, however, simply do not allow it to be pursued here, except to comment that novice and expert alike will not find it easy to discern the exact position taken in the volume. For example, the Alands speak of the "Alexandrian Egyptian" text, but elsewhere distinguish between the Alexandrian and the Egyptian texts (28).[31] Moreover, the differing meanings of "Western" text and "D text" are not easy to grasp. Yet, their general conviction about text types is firmly stated: "Remember that only the Alexandrian text, the Koine text, and the D text are incontestably verified" (67). In all of this, though, it is evident that church history drives their views on New Testament text types, rather than the other way around. For instance, no "Western" text in the geographical sense could ever have existed, they say, because:

> No important personality can be identified at any time or place in the early Western church who would have been capable of the singular theological achievement represented by the text of the Gospels and Acts in the ancestor of Codex Bezae Cantabrigiensis (D). (69)

But no one in recent times has argued that "Western" text means Western in a geographical sense. So the point is not well taken, not

---

[29] Esp. by J. Keith Elliott, e.g., "Rational Criticism and the Text of the New Testament," *Theology* 75 (1972) 339–40; idem, "Can We Recover the Original New Testament?" *Theology* 77 (1974) 345.

[30] See E. J. Epp, "Textual Criticism," in idem and George W. MacRae, S.J., eds., *The New Testament and Its Modern Interpreters* (Philadelphia: Fortress; Atlanta: Scholars Press, 1989) 97–100; and idem, "The Significance of the Papyri for Determining the Nature of the New Testament Text in the Second Century: A Dynamic View of Textual Transmission," in W. L. Petersen, ed., *Gospel Traditions in the Second Century* (Christianity and Judaism in Antiquity 3; Notre Dame: University of Notre Dame Press, 1989) 84–101.

[31] Hyphenated in the German edition; the two texts are distinguished on 56, 70–71.

only on that ground but also in proposing that a phenomenon is precluded simply because it is not possible to identify a specific, known personality who might have produced it. Should it not first be determined whether or not such an entity as a D-text existed in the early period, and should it not then—and only then—be asked whether a text with that particular character can be fitted into a specific church-historical situation? Even if no "important personality" can be found, that does not invalidate an otherwise established textual phenomenon. After all—to take a simple example—the Epistle to the Hebrews came into the New Testament canon and remained there even though, as Origen said, "God only knows" who wrote it (Eusebius *Hist. eccl.* 6.25.14).

The Alands' volume complains, by the way, that "New Testament textual criticism has traditionally neglected the findings of early Church History, but only to its own injury" (49; cf. 52, 66), yet here again the neglect of British and American New Testament text-critical work has diminished the accuracy and value of the Alands' book, for it was especially among English-speaking scholars that the transmission of the New Testament text was placed within its church-historical context. Beside Westcott-Hort (!), one need only mention Kirsopp Lake's seminal study, *The Influence of Textual Criticism on the*
Exegesis of the New Testament of 1904[32] or J. Rendel Harris's work, 228
where, already in 1914, he proposed adding to Hort's famous dictum that "Knowledge of documents should precede final judgment upon readings"[33] the further rule that "Knowledge . . . of Church History should precede final judgment as to readings."[34] To the names of Lake and Harris may be added an extensive list of other Anglo-American scholars who have emphasized the importance of pursuing New Testament textual criticism within the context of early church history.[35]

[32] Kirsopp Lake, *The Influence of Textual Criticism on the Exegesis of the New Testament* (Oxford, 1904) 3–4, 11–12.

[33] Westcott-Hort, *New Testament in the Original Greek*, 2.31.

[34] J. Rendel Harris, "New Points of View in Textual Criticism," *Expositor* VIII. 7 (1914) 322; cf. 319–23; idem, "The Mentality of Tatian," *Bulletin of the Bezan Club* 9 (1931) 8.

[35] Among others, Donald W. Riddle, "Textual Criticism as a Historical Discipline," *ATR* 18 (1936) 220–33; Merrill M. Parvis, "The Nature and Tasks of New Testament Textual Criticism: An Appraisal," *JR* 32 (1952) 165–74; Günther Zuntz, *The Text of the Epistles: A Disquisition upon the Corpus Paulinum* (Schweich Lectures, 1946; London:

New Testament Textual Criticism Future

The portrayal of New Testament textual criticism in the future commands little attention in the Alands' volume, and that is understandable given its nature. At least two statements, however, are somewhat disturbing and raise issues of general interest and of scholarly morale in the field. First, it is affirmed that "of course the new 'Standard text' itself is not a static entity" and that proposals for changes, if they are to be adopted, require only convincing arguments. The authors then state that "many will undoubtedly feel strongly inclined to make improvements here and there in the 'Standard text.' This temptation should be resisted" (35). It is clear, however, that we cannot have it both ways.

229 Their second statement, while not of great consequence, is perhaps incautious. In speaking of "the increasing number of manuscripts," the authors state: "After the impressive growth in the number of manuscripts recorded in the nineteenth century by Gregory and in the twentieth by the Institute for New Testament Textual Research, it is unlikely that the future will bring any comparable increases" (75). That may be so, and it is true that any buried papyri in Egypt are likely to be destroyed by the rising water table due to the High

Oxford University Press for the British Academy, 1953) 10–11; Kenneth W. Clark, "The Effect of Recent Textual Criticism upon New Testament Studies," in W. D. Davies and David Daube, eds., *The Background of the New Testament and Its Eschatology* (Cambridge: Cambridge University Press, 1956) 44–45; idem, "Textual Criticism and Doctrine," *Studia Paulina in honorem Johannis De Zwaan septuagenarii* (Haarlem: Bohn, 1953) 52–65; reprinted, respectively, in Clark's *The Gentile Bias and Other Essays* (ed. J. L. Sharpe III; NovTSup 54; Leiden: Brill, 1980) 82–83; 90–103; J. Neville Birdsall's masterful survey of New Testament textual criticism in a historical framework, "The New Testament Text," in P. R. Ackroyd and C. F. Evans, eds., *The Cambridge History of the Bible*, vol. 1: *From the Beginnings to Jerome* (Cambridge: Cambridge University Press, 1970) 311–16; 328–77. Other names could be added, to result in a list that would read almost like a litany in the discipline (K. Lake, J. R. Harris, B. H. Streeter, E. C. Blackman, G. Zuntz, J. N. Birdsall, D. W. Riddle, E. C. Colwell, M. M. Parvis, K. W. Clark, E. W. Saunders, L. E. Wright,), and this British-American emphasis could hardly be overlooked accidentally by anyone in the field. Europeans, specifically Germans, who emphasize this church-historical approach are fewer, but the small, influential volume by Erich Fascher is well known: *Textgeschichte als hermeneutisches Problem* (Halle [Saale], 1953); cf. M. Karnetzki, "Textgeschichte als Überlieferungsgeschichte," *ZNW* 47 (1956) 170–80. For discussion and pertinent quotations, see Eldon Jay Epp, *The Theological Tendency of Codex Bezae Cantabrigiensis in Acts* (SNTSMS 3; Cambridge/New York: Cambridge University Press, 1966) 14–21.

Dam at Assuan, yet who would have foreseen that either the Chester Beatty or Bodmer New Testament papyri would come to light in the 1930s and 1950s? The discipline of New Testament textual criticism, with or without new manuscript discoveries, has a promising and vibrant future, but let us hope that the pessimism regarding fresh discoveries will not find fulfillment and that younger scholars will be taught, rather, to look to the future with expectation and optimism.

Conclusion

What does all this mean for New Testament textual criticism? On the practical side, it means—at least for some—that we have a volume in hand to which all experts must and will refer constantly for information on the witnesses to the New Testament text, but a volume which most experts—on other grounds—would be extremely reluctant to place in the hands of uninitiated students in the field. The irony is that the book was designed for the novice and not the specialist, yet the novice is precisely the person who will receive from it a distorted impression of the history and theory of the New Testament text—if the first two chapters are read. Unfortunately, many may use it as their first introduction to the discipline, especially in its German original in German-speaking countries—perhaps less so in English—and such readers will both be ill-informed about history and also frustrated by the intricate detail in which the manuscripts, versional, and patristic material is presented. Most worrisome of all, however, will be the difficulty of correcting the misimpressions conveyed by a popular revisionist history—if indeed this volume is or becomes popular—and it is this realization that constitutes the primary motivation for the present analysis and critique.

As will be obvious from the foregoing, one comes away from the Alands' volume with an overwhelming sense of ambivalence, for so much of it is so excellent, yet other, smaller portions are seriously flawed. The excellent parts should by no means be lost sight of, yet it would be less than responsible to ignore those limited portions that appear to have been skewed by revisionist polemics. These flawed portions, while they fall short of being fatally flawed, nevertheless constitute a serious handicap and one that will lead many New Testament textual critics to recommend the book only with caution and with clear caveats, particularly in the English-speaking world, where the offense will be the greatest, but elsewhere as well.

Added Notes, 2004

This paper was first presented in the New Testament Textual Criticism Section at the 1988 Annual Meeting of the Society of Biblical Literature in Chicago. A decade and a half later, I stand by this harsh critique of several aspects of the Alands' book, though I would reemphasize that the criticism applies to a small portion and that, as I stressed in the article, the bulk of their volume contains a vast amount of important material that is indispensable for textual critics and convenient to find and to utilize. Indeed, it is a book that I use virtually on a daily basis. All of us owe a great debt to Kurt and Barbara Aland for their premier works on New Testament textual criticism—this handbook, the Nestle-Aland and United Bible Societies' Greek New Testaments, and the numerous reference works produced by the Münster Institute over the years. Without them, the discipline could not have flourished and the work of individual scholars would be hampered enormously.

The second edition of the Alands' book appeared in German in 1988, and the second English edition in 1989. The pagination of the two English editions varies by only a few pages throughout, and the content is essentially the same, except that the second edition contains an added chapter on "Categories and Text Types, and the Textual Analysis of Manuscripts" (pp. 317–37) by Barbara Aland.

On the Alands' classification of texts and manuscripts, i.e. their characterizations of "free text," "normal text" "strict text," and "D-text," and their five manuscript categories (pp. 224–26; cf. the added chapter in the second edition), see my "Issues in New Testament Textual Criticism: Moving from the Nineteenth Century to the Twenty-First Century," *Rethinking New Testament Textual Criticism* (ed. D. A. Black; Grand Rapids, MI: Baker Academic, 2002) 39–41; Bart D. Ehrman, "A Problem of Textual Circularity: The Alands on the Classification of New Testament Manuscripts," *Bib* 70 (1989) 377–88.

On the term "Standard Text," note that the term was dropped from the Alands' subsequent publications (cf., e.g., p. 30 in the first with the second English edition of their *Text of the New Testament*, where "new text" replaces it). See Ian A. Moir, "Can We Risk Another

'Textus Receptus,'?" *JBL* 100 (1981) 614–18; cf. Hans-Werner Bartsch, "Ein neuer Textus Receptus für das griechische Neue Testament?" *NTS* 27 (1980–1981) 585–92.

Some reviews of the Alands' *The Text of the New Testament* (first German and English editions): Birdsall, J. Neville, *BT* 39 (1988) 338–42; J. Keith Elliott," *TZ* 39 (1983) 247–49; idem, *ExpT* 100 (1988–1989) 183; E. J. Epp, "An Indispensable But Flawed Tool for Textual Critics," *Int* 44 (1990) 71–75; Michael W. Holmes, *JBL* 108 (1989) 139–44; Larry W. Hurtado, *CBQ* 50 (1988) 313–15; George D. Kilpatrick, *NovT* 25 (1983) 89–90; Frans Neirynck, *ETL* 58 (1982) 388–91; Jon Paulien, *AUSS* 29 (1991) 73–76; Stephen Pisano, *Bib* 66 (1985) 265–66; Moisés Silva, *WTJ* 50 (1988) 195–200; Daniel B. Wallace, *Grace Theological Journal* 8 (1987) 279–85.

CHAPTER TWELVE

THE NEW TESTAMENT PAPYRUS MANUSCRIPTS IN HISTORICAL PERSPECTIVE[1]

> The nineteenth century is the age of inscriptions; the twentieth will be the age of papyri.
>
> Theodor Mommsen[2]

I have two major interests in New Testament textual criticism: history and method. These may appear to be two separate interests, but I have never been able to keep them apart. Methodology in New Testament textual criticism is informed by its history, and its history, in turn, is informed by the study of method. This interaction of history and method is integral to this brief and somewhat simple paper, for the question that intrigues me is this: If the New Testament papyri are considered to be so extraordinarily important by virtually all textual critics, then why was their importance really not recognized—or at least not widely recognized—for something

[1] This paper draws a fair measure of material from the author's Kenneth Willis Clark Lectures at Duke University in April, 1986, "Papyrus Manuscripts of the New Testament: Treasure from the Past—Challenge for the Future," but its particular thrust was developed for presentation at the Annual Meeting of the Society of Biblical Literature in November of that year. Following that reading, Gordon D. Fee graciously alerted me to a serious deficiency, which I have corrected for this version, and I am grateful to him.

Professor Fitzmyer presided at the session in which I read my very first paper at a learned society—at the Society of Biblical Literature in December of 1960—and that paper became my first publication ("The 'Ignorance Motif' in Acts and Anti-Judaic Tendencies in Codex Bezae," *HTR* 55 [1962] 51–62). In the same year Professor Fitzmyer published an article on P75 (*CBQ* 24 [1962] 170–79)—noting some of the methodological points emphasized now in this paper—and his magisterial commentary on *The Gospel according to Luke* (2 vols.; AB 28; Garden City: Doubleday, 1981–85), unlike many, is fully informed by text-critical discussion. During Professor Fitzmyer's six-year term (1971–76) as Editor of the *Journal of Biblical Literature*, I was privileged to serve as Associate Editor for New Testament book reviews, and my already high admiration for him as a scholar was enlarged to include admiration also as a fair-minded and meticulous editor and as a good friend and colleague.

[2] See the following note.

like fifty or sixty years after the first discoveries? In exploring this issue, the intertwining of history and method will be both obvious and extensive.

This paper, then, has a simple thesis and a limited purpose. The thesis is that the New Testament papyri were surprisingly underappreciated until about twenty years ago, and the purpose is to attempt an explanation for this claim, as well as to shed some light both on the history of New Testament textual criticism and on text-critical theory. In the process, it will be of interest to ask, for example, what papyri were known at various critical points in New Testament text-critical work, to what extent they were utilized by researchers and editors, and how important they were at various historical junctures.

262 Theodor Mommsen (1817–1903), the great nineteenth century classical scholar and winner of the Nobel Prize for literature in 1902—the year before his death—referred to the nineteenth century as "the age of inscriptions"; "the twentieth," he said, "will be the age of papyri."[3] Certainly this prediction was "on target" for the ancient world generally, but no less so for the New Testament text—particularly from our present perspective near the end of that twentieth century. Yet, our understanding of the significance of the papyri for New Testament textual criticism cannot be complete unless we have walked, step by step and year by year, through the period of their discovery, use, and eventual triumph. This journey begins with a general account of the use of papyrus in antiquity, which will provide background and perspective for our subject.

I. The Ancient Use of Papyrus and Its Modern Rediscovery

Anyone vaguely familiar with antiquity knows how the freshly-cut lower stem of the papyrus plant can be peeled off in long strips, which are placed side by side—slightly overlapping—and are then covered by another set of strips laid crosswise, and how several blows

[3] E. G. Turner, *Greek Papyri: An Introduction* (Oxford: Clarendon Press, 1968) 23. [Actually, this "quotation" has not been located among Mommsen's writings, but Peter van Minnen, "The Century of Papyrology (1892–1992)," *BASP* 30 (1993) 5 n. 2, has traced its likely source to K. Preisendanz: "Mommsen once said. . . ."]

from a broad mallet or a flat stone fuse the two layers together into a sheet, which, when dried and polished with pumice, produces a writing material that is light-colored, strong, flexible, and durable.[4]

Durability, of course, is a relative term. Yet, those who doubt the strength and flexibility of the papyrus stems need only be reminded of the papyrus sailing ships built and used by Thor Heyerdahl in his attempt to replicate those of antiquity. Heyerdahl's second ship, the *Ra II*, was constructed of eight tons of papyrus, held together only by rope. As many will recall, in 1970 it completed the 3,270-mile trip from Morocco to Barbados in fifty-seven days. A year earlier the first ship, the *Ra I*, broke apart 600 miles short of its goal, but the failure was due, not to the papyrus itself, but to an inferior, segmented method of construction.[5] We know that light skiffs were made of papyrus in Egypt already in the 4th dynasty (around 2600
B.C.E.), as, for example, were sails and, in 480 B.C.E., the cables for 263
a bridge of boats across the Hellespont.[6] The Egyptian tombs also yield examples of papyrus rope.[7]

When prepared as a writing material, papyrus retained these same characteristics of strength and flexibility, contrary to the long-standing and popular misconception that it was an especially fragile substance that certainly—it is said—was inferior in durability to parchment. One striking confirmation that this is a misconception was the discovery that the Qumran leather scroll of Samuel (4QSam^{a}) had been strengthened on the back with a strip of papyrus, thereby significantly aiding the scroll's preservation. We know also that papyrus manuscripts already 250 years old were used again for new documents in the first century B.C.E.[8]

---

[4] Ibid., 3; H. Idris Bell, *Egypt from Alexander the Great to the Arab Conquest: A Study in the Diffusion and Decay of Hellenism* (Oxford: Clarendon Press, 1948) 6–7. For the *locus classicus* on the making of papyrus in antiquity (Pliny, *Natural History* xiii.74–82), see the text, commentary, and discussion in Naphtali Lewis, *Papyrus in Classical Antiquity* (Oxford: Clarendon Press, 1974) 34–69.

[5] Thor Heyerdahl, "The Voyage of *Ra II*," *National Geographic Magazine* 139 (January, 1971) 44–71, esp. 46–47.

[6] *Encyclopaedia Britannica* (1972) 19.614a; 17.296c.

[7] Ibid., 19.614a. A full account of uses of papyrus in antiquity can be found in Lewis, *Papyrus in Classical Antiquity*, 21–32; 95–97.

[8] T. C. Skeat, "Early Christian Book-Production: Papyri and Manuscripts," *Cambridge History of the Bible, Volume 2: The West from the Fathers to the Reformation* (ed. G. W. H. Lampe; Cambridge: University Press, 1969) 59–60.

Papyrus does, however, become fragile when it has been alternately wet and dry. If this occurs repeatedly, papyrus disintegrates at the slightest touch.[9] Actually, papyrus manuscripts survive only when protected from moisture, either by placement in protective caves, buildings, or jars, or when buried in ordinary ground in the virtually rain-free areas of Egypt, Palestine, and Mesopotamia—provided, however, that they are neither too close to the surface, nor too deeply buried so as to be affected by water rising from below.[10] Incidentally, the new high dam at Assuan and increased irrigation will result in the gradual raising of the water-table, not merely in the immediate area, but throughout Egypt, and—most regrettably—the continued survival of any buried papyrus is thereby forever threatened.[11]

Unfortunately, too, the conditions necessary for the survival of papyrus did not prevail in the vast Delta area of Egypt, including Alexandria, which contained the greatest library of the ancient world and was a city with extensive literary activity. Ancient Alexandria, in fact, is now below sea level.[12] Moreover, blowing sand often defaces papyrus text, and white ants may devour papyrus manuscripts.[13] With all of these natural hazards—ancient and modern—it is remarkable that any considerable quantity of papyrus has survived.

264 When human hazards are added to the natural ones, it is an even greater wonder that we have much papyrus remaining at all. One of the earliest stories of westerners securing papyrus manuscripts comes from the late 18th century (1778) and reports that a traveler was offered at a low price some forty or fifty papyrus rolls, but that he bought only one and that the others—so the story goes—were torn up and burned for their pleasant odor.[14] A century later, when scholars began to search systematically for papyri, masses of discarded documents were discovered in the rubbish heaps of Egypt. These were documents that had been discarded already in antiquity. Researchers, however, often discarded anew the top layers of Arabic, Coptic, and Byzantine papyri that they uncovered, and kept only the more interesting ones from earlier periods, or they discarded

[9] Turner, *Greek Papyri*, 3.
[10] Ibid., 18.
[11] Ibid., 40.
[12] Bell, *Egypt*, 10.
[13] Ibid., 61.
[14] Turner, *Greek Papyri*, 18–19.

papyri in general in favor of ancient artifacts that might have more artistic or intrinsic worth. E. G. Turner, currently perhaps the leading expert on papyri, estimates that "many thousands, perhaps millions of texts must have been destroyed" in this process.[15] He estimates, moreover, that "in the hit-or-miss ransacking of ancient sites for [artifacts] of intrinsic value, perhaps half the papyri they contained were ruined by the coarse methods employed."[16] But even when papyri were specifically sought and valued, disaster might strike: the ship containing the entire results of an 1898 German expedition caught fire in the harbor at Hamburg, and all the papyri were destroyed.[17] Who knows what may have been lost in that unforeseen destruction! When one recognizes the historical value that we now attach, for example, to a credit-card-sized papyrus of the Fourth Gospel, one shudders to think of what might—indeed, must—have been lost through natural causes or human negligence. I refer in this example, of course, to P52, a tiny fragment of John that can be dated to between 100 and 125 and shows that John's Gospel was written recently enough to have been transferred to Egypt and to have been copied and circulated there at that early period.[18]

If so much militated against the survival of papyrus manuscripts, what aided their preservation? There were, after all, tens of thousands of papyri recovered (if one counts fragments) and many thousands published.[19] It is difficult, by the way, to find statistics, but already by 1920 perhaps 20,000 papyri had been discovered, and about half of those had been published.[20] A recent estimate is that "somewhere between 15,000 and 20,000" Greek and Latin papyrus documents had been published by 1968, and that this represented 265
perhaps only half of those discovered.[21] Literary texts, of course, are far less numerous, and William H. Willis suggested as long ago as

[15] Ibid., 21.
[16] Ibid., 26.
[17] Ibid., 13; Bell, *Egypt*, 18.
[18] [See now E. J. Epp, "New Testament Papyrus Manuscripts and Letter Carrying in Greco-Roman Times," *The Future of Early Christianity: Essays in Honor of Helmut Koester* (eds. B. A. Pearson, in collaboration with A. T. Kraabel, G. W. E. Nickelsburg, and N. R. Petersen; Minneapolis, MN: Fortress, 1991) 35–56, esp., 52–56, on the speed with which letters could travel.]
[19] Bell, *Egypt*, 19.
[20] B. P. Grenfell, "The Present Position of Papyrology," *BJRL* 6 (1921–22) 155–56.
[21] Turner, *Greek Papyri*, 128.

1968 that "the number of literary papyri already published must now have exceeded 3,000."[22] Not only has much survived the hazards, but some discoveries will continue—though only tombs, or hiding places in the desert on the fringes of the Nile valley are likely to be safe preserves in the days ahead.[23]

In addition to the dry, natural conditions specified earlier, where would papyri best survive? Placing them in the semi-loose soil of a rubbish mound, or in a building partly filled with and buried in rubbish, or in a collapsed building filled with wind-blown sand, would significantly aid their survival. In 1896/1897, B. P. Grenfell and A. S. Hunt, who developed a calculated method for searching these kinds of sites for papyri, excavated the ancient town of Oxyrhynchus, which is on the edge of the desert 120 miles south of Cairo, where they recovered a huge quantity of papyrus from the rubbish heaps. During two of the best days, for example, thirty-six large baskets of papyri were recovered the first day, and twenty-five more the second.[24]

A cemetery unaffected by moisture—as already intimated—was another favorable location, and some papyri were buried with the dead. Papyrus was also one of the materials used for constructing mummy cases in certain periods and in certain parts of Egypt. Layers of used papyrus were glued together to form a kind of paper maché, which was molded into shape, plastered, and painted.[25] In 1900, Grenfell and Hunt, again, were searching a cemetery for mummy cases, hoping to find such papyrus with writing on it, when one of their workmen—disgusted at finding only mummified crocodiles—struck and broke one of the crocodile cases. It was wrapped in sheets of papyrus. Within a few weeks "several thousand" crocodiles were excavated, of which about 2% contained papyrus.[26]

Of particular interest, however, are the Jewish customs of preserving manuscripts by placing them in jars and of disposing of defective or worn-out manuscripts by burying them near a cemetery. The Dead Sea Scrolls represent the best-known example of this practice. It has been suggested recently that these habits were taken over from

---

[22] William H. Willis, "A Census of the Literary Papyri from Egypt," *GRBS* 9 (1968) 205.

[23] Turner, *Greek Papyri*, 40.

[24] Ibid., 27–30.

[25] Bell, *Egypt*, 13–14.

[26] Turner, *Greek Papyri*, 31–32; Bell, *Egypt*, 13–14.

Judaism by early Christians and that the preservation of some Christian documents must be attributed to this procedure. These views were developed by C. H. Roberts, who for a generation has been one of the premier palaeographers of the English-speaking world, though T. C. Skeat, another of that elite group, is skeptical of the theory.[27] 266
It is significant, however, that only one classical manuscript has been discovered in a jar—in an archive of family papers from the 6th century C.E.[28]—while some Christian papyri were discovered in jars or other hiding places in houses, presumably to preserve them during times of persecution.[29] If this is how some New Testament papyri were preserved, then—at the risk of an unworthy pun and to paraphrase Paul in 2 Cor 4:7—"we have these treasures in earthen vessels."

The majority of papyri, however, were recovered from rubbish heaps or ruined buildings, and the vast majority, of course, are not literary texts—much less biblical texts—but rather official documents, correspondence, and records; or land surveys, census lists, and legal documents and contracts of all kinds; or even schoolboys' exercises in penmanship.[30]

This profusion of material attests to the fact that at times papyrus as a writing material was quite inexpensive. For example, an account from Ptolemaic Egypt in 257 B.C.E. indicates that certain offices of the prime minister used 434 rolls in just thirty-three days.[31] Lest this evidence be discounted on the ground that government officials—then or now—can hardly be expected to set standards for the economical use of supplies, consider that papyrus was often used with wide margins and large unwritten spaces, or that papyrus could be easily reused in either or both of two ways: by washing off the original writing (thus producing a *palimpsest*) or by writing on the reverse side—and yet such reuse was infrequent. Rather, vast quantities of

---

[27] T. C. Skeat, [review of C. H. Roberts, *Manuscript, Society and Belief in Early Christian Egypt*, 1979] *JTS* 31 (1980) 186.

[28] Colin H. Roberts, *Manuscript, Society and Belief in Early Christian Egypt* (Schweich Lectures, 1977; Oxford: Oxford University Press for the British Academy, 1979) 6–7.

[29] Ibid., 8.

[30] Bell, *Egypt*, 20–21.

[31] Turner, *Greek Papyri*, 6. For more detail on this heavy use of papyrus in finance offices in Oxyrhynchus, see Naphtali Lewis, *Greeks in Ptolemaic Egypt: Case Studies in the Social History of the Hellenistic World* (Oxford: Clarendon Press, 1986) 51–55.

documents that might have been used again were thrown on the rubbish heaps of Oxyrhynchus and other sites. As T. C. Skeat says, "the consumption of papyrus in the ancient world was on a scale which almost passes belief" and it is a "major misconception" that papyrus was an expensive commodity.[32]

When did papyrus become a vehicle for writing, and how long was it in use? A papyrus roll for writing has been found from 3000
267 B.C.E.,[33] and papyrus was still being manufactured in Egypt in the 11th century C.E.[34]—a period of more than 4000 years. The earliest extant papyri with Greek writing on them go back to the 4th century B.C.E.,[35] and Greek papyrus manuscripts were used for literary works as late as the 6th century C.E. and for documents and letters into the early 8th century C.E.—some 1100 years overall.[36]

Greek literary works during this period were more commonly written on parchment or vellum manuscripts—carefully prepared from the skins of animals—which was probably a more expensive material and certainly a more elegant one.[37] In the pre-Christian era these Greek literary works were written on rolls. From the first century C.E. there are extant 253 such rolls, and only one writing in codex form—that is, in our form of the book as we know it, constructed of folded sheets bound at one edge. In fact, until 300 C.E., Greek literature is found on 1697 rolls and in only thirty-six codices.[38] A theory advanced thirty years ago and held with increasing certainty is that the Christians invented the codex form of the book and that the earliest codices were made of papyrus, or—if Christians did not invent the codex—they immediately adopted it as the only acceptable form for their writings. As we just observed, it is striking that Greek literary work is found on only one codex in the first century and on only four more before 200 C.E., and that the earliest Latin codex is dated about 100, with no others dating prior to about 300.[39]

---

[32] Skeat, "Early Christian Book-Production," 59. See also the careful assessment by Lewis, *Papyrus in Classical Antiquity*, 129–34.

[33] Turner, *Greek Papyri*, 1.

[34] Ibid., 16.

[35] Ibid., 1.

[36] Ibid., 16.

[37] On the "profitless debate" about which was more expensive, see Colin H. Roberts and T. C. Skeat, *The Birth of the Codex* (London: British Academy by Oxford University Press, 1983) 7.

[38] Ibid., 37.

[39] Ibid., 28.

There are, however, eleven biblical manuscripts that Roberts and Skeat would date in the second century: six are Old Testament texts made and used by Christians, and five are New Testament texts. These are "the earliest Christian manuscripts in existence. All are on papyrus and in codex form."[40] The natural conclusion that they draw is "that when the Christian Bible first emerges into history the books of which it was composed are always written on papyrus and are always in codex form."[41] This "instant and universal" adoption of the codex by the earliest Christians is all the more striking because, whether Jewish or Gentile, these early Christians would "be strongly prejudiced in favour of the roll by upbringing, education and environment."[42] Clear reasons for this Christian propensity for the codex are still matters of debate and speculation, but if their preference 268
achieved nothing else, it clearly differentiated Christian writings from both Jewish and secular writings, where the roll-form of the book persisted and was dominant for a considerable period.[43]

In this connection, it is interesting that Christians at about the same time invented Greek abbreviations, or—better—contractions for the so-called *nomina sacra*, or certain divine names or terms used in the New Testament. The contractions were marked with a superscript line, and the words so treated were GOD, LORD, JESUS, and CHRIST, but also SPIRIT, ANTHROPOS (MAN), CROSS, FATHER, SON, SAVIOUR, MOTHER, HEAVEN, ISRAEL, DAVID, and JERUSALEM. This was "strictly a Christian usage unknown to Jewish or pagan manuscripts,"[44] and was carried through the Christian biblical manuscripts with rigorous uniformity. It has recently been suggested that these *nomina sacra* were theologically motivated—that the most prominent terms represented the common beliefs of all Christians: GOD, FATHER; LORD, JESUS, CHRIST, SON, SAVIOUR, CROSS; and SPIRIT.[45] In any case, like the exclusive use of the papyrus codex form in the earliest period, the *nomina sacra* also set apart the Christian writings from those that were Jewish or secular. It might be said also that their development of

[40] Ibid., 40–41.
[41] Ibid., 42.
[42] Ibid., 53.
[43] See ibid., 60.
[44] Ibid., 57.
[45] Modified from Roberts, *Manuscript, Society and Belief*, 46–47.

the codex form of the book shows that the early Christians were pragmatic—looking for practical ways to place more of their writings (including the bulky Septuagint) in less space than would have been required in the scroll form of the book.

But this is to push ahead of our story. Though used over these long periods, papyrus was little known or thought about from the late middle ages (1100 on) through the Renaissance. Papyrus was rediscovered by the scholarly world, however, when 800 rolls turned up at Herculaneum in 1752. They had been buried in the volcanic ash from Mt. Vesuvius in 79 C.E. The elements, though, had turned them into hardened masses, and they could not immediately be unrolled in any fruitful manner.[46] In spite of this new interest, the first papyrus manuscript was edited and published only in 1787; though this publication did not meet the expectations that the discovery had generated, numerous Europeans searched for and collected papyrus manuscripts during the following century.[47] Yet, Greek (and Latin) papyri were not common: in 1891 only 200 had been
269 published, with very few literary texts among them,[48] and not even a half-dozen fragments of the New Testament were included. The fact remains, however, that papyri had been rediscovered in the late 18th century and that a hundred years of moderate interest in them then prepared the way for the great discoveries that were to burst upon us during the last few years of the 19th century and the first half of the 20th.

II. The Discovery and Publication of New Testament Papyri

The discovery of New Testament papyri and their publication had an inauspicious and bizarre beginning, for the first claim to have found New Testament papyri and the first publication of these papyri took place in 1861, when a volume in large format was issued in

[46] Turner, *Greek Papyri*, 17–18. For an extensive, popularized account of the discoveries at Herculaneum, see Leo Deuel, *Testaments of Time: The Search for Lost Manuscripts and Records* (Baltimore, MD: Penguin Books, 1970 [original, New York: Knopf, 1956]) 55–57.

[47] Turner, *Greek Papyri*, 18–20; see also Deuel, *Testaments of Time*, 90–93.

[48] Turner, *Greek Papyri*, 21.

London entitled, *Fac-Similes of Certain Portions of The Gospel of St. Matthew and of the Epistles of Ss. James & Jude Written on Papyrus in the First Century*. Its editor was Constantine Simonides, and the papyri were quickly exposed by recognized experts as forgeries—this was a genuine "pious fraud." Simonides had, in fact, perpetrated other manuscript forgeries several years earlier in Germany. The most curious aspect of this unusual story, however, developed in the following year, 1862, when Simonides claimed, in a letter to *The Guardian*, that he himself had written the famous parchment Codex Sinaiticus, which Constantin Tischendorf had recently found in St. Catherine's Monastery on Mount Sinai. Though Simonides vigorously denied forging the papyrus manuscripts of Matthew, James, and Jude, he just as vigorously claimed to have forged Codex Sinaiticus—obviously in an attempt to discredit Tischendorf, whose discovery of this mid-fourth century parchment manuscript was not only attracting attention in the world press but was promising to revolutionize biblical textual criticism.[49]

Several years later, in 1868, the first genuine New Testament papyrus text, now designated P11, was published by Tischendorf, about twenty years after he had discovered Codex Sinaiticus. Tischendorf and C. R. Gregory, who wrote the voluminous *Prolegomena* to Tischendorf's 8th critical edition (1864–1872; *Prolegomena*, 1884–1894), published a total of three New Testament papyri (P7, P8, P11), and two others (P3, P14) had been published by Carl Wessely and J. Rendel Harris prior to 1898. Of these five papyri, however, two date in the 7th century, two in the 5th, and one in the 4th century—and none is older than the great uncial manuscripts Sinaiticus
and Vaticanus, which had dominated the construction of the critical 270
New Testament texts of Tischendorf in 1869 and Westcott-Hort in 1881. Moreover, these five papyri contain a combined total of only 120 verses of the New Testament. It is not surprising, therefore, that they did not create great excitement in New Testament scholarship.

A sense of excitement was almost immediate, however, when Grenfell and Hunt, during their systematic searches for manuscripts,

[49] See J. K. Elliott, *Codex Sinaiticus and the Simonides Affair: An Examination of the Nineteenth Century Claim that Codex Sinaiticus Was Not an Ancient Manuscript* (Analecta Vlatadon, 33; Thessaloniki: Patriarchal Institute for Patristic Studies, 1982) 26–70; 131–70.

began to dig a low mound at Oxyrhynchus on January 11, 1897. They had purposely selected Oxyrhynchus as:

> a site where fragments of Christian literature might be expected of an earlier date than the fourth century, to which our oldest manuscripts of the New Testament belong; for the place was renowned in the fourth and fifth centuries on account of the number of its churches and monasteries.[50]

As Grenfell and Hunt began to dig, almost immediately two sheets of great significance appeared: first a leaf of "Sayings of Jesus" from an apocryphal gospel and then, nearby but "a day or two afterwards,"[51] a leaf containing parts of Matthew chapter 1, now designated P1 in the official list of New Testament papyri. It dates, as they had properly surmised, to the third century. When the first volume of *The Oxyrhynchus Papyri* appeared in 1898, the place of honor as their first published papyrus was given to the "Sayings of Jesus," but the papyrus of Matthew appears second, and at the time, as Grenfell and Hunt affirmed, "it may thus claim to be a fragment of the oldest known manuscript of any part of the New Testament."[52] Furthermore, it is clearly from a codex, that is, in our form of the book.

Papyrus manuscripts flowed from the Oxyrhynchus sites until they became a "torrent," and twenty-seven of our present eighty-six different New Testament papyrus manuscripts were found there. These Oxyrhynchus papyri contain portions of fifteen of our twenty-seven New Testament books; six contain portions of Matthew, four have portions of John's Gospel, three have Romans, two contain Hebrews, two have James, two have the Apocalypse, and one each has Luke, Acts, 1 Corinthians, Galatians, Philippians, 1 Thessalonians, 2 Thessalonians, 1 John, and Jude. The only major New Testament books not represented are Mark, 2 Corinthians, Ephesians, Colossians, and the Pastoral Epistles, though certainly that is of no significance in the kind of random situation that excavations in rubbish heaps provide.
271 What is remarkable, however, is that nineteen of the Oxyrhynchus

[50] Turner, *Greek Papyri*, 28, quoting the excavation report. See also the extended, but popular account of Grenfell and Hunt's excavations by Deuel, *Testaments of Time*, 132–64.

[51] Bernard P. Grenfell and Arthur S. Hunt (eds.), *The Oxyrhynchus Papyri* (London: Egypt Exploration Fund, 1898) I. 4.

[52] Ibid.

papyri [plus one uncial manuscript (0162) found there] were written in the second, third, or early fourth centuries, that is, prior to the great uncial manuscripts that have loomed so large for so long, such as Codices Sinaiticus, Vaticanus, Alexandrinus, and Bezae. Today there are forty-one such early papyri—and Oxyrhynchus provided almost half. These early papyri, of course, are all highly fragmentary.

But greater discoveries were yet to come, though not so much by systematic excavation and calculated searches. Such excavations are expensive, and already by 1920 Grenfell reached the conclusion "that the present time is more propitious for buying papyri found by native diggers [who are looking for] nitrous earth [to be used for fertilizer] than for digging at one's own expense."[53] He added that "America, owing to the favorable [currency] exchange, seems to be the only country which is just now in a position to face the heavy outlay for excavations in search of papyri in town sites."[54] Alas, America's "Great Depression" was only several years away.

It will be instructive to stop short of the next important discoveries in the early 1930s and to ask what papyri were available to the scholarly world in 1930. We mentioned earlier that only 200 papyri had been published by 1891, but by 1920, according to a survey of the entire scene of papyrology made by Grenfell, some sixty volumes containing nearly 10,000 texts had been published, though he estimated that this represented "probably less than half of the whole material which has been recovered."[55]

What interests us, of course, is the quantity of known *New Testament* papyri. By 1922, twenty-one of the twenty-seven Oxyrhynchus papyri of the New Testament had already been published, but then no more were edited until 1941, and the last two, P77 and P78, were not published until 1968. Of other New Testament papyri, twenty-one were edited and published by 1930 in addition to the Oxyrhynchus, for a total of forty-two (P1 through P44, minus P25 [1938] and P42 [1939]), or just under half the present number of known New Testament papyri. It must be emphasized again, however, that these forty-two papyri are highly fragmentary in nature. For example, many contain bits and pieces of a few or several verses; the only

[53] Grenfell, "Present Position," *BJRL* 6 (1921–1922) 161.
[54] Ibid.
[55] Ibid., 155–56.

ones with extensive text—say, of more than two dozen verses—are P4, with about ninety-six verses of Luke (3rd century); P5, with about thirty-seven verses of John (3rd century); P8, with about twenty-nine verses of Acts (4th century); P11, with about sixty-four verses of 1 Corinthians, though it dates in the 7th century; P13, with about seventy-nine verses of Hebrews (3rd/4th century); P15, with about twenty-seven verses of 1 Corinthians (3rd century); P27, with about thirty
272 verses of Romans (3rd century); P37, with about thirty-four verses of Matthew (3rd/4th century); P40, with about thirty-four verses of Romans (3rd century); and P41, with about fifty-two verses of Acts, but dated in the 8th century. Yet even sections thirty, sixty, or ninety verses in length are still mere fragments. This is clear when we are reminded that the entire Gospel of Matthew has about 1070 [1068] verses, Luke has about 1150 [1149] verses, and even our shortest gospel, Mark, has about 660 [661] verses.

Nevertheless, these ten longer papyrus texts, as well as the thirty-two that are still more fragmentary in nature, are of great significance, especially since twenty-three of them—more than half—are prior to the 3rd/4th century, that is, prior to the great parchment uncials upon which the New Testament text, by 1930, had been based already for several decades.

Now, it is this largely fragmentary character of the papyri known prior to 1930 that makes the discovery of the Chester Beatty papyri in 1930–31 and the Bodmer papyri about 1955–56 so extremely important. We know virtually nothing, however, about the origin of these and some similar collections of papyri, for they were purchased or obtained in some fashion other than excavation and other than discovery *in situ*. Sir Frederic Kenyon, who published the bulk of the Chester Beatty papyri in 1933–37, gives the following brief and often-repeated assessment of their likely place of origin:

> From their character, however, it is plain that they must have been discovered among the ruins of some early Christian church or monastery; and there is reason to believe that they come from the neighbourhood of the Fayum.[56]

[56] Frederic G. Kenyon, *The Chester Beatty Biblical Papyri: Descriptions and Texts of Twelve Manuscripts on Papyrus of the Greek Bible: Fasciculus I, General Introduction* (London: Emery Walker, 1933) 5.

Carl Schmidt, in reviewing Kenyon's work, reports that a Fayumic dealer told him in early 1933 that the manuscripts were found in a pot at Atfih, that is, ancient Aphroditopolis in the Fayum, about two-thirds of the way up the Nile from Alexandria to Oxyrhynchus.[57] Regardless of their places of origin, here for the first time were extensive portions of extraordinarily ancient New Testament codices. First to come to light were the three most famous Chester Beatty papyri:

> **P45**, from the first half of the 3rd century, contains thirty leaves (or 14%) of an original codex of perhaps 220 leaves, which originally held all of the four gospels and Acts. What has been preserved are sixty-one verses of Matthew; about six chapters of Mark; more than five chapters of Luke; most of John 10 and 11; and thirteen chapters of Acts.
> **P46**, from about the year 200, contains eighty-six leaves (or 84%) of 273
> an original 104. Ten epistles of Paul (but presumably not the Pastorals)[58] were originally included, and, though none of 2 Thessalonians has been preserved, the codex does have about eight chapters of Romans; virtually all of 1 and 2 Corinthians; all of Galatians; all of Ephesians; all of Philippians; all of Colossians; two of the five chapters of 1 Thessalonians; and all of Hebrews. The epistles, however, are not in the usual canonical order.
> **P47**, dating to the mid or latter 3rd century, contains ten leaves (or 31%) of an estimated thirty-two originally. It held the Book of Revelation, of which eight chapters from the middle survive.

Then, twenty-five years later, M. Martin Bodmer, founder of the Bodmer Library near Geneva, came into possession of four codices, of which three are in some respects even more extraordinary than the Chester Beatty:

> **P66**, which, like P46, dates from around 200, contains 104 pages of the text of the Gospel of John, to which fragments of forty-six other pages were later added. All but about twenty-five verses of the first fourteen and a half chapters of the Fourth Gospel are well preserved, as well as fragments of the remaining portions.
> **P72**, a small 3rd century codex which is the earliest known copy of 1 and 2 Peter and Jude, contains the entire text of these three epistles, as well as a half dozen other Christian writings.[59]

[57] Carl Schmidt, "Die Evangelienhandschrift der Chester Beatty-Sammlung," *ZNW* 32 (1933) 225–26; I was alerted to this by Roberts, *Manuscript, Society and Belief*, 7.

[58] [On whether P46 could have contained the Pastoral Epistles, see now E. J. Epp, "Issues in the Interrelation of New Testament Textual Criticism and Canon," *The Canon Debate: On the Origins and Formation of the Bible* (eds. L. M. McDonald and J. A. Sanders; Peabody, MA.: Hendrickson, 2002) 495–502.]

[59] [On the complex context of P72, now see ibid., 491–93.]

P75, from the early 3rd century—possibly earlier—contains 102 pages (or 71%) of its original 144, and it preserves portions of Luke 3, 4, and 5, all of chapters 6 through 17, half of chapter 18, and virtually all of chapters 22, 23, and 24. It also contains virtually all of John chapters 1 through 12, and portions of chapters 13, 14, and 15. This is the earliest known copy of Luke. As is now well known, the text of P75 is extraordinary in its identity with that of Codex Vaticanus.

P74, dating in the 7th century, contains portions of Acts, James, 1–2 Peter, 1–3 John, and Jude.

P73, also from the 7th century, is still unedited, but contains only 3 verses of Matthew.[60]

Given the unlikelihood of survival, the New Testament papyri are all genuine treasures, but they are far more than ancient artifacts that have survived the hazards and ravages of time, for they furnish us with texts that may help us unlock the secrets of the very earliest stages of our New Testament textual transmission. But what, more precisely, has been their reception and their influence?

274 III. The General Effect of the Papyrus Discoveries upon New Testament Textual Criticism

As is well known, from the early 18th century on, New Testament textual criticism attempted to overcome its long-standing reliance on the *textus receptus*—the text found in the mass of 8th century and later manuscripts. Slowly but surely textual critics shifted their allegiance, rather, to earlier manuscripts, and particularly to the great uncial manuscripts of the 4th and 5th centuries. From our present standpoint, therefore, we would naturally assume that when all the major New Testament papyri had been published, the scholarly world would revel in the extensive documentation that they provide for the early history of the New Testament text. After all, they fill in—from actual, datable texts—the critical period that reaches 150 to 200 years behind the great uncial manuscripts that had been the mainstay of the discipline at least since the grand days of Tischendorf and Westcott-Hort.

Moreover, these papyri seem to provide precisely what the landmark figures in textual criticism had been looking for ever since

[60] [P73 now has been published by Carsten Peter Thiede, "Papyrus Bodmer L: Das neutestamentliche Papyrusfragment p^{73} = Mt 25,43/26,2–3," *MH* 47 (1990) 35–40.]

1730, when *Bentley* and *Wettstein* enunciated the basic text-critical principle that the more ancient reading is preferable, and when *Bengel* insisted that textual witnesses must be weighed and not merely counted. This, moreover, is precisely the direction that *Lachmann* took in 1831 when he made the decisive break with the *textus receptus*—that is, when he broke the reliance on the mass of late manuscripts—and took as his aim the establishment of the New Testament text as it existed around 400 and, accordingly, devised his text entirely from the most ancient witnesses known to him. And it goes without saying that this is precisely the principle operative in the work of the greatest figures among textual critics, *Tischendorf* and *Tregelles* around 1850 and *Westcott-Hort* in 1881, for all of them based their work on the hard-won criterion that, as Tischendorf put it, "the text should be sought solely from ancient witnesses" and that "among disagreeing witnesses" "the oldest Greek codices" are to be placed first, for "those that excel in antiquity prevail in authority," or, as Hort put it, "older readings, manuscripts, or groups are to be preferred."[61] These firmly-held principles suggest that any newly-found documents of early date would play a highly important role as New Testament textual criticism continued to unfold.

Yet, when numerous fragmentary papyri from the 3rd/4th century appeared, and even when papyri containing extensive portions of text and dating from around the year 200 came to light in the 1930s and mid-1950s, much less changed than this history of textual criticism would lead one to expect. Obviously, the papyri, by any measure, are great treasures from the past, but—as we shall see momentarily—the papyri, including the Chester Beatty, were often
treated not so much as welcome illuminators of textual history, but 275
more as intruders and as irritants to an already firmly-established understanding of the history of the text. After all, textual critics in the first half of the 20th century had carefully and confidently reconstructed the early textual history of the New Testament in accordance with the elegant parchment codices of the 4th and 5th centuries,

[61] On these various textual critics and their views, see my "The Eclectic Method in New Testament Textual Criticism: Solution or Symptom?" *HTR* 69 (1976) 219–44; and "Decision Points in Past, Present, and Future New Testament Textual Criticism" [original title, "Textual Criticism"], *The New Testament and Its Modern Interpreters* (eds. E. J. Epp and †G. W. MacRae, S.J.; Philadelphia: Fortress; Atlanta, GA: Scholars Press, 1989) 75–84.

and many critics simply did not wish that structure to be jeopardized by these young papyrus interlopers—these ragged-edged documents written on what seemed to some of them to be an almost unworthy vehicle for the Scripture. Yet the papyri would not and could not be ignored, and they were gradually worked into the critical editions of the numerous Greek New Testaments that were produced in the 20th century. When the dust had settled, what was the result? I think that most will agree that the result was something unexpected rather than expected.

As noted earlier, the extraordinarily old but highly fragmentary papyri that came to light prior to about 1930 had relatively little impact on New Testament textual criticism. The great critical edition of Tischendorf in 1869, and the influential edition of Westcott-Hort in 1881, by the very fact of timing, could not have been much affected by papyri. Though Tischendorf published P11 (containing sixty-four verses of 1 Corinthians) a year before his 8th edition, he cites it in his apparatus (using the symbol "Q") only about six times (1 Cor 6:13, 14; 7:3, 13bis, 14). As for Westcott-Hort, they do not refer to the six papyri known before the second edition of their *Introduction* was issued in 1896, even though they do take special note of an Old Syriac manuscript discovered in 1892, and its readings were incorporated into their notes; also, they mention three uncial manuscripts reported by Gregory in his *Prolegomena* to Tischendorf's edition, but they do not mention the two papyri Gregory published for the first time in that very same work.[62]

The logical conclusion to be drawn from these sparse data is that in this early period the papyri did not make an impact as a new and important category of New Testament manuscripts. The reasons were obvious enough: these first six papyri to become available (P3 [6th/7th century]; P4 [3rd century, but considered 6th century when published; revised to 4th century in Gregory, 1909]; P7 [4th/6th centuries?]; P8 [4th century]; P11 [7th century]; and P14 [5th century]) were all dated at that time from the 4th to the 7th century (though one [as noted] was later revised to the 3rd century), with the result that they were viewed as being no older—and in most cases much later—than the great uncials upon which Tischendorf

[62] B. F. Westcott and F. J. A. Hort, *The New Testament in the Original Greek* (Cambridge/London: Macmillan, 1881–1882) 2.325–30.

and Westcott-Hort relied. Along with this perception were three others: First, the highly fragmentary nature of the papyri; second, the fact that they provided texts from only Luke, Acts, and 1 Corinthians; and, third, the difficulty of readily identifying them with the major 276
text-types recognized by the textual scholars of that period. All of this, then, combined to make these scraps of papyrus appear less than startling, and at the time they did not appear to be revolutionary discoveries. If one adds to this the extraordinary confidence possessed by the textual critics of that day—such as the almost total confidence that Westcott-Hort placed in the mid-fourth century Codices Vaticanus and Sinaiticus—then it is understandable that the papyri caused little excitement, either then or during the following years when that same confidence was the hallmark of the discipline.

Indeed, thirty years after Westcott-Hort, Sir Frederic Kenyon, who was later to edit the Chester Beatty papyri, spoke of the nineteen papyri known to him in 1912 as follows: "Valuable as such copies may be, chiefly on account of their age, we cannot look to them with any confidence for purity of text."[63] Why? Because, he went on to say, "The papyrus period . . . may be summarily characterized as the period when the textual problems came into being, which we have to try to solve with the help of the evidence afforded by the later periods." Then, just two paragraphs before Kenyon listed the nineteen known papyri, of which at least nine dated in the 3rd/4th century, he dared to say that "up to the present time, no evidence worth mentioning is extant which comes from within this [papyrus] period itself." Next, in a prophetic passage, Kenyon says that it is possible, even probable, "that Egypt . . . may yet bring to light a Gospel or an Epistle written in the second or third century"—which indeed happened only twenty years later. Kenyon goes on to remark, however, that "such a discovery would be full of interest . . .; but it would have to be received with caution . . . [for] it might contain a text inferior in quality to that of some existing manuscripts." Therefore, he concludes, "the best preparation for dealing judiciously with such new testimony is a sound knowledge of the evidence already in existence."[64] And what does he mean? He immediately begins to describe

---

[63] Frederic G. Kenyon, *Handbook to the Textual Criticism of the New Testament* (2nd ed.; London: Macmillan, 1912) 40.

[64] Ibid., 40–41.

in glowing terms the great uncial manuscripts of the 4th century. That is what the papyri were up against: the overwhelming dominance of the uncials and of their preeminent place in New Testament textual theory as it was then understood.

How were the papyri treated in the following years? When the next full critical edition appeared, that of von Soden in 1913, only twelve papyri were in his apparatus,[65] though twenty had been pub-
277 lished. George Milligan, the Scottish papyrologist, could list twenty-three New Testament papyri in 1913, but he is quite clear in stating that their real significance comes with the light they cast on the nature of the *koine* Greek language,[66] and even ten years later he states that the papyri "present us with no new readings of special interest."[67] The text-critical handbooks of Eberhard Nestle—the standard manuals of their time—follow the lead of Gregory and list the New Testament papyri at the end of the list of uncials. The second edition, which was translated into English in 1901, includes six papyri;[68] the third edition of 1909 lists fourteen papyri and calls attention to the fact that the author has added "an entirely new section, the papyri," to Gregory's conventional way of listing the New Testament manuscripts, and for the first time includes two plates of New Testament papyrus manuscripts (P1 and P10).[69] Yet, in these editions the papyri are still listed at the end of the uncial list. After Nestle's death in 1913, the authorship of the Nestle handbook eventually fell to Ernst von Dobschütz, and the fourth edition appeared in 1923. It reveals a significant change: von Dobschütz places the

[65] Apud Benedikt Kraft, *Die Zeichen fur die wichtigeren Handschriften des griechischen Neuen Testaments* (3rd ed.; Freiburg im Br.: Herder, 1955) 11–30. According to J. K. Elliott, *A Survey of Manuscripts Used in Editions of the Greek New Testament* (NovTSup 57; Leiden: Brill, 1987) 3–4, cf. xiii–xiv, twenty-one papyri were theoretically available to von Soden. Why P3 is included in neither list is unclear, for it was published by Wessely in 1882.

[66] George Milligan, *The New Testament Documents: Their Origin and Early History* (London: Macmillan, 1913) 60–62; 248–54.

[67] George Milligan, *Here and There among the Papyri* (London: Houghton and Stoughton, 1923) 121.

[68] Eberhard Nestle, *Introduction to the Textual Criticism of the Greek New Testament* (tr. from the 2nd German ed. by W. Edie; ed. A. Menzies; Theological Translation Library, 13; London: Williams and Norgate; New York: Putnam, 1901) xv, 74; 80; cf. 81–82.

[69] Eberhard Nestle, *Einführung in das Griechischen Neuen Testament* (3rd ed.; Göttingen: Vandenhoeck & Ruprecht, 1909) 61; 88–89; plates 11–12.

papyri at the head of the list of manuscripts, "in distinction," as he says, "from Gregory and Nestle" (and the two plates reproducing P1 and P10 also are dutifully moved to the beginning of that section at the end of the volume!). Then follow entries for thirty-two papyri.[70] Interestingly, Nestle is quick to point out—as was true at the time—that "our very oldest manuscripts" are the deluxe [parchment] codices of the fourth century.[71] Beyond this, very little attention is paid to the papyri by these handbooks of Nestle and von Dobschütz.

Edgar J. Goodspeed, in 1937, after the publication of the Chester
Beatty papyri, does refer to these and other papyrus discoveries as
"remarkable" and "sensational," but concludes that "it is not these
discoveries of Biblical papyri, however dazzling," that most affect the
biblical text; rather—again—it is the discovery of the thousands of
everyday papyrus documents that illuminate the New Testament language.[72] Kenyon, also writing in 1937, after he had himself pub- 278
lished the Chester Beatty papyri, still spoke of the previously discovered
New Testament papyri as follows: ". . . Small fragments, individually of slight importance, but collectively of some value," and "Though
their evidence with regard to particular readings does not amount
to much, they are of value as throwing a little light on the general
character of the . . . types of text current in Egypt during this period."
Naturally, he speaks more glowingly of the Chester Beatty, a discovery, as he puts it, "which threw all the others in the shade and
which is indeed only to be rivaled by that of the Codex Sinaiticus."[73]
Yet the *independent* significance of these papyri—as we shall observe
in a moment—was not championed even by Kenyon.

Continuing our assessment of critical editions of the Greek New Testament, it is understandable that the large critical apparatus of Mark by S. C. E. Legg in 1935 cited only one papyrus, the Chester Beatty P45, for Mark is poorly represented among the papyri. It is

[70] Ernst von Dobschütz, *Eberhard Nestle's Einführung in das Griechischen Neuen Testament* (4th ed.; Göttingen: Vandenhoeck & Ruprecht, 1923) 85–86; plates 1–2.

[71] The same comment is found in both of Nestle's editions referred to in nn. 68 and 69, above: English, p. 82; German, p. 90.

[72] Edgar J. Goodspeed, *New Chapters in New Testament Study* (New York: Macmillan, 1937) 92–101.

[73] Frederic G. Kenyon, *The Story of the Bible: A Popular Account of How It Came to Us* (New York: Dutton, 1937) 110–13.

found in only three: P45, which had been published only two years prior to Legg's edition; in another fragment published in 1972; and in one still unedited.[74] However, the succeeding volume by Legg on Matthew in 1940 cites only six papyri when nine of Matthew were known.[75] In the popular Nestle Greek New Testament (*Novum Testamentum Graece*), the 16th edition of 1936 cited only fifteen papyri, including the recently discovered Chester Beatty, though altogether nearly fifty were known at the time. The number of papyri cited increased rapidly, however, with each succeeding Nestle edition, so that twenty-eight appeared in the 21st edition of 1952; thirty-seven in the 25th of 1963, which was after the Bodmer papyri were published; and finally all eighty-six were cited in the current 26th edition of 1979, when completeness was finally considered a virtue and the papyri had come fully into their own.

But—perhaps to our considerable surprise—this "coming into their own" did not occur even with the finding of the extensive texts of the Chester Beatty papyri, for the nature of the text found in the early third century P45 did not conform to the type of text in either of the two text-types identified by Westcott-Hort as very early (i.e., the so-called "Neutral" and the so-called "Western"), nor, of course, to their later Syrian (or Byzantine) text-type. Rather, P45 appeared to fall midway between these two texts, and seemed at the time (that is, in the mid-1930s when it was found) to confirm the Caesarean text-type, which recently had been identified by textual critics as a text-type additional to those marked out by Westcott-Hort in their
279 depiction of New Testament textual history. The Caesarean text, though considered at the time to be an early, local text, was not thought to be as early as either the "Neutral" or the "Western" text-types; hence identifying P45 with the Caesarean text did not thereby confer on P45 any preponderant authority. There was no general agreement, however, as to the exact nature of the text of

---

[74] S. C. E. Legg (ed.), *Nouum Testamentum graece secundum textum Westcotto-Hortianum: Euangelium secundum Marcum* (Oxford: Clarendon Press, 1935). [The papyri in question would be P84, published only recently: S. Verhelst, "Les fragments du Castellion (Kh. Mird) des Évangiles de Marc et de Jean (P[84])," *Muséon* 116 (2003) 15–44; and P88: S. Daris, "Papiri letterari dell'Università Cattolica di Milano . . . 6. Marco, *Vangelo* 2, 1–26," *Aeg* 52 (1972) 80–88+2 pls.]

[75] S. C. E. Legg (ed.), *Nouum Testamentum graece secundum textum Westcotto-Hortianum: Euangelium secundum Matthaeum.* (Oxford: Clarendon Press, 1940).

P45 *vis-à-vis* the established text-types—the subject of a complicated and extended discussion in the mid-1930s by F. G. Kenyon, R. V. G. Tasker, M. J. Lagrange, P. L. Hedley, C. C. Tarelli, H. Lietzmann, and others, which was summarized by A. F. J. Klijn in 1949.[76] But that is the point: mostly these discussions of P45 were *vis-à-vis* the established text-types, rather than in terms of the *independent* significance of the papyrus for the history and method of the New Testament text. Lietzmann, for instance, in two articles in 1934 (on P46) and in 1935 (on P45), says in each that these very welcome discoveries confirm both the reliability of our textual tradition and of our present knowledge, and he states quite bluntly that they teach us neither anything radically new nor anything we did not already know.[77] Lagrange, in his 1935 analysis, does at one juncture assign methodological significance to P45 when he says that "the independence of the papyrus in relation to the D [text-]type is of the highest importance for the history of the text."[78] Yet, this judgment, too, is in the context of fitting the newly discovered manuscript into the current textual formulation—a pattern disclosed and reinforced almost invariably as one peruses the scores of assessments of P45 in the period preceding the discovery of the Bodmer papyri. Klijn, at the conclusion of his 1949 overview, seems almost apologetic when he states that "on the surface it may seem that this rather long discussion of the inquiry into the text of P45 may have originated in an overrating of a newly discovered text," but the statement that follows is one of the few that give P45 a right to independent status; he continues, "This is seen to be false once we grasp that Egypt appears to be more and more important for the history of the text, and since P45 takes a central place in the text of Egypt, it requires thorough study."[79] Here, at last, is a clear recognition that this papyrus and, by implication, the other early papyri have independent and funda-

---

[76] A. F. J. Klijn, *A Survey of the Researches into the Western Text of the Gospels and Acts* (Utrecht: Kemink, 1949) 132–46.

[77] Hans Lietzmann, "Die Chester-Beatty-Papyri des Neuen Testament," *Antike* 11 (1935) 147, reprinted in *Kleine Schriften, II: Studien zum Neuen Testament* (ed. K. Aland; TU 68; Berlin: Akademie-Verlag, 1958) 168–69; and "Zur Würdigung des Chester-Beatty-Papyrus der Paulusbriefe," SPAW, phil.-hist. Klasse, 25 (1934) 775, reprinted in his *Kleine Schriften II*, 171.

[78] M.-J. Lagrange, *Critique textuelle: II. La critique rationnelle* (EBib; Paris: Gabalda, 1935) 415.

[79] Klijn, *Survey*, 145.

mental significance in tracing out the history of the New Testament text.

For the most part, the second Chester Beatty papyrus, P46 of the
280 Pauline epistles, received treatment similar to that accorded P45 by most scholars: its readings were assessed in comparison with the prevailing manuscripts and within the traditional framework of text-types, yielding the general conclusion that P46 sides with the "Neutral" text over against the "Western." Yet, to Kenyon, the editor of the Chester Beatty papyri, P46's major significance appeared to be in sharpening the already well-established distinction between the Neutral and Western text-types, and his overall assessment is that the papyrus "in general confirms the integrity of the text that has come down to us, and offers no sensational variants." The concluding paragraph of his edition of P46 reads:

> It therefore seems clear that, while our modern texts are an advance on those which preceded them, we have not reached finality. The papyrus affects the balance of evidence in many cases; and while it can by no means claim a predominant authority (since, so far as we know, it is only a text circulating in provincial Egypt), it shows that the margin of doubt in details is greater than was supposed, and that the exercise of critical judgement and the search for further evidence are still required.[80]

Henry A. Sanders, in his publication of the forty then-known leaves of P46 (out of the eighty-six eventually recovered), follows the usual procedure of evaluating them against all the relevant later manuscripts and text-types.[81] It is of interest, too, that a footnote in a 1953 article by Kenneth Clark affirms that "the contribution [of P46] to the textual criticism of the New Testament has not been fully exploited"—and this was already twenty years after P46 was discovered and is another evidence that the significance of these extensive papyri had not been appreciated even by the mid-1950s.[82]

---

[80] Frederic G. Kenyon, *The Chester Beatty Biblical Papyri: Descriptions and Texts of Twelve Manuscripts on Papyrus of the Greek Bible: Fasciculus III Supplement, Pauline Epistles, Text* (London: Emery Walker, 1936) xxii.

[81] Henry A. Sanders (ed.), *A Third-Century Papyrus Codex of the Epistles of Paul* (University of Michigan Studies, Humanistic Series, 38; Ann Arbor: University of Michigan Press, 1935) 23–32.

[82] Kenneth W. Clark, "Textual Criticism and Doctrine," *Studia Paulina in honorem Johannis de Zwaan septuagenarii* (Haarlem: Bohn, 1953) 56, reprinted in K. W. Clark, *The Gentile Bias and Other Essays* (ed. John L. Sharpe, III; NovTSup 54; Leiden: Brill, 1980) 94.

There was, however, a notable—and perhaps singular—exception to all of this, a substantial work published in the same year as Kenneth Clark's comment: G. Zuntz's *The Text of the Epistles*.[83] Zuntz turned then-current procedures upside down: he began his study with "the oldest manuscript" of the Pauline corpus, P46, which he calls "the decisive material accession" to our resources,[84] and proposes to
employ it "as a foil in assessing the value of, and the interrelation 281
between, the other witnesses."[85] Then, for more than half of his large volume, he uses that papyrus as the standard against which all other manuscripts are measured. This is the "exception [as we say—though with questionable logic] that proves the rule." Still, it was 1953 before this quite reasonable approach appeared in print (even though Zuntz's Schweich Lectures were delivered originally in 1946), and it represents a direction and an emphasis taken by very few others in this period.

As to the third Chester Beatty codex, P47, containing the text of Revelation, Kenyon—as late as 1948—says merely that "the textual variants in Revelation are not of great importance, but the papyrus [P47] must take its place as one of the principal . . . authorit[ies] for the book," since it is the oldest.[86] Josef Schmid in 1955, in the leading work on the Greek text of the Apocalypse, did find that this most ancient, extensive manuscript permitted the older text of Revelation to be divided into two distinct text-groups, that it helped to confirm the mixed character of Codex Sinaiticus, and that it established more precisely the superior value of the Codices A and C group over the Sinaiticus-P47 group.[87] Yet, in his extensive investigations, the readings of P47 are largely fed into the existing textual classifications and utilized as would those of any other newly-found witness.

[83] G. Zuntz, *The Text of the Epistles: A Disquisition upon the Corpus Paulinum* (Schweich Lectures, 1946; London: British Academy by Oxford University Press, 1953).

[84] Ibid., 11.

[85] Ibid., 17.

[86] Frederic G. Kenyon, *The Text of the Greek Bible: A Student's Handbook* (Studies in Theology; 2nd ed.; London: Duckworth, 1949) 191; cf. 188–91.

[87] Josef Schmid, *Studien zur Geschichte des griechischen Apokalypse-Textes. 2. Teil: Die alten Stämme* (Münchener theologische Studien, 1. Ergänzungsband; Munich: Karl Zink, 1955) 12; 251. See now Kurt Aland and Barbara Aland, *The Text of the New Testament: An Introduction to the Critical Editions and to the Theory and Practice of Modern Textual Criticism* (tr. E. F. Rhodes; Grand Rapids, MI: Eerdmans; Leiden: Brill, 1987) 59: P47 is related to Codex Sinaiticus, not to codices A or C.

Such assessments of these three extensive papyri (with the notable exception of Zuntz's procedure) hardly suggest that they were considered revolutionary discoveries destined to change the world of textual criticism. And this lack of enthusiasm strikes us as rather surprising when the quantity of known New Testament text on papyrus had suddenly been multiplied many times over by the appearance of the Chester Beatty papyri and when the date of extensive documentary evidence had been pushed back 100 to 150 years behind the great uncials. We can understand, of course, why the other papyri then known attracted relatively little attention, for they were extremely fragmentary, and—due primarily to their fragmented state—did not solidify the currently identified textual configurations. They appeared, therefore, to be factors of confusion in the textual theory of the time, rather than vehicles for clarification. Yet, this would appear also to be the main reason why the Chester Beatty papyri did not generate as much excitement as we would have expected: in the Gospels,
282 Acts, and Epistles, these papyri introduced complicating factors rather than greater clarity in textual history and theory as they were then understood.

Hindsight might suggest, nevertheless, that these papyri all should have been viewed as more important than they were in the 1930s and 1940s—and even in the early 1950s—but the necessary catalyst for recognizing their critical importance came only with the discovery of the Bodmer papyri in the mid-1950s. P66, but especially P75, raised them all to a new level of visibility and significance. Why? Primarily because P75, a codex of John and Luke from around the year 200, contains a text extraordinarily similar to Codex Vaticanus (B) and yet dates a 150 years earlier. That made textual critics sit up and take notice, for the common view after Westcott-Hort had been that the text represented in Codex Vaticanus was the result of revision over time and thus presented a refined, smoothened version of an older, rougher text. Rather than confirming that hypothesis, P75 demonstrated—in an actual, datable document—that already around 200 this very text existed in Egypt. But P66 also attracted attention, though in a different way. This codex of John, also from about the year 200, was viewed as a mixed text "with elements that are typically Alexandrian and Western,"[88] that is, with textual char-

[88] As reflected, e.g., in the description of P66 offered by Bruce M. Metzger, *The*

acteristics that are typical of the two early but sharply distinguishable text-types that Westcott-Hort had identified. (This assessment was later modified and P66 is now usually linked with the P75–B kind of text, though recognizing that it is a rather "wild" member of that group.)[89] Here again, however—with respect to both P75 and P66—we encounter that almost universal shortcoming among textual critics who approach new papyri discoveries, which J. N. Birdsall so forcefully pointed out in 1958, when he spoke of the fault "common to many contemporary scholars who attempt to discuss and define such early evidence as this by standards of later witnesses." He continues:

> Beyond the fourth century the divisions of "Neutral," "Western," "Caesarean," "Byzantine" (or corresponding terms) are apposite: but in the early period, which such a papyrus as P66 reveals to us, these concepts are out of place. The task of present-day criticism is to inaugurate an era in which we begin from the earliest evidence and on the basis of its interpretation discuss the later.[90]

This statement has been widely quoted—and rightly so—but has not 283
yet been widely heeded. Less well known are similar sentiments expressed a decade earlier—before the Bodmer papyri had been discovered—by Kenneth Clark at a Chicago conference to honor Edgar J. Goodspeed. Referring to the Chester Beatty papyri, he reported that "the only studies made thus far seem to approach these texts by reversing the centuries. We require a new mental attitude, wherein we . . . approach these earliest materials *de novo*," and Clark offered the further admonition that "we should study the third-century witnesses in their own right."[91]

Text of the New Testament: Its Transmission, Corruption, and Restoration (2nd ed.; New York/Oxford: Oxford University Press, 1968) 40.

[89] See Gordon D. Fee, "P75, P66, and Origen: The Myth of Early Textual Recension in Alexandria," *New Dimensions in New Testament Study* (ed. R. N. Longenecker and M. C. Tenney; Grand Rapids, MI: Zondervan, 1974) 30–31; idem, *Papyrus Bodmer II (P66): Its Textual Relationships and Scribal Characteristics* (SD 34; Salt Lake City: University of Utah Press, 1968) 35.

[90] J. Neville Birdsall, *The Bodmer Papyrus of the Gospel of John* (Tyndale New Testament Lecture, 1958; London: Tyndale Press, 1960) 7.

[91] Kenneth W. Clark, "The Manuscripts of the Greek New Testament," *New Testament Manuscript Studies: The Materials and the Making of a Critical Apparatus* (eds. M. M. Parvis and A. P. Wikgren; Chicago: University of Chicago Press, 1950) 20–21.

As was the case with the Chester Beatty papyri, this faulty and illogical procedure of judging the earlier by the later was the one normally applied also to P66 and P75. Yet there was a difference here, as will be noted presently.

More significant than its textual character, however, was the observation that P66 contains four to five hundred scribal corrections, most of which are the scribe's own corrections of his errors, though others appear to be corrections made by comparison with another exemplar, that is, comparison of the finished product with another manuscript. Thus, P66 presents a kind of early textual history of its own, showing how scribes worked, how they made corrections, and how different textual complexions can be found in the same manuscript.[92]

These findings gave the Bodmer and all early papyri a new status: P75 connected Codex Vaticanus (B)—generally considered the preeminent New Testament manuscript—directly to the earliest level of textual history, thereby bestowing new significance on both manuscripts, but new significance not only as witnesses but also in terms of text-critical methodology. The same was true of P66: it acquired a fresh, independent importance for its disclosure of the character of the early transmission process. New Testament papyri, therefore, had finally come into their own with the analysis of the Bodmer discoveries. At last they could stand on their own merit and be judged on their own terms. It is no coincidence that the first entirely new critical edition to be produced after their appearance, the United Bible Societies *Greek New Testament* (UBSGNT), first issued in 1966, contained a list of all the known papyri—the first Greek New Testament to do so. Moreover, all the papyri were newly collated for this edition and cited in every case where they offer data for variant readings. This full citation of the textual evidence in the papyri is now standard procedure.

284 This is where this paper should end, for its purpose—as indicated in the title—was to provide historical perspective on the New Testament papyri. That included an assessment of papyrus as a writing material for manuscripts, a review of their discovery, but particularly a scrutiny of their reception and use by New Testament textual critics from

[92] See Fee, *Papyrus Bodmer II*, 35; 56; 76–83.

their first appearance down to the present time. Those tasks have been performed, though with what success is for the reader to judge.

At the very time, however, when the New Testament papyri seemed finally to have achieved independent status and to have been fully utilized in New Testament textual criticism, a quite unexpected and disquieting discovery made its appearance, raising serious questions about the actual, practical impact of the papyri upon New Testament text-critical method and upon the critical editions of our own time that have been the beneficiaries of these precious documents from the distant past. Were it not for this turn of events, the succeeding section might not be necessary.

IV. The Proper Place of the Papyri in New Testament Textual Criticism

The unexpected and disquieting development to which I refer can be quickly described. When these half dozen early and extensive New Testament papyrus manuscripts had finally been analyzed, utilized, and incorporated into the texts and into the textual apparatuses of our latest critical editions, what was the result? As demonstrated by several assessments of the post-Bodmer editions of the Nestle-Aland text and of the United Bible Societies text, as well as others, it was discovered that these New Testament texts in general usage actually differed only moderately from the Greek text of Westcott-Hort in 1881. Kenneth Clark demonstrated this already in a 1956 publication—before the Bodmer papyri had been worked into our critical texts—and again in 1968—after all the major papyri had been fully utilized.[93] The analysis done at Duke University led to the following forthright conclusion:

> Since 1881 [that is, since Westcott-Hort's text] twenty-five editors have issued about seventy-five editions of the Greek New Testament. The

[93] Kenneth W. Clark, "The Effect of Recent Textual Criticism upon New Testament Studies," *The Background of the New Testament and Its Eschatology* (eds. W. D. Davies and D. Daube; Cambridge: University Press, 1956) 33–36, reprinted in K. W. Clark, *The Gentile Bias*, 71–74; and idem, "Today's Problem with the Critical Text of the New Testament," *Transitions in Biblical Scholarship* (Essays in Divinity, 6; ed. J. C. Rylaarsdam; Chicago: University of Chicago Press, 1968) 158–60, reprinted in Clark, *The Gentile Bias*, 121–23.

> collation of these many "critical" texts consistently exposes the fact that each of them is basically a repetition of the Westcott-Hort text. . . . Indeed, we have continued for eighty-five years to live in the era of Westcott-Hort, our *textus receptus* [i.e., the text received by all].[94]

285 Now it is 107 years later than Westcott-Hort, and yet essentially the same statement must be made today. That is a striking conclusion to be drawn after a hundred years of vigorous text-critical work and after a hundred years of extraordinary papyrus discoveries, to say nothing of the discovery of numerous other influential manuscripts and versions. Indeed, it is a shocking and therefore sobering conclusion, and one not lost on a number of us who work in the field. *If Westcott-Hort did not utilize papyri in constructing their New Testament text, and if our own modern critical texts, in fact, are not significantly different from that of Westcott-Hort, then why are the papyri important after all?* And have they really "come into their own" and been fully and *appropriately* utilized in the text-critical discipline? While there is one sense, then, in which the New Testament papyri have come into their own—they have been fully incorporated into our critical editions—there is another real sense in which their expected impact has not yet been fully felt.

To raise this question in a different way, the great achievement of New Testament textual criticism over the past 250 years—since 1730—was the departure from and triumph over the *textus receptus*, that is, the long struggle to accredit the few older manuscripts as superior witnesses to the original text over against the mass of later manuscripts. That was achieved by the rudimentary and preparatory—and yet monumental—work of those mentioned earlier (Bentley, Wettstein, Bengel, and Griesbach), whose labors were characterized, for example, by the insistence that textual witnesses must be weighed and not merely counted (Bengel), followed by the decisive break with the *textus receptus* in Lachmann's Greek New Testament of 1831. During the succeeding fifty years—until the 1881 appearance of Westcott-Hort's *The New Testament in the Original Greek* (as they called it)—giants like Tischendorf and Tregelles pressed home the principles that "the text should be sought solely from ancient witnesses" (Tischendorf), that textual witnesses "that excel in antiquity prevail

[94] K. W. Clark, "Today's Problem with the Critical Text," 160, reprinted in Clark, *The Gentile Bias*, 123.

in authority" (Tischendorf), and that the New Testament text should be formed "on the authority of ancient copies without allowing the 'received text' any prescriptive rights" (Tregelles). Hort then produced the *tour de force* in his *Introduction* to the Greek New Testament, in which he effectively argued that the "original" text is to be found in the "best" manuscripts, and that the "best" manuscripts are, first, Codex Vaticanus (B) and, secondarily, Codex Sinaiticus (Aleph), the two great parchment codices that originated in the mid-fourth century. All of this was achieved without the assistance of the early papyri.

Textual criticism did not, of course, stand still during the intervening fifty years until the Chester Beatty papyri were discovered, yet little had occurred to alter the basic understanding of the development of the text as Hort had outlined it, except that a Caesarean text had been proposed as a type of text midway between Hort's two early text-types, the "Neutral" and the "Western." Moreover, really nothing had occurred to dislodge Codices Vaticanus and Sinaiticus from their preeminent place in the whole structure. The Chester Beatty papyri, as we have seen, provided readings that supported the general theory of these three earliest text-types, and then 286
later the Bodmer papyri attested an earlier stage of the Vaticanus text in P75, as well as another example, in P66, of a text basically supportive of the P75-B type of text, but also showing elements of other identifiable texts as they are found in the Westcott-Hort framework. It is only natural, then, to expect the critical texts of the New Testament to resemble Westcott-Hort's 1881 text, and that, essentially, is what they did, despite numerous claims that great advances had been made since the papyri had made their appearance.

I repeat, therefore, the question: *If Westcott-Hort did not utilize papyri in constructing their New Testament text, and if our own modern critical texts, in fact, are not significantly different from that of Westcott-Hort, then why are the papyri important after all?*

This point might have been made in another way. In the process of describing and extolling the work of Eberhard Nestle (1851–1913) and his son, Erwin Nestle (1883–1972) in producing their long series of hand-editions of the Greek New Testament, Kurt and Barbara Aland compare the early Nestle editions (that of 1898—the first—and those that quickly followed) with the so-called "Standard Text" in their own Nestle-Aland twenty-sixth edition of 1979. They say—somewhat surprisingly—that Nestle "produced a text that not only lasted seventy years, but on the whole truly represents the modern state of knowledge. It is significant that in its 657 printed pages the early Nestle text differs from the modern 'Standard text' in merely seven hundred passages."[95] By the nature of the circumstances, the papyri could play only the smallest role in these early Nestle editions, so the small difference between their text and that of the latest Nestle-Aland raises the same question: why should we attribute to the papyri such great importance?

So we are left with the somewhat disappointing conclusion that the significance of the strikingly early and even the strikingly extensive New Testament papyri has not yet been clarified by New Testament textual critics—contrary to the expectations so reasonably elicited as each new papyrus came to light. If this is the case, where do we go from here?

In contemporary New Testament textual criticism, nearly everyone talks about the "monumental" importance of the New Testament papyri, and Kurt Aland has claimed repeatedly in recent years that in the forty papyri prior to about 300 the history of the New Testament text "can be studied in the original."[96] More recently he has claimed that in the Nestle-Aland 26th edition "the goal of an edition . . . 'in the original Greek' seems to have been reached"[97]
287 Yet, this critical text that he has edited (most recently with Barbara Aland) also falls under the same judgment rendered a few moments ago: it is among those that differ little from the Westcott-Hort text of 1881,[98] which was constructed without benefit of the papyri. At

[95] Aland and Aland, *The Text of the New Testament*, 20.

[96] Kurt Aland, "The Twentieth-Century Interlude in New Testament Textual Criticism," *Text and Interpretation: Studies in the New Testament Presented to Matthew Black* (eds. E. Best and R. McL. Wilson; Cambridge/New York: Cambridge University Press, 1979) 11 [A reply, in German, to my Hatch Memorial Lecture of the same title, JBL 93 (1974) 386–414; cf. my response to Aland in "A Continuing Interlude in New Testament Textual Criticism?" *HTR* 73 (1980) 131–51].

[97] Kurt Aland, "Der Neuen 'Standard Text' in seinem Verhältnis zu den frühen Papyri und Majuskeln," *New Testament Textual Criticism: Its Significance for Exegesis: Essays in Honour of Bruce M. Metzger* (eds. E. J. Epp and G. D. Fee; Oxford: Clarendon Press, 1981) 274–75.

[98] The close relationship between the texts of Nestle-Aland^{25} (1963) and of Westcott-Hort (1881) is demonstrated vividly in a chart in Aland and Aland, *The Text of the New Testament*, 26–27. In a comparison of Nestle-Aland with the editions of Westcott-Hort, Vogels, Merk, and Bover (as well as Tischendorf), Nestle-Aland^{25} shows strikingly fewer variants from Westcott-Hort than from any of the others. The numbers of variants from Nestle-Aland^{25} are as follows: Westcott-Hort (1881) =

the same time, the Nestle-Aland text (which is identical to that of the UBS *Greek New Testament*) is widely accepted and, by some, is even acclaimed as the new "standard text"[99] of the New Testament.

So our discipline faces an interesting situation: on the one hand, we have a widely used and generally accepted New Testament text of good quality—no one denies that—but a text that would not be much different if the New Testament papyri had not been discovered; on the other hand, we have new manuscript treasures of great antiquity with extensive coverage of the New Testament text that—contrary to their intrinsic and expected worth—appear to be underutilized and even undervalued when one looks at their actual influence on text-critical history and method. So a pointed question arises: Should there not be a more *dynamic* relationship between the two—between the early papyri and the critical text? That is, should not current methodology be more *actively* and more *radically* affected by these startling new discoveries? And should not the current critical text be more *directly* based on principles and theories that issue more *immediately* from an assessment of the textual character of the earliest papyri? The challenge that results is this: Can we find a way, methodologically, to use these papyri to break through in a new fashion to an earlier state of the New Testament text? Some think that this has already happened—as noted above—but it would appear that the papyri have been fed into the critical editions almost in a passive manner and in accordance with theories of the New Testament text formulated before the early, extensive papyri were ever discovered. A more logical approach—as intimated above—would be to establish a history and theory of the New Testament text, or reconfirm 288

558 variants; Merk[9] (1965) = 770 variants; Bover[5] (1968) = 1161 variants; and Vogels[4] (1950) = 1996 variants [as a matter of interest, Tischendorf[8] (1869) differs by 1262 variants].

[99] Notice the pervasive use of the term "Standard Text" in Aland and Aland, *The Text of the New Testament*, especially pp. 20–36. They hasten to point out that "this name did not come from the editors but from reviews of the new Nestle-Aland[26] in the popular press and in scholarly journals" (p. 30). The matter is by no means undisputed, however, as evidenced, e.g., by Ian A. Moir, "Can We Risk another 'Textus Receptus'?" *JBL* 100 (1981) 614–18; or H.-W. Bartsch, "Ein neuer Textus Receptus für das griechische Neue Testament?" *NTS* 27 (1980–1981) 585–92, to which Kurt Aland replied, under the same title, in *NTS* 28 (1982) 145–53. [Note that the term was dropped from the Alands' subsequent publications: cf., e.g., p. 30 in the first and second English editions of their *Text of the New Testament*, where "new text" replaces it.]

an existing one, by beginning with the early papyri and then basing the critical text on the resultant theory. That, of course, is a highly complex subject, which I have treated, though only in a preliminary fashion, in more than one publication.[100] Space does not permit repetition of those proposals here, but suffice it to say that the papyri can and should play a fundamental role in at least three areas:

(1) The papyri can be employed to isolate the earliest discernible text-types, which is feasible because the papyri vary in their textual complexions and can be placed into groups.

(2) By using the resulting text-types, the papyri can help us to trace out the very early history of the New Testament text, thereby opening the way for more objective methods of judging the quality of witnesses than are presently available.

(3) Finally, the papyri can aid in refining the canons of criticism—the principles by which we judge variant readings—for they open to us a window for viewing the earliest stages of textual transmission, providing instances of how scribes worked in their copying of manuscripts.

All of this confirms our sense that the papyri are of extraordinary importance for writing the history of the New Testament text and for guiding the development of its proper methodology.[101]

Added Notes, 2004

Joseph A. Fitzmyer, S.J., is mentioned in n. 1 because the volume in which this essay appeared was a *Festschtrift* to honor him on his

[100] See E. J. Epp, "Decision Points" [see n. 61, above], 97–106; idem, "The Twentieth Century Interlude," 397–99.

[101] The issues raised here have been explored by the present writer also in a paper presented at the international conference on "Gospel Traditions in the Second Century" at the University of Notre Dame, 15–17 April 1988, entitled, "The Significance of the Papyri for Determining the Nature of the New Testament Text in the Second Century: A Dynamic View of Textual Transmission," *Gospel Traditions in the Second Century* (ed. W. L. Petersen; Studies in Christianity and Judaism in Antiquity, 3; Notre Dame, IN: University of Notre Dame Press, 1989) 71–103. [Cf. also E. J. Epp, "The Papyrus Manuscripts of the New Testament," *The Text of the New Testament in Contemporary Research: Essays on the* Status Quaestionis (ed. B. D. Ehrman and M. W. Holmes; Studies and Documents, 46; Grand Rapids, MI: Eerdmans, 1995) 3–21.]

seventieth birthday. Though not my mentor in any formal academic sense, he became my mentor for editorial work, which occupied me one way or another for the rest of my career. In 1971, Professor Fitzmyer, who had just become Editor of the *Journal of Biblical Literature*, asked me to serve as his Associate Editor for New Testament Book Reviews, which I did for the six years of his editorship. That, however, was only the beginning, for the next three editors, Victor Paul Furnish, John H. Hayes, and John J. Collins, reappointed me to the position until I had served for twenty years (1971–1990). At that point, I became editor of the then recently established *Critical Review of Books in Religion* from 1991–1994—a joint venture of the American Academy of Religion and the Society of Biblical Literature.

Joseph Fitzmyer did not provide an easy model to follow, for attention to accuracy, consistency, proper form, and to the finest details were simply part and parcel of his editorial nature. But these are far from the heart of his editorial skills, which consist in competence across virtually all biblical fields, keen judgment of quality—or the lack thereof—in considering material for publication, fairness in those considerations, and a wealth of wisdom in handling difficult issues. My hope has been that some of these qualities, at least, might have emerged in my own editorial ventures.

CHAPTER THIRTEEN

THE SIGNIFICANCE OF THE PAPYRI FOR DETERMINING THE NATURE OF THE NEW TESTAMENT TEXT IN THE SECOND CENTURY: A DYNAMIC VIEW OF TEXTUAL TRANSMISSION[1]

This is largely an exercise in historical-critical imagination. It is an 71
attempt to discover some things we do not know about the earliest stages of New Testament textual transmission by applying creative imagination to what we do know. The question, to be more specific, is whether we can take our limited knowledge of the earliest textual witnesses, combine it with the data we have about our later textual witnesses, and then think creatively about the process that must—or at least might—have produced it all. The approach proposed involves, first, exploring the dynamic relationships and movements (both secular and Christian) that must have occurred in the earliest centuries of textual transmission; second, utilizing textual complexions—commonly called text-types—to sort out the manuscripts; and, third, bringing into view the early textual spectrum that results from, and is reflected in, the array of manuscript witnesses. In pursuing the first of these tasks, it will be instructive to offer two brief sketches, one of the general situation in the first few centuries of Christianity, and another of the specific environment of the earliest New Testament manuscripts and papyri.

I. The Dynamic Historical Situation of the Early Church

In looking at the earliest centuries of Christianity, that period when the New Testament text originated and began its odyssey of transmission,

[1] This essay was prepared for an international conference at the University of Notre Dame (15–17 April 1988) on "Gospel Traditions in the Second Century" and was published in a volume under that title edited by William L. Petersen (Notre Dame, IN: University of Notre Dame Press, 1989), though with a subtitle of "Origins, Recensions, Text, and Transmission." The eight participants were Barbara Aland, Tjitze Baarda, J. Neville Birdsall, Sebastian P. Brock, Joël Delobel, Helmut Koester, Frederik Wisse, and the present writer, as well as Professor Petersen.

the word "dynamic" is constitutive. For too long the text of the New Testament has been conceived in static terms. It has often been assumed that one type of text existed only in one place and other types existed only somewhere else; or that one of these types on a rare occasion made its way solely to some other location; or that
72 distinctive and persistent "local texts" existed at a number of discrete localities; or that revisions and refinements of certain texts took place in isolated fashion in insulated locations. To be sure, all of these things probably happened, but much, much more was happening also—and simultaneously.

We focus, of course, on those first centuries when Christianity was expanding with rather phenomenal rapidity and in all directions within the vast Greco-Roman world until, already by the end of the second century, Christian centers existed from Edessa and Antioch and Caesarea in the East to Spain and Lyon and Rome in the West, and from Britannia and Sinope in the North to Carthage and Alexandria in the South.[2] This was not a static, but a dynamic world. And this was not an eastern world or a western world—it was both eastern and western; this was not a northern world or a southern—but both northern and southern. And things were happening: from its Judaean and Galilean origins, Jewish Christianity quickly spread to places like Antioch of Syria and Damascus, thence to Asia Minor and Macedonia, and to Greece and Rome.[3] As Mithraism spread to virtually every outpost of the Roman army, so—in the earliest generations—Christianity spread to innumerable Jewish settlements throughout that Greco-Roman world, and, of course, to non-Jewish centers as well.

The writings that were later to constitute the "New Testament"

---

[2] Compare the end paper maps in W. H. C. Frend, *The Rise of Christianity* (Philadelphia: Fortress, 1984). For much of the summary of early Christianity that follows, I have used this volume as a general resource. In addition, I have relied upon the more cautious—and, for the earliest period, undoubtedly more accurate—work of Helmut Koester, *Introduction to the New Testament. Volume Two: History and Literature of Early Christianity* (Philadelphia: Fortress; Berlin/New York: de Gruyter, 1982[1] [the 1st ed. is cited; 2nd ed. published in 2000]); and J. Neville Birdsall, "The New Testament Text" *The Cambridge History of the Bible: Volume 1: From the Beginnings to Jerome* (eds. P. R. Ackroyd and C. F. Evans; Cambridge: Cambridge University Press, 1970) 308–77, whose discussion is always in full awareness of the church-historical context.

[3] Koester, *Introduction to the New Testament*, 2.86–94.

were in circulation, along with other Christian documents. For example, Jewish-Christian Gospels (later to be designated "non-canonical") were appearing around the middle of the second century in Syria-Palestine and Egypt, and during that same period and in the same areas Christian "gnostic" groups were flourishing and came into conflict with the main-stream church.[4] In Rome in 144 C.E., Marcion—soon to be considered the arch-heretic of the church—was excommunicated by the church of Rome. Even before this, early doctrinal 73
definitions were underway, including—among a wide range of emerging issues—questions concerning the nature of Christ and his relation to God, the definition of church authority and organization, as well as liturgical practices and eschatological views, and the relation of church to empire. Differences in understanding these issues are reflected already in the New Testament writings and occur with increasing specification, for example, in *1 Clement, Didache, Epistle of Barnabas, Polycarp*, the *Letters* of Ignatius, the *Apocalypse of Peter*, the *Shepherd of Hermas*, as well as in Montanus, Tatian, Celsus, Hegesippus, and Irenaeus. The general heterodoxy of this initial period of Christianity is now well recognized, as is the early dominance in many areas of what the orthodox church would later call "heresies."[5] Certainly heterodoxy—"a syncretistic situation conducive to speculative thought without hierarchical control"[6]—was the mark of the earliest Egyptian period, which encompassed a variety of practices in Christianity, including "gnostic" forms of the young faith.

Meanwhile, forces outside Christianity were affecting it as well. Pliny the Younger, Governor of Bithynia in Asia Minor, wrote to the Emperor Trajan around 112 C.E. about "the contagious disease of this superstition" (10.96), and Christian apologists, beginning with

[4] Ibid., 2.201–03; 219–33, esp. 232; and also 236.

[5] For a convenient summary of these points, see Frederik W. Wisse, "The Use of Early Christian Literature as Evidence for Inner Diversity and Conflict," *Nag Hammadi, Gnosticism, & Early Christianity* (eds. C. W. Hedrick and R. Hodgson, Jr.; Peabody, MA: Hendrickson, 1986) 177–90.

[6] F. W. Wisse, "Prolegomena to the Study of the New Testament and Gnosis," *The New Testament and Gnosis: Essays in Honour of Robert McL. Wilson* (eds. A. H. B. Logan and A. J. M. Wedderburn; Edinburgh: T. & T. Clark, 1983) 142; see also A. F. J. Klijn, "Jewish Christianity in Egypt," *The Roots of Egyptian Christianity* (eds. B. A. Pearson and J. E. Goehring; SAC; Philadelphia: Fortress, 1986) 161–75; note the following statement: "Egypt is a fine example of burning questions dealing with orthodoxy and heterodoxy, and with Jewish Christianity and gnosis" (175).

Quadratus and Aristides, soon issued their "invitations to a philosophical way of life."[7] Justin also sought to demonstrate the truth of the Christian faith, and died around 165 C.E. for confessing it, as did the aged Polycarp.

Then, by the end of the second century, the Greek New Testament was being translated into Latin, undoubtedly also into Syriac, and
74 possibly into Coptic.[8] It is both of interest and of considerable significance to observe that "in the first two centuries all the theologians who achieved fame in the West were themselves from the East (from Marcion and the Apologists through Irenaeus and Hippolytus)," and, therefore, that "all the significant theologians of any influence in the West in the early period came from Eastern church backgrounds, bringing their New Testament texts with them."[9]

With the coming of the third century, issues of Christian theology and philosophy were pursued in increasingly sophisticated fashion by Clement of Alexandria, Tertullian, Origen, Cyprian and others, involving, for example, controversies over rebaptism, penance, Easter, the trinity, and christology. Influential centers of Christian scholarship existed, for example, in Alexandria and Caesarea, and Origen was influential in both. Manichaeism was a threat, but the greater threat in the middle of the third century was the brief Decian persecution, affecting Christians in cities throughout the empire, followed by a similar period under Valerian several years later.

In the midst of these varied activities, both positive for the church's development as well as negative, and occurring variously in the East and the West and from North to South, the earliest Christian writings were continuing to circulate. This can be documented in a number of ways. Colossians (4:16) shows that letters were exchanged between churches and read, and 2 Peter (3:15–16) confirms a knowledge of "all" of Paul's letters, indicating that they were in movement. The Apostolic Fathers (ca. 90–130) quoted from the earlier

---

[7] Koester, *Introduction to the New Testament*, 2.338–40.

[8] Birdsall, "The New Testament Text," 345–347; cf. Bruce M. Metzger, *The Early Versions of the New Testament: Their Origin, Transmission, and Limitations*. Oxford: Clarendon Press, 1977) 8; 287–90.

[9] Kurt Aland and Barbara Aland, *The Text of the New Testament: An Introduction to the Critical Editions and to the Theory and Practice of Modern Textual Criticism* (tr. Erroll F. Rhodes; Grand Rapids: Eerdmans; Leiden: Brill, 1987; 2nd ed., 1989) 68. [1987 ed. is cited—page numbers usually are identical in 1989 ed.] [German original, 1982.]

Christian writings. Justin (ca. 150) knows two or more of our four Gospels. Marcion not only limited his canon to the Gospel of Luke and ten letters of Paul, but edited them critically. Tatian produced his Diatessaron in Syria around 175, beginning a competition between a single, harmonized Gospel and the four separate Gospels. Succeeding Patristic writers quoted from a wide range of writings, many of which were to become canonical. Final settlement of the New Testament canon was to come more than two centuries after the days of Justin and Marcion, though the collection and authority of the four-fold 75
Gospel and of the Pauline Corpus were clear enough by Irenaeus's time (ca. 180).

Though we can never know the actual extent of the circulation of Christian writings throughout the Roman world, the process was dealt a severe blow during the Diocletian persecution at the outset of the fourth century, when—beginning perhaps in 303—copies of Christian Scripture were confiscated and destroyed. Over the following two decades, events significant for the church—both positive and negative—continued, culminating in Constantine's opening of the Council of Nicaea in 325 and his establishment of the "new Rome" at Constantinople in 330, and, of course, in the achievement by Eusebius of an *Ecclesiastical History*.

The point of this hasty and quite inadequate survey of activities and movements in the first few centuries of Christianity is simply to recall the multifarious interactions in these tumultuous times and to suggest that copies of New Testament books—as well as those of other early Christian writings—were circulating within these complex situations and were interactive with the circumstances described and with innumerable others like them. Unfortunately, we cannot with certainty link any specific early New Testament manuscript with any specific event or person. Yet we can imagine—quite legitimately—the importance of biblical manuscripts again and again in this early Christian world. We can well envision their role in worship and homily, in teaching and polemic, in church consultations, and in times of persecution; and we can postulate their certain transfer from congregation to congregation, from church leader to church leader, and from scholar to scholar, within both orthodox and heterodox Christianity.

It is within this background of dynamic movement, development, and controversy that the earliest New Testament manuscripts must be examined, for—as has long been asserted but too little appropriated—the text of the New Testament in its earliest stages was a vibrant, living text that functioned dynamically within the developing church. Textual criticism, therefore, can never be understood apart from the history of the church.[10]

76 II. The Environment of the Earliest New Testament Manuscripts

In addition to this ecclesiastical background, we need also to sketch not only the situation with respect to the earliest manuscripts, including something of the environment they shared in the places where they were found, but also their general life setting in Christianity's dynamic first centuries. There are innumerable difficulties attending these tasks, as everyone recognizes, yet this is a crucial step if we are to make progress. One of the difficulties is that we know almost nothing about the specific provenance of our early manuscripts, except—of course—that the forty-five earliest ones virtually all come from Egypt and that twenty of these (as well as seven others) were unearthed at Oxyrhynchus.[11] Very little, however is known about Christianity at Oxyrhynchus at the time these manuscripts were used and finally discarded—although this general area of Egypt is known

[10] On the study of New Testament textual criticism in the context of church history, see especially Birdsall, "The New Testament Text," 311–16; 328–77; see also note 2, above, and K. and B. Aland, *The Text of the New Testament*, 49–54; 67–71. The latter work, however, exaggerates the lack of attention to church history by New Testament textual critics, for viewing textual variants as products of the church's tradition is a theme that has been pursued by a number of scholars over the past sixty years, though most notably by American and British textual critics; for a summary, see E. J. Epp, *The Theological Tendency of Codex Bezae Cantabrigiensis in Acts* (SNTSMS 3; Cambridge/New York: Cambridge University Press, 1966) 15–21. [Much has transpired since this essay was written: see esp. Bart D. Ehrman, *The Orthodox Corruption of Scripture: The Effect of Early Christological Controversies on the Text of the New Testament* (New York: Oxford University Press, 1993); idem, "The Text as Window: New Testament Manuscripts and the Social History of Early Christianity," *The Text of the New Testament in Contemporary Research: Essays on the* Status Quaestionis (eds. B. D. Ehrman and M. W. Holmes; SD 46; Grand Rapids, MI: Eerdmans, 1995); David C. Parker, *The Living Text of the Gospels* (Cambridge/New York: Cambridge University Press, 1997).]

[11] [These figures, of course, have been altered by recent discoveries: see the articles on the Oxyrhynchus papyri, below.]

to have been a center of Christian activity at a later time, that is, in the fourth and fifth centuries.[12]

Of the provenance of the other earliest papyri, such as the famous Chester Beatty (P^{45}, P^{46}, P^{47}) and the Bodmer papyri (P^{66}, P^{72}, P^{75}), still less is known, though it was reported at the time of their purchase that the Chester Beatty papyri were discovered in a pitcher in a ruined church or monastery near Atfih (Aphroditopolis) in the Fayum,[13] about one-third of the way down the Nile River from Oxyrhynchus toward Alexandria. A similar statement accompanied the purchase of P^{52}, most likely the earliest New Testament fragment of all, which was assumed to have come either from the Fayum or from Oxyrhynchus.[14] It has also been surmised that the Beatty and Bodmer codices may have come from the same church library, though there is no proof.[15] Among the famous uncial manuscripts, it has been suggested on occasion that Codices Vaticanus (B) and Sinaiticus (א) represent
two of the fifty parchment manuscripts that, according to Eusebius, 77
were ordered by Constantine around 331 for his new churches in Constantinople, but this identification is based, most tenuously, on Eusebius's reference to "volumes of threefold and fourfold forms," which could, of course, fit the respective three-column and four-column formats of the two codices. However, Eusebius's words can be interpreted in other ways, and there are some reasons to think that Codex Vaticanus may have originated in Egypt.[16] Likewise, though Codex Alexandrinus (A) is usually assumed to have originated in

---

[12] Eric G. Turner, *Greek Papyri: An Introduction* (Oxford: Clarendon Press, 1968) 28. [On knowledge of Christianity at Oxyrhynchus, see now my "The Oxyrhynchus New Testament Papyri: 'Not without honor except in their hometown'?" *JBL* 123 (2004) 5–55.]

[13] Colin H. Roberts, *Manuscript, Society and Belief in Early Christian Egypt* (Schweich Lectures, 1977; London: Oxford University Press, 1979) 7.

[14] C. H. Roberts, *An Unpublished Fragment of the Fourth Gospel in the John Rylands Library* (Manchester: Manchester University Press, 1935) 24–25; H. Idris Bell and T. C. Skeat, *Fragments of an Unknown Gospel and Other Early Christian Papyri* (London: Oxford University Press, 1935) 7.

[15] C. H. Roberts, "Books in the Graeco-Roman World and in the New Testament," *The Cambridge History of the Bible. Volume 1: From the Beginnings to Jerome* (eds. P. R. Ackroyd and C. F. Evans; Cambridge: Cambridge University Press, 1970) 56.

[16] See Bruce M. Metzger, *The Text of the New Testament: Its Transmission, Corruption, and Restoration* (2nd ed.; Oxford/New York: Oxford University Press, 1968) 7–8; see also Birdsall, "New Testament Text," 359–60. [On B and א, see now T. C. Skeat, "The Codex Sinaiticus, the Codex Vaticanus and Constantine," *JTS* 50 (1999) 583–625; both were written in Caesarea (603–4).]

Alexandria, it might have come from Constantinople or Caesarea.[17] All of this is to suggest that our knowledge of the provenance of early New Testament manuscripts is scant.

Accordingly, these sparse data would appear to offer precious little assistance in an effort to link our early manuscripts in some direct way with early church history. Difficult as the process is, the fact that virtually all of the earliest manuscripts come from Egypt makes worthwhile any and every conceivable form of investigation of the Egyptian environment. Artifacts and manuscripts from Alexandria certainly would help, but papyri from Alexandria and the Delta region have not survived, and the ancient city of Alexandria is now below sea level,[18] raising several critical questions. For instance, were the cities in the Fayum or those farther removed from Alexandria, like Oxyrhynchus, Antinoe, or Hermopolis, in close touch with Alexandria or largely isolated from it? With what ease or difficulty did letters and literature circulate in these areas? What was the general level of cultural and literary activity in such places? Information on these matters will help us to assess the role that the papyrus books originating in these localities might have played in society and the extent to which such books circulated within Egypt and in the Greco-Roman world generally.

We begin, then, by asking what we know of Christianity in Egypt in this period. Statements about our lack of knowledge are classic,[19]
78 but the beginnings of Christian faith in Alexandria and in other parts of Egypt must reach back to the first half of the second century, even though that cannot easily be documented. One might, however, argue for that conclusion from what is perhaps our earliest New Testament manuscript, P^{52}. This tiny fragment of the Fourth Gospel was written in the first quarter of the second century, but probably nearer 100 than 125;[20] the same may be said for the

[17] Burnett H. Streeter, *The Four Gospels: A Study of Origins, Treating of the Manuscript Tradition, Sources, Authorship, & Dates* (London: Macmillan, 1924) 120 n. 1.

[18] H. I. Bell, *Egypt from Alexander the Great to the Arab Conquest: A Study in the Diffusion and Decay of Hellenism* (Oxford: Clarendon Press, 1948) 10.

[19] For statements from Adolf Harnack and B. H. Streeter, see Klijn, "Jewish Christianity in Egypt," 161; from C. H. Roberts, see the opening sentence of his *Manuscript, Society and Belief*, 1, also quoted by Birger A. Pearson, "Earliest Christianity in Egypt: Some Observations," *The Roots of Egyptian Christianity* (eds. B. A. Pearson and J. E. Goehring; SAC; Philadelphia: Fortress, 1986) 132.

[20] Roberts, *Unpublished Fragment of the Fourth Gospel*. Though at an earlier time

"Sayings of Jesus" fragment from Oxyrhynchus[21] and of Papyrus Egerton 2, usually referred to as "the Unknown Gospel."[22] The precise provenance of neither P^{52} nor Egerton 2 is known, but doubtless they are from the Fayum or Oxyrhynchus,[23] and the "Sayings of Jesus" fragment is from Oxyrhynchus. In fact, certain affinities between the latter papyrus and P^{52} suggest to some that they could have come from the "the same early Christian community in Middle Egypt."[24]

Looking at the early date of these papyrus fragments and their likely provenance in the Fayum or Oxyrhynchus—that is, in Middle Egypt 150 to 200 miles up the Nile from Alexandria—suggests that Christianity was well established in those areas by around 100 C.E. In addition, the very likelihood that a number of the very early Oxyrhynchus Christian papyri were private copies—copies belonging to individual Christians rather than to communities or churches[25]—
reinforces the early presence of Christianity in Egypt, for the following 79
reason: though possibly debatable, it is logical to assume that copies of authoritative books would first be in the possession of a church or community (for liturgical and instructional use) and only later be copied for private use. If so, the existence of private copies so far from Alexandria at so early a period suggests the early origin, rapid expansion, and significant saturation of Christianity in at least the lower third of Egypt at an early time.

Though this scenario is the most likely one, a *caveat* is in order. It is possible—following the line of argument to be presented below—that one or even all of these early Christian papyri could have been written elsewhere and brought into Egypt for use there, and such

dated 125–150, recent opinion moves it back into the 100–125 period, perhaps very early in that quarter century (12–16); Aland and Aland, *Text of the New Testament*, 85.

[21] Bernard P. Grenfell and Arthur S. Hunt, *The Oxyrhynchus Papyri* (London: Egypt Exploration Fund, 1898) I.1–3 + pl., who gave it the first position in this first published volume of *The Oxyrhynchus Papyri*.

[22] Bell and Skeat, *Fragments of an Unknown Gospel*; Koester, *Introduction to the New Testament*, 2.222. Roberts, "Books in the Graeco-Roman World," 62, dates it "about the middle" of the 2nd century.

[23] Roberts, *Unpublished Fragment of the Fourth Gospel*, 24–25.

[24] Ibid., 25.

[25] Roberts, *Manuscript, Society and Belief*, 9. He says "many, but not all" of our papyri may have belonged to individual Christians. For more on the non-professional quality of these papyri, see Roberts, "Books in the Graeco-Roman World," 62–63.

an event could have occurred immediately after the production of a papyrus manuscript or considerably thereafter. Should this have taken place many decades or as much as a century or more after their writing, these manuscripts could not so easily be used to document the presence of Christianity in Egypt in the early second century.

Yet it must be remembered that virtually all of the New Testament papyri are from Egyptian rubbish heaps and presumably, therefore, were in extended use—most likely in Egypt—prior to being discarded. Nevertheless, the possibility that manuscripts like P^{52} could have been produced elsewhere and imported into Egypt is a further complicating factor and gives the whole matter an ironic twist: In determining the presence of Christianity in Egypt, the date that a papyrus manuscript was discarded may be more important than the date of its copying.[26] If, for example, it could be determined that P^{52} was discarded in 175 or 200 or 250, and if we knew more about how long manuscripts were used in early Christian congregations before they were "retired" and replaced, we could work backward from the date of discard to the date of a probable presence of Christianity in Middle Egypt. Unfortunately, much less is known about when the manuscripts were cast on the rubbish heaps than about the date and provenance of writing—which is itself precious little—and the useful life of a papyrus manuscript in a liturgical setting is something I have not seen discussed.[27]

81 The non-Christian Egyptian papyri in general, however, provide information on two other factors highly relevant to our discussion and here there is greater clarity: first, the papyri attest extensive and lively interactions between Alexandria and the outlying areas, and also between the outlying areas and other parts of the Roman world, including Rome itself; and, second, they provide evidence of the wide circulation of documents in this early period. The following are a few examples. Papyri indicate that Jews were in touch with each other in the provinces.[28] One papyrus shows that of 325 Philadelphians

[26] I owe this point to Frederik Wisse, in discussion at the conference.

[27] Contrary to common opinion, papyrus is a durable substance: see E. J. Epp, "The New Testament Papyrus Manuscripts in Historical Perspective," *To Touch the Text: Studies in Honor of Joseph A. Fitzmyer, S.J.* (eds. M. P. Horgan and P. J. Kobelski; New York: Crossroad, 1989) 262–66 for a summary of the issue.

[28] Roberts, *Manuscript, Society and Belief*, 4, who refers, of course, to Victor A. Tcherikover and Alexander Fuks (eds), *Corpus Papyrorum Judaicarum* (3 vols.; Cambridge, MA: Harvard University Press, 1957–1964) vols. 1 and 2.

registered as resident outside that village, sixty-four were resident in Alexandria.[29] Tax registers from Karanis suggest a population of five or six thousand there and "a small minority of Alexandrian citizens, who are probably absentee landlords," as well as Greeks from Alexandria and Roman veterans; and literary texts there include Homer's *Iliad* and Chariton's romance, *Chaereas and Callirhoe.*[30] Hermopolis (up the Nile from Oxyrhynchus) yielded an official letter of congratulation to a certain Plution upon his return from Rome, including quotations from Euripides and *Poimandres.*[31] A number of members of the Museum at Alexandria are connected by the papyri with estates in the outlying country. One prominent member of this scholarly group, around 200 C.E. in Philadelphia, can also be connected with Rome, leading E. G. Turner to remark that he was "a person therefore who might have carried books from Rome to Philadelphia."[32] Other members of this Museum elite can be documented in Antinoe (near Hermopolis) and in Oxyrhynchus. Documents from Oxyrhynchus, dating from around 173 C.E., involve people who were obviously Alexandrian scholars (at least one of whom is known otherwise) and who discuss the procurement of books. Turner's conclusion on this is of interest:

> Here, for Oxyrhynchus at least, we tread firm ground: a circle of per- 82
> sons exchanging notes on how to procure and get copies made of works of scholarship, who are themselves professional scholars.[33]

In addition, there is extensive papyrus evidence that documents and letters were brought to Egypt from a wide range of localities and from considerable distances, including Ravenna, Macedonia, Seleucia, Ostia, Rome, and Constantinople, eliciting Turner's rhetorical question, "What books or Christian texts might not have been carried in?" He adds that these data serve to "alert the searcher to the possibility that other literary (and religious) books, Latin or Greek, found

---

[29] Roberts, *Manuscript, Society and Belief,* 4.
[30] Turner, *Greek Papyri,* 80–81.
[31] Ibid., 85–86.
[32] Ibid., 86.
[33] Ibid., 87. [Though both Turner and Roberts think that a "circle of friends" is implied here, that has been called into question: see my discussion under "General literary activity in Oxyrhynchus," in "The New Testament Papyri at Oxyrhynchus: Their Significance for Understanding the Transmission of the Early New Testament Text," *Oxyrhynchus: A City and Its Texts* (ed. Peter Parsons, et al.; London: Egypt Exploration Society, forthcoming).]

in Egypt were the products of scriptoria outside Egypt," though he admits that a desideratum in the field is a criterion for identifying manuscripts copied outside Egypt.[34]

Oxyrhynchus also yielded an account of fees paid to a scribe for copying. There were letters asking friends in Alexandria to buy paper for them, or telling family members that inkwells and pens have been left for their use, or revealing fine expression and writing style. An interesting papyrus scrap lists subjects for student declamations that would require the reading of Thucydides or Euripides.[35] In the villages in the Fayum generally, Homer, Plato, Sophocles, and other Greek authors are well represented.[36] Moreover, the papyrus texts of the "Acts of the Alexandrian Martyrs," stemming from the first three centuries, represent a "pamphleteering literature, probably passed from hand to hand,"[37] and there is evidence of wide circulation since specimens have been found as far as 200 miles apart, beginning more than 150 miles from Alexandria at Arsinoe, then at Oxyrhynchus, and perhaps also at Panopolis, 160 miles up the Nile from Oxyrhynchus.[38] From these data, C. H. Roberts concludes:

> 83 With this analogy in mind, we shall not be inclined to accept the view of some scholars that until the third century Christianity was confined to Alexandria when Christian manuscripts of second century date have been found in Middle and Upper Egypt.... There is abundant evidence of a close and continuous relationship between the Greeks of Alexandria and the Greek middle class in the provincial towns and villages at all levels—economic, cultural, and personal.[39]

It is not easy, however, to determine precisely what economic, cultural, and personal life was actually like in a district capital such as Oxyrhynchus, where archaeological finds were minimal. It is, however, of interest—as we have already observed—how much can be discerned from "philological archaeology," that is, from the papyrus documents. We know something of the number of public buildings

[34] Turner, *Greek Papyri*, 50–51; 96; see also C. H. Roberts and T. C. Skeat, *The Birth of the Codex* (London: Oxford University Press, 1983) 35.

[35] Turner, *Greek Papyri*, 83–85; 87.

[36] E. G. Turner, *Greek Manuscripts of the Ancient World* (Oxford: Clarendon Press, 1971) 96.

[37] Roberts, *Manuscript, Society and Belief*, 3.

[38] Ibid.

[39] Ibid., 4; see also Roberts and Skeat, *Birth of the Codex*, 35.

Sites of Papyrus Finds in Egypt 80

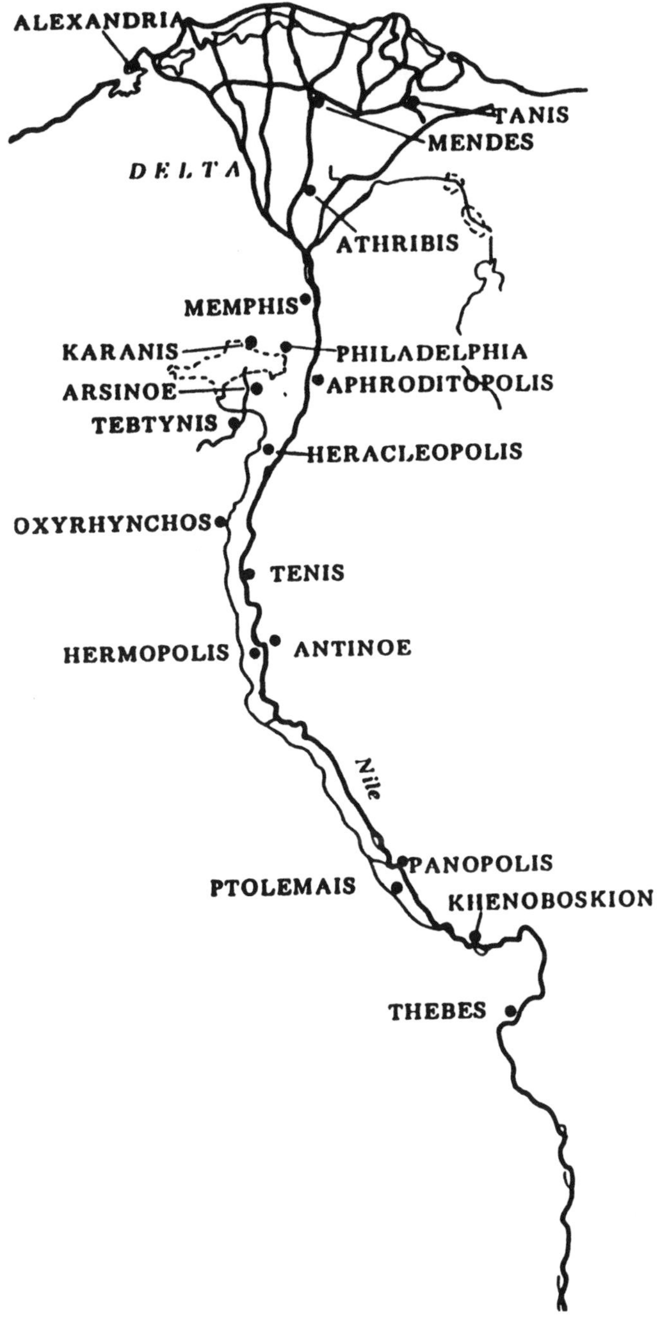

from records of a night watchman's rounds, including temples and two Christian churches; we have evidence, actually, of twenty temples, of gymnasia, of courts for playing ball and a race course, of a theater—seating 8,000 to 12,000 people—as well as a script on papyrus for a play of Euripides; and we have records of money allocated for a new street, of residents' addresses in named quarters of the city, and of soldiers stationed in Oxyrhynchus.[40] This is in addition to the correspondence and literary activity alluded to earlier, all of which adds up to a city full of cultural and intellectual pursuits, not to mention, of course, the everyday activities of life.

Similar data could be compiled for other cities, in the Fayum or farther up the Nile, where papyri have been found, but what we have outlined will be sufficient to make the point that these were places not only of literacy but of literary activity and that they were in frequent and relatively easy communication—both through travel and letter writing—with Alexandria and other major areas in the Greco-Roman world. As further documentation, reference might be made, for example, to P. Mich. Zenon 10, a letter dated 257 B.C.E., which reports a two-month adventure by ship from Alexandria to southern Asia Minor; but the letter itself which told of the trip "took only nineteen days to get back to the village of Philadelphia in the
84 Arsinoite nome, some 250 kilometers up-river from Alexandria."[41]
In addition, mundane commercial documents on papyrus show that the business dealings of the Philadelphian banker, Zenon, reached not only nearby Memphis, but all the way into the Nile Delta to places like Athribis, about seventy miles from Philadelphia, and Mendes, forty miles farther into the Delta near the Mediterranean Sea.[42]

Though one would not hastily equate the Christian production

---

[40] Turner, *Greek Papyri*, 81–82; see also 78–88 for other localities and cultural information.

[41] Naphtali Lewis, *Greeks in Ptolemaic Egypt: Case Studies in the Social History of the Hellenistic World* (Oxford: Clarendon Press, 1986) 12.

[42] Ibid., 53–54. Note, incidentally, that the Zenon correspondence refers to the acquisition of papyrus rolls from the Delta region (54). [See the much more detailed study of the Zenon archive and its relation to letter carrying in my essay, "New Testament Papyrus Manuscripts and Letter Carrying in Greco-Roman Times," *The Future of Early Christianity: Essays in Honor of Helmut Koester* (eds. B. A. Pearson, with A. T. Kraabel, G. W. E. Nickelsburg, and N. R. Petersen; Minneapolis, MN: Fortress, 1991) 35–56.

and use of books with the cultural literary activity of the Greco-Roman world, yet the Christian papyri—in our case the New Testament papyri—must be viewed within this active, vibrant world, and viewed with every degree of legitimate historical and creative imagination that can be brought to bear on the subject.

III. Textual Clusters and the Early Spectrum of the New Testament Manuscripts

It is time, now, to look at the early New Testament text within this two-fold background of the church-historical context and the Roman-Egyptian cultural setting as revealed through the papyri. We must explore how our knowledge of the New Testament manuscripts might be combined with the information gained from their historical-cultural environment and then break through, if possible, to new insights into the earliest period of textual transmission. Should that elude us, we may hope at least for greater clarity on the issues that confront us in the early formative period.

A. *Designations for the Textual Clusters*

A first step (though by no means an indispensable one) is to take seriously the clarion call from the early post-World War II era that we abandon the anachronistic terminology used in the period prior to the discovery of the Chester Beatty and Bodmer papyri. Kenneth W. Clark issued that call already in 1948, before the Bodmer papyri were known, by saying that "the only studies made thus far [of the Chester Beatty Papyri] seem to approach these texts by reversing the centuries. We require a new mental attitude, wherein we . . .
approach these earliest materials *de novo*," adding that "we should 85
study the third-century witnesses in their own right."[43] More widely quoted—and rightly so—has been the statement of J. Neville Birdsall in 1958, who pointed out the fault "common to many contemporary scholars who attempt to discuss and define such early evidence as this by standards of later witnesses," adding specifically:

[43] Kenneth W. Clark, "The Manuscripts of the Greek New Testament," *New Testament Manuscript Studies: The Materials and the Making of a Critical Apparatus* (eds. M. M. Parvis and A. P. Wikgren; Chicago: University of Chicago Press, 1950) 20–21.

> Beyond the fourth century the divisions of "Neutral," "Western," "Caesarean," "Byzantine" (or corresponding terms) are apposite: but in the early period, which such a papyrus as p^{66} reveals to us, these concepts are out of place. The task of present-day criticism is to inaugurate an era in which we begin from the earliest evidence and on the basis of its interpretation discuss the later.[44]

So, we shall abandon the long-standing but largely anachronistic and partially misleading designations of the past when discussing the earliest textual period, especially the terms "Neutral," "Western," and "Caesarean," and we shall try some new terms. Departure from the old categories is particularly important when dealing with the papyri, but we should go a step farther and abandon also, at least for the moment, the term "text-type," since the existence of such entities in the early centuries has been questioned in some quarters.[45] We shall substitute "textual group" or "textual cluster," assuming that these terms lack the offensive implications of a rigidly fixed form or a
86 tightly integrated character and that they avoid the attribution to textual groups of an officially conveyed status. Then, if and as appropriate, we may bring back the term "text-type" in the course of the investigation.

It will be obvious to all that proposing new symbols in the field of New Testament textual criticism is an extremely hazardous venture, as witnessed by the fate accorded the schemes of Westcott-Hort, or von Soden, or F. G. Kenyon—all of which seemed appropriate

---

[44] J. Neville Birdsall, *The Bodmer Papyrus of the Gospel of John* (Tyndale New Testament Lecture, 1958; London: Tyndale, 1960) 7.

[45] Most prominently Kurt Aland; see "The Significance of the Papyri for Progress in New Testament Research," *The Bible in Modern Scholarship: Papers Read at the 100th Meeting of the Society of Biblical Literature, December 28–30, 1964* (ed. J. Philip Hyatt; Nashville/New York: Abingdon, 1965) 334–37 (and the updated German version, "Die Konsequenzen der neueren Handschriftenfunde für die neutestamentliche Textkritik," in his *Studien zur Überlieferung des Neuen Testaments und seines Textes* [ANTF 2; Berlin: De Gruyter, 1967] 188–89); more recently, see Aland and Aland, *Text of the New Testament*, 59–64; 103, who distinguish between "different forms" of the text (which they say did exist prior to the 3rd/4th century) and "text types" (which they say existed only in the 4th century and after); cf. Ernest C. Colwell, "The Origin of Texttypes of New Testament Manuscripts," *Early Christian Origins: Studies in Honor of Harold R. Willoughby* (ed. A. Wikgren; Chicago: Quadrangle, 1961) 138; repr. as "Method in Establishing the Nature of Text-Types of New Testament Manuscripts," in Colwell, *Studies in Methodology in Textual Criticism of the New Testament* (NTTS 9; Leiden: Brill, 1969) 55: "Very few, if any, text-types were established by that time [200 C.E.]."

enough in their respective periods of research, but, as scholarship passed them by, were soon out of date. Nor do I wish to suggest that proposing new terminology is either the burden of this paper or, for that matter, of any intrinsic importance. Yet, reluctance to start anew is, by default, to permit the perpetuation of anachronistic labels and to necessitate the repeated explanation of terms that already are used by all of us only with surrounding quotation marks.

In forming new designations, ideally we should begin with terms or symbols that are both simple and unbiased, or—alternatively—with terminology that has a genuine historical basis. On the latter approach, natural designations for New Testament textual clusters, for example, would be "the P^{75} text," "the P^{45} text," etc., but the obvious danger here is the same as that which brought about our present terminological crisis: who can say that even manuscripts like P^{75} will remain either the earliest or the most distinctive representative of that particular textual cluster?[46] Rather, the use of arbitrary symbols is preferable, though it would be advantageous if we could employ some symbols that, at the same time, would also recognize and recall certain aspects of our past scholarship that are generally recognized as valid. That would make the symbols both more meaningful and easier to remember. So, rather than merely selecting in an arbitrary fashion the numbers 1, 2, 3, 4; or the Greek letters, alpha, beta, gamma, delta (as Westcott-Hort and Kenyon did, though
with different meanings),[47] I would suggest that we keep matters as 87
simple as possible and use the letters A, B, C, and D, when probing for the basic New Testament textual groups of the early period. These are symbols that will easily justify themselves, and yet will

[46] As to the likelihood of discovering additional New Testament papyri of importance, see the pessimistic statement in Aland and Aland, *Text of the New Testament*, 75: "After the impressive growth in the number of manuscripts recorded in the nineteenth century by Gregory and in the twentieth century by the Institute for New Testament Textual Research, it is unlikely that the future will bring any comparable increases," though they go on to allow that recent finds at St. Catherine's Monastery on Mt. Sinai "could change the situation." Of course, the rising water table throughout Egypt, as a result of the high dam at Assuan, threatens the survival of any buried papyri; yet, the long-standing pessimism in the past about new finds in Egypt was repeatedly falsified by fresh discoveries (see Turner, *Greek Papyri*, 40).

[47] See Vincent Taylor, *The Text of the New Testament: A Short Introduction* (2nd ed.; London: Macmillan, 1963) 6–7; F. G. Kenyon, *The Text of the Greek Bible* (rev. ed.; London: Duckworth, 1949) 197.

remain essentially unbiased regardless of future discoveries and developments. In this way we can make a fresh start—at least in appearances—with respect to our terminology, and yet retain connections that are sufficiently reminiscent of certain significant scholarly achievements in our evolving history of the text as to give the system immediate credibility. The four proposed groups are set forth in what follows.

Textual Group "A"—On this scheme, "A" would designate what is variously called the Majority text, or the Koine, or the later Byzantine; with the letter "A" suggesting such words as the "average" text (in the sense of ordinary or common), or the "accepted" text (with affinities to *textus receptus*), or the "ascendant" text (since it became the text that prevailed, though wrongly so), but also calling to mind Codex Alexandrinus (A), which is the oldest representative of this textual group—though only in the Gospels—and, of course recalling Westcott-Hort's designation, "Antiochian"[48] (We could use "K" for Koine, or "M" for Majority, but there is a nice symmetry in using four consecutive letters of the alphabet.)

Textual Group "B"—The symbol "B" would be used to represent the character and quality of the text found in P^{75} and Codex Vaticanus (B), which are the major representatives of this textual cluster. Of the close relationship of the texts in these two specific manuscripts there can be no doubt. The symbol "B," while it may appear to perpetuate anachronistic procedures of the past—in that it appears to use a later manuscript's designation for an earlier textual phenomenon—is in reality quite neutral when it is seen simply as one of several consecutive letters of the alphabet. Yet, it has the advantage of easy recognition.

Textual Group "D"—The letter "D" (to skip group "C" for the moment) would designate the kind of text found in P^{48}, P^{38}, and P^{69}, which in a later form is found in Codex Bezae (D). The use of "D" would rid us of the largely misleading term "Western," but would
88 leave us with a well-established symbol for this textual cluster and—again—place it in a more unbiased setting.

Textual Group "C"—Finally, the letter "C," which conveniently

[48] Brooke Foss Westcott and Fenton John Anthony Hort, *The New Testament in the Original Greek* (2 vols.; Cambridge/London: Macmillan, 1881–1882 [2nd ed., 1896]) 2.142–46.

stands between "B" and "D," would represent the "in-between" text that occurs, for example, in P[45] and in parts of Codex Washingtonianus (W). The letter "C," of course, recalls the term "Caesarean," though this is a name that should no longer be perpetuated; yet no harm will be done if, for some, it serves to recall the general kind of text found in this cluster.

Before offering further explanations of this scheme, it should be observed that those who eschew the identification of text-types in the early period of New Testament textual transmission[49] will object to the entire enterprise, though such an approach appears to reflect more an obscurantism than a realistic attempt to come to terms with the early data, limited though it is. It seems to me that we should use as judiciously and as creatively as possible the data we have and venture boldly toward some scholarly progress—we should take risks, forge new paths—rather than close off the future by preemptive decisions or through judgments that by their very nature preclude advances in our knowledge of the past.

B. *Definitions of Textual Clusters*

The next steps are to define these textual clusters in greater detail (using the fresh symbols) and then to show how they are to be viewed dynamically within their general life setting in those earliest centuries of Christianity. Naturally, there is a fair measure of tentativeness in all of this, but that—as we say—"goes with the territory." Though textual criticism has shown itself to be, by its very nature, a highly conservative discipline, an overly cautious attitude when exploring theoretical issues will forestall the progress so urgently required in the field. We need to open some new windows, and—if possible—a few doors as well! A general survey of the situation of the text in the earliest known period will set the stage for these closer definitions of textual groups.

The forty-five[50] earliest New Testament manuscripts that are currently known, that is those dating up to and including the turn of

---

[49] See n. 45, above.

[50] [The current figure is sixty-one, updated from Aland and Aland, *Text of the New Testament*, 57 (where there were 43 papyri plus 5 majuscules = 48), by adding P[98], P[104] (2nd c.); P[103] (2nd/3rd c.); P[101], P[106], P[107], P[108], P[109], P[111], P[113], P[114] (3rd c.); P[99], P[100], P[102], P[115] (3rd/4th c.) = 63, but then combining P[4] with P[64+67] and subtracting 0212 (Diatessaron) = 61.]

the third/fourth centuries, present us with a number of differing textual complexions. Everyone recognizes this, though not all agree on
89 how they are to be differentiated or what to call them or what the range of difference means. These and other difficulties abound as we try to interrogate these aged witnesses and as we attempt to use them in theorizing procedures. Perhaps the most obvious difficulty is that most are highly fragmentary in nature. Yet, the first principle to be adopted in assessing the fragmentary papyri is clear enough: "If a fragment preserves a passage where there is any variation in the tradition, it is quite sufficient to signal the textual character of the whole manuscript," as Kurt and Barbara Aland affirm in their recent book.[51]

A second difficulty is that virtually all forty-five of these earliest manuscripts—as well as the vast majority of all the other New Testament papyri—are from Egypt. Does this mean that the array of textual complexions they present all originated in Egypt? In answering that question, we should resist the temptation to look to later New Testament manuscripts that may represent other places and draw any conclusions; rather—at least at this stage of investigation—we should stay with the earliest manuscripts only and restrict our analysis to them alone. But does that not preclude the possibility of offering any sort of answer as to whether all the New Testament texts found on papyri in Egypt originated in Egypt? No, for it seems to me that we do have a path toward an answer, though—by the nature of the case—it cannot be decisively demonstrated.

The answer as to whether the varying textual complexions of the earliest Egyptian papyri all originated in Egypt—and, therefore, the answer to the more substantive question as to whether Egypt is representative of the entire early history of the New Testament text—was implicit in our description of the movement of population and the circulation of letters and literature throughout Egypt in the first centuries of the Christian era. That is, if—as we have shown—there existed a lively and vigorous movement of people back and forth between Alexandria and the Greco-Roman world to the east and west and north, and also between Alexandria and the upper regions

[51] Aland and Aland, *Text of the New Testament*, 58. They support the principle with the everyday analogy that "there is no need to consume a whole jar of jelly to identify the quality of its contents—a spoonful or two is quite enough!"

of Egypt, especially the Fayum and centers like Oxyrhynchus, and
if—as we have shown—there was a brisk circulation of letters and
of literature in these same areas, then we are compelled to give up,
first, the notion that all of these textual complexions necessarily originated in Egypt, and, second, that they remained in or were confined
to Egypt. In fact, the evidence from the non-New Testament papyri
that reveals dynamic interchanges of people, letters, and books to 90
and from Egypt, as well as within Egypt, actually would permit us
to go to the logical extreme—if we wished—of asserting that *none* of
the New Testament textual complexions necessarily originated in
Egypt, though there is no reason to carry the matter that far. Suffice
it to say that the breadth and intensity of the intellectual commerce
between Egypt—even Middle and Upper Egypt—and the rest of the
vast Mediterranean region between 30 and 300 C.E.[52] supports the
strong possibility—indeed the strong probability—that *the various textual*

---

[52] [The case for the widespread and speedy transfer of letters in the Greco-Roman world has now been presented, with detailed documentation, in my "New Testament Papyrus Manuscripts and Letter Carrying in Greco-Roman Times," 35–56, especially in the section on "The Speed of Transferring Letters" (52–55). Here it is shown, from dated and docketed papyrus letters—i.e., letters containing both the date of writing and the date of receipt—that letters could travel some 800 miles in two months; or some 350 miles in thirty-six days; or 125 miles in three weeks, or some 400 miles in fourteen days; or 150 miles in four, six, or seven days; or fifteen miles in the same day, to cite several actual examples. The study concludes that:

> The evidence sampled here—and there is much more—documents . . . the prompt transfer of letters throughout the Greco-Roman world. This lively activity occurred not only within Egypt (i.e., between the Delta, the Fayum, and upper Egypt), but between Egypt and places as far removed as Ostia in Italy, Cilicia in Asia Minor, Sidon in Syria, and Arabia—to mention only a few specific examples cited above. This data can be combined with other evidence of brisk "intellectual commerce" and dynamic interchanges of people, literature, books, and letters between Egypt and the vast Mediterranean region during the broad New Testament period to permit at least two claims about the early New Testament manuscripts: (1) the various textual complexions (usually called "text-types") represented by the earliest New Testament papyri—virtually all of which were found in Egypt—did not have to originate there, but could easily, in a matter of a few weeks, have moved anywhere in the Mediterranean area. Moreover, if some of these textual complexions did originate in Egypt, the dynamic situation meant that they would not—could not—have been confined to Egypt. Therefore, (2) it is not only theoretically possible, but quite probable that the present array of text-types represented in the Egyptian New Testament papyri do, in fact, represent text-types from the *entire* Mediterranean region, and, furthermore, that they could very likely represent *all* of the existent text-types in that large region in the early period of New Testament textual transmission. (55–56)]

groups presented by our Egyptian papyri represent texts from the entire Mediterranean region (including, of course, those texts that might have originated in Egypt itself).

A dynamic view of New Testament textual transmission, then, envisions considerable movement of New Testament manuscripts to and from Egypt and within Egypt, at least in the period up to the Diocletian persecution beginning around 303. It also permits us, by inference, to put to rest the question as to whether Egypt adequately represents the textual spectrum of earliest Christianity—we may presume that it does.

Another line of argument can be employed to support the same conclusion in a more explicit fashion. Recently C. H. Roberts (with T. C. Skeat) has made a case that the *nomina sacra* (the uniform abbreviations of divine names and sacred terms in manuscripts) were a Christian creation established either by the church at Jerusalem before 70 C.E., or by the church at Antioch slightly later—as a kind of "embryonic creed" of the first church—and that from there they "spread to Egypt and everywhere where Greek was written." This system, Roberts says, "was too complex for the ordinary scribe to operate without either rules or an authoritative exemplar"—because without one or the other it would have been difficult, even in a small Christian community, to determine which usages (of the secondary *nomina sacra*) were secular and which were sacred.[53] In addition, a case can be made that the *nomina sacra* and the codex form of book not only were both Christian inventions,[54] but that both came into existence at the same place at about the same time. Moreover, both phenomena share the same characteristic: each serves effectively to differentiate Christian books from both Jewish and secular books.[55]

91 The presence in Egypt of "this remarkably uniform system of *nomina sacra*" in the earliest Christian manuscripts (all but four of which were codices) only slightly more than a century after their invention

---

[53] The basic case is made in Roberts, *Manuscript, Society and Belief*, 44–46, where he argued for Jerusalem, but it is revised and supplemented in Roberts and Skeat, *Birth of the Codex*, 57–61, where Antioch is favored.

[54] [I would be more cautious now about asserting that Christians "invented" the codex or the *nomina sacra*; both are much debated currently and remain open questions.]

[55] Roberts and Skeat, *Birth of the Codex*, 57–58.

calls for explanation. Roberts's conclusion is that already "at an early date there were standard copies of the Christian scriptures."[56] On this theory, such standard copies would have to have been established in Jerusalem or Antioch and transmitted, either directly or through other centers, to Egypt. Others think that the *nomina sacra* (and also the codex form) might have originated at Alexandria or even Rome.[57] The point is that a highly technical, rigidly practiced *Christian* procedure was well established in Middle Egypt prior to the time of our earliest New Testament papyri, which in a rather striking fashion, regardless of its place of origin, attests to the active movement of New Testament manuscripts within the eastern Greco-Roman world—and at very least attests to early and active textual transmission within Egypt itself.

Though no one yet is asserting that the *nomina sacra* procedures and practices suggest that Christian scriptoria existed prior to 200, that is at least a possibility. What these practices do suggest with more certainty, however, is that the churches in this earliest period, at least in the East, were perhaps not as loosely organized as has been assumed,[58] and, therefore, they also were not as isolated from one another as has been affirmed. Indeed, at least one "program of standardization"[59]—the *nomina sacra*—was certainly functioning with obvious precision and care. Moreover, the nearly exclusive use of the codex by Christians for biblical books in the earliest period[60] evidences a second standardization program—the very form that the books assumed appears to have been a matter of policy. We should not, then, "rule out of court" the likelihood that additional standard textual procedures were in operation at this very early time.

When—at long last—we now analyze the textual characteristics 92
of our earliest New Testament witnesses, noting differences among readings that are sufficient to distinguish separate textual complexions,

[56] Roberts, "Books in the Graeco-Roman World," 64. See n. 60, below.

[57] See Roberts, *Manuscript, Society and Belief*, 42–44; for arguments against Alexandria especially, see Roberts and Skeat, *Birth of the Codex*, 54–57.

[58] These two points are made against views taken in Aland and Aland, *Text of the New Testament*, 55–56; 59.

[59] The phrase is from ibid., 59, where, in the Alands' discussion of P^{45}, P^{46}, and P^{66}, they do at least allow for the possibility that the manuscripts could have been "imported from elsewhere."

[60] Roberts and Skeat, *Birth of the Codex*, 42. P^{12}, P^{13}, P^{18}, and P^{22} are from rolls, but are either opisthographs or on reused papyrus.

and when we subsequently trace lines of connection with later manuscripts of similar textual complexions, we must take these factors into account. Other significant observations will arise in the process of sketching the composition of the various textual clusters, to which we now turn.

Members of the "A" text group—The "A" text cluster, that is, the "accepted" text or the Koine or later Byzantine textual group, need not be further considered here, for the early papyri are not involved (although a few papyri of the sixth and seventh centuries do represent the "A" text). Furthermore, everyone recognizes that this textual group exists, though not until the fourth century—that is, after the period of the earliest papyri. Moreover, everyone also acknowledges that this can actually be called a "text-type."[61] The recognized constituent members can be found in the standard handbooks.[62]

Members of the "B" text group—The place to begin a description of the "B" textual cluster is with the striking and highly significant fact that the texts of P^{75} and Codex Vaticanus (B) are almost identical, a fact that demonstrates that there is virtually a straight line from the text of a papyrus dated around 200 to that of a major, elegant manuscript of 150 years later.[63] Does this permit us to expect—or to require—that similarly direct connections will be found between other early papyri and certain later manuscripts? Not necessarily, for both the discovery of the New Testament papyri and the survival of later manuscripts are random phenomena, and no uniform or complete representation of the textual spectrum can be expected to have been preserved for us. So we take what we have, both of the early papyri and the later witnesses, and attempt a creative reconstruction of the transmission process, recognizing that it will always be partial and less than fully satisfying. Precisely because this is the
93 situation, the close affinity of P^{75} and B is all the more striking, for

[61] See, e.g., Aland and Aland, *Text of the New Testament*, 51; 64–69.

[62] E.g., Bruce M. Metzger (ed., for the Editorial Committee) *A Textual Commentary on the Greek New Testament: A Companion Volume to the United Bible Societies' Greek New Testament (Third Edition)* (London/New York: United Bible Societies, 1971 [2nd ed., 1994]) xxx–xxxi [2nd ed., 15*–16*]; idem, Metzger, *Text of the New Testament*, 213.

[63] This hardly requires documentation, but both references and evidence may be found in G. D. Fee, "P^{75}, P^{66}, and Origen: The Myth of Early Textual Recension in Alexandria," *New Dimensions in New Testament Study* (eds. Richard N. Longenecker, and Merrill C. Tenney; Grand Rapids, MI: Zondervan, 1974) 24–28.

it demonstrates that an early papyrus can stand very near the beginning point of a clearly identifiable and distinctive textual group that has been preserved with a high degree of accuracy over several generations and through a period that often has been assumed to have been a chaotic and free textual environment.

If we had several pieces of evidence like the P^{75}-B relationship, it would be plausible to argue that the situation was not chaotic, but quite orderly. Although that evidence eludes us due to the randomness of the survival of papyrus, the evidence we have does, to a certain extent, move in that direction. For it was more likely a semblance of standardization, rather than accident, that permitted the text of Vaticanus—over several generations—to maintain its close affinity to that represented in P^{75}. Vaticanus was not copied from P^{75}—they had a common ancestor[64]—so one must ask about the transmission process that would have produced this very similar resultant text. To answer that P^{75} is a manuscript with a "strict" text[65] may be descriptive, but it does not answer the question "*Why?*" Indeed, the very employment of the term "strict" in describing some early New Testament papyri implies—though it does not prove—that a form of standardization was operative in the transmission process already at an early time.

As a matter of fact, the discovery of P^{75} nullified an older view of standardization, for the close affinity of P^{75} with Codex Vaticanus swept away the cobwebs of a long-standing and commonly-held notion that Codex Vaticanus reflects only a third/fourth century recension. On the contrary, it can be demonstrated that P^{75}-B textual tradition represents a relatively pure form of preservation of the text of a common ancestor,[66] and that P^{75}, therefore, is not itself an editorial adaption or recension.[67] We are left, then, with the undoubted fact that a distinctive kind of text, *with both antecedents and descendants*, existed in the very early period of New Testament textual transmission. 94
That text actually exists in an extant document from around 200 C.E.

[64] Fee, "P^{75}, P^{66}, and Origen," 33–40.

[65] Aland and Aland, *Text of the New Testament*, 64; 93; 95.

[66] See the compelling series of arguments that lead to this conclusion in Fee, "P^{75}, P^{66}, and Origen"; on the recension view, see 20–24; on the view that there is a common ancestry of the manuscripts, see 33–40.

[67] Ibid., 32–33; cf. Aland and Aland, *Text of the New Testament*, 64; 93; 95, where the term "strict" implies the same conclusion.

It also had earlier antecedents, although it is difficult to specify their dates. However, a dynamic view of textual transmission—combined with the *nomina sacra* evidence—would suggest that not only the text of P^{75} and its antecedents, but also other early New Testament papyri have a significantly earlier history in Judaea or Syria, as well as in Egypt. Moreover, there are enough hints that some early procedures of standardization were involved in the process to warrant calling the P^{75}-B cluster a "text-type." Therefore, I would not hesitate to affirm the existence of at least one text-type—which we can designate the "B text-type"—*in the second century*.

The slightly earlier P^{66} is usually associated with P^{75} and the later Vaticanus in this textual group. It has been argued that P^{66} is the product of a scriptorium.[68] Whether or not this is the case, the papyrus was produced by a "scribe-turned-recensor," who (though a careless workman) was himself correcting his text against a second exemplar and, in addition, appears intent on producing a more readable, common Greek style by abandoning Johannine style on numerous occasions (Johannine style, that is, as it is found in P^{75} and B). Thus, his text moves away from that of P^{75} (and toward the kind of readings later seen in the "A" type of text), though overall the text of P^{66} still is closer in character to that of P^{75} (and B) than it is to other manuscripts,[69] though it falls short (by at least ten percentage points) of the seventy percent agreement required by current practice to demonstrate textual affinity (see below). Yet, to place a text like P^{66} in a "text-type" like "B" does not diminish "B" as an actual text-type, for the motivations of the scribe of P^{66}—both his efforts to make the text readable and his quasi-scholarly activity in comparing and correcting his copy to a second exemplar—can be adequately recognized, providing thereby an explanation for his departures from his text-type norm. It may be a "wild" member of the group, but it is a group member nonetheless.[70]

---

[68] E.g., by Ernest C. Colwell and Gordon D. Fee; for documentation and arguments, see Fee, "P^{75}, P^{66}, and Origen," 30–31. On the "impossibility" of Christian scriptoria before 200 (except perhaps in Alexandria "about 200"), see Aland and Aland, *Text of the New Testament*, 70.

[69] Fee, "P^{75}, P^{66}, and Origen," 30–31; cf. Fee, *Papyrus Bodmer II (P^{66}): Its Textual Relationships and Scribal Characteristics* (SD 34; Salt Lake City, UT: University of Utah Press, 1968) 9–14; 35; 76–83.

[70] A. F. J. Klijn's description of P^{66} as "Neutral in a non-pure way" is accepted and confirmed by Fee, *Papyrus Bodmer II (P^{66})*, 35.

If this is an adequate analysis of P^{66} and of its relationship to P^{75} 95
and Vaticanus, then we learn something significant about "text-types." A text-type is not a closely concentrated entity with rigid boundaries, but it is more like a galaxy—with a compact nucleus and additional but less closely related members which range out from the nucleus toward the perimeter. An obvious problem is how to determine when the outer limits of those more remote, accompanying members have been reached for one text-type and where the next begins. We shall return to this issue in a moment.

To these witnesses for the "B-text"—P^{75}, Vaticanus (B), and P^{66}—can be added others, both among the papyri and among later manuscripts that share a similar textual complexion. These identifications necessarily must be quite tentative with respect to the fragmentary papyri. In addition, the classifications for all manuscripts should really be structured separately for various sections of the New Testament, particularly for the Gospels, for the Pauline letters, for Acts and the General Epistles, and for Revelation, because many manuscripts confine their contents to one of these groups. The matter is more complex, however, for "the textual history of the New Testament differs from corpus to corpus, and even from book to book; therefore the witnesses have to be re-grouped in each new section."[71] This is primarily the result of the way in which books were grouped in the transmission process, for the make-up of manuscripts varies vastly and many different combinations of books are to be found as one moves from manuscript to manuscript.[72] In addition, a number of manuscripts show "block mixture," that is, they contain sections reflecting one distinctive kind of text, and other sections reflecting another. Thus, any classification of manuscripts will lack the desired precision and neatness.

By definition, textual clusters, and especially text-types, can only become visible and be identified when lines of connection can be drawn between and among a number of manuscripts that share a similar textual complexion. Furthermore, standards must be established both to determine relationships between manuscripts and to differentiate distinctive textual groups from one another. These standards cannot

[71] E. C. Colwell, "The Origin of Texttypes," 138; repr. in his *Studies in Methodology*, 55.

[72] See Aland and Aland, *Text of the New Testament*, 78–79, for statistics.

be impressionistic or based on random samples, but must be grounded in a scientific and full comparison of agreement/disagreement in
96 variation-units (or in test readings, when large numbers of manuscripts are under consideration). The isolation of the variation-units (or test readings) must then be followed by quantitative measures of textual similarities and differences. These methods have been extensively explored and utilized, as well as substantially refined, in the current generation of New Testament textual criticism.[73] As to the definition of "text-type," no one yet has surpassed that offered by Ernest C. Colwell:

> The quantitative definition of a text-type is a group of manuscripts that agree more than 70 percent of the time and is separated by a gap of about 10 percent from its neighbors.[74]

Although highly fragmentary manuscripts do not lend themselves readily to this process, yet the readings within their variation-units can be fully compared with those of any other manuscript. To such results the criterion earlier quoted must be applied:[75] the textual character of a whole manuscript can be signaled even by a fragment's agreement with a variation in the textual tradition; therefore significant agreement with other manuscripts should qualify even a fragmentary witness as a member of a textual cluster. The randomness of the fragmentary papyri raises additional questions, however. For example, in these situations is seventy per cent agreement still the minimum to qualify as a "fellow member" of a textual group?

In spite of all these contingencies, the process of assessing textual complexions can go forward and relationships can be established. In the case of the B-text, the later "trajectory" of transmission would

[73] See the important theoretical work, and its application, by Gordon D. Fee, especially "Codex Sinaiticus in the Gospel of John: A Contribution to Methodology in Establishing Textual Relationships," *NTS* 15 (1968/69) 23–44.

[74] E. C. Colwell (with Ernest W. Tune), "The Quantitative Relationships between MS. Text-types," *Biblical and Patristic Studies in Memory of Robert Pierce Casey* (eds. J. N. Birdsall and R. W. Thomson; Freiburg/Basel/New York: Herder, 1963) 29; reprinted as "Method in Establishing Quantitative Relationships between Text-Types of New Testament Manuscripts," in Colwell, *Studies in Methodology*, 59. [See now the critique of Colwell's formula and other aspects of his method by Klaus Wachtel, "Colwell Revisited: Grouping New Testament Manuscripts," *The New Testament Text in Early Christianity: Proceedings of the Lille Colloquium, July 2000* (eds. C.-B. Amphoux and J. K. Elliott; HTB 6; Lausanne: Zèbre), 31–43.]

[75] See note 51, above.

include—beyond P^{75}, Vaticanus (B), and P^{66}—the fourth century
Codex Sinaiticus (א) (though not in John 1–8), Codex L (eighth century), and minuscules 33 (ninth century), 1739 (tenth century) (except 97
in Acts), and 579 (thirteenth century), to mention only the most
obvious.

Members of the "C" text group—In line with our stated principle of beginning at the beginning, we start with one of the early papyri that clearly differs in its textual complexion from that represented in the "B" text, namely, P^{45}. Since textual groupings can be defined only when lines of connection can be drawn to other similar manuscripts, we want to know if such connections exist for P^{45}. Since the time of its discovery and initial analysis, its most interesting connections have been found to be with Codex Washingtonianus (W) of the fifth century, but only in Mark 5:31–16:20 (since W is a classic example of block mixture). Elsewhere in the Gospels, its text has been described as "intermediate" between the Alexandrian (= "Neutral") and "Western," to use the usual designations[76] and the usual methods,[77] or—to use our designation—its text stands between the "B" and "D" textual groups. Thus, P^{45} was linked to a textual group called "Caesarean," a text-type considered, until recently, as a well-established one standing midway between "B" and "D." This is not the place to review the exigencies of the so-called "Caesarean" text,[78] but it is sufficient to say that the P^{45}—W kind of text cannot be described as either "Caesarean" or "pre-Caesarean" in Mark. Rather, it constitutes its own group, with further developments evident in f^{13}, but with no significant connections with its previously regarded "Caesarean" fellow members, chief among which were Codex Koridethi (Θ) and minuscule 565.[79] Yet the affinity of variation-units between P^{45} and W in Mark virtually reaches the seventy percent mark (68.9%), with P^{45} and f^{13} registering 55.3% agreement, but no other manuscript reaching more than 44% agreement with P^{45}.[80] Hence, the line or

---

[76] Metzger, *Text of the New Testament*, 37.

[77] See E. J. Epp, "The New Testament Papyrus Manuscripts in Historical Perspective," *To Touch the Text: Studies in Honor of Joseph A. Fitzmyer, S.J.* (eds. M. P. Horgan and P. J. Kobelski. New York: Crossroad, 1989) 261–88, where the treatment of the papyri in the history of New Testament textual criticism is treated in detail.

[78] See Larry W. Hurtado, *Text-critical Methodology and the Pre-Caesarean Text: Codex W in the Gospel of Mark* (SD 43; Grand Rapids, MI: Eerdmans, 1981).

[79] Ibid., 88–89.

[80] Ibid., 63; cf. 86–87.

"trajectory" of the P^{45} or "C" text, to the extent that it can be recognized at present, extends from P^{45} to W (in Mark) and secondarily to f^{13}. Codex W, by the way, appears to have been written in Egypt,[81]
98 but—on the basis of principles earlier enunciated—it would be premature and unwarranted to draw the conclusion that it might represent a text-type of Egyptian origin.

In the case of the "C" text, we cannot readily refer to the standard handbooks to find its constituent members. This is due to the fact that so much has changed in the discipline in the past decades.[82]

Members of the "D" text group—Finally, four or five manuscripts (including one uncial) from the third or fourth century form another early cluster: P^{48}, P^{69}, P^{38}, 0171, and perhaps P^{29}. These have an affinity with Codex Bezae (D) of the early fifth century. The reality of a D-text (long known as the "Western" text) is not doubted, although it has been asserted recently that its existence "as early as the second century" is "quite inconceivable."[83] Admittedly, the chrono-

[81] Henry A. Sanders, *Facsimile of the Washington Manuscript of the Four Gospels in the Freer Collection* (Ann Arbor, MI: University of Michigan Press, 1912) v, though he gives no reason or explanation for his 4th century date.

[82] See E. J. Epp, "The Twentieth Century Interlude in New Testament Textual Criticism," *JBL* 93 (1974) 393–96, on the status of the Caesarean text in current criticism. [The diminution and likely demise of the "Caesarean" text-type finds striking confirmation in a comparison of the "List of Witnesses according to Type of Text" in Metzger, *Textual Commentary*, 1st ed. of 1971 (xxix–xxx) under four headings: Alexandrian, Western, Caesarean, and Byzantine, with the same list in the 2nd ed. of 1994 (15*–16*), where there are only three: Alexandrian, Western, and Byzantine—the Caesarean has disappeared altogether!]

[83] Aland and Aland, *Text of the New Testament*, 55. However, their conception of the D-text is not clear, as appears from their several statements on the subject: (1) The claim that "it is quite inconceivable that the text of Codex Bezae Cantabrigiensis could have existed as early as the second century" (55). (2) The assertion that Codex Bezae's "tendentious revision (or more probably that of its ancestor of the third/fourth century) is based on a papyrus with an 'early text' of this kind" (51). (3) The reference to "the phantom 'Western' text" (55). (4) The statement, while speaking of the "Early Text" (prior to the third/fourth century), that "we also find manuscripts, although only a few, which approach the neighborhood of the D text" (64). (5) The affirmation that these pre-third/fourth century manuscripts include "some which anticipated or were more closely akin to the D text, but not until the fourth century . . . did the formation of text types begin" (64). (6) Finally, the claim that "the text found in Codex Bezae . . . represents (in its exemplar) the achievement of an outstanding early theologian of the third/fourth century" (69).

Apparently the Alands wish to differentiate between the "D text" and the "Western" text (as a geographical designation) (67–69), insisting that the latter is a "phantom" [yet for generations no one has seriously suggested that the "Western" text was western]. A curiosity, therefore, is their repeated emphasis that there could be no

logical gap between the earliest representatives and the major man- 99
uscript that connects with them is greater than the gap between P^{75} and Vaticanus (B), yet it is no greater than that between P^{45} and Washingtonianus (W). Of course, no one will claim that if we had extensive portions of P^{48} or P^{38}, or of the other early manuscripts in this group, they would be virtually identical to Codex Bezae. This later manuscript, Codex Bezae, has a complex history of its own, and the text it contains has evolved over more time and perhaps through greater exigencies than did the text of Vaticanus, though it has been almost impossible to determine the nature and scope of those situations. Yet—and this is crucial—lines of connection can be drawn from the four or five early manuscripts to Codex Bezae, and a further "trajectory" can be traced into the tenth century in minuscule 1739 (Acts only) and to the thirteenth century with minuscules 614 and 383.

It is significant that all five of the early manuscripts placed in this category contain portions of Luke-Acts (P^{69} and 0171 with Luke, though the latter also contains a portion of Matthew), and that three of them contain only portions of Acts (P^{29}, P^{38}, P^{48}). It is well known that the textual distincitves of Codex Bezae are more prominent in Luke-Acts (and especially in Acts) than in Matthew, Mark, or John. Though accidental, it is nonetheless extraordinary that it is precisely

early "Western" text because "no important personality can be identified at any time or place in the early Western church who could have been capable of the singular theological achievement represented by the text of the Gospels and Acts in the ancestor of Codex Bezae Cantabrigiensis (D)" (69; cf. 54). Indeed, if one wanted to make the case (though no one does) that the "Western" text was western, it would not be essential to identify a specific, known individual capable of producing it; after all, the canonical Epistle to the Hebrews was produced by someone not only unknown to us now, but also unidentified in antiquity (witness Origen). In the final analysis, the Alands affirm that "only the Alexandrian text, the Koine text, and the D text are incontestably verified" (67; cf. 243), but this apparently means the D text only after the second century (if we take seriously the strong statement on p. 55). Of these six statements, it seems that numbers 2, 4, and 6 are correct.

At the Notre Dame conference, Barbara Aland appeared to accept the term "proto" or "pre-D-Text" to describe the kind of text in manuscripts like P^{48}, P^{69} and P^{38}, implying that the D-text (though in her view not in existence until the beginning of the third century) represents a *process*, developing from a "proto D-Text" to a later, established "D-Text." In their book (p. 93), the Alands do refer to P^{38}, P^{48}, and P^{69} as "precursors or branches of the D text." Yet, note their caution about using the prefix "pre-" for any textual group (67).

these most noteworthy portions (Luke-Acts) of the later representative, Codex Bezae, that—relatively speaking—are so numerously represented by very early manuscripts. Certainly that lends more credibility to their affinity with Codex Bezae than would otherwise be the case, and just as certainly it lends greater credibility to the identification of a "text-type" that includes Codex Bezae as a prominent member.

The preceding is simply a sketch of the constituent members of each group; many more could be added to the "A," "B," and "D" clusters (though not so easily to the "C" cluster [but see below]).[84] However, our interest lies in the New Testament *papyri* and whether more of them can be fitted into the textual scheme outlined above. It would be premature—and presumptuous—for me to imply that independent judgments permit me to place the various remaining papyri into these groups, but many of them have been categorized by other individuals according to their textual complexions, and the following is at least suggestive of the result (though new assessments
100 and measurements undoubtedly are in order).[85]

(1) *The "A" group*: P^{63} (ca. 500); P^{84} (6th); P^{68}, P^{73}?, P^{74}? (7th); P^{42} (7th/8th)
(2) *The "B" group*: P^{52} (2nd); P^{46},P^{64+67}, P^{66} (2nd/3rd); P^{1}, P^{4}, P^{15}, P^{20}, P^{23}, P^{28}, P^{39}, P^{40}, P^{47}, P^{49}, P^{53}, P^{65}, P^{75}, P^{91} (3rd); P^{13}, P^{16}, P^{72} [in Peter], P^{92} (3rd/4th); P^{10}, P^{62}, P^{71}, P^{86} (4th); P^{50}, P^{57} (4th/5th); P^{14} (5th); P^{56} (5th/6th); P^{33+58} (6th); P^{3}, P^{43}, P^{44}, P^{55} (6th/7th); P^{11}, P^{31}, P^{34} (7th); P^{60}, P^{61}? (7th/8th).
(3) *The "C" group*: P^{45} (most of Mark). In addition, though fresh assessments must be made, the following papyri are identified as mixed, with elements of "B" and "D": P^{27} (3rd); P^{37}? (3rd/4th); P^{8}, P^{35} (4th); P^{36} (6th).
(4) *The "D" group*: P^{5}, P^{29}?, P^{48}, P^{69} (3rd); P^{37}?, P^{38}, P^{72} [Jude], 0171 (3rd/4th); P^{25}? (4th); P^{19}? P^{21}? (4th/5th); P^{41} (7th/8th).

Though the placement of each papyrus in these categories is tentative and subject to review and possible revision, this is a beginning. These lists take into account the papyri through number 76, with the addition of P^{84}, P^{86}, P^{91}, and P^{92}, for decisions on textual groupings are

[84] [See now n. 82, above.]

[85] I simply rely on Metzger, *Textual Commentary*, xxix–xxx [but see n. 82, above], and his earlier groupings in *Text of the New Testament*, 247–55, with modifications from other sources. I have consulted the original publications of the most recently available papyri and have adopted the editors' judgments when given. [See the added note, below, on "Papyri in the A, B, C, and D groups."]

not readily available for the rest. Yet, sixty-one of these eighty papyri can be placed into various textual groupings, or seventy-six percent of them. If their respective categorizations can be sustained, then seventy-six percent is a significant proportion. The textual complexion of the remaining ones will need to be clarified or initially determined (if possible). An obvious difficulty is that the procedure of classifying textual fragments really works only when there is a later comparative basis in larger bodies of surviving text that permits us to identify the kind or character of text that a particular papyrus represents. Small fragments that issue in no clear lines of connection to later materials are difficult to classify.

Can this proposal on early textual groupings be buttressed in any 101
other way? Certainly the quotations of Patristic writers from the same period are essential aspects of the data and should be utilized in the process of discriminating among early textual groups, and—though more complex and difficult—the early versions should be employed in the same way. The standard handbooks will indicate the textual groups that the various early Patristic authors and the versions support, but such a discussion would take us well beyond the reasonable scope of the present paper.

IV. Conclusion

Did "text-types" exist in the first two centuries of Christianity? If so, how early and where? Though exact answers cannot be given to the latter questions, I have established reasonable grounds for concluding that three identifiable text-types were in existence around 200 C.E. or shortly thereafter: a "B" text-type, a "C" text-type, and a "D" text-type. I have also furnished reasons for justifying the existence of these text-types already in the second century. Though some may consider the "reasonable grounds" to be "speculative," I would rather call them "creative." Essentially, I have argued as follows:

(1) The dynamism of the early Christian environment in the first three centuries stimulated the movement of Christian writings (whether later to become "canonical" or "non-canonical") over wide areas of the Greco-Roman world and encouraged their use in various aspects of the liturgical and theological/intellectual life of the church.

(2) The dynamism of life in the Greco-Roman world—even in the outlying areas of Egypt (where most of the New Testament papyri

were discovered)—permitted relatively easy travel and rather free transmission of letters and documents, so that the earliest New Testament papyri—though they have survived accidentally and randomly—are generally representative of the earliest New Testament texts used by the Christianity of the time in all parts of the Greco-Roman world. Incidentally, it is of more than passing interest that the New Testament papyri contribute virtually no new substantial variants, suggesting not only that virtually all of the New Testament variants are preserved somewhere in our extant manuscript tradition, but also that representatives of virtually all textual complexions have been preserved for us in the papyri.

(3) Several hints, found in the New Testament (and in other Christian) papyri themselves, suggest that standardization procedures
102 were in existence already in the late first or early second century for the transmission of Christian texts, such as the codex form, the *nomina sacra* techniques, and the possible presence of scriptoria. These standardization procedures permit us to claim that our very earliest New Testament papyri had antecedents or ancestors as much as a century earlier than their own time. This point is supported by the demonstration that P^{75}-B text had a common ancestor earlier than the third century P^{75} itself.

(4) By tracing lines of connection from the earliest papyri to later manuscripts with similar textual complexions, the broad *spectrum* of the early New Testament text can be viewed, revealing a range of differing textual complexions, which—at their extremes—merge with or blend into one another. To employ another model alluded to earlier, a number of distinctive textual streams or *trajectories* present themselves. This model has the advantage of envisioning, in a chronological, developmental fashion, extended series of related manuscripts in distinctive groups. Such trajectories not only begin with one or more papyri and extend forward for several—and sometimes many—centuries, but they also extend backward to the hypothetical antecedent manuscripts/texts that preceded the earliest papyri. As we have observed, P^{75} had an antecedent whose existence can be established even though that manuscript itself is not extant, and the same kind of text appears later in Codex Vaticanus. The result is that a genuine trajectory can be drawn from a very early (though non-extant) manuscript to P^{75}, and then to Codex Vaticanus, and on to later witnesses. Moreover, since no canonical New Testament books were

authored in Egypt, the texts had to travel to Egypt; hence, manuscripts copied anew in Egypt have trajectories reaching back to their antecedents in other parts of the very early Christian world.

What is striking in this process is that one or more of the earliest papyri almost immediately can be connected with an early major uncial manuscript that has a similar textual complexion. The major, non-fragmentary uncials from the fourth and fifth centuries are Sinaiticus (א), Vaticanus (B), Alexandrinus (A), Ephraemi (C), Washingtonianus (W), and Bezae (D). Four of these connect with earlier papyri to form our distinctive early textual groups: Vaticanus and Sinaiticus for the "B" text-type; Washingtonianus for the "C" text-type; and Bezae for the "D" text-type. Another uncial, Alexandrinus, represents the later "A" text-type and, not surprisingly, connects with some sixth and seventh century papyri; the remaining uncial, Ephraemi Rescriptus, is a mixed, composite manuscript. If such lines of connection could not be drawn, the claim for early "text-types" would be less credible, though by no means discredited.

If all the groups presented as neat a picture as the B-text trajec- 103
tory described earlier, the trajectory model would be the most appropriate one, especially if the manuscripts representative of each text-type showed the requisite seventy percent agreement among themselves and also the required ten percent difference in the percentage of agreements with the members of the adjacent text-types. Such a ten percent gap generally can be shown when measuring manuscripts that have extensive portions of text (whether papyri, uncials, or minuscules), but such measurements are difficult and less significant when attempted with the fragmentary papyri. Therefore, unless measurements of the latter can be refined, it may be preferable to employ the "spectrum" model when describing the early text-types.

On the spectrum model, the primary colors (distinct text-types) can be seen immediately, namely, the B, C, and D text-types in the earliest period. As we look farther along in time, the A text-type presents itself as an identifiable hue on the textual spectrum. Many of the fragmentary papyri (as specified in the lists for the various textual groups above) will reveal the same strong colors that identify a text-type, but others will appear as shades of the brighter hues, and the early papyri will range broadly across the spectrum. Yet a spectrum is a spectrum: it has concentrations of primary and secondary colors, with gradations of merging and blending hues between them. This very well portrays the early textual situation, with three (or four) primary concentrations that represent clearly identifiable early text-types and a spread of manuscripts between them.

(5) Therefore, (a) since clear concentrations of manuscripts with similar textual character existed in the earliest period of transmission accessible to us, and—to change the figure—since lines of connection can be drawn from the papyri to major manuscripts with recognizable textual complexions, and (b) since these concentrations or lines of trajectory identify clusters that in turn differentiate themselves sufficiently from other clusters, the claim that at least three "text-types" existed in the dynamic Christianity of the second century may be made with considerable confidence.

Added Notes 2004

I stand by the four points argued in the paper and outlined in the conclusion, and I have tried subsequently to expand on the dynamism in the transmission and use of early Christian writings, particularly in the essays below on "New Testament Papyrus Manuscripts and Letter Carrying in Greco-Roman Times," in the three articles involving the New Testament papyri and Oxyrhynchus, and in "The Multivalence of the Term 'Original Text.'" I hold also to the notion of three early "textual clusters," commonly called text-types, a topic I have pursued in various publications for thirty years or more. See, most recently, my "Issues in New Testament Textual Criticism: Moving from the Nineteenth Century to the Twenty-First Century," *Rethinking New Testament Textual Criticism* (ed. D. A. Black; Grand Rapids, MI: Baker Academic, 2002) 41–43, esp. n. 63. Yet, I have never pursued to the extent that I had hoped the detailed make-up of the various text groups that I specify, namely:

Papyri in the A, B, C, and D groups. Though several statements of tentativeness accompanied my discussion, I wish to emphasize again that the placement of various papyri in the four text groups on p. 100 is certainly open to question in much of its detail. My plan to seek a more solid basis for placing the various papyri in these groups never was carried through. The difficulties, of course, are great, particularly with the many highly fragmentary manuscripts. I was pleased, however, to see the recent article by J. Keith Elliott, "Codex Bezae and the Earliest Greek Papyri," *Codex Bezae: Studies from the Lunel*

Colloquium, June 1994 (eds. D. C. Parker and C.-B. Amphoux; NTTS 22; Leiden: Brill, 1996) 161–82. He, too, is modest about the study, indicating some of the attendant difficulties (162) and its largely negative results (182). Yet, it is an attempt, as he says elsewhere, "to see what support distinctly Western readings had in early papyri," concluding that there is "evidence there of early Western-type readings": see "The Nature of the Evidence Available for Reconstructing the Text of the New Testament in the Second Century," *The New Testament Text in Early Christianity: Proceedings of the Lille Colloquium, July 2000* (eds. C.-B. Amphoux and J. K. Elliott; HTB 6; Lausanne: Zèbre), 17.

I have not attempted a revision of my highly provisional list, but perhaps others will be challenged to undertake such an exploration. It is clear to me, however, that—with respect at least to the D-text—determining its complexion or character cannot be done on the basis of Greek manuscripts alone, that is, by measurements of agreements between and among Greek witnesses only, no matter how sophisticated the quantitative methods might be. Rather, due to the nature of the D-text—however it is viewed—its adherents and supporters can only be identified by assessing both the relevant Greek manuscripts and the Old Latin, Old Syriac, and Coptic witnesses. A manuscript like Coptic G67, for example, must be taken fully into account (as Hans-Martin Schenke has shown). See the discussion below in my "Toward the Clarification of the Term 'Textual Variant,'" 163–66, and the recent "Anti-Judaic Tendencies in the D-Text of Acts: Forty Years of Conversation," esp. 117–22, and elsewhere as I attempt to clarify the method used to establish the presumably early D-text in its relation to or distance from the text of Codex Bezae.

CHAPTER FOURTEEN

NEW TESTAMENT PAPYRUS MANUSCRIPTS AND LETTER CARRYING IN GRECO-ROMAN TIMES[1]

I. Issues, Purpose, and Limitations

It is well known that the earliest extant manuscripts of the New 35
Testament were written on papyrus and that virtually all were found in Egypt. The first was published in1868 (P11), but B. P. Grenfell and A. S. Hunt's 1897 discoveries at Oxyrhynchus occasioned the first genuine excitement over such finds, and eventually thirty-one fragmentary New Testament papyri were recovered from that site alone. More significant discoveries, in terms of extensive manuscripts of early date, were to come from other locales in the 1930s and 1950s, and currently some ninety-three different New Testament papyrus manuscripts are known. These manuscripts reflect a variety of textual complexions, which has given rise to the intractable questions as to whether or not the papyri represent an array of early "text-types" and—even more basic—whether there were or could have been "text-types" in Egypt in the period of the earliest group of New Testament papyri—those dating prior to ca. 300 C.E.

There also are subsidiary questions, whose answers could help resolve these larger issues, including the following: Though virtually all New Testament papyri were found in Egypt, did they actually originate in Egypt? If not, how easily and quickly could they or their ancestors have been transferred to Egypt from other parts of the Greco-Roman world? And how readily did written documents in general—but especially letters and literature—move from place to place in that period?

The issue can be exemplified in the customary treatment of P52 (likely the oldest New Testament manuscript) when it is invoked in

[1] To Helmut Koester, a demanding but always supportive mentor and a career-long colleague in Hermeneia, I owe far more than can be conveyed in a brief statement—that he inspired his students to seek out important issues in early Christianity, to pursue them armed with a thorough grasp of the Greco-Roman world, and to persist in their resolution despite obstacles or opposition.

determining the date of the composition of the Fourth Gospel. Numerous scholars have voiced the opinion that the existence of P52 in Egypt very early in the second century means that the *terminus ad quem* for the writing of the Fourth Gospel was some years or decades earlier because—to use a common phrase—it would take some time for the manuscripts to circulate into Middle Egypt (where P52 no doubt was found). Treatments of the Gospel of John commonly contain a statement similar to this one from Raymond Brown:

> Thus, it is quite clear that John circulated in many copies in Egypt in the period 140–200 [though we might now say 100/125–200]. The theory that John was composed in Egypt has had little support. If, as is generally supposed, it was composed in Asia Minor (or even Syria), we must allow time for it to have reached Egypt and to have passed into common circulation there. Moreover, the Bodmer Papyri reflect partially different textual traditions of the Gospel, that is, P66 is close to the text we later find in Codex Sinaiticus; P75 is almost the same as the text of Codex Vaticanus. The development of such variation must have required time.[2]

The issue for us, then, is whether an extended period of time was required for a text to move to Egypt from Palestine, Syria, Asia Minor, and even from Greece and Rome, and the answer may have significant implications for the questions about early "text-types" in Egypt.

36 These topics require exploration of the social context of our New Testament papyri, something the present writer, in a recent article, undertook in a preliminary way, and the simple intention of the present exploratory essay is to attempt a further step in that investigation—though the arguments presented there will not be repeated here.[3]

A. *The New Testament papyri in their setting*

The papyrus manuscripts of the New Testament did not exist in a vacuum, but were part of an active, vibrant world of agriculture,

[2] Raymond E. Brown, S.S., *The Gospel according to John* (2 vols.; AB 29–29A; Garden City, NY: Doubleday, 1966–70) lxxxiii. Cf. A. H. McNeile, *An Introduction to the Study of the New Testament* (2nd ed., rev. by C. S. C. Williams; Oxford: Clarendon Press, 1953) 294. [Bracketed statement not in original.]

[3] E. J. Epp, "The Significance of the Papyri for Determining the Nature of the New Testament Text in the Second Century: A Dynamic View of Textual Transmission," *Gospel Traditions in the Second Century: Origins, Recensions, Text, and Transmission* (ed. William L. Petersen; Christianity and Judaism in Antiquity, 3; Notre Dame, IN: University of Notre Dame Press, 1989) 76–84, esp. 81–84 and 89–90.

commerce, travel, education, literary activity, medicine, religion, law, and everyday life in the society of the day. All of this—and more—is abundantly attested by the papyrus documents and letters that have come down to us from ancient Egypt. Among the activities of business, legal, and public life that have been documented for us by the papyri are edicts, codes, reports, declarations, and announcements of government officers; applications, nominations, and appointments to official positions; petitions, summonses, depositions, minutes, and judgments in legal proceedings; and business orders, contracts, statements, receipts, accounts, and audits. Education, literature, and philosophy are attested by copies of works by Homer, Hesiod, Sappho, Pindar, Bacchylides, Sophocles, Euripides, Menander, and Callimachus, to mention only the most prominent poets and playwrights; by portions of the historical writings of Herodotus and Thucydides, of orations by Aeschines, Demosthenes, and Hyperides, of philosophers such as Plato, Theophrastus, and various Sophists, Cynics, and Stoics; as well as by school exercises, folk poetry, and an array of miscellaneous literary texts. Among the myriad events and social interactions of everyday life that are reflected in this material are marriage and divorce; birth, adoption, civil rights, death, wills, bequests, and even the exposure of children; sons in military service and children away at school; concern about health, safety, and welfare; invitations to visit and the sending of gifts; crime, fraud, and vandalism; and prayers, charms, and horoscopes. In addition, this real-life, flesh-and-blood world that the papyri reveal to us is replete with the wide array of human perceptions and emotions, including feelings of accomplishment and disappointment, anger and approval, estrangement and reconciliation, loneliness and comfort, anxiety and relief, depression and elation, and joy and sorrow. The papyri were sent, received, 38
and employed in a down-to-earth, everyday social environment, and it was within this same world that the New Testament papyrus texts were transmitted and used.

The quantity of this variegated material is immense.[4] In the New Testament field, it has been used since its discovery to explore the

[4] For a convenient summary, see E. J. Epp, "The New Testament Papyrus Manuscripts in Historical Perspective," *To Touch the Text: Biblical and Related Studies in Honor of Joseph A. Fitzmyer, S.J.* (eds. Maurya P. Horgan and Paul J. Kobelski; New York: Crossroad, 1989) 264–65 and the references there. Some of the relevant material can be found conveniently, e.g., in A. S. Hunt and C. C. Edgar,

nature of the vocabulary, diction, and syntax of New Testament Greek and to locate parallels to the content of the New Testament. Yet this social world of the New Testament papyrus manuscripts has seldom been related directly to those New Testament papyri themselves in an effort to discover how such texts were transmitted; from where, to where, and by whom they were carried; and how and how fast they traveled. To be sure, this analysis may not—in any specific fashion—illumine the New Testament papyri text-critically, or even assist in locating them precisely and individually in their own immediate settings, but it can help us to see them for what they are: artifacts of a real-life setting that was in no way isolated from the daily flow of people and events. Above all, we are permitted—indeed, compelled—to see that the New Testament papyri neither originated nor functioned in a vacuum, nor did they move in and through the Greco-Roman world via a kind of sacred superhighway, as if unrelated or insensitive to the world around.

That the New Testament papyrus manuscripts were part of and participants in this vibrant social environment is perhaps in no way so poignantly confirmed as by the fact that the vast majority of the New Testament papyri appear to have been discovered in the rubbish heaps of Egypt—one of the great levelers in society short of death itself. Contrary to what a pious Christian might believe or wish to believe, these priceless portions of "sacred scripture" suffered the same ignominious fate that befell thousands of legal, official, and business documents, personal letters, and school exercises, and also copies of the works of great secular writers, historians, and philosophers of antiquity that have been mentioned earlier. Whether the biblical papyri were worn out by use and discarded, or were abandoned because of neglect and non-use, they rested unceremoniously for hundreds upon hundreds of years along with other remnants and cast-offs of an active social milieu. As a matter of interest, some of our more extensive New Testament papyri—the Chester Beatty—were rumored to have been found in a pitcher in a ruined church

---

Select Papyri: I. Non-Literary Papyri, Private Affairs and *II. Public Documents*, and Denys L. Page, *Select Papyri III: Literary Papyri, Poetry* (LCL 266, 282, 360; Cambridge, MA: Harvard University Press, 1932–42) [cited as LCL, 1, etc.], and in John L. White, *Light from Ancient Letters* (Foundations and Facets; Philadelphia: Fortress, 1986).

[Abbreviations of papyri follow the *Checklist of Editions of Greek, Latin, Demotic, and Coptic Papyri, Ostraca and Tablets* (eds. John F. Oates, Roger S. Bagnall, *et al.*; 5th ed.; BASP Supplements, 9; Oakville, CT: David Brown; Oxford: Oxbow, 2001).]

or monastery near Aphroditopolis in the Fayum, which might sug- 39
gest that they, too, had outlived their usefulness and were given a customary form of "burial" for unwanted manuscripts.[5] Over all, rubbish heaps, collapsed and rubbish-filled buildings, ruined structures filled with wind-blown sand, and an occasional jar have been the common resting places for New Testament papyri and for the tens of thousands of other literary and non-literary manuscripts from Egypt. Others, no more nobly treated, were reused in the bindings of later books or by turning them into cartonnage or "paper maché" for wrapping mummies.[6]

This, then, constitutes the general setting and the larger context for the treasured fragments of papyrus that carry texts of the New Testament writings.

B. *Scholarly attitudes toward non-literary papyri*

It has long been customary for New Testament textual critics to pick up (so to speak) the New Testament papyrus documents as precious, independently existing artifacts, dust them off, and then utilize them for text-critical purposes largely in isolation both from the immediate environment out of which they were "rescued" (a common expression that itself makes the point!) and from the social-world setting in which they originated and functioned. This attitude is perhaps understandable when one recalls that early archaeologists discarded untold numbers of papyri in favor of finding intrinsically valuable artifacts or those of museum quality,[7] and that classical scholars in the first half of the nineteenth century were dismayed that Greek papyrus discoveries throughout that period were predominantly documentary rather than literary. Overall, until the twentieth century little attention was paid to those non-literary documents that reflected the socioeconomic history of the Hellenistic and Roman periods, for "papyri were rated according to literary content, and these were regarded as pretty mediocre."[8]

---

[5] Colin H. Roberts, *Manuscript, Society and Belief in Early Christian Egypt* (Schweich Lectures, 1977; London: Oxford University Press, 1979) 7.

[6] To complete the picture, it should be added that tombs also yielded a few Greek papyrus manuscripts that had been buried with the dead.

[7] Leo Deuel, *Testaments of Time: The Search for Lost Manuscripts and Records* (Baltimore, MD: Penguin Books, 1970 [original, New York: Knopf, 1965]), 92; cf. 88.

[8] Ibid., 92–93.

This preference for literary papyri over the non-literary continued into the twentieth century, so that Adolf Deissmann in 1922 could say "it is regrettable, therefore, to see the merest scrap of an ancient book [i.e., a literary papyrus] treated as if it were something sacred—immediately published with notes and facsimile, even it be a fragment of some forgotten scribbler who deserved his fate—while on
40 the other hand the non-literary items are often not even printed in full."[9] Papyrologists, when publishing papyri, routinely make the same distinction between literary papyri and documentary or non-literary papyri, further subdividing the latter into private documents (including letters) and public documents (as is done, e.g., in LCL, 1 and 2, respectively). Further, when publishing literary papyri, papyrologists often assign biblical fragments to a category different from that given to texts of classical authors. All of these procedures and attitudes tended not only to separate the documentary papyri from the literary, but at times even to separate biblical from classical texts.

Naturally, these characterizations are not meant to suggest any reform in how the papyri are classified or published. The point is a much simpler one, though not thereby any less important: the attitude that separated documentary from literary papyri, or personal letters from literary works, or biblical papyri from secular manuscripts has impoverished the study of the New Testament papyri by abstracting them from their "bedfellows" in the rubbish heaps and thereby isolating and insulating them from their proper social environment or life-setting. Rather, the New Testament papyri need to be studied in their proper social context.

C. *Purpose and limitations of the present study*

The proper procedure—restoring the New Testament papyri to their life-setting—not only can enlighten us about their immediate social context, but also can help in answering the questions posed earlier—how far, how easily, and how quickly New Testament manuscripts might have moved around the Greco-Roman world of earliest Christianity, and by what means of transfer. Answers to these puzzles are directly relevant to the other questions raised earlier about New Testament textual criticism: (1) Were there distinctive and identifiable

[9] See Adolf Deissmann, *Light from the Ancient East* (New York: Harper, 1927 [German original, 4th ed., 1922]) 39.

37

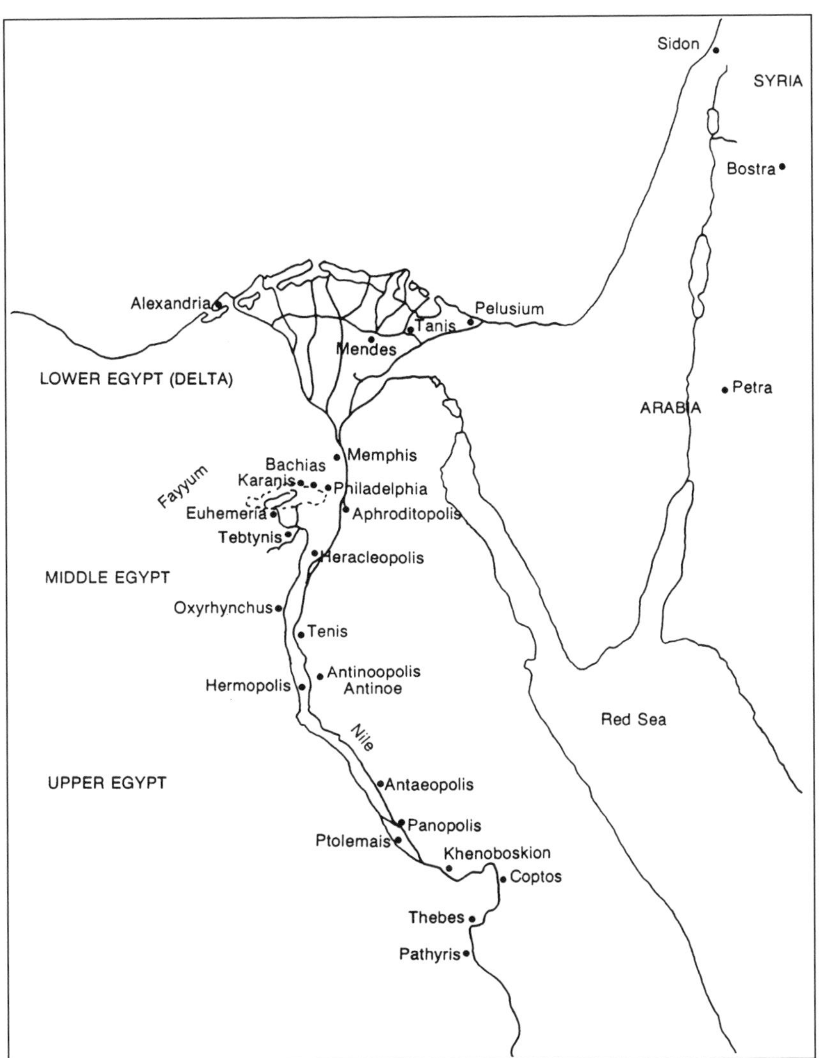

Sites involving letter carrying

text-types in the earliest period of New Testament textual transmission? (2) If so, to what extent are the Egyptian papyri representative of that spectrum of texts? (3) And did they originate only in Egypt?

This present effort is only a beginning, and space restrictions further require that the investigation be limited to a single facet of the New Testament papyri's social world: *letter carrying*. The purpose of these limited pages, then, will be to show how Greco-Roman letters and their movement reveal aspects of the social-world environment of the time that are relevant to answering the basic but intractable questions just posed about the New Testament papyri.

41 The illustrative material will be restricted to private letters (though with occasional reference to public documents), and it will range over papyri originating in the broad Greco-Roman period (generally, from Alexander to Constantine). Obviously, the random nature of the data—tens of thousands of manuscripts found but hundreds of thousands lost, with the survivors offering mainly a selection of documents discarded in antiquity—leaves us in a far less than desirable situation, though we remain immensely grateful for what we do possess. We quickly discover, however, how important letters were. For example, a slave writes to her master in the second century C.E., "I beg you, my lord, if it seems good to you, to send us a letter also, since we die if we do not see you daily. Would that we could fly to you and greet you. . . ." (P.Giss. 17; LCL 1.115).[10] Or a marine writes from Misenum, a port near Naples, to Philadelphia in the Fayum (second century C.E.), begging his father to write even "a little letter, telling me first of your welfare, secondly of my brother's and sister's, and enabling me thirdly to make obeisance before your hand[writing]" (BGU 423; LCL 1.112). The son, newly settled at his naval assignment, thinks of his family, and even a "little letter" written in his father's own hand would bring to him all the warmth of home and hearth. "And do not hesitate to write letters," a man writes to his brother in Karanis (in the Fayum) on 23 August, 133, "since I rejoiced exceedingly, as if you had come. From the day that you sent me the letter I have been saved" (P.Mich. VIII 482), and it goes on, incidentally, to report that "Peteeus, who is writing this

[10] For this translation, see John Garrett Winter, *Life and Letters in the Papyri* (Jerome Lectures; Ann Arbor, MI: University of Michigan Press, 1933), 130.

letter for me, salutes you repeatedly as well as your wife and your daughter and Bassus your horse"(!).

In addition, the extant papyri provide evidence covering the full range of human endeavor and of human emotion. Human feelings emerge with special force and poignancy, of course, in papyri of a private nature, and it is impossible to avoid the impression that most social interactions of everyday life in the Egypt of the period surrounding the earliest Christian era bear close resemblance to aspects of modern life. A few examples must suffice. Disease and calamity occur: "I beg you, brother, to write to me about your being all well, as I heard at Antinoopolis that there has been a plague in your neighborhood. So do not neglect to write, that I may feel more cheerful about you," writes Pausanias to Heraclides in Oxyrhynchus in the third century (P.Oxy. 1666; LCL 1.149). Another letter, from 95 B.C.E., says, "We heard that mice have eaten up the crop. Pray come to us and buy wheat here . . . (P.Grenf. II 36; LCL 1.103). Bills were sometimes hard to collect: "Let me tell you that you owe me seven years' rents and revenues, so unless you send remittances you know the risk you run" (late third century; P.Tebt. 424; LCL 1.154). Caution is needed during travel: "When you come, bring
your gold ornaments, but do not wear them on the boat," writes 42
Paniskos to his wife in 296 C.E. (P.Mich. III 214). Propriety triumphs over feelings in this postscript to a second-century letter from mother to son: "At your wedding the wife of my brother Discas brought me 100 drachmae; and now that her son Nilus is about to marry, it is right that we should make a return gift, even if we have grievances against them still pending" (P.Flor. 332; LCL 1.114). Above all, family conflicts occur, as in the second-century C.E. letter from one brother to another:

> Sempronius to Maximus his brother, very many greetings. . . . I learned that you are treating our revered mother harshly as if she were a slave. Please, dearest brother, do not distress her in anything. If any one of the brothers talks back to her, you ought to box their ears. . . . For we ought to reverence her who bore us as a god, especially when she is so good. This I have written to you, brother, since I know the sweetness of dear parents. Please write me about your health. Farewell, brother. (LCL 1.121)[11]

---

[11] Ibid., 48–49 for the translation.

A daughter, Plutogenia, writes from Alexandria to her mother in Philadelphia (ca. 296 C.E.) in severe language: "It is already eight months since I came to Alexandria, and not even one letter have you written to me. Again then you do not regard me as your daughter but as your enemy" (P.Mich. III 221), and the phraseology indicates that the problem is not mere delinquency in letter writing. Then, too, a mother (who happens to be a Christian) writes to her son (fourth/fifth century C.E.), referring to herself:

> ... Your mother Cophaena is ill, look you, thirteen months, and you had not the good grace even to write me a letter, since you yourself know that I have dealt more kindly with you than my other children [?], and you had not the grace, on hearing that I am ill, you had not the grace to send me at once anything at all.... I pray for your welfare for many years. (BGU 948)[12]

A son can chastise a father just as effectively, as in this tantrum, though by the time one reaches the last line it seems to be good natured and written out of serious concern (January, second or third century C.E.):

> Theon to Theon his father, greeting. You did a fine thing; you didn't take me with you to the city. If you do not wish to take me with you to Alexandria, I'll not write you a letter or talk to you or wish you good health. What's more, if you go to Alexandria, I won't take a hand from you or greet you again. So if you do not wish to take me with you, that's that!... But you did a fine thing; you sent me presents, big ones, locust beans!... But send for me, I beg you. If you do not send, I won't eat, won't drink! There! I pray for your good health. (P.Oxy. 119)[13]

A son away at school reassures his father (third century C.E.): "Now do not be uneasy, father, about my studies; I am working hard and
43 taking relaxation; I shall do well" (P.Oxy. 1296; LCL 1.137). Finally, the famous second century C.E. letter from a penitent son, Antonius Longus, to Nilous, his mother, deserves quotation, at least in part: "I was ashamed to come to Karanis, because I go about in filth. I wrote to you that I am naked. I beg you, mother, be reconciled to me. Well, I know what I have brought on myself. I have received a fitting lesson. I know that I have sinned" (BGU 846; LCL 1.120).

[12] Ibid., 154–55.
[13] Ibid., 60.

These glimpses into real life—which are abundant in the papyri—serve to highlight the enmeshment of the New Testament papyri in that same day-by-day, week-by-week routine, and as we explore the evidence on sending and receiving letters in the Greco-Roman world, this view of the social world for its own sake will in itself be an attendant benefit, even though available space often will prevent us from quoting the full text of the letters cited.

II. Letter Carrying as Disclosed in the Papyri

It is common knowledge that letters in late antiquity were carried by family members, friends, acquaintances, employees, slaves, and soldiers; by business men or passing travelers headed for places of the letters' destinations; by soldiers given a letter-carrying commission; and by government postal services. Sometimes, too, letters were sent to an intermediary place or person, whence they would be forwarded to the addressee.

A. *Official and private transfer of letters*

Apart from government postal service, letter carrying was personal and unstructured. Expressions such as "many people have sailed down" or "if I find someone going to you . . ." are common, and the occasions for sending letters were obviously frequent, for we often hear complaints that "I have sent you three letters this month" or "I have sent you so many letters and you have written none in return." As for letter carriers:

> Engaged in their own concerns, they passed up and down the land in never-ceasing motion, executing minor commissions and stolidly bearing, after the manner of modern postmen, the business of a great people, as well as a people's cares and joys. They carried the letters entrusted to them, but they were unlike our postmen in that they had no official status except in the case of the imperial post.[14]

The Roman imperial postal service, as E. G. Turner notes, "must have been well organized; but so was that of the Ptolemaic kings," and he documents both points from papyri evidence.[15] First, regarding

[14] Ibid., 82.

[15] E. G. Turner, *Greek Papyri: An Introduction* (Oxford: Clarendon Press, 1968) 139–40.

44 the Ptolemaic post, there is extant a fragment (of sixty-three lines) from a postal register dating about 255 B.C.E., which comes from a day-book listing postal items that have passed through an intermediate station on the government's postal service. It shows items checked in by day and hour, the names of the carrier, the receiver, and the subsequent carrier, as well as the sender and designated recipient. Seven times King Ptolemy is recorded as the sender and twice as the recipient of papyrus rolls in this particular list (LCL 2.397). Second, concerning the later Roman imperial post, a file of papyrus copies of letters sent from the strategus of the Panopolite nome in September of 298 C.E. reveals that this official had six clerks writing his letters and that as many as seventeen letters were sent in a single day (P.Panop.Beatty 1). In addition, a file of letters that came to the same stategus from the procurator, covering January–February of 300 C.E., lists the dates when the letters were sent and received. Many of these were meant to be forwarded to other destinations, but the interesting point is that some letters arrived in Panopolis the same day they were sent—120 miles away—(P.Panop. Beatty 2), if one assumes that the procurator was stationed at Hermopolis.[16]

Government postal service—Hellenistic and Roman—was patterned after the highly successful Persian relay service. The Ptolemies, for example, set up two major routes in Egypt, one following the Nile, using mounted couriers operating in relay, the other across country using foot messengers. Boats on the Nile and camels across land carried parcels. In the Roman Empire, the *cursus publicus* functioned by messengers changing horses at fixed posts or stations and later by using chariots on the highway network. These Greek and Roman systems were efficient, but almost exclusively for state and military purposes.[17]

But private correspondence lacked this organization and support, to say nothing of the efficiency of the government post. Yet private communication, which would be the usual mode of travel for Christian letters and New Testament papyri, was a widespread and everyday practice:

[16] Ibid., 139.

[17] White, *Light from Ancient Letters*, 214–15; *OCD*^{2}, 869 [see now *OCD*^{3}, 1233–34].

> It was an easy matter to take a sheet of papyrus (the back of a business document would do), write on it, roll or fold it, pull out a fibre to act as a wrapping string, and close it with a lump of clay impressed with one's seal ring; it was more difficult to find a friend or messenger to carry it to its destination, and no doubt letters often went astray.[18]

Yet the degree of difficulty encountered in sending and receiving letters remains a relative matter and it should be assessed from the papyri themselves.

B. *Ease and difficulty of private correspondence* 45

That the writer of private letters had to find his or her own letter carrier is abundantly illustrated from the papyrus letters themselves. Often the carrier is nameless and, apparently, merely a chance or casual acquaintance. For example, a late third century C.E. letter begins, "Having chanced on someone going up to you, I have been moved to write and tell you of my plight, how I was afflicted with illness for a long time so that I could not even stir." This papyrus, however, contains a fragmentary postscript along its margin, which refers to the receipt (and perhaps forwarding) of an earlier letter, "a letter sent from the praefect," and it mentions "our friend Morus the letter-carrier" (PSI 299; LCL 1.158). If the latter is a reference to a professional carrier, this single letter would attest both the chance private letter carrier and the imperial-post professional. Almost identical is a third/fourth century C.E. explanation for a father writing his son: "Having had the luck to find someone going up to you I felt obliged to address you. I am much surprised, my son, that to date I have received from you no news of your welfare. . . . Reply to me promptly, for I am quite distressed at having no letter from you" (P.Oxy. 123; LCL 1.159).

A happier report goes from a son to his father in Hermopolis about 117 C.E.: "Heliodoros to his father Sarapion, greeting. I have just received your letter, and I rejoiced that you are well. . . . I am always glad to send you greetings by anyone I find sailing up-river, even when there is no news to tell you" (P.Bad. 36; C.Pap.Jud. II 440). The same Heliodorus, however, encounters some difficulty in

[18] Turner, *Greek Papyri*, 130.

communicating with two corespondents, as shown in two other letters of the same general date (P.Bad. 39; C.Pap.Jud. II 441): "For there has still been no one sailing up to bring you letters except [. . .]" and "I am very glad that you get the letters I send. I greet you at least in writing. That is why I watched wearily for anyone who is sailing up." Possibly these communication difficulties were due to the Jewish revolt in Egypt and elsewhere during 115–17 C.E.[19]

A third century C.E. letter, found at Oxyrhynchus and sent from Serenus to Diogenes, reports that "I had been intending to come up myself . . ., since Sarapion's people said that he was ill; wherefore I am writing to you to write me news of him from time to time by anyone you can send" (P.Oxy. 935; LCL 1.136). A later Oxyrhynchus papyrus of the fifth century C.E. (P.Oxy. 2156) refers—in similar fashion—to the writing of a letter because of "a favorable opportunity by a man who is going to you."

46 Frequently the letter carrier is named, as in this papyrus of 41 C.E., which reports sending letters to Alexandria by two individuals and receiving another:

> Sarapion to our Heraclides, greeting. I sent you two other letters, one by Nedymus and one by Cronius the sword-bearer [or: police officer]. For the rest, I received the letter from the Arab, read it, and was grieved. (BGU 1079; LCL 1.107)

Naming the letter carrier, of course, does not mean that we are thereby any better informed about the relationship of letter writer to letter carrier, but the examples are numerous. In 168 B.C.E., a wife expresses relief at learning that her husband is safe in a retreat at the Serapeum at Memphis, but then complains bitterly that he has not returned home to rescue her and his son from virtual bankruptcy and starvation, concluding "now that Horus who brought the letter has told us about your having been released from your retreat, I am utterly distressed" (P.Lond. 42).[20] A fourth century C.E. letter

[19] Victor A. Tcherikover and Alexander Fuks (eds.), *Corpus Papyrorum Judaicarum* (3 vols.; Cambridge, MA: Harvard University Press, 1957–64) 2.242–43 [= C.Pap.Jud.] This view is based largely on the words "harm" and "danger" at the end of the second letter: "May the gods preserve you from harm and make you prosper among every danger." Cf. P.Brem. 11; C.Pap.Jud II 249–51, col. II. 24–26, though the text lacks most of a line: "We took much trouble to write to one another [. . .], however, because of the Jewish disturbances."

[20] George Milligan, *Selections from the Greek Papyri* (Cambridge: Cambridge University Press, 1910) 8–11.

concerns a woman reported seriously ill in earlier correspondence who has now improved: “But as she seems to have taken a turn for the better, I have made haste to have another letter brought to you by Euphrosynus, in order to cheer you” (P.Oxy. 939; LCL 1.163). A wife (who happens to be a Christian) writes to her husband in the same century: “I send you through Apon [= Apion?] your fellow-soldier a letter and a cloak” (P.Grenf. I.53).[21] Other letters naming the carrier include P.Bour. 12 (88 B.C.E.); and P.Fay. 123 (110–11 C.E.): “your man Mardon.”

In at least one case, however, a letter carrier—though not named—is recommended to the addressee as qualified to expand on the situation treated in the letter: a woman seeks Zenon’s help against a third party who allegedly is mistreating her son, and her letter concludes, “The rest please learn from the man who brings you this letter. He is no stranger to us” (P.Col. III 6).

Other letters show that various named and unnamed messengers were used: a second century C.E. letter: “I sent you many letters both through the slave of Sarapion and by means of the son of the crown scribe” (P.Amh. II 131); or a third century C.E. letter, written by Herculanus to Aplonarion: “I rejoiced greatly on receiving your letter which was given to me by the cutler, though I have not yet received the one which you say you have sent me by Platon the dancer’s son” (P.Oxy. 1676; LCL 1.151), or a Tebtynis papyrus from late in that century, in which Sarapammon, the writer, says to Piperas, “I sent you a letter by the baker” (P.Tebt. 424; LCL 1.154).

Occasionally we discover an effort to increase letter-carrying efficiency, as in a 256 C.E. letter from a landowner to his steward, reporting that “the agent at Euhemeria has sent another carrier with
a few things, though both of you could send by the same man after 47
notifying each other” (P.Flor. 176; LCL 1.141). The reference here seems to be to carrying goods rather than merely letters, but the same principle applies. Alternatively, the writer could specify a carrier for the reply: “Send me a letter quickly by means of Polydeukes . . .” (UPZ I 68).

The availability of letter carriers, then, presents a mixed picture. Yet, even in the Roman frontier province of Arabia, a soldier stationed at Bostra finds frequent letter carriers to Karanis, though that

[21] See Winter, *Life and Letters in the Papyri*, 157–58.

does not prevent him from registering a complaint—that his father still does not write back (19/20 February, 107 C.E.):

> . . . But this has troubled me, that I have very often written to you through Saturninus the standard-bearer, likewise through Julianus the son of Longinus [and through Dius], and not yet have you answered me concerning your health. But nevertheless, now that you have been asked, do give your attention necessarily before all else to writing to me concerning your health. A number of times I asked Longinus, who brings you the letter, to take something for you, and he refused, saying he was unable. . . . If, then, you love me, you will straightway take pains to write to me concerning your health. . . . (P.Mich. VIII 466)

At the same time, the arrival of numerous travelers from a location can be used more directly to chide the non-writer of letters, as in this second century C.E. letter from a centurion of the Alexandrian (?) legion to his brother in Karanis:

> Julius Clemens to Arrianus his brother, greeting. This is now the third letter I am writing to you, and you have sent no reply, although you know that I am worried if you do not write me frequently about your affairs, and in spite of the fact that many persons come here from your vicinity. I therefore ask you, brother, . . . to write to me about your well-being, which is my prayer to all the gods. I pray for your good health. (P.Mich. VIII 484)

From the same century, though more succinct, is the complaint of a son to his mother: "How many letters have I sent you and not one have you written me in reply, though so many people have sailed down!" (LCL 1.121), and a pregnant woman, in two letters to her family around 200 C.E., speaks of several people going to or from them; yet she complains bitterly: "You have not even thought fit to write me one letter" (P.Mich. VIII 508).

On the other hand, the lack of a readily available letter carrier can be an excuse for not writing, as in this otherwise touching letter with deep personal affection, probably from father to son (second century C.E.):

> . . . I received Antinus' letter and yours, in which I seemed to see you.
> Wherefore I beseech you to do the same [i.e., to write] continually,
> 48 for so our love will be increased. . . . When I am slow in writing to
> you, this is easily accounted for by the fact that I can find no one
> who is going to you." (P.Mich. Inv. No. 241)[22]

[22] Ibid., 60; 82.

At least one letter writer complains of negligent letter carriers who excuse themselves by accusing the letter writers of negligence (second century C.E., found at Karanis): "I have written to you often, and the negligence of those who carry [the letters] has slandered us as negligent" (P.Mich. VIII 499).

There are, however, other ways to reprimand a lax correspondent (second century C.E., Karanis):

> Apol[. . .] to Apollinarius, his brother greeting. Having learned that you are in Bacchias I salute you, brother, and I urge you to write to us immediately concerning your health. For I have already used up a papyrus roll in writing to you, and I received barely one letter from you. . . . (P.Mich. VIII 496)

The writer adds, at the end, that Bacchias is only two hours away(!) from Karanis, indicating that letter writing was not only used for bridging long distances. And a son away at school sends a scolding but plaintive letter to his father (early third century C.E.):

> To my lord and father Arion from Thonis greeting. . . . Look you, this is my fifth letter to you, and you have not written to me except only once, not even a word about your welfare, nor come to see me; though you promised me saying, "I am coming," you have not come to find out whether the teacher is looking after me or not. . . . If you had come up with me, I should have been taught long ago. And when you come, remember what I have often written you about. [postscript] Remember our pigeons. (LCL 1.133)

A business man anxious to conclude a deal tries to get his associate to act by referring to menacing letters from his father (first century C.E., Alexandria [?] to Philadelphia):

> . . . Please do not neglect to write me, through anyone you may find, what you decide about the thirty items. Since, from when I sailed down river, this is the fifth letter my father will be writing me about them, and he is growing angry, and I am going to buy them, and will you make up your mind? Tell me through anyone you can . . ., and please be sure to write me . . . (P.Col. Inv. 316)[23]

If recipients do not respond, one remedy is to send them papyrus, as did the writer of an early second century C.E. letter from Alexandria

[23] Jacqueline Long, "Confidential Business: P.Col. Inv. 316," *BASP* 24 (1987) 9–12.

49 (?) to Karanis: "I sent you papyrus so that you might be able to write me concerning your health" (P.Mich. VIII 481). A third century C.E. letter has the same theme:

> Aurelius Theoninus to the most honorable Didymus, greeting. . . . For though I have often written to you and sent you papyrus for letter-writing, to enable you to write to me, you have never deigned to remember me in any way; but evidently your pride in your wealth and the great abundance of your possessions make you look down on your friends. Now do not behave in this sort towards your brother Theoninus, but write to me more frequently that by means of your letters your friend may be fully informed about your affairs. (P.Flor. 367; LCL 1.147)

Yet, there were more ingenious ways than these to solicit replies. For example, a fifth century C.E. letter carrier apparently has been instructed to "bribe" the recipient for a response: "Please ask the letter carrier for six melons. Do not fail to send me a reply" (P.Mich. Inv. No. 497),[24] but perhaps the most unusual pressure placed upon the non-communicating addressee is found in this Karanis letter from the second century C.E., from a soldier seeking to be reconciled to his brother: "I ask you to write to me, and the gods ask the same thing of you" (P.Mich. VIII 502).

What steps could be taken to insure delivery? Normally a letter was addressed by writing the name of the addressee on the outside of the folded letter. This might be simply "To Ptolemaeus" or "To Ptolemaeus and Apollonius" (LCL 1.98, 99); or with a title, "To Apollonius the strategus" (LCL 1.115); or with the location, "To Zenon. To Philadelphia" (LCL 1.93) or "Deliver at Pathyris to my father" (LCL 1.101); or with a return address, "Deliver at Karanis to Taesis, from her son Apollinarius of Misenum" (LCL 1.111) or "Deliver the letter to Horina sister of Apollonius, of Coptos, from Tare daughter of her sister, of Apamea" (LCL 1.165) or, more elaborately, "To Apion, gymnasiarch and ex-strategus of the Antaeopolite nome, from Philosarapis, holding office as sacrificial magistrate of Antaeopolis" (LCL 1.148); or "To Dionysios, who is also called Amois, son of Ptolemy and brother of Apollonios the village secretary

[24] See Winter, *Life and Letters in the Papyri*, 82.

of Tholthis, who is staying near Theon, the son of Ischyrion" (P.Oxy. VII 1061, 22 B.C.E.); or with special instructions, "Deliver in Alexandria in the Imperial Market . . . to Heraclides from Sarapion" (LCL 1.107); or "At the gymnasium. To Theon the son of Nikoboulos, the olive supplier" (P.Oxy. II 300, late first century C.E.). (See also P.Oxy. VII 1061, 22 B.C.E.; P.Mert. II 63, 57 C.E.) In general, however, the simpler forms of address predominate.

The papyri, though, do furnish an interesting additional example of care in assuring delivery. A church official in the early third century began to draft some instructions for a letter carrier, then revised them in the second part of the surviving papyrus. Although the instructions remain problematic, here we catch a glimpse of someone struggling to provide full directions for transmitting an obviously important letter to the famous bishop, Theodotus (though the letter itself did not survive):

> I wish to send a letter to Antioch. . . . Deliver [it] so that it comes into the hands of him whom I wish, to this end, that it be delivered to the bishop of Laodicea, which is two stations before Antioch . . . . [Revision:] Go to the bishop of Antioch and place this letter in his own hands . . . in order that he may deliver it into the hands of Theodotus, the bishop of Laodicea. For such is in fact the address. But since there are two Laodiceas, one in Phrygia and one in Syria, he will dispatch it to Laodicea of Coelesyria, two stations before Antioch. Theodotus is the bishop there. Deliver it now to . . . incomparable brother. (PSI 311)[25]

These various forms of address may tell us something about letter carriers: the presence of the addressee's name only, especially on a family letter, may suggest that the letter carrier was well known to the writer or addressee, while a more complete address may imply a stranger or a chance carrier. However, a more detailed or formal address, complete with titles, may indicate the status or measure of respect afforded the addressee and should not be understood to mean that the person was more difficult to find—the opposite would be the case. Overall, therefore, the relative simplicity of addresses suggests and supports the view that letters moved with general ease throughout the Greco-Roman world.

In the event that a direct letter carrier is not readily available, a letter might be sent to an intermediary for forwarding, as was done

---

[25] Ibid., 170–71; see the discussion there of the textual problems.

by a second century C.E. Egyptian marine stationed at Misenum (near Naples) when trying to reach his father. The letter's additional address directed that it be sent (presumably by military post) to the camp of the cohort in Egypt (doubtless at Alexandria) and then forwarded to the father in Philadelphia (BGU 423; LCL 1.112). Another writer, perhaps in the third century C.E., reports that "the letter which you forwarded to me to deliver to Bolphius I have delivered" (PSI 1080; LCL 1.132), and a sailor writing to his mother in Karanis from Ostia in Italy (second century C.E.) suggests to her that she send her letter to an intermediary for forwarding:

> Apollinaris to Taesion, his mother, many greetings.... From Cyrene, where I found a man who was journeying to you, I deemed it necessary to write to you about my welfare.... And now I am writing to you from Portus [two miles north of Ostia], for I have not yet gone up to Rome and been assigned [to a fleet].... Do not delay to write about your health and that of my brothers. If you do not find anybody coming to me, write to Socrates and he forwards it to me. (P.Mich. VIII 490)[26]

51 Interestingly, this letter was found excellently preserved in a house, presumably the mother's, along with a second written by the same son a short time later from Rome, in which he reports his safe arrival there and his assignment to the fleet at Misenum. "Please write to me about your welfare and that of my brothers and all your kinfolk," he says, "And for my part, if I find someone [to carry the letters], I will write to you; I will not delay to write to you" (P.Mich. VIII 491; LCL 1.111).

Another military son writes to his mother in the same city of Karanis (early second century C.E.) and hopes to visit her under a military commission to carry letters, though he has some fears of losing the opportunity:

> Saturnalus to Aphrodous his mother, very many greetings.... I wish you to know that I sent you three letters this month.... If I find an opportunity of putting my plan into effect, I am coming to you with letters [i.e., he has a commission for carrying letters].... I was afraid to come just now because they say: "The prefect is on the route," lest he take the letters from me and send me back to the frontier, and I incur the expense in vain.... You wish to see me a little; I wish it

[26] See ibid., 40–41.

> greatly and I pray daily to the gods how I may find a good chance to come. . . . (SB 7356)[27]

The "expense" to which Saturnalus refers is undoubtedly the bribe he would have paid for the letter-carrying assignment, for "in the army everything depends on the right opportunity."[28]

Finally, on occasion a copy was made of a letter and both were sent, presumably by different carriers, as appears to be indicated in this sentence of a second century C.E. Karanis papyrus: "I sent you a copy so that it might not go astray" (P.Mich. VIII 500).

All of these examples suggest that, in spite of occasional difficulties, letters moved with frequency and ease throughout the Hellenistic and Roman worlds. If papyrus was needed, it could be sent; if forwarding was required, that could be arranged; if detailed delivery instructions were essential, they could be provided; if a reply was urgent, a return letter carrier might be designated. Apparently addressees were easily enough located, both by the letter writer and by the carrier; certainly letters were lost, but important communications could be sent in copies via different carriers; and it appears that human failure far more commonly was that of the letter writer—the failure to write—and not of the letter carrier.

C. *The speed of transferring letters* 52

How fast did letters like these travel? We reported earlier that governmental mail could move letters more than a hundred miles the same day. What about private letters? A third century C.E. letter from Isis to Thermouthion, her mother, says, "I wish you to know that I have arrived in Alexandria safe and sound in four days" (BGU 1680). This letter was found at Philadelphia in the Fayum, some 150 miles from Alexandria, presumably the daughter's home. Even to and from out-of-the-way places, there was daily traffic available for mail transfer. A letter (mentioned earlier) written by a soldier stationed on the frontier at Bostra ("eight days' journey from Petra," the letter itself tells us) to his father in Karanis on March 27, 107

---

[27] Ibid., 50–51.

[28] For this interpretation, see M. P. Speidel, "Furlough in the Roman Army," *Papyrology* (ed. Naphtali Lewis; YCS 28; Cambridge/New York: Cambridge University Press, 1985) 292–93.

C.E., complains that his father has not answered his numerous letters sent through various named individuals, and then he says, "If, then, you love me, you will straightway take pains to write me concerning your health and, if you are anxious about me, to send me linen garments through Sempronius, *for merchants come to us from Pelusium every day*" (P.Mich. VIII 466 [italics added]).

The possibility of replying the same day as the receipt of a letter appears to be documented in the impassioned communication between a husband and his wife in the second century C.E.; the wife seems to have run off with a man named or nick-named "Bobtail" (*Kolobos*), and strong emotion is conveyed in striking ways, though we possess only the husband's (uneducated and therefore at points obscure) response:

> Serenus to Isidora, his sister and wife, very many greetings. . . . I want you to know that ever since you left me I have been in mourning, weeping at night and lamenting by day. After I bathed with you on Phaophi [= month] 12th I had neither bath nor oil-rub till Hathyr 12th [= the next month], when I received from you a letter that can shatter a rock, so much did your words upset me. I wrote you back on the instant, and sent it on the 12th with your letter enclosed. . . . But look, I keep writing you and writing you. Are you coming [back] or not coming? Tell me that. (P.Oxy. 528; LCL 1.125)[29]

Not only has he responded on the very day of receipt but has returned her letter as well—perhaps so that his wife can reread the letter that has so disturbed him and be brought to her senses.

In addition, there are invitations to dinners and weddings, asking the invitee to come "today" or "tomorrow" (see P.Oxy. 1485, 1487; LCL 1.172, 174), though undoubtedly these would be invitations to local events. There also are letters ordering items for specific dates, such as birthdays or festivals. For example, on the 18th of the month
53 Choiak in 100 C.E., Gemellus, a land-owner in the Fayum, writes an order: "And send the fish on the 24th or 25th for Gemella's birthday feast" (P.Fay. 114; LCL 1.109), presumably six or seven days after the letter was written; of course, we do not know where in the Fayum this letter originated or was sent, but the interval between order and delivery is relatively short.

[29] For this translation, see Naphtali Lewis, *Life in Egypt under Roman Rule* (Oxford: Clarendon Press, 1983) 56.

The best and most detailed evidence on the transfer of private letters, however, comes from the famous Zenon archives, consisting of the papers of a certain Zenon, manager of the 6,800-acre Philadelphia estate of Apollonius, the finance minister under Ptolemy II. It is the largest single papyrus archive ever found, consisting of nearly two thousand items very well preserved and covering the years 260–240 B.C.E. It is of interest that these papers include not only lists, inventories, accounts, records of deposits, petitions, and letters from court officials and of a business nature, but more personal letters and some ten works of literature; in addition, they place us in contact with Zenon's home town of Caunus (or Kaunos) on the coast of Caria in Asia Minor.[30] Zenon, we learn, even employed a commercial traveler, Promethion, who—among other duties—bought papyrus rolls for Zenon.[31] Zenon himself traveled widely, and in 256 B.C.E., when he settled permanently in Philadelphia, he brought with him the documents he had carefully collected over the preceding four years.[32] This is significant, of course, because it preserves for us far more than might normally have been expected, but also because it shows how a group of documents might have been collected and circulated in antiquity.

What interests us most, however, is that Zenon frequently dockets his incoming letters, noting (on the outside) the contents and/or the date of receipt. If a letter carries its date of sending (as is the usual practice), a comparison with the docket's date of receipt will indicate the time required for delivery, and if places of origin and destination are stated or known, additional information of value is gained.[33]

A first example is an order for logs for the Isis festival in 256 B.C.E. (P.Cair.Zen. 59154; LCL 1.90): "Apollonius to Zenon greeting. From the dry wood put on board a boat as many of the thickest

[30] Turner, *Greek Papyri*, 35; 48; 77–78; Naphtali Lewis, *Greeks in Ptolemaic Egypt: Case Studies in the Social History of the Hellenistic World* (Oxford: Clarendon Press, 1986), 42–43; 52–55; for a full description, see Campbell Cowan Edgar, *Zenon Papyri in the University of Michigan Collection* (Ann Arbor, MI: University of Michigan Press, 1931), 1–50; P. W. Pestman, *A Guide to the Zenon Archive: A. Lists and Surveys and Indexes and Maps* (Papyrologia Lugduno-Batava, 24A–B; Leiden: Brill, 1981).

[31] Lewis, *Greeks in Ptolemaic Egypt*, 54–55.

[32] Edgar, *Zenon Papyri*, 25–26. On the Zenon letters, see White, *Light from Ancient Letters*, 27–52.

[33] See J. L. White, "A Note on Zenon's Letter Filing," *BASP* 13 (1976) 129–31.

logs as possible and send them immediately to Alexandria that we may be able to use them for the festival of Isis. Goodbye." The letter is dated Phaophi 23 (= 17 December 256 B.C.E.), and it was
54 received on Hathur 18 (= 11 January 255 B.C.E.), or 25 days later; unfortunately, however, something went awry with the letter delivery, and it arrived too late, for the festival ran from Hathur 17–20. Perhaps it was sent at the last minute, for the address (on the outside) says "To Zenon. At once," indicating that the letter should be immediately dispatched.

More information can be garnered from a letter in the Zenon archive written a year earlier, in 257 B.C.E., which tells of a trip by two travelers, Ariston and his sister (presumably the Doris mentioned in the letter's docket), from Alexandria to southern Asia Minor, who experienced delays in their ship passage and spent two months before reaching their destination (cf. P.Cair.Zen. 59029). Their host in Cilicia, a certain Sosipatros, reports their arrival to a certain Antimenes, who (presumably) lives in Alexandria, and this letter, dated Apellaios 26 (= 31 January 257 B.C.E.), reaches Antimenes about two months later, having traveled perhaps some eight hundred 800 miles. At that time, on Peritios 28 (= 1 April 257 B.C.E.), Antimenes sends to Zenon a copy of Sosipatros's letter, with a covering note (P.Mich. I 10; cf. P.Cair.Zen. 59052). Zenon receives this double letter nineteen days later in the city of Mendes (in the Delta), that is, on Dystros 17 (= 20 April 257 B.C.E.), which we learn from Zenon's docketing of its receipt. Since Mendes is about eighty miles from Alexandria, we obtain some definite information on the time required to move letters not only from Asia Minor to Alexandria, but also from Alexandria to Mendes.[34]

A letter to Zenon in Philadelphia from Artemidorus, a physician writing from Sidon in Syria, was written on Peritios embolimos [intercalary] 6 (= 14 April 252 B.C.E.) and was docketed by Zenon in Philadelphia on Phamenoth 6 (= 28 April 252 B.C.E.), after traveling some four hundred miles, more or less, in fourteen days (P.Cair.Zen. 59251).[35] Two letters of Toubias to Apollonios, sent

[34] Edgar, *Zenon Papyri*, 69–71; Pestman, *Guide*, 266. It is not clear why Lewis (*Greeks in Ptolemaic Egypt*, 12) states that the letter came to Zenon in Philadelphia rather than Mendes—the latter is clear enough in the docket.

[35] See Pestman, *Guide*, 234–35.

from Transjordan to Alexandria (perhaps 350 miles) reached Zenon in thirty-six days (C.Pap.Jud. I 4–5 = P.Cair.Zen. 59075 and 76), for they were sent on Xandikos 10 (= 13 May 257 B.C.E.) and docketed in Alexandria on Artemisios 16 (= 17 June 256 B.C.E.). In addition, we know that PSI V 514 moved the one hundred and fifty miles from Alexandria to Philadelphia in four days. It was written on Peritios 28 (= 25 April 251 B.C.E.) and docketed on Phamenoth 7 (= 29 April 251 B.C.E.).[36] PSI V 502 traveled between the same two points in seven days, and P.Mich. I 48 also may have been sent from Alexandria to Philadelphia; if so, it traveled there in six days (double-dated Panemos 28 and Epeiph 30 = 20 September 251 B.C.E. to Mesore 7 = 26 September 251 B.C.E.).[37] Lastly, a brief letter about 55
two rams' fleeces is sent from Memphis by Nikon to Zenon in Alexandria on Pharmouthi 25 (= 17 June 257 B.C.E.), and its receipt was docketed on Daisios 11 (= 11 July 257 B.C.E.), indicating a delivery time of about three weeks for the one hundred twenty-five mile distance (P.Mich. I 16).[38]

Actually, more than 150 of the Zenon papyri have been docketed as to their date (and often place) of receipt; these cover the years 258–247 B.C.E. Many, however, did not or no longer contain their dates of composition, and often the places of origin and/or of destination cannot be determined. We do have examples, however, of letters received within a day or two, such as a letter from Sosos in Aphroditopolis, which is dated Mecheir 5 [Egyptian year] (= 29 March 256 B.C.E.) and was docketed by Zenon near or in Philadelphia on Peritios embolimos 6 (= 29 March 256 B.C.E.)—the same day—after covering a distance of something like fifteen miles (P.Mich. I 28).[39] Other letters that were sent and received on the same day include P.Mich. I 32, circulating somewhere in the Fayum; P.Lond. VII 1951, in the Delta; P.Mich. I 35; P.Hib. I 43; and P.Col. IV 121. At least the following letters moved within the Delta region in two days: P.Hib. I 44 = P.Yale 33; P.Ryl. IV 560; P.Col. III 16; and P.Mich. I 18. Finally, P.Col. III 10 was received in Memphis five days after it was written (probably) in the Fayum.

---

[36] Edgar, *Zenon Papyri*, 119, says "within seven days"; see Pestman, *Guide*, 236.

[37] See Pestman, *Guide*, 238–39.

[38] We know Nikon's location from P.Mich. I 14. For dates, see Pestman, *Guide*, 267.

[39] See Pestman, *Guide*, 226–27; 268.

III. Conclusion

The evidence sampled here—and there is much more—documents both the vibrant, every-day quality and the prompt transfer of letters throughout the Greco-Roman world. This lively activity occurred not only within Egypt (i.e., between the Delta, the Fayum, and upper Egypt), but between Egypt and places as far removed as Ostia in Italy, Cilicia in Asia Minor, Sidon in Syria, and Arabia—to mention only a few specific examples cited above. This data can be combined with other evidence of brisk "intellectual commerce"[40] and dynamic interchanges of people, literature, books, and letters between Egypt and the vast Mediterranean region during the broad New Testament period to permit at least two claims about the early New Testament manuscripts: (1) the various textual complexions (usually called "text-types") represented by the earliest New Testament papyri—virtually all of which were found in Egypt—did not have to originate there, but could easily, in a matter of a few weeks, have moved
56 anywhere in the Mediterranean area. Moreover, if some of these textual complexions ("text-types") did originate in Egypt, the dynamic situation meant that they would not—could not—have been confined to Egypt. Therefore, (2) it is not only theoretically possible, but quite probable that the present array of text-types represented in the Egyptian New Testament papyri do, in fact, represent text-types from the *entire* Mediterranean region, and, furthermore, that they could very likely represent *all* of the existent text-types in that large region in the early period of New Testament textual transmission.

Added Notes, 2004

This article was first presented in the New Testament Textual Criticism Section at the 1990 Annual Meeting of the Society of Biblical Literature.

Recent studies of mail delivery in Ptolemaic, Hellenistic, and Roman times. Since this essay was published, Stephen Robert Llewelyn (Macquarie University, Sydney) has gained a reputation as an expert on ancient

[40] See Epp, "Significance of the Papyri," 81–84; 89–91 [and the essays below on the Oxyrhynchus papyri and the New Testament].

mail service. The present essay would have profited much from the following:

"Did the Ptolemaic Postal System Work to a Timetable?" *ZPE* 99 (1993) 41–56.

"The εἰς (τὴν) οἰκίαν Formula and the Delivery of Letters to Third Persons or to Their Property," *ZPE* 101 (1994) 71–78.

"The Function of the ΣΗΜΑΣΙΑ-Texts, P.Oxy. XXXIV 2719 and SB XVI 12550," *ZPE* 104 (1994) 230–32

"Directions for the Delivery of Letters and the Epistles of St Paul," *Ancient History in a Modern University, Volume 2: Early Christianity, Late Antiquity and Beyond* (eds. T. W. Hillard, R. A. Kearsley, C. E. V. Nixon, and A. M. Hobbs; Macquarie University: Ancient History Documentary Research Centre; Grand Rapids, MI: Eerdmans, 1998) 184–94.

"The Conveyance of Letters," *NewDocs* 7 (1994) 1–57 [A wealth of information].

"Sending Letters in the Ancient World: Paul and the Philippians," *TynBul* 46 (1995) 337–56.

On family terms. Terms such as "mother," "father," "sister," and "brother" occur frequently in papyrus letters, but more often than not they are terms of respect and not to be understood literally. In the letters quoted above, we have tried to assess from the context whether or not a literal family relationship is intended; if so, we have spoken, e.g., of "a son writes to his father," etc. Also, wives often are referred to as "sister," or "my lady sister."

CHAPTER FIFTEEN

THE PAPYRUS MANUSCRIPTS OF THE NEW TESTAMENT

I. Introduction

The papyrus manuscripts of the New Testament[1] constitute the first 3
category in our conventional listing of the witnesses to the New Testament text. They share, of course, a common writing medium: papyrus, a resilient material (except when it has been alternately wet and dry)[2] that was used for New Testament manuscripts into the eighth century, and exclusively so until around 200, when parchment began to be used. Naturally, the New Testament papyri occupy this primary category because of their antiquity—our oldest manuscripts

[1] See the standard handbooks for data on the New Testament papyri, notably Kurt Aland and Barbara Aland, *The Text of the New Testament: An Introduction to the Critical Editions and to the Theory and Practice of Modern Textual Criticism* (trans. E. F. Rhodes; Grand Rapids: Eerdmans; Leiden: Brill, 1987; 1989²) [page numbers in the two editions are generally the same] and Bruce M. Metzger, *The Text of the New Testament: Its Transmission, Corruption, and Restoration* (New York/Oxford: Oxford University Press, 1968²; 1992³). For a description and bibliography of the New Testament papyri 1–88, see K. Aland (ed.), *Repertorium der griechischen christlichen Papyri: I: Biblische Papyri: Altes Testament, Neues Testament, Varia, Apokryphen* (PTS 18; Berlin/New York: de Gruyter, 1976) 215–322. For a display of the text of the papyri over against Nestle-Aland²⁶ (NA²⁶), see K. Junack and W. Grunewald (eds.), *Das Neue Testament auf Papyrus: I. Die katholischen Briefe* (ANTF 6; Berlin/New York: de Gruyter, 1986); K. Junack, E. Güting, U. Nimtz, and K. Witte (eds.), *Das Neue Testament auf Papyrus: II. Die paulinischen Briefe, Teil 1: Röm., 1. Kor., 2. Kor.* (ANTF 12; Berlin/New York: de Gruyter, 1989) and forthcoming volumes. For further perspective, discussion, and the present writer's views, see E. J. Epp and Gordon D. Fee, *Studies in the Theory and Method of New Testament Textual Criticism* (SD 45; Grand Rapids, MI: Eerdmans, 1993), esp. chaps. 2, 5, 6, and 14; E. J. Epp, "The New Testament Papyrus Manuscripts in Historical Perspective," *To Touch the Text: Studies in Honor of Joseph A. Fitzmyer, S.J.* (ed. M. P. Horgan and P. J. Kobelski; New York: Crossroad, 1989) 261–88; idem, "New Testament Papyrus Manuscripts and Letter Carrying in Greco-Roman Times," *The Future of Early Christianity: Essays in Honor of Helmut Koester* (ed. B. A. Pearson, A. T. Kraabel, G. W. E. Nickelsburg, and N. R. Petersen; Minneapolis, MN: Fortress, 1991) 35–56; idem, "Textual Criticism (NT)," *ABD* 6:412–35.

[2] For a summary of the nature and survival of papyrus manuscripts, see E. J. Epp, "The New Testament Papyrus Manuscripts in Historical Perspective, 261–69.

are among them—and because of the general assumption that they are first in importance as well. It was not always so, for even Frederic Kenyon, the discoverer of the Chester Beatty papyri, could say of all previous papyri that they only "are of value in throwing a little light on the general character of the . . . types of text current in Egypt
4 during this period."[3] As the number and quality of New Testament papyri increased, however, so did their role in New Testament textual criticism, until today they occupy a highly visible and significant position among the witnesses to the New Testament text. Indeed, most textual critics consider those papyri dating prior to the mid-fourth century as decisive in text-critical matters, *mutatis mutandis*. Yet, having come into their own, the place of the New Testament papyri in present and future textual criticism not only remains a matter of debate but also of urgency as scholars seek to solve the often intractable problems of the New Testament text.

II. Discovery and Description of the Major New Testament Papyri

The first New Testament papyrus came to light in 1868 when Constantin von Tischendorf—some twenty years after he had discovered Codex Sinaiticus—published a sixty-two verse fragment of 1 Corinthians 1–7, later designated P11. Over the following thirty years, C. R. Gregory, Carl Wessely, and J. Rendel Harris published four more New Testament papyri, though none of these predated the great majuscule manuscripts Sinaiticus and Vaticanus, which had dominated the critical editions of Tischendorf (1869) and Westcott-Hort (1881). Since these five papyri were of relatively late date (4th–7th centuries) and contained only 120 verses of the New Testament, it is understandable that they created little excitement among New Testament scholars.

[3] Frederic Kenyon, *The Story of the Bible: A Popular Account of How It Came to Us* (New York: Dutton, 1937) 110–13. In a similar vein—and at the same time (1937)—Edgar J. Goodspeed, while speaking of the Chester Beatty and other papyri as "remarkable" and "sensational," saw the real significance for understanding the biblical text, not in these biblical papyri, but in the thousands of everyday documentary papyri that illuminate the New Testament language (*New Chapters in New Testament Study* [New York: Macmillan, 1937] 92–101).

Excitement, however, accompanied the 1897 discovery by B. P. Grenfell and A. S. Hunt of the first Oxyrhynchus papyri. Almost immediately they uncovered a fragment containing "Sayings of Jesus," though this was part of an apocryphal gospel and not the New Testament. But very soon they turned up a fragment of a codex with portions of Matthew 1 (designated P1), which dated from the third century and which, at that time, was "the oldest known manuscript of any part of the New Testament."[4] Thereafter, a virtual "torrent" of papyri flowed from Oxyrhynchus, and now thirty-one of our ninety-three or ninety-four different New Testament papyri have their origin there. Their canonical coverage is striking, for Oxyrhynchus papyri contain portions of fifteen of our twenty-seven New Testament books, and the only major New Testament writings or groups not represented there are Mark, 2 Corinthians, Ephesians, Colossians, and the Pastoral Epistles. These gaps in the distribution are not, of course, of significance in the random situation offered by excavations in rubbish heaps. Of great significance, however, is the fact that twenty-one of these Oxyrhynchus papyri date to the second, third, or early fourth centuries—that is, prior to the great majuscule manuscripts (such as Codices Sinaiticus, Vaticanus, Alexandrinus, and Bezae) that have been so prominent in New Testament textual criticism both before and after the papyri discoveries.

While many of the Oxyrhynchus papyri are of early date, they also are highly fragmentary. Indeed, if one looks back to 1930, a total of forty-two New Testament papyri had been edited and published (including twenty-one from Oxyrhynchus), most contain bits
and pieces of a few or several New Testament verses, and only ten 5
contain portions of text as extensive as thirty to ninety verses. Yet, twenty-three of the forty-two—more than half—can be dated prior to the early fourth century.

This state of affairs in 1930—the preeminent majuscule manuscripts of the mid fourth to sixth centuries standing out like volcanic mountains amidst a sea of minuscules and an increasing array of old but fragmentary papyri—provided the environment for the emergence of the Chester Beatty New Testament papyri in 1930–31. Designated P45, P46, and P47, they were published in 1933–37 by

[4] Bernard P. Grenfell and Arthur S. Hunt (eds.), *The Oxyrhynchus Papyri*, Part I (London: Egypt Exploration Fund, 1898) I.4.

Sir Frederic Kenyon and presented a striking combination of extensive text and early date not seen hitherto. Dating from about 200 to 250, the three manuscripts contained, respectively, thirty leaves (14%) of an original codex of about 220 leaves (P45); eighty-six (84%) of an original 102 (P46); and ten leaves (31%) of an original estimated at thirty-two (P47). More specifically, P45 once contained the gospels and Acts, of which sixty-one verses of Matthew, about six chapters of Mark, five-plus chapters of Luke, most of John 10–11, and thirteen chapters of Acts survive; P46 originally had ten Letters of Paul (but not the Pastorals[5]), though none of 2 Thessalonians is extant; preserved are about eight chapters of Romans, virtually all of 1–2 Corinthians, Galatians, Ephesians, Philippians, Colossians, and Hebrews, and five chapters of 1 Thessalonians; finally, P47, which originally held the Revelation of John, now preserves about eight chapters from its central section.

Suddenly the papyri gained a measure of respect not enjoyed earlier, and their prestige received a further striking boost when five codices (three as early as the Chester Beatty and with very extensive text) appeared in the mid-1950s: the Bodmer papyri. P66 (around 200) preserves all but about twenty-five verses of the first fourteen and a half chapters of John and fragments of the rest. P72 (third century) contains the entire text of 1–2 Peter and Jude and is the earliest known copy of these epistles.[6] P74, though it dates to the seventh century, has portions of Acts, James, 1–2 Peter, 1–3 John, and Jude. P75 (very early third century) is the earliest copy of Luke, containing portions of chapters 3–5 and all of 6–17, half of 18, and virtually all of 22–24, as well as nearly all of John 1–12 and portions of 13–15; its text is noteworthy for its extraordinary similarity to that of Codex Vaticanus. A fifth Bodmer papyrus, P73, also of the seventh century, contains only three verses of Matthew 25 and 26.

Today New Testament papyri total ninety-nine, representing ninety-six different manuscripts (since P11 = P14; P33 = P58, and P64 = P67[7]); all but four are from codices (and the four that are written

[5] [On whether P46 could have contained the Pastoral Epistles, see now E. J. Epp, "Issues in the Interrelation of New Testament Textual Criticism and Canon," *The Canon Debate: On the Origins and Formation of the Bible* (eds. L. M. McDonald and J. A. Sanders; Peabody, MA.: Hendrickson, 2002) 495–502.]

[6] [On the complex context of P72, now see ibid., 491–93.]

[7] Or 95 different papyri, if one agrees that P4 is from the same manuscript as

on scrolls, P12, P13, P18, and P22, are exceptional in that they were
either written on both sides or on reused papyrus); and together the
papyri contain portions of all New Testament books except 1–2
Timothy. Their dates run from shortly after 100 to the eighth century, but, as a whole, they constitute less than 2% of all Greek New
Testament manuscripts. All of the papyri are continuous-text manuscripts, that is, manuscripts containing (originally) at least one New
Testament writing in continuous fashion from beginning to end (to
be distinguished, therefore, from lectionary manuscripts, which bring
together various portions of Scripture to be read in church services 6
at appointed times), and all of the papyri are written in large, unconnected letters (uncials).

Premier among these ninety-six different papyri, however, are forty-five[8] that are dated prior to or around the turn of the third/fourth centuries, with twenty-seven of them furnished by the three major finds: Oxyrhynchus providing twenty-one, Chester Beatty three, and Bodmer three. Of equally early date, though written on parchment and therefore classified as "majuscules," are four additional manuscripts (0189, second/third century; 0220, third; and 0162 and 0171, both third/fourth) that belong in this elite group, bringing its total membership to forty-nine.[9] The oldest manuscript of the New Testament is likely P52, containing portions of only five verses of John 18 (31–33, 37–38) and usually dated ca. 125, though possibly it is

P64 and P67, as argued by Colin H. Roberts, *Manuscript, Society and Belief in Early Christian Egypt* (Schweich Lectures, 1977; Oxford: Oxford University Press for the British Academy, 1979) 13; cf. 8 n. 1. [Now see also T. C. Skeat, "The Oldest Manuscript of the Four Gospels?" *NTS* 43 (1997) 1–34, esp. 8–9; 30.] [Since 1997, sixteen additional Oxyrhynchus papyri have been added (P100–P115), plus P116, for a total of 113 different papyri (or 112 if P4 goes with P64+P67). The official list of New Testament manuscripts is Kurt Aland (ed.), *Kurzgefasste Liste der griechischen Handschriften des Neuen Testaments* (ANTF 1; 2d ed., rev. and enl.; Berlin/New York: de Gruyter, 1994). Aland's list is continued, for P100–P115, majuscules 0307–0309, and minuscules 2857–2862, in *Bericht der Hermann Kunst-Stiftung zur Förderung der neutestamentlichen Textforschung für die Jahre 1995 bis 1998* (Münster/Westfalen, 1998) 14–16; and for P116, majuscules 0310–0316, and minuscules 2863–2877, in *Bericht der Hermann Kunst-Stiftung zur Förderung der neutestamentlichen Textforschung für die Jahre 1998 bis 2003* (Münster/Westfalen, 2003) 74–79].

[8] Or forty-four if P4 is joined with P64+67. [Since 1997, 13 new Oxyrhynchus papyri dating up to around the turn of the 3rd/4th centuries have been added, bringing the total early papyri up to 58 (or 57 without P4); with the four early majuscules, the total is 62 (or 61).]

[9] [See the preceding note. This list has been updated from Aland and Aland, *Text of the New Testament*, 57.]

earlier in that first quarter of the second century.[10] These forty-five oldest papyri, by century, are P52, P90, P98 (2nd); P32, P46, P64/67, P66 (ca. 200); P77 (2nd/3rd); P1, P4, P5, P9, P12, P15, P20, P22, P23, P27, P28, P29, P30, P39, P40, P45, P47, P48, P49, P53, P65, P69, P70, P75, P80, P87, P91, P95 (3rd); and P13, P16, P18, P37, P38, P72, P78, P92, P99 (3rd/4th), to which the four majuscules mentioned above should be added.[11]

III. Provenance of the New Testament Papyri

As noted earlier, papyrus manuscripts survive only when protected from moisture—when placed in protective caves, jars, or buildings, or when buried in the soil of virtually rain-free regions of Egypt, Palestine, or Mesopotamia (though papyri must neither be too near the surface nor so deeply buried as to be affected by a rising water table). Blowing sand can deface papyrus manuscripts and white ants can devour them. Yet, thousands of documents on papyrus survive—perhaps twenty thousand have been published, mostly documentary, but including some three thousand or more literary papyri—and they survived largely in the semi-loose soil of Egyptian rubbish heaps, or in ruined buildings filled with refuse or wind-blown sand, or as material used in constructing mummy cases.[12]

How and where were the New Testament papyri preserved? Virtually all stem from Egypt, but exact geographical locations or specific discovery sites are rarely known, except for those found in the rubbish heaps and building ruins of Oxyrhynchus, the Fayum, and in similar situations. In such cases, though, we know more certainly their places of *discard* than of their origin. Yet, to know the villages where many papyri had been utilized by Christians—whether as individuals or as a church—is not to say that much is known

[10] Though earlier dated 125–150, recent opinion moves it back into the 100–125 period, perhaps very early in that quarter century. See Colin H. Roberts, *An Unpublished Fragment of the Fourth Gospel in the John Rylands Library* (Manchester: Manchester University Press, 1935) 12–16; and Aland and Aland, *Text of the New Testament*, 85–87.

[11] For descriptions and discussion of the papyri, see Aland and Aland, *Text of the New Testament* (1989²) 56–57; 95–102; and his *Repertorium der griechischen christlichen Papyri*, 215–322.

[12] For data and references on these issues, see Epp, "The New Testament Papyrus Manuscripts in Historical Perspective," 262–66.

about Christianity in those locations. Speculation has it, for example, that the Chester Beatty papyri, "acquired through the hands of natives and dealers, . . . must have been discovered among the ruins of some early church or monastery; and there is reason to believe that they come from the neighbourhood of the Fayum."[13] A similar
statement accompanied the purchase of P52, likely the earliest New 7
Testament fragment of all, which was assumed to have come either from the Fayum or from Oxyrhynchus.[14] It has also been surmised that the Beatty and Bodmer codices may have come from the same church library.[15] These identifications lack confirmation, and rarely elsewhere do we possess certain knowledge of the provenance of early New Testament manuscripts; indeed, the whole matter of the provenance of papyrus manuscripts is fraught with difficulties, as E. G. Turner pointed out, not the least of which is the unreliability of dealers's reports on their places of discovery.[16] Even finds *in situ* are not particularly enlightening. For example, P4 (with very early fragments of Luke) was found in a jar walled up in a house at Coptos (modern Qift, just below [north of] Thebes in upper Egypt), but it was in the binding of a (presumably Christian) codex of Philo and in a house with no evident connection to a church.[17] In 1969, P92 was found at Madīnat Mādī (modern Narmouthis—between Theadelphia and Tebtunis in the Fayum) in a rubble-filled structure near a racing-course;[18] again, this throws no light on the origin or use of this manuscript. In the final analysis, this lack of context for our New Testament papyri does not greatly affect their use in establishing the New Testament text on a case-by-case basis, though we would be helped particularly in matters of text-critical theory if we knew more of their life-setting.[19]

---

[13] Frederic G. Kenyon, *The Chester Beatty Biblical Papyri: Descriptions and Texts of Twelve Manuscripts on Papyrus of the Greek Bible: Fasciculus I, General Introduction* (London: Emery Walker, 1933) 5. See further, Roberts, *Manuscript, Society and Belief*, 7.

[14] Roberts, *Unpublished Fragment of the Fourth Gospel*, 24–25; H. Idris Bell and T. C. Skeat, *Fragments of an Unknown Gospel and Other Early Christian Papyri* (London: British Museum by Oxford University Press, 1935) 7.

[15] C. H. Roberts, "Books in the Graeco-Roman World and in the New Testament," *Cambridge History of the Bible, Volume 1: From the Beginnings to Jerome* (eds. P. R. Ackroyd and C. F. Evans; Cambridge: Cambridge University Press, 1970) 56.

[16] Eric G. Turner, *Greek Papyri: An Introduction* (Oxford: Clarendon, 1968) 51–53.

[17] C. H. Roberts, *Manuscript, Society and Belief*, 8, 13.

[18] Claudio Gallazzi, "Frammenti di un codice con le Epistole di Paoli," *ZPE* 46 (1982) 117.

[19] [See now my articles on the Oxyrhynchus papyri, below, esp. "The Oxyrhynchus

Oxyrhynchus may provide a more interesting and perhaps useful example. The general area around Oxyrhynchus is known to have been a center of Christian activity in the fourth and fifth centuries, when Rufinus reported thirty churches there, but only two are known around the turn of the third/fourth centuries.[20] Yet, in view of the large number of New Testament papyri turned up in Oxyrhynchus, it is intriguing to wonder how many different discarded codices containing portions of the New Testament one might expect to find in a district capital in Upper Egypt, where, e.g., the names of some fifty-seven hundred individuals who likely lived there between 30 B.C.E. and 96 C.E. can also be gleaned from the papyri,[21] and where some twenty temples existed, along with a theater that may have accommodated between eight and twelve thousand people, and where a Roman garrison was stationed in the second century?[22] Oxyrhynchus was also a city, as the papyri show, where copying and securing works of scholarship were subjects of letters by scholars and where critical editing and annotating of literary texts took place, with much of this evidence from the second century.[23]

8 Presumably the Oxyrhynchus New Testament papyri constitute merely a random selection of survivors among many more that are now lost, but what inferences may be drawn from them? Do they imply that many Christians and/or numerous churches were present at Oxyrhynchus; or that collections or even libraries of New Testament writings existed in one or more churches; or that many copies of New Testament writings were coming to and going from Oxyrhynchus; or perhaps that a Christian school or other scholarly activity, including text-critical work were part of that environment? We do not have these answers,[24] though some of them would help us immensely

New Testament Papyri: 'Not without honor except in their hometown'?" *JBL* 123 (2004) 5–55.]

[20] Turner, *Greek Papyri*, 28; 150.

[21] B. W. Jones and J. E. G. Whitehorne, *Register of Oxyrhynchites 30 B.C.–A.D. 96* (ASP 25; Chico, CA: Scholars Press, 1983).

[22] Turner, *Greek Papyri* 81–82.

[23] Ibid. 86–88; 116–18; 121–22.

[24] [I broached some of these issues in "The New Testament Papyri at Oxyrhynchus in Their Social and Intellectual Context," *Sayings of Jesus: Canonical and Non-Canonical. Essays in Honour of Tjitze Baarda* (eds. W. L. Petersen, J. S. Vos, and H. J. de Jonge; NovTSup 89; Leiden: Brill, 1997) 47–68; idem, "The Codex and Literacy in Early Christianity and at Oxyrhynchus: Issues Raised by Harry Y. Gamble's *Books and Readers in the Early Church*," *CRBR* 11 (1998) 15–37; idem, "The New Testament

in understanding the meaning of this array of very early New Testament manuscripts existing in a specific location such as Oxyrhynchus during the first few centuries of the Christian era.

IV. Transmission of Papyrus Documents in Early Christian Times

Since nearly all of our New Testament papyri were found in Egypt—though with few clues about their specific origin or precise use—the question has been raised whether they (and their texts) all originated in Egypt. Generally, this has been the assumption in the past, for the terms "Egyptian" or "Alexandrian text" to identify the "B" or so-called "Neutral" text really meant "the text of/from/characteristic of Egypt." Recently, however, it has been shown from the non-Christian papyri that in Egypt, during the first centuries of the Christian era, there was a lively and vigorous movement of people back and forth between Alexandria and the Greco-Roman world to the east and west and north, and also (of course) between Alexandria and the upper regions of Egypt, especially the Fayum and centers like Oxyrhynchus, and—in addition—that there was also a brisk circulation of letters and of literature in these same areas. This means that the several differing textual complexions contained in the New Testament papyri did not necessarily have to originate in Egypt, nor would they necessarily have remained in or been confined to Egypt once they arrived there—and the same would apply had they originated in Egypt. In fact, these dynamic interchanges of people, letters, and books to and from Egypt, as well as within Egypt, could allow the extreme assertion—though no one would wish to make it—that *none* of the New Testament textual complexions represented in our papyri necessarily had to originate in Egypt; they could have been carried there from anywhere in the Mediterranean world.[25]

Papyri at Oxyrhynchus: Their Significance for Understanding the Transmission of the Early New Testament Text," scheduled for publication in *Oxyrhynchus: A City and Its Texts* (eds. Peter Parsons, *et al.*; London: Egypt Exploration Society). See also n. 19, above.]

[25] The evidence, with references, is summarized in Epp, "The Significance of the Papyri for Determining the Nature of the New Testament Text in the Second Century: A Dynamic View of Textual Transmission," *Gospel Traditions in the Second Century: Origins, Recensions, Text, and Transmission* (ed. William E. Petersen; Christianity

It has also been shown from the non-Christian papyri that letters traveled with rather considerable speed in Greco-Roman times, even if examples are used only from the informal "mail service" and not the imperial post (since it may be assumed that Christian writings would have circulated by informal means). This speed is demonstrated by extant papyrus letters that show both their date of writing and their docketed date of receipt, generally with records also of their place of origin and destination. The major evidence is found in the archives of Zenon, an estate manager in Philadelphia at the time of Ptolemy II; the horde consists of nearly two thousand items
9 covering 260–240 B.C.E. A few examples will make the point: letters traveled 800 miles from Asia Minor to Alexandria in two months; from Transjordan to Alexandria, about 350 miles, in thirty-six days; from Philadelphia to Syria, some 400 miles, in fourteen days; 150 miles from Alexandria to Philadelphia in four days and another in seven days; from Alexandria to another Delta city in nineteen days; and from Memphis to Alexandria, about 125 miles, in three weeks. Thus, this prompt transfer of letters by casual means—finding. e.g., someone sailing up the river to the destination of your letter—operated not only within Egypt (i.e., between the Delta, the Fayum, and upper Egypt), but also between Egypt and places far removed, such as Ostia in Italy, Cilicia in Asia Minor, Sidon in Syria, and Arabia (to use some actual examples in addition to those cited earlier), and it functioned both in the Hellenistic and Roman periods.[26]

This demonstration permits us to argue that New Testament writings, wherever they might have originated in the vast Mediterranean region, could very rapidly have made their way to any other part of that Roman world—and this could have been accomplished in a matter of days or weeks. No longer, therefore, do we have to assume a long interval of years between the time a New Testament letter or Gospel was written and its appearance in another place—even a far-off place. Wherever the Gospel of John, for example, was written, its text—whether in a form like that in P52 or P66 or P75—could have reached Egypt quickly. If New Testament texts reaching

and Judaism in Antiquity, 3; Notre Dame, IN: University of Notre Dame Press, 1989) 81–84, reprinted in Epp and Fee, *Studies in the Theory and Method*, 280–83.

[26] The detailed evidence, with references, is summarized in Epp, "New Testament Papyrus Manuscripts and Letter Carrying," 52–55 (cf. 43–51 on papyrus letters more generally).

Egypt were modified during Christian use there, those "revisions," again, could quickly be transferred to another part of the Christian world anywhere in the Roman Empire. Indeed, in the nature of things, it must be granted that various forms of text in the early Christian world could not have been confined to one region for any length of time in any single form.

This analysis, moreover, permits us another assertion—though one that cannot be proved: the intellectual commerce demonstrable in the Mediterranean area, particularly to and from Egypt, supports the strong possibility—if not probability—that the various textual complexions evident in our Egyptian papyri represent texts from that *entire Mediterranean region* (including, of course, texts that might have originated in Egypt itself). Thus, in contrast to the common view that the papyri represent "only" the text of "provincial Egypt,"[27] it is much more likely that they represent an extensive if not the full textual spectrum of earliest Christianity.

The letters of Paul and other New Testament and early Christian writings support this view, for they adequately document the use of amanuenses to write and emissaries to carry Christian letters in that period,[28] and Christian private letters among the extant papyri—
though few and relatively late—attest to the Christian utilization of 10
the usual letter-posting procedures of the time.[29] Beyond this, the

[27] Applying more broadly the words used of P46 by Frederic G. Kenyon, *The Chester Beatty Biblical Papyri: Descriptions and Texts of Twelve Manuscripts on Papyrus of the Greek Bible: Fasciculus III Supplement, Pauline Epistles, Text* (London: Emery Walker, 1936) xxii.

[28] On amanuenses, see e.g., the *greeting* [and, therefore, not the whole letter] written in Paul's own hand (1 Cor 16:21; 2 Thess 3:17; Phlm 19; cf. Gal 6:11) or the writer's own hand (Col 4:18); self-reference by an amanuensis (Tertius: Rom 16:22). For references to letter-carriers, see e.g., Phlm 12; 17, implying that Onesimus carried the letter to Philemon; Silvanus in 1 Pet 5:12; possibly Phoebe in Rom 16:1, and Titus (plus two "brothers") in 2 Cor 8:16–24; Tychicus is at least implied in Eph 6:21–22 and Col 4:7–9 (though this evidence would largely disappear if these post-Pauline "letters" are really imitative literary works; in that case the writer would show knowledge of the customary means of letter-carrying); three individuals in *1 Clem.* 65.1; Burrhus in Ign. *Phld.* 11.2; *Smyrn.* 12.1; cf. William R. Schoedel, *Ignatius of Antioch* (Hermeneia; Philadelphia: Fortress, 1985) on Ign. *Rom.* 10:2; and, finally, Crescens in Pol. *Phil.* 14.1.

[29] See, e.g. a 330–340 C.E. letter from a Meletian Christian to a presbyter requesting help in recovering children taken from a fellow Christian (along with all his possessions) to pay a debt (*Select Papyri I* [Loeb] 378–81); or one from Apamea [Syria?] to Coptos (also 4th century) telling an aunt of her sister's death (ibid., 388–89).

specific motivations and mechanisms by which New Testament writings were transmitted in the early centuries are still obscure, though understandable enough in their broad outlines. We may assume, for example, that in the early decades of Christianity an apostolic letter or, slightly later, portions of a Gospel would be read in a worship service and that visiting Christians, on occasion, would take copies back to their own congregations, or writings would be shared in some other way with other Christians or other churches—sometimes at the request of the writer (cf. 1 Thess 5:27; Col 4:16). Soon some churches would possess several of these early writings and small collections of Gospels and/or apostolic works would emerge, perhaps even through the conscious effort, for instance, of a devoted follower of Paul. Apart from this sort of historical imagination (backed by bits of evidence), we know extremely little about such transmission processes, though we do know that the earliest New Testament manuscripts (as well as Old Testament writings copied for Christian use) were in codex form (as opposed to the rolls or scrolls that constitute the format used for Jewish and secular literature prior to Christianity). Indeed, it is possible that Christians invented the codex for the presentation and preservation of their writings or, at very least and more likely, capitalized upon this recent invention as a convenient and space-saving format[30]—and this less cumbersome format further aided (if only slightly) the rapid and quite efficient transfer of Christian literature in the first centuries.

V. Utilization of the Papyri in New Testament Textual Criticism

As intimated earlier, the first series of New Testament papyri did not produce instant or widespread changes in the critical texts of the New Testament; on the contrary, even after the discovery of the Chester Beatty papyri (and, remarkably, to some extent after the Bodmer), these early papyrus artifacts of the New Testament text were often treated not so much as welcome illuminators of textual

[30] The main reference here is Colin H. Roberts and T. C. Skeat, *The Birth of the Codex* (Oxford: Oxford University Press for the British Academy, 1983) 35–61; see Epp, "The New Testament Papyrus Manuscripts in Historical Perspective," 267–68.

history, but more as intruders or even irritants to an already well-established and quite satisfactory understanding of the history of the text.
After all, textual critics in the first half of the twentieth century had
carefully and confidently reconstructed the early textual history of
the New Testament—and the text itself—in accordance with the elegant fourth and fifth century parchment codices, and many critics
simply did not wish that structure to be jeopardized by these youth-
ful papyrus interlopers—these ragged-edged documents written on
what may have seemed to some of them an almost unworthy vehi- 11
cle for Sacred Scripture. Yet, had not Lachmann, Tischendorf,
Tregelles, and Westcott-Hort called for the New Testament text to
be established (as Tischendorf put it) "solely from ancient witnesses,"
for "those that excel in antiquity prevail in authority"?[31] And were
not such ancient witnesses more and more coming to light? So, the
papyri would not and could not be ignored, and gradually they were
worked into the critical editions of the numerous Greek New Testaments produced in the 20th century.[32]

"Gradually," however, is the governing word here. Naturally, the earliest published papyri could have relatively little impact on critical editions such as Tischendorf's in 1869 or Westcott-Hort's in 1881. Yet von Soden's edition (1913) cited only twelve papyri out of twenty then known; Legg's edition of Mark (1935) cites only P45 (though that was, at the time, the only known papyrus containing Mark); his edition of Matthew (1940) uses six (when nine were known); and Nestle's 16th edition (1936) cites fifteen papyri (when nearly fifty were known). Succeeding Nestle editions cited twenty-eight in 1952 (21st); thirty-seven in 1963 (25th, when seventy-five had been published); and finally in 1979 (26th) and following, all the papyri are cited. Actually, the first Greek New Testament to list all known papyri was also the first completely new critical edition to be produced after the Bodmer papyri appeared: the first edition of the United Bible Societies *Greek New Testament* (1966), signifying that the papyri now had fully and officially come into their own.[33]

[31] In Tischendorf's 2nd ed. of 1849, but quoted in C. R. Gregory's *Prolegomena* to Tischendorf, *Novum Testamentum Graece* (8th major ed.; 3 vols.; Leipzig: Hinrichs, 1869–94) 3.47–48.

[32] For detailed consideration, with full references, see Epp, "The New Testament Papyrus Manuscripts in Historical Perspective," 274–83.

[33] Ibid., 275–78; 283.

The slowness to utilize the papyri is even more obvious in handbooks to textual criticism in the first quarter of the twentieth century (e.g., those by George Milligan, Eberhard Nestle, and Ernst von Dobschütz),[34] but especially by analysts and even editors of the papyri—an attitude that persisted to some extent even after the Chester Beatty documents came to light. The basic problems were two: first, the new discoveries were fragmentary, especially the earliest ones; and, even though the Chester Beatty P45 contained 14% of the original leaves of its codex (though less than that of its original text), and even though P46 had 84% of its codex, and P47 had 31%, they could not compare with the mid-fourth century majuscule manuscripts (primarily Codices Vaticanus and Sinaiticus) in coverage or consistency of text. Second, the new papyrus discoveries—even those as spectacular as the Chester Beatty—continued to be judged by these later, grand majuscules. A main reason was that a manuscript like P45, for example, did not coincide with the Vaticanus-Sinaiticus (or B-text)—which was dominant in the editions of Tischendorf and Westcott-Hort—nor did it fit the other clearly-established, early text-type of Westcott-Hort: the D-text. It was thought at the time, however, that P45 confirmed the recently-established "Caesarean" text, which was considered to be later than both the B and D-texts; therefore, its support by P45 did not confer on P45 any distinctive authority over against the earlier B and D-texts. In
12 the mid-1930s, Hans Lietzmann stated quite bluntly that P45 and P46 do not teach us anything radically new or anything we did not already know.[35] And Kenyon—who edited P45, P46, and P47—said of P46 that it "in general confirms the integrity of the text that has come down to us, and offers no sensational variants" and, therefore, it has no predominant authority "since, so far as we know, it is only a text circulating in provincial Egypt."[36] Thus, the papyri gave rise to no new rationale that would unseat the textual theory that had elevated the witnesses supporting the B-text to their position as the "best" manuscripts and "best" text.

---

[34] Ibid., 277.

[35] Hans Lietzmann, "Zur Würdigung des Chester-Beatty-Papyrus der Paulusbriefe," SPAW, phil.-hist. Klasse, 25 (1934) 775, reprinted in his *Kleine Schriften, II: Studien zum Neuen Testament* (ed. K. Aland; TU 68; Berlin: Akademie-Verlag, 1958) 171; and "Die Chester-Beatty-Papyri des Neuen Testament," *Antike* 11 (1935) 147, reprinted in *Kleine Schriften*, II.168.

[36] Kenyon, *The Chester Beatty Biblical Papyri: III Supplement, Pauline Epistles, Text*, xxii.

Two subsequent events are symptomatic—if not causative—of a profound change. First, it was only when Günther Zuntz turned the customary procedure upside down by beginning his study of *The Text of the Epistles* with the "oldest manuscript of the Pauline corpus" (P46) and employing it "as a foil in assessing the value of, and the interrelation between, the other witnesses"[37] that an early New Testament papyrus became the standard against which all other relevant manuscripts were measured. Second, a striking catalyst appeared in the discovery of the Bodmer papyri in the mid-1950s. P66, P72, and P75 raised the papyri in general to a new level of visibility and significance, though it was P75 that played the major role. Here was a very early third century manuscript of John and Luke that turned out to have a text extraordinarily close to that of Codex Vaticanus (B) and yet dates 150 years earlier. That made textual critics sit up and take notice, for ever since Westcott-Hort it had commonly been held that the text of B was the result of revision over time and therefore presented a refined, smoothened version of an older and rougher text. But P75 did not confirm that hypothesis; rather, it demonstrated—in an actual, datable document—that already around 200 this very text was being used in Egypt.

Attention in the 1960s turned also to P66 (ca. 200), though not in the same way. This codex of John was judged at the time to be a mixed text, sharing typical B-text and D-text characteristics, that is, with textual features of the two early but sharply distinguishable text-types identified by Westcott-Hort. Here again, however, textual critics were judging a new, very early manuscript by later manuscripts that held well-established positions in current text-critical theory. We now recognize, of course, that significant new manuscripts of great antiquity should be studied *de novo* and should "set the stage" rather than be pulled into an existing "drama" or "plot" of textual theory [though we have yet to implement this insight fully]. So, this early assessment of P66 left it somewhat in the position that P45 had assumed earlier: a source of confusion over against current theory—which it did not seem to fit—and hence P66 was viewed much as was P45: a very early but enigmatic treasure. (The judgment that

[37] G. Zuntz, *The Text of the Epistles: A Disquisition upon the* Corpus Paulinum (Schweich Lectures, 1946; London: British Academy by Oxford University Press, 1953), 11; 17.

P66 was a "mixed" text (B and D) was later modified, and it is now
13 usually linked with the P75-B kind of text, though recognizing that
it is a rather "wild" member of that group.[38])

P66 acquired independent significance, however, through the observation that it contained four to five hundred scribal corrections of two kinds: most of them corrections by the scribe of his own errors, but others that appear to be corrections made upon comparison with another exemplar—the scribe checking his finished product against another manuscript. P66, therefore, showed a kind of microcosmic textual history of its own—revealing how scribes worked, how they might make corrections, and how different textual complexions might appear in a single manuscript.[39]

By the mid- to late-1960s, then, the papyri has secured their position in the formation of text-critical theory and were fully utilized in establishing a critical text of the New Testament—as attested also by their fresh collation and full use in the first edition of UBS*GNT* (1966).

VI. Significance of the Papyri for the New Testament Text: Past and Future

How have the papyri altered the critical text of the New Testament or our understanding of the theory behind it—or how should the papyri affect these matters? After the Bodmer papyri—and all the other major papyrus discoveries—had been worked into our critical texts, several analyses of these post-Bodmer critical editions revealed that, in actuality, their texts (including those of Nestle-Aland and of the United Bible Societies) differed only moderately from the 1881 Greek text of Westcott-Hort. One such analysis, performed at Duke University around 1968, concluded:

---

[38] See Gordon D. Fee, "P75, P66, and Origen: The Myth of Early Textual Recension in Alexandria," *New Dimensions in New Testament Study* (eds. R. N. Longenecker and M. C. Tenney; Grand Rapids, MI: Zondervan, 1974) 30–31, reprinted in Epp and Fee, *Studies in the Theory and Method*, 258–59; idem, *Papyrus Bodmer II (P66): Its Textual Relationships and Scribal Characteristics* (SD 34; Salt Lake City: University of Utah Press, 1968) 35.

[39] See Fee, *Papyrus Bodmer II*, 35; 56; 76–83; idem, "P75, P66, and Origen," 30–31, reprinted in Epp and Fee, *Studies in the Theory and Method* 258–59, and the further discussion below.

> Since 1881 twenty-five editors have issued about seventy-five editions of the Greek New Testament. The collation of these many "critical" texts consistently exposes the fact that each of them is basically a repetition of the Westcott-Hort text. . . . Indeed, we have continued for eighty-five years to live in the era of Westcott-Hort, our *textus receptus* ["the text received by all"].[40]

Now it is 113 years later than Westcott-Hort, and yet essentially the
same situation obtains today. This is confirmed by an assessment of
Nestle editions over time: Kurt and Barbara Aland (the current editors of Nestle-Aland), in a comparison of Nestle's early editions (that
of 1898—the first—and those that quickly followed) with the text in
their own twenty-sixth edition of 1979 (whose text is identical to
UBS*GNT*^{3}), concluded that the early Nestle text differs from its most 14
recent counterpart "in merely seven hundred passages."[41] They also
provided a detailed comparison of Nestle-Aland^{25} (1963) with the
editions of Tischendorf, Westcott-Hort, von Soden, Vogels, Merk,
and Bover; that analysis demonstrated that Nestle-Aland^{25} differed
most from von Soden (2,047 variants), then (in descending order)
from Vogels (1,996), Tischendorf^{8} (1,262), Bover (1,161), Merk (770),
and, finally—with the fewest variants—Westcott-Hort (558).[42]

Of course, the papyri could play virtually no role in the early Nestle editions and in Tischendorf and Westcott-Hort, but that is precisely the point: If the papyri were not utilized by Westcott-Hort in constructing their New Testament text, and if our own modern critical texts—which do use the papyri fully—are not significantly different from Westcott-Hort, why are the papyri considered to be so important? This is a sobering question when we attempt to determine the role of the papyri over the past century—have they had any substantive influence on the New Testament text itself?

---

[40] K. W. Clark, "Today's Problem with the Critical Text of the New Testament," *Transitions in Biblical Scholarship* (Essays in Divinity, 6; ed. J. C. Rylaarsdam; Chicago: University of Chicago Press, 1968) 160, reprinted in K. W. Clark, *The Gentile Bias and Other Essays* (ed. J. L. Sharpe III; NovTSup 54; Leiden: Brill, 1980), 123.

[41] Aland and Aland, *Text of the New Testament*, 20. Curiously, several pages later (26) they say that the Nestle text, for eighty years, "remained the same (apart from a few minor changes adopted by Erwin Nestle—no more than a dozen at most)."

[42] Ibid., 26–27. For discussion and references on various comparisons, see Epp, "The Twentieth Century Interlude in New Testament Textual Criticism," *JBL* 93 (1974) 388–90, reprinted in Epp and Fee, *Studies in the Theory and Method*, 85–86; Epp, "The New Testament Papyrus Manuscripts in Historical Perspective" 284–86.

On the other hand, why should this close similarity between the texts of Westcott-Hort and our modern editions be surprising? After all, none of these new discoveries had dislodged Codices Vaticanus and Sinaiticus from their preeminent place in the whole structure, for the Chester Beatty papyri provided readings that left untouched the generally-held theory of the time that three early text-types existed (the "Neutral" [B], the "Western" [D], and the more recently established [though later questioned] Caesarean text), for P45 appeared to fall midway between the B- and D-texts (hence, not threatening their existence), while P46 stood with the B-text. Subsequently, the Bodmer papyri provided an even earlier witness to the Vaticanus or B-text, namely P75, as well as another example, in P66, of a text basically supportive of the P75-B type of text—though at the same time moving away from it ("neutral, in a 'non-pure' way," Klijn called it).[43] It is only natural, then, to expect the post-Bodmer critical texts of the New Testament to resemble Westcott-Hort's 1881 text, and that, essentially, is what they did, despite numerous claims and a broad assumption that the New Testament papyrus treasures had changed everything. This is a striking conclusion to be drawn after a hundred years of extraordinary discoveries and vigorous text-critical work.

Have the papyri, then, really "come into their own" and have they been utilized fully and appropriately in textual criticism? They have, of course, been *fully* incorporated into our critical editions, but perhaps that is not where their major significance is to be found.

The forty-nine manuscripts dating up to the turn of the third/fourth centuries certainly are of paramount importance—perhaps even of "automatic significance"[44]—for establishing the text. A problem, however, is that these earliest witnesses do not reflect a unitary textual complexion, but rather a few if not several differing complexions. It remains doubtful, therefore, whether it can be said that in these forty-nine manuscripts the New Testament text "can be studied in

[43] A. F. J. Klijn, "Papyrus Bodmer II (John I–XIV) and the Text of Egypt," *NTS* 3 (1956–57) 333; cf. Fee, *Papyrus Bodmer II*, 9–14; 35; 76–83; Epp, "Significance of the Papyri," 94–96, reprinted in Epp and Fee, *Studies in the Theory and Method*, 290–91.

[44] In the "Introduction" of Nestle-Aland^{26}, 12* ("automatisch Bedeutung"); 49* ("intrinsic significance"). In Aland and Aland, *Text of the New Testament*, 93, the 1982 German edition's "automatisch Bedeutung" is translated "inherent significance."

the original,"[45] for the question regarding these textual witnesses—as in all other cases of textual variation—is still "*which* is original?" Nor does it seem helpful to designate a papyrus manuscript's fidelity to or deviation from the "original" in terms of "normal," "free," or "strict text,"[46] for these characterizations can hardly escape the charge of question begging.[47] Hence, the papyri may have greater impact when employed to solve major methodological issues in that they can (1) provide clues to modes of textual transmission, (2) assist in describing early scribal habits and the phenomena of textual alteration, and (3) aid in defining the earliest forms of the New Testament text and provide a basis for clarifying the existence and nature of the earliest identifiable textual complexions (or "text-types," as they have been called traditionally). Thus, for the future, the papyri may serve in these ways as keys to unlock the abiding mysteries of the early history of the New Testament text and of text-critical theory.

1. The manner in which the papyri may help our understanding of the early Christian transmission processes has been sketched earlier: the rapid movement of texts in the Mediterranean world and the representative nature of the Egyptian papyri.

2. Early scribal habits are illuminated in a striking fashion and for a very early stage of New Testament transmission by P66. This

[45] Kurt Aland, "The Twentieth-Century Interlude in New Testament Textual Criticism," *Text and Interpretation: Studies in the New Testament Presented to Matthew Black* (eds. E. Best and R. McL. Wilson; Cambridge/New York: Cambridge University Press, 1979) 11 (A reply, in German, to my Hatch Memorial Lecture of the same title, published in *JBL* 93 (1974) 386–414; cf. my response, "A Continuing Interlude in New Testament Textual Criticism?" *HTR* 73 (1980) 131–51; both reprinted in Epp and Fee, *Studies in the Theory and Method*, 83–108; 109–23).

[46] These designations are those of Aland and Aland, *Text of the New Testament*, 93–95.

[47] See the brief critique in Bart D. Ehrman, "A Problem of Textual Circularity: The Alands on the Classification of New Testament Manuscripts," *Bib* 70 (1989) 381 n. 19. Ehrman points out, too (esp. 383–84), the severe limitations of the five "categories" that the Alands use to classify the New Testament papyri, uncials, and numerous minuscules (Aland and Aland, *Text of the New Testament* 106–7; 159–63; 332–37). E.g., the earliest papyri all fall into Category I—manuscripts, according to the Alands, with a very high proportion of readings of the original text—which is ("as a working hypothesis" [p. 333]) the text of Nestle-Aland[26]; thus, manuscripts most useful for establishing the original text are those with the highest proportion of original (i.e. Nestle-Aland) readings—again, begging the question. On both classification proposals, see Epp, "New Testament Textual Criticism Past, Present, and Future: Reflections on the Alands' *Text of the New Testament*," *HTR* 82 (1989) 224–26.

manuscript is possibly, though certainly not clearly, the product of a scriptorium,[48] yet its scribe was a careless worker. More to the point, P66 was copied by a "scribe-turned-recensor," who was correcting his own text against a second manuscript (in addition to his exemplar) and who, by abandoning Johannine style [as found in P75 and B] in a variety of places, seemed determined to produce a more readable, common Greek style. Thus, he moved his text away from
16 that found in P75 and toward the sort of readings found later in the Byzantine or A-text, thereby revealing at a very early period a scribal attitude that removes difficulties and seeks the best sense of the text rather than showing a rigid concern for the preservation of the "original text."[49] Recently, too, an analysis of scribal habits in the early papyri has challenged the validity of the old "rule" that the shorter reading is more likely to be original,[50] signaling ways in which the papyri can inform our understanding of the long-standing criteria for the originality of readings.

3. The papyri can aid in defining the earliest forms of the New Testament text and, in turn, help to establish the existence and to clarify the nature of the earliest identifiable textual complexions (or

---

[48] Suggested, e.g., by Ernest C. Colwell and Gordon D. Fee; for evidence and arguments, see Fee, "P^{75}, P^{66}, and Origen," 30–31, reprinted in Epp and Fee, *Studies in the Theory and Method*, 258–59. One might ask whether the obvious carelessness of this scribe does not militate against its being the product of a professional scriptorium. On the "impossibility" of Christian scriptoria before 200 (except perhaps in Alexandria "about 200"), see Aland and Aland, *Text of the New Testament*, 70. On some ways to argue that standardized procedures were being employed already in the earliest New Testament papyri, and even for the existence of scriptoria, see Epp, "Significance of the Papyri" 90–91; 101–2, reprinted in Epp and Fee, *Studies in the Theory and Method*, 287–89; 295–96. [Harry Y. Gamble, *Books and Readers in the Early Church* (New Haven, CT: Yale University Press, 1995) 120–22; 158–59, makes perhaps the best possible case for Christian scriptoria before 200; cf. Epp, "Codex and Literacy in Early Christianity," 25.]

[49] Fee, "P75, P66, and Origen," 30–31, reprinted in Epp and Fee, *Studies in the Theory and Method*, 258–59; cf. Fee, *Papyrus Bodmer II*, esp. 9–14; 35; 76–83.

[50] James R. Royse, "Scribal Habits in the Transmission of New Testament Texts" *The Critical Study of Sacred Texts* (ed. W. D. O'Flaherty; Berkeley Religious Studies Series, 2; Berkeley, CA: Graduate Theological Union, 1979) 150–55; Peter M. Head, "Observations on Early Papyri of the Synoptic Gospels, Especially on the 'Scribal Habits,'" *Bib* 71 (1990) 240–47. [See now James R. Royse, "Scribal Tendencies in the Transmission of the Text of the New Testament," *The Text of the New Testament in Contemporary Research: Essays on the* Status Quaestionis (eds. B. D. Ehrman and M. W. Holmes; SD 46; Grand Rapids, MI: Eerdmans, 1995) 242–47; idem, *Scribal Habits in Early New Testament Papyri* (SD 47; Grand Rapids, MI: Eerdmans, 2005).]

"text-types"). A first step is to accord to the more extensive, early papyri their rightful role as *definers* of textual character and textual streams, rather than forcing them—often arbitrarily and sometimes prematurely—into Procrustean beds constructed on the basis of later, more prominent manuscripts. A concomitant step is to permit papyri of various textual complexions to draw similar manuscripts into their particular constellations so as to form distinguishable clusters and then to observe how the manuscripts sort themselves out. This is not as simple as it sounds for at least three reasons. First, the highly fragmentary papyri are often difficult to classify; second, classifications must be made for each section of the New Testament (i.e., for each circulating unit), such as the Gospels or the Gospels plus Acts, the Pauline letters, the general epistles (sometimes with Acts), and the Apocalypse—and at times for each New Testament book; and, third, there is often block mixture in manuscripts, some sections of a single manuscript reflecting one distinctive kind of text and other sections reflecting another.

Moreover, the existence of "text-types" in the earliest period of New Testament textual history is not acknowledged by all.[51] This is partly—but only partly—a matter of defining terms, for "text-types" may imply rigidly fixed forms with closely integrated characteristics—something difficult to demonstrate on a broad scale for the earliest period due to the fragmentary nature of the papyri. As a working definition, a text-type may be defined as an established textual cluster or constellation of manuscripts with a distinctive textual character or complexion that differentiates it from other textual constellations. Such differentiations must be based, not on general impressions or

[51] Especially Kurt Aland; see his "The Significance of the Papyri for Progress in New Testament Research," *The Bible in Modern Scholarship* (ed. J. P. Hyatt; Nashville: Abingdon, 1965) 334–37; updated in Aland, "Die Konsequenzen der neueren Handschriftenfunde für die neutestamentliche Textkritik," *Studien zur Überlieferung des Neuen Testaments und seines Texts* (ANTF, 2; Berlin: de Gruyter, 1967) 188–89; more recently, see Aland and Aland, *Text of the New Testament*, 59; 64; 103, who distinguish between "different forms" of the text (which they say did exist prior to the third/fourth century) and "text types" (which they say existed only in the fourth century and after); cf. Ernest C. Colwell, "The Origin of Texttypes of New Testament Manuscripts,"*Early Christian Origins: Studies in Honor of Harold R. Willoughby* (ed. A. Wikgren; Chicago: Quadrangle, 1961) 138; repr. as "Method in Establishing the Nature of Text-Types of New Testament Manuscripts," 55: "Very few, if any, text-types were established by that time" [A.D. 200].

17 on random samples, but on a full quantitative comparison of agreement/disagreement in variation-units (or test readings when large numbers of manuscripts are being considered). To be more specific, a prominent working hypothesis states that "the quantitative definition of a text-type is a group of manuscripts that agree more than 70 per cent of the time and is separated by a gap of about 10 per cent from its neighbors."[52] The few instances where New Testament papyri have been employed in such full comparisons, P75 and B in John, for example, show this kind of statistical distinctiveness in their relationship,[53] as do P45 and W in Mark, though P45 is highly fragmentary here.[54] Until more detailed analyses have been made, some may prefer to speak of "textual groups" or "textual clusters" rather than "text-types" in the early period.

Yet, what makes this sorting process so natural—and attractive—is that several early papyri draw to themselves other later manuscripts and form three reasonably separable constellations with similar textual characteristics. Most significant is the fact that the papyri in each group can be identified textually with one or more major majuscule manuscripts. Though it may appear that this procedure comes perilously close to classifying manuscripts on the basis of the great majuscules, it avoids that classic fault by first differentiating various papyri from one another according to their differing textual character, and only then seeking partners for them farther down the stream of New Testament manuscripts—partners with similar textual complexions. Thus, one can argue plausibly that three textual clusters or constellations emerge in our stream of transmission, each

[52] E. C. Colwell (with Ernest W. Tune), "The Quantitative Relationships between MS Text-Types," *Biblical and Patristic Studies in Memory of Robert Pierce Casey* (eds. J. N. Birdsall and R. W. Thomson; Freiburg/Basel/New York: Herder, 1963) 29, reprinted as "Method in Establishing Quantitative Relationships between Text-Types of New Testament Manuscripts," in Colwell, *Studies in Methodology in Textual Criticism of the New Testament* (NTTS 9; Leiden: Brill, 1969) 59. [See now the critique of Colwell's formula and other aspects of his method by Klaus Wachtel, "Colwell Revisited: Grouping New Testament Manuscripts," *The New Testament Text in Early Christianity: Proceedings of the Lille Colloquium, July 2000* (eds. C.-B. Amphoux and J. K. Elliott; HTB 6; Lausanne: Zèbre), 31–43.]

[53] See G. D. Fee, "Codex Sinaiticus in the Gospel of John: A Contribution to Methodology in Establishing Textual Relationships," *NTS* 15 (1968–69) 25–36; 44, reprinted in Epp and Fee, *Studies in the Theory and Method*, 223–34; 243.

[54] Larry W. Hurtado, *Text-Critical Methodology and the Pre-Caesarean Text: Codex W in the Gospel of Mark* (SD 43; Grand Rapids, MI: Eerdmans, 1981) 63–66; 88–89; 94.

with roots in the earliest period. First, the clearest cluster can be identified (for example, in the Gospels) in the P75-Codex B line (along with P66, Sinaiticus [except in John], and the later L and 33—as well as P46 and 1739 for Paul, etc.), which might be called the *B-text-group* (traditionally known as Egyptian, Alexandrian, or "Neutral"). Second, three or four papyri and one majuscule prior to the fourth century containing portions of Luke-Acts (P48, P38, P69, 0171, and perhaps P29) form a cluster that can be connected to Codex D, and later with 1739 and 614, 383. This has long been called—though incorrectly in the geographical sense—the "Western" kind of text, which might better be designated the *D-text-group*. Third, a cluster (for the Gospels) exists in P45 and Codex Washingtonianus (with, e.g., f^{13}), which might be called the *C-text-group* because it stands midway between the B and D text-groups [though no longer to be called Caesarean]. In addition, though not among the early clusters and therefore with no early papyrus representatives, there is the later Majority or Byzantine text-group, whose earliest major witness is Codex A (though only in the Gospels). Therefore, this might be called the *A-text-group* in recognition of Codex Alexandrinus. This cluster does have supporting witnesses among the papyri, but only from the sixth (P63, P84), seventh (P68, perhaps P73 and P74), and seventh/eighth centuries (P42), and it is the only "text-type" that the Alands recognize before the fourth century.[55]

Yet, once the nature of text-types is understood, it is plausible to 18
argue that the three textual constellations (in addition to the A-text) also constitute three distinguishable "text-types" as early as the second century (with the C-text-group, however, ceasing with Codex W). Again, the relationship of P75 and P66 may point the way. As noted earlier, the text of P66, through its corrections, moves toward the A-text and away from P75 (and B), but it is still closer to the latter manuscripts than to any other group[56] (though it misses by at least ten percentage points the seventy percent requirement for text-type affinity). What this tells us is that a text-type is not a closely concentrated entity with rigid boundaries, but is more like a galaxy—with a compact nucleus and additional but less closely related members that range out from the nucleus toward the perimeter. An

[55] Aland and Aland, *Text of the New Testament*, 64–69.
[56] Fee, *Papyrus Bodmer II*, 14; 35; 80–83.

obvious problem is how to determine when the outer limits of those more remote members have been reached for one text-type and where the next begins. To change the figure, text-types appear on a spectrum: the primary colors stand out (corresponding, in the early period, to the major manuscripts in the B, C, and D texts), with a spread of other manuscripts (secondary colors) between them.

The case made here for early text-types may be summarized as follows: The dynamic intellectual commerce demonstrated by the many papyrus documents—to say nothing of other evidence—permits us to envision a rather free and speedy transmission of letters and documents in the Greco-Roman world, including the New Testament writings on papyrus. This, in turn, permits us to postulate that the New Testament manuscripts unearthed in Egypt—presuming the movement of their texts to and from and within Egypt—may be judged to be representative of the entire spectrum of New Testament texts in the Mediterranean area in the first centuries of Christianity. Allowing these representative papyri to sort themselves into groups with similar textual complexions reveals three primary concentrations on the earliest textual spectrum, whose chief members connect readily with major majuscules of the fourth and fifth centuries and with other later manuscripts. Therefore, the existence, as early as the second century, of the B, C, and D text-types, followed by the later A-text, seems beyond a reasonable doubt, and all of this finds its basis in the New Testament papyri.

Added Notes, 2004

This essay was commissioned as a "state of the discipline" chapter on the New Testament papyri for a volume on *The Text of the New Testament in Contemporary Research: Essays on the* Status Quaestionis. Naturally, then, it draws on the preceding three essays, which treated the papyri from different aspects and, therefore, were relevant for the present task. The downside for this volume of collected essays is that numerous portions are similar in two or more essays, sometimes explicitly repeating material. I have reprinted this article, how-

[57] For a fuller discussion, cf. Epp, "Significance of the Papyri" 84–103, reprinted in Epp and Fee, *Studies in the Theory and Method*, 283–97.

ever, because it is a succinct statement that both summarizes where scholarship stood in 1995 and permits an expression of my own considered judgments on an array of critical issues. Detailed evidence and discussion of most points will be found in the earlier essays.

Relevant bibliography or additional material has been added to the footnotes in square brackets.

This essay was read in the New Testament Textual Criticism Section of the Society of Biblical Literature at its Annual Meeting in 1994, along with four other contributors to *The Text of the New Testament in Contemporary Research: Essays on the* Status Quaestionis (ed. B. D. Ehrman and M. W. Holmes; SD 46; Grand Rapids, MI: Eerdmans, 1995), when the volume, which honors Bruce M. Metzger, was presented to him.

CHAPTER SIXTEEN

THE INTERNATIONAL GREEK NEW TESTAMENT PROJECT: MOTIVATION AND HISTORY*

The International Greek New Testament Project (IGNTP)—a title 1
used since 1951[1]—will soon celebrate its fiftieth anniversary (1998), and this half-century has been a time of good intentions, good will, and good work, hampered, however, by uncertain financial support, lost opportunities for international cooperation, and unexpected delay after unexpected delay.

I. The Prehistory of the IGNTP: The 1920s to 1948

The more remote background or prehistory of the IGNTP is to be found in the push for a "new Tischendorf" that had emerged as early as the mid-1920s when a number of British and German scholars were separately considering the compilation of a major new critical apparatus to the Greek New Testament. On the German side, the Neutestamentler-Tagung as early as 1922 was considering whether to reprint Tischendorf's edition, with corrections and supplements, or to undertake an entirely new large critical edition, though subsequent meetings turned the discussion toward manuscript symbols and to the most efficient uses of signs in the Nestle apparatus.[2] More serious discussion of the options for a base-text for new manuscript collation and for the display of variants took place in 1925 and 1926, as reported by Ernst von Dobschütz and Otto Stählin. Should that base-text be the Tischendorf edition, or that of Nestle, or a single

* Revised version of a paper presented in the Textual Criticism Section at the Annual Meeting of the Society of Biblical Literature, Philadelphia, 1995, in a session devoted to the International Greek New Testament Project on the Gospel of John.

[1] See the "Report of the American Textual Criticism Seminar" for December 1951 in *JBL* 71 (1952) xxv, and beyond.

[2] E. von Dobschütz, "Die Neutestamentler-Tagung in Würzburg," *ZNW* 22 (1923) 147–149; cf. 310–311; 23 (1924) 312.

manuscript like B or A (which, as Lietzmann suggested, would parallel the LXX project of the time)?[3] But, said von Dobschütz,
2 Tischendorf's text "must once again be entirely revised"; and the
use of "a single manuscript, whether B or another, seems to us Germans too mechanical."[4] Both von Dobschütz and Stählin, therefore, preferred the Nestle edition of the time as a collation base; indeed, both spoke of Nestle as "a kind of modern *textus receptus*."[5]

Beyond the issue of the collation base, however, Stählin made the (correct) assumption that, in such a project, "the new Tischendorf would not be a definitive text-critical edition, but would bring into view the text-critical material as completely and reliably as possible."[6]

Meanwhile, on the British side, by 1926 a New Testament committee had been formed for a "Proposed Edition with full Critical Apparatus," chaired by A. S. Headlam, with S. C. E. Legg as secretary and editor. Among the other members of this "Central Committee in England" were Sir Frederic G. Kenyon, Alexander Souter, F. C. Burkitt, and B. H. Streeter.[7]

Sometime between September 1925 and October 1926, the British committee proposed to the Germans that American and German affiliated committees be established,[8] and then British members discussed their proposal with German representatives at the October 1926 Breslau Neutestamentlertagung.[9] Von Dobschütz, in his report of that conference, carried further the discussion of the collation base, now addressing additional options arising from the British side, namely the possible use of Westcott-Hort or the *textus receptus*. The latter had been proposed by Streeter, but, as von Dobschütz reports,

---

[3] Otto Stählin, "Zur Vorbereitung des neuen Tischendorf," *ZNW* 25 (1926) 165; Ernst von Dobschütz, "Neutestamentlertagung zu Erlangen am 29. und 30. September 1925," *ZNW* 25 (1926) 172.

[4] von Dobschütz, *ZNW* 25 (1926) 172.

[5] Ibid., 170; cf. 172; von Dobschütz, "Neutestamentlertagung zu Breslau am 4. und 5. Oktober 1926," *ZNW* 25 (1926) 318; Stählin, *ZNW* 25 (1926) 165–166.

[6] Stählin, *ZNW* 25 (1926) 165–166.

[7] Printed brochure titled, *The New Testament: Proposed Edition with Full Critical Apparatus* (Oxford, 1929) 8pp. Description by S. C. E. Legg (pp. 1–5); financial information by H. J. White (pp. 6–8).

[8] von Dobschütz, *ZNW* 25 (1926) 317.

[9] American and British Committees of the International Greek New Testament Project, *The New Testament in Greek: The Gospel according to St. Luke, Part One: Chapters 1–12; Part Two: Chapters 13–24* (2 vols.; New Testament in Greek, 3; Oxford: Clarendon Press, 1984–87) 1.v.

"to us Germans a reaching back to the *textus receptus* of the past appears to be an unbearable anachronism, so much so—on this unanimity reigns—that we would make the promise of our collaboration contingent upon this, that the *textus receptus* not become the basis."[10] On the positive side, however, the Germans also insisted 3
that the apparatus—which they (rightly) considered more important than the text—function on the "opposition principle" found in Tischendorf, namely, the presentation of witnesses both for and against a given variant, rather than on the "subtraction principle" of von Soden, which meant citing only the supporting witnesses for a reading.[11]

A plan for international collaboration resulted from the British-German discussions, and Advisory Committees in America and Germany were established, as well as one representing France and Switzerland; von Dobschütz was named Correspondent in Germany and James Hardy Ropes Correspondent in America. These Advisory Committees reacted to specimen sheets that had been completed by the end of 1926, and early in 1927 a decision was made to use the Westcott-Hort text as the base. Also, it was estimated in Britain that no less than £10,000 would be required to support the project—for the editor's annual salary of £250; to pay two or three assistants, as well as others who would collate or photograph manuscripts and versions; and to purchase books, especially critical editions of the Fathers. By the end of 1928, eighty-two contributions had been made to the fund, totaling £1,332 and ranging in size from 5 shillings [!] to the largest gift of £204 (i.e., $1,000) from the only American on the list, a New York City attorney. Yet the secretary-editor, Mr. Legg, felt compelled to complain that "the general response has so far been quite inadequate to enable the work to be carried on to any satisfactory extent and with any reasonable progress."[12] [Alas! the lack of funds was destined to hamper the project from then until the present time.] The British Academy did, however, begin a series of modest contributions to support "The Critical Edition of the New

[10] von Dobschütz, *ZNW* 25 (1926) 318.

[11] Ibid., 318. That a "reliable and complete" apparatus is more important than "the text as such" was emphasized already four years earlier, as reported by von Dobschütz in "Die Neutestamentler-Tagung in Würzburg," *ZNW* 22 (1923) 148.

[12] Oxford brochure (1929) p. 5.

Testament," providing grants quite consistently for a thirty-year period (1927 through 1956), though with the exception of seven years.[13]

4 What international collaborative work, if any, was carried on between 1927 and the appearance, in 1935, of the *Euangelium secundum Marcum* (Oxford: Clarendon Press), a textual apparatus of the Gospel of Mark edited by Legg, is not clear—at least to this writer. Alexander Souter's brief "Prologus" to the Mark volume did contain a ten-line paragraph acknowledging German and American supporters, while at the same time noting that "the Germans themselves are resolved to prepare a new edition of the Greek New Testament"; special thanks were extended to von Dobschütz, and Ropes's recent death (1933) was lamented. The 1940 companion volume on Matthew, *Euangelium secundum Matthaeum* (Oxford: Clarendon Press), whose printing had been delayed for two years by war,[14] did not have its own introduction, but by that time World War II had removed any possibility of German cooperation.

While waiting for the Matthew volume to emerge from Oxford University's Clarendon Press, Legg, assisted by R. V. G. Tasker, had begun to work on the Gospel of Luke, though Oxford had indicated "that it is out of the question to start printing another volume in war time."[15] When the Matthew volume did appear at the end of 1940, however, the *Proceedings of the British Academy* for 1941 contained the ominous news that Mr. Legg's eyes "have given way under the strain" and that, "in these circumstances it has been necessary to suspend the work being done on St. Luke. . . ."[16] More problems were reported the following year, 1942:

> Advantage has been taken of the enforced suspension of progress with this work, due both to the lack of funds and to the state of Mr. Legg's eyesight, to consider its future conduct in the light of criticisms made on the two published volumes.[17]

---

[13] No grants were provided in 1928, 1929, 1931, 1933, 1949, 1950, and 1952. The norm for grants became £100 through 1948, rising to an average of £200 for 1951 to 1956; with the exception of 1961, no grants were provided from 1957 to 1970, but from 1971 through 1978, a total of nearly £35,000 was granted "for the editorial expenses of this international project" (*Proceedings of the British Academy* 57 [1971] 30). The amount may have been larger since no annual report was published for 1977, though the annual contribution was £6,426 in both 1976 and 1978. See the annual reports in the *Proceedings* for the various years.

[14] *Proceedings of the British Academy* 26 (1940) 15.

[15] Ibid., 26 (1940) 15–16.

[16] Ibid., 27 (1941) 15.

[17] Ibid., 28 (1942) 10.

As it turns out, the Legg volumes on Mark and Matthew were ill-fated, for two devastating reviews had appeared in 1942, one by G. D. Kilpatrick and the other by T. W. Manson.[18] Kilpatrick referred to "serious defects," and "unsatisfactory features in the two parts which awaken disquiet in all who have to use them," including "defects in the citation of the patristic evidence" and "very unreliable" representation of the Syriac authorities.[19] He went on to recommend Streeter's earlier suggestion that the Byzantine text be used as a collation base; "indeed it might save considerable pains and possibly some mistakes if the Textus Receptus were printed above the apparatus."[20] He concluded that "the halt that has at present probably to be called in producing this work may well be used in considering the method and results of the venture. . . . Above all we cannot have too much accuracy."[21]

If Kilpatrick was blunt, Manson was unmerciful in his critique:

> The publication of the first volume of this most elaborate edition of the New Testament in Greek raised in the minds of many scholars doubts and misgivings which the appearance of the second volume does nothing to allay. Before the printing of the third Gospel is taken in hand there are questions which imperatively demand an answer, questions concerning both the plan of the undertaking and its execution. A work of this magnitude is not, indeed cannot be, produced without receiving considerable subsidies from trust funds as well as a high price from the purchaser. Both those who provide the subventions and those who buy the finished article are entitled to value for their money, and all the artistic excellence of Clarendon Press typography will not compensate if the work is ill planned and the execution faulty.[22]

Therefore, Manson argued, ". . . it does not seem too much to ask that the entire scheme be subjected to thorough reconsideration and, if necessary, drastic revision forthwith," and he, like Kilpatrick, called for separating the task of creating a critical text from that of producing an apparatus, followed by an appeal to use the Byzantine

[18] *JTS* 43 (1942) 30–34; and 83–92, respectively. See also the reviews by Ernest Cadman Colwell, *JR* 16 (1936) 234–236; *CP* 33 (1938) 112–115; 39 (1944) 67–68; following his two negative reviews of the 1935 Mark volume, he begins his review of the 1940 Matthew apparatus with, "This has gone far enough" and then points to its inconsistencies and inaccuracies.

[19] *JTS* 43 (1942) 32.

[20] Ibid., 33.

[21] Ibid., 34.

[22] Ibid., 84.

text as a collation base, which would save space, increase accuracy, and assure that only "really significant" variants appeared in the apparatus.[23] In addition, both reviewers indicated that "the task which Mr. Legg has undertaken is completely beyond his strength, or indeed that of any individual. . . . Mr. Legg has essayed to do the job single-handed, and has proved with immense labour and at considerable expense that it cannot be done that way."[24]

Meanwhile, Legg's eyesight improved, and he continued his work during 1942 and 1943, completing most of the material for a Luke volume, still, of course, employing the Westcott-Hort base and utilizing, as for Matthew and Mark, a similarly restricted number of manuscripts. The *Proceedings of the British Academy* printed Legg's progress reports for the years 1943 to 1948. For example, in 1943–1944, he indicated that, due to the efforts of H. A. Sanders, T. W. Manson, Matthew Black, and R. P. Blake, material for the first twelve chap-
6 ters of Luke had been assembled and that the first seven chapters had reached "a possible final form." However, "under the present difficult conditions caused by the war it seems hardly wise or necessary to call a Committee at the present time," he writes, and "the inaccessibility of certain books and original manuscripts for reference is causing a good deal of difficulty."[25] The next year, 1944–1945, Legg reported "real progress" with "at least twelve chapters" completed, though much checking and revision "can only be done when manuscripts and rare books have returned from their war-time hiding places"—something then expected very soon since the war was over.[26] The 1945–1946 report, however, was less optimistic: manuscripts had been "slow in returning from their war shelters" and, although sixteen chapters were now finished, it appeared that the Oxford University Press would not be ready to undertake publication for a year or two.[27] Along with the welcome news that the entire Luke volume had been completed and could go to press in 1948, the next two extremely brief annual reports carried more ominous news. First was the report that Mr. Legg could not continue and another editor must be sought by the now enlarged Committee,

[23] Ibid., 87; 89.
[24] Ibid., Manson, 84; Kilpatrick, 32.
[25] *Proceedings of the British Academy* 30 (1944) 11.
[26] Ibid., 31 (1945) 10–11.
[27] Ibid., 32 (1946) 9–10.

chaired by R. H. Lightfoot.[28] Second was the 1947–1948 report that "progress has been suspended" on the now complete Lukan material:

> in view of the announcement of the undertaking in America (with headquarters at the University of Chicago) of a full-scale critical edition of the New Testament. Communications are in progress with a view to ascertaining whether co-operation between this country and America is practicable.[29]

It was at this point that Legg retired from the editorship that he had held for some twenty-two years. Also, the British Academy's financial support, continuous during the war years, now became more erratic.[30]

The British reference to an American proposal for a "full-scale *critical edition* of the New Testament" was, of course, incorrect; rather, the proposal was for "a new critical apparatus of the Greek New Testament"[31] or, as stated in a project description from 1955, "a new edition of the manuscript evidence for the text of the Greek New Testament."[32]

Thus, recognition of the inadequacy of the Legg volumes would 7
lead, after World War II, to a new British-American undertaking, though now with revised principles, including a different base-text, a broader range of witnesses to be cited, and a vastly expanded, largely volunteer work force. And, for practical reasons, it would begin where Legg left off—with the Gospel of Luke.

This, however, is to jump ahead of our story, for the more direct origins of what later was to become the IGNTP reside in plans drafted already in 1942 by Merrill Parvis in consultation with his colleagues Ernest Colwell and Allen Wikgren at the University of Chicago. A set of principles and rules of procedure were circulated to American and British scholars, "with the understanding that the coöperation of scholars in other countries would be sought as

[28] Ibid., 33 (1947) 17.

[29] Ibid., 34 (1948) 14.

[30] See n. 13, above.

[31] *JBL* 68 (1949) xxv; 69 (1950) xxv; *New Testament Manuscript Studies: The Materials and the Making of a Critical Apparatus* (ed. M. M. Parvis and A. P. Wikgren; Chicago: University of Chicago Press, 1950) ix.

[32] *Emory Alumnus* (December 1955) 8; much of this material was reproduced in a later mimeographed project description, undated, but ca. 1958, with appropriate updating.

opportunities developed in the postwar years."[33] However, as we have noted earlier, British scholars at the time generally were still committed to the Luke volume to be edited by Legg—in spite of devastatingly negative reviews of his Mark and Matthew volumes that have been summarized above. In 1945 in North America, the Society of Biblical Literature approved a Textual Criticism Seminar (which, by 1947, was called the American Textual Criticism Seminar) to discuss "the proposed production of an adequate critical apparatus of the Greek New Testament."[34]

II. The IGNTP Proper: 1948 to the Present

The more formal beginnings of the IGNTP, however, lie in a 1948 conference at the University of Chicago, exactly midway in the six-year term of Ernest Cadman Colwell as President of that distinguished university. Actually, that October meeting of American textual critics had two related purposes: first, to honor Edgar J. Goodspeed, who had brought together an impressive New Testament manuscript collection there, which—on this occasion—was formally named for him; second, the meeting was called "to discuss matters preliminary to the preparation of a new critical apparatus of the Greek New Testament,"[35] to which were devoted most of the chapters of the resultant publication: *New Testament Manuscript Studies: The Materials*
8 *and Making of a Critical Apparatus* (ed. Merrill M. Parvis and Allen P. Wikgren; Chicago: University of Chicago Press, 1950). Three chapters, for example, discussed the New Testament Greek manuscript evidence, the versional evidence, and the Patristic evidence, respectively, followed by three chapters on methods of citing these three bodies of evidence in an apparatus.

By coincidence, just two weeks or so before the Chicago conference opened, G. D. Kilpatrick of Oxford University had written to Colwell indicating that the Critical Greek New Testament Committee

[33] Parvis, "The International Project to Establish a New Critical Apparatus of the Greek New Testament," *Crozier Quarterly* 27 (1950) 302; cf. his "Greek's Not Greek to Them," *Emory Alumnus* (December 1955) 9.

[34] *JBL* 65 (1946) ii–iii; Parvis's 1945 article, "The Need for a New *apparatus criticus* to the Greek New Testament," *JBL* 65 (1946) 353–369, clarifies the need and outlines a plan for the new apparatus.

[35] *New Testament Manuscript Studies*, ix.

supervising the Legg edition of Luke "had reached a point where it wished to consider its future plans and activities and inquiring as to the possibility of international cooperation and preparation of an edition of the manuscript evidence for the text of the Greek New Testament,"[36] and so, when this proposal was presented to the delegates at the Chicago conference and was endorsed unanimously, the joint cooperation of the British and Americans in the newly constituted project was established. President Colwell offered the University of Chicago as the Project's administrative home "provided the necessary financial support could be obtained";[37] a grant of $12,500 from the Rockefeller Foundation permitted the work to begin in 1949, and negotiations were soon completed for publication of the results by Oxford University Press,[38] which (including the already-published Legg editions) were to comprise eight volumes of apparatus and two (later) volumes of prolegomena.[39]

The Project, of course, needed "intellectual" sponsorship, and this was assured from the North American side when, at its December 1948 Annual Meeting, the Society of Biblical Literature and Exegesis appointed an Editorial Board of eighteen members and an American Executive Committee of six members, with Colwell as chair, A. P. Wikgren as vice-chair, and Parvis as executive secretary (of both the Editorial Board and the Executive Committee), plus K. W. Clark, B. M. Metzger, and R. P. Casey [who—when he returned to Cambridge (where he received his Ph.D.)—was replaced in 1950 by Paul Schubert]. Four American subcommittees (each headed by an Executive Committee member) were established: Greek Manuscripts (Clark), Lectionary Manuscripts (Wikgren), Versions (Metzger), and
Patristic Quotations (Casey, later Schubert).[40] Also, the *textus receptus* 9
was adopted as the collation base, selecting the 1873 Oxford edition, which was quickly reprinted for use by collators.

---

[36] A paraphrase of Kilpatrick's letter by Parvis in *Emory Alumnus* (December 1955) 10; augmented in mimeographed description of the Project, ca. 1958, p. 9.

[37] Parvis, *Emory Alumnus* (December 1955) 10; cf. Parvis, *Crozier Quarterly* 27 (1950) 302.

[38] *JBL* 69 (1950) xxv.

[39] Parvis, *Crozier Quarterly* 27 (1950) 308; Parvis, *Emory Alumnus* (December 1955) 9.

[40] *JBL* 69 (1950) xxvi; Parvis, *Crozier Quarterly* 27 (1950) 303; cf. *New Testament Manuscript Studies*, xi; *NTS* 16 (1969–70) 180 n. 2; Colwell, *What Is the Best New Testament?* (Chicago: University of Chicago Press, 1952) 107–108; Colwell, "Restoring the Text of the Greek New Testament", *Emory University Quarterly* 8 (1952) 149.

In Spring 1949, Kilpatrick spent a month on the American side of the Atlantic in consultation with American Board members, while Parvis, beginning that summer, conferred for five months with British and Continental scholars and attended six meetings of the British Committee. That Committee had eleven members (by 1950, including Casey), chaired by R. H. Lightfoot, with Kilpatrick as Secretary; its Working Committee (i.e., executive committee) consisted of Kilpatrick, W. D. McHardy, T. W. Manson, and H. F. D. Sparks. Merrill Parvis, as part of the Project from its outset, and as executive secretary, became for all practical purposes the director if not the everyday "life" of the American Project for many years.

The budget for the American work in 1950 was $26,500, plus in-kind contributions for a total of about $50,000. All funds were administered by the Society of Biblical Literature.[41]

On the British side, however, no report on the "Critical Edition of the Greek New Testament" could be found for several years in its customary place in the *Proceedings of the British Academy* (1944 through 1950) until a 1951 notation of four lines, indicating that "co-operation having now been established between the British and American Committees for the production of a joint edition, work on this undertaking has been resumed, and an edition of Luke will be the first to appear under the new arrangement,"[42] followed by news of a 1952 meeting of the American Executive Committee with the British Committee. On that occasion, the two committees agreed that the joint project should be pursued and that the Gospel of Luke should be their focus, though now under the post-Legg guidelines.[43] Another joint decision at that time was to construct an "index of Greek readings to Luke," which was completed in 1956.[44] This "Index of Readings" was a massive mimeographed document of 864 pages designed merely to provide a catalog of existent variant readings
10 identified at that stage of the joint Project; that is, variation unit by variation unit, it listed for the entire Gospel of Luke all variant readings found (1) in the editions by Legg (the unpublished Luke volume), von Soden, Tischendorf (8th major ed.), or Tregelles; (2) in

[41] Parvis, *Crozier Quarterly* 27 (1950) 305. On financial difficulties, see Colwell, *Emory University Quarterly* 8 (1952) 151–153.

[42] *Proceedings of the British Academy* 37 (1951) 10.

[43] *The New Testament in Greek: The Gospel according to St. Luke*, 1.v.

[44] *Proceedings of the British Academy* 43 (1957) 12.

patristic quotations listed in those editions; and (3) in any of the eighteen uncials or eighty-one minuscules collated for the Project files up to 1 July 1956. Since the "Index" likely contained the vast majority of the important variation-units in Luke, the organization of the variants that would emerge from subsequent manuscript collations would be greatly facilitated.

Work on both sides of the Atlantic had picked up since the joint venture had been established—possibly spurred on also by the startling discovery of P66 and its publication just weeks before the 1956 meeting of Society of Biblical Literature and its American Textual Criticism Seminar. The latter had been established by the Society in 1945 (as noted earlier) and quickly had become the regular forum for discussing text-critical issues and for reporting the progress of the IGNTP.[45] On the British side, numerous scholars were working on the Latin, Syriac, Coptic, and other early versions, as well as on the Diatessaron and selected patristic writers—the volume of activity is obvious from the comparatively lengthy annual reports from most of the years 1953–1959.[46] Curiously, though, funding from the British Academy dropped off completely from 1957 through 1970 (the only exception was a £100 contribution in 1961). In 1960, however, the American branch of the Project received a three-year grant of $5,000 per year from the Bollingen Foundation.[47]

As this well-organized joint project had moved through its first decade of work, optimism had run high, in part because nearly 300 people from twenty-five countries and all brands of Christianity had already become involved in the Project. By 1955, the American side of the Project had collated 193 Greek manuscripts, checked eighty-four of them, and recorded forty-five in the Project's master file; had completed collations of twenty-nine lectionaries; various editions and manuscripts of several versions had been collated against the base-text; and the "slipping" of Patristic quotations had progressed.[48]

The Project's meticulous plans and careful organization perhaps 11
justified, at the time (1950), the confident, euphoric predictions from

[45] *JBL* 66 (1947) iii–iv; cf. *JBL* 65 (1946) ii–iii; and succeeding reports in *JBL* from 67 (1948) through 80 (1961).

[46] *Proceedings of the British Academy* reports for those years.

[47] *JBL* 80 (1961) xvi.

[48] Bruce M. Metzger, "Report of Progress of the American Section of the International Greek New Testament Project," *NTS* 2 (1955–56) 222–223.

the North American side: "We have set 1954 as the time when the Luke volume will go to press. . . . The entire Project should be completed in about fifteen years."[49] In spite of vigorous activity, this target date had to be modified by 1955:

> Sept. 30, 1956 has been set as the time when all material for the Gospel of Luke . . . is to be in the Emory University office of the project. One year has been allowed for the final editorial work. Thus, the first volume should go to press late in 1957. The remainder of the New Testament should be completed within another decade and a half.[50]

About three years later, the text of this 1955 report was reprinted in modified form with revised dates: September 30, 1959 for all Lucan materials to come in; first volume to the press in 1960; and completion of the entire New Testament "in another fifteen years."[51]

In the meantime, along with the collation of available manuscripts, it was essential to find ways to make hitherto inaccessible manuscripts available, and it was desirable to locate new manuscripts as well. Photographs, photostats, and microfilms of manuscripts in Western European libraries were being purchased for the Project, and further microfilming was urgently required. We may have forgotten that microfilm technology was relatively new at the time that the IGNTP was established. Although the Recordak system was developed in 1928 by Eastman Kodak, primarily using 16mm. film to record checks in bank transactions—and later using 35mm. film—it was only in 1941 that the V-Mail process was designed to deliver mail to British and American armed forces overseas.[52] Thus, an early description of the Project highlighted the fact that:

> there is available now for the first time the means of recording manuscripts on microfilm that makes it possible to bring together in one center facsimiles of all of the known copies of the New Testament at a relatively low cost. This has never been done, but it must be done to make accessible the materials that will enable scholars to reconstruct the earliest text of the New Testament and to understand its textual history and to preserve the manuscripts against the destruction of another World War.[53]

---

[49] Parvis, *Crozier Quarterly* 27 (1950) 308.
[50] *Emory Alumnus* (December 1955) 10; cf. *JBL* 74 (1955) xix.
[51] Mimeographed Project description (ca. 1958) 11.
[52] *Encyclopaedia Britannica* (1972) 17.954.
[53] *Emory Alumnus* (December 1955) 10.

Accordingly, we owe much to three early members of the Project, 12
Silva Lake, Kenneth W. Clark, and Ernest W. Saunders, who (respectively) led expeditions to libraries in Western Europe and the Near East in 1949; to monasteries on Mount Sinai and to libraries in Jerusalem in 1949–1950; and to Mount Athos in 1952–1953. They were sponsored largely by the United States Library of Congress and the American Schools of Oriental Research and made available on microfilm, for example, 1,687 manuscripts from St. Catherine's Monastery, 1,030 from two libraries in Jerusalem, and 253 from Mount Athos. Among these, biblical manuscripts were abundant, including, for example, 209 out of the 253 from Mount Athos. As Saunders noted, the chief purpose of the Mount Athos expedition was to photograph New Testament manuscripts "which were representative of Von Soden's subdivisions of the Koine recension, the readings of which might ultimately be incorporated into the *apparatus criticus* now being compiled by the International Greek New Testament Project."[54] Items listed in the three *Checklist*s by Clark and Saunders include the length of microfilm for each: for example, Codex Ω (Gregory 045) of the gospels required thirty-nine feet of film. The scope and achievement of these projects may be judged from the report that a year's work by K. W. Clark in the libraries in Jerusalem recorded 1,270,000 pages of manuscripts. Slightly later, around 1957, the United States Department of State had assisted the IGNTP in securing microfilms of some fifty manuscripts in the USSR.[55] At about the same time, on the British side, J. A. Spranger was microfilming manuscripts in Italian libraries during 1952–1955.[56]

"And the work progressed" might well be the refrain of the Project's lengthy story. Ernest Colwell, original and continuing chair of the American Executive Committee, moved from Chicago to an administrative position at Emory University in 1951 and the American side of the Project—as well as Merrill Parvis—followed him there in 1955,

[54] Ernest W. Saunders, *A Descriptive Checklist of Selected Manuscripts in the Monasteries of Mount Athos* (Washington, DC: Library of Congress Photoduplication Service, 1957) xi; see K. W. Clark, *Checklist of Manuscripts in St. Catherine's Monastery, Mount Sinai* (Washington, DC: Library of Congress Photoduplication Service, 1952) and *Checklist of Manuscripts in the Libraries of the Greek and Armenian Patriarchates in Jerusalem* (Washington, DC: Photoduplication Service, Library of Congress, 1953); cf. Parvis, *Crozier Quarterly* 27 (1950) 304–305.

[55] *JBL* 77 (1958) xxviii.

[56] *Proceedings of the British Academy* 39 (1953) 8; 40 (1954) 8; 41 (1955) 10.

though Duke University hosted a portion of the work beginning in 1963. Then, several years after Colwell's move to head the School
13 of Theology at Claremont (1958), the project files and headquarters were transferred, in 1966, to the newly-established Institute for Antiquity and Christianity within the Claremont Graduate School, where the Claremont Profile Method was developed.[57] Today the Project's collection of manuscript microfilms resides in the Claremont Ancient Biblical Manuscript Center.

The American Committee continued the pursuit of its assigned tasks through the 1950s and 1960s, while on the British side, G. G. Willis had been appointed Executive Editor in 1962; most unfortunately, however, in 1969 he developed glaucoma and it was determined, within a few months, that he had no prospect of regaining his sight.[58]

It is appropriate to interrupt this story for a moment to report that, in 1965, a high point in progress long-delayed was reached when finally a specimen of the proposed *apparatus criticus* was printed by the Clarendon Press and circulated in June 1965 to some forty scholars, with a request to respond to the format design—a high point that very quickly became a notorious point of international contention. The preparation of this sample apparatus by the joint Committees had involved decisions on scores of major and minor issues that pertain to the *display* of textual variants. These decisions, some provisional, were described in a three-page document accompanying the specimen, which contained an appropriate caveat: "The specimen is provisional, and it is not claimed that it is accurate in

[57] On the development of this method, see E. J. Epp, "The Claremont Profile-Method for Grouping New Testament Minuscule Manuscripts," *Studies in the History and Text of the New Testament in Honor of Kenneth Willis Clark, Ph.D.* (ed. B. L. Daniels and M. J. Suggs; SD 29; Salt Lake City, UT: University of Utah Press, 1967) 27–38; reprinted in E. J. Epp and G. D. Fee, *Studies in the Theory and Method of New Testament Textual Criticism* (SD 45; Grand Rapids, MI: Eerdmans, 1993) 211–220; and E. C. Colwell, with I. A. Sparks, F. Wisse, P. R. McReynolds, "The International Greek New Testament Project: A Status Report," *JBL* 87 (1968) 191–197. For works by the principal developers of the method, see Frederik Wisse and Paul R. McReynolds, "Family E and the Profile Method," *Bib* 51 (1970) 67–75; P. R. McReynolds, "Establishing Text Families," *The Critical Study of Sacred Texts* (ed. W. D. O'Flaherty; Berkeley: Berkeley Religious Studies Series; Berkeley, CA: Graduate Theological Union, 1979) 97–113; and F. Wisse, *The Profile Method for the Classification and Evaluation of Manuscript Evidence as Applied to the Continuous Greek Text of the Gospel of Luke* (SD 44; Grand Rapids, MI: Eerdmans, 1982).

[58] British Committee report (1971)—unsigned.

all details. Rather it is designed to demonstrate the form and arrangement of the material." At the end came the request for advice—to assist the editors, Parvis and Willis, and the Committees in their final decisions. To the surprise of all, almost immediately (January 1966) Kurt Aland made a public response in a lengthy article in *New Testament Studies*.[59] Apparently, however, he had not understood the
stated nature and purpose of the sample and, instead of focusing on 14
format, pursued at length matters of its completeness and accuracy—more specifically, its incompleteness and inaccuracy; moreover, he spoke throughout of the "edition" or the "new edition," (rather than of a "critical apparatus"), and at the end he expressed his astonishment over the use of the *textus receptus* as a base-text, referring to it, in view of our advanced knowledge of the New Testament text, as an "anachronism"[60]—precisely the term von Dobschütz had used in 1926 when reacting to Streeter's proposal to use the *textus receptus* as the base-text. So, history repeats itself, though a tally made in 1965 of the responses to the specimen from scholars in North America, the United Kingdom, and the Continent "showed that 'no one questions the use of the Textus Receptus.'"[61] Today, we may be very grateful indeed that the long-debated issue of a base-text for collation has become moot, for the computer technology employed for the current phase of the IGNTP—the Gospel of John—will enable us to call up and to display the apparatus of variants against any text we choose—any edition or any manuscript that has been entered into the system—just as we can reconstruct from its variants any

[59] "Bemerkungen zu Probeseiten einer grossen kritischen Ausgabe des Neuen Testaments," *NTS* 12 (1965–66) 176–185; expanded and updated in his *Studien zur Überlieferung des Neuen Testaments und seines Textes* (ANTF 2; Berlin: de Gruyter, 1967) 81–90. See a lengthier discussion in Epp, "The Twentieth Century Interlude in New Testament Textual Criticism," *JBL* 93 (1974) 402–3; reprinted in E. J. Epp and G. D. Fee, *Studies in the Theory and Method of New Testament Textual Criticism* (SD 45; Grand Rapids, MI: Eerdmans, 1993) 97–98.

[60] Aland, "Bemerkungen zu Probeseiten," 184; cf. ibid., *Studien zur Überlieferung*, 89–90. This action prompted an assessment of the Project by Jean Duplacy, "Une tâche importante en difficulté: L'édition du Nouveau Testament grec," *NTS* 14 (1967–68) 457–468.

[61] Jean Duplacy and M. Jack Suggs, "Les citations grecques et la critique du texte du Nouveau Testament: Le passé, le présent et l'avenir," *La Bible et les Pères: Colloque de Strasbourg (1er–3 octobre 1969)* (ed. André Benoit and Pierre Prigent; Bibliothèque des centres d'Etudes supérieures spécialisés; Paris: Presses Universitaires de France, 1971) 189 n. 4.; cf. 204–206.

manuscript collated for the Project [in John only, of course, at this juncture]. Yet, wisdom dictates that we collate—that is, enter the variants—against the text that facilitates the greatest degree of accuracy, economy, and efficiency, and—especially when numerous minuscules are involved—that the most desirable base-text consist of a "full text," such as our selected edition of the *textus receptus*. Then, if one wishes, the apparatus can be displayed, for example, against the current Nestle-Aland text.

This incident involving the late—and most highly distinguished—Kurt Aland (1915–1994) may veil some missed opportunities in the so-called *International* Greek New Testament Project, for its title frequently has raised questions of appropriateness, since (with *very few* exceptions until the current phase) only North American and British scholars were directly related to it. Parvis, in 1950, mentions that numerous European scholars with whom he had visited or corresponded, expressed "genuine interest" in the Project, and among them—last on his list—was Kurt Aland of Berlin.[62] Later, around 1958 and—as far as I can discover—in mimeographed form only, a General Editorial Board was listed that included, in addition to twenty-one British and Americans, also two Germans, Kurt Aland and Bonifatius Fischer, and Maurice Brière of France. Was this a brief "moment" when the Project was genuinely "international" and did we miss that possibility again in the mid-1960s, following Aland's response to the specimen? Colwell, in a letter to the American Executive Committee (dated 7 November 1966), among reports of significant Project activity on the American side and in UK, reported that he had held:

> an hour and a quarter's discussion with Mr. Aland on the possibility of his suggesting material to be included, or supplying material to be included, or becoming a member of an advisory panel of European scholars. In the course of the conversation Mr. Aland said he had had a letter from Plumley [chair of the British Committee; letter dated 11 August 1966] but he felt it was a very meager letter—the implication being that it was too meager to be answered. He made it quite clear to me that unless he were a member of a centrally powerful committee he would not be interested in any cooperation with the Project. I regret this very much, for I feel that if he had answered Plumley and were willing to take this half-step toward complete involvement,

[62] Parvis, *Crozier Quarterly* 27 (1950) 308.

> his complete and significant involvement in the future would become a reality. In short, then, the result of my interview was that Mr. Aland's answers to all three questions at the beginning of this paragraph were negative.

As a matter of fact, Aland did finally answer J. M. Plumley—probably as a direct result of his conversations with Colwell—but only on 24 January 1967, after a four-and-a-half month delay. Following a highly apologetic opening paragraph regretting and explaining the lateness of his reply, Aland indicates that his positive response to involvement with the Project would require a seat and voting powers ("Sitz und Stimme") in both committees. The American Executive Committee, at a 29 December 1967 meeting in New York, made the following recommendation: "That Professor Aland not be invited to join our committee or the British committee." The main reason given was Aland's intention to publish his apparatus of the Pauline corpus—leaving the four gospels, at least, to the British-American group.[63] Just prior to the American decision, the British Committee's Minutes (for 16 November 1967) report a majority vote to postpone a decision on Aland's membership until 7 February 1968—after the 16
American decision was known. At that February meeting, the British decision was unanimous "that it would be inappropriate for a Continental scholar to be a full member of the British Committee," and it too refers to "an agreed division of the New Testament field."[64] A covering letter from the British editor, Willis, explains further that, if Aland is "getting on" with the Pauline Epistles, and "if your committee and ours get on . . . with Luke, followed by John, we shall steer clear of the German Committee's field." It is not coincidental, but quite understandable, that the same letter carries the following note (detached from the Aland paragraph above):

> Our official title has always been "The Critical Greek New Testament Committee," and it has come to our ears that the usual American title, "The International Greek New Testament Project" has given rise on the Continent, e.g. in Aland's mind, to misconceptions. They think that the adjective "International" means "from all sorts of nations, including the Continent" and that it is a misleading description of a

[63] Recommendations made by the American Committee, 29 December 1967, accompanied by a letter of 8 January 1968 from Colwell to the American Executive Committee.

[64] Minutes of the British Committee, 7 February 1968.

> committee including only British and Americans. Of course *we* know that "International" means "between two or more nations" and it is a perfectly fair description of a committee, or associated committees' project, embracing Britain and U.S.A.[65]

In the meantime, at a joint meeting of the British and American executive committees in Cambridge, UK, in September 1966, a "tentative date" of 1971 was put forward for the completion of Luke, with the further notation that publication for the centennial of Tischendorf's eighth major edition in 1972 would be "a happy coincidence."[66] However, another recycling of the Project description cited earlier occurred in late 1967, and its prediction was even more muted: "If adequate funds are made available, the publication of Luke could be expected within a few years. The succeeding volumes would follow in much more rapid sequence, since they would use materials already assembled."[67] Two years later (1969), the expectation of the American Executive Committee continued to be that "the evidence for Luke will be complete early in 1970" and that the volume could be sent to the publisher in 1971.[68] When it was time to report on activities for the period 1969 to 1971, after the American
17 Executive Committee had elected four new and younger members (E. J. Epp, G. D. Fee, P. R. McReynolds, I. A. Sparks) and new officers (Bruce Metzger had replaced Colwell as chair), the Project expected that its American executive editor, K. W. Clark, should be able to complete work on the typescript of the Greek evidence (continuous-text Greek manuscripts, lectionaries, several ancient versions, and Greek patristic quotations)—the American responsibility—by early 1972 and that recent financial support from the British Academy would enable the newly-appointed British Executive Editor, J. Neville Birdsall, to devote himself full-time to the Project beginning October 1971.[69] Indeed, this encouraging prospect for the editorial work led

[65] Letter of G. G. Willis to Colwell, 10 February 1968.

[66] K. W. Clark, "The International Greek New Testament Project: A Status Report," Annual Meeting of SBL/American Textual Criticism Seminar (29 December 1966) [unpublished report].

[67] Mimeographed report dated 1 August 1967. It was at this juncture that Jean Duplacy warned that a project of this kind cannot be completed quickly—or without broad collaboration: "Une tâche importante en difficulté," 457–468, esp. 459–462.

[68] James M. Robinson, et al., "The Institute for Antiquity and Christianity," *NTS* 19 (1969–70) 180–82 ["International Greek New Testament" by E. C. Colwell].

[69] *Proceedings of the British Academy* 58 (1972) 11; "Institute for Antiquity and

the British Academy, in 1971–72, to "adopt" the Critical Edition of the Greek New Testament as one of its Major Projects; to constitute its Committee as a Committee of the Academy; and to take on the obligation to pay Dr. Birdsall's salary during a three-year period of "secondment."[70] The following year's report stated confidently that "completion of the publication is now assured."[71] Unfortunately, Birdsall's otherwise productive three-year period—during which great progress had been made—quickly passed, and "correcting certain deficiencies . . . in the materials," "largely unforeseen," had once again slowed down the editorial process;[72] he continued as "caretaker Editor" until March 1978,[73] and in September of that year J. Keith Elliott was appointed Executive Editor;[74] Elliott brought to completion volume 1 of Luke (chaps. 1–12) for its publication in 1984, and volume 2 appeared in 1987.[75]

The Luke volumes involved (1) the efforts of some 283 scholars and graduate students, mostly from North America, who collated Greek manuscripts and collected data from Greek patristic writers and (2) prodigious labors by many scholars from the United Kingdom who collected and processed versional evidence and the non-Greek
patristic material. In addition, the resources of the Vetus Latina 18
Institut at Beuron and of the Institut für neutestamentliche Textforschung at Münster were made available to the Project's researchers. Of utmost importance, of course, were (3) the contributions of the British and American committee members and especially the various officers and editors over a forty-year period.[76]

Christianity, Annual Report 1969–70 and 1970–71," *Bulletin of the Institute for Antiquity and Christianity* 3 (No. 3, June 1972) 1–2.

[70] *Proceedings of the British Academy* 58 (1972) 5, 11.

[71] Ibid., 59 (1973) 21.

[72] Ibid., 59 (1973) 20–21.

[73] Ibid., 64 (1978) 554.

[74] Ibid., 65 (1979) 56.

[75] American and British Committees of the International Greek New Testament Project, ed. *The New Testament in Greek: The Gospel according to St. Luke: Part One: Chapters 1–12. Part Two: Chapters 14–24* (2 vols.; Oxford: Clarendon Press, 1984–87). Cf. J. K. Elliott's description of the project just prior to the publication of vol. 1: "The International Project to Establish a Critical Apparatus to Luke's Gospel," *NTS* 29 (1983) 531–538; and his "Why the International Greek New Testament Project is Necessary," *ResQ* 30 (1988) 195–206; cf. idem, "The Purpose and Construction of a Critical Apparatus to the Greek New Testament," *Studien zum Text und zur Ethik des Neuen Testaments: Festschrift zum 80. Geburtstag von Heinrich Greeven* (ed. W. Schrage; BZNW 47; Berlin/New York: de Gruyter, 1986) 125–43.

[76] For a complete list of the committees and contributors, see *The New Testament*

When these collected materials, the result of forty years of tangled history, finally were frozen in print and presented to the scholarly public, what was the reaction? History repeated itself—what else? A series of reviews, all thoughtful and—as reviews go—some of astounding length and with substantial critique, assessed the format, as well as the completeness and accuracy of the volumes—and not always positively. Noteworthy perhaps were those reviews of part 1 by Kurt Aland in 1984[77] and Barbara Aland in 1991;[78] of part 2 by J. Neville Birdsall [its penultimate editor, 1970–77] in 1989[79] and Carroll D. Osburn [current member of the North American Committee] in 1990;[80] and of parts 1 and 2 by William L. Petersen [current member of the North American Committee] in 1988[81] and Mikeal Parsons in 1991.[82] As in 1935 and 1940, the lessons learned are being applied (or should be) to the current phase of the IGNTP.[83]

III. The IGNTP Currently: The Gospel of John

Is there IGNTP life beyond Luke? After the publication of the Luke volumes, the British Committee was reorganized and currently consists of T. S. Pattie (Chair), J. K. Elliott (Secretary), W. J. Elliott
19 (Co-Editor), D. C. Parker (Co-Editor), C.P. Hammond-Bammel, J. L. North, and J. D. Thomas (G. D. Kilpatrick was a member until his death in 1989). In early 1987, J. Keith Elliott wrote to Bruce Metzger—still the titular chair of the American Executive Committee—about his interest, and that of the American Committee (if it still

in Greek [cited in the preceding note], 1.xiv–xvi. For a recent, brief description of the Project, see J. Neville Birdsall, "The Recent History of New Testament Textual Criticism (from Westcott and Hort, 1881, to the Present)," *ANRW* II:26:1 (1992) 181–184.

[77] *Gnomon* 56 (1984) 481–497.

[78] *JTS* 42 (1991) 201–215.

[79] *Classical Review* 39 (1989) 198–200.

[80] *SJT* 43 (1990) 524–526.

[81] *JBL* 107 (1988) 758–762.

[82] *CBQ* 53 (1991) 322–325. Other reviews are listed in D. C. Parker, "The International Greek New Testament Project: The Gospel of John," *NTS* 36 (1990) 157 n. 2; Parker responds to some points of criticism in that article.

[83] See now, e.g., the programmatic assessment by T. Baarda, "What Kind of Critical Apparatus for the New Testament Do We Need? The Case of Luke 23:48," *New Testament Textual Criticism, Exegesis, and Early Church History: A Discussion of Methods* (ed. B. Aland and J. Delobel; Kampen: Kok Pharos, 1994) 37–97.

existed), in continuing the Project into the Gospel of John.[84] Metzger replied that, for himself, he could no longer continue, but he polled the remaining members of the American Committee to assess their interest, individually and collectively. My own view, for what it was worth, was that I did not wish to support a project that would involve another forty years in constructing the apparatus of just one more gospel, but that, if computer programs were available or could be devised to assist in collations and to record and to maintain the textual data in ways that could usefully manipulate them for our purposes, I would surely support the continuance of the Project.

In North America the following year, 1988, the Textual Criticism Section of the Society of Biblical Literature nominated and elected a new North American Committee of the IGNTP, consisting of Gordon D. Fee (Chair), Carroll D. Osburn (Vice-Chair), Thomas C. Geer (Secretary), James A. Brooks, Bart D. Erhman, Eldon Jay Epp, Michael W. Holmes, and Paul R. McReynolds. By the second meeting of the Committee (1989), William L. Petersen had been invited and had accepted membership in the Committee. In that same year, Holmes was appointed North American Editor, as the counterpart to the British editors. Mr. Bruce Morrill, who played a major role in the development of the electronic program used in collation, serves as Consultant to the Committee on computer technology and became a member of the Committee in 1992. Geer resigned from the Committee in 1994; Fee remains as Chair, with Holmes as Executive Chair and Editor, while Osburn has become Secretary.

A division of labor between the British and North American committees was early agreed upon, with the North Americans assuming responsibility for the Greek minuscules, the Greek patristic writers, the Diatessaron, and the Armenian, Coptic, Gothic, and Slavonic versions, while the British would supervise work on the papyri, the uncials, the lectionaries, and the other versions (including the Latin, Syriac, Nubian, Ethiopic, and Georgian, and the Latin and Syriac patristic writers). A fair number of continental scholars have been engaged to assist with the tasks of the two committees; cooperation has been arranged with the Vetus Latina Institut at Beuron; and

[84] See D. C. Parker, "The International Greek New Testament Project: The Gospel of John," *NTS* 36 (1990) 157–160.

conversations with Barbara Aland, director of the Institut für Neutestamentliche Textforschung at Münster have been initiated—giving new validity to the long standing term "international" in the Project's title.

20 "And the work goes on." Many scholars are collating Johannine manuscripts and assessing versions and patristic quotations, but many more collators are needed. Small grants have been received, but large grants, so far, have eluded us. Target dates cannot be established in such circumstances, but we trust that good intentions, good will, and good work—now including electronic technology—will bring us to the next goal in a more timely fashion. Indeed, a major milestone was reached in late 1995 when the present IGNTP Committees published their first collaborative result, *The New Testament in Greek IV: The Gospel according to St. John, Volume One, The Papyri* (ed. W. J. Elliott and D. C. Parker; NTTS 20; Leiden: Brill, 1995). This large volume presents an introduction, and (1) transcriptions of the twenty-three papyri containing John, except the extensive P66 and P75, (2) a complete *apparatus criticus*, and (3) a complete set of plates for all papyri except P66 and P75. Its very appearance bodes well for the future of the IGNTP.

Added Notes, 2004

The work of IGNTP has continued since the publication of the preceding article, with increased consultation and cooperation between the British and North American committees, and with two significant developments. First, facilitated by a mutual desire for cooperation after years of competition and by enhanced computer capabilities, the IGNTP and the Münster Institut für Neutestamentliche Textforschung signed a joint agreement in October 2000 to collaborate fully on the Editio Critica Maior of the Gospel of John. The two projects would maintain their separate identities, but the IGNTP would no longer insist that the apparatus be displayed under the *textus receptus*, and the Institut would agree to a joint comparison and assessment of both the Claremont Profile Method and their own use of Teststellen and the COLLATE computer program for grouping Johannine manuscripts. In view of the lengthy battle over an appropriate collation base, this new collaborative arrangement represents an historic event, but one doubtless impossible apart from modern electronic technology (see further below on computer programs).

Second, significant new funding in the United Kingdom for support of IGNTP has brightened the future of the entire enterprise. The vehicle for this support—and for a major portion of the work—is the Principio Project in the Centre for Editing Texts in Religion at the University of Birmingham (UK), organized and headed by David C. Parker and funded by the UK Arts and Humanities Research Board. It will carry out its work in close consultation with the British and North American Committees of IGNTP and with the Münster Institut. See a full report in D. C. Parker, "The Principio Project: A Reconstruction of the Johannine Tradition," *Filologia Neotestamentaria* XIII (2000) 111–18.

To back up briefly, in 1990 Bruce Morrill and Jerry Lewis, working with Paul R. McReynolds, began to develop a computer program for the recording and display of manuscript evidence for IGNTP; by 1992 the software, called MANUSCRIPT was in use by collators, greatly simplifying the registration of data and obviously enhancing accuracy. Among other advantages, the program will allow the printing of the complete text of any collated manuscript; the electronic construction of a critical apparatus; the presentation of manuscript variants against any desired base or in comparison with any other collated manuscript; and the discovery of percentages of agreement among manuscripts. Naturally, it also offers the possibility of online access and use, and continuous updating.

Recent changes in IGNTP personnel include the addition of Kim Haines-Eitzen to the North American Executive Committee in 2000. On the British side, J. David Thomas and Caroline Hammond Bammel became members in 1990 (though the latter died in 1996), and Philip Burton, Peter Head, and C. M. Tuckett joined the Committee in 2001.

Subsequent publications relevant to IGNTP include David C. Parker, "The International Greek New Testament Project: The Gospel of John," *NTS* 36 (1990) 157–60; idem, "The Principio Project: A Reconstruction of the Johannine Tradition," cited above; idem, "Manuscripts of the Gospels in the Electronic Age," *ResQ* 42 (2000) 221–31; idem, "A Comparison between the *Text und Textwert* and the Claremont Profile Method Analyses of Manuscripts in the Gospel of Luke," *NTS* 49 (2003) 108–38; idem, "Through a Screen Darkly: Digital Texts and the New Testament," *JSNT* 25 (2003) 395–411.

CHAPTER SEVENTEEN

TEXTUAL CRITICISM IN THE EXEGESIS OF THE NEW TESTAMENT

I. The Role of Textual Criticism in New Testament Interpretation

In the broad sweep of biblical interpretation, textual criticism 45
logically and traditionally has preceded "higher criticism"; hence, textual criticism is known as "lower criticism"—though these two hierarchical terms, while instructive, are no longer widely used. "Higher criticism" encompasses all other forms of biblical criticism, interpretation, and exegesis; during the modern period, it culminated in source, form, and redaction criticism and has mushroomed in recent decades as several new modes of criticism and interpretation have emerged, notably perhaps the various rhetorical, literary, ideological, and sociological methodologies employed to illuminate and to interact with the New Testament texts.

This accumulation of interpretive methodologies over the past century and a half has increasingly pushed textual criticism into the background of the exegesis process when, in fact, no hermeneutical procedure that takes seriously the ancient New Testament text can logically or legitimately do so. Part of this eclipse is due to the "information explosion," which has pushed scholars constantly toward greater specialization and, in turn, toward an increasing neglect of specializations not their own, notably ones as complex as textual criticism. As a result, only a minority of commentators on New Testament writings, for example, *independently* treat text-critical issues in the texts they interpret; rather—if they explore textual variations at all—many rely on the data provided and even the decisions made for them by the popular critical hand-editions of the Greek New Testament, the so-called Nestle-Aland Greek text (27th ed., 1993) and that of the United Bible Societies (4th ed., 1993), both with the same text but with varying apparatuses of variant readings. In addition to these excellent resources, exegetes commonly—and wisely—will use the companion volume to the latter text, *A Textual Commentary on the Greek*

New Testament,[1] which provides text-critical analyses of some 2,050
46 sets of variation units in the New Testament that are of both textual and exegetical significance, providing reasons for the adoption or rejection of variant readings.

That this is a realistic assessment of the use—or non-use—of textual criticism in New Testament scholarship is confirmed by a perusal of the hundreds upon hundreds of books and articles that appear annually on myriad topics across the vast range of New Testament studies, including investigations of the historical Jesus, treatments of biblical theology, literary and sociological studies, and even commentaries, to mention only a few broad categories. How many of these, after all, move beyond the text presented in Nestle-Aland and the UBS*GNT*? How many pause to consider the options and probabilities concerning what the author most likely wrote or, as we usually say, the most likely "original" text of passages under study? How many stop to ask how the other readings in a given variation unit might disclose different socio-cultural contexts and various ancient interpretations of that text?

Text-critical specialists will have mixed feelings about the shortcuts and compromises made by many exegetes. On the one hand, they will applaud at every turn the utilization of textual variants in interpreting crucial passages, while, on the other, lamenting the pandemic lack of serious engagement with the theory and principles of New Testament textual criticism and the consequent infrequence of independent text-critical judgments. Textual critics, of course, are well aware that neither they nor those who emphasize one or another of the numerous subspecialties in New Testament criticism can master everything, and they will continue to offer the requisite handbooks with their principles and examples, all the while hoping to draw more exegetes into those substantive text-critical discussions that would not only enlighten but enliven their interpretive endeavors.

This may appear to be a highly arrogant view of the current situation—a view of textual criticism, on the one hand, as a basic discipline that ideally all exegetes should master, yet, on the other hand, as an esoteric field that only an elite few will be willing or able to

[1] Bruce M. Metzger (ed.), *A Textual Commentary on the Greek New Testament: A Companion Volume to the United Bible Societies' Greek New Testament (Fourth Revised Edition)* (2nd ed.; Stuttgart: Deutsche Bibelgesellschaft/United Bible Societies, 1994).

comprehend, let alone practice! In adopting such a stance, are not textual critics isolating themselves and, in the process, encouraging exegetes to ignore them? While discussing merits and demerits of basic text-critical theory and debating the validity of criteria for determining the priority of readings, should textual critics not be more attentive to the practical needs of exegetes? Should they not be more eager to be servants of exegesis by providing, for example, compendia of predigested decisions on hundreds of variation units?

A quick example may suggest an answer. Mark's opening words 47
as usually given, "The beginning of the gospel of Jesus Christ, the Son of God," veil a rather evenly divided textual tradition regarding these divine titles. On one hand, Codex Sinaiticus (א) and others have the full phrase, "Jesus Christ, Son of God," while Codices Vaticanus (B), Bezae (D), and Washingtonianus (W), and other witnesses, have only "Jesus Christ." A decision made solely on the basis of manuscript evidence (external evidence) would have to cope with the unsettling fact that the two manuscripts generally deemed "best," א and B, go their separate ways in this instance. With closely divided manuscript evidence, however, the textual critic would move immediately to internal evidence (evidence from the transcriptional process—how scribes worked—and from the immediate and larger context of the variation unit). Assessing rudimentary transcriptional evidence likely would support the shorter reading in this case ("Jesus Christ" without "Son of God"), for Christian scribes, especially when encountering divine names, would be more likely to add the common words, "Son of God," to an existing "Jesus Christ" than to remove the former phrase if it were in the manuscript being copied. But the larger issue is context—here perhaps the *entire* Gospel of Mark! Are the words "Son of God" likely to have been part of the author's original text because Jesus as "Son of God" or Jesus' sonship is a major or even a crucial theme of the Gospel? If so, to rule it out by various other text-critical criteria might be to remove from the opening sentence the author's dramatic announcement of a major theme for the entire work that follows. Naturally, whether "Son of God" serves Mark's Gospel in this way is a question for exegetes to answer, and indeed they have answered it both ways.

The point, however, is that a compendium approach to textual criticism—helpful as the *Textual Commentary*, for example, might be—is not always adequate. Just as exegesis often involves and needs textual criticism, so textual criticism often involves and needs exegesis.

Decisions frequently cannot be made merely on external evidence, or by using internal criteria such as preference for the harder reading (since scribes tend to smooth out difficulties), or even by assessing the immediate context; rather, larger issues of conformity of a variant to the writing's entire ideological context or to the author's distinctive style or theology, or a reading's conformity to extrinsic heterodox or orthodox doctrinal views must be taken into account.

Another complicating, though nonetheless positive, aspect of the
48 overlap of textual criticism and exegesis that should not be overlooked is that competing readings—even those judged not the most likely original—often have the power to illuminate a text by disclosing alternative "readings" or interpretations of that text in the early church. These interpretations (when it can be assumed that they were conscious alterations) may reflect either the solo view of a thinking scribe or the convictions of a local or regional church or of an entire doctrinal tradition. Thus, textual criticism, often conceived as having a singular goal of establishing the "original" text, is in reality a discipline with broader goals, including the display of the variety of opinions and convictions that enlivened the life of the church throughout its early history. Exegetes, therefore, should never consider the New Testament text to be static or inert, for it was and remains a *living text* that, in turn, reveals the living church that transmitted it.[2]

Two additional examples of the intersection of exegesis and textual criticism involve a contemporary issue in much of Christianity. First, the paragraph comprising 1 Cor. 14:34–35 contains the vexing words, "Women should be silent in the churches," followed by a further statement of submission to husbands and a reinforcement of silence by asserting that "it is shameful for a woman to speak in church." Exegetes for generations have observed the difficulties in defending these verses as consistent with Paul's preceding and following arguments, giving rise to a variety of interpretations that attempt, on the one hand, to justify its place in this context and, on

---

[2] [This is vividly exemplified in a book appearing after the present article was written: David C. Parker, *The Living Text of the Gospels* (Cambridge: Cambridge University Press, 1997). I have displayed his striking illustrations in Epp, "The Multivalence of the Term 'Original Text' in New Testament Textual Criticism," *Harvard Theological Review* 92 (1999) 264–66; idem, "The Oxyrhynchus New Testament Papyri: 'Not without honor except in their hometown'?" *JBL* 123 (2004) 7–8.]

the other, to dismiss it as an interpolation into the text—whether by Paul but not belonging here or not Pauline at all. Can textual criticism contribute to a solution?

At first glance, the expected answer might be negative, for these two verses are present in all extant textual witnesses—no divided tradition here and no textual variants in the usual sense. However, a group of Greek and Latin manuscripts including Codex Claromontanus—D^{Paul}—(the so-called "Western" manuscripts—but better, the D-text) place the two verses after v. 40, that is, between the conclusion of a lengthy, connected argument by Paul and the abrupt beginning of a new discussion (chap. 15). Already this dislocation in the textual tradition suggests some uncertainty among scribes about the appropriate place for vv. 34–35 in 1 Corinthians. Moreover, recent investigation shows that vv. 34–35 are invariably treated as a separate paragraph—and not connected with v. 33b—in early Greek manuscripts (including P46, B, ℵ, A, D^{Paul}, 33). More telling,
in the Latin Codex Fuldensis (F, 547 C.E.), which contains vv. 34–35 49
in its usual place, the original scribe placed a siglum after v. 33 that referred the reader to a portion of text in the bottom margin, namely, vv. 36–40 recopied *in toto*. This almost certainly indicates that vv. 34–35 are to be omitted; the scribe (or more likely Bishop Victor, whom we know to have supervised the copying of Fuldensis) had evidence or was otherwise convinced that these verses were not part of the 1 Corinthians text. More significant still, the original scribe of perhaps our most important uncial manuscript, Codex Vaticanus (B, 4th century), used distinctive sigla to mark vv. 34–35 as a known textual problem, strongly supporting the view that vv. 34–35 is an interpolation and may not be Pauline at all.[3] In this striking example, we observe exegesis alerting us to a text-critical problem and textual criticism, in turn, assisting in a solution to the exegetical difficulty.

[3] See Philip B. Payne, "Fuldensis, Sigla for Variants in Vaticanus, and 1 Cor 14.34–5," *NTS* 41 (1995), pp. 240–62; [now also P. B. Payne and Paul Canart, "The Originality of Text-Critical Symbols in Codex Vaticanus," *NovT* 42 (2000) 105–13]. On the whole issue, see also Gordon D. Fee, *The First Epistle to the Corinthians* (NICNT; Grand Rapids, MI: Eerdmans, 1987) 699–708; Jacobus H. Petzer, "Reconsidering the Silent Women of Corinth—A Note on 1 Corinthians 14:34–35," *Theologia Evangelica* 26 (1993) 132–38. [For a full treatment, see now E. J. Epp, "Text-Critical, Exegetical, and Socio-Cultural Factors Affecting the Junia/Junias Variation in Romans 16,7," *Textual Criticism and Exegesis: Festschrift J. Delobel* (BETL, 161; ed. A. Denaux; Leuven: Leuven University Press/Peeters, 2002) 237–42.]

A second example involves the mere difference of a Greek accent in a proper name in Rom. 16:7, which—depending on the decisions made—could offer the one text in which Paul used the word "apostle" to describe a woman. Again there are both text-critical and exegetical complications. Paul here requests his readers to "Greet Andronicus and 'IOYNIAN [accusative case] . . .; they are prominent among the apostles." The accusative singular form 'IOYNIAN can be either 'Ιουνιᾶν (masculine, "Junias," a hypothetical shortened form of Junianus[4] or 'Ιουνίαν (feminine, "Junia"). Accents, however, seldom occur before the seventh century in New Testament manuscripts, but the second correctors (in the sixth/seventh and ninth centuries, respectively) of two major manuscripts, B [fourth century] and D^{Paul} [sixth century], accent the word as feminine, as do many of the later Greek manuscripts, and the Sahidic Coptic[5] and Chrysostom also understand it as feminine. Indeed, the latter (ca. 390 C.E.) comments on Junia, "How great the wisdom of this woman that she was even deemed worthy of the apostles' title."[6]

Normal text-critical procedure, such as relying heavily on the earliest manuscripts, is not particularly helpful here because of their lack of accents, and Chrysostom's statement becomes the earliest useful witness, affording confirmation to the feminine form that appears as soon as accents come into play.

Contemporary social usage and Greek grammar, however, must also be applied in this case: "Junias" as a male name is nowhere to be found, but "Junia" as a Latin woman's name is common in Roman literature and occurs more than 250 times in inscriptions in Rome alone.[7] Grammatically, the rendering, "they are prominent among the apostles" [i.e., "as apostles"], is preferable to "they are esteemed *by* the apostles" [but are not apostles].[8]

[4] But see Richard S. Cervin, "A Note regarding the Name 'Junia(s)' in Romans 16.7," *NTS* 40 (1994) 468–70.

[5] See U. K. Pilsch, "Die Apostelin Junia: Das exegetische Problem in Röm 16.7 im Licht von Nestle-Aland^{27} und der sahidischen Überlieferung," *NTS* 42 (1996) 477–78.

[6] *In ep. ad Romanos* 31.2 (PG 60:669–670).

[7] Metzger, *Textual Commentary*, 475; Cervin, "Note regarding the Name 'Junia(s),'" 466–69.

[8] See Cervin, ibid., 470; cf. Joseph A. Fitzmyer, *Romans* (AB 33; New York: Doubleday, 1993) 739–40.

Though evidence for apostleship of women in the early church is not restricted to this passage, the term "apostle" applied to a woman is found only here. Elsewhere in the same chapter (16:6, 12), four women are said to have "worked very hard" (κοπιάω), a term Paul uses of his own apostolic ministry (1 Cor. 4:12; 15:10; Gal. 4:11; Phil. 2:16) and that of others (1 Cor. 16:15–16; 1 Thess. 5:12), and other women are called Paul's "coworkers" (Rom. 16:3; Phil. 4:2–3) or "deacon" (*NRSV*, "minister," Rom. 16:1)[9] Exegetes must determine what these expressions imply in their various contexts, but the female apostle Junia seems well established through a combination of textual criticism, contemporary Roman evidence, Greek grammar, and plausibly complementary passages in Paul.[10]

These various examples illustrate the broad scope and extensive relevance of New Testament textual criticism to interpretation, but especially its formidable complexity. Indeed, this complexity of the text-critical enterprise is a prominent reason (1) why textual critics resist the prepackaging and isolation of most text-critical decisions, why they insist that the panoply of text-critical principles be brought to bear on each case, and why many textual "decisions" remain open to new evidence, new methods, and new exegetical interpretations—and also (2) why interpreters tend to neglect textual criticism. This scholarly discipline, sometimes viewed as merely mechanical and perfunctory, in reality has both (1) objective, empirical, and "scientific," aspects (quantitative measurement of manuscript relationships, for instance) and (2) subjective and qualitative aspects—aspects of "art" (such as balancing the probabilities when manuscript evidence is evenly divided or when a reading in a variation unit is both the smoother and yet conforms to the author's style [see further below]). In actuality, therefore, the lengthy history of text-critical studies to date has yielded few if any definitive methods or principles that function independently—much less automatically—
and only occasionally provides "right" or "wrong" answers in indi- 51
vidual cases. Debate is lively between rival brands of eclecticism, on

[9] See David M. Scholer, "Paul's Women Coworkers in Ministry," *Theology, News and Notes* (Pasadena, CA: Fuller Theological Seminary) 42 (no. 1, March, 1995) 20–22.

[10] [See now the comprehensive treatment of the entire Junia matter in Epp, "Text-Critical, Exegetical, and Socio-Cultural Factors Affecting the Junia/Junias Variation in Romans 16,7," 242–91.]

the notions of "best" manuscripts and "best" groups of manuscripts, and on the date and even existence of various major text-types. In fact, text-critics have yet to reach agreement on two very basic matters: the reconstruction of the history of the New Testament text—showing its chronological evolution in relation to extant manuscripts—and the methods by which to do so. If that were not enough, research surprises us with increased complexity when it can be demonstrated—as has been done so well recently—that ancient textual alterations often issued from the will to support not only *heterodox* teaching (a view well established a century ago) but also *orthodox* theology.[11]

Thus, rather than merely dispensing simple or simplified principles or operating with "cut-and-dried" methods—luxuries the discipline does not enjoy—New Testament textual criticism must attempt (1) to determine the most likely original reading through an eclectic (and thereby complex) methodology, one that utilizes an array of criteria that include both objective and subjective—and at times conflicting—guidelines, and (2) to elicit from variants their scribal or community motivations and their socio-cultural contexts in an effort to illuminate the thought and life of the church.

This is not to say, however, that New Testament textual criticism is paralyzed and unable to function, or incapable of making useful decisions that will facilitate the exegete's work. It only means that it is often harder than might have been expected and that results are less definitive than might have been wished—and also that a high degree of sophistication in the discipline and a fair measure of courage to apply it are required.

II. The Nature and Major Issues of New Testament Textual Criticism

In view of these introductory remarks, New Testament textual criticism may be defined as the science and art of assessing the trans-

[11] For numerous examples, see Bart D. Ehrman, *The Orthodox Corruption of Scripture: The Effect of Early Christological Controversies on the Text of the New Testament* (New York/Oxford: Oxford University Press, 1993); idem, "New Testament Manuscripts and Social History," *The Text of the New Testament in Contemporary Research: Essays on the* Status Quaestionis (eds. B. D. Ehrman and M. W. Holmes; SD 46; Grand Rapids, MI: Eerdmans, 1995) 361–79.

mission of the New Testament text by (1) evaluating its variations, alterations, and distortions, and then attempting its restoration—its earliest recoverable forms—and (2) seeking to place variants within the history and culture of the early church, both to determine the age, meaning, and motivation of variants and to extract from them some knowledge of the development and character of early Christian theology, ecclesiology, and culture. 52

The requirements for pursuing these goals are essentially twofold: (1) familiarity with the textual transmission process, including the full range of scribal habits and other phenomena of textual variation that influenced it, and (2) knowledge both of the Greek manuscripts that preserve and transmit to us the New Testament text-forms and also of the early versions that delivered these Christian writings to non-Greek speaking areas. Meeting the first prerequisite will require, in turn, the formulation of criteria for isolating the most likely original readings, while acquaintance with the thousands of manuscripts will require grouping them in some fashion according to shared characteristics. In most of these aspects, New Testament textual criticism is no different from that applied to other ancient literature, but in some ways it presents a special case.

It is well known that numerous writings of classical Greek and Latin authors are preserved in only a small number of manuscripts—often the earliest ones dating some centuries later than the origin of the documents—and that frequently these relatively few textual witnesses quite conveniently can be employed to construct stemmata (or family trees) of the manuscripts, thereby isolating the earliest forms of the text and facilitating the construction of critical editions—though often with the help of considerable textual emendation. However, in the case of the New Testament—or even its individual parts—a different situation dictates a different solution. The difference arises chiefly from the number and age of the extant manuscripts of the New Testament: Greek manuscripts alone run between 5,000 and 5,500 in number; at least one fragment (P52) dates as early as one generation after the date of composition, while others, including a fair number extensive in their coverage of text, date from around 200 and into the third century (e.g., P45, P46, P66, P75). These earliest manuscripts, dating up to and around the turn of the third/fourth centuries, still number about sixty, with about 250 more up to the ninth century, and then the manuscripts burgeon in number so that nearly 4,800 date from the ninth through the sixteenth centuries. Versional manuscripts are also numerous, especially Latin, with about fifty early ones (Old Latin) and more than 10,000 of the Vulgate revision.

This situation—the vast breadth and depth of manuscript materials—affords us both opportunities and difficulties. An opportunity arises from the very mass of extant witnesses, for we may reasonably assume that somewhere among the estimated 300,000 variant
53 readings reside virtually all of the original readings. Thus, the necessity for conjectural emendation is almost entirely ruled out.[12] Another advantage in the richness of variation is the greater ease with which we should be able to trace out the development and history of the text and also the ideological and doctrinal variants that illumine for us the history of the church. On the other hand, the inherent negatives are obvious enough: the sheer quantity of witnesses and of textual variants vastly complicates the process of determining the most likely original text. For one thing, because of extensive textual mixture among the extant manuscripts, the genealogical method (forming stemmata) is not a viable procedure; hence, it is rarely used in New Testament criticism—except, importantly, at the level of an *individual variation unit*, where an attempt is made to identify the one reading in each circumscribed group of variants that best explains the rise of all the others.

What is required (as earlier intimated) is, first, to group manuscripts that share similar textual complexions and to establish time-frames for each group. Smaller groups are called families and the largest groups are called text-types, though the process is not as easy as it sounds. In simplest terms, however, if early groupings can be isolated, it is more likely that their readings stand closer, not only in time but also in quality, to those of the original compositions.[13] Second, what used to be called "canons of criticism," that is, criteria for determining the earliest or most likely original readings, need to be (and currently are being) refined so that they can be applied

[12] But see Joël Delobel, "Textual Criticism and Exegesis: Siamese Twins?" *New Testament Textual Criticism, Exegesis, and Early Church History: A Discussion of Methods* (eds. B. Aland and J. Delobel; CBET 7; Kampen: Kok Pharos, 1994) 98–117; and cf. Michael W. Holmes, "Reasoned Eclecticism in New Testament Textual Criticism," in Ehrman and Holmes (eds.), *Text of the New Testament in Contemporary Research*, 347–49.

[13] See further under "External Evidence," below.

to individual variant units with more confident results. The massive quantity of variant readings—often with several in an individual variation unit—will on numerous occasions, however, yield closely competitive variants, each of which will command support from one or more criteria that, in a simpler situation, would accredit that particular variant as *the one* most likely original. But now we may have two or three readings, each one meeting different criteria, so that more than one possesses a plausible claim to originality. For instance, Luke 10:41–42 reads (*NRSV*):

> Martha, Martha, you are worried and distracted by many things; there is need of only one thing. Mary has chosen the better part, which will not be taken away from her.

What words of Jesus to Martha did the author of Luke most likely write? Four basic readings survive: (1) The shortest reading (in the
so-called "Western" textual tradition) omits everything between 54
"Martha" and "Mary." (2) The second (found in one Greek manuscript and some early versions) has "Martha, Martha, a few things are needed. . . ." This, in the context, is the most difficult reading. (3) The third, "one thing is needed" (found in two very early papyri and numerous other witnesses), is adopted in the *NRSV* above and selected by several modern critical editions because it has often been judged as best explaining the other variants and hence must have preceded them. (4) However, the fourth reading, "a few things are needed, or only one" (found in two prominent codices, ℵ and B), is also seen as capable of explaining all the others.

So, at first glance, we have a shortest reading, meeting a longstanding criterion of authenticity [but see below]; a most difficult reading, meeting another criterion suggesting authenticity; and two readings thought capable of explaining the others. Where does one turn? In this case, a fuller analysis shows that reading number 1 most likely involves an accidental omission that leaves little sense in the passage, so it drops out of contention. (The "shorter reading" criterion has recently been questioned, though it never was accorded authority when an accidental omission could be argued.) Externally, reading number 2 is very weakly attested and likely represents a late corruption of either reading 3 or 4—both of which, by the way, are attested within and outside of Egypt at an early date. The decision rests, then, on whether reading 3 arose from 4 or vice versa, a decision that, in turn, rests on judgments about transcriptional probabilities (what would a scribe most likely write?), on Lucan grammatical usage, and on the degree of sense in the context—an exegetical consideration. Taking these criteria into account, a case can be made that reading 4 is the more difficult of the two yet makes sense and that reading 3, though the shorter, can plausibly have been derived from 4. Hence, reading 4 may best explain the rise of all the others.[14]

New Testament textual critics, then, have to cope with complexity and conflict—and no easy answers—at almost every turn. Yet, they rejoice in the embarrassment of manuscript riches and much prefer that—with all of the complicating factors—to the situation in which their classical colleagues (or those in Mishnah and Talmud studies) find themselves.

55 III. The Transmission of the New Testament Text and Text-Critical Practice

It is clear, however, that neither the grouping of manuscripts nor the clarification of criteria for assessing variants can be accomplished apart from a grasp of the process by which the New Testament text has been transmitted to us. Hence, textual critics—and exegetes—need to rehearse that story of transmission, understand its inner dynamics, and "get the feel" of it in its ancient context. To do so requires acquaintance with the manuscripts themselves and knowledge of Greco-Roman writing materials, palaeography (or handwriting), scribal habits, scriptoria (where manuscripts were copied), ways that manuscripts were carried from place to place—and a bit of historical imagination.

Though we do not know much about early Christian worship services—except that they would likely follow the format of synagogue services (about which, in turn, all too little is known)—we may be sure that early Christian writings were preserved and transmitted in ways that facilitated their use in the worship and life of the church. Of course, as with all ancient literature, no autographs survive, but we may safely assume that in the early decades of Christianity a let-

[14] See Gordon D. Fee, "'One Thing is Needful'?" *New Testament Textual Criticism: Its Significance for Exegesis: Essays in Honour of Bruce M. Metzger* (ed. E. J. Epp and Gordon D. Fee. Oxford: Clarendon Press, 1981) 61–75.

ter of Paul or, shortly thereafter, portions of a gospel would be read in worship services and that, on occasion, visiting Christians would request copies and carry these hitherto unfamiliar documents to their own congregations. At other times, writings would be shared with other churches—sometimes at the request of the writer (cf. 1 Thess. 5:27; Col 4:16)—and we may assume that a natural way to do this would be to produce copies (papyrus was the normal writing material of the ancient world and at times it was relatively inexpensive). As New Testament manuscripts were used and reused—and sometimes wore out—they were copied and recopied, whether privately, in churches, or later in scriptoria (ca. 200 C.E. and after). Soon, we may imagine, some churches would possess several of these early Christian writings, and rudimentary collections of gospels and/or apostolic letters would emerge, some possibly by the conscious act, for example, of a devoted pupil of Paul. In ways such as these, the centuries-long process of Christian manuscript copying and circulation began, followed by copies of copies of copies, eventually leaving for us the rich, 5,000-plus legacy of widely divergent Greek manuscripts, plus the thousands of versional manuscripts and quotations of New Testament passages in patristic writings.

Beyond this sort of reasonable historical imagination (backed by 56
fragments of evidence), we know precious little about the beginning stages of transmission, though the earliest New Testament manuscripts (as well as Old Testament Scriptures copied for Christian use) were in codex form, that is, our book form as opposed to the scrolls that functioned as the format for Jewish and secular literature prior to Christianity. If Christians did not invent the codex—a debated issue—they at least capitalized upon this recently invented medium as a more convenient and space-saving format for the preservation and circulation of their writings, thereby enhancing the transmission process.

In this process, however, numerous early manuscripts were poorly preserved and now are highly fragmentary—often a single leaf or only a few leaves remain—and very often they contain only a small portion of a single book. Actually, two-thirds of the papyri and nearly one-third of the majuscule manuscripts are preserved in only one or two leaves. Nearly all of the very early, more extensive manuscripts (such as P45, P46, P72, P75—but not P66) contain more than one writing. It is significant, however, that, among the forty-eight earliest manuscripts, four of those that contain no more than two leaves nonetheless contain portions of two New Testament books (P30, P53, P92, and 0171). This opens the possibility—not yet subject to proof—that many, perhaps very many, of the fragmentary papyri originally comprised multiple writings, for when we move away from the third/fourth century, some sixty extant codices contain the entire New Testament and many other manuscripts demonstrate that early Christian writings circulated in certain quite regular combinations rather than individually. Most often, for example, the four gospels circulated together in a single codex (as in the third century P45), as did the Pauline letters (see the very early P46), though Acts might join either group (as in P45); or Acts and the General Epistles might form another group (as in P74)—and there were other combinations. (These conventions in the circulation of groups of early Christian writings, as well as the contents of manuscripts and the sequence of books in them, have implications, of course, for the lengthy process by which the New Testament canon was formed.[15])

How did documents actually move about in the Greco-Roman world? The New Testament letters confirm what is abundantly evident from many hundreds of private papyrus letters preserved in Egypt, that letter writers frequently utilized secretaries to write for
57 them and then used the informal "mail service" to secure delivery to their addressees. The latter typically consisted in finding someone sailing up the river or traveling the Roman roads to the destination of one's letter. This process is abundantly illustrated in the everyday Egyptian papyri, but also in the New Testament letters: Paul in his own hand, for example, adds his "greeting" to letters otherwise written by amanuenses (1 Cor. 16:21; 2 Thess. 3:17; Phlm. 19; cf. Gal. 6:11), and in Rom. 16:22 the amanuensis refers to himself—"Tertius." And presumably (according to Phlm19) Onesimus carried Paul's letter to Philemon; Silvanus carried 1 Peter (5:12); and possibly Phoebe was the carrier for Romans (16:1) and Titus (plus two "brothers") for 2 Corinthians (8:16–24). Other early Christian writers reflect the same practices: Burrhus carried Ignatius, *Philadelphians*, and Crescens Polycarp's *Philippians*.

More significant for the transmission of the New Testament, however, is the speed with which private letters (and other documents)

[15] [See now Epp, "Issues in the Interrelation of New Testament Textual Criticism and Canon," *The Canon Debate: On the Origins and Formation of the Bible* (ed. Lee M. McDonald and James A. Sanders; Peabody, Mass.: Hendrickson, 2002) 485–508.]

traveled in the Greco-Roman world. It can now be documented from extant papyrus letters that show both their date of writing (a customary feature) and their docketed date of receipt (much less commonly done) that letters traveled, for example, 800 miles from Asia Minor to Alexandria in two months; from Transjordan to Alexandria, about 350 miles, in thirty-six days; from Philadelphia to Syria, some 400 miles, in fourteen days; 150 miles from Alexandria to Philadelphia in four days and another in seven days; from Alexandria to another Delta city in nineteen days; and from Memphis to Alexandria, about 125 miles, in three weeks. This casual but prompt transfer of letters functioned both in the Hellenistic and Roman periods and operated not only within Egypt (between the Delta, the Fayum, and upper Egypt), but also between Egypt and places far removed, such as Ostia in Italy, Cilicia in Asia Minor, Sidon in Syria, and Arabia (taking some actual examples in addition to those cited above).[16]

From data of this kind we can draw important conclusions about the transmission of the early Christian writings and the kinds of text they contained. First, wherever they might have originated in the broad Mediterranean region, the writings that were to form the New Testament could very rapidly have made their way to any other part of the Roman world, and—more significant—this could have been accomplished in a matter of days, weeks, or a few months. Indeed, it is no longer necessary to assume a long interval of years between the time a New Testament letter or gospel was written and its appear- 58
ance in other places—even far-off places. The Gospel of John, extant in several very early manuscripts, is a good example; wherever it may been written, its text (whether in a form like that now in P52 or P66 or P75—all, of course, Egyptian papyri) could have reached Egypt quickly. If such a text were then modified during Christian use there, those "revisions," again, could rapidly be transported to another part of the Christian world anywhere in the Roman Empire. In view of this situation, it must now be granted that various forms of text in the early Christian world could not have been confined to one region for any length of time in any single form; or, to put

[16] For the data and full discussion, see E. J. Epp, "New Testament Papyrus Manuscripts and Letter Carrying in Greco-Roman Times," *The Future of Early Christianity: Essays in Honor of Helmut Koester* (ed. B. A. Pearson, in collaboration with A. T. Kraabel, G. W. E. Nickelsburg, and N. R. Petersen; Minneapolis, MN: Fortress, 1991) 35–56.

it more positively, early Christian writings, regardless of their place of origin, could very quickly move to all other Christian areas, burdened or blessed with all of the unintended and intended or conscious alterations that accumulated during their active use in a vibrant church.

Second, as a consequence of the quick-paced intellectual commerce demonstrable in the Mediterranean area (but especially to and from Egypt), we may posit the reasonable assertion—though one that cannot yet or easily be proved—that the various textual complexions evident in our very earliest manuscripts, namely, the Egyptian papyri, very possibly and quite plausibly represent texts from that *entire Mediterranean region* (including, of course, forms of text that might have originated in Egypt itself). Thus, in contrast to the common view that the papyri represent only the text of provincial Egypt, it is much more likely that they represent an extensive range, if not the full textual spectrum, of earliest Christianity.[17]

This in many ways is an enlightened and enlightening view of the transmission of the New Testament writings in the period of earliest Christianity, for it brings us into closer touch with the dynamic, vibrant activity within the emergent church that, in turn, was situated in a real Greco-Roman life-setting that was equally vigorous and robust in its intellectual commerce. We can well imagine the excitement of discovery when Christians of different localities encountered new apostolic letters or gospels, whether personally when visiting another church or through private exchange of letters and documents. We can imagine the strength and comfort that arose from knowledge that others, near and far, held the same spiritual convictions and doctrinal beliefs and were eager to share the docu-
59 ments in their possession that embodied and expressed those convictions. We can imagine the justifiable pride that congregations would develop as they acquired increasing numbers of these documents—which they would be quick to test by reading from them in services and utilizing them in their teaching, evangelism, and defense.

[17] On the preceding several paragraphs, in addition to ibid., 43–56, see Epp, "The Significance of the Papyri for Determining the Nature of the New Testament Text in the Second Century: A Dynamic View of Textual Criticism," *Gospel Traditions in the Second Century* (ed. William L. Petersen; Studies in Christianity and Judaism in Antiquity, 3; Notre Dame, IN: University of Notre Dame Press, 1989) 71–83; idem, "The Papyrus Manuscripts of the New Testament," in Ehrman and Holmes (eds.), *Text of the New Testament in Contemporary Research*, 8–10.

This combination of data and scholarly speculation may stretch our minds in other ways. Virtually all the New Testament papyri issue from Egypt, but exact geographical locations of their use or even of their discovery elude us a great deal of the time. The town of Oxyrhynchus, however, yielded thirty-one of our current ninety-six different New Testament papyri; while fragmentary, they contain portions of fifteen of our twenty-seven books; and twenty-one of them date in the second, third, and early fourth centuries. What do these random discoveries from the rubbish heaps and ruined buildings of this district capital in Upper Egypt tell us about its Christian churches or the role of the Christian writings in those churches? We know from other papyri found there that this small city had twenty temples, a theater accommodating eight to twelve thousand people, and a Roman garrison in the second century. And the papyri attest the names of some 5,700 individual inhabitants between 30 B.C.E. and 96 C.E. Yet we know virtually nothing about Christianity there and very little about Christianity in Egypt in general at this time. Does the sizable horde of randomly surviving New Testament papyri indicate many Christians and/or several churches in Oxyrhynchus, or a significant collection or even a library of Christian documents, or that numerous copies were moving to and from Oxyrhynchus, or perhaps that it was a center of Christian scholarship or even text-critical activity (because we have evidence there of critical editing and annotation of Greco-Roman literary works)? These are tantalizing questions, but currently they do not have answers.[18] Yet, the mere raising of the questions in a real socio-historical context gives a "feel" for the transmission process of our New Testament text and provides agenda for further research.

We do, however, have better knowledge of the technical and mechanical aspects of the process—the nature of scribal activity in copying manuscripts.

[18] [I have tried to provide some answers in subsequent work: "The New Testament Papyri at Oxyrhynchus in Their Social and Intellectual Context," *Sayings of Jesus: Canonical and Non-Canonical. Essays in Honour of Tjitze Baarda* (eds. W. L. Petersen, J. S. Vos, and H. J. de Jonge; NovTSup 89; Leiden: Brill, 1997) 47–68; idem, "The Codex and Literacy in Early Christianity and at Oxyrhynchus: Issues Raised by Harry Y. Gamble's *Books and Readers in the Early Church*," *CRBR* 11 (1997) 15–37; but especially in "The Oxyrhynchus New Testament Papyri: 'Not without honor except in their hometown'?" *JBL* 123 (2004) 5–55.]

A. *The Role of Scribes in Textual Transmission*

Crucial in the whole New Testament transmission process prior to the invention of movable type in the mid-fifteenth century was the influence of the scribes or copyists, for, as they churned out copies
60 of New Testament writings, both their inadvertent errors and their quite conscious improvements (as they would view them) created the tens upon tens of thousands of textual variants that now present themselves to us for analysis and decision. Scribal "errors" (better: scribal alterations), however, must be seen in proper perspective because the copying of manuscripts by its very nature is a conservative process (in both senses of "conservative") and the overwhelming majority of copying was accurately accomplished. Nonetheless, the most attentive and dedicated scribe—even the slavish scribe—suffered inattentive moments and lapses of connection between eye or mind and hand. Subtle influences—parallel passages, especially in the Synoptic Gospels, or daily familiarity with liturgical forms of biblical passages—led scribes to conform the texts they were producing to those more familiar parallel forms that were fixed in their minds. A greater threat [if that is the appropriate word] to the transmission process, however, was the "thinking" scribe who felt compelled to assess the meaning or meaningfulness of the text being copied rather than merely to do the job; thus, some were bold enough to "correct" the text before them or to include extraneous material familiar to them from other contexts or manuscripts or even from the margins of manuscripts. Numerous variant readings arose in these ways, yet we should not miss noticing that this scribal activity is another vivid evidence that the New Testament text was a living text subject to the vicissitudes of existence—a living, breathing organism reflecting and reacting to its social and theological environment as it moved along in the stream of the vibrant Christian community of which it was a part.

Technically, scribal alterations customarily are placed under the two categories implied above. First, *unintentional scribal alterations* comprise what are often characterized as errors of the eye, of the ear (if copying by dictation), and of the memory or (unthinking) judgment, including (1) confusion of letters or letter-combinations having similar appearance (or sound); (2) mistaken word division (since uncial manuscripts, including the papyri, were written without spaces or punctuation); (3) misread abbreviations or contractions; (4) inter-

changes in the order of letters or words (metathesis); (5) substitution of a more familiar word for a less familiar one, or writing a synonym when the meaning but not the exact word is in the copyist's mind; (6) omission of one word when it occurred twice, or skipping material between two similar words or letter-groups (haplography); 61
(7) repetition of a letter, word, or passage when the eye returns to a place already copied (dittography); (8) careless spelling and failure to correct such errors; and (9) unconscious assimilation to similar wording in a parallel passage or lection (on occasion this may be intentional), or harmonization with wording in the immediate context.

Second, *intentional scribal alterations*, inevitably *well* intentioned, correct or otherwise improve the text in accordance with what the scribe believed to be its original (or intended) form or meaning—or even a meaning more relevant to the scribe's present ecclesiastical context or theological orientation. Thus, sometimes, though still with worthy motives from the scribe's standpoint, changes were made to promote a doctrinal or ideological view not in the text being copied, making the text say what the scribe "knew" it to mean.[19] These conscious alterations, to be sure, are usually subtle in nature and modest in scope; yet inevitably they will shape the transmission process more than do accidental alterations.

Intentional alterations include (1) changes in grammar, spelling (often proper names), and style; (2) conscious harmonization with parallel passages (often in the Synoptic Gospels, in Old Testament quotations, or in lectionaries)—motivated perhaps by the wish to present the "complete" text in a given context; (3) clarification of geographical or historical points (e.g., time or place; or authorship of Old Testament quotations); (4) conflation of differing readings in two or more manuscripts known to the copyist—again, to be complete; (5) addition of seemingly appropriate material (such as expanding "Jesus" to "Jesus Christ" or to the "Lord Jesus Christ"); and (6) theological or ideological alterations, often small changes in the interest of supporting accepted doctrine, especially issues of christology or Trinity, or the Virgin Birth, asceticism, etc., or longer additions such as found in manuscripts of the D-text or "Western" textual tradition, where anti-Judaic, antifeminist, pro-apostle, and other tendencies have been detected.

---

[19] The expression is from Ehrman, *The Orthodox Corruption of Scripture*, xii; 276.

B. *Internal Criteria*

Making textual decisions depends very directly on acquaintance with these scribal habits as they functioned in the copying process, for textual critics move from that knowledge to the formulation of *internal criteria* that will assist in distinguishing the most likely original reading among those in a given variation unit. The criteria in this category are labeled "internal" because they relate to factors or char-
62 acteristics *within* the text itself (as opposed to "external" criteria, which relate to the nature of manuscripts [e.g., date and provenance] as something "outside" or separate from the texts they enshrine). Text-critical criteria have evolved over nearly the whole history of Christianity, for rudimentary "rules" can be found as early as Origen in the third century, with their modern history beginning in the early eighteenth century.

Essentially, the criteria ask various questions of each variant reading in a variation unit: Can this variant account for the rise of all the others? Does this variant agree with the writer's literary style, or theology? Is this variant "harder," that is, rough or unrevised when compared with others in the unit? And so forth. Not all criteria will be relevant in all cases, so they are tested for relevance and the results compared. Not infrequently (as noted earlier) one variant will be supported as the most likely original by one or more of the criteria, while a competing variant is supported by other criteria, or one criterion may support a reading while another discredits it. (An example is Matt 6:33, where a reading that explains the others competes with one that conforms better to Matthew's style.) At the same time, not all criteria carry the same weight—and the validity of some is now under debate (notably numbers 2 and 6 below). So, after analysis, the decision will often have to be made on the basis of "the balance of probabilities" as we say. There is, however, general agreement on what Constantin Tischendorf noted long ago, that the first criterion below takes precedence over all the others—if it works in a given case.[20]

The criteria that follow are phrased so that, *if a criterion accurately describes a textual variant (other things being equal), that variant would have the presumption of being the most likely original.*

---

[20] For general discussion and references, see Epp, "The Eclectic Method in New Testament Textual Criticism: Solution or Symptom?" *HTR* 69 (1976) 211–57,

Criteria related to internal evidence

1. A variant's fitness to account for the origin, development, or presence of all other readings in the variation-unit. [Because such a variant logically must have preceded all others that can be shown to have evolved from it; K. Aland calls this the "local genealogical method."]
2. A variant's status as the shorter/shortest reading in the varia- 63
tion-unit. [Because scribes tend to expand the text rather than shorten it—though this is now debated.][21]
3. A variant's status as the harder/hardest reading in the variation-unit. [Because scribes tend to smooth or fix rough or difficult readings.]
4. A variant's conformity to the author's style and vocabulary. [Because the "original" reading is likely to follow the author's style as observed in the bulk of the writing.][22]
5. A variant's conformity to the author's theology or ideology. [Because the "original" reading is likely to display the same convictions or beliefs found in the bulk of the work. A scribe, however, might "correct" an author's statement to conform it more closely to that author's theology, thus altering what would have been a "harder" reading to a smoother reading).]
6. A variant's conformity to Koine (rather than Attic) Greek. [Because scribes show a tendency to shape the text being copied to the more elegant Attic Greek style.][23]

---

reprinted in E. J. Epp and G. D. Fee, *Studies in the Theory and Method of New Testament Textual Criticism* (SD 45; Grand Rapids, MI: Eerdmans, 1993) 141–73; Epp, "New Testament Textual Criticism," *ABD* 6.412–35. For example, see James R. Royse, "Scribal Habits in the Transmission of New Testament Texts," *The Critical Study of the Sacred Texts* (ed. Wendy Doniger O'Flaherty; Berkeley, CA: Berkeley Religious Studies Series, 1979) 154–55; idem, "Scribal Tendencies in the Transmission of the Text of the New Testament," in Ehrman and Holmes (eds.), *Text of the New Testament in Contemporary Research*, 239–52; [idem, *Scribal Habits in Early New Testament Papyri* (SD 47; Grand Rapids, MI: Eerdmans, 2005)].

[21] See J. R. Royse, "Scribal Tendencies," 242–43; 246–47. Thoroughgoing eclectics, such as J. Keith Elliott, are inclined to prefer the longer reading: Elliott, "Thoroughgoing Eclecticism in New Testament Textual Criticism," in Ehrman and Holmes (eds.), *Text of the New Testament in Contemporary Research*, 327–28.

[22] Challenged recently by Jacobus H. Petzer, "Author's Style and the Textual Criticism of the New Testament," *Neot* 24 (1990) 185–97.

[23] This canon, suggested by George D. Kilpatrick, "Atticism and the Text of the Greek New Testament, *Neutestamentliche Aufsätze: Festschrift für Prof. Josef Schmid zum 70. Geburtstag* (eds. J. Blinzler, O. Kuss, and F. Mussner; Regensburg: Pustet, 1963)

7. A variant's conformity to Semitic forms of expression. [Because the New Testament authors, being either Jewish or familiar with Septuagint/Greek Old Testament style, are likely to reflect such Semitic expressions in their writings.]
8. A variant's *lack* of conformity to parallel passages or to extraneous items in the context generally. [Because scribes tend, consciously or unconsciously, to shape the text being copied to familiar parallel passages in the Synoptic Gospels or to words or phrases just copied.]
9. A variant's *lack* of conformity to Old Testament passages. [Because scribes, who were familiar with the Jewish Bible, tend to shape their copying to the content of familiar passages.]
10. A variant's *lack* of conformity to liturgical forms and usages. [Because scribes tend to shape the text being copied to phraseology in the familiar liturgical expressions used in devotion and worship.]
11. A variant's *lack* of conformity to extrinsic theological, ideological, or other socio-historical contexts contemporary with and congenial to a text's scribe. [Because scribes unconsciously, but more likely consciously, could bring a text into conformity with their own or their group's doctrinal beliefs or with accepted socio-cultural conventions.[24] Naturally, difficulties exist in identifying both the contemporary context and the copyist's time frame and provenance.]

64 The judicious application of these criteria to competing readings within each variation unit fulfills a major part—but only one part—of the twofold methodological process for decision-making: treating

125–37, is now debated: see Gordon D. Fee, "Rigorous or Reasoned Eclecticism—Which?" *Studies in New Testament Language and Text: Essays in Honour of George D. Kilpatrick on the Occasion of His Sixty-fifth Birthday* (NovTSup 44; Leiden: Brill, 1976) 184–91, reprinted in Epp and Fee, *Studies in the Theory and Method*, 131–36; Carlo M. Martini, "Eclecticism and Atticism in the Textual Criticism of the Greek New Testament," *On Language, Culture, and Religion: In Honor of Eugene A. Nida* (eds. M. Black and W. A. Smalley; The Hague/Paris: Mouton, 1974) 149–56.

[24] See Ehrman, *The Orthodox Corruption of Scripture*, 1993; idem, "New Testament Manuscripts and Social History," 361–79; but contrast Frederik Wisse, "The Nature and Purpose of Redactional Changes in Early Christian Texts: The Canonical Gospels," *Gospel Traditions in the Second Century: Origins, Recensions, Text, and Transmission* (ed. W. L. Petersen; Christianity and Judaism in Antiquity, 3; Notre Dame, IN: University of Notre Dame Press, 1989) 39–53.

phenomena *within* the transmitted text. The *externals* of the matter, the manuscripts themselves as artifacts and each treated as an entity, a "whole," are the focus of the other major task.

C. *The Source Materials of Textual Transmission*

Just as "internal evidence" must be analyzed and evaluated by "internal criteria," so "external evidence" must be subjected to "external criteria." This involves scrutiny and assessment of the manuscripts, especially with respect to their age, their provenance, the nature of the text they contain, and the manuscript company that they keep: Is the text rough, or smooth and/or revised? Was it copied with care, corrected? Does it share distinctive readings with other manuscripts? Can it be placed into a family or text-type with other similar manuscripts? It is, of course, the scribal process just described that has brought us the Greek manuscripts, which now constitute the primary sources for establishing the New Testament text—along with the versional manuscripts, which, in their respective traditions, have experienced the same phenomena of shaping and alteration. Only a very brief survey of these primary sources can be provided here.

1. *Greek manuscripts of the New Testament*

Since the New Testament books were composed in Greek, the Greek manuscripts that preserve them are of primary importance. Unfortunately, some unnecessary complexity has crept into their classification: Greek manuscripts take two forms and are written in two kinds of handwriting on three different writing materials.

a. *Format*

The two basic forms are *continuous-text* manuscripts, which contain (or originally contained) at least one New Testament writing in continuous fashion from beginning to end, and *lectionary* manuscripts, which developed later and bring together those portions of Scripture appointed to be read in services. Lectionaries do not have the New Testament text in continuous form or in canonical order, but provide readings arranged either according to the church year or the calendar year. Often an introductory phrase (*incipit*) had to be added to adapt the selected portion to liturgical use (e.g., "Jesus said. . . ." or "In those days . . .").

b. *Palaeography*

As to handwriting, New Testament manuscripts were written in large,
unconnected letters (uncials or, better, majuscules) into the tenth cen-
65 tury, using both papyrus and parchment. Beginning in the ninth century, smaller (minuscule) and cursive ("running") or connected letters
were used, employing parchment and paper.

c. *Media*

With respect to writing materials, papyrus was used from the beginning into the eighth century, though nearly 75% of New Testament manuscripts were written on parchment (also called vellum) from the eighth century to the sixteenth; and paper was employed from the twelfth to the nineteenth centuries. Papyrus manuscripts are all continuous-text manuscripts (ninety-nine currently—some ninety-five different ones), while parchment was the vehicle for both continuous-texts (about 2,400) and lectionaries (about 1,700). Paper manuscripts, used for minuscules and lectionaries, total about 1,300.

d. *Current classifications*

To add to the confusion, textual critics ignore some of these categories (continuous-text, parchment, paper) and classify Greek manuscripts using four terms: *papyri*, *uncials* or *majuscules*, *minuscules*, and *lectionaries*. The papyri are in majuscule script (though not counted among the majuscules!), but have been placed in a separate category due to their early date and greater significance—and also for historical reasons: the first was not published until 1868. Reckoned in these categories, different "papyri" number ninety-five,[25] "majuscules" more than 260, "minuscules" more than 2,800, and "lectionaries" nearly 2,300. Papyri, majuscules, and minuscules are all continuous-text manuscripts, while lectionaries are written in both majuscule (numbering about 270) and minuscule hands and on both parchment and paper and date from the fourth century on (though only ten originated before the eighth century). To complicate matters further, some manuscripts are bilingual, mainly Greco-Coptic

[25] Depending on whether P4 is considered a part of the same manuscript as P64+P67; if not, there currently are ninety-six different papyri. K. Aland considers P4 a separate manuscript; T. C. Skeat joins it with P64 and P67: see Skeat, "The Oldest Manuscript of the Four Gospels?" *NTS* 43 (1997) 1–34. Also from the same manuscript are P11+P14 and also P33+P58, hence, ninety-nine minus three equals ninety-six different papyri; ninety-nine minus four accounts for ninety-five.

and Greco-Latin (including thirty-four majuscules), while others are palimpsests—manuscripts, usually parchment, reused by scraping off their original texts and writing on the newly prepared surface. There remain more than a hundred New Testament majuscules and lectionaries that have been overwritten in this fashion.

In summary, then, the term "papyri" includes only manuscripts written on papyrus; "majuscule" means only non-papyrus continuous-text manuscripts written in majuscule hand (and does not include the lectionaries so written); "minuscule" includes only continuous-text manuscripts written in cursive hand (and not the many lectionaries so written); and "lectionary" means portions for liturgical use regardless of the script or writing material employed. Although many statistics are cited above, the total number of different Greek
manuscripts of the New Testament is difficult to determine, since 66
some thirty papyri and majuscules are actually portions of others, as are numerous minuscules and lectionaries. Raw numbers for manuscripts in the latest lists total more than 5,660,[26] but when duplicates are noted and improperly classified lectionaries are subtracted the actual total is reduced by perhaps a few hundred, and the safest statement, therefore, is that more than 5,000 different Greek New Testament manuscripts are presently extant.

More important than script, writing materials, and format is the value placed on these Greek witnesses. Simply put, beginning in the early eighteenth century and decisively by mid-century, it was agreed that early manuscripts, though fewer, are generally to be preferred to the agreement of a larger number of later manuscripts; hence, the papyri and early majuscules assumed the position of prominence. Two groups stand out in importance: first, the forty-eight oldest manuscripts (forty-four papyri plus the four oldest uncials), all of which date up to the early 4th century; and, second, the great majuscule manuscripts of the fourth and fifth centuries, primarily Codices Sinaiticus (א, fourth), Alexandrinus (A, fifth), and Vaticanus (B, fourth), which contain all or most of the New Testament—but also Codex Bezae (D, around 400), containing the gospels and Acts, and Codex Washingtonianus (W, fifth), with the four gospels. The standard

---

[26] Kurt Aland, *Kurzgefasste Liste der griechischen Handschriften des Neuen Testaments* (2nd ed.; ANTF 1; Berlin: De Gruyter, 1994 [1st ed., 1963.]), which is the official list of New Testament manuscripts.

handbooks describe these manuscripts and many others of importance.[27]

As for the minuscules, about 80% of them are solid representatives of the Majority text (i.e., the Byzantine or Koine text), a text-type that developed in the fourth century and beyond and become the official ecclesiastical text of the Byzantine Church. While it may contain some early readings, it is a full or conflate text that collected numerous expansive and harmonizing readings and developed over time into a smooth and refined text that has been preserved in hundreds upon hundreds of mostly late manuscripts. However, about 10% of the minuscules are important in establishing the original text because they preserve elements of the early text.[28]

To a high degree, though not exclusively, the lectionaries also represent the Byzantine text-type and have not been considered of pri-
67 mary importance in establishing the most likely original text. Still, they are likely to have been preserved with a high degree of conservatism because of their official role in church services, doubtless carefully preserving texts much older than their own generally late dates; hence, they assist in tracing the transmission of the New Testament text and cannot be overlooked in seeking the most likely original.[29]

It took generations of fierce intellectual struggle to reach the conclusion that textual critics will want to devote their best efforts to readings and variants of the papyri and of the majuscules up to about the tenth century, for the presumption is that (1) the most likely original readings are apt to be found there, as are (2) the earliest and most important theological alterations to the text.[30] Always, however, the early versions and patristic citations must be checked in comparison with the Greek witnesses.

---

[27] See Bruce M. Metzger, *The Text of the New Testament: Its Transmission, Corruption, and Restoration* (3rd edition; New York/Oxford: Oxford University Press, 1992; 1st ed., 1964; 2nd ed., 1968); Kurt Aland and Barbara Aland, *The Text of the New Testament: An Introduction to the Critical Editions and to the Theory and Practice of Modern Textual Criticism* (2nd ed.; Grand Rapids, MI: Eerdmans, 1989). See also Ehrman and Holmes, (eds.), *Text of the New Testament in Contemporary Research*, the chapters on "The Greek Witnesses": Epp on papyri (3–21); D. C. Parker on majuscules (22–42); Barbara Aland and Klaus Wachtel on minuscules (43–60); and Carroll D. Osburn on lectionaries (61–74).

[28] Aland and Aland, *Text of the New Testament*, 128; Ehrman and Holmes, (eds.), *Text of the New Testament in Contemporary Research*, the chapter by Barbara Aland and Klaus Wachtel on the minuscules (43–60).

[29] Ibid., Carroll D. Osburn on lectionaries (61–74).

[30] For a summary of the long history that led to the triumph of the older manuscripts over the *textus receptus*, the "text received by all," see Epp, "Decision Points

2. *Versions of the New Testament*

Textual criticism would be much simpler—but also much impoverished—if the New Testament text were preserved only in Greek manuscripts. The earliest translations were the Latin, Syriac, and Coptic versions (though not necessarily in that order) and they retain the greatest importance. Though the actual origins and early histories are obscure, Latin, Syriac, and Coptic versions of the gospels and other parts of the New Testament were widely circulated in the third century—though the earliest extant manuscripts date only in the fourth, and late in that century for Latin and Syriac.

Difficulties arise in the use of these and other versions, for no language mechanically reproduces another. For instance, Syriac has no comparative or superlative; Syriac and Coptic have no case endings and the latter employs strict word order to show subject, object, indirect object, etc.; Gothic has no future form; and even Latin—generally a fine medium for translating Greek—cannot distinguish between the aorist and perfect tenses or the lack of a definite article. Such factors diminish the certainty of recognizing exactly the Greek text behind the versions. Also, some translations are secondary—that is, not translated directly from the Greek text, but from another translation. For example, the Armenian and Georgian possibly have been based on the Greek, but more likely the Armenian stems from Syriac and the Georgian either from Armenian or Syriac or both jointly. In spite of these hindrances, the ancient versions are significant in
the search for the most likely original Greek text, especially the three 68
earliest ones.

Actually, the earliest version of the gospels was not a straight-text translation but the famous *Diatessaron* of Tatian, most likely composed in Syriac about 172 C.E.—a harmony of the gospels with a complex history, since it influenced all further Syriac texts and then appears in Persian, Armenian, Arabic, and Georgian forms in the East and in Latin, Middle Dutch, Old French, Old and Middle German, Middle English, and Middle Italian in the West.[31]

---

in Past, Present, and Future New Testament Textual Criticism" [originally "Textual Criticism"] *The New Testament and Its Modern Interpreters* (eds. E. J. Epp and †G. W. MacRae, S.J.; Philadelphia: Fortress Press; Atlanta, GA: Scholars Press, 1989) 75–84, reprinted in Epp and Fee, *Studies in the Theory and Method*, 17–25; idem, "Textual Criticism: New Testament," *ABD* 6.427–30.

[31] See William L. Petersen, *Tatian's Diatessaron: Its Creation, Dissemination, Significance,*

The *Latin versions*, the largest tradition of any version, comprise more than 10,000 manuscripts. More than fifty of these (dating from the fourth to the thirteenth centuries) represent the Old Latin version, known from the earliest period in both North Africa and in Europe, and perhaps originating in North Africa in the late second century—though these matters are highly debated. The language of the Old Latin was rough and no unitary form of text existed; this was recognized already by Jerome, who was asked by Pope Damasus to prepare a revision of these diverse texts, and Jerome and others completed the task in 383. This "common" version was known as the Vulgate. Old Latin manuscripts continued to be used, however, long after Jerome's time, and these Old Latin texts are particularly useful in understanding the history of the Greek text of the New Testament.[32]

The *Syriac versions*, like the Latin, have an earlier phase followed by a "common" edition, the Peshitta (fifth century). Opinions on the version's origin vary from the end of the second century to the mid-fourth. For the gospels, Acts, and Pauline letters (the limits of the canon in the early Syriac church), an Old Syriac form survives in continuous-text manuscripts for the gospels (the Curetonian and the Sinaitic), but virtually only in patristic quotations for the Acts and Paul. Like the Latin, the Old Syriac is more useful in textual criticism than the Peshitta.[33]

The *Coptic versions* are known from third century Egypt in several dialects: Sahidic, the language of Upper (southern) Egypt; Bohairic from the Delta region of Lower (northern) Egypt; and lesser dialects, such as the Achmimic, sub-Achmimic, Middle Egyptian, and Fayyumic. The manuscripts are largely fragmentary or late, though a few extensive ones from the fourth-fifth centuries are extant for Matthew,
69 John, and Acts.[34]

and History in Scholarship (VCSup 25; Leiden: Brill, 1994); idem, "The Diatessaron of Tatian," in Ehrman and Holmes (eds.), *Text of the New Testament in Contemporary Research*, 77–96.

[32] See Jacobus Petzer, "The Latin Version of the New Testament," in Ehrman and Holmes (eds.), *Text of the New Testament in Contemporary Research*, 113–30.

[33] See Tjitze Baarda, "The Syriac Versions of the New Testament," in Ehrman and Holmes (eds.), *Text of the New Testament in Contemporary Research*, 97–112.

[34] See Frederic Wisse, "The Coptic Versions of the New Testament," in Ehrman and Holmes (eds.), *Text of the New Testament in Contemporary Research*, 131–41.

Other early versions of significance include the *Armenian*, probably made in the early fifth century; the *Georgian*, closely akin to the Armenian in origin and character and known from the fifth century; and the *Ethiopic*, perhaps stemming from the fourth or fifth century. Less important ancient versions are in *Arabic*, *Nubian*, and *Sodgian* (Middle Iranian) in the East and in *Gothic*, *Old Church Slavonic*, and *Old High German* in the West.[35]

3. *Patristic Quotations*

A final body of source material for establishing the text—and an important source if properly used—is comprised of New Testament quotations found in church authors of the first several centuries, not only in Greek, but in all relevant languages. They are of special significance for providing closely dated and geographically located textual readings—thus indicating the form that a reading or a text had at a rather definite place and time. Moreover, a comparison with similar readings in continuous-text manuscripts enables us to specify the antiquity of such readings in the textual tradition and, though less clearly, the possible provenance of the manuscripts containing them. Hence, patristic quotations are valuable evidence in individual cases and can be especially useful in establishing text-types.

Regrettably, however, the use of patristic quotations is not a simple matter, for the entire text-critical process must first be applied to each of these church writings to establish the text most likely written. Even the best critical editions, however, do not solve the further problems, for we need to determine whether the writer is (a) quoting the text of a New Testament book directly and exactly as it occurs in the text being used (a *citation*); or (b) paraphrasing the text by adapting it to the discussion or to the writer's own syntax while generally maintaining verbal identity with the text being used (an *adaptation*); or (c) merely alluding to a text's content without substantial verbal correspondence (an *allusion*). Only when these questions are answered and we know each writer's citing habits and the type of citation in each separate case can patristic quotations be used

[35] In Ehrman and Holmes (eds.), *Text of the New Testament in Contemporary Research*, see Rochus Zuurmond, "The Ethiopic Version of the New Testament," 142–56; Joseph M. Alexanian, "The Armenian Version of the New Testament," 157–72; and J. Neville Birdsall, "The Georgian Version of the New Testament," 173–87.

as evidence for the New Testament text. It is more likely, for example, that long quotations were copied from a manuscript than cited from memory, but it will be obvious how complex and difficult the entire matter is.[36]

70 D. *External Criteria*

From knowledge of these various sources arise two critical exercises: First, an attempt to reconstruct the history and evolution of the New Testament text. This would involve sorting the manuscripts according to their distinctive textual characteristics and then placing the groups or clusters of manuscripts into a chronological/historical continuum, which, in turn, would display temporally the various textual complexions inherent in each group. Families (such as Family 1 and Family 13) can occasionally be established, followed by attempts to identify the larger "text types," classically defined in quantitative terms as "a group of manuscripts that agree more than 70 percent of the time and is separated by a gap of about 10 percent from its neighbors."[37]

---

[36] Lists of patristic writings cited in critical editions can be found in Nestle-Aland^{27} and UBS*GNT*^{4}. On the whole subject, see Gordon D. Fee, "The Use of Greek Patristic Citations in New Testament Textual Criticism: The State of the Question," *ANRW* II/26/1.246–65, reprinted in Epp and Fee, *Studies in the Theory and Method*, 344–59; idem, "The Use of the Greek Fathers for New Testament Textual Criticism," in Ehrman and Holmes, *Text of the New Testament in Contemporary Research*, 191–207; Ehrman, "The Use and Significance of Patristic Evidence for New Testament Textual Criticism," *New Testament Textual Criticism, Exegesis, and Early Church History: A Discussion of Methods* (eds. B. Aland and J. Delobel; CBET 7; Kampen: Kok Pharos, 1994) 118–35; and Petersen, "What Text Can New Testament Textual Criticism Ultimately Reach?" in B. Aland and Delobel (eds.), *New Testament Textual Criticism, Exegesis, and Early Church History*, 136–52. On Latin and Syriac patristic writers, see J. Lionel North, "The Use of the Latin Fathers for New Testament Textual Criticism" (208–23) and Sebastian P. Brock, "The Use of the Syriac Fathers for New Testament Textual Criticism" (224–36) in Ehrman and Holmes, *Text of the New Testament in Contemporary Research*.

[37] E. C. Colwell (with Ernest W. Tune), "The Quantitative Relationships between MS. Text-types," *Biblical and Patristic Studies in Memory of Robert Pierce Casey* (eds. J. N. Birdsall and R. W. Thomson; Freiburg/Basel/New York: Herder, 1963) 29; reprinted as "Method in Establishing Quantitative Relationships between Text-Types of New Testament Manuscripts," in Colwell, *Studies in Methodology*, 59. See also Thomas C. Geer, "Analyzing and Categorizing New Testament Greek Manuscripts: Colwell Revisited," in Ehrman and Holmes, *Text of the New Testament in Contemporary Research*, 253–67. [See now the critique of Colwell's formula and other aspects of his method by Klaus Wachtel, "Colwell Revisited: Grouping New Testament Manuscripts," *The New Testament Text in Early Christianity: Proceedings of the Lille Colloquium, July 2000* (eds. C.-B. Amphoux and J. K. Elliott; HTB 6; Lausanne: Zèbre), 31–43.]

Though identifying text-types is a subject of current debate, all agree on the *Byzantine text type*, or Majority text, represented by Codex Alexandrinus (A, fifth century)—but only in the gospels—and by the vast majority of all our manuscripts; it originated in the fourth century and, with rare exceptions, does not *exclusively* contain readings with high claims to represent the original text, though it can help us trace points of theology and ecclesiology during its long reign as the official text of the church.[38]

Most agree that two early—and therefore highly significant—text types have their roots in the second century and are represented in identifiable groups or clusters: (1) the *Alexandrian text type* (or B-text, formerly called "Neutral"), exemplified predominantly in P75 (third century) and Codex Vaticanus (B, fourth century), along with P66 (ca. 200), Sinaiticus (א, fourth century), and later Codex L (eighth century), and (2) the *"Western" text type* (or D-text), represented by Codex Bezae (D, fifth century) and by the fragmentary P38, P48, P69, 0171, perhaps P29, and later (for Acts), 1739, 614, 383.

In addition, there exists an abortive text type, which we may call the C-text (formerly called the "Caesarean") that presents a textual complexion midway between the Alexandrian and "Western" (i.e., 71
midway between B and D, hence C-text). It is represented by P45 (third century) and Codex Washingtonianus (W, fifth century) in Mark, with origins certainly as early as P45, though its line does not move unambiguously beyond Codex W.

Textual critics, acting on their penchant for early manuscripts and groups, place the most weight on text types B, C, and D, though most recognize B and D as the earliest even if no definitive decision has been reachable as to which of the two had priority. Because of the high quality of text found in the B group in contrast to the often rough form in the D group, most critics favor B as the "best" kind of text and generally accord to it preeminent authority in textual decisions. Others, recognizing the internal criterion favoring the "harder" reading, suggest that D's rougher text implies greater antiquity—and the debate goes on. The 1950s discovery of P75 is often taken, however, as supporting the former view—the superior quality

---

[38] See Gordon D. Fee, "The Majority Text and the Original Text of the New Testament," in Epp and Fee, *Studies in the Theory and Method*, 183–208; Daniel B. Wallace, "The Majority Text Theory: History, Methods, and Critique," in Ehrman and Holmes, *Text of the New Testament in Contemporary Research*, 297–320.

of the B-text: Codex Vaticanus, because of its smooth, refined text, had often been viewed as a revised text, but the virtual identity of P75's text with that of Vaticanus, though P75 is perhaps a century and a half earlier, automatically ruled out a fourth century revision as the source of the B-text and pushed the existence of that high quality textual complexion back already to the beginning of the third century.

In summary and despite much uncertainty and debate, knowledge of the manuscripts permits fairly confident groupings, yielding earlier and later text types, with the presumption of originality *ceteris paribus* resting somewhere in the readings of the early groups, predominantly the B-text, but also the D-text and the P45–W combination (C-text). This rough reconstruction of the history of the New Testament text and its groupings leads to the second set of criteria for originality of readings, which we call "external criteria."

Again, these are phrased so that *if a criterion describes the situation of one reading within a variation unit, that reading may be reckoned the most likely original.*

Criteria related to external evidence

1. A variant's support by the earliest manuscripts, or by manuscripts assuredly preserving early texts. [Because historians of the text conclude that old manuscripts have been less subject to conflation and other scribal alterations.]

72 2. A variant's support by the "best quality" manuscripts. [Because manuscripts evidencing careful copying are less likely to have been subject to textual corruption or contamination, and because manuscripts that frequently and consistently offer readings accredited as most likely "original" thereby acquire a reputation of general high quality—but it must be recognized that internal criteria are utilized to reach the conclusion that certain manuscripts are "best."]

3. A variant's support by manuscripts with the widest geographical distribution. [Because readings attested in more than one locality are less likely to be accidental or idiosyncratic.]

4. A variant's support by one or more established groups of manuscripts of recognized antiquity, character, and perhaps location, i.e., of recognized "best quality." [Because, not only individual manuscripts, but families and text-types can be judged as to age and quality—again, internal criteria contribute to these judgments.]

Naturally, what is true of internal criteria is also the case with the external: conflicting judgments on a single reading may arise from application of these various external criteria, or two competing readings may be supported by different criteria. More often, however, conflicts arise *between the internal and external criteria*: an external criterion may support one reading as original, while an internal criterion supports another, as when a variant in a very early manuscript (or group) is also the smoother reading or contains material from a parallel passage—or many other possibilities. For example, in Matt. 27:17, was Barabbas's name really Jesus Barabbas? There is strong and widespread external support for "Barabbas" only, but is it highly plausible that the most likely original is "Jesus Barabbas" even though this reading has weak external support. Why? Because, on internal grounds (reverence for Jesus Christ), "Jesus" was doubtless dropped from the text because (as Origen in fact says) "no one who is a sinner [is called] Jesus."[39]

Thus, the resolution, though rarely simple, is sought once again in the balance of probabilities—by using all relevant criteria and assessing their relative merits in answering the question, What would the author most likely have written? This last sentence describes the method currently dominant: "reasoned eclecticism." It represents middle ground between what might be called a "historical-documentary" method—basically reliance upon documents or manuscripts, that is, external criteria—and "thoroughgoing eclecticism"—a virtually exclusive reliance upon transcriptional probability, that is, internal crite- 73
ria. "Reasoned eclecticism," then, combines the two approaches and employs all relevant criteria for a given case (external and internal) and attempts a resolution by weighing (over against one another) the various criteria, once again invoking the phrase, relying on "the balance of probabilities" when trying to decide on the most likely original reading.[40]

---

[39] See Metzger, *Textual Commentary*, 56.

[40] On "thoroughgoing [or: rigorous] eclecticism," see J. Keith Elliott, "Thoroughgoing Eclecticism in New Testament Textual Criticism," in Ehrman and Holmes, *Text of the New Testament in Contemporary Research*, 321–35; on "reasoned eclecticism," see M. W. Holmes, "Reasoned Eclecticism in New Testament Textual Criticism," ibid., 336–60; on both, see Fee, "Rigorous or Reasoned Eclecticism—Which?" in Elliott (ed.), *Studies in New Testament Language and Text*, 174–97, reprinted in Epp and Fee, *Studies in the Theory and Method*, 124–40; Epp, "Eclectic Method," reprinted in ibid.,

IV. Conclusion

In this essay we have journeyed through the relevance of textual criticism for interpreting the New Testament; through the lively story of how its text was transmitted to us, with all of its scribal exigencies that must be understood, evaluated, and often countervailed; through the oft-competing principles that apply both to the internal transcriptional and to the external documentary aspects of manuscripts; and through the description of these documents themselves. Viewing the textual variants of each New Testament writing within this broad context, we discern multiple voices arising from within the fabric of the text—voices of an ancient author; of the oldest attainable text; of a harmonistic amplifier; of a grammarian or stylist seeking improvement; of a heterodox propagandist or an orthodox "corrector"; of an otherwise culturally conditioned interpreter; and even the voice of an editor or possibly a revisionist responsible for composition levels that may lie behind some of our present New Testament writings. Discerning a particular voice is not easy and often nigh impossible, but each attempt enlightens us about the richness, the diversity, and the dynamism of the early church and its authoritative collection of ancient writings.

Added Notes, 2004

Original published essay. This article originally was published with an "Excursus: The Intersection of Textual Criticism and Canon" (73–91). That preliminary statement has been dropped because almost immediately I began to develop two long articles on the subjects raised there, which now supersede the Excursus, namely:

"The Multivalence of the Term 'Original Text' in New Testament Textual Criticism," *HTR* 92 (1999) 245–81.

"Issues in the Interrelation of New Testament Textual Criticism and Canon," *The Canon Debate: On the Origins and Formation of the Bible* (eds. Lee M. McDonald and James A. Sanders; Peabody, MA: Hendrickson, 2002) 485–515.

141–82. Numerous examples of how the various criteria function can be found in Metzger, *Text of the New Testament*, 207–46; and in Aland and Aland, *Text of the New Testament*, 280–316.

On internal and external criteria. In addition to bibliography added to various footnotes, see the discussion and references in my "Issues in New Testament Textual Criticism: Moving from the Nineteenth Century to the Twenty-First Century," *Rethinking New Testament Textual Criticism* (ed. D. A. Black; Grand Rapids, MI: Baker Academic, 2002) 20–34.

The two lists of "Criteria" on pp, 62–63 and 71–72 have been enhanced, and I think improved, in their phraseology, by slight re-ordering in terms of priority, and especially by providing a succinct rationale for each principle enunciated. Cf. with the lists of nearly thirty years ago in my "The Eclectic Method in New Testament Textual Criticism: Solution or Symptom?" *HTR* 69 (1976) 243.

CHAPTER EIGHTEEN

THE NEW TESTAMENT PAPYRI AT OXYRHYNCHUS IN THEIR SOCIAL AND INTELLECTUAL CONTEXT

I. At the Outset: Sayings of Jesus and New Testament Papyri at Oxyrhynchus

Collections of sayings of Jesus might well serve as a hallmark of New 47
Testament discoveries in Egypt in the five decades or so from the last years of the nineteenth century until the middle of the twentieth, and, were it not for Nag Hammadi, the focal point might well have been Oxyrhynchus, where fragments of at least three such lists were discovered in 1897 and 1903 (Oxyrhynchus papyri 1, 654, and 655), all dating in the third century and together preserving portions of seventeen sayings. Of course, nearly a half century later these fragments were identified as portions, in Greek, of the Coptic *Gospel of Thomas*—when the latter was discovered about 1945.[1] In addition, Oxyrhynchus yielded P.Oxy X.1224 (early 4th C.E.), which is a highly fragmentary, poorly preserved papyrus with three sayings. The genre of the document, however, cannot be determined, nor can it be identified with any known gospel.[2] The latter is the case also with P.Oxy V.840 (4th/5th C.E.), a dialogue of Jesus with a chief priest in the Temple,[3] and with P.Oxy XI.1384 (5th C.E.), containing a saying of Jesus on healing. Sayings of Jesus occur also, of course, in eleven other papyri from Oxyrhynchus (New Testament P5, P19,

[1] P.Oxy IV.654 = Coptic introduction and sayings 1–5; P.Oxy I.1 = sayings 27–31 plus the end portions of 77, 32, 33, 34; and P.Oxy IV.655 = sayings 37–40.

[2] [See now François Bovon, "Fragment Oxyrhynchus 840, Fragment of a Lost Gospel, Witness of an Early Christian Controversy over Purity," *JBL* 119 (2000) 705–28, who marshals substantial evidence to show that it reflects an intra-Christian dispute: cf. 728.]

[3] See W. Schneemelcher and R. McL. Wilson (eds.), *New Testament Apocrypha* (rev. ed.; 2 vols.; Louisville, KY: Westminster/John Knox; London: James Clarke, 1991–92) 1.100. P. Egerton 2 possibly came from Oxyrhynchus: it was purchased along with other papyri among which nearly all whose provenance could be identified were from Oxyrhynchus. This, however, falls far short of proof: H. I. Bell and T. C. Skeat, *Fragments of an Unknown Gospel and Other Early Christian Papyri* (London: British Museum, 1935) 7.

48 P21, P22, P28, P39, P69, P70, P71, P77, and P90), though these are randomly preserved portions of the four gospels.

The story of the discovery of P.Oxy I.1, the first of these collections of sayings of Jesus to turn up, and of P.Oxy I.2, the first papyrus to be uncovered at Oxyrhynchus, is well enough known, but neither the drama of those moments nor their significance for New Testament scholarship can be appreciated apart from a thumbnail sketch of the papyrus discoveries that preceded them.

Travelers to Egypt had brought papyrus documents back to Europe since the sixteenth century, but the 1752 discovery of 800 carbonized scrolls at Herculaneum attracted the attention even of King George IV of England—though the scrolls could not be unrolled. Other papyri were studied by Napoleon's scholars and then by numerous other Europeans during the first half of the nineteenth century, but when Ulrich Wilcken brought together and reedited the Greek and Latin papyri of the Ptolemaic period that had been published up to 1891, there were only about 200. In the 1870s, however, a new phase began for the discovery of papyri as Egyptian farmers, seeking fertilizer, began to haul away nitrate-rich soil from ancient villages, thereby uncovering large quantities of papyri that had been deposited in rubbish heaps in the Byzantine period and earlier. Notable sites were Arsinoe (the Fayum capital), as well as Hermopolis, Heracleopolis, and elsewhere.[4]

The 1890s saw increased activity, particularly in the purchase of papyrus documents, but also in a more systematic and rational approach to finding additional Greco-Roman papyri, and another fresh phase of discovery was opened when the Egypt Exploration Fund commissioned B. P. Grenfell, A. S. Hunt, and D. G. Hogarth, in 1895, to explore and excavate promising sites, first in the Fayum, then Karanis, and, in 1896–97, Oxyrhynchus. They had quite deliberately chosen Oxyrhynchus, where Grenfell and Hunt took over following a brief preliminary survey by Flinders Petrie; notice the opening paragraph of Grenfell's full account of the dramatic first season:

> I had for some time felt that one of the most promising sites in Egypt for finding Greek manuscripts was the city of Oxyrhynchus, the modern

[4] On this early period, see E. G. Turner, *Greek Papyri: An Introduction* (Oxford: Clarendon, 1968) 20–27.

> Behneseh, situated on the edge of the western desert 120 miles south
> of Cairo. Being the capital of the Nome, it must have been the abode 49
> of many rich persons who could afford to possess a library of literary
> texts. Though the ruins of the old town were known to be fairly exten-
> sive, and it was probable that most of them were of the Graeco-Roman
> period, neither town nor cemetery appeared to have been plundered
> for antiquities in recent times. Above all, Oxyrhynchus seemed to be
> a site where fragments of Christian literature might be expected of an
> earlier date than the fourth century, to which our oldest manuscripts
> of the New Testament belong; for the place was renowned in the
> fourth and fifth centuries on account of the number of its churches
> and monasteries, and the rapid spread of Christianity about Oxyrhynchus,
> as soon as the new religion was officially recognized, implied that it
> had already taken a strong hold during the preceding centuries of per-
> secution.[5]

When Grenfell and Hunt began to dig a low mound on January 11, 1897, papyrus fragments became abundant, with most of them retrievable from near the surface. Grenfell increased the number of workmen from seventy to 110 as "the flow of papyri soon became a torrent" so that the two men assigned to making tin boxes for storing the papyri could barely keep up during the next ten weeks. When the discoveries of the second day were being assessed, Hunt's eye caught the uncial letters, ΚΑΡΦΟϹ ("speck"), reminding him of the "mote" and "beam" passage in Matt 7:3–5 par. Luke 6:41–42, though it soon became apparent that four others among the fragment's eight sayings differed radically from the canonical gospels and that the remaining three had only partial parallels. This portion of a collection of "Sayings of Jesus," dated ca. 200, was designated P.Oxy 1 and given the place of honor as their first published papyrus when the volumes of *The Oxyrhynchus Papyri* began to appear in 1898.

The next day Hunt identified another majuscule papyrus, part of a sheet from a codex containing most of Matthew 1. Dating in the third century, it was designated P.Oxy 2, but became the frontispiece in volume 1 of the *Oxyrhynchus Papyri*; it later was accorded the distinction of being Papyrus 1 in the official list of New Testament papyri[6]—which was to grow to nearly 100 items over the succeeding

---

[5] B. P. Grenfell, "Oxyrhynchus and Its Papyri," Egypt Exploration Fund, *Archaeological Report 1896–1897* (ed. F. Ll. Griffith; London: Egypt Exploration Fund, 1897) 1. Our following paragraphs summarize 5–7.

[6] In C. R. Gregory, *Die griechischen Handschriften des Neuen Testaments* (Leipzig, 1908) 45. Note that the papyri follow the majuscules, both here and in Gregory, *Textkritik*

50 century. Although the Matthew papyrus was not the first New Testament papyrus to be discovered or published, its first position was justified because at the time, as Grenfell and Hunt affirmed, "it may . . . claim to be a fragment of the oldest known manuscript of any part of the New Testament."[7] Already in 1868, about twenty years after discovering Codex Sinaiticus, Constantin Tischendorf published what was to become P11, followed by those designated P7 and P8 in the official list.[8] Meanwhile, P3 had been published by Carl Wessely in 1882 and P14 by J. Rendel Harris in 1890. These first five New Testament papyri to be presented to the public did not attract much attention, however, because two of them dated in the seventh century, two in the fifth, and one in the fourth—and none, therefore, was older than the two famous mid-fourth century majuscule manuscripts, Sinaiticus and Vaticanus, that had led the way in the construction of the critical New Testament texts of Tischendorf in 1869 and of Westcott-Hort in 1881. Not only that, but these five papyri together contained only 120 New Testament verses. Thus, the lack of excitement over them is not surprising, but the Oxyrhynchus papyri changed all that, primarily because of their early dates and partly because they issued from a known provenance.

The provenance of early New Testament manuscripts is all too rarely known. This is the case with nearly all of the major fourth and fifth century majuscule manuscripts like Codices Sinaiticus (א), Vaticanus (B), Alexandrinus (A), Bezae (D), and Washingtonianus (W).[9] As for the papyri, naturally they come almost entirely from
51 Egypt, but where exactly? One major group, the Chester Beatty

des Neuen Testamentes (Leipzig, 1909) 1,084–92. The catalogued papyri totaled fourteen at this time.

[7] Bernard P. Grenfell and Arthur S. Hunt (eds.), *The Oxyrhynchus Papyri* (London: Egypt Exploration Fund, 1898–) I, p. 4.

[8] Published at that time in C. R. Gregory's *Prolegomena* to Tischendorf's *Novum Testamentum Graece* (8th major ed.; 3 vols.; Leipzig: Giesecke & Devrient, 1869–72; *Prolegomena* (Leipzig: Hinrichs, 1894).

[9] א, B, and A could have originated in Constantinople, though B could have originated in Egypt and A in Caesarea; A, however, is usually assumed to be from Alexandria; for references, see Epp, "The Significance of the Papyri for Determining the Nature of the New Testament Text in the Second Century: A Dynamic View of Textual Transmission" *Gospel Traditions in the Second Century: Origins, Recensions, Text and Transmission* (ed. W. L. Petersen; Christianity and Judaism in Antiquity, 3; Notre Dame, IN: Notre Dame University Press 1989) 76–77; reprinted in E. J. Epp and G. D. Fee, *Studies in the Theory and Method of New Testament Textual Criticism* (SD 45; Grand Rapids, MI: Eerdmans, 1993) 278; D. C. Parker, summarizing other views, constructs an elaborate case that D originated in Berytus (Beirut): *Codex Bezae: An*

(P45, P46, P47) carried with it rumors at the time of purchase that these papyri were found in a pitcher in a ruined church or monastery near Atfih (Aphroditopolis) in the Fayum,[10] about a third of the way down the Nile River from Oxyrhynchus toward Alexandria, and it has been surmised that both the Chester Beatty and the other major group, the Bodmer papyri (P66, P72, P75) may have come from the same church library, though proof is lacking.[11] A report accompanying the purchase of P52, likely the oldest New Testament fragment, places its origin either in the Fayum or in Oxyrhynchus.[12] P4 of Luke actually was found *in situ* in a jar walled up in a house at Coptos (modern Qift, just below [north of] Thebes in upper Egypt); it was, however, in the binding of a (presumably Christian) codex of Philo and the house had no evident connection to a church.[13] P92 was found in 1969 at Madīnat Mādī (modern Narmouthis, between Theadelphia and Tebtunis in the Fayum) in a rubble-filled structure near a racing-course,[14] but this does not enlighten us about the origin or use of this manuscript.

The situation is much clearer, of course, regarding the papyri excavated at Oxyrhynchus, though it must be recognized that some of the documents might have been transported for use there from other places in Egypt or beyond.[15] Nevertheless, we have thirty-one

Early Christian Manuscript and Its Text (Cambridge: Cambridge University Press, 1992) 261–78; and H. A. Sanders provides evidence that W was found near the ruined Monastery of the Vinedresser, near Gizeh, near Cairo, in Egypt: *The New Testament Manuscripts in the Freer Collection: Part I: The Washington Manuscript of the Four Gospels* (New York: Macmillan, 1912) 1–4.

[10] Colin H. Roberts, *Manuscript, Society and Belief in Early Christian Egypt* (Schweich Lectures, 1977; London: British Academy by Oxford University Press, 1979) 7.

[11] C. H. Roberts, "Books in the Graeco-Roman World and in the New Testament," *Cambridge History of the Bible, Volume 1: From the Beginnings to Jerome* (ed. P. R. Ackroyd and C. F. Evans; Cambridge: Cambridge University Press, 1970) 56.

[12] Colin H. Roberts, *An Unpublished Fragment of the Fourth Gospel in the John Rylands Library* (Manchester: Manchester University Press, 1935) 24–25; Bell and Skeat, *Fragments of an Unknown Gospel*, 7.

[13] Roberts, *Manuscript, Society and Belief*, 8; 13.

[14] Claudio Gallazzi, "Frammenti di un codice con le Epistole di Paoli," *ZPE* 46 (1982) 117.

[15] On the rapid transfer of letters, documents, and literature, see Epp, "New Testament Papyrus Manuscripts and Letter Carrying in Greco-Roman Times," *The Future of Early Christianity: Essays in Honor of Helmut Koester* [eds. B. A. Pearson, A. T. Kraabel, G. W. E. Nickelsburg, and N. R. Petersen; Minneapolis, MN: Fortress, 1991) esp. 55–56. E. G. Turner, *Greek Manuscripts of the Ancient World* (Oxford: Clarendon, 1971) 20–21; idem, *Greek Papyri*, 49–53; 87; 90; 137, discusses principles for identifying copies made in Oxyrhynchus and the place of finding a text in relation to the place of its writing.

52 New Testament papyri discovered at one locality; that represents thirty-three percent of some ninety-five different New Testament papyri currently known. More remarkable is the fact that twenty-one of these (plus one majuscule found there) are among the forty-eight oldest New Testament manuscripts—those dating prior to or around the turn of the third/fourth centuries, namely, forty-four papyri and the four oldest majuscules, all of which are of special significance because (as noted earlier) they predate the great majuscule manuscripts that occupy so prominent a position in New Testament textual criticism: ℵ, B, A, W, and D. That Oxyrhynchus should have provided forty-six percent of the earliest and most valuable group of papyri is particularly noteworthy.

In addition, the number of New Testament books covered by the Oxyrhynchus papyri is impressive, for, although highly fragmentary, they contain sections of fifteen of our twenty-seven New Testament books. Portions of Matthew are found in six papyri; John's Gospel in five; Romans in three; Hebrews, James, and the Apocalypse of John each in two; and Luke, Acts, 1 Corinthians, Galatians, Philippians, 1–2 Thessalonians, 1 John, and Jude are each found in one papyrus. The twelve books not represented are Mark, 2 Corinthians, Ephesians, Colossians, the Pastoral Epistles, Philemon, 1–2 Peter, and 2–3 John, though that is of little significance given the random situation that obtains in excavating rubbish heaps. [1 Peter is found in the majuscule P.Oxy XI:1353 (4th C.E.) = 0206.] The twenty papyri (plus 0162) among the forty-eight earliest manuscripts cover Matthew, Luke, John, Acts, Romans, Philippians, 1–2 Thessalonians, Hebrews, James, 1 John, Jude, and Revelation. Yet, among them, only four preserve more than about two dozen verses: P5, with about thirty-seven verses of John (3rd C.E.); P13, with about seventy-nine verses of Hebrews (3rd/4th); P15, with about twenty-seven verses of 1 Corinthians (3rd); and P27, with about thirty verses of Romans (3rd). Compared, for example, with our longest gospel, Luke (1,149 verses) or even with our shortest gospel, Mark (661 verses), these papyri are still mere fragments.

53 Despite this fragmentary nature of the Oxyrhynchus papyri, they do constitute a remarkable cache of valuable material with a known provenance and they should be allowed, therefore, to inform us about the real-life context in which they were used. Hence, the purpose of this investigation is to place not only the papyrus sayings of Jesus but, more than that, all of the New Testament papyri found at

Oxyrhynchus within the historical and socioeconomic, but particularly the literary, intellectual, and religious environment of the location where they were discovered. This will be attempted through a case study of the city of Oxyrhynchus and its surrounding area as revealed through the other papyri found there, of which about 4,000 have been published in the multi-volume *Oxyrhynchus Papyri* (1898–; a total of sixty-four volumes to date), and many others elsewhere, especially in the Italian series, *Papiri greci e latini* (= PSI, 1912–; fifteen volumes to date), since Pistelli and Breccia succeeded Grenfell and Hunt in 1910. For documentation and illustrative purposes, papyri dating in the fourth century and earlier will serve as our primary sources for the obvious reason that we wish to understand the nature of the Oxyrhynchite area in the period when our earliest forty-eight New Testament manuscripts were current.

II. The General Sociocultural Context Provided by Oxyrhynchus

Ancient Oxyrhynchus covered an area about one and a quarter miles long by one-half mile wide, but its ancient buildings have all but disappeared, for they served during a millennium as a quarry for bricks and limestone, with buildings peeled away down to their foundations. Also, both the city's cemeteries, normally expected to yield papyrus mummy-cases or papyrus rolls in their owners' tombs, proved disappointing, for the Roman cemetery had been situated in a low area and almost all tombs had been affected by dampness; moreover, most bodies had not been mummified. And the ancient Egyptian cemetery had been robbed long ago and dampness had affected the mummies that remained so that they turned to dust when touched. This situation drove Grenfell and Hunt to the rubbish heaps in their search for papyri,[16] and requires that Oxyrhynchus, where archaeological data are sparse, must be understood mainly on the basis of "philological archaeology"—that is, the papyrus documents.[17] 54

[16] Grenfell, "Oxyrhynchus and Its Papyri," 2–6.

[17] Turner, *Greek Papyri*, 80; cf. Roger S. Bagnall, *Egypt in Late Antiquity* (Princeton: Princeton University Press, 1993) 6–7.

The picture of Oxyrhynchus arising in this fashion can only be hinted at in this present, brief presentation. In recent publications, I have asked but not answered what it might mean for the New Testament papyri at Oxyrhynchus when it is recognized that they were found in a city that we know contained at least two churches around the turn of the third/fourth centuries—ascertained from records of a night watchman's rounds (see below)—but a city that was known to have been a significant center of Christian activity in the fourth and fifth centuries, when Rufinus reported thirty churches there,[18] and in the early sixth century, when a bishop and some forty churches are evidenced by P.Oxy XI.1357 (535–36 C.E.), a calendar of church services at Oxyrhynchus.

The extended question concerns what it might mean for the New Testament manuscripts used and preserved there when we realize that from the papyri the names of some 5,700 residents of the Oxyrhynchite nome can be identified already in the period from ca. 30 B.C.E.–96 C.E.[19] and that the city had some twenty temples and a theater that seated some eight to twelve thousand people,[20] permitting a presumption that in Roman times the population was around 30,000.[21]

The importance of Oxyrhynchus in antiquity is attested by P.Oxy X.1264 (272 C.E.), where the city is termed λαμπρὰ καὶ λαμπροτάτη ("illustrious and most illustrious"), the first of many occurrences of this two-fold description that replaces the earlier λαμπρά. Possibly the new title arose in view of the world games, the *Iso-Capitolia*, that were first held in Oxyrhynchus in the following year, 273.[22] Other

[18] *Oxyrhynchus Papyri*, XI, p. 26; Turner, *Greek Papyri*, 81; 150; cf. 28.

[19] B. W. Jones and J. E. G. Whitehorne, *Register of Oxyrhynchites 30 B.C.–A.D. 96* (ASP 25; Chico, CA: Scholars Press, 1983).

[20] Turner, *Greek Papyri*, 81; idem, "Roman Oxyrhynchus," *JEA* 38 (1952) 81, reports that Flinders Petrie, the excavator in 1922, estimated that the theater would hold 11,200 spectators; for a catalogue of temples, see Turner, ibid., 82–83.

[21] Julian Krüger, *Oxyrhynchos in der Kaiserzeit: Studien zur Topographie und Literaturrezeption* (European University Studies, III, vol. 441; Frankfurt am Main/New York: Peter Lang, 1990) 8. Itzhak F. Fichman [otherwise Fikhman], "Die Bevölkerungszahl von Oxyrhynchos in byzantinischer Zeit," *APF* 21 (1971) 111–20, on extensive evidence, suggests 15,000 to 25,000. [Recently Dirk Obbink, *Egyptian Archaeology* 22 (Spring, 2003) 3, speaks of "perhaps 20,000 inhabitants of the Greek-speaking settler class, Egyptian Greeks, and their later Roman counterparts."]

[22] Turner, "Roman Oxyrhynchus," *JEA* 38 (1952) 78. Cf. P.Oxy IX.1199 (3rd C.E.).

indications of importance include the following: (1) The presence of 55
a Roman garrison at Oxyrhynchus at the outset of the second century, attested by the Latin P.Oxy VII.1022 (103 C.E.), which provides the names, ages, and distinguishing marks of six new recruits to be added to the third Ituraean cohort. (Curiously, the first recruit, Veturius Gemellus, reappears forty years later in P.Oxy VII.1035 [143 C.E.] as a "veteran" whose son enters into a rental contract for an iron wool comb or shears.) (2) The recognition of Oxyrhynchus in 202 C.E. by the Emperors Septimius Severus and Marcus Aurelius Antoninus as having a status second to Pelusium but above Memphis in access to imperial benefactions, as shown in two petitions to the Emperors by Aurelius Horion, a high official of the "most illustrious city of Alexandria" who had large landholdings in Oxyrhynchus (P.Oxy IV.705 [200–202 C.E.]). (3) An early fourth century levy upon the city and the Oxyrhynchite nome of thirty-eight pounds of gold (P.Oxy XVII.2106); in the same period, an average of only ten pounds was exacted from seven nomes in the Delta region.[23]

The character of the city can be assessed further, for example, from P.Oxy I.43 (verso), a list from after 295 C.E. of watchmen who made the rounds of the main streets and public buildings, including the temples of Sarapis, Isis, Thoëris, and Caesar; two churches, north and south; the theater; the capitol; three baths; the gymnasium; a Nilometer—to measure the annual floods—and four city gates.[24] Already in the late second century, an Oxyrhynchus municipal account of payments specifies 2,000 drachmai "to Dionysius . . . in command of the 50 night watchmen" (P.Oxy XVII.2128). Also, the city had "quarters" or regions, perhaps as many as twenty, named for various inhabitants, such as Cretens and Jews (P.Oxy II.335: sale of a house in the Jewish quarter ca. 83 C.E.); trades or occupations (gooseherds, shepherds, equestrian camp); temples (Sarapis, Thoëris); public buildings (theater, gymnasium, warm baths); and streets or location (South Broad Street quarter, north quarter, south quarter).

Along with the two Christian churches mentioned earlier, P.Oxy IX.1205 refers to a Jewish synagogue (i.e., congregation) that, in 291 C.E., paid fourteen talents of silver (a large sum) to free a woman

[23] See Turner, "Roman Oxyrhynchus," *JEA* 38 (1952) 79. I owe both of the last two Oxyrhynchus references to Turner.

[24] *Oxyrhynchus Papyri*, I, p. 89.

and her two small children, one of whom was named Jacob.[25] Of course, religion in Oxyrhynchus was dominated by Greek and Roman practices and cults, and by the continuance of traditional Egyptian rites, as attested by innumerable references in the papyri to temples, deities, officiants, festivals, and sacrifices, to say nothing of the inevitable prayers and invocations of the gods in private letters—too numerous to document here.[26]

In addition to religion, the papyri open to us the entire gamut of life and livelihood in Oxyrhynchus through documentary and literary papyri, and through private correspondence. The variety and breadth of classical literature available would have been hard to imagine had the papyri remained undiscovered, as would the range of commerce and agriculture, of transportation, of legal transactions and court activity, of military matters, of politics and government, of cultural and social characteristics, and of work and leisure, as well as the everyday involvements in child rearing, education, marriage and divorce, family joys and sorrows, health and sickness, and natural disasters, all of which are abundantly documented for us at this one location in Egypt.[27]

The location within this socio-economic-cultural milieu of so large a proportion of our extant New Testament papyri raises again intriguing questions as to how this kind of community impacted upon Christianity up to the fourth century period—and what Christianity's impact upon Oxyrhynchus might have been.

III. The Intellectual Environment at Oxyrhynchus

More directly relevant to the New Testament papyri than this brief foray into the sociocultural environment of Oxyrhynchus are the remains and other evidences of intellectual life, particularly the

[25] See *Oxyrhynchus Papyri*, IX, pp. 239–42, and *C.PapJud.* 1.94.

[26] See, e.g., Turner, "Roman Oxyrhynchus," *JEA* 38 (1952) 82–83.

[27] Space does not permit detailed documentation; perusal of the volumes of *Oxyrhynchus Papyri* will furnish myriad examples; others may be found in Hugh MacLennan, *Oxyrhynchus: An Economic and Social Study* (Chicago, 1968) [though many question his interpretations], and in my recent, but highly popularizing article, "*Humanitas* in the Greco-Roman Papyri," *Biblical and Humane: A Festschrift for John F. Priest* (eds. L. Bennett Elder, D. L. Barr, and E. Struthers Malbon; Homage Series; Atlanta, GA: Scholars Press, 1996) 189–213.

literary works found there and evidences of literary activity, of scholarly editing, and of other literary-critical endeavors. General indications of such activity at Oxyrhynchus are many, including the following: 57
Already in the third century B.C.E., the peripatetic biographer Satyrus wrote in Oxyrhynchus (notice the extensive P.Oxy IX.1176 [2nd C.E.], *Life of Euripides*), as did the writer and epitomizer, Heraclides Lembus (2nd B.C.E.). In our period, P.Oxy XXIV.2400 (3rd C.E.) lists subjects for student declamations that would require the reading of Thucydides or Euripides, and some Oxyrhynchus private letters contain fine expression and writing style, such as P.Oxy XVIII.2190 (1st C.E.) and PSI 1248.[28] The list of titles of Hyperides' speeches in P.Oxy XLVII.3360 = P.Coll.Youtie I.3 (2nd/3rd C.E.), written in Oxyrhynchus (because it is on the back of a money account), "may illustrate the copying of that author's speeches and their study in that town," and it may, moreover, be a list of books available in someone's library, or a list of books sought, or an account for a scribe's copying work;[29] and P.Oxy VIII.1153 (1st C.E.), a private letter, reports, "I have received through Heraclas the boxes with the books" sent (as the address shows) from Alexandria.

More significant, however, are documents found at Oxyrhynchus identifying individuals as members of the Alexandrian Museum—the most famous among such institutions (originally connected with the arts inspired by the Muses) that housed and provided generous stipends to a group of literary scholars engaged in lecturing and research. For example, P.Oxy XXVII.2471 (ca. 50 C.E.), which confirms a loan repayment to two brothers, Demetrius and Isidorus, describes Demetrius as "one of those exempt from taxes and maintained in the temple of the Muses." Another Oxyrhynchus document, P.Mert. I.19 (31 March 173 C.E.) records the sale of a river boat to Valerius Diodorus, "member of the Museum," and the significant "letter about books" (P.Oxy XVIII.2192), sent to Oxyrhynchus in the second century C.E., also mentions a Diodorus in the context of private book acquisition. The names of both sender and receiver are lost; the three different hands of the fragments complicate the interpretation. The main part of the document was

[28] Cf. Turner, *Greek Papyri*, 84–85; 88; idem, *Greek Manuscripts*, 126.

[29] *Collectanea Papyrologica: Texts Published in Honor of H. C. Youtie* (ed. A. E. Hanson; 2 vols.; PTA 19; Bonn: Habelt, 1976) 1.53; 57.

written in a large, flowing, semi-literary hand and in a literary style; following that, the writer in his own hand adds:

58 I pray for your health, my lord brother. . . . Make and send me copies of books 6 and 7 of Hypsicrates' *Characters in Comedy*. For Harpocration says that they are among Polion's books. But it is likely that others, too, have them. He also has prose epitomes of Thersagoras' work on the myths of tragedy.

At this point a third hand inserts:

> According to Harpocration, Demetrius the bookseller has them. I have instructed Apollonides to send me certain of my own books which you will hear of in good time from Seleucus himself. Should you find any, apart from those which I possess, make copies and send them to me. Diodorus and his friends also have some which I do not have. . . .

The third hand, suggest the editors, may be "a note by another member of the family or circle, correcting and adding to the preceding note." It is now accepted that Harpocration of Alexandria, the author of the *Lexicon of the Ten Orators*, is referred to here, showing that "he was in touch with an intellectual circle in Oxyrhynchus."[30] Turner asserts that the Diodorus here and in P.Merton (above) are the same person, who is to be identified with Valerius Diodorus, the son of Valerius Pollio (= Polion of the papyrus)—two known Alexandrian writers on lexicography.[31] The Merton papyrus makes it likely that Diodorus owned land in Oxyrhynchus, and P.Oxy 2192 could be read to mean that Polion and Diodorus were living in Oxyrhynchus or, more likely, spent time at their property there—and that Harpocration may have visited Polion.[32] It has also been suggested that Seleucus is to be identified with the Alexandrian gram-
59 marian.[33] In sum, "the interest of the letter lies in the picture it suggests of a circle of friends at Oxyrhynchus all interested in the acquisition of books and getting their friends to have copies made of works not in their possession. Side by side with this system of

[30] *OCD*[3], in loc.; this is not in *OCD*[2] and may be based on Turner's work: "Roman Oxyrhynchus," 91–92 and *Greek Papyri*, 87.

[31] Turner, "Roman Oxyrhynchus," 92; idem, *Greek Papyri*, 86–87; idem, *Greek Manuscripts*, 114.

[32] Turner, "Roman Oxyrhynchus," 92. He notes (85) that some twenty-four Alexandrian citizens are attested as owning property in Oxyrhynchus during the first three centuries.

[33] By B. Hemmerdinger, "Deux notes papyrologiques," *REG* 72 (1959) 107–9 (*apud* Turner, *Greek Manuscripts*, 114).

private borrowing and copying, we have . . . an allusion to the book trade."[34]

The natural question, again, is what does it mean for the New Testament papyri at Oxyrhynchus when it is recognized that they were found in a city where vast numbers of literary texts were in use and were subjected to scholarly analysis and editing?

Actually, the quantity and range of literary works preserved at Oxyrhynchus is enormous, for its rubbish heaps yielded 1,435 papyrus remnants of known and previously unknown classical authors (as catalogued by Krüger).[35] These rolls and codices cover the period from around the turn of the second/first centuries B.C.E. to the turn of the sixth/seventh centuries C.E.—more than 700 years. It would not be fair, therefore, to use the entire lot to characterize Oxyrhynchus at any given point during these centuries, so some reasonable representation must be determined. Since books often last longer than people—papyrus, when kept dry, is very resilient and durable—and since our interest lies mainly in the period from the turn of the first/second to that of the third/fourth centuries C.E. (the period coinciding with our earliest forty-eight New Testament manuscripts), we can select that 200-year period for investigation. This may suggest that we have in mind the literature available during the lifetime of 60
a 200-year-old Oxyrhynchite and that it would be better to choose a single century, but that difficulty is mitigated if we list the material period by period, so that either the time-frame from about 80–200 or that from 200 to about 325 may be observed separately.

[34] P.Oxy XVIII, p. 150. [Note that this common interpretation—that a circle of literary friends is implied here—may be overstated, and the phrase may be only an honorific form of address to Diodorus (conveyed to be by Dirk Obbink at Oxford).]

[35] Krüger, *Oxyrhynchos in der Kaiserzeit*, 227–45; 313–50; cf. the list of Christian and Jewish papyri, 351–54. In 1922, F. Kenyon, "The Library of a Greek of Oxyrhynchus," *JEA* 8 (1922) 130–34, could reckon only 390 literary manuscripts of the Greco-Roman period at Oxyrhynchus (though not counting Homer): 38 from the 1st century, 113 from the 2nd, 121 from the 3rd, 51 from the 4th, etc. The *OCD*[3], 1088, asserts that "over 70 per cent of surviving literary papyri come from Oxyrhynchus."

Though it is difficult to offer a modern comparison with Oxyrhynchus, a city of some 25,000 to 30,000, residents of the United States might think of a city the size of Fairbanks (30,800) or Juneau, Alaska (26,750), New Castle, PA (28,330), Paducah, KY (27,250), Del Rio (30,700) or Texarkana, TX (31,650), or Walla Walla, WA (26,500)—recognizable small cities but certainly not major urban centers—and ask about the range and quantity of literary works that might be available there (subtracting the benefits of the printing press and modern distribution methods—and of a system of public education).

A very quick summary shows that in the period of about 80–200 Oxyrhynchus possessed the following number of copies of works by well-known authors—selected from a much longer list:

Aeschylus	24
Apollonius of Rhodes	10
Aristophanes	3
Aristotle	2
Callimachus	28
Demosthenes	18
Euripides	18
Herodotus	11
Hesiod	34
Homer	55
Isocrates	8
Menander	14
Pindar	13
Plato	28
Plutarch	1
Sappho	8
Sophocles	10
Theocritus	9
Theophrastus	1
Thucydides	11
Xenophon	6

In addition, the Oxyrhynchus papyri in this period include many other known authors, some 100 anonymous literary works, and three dozen miscellaneous works.

If one moves to the period from about 200 to 325, most of the authors are represented by additional copies (as examples among many others):

Demosthenes	16
Euripides	16
Herodotus	12
Hesiod	30
Homer	121
Menander	17
Pindar	8
Plato	21
Sappho	7
Sophocles	5
Thucydides	13
Xenophon	6

In addition, there are Latin authors like Livy, Sallust, and Virgil, plus many other known authors and nearly 100 each of anonymous literary works and of historical and scientific works.

Literature at Oxyrhynchus, of course, was not limited to classical authors, but the papyri preserve some Jewish writings and numerous copies of Christian writings in addition to New Testament texts, that is, beyond the thirty-one New Testament papyri and twelve uncials (069 [P.Oxy I.3], 071 [III.401], 0162 [VI.847], 0163 [VI.848],
0169 [VIII.1080], 0170 [IX.1169], 0172 [PSI 1.4], 0173 [PSI 1.5], 61
0174 [PSI 2.118], 0176 [PSI 3.251], 0206 [XI.1353]), and 0308 [LXVI.4500], of which twenty-one papyri and the parchment codex 0162 fall into the period up to the turn of the third/fourth centuries. The apocryphal sayings of Jesus have been discussed above (P.Oxy I.1; IV.654, 655; and X.1224), and they date from the same early period. Also within our selected time-frame are portions of Greek (and Latin) Jewish Scripture made for Christian use, though it is difficult to know for certain which were of Christian origin),[36] and various Christian theological texts and treatises, as well as devotional materials. A quick survey, again only through the turn of the third/fourth centuries, shows that some two dozen items of non-New Testament Christian literature survive at Oxyrhynchus,

[36] Here is a list complied from Krüger, *Oxyrhynchos in der Kaiserzeit*, 351–54:
P.Oxy VII.1010 (4th): 6 Ezra (vellum codex).
P.Oxy VIII.1073 (4th): Old Latin Genesis (vellum codex).
P.Oxy VIII,1074 (3rd): Exodus (papyrus codex).
P.Oxy VIII,1075 (3rd): Exodus (papyrus roll).
P.Oxy IX.1167 (4th): Genesis (papyrus codex).
P.Oxy IX.1168 (4th): Joshua (vellum codex).
P.Oxy X.1226 (3rd/4th): Psalms (papyrus codex).
P.Oxy XI.1351 (4th): Leviticus (vellum codex).
P.Oxy XI.1352 (early 4th): Psalms (vellum codex).
P.Oxy XIII.1594 (late 3rd): Tobit (vellum codex).
P.Oxy XV.1779 (4th): Psalm 1 (papyrus codex).
PSI 1163 (4th): Job (papyrus codex).
P.Harr.31 (4th): Psalm 43 (papyrus codex).
P.Mil.R.Univ 1.22 (4th): Exodus (vellum codex).
P.Oxy XXXVI.2745 (3rd/4th): Onomasticon of Hebrew Names (verso of land register).
P.Oxy IX.1173+XI.1356+XVII.2158 (3rd) Philo (papyrus codex—very extensive).
In addition, according to Roberts (*Manuscript, Society and Belief*, 74–78), P.Oxy IV:656 (3rd C.E.), Genesis (papyrus codex), is Jewish, while P.Oxy VII.1007 (3rd C.E.), Genesis (parchment codex); P.Oxy IX.1166 (3rd C.E.), Genesis (papyrus roll); and P.Oxy X.1225 (1st half 4th C.E.), Leviticus (papyrus roll) could be either Jewish or Christian.

including eight manuscripts with apocryphal gospels or sayings of Jesus (*Gospel of Thomas* [I.1; IV.654, 655]; *Sophia Jesu Christi* [VIII.1081]; *Gospel of Mary* [L.3525; P.Ryl III.463]; X.1224; P.Lond.Christ.1); four copies of the *Shepherd of Hermas* (III.404; XV.1828; L.3527; L.3528); two doubtless of the *Gospel of Peter* (XLI.2949; LXIV.4009); and single copies of the *Acts of Peter* (VI.849), possibly of the *Apocalypse of*
62 *Peter* (P.Vindob.G); and of Irenaeus's *Against Heresies* (P.Oxy III.405, but see IV, pp. 264–65); an apologetic work (XVII.2072); an anti-Jewish dialogue (XVII.2070); a prayer (III.407); and a hymn with musical notation (XV.1786), as well as some "gnostic" (I.4; XII.1478; P.Harr.107) and other miscellaneous material (II.210).

Incidentally, nearly twenty additional items are added if the full fourth century is taken into account, including three more copies of *Hermas* (IX.1172+3526; XIII.1599; XV.1783); copies of the *Didache* (XV.1782), the *Acts of John* (VI.850), Aristides' *Apology* (XV.1778), the *Passion of St. Dioskorus* (L.3529), and the *Apocalypse of Baruch* (III.403); an apocalyptic fragment (XVII.2069); a liturgical fragment (XVII.2068); a prayer (VII.1058); three sermons (XIII.1601; 1602; XVII.2073); three amulets (PSI.719; P.Amst 26; SB 10762); and a "gnostic" charm (VI.924) and a prayer (XII.1566).[37] The anti-Jewish dialogue (P.Oxy XVII.2070 [late 3rd C.E.]) may support Oxyrhynchus as "a Christian intellectual center"[38] at the time, not—to be sure—because of its subject-matter(!), but because the papyrus appears to be an autograph by a local writer, as evidenced by frequent corrections, but especially by alterations to the text by the original hand, which "are difficult to explain except on the hypothesis that we here have a fragment of the author's own manuscript."[39]

[37] Though inferences are risky when assessing randomly preserved data, it is tempting to ask whether apocalyptic interests ran high in Christian Oxyrhynchus because of the large proportion of such literature: ten items out of this list of forty-some. Notice also that two out of the six New Testament majuscule fragments contain the Apocalypse of John (one 4th century, though the other is 5th). It is known, of course, that *Hermas* was used in instructing catechumens—see Tertullian, *de Pud.* 10.39 (Roberts, *Manuscript, Society and Belief*, 22).

[38] Ibid., 24 n. 5. [For the subject, content, and nature of this anti-Jewish dialogue, see E. J. Epp, "The Oxyrhynchus New Testament Papyri: 'Not without honor except in their hometown'?" *JBL* 123 (2004) 40–42.]

[39] P.Oxy XVII, p. 9. P.Oxy VII.1015 (later 3rd C.E.) may be another autograph (though not Christian), probably of a prize poem (Turner, *Greek Manuscripts*, 90–91).

Though hardly comparable to the huge classical corpus that had
been built up over several centuries, this range—if not the quantity—of Christian literature from within a restricted time-frame is
impressive nonetheless, and it suggests an active interaction of the
churches there with the young faith's written traditions.[40] Even the
limited quantity, however, seems sufficient for C. H. Roberts to sus- 63
pect that a Christian scriptorium at Oxyrhynchus by or in the third
century is "not unlikely."[41]

IV. Literary-critical Activity at Oxyrhynchus and the New Testament Papyri

In view of the extensive documentation of literary-critical activity at Oxyrhynchus, the next appropriate question is whether the New Testament papyri and early majuscules at that locality were subject to any scholarly analysis or critical editing.

First, however, it is essential to clarify the evidence sought. We are not concerned with *scribal activity* per se, that is, normal/routine manuscript corrections[42] or lection marks, including punctuation, paragraph marks (the *paragraphus*), accent and breathing marks, the

[40] Recently Harry Y. Gamble, *Books and Readers in the Early Church: A History of Early Christian Texts* (New Haven, 1995), estimates a 10%–20% literacy rate at this time for the Greco-Roman world in general, and for Christians "ordinarily not more than about ten percent in any given setting, and perhaps fewer in many small and provincial congregations that were characteristic of early Christianity" (4, see n. 8; 5–7). The surveys of classical and Christian literature presented above raise the question as to the appropriateness of these figures for Oxyrhynchus; see my "The Codex and Literacy in Early Christianity and at Oxyrhynchus: Issues Raised by Harry Y. Gamble's *Books and Readers in the Early Church*," *CRBR* 11 (1998) 28–32 [and now my "Oxyrhynchus New Testament Papyri: 'Not without honor except in their hometown'?" 31–34.]

[41] Roberts, *Manuscript, Society and Belief*, 24. Note also that a number of scribes can be identified as producing more than one manuscript (Turner, "Roman Oxyrhynchus," 91; idem, *Greek Papyri*, 92; idem, *Greek Manuscripts*, 20), though it is not certain whether such items were copied in Oxyrhynchus or, e.g., at Alexandria.

[42] To be sure, it is not always easy to distinguish "normal" or "routine" copying corrections from an activity that might be described as "critical corrections" or "critical editing." For example, the kind of editorial correction applied to P66 by its scribe—which moves the text of his exemplar toward a Byzantine type of reading (see Fee, *Papyrus Bodmer II (P66): Its Textual Relationships and Scribal Characteristics* [SD 34; Salt Lake City, 1968] 76–83)—appears to be right on the line between the two categories of correction, though perhaps leaning toward a critical editing activity. See below, e.g., on signs for "this is what stood in the exemplar."

trema or *diairesis,* the *apostrophe*, etc. P5 (P.Oxy II.208+XV.1781 [3rd C.E.]) may serve as a random but typical example, for it shows a few corrections written above the line and an omission due to homeoteleuton placed at the foot of the page, the usual *nomina sacra*, blank spaces as punctuation, and a few rough breathings.

Rather, our search is for editing marks—beyond the copying process—that reveal primarily a *reader's* use and critical reaction to or interaction with the text. Specifically, we are interested in edi-
64 tor's or scholar's notations or critical marks, such as *glosses* or *scholia* (marginal notes, respectively, for explanation and illustration or for elucidating the meaning of difficult passages); *onomastica* (glosses explaining the meaning of names and places); notes of *commentary*, pointers to a commentary, or indications of a need for a commentary to a portion of text; and very specific *critical marks* or signs, most commonly the χ sign and the > or diple (διπλῆ), but also the obelus and antisigma, and others.[43] These notes and signs are employed in literary manuscripts, both poetry and prose, though not in documentary texts or private letters (with some rare exceptions).

Both of the common signs, χ and >, as well as others, were prefixed to a line and apparently were used to indicate a point in the text that required a clarifying commentary, but each served a number of other purposes, as observed in the papyri.[44] The χ sign was employed to indicate something noteworthy in a line, such as dissent from a reading, an inconsistency, a quotation or a parallel, an unusual word or form of a word, and other general uses or

---

[43] For a convenient discussion, see Turner, *Greek Papyri*, 112–18; cf. 92–95, on commentaries and scholia, 118–24; idem, *Greek Manuscripts*, 17–18. Cf. B. M. Metzger, *Manuscripts of the Greek Bible: An Introduction to Greek Palaeography* (Oxford: Oxford University Press, 1981) 46–48. On the invention of the first critical sign, the obelus (probably to mark passages whose authenticity was suspect), by Zenodotus of Ephesus (b. ca. 325 B.C.E.), see Rudolf Pfeiffer, *History of Classical Scholarship from the Beginnings to the End of the Hellenistic Age* (Oxford: Clarendon, 1968; repr. 1978), 115; on the additional signs of Aristophanes of Byzantium (fl. 200 B.C.E.), see 178; cf. 173–75; on the system of critical signs perfected by Aristarchus (ca. 216–144 B.C.E.) for his editions of Homer and on Alexandrian editing practices, see L. D. Reynolds and N. G. Wilson, *Scribes and Scholars: A Guide to the Transmission of Greek and Latin Literature* (3rd ed.; Oxford: Clarendon, 1991) 10–16; 317; cf. Pfeiffer, *History*, 218.

P.Oxy VIII.1086 (1st B.C.E.) is the oldest extant commentary, and it contains Aristarchean critical signs (e.g., the diple in ll. 27, 54, 97). For examples of extended scholia, see P.Oxy V.841 (1st C.E.); P.Oxy XX.2258 (ca. 6th C.E.)—Turner, *Greek Manuscripts*, 67–69.

[44] The following is summarized from Turner, *Greek Papyri*, 116–18.

specialized uses in certain authors, e.g., Homer, Pindar, or Plato. The > was used to expose wrong glosses, to mark disputed words or passages, among other queries. The presence of these two signs in a text, says Turner, “suggests either that the papyrus was being marked by a reader who had access to a commentary (or was making one for himself); or else that it was a copy of a text so marked,” 65
and he points to an instance in P.Oxy 2427 (2nd/3rd C.E.), fr. 53, as evidence that a commentary on Epicharmus existed, for the marginal note there reads “the χ was not in Theon’s [copies].”[45] Sometimes scholia are introduced by ὅτι . . . following a lemma, meaning “the sign is placed because. . . .”[46] Closely related are marks, notations, or abbreviations of notations that indicate whether a word or portion of text stood in the exemplar, most commonly ὃ = οὕτως or ὃῆ = οὔ(τως) ἦν, the equivalent of *sic*, meaning “this is what stood in the exemplar.[47] The clear implication is that the annotator has checked a manuscript exemplar or a commentary.

In short, these critical marks and notations in a literary text indicate literary criticism and other scholarly activity, such as *critical* corrections (as opposed to routine), and there are many instances of such marks in the literary papyri at Oxyrhynchus. Turner provides lists that include twenty-seven manuscripts,[48] and my perusal of the texts and plates of Oxyrhynchus papyri disclosed many more.[49]

---

[45] Turner, *Greek Papyri*, 117 and 184 n. 37; cf. 93–94 and 182 n. 55. See P.Oxy XXIV.2387 (1st B.C.E./1st C.E.) and Turner, *Greek Manuscripts*, 42–43.

[46] See Turner, *Greek Papyri*, 114–15 and his Oxyrhynchus examples: P.Oxy II.221 (1st C.E.), esp. x.24 and pl. VI; and P.Oxy VIII.1086 (1st B.C.E.), ii.55: διπλῆ ὅτι. . . .

[47] Turner, *Greek Manuscripts*, 17; *Greek Papyri*, 93 and 182 n. 55, referring to P.Oxy XXIV.2387 (1st B.C.E./1st C.E.) *fr.* 1. See also P.Oxy IX.1174 (late 2nd C.E.), cols. iv, v, vi, viii, ix, xi, xiii, xv; P.Oxy IX.1175, *fr.* 5, I.20 and pl. III; and Turner, *Greek Manuscripts*, 66. For its rare occurrence in a documentary papyrus, see P.Oxy III.478 (132 C.E.), *l.* 28.

[48] Turner, *Greek Papyri*, 116–17. Oxyrhynchus examples constitute twenty-seven of the thirty-four in his lists.

[49] Some random examples into the fourth century C.E.:
P.Oxy IV.687 (two diples where other scholia exist)
P.Oxy VIII.1082 (marginalia and variants added by different person)
P.Oxy VIII.1086 (κρηστόν, diple, etc.)
P.Oxy XI.1371 (sign and marginal notes—see pl. VII)
P.Oxy XIII.1620 (several signs and marginal notes—see pl. VI)
P.Oxy XIII.1624 (many corrections, alternative readings by another hand—see pl. VI)
P.Oxy XV.1808 (signs and marginalia by different hand—see pl. IV)
P.Oxy XV.1809 (several signs and marginalia by different hand)

66 "Critical marks of this kind, used scrupulously, are one of the strongest and best indications that the texts in question were scholars' copies."[50]

From the outset of my investigation, I wondered whether such marks were to be found in our early New Testament papyri—which, if they were, would indicate early critical assessment and scholarly work in the Christian community in those early generations. I have located virtually no discussions of this matter and examination of the published texts and of available plates of the Oxyrhynchus New Testament papyri so far has turned up few if any certifiable specialized critical marks of this kind, even though a significant number of lines with left margins preserved—where these marks usually occur—are found in the twenty-eight Oxyrhynchus papyri and the six uncials containing the New Testament.

The most obvious testing ground would be any New Testament papyri that possess a clear literary character. Among the fourteen earliest Christian papyri (from the second and second/third centuries), C. H. Roberts identified three that are "incontrovertibly literary in style,"[51] two of which are from Oxyrhynchus, though only one contains New Testament text. The first is P.Oxy III.405 [but see P.Oxy IV, p. 264] (late 2nd C.E.), a portion of a Greek papyrus roll containing fragments of Irenaeus's *Adversus Haereses*, which has a series of diple signs marking the quotation of Matt 3:16–17; if these were made by a user of the text rather than a copyist—apparently unclear (see pl. I)—they would border on critical notations (yet would be of no great significance). The second example is the New Testament P77 (P.Oxy XXXIV.2683 [later 2nd or 2nd/3d C.E.], a leaf with Matt 23:30–39 in an elegant hand, with chapter divisions, punctuation, and breathing marks—all short of the critical signs we are seeking. The third, not from Oxyrhynchus, makes up P64+P67+P4 [Aland does not include P4] (ca. 200 C.E.), with portions of Matthew (and Luke), which also has section divisions, as well as punctuation and omission and quotation signs,[52] though judging from the transcriptions and plates, nothing here moves beyond the copyist realm.

P.Oxy XVIII.2174, *fr.* 16 (diple and antisigma—see pl. X)
P.Oxy XXIV.2394, *fr.* 1 (signs—see pl. XI)
P.Oxy XXV.2430 (marginal notes/corrections by different hand—see pl. V)

[50] Turner, *Greek Papyri*, 118.

[51] Roberts, *Manuscript, Society and Belief*, 23.

[52] Ibid.

Examining transcriptions and available plates of other Christian literature from Oxyrhynchus within our time-frame led to the same result, as did a perusal of numerous folios of non-Oxyrhynchus papyri,
such as P45, P46, P47, P66, P75, and others.[53] Naturally, it is always 67
risky to assert that no instances of a given phenomenon exist across a sizable body of literature, so any conclusions remain preliminary at this time and subject to further analysis. At very least, however, it seems safe to say that critical signs indicating scholarly editing—those moving beyond the copying process—rarely if ever occur in the New Testament papyri at Oxyrhynchus or in other Christian literature there from the early period.

At first this lack of evidence was disconcerting, for would it not have been enlightening to have found in our earliest New Testament manuscripts some technical marks of literary-critical scholarship and text-critical editing? Would not such marks of scholarly attention, including notice of text-critical judgments, have clarified the origin or development of some textual variants? And would we not have been the richer for such information? Perhaps, but the essentially negative result with respect to critical marks provides clarity about our earliest New Testament manuscripts in another way—the nature of the codex form as employed in Christianity.

That early Christians very quickly adopted the codex form for their writings—when the roll was normal for literary works—is well established, though the possible reasons for the practice cannot be rehearsed here. What is relevant, however, is that early Christian books were essentially *practical* and produced for use in the life of the Christian community. Included would be New Testament texts and—even earlier—portions of the Jewish Bible prepared for Christian use. Evidences of this practicality and utilitarianism of our earliest Christian manuscripts are several practices carried over from docu-

[53] A quick reading of Roberts, *Manuscript, Society and Belief*, 9–10; 14; 21–25, may give the impression that early Christians frequently placed marks, including "critical signs," in their manuscripts. For the most part, however, he is speaking of lectional or reading aids—punctuation, accents, breathings, diaereses, etc.—as well as customary spacing and paragraph marks. The exceptions include P.Ryl I.1, a copy of Deuteronomy from ca. 300 and presumably made for Christian use, that has two χ-marks before ll. 48–49 (though their purpose is not clear); see A. S. Hunt, *et al.*, (eds.), *Catalogue of the Greek Papyri in the John Rylands Library* (3 vols.; Manchester: Manchester University Press, 1911–1938], I.1–3); and P.Grenf. I.5, a copy of Origen's hexaplaric signs (Roberts, *Manuscript, Society and Belief*, 25).

mentary papyri—and distinct from normal literary conventions—among them the consistent use of the codex form (see below), the
68 virtual absence of a calligraphic hand, a lack of strict *scriptio continua*, an enlarged initial letter or one extruded into the margin, the use of symbols rather than words for cardinal numbers, and the use of contractions (notably the *nomina sacra*).[54]

The lack of literary editing in early Christian texts can be explored (and explained) further by considering the very format employed so consistently: the codex. Harry Gamble places the earliest Christian books in the "intermediate phase in the evolving status of the codex—in the late first and early second centuries" and affirms that "the Christians who made them and made use of them did not regard them either as notebooks [the earliest phase] or as fine literature" [the final phase]—"they were practical books for everyday use."[55] Thus, the Oxyrhynchus literary papyri exhibit the critical marks of scholarly editing and literary criticism, as they should, while the New Testament codices found there do not, which is also as it should be, for they have not yet evolved to the final, literary stage of the codex form, but stand midway in the evolutionary process by virtue of their utilitarian character as writings designed for use in the church.

Appended Note on the New Oxyrhynchus New Testament Papyri

Since the completion of the preceding article at the end of 1996, sixteen new Oxyrhynchus papyri containing portions of the New Testament have been published in *The Oxyrhynchus Papyri*, vols LXIV (1997) 1–13 (P101–P105); LXV (1998) 10–25 (P100, P106–P109); and LXVI (1999) 1–35 (P110–P115).

The contents of these newly-published manuscripts (P100–P115 in the official New Testament list) and their assigned dates are as follows (in canonical order): MATTHEW: P101 (P.Oxy. 4401) 3rd; P102 (P.Oxy. 4402) 3rd/early 4th; P103 (P.Oxy. 4403) 2nd/3rd; P104 (P.Oxy. 4404) late 2nd; P105 (P.Oxy. 4406) 5th/6th; and P110 (P.Oxy. 4494) 4th; LUKE: P111 (P.Oxy. 4495) 3rd; JOHN: P106

[54] Roberts, *Manuscript, Society and Belief*, 12–22; 29.
[55] Gamble, *Books and Readers*, 66; cf. 77–78.

(P.Oxy. 4445), P107 (P.Oxy. 4446), P108 (P.Oxy. 4447), and P109 (P.Oxy. 4448), all dating in the 3rd century; ACTS: P112 (P.Oxy. 4496) 5th; ROMANS: P113 (P.Oxy. 4497) 3rd; HEBREWS: P114 (P.Oxy. 4498) 3rd; JAMES: P100 (P.Oxy. 4449) 3rd/4th; and the REVELATION OF JOHN: the extensive P115 (P.Oxy. 4499) 3rd/4th. In addition, a new fragment of P77 (P.Oxy. 2683) was published as P.Oxy. 4405, and an uncial fragment of the Revelation of John as P.Oxy. 4500 (= New Testament 0308) 4th. All are from codices.

Naturally, these new papyri alter the statistics in the preceding article (p. 52) Therefore, Oxyrhynchus to date accounts for forty-seven or 42% of all New Testament papyri (which, though they now number 116, probably consist of 112 different papyri). Moreover, since thirteen of these sixteen newly-published papyri date at or prior to the turn of the 3rd/4th centuries, Oxyrhynchus now provides thirty-five of the group of sixty-one earliest New Testament manuscripts, or 57%. Finally, P115 must now be added to the small group of Oxyrhynchus papyri that contain more than about two dozen verses (p. 52 above), for this newest papyrus of the Revelation of John contains some 317 lines from twelve chapters of the apocalypse.

Though no New Testament writings are represented for the first time among these papyri (p. 52 above), the enhanced quantity of Matthean and Johannine papyri is impressive. Fifteen of the twenty-seven books of the New Testament are still to be found among the forty-seven Oxyrhynchus papyri, but distributed as follows: Matthew in 13 papyri; John in 10; Romans in 4; Acts, Hebrews, James, and the Revelation of John in 3 each; Luke in 2; and 1 Corinthians, Galatians, Philippians, 1–2 Thessalonians, 1 John, and Jude in 1 papyrus each.

Added Notes, 2004

The two articles on the New Testament papyri in relation to Oxyrhynchus are closely related and overlap considerably: (1) "The New Testament Papyri at Oxyrhynchus in Their Social and Intellectual Context" (1997); (2) "The Codex and Literacy in Early Christianity and at Oxyrhynchus: Issues Raised by Harry Y. Gamble's *Books and Readers in the Early Church*" (1997). The explanation is simple enough: in 1989 I had utilized materials from Oxyrhynchus to illustrate dynamic literary activity in the Roman world for my study on "The

Significance of the Papyri for Determining the Nature of the New Testament Text in the Second Century: A Dynamic View of Textual Transmission." This ignited my interest in this Egyptian locality that yielded so large a proportion of our New Testament papyri. The opportunity for further exploration came with an invitation to contribute an article to a *Festschrift* for Tjitze Baarda (the first article), accompanied by a request to prepare a review article on Harry Gamble's significant and perceptive volume on *Books and Readers in the Early Church* (the second article). It became obvious to me that some of the data developed for the Baarda essay could be employed in what I hoped would be a constructively critical assessment of selected portions of Gamble's multifaceted volume. So the overlapping material had largely different purposes in the two articles.

CHAPTER NINETEEN

THE CODEX AND LITERACY IN EARLY CHRISTIANITY AND AT OXYRHYNCHUS: ISSUES RAISED BY HARRY Y. GAMBLE'S *BOOKS AND READERS IN THE EARLY CHURCH*

Harry Gamble's *Books and Readers in the Early Church*[1] is a fine sur- 15
vey, a skilled and convenient summary, and an intelligent and critical synthesis of current information on the making of books, on their circulation, collection, and use in the world of early Christianity, and on research and scholarship in that broad field. It is a fitting successor to and a far more comprehensive volume than Frederic Kenyon's *Books and Readers in Ancient Greece and Rome*[2]—itself a remarkable book for the early 1930s. Gamble's coverage of the topics is broader and deeper and, of course, benefits from sixty-five years of discoveries and analysis of data. His use of primary and secondary sources is extensive and his evaluation of past scholarship is careful and judicious. His own hypotheses, which appear on appropriate occasions, are meticulously argued and well supported by relevant evidence. Quite obviously the book is written both for scholars and for a wider audience, and the latter accommodation accounts for the substratum of explanations to the non-expert of terms, concepts, and situations. This is all well done, and we should be grateful that his subjects of investigation, often highly technical, are thereby more accessible to many.

These general assessments should be sufficient to indicate that, overall, I have little negative criticism of the book. I would like, however, to apply constructive criticism to a few selected points by raising some questions and by offering what, I trust, will be seen as supportive information or as alternative explanations.

---

[1] Harry Y. Gamble, *Books and Readers in the Early Church: A History of Early Christian Texts* (New Haven/London: Yale University Press, 1995) xiii+337. References to this book usually are given in brackets, e.g., (52).

[2] Frederic G. Kenyon, *Books and Readers in Ancient Greece and Rome* (Oxford: Clarendon Press, 1932, 1951[2]).

I. The Codex Format and Its Christian Use

Gamble's hypothesis on what occasioned the first and quickly expanding Christian use of the codex constitutes a major thrust of his second chapter, "The Early Christian Book." This is a topic of continuing
16 interest, though one that resists resolution. Indeed, because of Gamble's discussion, I would be more restrained now than I was in a couple of publications about the probability that Christians invented the codex.[3] At the same time, however, I would suggest that the question may not yet be finally closed, for it depends so heavily on paleographic dating of manuscripts—something so few are competent to do.

For example, P.Oxy I.30, a Latin historical fragment on parchment, is taken by Gamble to be "the earliest known codex" (52). Its first editors pointed to paleographic features resembling those in a Herculaneum papyrus (hence, prior to 79 C.E.) and to other features typical of the first century and the first half of the second century; yet they dated it in the third century because of still other paleographic features but perhaps primarily because it was on vellum and because it was, in fact, a codex, which could not by its very nature—as was assumed at the time—be extremely early.[4] According to E. G. Turner, the papyrus [497 in his numbering] currently is "acceptably dated" to early in the second century,[5] though J. Mallon, who also offers this early dating, thought it might stem from near the beginning of the second century or even from the end of the first.[6]

Paleographic dating is crucial also in the issue of the earliest extant New Testament manuscript, usually assumed to be P52, which con-

---

[3] As in Epp, "The Significance of the Papyri for Determining the Nature of the New Testament Text in the Second Century: A Dynamic View of Textual Transmission," *Gospel Traditions in the Second Century: Origins, Recensions, Text and Transmission* (ed. W. L. Petersen; Christianity and Judaism in Antiquity, 3; Notre Dame, IN: University of Notre Dame Press, 1989) 90 [= E. J. Epp and Gordon D. Fee, *Studies in the Theory and Method of New Testament Textual Criticism* (SD 45; Grand Rapids, MI: Eerdmans, 1993) 288]; Epp, "Textual Criticism (NT)" *ABD* 6.417.

[4] Bernard P. Grenfell and Arthur S. Hunt, eds., *The Oxyrhynchus Papyri* (London: Egypt Exploration Fund I (1898), 59–60.

[5] Eric G. Turner, *The Typology of the Early Codex* (Haney Foundation Series 18; Philadelphia: University of Pennsylvania Press, 1977) 38; cf. 93.

[6] See Gamble, *Books and Readers*, 269 n. 42; Turner, *Typology of the Early Codex*, 128.

tains a fragment of John 18 and is from a codex. C. H. Roberts (its first editor), T. C. Skeat, and Turner[7] all date it in the first half of the second century, while Kurt Aland[8] places it in the first quarter of that century. More recently, van Haelst[9] has disputed this and other early second century dates for Christian codices, assigning them rather to the second half of the second or even the beginning of the third century. Yet, Turner (in 1977), who—as just noted—accepted P.Oxy 30 as stemming from the early second century, after surveying some 236 papyrus and parchment codices of the second to the third/fourth centuries, said of P52:

> It is the only codex in my list that I would place so early, for I would not be willing to admit any of the others to a date earlier than the second half of the [second] century.[10]

So the debate will likely go on about which extant codex is the earliest—a Roman historical writing or a New Testament book—but whether this will assist us in determining where the codex actually originated and why is unclear. What is clear, as others have established and Gamble repeats, is that early Christians picked up quickly on the use of the codex for their writings. Yet, it remains unclear when and why this happened. Gamble faces the issue directly, and his explanation will occupy us shortly; for the moment, however, we turn to a brief discussion of previous views on the subject.

A. *Previous Explanations for the Christian Adoption of the Codex: Roberts and Skeat* 17

C. H. Roberts[11] previously had asserted that the early and extensive use of the codex in Christianity required a substantial cause, and he proposed that Mark was first written in a parchment codex in Rome

---

[7] Turner, *Typology of the Early Codex*, 100.

[8] Kurt Aland, ed. for the Patristischen Arbeitsstelle of Münster, *Repertorium der griechischen christlichen Papyri: I: Biblische Papyri: Altes Testament, Neues Testament, Varia, Apokryphen* (PTS 18; Berlin/New York: De Gruyter, 1976) 282; Kurt Aland and Barbara Aland, *The Text of the New Testament: An Introduction to the Critical Editions and to the Theory and Practice of Modern Textual Criticism* (Grand Rapids: Eerdmans; Leiden: Brill, 1989^2) 85, 99.

[9] As Gamble reports (*Books and Readers*, 54).

[10] Turner, *Typology of the Early Codex*, 100.

[11] Colin H. Roberts, "The Codex," *PBA* 40 (1954) 187–89; restated in C. H. Roberts and T. C. Skeat, *The Birth of the Codex* (London: Oxford University Press, 1983) 54–55.

and that, in this form, it acquired "a sentimental and symbolic value"[12] that carried over to the further, widespread use of the codex format in Christian writings. Yet, there was little evidence to support such a role for Mark (a writing that is preserved—for what it is worth—in only three papyri out of our ninety-five, or 3%). Later, Roberts[13] recognized the weaknesses of this theory and proposed another, only somewhat less speculative: Isolated rabbinic decisions and rabbinic sayings are known to have been written down on tablets, including those made of wax, polished surfaces, and papyrus; therefore, sayings of Jesus might also have been recorded on papyrus tablets (not wax—as Gamble reports it [57]), which then developed into "a primitive form of codex." Roberts and Skeat[14] argued that this most likely happened at Antioch. Gamble (57–58) rightly points to the flaws in this revised hypothesis.

Indeed, very recently (but too late to be observed by Gamble) Skeat[15] also acknowledged the failure of this hypothesis but pointed out that the number of papyrus manuscripts of the New Testament gospels has virtually doubled since 1954 (when Roberts first published his views in "The Codex") and that all are in codex form. He then proposed that the powerful motive for Christians to adopt the codex as a vehicle for their writings was the fact that only a codex—and not a roll—could hold the four gospels. He proceeded, in a complex argument, to search for evidence of a four-gospel codex in the second century; lacking direct evidence, he speculated that "P75 [early 3rd century, containing portions of Luke and John] was originally a four-Gospel codex . . . [consisting] of two single-quire codices sewn together" which, "of course, must also have had ancestors."[16] More recently still, Skeat published his conclusions on P64, P67, and P4, providing full argumentation (1) that they all come from the same codex, which was almost certainly a four-gospel codex[17]

---

[12] Roberts, "The Codex," 189; cf. Gamble, *Books and Readers*, 56–57.

[13] Roberts, with Skeat, *Birth of the Codex*, 55–57.

[14] Ibid., 58–60.

[15] Theodore C. Skeat, "The Origin of the Christian Codex," *ZPE* 102 (1994) 263–64.

[16] Ibid., 264; cf. idem, "The Oldest Manuscript of the Four Gospels?" *NTS* 43 (1997) 30–32 [square brackets not in original]; on 31 he asks whether they might have been two separate volumes.

[17] See T. C. Skeat, "Oldest Manuscript of the Four Gospels?" 16–19.

and (2) that the codex dates from the "late 2nd century."[18] If so, P64+67+4 would be our oldest manuscript of the four gospels, with P75 being "the only possible rival."[19]

Finally, referring to P52, a codex of the Fourth Gospel and the earliest extant New Testament papyrus (early 2nd century), Skeat suggested that the "key" to the early Christian choice of the codex over the roll was the publication of the Gospel of John about 100 C.E.—an event that forced the church "to consider any physical
means by which the four Gospels could be brought together and at 18
the same time additions to their number could be discouraged," resulting in a decision "to include all four in a codex, the new form of book recently developed in Rome."[20] Thus, it is no longer the Gospel of Mark (as proposed earlier) that was the catalyst, but the Gospel of John.

B. *Gamble's Explanation for the Christian Adoption of the Codex*

Gamble rightly moves beyond these theories of Roberts and Skeat—though he could not have dealt with Skeat's revised hypothesis that the fourfold gospel in a single-book format provided the occasion that solidified the Christian use of the codex. Gamble's approach to the issue of how and why the early Christians adopted the codex format is, so to speak, to leap-frog over all of the controversy about earliest extant codices and to move to a slightly earlier period of Christianity—that is, he takes a sizable step backward in time that he hopes will be a major leap forward in answering how the codex became so major a feature of earliest Christianity. In short, he argues (49–66) that the Pauline letters occasioned the Christian use of the codex. More specifically, he postulates an early collection of Paul's letters, arranged according to the number, not of letters written, but of churches to which he wrote, namely seven churches, and he maintains that the letters were arranged in the edition by decreasing length. The publication of such a collection could only have been achieved, he argues, by placing them in a single book—namely a codex. If not a codex, a roll eighty feet long would have been

[18] Ibid., 30; cf. 26–31.
[19] Ibid., 30; cf. now Graham N. Stanton, "The Fourfold Gospel," *NTS* (1997) 326–29.
[20] Skeat, "The Origin of the Christian Codex," 266–67.

required—double the maximum length and triple the normal length of Greek rolls (58–63). Gamble brings an array of support to his proposal that esteem for Christian documents in the early second century sufficient to warrant imitation of their format can only be found in connection with the Pauline corpus (63). He does not claim that this Pauline codex was the first use of a codex in Christianity; rather, it is "likely," he says, that the codex's earliest use by Christians was for collections of texts or "testimony books" from Jewish Scripture. He bases this on the earliest known function for the codex, namely as a notebook. That, however, would not have been a sufficiently significant catalyst to lock in the codex format as the Christian standard—a role Gamble reserves exclusively for the Pauline seven-church corpus (65).

Gamble's argument, which cannot be further reviewed here, is
meticulously documented and progresses logically toward his conclusion; yet, it is complex and is not without its speculative aspects.
For one thing, in spite of its advantages over Roberts's and Skeat's
original views of a single book as catalyst for the adoption of the
codex, Gamble's assertion that an early Pauline collection served as
that catalyst must face up to the actual evidence for codices in the
earliest period of Christianity that contain two or more writings—
or, rather, the paucity of such codices containing letters of Paul as
19 compared with those containing more than one gospel. These data
will be presented later.

C. *Alternative Views on the Christian Adoption of the Codex*

In the meantime, I wonder whether a simpler—perhaps almost simple-minded—explanation is not more likely in the pragmatic and spontaneous evangelistic environment of earliest Christianity. Focusing again on Paul, the first known Christian writer, I am still inclined to give more weight than Gamble does to a 1985 review of Roberts and Skeat's *The Birth of the Codex* by Michael McCormick of Dumbarton Oaks and Johns Hopkins University.[21]

McCormick utilized two items, the first from the book he was reviewing, namely, its list of the seventeen non-Christian codices

[21] Michael McCormick, "The Birth of the Codex and the Apostolic Life-Style," *Scriptorium* 39 (1985) esp. 154–58.

assigned to the second century, and the second from Eric Turner's *Typology of the Early Codex*, which cataloged the sizes of nearly 250 papyrus codices. McCormick noted that ten of the early non-Christian codices contained works prominent in Hellenistic education and that two others were medical treatises;[22] he then suggested that "geographical mobility" was a common characteristic of ancient doctors and teachers—who were often on the move—and, further, that Turner's lists reveal that early papyrus codices tend to be modest in size but especially narrower than later codices;[23] indeed, a group of some forty codices are twice or more as tall as they are wide; nearly 80% of these date from the second to the fourth centuries and, in addition, they include three out of the nine very earliest codices (2nd or 2nd/3rd century) in the entire list of some 250.[24] (The four earliest parchment codices, also all dating to the 2nd or 2nd/3rd centuries, also are modest in size though squarish.[25]) Such modest sized codices, and especially narrow ones, would be convenient for travel.

What sizes are we talking about? The largest papyrus codex (from the 6th/7th century) is nearly fifteen inches wide and eleven inches high, but the average large codex is more like ten inches wide by fourteen inches, while a "modest" codex might average about five or six inches wide with heights varying from six to eight inches, though more normally from nine to ten inches and not infrequently as much as eleven or twelve inches high. What sizes are our New Testament manuscripts up to the year 200 C.E.? Giving width first and then height, P52 is about 7¼ × 8½ inches; P46 is 6½ × 10¾; P32 is 6 × 8½; P64+67+4 is about 5¼ × 7½; and P66 and P90 are only 5½ or 5 × 6½ inches. The page sizes of P77 and P98 have not been determined. If we add two New Testament codices dated in the early third century by Aland,[26] we increase the number of early Christian codices of modest size, for P23 measures only 4½ × 8 inches (though Turner dates it 3rd or 4th century rather than early third)[27] and P75 is 5¼ × 10½. Indeed, if we observe

---

[22] Ibid., 156–57.
[23] Ibid., 157–58.
[24] See Turner, *Typology of the Early Codex*, 14–25.
[25] Ibid., 39.
[26] Kurt Aland, *Kurzgefasste Liste der griechischen Handschriften des Neuen Testaments* (2nd ed.; ANTF 1; Berlin/New York: de Gruyter, 1994) 30, 33.
[27] Turner, *Typology of the Early Codex*, 146.

where our earliest New Testament papyri are to be found in Turner's
20 convenient analysis of codex dimensions, McCormick's point is the more impressive: Turner placed papyrus codices into eleven categories, beginning with the broadest (fifteen inches) and moving down to the narrowest (one inch!); of course, anyone consulting his tables[28] will quickly discover that the matter is not as simple as it sounds. The results, however, can be simply enough stated: Twenty-three New Testament papyri are included in the list of 248 papyrus codices and sixteen of these are dated (by Aland—though not always by Turner) to the turn of the third/fourth centuries or earlier. Of these sixteen earliest manuscripts, none appears in the first three groups (those listing the widest and largest codices), while P45 (8 x 10 inches) falls into Group 4, P52 (7¼ × 8½) in Group 5, and P39 (6½ × 10½) in Group 6. As the widths decrease (and often the heights increase), we find P28, P32, and P47 (ca. 5¼ × 8½ to 10¾) in Group 7; then P1, P5, P37, P46, P69, and P75 (all of them between 5⅛ to 6½ × 10 to 10¾) in Group 8. This eighth group is special for Turner because twenty-five of its forty-five codices are twice as high as they are wide, while the other twenty codices are also narrow and tall; in addition, fifteen are certainly single-quire volumes and the other ten may be also; finally, thirty-eight of the forty-five are of fourth century or earlier date, with sixteen of the forty-five dating to the turn of the third/fourth centuries or earlier; moreover, three of the group members stem from the second or second/third centuries. This leads Turner to theorize that the earliest format of the papyrus codex is represented by this group—or possibly by Group 9.[29] The latter consists of more or less square codices, including New Testament P4, P64+67, and P66 (all in the 5 or 5½ × 6½ or 7½ range); eleven out of the twenty-one codices date at or before the turn of the third/fourth centuries. Incidentally, P23 (Aland, early 3rd, but Turner, 3rd/4th) would fit Group 8, and P90 (Aland, 2nd [= P.Oxy L.3523, published in 1983]) would fall into Group 9. Finally, no New Testament papyri appear in Group 10, though P78 (2 × 1¼) fits the "miniature" category of Group 11. So, of the eighteen of our earliest New Testament papyri in these lists, only one (P45, which is 8 × 10 inches) may exceed the "modest" size, for the

[28] Ibid., 13–25.
[29] Ibid., 24–25.

other seventeen are no wider than about seven inches—and are mostly narrow and tall or narrow and "squarish"—and eleven fall into the two groups most likely representative of the earliest codex form.

We return to McCormick's discussion: After noting that the codex was attractive to itinerant teachers and doctors for its transportability and for the protection provided to the texts between its covers (though no covers survive from codices of the first three centuries[30]), he asked a leading question:

> Is it impossible then that the transient life-style of the first generations of Christian evangelizers encouraged them to adopt a novel form of the book, one which appealed mainly to contemporaries whose life-style also involved frequent movement?[31]

His answer, naturally, was negative—that it is altogether possible 21
that first generation Christians "on the move" would adopt the new codex format. McCormick then appealed to Martial's reference from 84–86 C.E. about codices being more compact and convenient for travelers (I.2) and to the fictive 2 Tim 4:13–as does Gamble (quoting McCormick) for his theory. The 2 Timothy passage shows that Paul and books in codex form were linked together in the minds of slightly later Christians, and it also put into the mix a "cloak" (φαιλόνης) typical of travelers.[32] For what it is worth, 2 Timothy likely appeared in the same general period that produced P52-depending again on the dating of P52 by paleographers and of 2 Timothy by New Testament scholars.

Thus, rather than the "big bang" theories of Roberts and Gamble (and lately Skeat)—who require a powerful event involving a Christian document of high authority in codex form to establish this format as the standard for subsequent Christian writings—it may be that simple *portability* of writings for the practical evangelistic and teaching purposes of the new faith loomed much larger than other factors in the Christian readiness to adopt the codex at a very early time.

At once, of course, I can hear the highly appropriate question from Roberts, Gamble, and Skeat: "Portability of what?" What early Christian documents would need to accompany an early itinerant

---

[30] See Gamble, *Books and Readers*, 69.

[31] McCormick, "Birth of the Codex," 158.

[32] Ibid., 155, 157; cf. Gamble, *Books and Readers*, 64–65.

teacher/missionary? Roberts would say, "Mark, the earliest gospel!" Gamble might answer, "Prior to the Pauline corpus, *testimonia* would be carried about," and then he would add, "The seven-church Pauline corpus!"—especially since we have fairly early evidence that letters contained in that corpus were read in other churches (witness Col 4:16). Skeat would respond, "A four-gospel codex!" Has this lengthy discussion of portability, then, taken us no farther than when we undertook it? Not necessarily.

My own answer as to what might have been between the covers of a Christian traveler's codex would be quite muted; I would simply postulate that somewhere in the first century and a half of Christianity, some traveling leader (or leaders) utilized the codex for carrying writings important to such a person in the early Christian mission—whatever those writings might have been. In a time of relatively few personal possessions, a respected visitor's "props" (so to speak) would be strikingly visible to the congregation visited and doubtless would be readily imitated—since papyrus was relatively plentiful and inexpensive.[33] In contrast to the expected roll, the fairly new codex would be memorable. Witness again the stereotypical "props" of the itinerant Paul as imagined by the author of 2 Timothy (4:13): "the cloak . . ., also the books, and above all the parchments." So, in my view, the likely content of the traveling codex is less important than its mere presence and use in the highly charged setting of evangelism and edification in pristine Christianity—especially when a respected visitor is present with this new mark of his/her calling.

22 Does this, however, move the issue at all beyond the view of Roberts—that the codex of Mark "acquired a sentimental and symbolic value as well as a practical one"?[34] The answer is "yes" when it is observed that the present view obviates the notion that a copy of Mark must have been in the codex—which was unconvincing—just as it renders unnecessary the presence of a specific writing or collection of writings, such as the fourfold gospel or the sevenfold Pauline corpus. These views all have their highly speculative aspects. Yet, by retaining Roberts's aptly phrased "sentimental," "symbolic," and "practical" characteristics of the new codex format and stressing

[33] On the availability and cost of papyrus, see T. C. Skeat, "Was Papyrus Regarded as 'Cheap' or 'Expensive' in the Ancient World?" *Aeg* 75 (1995) 75–93.

[34] Roberts, "The Codex," 189.

their nature as a galvanizing combination when an itinerant Christian leader very visibly displayed his/her "book" and employed it in heart-stirring proclamation, in compelling paraenesis, or in urgent debate, perhaps some progress may be claimed.

After all, we know well enough from Paul's genuine letters, from the Deutero-Paulines, and from Acts—recognizing all of its historical problems—that leaders in early Christianity were traveling about from the first generation of the new faith. Of course, no Christian writings are known until those of Paul in the sixth decade of the first century, but in the succeeding three or four decades our four gospels were produced, and by the first half of the second century a codex of the Gospel of John (P52) was in use in Egypt. By the late second century or the turn of the second/third centuries, other codices of John (P90, P66, P75), of Acts (P98), of Pauline letters (P32 [Titus], P46), of Matthew (P77), of Luke (P75), and of Matthew and Luke (P64+67+4) were in circulation (as we can document from among the randomly preserved Egyptian papyri). At this very time the *Gospel of Peter*, for instance, was being used in Egypt, as witnessed by two fragments from Oxyrhynchus (P.Oxy XLI.2949).[35] Certainly other Christian writings were circulating as well, some destined for the canon and others not, including Jewish Christian and other gospel materials and apocryphal apocalypses, though it is not until the third century that we have documentary evidence for the circulation of collected Greek sayings of Jesus: PEgerton 2 (ca. 200);[36] P.Oxy I.1 and IV.654, 655 (all third century, though only I.1 is a codex), later identified, of course, as portions of the Coptic *Gospel of Thomas*; and, slightly later (early 4th century), the enigmatic P.Oxy X.1224, a codex with three otherwise unknown sayings of Jesus. Codices containing New Testament portions bloom in the third century through the turn of the third/fourth centuries, with thirty-five beyond the nine already mentioned (30 papyri + 5 on parchment, if one includes the Diatessaron majuscule, 0212).

Altogether, the New Testament manuscripts to which we have just referred number forty-four and they all date up to the turn of the

---

[35] See Dieter Lührmann, "POx 2949: EvPt 3–5 in einer Handschrift des 2./3. Jahrhunderts." *ZNW* 72 (1981) 216–26; cf. Helmut Koester, *Ancient Christian Gospels: Their History and Development* (Philadelphia: Trinity Press International, 1990) 216–17.

[36] See Koester, *Ancient Christian Gospels*, 205–16.

third/fourth centuries or earlier. Four other New Testament papyri are from rolls (P12, P13, P18, and P22, though all are exceptional cases, for they were written either on reused papyrus or on the back of a roll containing another writing:[37] e.g., P13 is on the reverse of an epitome of Livy and P18 on the verso of a roll with Exodus).
23 Together these forty-eight manuscripts (with 0212) are our earliest documentary witnesses to the New Testament texts. Their coverage of the New Testament is impressive—recognizing again the random nature of their preservation. Subtracting the four fragments from rolls and thereby, for our present purpose, counting only the forty-four earliest codices, twenty (or 45.5%) contain gospels (including 0212, the Diatessaron parchment), twelve (or 27.5%) contain Pauline letters, six (or 13.5%) contain the Acts (plus two others that also have gospel portions), five (11.5%) have catholic epistles, one (2%) has the Apocalypse of John, and Hebrews is found along with Pauline letters in P46.

Now, why have I offered all this tedious detail on codices of the third/fourth centuries and earlier? For two reasons. First, to show, for what it may be worth, that extant codices containing letters of Paul in this early period do not constitute a majority of the texts preserved but only about 27%. Similar proportions result when the gospel and Pauline papyri are sorted out from the entire list of our ninety-five different papyri, or, better, ninety-one when we subtract the four rolls: the gospels appear in forty-four papyri, comprising 48%, while Pauline letters are found in twenty papyri, or 23%.

Second, these data assist in responding to a statement from Gamble that:

> The large majority of Christian codices in the earliest period contain the text of only a single document. With the exception of the letters of Paul, the practice of collecting discrete texts within a single codex was limited. (67)

There is no quarrel with the first sentence, for, as far as we can tell, fewer than one-fourth of the earliest group combine two or more writings; however, the implication of the second sentence is that it supports his preceding theory that a seven-church edition of Paul established the codex format in Christianity. To be more specific, of

[37] See Aland and Aland, *Text of the New Testament*, 102.

the forty-five earliest papyri and majuscules in codex form (through the turn of the 3rd/4th centuries), eleven contain two or more New Testament writings. This assumes that 1–2 Thessalonians count as two writings (P30); that the identification of P4 with P64+P67 is accepted (as discussed above and adopted by Gamble), which would make this a manuscript that contained Matthew and Luke; and that the Diatessaron codex (0212) is included. Incidentally, Skeat, when examining P90, a second century codex with portions of John 18–19, concluded that "a combination of two [gospels], like the Bodmer Luke and John (P75) cannot be ruled out."[38] Of these eleven [or twelve—if the Diatessaron manuscript is excluded] codices with two or more writings, only four are Pauline (P30, P46, P92, P99), that is, 36% [or 33%], compared with six [or seven] of the gospels, that is, 55% [or 58%]. The remaining codex with multiple writings has Jude and 1–2 Peter (P72).[39]

The result is that, on three counts now, we have similar—and 24
smaller—percentages of our earliest manuscripts that contain Paul. First, among all of these forty-five oldest codices, 27% contain Pauline materials compared with 44% containing gospels; second, among all ninety-one New Testament papyrus codices, 23% contain Paul, while 48% have gospels; third, of the eleven codices of the third/fourth centuries or earlier that have two or more New Testament writings, 36% are Pauline, while 55% are gospels (or in one case Matthew plus Acts [P53]). Therefore, the implication that the collecting of Pauline letters in a single codex was more common than collecting non-Pauline New Testament writings is difficult to sustain, at least on the basis of the earliest surviving papyrus and parchment codices.[40] The various comparisons referred to can be displayed as follows:

[38] T. C. Skeat in his edition of P.Oxy L.3523: *The Oxyrhynchus Papyri* (Graeco-Roman Memoirs, 70; London: British Academy, 1983) L, p. 4.

[39] [On the content and arrangement of P72, see now E. J. Epp, "Issues in the Interrelation of New Testament Textual Criticism and Canon," *The Canon Debate* (ed. Lee Martin McDonald and James A. Sanders; Peabody, MA: Hendrickson, 2002) 491–93.]

[40] See now also Stanton, "The Fourfold Gospel," 339 n. 79.

Proportions of Gospel and Pauline Manuscripts

Basis of Comparison	Gospels	Paul
11 multi-writing codices	6 manuscripts = 55%	4 manuscripts = 36%
48 oldest manuscripts	21 manuscripts = 44%	12 manuscripts = 25%
45 oldest codices	20 manuscripts = 44%	12 manuscripts = 27%
95 different papyri	45 manuscripts = 47%	21 manuscripts = 22%
91 different codices	44 manuscripts = 48%	21 manuscripts = 23%

Do these statistics disprove Gamble's theory? Not at all, for we may be dealing with quite random and accidental data, but they do, I think, allow for other explanations, including the one offered above—that the codex as a new and memorable property of early traveling Christian leaders (chosen in the first instance for convenience) quickly became a trademark of early Christian teachers and preachers and was rapidly and widely adopted as the format for writings used in the worship and life of the Christian community.

Another recent suggestion deserves discussion. The Annual Meeting of the Society of Biblical Literature in November 1996 was the occasion for my presentation of the preceding information and views; some six months later, Graham Stanton's informative and incisive Presidential Address for the Studiorum Novi Testamenti Societas (August 1996) on "The Fourfold Gospel" first came to my attention when it appeared in *New Testament Studies* (1997). Working independently and to somewhat different ends, we nonetheless approached several issues in similar fashion and developed generally similar views, sometimes using strikingly similar expressions (e.g., "big bang" theory). Stanton, whose aim was to account for the rise of the fourfold gospel, asked "Which form of explanation is preferable, a 'big bang' theory or a theory of gradual development?"[41] He engaged the views of David Trobisch[42] and Skeat,[43] and he concluded (à la Skeat) that the emergence of the four-gospel format must be tied to the "Christian
[25] adoption of the codex, for no roll could contain four gospels."[44] But, in contrast to Skeat's crisis explanation—the appearance of the Fourth

[41] Ibid., 336.

[42] David Trobisch, *Die Endredaktion des Neuen Testaments: Eine Untersuchung zur Entstehung der christlichen Bibel* (NTOA 31; Freiburg: Universitätsverlag; Göttingen: Vandenhoeck & Ruprecht, 1996).

[43] Skeat, "The Origin of the Christian Codex."

[44] Stanton, "The Fourfold Gospel," 337; see 338–39.

Gospel (see above)—he preferred to postulate a gradual endorsement of the codex form, envisioning Christian scribes who "experimented with single-gospel codices" by following the pattern of the pocket-sized parchment codices of Roman invention recommended by Martial for travelers.[45] Stanton further imagined the process in this interesting fashion:

> Christian scribes preparing writings to be carried by missionaries, messengers, and travellers over long distances would have readily appreciated the advantages of the codex. Their general counter-culture stance would have made them more willing than their non-Christian counterparts to break with the almost unanimous preference for the roll and experiment with the unfashionable codex. (338–39)

He added:

> The earliest Christian experiments with the codex took place at a time when Christians were adopting a distinctive identity as a *tertium genus* over against both Judaism and the pagan world.[46]

The new format, then, was their way of expressing their sense of newness and distinctiveness.[47]

Stanton's suggestion of conscious, deliberate experiments with the codex format by Christian scribes around 150 in an effort to prepare suitable and convenient writings for traveling missionaries has its appeal, though it may strike some as presuming more formal, more organized, and more professional Christian scribal activities than can yet be documented in this period—and perhaps also more calculation and intentionality by these scribes than might be likely in the early Christian situation. How much, after all, do we know about Christian scriptoria in this early period? Gamble (120–22; 158–59) skillfully pulls together the evidence and makes perhaps the best possible case for Christian scriptoria in the second century, though one based—of necessity—on inference and speculation, and C. H. Roberts inferred from the large quantity of Christian texts, including an autograph, found at Oxyrhynchus that a Christian scriptorium there in the third century or even the late second is "not unlikely."[48] At the same time, Kurt Aland's view is well known:

---

[45] Ibid., 338; he also refers to McCormick, "Birth of the Codex."

[46] Stanton, "The Fourfold Gospel," 338–39.

[47] Ibid., 339.

[48] C. H. Roberts, *Manuscript, Society and Belief in Early Christian Egypt* (Schweich

"There were no scriptoria . . . before A.D. 200 at the earliest."[49]

Stanton's view, nonetheless, has the distinct virtue of envisaging the Christian codex format emerging out of practical, real-life situations, as assuredly must have been the case. My view, though no less speculative, also seeks to identify an appropriately practical set
26 of circumstances for the adoption of the codex. As described above, my suggestion, however, may have the advantage of envisioning (1) a less conscious and calculated adaptation and adoption of the codex as a format for writings useful to itinerant Christian leaders and (2) a more *dynamic* and spontaneous situation in which the new format took hold in earliest Christianity: the codex's simple portability and therefore practicality when such traveling teachers required a portion of the Septuagint, an apostolic letter, or a gospel that might serve evangelistic purposes or deeply felt needs for paraenesis and edification in the life of a developing but vibrant church. Then, once used in an impassioned, life-altering context by a person of accepted authority, the codex became a memorable attribute and acquired a symbolic value.

II. Literacy and Literary Criticism

Next, I wish to follow a suggestion made early in Gamble's work. He speaks of the desirability of "a sociology of early Christian literature" and calls the book "a social artifact" (p. 43): "All aspects of the production, distribution, and use of texts presuppose social functions and forces" (p. 43). I agree heartily and wish to explore and illustrate his point further in a constructively critical fashion.

A. *Oxyrhynchus as a Test Case*

The approach I would like to take may seem arbitrary at first, but is logical enough upon reflection. Where, in a single geographical location, can the socio-cultural setting of a sizable number of our earliest New Testament manuscripts be observed? The obvious answer

Lectures, 1977; London: Oxford University Press, 1979) 24; for another inferential approach, see Epp, "Significance of the Papyri," 91 [= Epp-Fee, *Studies in the Theory and Method*, 288–89].

[49] Aland and Aland, *Text of the New Testament*, 55.

is Oxyrhynchus, an Egyptian district capital some 200 miles up the Nile from Alexandria, where thirty-one New Testament papyri were discovered.[50]

1. *New Testament Manuscripts at Oxyrhynchus*

These thirty-one papyrus manuscripts constitute thirty-three percent of the ninety-five different New Testament papyri currently known. (Papyri total ninety-nine, but four should be subtracted because three pairs or groups among them each represent a single manuscript: P11+14, P33+58, and P64+67+4.) Moreover, twenty-one of these (twenty-two if we count uncial 0162 from Oxyrhynchus [P.Oxy VI.847]) are among the forty-seven oldest New Testament manuscripts (or forty-eight if uncial 0212 of the Diatessaron is counted), that is, those dating prior to or around the turn of the third/fourth centuries. Included in this ancient cohort are forty-three papyri and four or five uncials (0189, 0220, 0162, 0171, and five if we count 0212)—all of which are accorded special significance by textual critics because they predate the grand majuscule manuscripts long prominent in New Testament textual criticism: ℵ, B, A, W, and D. It is particularly noteworthy, then, that Oxyrhynchus has furnished us with 45% of the earliest group of New Testament manuscripts.

Of additional significance is the proportion of New Testament 27
writings included among the Oxyrhynchus papyri; most, of course, are highly fragmentary, but portions of fifteen of our twenty-seven New Testament books are attested, in spite of the quite random preservation factors in the rubbish heaps of Oxyrhynchus. Some books, like Matthew and John, are represented in seven and six different papyri, respectively; Romans occurs in three; Acts, Hebrews, James, and John's Apocalypse are found each in two; and the following each in a single papyrus: Luke, 1 Corinthians, Galatians, Philippians, 1–2 Thessalonians, 1 John, and Jude. One of them (P30) contains two writings—1–2 Thessalonians (as perhaps P90 did originally—as discussed above). Overall, the gospels comprise 45%, while Paul accounts for 23% of the Oxyrhynchus New Testament papyri. It is perhaps only a curious coincidence that these proportions are

[50] Twenty-eight were published in *The Oxyrhynchus Papyri*; three as PSI 1 (P35, 4th), PSI 3 (P36, 6th), and PSI 1165 (P48, 3rd).

exceptionally close to the percentages shown earlier for the gospels (44%) and for Paul (25%) when the larger group of the forty-eight earliest New Testament manuscripts is analyzed, or when all ninety-five papyri are considered. These statistics may be displayed for clarity:

Proportions of Gospel and Pauline Manuscripts

Basis of Comparison	Gospels	Paul
31 oxyrhynchus papyri	14 manuscripts = 45%	7 manuscripts = 23%
48 oldest manuscripts	21 manuscripts = 44%	12 manuscripts = 25%
95 different papyri	45 manuscripts = 47%	21 manuscripts = 22%

This may well suggest that Oxyrhynchus, even in its random preservation of papyri, is, in this respect at least, a fine representative of the New Testament papyri as a whole. Be that as it may, the Oxyrhynchus papyri constitute an invaluable laboratory where statistically significant materials of known provenance can be examined, and we have every right to expect them to provide useful insights into the real-life context in which they were used.

2. *The Socio-cultural Setting of Oxyrhynchus*

Actually, we know a good deal about Oxyrhynchus with respect to its socio-cultural-economic characteristics from the 4,400 or more published papyri found there. It was a city that, in Roman times, had a population of perhaps 30,000,[51] and the papyri provide us with the actual names of some 5,700 residents that can be identified already in the period from ca. 30 B.C.E.–96 C.E.[52] As is also known from its papyri and from excavation, the city had some twenty temples and a theater with a capacity in the range of eight to twelve thousand people.[53] For example, P.Oxy I.43 (verso), dating after 295 C.E., provides a report of watchmen and their rounds of Oxyrhynchus's

[51] Julian Krüger, *Oxyrhynchos in der Kaiserzeit: Studien zur Topographie und Literaturrezeption*; European University Studies, III. 441; Frankfurt am Main/New York: Peter Lang, 1990) 8.

[52] B. W. Jones and E. G. Whitehorne, *Register of Oxyrhynchites 30 B.C.–A.D. 96* (ASP 25; Chico, CA: Scholars Press, 1983).

[53] Eric G. Turner, *Greek Papyri: An Introduction* (Oxford: Clarendon Press, 1968) 81.

main streets and public buildings, and we learn of the temples of
Sarapis, Isis, Thoëris, and Caesar; of two churches, north and south;
of the aforementioned theater, the capitol, three baths, the gymna- 28
sium, a Nilometer (measuring the annual floods), and four city gates.[54] We discover something else about the city's night watchmen from a municipal account of payments about a century earlier: it records an allocation of 2,000 drachmai "to Dionysius . . . in command of the fifty night watchmen" (P.Oxy XVII.2128). The residents of multicultural Oxyrhynchus lived in "quarters" or regions that might have numbered as many as twenty, some named for various groups of inhabitants, such as Cretans or Jews (P.Oxy II.335 records the sale of a house in the Jewish quarter ca. 83 C.E.; cf. P.Oxy IX.1205's mention of an affluent synagogue in 291 C.E.); others for trades or occupations, including gooseherds, shepherds, and an equestrian camp; still others bear the names of temples (Sarapis, Thoëris), public buildings (theater, gymnasium, warm baths), and streets or location within their boundaries (South Broad Street, north quarter, south quarter).

There is no time to pursue the almost endless socio-cultural, economic, and political insights that we gain from some 3,000 business and legal documents and private letters that the papyri from the rubbish heaps preserve for us in this "illustrious and most illustrious" city of Oxyrhynchus (P.Oxy X.1264, among many others), which already at the beginning of the second century quartered a Roman garrison (P.Oxy VII.1022 [Latin]). This brief survey, however, may serve adequately the present purpose.[55]

B. *Classical Writings at Oxyrhynchus and Literacy*

More important for our present purposes are the remnants of known and previously unknown classical authors that pervaded these same rubbish heaps. As catalogued by Julian Krüger in his1990 volume,[56] the classical works numbered 1,435 (though many more have been published since then), and these rolls and codices stem from the period around the turn of the second/first centuries B.C.E. to the turn of the sixth/seventh centuries C.E.—more than 700 years. To

[54] *Oxyrhynchus Papyri* I, p. 89.

[55] See Epp, "The Significance of the Papyri," 54–62, for details on the foregoing and for fuller data on what follows.

[56] Krüger, *Oxyrhynchos in der Kaiserzeit*, 313–48.

pursue our goal of placing the early Oxyrhynchus New Testament manuscripts within their socio-cultural and intellectual context requires, however, the narrowing of the comparative base to the period encompassed by the earliest forty-eight New Testament manuscripts, namely the period from the turn of the first/second centuries to the third/fourth centuries—a span of some 200 years rather than 700. However, this is still too long a period to provide a realistic picture of classical literature present and available in Oxyrhynchus during a typical lifespan, so shorter time-frames ought to be delineated. Literary works, however, cannot often be dated precisely—either as to their time of production or of use—so literature available during periods of fifty years, for example, would be difficult to determine. Methodologically then, since books usually outlast people, we may settle on examining literature falling into two periods: one from about 80–200 C.E. and another from 200 to about 325 C.E.

29 A cursory summary—requiring updating since Krüger—shows that in the 80–200 period, Oxyrhynchus held twenty-four copies of works by Aeschylus, ten of Apollonius of Rhodes, three of Aristophanes, two of Aristotle, twenty-eight of Callimachus, eighteen of Demosthenes, eighteen of Euripides, eleven of Herodotus, thirty-four of Hesiod, fifty-five of Homer, eight of Isocrates, fourteen of Menander, thirteen of Pindar, twenty-eight of Plato, one of Plutarch, eight of Sappho, ten of Sophocles, nine of Theocritus, one of Theophrastus, eleven of Thucydides, and six of Xenophon, plus many other known authors and some 100 anonymous literary works and three dozen miscellaneous works.

A similar assessment of the succeeding period of about 200 to 325 reveals that most of these authors are represented by additional copies, for instance, sixteen more copies each of Demosthenes and Euripides, twelve of Herodotus, thirty of Hesiod, 121 of Homer, seventeen of Menander, eight of Pindar, twenty-one of Plato, seven of Sappho, five of Sophocles, thirteen of Thucydides, and six of Xenophon, plus Latin authors such as Livy, Sallust, and Virgil, plus many other known authors and nearly 100 each of anonymous literary works and of historical and scientific works.

How does all this apply to Gamble's book? First, it occasions a question—though no answer—about literacy, and, second, it provides an opportunity to support his position on the generally non-literary character of Christian books. Though it is difficult and risky to compare Oxyrhynchus, a city of some 30,000, with modern cities of similar size, North Americans may think of a city the size of Fairbanks, Alaska (30,800), or New Castle, Pennsylvania (28,330), or Paducah, Kentucky (27,250), or Del Rio, Texas (30,700), or Walla Walla, Washington (26,500), and ask about the breadth, depth, and general quantity of literary works that might be available there, at the same time discounting the benefits of the printing press, modern distribution methods, and a system of public education.

Assessing literacy in the Greco-Roman and early Christian worlds is fraught with difficulties.[57] The vast breadth but also depth in classical authors found in either the second or the third century in Oxyrhynchus suggests at least a questioning of the 10% to 20% average literacy rate for the entire Greco-Roman world that Gamble accepts from William Harris.[58] Those figures may be perfectly justifiable, and certainly I am neither trained nor qualified to alter them, but the instance of Oxyrhynchus, with its extensive literary activity and also the evidence from its vast array of documents and letters, causes one to wonder about them. To be sure, time and time again the papyrus documents indicate that their originators are illiterate and that others are writing for them. In Roman Egypt, families with literate men commonly had illiterate women, yet, an Oxyrhynchus papyrus provides a rare exception, for it reveals a literate Oxyrhynchite woman, whose Alexandrian (!) husband and his brother were illiterate (P.Oxy XII.1463 [215 C.E.]);[59] and in 263 C.E. a female petitioner supports her argument by claiming that she is "able to write with the greatest ease"(P.Oxy XII.1467). Harris takes this as evidence that even among affluent women like these literacy was the exception,[60] but the woman petitioner is writing to the Prefect of Egypt and her appeal to writing may indicate, rather, that literate Oxyrhynchite women were more numerous than at other localities (cf. also P.Oxy XII.1473, line 21).

Interestingly, Harris also affirms that "there is little to suggest that any ordinary Greek city of this period took the large extra step of publicly financing elementary education,"[61] but then he points to

[57] See Gamble, *Books and Readers*, 2–10.

[58] Ibid., 4, see n. 8. He is referring to William V. Harris, *Ancient Literacy* (Cambridge, MA: Harvard University Press, 1989).

[59] See Harris, *Ancient Literacy*, 279–80.

[60] Ibid., 280.

[61] Ibid., 245.

the only known example of such financing—and where is it? At Oxyrhynchus in the mid-third century, in a petition to the Emperors Valarian and Gallienus, from a certain Lollianus, who describes himself as a "public grammaticus of the City of the Oxyrhynchites." Here is how he registers his complaint:

> Your heavenly magnanimity, which has irradiated your domain, the whole civilized world, and your fellowship with the Muses (for Education sits beside you on the throne) have given me confidence to offer you a just and lawful petition. It is this: . . . For though I was elected public grammaticus here by the city council, it is not at all the case that I receive the usual salary, on the contrary, if at all, it is paid in sour wine and worm-eaten grain. . . . (P.Oxy LXVII. 3366 [253–60 C.E.])

He follows this with a request for an orchard in lieu of the salary owed, so that he may "have ample time for teaching the children." This sparse evidence, of course, applies to publicly supported education, and not to the private education or schools paid for by parents—which were likely to be found in every Greek or Hellenized city,[62] as witnessed also by P.Oxy XXXI.2595, line 10, which speaks of a "governess" or teacher in the household [τὴν δέσκαλον = διδάσκαλος]. So, is the estimate of 10% to 20% literacy high enough in this kind of city?

C. *Christian Literature at Oxyrhynchus and Literacy*

More relevant to Gamble's interest is Christian literacy. He assumes, perhaps quite correctly, the view that literacy in Christian circles during the first three centuries would not exceed—and more likely would not even attain—the level of literacy of its surrounding Greco-Roman culture, especially since Christians would likely have drawn a smaller percentage of its members from the upper (and more highly educated) classes and because the early church did not create its own alternative education system. He judges literacy among Christians in the first several centuries to have been "ordinarily not more than about 10 percent in any given setting, and perhaps fewer in many small and provincial congregations that were characteristic of early Christianity" (5; cf. 6–7).

It may be worth asking, again, whether Oxyrhynchus is likely to have followed this literacy pattern. What do we know about Christianity

[62] Ibid.

at Oxyrhynchus at the turn of the third/fourth centuries, the cut- 31
off date for our oldest group of New Testament papyri? Very little, actually—just as little is known about Christianity in Egypt as a whole in the earliest period. We know, however, from the night watchmen's records (mentioned earlier) that, as they made their rounds sometime after 295 C.E., there were at least two churches in Oxyrhynchus (P.Oxy I.43; cf. XI, p. 26); Rufinus reported thirty churches there in the fourth and fifth centuries, and in the early sixth century a bishop and some forty churches are evidenced by P.Oxy XI.1357 (535–36 C.E.)—a calendar of church services at Oxyrhynchus. [Though not relevant to Christianity, it is of interest that P.Oxy IX.1205 refers to a Jewish synagogue that, in 291 C.E., paid fourteen talents of silver (a large sum) to free a woman and her two small children, one of whom was named Jacob.][63]

Another source of information about Christianity at Oxyrhynchus is its literature, not only the twenty-eight New Testament papyri—of which twenty and a parchment codex (0162) fall into the period up to the turn of the third/fourth centuries—but also the apocryphal sayings of Jesus discussed earlier (P.Oxy I.1; IV.654, 655 [= portions of the Coptic *Gospel of Thomas*] and P.Oxy X.1224). Yet, there is much more within our selected time-frame, including some fifteen portions of Greek Jewish Scripture made for Christian use[64] and various Christian theological texts and treatises. A quick survey, first through the turn of the third/fourth centuries, reveals that some twenty more items of non-New Testament Christian literature survive at Oxyrhynchus, including gospels like the *Sophia Jesu Christi* (VIII.1081), the *Gospel of Mary* (L.3525; P.Ryl. III.463), and others (LXI.2949; P.Lond.Christ.1); four copies of the *Shepherd of Hermas* (III.404; XV.1828; L.3527, 3528); and one each of the *Apocalypse of Peter* (P.Vindob.G), the *Acts of Peter* (VI.849), Irenaeus's *Against Heresies* (III.405, but see IV, pp. 264–65), another apologetic work (XVII.2072),

---

[63] See P.Oxy IX, pp. 239–42, and *CPJ* 1.94. For the latter, see Victor A. Tcherikover and Alexander Fuks, eds., *Corpus Papyrorum Judaicarum* (3 vols.; Cambridge, MA: Harvard University Press, 1957–1964) 3.33–36.

[64] See a summary in E. J. Epp, "The New Testament Papyri at Oxyrhynchus in Their Social and Intellectual Context," *The Sayings of Jesus: Canonical and Non-canonical. Essays in Honour of Tjitze Baarda* (ed. W. L. Petersen, J. S. Vos, and H. J. de Jonge; NovTSup 89; Leiden: Brill, 1997) 60 n. 35 (where it is noted that "it is difficult to know for certain which were of Christian origin").

an anti-Jewish dialogue (XVII.2070), a prayer (III.407), and a hymn with musical notation (XV.1786), as well as some "gnostic" (I.4; XII.1478; P.Harr. 107) and other miscellaneous material (II.210). Twenty-some additional items would be added if the full fourth century is assessed, including three more copies of *Hermas* (IX.1172+3526; XIII.1599; L.3527), one each of the *Didache* (XV.1782), the *Acts of John* (VI.850), Aristides' *Apology* (XV.1778), the *Passion of St. Dioskorus* (L.3529), and the *Apocalypse of Baruch* (III.403), as well as an apocalyptic fragment (XVII.2069), a liturgical fragment (XVII.2068), a prayer (VII.1058), three sermons (XIII.1601; 1602; XVII.2073), three amulets (PSI 719; P.Amst. 26; SB 10762), and a "gnostic" charm (VI.924) and prayer (XII.1566).

What might this body of Christian literature imply about literacy within the Christian community (or communities) at Oxyrhynchus? That question would lend itself more easily to an answer if we had better knowledge of how large the Christian population was in the first three centuries or in the fourth. Or is that question better answered by asking what size community would produce or require
32 this array of Christian writing, recognizing that the surviving fragments are only partially representative of a larger quantity of books—and only of books discarded after use? What does it mean for the density of Christians in a city of 30,000 if at least two churches existed around 300 C.E. (P.Oxy I.43)? What size were such congregations? Or, again, are we not more likely to answer this question, too, on the basis of the quantity of Christian writings in use? Does it help any that we know of thirty churches in the next two centuries, or forty in the sixth century (P.Oxy XI.1357)? Also, we recognize fully that most reading in the Greco-Roman context was aloud[65] and that Christians who were illiterate thereby could still hear and interact with the written word. Thus, "literacy"—especially in a community where proclamation and teaching are intrinsic to its very life—is extended even to the illiterate, and such a community conceivably might even require or find useful a larger complement of literature than a smaller, purely literate congregation. Yet, with this caveat and in spite of many unanswerable questions, is it not appropriate to suggest that the Christian literacy rate at Oxyrhynchus was higher than 10%?

[65] See Gamble, *Books and Readers*, 203 and n. 1; but cf. Frank D. Gilliard, "More Silent Reading in Antiquity: *non omne verbum sonabat*," *JBL* 112 (1993) 689–96.

D. *Literary Criticism at Oxyrhynchus*

The data on literature and literacy at Oxyrhynchus also may help us to assess the literary character and quality of the New Testament writings there, and to determine whether literary-critical activity is evidenced in the New Testament manuscripts. Gamble places the earliest Christian books in the "intermediate phase in the evolving status of the codex—in the late first and early second centuries" and affirms that "the Christians who made them and made use of them did not regard them either as notebooks [the earliest phase] or as fine literature" [the final phase]—"they were practical books for everyday use" (66; cf. 77–78). I think that this is correct, and that it can be supported when the Oxyrhynchus literary papyri are compared with the New Testament papyri found there.

At Oxyrhynchus, there is much evidence of literary activity beyond the presence and presumed use of the myriad writings already surveyed. For example, an interesting third century papyrus scrap (P.Oxy XXIV.2400) lists subjects for student declamations that would require the reading of Thucydides or Euripides, and even some private letters (e.g., PSI 1248, early 3rd century) reveal fine expression and writing style.[66] More significant are documents dating around 173 C.E. that involve people who obviously are Alexandrian scholars (one of whom is known otherwise) who either are living in Oxyrhynchus or, more likely, spend time at their property there and who discuss the procurement of books and allude to a bookseller (P.Mert. I.19 and P.Oxy XVIII.2192)—"a circle of persons exchanging notes on how to procure and get copies made of works of scholarship, who are themselves professional scholars."[67] To these few examples, much more can be added to show that Oxyrhynchus was a city where numerous literary texts not only were in use but were subject to 33
editing and critical analysis.[68]

As Turner has pointed out, certain conventional critical marks or marks used in editing reveal that a reader has made use of a text, but they also display a reader's critical reaction to or interaction with the text. These are marks that move beyond the copying process,

---

[66] See Turner, *Greek Papyri*, 66–67; 84–85.

[67] Ibid., 87; cf. P.Oxy XVIII, p. 150.

[68] For a survey of further evidence, see Epp, "New Testament Papyri at Oxyrhynchus," 56–68.

so the concern here is not with *scribal* activity per se, that is, punctuation, lection marks, paragraph marks (the *paragraphus*), or even normal, simple, or routine manuscript corrections. Rather, the interest is in editor's or scholar's notations or critical marks, such as *glosses* or *scholia* (marginal notes, respectively, for explanation or illustration or for elucidating the meaning of difficult passages); *onomastica* (glosses explaining the meaning of names and places); notes of *commentary*, pointers to a commentary, or indications of the need for a commentary to a portion of text; and very specific *critical marks* or signs, most commonly the χ sign and the > or *diple* (διπλῆ), but also the obelus and antisigma, among others.[69] Such notes and marks are employed in prose and poetic literary manuscripts, but not—with rare exceptions—in documentary texts or private letters.

Many critical marks, especially the common signs χ and >, were prefixed to a line, apparently to indicate a point in the text that required a clarifying commentary, though they could serve other purposes as well, a number of which can be observed in the papyri. The χ sign was employed to call attention to something noteworthy in a line, including dissent from a reading, an inconsistency, a quotation or a parallel text, an unusual word or form of a word, and other general or specialized uses in certain authors, such as Homer, Pindar, or Plato. The > could expose wrong glosses, mark disputed words or passages, or raise other queries. Finding these two signs in a text, says Turner, "suggests either that the papyrus was being marked by a reader who had access to a commentary (or was making one for himself); or else that it was a copy of a text so marked," and he cites an instance in P.Oxy 2427, fr. 53, as evidence for the existence of a commentary on Epicharmus, because of the marginal note that reads "the χ was not in Theon's [copies]."[70]

In short, these critical marks in a literary text indicate literary criticism and other scholarly activity. There are many instances in the literary papyri at Oxyrhynchus: Turner, for example, in a list of

[69] See summaries in Turner, *Greek Papyri*, 112–18; cf. 92–95; idem, *Greek Manuscripts of the Ancient World* (2nd ed. rev. by P. J. Parsons; Bulletin Supplement, 46; London: University of London, Institute of Classical Studies, 1987 [original: Oxford: Clarendon Press, 1971], 14–16.

[70] Turner, *Typology of the Early Codex*, 117 and 184 n. 37; cf. 93–94 and 182 n. 55; for a similar marginal note, see P.Oxy XXIV.2387 and Turner, *Greek Manuscripts of the Ancient World*, 42–43.

thirty-four includes twenty-seven from Oxyrhynchus literary texts, and in a cursory perusal of the texts and plates in *The Oxyrhynchus Papyri* I discovered many additional examples into the fourth century.[71]

My next search was of the New Testament papyri from Oxyrhynchus, remembering Turner's challenging words: "Critical marks of this kind, used scrupulously, are one of the strongest and best indications that the texts in question were scholars' copies."[72] Were there any scholars' copies of New Testament books in Oxyrhynchus? 34
Incidentally, this question is not unrelated to the issue of scriptoria, yet it is a distinctly different matter, for Christian professional copying—if it were to be found in the early Christian generations at Oxyrhynchus—is still a step removed from literary and textual criticism (though it must be granted that a number of early scribes slipped across the line separating the two functions).[73] As far as *formal* literary-critical marks in our early New Testament papyri are concerned—which, if they were found, would indicate critical, scholarly work on those Christian writings—I have neither located studies on the matter nor has my own examination of available plates of numerous New Testament papyri, but especially those from Oxyrhynchus, disclosed certifiable instances of the specialized signs described earlier. They usually occur in the left margin, and a significant number of lines with left margins preserved survive among the twenty-eight Oxyrhynchus papyri (as well as the six New Testament uncials). The marks that do occur are lectional or reading aids (punctuation, accents, breathings, etc.) and the customary spacing and paragraph signs.[74] A few critical marks occur in manuscripts of the Bible presumably made for Christian use, including P.Ryl. I.1 of Deuteronomy, though the purpose of the signs is unclear there, and in P.Grenfell I.5, where Origen's hexaplaric signs occur in a copy of Ezekiel.[75] Cursory examination of extra-New Testament Christian literature from Oxyrhynchus did not provide instances of editing marks.

---

[71] Epp, "New Testament Papyri at Oxyrhynchus," 65 n. 48.

[72] Turner, *Greek Papyri*, 118.

[73] For examples, see E. J. Epp, *The Theological Tendency of Codex Bezae Cantabrigiensis in Acts* (SNTSMS 3; Cambridge: Cambridge University Press, 1966); Bart D. Ehrman, *The Orthodox Corruption of Scripture: The Effect of Early Christological Controversies on the Text of the New Testament* (New York/Oxford: Oxford University Press, 1993).

[74] For examples, see Epp, "New Testament Papyri at Oxyrhynchus," 20–21.

[75] See ibid., 20 n. 52.

In one sense, this lack of critical marks in New Testament and related early papyri was a disappointment, for discovery of such professional literary-critical activity and scholarly editing in early New Testament manuscripts would provide an opening for explaining the origin and development of any number of variant readings, accounting for aspects of the New Testament's tendentious textual variation, and answering long-intractable questions about early textual revisions, to give a few examples. But there is also a positive—and quite sensible—contribution, for these preliminary findings do support Gamble's view that the earliest Christian books represent the "intermediate phase" in the evolving codex, for they were regarded neither as notebooks nor as fine literature, but as "practical books for everyday use" (p. 66; cf. 77–78). That seems also to have been the case in the churches at Oxyrhynchus.

Appended Note: The Discovery of new Oxyrhynchus Papyri of the New Testament

Following the completion and submission of this article, Dr. J. David Thomas, paleographer and long-time editor of Oxyrhynchus papyri, who recently was named a general editor of *The Oxyrhynchus Papyri*, announced at the 1997 meeting of the Studiorum Novi Testamenti Societas in Birmingham, UK, the discovery and forthcoming publication of several new papyri of the New Testament from Oxyrhynchus—which were to total sixteen (P100–P115), published in *Oxyrhynchus Papyri* LXIV (1997); LXV (1998); and LXVI (1999). Relevant to the present study, six of these papyri contain portions of Matthew, one of Luke, four of John, and one of Romans, and all of these date from the 3rd/4th century or earlier.

For clarification and completeness, all sixteen newly-published manuscripts (P100–P115 in the official New Testament list) and their assigned dates are given here (in canonical order): MATTHEW: P101 (P.Oxy 4401) 3rd; P102 (P.Oxy 4402) 3rd/early 4th; P103 (P.Oxy 4403) 2nd/3rd; P104 (P.Oxy 4404) late 2nd; P105 (P.Oxy 4406) 5th/6th; and P110 (P.Oxy 4494) 4th; LUKE: P111 (P.Oxy 4495) 3rd; JOHN: P106 (P.Oxy 4445), P107 (P.Oxy 4446), P108 (P.Oxy 4447), and P109 (P.Oxy 4448), all dating in the 3rd century; ACTS: P112 (P.Oxy 4496) 5th; ROMANS: P113 (P.Oxy 4497) 3rd; HEBREWS: P114 (P.Oxy 4498) 3rd; JAMES: P100 (P.Oxy

4449) 3rd/4th; and the REVELATION OF JOHN: the extensive P115 (P.Oxy 4499) 3rd/4th. In addition, a new fragment of P77 (P.Oxy 2683) was published as P.Oxy 4405, and an uncial fragment of the Revelation of John as P.Oxy 4500 (= NT 0308) 4th. All are from codices and none gives clear evidence of having contained more than one New Testament writing.

Though no New Testament writings are represented for the first time among these papyri, the enhanced quantity of Matthean and Johannine papyri is impressive. Fifteen of the twenty-seven books of the New Testament are still represented among the 47 Oxyrhynchus papyri, but distributed as follows: Matthew in 13 papyri; John in 10; Romans in 4; Acts, Hebrews, James, and the Revelation of John in 3 each; Luke in 2; and 1 Corinthians, Galatians, Philippians, 1–2 Thessalonians, 1 John, and Jude in 1 papyrus each.

The significance of these remarkable finds for the present article will be obvious enough. We now possess 116 New Testament papyri, representing perhaps 112 different manuscripts; thirteen of the sixteen new papyri join the elite, early group (those up to and around the turn of the 3rd/4th centuries), and eleven contain portions of the gospels, while one contains Paul. Altogether, Oxyrhynchus New Testament papyri now number forty-seven of our 112 different New Testament papyri (42%) and constitute thirty-five of the sixty-one earliest New Testament manuscripts (57%).

Thus, in part 1 above on "The Codex Format," numerous statistics change in favor of our position. It would not be fair, however, to employ these data in our critique of Gamble's views, for the new manuscripts were not available to him for his book. An item that does not change is the proportion of multi-writing codices containing the gospels over against Paul, but—since all sixteen new Oxyrhynchus papyri are from codices—the proportion of gospel codices versus Pauline codices changes significantly both among our earliest witnesses and among all of our papyri: Among the fifty-seven oldest *codices* twenty-eight (49%) now are gospels and thirteen (22.8%) are Pauline, while among our 107 different *codices*, fifty-four (50.5%) contain gospels and twenty-two (20.6%) have Paul. The chart on p. 24, then, should be altered as follows:

PROPORTIONS OF GOSPEL AND PAULINE MANUSCRIPTS

BASIS OF COMPARISON	GOSPELS	PAUL
11 MULTI-WRITING CODICES	6 MANUSCRIPTS = 54.6%	4 MANUSCRIPTS = 36.4
61 OLDEST MANUSCRIPTS	29 MANUSCRIPTS = 47.5%	13 MANUSCRIPTS = 21.3
57 OLDEST CODICES	28 CODICES = 49%	13 CODICES = 22.8%
111 DIFFERENT PAPYRI	55 MANUSCRIPTS = 49.6%	22 MANUSCRIPTS = 19.8%
107 DIFFERENT CODICES	54 CODICES = 50.5%	22 CODICES = 20.6%

The chart on p. 27 (which repeats some of the preceding data) should be altered as follows:

PROPORTIONS OF GOSPEL AND PAULINE MANUSCRIPTS

BASIS OF COMPARISON	GOSPELS	PAUL
47 OXYRHYNCHUS PAPYRI	24 MANUSCRIPTS = 51%	8 MANUSCRIPTS = 17%
61 OLDEST MANUSCRIPTS	29 MANUSCRIPTS = 47.5%	13 MANUSCRIPTS = 21.3
111 DIFFERENT PAPYRI	55 MANUSCRIPTS = 49.6%	22 MANUSCRIPTS = 19.8%

These new papyrus discoveries frustrate and at times confuse previous analyses, but their contributions to paleography, codicology, and textual criticism are enormous and much to be welcomed. Certainly these new papyri and the role of Oxyrhynchus in early Christian history will command increasing attention over the near term.

CHAPTER TWENTY

THE MULTIVALENCE OF THE TERM "ORIGINAL TEXT" IN NEW TESTAMENT TEXTUAL CRITICISM[1]

I. Introduction

One hundred and ninety-one years ago, in 1808, Johann Leonhard 245
Hug's *Introduction to the New Testament* carried statements that, in part, may strike textual critics as being far ahead of their time. Hug laments the loss of all the original manuscripts of the New Testament writings "so important to the church" and wonders "How shall we explain this singular fact?" Next, he observes that Paul and others employed secretaries, but Hug views the closing salutation, written in the author's own hand, as "sufficient to give them the value of originals." Then, referring to the further role that scribes and correctors must have played after such a Christian writing had been dictated by its author, he says:

> Let us now suppose, as it is very natural to do, that the same *librar-* 246
> *ius* [copyist] who was employed to make this copy, made copies likewise for opulent individuals and other churches—and there was no original at all, or there were perhaps ten or more [originals] of which none could claim superiority.[2]

A writing with no original? Or with ten originals? And proposed by a scholar at the outset of the nineteenth century? Later Hug asserts that "the New Testament has had the peculiar fate of suffering more

[1] This article is based on a paper presented in the New Testament Textual Criticism Section, Society of Biblical Literature Annual Meeting, Orlando, Florida, November 1998. An earlier exploration of several of the issues appeared in an excursus on "The Intersection of Textual Criticism and Canon" (73–91) in Eldon Jay Epp, "Textual Criticism in the Exegesis of the New Testament, with an Excursus on Canon," in Stanley E. Porter, ed., *Handbook to Exegesis of the New Testament* (NTTS 25; Leiden: Brill, 1997) 45–97. The author wishes to thank ElDoris B. Epp, Ph.D., for her critique and suggestions at crucial points in the writing of this article.

[2] Johann Leonhard Hug, *Hug's Introduction to the New Testament* (trans. from the German 3d ed. by David Fosdick Jr. with notes by Moses Stuart; Andover, MA: Gould & Newman, 1836) 70–71. [German original, 1808; 3d ed., 1826.] I have not found the 1808 ed., but I have checked the 2d (1821) and 4th (1847) German eds., where the language is identical to that translated in the English ed.

by intentional alterations than the works of profane literature . . . and the heretics, to whom it would perhaps be attributed, had no share in it."[3] What he is saying by both assertions is that, because "strange things had happened in individual MSS, even at this early period"[4] (that is, before the mid-third century), the originals of the New Testament writings, through such alterations, have been obscured and the very notion of an "original" has been confounded.

This illustration from an early generation of modern criticism is hardly necessary to remind current textual critics that the question of "original text" in the New Testament is not only complex and tangled, but is also an issue that confronts one with increased intensity and urgency in this generation when, quite understandably, ambiguity is pervasive and multiple meanings are endemic to this multicultural world. The issue of "original text" is, for example, more complex than the issue of canon, because the former includes questions of both canon and authority. It is more complex than possessing Greek gospels when Jesus spoke primarily Aramaic, because the transmission of traditions in different languages and their translation from one to another are relevant factors in what is "original." It is more complex than matters of oral tradition and form criticism, because "original text" encompasses aspects of the formation and transmission of pre-literary New Testament tradition. It is more complex than the Synoptic problem and other questions of compositional stages within and behind our New Testament, because such matters affect definitions of authorship, and of the origin and unity of writings. More directly, it is more complex than making a textual decision in a variation unit containing multiple readings when no "original" is readily discernible, because the issue is broader and richer than merely choosing a single "original" and even allows making no choice at all. Finally, what "original text" signifies is more complex than
247 Hermann von Soden's, or Westcott-Hort's, or any other systems of text-types, or B. H. Streeter's theory of local texts, or various current text-critical methodologies, including the criteria for originality of readings, or "rigorous" versus "reasoned" eclecticisms, or claims of theological tendencies or ideological alterations of readings and manuscripts, because the question of "original text" encompasses all of these and much more.

[3] Ibid., 85.
[4] Ibid., 86.

To be sure, New Testament textual critics recently have placed the words "original text" in quotation marks, but do they really understand what is signified thereby? Actually, those tiny marks protect against full disclosure, for—while conveying little by way of specifics—they appear to provide a generalized caution against expecting overly precise or fully confident conclusions, and thereby for most textual critics they signal a measure of humility in the face of our awesome task of accommodating and analyzing the thousands of manuscripts and the few hundred thousand variant readings that transmit a very small body of ancient writings. Why, then, should textual critics be expected to define and to disclose their purposes in fine detail when already they are overwhelmed by data and are struggling to find the way out of this textual morass? Yet, to the extent that the use of quotation marks around the words "original text" represents a flight from forthrightness in the statement of text-critical goals, is it not time that textual critics scrutinize those aims and intentions, evaluate them realistically, and then articulate them as clearly as possible?

At this point textual critics may well be tempted to turn and run away—perhaps like the young man of Mark 14:51–52, because, like him, they feel caught in the face of a difficult and intractable situation and they wish to flee, as it were, even if naked into the night. Yet, while textual critics may flee from the issue, the issue itself will not go away. Indeed, New Testament textual critics have been both slow and reticent to face what the term, "original text" might mean or what implications might flow from any given definition of it, and they have been much more reluctant than their text-critical colleagues in Hebrew Bible or Septuagint studies to confront this issue.[5]

[5] See the extensive discussion in Emanuel Tov, *Textual Criticism of the Hebrew Bible* (Minneapolis, MN: Fortress; Assen/Maastricht: Van Gorcum, 1992), esp. chap. 3B on "The Original Shape of the Biblical Text," 164–80. Note Tov's comments elsewhere: "Textual criticism deals with the origin and nature of all forms of a text, in our case the biblical text. This involves a discussion of its putative original form(s). . . ." (1); and ". . . the concept of an 'original text' necessarily remains vague" (11). For various views of "original" text, with critique, see James A. Sanders, "The Task of Text Criticism," in Henry T. C. Sun, Keith L. Eades, *et al.*, eds., *Problems in Biblical Theology: Essays in Honor of Rolf Knierim* (Grand Rapids, MI: Eerdmans, 1997) 315–27, esp. 319–22; 325; and idem, "Stability and Fluidity in Text and Canon" in Gerard J. Norton and Stephen Pisano, eds., *Tradition of the Text: Studies offered to Dominique Barthélemy in Celebration of His 70th Birthday* (OBO 109; Göttingen: Vandenhoeck & Ruprecht, 1991) 205–6; 213–14; 217. It would be fruitful to compare

Rather than using such negative terms, however, I much prefer to put a positive and forward-looking slant on the matter and to say
248 that New Testament textual critics now have an opportunity to view afresh the richness and the possibilities for insights into the tradition and the theological culture of early Christianity that arise out of an analysis of "original text."[6]

II. The Use of the Term "Original Text" Past and Present and Its Multivalence

It is not only appropriate but helpful to place any discussion of original text in its historical and disciplinary setting. Two phases may be identified in the evolving understanding of "original text," one that may be designated simply as the past, and another that may be characterized as a current, emerging use of the term, though there were preparatory developments for this latter phase that require elucidation as well.

A. *The Past Use of "Original Text"*

One might assume that all older text-critical manuals state simply and without reservation that the object of New Testament textual criticism is to establish the original text, that is, what the writers originally wrote—the autographs. A few handbooks do just that. For instance, long ago, in his text-critical manual of 1815, Frederick Nolan spoke of determining "the authentik readings" and of "ascertaining the genuine text of the sacred canon,"[7] and in 1878 Thomas

---

these views with those in New Testament textual criticism, but that is beyond the scope of the present discussion.

[6] I was struck by one of Hort's emphases in his three-page description of textual criticism: "textual criticism is always negative, because its final aim is virtually nothing more than the detection and rejection of error" (Brooke Foss Westcott and Fenton John Anthony Hort, *The New Testament in the Original Greek* (2 vols.; Cambridge/London: Macmillan, 1881–82; 2d ed., 1896) 2. 3. Perhaps this statement or at least such sentiment—repeated too often—has contributed to the morosity of some practitioners and to the view of many outsiders that textual criticism is a dull if not moribund discipline. A subsidiary purpose of the present paper is to demonstrate the broad relevance, the deep vitality, the high excitement, and the positive reach forward of current New Testament textual criticism.

[7] Frederick Nolan, *An Inquiry into the Integrity of the Greek Vulgate or Received Text of the New Testament: In Which the Greek Manuscripts Are Newly Classified, the Integrity of the*

R. Birks sought the principles that would show "what is the true and genuine form of the original text of the New Testament."[8] It would be natural to expect a simple, straightforward goal from F. J. A. Hort, who characterizes the Westcott-Hort critical edition (1881) 249
as "an attempt to present exactly the original words of the New Testament, so far as they can now be determined from surviving documents," echoing, of course, the title of the Westcott-Hort edition, *The New Testament in the Original Greek.*[9] As all will recognize, however, the Westcott-Hort text and the theory behind it are not as simple matters as this statement suggests. It is interesting to note, however, that C. R. Gregory specifically names the Westcott-Hort "pre-Syrian" text the "Original Text," repeating that it is "to all intents and purposes the Original Text. No one has been doctoring it. No one has set about changing it."[10] Thus, "original" (at least for Gregory) can signify a critical text established on certain methodological grounds. Notice also the first sentence in Alexander Souter's 1913 handbook: "Textual criticism seeks, by the exercise of knowledge and trained judgment, to restore the very words of some original document which has perished. . . ." Here "original" means autograph. Souter then appends a further assertion, frequently echoed elsewhere: "If we possessed the twenty-seven documents now comprising our New Testament exactly in the form in which they were dictated or written by their original authors, there would be no

Authorised Text Vindicated, and the Various Readings Traced to Their Origin (London: Rivington, 1815) 2–3.

[8] Thomas Rawson Birks, *Essay on the Right Estimation of Manuscript Evidence in the Text of the New Testament* (London: Macmillan, 1878) 1; compare v. Also, in the strongly apologetic, biased writings of John William Burgon (and of his followers up to the present time), clear-cut definitions are to be expected. Burgon writes, "The object of textual criticism . . . is to determine what the Apostles and Evangelists of Christ actually wrote—the precise words they employed, and the very order of them" (Burgon's posthumous work, Edward Miller, ed., *The Traditional Text of the Holy Gospels Vindicated and Established* [London: Bell, 1896] 19). Elsewhere Burgon refers to establishing "the true text" (p. 6).

[9] Westcott and Hort, *The New Testament in the Original Greek*, 2. 1. Further on the relationship between autograph and original text, see 2. 66–68. The progress of textual criticism, Hort says, consists "in approximation towards complete ascertainment of definite facts of the past, that is, towards recovering an exact copy of what was actually written on parchment or papyrus by the author of the book or his amanuensis" (p. 3).

[10] Casper René Gregory. *Canon and Text of the New Testament* (International Theological Library; Edinburgh: T. & T. Clark, 1907) 485.

textual criticism of the New Testament."[11] Of course, textual critics know how shortsighted is this latter statement, how much better they now understand the breadth of the discipline, and what it can tell them of the history of the church, its doctrine, and its culture. Perhaps it is unfair to make an example of Souter in this way, for both his small volume and his other works are sophisticated contributions.
250 Yet it is of interest to discover just how few handbooks of New Testament textual criticism so simply define its task. A final, more recent example is found in J. H. Greenlee's manual: "Textual criticism is the study of copies of any written work of which the autograph (the original) is unknown, with the purpose of ascertaining the original text."[12] Again, "original" means autograph.

But elsewhere (besides Hug), the matter is far more complicated. At first glance, for example, Frederic Kenyon in 1901 appears to have stated the same simplistic goal for textual criticism: "the ascertainment of the true form of a literary work, as originally composed and written down by its author." A page later, however, he explains that once "the original autograph" is gone, anyone who wishes to "know exactly what an author wrote has to discover it by examination of later copies, of which the only fact certain *a priori* is that all will be different and all will be incorrect."[13] Where does that leave the search for the original text?

Surprisingly, other handbooks virtually ignore the entire issue and move directly to describing the witnesses available, the making of printed editions, and the practice of textual criticism—that is, how variant readings are to be evaluated. M.-J. Lagrange does this (though

[11] Alexander Souter, *The Text and Canon of the New Testament* (1913; 2d ed., London: Duckworth, 1954) 3. Similarly, Frederic G. Kenyon, *The Text of the Greek Bible: A Student's Handbook* (2d ed.; London: Duckworth, 1953) 12: "If the author's original manuscript had survived, it would of course be unnecessary to trouble about later and less accurate copies of it, or the work of revising editors. . . ." This sentiment is echoed, for example, in J. Harold Greenlee, *Introduction to New Testament Textual Criticism* (1964; rev. ed.; Peabody, MA: Hendrickson, 1995) 2.

[12] Greenlee, *Introduction*, 1.

[13] Frederic G. Kenyon, *Handbook to the Textual Criticism of the New Testament* (1912; 2d ed., London: Macmillan, 1926) 1–2. A qualified statement appears in his *Text of the Greek Bible*, 9. Günther Zuntz, *The Text of the Epistles: A Disquisition upon the Corpus Paulinum*. (Schweich Lectures, 1946; London: British Academy, 1953), reports that "the optimism of the earlier editors has given way to that scepticism which inclines towards regarding 'the original text' as an unattainable mirage," though he thinks that the "contamination" in the New Testament textual tradition can be overcome (p. 9).

the aim of textual criticism can be found in his preface: "to determine as nearly as possible the original text of the manuscript delivered to the public by the author").[14] It is nonetheless surprising that the two manuals most widely used today—those of Bruce Metzger and of Kurt and Barbara Aland—also fall into this category. Both of these manuals proceed quickly to the materials of criticism, to critical editions and the history of the text, and to the practice of evaluating readings. Hence, in both manuals the search is rather lengthy for a definition or goal of textual criticism.

The Alands' handbook on *The Text of the New Testament* aims to provide "the basic information necessary for using the Greek New Testament and for forming an independent judgment on the many kinds of variant readings characteristic of the New Testament textual tradition,"[15] but it is only after 279 pages, when the authors turn to the praxis of textual criticism, that statements relevant to its aim appear. The Alands then set down as the first of twelve basic principles that "only *one* reading can be original, however many variant readings there may be."[16] A dozen pages later they assert that: "It is precisely the overwhelming mass of the New Testament tex- 251
tual tradition . . . which provides an assurance of certainty in establishing the original text" for ". . . there is still the evidence of approximately 3,200 manuscripts of the New Testament text, not to mention the early versions and the patristic quotations [and]—we can be certain that among these there is still a group of witnesses which preserves the original form of the text. . . ."[17] We know from other writings of Kurt Aland that, on one hand, he can identify the "original text" with the kind of text that can be abstracted from the forty-eight earliest papyri and uncials[18]—those dating up to and

[14] Marie-Josèphe Lagrange, *Critique textuelle, II: La critique rationnelle* (2d ed.; EBib; Paris: Gabalda, 1935) vii.

[15] Kurt Aland and Barbara Aland, *The Text of the New Testament: An Introduction to the Critical Editions and to the Theory and Practice of Modern Textual Criticism* (trans. Erroll F. Rhodes; 2d ed.; Grand Rapids, MI: Eerdmans; Leiden: Brill, 1989) v.

[16] Ibid., 280. This principle is reminiscent of Hort: "Where there is variation, there must be error in at least all variants but one; and the primary work of textual criticism is merely to discriminate the erroneous variants from the true" (Westcott and Hort, *The New Testament in the Original Greek*, 2. 3).

[17] Aland and Aland, *Text of the New Testament*, 291–92.

[18] With the discovery and publication of sixteen additional New Testament papyri from Oxyrhynchus (P100–P115), of which thirteen date at or prior to the turn of

around the turn of the third/fourth century—when he states that here the early history of the New Testament text "can be studied in the original."[19] On the other hand, elsewhere Aland equates the original with the text of the latest Nestle-Aland and United Bible Societies' Greek New Testament, when, in referring to this common text, he asserts that it "has passed the test of the early papyri and uncials. It corresponds, in fact, to the text of the early time." This leads Aland to the conclusion that "a hundred years after Westcott-Hort, the goal of an edition of the New Testament 'in the original Greek' appears to have been reached."[20] Hence, the aim is to attain the "original" text, but what precisely is it?

Finally, Bruce M. Metzger's *Textual Commentary* puts the goal in the form of a question: "What is the original text of the passage?"[21]
252 The title of his widely used handbook, of course, implies a text-critical goal: *The Text of the New Testament: Its Transmission, Corruption, and Restoration*."[22] But it is only well into the latter volume that Metzger refers to "efforts to ascertain the original text of the New Testament,"[23] and later appears the insistence that the textual critic must "rectify the errors."[24] Little else of this nature appears in Metzger's text, although the diligent reader will find a clearer definition tucked away

---

the third into the fourth century (P100–P104; P106–P109; P111; and P113–115), this important group now numbers sixty-one. For the forty-eight listed in 1989, see Aland and Aland, *Text of the New Testament*, 56–57; 93. For the new papyri, see the listing in *Bericht der Hermann Kunst-Stiftung zur Förderung der neutestamentlichen Textforschung für die Jahre 1995 bis 1998* (Münster/Westfalen: Hermann Kunst-Stiftung, 1998) 14–18; for the texts, see vols. LXIV (1997), LXV (1998), and LXVI (1999) of *The Oxyrhynchus Papyri* (Greco-Roman Memoirs, 84–86; London: The British Academy by the Egypt Exploration Society).

[19] Kurt Aland, "The Twentieth-Century Interlude in New Testament Textual Criticism," in Ernest Best and Robert McLachlan Wilson, eds., *Text and Interpretation: Studies in the New Testament Presented to Matthew Black* (Cambridge: Cambridge University Press, 1979) 11.

[20] Kurt Aland, "Der neue 'Standard-Text' in seinem Verhältnis zu den frühen Papyri und Majuskeln," in Eldon J. Epp and Gordon D. Fee, eds., *New Testament Textual Criticism: Its Significance for Exegesis: Essays in Honour of Bruce M. Metzger* (Oxford: Clarendon Press, 1981) 274–75.

[21] Bruce M. Metzger on behalf of and in cooperation with the Editorial Committee of the United Bible Societies' Greek New Testament, *A Textual Commentary on the Greek New Testament* (1971; 2d ed., Stuttgart: United Bible Societies, 1994), orig. ed., xiii; 2d ed., xv.

[22] Bruce M. Metzger, *The Text of the New Testament: Its Transmission, Corruption, and Restoration* (1964; 1968; 3d ed., Oxford/New York: Oxford University Press, 1992).

[23] Ibid., 150.

[24] Ibid., 186.

in the preface: "The textual critic seeks to ascertain from the divergent copies which form of the text should be regarded as most nearly conforming to the original."[25]

Now, it is this last kind of *qualified* statement of the aim of New Testament textual criticism, namely, to establish the text "most nearly conforming to the original" or "as close to the original as possible" that is typical of what one finds elsewhere in numerous handbooks, though in varying forms and occasionally but not often, with more explicit caveats. For instance, as far back as 1854 Samuel P. Tregelles asserted that:

> The object of all Textual Criticism is to present an ancient work, as far as possible, in the very words and form in which it proceeded from the writer's own hand. Thus, when applied to the Greek New Testament, the result proposed is to give a text of those writings, as nearly as can be done on existing evidence, such as they were when originally written in the first century.[26]

Nor should we neglect to point out that Hort's statement cited earlier spoke of presenting "exactly the original words . . . *so far as they can now be determined from surviving documents*.[27] Even Benjamin Warfield's
frequently repeated statement regarding "original text" has a qualifier 253
at the end—though it is not always quoted. Warfield wrote: "The autographic text of the New Testament is distinctly within the reach of criticism *in so immensely the greater part of the volume*, that we cannot despair of restoring . . . His Book, word for word, as He gave it by inspiration to men."[28] It is not necessary to multiply exam-

[25] Ibid., v.

[26] Samuel Prideaux Tregelles, *An Account of the Printed Text of the Greek New Testament; With Remarks on Its Revision upon Critical Principles* (London: Bagster, 1854) 174. Tregelles's preface is less cautious, however: through textual criticism "we know, on grounds of ascertained certainty, the actual *words* and *sentences* . . . in the terms in which the Holy Spirit gave it" (viii [italics in original]). Yet, on the first page of his large handbook, a rewriting and revision of Thomas Hartwell Horne's *An Introduction to the Critical Study and Knowledge of the Holy Scriptures* (11th ed. by Horne, John Ayre, and S. P. Tregelles; 4 vols.; London: Longman, Green, Longman, and Roberts, 1860) 4. 1, Tregelles defines textual criticism as "that species of criticism which has to do with the ascertainment, as far as is practicable, of what it was that the writer of any ancient work actually wrote." Tregelles's work appeared earlier and separately, with the same definition, as *An Introduction to the Textual Criticism of the New Testament* (London: Longman, Green, *et al.*, 1856) 1.

[27] Westcott and Hort, *The New Testament in the Original Greek*, 2. 1; my emphasis.

[28] Benjamin Breckinridge Warfield, *An Introduction to the Textual Criticism of the New*

ples,[29] for in expressing the text-critical goal some kind of qualifying phrase, usually along the lines of "the most likely original text," is also what most in the field have said or still say.

It should be clear that this review of handbooks on New Testament textual criticism has yielded little clarity regarding the use or meaning of "original text," and it is for this reason that I have pursued the matter at length—precisely to make the point that over the greater part of two centuries virtually no discussion of this matter is to be found in the very volumes that have been the major guides in the theory and practice of the discipline. At times, as has been

---

Testament (1886; 7th ed., London: Hodder & Stoughton, 1907) 15; my emphasis. The omission of the italicized portion may be found, as a random example, in Brevard S. Childs, *The New Testament As Canon: An Introduction* (Philadelphia: Fortress, 1985) 522 (see note 109, below). Warfield also speaks of the need to restore the texts "substantially to their original form" (11).

[29] See, e.g., the following: Frederick Henry Ambrose Scrivener, *A Plain Introduction to the Criticism of the New Testament for the Use of Biblical Students* (2 vols.; 4th ed. by Edward Miller; London: Bell, 1894) 1. 5. Eberhard Nestle, *Introduction to the Textual Criticism of the Greek New Testament* (trans. from 2d German ed.; London: Williams and Norgate, 1901) 156: "The task is to exhibit what the original writer intended to communicate to his readers, and the method is simply that of tracing the history of the document in question back to its beginning, if, and in so far as, we have the means to do so at our command." Compare Nestle's *Einführung in das griechische Neue Testament* (1897; 1899; 1909 [p. 168]; 4th ed., Göttingen: Vandenhoeck & Ruprecht, 1923, ed. by Ernst von Dobschütz [p. 118]); E. Jacquier, *Le Nouveau Testament dans l'église chrétienne, tome second: Le texte du Nouveau Testament* (2d ed.; Paris: Gabalda, 1913) 1; Heinrich Joseph Vogels, *Handbuch der Textkritik des Neuen Testaments* (1923; 2d ed.; Bonn: Hanstein, 1955) 1; Archibald Thomas Robertson, *An Introduction to the Textual Criticism of the New Testament* (Nashville, TN: Broadman, 1925) has no direct, introductory statement, but see p. 173 and esp. p. 221; Kirsopp Lake, *The Text of the New Testament* (6th ed., rev. by Silva New; Oxford Church Text Books; London: Rivingtons, 1928) 1; Vincent Taylor, *The Text of the New Testament: A Short Introduction* (2d ed.; London: Macmillan, 1963) 1; Leon Vaganay, *An Introduction to New Testament Textual Criticism* (2d ed., rev. by Christian-Bernard Amphoux (Cambridge: Cambridge University Press, 1991) 1: textual criticism "aims to retrieve the original form of a text or at least the form closest to the original" (compare 1st English ed., 1937, p. 9; French eds., 1934; rev. ed., 1986, p. 15.). David Alan Black, *New Testament Textual Criticism: A Concise Guide* (Grand Rapids, MI: Baker, 1994) 12: ". . . to recover the original text of the New Testament from the available evidence"; J. Keith Elliott and Ian Moir, *Manuscripts and the Text of the New Testament: An Introduction for English Readers* (Edinburgh: T & T Clark, 1995) 1.

Finally, the life-goal of Lobegott Friedrich Konstantin von Tischendorf, as stated in a letter to a patron in 1844 (after he had outlined his plans to collect and to publish pre-tenth century manuscripts, ancient Latin manuscripts, and the Patristic quotations), was to form "a text that will approach as closely as possible to the very letter as it proceeded from the hands of the Apostles" (cited in Matthew Black and Robert Davidson, *Constantine von Tischendorf and the Greek New Testament* [Glasgow: University of Glasgow Press, 1981] 7).

shown, the term "original text" may be given an equivalent, such as "autograph," but discussion of the concept is lacking. Although I shall continue my search, the same judgment, I think, can be rendered on virtually all monographs and articles in the field up to the present time—with the exception of the several recent and current items to be discussed presently. It is significant also that nowhere in any of the examples cited above does "original text" appear in quotation marks.[30] At the same time, simply to speak of "the most likely original text" or that which is "as close as possible to the original," or to use similar qualifiers is clearly another way of putting quotation marks around the term. To reverse the image, these qualifying phrases doubtless represent what most textual critics signify by placing quotation marks on the term, "original." Neither the qualifying phrases, nor the caveats, nor quotation marks, however, clarify or define "original" in any meaningful fashion. Most important of all, the term "original" in all of these formulations appears to have in view a *single* original text of the New Testament writings, with the assumption, I presume, that this "original" is to be identified with the autograph (at least ideally) and apparently with little thought given to questioning this assumption.

Now, "original" used in this sense of a single entity or a singular target automatically invokes the notion of "canon," that is, of authority.[31] While many text critics have in the past and still may employ the term with that unspoken bias, others have used the term "original text" to designate an elusive, unrealistic target, for which was then substituted "the earliest attainable or recoverable text" as a reasonable goal for the discipline. Yet, even this redefinition of "original text," unaccompanied as it was by any close analysis, clarifies the problem only slightly, if at all, and only at a superficial level.

In view of the preceding survey, I choose to categorize these manuals and other similar text-critical studies as representative of the *past* as far as this issue of "original text" is concerned, and to name as

[30] I am not surprised now to discover that I used the term in quotation marks already in 1966 (though not consistently) in *The Theological Tendency of Codex Bezae Cantabrigiensis in Acts* (SNTSMS 3; Cambridge/New York: Cambridge University Press) e.g., 13[bis], 18[bis], 36.

[31] See discussion on "The Relation of an Elusive, Multivalent 'Original Text' to the Concept of 'Canon'" and "Textual Variants as Canonical/Authoritative" later in the article.

the *present* or *current* view a change that is emerging in a small corner of New Testament textual criticism.

255 B. *An Emerging Use of "Original Text"*

As far as I can discover, the pursuit by New Testament textual critics of a more specific, more clearly defined and more critically scrutinized, and hence a more honest meaning for the term "original" has appeared only in the past decade, and primarily in the work of a few members of the Society of Biblical Literature's New Testament Textual Criticism Group and of a creative and forward-looking scholar in the United Kingdom. Basic in their work are two relevant and crucial factors: first, their willingness to examine the assumptions underlying the notion of "original text" and to face the daunting implications of such an analysis; and, second, their insistence that the New Testament text and its myriad variant readings be scrutinized within the theological and sociocultural settings in which they were employed and manipulated. I begin, however, by defining what appears to me to have been a major stimulus for the new phase in our understanding of "original text."

1. *Stimulus from Helmut Koester*

The impetus for this new exploration came to some of us during a 1988 Notre Dame University conference on "Gospel Traditions in the Second Century," organized by William L. Petersen,[32] and specifically from a challenge launched there by Helmut Koester. Koester's discussion of "The Text of the Synoptic Gospels in the Second Century,"[33] was introduced by the fully acceptable observa-

[32] The conference papers were published by William L. Petersen, ed., *Gospel Traditions in the Second Century: Origins, Recensions, Text, and Transmission* (Christianity and Judaism in Antiquity, 3; Notre Dame, IN: University of Notre Dame Press, 1989). See Zuntz, *Text of the Epistles*, 11: "The recovery of the original text, if it is to be attempted scientifically, depends upon the illumination of its history in the second century."

[33] Helmut Koester, "The Text of the Synoptic Gospels in the Second Century," in Petersen, ed., *Gospel Traditions in the Second Century*, 19–37. It is of interest that among the nine conference participants (from six nations) only Koester, though he works in the text-critical field (for example, "The Text of 1 Thessalonians," in Dennis E. Groh and Robert Jewett, *The Living Text: Essays in Honor of Ernest W. Saunders* [Lanham, MD: University Press of America, 1985] 219–27), would not be first identified as a "textual critic"; he chooses the term "exegete" (ibid., 219).

tion that (except for the fragment, P^{52}) no second century manuscript evidence for the New Testament exists[34] and, therefore, severe problems attend the reconstruction of the textual history of the gospels in the first century of their transmission. Koester then startled many by turning on its head the New Testament textual critics' standard claim that they are fortunate to have so many early manuscripts so close to the time the writings originated. In contrast, he aptly observed 256
that "the oldest known manuscript archetypes are separated from the autographs by more than a century. Textual critics of classical texts know that the first century of their transmission is the period in which the most serious corruptions occur." He then added the provocative note that "textual critics of the New Testament writings have been surprisingly naïve in this respect."[35]

Working from textual agreements between Matthew and Luke when they use Mark, and from comparisons of the *Secret Gospel of Mark* with canonical Mark, Koester argued that an earlier form of Mark can be discerned behind the canonical Mark; that the latter represents a revision; and that the former becomes the "oldest accessible text of the Gospel of Mark"—accessible, that is, through the comparisons adduced. Next, using the gospel material quoted by Justin Martyr (ca. 150), Koester postulated that Justin's aim was to produce "*one* inclusive new Gospel" by harmonizing or by using a harmony of Matthew and Luke; as he proceeded, Justin reveals a freedom to modify this material (to demonstrate, for example, a more complete fulfillment of prophecy in the events of Jesus).[36] Koester's view is much more complex than this quick summary, but his point—whether or not his hypothesis is sustained in all of its detail—is clear and sharp:

> . . . [T]he text of the Synoptic Gospels was very unstable during the first and second centuries. With respect to Mark, one can be fairly certain that only its revised text has achieved canonical status, while the original text (attested only by Matthew and Luke) has not survived.

[34] To P^{52} (a fragment of John) now should be added the fragmentary P^{90} (*P.Oxy.* 3523, second century, John); P^{104} (*P.Oxy.* 4404, second half of the second century, Matthew); and probably P^{98} (second century [?], Apocalypse of John). Three other papyri date "around 200": P^{46}, P^{64+67}, and P^{66}, while two others (both with portions of Matthew) stem from the late second/early third century: P^{103} (*P.Oxy.* 4403) and P^{77} (*P.Oxy.* 2683+4405). [For P^{103} and P^{104}, see n. 18, above.]

[35] Koester, "The Text of the Synoptic Gospels in the Second Century," 19.

[36] Ibid., 21, 30–33.

> With respect to Matthew and Luke, there is no guarantee that the archetypes of the manuscript tradition are identical with the original text of each Gospel. The harmonizations of these two Gospels demonstrate that their text was not sacrosanct and that alterations could be expected. . . . New Testament textual critics have been deluded by the hypothesis that the archetypes of the textual tradition which were fixed ca. 200 C.E. . . . are (almost) identical with the autographs. This cannot be confirmed by any external evidence. On the contrary, whatever evidence there is indicates that not only minor, but also substantial revisions of the original texts have occurred during the first hundred years of the transmission.[37]

Whether or not textual critics acquiesce in all of these charges, a strong challenge remains, for they are left not only with text-critical
257 questions—for example, which variants of Mark are most likely original?—but also with penetrating canonical questions, such as, which Mark is original?

Similar issues arise with respect to the composition of the other Synoptics, the Fourth Gospel, the Pauline letters, and other portions of the New Testament. The relation to the Fourth Gospel of the well-known Egerton Papyrus 2 (currently dated ca. 200) is one such example. Although usually understood as a later excerpt from all four gospels, Koester (retaining a dating in the first part of the second century) views the papyrus as representing a text older than John because, "with its language that contains Johannine elements but reveals a greater affinity to the Synoptic tradition, it belongs to

[37] Ibid., 37; compare idem, *Ancient Christian Gospels: Their History and Development* (London: SCM; Philadelphia: Trinity Press International, 1990) 275–86, 295–302, 360–402. A description and assessment of Koester's view may be found, for example, in Philip Sellew, "*Secret Mark* and the History of Canonical Mark," in Birger A. Pearson, et al., eds., *The Future of Early Christianity: Essays in Honor of Helmut Koester* (Minneapolis, MN: Fortress, 1991) 242–57. Note that Sellew proposes terminology for four stages in Mark's history that, in three cases, have parallels to my proposed "dimensions of originality" (below): Original Mark, Augmented Mark, Secret Mark, and Canonical Mark (243 n. 6). For a critique of Koester's view, see David C. Parker, *The Living Text of the Gospels* (Cambridge: Cambridge University Press, 1997) 107–10.

François Bovon, "The Synoptic Gospels and the Noncanonical Acts of the Apostles," *HTR* 81 (1988) 19–36, provides a new perspective on "the alterations of older sources made by the Evangelists as well as the subsequent modifications of their work made by those who came later" (21) by comparing such literary activities with their parallels in the transmission of the Christian apocryphal literature. In the process he relies on codicological data; citation, imitation, and adaptation techniques; redactional tendencies; the witness of early church writers; etc. to conclude,

a stage of the tradition that preceded the canonical gospels."[38] If so, the gospel of which these surviving fragments were a part would have been read, without question, as authoritative in some early church(es) and possibly also could have played a role in the composition of our gospels. Again, the question arises, what or where is the original Mark? Or Matthew? Or Luke? Or John?

Now, if the goal of textual criticism is to recover the most likely "original" text, what in actuality is the object of textual critics' research—a text of the gospels that is somewhat earlier than but very likely similar to the text of our earliest manuscripts, or a text of even earlier and now largely lost predecessor forms of these gospels?
In other words, textual critics face two or more questions rather than 258
one: first, a prior question as to which Mark (or John, or Corinthian letters, or Ephesians, etc.) is "original," followed by the more traditional inquiry as to which variant readings of a particular work are "original." More clearly than before, the multivalence of the term "original text" emerges and confronts textual critics with its complexity.

Incidentally, should the illustrative examples employed here be rejected by some, there are others that could be adduced, given that hypotheses about pre-literary or predecessor literary layers behind many of the present New Testament writings are numerous and of

---

for example, that "perhaps Matthew and Luke used a version of the Gospel of Mark that was earlier than, and different from, our canonical Mark" (27).

Very recently and (like Bovon) by using noncanonical gospel material, James McConkey Robinson, "A Written Greek Sayings Cluster Older than Q: A Vestige," *HTR* 92 (1999) 61–77, demonstrates from a textual variant in *P.Oxy*. 655 (supported by the first hand of ℵ), namely οὐ ξαίνει for αὐξάνει, that this Oxyrhynchus fragment of the *Gospel of Thomas* carries a text that is not only pre-Matthew and pre-Luke, but clearly pre-Q as well. Thus, a "very ancient tradition" is exposed that "obviously originated prior to Q and the canonical gospels written in the last third of the first century" because it was "not contaminated by the scribal error that made its way already into Q and thus into the canonical gospels" (67). This evidence, not insignificantly, also confirms that "Q was indeed a written Greek text, behind which stood an older written Greek text as *Vorlage*" (61). Cf. J. M. Robinson and Christoph Heil, "Zeugnisse eines schriftlichen, griechischen vorkanonischen Textes: Mt 6,28b ℵ*, P.Oxy. 665 I,1–17 (EvTh 36) und Q 12,27," *ZNW* 89 (1998) 30–44.

[38] Helmut Koester, *Introduction to the New Testament. II. History and Literature of Early Christianity* (Philadelphia: Fortress, 1982) 2. 182. Koester more recently (*Ancient Christian Gospels*, 206–16) endorsed the argument of J. B. Daniels's dissertation that the synoptic parallels in P. Egerton 2 represent "a separate tradition which did not undergo Markan redaction" and that the author of the papyrus "did not make use of the Gospel of John in canonical form" (207).

long-standing. I have employed these examples from Koester, however, for two compelling reasons. First, his examples were educed in a specifically text-critical context that, as a matter of course, invited scrutiny of the term "original text" in a fresh and provocative fashion, and, second, these examples very directly "jump started" my own ruminations on the meaning of "original text" and without doubt influenced others as well.[39]

I wish now to invoke, in chronological order, four contemporary views that appear to have departed decisively from the notion of a single "original" text and that favor the multivalence of the term.

2. *Bart D. Ehrman*

Bart D. Ehrman's 1993 volume on *The Orthodox Corruption of Scripture*[40] raises relevant questions about the term, "original text." Ehrman's impressive and startling thesis is now well known, to trace "the ways scribes modified their texts of Scripture in light of the polemical contexts within which they worked, altering the manuscripts they reproduced to make them more orthodox on the one hand and less susceptible to heretics on the other."[41] Ehrman is concerned with scribes of the second and third centuries who were what he calls
259 "proto-Orthodox Christians" concerned to advance their own christological views against three main groups of detractors: adoptionists, docetists, and separationists. As scribes introduced intentional changes into their texts of writings that were to become the New Testament,

[39] It is obvious to me that Koester's Notre Dame paper also was a direct influence on William L. Petersen's views in his "What Text Can New Testament Textual Criticism Ultimately Reach?" in Barbara Aland and Joël Delobel, eds., *New Testament Textual Criticism, Exegesis, and Early Church History* (Contributions to Biblical Exegesis and Theology; Kampen: Kok Pharos, 1994) 136–52, esp. 136–37, inasmuch as Petersen edited the volume of conference papers (see note 32, above) and uses similar examples. Also, Bart D. Ehrman and Michael W. Holmes were among the very few non-local attendees at the Notre Dame conference. Holmes twice refers to Koester's views from that conference in his extremely brief discussion of the emerging issue of what really is meant by terms such as "autograph" and "original" in his chapter, "Reasoned Eclecticism in New Testament Textual Criticism," in Bart D. Ehrman and Michael W. Holmes, eds., *The Text of the New Testament in Contemporary Research: Essays on the* Status Quaestionis (SD 46; Grand Rapids, MI: Eerdmans, 1995) 353–54.

[40] Bart D. Ehrman, *The Orthodox Corruption of Scripture: The Effect of Early Christological Controversies on the Text of the New Testament* (New York: Oxford University Press, 1993).

[41] Ibid., 15, compare 275.

they would, as Ehrman says, "make them *say* what they were already known to *mean*," thus "corrupting" their texts for theological reasons—hence, the title of his book.[42] I call this a startling thesis, not because textual critics were unaware that scribes made such alterations in their manuscripts, but because of the *direction* in which Ehrman shows these changes to have moved—toward supporting and emphasizing the emerging main-stream theology, or orthodoxy, of the time—rather than following the previously common theme in textual criticism that *heretics* twisted the text to accredit their views. In the process, Erhman treats just short of 180 variation-units;[43] needless to say, one need not agree with all of his analyses to recognize his point, nor will the implications for "original text" be missed by many. The issue arises implicitly throughout the work but emerges explicitly in the final paragraphs:

> ... [U]nderstanding a text ... involves putting it "in other words." Anyone who explains a text "in other words," however, has altered the words.
>
> This is exactly what the scribes did: they occasionally altered the words of the text by putting them "in other words." To this extent, they were textual interpreters. At the same time, by *physically* altering the words, they did something quite different from other exegetes, and this difference is by no means to be minimized. Whereas all readers change a text when they construe it in their minds, the scribes actually changed the text on the page. As a result, they created a new text ... over which future interpreters would dispute, no longer having access to the words of the original text, the words produced by the author.[44]

Therefore, which is the "original," the texts altered by the scribes—now much obscured—or the scribes' altered texts? Subsequently, Ehrman comments that "[t]he ultimate goal of textual criticism, in the judgment of most of its practitioners, is to reconstruct the original text of the New Testament," but he quickly modifies this statement in a footnote, emphasizing that:

> [I]t is by no means self-evident that this *ought* to be the ultimate goal 260
> of the discipline, even though most critics have typically, and somewhat unreflectively, held it to be. In recent years, however, some schol-

[42] Ibid., xii [italics in original]; compare 276.
[43] Review of Ehrman by David C. Parker, *JTS* 45 (1994) 707.
[44] Ehrman, *Orthodox Corruption of Scripture*, 280 [italics in original].

> ars have recognized that it is important to know not only what an author wrote (i.e., in the autograph), but also what a reader read (i.e., in its later transcriptions). . . . Thus it is important for the historian of Christianity to know *which* form of the text was available to Christians in different times and places. . . . Given these historical concerns, there may indeed be scant reason to privilege the "original" text over forms of the text that developed subsequently.[45]

3. *William L. Petersen*

A second example of new views regarding the notion of "original text" appears in a 1994 article by William L. Petersen on "What Text Can New Testament Textual Criticism Ultimately Reach?[46] Beginning with the classical scholar Paul Maas's statement: "The business of textual criticism is to produce a text as close as possible to the original,"[47] Petersen says that first among the problems in New Testament textual criticism is "the difficulty of defining 'original.'" Using Mark as an example, he asks a series of penetrating questions:

> Is the "original" Mark the Mark found in our fourth-century and later manuscripts? Or is it the Mark recovered from the so-called "minor agreements" between Matthew and Luke? And which—if any—of the four extant endings of "Mark" is "original"? And how does the "Secret Gospel of Mark" . . . relate to the "original" Mark.? It is clear that, without even having to consider individual variants, determining which "Mark" is "original" is a difficult—and perhaps even impossible—task.[48]

The burden of his article, however, runs parallel to these particular issues, namely, if the goal of New Testament textual criticism is to produce a text "as close as possible to the original," then it should employ the sources that will facilitate that goal. The papyri, he says, will not do, for they contribute no new readings to the critical text of the gospels (that is, to the gospel text of Nestle-Aland/UBS),

---

[45] Bart D. Ehrman, "The Text as Window: New Testament Manuscripts and the Social History of Early Christianity," in B. D. Ehrman and Michael W. Holmes, eds., *The Text of the New Testament in Contemporary Research: Essays on the* Status Quaestionis (SD 46; Grand Rapids, MI: Eerdmans, 1995) 361 and n. 1 [italics in original].

[46] William L. Petersen, "What Text Can New Testament Textual Criticism Ultimately Reach?" 136–37.

[47] Paul Maas, *Textual Criticism* (Oxford: Clarendon Press, 1958) 1.

[48] Petersen, "What Text Can New Testament Textual Criticism Ultimately Reach?" 136–37.

though they do frequently extend other manuscript evidence from the fourth century back to the third.[49] Petersen is asserting, I gather,
that the early papyri, by themselves, do not/cannot establish a text 261
any closer to the original than already exists in the B-text. The abundant Patristic evidence, he continues, "has been largely ignored," especially compared to the papyri; the evidence for this is in the gospel text of Nestle-Aland/UBS, which, again, "shows not a *single* instance where the text is based solely—or even principally—upon Patristic evidence"; rather, Patristic evidence enters the critical text only when supported by the uncials.[50] Is this, Petersen asks, the proper use of Patristic evidence?

Petersen offers three examples that "demonstrate that by using multiple sources we can both readily and reliably triangulate readings from the second century,"[51] that is, readings solidly attested by second century Patristic sources that are multigeographic and multilanguage in nature. His exhibits[52] first show that methodologically one can move behind our earliest manuscript tradition—the entirety of which (except for P52)[53] is from the third century or later. Secondly, Petersen raises the likelihood that some very early readings were excised from the gospel text, doubtless because they were "no longer theologically acceptable,"[54] and therefore did not survive long enough to appear in the manuscript tradition. A telling example is a variant of Matt 19:17 found in Justin ("One is good, [then Justin's variant] *my father in the heavens*"), which is attested twice more in the second century, as well as in other early sources. Petersen argues impressively that this reading—at an early time—must have been well attested in manuscripts, but once it was "redacted away," "excised" from Matthew, it virtually disappeared from our manuscripts [it is in two Old Latin manuscripts of the fifth century], and that it thereby discloses an earlier level of gospel text. Petersen's question, then, is pertinent: "If these readings do indeed reflect a pre-180 manuscript tradition, then why do we not occupy ourselves

[49] Ibid., 138–39. Petersen's claim concerns the 27th ed. of Nestle/Aland = 4th ed. of UBSGNT.

[50] Ibid., 139–40 [italics in original].

[51] Ibid., 148.

[52] Ibid., 140–47.

[53] But see n. 34, above.

[54] Petersen, "What Text Can New Testament Textual Criticism Ultimately Reach?" 148; compare 150.

with its reconstruction?"[55] What he has exposed here is a layer of text beneath what most would consider the "original text" that traditionally has been the object of textual criticism—that is, he documents a layer constituting an earlier "original" or "originals" that are open to restoration.

4. *The author's preliminary exploration*

In 1997 I published an excursus on "The Intersection of Textual Criticism and Canon" in a larger article in Stanley Porter's *Handbook to Exegesis of the New Testament*,[56] in which Koester's Notre Dame paper
262 was invoked in the manner that I have used it, in opening the issue of multiple "originals." In that article, I also utilized an extended example from Nils A. Dahl on the Pauline corpus. Dahl's example moves in the same direction, and it concerns early recensional activity within that corpus.

As is well known, the phrase, "in Ephesus," is lacking in a small number of witnesses at Eph 1:1, though these witnesses include P^{46}, א*, and B*. Based on the reading of these witnesses and the general or "catholic" nature of Ephesians, several theories were developed regarding the omission. These theories include the seventeenth century view of Archbishop Ussher that Ephesians was a circular letter intended for several churches and that a blank was left in 1:1 for names of churches using it, as well as the well-known theory of E. J. Goodspeed (1933) that "Ephesians" was written to introduce the first Pauline collection. Dahl, however, interprets this textual variant differently, first by rejecting the reading of the oldest manuscripts, suggesting that the context within Eph 1:1 requires a geographical designation, but then by allowing the possibility that:

> [T]he letter was originally issued in several copies with a special address in each of them. In any case, the letter must have had a pre-history before it was published as part of the Pauline corpus. The text without any concrete address is to be understood as a result of a secondary "catholicyzing," to which we have an analogy in the textual tradition of Romans.[57]

---

[55] Ibid., 149.

[56] Eldon Jay Epp, "Textual Criticism in the Exegesis of the New Testament," 45–97; the "Excursus" occupies pp. 73–91.

[57] Nils A. Dahl, "The Particularity of the Pauline Epistles as a Problem in the Ancient Church," in W. C. van Unnik, ed., *Neotestamentica et Patristica: Eine Freundesgabe,*

The latter reference, of course, is to Rom 1:7 (and Rom 1:15), where "in Rome" is absent from a few witnesses. Dahl, in an elaborate argument, contends that the short, fourteen-chapter version of Romans—ending with 14:23 plus the doxology of 16:25–27 placed there by a number of manuscripts—circulated "in early days" without geographical designation and as another "catholic" epistle of Paul. The well-known text-critical problems involving the doxology serve, in Dahl's view, as "further evidence of the existence of more than one recension of Romans."[58] Like Ephesians, this fourteen-chapter version of Romans "will have to be explained as the result of editorial activity . . . between the times of Paul and Marcion."[59] Dahl then points out that the earliest Patristic references do not easily support "a standard edition of the Pauline corpus before 100 A.D." and 263
that "the question whether our whole textual tradition goes back to one archetypical manuscript of the whole collection will need further investigation."[60] What text, then, of Ephesians or Romans is designated by the term "original"?

These issues might well have been explored also by reference to Harry Y. Gamble's *The Textual History of the Letter to the Romans*,[61] with its extensive utilization of text-critical data.

My earlier exploration went on to raise matters of canon and authority that are parallel to or interactive with issues of multiple originals, and some of these issues will be revisited later in article.

Before the final example of this emerging new view, a brief summary may be useful. Very recently the tasks of New Testament textual criticism have become more intriguing and more challenging as the discipline turns its attention, for example, away from the search for merely one "original text" to an understanding of earlier stages of composition and to earlier texts—earlier "originals"—that lie behind what textual critics have become accustomed to consider *the* "original." In addition, various other "original" texts may have been defined

---

Herrn Professor Dr. Oscar Cullmann zu seinem 60. Geburtstag überreicht (NovTSup 6; Leiden: Brill, 1962) 267.

[58] Ibid., 268.

[59] Ibid., 269.

[60] Ibid., 271 n. 2.

[61] Harry Y. Gamble, *The Textual History of the Letter to the Romans: A Study in Textual and Literary Criticism* (SD 42; Grand Rapids, MI: Eerdmans, 1977) esp. 11–35; 96–142. Compare idem, *Books and Readers in the Early Church: A History of Early Christian Texts* (New Haven, CT: Yale University Press, 1995) 58–65.

by and during the lengthy canonization process, perhaps, for example, at the point when the gospels or the Pauline letters were formed into collections. Finally, additional "original" texts were created as theologically motivated scribes altered the texts that were their "originals" by making the latter say what they knew them to mean. As a result, on the one hand, textual critics have extended the process of textual transmission farther into the past as they postulate the displacement of a previously conceived "original" by one or more preceding "originals," so that a text long thought of as "original" suddenly is recognized as derivative. On the other hand, textual critics have pushed the notion of "original" forward in time, beyond what they have usually conceived as the autographs, to encompass more recent reshapings of the texts, so that the original "original" is now replaced by a new, successor "original" that circulates in the church and thereby often obscures the earlier, now dethroned original. Within this complex tangle of texts and revisions that find their life settings in a vibrant, developing, and theologically multifaceted church, what, indeed, does "original text" mean? Which "original" or "originals" ought we seek? Or, to anticipate a more radical question to be raised presently, ought textual critics to seek or to emphasize the search
264 for an "original" at all? Finally, as a new dimension, what meanings are carried by the words "canon" and "canonical" as they relate to these newly recognized multiple "originals"?

5. *David C. Parker*

My final example of a new current in the discussion of "original text" is the work of David Parker, who comes to this issue from a different perspective in his introductory volume, *The Living Text of the Gospels*.[62] Parker begins by challenging the common belief that "the purpose of textual criticism is to recover the original text," followed by a call to examine whether there is an original text to be recovered.[63] Indeed, this question is "the principal theme" of his book.[64] But Parker does not eschew the "attempt to recover early text forms"; he does not[65] because such a search is "a necessary part of that

[62] David C. Parker, *The Living Text of the Gospels* (Cambridge: Cambridge University Press, 1997).
[63] Ibid., 3–4.
[64] Ibid., 7.
[65] Ibid., 132–37.

reconstruction of the history of the text without which . . . nothing can be understood."[66] Yet Parker does distinguish the recovery of "earlier forms of the text" from the "original," asserting that "it does not follow that it is also necessary to recover a single original text."[67] He states, "The question is not whether we *can* recover it, but why we want to,"[68] To the question "whether the task of textual criticism is to recover the original text," Parker replies, "[I]t may be, but does not have to be,"[69] and he chooses not to emphasize and often not to seek a single original.

The reasons are clear enough from the several chapter-length examples that he gives and from the larger context of his book. First, the diversity of readings in the manuscript tradition of the gospels (to which he restricts his study) reveals a text that from the beginning grew freely,[70] for "sayings and stories continued to be developed by copyists and readers."[71] Parker affirms that the most dramatic changes in the text occurred in the first 150 years—"initial fluidity followed by stability."[72] Hence, he characterizes the text of the gospels "as a free, or perhaps, as a living, text,"[73] and he asks again "whether the attempt to recover a single original text is consonant with the
character of a free manuscript tradition."[74] The gospels are "not 265
archives of traditions but living texts,"[75] and, therefore, "the concept of a Gospel that is fixed in shape, authoritative, and final as a piece of literature has to be abandoned."[76] As he says elsewhere, "The [free] text indicates that to at least some early Christians, it was more important to hand on the spirit of Jesus' teaching than to remember the letter. . . . [T]he material about Jesus was preserved in an interpretive rather than an exact fashion."[77]

This conclusion bears on Parker's second reason for choosing not to pursue an original text, one that arises out of important cases

[66] Ibid., 211.
[67] Ibid., 208.
[68] Ibid., 209.
[69] Ibid., 182.
[70] Ibid., 203.
[71] Ibid., 45–46.
[72] Ibid., 70; compare 200.
[73] Ibid., 200.
[74] Ibid., 209.
[75] Ibid., 119.
[76] Ibid., 93.
[77] David C. Parker, "Scripture is Tradition," *Theology* 94 (1991) 15.

where the readings in a variation unit are multiple and do not yield an easily determined original reading, or any plausible original at all. Two examples include the gospel sayings on marriage and divorce, and the Lord's Prayer. Parker's text-critical analysis of the gospel sayings on marriage and divorce lead him to conclude that "the recovery of a single original saying of Jesus is impossible"; rather, "[w]hat we have here is a collection of interpretive rewritings of a tradition"[78]—"the early church rewrote the sayings in their attempt to make sense of them."[79] As Parker says of a similar example, the Lord's prayer, which has six main forms in the manuscript tradition:

> [A]ll six forms contribute to our understanding. Once we have discovered their existence, they will be part of the way in which we read and interpret the Lord's Prayer. We shall not be able to erase them from our minds, and to read a single original text as though the others had never existed.[80]

His point, of course, is that the church has been and continues to be instructed by all meaningful multiple variants, because these variants disclose how the early church dealt with or thought about theological or ethical issues.

Later, Parker treats an extended passage from Luke (the last three chapters), instead of merely small blocks of material, and finds that variants in some forty verses out of the last 167 provide, as he says, "incontrovertible evidence that the text of these chapters was not fixed, and indeed continued to grow for centuries after its composition,"[81] including "a significant number of passages which were added to the Gospel in order to emphasize its orthodoxy."[82] "We might say," he concludes, "that Luke is not, in these early centuries, a
266 closed book. It is open, and successive generations write on its pages."[83]
So, when Parker says that "the Gospel texts exist only as a manuscript tradition"[84] and not in an early, fixed form, he means that

[78] Parker, *The Living Text of the Gospels*, 92–93.

[79] Ibid., 183. Compare Hans Dieter Betz, *The Sermon on the Mount* (Hermeneia; Minneapolis, MN: Fortress, 1995): ". . . there was never only *one original written* Lord's Prayer" (p. 370 and n. 320 [italics in original]).

[80] Parker, *The Living Text of the Gospels*, 102.

[81] Ibid., 172.

[82] Ibid., 183.

[83] Ibid., 174.

[84] Ibid., 203.

statement to apply not only to the past but to the present as well, allowing the richness of the manuscripts, with all of their variants and with the interpretations and insights that they offer, to illuminate not only the culture of the early church but the culture of today as well. Parker is affirming that the full manuscript tradition brings vastly more than restriction to a single original reading or text could ever provide, but this approach does not mean that all variants on divorce, for example, now have the authority traditionally ascribed only to one of those readings. "The tradition is manifold. . . . There is no authoritative text beyond the manuscripts which we may follow without further thought"; thus, ". . . the people of God have to make up their own minds. There is no authoritative text to provide a short-cut."[85]

Parker's bold statements carry us beyond merely the issue of multiple "originals" to a firm de-emphasis on the necessity or desirability of seeking a single "original text" of the New Testament or a single "original" reading in a given variation unit. In all of this discussion, however, a strong, positive thrust remains. Textual critics are encouraged to permit the New Testament's fluid and living text of the past to sustain its free, vital, unbroken, multifaceted tradition in the present and into the future—with the multiplicity of text-forms presenting "a collection of interpretive rewritings"[86] of that tradition and sweeping textual critics up into the flow that makes them part of that ongoing tradition and also confirms that ancient tradition as very much our own.

C. *Have We Moved beyond the Legitimate Domain of Textual Criticism?*

As I pursued these current, progressive viewpoints and contemplated the increasing complexity in trying to define "original text," I was caught short by my review of a passage I had long ago marked in the Alands' *Text of the New Testament*:

> [T]he competence of New Testament textual criticism is restricted to the state of the New Testament text from the moment it began its literary history through transcription for distribution. All events prior to this are beyond its scope.[87]

---

[85] Ibid., 212.
[86] Ibid., 93.
[87] Aland and Aland, *Text of the New Testament*, 297. See the statement in *Der Text*

Do the views described above violate the parameters of textual criticism? On this definition in the Alands' handbook, any precursor
267 compositional levels, as usually understood and as employed above for illustrative purposes, would appear to be beyond the scope of the discipline. The context of the Alands' statement confirms this exclusion, for they refer to such matters as "composition theories" concerning the Pauline letters and the Fourth Gospel:

> None of the composition theories advanced today in various forms with regard to the Pauline letters, for example, has any support in the manuscript tradition. . . . At no place where a break has been posited in the Pauline letters does the critical apparatus show even a suspicion of any interference with the inevitable deposit of telltale variants. In other words, from the beginning of their history as a manuscript tradition the Pauline letters have always had the same form that they have today.[88]

Yet the context leading directly to this statement in the handbook describes the "utter chaos" of the textual tradition of the end of Romans (that is, the varying placement of the doxology), precisely the text-critical data that form the basis for the predecessor composition theories of Dahl and also of Gamble regarding both Romans and the larger Pauline corpus. Quite clearly, then, such explorations of prior compositional levels in the Pauline letters and elsewhere in the New Testament have been regarded as legitimate text-critical enterprises by various scholars, whenever textual variants, manuscript marks, or other text-critical factors appear to reflect some kind of previous textual or literary layers or some textual disruption.[89] My own judgment also is that such explorations remain within the proper domain of textual criticism.

---

des Neuen Testament (Stuttgart: Deutsche Bibelgesellschaft, 1982[1]) 298: "Denn die neutestamentliche Textkritik kann über den Textbestand der neutestamentlichen Schriften nur urteilen von dem Augenblick an, wo sie durch Abschriften ihre literarische Existenz beginnen, zu dem, was voher war, hat sie keinen Zugang."

For a discussion of the task and boundaries of Old Testament textual criticism, see James A. Sanders, "The Task of Text Criticism," 319–22, and his further references; idem, "Stability and Fluidity in Text and Canon," 205–6; and Ferdinand E. Deist, "Text, Textuality, and Textual Criticism," *JNSL* 21 (1995) 59–67, who treats implications of textual criticism, defined as "text-restoration," for recent literary theory. See also note 5 of this article, above.

[88] Aland and Aland, *Text of the New Testament*, 296.

[89] See discussion on Bovon and Robinson in n. 37. Jacobus H. Petzer, "Reconsidering the Silent Women of Corinth—A Note on 1 Corinthians 14:34–35,"

Moreover, do we not encounter some of the same issues that are involved in the term "original text," when we analyze the phrase in the Alands' previously cited quotation that refers to "the state of the 268
New Testament text from the moment it began its literary history [or existence] through transcription [or copies] for distribution"? When does a writing's literary existence begin? Can the beginning of a writing's literary history be limited to the moment when copies were made and circulated (that is, the time of its "publication")? And if earlier composition levels can be detected, especially when signaled by textual variants, have textual critics not uncovered an earlier "beginning" of that writing's literary history? Or, to move forward in time, could not a literary process (such as revision or rearrangement of the text) have taken place after the first copies were made and released, thereby turning the earlier, copied version itself into a predecessor literary layer of the writing? Hence, the term "beginning" begins to take on multiple dimensions, just as "original" does, and textual critics face the possibility that the text of a writing that has been transmitted, which they presume to have stood at the beginning of that particular writing's history, now can be shown (triggered by textual variants) to have evolved from an earlier "beginning"—an "original" has had earlier "originals."

Without pursuing this farther, perhaps most will agree on the following principle regarding what, in addition to the traditional investigations, falls within the proper domain of textual criticism:

Theologia Evangelica (Pretoria) 26 (1993) 132–38; esp. 135–37, uses this text to illustrate his view of an "original text" and a later-developed but oldest "received text" of the Epistle—indicating, in our present language, two levels of originality.

On the complex issue of interpolations, see William O. Walker Jr., who has suggested both principles for and examples of possibly interpolated passages in the New Testament, always insisting that "text-critical considerations should play a significant role in the identification of interpolations" ("Is First Corinthians 13 a Non-Pauline Interpolation?" *CBQ* 60 [1998] 496; but see esp. his "The Burden of Proof in Identifying Interpolations in the Pauline Letters," *NTS* 33 [1987] 610–18; "Text-Critical Evidence for Interpolations in the Letters of Paul," *CBQ* 50 [1988] 622–31; "1 Corinthians 11:2–16 and Paul's Views regarding Women," *JBL* 94 [1975] 94–110; and "1 Corinthians 2.6–16: A Non-Pauline Interpolation?" *JSNT* 47 [1992] 75–94.) For a critique of Walker's views, see Frederik W. Wisse, "Textual Limits to Redactional Theory in the Pauline Corpus," in James E. Goehring, Charles W. Hedrick, Jack T. Sanders, with Hans Dieter Betz, eds., *Gospel Origins & Christian Beginnings in Honor of James M. Robinson* (Forum Fascicles, 1; Sonoma, CA: Polebridge Press, 1990) 172–78.

> Any search for textual *pre*formulations or *re*formulations of a literary nature, such as *prior* compositional levels, versions, or formulations, or *later* textual alteration, revision, division, combination, rearrangement, interpolation, or forming a collection of writings, legitimately falls within the sphere of text-critical activity *if such an exploration is initiated on the basis of some appropriate textual variation or other manuscript evidence.*[90]

"Other manuscript evidence" would include marginal or other sigla in manuscripts indicating uncertainty regarding placement of a passage or pointing to another textual problem. The principle enunciated here might be exemplified further under two "categories," with some random examples (though items may slip from one category to the other).

Category 1 looks behind our transmitted texts to preformulations (that is, to "pre-original" compositional levels):

269 1. Textual variants signaling *predecessor literary activity*, such as prior compositional levels, versions, or formulations, would provide legitimacy for, among others, the following:

Hypotheses about early sayings traditions or sources, or about early gospel harmonies—because of variant readings in the sayings of Jesus tradition (including agrapha, the *Gospel of Thomas*, etc.).

Theories about varying versions, revisions, formulations, partitions, or combinations behind, or interpolations into, or collections of the Pauline letters—because of variant readings concerning a letter's addressees, the placement of doxologies, etc., and because of manuscript sigla indicating textual problems. (These and similar phenomena might fall into category 2.)

Consideration of dual versions of Acts or Luke-Acts—because of extensive textual variation in the B and D textual traditions. Hypotheses about the ending of Mark—because the (later) textual tradition provides various endings to adjust for the perceived abruptness in ending the gospel with Mark 16:8. (Could be category 2.)

Consideration of the *pericope adulterae* (John 7:53–8:11), its authenticity/inauthenticity, and whether it was part of John, etc.—because

[90] I offer this definition of the proper sphere of New Testament textual criticism and the descriptions of two subcategories as the first such attempts; they aim to clarify the issues but also to stimulate further consideration of these complex subjects.

of its several locations in manuscripts of John and Luke, its varying text forms, its absence from early manuscripts, and because scribal sigla in other manuscripts indicate uncertainty. (Might be placed in category 2.)

Category 2 largely looks at reformulation, the interpretive recasting of books, but especially of passages, already in circulation and use (that is, at "post-original" literary activity), which, when accepted, may obscure the readings of the circulating text or, conversely, when neglected or suppressed, may be obscured by the dominant circulating textual tradition:

2. Textual variants signaling *successor literary activity*, such as reformulation or adaptation of an earlier level of composition, would provide legitimacy for the following:

   Hypotheses about alterations to writings in the interest of orthodox or heretical theology or in the interest of pro- or anti-Judaic sentiments or pro- or anti-female views, etc.—because of numerous textual variants inviting such inquiries.

   Consideration of rearrangements, additions, dislocations, and 270
   interpolations in already circulating writings, such as endings of Mark, portions of John or Pauline letters, etc.—because of variant readings and varying positions or sigla in manuscripts.[91]

---

[91] On interpolations, see n. 89. Extensive literature has developed on the possible interpolation (thus, doubtless non-Pauline) or dislocation of 1 Cor 14:34–35; it is found after 14:40 in D^{Paul} 88 et al., is treated as a separate paragraph in P^{46} B ℵ A D^{Paul} 33, and is marked in various manuscripts by sigla interpreted by some to indicate either that it was lacking in those manuscripts or dislocated. See, for example, Gordon D. Fee, *The First Epistle to the Corinthians* (NICNT; Grand Rapids, MI: Eerdmans, 1987) 699–708; Walker, "1 Corinthians 11:2–16," 95 n. 6; 109; Philip B. Payne, "Fuldensis, Sigla for Variants in Vaticanus, and 1 Cor 14.34–5," *NTS* 41 (1995) 240–62; idem, "MS. 88 as Evidence for a Text without 1 Cor 14.34–5," *NTS* 44 (1998) 152–58. For a contrary view, see Curt Niccum, "The Voice of the Manuscripts on the Silence of Women: The External Evidence for 1 Cor 14.34–5," *NTS* 43 (1997) 242–55. [See now Philip B. Payne and Paul Canart, "The Originality of Text-Critical Symbols in Codex Vaticanus," *NovT* 42 (2000) 105–13; E. J. Epp, "Text-Critical, Exegetical, and Socio-Cultural Factors Affecting the Junia/Junias Variation in Romans 16,7," *Textual Criticism and Exegesis: Festschrift J. Delobel* (BETL, 161; ed. A. Denaux; Leuven: Leuven University Press/Peeters, 2002) 237–42.]

Alistair Stewart-Sykes, "Ancient Editors and Copyists and Modern Partition Theories: The Case of the Corinthian Correspondence," *JSNT* 61 (1996) 53–64, argues that *complex* compilation or partition theories regarding the Pauline letters

Theories about liturgical embellishments to the Lord's prayer, the Last Supper, etc.—because of multiple forms in the textual tradition.

Deliberations over the marriage and divorce sayings in the synoptic gospels—because of their tangled textual tradition.

As with the examples cited under category 1, many more examples could be cited here.

The explorations exemplified in these lists—and numerous others that might be added—directly and indirectly invoke the multivalence of the term "original text" and thereby enrich the text-critical discipline by opening the way for fresh insights from the varying interpretations of early Christian thought and life that they reveal. Moreover, recognizing the multivalence of "original text" insures that New Testament textual criticism will certainly diminish and possibly relinquish its myopic concentration on an elusive and often illusive target of a single original text. Clearly, for some, these investigations of both predecessor and successor compositional activities will challenge not only the traditional object, but also the customary boundaries of New Testament textual criticism; yet, that challenge should be understood as expanding our horizons and making our discipline more broadly relevant than previously to related fields, such as literary-critical, hermeneutical, and church-historical studies.

III. The Relation of an Elusive, Multivalent "Original Text" to the Concept of "Canon"

Text and canon have been treated together for generations, as scores of books and encyclopedia articles will attest, but more often than not their relationship has been one merely of juxtaposition rather

would have been "a virtual physical impossibility" on the assumption that Paul's letters were both written and preserved on rolls—because rolls could not be manipulated in a fashion that would permit such literary rearrangements. Nowhere, however, does he discuss the large issue of the codex in early Christianity, nor does he refer, e.g., to the palaeographic and codicological work of C. H. Turner, C. H. Roberts, or T. C. Skeat, or to recent work, like Gamble, *Books and Readers in the Early Church*; cf. my "The Codex and Literacy in Early Christianity and at Oxyrhynchus: Issues Raised by Harry Y. Gamble's *Books and Readers in the Early Church*," *Critical Review of Books in Religion* 10 (1997) 15–37, esp. 15–26.

than of interaction.[92] Our concern here is not so much with the long-standing and quite static juxtaposition of the two fields, but rather with the parallels or interaction between canon and text in 271
the sphere of "authority." "Canon" by nature embraces authority, for it involves "measure," or "standard"—something measured and meeting a standard. When a Jewish or Christian writing has been measured and accepted as canonical (whether formally by leaders in a given region or informally in the life of a community), that writing and its text acquire authority. The "original text" of the New Testament—in its common understanding—also has been viewed as authoritative, and this point at which canon and text cross paths gives rise to some penetrating questions. One example might be, if "original" is multivalent, can "canon" escape multivalence?

A. *Textual Variants as Canonical/Authoritative*

Several issues raised by the scholars whose views have been discussed in this article lead directly to this interaction between textual criticism and canon, that is, to the point at which they intersect over the concept of authority. We may begin by noting the extensive similarity between Parker's view of "the living text" and the emphasis developed by the "Chicago School" of New Testament textual criticism in the years before and after World War II, for, as I will discuss later in this section, those scholars also viewed the New Testament text as "a living body of literature," which, through scribal changes in a vibrant theological and practical context, opened a window upon the history of the church and its doctrine. I refer especially to the studies of Donald W. Riddle, Ernest C. Colwell, and Merrill M. Parvis, surrounded by their distinguished Chicago colleagues, Edgar J. Goodspeed, Harold R. Willoughby, and Alan Wikgren, and, by extension, to graduates of this University of Chicago program, notably Kenneth W. Clark. The relevant view was summarized and high- 272
lighted in ten pages of the introduction to my 1966 monograph on Codex Bezae,[93] in which I labeled it, "Present-day Textual Criticism." This designation, I fear, was a quarter-century premature, for it was

[92] For an earlier, brief attempt to clarify this relationship, see my "Textual Criticism in the Exegesis of the New Testament," 73–84.

[93] Eldon Jay Epp, *The Theological Tendency of Codex Bezae Cantabrigiensis in Acts* (SNTSMS 3; Cambridge: Cambridge University Press, 1966) see 12–21.

that long before the major work of Bart Ehrman exemplified this new understanding of textual criticism and nearly thirty years until David Parker engaged in it—though quite independently, it would appear. What exactly was the view that emerged from Chicago?

Its roots can be traced back directly to Kirsopp Lake in 1904, in the context of his often-quoted evaluation of Westcott-Hort, though many readers may fail to move beyond that to Lake's programmatic statement. Lake characterized Westcott-Hort's edition a "failure"—"... it was one of those failures which are more important than most successes."[94] As a result, Lake continues, it can no longer be supposed that the textual critic can immediately edit the original text; editing of local texts must come first, and this step complicates the task because the exegete must now "... expound the meaning, not of Westcott and Hort's text, but of the ecclesiastical Bibles in use at different times.... We need to know what the early Church thought [a passage] meant and how it altered its wording in order to emphasize its meaning."[95] Thirty-some years after Lake's assessment, Riddle wrote this impassioned paragraph:

> The legitimate task of textual criticism is not limited to the recovery of approximately the original form of the documents, to the establishment of the "best" text, nor to the "elimination of spurious readings." It must be recognized that every significant variant records a religious experience which brought it into being. This means that there are no "spurious readings": the various forms of the text are sources for the study of the history of Christianity.[96]

273 Later Riddle refers to "the unreality of that common abstraction ..., the 'original' text from which all variants were derived." He continues:

[94] Kirsopp Lake, *The Influence of Textual Criticism on the Exegesis of the New Testament* (Oxford: Parker, 1904) 3–4.

[95] Ibid., 11–12. Compare Lake's earlier, similar, but less well-developed suggestions in "The Practical Value of Textual Variation Illustrated from the Book of Acts," *Biblical World* 19 (1902) 361–69, esp. 363–64, 369. How forward-looking this view of Lake was in his day can be seen by contrasting it with what Warfield was still saying in 1907 in the 7th ed. of his *Introduction to the Textual Criticism of the New Testament*, p. 11: "The text conveys the sense; but the textual critic has nothing to do, primarily, with the sense. It is for him to restore the text, and for the interpreter who follows him to reap the new meaning." But when Lake speaks of the "textual critic" and the "exegete," they are intimately related, if not identified, as he brings the interpretive task virtually into the textual criticism enterprise. Certainly the two tasks become one in the views of Riddle and Parvis.

[96] Donald W. Riddle, "Textual Criticism as a Historical Discipline," *AngThR* 18 (1936) 221.

> Of course the New Testament writers wrote something. But what is the use of picturing this original copy? It had no status as a sacred document; no reverence for it as Scripture was accorded it until a century after its writing; it was valued only for its practical value; it was early and frequently copied.[97]

Merrill Parvis echoes these notions regarding so-called spurious readings:

> All are part of the tradition; all contribute to our knowledge of the history of Christian thought. And they are significant contributions because they are interpretations which were highly enough thought of in some place and at some time to be incorporated into the Scripture itself.[98]

Thus textual variants and canon meet in dynamic fashion—but not only are the variants that find their way into the canonical text of the church designated canonical, but also those that did not. "Canon" suddenly takes on more than one meaning or level. Parvis, however, goes further. Even when we have approached the autographs, he says, we still have only one form of the tradition. Then, almost lamenting the invention of printing, he states that prior to its use ". . . the Scripture was a living body of literature, which was constantly being enriched as it was interpreted and reinterpreted by each succeeding generation."[99]

A year later, across the Atlantic, Erich Fascher spoke of reflective scribes of the New Testament in this fashion: "The interpreting copyist moves between text and copy and forces his interpretation upon his later readers, since he has yet no knowledge of an authoritative text."[100] This assertion regarding the lack of an authoritative text, and the similar one by Riddle quoted above, were not, however, to be tolerated by another Chicago scholar, Ernest Colwell. After strong statements that "most variations . . . were made deliberately," and that "[t]he majority of the variant readings in the New Testament

[97] Ibid., 227.

[98] Merrill M. Parvis, "The Nature and Tasks of New Testament Textual Criticism," *JR* 32 (1952) 172. Compare Zuntz, *Text of the Epistles*, 10: ". . . this [New Testament] tradition is embedded in a vast historical process: it is part and parcel of the life of Christianity."

[99] Ibid., 173.

[100] Erich Fascher, *Textgeschichte als hermeneutische Problem* (Halle [Saale]: Max Niemeyer, 1953), 12.

were created for theological or dogmatic reasons," he turns an old assumption on its head:

> Most of the manuals and handbooks now in print (including mine!) will tell you that these variations were the fruit of careless treatment which was possible because the books of the New Testament had not yet attained a strong position as "Bible." The reverse is the case. It was because they were the religious treasure of the church that they were changed.[101]

274 Colwell adds:

> The paradox is that the variations came into existence because these were religious books, sacred books, canonical books. The devout scribe felt compelled to correct misstatements which he found in the manuscript he was copying.[102]

Colwell's statements suggest that textual alteration was encouraged rather than discouraged by the notion of canonicity, which would suggest, in turn, that when effecting a theologically motivated textual reformulation, a scribe was actually making a canonical decision—an independent (or perhaps a community) enhancement to the New Testament canon. This hypothesis suggests, finally, that canon formation was a process operating at two quite distinct levels: first, at the level of church leaders in major localities or regions of Christianity, who were seeking broad consensus on which *books* were to be accepted as authoritative; and, second, also at the level of individual scribes (though it might be assumed that usually they would represent a monastic or some other small community), whose interest would be in *individual variants* that would express appropriately their theological or liturgical understanding of portions of their already authoritative church writings.

From these notions flows a torrent of questions that can be treated here only by referring quickly to some examples, mostly discussed or alluded to in the preceding text of this article. First, however, it might be helpful to remember that gospels and epistles, though scribes copied them word by word, undoubtedly were read holistically in early Christian worship and use, and not discretely as is the ten-

[101] Ernest Cadman Colwell, *What Is the Best New Testament?* (Chicago: University of Chicago Press, 1952) 52–53.
[102] Ibid., 52.

dency in critical scholarship. Early Christians, therefore, would not likely raise the "canonical" questions illustrated here, but would have treated as "canon" whatever text-form of a gospel or letter had reached them in the transmission process. For instance, if they possessed a gospel expanded by harmonization or by liturgical embellishment, they would not likely have noticed or been concerned—unless the reader or hearer were, for example, an Origen![103] Consider the following inquiries:

First, in what sense were or are competing variant readings "canonical" (for example, in the marriage and divorce sayings), or to what extent were or are variants "canonical" that textual critics now reject but that were once authoritative scripture in the fourth or fifth centuries or even the seventeenth century (for example, additional endings of Mark, or numerous readings of the *textus receptus* preserved in the King James Version)?

Second, was or is the doxology in Romans "canonical" after 14:23, 275
after 15:33, or after 16:23, or after both 14:23 and 16:23 where several manuscripts put it? Or was this doxology never part of Romans, as attested by other manuscripts and church writers? And if a fourteen-chapter Romans was a literary successor to a sixteen-chapter Romans, which form of Romans is "original" and which is "canonical"?[104]

Third, was or is Romans "canonical" or "original" with or without "in Rome" in Rom 1:7 and 1:15? Or are both in some sense canonical and in some sense original? The same questions arise about "in Ephesus" in Eph 1:1.

Fourth, the Lord's prayer has six main forms in our textual tradition. Was, for instance, the Matthean phrase (6:13), "but rescue us from evil," "canonical" also in the Gospel of Luke for the numerous manuscripts that have it in their texts of Luke 11:14? Was the

103 On Origen as a textual critic, see Epp, "Textual Criticism in the Exegesis of the New Testament," 83.

104 For these views of Romans, see Gamble, *Textual History of the Letter to the Romans*, 15–35; 96–129; compare John J. Clabeaux, *A Lost Edition of the Letters of Paul: A Reassessment of the Text of the Pauline Corpus Attested by Marcion* (CBQMS 21; Washington, DC: Catholic Biblical Association, 1989) 1–4, for a summary; Ulrich Schmidt, *Marcion und sein Apostolos: Rekonstruktion und historische Einordnung der marcionitischen Paulusbriefausgabe* (ANTF 25; Berlin: de Gruyter, 1995) 284–94; and Peter Lampe, "Zur Textgeschichte des Römerbriefes," *NovT* 27 (1985) 273–77.

final phrase in Matthew's version (at 6:13), "For the kingdom and the power and the glory are yours forever," "canonical" for the many witnesses carrying it (despite the clear evidence that it represents a successor, liturgical rewriting)?

Fifth, was or is the Book of Acts "canonical" in its B-text form or its D-text form, or both?

Finally, to change the focus of these questions and to return to one raised at the outset of this discussion, if "original" is multivalent, can "canon" escape multivalence? What does "canon" or "canonical" mean? Just as each of the 5,300 Greek New Testament manuscripts and the perhaps 9,000 versional manuscripts is an "original," so each of these thousands of manuscripts likely was considered "canonical" when used in the worship and teaching of individual churches—and yet no two are exactly alike. Consequently, each collection or "canon" of early Christian writings during the centuries-long process of canonization was likewise different, whether in the writings it included and excluded or—more likely—in the detailed content of those writings as represented in their respective manuscripts, with their varying textual readings. As for the latter—if we follow the insights of the Chicago school—interpretive variant readings had authority in one Christian community or another. So "canon" and "canonical," which inherently involve authority, have varying dimensions of meaning at various times and in diverse places, and "canon" is no less polyvalent than "original text."

276 B. *Proposed Dimensions of Meaning in the Term, "Original Text"*

It is clear that the notion of multiple "originals" is implicit in some and explicit in others of the several new views surveyed. These various "originals" or, better, "dimensions of originality" might be viewed as functioning in four ways with respect to the New Testament text. However, because the term "original" no longer has its apparent or traditional meaning, an alternate terminology—terms that do not confuse the issue (as "original" does) but that clarify or at least are neutral—is required. I shall try the term "text-form" as the common designation in all of the proposed dimensions:

First, a *predecessor text-form*, that is, a form of text (or more than one) discoverable behind a New Testament writing that played a role in the composition of that writing. Such a predecessor might have affected either larger or smaller portions of a writing. In less careful language,[105] this predecessor is a "pre-canonical original" of the text of certain books, representing an earlier stage in the composition of what became a New Testament book.

Second, an *autographic text-form*, that is, the textual form as it left the desk of a Paul or a secretary, or of other writers of portions of what became our New Testament. Whole books in this dimension of originality hypothetically would be close in form to the New Testament writings as we possess them—except in two important and frequent cases: when they have been subject to reformulation by the forces operative in the next two dimensions of originality. Most often, later reformulations of this autographic form would have affected some or many of its individual variation units rather than the entire book in wholesale fashion. So this text-form may be largely an ideal.

Third, a *canonical text-form*, that is, the textual form of a book (or a collection of books) at the time it acquired consensual authority or when its canonicity was (perhaps more formally) sought or established, such as when a collection was made of the Pauline letters or of the four-fold gospel, or—at the level of detail—when phrases like "in Rome" or "in Ephesus" might have entered or been removed from the text. A major difficulty, of course, is determining the point at which "canonicity"—however defined—was attributed to a writing. ("Canonical original" may be a tolerable label, but then it really should be designated "'canonical' 'original,'" because of the multivalence of both terms. Thus the complexities multiply!) 277

Fourth, an *interpretive text-form*, representing any and each interpretive iteration or reformulation of a writing—as it was used in the life, worship, and teaching of the church—or of individual variants so created and used. Actually, then, the interpretive text-form is a newly interpreted text that replaces the prior "original" upon which it has imposed its fresh reformulation. Examples abound in the works of Ehrman and Parker (noted earlier) and in those of many other textual critics who have explored text-critical reformulations motivated by theological, liturgical, ideological, historical, stylistic, or other

[105] The terms "pre-canonical original," "canonical original," and "interpretive original" were used in my earlier attempt to describe levels or, better, dimensions of originality ("Textual Criticism in the Exegesis of the New Testament," 89), but obviously I prefer the terminology and refinements adopted for the present paper.

factors. There is, then, a real sense in which every intentional, meaningful scribal alteration to a text creates a new text-form, a new "original," though we may not wish to carry the matter to this extreme (if only out of practical considerations).

A series of distinctions such as this one veils numerous complexities. Of first importance is the caveat that, while these characterizations describe ways in which the various text-forms may have functioned and how they may be related to one another, they should not be understood as being discrete entities or as having a linear relationship. Nor will every writing or variation unit have incarnations in all of these text-forms: some will have one, others more. For example, an autographic text-form may really be, as far as one can tell, a canonical text-form and/or an interpretive text-form. That is, if an autographic text-form has predecessor text-forms, it is simultaneously an interpretive text-form, or, if it has emerged from the canonical process without reformulation, it will be identical with its canonical text-form. It should be clear also that, despite some 300,000 variant readings in the New Testament manuscript tradition, there will not always be sufficient variants or other manuscript indications to provide clear knowledge of what a given text represents among these possibilities. For instance, it seems fair to say that something both mechanical and creative has happened prior to, during, and after the composition of our various gospels and that a letter like Romans has a complex history of transmission; thus there is sufficient warrant for one or another of our labels in these cases, and certainly something has happened to yield two noticeably divergent textual streams in Acts, and so forth. Yet, in some larger pieces and in innumerable smaller ones, little may have affected the texts or, where a text has been altered for one reason or another, the reformulation may have left no trace in the manuscript tradition, forever obscuring the earlier "original." Textual critics should not expect, therefore, that a search for one or more of the multivalent "originals" or text-forms will be easy or certain—should they choose to launch it. Yet, in so many instances textual critics have adequate data in their long and rich New Testament textual tradition to make the search for dimensions and functions of "originality" a worthwhile and fruitful one. In any event, the multivalence of the term "original" is a reality not to be denied.

C. *The Distance between the Disciplines of Textual Criticism and Canon* 278

Text and canon may be juxtaposed quite properly as twin disciplines that are in some sense foundational or basic to the biblical fields, and they may also be seen, quite correctly, as interactive in areas where the notion of "authority" is present. It is at the latter point, however, that I think a distinction must be drawn between the two, showing that in essence text and canon stand at a distance from one another. Canon, by definition, is concerned with and contains authoritative material—in the case of Christianity, authoritative writings that were or became normative for faith and practice. Canon by definition also involves limitations, even if the placing of limits was not accomplished immediately in the early church or by easily recognized criteria. Thus canon in its essence involves authority.

Our earlier survey of the use of the term "original text" in text-critical handbooks permits the deduction that over several generations New Testament textual critics have been socialized into thinking of a single original text as its object. That approach, in turn, may suggest at first glance that the text-critical discipline, too, is necessarily concerned with authority. After all, in simpler times, this single "original text" was more often than not identified with the autographs, and the autographs with the canonical, authoritative New Testament text that was the standard for Christian faith and practice (as, for example, in Nolan [discussed above]: "the genuine text of the sacred canon").[106] Recent and current views are making it clear, however, that there is no easy equivalence between "original" texts and "canonical" texts, because each term is multivalent. Thus, there is no more a single "canonical" text than there is a single "original"; our multiplicities of texts may all have been canonical (that is, authoritative) at some time and place. To paraphrase Parker, the canon of the New Testament should be viewed "as a free, or perhaps, a living *canon*" and therefore "the concept of a *canon* that is fixed in shape, authoritative, and final as a piece of literature has to be abandoned."[107] The same vitality, the same fluidity that can be observed in textual variation carries over to canonicity.

---

[106] Nolan, *An Inquiry into the Integrity of the Greek Vulgate*, 2–3.

[107] Parker, *The Living Text of the Gospels*, 200, 93, refers to the New Testament "text" in these statements, and it should not be assumed that he would approve my substitution of "canon" for "text."

As a result of this conclusion, textual criticism as a discipline is not automatically and necessarily concerned with authority. For example, difficult though it may be, if one can establish a text or reading to be "as close as possible" to an autographic text-form that appears unaffected by predecessor or successor text-forms, does that text-critical decision in fact create an authoritative text or reading?—"authoritative" in the sense of theologically normative? My answer
279 is clearly negative; rather, it only means that a scholarly decision has been reached that affirms a given text or reading to be "as close as possible" to an apparently un-preformulated and un-reformulated text-form. The text-critical discipline per se carries with it no normative implications and imposes no theological overlay onto such a text or variant. As I have emphasized earlier,[108] some (perhaps many) textual critics may be seeking an authoritative "original" New Testament text and may choose to identify it with an authoritative "canon," but such a goal is neither intrinsic to textual criticism as a historical-critical discipline, nor is it within the domain of textual criticism to place a theological overlay on either its purposes or its results. In the same breath, however, I wish also to emphasize that every textual critic has full freedom to perform his or her text-critical work within any chosen theological framework, but that choice constitutes a fully separate, voluntary, additional step and one not intrinsic to or demanded by the discipline.[109]

[108] See "Textual Criticism in the Exegesis of the New Testament," 91.

[109] Brevard S. Childs, *New Testament as Canon*, applies his "canonical approach" to the entire New Testament, and his excursus on "The Hermeneutical Problem of New Testament Text-Criticism" (pp. 521–30) is equally ideological. I cannot do justice to it here (nor am I confident that I understand all of its many nuances), though its relevance to our discussion is frequent and considerable. For example, Childs recognizes that "[t]he selection and shaping of the books of scripture took place in the context of the worship of the struggling church as it determined canonicity by the use and effect of the books themselves" (p. 31); and he also affirms ". . . the effect of the canonical collection in its final form on the shaping of the tradition for those who treasured these writings as scripture" (p. 32). In Childs's view, "[t]he earliest levels of textual witness reveal a state of wide multiplicity" and the goal of restoring the "original autographs" "seems increasingly one-sided" (p. 524). For him, the term canon also has different uses (p. 41), yet the New Testament canon is "that corpus received as scripture. . . . The canonical form marks not only the place from which exegesis begins, but also it marks the place at which exegesis ends. The text's pre-history and post-history are both subordinated to the form deemed canonical" (p. 48). And the "canonical vision" involves "interpreting the New Testament as sacred scriptures of the church" (p. 53). As for New Testament textual criticism, it is "part of the larger canonical process" (p. 523), and Childs

Conclusion 280

As New Testament textual criticism moves into the twenty-first century, it must shed whatever remains of its innocense, for nothing is simple anymore. Modernity may have led many to assume that a straightforward goal of reaching a single original text of the New Testament—or even a text as close as possible to that original—was achievable. Now, however, reality and maturity require that textual criticism face unsettling facts, chief among them that the term "original" has exploded into a complex and highly unmanageable multivalent entity. Whatever tidy boundaries textual criticism may have presumed in the past have now been shattered, and its parameters have moved markedly not only to the rear and toward the front, but also sideways, as fresh dimensions of originality emerge from behind the variant readings and from other manuscript phenomena.

Nor (for those who choose to work within a theological framework) is textual criticism a "safe" discipline—a phrase I have heard for four decades—that can be practiced without challenge to theological convictions or without risk to faith commitments or truth

---

sees a crucial need to "redefine the task of New Testament textual criticism in such a way as to do justice to the text's peculiar canonical function within the Christian church," that is, "establishing the church's received and authoritative text" and "to recover that New Testament text which best reflects the true apostolic witness found in the church's scripture" (p. 527). Methodologically, he asserts, this is done by starting with the *textus receptus* because it describes "a full range of textual possibilities which actually functioned in the church," from which one discerns, critically, "the best received, that is, canonical text"—"that text which best reflects the church's judgment as to its truth" (p. 528). Childs recognizes the "element of subjectivity" in this "continuing process," for "the discipline of text criticism is not a strictly objective, or non-theological activity" (p. 529).

Of course, textual criticism is not a strictly objective exercise, but I differ in thinking that it is preferable to begin the enterprise with the earliest witnesses/texts rather than later ones, (though for me that is more a matter of convenience than ideology) and that canon and text should be distanced rather than integrally joined. The many references by Childs, within the last few pages of his excursus, to the text best reflecting "the true apostolic witness" (p. 527) or "the church's judgment as to its truth (p. 528) or "the truest witness to the gospel" or the best received text's "purity" (p. 529) or, finally, to "the truest textual rendering" (p. 530) heighten his unification of text and canon as jointly a theological enterprise. I would seek ways, rather, to distance them one from the other as an essential aspect of textual criticism as a scholarly discipline.

Further on "canonical criticism," including interaction with Childs's views, see the works of James A. Sanders, esp. *From Sacred Story to Sacred Text: Canon as Paradigm* (Philadelphia: Fortress, 1987).

assertions. I doubt that it ever was "safe"—at least for any who have thought through the implications of our myriad variation units, with their innumerable competing readings and conceptions, as well as the theological motivations that are evident in so many. But if it has been a "safe" discipline, it is safe no more. And if it has been or is now conceived to be a "narrow" or neatly circumscribed discipline, either by those inside or outside the field, it is narrow no more. Any who embrace it as a vocation will find its intellectual challenges to have been increased a hundredfold by its enlarged boundaries and broadened horizons, which extend into codicology and papyrology and also into related early Christian, classical, literary, and sociological fields, all of which favor accommodation of the richness of the manuscript tradition, with its multiplicity of texts and its multivalent originals, rather than the myopic quest for a single original
281 text. Both broad training and knowledge, and a capacity to tolerate ambiguity will be high on the list of requisite qualifications for its practitioners. A decade ago François Bovon warned that "[s]pecialization is already revealing its limitations. Textual critics should reach back into the discipline of codicology and forward into the field of hermeneutics,"[110] and Martin Hengel, in his 1993 presidential address before the Studiorum Novi Testamenti Societas, also regretted that New Testament textual criticism has become highly specialized and insisted that "it must again become a shared task, especially since burning theological and historical issues lurk behind it."[111] Though not all will agree, it appears to me that promising avenues of cooperative research have been opened by these recent and current viewpoints and that New Testament textual criticism now is poised to contribute to the understanding of early Christianity more broadly and more richly than ever before.

Added Notes, 2004

On note 37. James M. Robinson's article advocating a written text prior to Q, which I used to illustrate layers of text and tradition

[110] François Bovon, "The Synoptic Gospels and the Noncanonical Acts of the Apostles," *HTR* 81 (1988) 35.

[111] Martin Hengel, "Aufgaben der neutestamentlichen Wissenschaft," *NTS* 40 (1994) 341–42. A slightly revised version appeared in *Bulletin for Biblical Research* 6 (1996) 76–86; see 79.

behind our gospels, quickly generated an array of articles, including further studies by Robinson and his collaborator, Christoph Heil:

"The Pre-Q Text of the (Ravens and) Lilies, Q 12:22–31 and P.Oxy. 655 (*Gos. Thom.* 36)," *Text und Geschichte: Facetten theologischen Arbeitens aus dem Freundes- und Schülerkreis: Dieter Lührmann zum 60. Geburtstag* (eds. S. Maser and E. Schlarb; MThSt 50; Marburg: Elwert, 1999) 143–80.

"The Lilies of the Field: Saying 36 of the *Gospel of Thomas* and Secondary Accretions in Q 12.22b–31," *NTS* 47 (2001) 1–25.

"Noch einmal: Der Schreibfehler in Q 12,27," *ZNW* 92 (2001) 113–22;

"P.Oxy. 655 und Q. Zum Diskussions-Beitrag von Stanley E. Porter," *For the Children, Perfect Instruction: Studies in Honor of Hans-Martin Schenke on the Occasion of the Berliner Arbeitskreis für koptisch-gnostische Schriften's Thirtieth Year* (eds. H.-G. Bethge, S. Emmel, K. L. King, and I. Schletterer; NHMS 54; Leiden: Brill, 2002) 411–23.

Critiques include the following:

Jens Schröter, "Vorsynoptische Überlieferung auf P.Oxy. 655? Kritische Bemerkungen zu einer erneuerten These," *ZNW* 90 (1999) 265–72.

Idem, "Verschrieben? Klärende Bemerkungen zu einem vermeintlichen Schreibfehler in Q und tatsächlichen Irrtümern," *ZNW* 92 (2001) 283–89.

Stanley E. Porter, "P.Oxy. 655 and James M. Robinson's Proposals for Q: Brief Points of Clarification," *JTS* 52 (2001) 84–92.

CHAPTER TWENTY-ONE

ISSUES IN THE INTERRELATION OF NEW TESTAMENT TEXTUAL CRITICISM AND CANON

The lengthy and complex process that brought about the final con- 485
sensus on what writings would constitute the canon of the New Testament is the province of other contributions in the present volume. The task of this essay is different and twofold: first, to expose ways in which manuscripts that preserve those writings were factors in or reveal aspects of that process, but also, second, to explore "canonical" issues that arise from the very fact of textual variation in and among these "New Testament" manuscripts, whether they were transcribed before or after the canon (or segments thereof) had been resolved. Naturally, "canonical" issues involving variant readings are also concerned with authority, for that is what canon is all about.[1] We begin, however, by examining rather matter-of-fact features of our "New Testament" manuscripts that have implications for canon, broadly defined.

I. Manuscript Contents with Implications for Canon

The varying content of manuscripts carrying writings that were to become part of the New Testament contribute to our understanding of how the early church was dealing with the issue of authority or canon. For example, what does it mean when manuscripts contain books ultimately not retained in the New Testament, or when certain manuscripts do not carry writings normally expected there, or, finally, when books are found in various manuscripts in different

---

[1] An excursus on "The Intersection of Textual Criticism and Canon," published in 1997, provides the core for the present essay, which, however, is much revised and vastly expanded: E. J. Epp, "Textual Criticism in the Exegesis of the New Testament, with an Excursus on Canon," *Handbook to Exegesis of the New Testament* (NTTS 25; ed. S. E. Porter; Leiden: Brill, 1997) 73–91. Part of this earlier excursus evolved into an extensive treatment of *The Multivalence of the Term 'Original Text' in New Testament Textual Criticism*, in *HTR* 92 (1999) 245–281.

groups or in differing sequences? And what role did the conventional groupings in which early Christian writings circulated play in the formation of the canon? These, of course, are all features extraneous to the actual texts of the manuscripts, yet they provide valuable raw data useful in exploring matters of canon, though inevitably they require critical analysis and interpretation. Moreover, the rea-
486 sons for the inclusion or exclusion of writings, or for the order or combination of writings in our manuscripts are not always apparent, often leaving investigators with a fair measure of uncertainty if not a sense of mystery.

We will treat these issues under three headings: (a) the presence of unexpected books in "New Testament" manuscripts, (b) the absence of expected books in "New Testament" manuscripts, and (c) the varying order of books in "New Testament" manuscripts. Yet, to speak, as we have, of *expected* or *unexpected* writings in *New Testament* manuscripts is, of course, to take a modern stance toward an ancient situation, which is one of the difficulties in this entire subject: the risk of imposing on early Christianity the results of a canon process not yet completed at the time. Therefore, considerable freedom is used when referring to manuscripts of the first several centuries of Christianity as "New Testament" manuscripts, or when characterizing certain writings as "expected" or "unexpected," "canonical" or "non-canonical," or as "apocryphal." And anomalies persist—indeed, anomalies multiply—when certain conventional time frames are adopted for recognition of the authoritative status, for instance, of the Pauline corpus (ten letters collected early in the second century, expanded by adding the Pastorals, and achieving scriptural status over a wide area by the end of the second century), the fourfold gospel (collected in the late second century and broadly accepted by the mid-third century), the Catholic Epistles (collected perhaps in the third century, and debated into the fourth), or the twenty-seven book New Testament as we know it (so listed first by Athanasius in 367 and authoritative at least in Alexandria, though much later in the East).[2]

---

[2] See Harry Y. Gamble, "Canon: New Testament," *ABD* 1.853–56; idem, "The Canon of the New Testament," *The New Testament and Its Modern Interpreters* (ed. E. J. Epp and G. W. MacRae; SBLBMI 3; Philadelphia: Fortress; Atlanta, GA: Scholars Press, 1989) 205–12; Helmut Koester, *Introduction to the New Testament: History and Literature of Early Christianity* (2 vols.; 2d ed.; New York/Berlin: de Gruyter,

First, however, a listing and analysis of the groups in which early Christian writings circulated will provide perspective for later discussion.

A. *Grouping of Manuscripts in the Circulation Process*

Manuscripts containing writings that would eventually be recognized as canonical were transmitted in fairly well-defined groups, but not consistently. The conventional groupings, with the approximate totals of Greek manuscripts of each, are as follows: the four gospels are found in 2,361 manuscripts; the Acts and the Catholic Epistles in 662; the Pauline letters in 792; and the Revelation to John in 287.[3] However, when details about these various groups are tabulated, the situation is much more complex than these figures and groupings imply. Leaving out the even more problematic papyri for the moment, Kurt and Barbara Aland reported in 1989 the following array of
majuscule and *minuscule* manuscript contents (with the majuscules updated 487
to 1998),[4] though not all actual combinations are included in the list:

a. Entire New Testament (as finally defined in twenty-seven books): three majuscules (א, A, C[5]), some fifty-six minuscules.

1995–2000) 2.6–12; cf. Lee M. McDonald, *The Formation of the Christian Biblical Canon* (rev. and enl. ed.; Peabody, MA: Hendrickson, 1995) 189–90; 250–54.

[3] These figures and the following data are taken from Kurt Aland and Barbara Aland, *The Text of the New Testament: An Introduction to the Critical Editions and to the Theory and Practice of Modern Textual Criticism* (2d ed.; trans. Erroll F. Rhodes; Grand Rapids, MI: Eerdmans; Leiden: Brill, 1989) 78–79. Since then, twenty new papyri and eighteen majuscules have been published (see the following note), as well as some sixty-five new minuscules. Note that the statistics presented here and in the following list do not add up, because the latter does not contain all actual combinations.

[4] For papyri numbers 97–99, majuscules 0299–0306, and newly added minuscules [as well as all the preceding manuscripts], see the official list of New Testament manuscripts: Kurt Aland (ed.), *Kurzgefasste Liste der griechischen Handschriften des Neuen Testaments* (ANTF 1; 2d ed., rev. and enl.; Berlin/New York: de Gruyter, 1994) 16, 44; this is updated, for P100–P115, majuscules 0307–0309, and minuscules 2857–2862 in *Bericht der Hermann Kunst-Stiftung zur Förderung der neutestamentlichen Textforschung für die Jahre 1995 bis 1998* (Münster/Westfalen: Hermann Kunst Stiftung, 1998) 14–16; [and for P116, majuscules 0310–0316, and minuscules 2863–2877 in *Bericht der Hermann Kunst-Stiftung zur Förderung der neutestamentlichen Textforschung für die Jahre 1998 bis 2003* (2003) 74–79].

[5] Codex C, a palimpsest, which has portions of every book except 2 Thessalonians and 2 John, has many lacunae throughout its text, though there is no reason to doubt its original completeness. For the lacunae, see Frederick Henry Ambrose Scrivener, *A Plain Introduction to the Criticism of the New Testament for the Use of Biblical Students* (4th ed., ed. Edward Miller; 2 vols.; London: George Bell, 1894) 1.121 n. 1.

b. All books except gospels: one majuscule (P^{apr}), seventy-five minuscules.
c. All books except Revelation: two majuscules (B,[6] Ψ), 147 minuscules.
d. Four gospels: 193 majuscules (119 fragmentary), 1,896 minuscules (fifty-seven fragmentary).
e. Gospels + Acts + Catholic Epistles: one majuscule (D), eight minuscules.
f. Gospels + Acts + Catholic Epistles + Revelation: two minuscules.
g. Gospels + Pauline letters: five minuscules.
h. Gospels + Revelation: eleven minuscules.
i. Acts + Catholic Epistles (= Apostolos): thirty majuscules (twenty-eight fragmentary), forty minuscules (five fragmentary).
j. Acts + Catholic Epistles + Pauline Letters: eight majuscules, 256 minuscules.
k. Acts + Catholic Epistles + Revelation: three minuscules.
l. Pauline Letters: fifty-eight majuscules (forty-six fragmentary), 138 minuscules (six fragmentary).
m. Pauline Letters + Revelation: six minuscules.
n. Revelation to John: eight majuscules (four fragmentary), 118 minuscules (one fragmentary).

Placing the "New Testament" papyri in these same categories would involve undue speculation as to the nature and size of the codices of which nearly all were a part, especially since only fourteen papyri presently contain more than one writing. Many more than these fourteen certainly contained books in addition to those they now preserve, and the approximate or even exact original size of some papyri can be calculated, especially those with substantial text, such as P45, P46 (see below), P74, and P75, and even some fragmentary
488 papyri, such as P64+P67+P4 (see below). At other times, the size of
a quire can be determined, for example, the recently published P115,[7] though it cannot be known in this case whether such a quire stood alone or had been bound with others. Also, the likely original contents can now and again be projected; for example, T. C. Skeat has

[6] It is generally assumed that Codex B originally had all twenty-seven books, but actually the Pastorals, Philemon, and Revelation are not extant (see discussion below).
[7] P.Oxy. LXVI.4499.

suggested that P75, which preserves extensive portions of Luke and John, was originally a volume made up of two single quires, or maybe P75 was one of two separately bound single quire codices, one with Matthew and Mark, and the other (P75) with Luke and John.[8] Skeat, on more solid grounds, argued persuasively that P64+P67+P4 (demonstrated to be the same manuscript),[9] now containing portions of Matthew and Luke, was a single quire volume that can be shown to have contained all four gospels originally.[10] On the other hand, a papyrus text like P46 defies certainty or even reasonable guesses as to its original content, even though its exact size can be determined (see below). Incidentally, as just noted regarding P64+P67+P4, some fragments of papyri have been identified as portions of the same manuscript; other instances are P14+P11 and P33+P58. Additional such identifications among our 116 papyri are unlikely, though new fragments of some could well be found (as with the recent case of P.Oxy. LXIV.4405, which was identified as a new fragment of P77 [P.Oxy. XXXIV.2683]).[11]

The content of our 116 "New Testament" papyri, representing 112 different manuscripts (most of which are fragmentary), might be summarized as follows (with some duplications, and considering only writings in Greek):[12]

a. More than one writing: fourteen papyri.
   (1) More than one gospel: five papyri: P44 (Matthew + John); P45 (four gospels + Acts); P64+P67+P4 (Matthew + Luke); P75 (Luke + John); P84 (Mark + John).

[8] T. C. Skeat, "The Origin of the Christian Codex," *ZPE* 102 (1994) 264.

[9] Idem, "The Oldest Manuscript of the Four Gospels?" *NTS* 43 (1997) esp. 1–9.

[10] Ibid., 9–19; see also Graham N. Stanton, "The Fourfold Gospel," *NTS* 43 (1997) 327–28.

[11] J. David Thomas observed that P103 of Matthew (P.Oxy. LXIV.4403) and P.Oxy. LXIV.4405 (now P77, with P.Oxy. 2683) might be from the same codex, but considered it safer to treat them as from different codices (P.Oxy. LXIV, p. 6).

[12] P2 contains portions of Luke and John in Coptic, in addition to Greek parts of John; P6, with segments of John in Greek, also has Coptic portions of John and James; P41 has both Greek and Coptic portions of Acts; P42 likewise has portions of Luke in Greek and Coptic (and also some Coptic Old Testament odes); P62 has the same six verses of Matthew in Greek and Coptic; P96 also has a few verses of Matthew in Greek and Coptic; and P99 contains parts of Romans, 2 Corinthians, Galatians, and Ephesians in Greek and Latin. Though P2 and P6 each has a single writing in Greek but additional writings in Coptic, they are not counted as papyri with more than one writing.

(2) One or two gospels + another writing: two papyri: P45 (four gospels + Acts, see above); P53 (Matthew + Acts).

(3) Acts + other writings: three papyri: P45 (above); P53 (above); P74 (Acts + 1–2 Peter + 1–3 John + Jude).

(4) Two or more Catholic Epistles: two papyri: P72 (1–2 Peter + Jude); P74 (above).

(5) Two or more Pauline Letters: six papyri: P30 (1–2 Thessalonians); P34 (1–2 Corinthians); P46 (Romans + Hebrews + 1–2
489 Corinthians + Ephesians + Galatians + Philippians + Colos-
sians + 1 Thessalonians); P61 (Romans + 1 Corinthians + Philippians + Colossians + 1 Thessalonians + Titus + Philemon); P92 (Ephesians + 2 Thessalonians); P99 (Romans, Galatians, Ephesians).

b. Portions of a single writing: ninety-eight papyri.

(1) Portions of one gospel only: fifty papyri: twenty-one with Matthew; one with Mark; seven with Luke; twenty-one with John.

(2) Portions of Acts only: eleven papyri (P8; P29; P33+P58; P38; P41; P48; P50; P56; P57; P91; P112).

(3) Portions of Hebrews only: seven papyri (P12; P13; P17; P79; P89; P114; P116).

(4) Portions of one Catholic Epistle only: seven papyri: James (P20; P23; P54; P100); 1 Peter (P81); 1 John (P9); Jude (P78).

(4) Portions of one Pauline Letter only: sixteen papyri: Romans (P10; P26; P27; P31; P40; P94; P113); 1 Corinthians (P11+P14; P15; P68); Galatians (P51); Ephesians (P49); Philippians (P16); 1 Thessalonians (P65); Titus (P32); Philemon (P87).

(5) Portions of Revelation to John only: seven papyri (P18; P24; P43; P47; P85; P98; P115).

These papyri, of course, include the numerous earliest witnesses to the text of the eventual New Testament, among them the sixty-one that date up to and around the turn of the third/fourth century. Obviously, the units in which the early manuscripts circulated have significance for canon; yet, it is only occasionally possible to offer strong evidence that fragmentary papyri containing, for example, portions only of Matthew and Luke (P64+P67+P4) or only of Luke and John (P75) came from codices containing the four gospels, as noted earlier. More often, however, such statements are based upon

assumptions, reflected in claims such as "a codex containing only Luke and John [P75] is unexpected" or "we have no other example [beside P75] of a two-gospel codex,"[13] or "a codex containing three gospels is unthinkable" [P64+P67+P4],[14] hence, "the only possible conclusion is that the manuscript *originally contained all four Gospels*."[15] As already noted, plausible arguments have been made that both P67+P64+P4 and P75 are parts of original fourfold gospel manuscripts, but such claims for papyri (or fragmentary majuscules) now preserving only a portion of a single writing are more difficult to accredit. Sometimes the claim rests upon the mere fact that the 490
fragment is from a codex (the format of all the papyri except four),[16]

---

[13] Stanton, "The Fourfold Gospel," 326, is describing Skeat's view of P75, though in a footnote Stanton cites P53 as presumably a two-gospel codex, based on K. Aland's description of that papyrus; it contains portions of Matthew and Acts, noting that it would be unlikely for the codex to have held four gospels plus Acts; see K. Aland (ed., *Repertorium der griechischen christlichen Papyri: vol. I: Biblische Papyri: Altes Testament, Neues Testament, Varia, Apokryphen* (PTS 18; Berlin/New York: de Gruyter, 1976) 283.

[14] Skeat, "The Oldest Manuscript of the Four Gospels?" 15. This statement appears in the process of argumentation: a third gospel must have existed between Matthew and Luke, etc. In actuality, no papyri contain three gospels, but only four (P45) or two in varying combinations: P44: Matthew and John; P64+P67+P4: Matthew and Luke; P75: Luke and John; P84: Mark and John. Nor are more than two gospels found in any of the majuscules until after the turn of the third/fourth century: 0162: only John; 0171: Matthew and Luke.

[15] Ibid. [italics in original].

[16] P12, P13, P18, P22. As the Alands indicate, all four "are either opisthographs or written on reused materials" (Aland and Aland, *Text of the New Testament*, 102). An opisthograph is a roll with writing on both sides (an unusual occurrence), of which P18 (P.Oxy. VIII.1079) is one example; it contains Ex 40:26–32 on the recto, and, on the verso—written in the reverse direction—is Rev 1:4–7. P13 (P.Oxy. IV.657) contains extensive portions from five chapters of Hebrews on the verso of a roll with portions of a Latin epitome of a history of Rome by Livy on the recto. P12 (P.Amh.I.IIIb, pp. 30–31) has part of Heb 1:1 on the recto in a third or early fourth century hand, followed by a Christian letter which, however, is in an earlier hand; on the verso, which was blank when the writer of the Hebrews verse used it, is Gen 1:1–5. Thus, the scribe who placed Heb 1:1 at the top of the letter was employing an already used papyrus—and also may have written the Genesis verses on the reverse: see Kenneth W. Clark, *A Descriptive Catalogue of Greek New Testament Manuscripts in America* (Chicago: University of Chicago Press, 1937) 170.

By their nature, these papyri do not enter into the roll *versus* codex discussion, for the scribe of P12 was reusing a papyrus letter, while P13 and P18 each utilized the verso of a roll whose recto had been used already; hence, a codex could not have been formed for the New Testament material. P22 (P.Oxy. X.1228) may at first appear to be an exception, for the reverse of both of its small fragments of John (from two consecutive columns) are blank, but John is written on the verso, and the blank portions are the recto. Obviously, more of John than several verses

which is taken as an automatic indication of the existence of a larger unit: a gospel portion implies a fourfold gospel codex, a Pauline fragment implies a codex with the Pauline corpus, etc. Undoubtedly this is often the case, yet caution may be advisable in citing statistics. For example, the Alands indicate that the "Four Gospels manuscripts" include forty-three papyri[17] [the comparable number now would be fifty-five], yet only one of these papyri has portions of all four gospels (P45, which includes Acts also), and only four others have parts of two gospels in various combinations, while fifty have one gospel only.[18] Similarly, it is stated that "the Apostolos (i.e., Acts and the Catholic letters) is found alone in 18 papyri,"[19] [the figure now would be twenty-one], but, while twelve of these papyri have portions of Acts, only one of them has Acts plus any Catholic Letters (P74, with Acts, James, 1–2 Peter, 1–3 John, and Jude). Finally, the Pauline Letters (including Hebrews) are said to occur in twenty-six papyri [now thirty-two], and P46 indeed has portions of nine Letters, P61 has seven, and P99 three, but of the rest three have two letters and sixteen have only one. The picture indeed differs significantly for the first three score or so majuscules, plus a half-score others down the list, which are extensive and offer greater numbers of manuscripts with all four gospels, or with both the Acts and Catholic Epistles, or with the Pauline Letters; yet, the two hundred and more remaining majuscules mostly are fragmentary with parts of one or a few writings. We end, then, with a note of caution about claims for regular and consistent combinations or groupings of writings in
491 manuscripts, especially the earlier ones, for—as noted in the lists above—a vast array of groupings are present.[20]

from chaps. 15 and 16 were written originally, and the other side of the roll elsewhere—and doubtless extensively—was occupied by text of some kind; if not, the scribe of John certainly would have used the customary and smoother recto of the roll. (For another explanation, see Aland, *Repertorium der griechischen christlichen Papyri: I*, 242). For details on Oxyrhynchus papyri, see the designated volume and text number in B. P. Grenfell and A. S. Hunt, eds., *The Oxyrhynchus Papyri* (London: Egypt Exploration Society, 1898–), 67 vols. to date.

[17] Aland and Aland, *Text of the New Testament*, 78.

[18] See the lists above.

[19] Aland and Aland, *Text of the New Testament*, 78.

[20] Aspects of these issues are treated in the important, seminal book of Harry Y. Gamble, *Books and Readers in the Early Church: A History of Early Christian Texts* (New Haven/London: Yale University Press, 1995), especially chaps. 2–3 on "The Early Christian Book" (42–81) and "The Publication and Circulation of Early Christian

B. *The Presence of Unexpected Books in "New Testament" Manuscripts*

It is commonplace that some of the manuscripts relevant to our considerations contain writings that did not become constituent parts of the New Testament. The codex containing P72 is the most ancient example.

1. *P72 and 1–2 Peter and Jude*

P72 (third/fourth century) contains the oldest known copy of Jude and 1–2 Peter, but these epistles are interspersed among an array of other Christian writings and two Psalms, all bound into a single codex, though each section was designated a separate Bodmer papyrus, as follows: the *Nativity of Mary* (or *Apocalypse of James*) [Bodmer V]; the Corinthian correspondence with Paul and *3 Corinthians* [Bodmer X]; the eleventh *Ode of Solomon* [Bodmer XI]; then Jude [Bodmer VII]; the *Homily on the Passover* by Melito (ca. 170) [Bodmer XIII]; a hymn fragment [Bodmer XII]; the *Apology of Phileas* [Bodmer XX]; Psalms 33 and 34 [Bodmer IX]; and, finally, 1–2 Peter [Bodmer VIII]. These nine works are quite separate sections bound together into one codex in the fourth century, though not all were copied by the same scribe or at the same time. Even Jude and 1–2 Peter (which together constitute P72 and were each copied around the turn of the third/fourth century) probably were not produced by the same scribe,[21] though they and the other writings still bear older page

Literature" (82–143); cf. E. J. Epp, "The Codex and Literacy in Early Christianity and at Oxyrhynchus: Issues Raised by Harry Y. Gamble's *Books and Readers in the Early Church*," *Critical Review of Books in Religion* 10 (1997) 15–37.

[21] Judgments about the scribe(s) of Jude and 1–2 Peter are hampered by the lack of a full photographic reproduction of Jude, of which only a single plate is available in the *editio princeps*: Michel Testuz, *Papyrus Bodmer VII–IX* (Cologny-Genève: Bibliotheca Bodmeriana, 1959) 12. He argued that the same scribe copied both Jude and 1–2 Peter (8; 29), followed by Floyd V. Filson, "More Bodmer Papyri," *BA* 25 (1962) 51–54, and though tentatively—awaiting photographs—by (the now late) Kurt Aland, *Repertorium der griechischen christlichen Papyri, vol. 2, Kirchenväter—Papyri, Teil 1, Beschreibungen* (PTS 42; Berlin/New York: de Gruyter, 1995) 366–68, 377, n. 14, cf. 374, n. 2. Postulating different scribes are Francis W. Beare, *The First Epistle of Peter* (3d ed.; Oxford: Blackwell, 1970) 9, n. 1; Eric G. Turner, *The Typology of the Early Codex* (Haney Foundation Series 18; Philadelphia: University of Pennsylvania Press, 1977) 79–80; and Kim Haines-Eitzen, *Guardians of Letters: Literacy, Power, and the Transmitters of Early Christian Literature* (Oxford/New York: Oxford University Press, 2000) 97–99, 173, nn. 87–90, who presents the most extensive and formidable evidence.

numbers showing that they may have been parts of four codices that were utilized to construct the present ninety-sheet composite Bodmer volume.[22] Notice that 1–2 Peter and Jude are separated in the pre-
492 sent, larger codex by four writings, but also were separate in their predecessor codices. This odd arrangement causes one to wonder, with Floyd Filson, whether 1–2 Peter and Jude "were really considered to be fully canonical by the fourth century Christian who made up this codex."[23]

As for the unit made up of the Corinthian correspondence with Paul and of *3 Corinthians*, the latter was written in the late second century and not only appears in Greek for the first time in the Bodmer papyrus but the latter is also its oldest copy. It is of interest that this (apocryphal) correspondence between the Corinthians and Paul was treated as canonical in the Syrian church by Aphraat (ca. 340) and Ephraem (d. 373), and also, through the Syriac, by the Armenian church at least by the fourth century and for several centuries thereafter.[24] Beyond this, it is difficult (a) to assess the significance for canon either of the later multisectioned codex with its variously dated, diverse contents, or (based on the continuous pagination that remains) of a similarly diverse codex that earlier contained the *Nativity of Mary*, *3 Corinthians*, the eleventh *Ode of Solomon*, and Jude, or (b) to explain the order chosen for 1–2 Peter and for Jude by the later compiler, or (c) to account for the separation of

[22] On paginations, Turner's scheme (*Typology of the Early Codex*, 80) is followed by K. Junack and W. Grunewald (*Das Neue Testament auf Papyrus, vol. 1, Die Katholischen Briefe* [ANTF 6; Berlin/New York: de Gruyter, 1986] 18) and Haines-Eitzen (*Guardians of Letters*, 100, 174, nn. 94–96), namely four pagination series: (1) *Nativity of Mary*, *3 Corinthians*, *Ode*, and Jude; (2) Melito and hymn; (3) *Phileas* and Psalms 33–34; and (4) 1–2 Peter. David Trobisch (*Die Endredaktion des Neuen Testaments: Eine Untersuchungen zur Entstehung der christlichen Bibel* [NTOA 31; Freiburg: Universitätsverlag; Göttingen: Vandenhoeck & Ruprecht, 1996] 49) appears to have a different scheme: (1) *Nativity*; (2) *3 Corinthians, Ode*, and Jude; (3) Melito and hymn, *Phileas*, and Psalms; and (4) 1–2 Peter. See his chart, 49.

[23] Floyd V. Filson, "More Bodmer Papyri," 57. Cf. Wolfgang Wiefel, "Kanongeschichtliche Erwägungen zu Papyrus Bodmer VII/VIII (P^{72})," APF 22/23 (1974) 292–93.

[24] See Bruce M. Metzger, *The Canon of the New Testament: Its Origin, Development, and Significance* (Oxford: Clarendon Press, 1987) 219, 223, cf. 7, 176, 182; Wilhelm Schneemelcher, ed., *New Testament Apocrypha* (2 vols.; rev. ed. of Edgar Hennecke and Wilhelm Schneemelcher, *Neutestamentliche Apokryphen* [6th ed.; Tübingen: Mohr-Siebeck, 1989–1990]; ET, ed. R. McL. Wilson; Louisville, Ky.: Westminster/John Knox, 1991–92) 2.217, 228–29, 254–57; and earlier, A. F. J. Klijn, "The Apocryphal Correspondence between Paul and the Corinthians," *VC* 17 (1963) 2–23, esp. 2–16.

1–2 Peter from Jude. It will be obvious, however, that both the third/fourth-century copying of 1–2 Peter and of Jude and the fourth-century compilation and binding of the present codex place these events clearly within the period when considerations of canon were most active, especially regarding the shorter Catholic Epistles.

While the history of canon formation for the Catholic Epistles shows that only 1 Peter and 1 John were quite well established in the third century, and that James, Jude, 2 Peter, and 2–3 John were still striving for acceptance, the history of the text of these epistles reveals that often they do not share a uniform textual character in a single manuscript, especially when such a document holds the conventional Apostolos group (Acts plus Catholic Epistles). Rather, each writing may have a text quite different in complexion from the others. This suggests that they had earlier circulated as independent writings and, therefore, that their differing textual character in a manuscript that brought them together stems from the earlier, most likely separate manuscripts from which they were copied.[25] Jude in P72 exemplifies aspects of this phenomenon. Even though this is the earliest manuscript containing Jude, it already shows a complex textual history for that Epistle.[26] Moreover, as noted earlier, the larger 493
Bodmer codex contains not only 1–2 Peter and Jude, but a half dozen other early "non-canonical" Christian writings or writings used liturgically by Christians. Thus, not only might a book's presence in a manuscript that contains "unexpected" writings reflect fluidity in canon formation, but fluidity can be inferred also from the varying textual complexions of books in a single grouping or collection, implying, for instance, that writings valued by some were copied and used as individual books until they were more broadly accredited by inclusion in a regular canonical grouping.[27]

[25] Aland and Aland, *Text of the New Testament*, 49–50. Cf. Beare, *First Epistle of Peter*, 8–9.

[26] Aland and Aland, *Text of the New Testament*, 50, where this general statement is made but without a rationale; for the latter, see Édouard Massaux, "Le Texte de l'Épître de Jude du Papyrus Bodmer VII (P^{72})," ALBO, Ser, III, fasc. 24 (1961) 108–25, who concludes by characterizing the text as "wild" (125); J. Neville Birdsall, "The Text of Jude in P^{72}," *JTS* 14 (1963) 394–99, shows, however, that these "wild" aspects of the text in P72 are shared by other witnesses, and he asks then whether "variant exegetical traditions" are reflected in P72's version of the text (398).

[27] Aland and Aland, *Text of the New Testament*, 49–50.

2. *Other manuscripts with "unexpected" writings*

The venerable Codex Sinaiticus (א, mid-fourth century) preserves the Old and New Testaments and, following the twenty-seven books of the latter, the *Epistle of Barnabas* and the *Shepherd of Hermas* (part of which is lost; it is not clear whether additional works were included originally in the volume). That the missing portions of Codex Vaticanus (B, mid-fourth century) also originally contained some Apostolic Fathers is speculation based on analogy with א and A.[28] Codex Alexandrinus (A, fifth century) likewise has the Old and New Testaments (the latter beginning at Matt 25:6) plus *1–2 Clement* (though the last two leaves are missing). Originally, as indicated by a table of contents, the eighteen *Psalms of Solomon* followed *Clement*.[29] It is noteworthy that this table of contents, prefixed to the Old Testament portion and under the heading Η ΚΑΙΝΗ ΔΙΑΘΗΚΗ, includes the two epistles of *Clement* immediately after Revelation, as if part of the canon, though the *Psalms of Solomon* appear to be separated from the preceding writings, as if not part of the canon, by a notation of the number of books.[30] This treatment of *1–2 Clement* agrees with their place in the "Apostolic Canons" 85, where (since Revelation is not included) they follow Jude.[31]

A very late papyrus, P42 (seventh/eighth century, though its editors[32] dated it in the sixth), contains tiny portions of Luke 1 and 2 in Greek and Coptic, which are part of an extensive series of odes

---

[28] Eberhard Nestle (*Introduction to the Textual Criticism of the Greek New Testament* [London: Williams and Norgate, 1901] 60) reports the view of Alfred Rahlfs that *Didache* and *Shepherd of Hermas* were included; Aland and Aland (*The Text of the New Testament*, 109) suggest that "texts of the Apostolic Fathers" were probably present "as in א and A."

[29] Casper René Gregory, *Canon and Text of the New Testament* (International Theological Library; Edinburgh: T. & T. Clark, 1907) 343.

[30] This is the interpretation of Scrivener-Miller, *Plain Introduction to the Criticism of the New Testament*, 1.99. The same view is found in Eberhard Nestle, *Introduction to the Textual Criticism of the Greek New Testament*, 59; idem, *Einführung in das Griechische Neue Testament* (3d ed.; Göttingen: Vandenhoeck & Ruprecht, 1909) 67; cf. Trustees of the British Museum, *The Codex Alexandrinus (Royal MS. 1 D v–viii) in Reduced Photographic Facsimile: New Testament and Clementine Epistles* (London: British Museum, 1909 ["Introduction" by F. G. Kenyon]) 8.

[31] English text in Metzger, *Canon of the New Testament*, 313; see discussion on 225; Greek text in Brooke Foss Westcott, *A General Survey of the History of the Canon of the New Testament* (4th ed.; London: Macmillan, 1875) 534–35.

[32] Walter Till and Peter Sanz, *Eine griechisch-koptische Odenhandschrift (Papyrus Copt. Vindob. K 8706)* (Monumenta biblica et ecclesiastica, 5; Rome: Päpstliches Bibelinstitut, 1939) 16–17 ("second half of the 6th century").

or hymns taken from the Jewish Bible and apocrypha, fragments of which are extant for thirteen selections in addition to those from Luke. The codex was designed for Christian liturgical purposes, and, 494
since it is very late and not a continuous text manuscript, it is not significant for canon.

The still later Greek and Latin majuscule, Codex Boernerianus (G^p, ninth century) of the Pauline Epistles, originally contained the *Epistle to the Laodiceans*, though only the superscription remains ("The Epistle to Laodiceans begins"), not the text. Curiously, this obviously spurious letter also appears in more than a hundred Latin Vulgate manuscripts, beginning with the mid-sixth century Fuldensis, and in Arabic and other manuscripts, as well as in all eighteen German Bibles prior to that of Luther, where it is found between Galatians and Ephesians.[33]

Another ninth century majuscule, P^{apr} (or P_2, a palimpsest), has Acts, all Catholic and Pauline Epistles, and the Revelation to John, but also fragments of *4 Maccabees*. As a final example, a twelfth century Harklean Syriac New Testament contains *1–2 Clement* and locates them between the Catholic Epistles and the Pauline, specifically between Jude and Romans.[34]

At certain times in certain places, as known from patristic sources and several canon lists, books like *1–2 Clement*, the *Epistle of Barnabas*, the *Epistle to the Laodiceans*, and many others, but especially the *Apocalypse of Peter* and the *Shepherd of Hermas*, were treated as authoritative (or "canonical").[35] It is well documented that the latter two apocalypses, along with the Revelation to John, vied over a long period of time for a place among the authoritative writings. All three were mentioned in the Muratorian Canon,[36] with doubt expressed about the *Apocalypse of Peter* and clear rejection assigned to *Hermas*.

[33] Metzger, *Canon of the New Testament*, 183, 239–40. J. B. Lightfoot (*Saint Paul's Epistles to the Colossians and to Philemon* [9th ed.; London: Macmillan, 1890; originally 1875] 272–98, esp. 279–98) provides a full discussion of this Epistle, including a Latin critical edition and a history of its inclusion in Latin, Albigensian, Bohemian, German, and early English Bibles over a period from the sixth to the fifteenth centuries. In general, see Schneemelcher, *New Testament Apocrypha*, 2.42–46.

[34] Metzger, *Canon of the New Testament*, 222.

[35] See the summary in McDonald, *Formation*, 223–25. On the *Shepherd*, see Metzger, *Canon of the New Testament*, 65.

[36] The text in English translation may be found in Metzger, *Canon of the New Testament*, 305–7.

Oddly, the *Apocalypse of Peter* has not been found as part of a "New Testament" manuscript, though it is included in the canon list attached to Codex Claromontanus (D^{p}, sixth century, but the list is thought to be earlier); this canon, by the way, also includes the *Shepherd of Hermas*, as well as the *Epistle of Barnabas* and the *Acts of Paul*, though the scribe has placed a dash to the left of these three, as well as the *Apocalypse of Peter*, to indicate that they are in some sense exceptional.[37]

We come now to some obvious questions: To what extent do our "New Testament" manuscripts reflect the status of canon formation in their times? Did they influence that process? One may assume effects in both directions, though proof is elusive. In the first two centuries of Christianity, books like *1 Clement, Epistle of Barnabas, Apocalypse of Peter, Shepherd of Hermas*, and others were treated as author-
495 itative by various patristic writers, especially Clement of Alexandria. In the third century, books like these were known, used, and valued by leaders such as Origen (185–254), Hippolytus (170–235), and Eusebius (ca. 265–240). At the same time, Origen is reported to have "doubted" 2 Peter and to have deemed 2–3 John questionable, while Eusebius, who placed *Barnabas, Apocalypse of Peter*, and *Hermas* in the "disputed books" category, also relegated to that same category James, Jude, 2 Peter, 2–3 John, and perhaps the Revelation to John. At the end of the third century, of course, P72 appeared with 1–2 Peter and Jude among the codex's mixed contents. Naturally, all of this attests to the fair measure of fluidity that remained on the fringes of the New Testament canon in the early and mid-fourth century—when Codex ℵ was produced, with its *Barnabas* and *Hermas*. Movement toward the twenty-seven-book canon accelerated as the fourth century closed, but not in all localities, for certainly there was no uniformity across the entirety of Christendom on these matters, especially between East and West and especially on books like Hebrews, Revelation, and *Apocalypse of Peter*.[38] So mysteries remain when attempting to spell out the significance of "unexpected" books in "New Testament" manuscripts, including P72's *3 Corinthians*, given this writing's later history, which might be significant were it not for the

[37] For the text in English translation and discussion, see ibid., 230, 310–11. See also Geoffrey Mark Hahneman, *The Muratorian Fragment and the Development of the Canon* (Oxford: Clarendon, 1992) 140–43.

[38] See Harry Y. Gamble, *The New Testament Canon: Its Making and Meaning* (GBS; Philadelphia: Fortress, 1985) 48–56.

apparently haphazard collection in which it appears. Then too, Codex ℵ's inclusion of *Barnabas* and *Hermas* in the mid-fourth century is a puzzle, but more so *1–2 Clement* in Codex A in the following century. Yet the greatest puzzle is the lengthy virulence of the *Epistle to the Laodiceans*, reinforced in the mid-sixth century with the Vulgate Fuldensis and carried by G^{p} through the ninth and then until the Reformation as part of the canon in certain areas.

C. *The Absence of Expected Books in "New Testament" Manuscripts*

If some "New Testament" manuscripts held writings that did not end up in the New Testament, there were other manuscripts that lacked certain books that might have been expected in their particular groupings, as well as manuscripts whose exact contents are difficult to discern. The earliest instance merits a thorough assessment; other examples will be treated more briefly.

1. *The disputed contents of P46*

Dating to ca. 200, this is the earliest example of an important manuscript whose contents are disputed. For that reason, it has also become highly controversial. It has been customary to say something like the following: P46 originally had ten letters of Paul, including Hebrews, but not Philemon, and it never contained the Pastoral Letters, for there is no room for them in the single quire codex when its missing first and last sections are reconstructed. I have twice made such statements,[39] based on secondary sources, as have others. Recent studies of the matter, however, require that we be more cautious, and our caution should begin by stating *positively* what P46 contains and not by reporting what it is variously assumed *not* to
have contained. P46 preserves, in this order, Rom 5:17–6:14; 8:15-end; 496
Hebrews; 1–2 Corinthians; Ephesians; Galatians; Philippians; Colossians; and 1 Thessalonians (with lacunae) through 5:28. Since most pages of this single quire codex are numbered, it is clear that seven leaves

[39] E. J. Epp, "The Papyrus Manuscripts of the New Testament," *The Text of the New Testament in Contemporary Research: Essays on the* Status Quaestionis (SD 46; ed. B. D. Ehrman and M. W. Holmes; Grand Rapids, MI: Eerdmans, 1995) 37; idem, "Textual Criticism in the Exegesis of the New Testament, with an Excursus on Canon," *Handbook to Exegesis of the New Testament* (NTTS 25; ed. S. E. Porter; Leiden: Brill, 1997) 76.

or fourteen pages from the beginning of the codex have not survived, and there is no dispute that Romans 1:1–5:17 would fit onto those pages and originally occupied them. This means, of course, that fourteen pages also are missing from the end, and the difficult question arises, what writing(s) followed 1 Thessalonians?

It may appear self-evident that 2 Thessalonians followed 1 Thessalonians, but the question at least should be raised. One relevant approach would be to ask whether the two letters ever circulated separately, either in the known papyri or majuscules. The papyri evidence is extremely limited, but 1 and 2 Thessalonians are together in P30 (third century); it is, in fact, the only papyrus with portions of both Epistles. But three other papyri have one of the Thessalonian letters: P61 (ca. 700) has small fragments of seven Pauline letters, including parts of 1 Thess 1:2–3 on the verso of a leaf that has parts of Col 4:15 on the preceding recto, but no immediately following leaves have survived.[40] P65 (third century) contains most of chapter 1 and half of chapter 2 of 1 Thessalonians, but nothing else, so (as with P61) it is inappropriate to assume that 2 Thessalonians followed,[41] since there is no possibility of knowing. Finally, P92 (third/fourth century) has survived in two tiny fragments, one with a few verses of Ephesians 1 on either side, and the other leaf, *quite separate from the Ephesians fragment*, contains 2 Thess 1:4–5 on the recto and 2 Thess 1:11–12 on the verso.[42] As to P61 and P65, then, we have no evidence of what followed the fragments of 1Thessalonians, and for P92 no evidence of what came before 2 Thessalonians, leading to the conclusion that 1 and 2 Thessalonians are together in the papyri wherever an appropriate test can be made (i.e., only in P30). Moreover, twelve Pauline majuscules with Thessalonians contain both epistles: ℵ A B D^{p} F^{p} G^{p} I K^{ap} L^{ap} P^{apr} Ψ 0278. Seven others, however, contain only portions of one or the other, but all of these manuscripts are fragmentary, most highly so, and in every case there is no evidence of what came immediately after the fragment of 1 Thessalonians or, if it is a fragment of 2 Thessalonians that is preserved, of what immediately preceded it: C H^{p} 048, 0111, 0183,

[40] See Lionel Casson and Ernest L. Hettich, *Excavations at Nessana, Volume 2: Literary Papyri* (Princeton: Princeton University Press, 1950) 118–119.

[41] See PSI XIV.1373 (pp. 5–7).

[42] See Claudio Gallazzi, "Frammenti di un codice con le Epistole di Paoli," *ZPE* 46 (1982) 117–22+plates.

0208, and 0226.[43] Hence, as in the case of the papyri, there is no instance where it can be demonstrated that 2 Thessalonians does not follow 1 Thessalonians. Therefore, it is fair to assume that 2 Thessalonians followed 1 Thessalonians in P46, especially in view of the 497
regular series of Pauline letters that there precede 1 Thessalonians.

In speculating about what P46 contained after 1–2 Thessalonians, certain data must be taken into account. First, it is self-evident that, in a single quire manuscript, pages at the beginning and at the end will be wider and therefore capable of carrying more text than those in the center, where all the sheets have been folded and where pages then were trimmed to provide an even right-hand edge for the codex. Second, it is observable that the scribe of P46 used smaller letters as the copying progressed beyond half of the codex and that the lines per page increased from twenty-six in the first half to twenty-eight, thirty, and finally to thirty-two lines per page at the end.[44] Third, the calculated space on the missing fourteen leaves following 1 Thessalonians is inadequate to accommodate the remaining writings of the Pauline corpus as we know it, namely, 1–2 Timothy, Titus, and Philemon (Hebrews, as already mentioned, is present earlier in P46, between Romans and 1 Corinthians).[45]

[43] Those that have only one are C (a palimpsest, with portions of every book except 2 John and 2 Thessalonians; After Colossians comes 1 Thess 1:1–2:9, but the next extant portion is Heb 2:4ff.); H^{p} (its leaves are scattered in eight different archives; nothing is extant between Col 3:11 and 1 Thess 2:9–13, and nothing after 1 Thess 4:11 until 1 Tim 1:7); 048 (part of 1 Thess 1, then nothing until 1 Tim 5); 0111 (fragment: 2 Thess 1:1–2:2); 0183 (fragment: 1 Thess 3:6–9; 4:1–5); 0208 (fragment of Col 1–2, then 1 Thess 2:4–7, 12–17, then nothing); 0226 (fragment: 1 Thess 4:16–5:5). Incidentally, the Muratorian Canon (English text in Metzger, *Canon of the New Testament*, 306–7) speaks of Paul's letters to the seven churches, first to the Corinthians . . . sixth to the Thessalonians, as if there were one each, but then adds that Paul wrote once more to each "for admonition." There is here no reason to think that the two letters to Thessalonians did not circulate together.

[44] See Henry A. Sanders, *A Third-Century Papyrus Codex of the Epistles of Paul* (University of Michigan Studies: Humanistic Series, 38; Ann Arbor, MI: University of Michigan Press, 1935) 5–6; Frederic G. Kenyon, *The Chester Beatty Biblical Papyri: Descriptions and Texts of Twelve Manuscripts on Papyrus of the Greek Bible, Fasciculus III Supplement: Pauline Epistles, Text* (London: Walker, 1936) ix; Robert M. Grant, *A Historical Introduction to the New Testament* (Touchstone Book; New York: Simon and Schuster, 1972 [original, 1963]) 210; David Trobisch, *Paul's Letter Collection: Tracing the Origins* (Minneapolis, MN: Fortress, 1994) 13–17.

[45] For various calculations, see Sanders, *A Third-Century Papyrus Codex*, 10–11, who suggests that, "if I and II Timothy were included, they were in an abbreviated form," and that all three Pastorals could be included with "more crowding than on the existing leaves and at least three extra pages added"; Kenyon, *The Chester*

Naturally, numerous possibilities have been offered as to how the approximately fourteen pages might have been filled, always allowing nearly five pages for 2 Thessalonians, and therefore leaving some nine pages with unknown contents. Without Philemon, 1 Timothy alone would fit with only a portion of a page left blank, but that has not been proposed; 2 Timothy with Philemon would fit; and 2 Timothy and Titus might be squeezed in, but these are unlikely combinations and have not been suggested, nor has the duo of 1 Timothy and Philemon, which would really require an additional page and is also an unlikely pair. It is clear, however, that 1–2 Timothy would require more than five extra pages, and with Titus a total of almost nine extra; if Philemon were included with the Pastorals, some ten extra pages would be needed.[46] On the other hand, if only Philemon were added after 2 Thessalonians, at least seven pages would be left blank.

Several scholars, however, have argued that P46, by design, contained only letters of Paul addressed to church communities, not personal letters, a distinction evident in the Muratorian Canon, which separates church letters from personal ones.[47] This would presume
498 that P46, in the missing end portions, contained 2 Thessalonians but no other letters beyond it. As noted earlier, however, about nine pages then would be left blank at the end of the codex. So a difficult problem remains.

A single quire codex, of course, places heavy demands on the ability of the scribe to estimate in advance the adequacy of space available for what is to be included, though—in the event of mis-

---

Beatty Biblical Papyri . . . Pauline Epistles, Text, x–xi; Grant, *Historical Introduction,* 209–11; and Jeremy Duff, "P46 and the Pastorals: A Misleading Consensus?" *NTS* 44 (1998) 581–82 (to be discussed below).

[46] I use the figures of Duff, "P46 and the Pastorals," when available, but consulting also those of Kenyon, *The Chester Beatty Biblical Papyri . . . Pauline Epistles, Text,* x; and Grant, *Historical Introduction,* 210; see preceding note. The assumption at this point is that the average of 1,050 letters per page in the last extant section of P46 continued in the missing pages. This will be adjusted slightly in the ensuing discussion.

[47] See the references in Duff, "P46 and the Pastorals," 582 n. 11, who, among others, refers to Jerome D. Quinn, "P46—The Pauline Canon?" *CBQ* 36 (1974) 379–85; see also Raymond E. Brown, S.S., *An Introduction to the New Testament* (Anchor Bible Reference Library; New York: Doubleday, 1997) 664. Quinn raises the intriguing possibility, but it is only that, of a comparable collection of Paul's personal letters, asking whether P32 (ca. 200, the same date as P46) could have been part of such a codex (380–82). Note that P87 (early third century) contains only Philemon.

calculation—the options remain (a) to leave blank pages at the end or (b) to glue on one or more pages and complete the copying. No such additional pages for P46 exist, nor is there any way to tell whether any were added.

Recently Jeremy Duff presented a review of these aspects of P46, including fresh calculations of the space used but especially of that remaining in the (reconstructed) codex, and he argues that the scribe of P46 "was always intending to include all fourteen Pauline epistles," though the attendant difficulties require Duff then to offer not one but two alternative hypotheses regarding the missing pages. The first hypothesis stipulates that the scribe intended to include the Pastoral Epistles but, due to lack of space, did not after all do so.[48] Duff's second hypothesis states that, after copying past the center of the single quire codex, it was clear that space was limited, and the scribe then gradually increased the amount of text on each page; yet, in Duff's view, even this good faith effort meant that only half of 2 Timothy would have been transcribed before the codex ended. At this point, Duff suggests, the scribe added about four[49] extra pages to accommodate the rest of 2 Timothy and Titus, or perhaps an additional small quire. Duff prefers the second alternative, though he insists that both options are viable and "point to a scribe who produced P46 assuming that the Pastorals were a constituent part of the Pauline corpus."[50]

Duff bases his hypotheses primarily on the scribe's increased number of lines per page and letters per line as the copying proceeded once the middle of the quire had been passed. To be sure, Duff's obviously careful counting of the number of letters on each page of P46 is both impressive and helpful, yet questions need to be raised

[48] Here Duff is quite unclear, for his hypothesis is that "P46 did not contain the Pastorals but was intended to do so" ("P46 and the Pastorals," 586), yet, he immediately goes on to say that "the scribe then left the codex full but, in his own eyes, incomplete" (ibid.). How can this codex be full and yet not contain (part of) the Pastorals? If he stopped after 2 Thessalonians, some eight to nine pages would be blank; if Philemon was added, there would be seven empty pages. Clear or not, this hypothesis is very far from compelling.

[49] According to the figures we have been using and Duff's own letter count, the Pastorals would require 18,900 letters, or eighteen 1,050-letter pages; hence, at least *nine* additional pages would appear to be requisite at this point (assuming, as Duff does, that Philemon had been copied after 2 Thessalonians).

[50] Duff, "P46 and the Pastorals," 585–89.

on some crucial matters. For instance, he correctly observes that "not long after the scribe passed the half-way point in the codex, he started fitting more and more text on each page," but two sentences later Duff asserts that the final section of the codex has some 50 percent more letters per page than in the middle.[51] These are
499 not inaccurate statements in themselves, but have the proper comparisons been made? If we take the average number of letters per page by using Duff's graph[52] and compare the first half of the extant codex with the second half, we find that the first half averages around 755 letters per page, while the latter half averages about 870, for a 15% increase of letters per page in the second part over the first. A better comparison (due to the changing widths of pages in a single quire) would be quarter by quarter: the first fourth of P46 averages 875 letters per page, the second 700 (for a decline of 20 percent); the third quarter (beginning at the center of the codex) averages 760 (an increase of 8.6 percent over the second), and the fourth quarter averages 1000 letters per page (an increase of 32 percent over the third quarter). However, even these comparisons are not particularly useful inasmuch as the central pages in a single quire codex, as noted earlier, will be more narrow than the earlier and later pages due to trimming—the more so the thicker the codex. P46 originally contained 52 papyrus sheets folded in the middle to form 104 leaves, that is, 208 pages. Hence, for such a single quire codex, the most appropriate comparison would be between the later pages, and not the most narrow middle leaf, but the comparable leaves at the beginning of the codex. Such a comparison, again using Duff's graph of letters per page, would begin with the pages showing the sharpest increase in letters and lines over preceding portions of text (namely, the last thirty-seven or so extant pages, but including also the missing pp. 188–191, for a total of some forty-four pages, i.e., roughly pages 150–193) and would compare them with the comparable extant

[51] Ibid., 584.

[52] Ibid., 583. My comparisons were made by enlarging Duff's graph and assigning the appropriate number of letters to each bar in the graph, using the graph's scale on the left. I then averaged the letters per page for each quarter of the graph. The fourth quarter happens to begin where the scribe's most dramatic compression of the text also begins. Comparisons, which I presume are reasonably accurate, were then made between and among the extant halves, quarters, and other sections of P46.

portion at the beginning of the codex (consisting of some forty-five pages, i.e., pages 20–64). This exercise yields a more appropriate result, showing that when the scribe began to add lines and to compress more letters into the available space, the latter forty-four pages contained 24 percent more letters than their extant counterparts in the front of the codex. Hence, while technically accurate, it is at the same time misleading to refer to a 50 percent increase at the end of the codex as measured against the middle, when in actuality the relevant portions show an expansion of text around half of that percentage when pages of roughly the same width are compared. To be still more specific about the second half of the codex, Duff's graph shows that after passing the middle the scribe compressed 7.6 percent more text per page into pages 105–129 than in the very central pages of the volume (pages 104–105); that pages 130–149 had 9 percent more than the preceding twenty-five pages; but that the final pages (150–193, i.e., the fourth quarter of the codex) crammed in 26 percent more text than pages 130–149. For this last reason, I chose to compare pages 150–193, the most strikingly compressed section of text, with the comparable pages at the outset of the scribe's extant work (pages 20–64). To repeat, this appropriate comparison showed a 24 percent increase in letters per page.

What does this all mean for Duff's hypotheses about the missing fourteen pages? According to his count—which is not being questioned—1 Thessalonians (5:28–end) plus 2 Thessalonians and Philemon would consist of 5,750 letters; the last extant pages of P46 average 1,050 letters each, and, arbitrarily allowing the scribe another 10 500
percent expansion in number of letters on the increasingly wider outer pages, five of the fourteen missing pages (each now with about 1,155 letters) would be required to accommodate the rest of the Thessalonian letters and Philemon. That would leave nine pages for whatever else the scribe had in mind, permitting writings totaling about 10,400 letters to be included. 1–2 Timothy and Titus, however, consist of 18,900 letters and would require sixteen and a half 1,155-letter pages, or seven and a half pages more than the single quire P46 contained; stating it differently, only 55 percent of the Pastorals could be included on the nine available pages and seven or eight additional pages would have to be glued on to contain all three.[53]

[53] In this discussion and in our earlier assessment, the discrepancies in the number

This assumes that Philemon was included, which (as noted above) some scholars have doubted; without Philemon, another page and a half would be available—still not enough to accommodate all the Pastorals. It is doubtful, however, that the personal letter, Philemon,[54] would have been excluded if the personal Timothy and Titus letters were included.

The addition of extra pages or a small additional quire is not unknown in the manuscript tradition,[55] but one wonders whether a scribe who, we might assume, had such an option in mind would undertake so seriously a program of compression of the text that is obvious in P46; why not continue in the fashion of the first portions knowing that a few or several pages might be added if required? On the other hand, one might suppose (since extra pages in manuscripts are not everyday experiences) that a scribe's pride might be at stake if calculations of space are excessively off the mark. The scribe of P46 has received mixed reviews and is described by H. A. Sanders as "well trained in his method" of producing blocks of writing with more or less the same margins;[56] by F. G. Kenyon as employing a script that, in contrast to P45, is "more calligraphic in character . . . with some pretensions to style and elegance";[57] while Günther Zuntz, who extolls the quality of the text in P46, nonetheless speaks of the "the very poor work of the scribe who penned it," for "P[46] abounds with scribal blunders, omissions, and also

---

of pages required due to the (perhaps overly generous) allowance of more letters per page as the pages widened nearer the end of the codex, i.e., when 1,050-letter pages are assumed for the Pastorals, eighteen pages would be required in P46, but if 1,155-letter pages are in view, sixteen and a half would be required; hence, with Philemon taking one and a half pages of the nine available, in the first instance (1,050-letter pages) more than ten extra pages would be required for the Pastorals, while in the second case (1,155-letter pages) only seven or eight extra pages would be needed. After making these calculations, I rechecked Kenyon (*The Chester Beatty Biblical Papyri . . . Pauline Epistles, Text*, x), who had virtually the same projection: "The space required [for Philemon and the Pastorals] is therefore nearly twice as much as is available," i.e., eighteen pages. Similarly, Trobisch's calculation estimates the need for nine more pages (*Paul's Letter Collection*, 16).

[54] Trobisch (*Paul's Letter Collection*, 25), however, suggests that Philemon could be placed among letters to congregations because it "actually is addressed 'to Philemon our dear friend and fellow worker, to Apphia our sister, to Archippus our fellow soldier and to the church that meets in your home' (Phlm 1–2)."

[55] Duff, "P46 and the Pastorals," 582, gives a number of examples.

[56] Sanders, *Third-Century Papyrus Codex of the Epistles of Paul*, 5–6.

[57] Kenyon, *The Chester Beatty Biblical Papyri . . . Pauline Epistles, Text*, xiii.

additions."[58] Whether praised or castigated, however, the scribe
appears to have miscalculated in grand style, at least as long as it 501
is assumed that the Pastoral Epistles and possibly Philemon were
intended for inclusion.

But what if the scribe of P46 used the missing pages, following 2 Thessalonians, for some "non-canonical" writing(s)? After all (as already reported), the codex containing P72 (turn of the third/fourth century) preserved 1–2 Peter and Jude surrounded by an array of such writings—a hundred years later than P46! Of course, the codex containing P72 may be a special case (see above), but then codices ℵ and A included assorted writings of the Apostolic Fathers fifty years after P72. Hence, the possibility must be kept open. The P72 codex, by the way, includes correspondence allegedly from Corinth to Paul, followed by an (apocryphal) Pauline *church* epistle, *3 Corinthians.* This Corinthian correspondence dates from the late second century and is now judged to have had an origin independent of the *Acts of Paul*, where it is most frequently preserved.[59] It would have been a relatively new work around 200 and would have fit with the other church letters in P46—if that was what the scribe intended for the codex. Yet, both pieces of the Corinthian correspondence would have filled fewer than four pages in P46—rendering the scribe's obvious compression of text no more meaningful than if only Titus had been added. Another church letter that could be a candidate for a Pauline codex (especially one comprised of letters to churches) is the *Epistle to the Laodiceans*,[60] which was attached to the Pauline Codex G^{p}, but it would occupy only about a page and a half (the size of Philemon) in P46, and even with the (apocryphal) Corinthian correspondence, some four and a half pages would remain unused. The Apostolic Fathers, of course, would be unlikely in an exclusively Pauline collection and, moreover, each would be too long: the *Didache*, for example, would fill the nine remaining pages and would require about four more added to the quire. So, we are left with the same situation that existed before Duff argued for the inclusion of the Pastoral Epistles: no reasonable combination of "canonical" or "non-canonical" writings fits the space remaining in the single quire codex P46.

---

[58] Günther Zuntz, *The Text of the Epistle: A Disquisition upon the* Corpus Paulinum (Schweich Lectures, 1946; London: British Academy, 1953) 212.

[59] Schneemelcher, *New Testament Apocrypha*, 2.228–29.

[60] See ibid., 42–46.

Has Duff made the case or at least made it more likely that the scribe of P46 intended to include 1–2 Timothy and Titus? Not really, for the Pastorals do not fit the space available, nor does either of his hypotheses provide a more likely solution than our proposals above. If the Pastorals would fit the space, it might be different, but both his hypotheses are arguments from silence and not compelling. To claim that a scribe intended to fill nine pages with eighteen pages of material with no evidence other than the compression of the text in the last quarter of the extant portion of the manuscript, at a rate of compression that by a very large measure could never succeed, is not credible. And to theorize that the scribe made a concerted effort to include "all fourteen Pauline epistles" by an increasing compression of the text, but walked away from the task without including the Pastorals when it became clear that space was insufficient is even less convincing. It may be more believable that the scribe glued on pages for the extensive remaining text, but it raises the unsettling question of why he compressed text as long and as intently as he did, when that enterprise was destined from the outset to fail, given the amount of space he needed. This clearly observable compression of text does not make sense if the scribe expected to insert
502 Philemon and all three Pastoral letters. A glance at the plates of P46 shows a scribe who is both well trained and experienced in the technique of ink on papyrus, for the result is precise and uniform. So great a miscalculation regarding space, if the Pastorals were in mind, is unlikely except by a novice in the trade or a rank amateur.

Yet, for a scribe to compress the text and still leave some nine blank pages does not make sense either. Hence, it would be far more reasonable to suggest that the scribe had the task of including one or more shorter writings. Indeed, my proposals above were intended less to be taken seriously and more to show that neither Duff nor anyone else yet has a feasible answer to what occupied the end of P46, for it must be admitted that what has become the traditional view—that P46 did not contain the Pastoral Epistles—is also based on an argument from silence. Duff's proposals are what he calls them: hypotheses. At the end, though reaffirming the viability of his hypotheses, he actually admits, "It may be wise to refuse to speculate as to what was on the missing pages."[61] This was also the judg-

[61] Duff, "P46 and the Pastorals," 589.

ment, for example, of Robert M. Grant[62] and more recently David Trobisch,[63] and our lengthy discussion here confirms the wisdom of that approach, at least until some new evidence appears.[64]

Finally, I am grateful to Duff for warning us about making less than careful statements about P46 and for raising a series of pertinent questions about this important manuscript. Yet, after repeated readings, it appears to me that from the very outset Duff is intent on providing any framework possible that would include the Pastorals in the early Pauline corpus. In this connection, it must be stated that our understanding of the nature of the Pastoral Epistles and of their place in early collections of Pauline letters and, consequently, their place in the early New Testament canon, is not dependent on whether P46 did or did not contain them. Rather, the character and rôle of the Pastorals will be determined primarily by other external evidence and especially by the extensive internal evidence present, including (a) linguistic peculiarities shared with second century Christianity, among them soteriological terminology parallel to that in Hellenistic religions and the emperor cult; (b) a lack of connection between the situations portrayed and what is known of Paul's life and ministry; (c) the adoption of a literary genre of Paul the martyr, providing "Paul's Testament" in defense of his heritage (especially 2 Timothy); and (d) the use of a church order and Christian conduct genre without an eschatological motivation (especially 1 Timothy and Titus), all reflecting an early to mid-second century period for the Pastorals' composition.[65] We might all wish that P46 provided the definitive answer to the presence or absence of the Pastorals in our earliest manuscript of the Pauline letters, but so far it does not.

---

[62] Grant, *Historical Introduction*, 210–11: "we do not know that [P46] did not include the Pastorals."

[63] Trobisch, *Paul's Letter Collection*, 16.

[64] Though the common assumption, as noted at the outset, has been that P46 does not contain the Pastorals, few scholars who have investigated more thoroughly have given a definite affirmative or negative answer. An exception is Quinn ("P46—The Pauline Canon?" 385), who says it did not have the Pastorals, based on his carefully argued proposals for three second-century collections of Pauline letters, concluding that "the scribe of P^{46} intended a collection of Pauline letters to churches. His inclusion of Hebrews witnesses to this concern."

[65] See, e.g., Koester, *Introduction to the New Testament*, 2.300–8.

503 2. *Codex Vaticanus and the Pastorals—an idle question?*

It may surprise many to suggest that the venerable Codex B presents a case analogous to P46 and the Pastorals. It is universally assumed that B's "New Testament" section contained all of our twenty-seven books, based, I suppose, on the fact that the other great majuscules of this general period that have the entire Bible (ℵ and A) have our twenty-seven books (plus some Apostolic Fathers). Actually, B contains the four gospels, followed by Acts, the Catholic Epistles, the Pauline letters from Romans through 2 Thessalonians, and then Hebrews, where B breaks off in the middle of Heb 9:14. A fifteenth-century supplement (designated minuscule 1957) fills in the missing portion of Hebrews and the Revelation of John, but this late substitute is of no significance. Although B has ancient page numbers—a rarity among Greek manuscripts—that permit a calculation of the number of pages lost at the beginning (some forty-six chapters of Genesis), there is no way of telling how many leaves were lost at the end—since, of course, this is a multiquire volume.[66] Alfred Rahlfs in 1889 surmised that B, in addition to the "New Testament," may have contained the *Didache* and the *Shepherd of Hermas*,[67] and the Alands also think it probable that, like ℵ and A, Codex B contained writings of the Apostolic Fathers.[68] Books of our New Testament that are missing from B as it stands (in addition to the rest of Hebrews) are 1–2 Timothy, Titus, Philemon, and the Revelation to John. However, given the mid-fourth century date of both B and ℵ, it is a fair assumption that these writings were indeed in B. Yet no one seems ever to have raised the question. And that is the reason I mention it here. Though any connection is implausible, it is curious that 1–2 Timothy, Titus, and Philemon are the same Pauline letters that are in dispute in P46 where, as we have seen, the three Pastorals do not fit in the available space and are unlikely to have been in P46. In the case of B, we lack any comparable evidence about space so that any proposals are mere speculation, except that the date of B a century and a half after P46 makes it reasonable to guess, as every one has, that the rest of our New Testament writings were there originally.[69]

[66] Gregory, *Canon and Text*, 344–45.
[67] Reported in Nestle, *Introduction*, 60.
[68] Aland and Aland, *Text of the New Testament*, 109.
[69] T. C. Skeat ("The Codex Sinaiticus, the Codex Vaticanus and Constantine,"

3. *Codex Bezae and the Catholic Epistles/Revelation*

A similar puzzle exists in Codex Bezae (D, Greek-Latin diglot, ca. 400), which contains Matthew, John, Luke, Mark (in that order), followed by a lacuna of sixty-six leaves. The next extant texts are 3 John 11–15 (in Latin only) and Acts through 22:29 (in Greek), where the codex breaks off. Since the codex is composed of quires of four sheets, its original length and contents are unknown. Because the last verses of 3 John are extant, the common assumption has been that the Catholic Epistles occupied the missing pages, but it is clear that they would not fill the space between Mark and Acts. Also, placement of the Catholic Epistles before Acts is curious.[70]

As in the case of P46, it is difficult to specify what occupied the sizable lacuna and whether any additional writings followed Acts, though no one doubts that Acts was complete in the codex. David Parker accepts John Chapman's case as the most probable, that 1–3 John and the Revelation to John filled the missing leaves, since that combination would provide "an accurate match" for the space.[71] Yet, there is no other compelling reason for this solution. Could one or more "non-canonical" writings have been included in the codex? In short, this is another case where current evidence fails to provide a solution.

4. *Hebrews, Catholic Epistles, and Revelation*

Finally, questions are raised also (a) by the lack of Hebrews in the ninth century Codex G^p (but see below), although Hebrews' place in the canon was firm by the end of the fourth century, and (b) by the lack of the Revelation to John in numerous manuscripts where it might be expected. The whole "New Testament" (i.e., our twenty-seven books) is preserved in three majuscules (ℵ, A, and C) and fifty-six minuscules, but two other majuscule manuscripts (B and Ψ) and

JTS 50 [1999] 600), asserts that "there can be no doubt that the Pastoral Epistles and the Apocalypse would have followed."

[70] For data and discussion, see David C. Parker, *Codex Bezae: An Early Christian Manuscript and Its Text* (Cambridge: Cambridge University Press, 1992) 8–9; John Chapman, "The Original Contents of Codex Bezae," *Expositor* VI: 2 (1905) 46–53; Gregory, *Canon and Text*, 351–53; Scrivener-Miller, *Plain Introduction*, 1.124–30. On the date of D, see Parker, *Codex Bezae*, 30, 280–81.

[71] Parker, *Codex Bezae*, 8–9. Chapman bases his conclusion on syllable counts: see "Original Contents of Codex Bezae," 49–51. Wilhelm Bousset proposed the same view: see Gregory, *Canon and Text*, 352.

147 minuscules (including the notable 33 of the ninth century) have the entire collection *except* the Revelation.[72] All who are acquainted with the history of canon will recognize that these two writings, Hebrews and the Revelation to John, along with several others, are among those that faced the strongest barriers in their paths to full acceptance.

504 a. *Hebrews*

Hebrews, though it became part of the Pauline collection, could not be linked to Paul or to any apostolic author, and it is not mentioned in the Muratorian Canon. While only *1 Clement* (36.2–5; 17.1) appears to quote Hebrews prior to its appearance in the oldest extant manuscript containing it, namely P46 (ca. 200), Hebrews is nonetheless firmly a part of the Pauline collection in that papyrus manuscript, standing between Romans and 1 Corinthians. The unusual position of Hebrews in this very early manuscript may reflect a conviction of Pauline authorship and, in addition, may constitute a canonical claim contemporary with Clement of Alexandria (ca. 200), who quotes Hebrews authoritatively and thought that Paul was in some way responsible for its content.

Codex G^p, a Greek-Latin diglot, however, requires a brief comment, for, once again, it is stated routinely that "it contains the Epistles of Paul but not Hebrews,"[73] implying that Hebrews might have been expected. Three majuscules (the Greek-Latin D^p [of which two extant copies, D^{abs1} and D^{abs2}—ninth and tenth centuries, also exist], K^{ap}, and L^{ap}) and at least 329 minuscules have Hebrews immediately after Philemon.[74] It is relevant that while D^p is sixth century, both K^{ap}, and L^{ap} are, like G^p, from the ninth century, possibly supporting the notion that G^p contained Hebrews. F^p, another ninth century Greek-Latin manuscript and doubtless stemming from the same archetype as G^p,[75] does have Hebrews, though in F^p, which has Latin

[72] See the statistics presented earlier and note 3, above; on codices C and B, respectively, see also notes 5 and 6, above.

[73] Casper René Gregory, *Textkritik des Neuen Testamentes* (Leipzig: Hinrichs, 1909) 112; Gregory, *Canon and Text*, 367; cf. Metzger, *Canon of the New Testament*, 238.

[74] This figure is from William H. P. Hatch, "The Position of Hebrews in the Canon of the New Testament," *HTR* 29 (1936) 143 n. 43, and is doubtless much out of date.

[75] See William H. P. Hatch, "On the Relationship of Codex Augiensis and Codex Boernerianus of the Pauline Epistles," *HSCP* 60 (1951) 187–99, esp. 195–97. The

in one column of each page and Greek in the other, Hebrews is only in Latin, employing both columns of each page and perhaps suggesting that a Greek text of Hebrews was not readily available. This anomaly undoubtedly dilutes the support of F^p for any claim that Hebrews stood in G^p. Actually, as noted earlier, after Philemon G^p inscribes the title for the *Epistle to the Laodiceans*, but not its text; rather, what follows is a Latin explanation of portions of Matthew and a Greek treatise "On Spiritual Law" with interlinear Latin.[76] In fact, F^p has no trace of *Laodiceans*.)[77] So, was the text of *Laodiceans* copied into G^p but is now lost, and is it likely that Hebrews once stood after it? Or, as appears more likely, was the remaining space in G^p left blank, in spite of the scribe's intention to insert *Laodiceans*, and then filled in subsequently with the additional material? From all of this, an argument might be made for the presence of Hebrews in G^p, though it would be anything but definitive.

b. *Catholic Epistles*

Though the manuscript transmission of the Catholic Epistles does not so readily or so often involve canon issues, Codex Vaticanus contains chapter divisions that are revealing. As C. R. Gregory noted, ". . . An old division found in the [Catholic] Epistles . . . does not 505
appear to take any notice of Second Peter, and seems therefore to be the work of someone who rejected that Epistle."[78]

c. *Revelation*

The Revelation to John, though widely used in both West and East during the second century, faced difficulties in the third in the East with respect to apostolic authorship and in the West because of its

manuscripts may have been copied mediately or immediately from the common ancestor.

[76] Alexander Reichardt, *Der Codex Bœrnerianus der Briefe des Apostels Paulus (Msc. Dresd. A 145^b) in Lichtdruck nachgebildet* (Leipzig: Hiersemann, 1909) 7; cf. Gregory, *Textkritik*, 112. Gregory says the additional material is later; Reichardt agrees that the comments on Matthew are later, but states that the treatise could be by the same hand as the Pauline letters.

[77] Hatch, "On the Relationship of Codex Augiensis and Codex Boernerianus," 192.

[78] Gregory, *Canon and Text*, 344; idem, *Textkritik des Neuen Testamentes*, 33. Cf. Scrivener-Miller, *Plain Introduction*, 1.181; Frederic G. Kenyon, *Handbook to the Textual Criticism of the New Testament* (2d ed.; London: Macmillan, 1926) 104; Heinrich Joseph Vogels, *Handbuch der Textkritik des Neuen Testaments* (2d ed.; Bonn: Hanstein, 1955) 50; Aland and Aland, *Text of the New Testament*, 110.

use by Montanists (though it still was used significantly in the West). It also had strong rivals in the *Shepherd of Hermas* and especially the *Apocalypse of Peter*. Consequently, the place of the Revelation to John in the canon of Eastern Christianity was not certain until the late fourth century, and even later in some areas.[79] The comparative paucity of extant Revelation manuscripts may reflect uncertainty about its authority and canonicity, though there could be other reasons for the phenomenon. There are only 287 manuscripts containing the Revelation to John over against 662 with Acts and Catholic Epistles, 792 with Paul, and 2,361 that contain gospels.[80]

Should one wish to claim that the comparatively small number of manuscripts transmitting Revelation is due to the fact that it was not part of the conventional groupings discussed earlier, and so probably circulated alone, the actual figures show that 133 papyri,[81] majuscules, and minuscules have only Revelation, which is fewer than half of the 287 manuscripts preserving Revelation. Hence, the majority of extant copies of Revelation circulated with other, more widely disseminated "New Testament" writings, which should have enhanced Revelation's chances of use and recognition. So quantity of manuscripts in circulation may have been a factor in the canonical acceptance of Revelation, but not the only one; another factor is that Revelation was never a part of the official lectionary of the Greek Church,[82] though this in turn undoubtedly affected the number of manuscripts preserving it.

D. *The Varying Order of Books in "New Testament" Manuscripts*

The arrangement of "New Testament" writings in some manuscripts differs from the traditional order, as mentioned above, and these differences may have affected or may reflect canon considerations, though the degree to which they do so is not easy to determine. For example, the four gospels occur in twelve different sequences across

[79] See Gamble, "Canon: New Testament," *ABD* 1.853–56 and n. 2, above.

[80] Aland and Aland, *Text of the New Testament*, 78–79, 83.

[81] P47 would appear to be a papyrus codex that contained only Revelation, though there is no certainty; the recently published P115 is extensive, but its editors say it is not possible to know whether it contained only Revelation or also other writings (P.Oxy LXVI: 4499, esp. 11); the others are highly fragmentary and the full extent of their original contents cannot be determined.

[82] Metzger, *Canon of the New Testament*, 217.

the manuscript tradition.[83] While most follow the traditional order, the deviation that has attracted the greatest attention, the so-called "Western" order, occurs in codices D (late fourth century) and W (fifth century), where the order is Matthew, John, Luke, and Mark. Perhaps this order is intended to highlight the first two apostles, who
then are followed by the two Evangelists who are associated with 506
apostles.[84] Beyond these, three other arrangements begin with Matthew, two with John, and two with Mark, but Luke, the longest gospel, is never first.[85] This would rule out descending length as an ordering principle. Acts nearly always follows the Gospels, but in א and the Latin Codex Fuldensis (F, sixth century) Acts follows the Pauline letters. Hebrews is very frequently included among the Pauline letters; Greek manuscripts commonly place it after Philemon (D^{p} L^{ap} Ψ, other majuscules, most minuscules) or between 2 Thessalonians and the Pastorals, that is, between letters to churches and those to individuals (א A B C H^{p} I K^{ap} P^{apr} and many others), though chapter numbers remaining in B show that Hebrews followed Galatians in the manu-script from which these section numbers were taken.[86]

[83] See the latest inventory in P.-M. Bogaert, "Ordres anciens des évangiles et tétraévangile en un seul codex," *RTL* 30 (1999) 298–307.

[84] Further, see Gregory, *Canon and Text*, 468.

[85] In a study of the length of the gospels and Acts in P45, Luke is the longest in all counts, except for T. C. Skeat's final figures, in which Matthew is shown to have occupied a page more than Luke: T. C. Skeat, "A Codicological Analysis of the Chester Beatty Papyrus Codex of Gospels and Acts (P45)," *Hermathena* 155 (1993) 27–43.

[86] Gregory, *Textkritik*, 33; idem, *Canon and Text*, 344, whose statement is careful and does not say the section numbers are older than B; yet, most publications I have seen claim that "the scribe of codex Vaticanus copied" the chapter numbers from "an ancestor of codex Vaticanus" (Metzger, *Textual Commentary*, 591 n. 2) or from its "archetype" (Hatch, "Position of Hebrews," 135–36). However, Skeat ("Codex Sinaiticus, the Codex Vaticanus and Constantine," 601) states that his examination of the section numbers makes it "obvious that they are *not* the work of either of the two scribes of the manuscript" and that "these numbers were *not* added in the scriptorium but after the manuscript had left it" (601). He reports that Carlo M. Martini, in the introduction to the 1968 Vatican facsimile edition of B, already understood these numerals as "subsequent additions" (601, n. 23). Hence, we face two unknowns: exactly how long after B had been produced these section marks were inserted and, more critical, whether the source was a manuscript older or younger than B. These uncertainties preclude such tempting speculations as (a) B's section markers preserve an older placement of Hebrews than B and a position more centrally among the Pauline letters, and (b) they reveal both an earlier conviction of Pauline authorship and perhaps a stronger view of canonicity for Hebrews.

However, as already noted, P46 (and some nine minuscules) put Hebrews after Romans. Altogether Hebrews is found in nine different sequences in our manuscripts.[87] P46 also has Ephesians before Galatians; in fact, Greek and versional manuscripts and patristic sources have arranged the Pauline letters in some twenty different sequences.[88] Finally, the Catholic Epistles, named for their presumed authors, are preserved in some seven sequences, though organizing principles are not often obvious, except that in the West Peter's primacy among the attributed authors may be reflected in four of the sequences, where 1–2 Peter stand first. Descending length does not work, for, when ancient *stichoi* are applied, 1 John is the longest, followed by James and 1 Peter; or, grouped by author, 1–2 Peter are the longest, followed by 1–2–3 John, then James, and then Jude. The latter order is found in the Council of Carthage list (397) and in Apostolic Canon 85 (sixth/seventh century).[89]

507 The relevance of these data to canon is more complex and with more subtle implications than in some of the preceding issues. As just intimated it is often claimed that "New Testament" books frequently were arranged according to length, usually from the longest to the shortest in their groups (using the occasionally recorded *stichoi* in manuscripts). Sometimes the writings of one author are counted as one work, and nearly always the Pauline church letters are separated from those to individuals.[90] Such an ordering by descending length appears to be operative at times, for example, with respect to 1–2 Timothy, Titus, and Philemon, but not often enough elsewhere to be a satisfactory overall explanation. For example, as already noted, the gospels never occur with the longest gospel, Luke, first; Galatians-Ephesians is a common order, yet Galatians is shorter than Ephesians; and, finally, the length of Hebrews should place it between 1–2 Corinthians, but it is never found there because, of course, 1–2 Corinthians would not be separated. If diminishing length is to be

[87] Metzger, *Canon of the New Testament*, 295–300; Bruce M. Metzger (for the Editorial Committee), *A Textual Commentary on the Greek New Testament* (2d ed., Stuttgart, Deutsche Bibelgesellschaft/United Bible Societies, 1994) 591–92. For a chart of all positions of Hebrews, see Hermann Josef Frede, ed., *Epistulae ad Philippenses et ad Colossenses* (Vetus Latina, 24:2; Freiburg: Herder, 1966–1971) 292–303; cf. Trobisch, *Paul's Letter Collection*, 20–21).

[88] Frede, *Epistulae ad Philippenses et ad Colossenses*, 292–303.

[89] Metzger, *Canon of the New Testament*, 299–300.

[90] Ibid., 296–300.

the criterion, Hebrews would likely follow immediately after 1–2 Corinthians, as in fact it does in several minuscules. David Trobisch claims, however, that P46, with its two anomalies—Hebrews between Romans and 1 Corinthians, and Ephesians before Galatians—has arranged Paul's letters "strictly according to their length," asserting (questionably, I think) that placing Hebrews *before* 1–2 Corinthians was the appropriate way to deal with Hebrews' greater length than 2 Corinthians.[91] Alternatively, in the case of Hebrews in P46, W. H. P. Hatch suggests that its placement immediately after Romans was "on grounds of doctrine."[92] Hence, interpreting the manuscript data on the order of books may be difficult.

It is also possible that fluctuating sequences of books may indicate canonical fluidity or uncertainty. It has been suggested above that placing Hebrews deep into the clearly Pauline letters (as in P46) may show a desire to accredit its Pauline authorship, and thereby perhaps its canonical authority. Or Hebrews' varying positions may reflect not only uncertainty about authorship, but also about its destination or addressees, revealing, in turn, uneasiness about its canonicity. Trobisch points to minuscule 794, which copies Hebrews twice, once after 2 Thessalonians and again after Philemon.[93] Placing Hebrews between the Pauline letters to churches and those to individuals, rather than *within* the former group, may have been prompted by the view, well established by the third/fourth centuries, that Paul wrote to seven churches, not eight.[94] In sum, this situation may have been a two-way street: on the one hand, questions about the canonicity of Hebrews may have motivated some to place it within the Paulines, and, on the other hand, its varying locations may themselves have raised the very same kinds of questions.

Finally, we note that Codex B's order of books is identical to that of Athanasius of Alexandria's famous list in 367, the first such list
known to contain all and only our twenty-seven New Testament 508
writings. On the assumptions that B originated in Egypt (Kirsopp

[91] Trobisch, *Paul's Letter Collection*, 16–17. Cf. Quinn, "P46—The Pauline Canon?" 379: "The letters that had been chosen were ordered on a stichometric principle."

[92] See Hatch, "Position of Hebrews," 133–34.

[93] Trobisch, *Paul's Letter Collection*, 21–22.

[94] See Nils Alstrup Dahl, "The Particularity of the Pauline Epistles as a Problem in the Ancient Church," *Neotestamentica et Patristica: Eine Freundesgabe, Herrn Professor Dr. Oscar Cullmann zu seinem 60. Geburtstag überreicht* (ed. W. C. van Unnik; NovTSup 6; Leiden: Brill, 1962) 261–64.

Lake)[95] or in Alexandria itself (J. Neville Birdsall)[96] and that it contained all twenty-seven books, B on occasion has been understood as supporting this fourth century canon of Athanasius. B's provenance, however, is disputed, though Skeat's recent, elaborate re-defense of Caesarea[97] undoubtedly will carry the day. Therefore, rather than a more precise claim, it is safer to say that Codex B documents a fourth-century view of canon, but not likely that of Egypt.

As the Alands affirm regarding the sequence of writings, "[t]he only characteristic common to the whole manuscript tradition (extending also to canon lists, patristic references, and other sources which allude to the sequence of the writings) is that the Gospels stand at the beginning and Revelation at the end."[98]

II. Manuscript Aids to Readers with Implications for Canon

Aids to readers of manuscripts take numerous forms, including punctuation, chapter and book titles, chapter divisions; glosses (explaining words or phrases), scholia (instructive comments of a teacher), catenae ("chains" of remarks from other writers), onomastica (providing etymology of names), and other marginal notations or marks; copying a text in sense lines; lection notes (designating portions to be read in worship); the Eusebian canons (markings and a table developed by Eusebius to help find parallel gospel passages), the Euthalian apparatus (aids for the Acts and epistles attributed to a certain Euthalius or Evagrius, including a sketch of Paul's life and martyrdom, a list of Old Testament citations, etc.),[99] the so-called Marcionite prologues, and, I would add, the codex format. Some of these are relevant to canon, others are not.

---

[95] For a thorough discussion of Lake's views, see Skeat, "Codex Sinaiticus, the Codex Vaticanus and Constantine," 586–92.

[96] J. N. Birdsall, "The New Testament Text," *The Cambridge History of the Bible, Volume 1: From the Beginnings to Jerome* (3 vols.; ed. P. R. Ackroyd and C. F. Evans; Cambridge/New York: Cambridge University Press, 1970) 359–60;

[97] Skeat, "Codex Sinaiticus, the Codex Vaticanus and Constantine," 598–604, esp. 603–4.

[98] Aland and Aland, *The Text of the New Testament*, 79.

[99] Summarized from Bruce M. Metzger, *The Text of the New Testament: Its Transmission, Corruption, and Restoration* (3d ed.; New York/Oxford: Oxford University Press, 1992) 21–31.

Earlier we have shown (a) how a table of contents in Codex A points to material now lost and suggests that some writings it contained were more authoritative than another; (b) how section divisions in Codex B in one place indicate a different position for Hebrews and in another imply that someone rejected 2 Peter; and (c) how a title in Codex G^{p} ("the Epistle to the Laodiceans begins") identifies content even when its text had not been copied there. Three other topics require brief treatment.

A. *"Marcionite" Prologues*

Some manuscripts possess what usually are called "Marcionite" prologues. A number of Latin Vulgate manuscripts (including the prominent Codex Fuldensis, F, sixth century) contain them, and they 509
provide, for the Pauline letters, short descriptions of the addressees and reasons for writing, with an emphasis on Paul's conflict with false apostles. Currently, however, these are viewed as not of Marcionite origin, but as written for a Pauline corpus to seven churches that was not connected with Marcion's canon and which later gave way to the fourteen-letter corpus; moreover, the prologues presuppose an earlier "seven church" corpus that began with Galatians, 1–2 Corinthians, and Romans, which, to be sure, is the same order found in Marcion's canon, though the order is no longer thought to be attributable to Marcion.[100]

These prologues are difficult to assess, but they can provide help in understanding some aspects of the canon process and some controversies involved, such as the elusive role of Marcion, whose differing text of Paul was most likely not a new creation but "the adaptation of an already existing Pauline Corpus that began with Galatians,"[101] and the development of various collections of Pauline letters, as noted in the preceding paragraph.

The so-called anti-Marcionite prologues to the Gospels (Mark, Luke, and John only) are found in nearly forty Latin biblical manuscripts of the fifth to the tenth centuries; the prologue for Luke is

---

[100] See John J. Clabeaux, *A Lost Edition of the Letters of Paul: A Reassessment of the Text of the Pauline Corpus Attested by Marcion* (CBQMS 21; Washington, DC: Catholic Biblical Association, 1989) 1–4; Ulrich Schmid, *Marcion und sein Apostolos: Rekonstruktion und historische Einordnung der marcionitischen Paulusbriefausgabe* (ANTF 25; Berlin/New York: de Gruyter, 1995) 287–89; Metzger, *Canon of the New Testament*, 94–97.

[101] Clabeaux, *Lost Edition of the Letters of Paul*, 4.

extant also in Greek. They were independently composed, and date from the fourth century, though that for Luke perhaps from the second. Their relevance to canon is negligible, though the early Lucan portion does refer to Luke as a follower of Paul, and that relationship could or might have been a factor in the canon process.[102]

B. *Indicators of Textual Problems within Manuscripts*

Scribes on occasion obviously had reservations about portions of text present in or absent from their exemplars, especially when they were aware of other manuscripts or traditions that differed from what appeared before them. Thus, it is relevant to ask how our manuscripts reveal textual uncertainties, since, in turn, they very likely indicate uncertainty as to the authority of problematic passages. Such passages commonly were marked with various scribal sigla; or blank spaces were left to indicate a passage that stood in the exemplar but was omitted by the scribe, or that the scribe knew existed in another manuscript but not in the exemplar; or a questionable section of text might be placed in an alternate position or in the margin, or a marginal note might be added.

For instance, all of these indicators appear in connection with the Pericope of the Adulteress (John 7:53–8:11). Most striking are the multiple locations in which scribes placed this paragraph: after 7:52 (most manuscripts), after 7:36, after 7:44, after 21:25, or in Luke, after 21:38. Also, a scribal asterisk or obelus alongside the passage—customary signs of a questionable portion of text—was placed in
510 scores of manuscripts, occasionally with additional marginal comments. A few scribes (e.g., of L and Δ) left a small blank space—too small for the passage but an obvious signal that a portion of questionable text was known to these scribes.[103] Likewise, in Codex B, contrary to the scribe's practice when coming to the end of a writing, an entire column has been left blank after Mark 16:8, "evidently because one or other of the two subsequent endings was known to him personally, while he found neither of them in the

[102] See Helmut Koester, *Ancient Christian Gospels: Their History and Development* (London: SCM; Philadelphia: Trinity Press International, 1990) 243, 335–36.

[103] For details, see Metzger, *Textual Commentary*, 187–89; Scrivener-Miller, *Plain Introduction to the Criticism of the New Testament*, 2.364–68.

exemplar which he was copying."[104] But Scrivener-Miller[105] interprets the vacant column to mean that the scribe was "fully aware" of the existence of the last twelve verses "or even found them in the copy from which he wrote." Similarly, manuscripts with Mark 16:9–20 often contain such sigla or even comments that older Greek manuscripts do not have the passage (see, e.g., minuscule 1).[106]

C. *The Codex Format*

The preceding items involve notations, additional marks, or spaces in manuscripts that assist the reader, but the very form of the book—the codex, adopted extremely early in Christianity as the vehicle for its valued writings—may well be treated as an "aid to the reader," even allowing for the fact that the scroll, in the hands of a skilled copyist, reader, or scholar, afforded remarkable efficiency in finding and checking points of inquiry.[107] Yet, the codex format was more convenient in general and certainly traveled more easily. These matters and the early Christian use of the codex have been much in discussion in recent decades and an extensive literature has resulted.[108]

One of the major emphases in the relationship between codex and canon involves the early and thorough adoption by Christianity of the codex format for its writings and, therefore, its possible influence upon the canonization, particularly, of the Pauline letters and of the fourfold Gospel, but of other portions of the "New Testament." To raise only the dominant issue, did the new codex form facilitate the collection of authoritative writings and the actualization of the canon? More specifically, what was it about the codex that initially appealed

[104] Brooke Foss Westcott and Fenton John Anthony Hort, *The New Testament in the Original Greek* (2 vols.; London, Macmillan, 1881–1882 [vol. 2, 2d ed., 1896]) 1.29 [*Notes*]).

[105] Scrivener-Miller, *Plain Introduction*, 1.108. Scrivener and Miller, of course, advocated the authenticity of the "longer ending" of Mark (1:7; 2:337–44). Their claim that the blank space in some way authenticates that ending is highly suspect, for the space, on any view, still expresses scribal doubt about what might have occupied it elsewhere

[106] Metzger, *Text of the New Testament*, 226; idem, *Textual Commentary*, 103.

[107] See T. C. Skeat, "Roll versus Codex—A New Approach?" *ZPE* 84 (1990) 297–98; and idem, "The Origin of the Christian Codex," *ZPE* 102 (1994) 265.

[108] For discussion and further references, see Gamble, *Books and Readers in the Early Church*, 42–81; Epp, "Codex and Literacy in Early Christianity and at Oxyrhynchus," 15–26. More recent discussions include E. Randolph Richards, "The Codex and the Early Collection of Paul's Letters," *BBR* 8 (1998) 151–66.

to the Christians who utilized it? Several answers have been offered recently, but no definitive solution is possible.[109] And were there per-
511 haps common sizes of codices that seemed to many to be the most efficient and convenient, and did those sizes perchance best accommodate a certain number of gospels (four?), or the gospels plus Acts, or a certain sized collection of Paul's letters (seven, or ten, or thirteen?)? If so, the codex may well have had an effect upon canon.

The fragmentary nature of our early papyri makes answers difficult, but among the papyri up to and around the turn of the third/fourth century, P45 has the four gospels and Acts, and P53 has Matthew plus Acts (possibly suggesting that it, like P45, contained the four gospels and Acts),[110] while P64+P67+P4 and P75 have portions of two gospels,[111] but the vast majority now preserve portions of only one gospel. And P46 has portions of nine Pauline Letters, P30 and P92 have two letters, and the rest only one. Finally, there is no early codex that contains more than one Catholic Epistle in sequence.[112] Hence, there is little ground on which to argue that codices up to the early fourth century held to any rigid pattern of contents, though the preservation of writings in categories such as Gospels, or Gospels and Acts, or Pauline Letters has some support. Harry Y. Gamble argues that only the codex format would allow for the collection of the Pauline Letters in one volume, because an eighty-foot roll would be required to contain them, which is twice the maximum length and three times the normal length of Greek rolls![113] Similarly, Graham Stanton, following the lead of T. C. Skeat, concluded that the emer-

---

[109] For a summary of several recent views, as well as a new proposal, see Epp, "Codex and Literacy in Early Christianity and at Oxyrhynchus," 15–26. [See now Graham Stanton, *Jesus and the Gospel* (Cambridge: Cambridge University Press, 2004) 169–72.]

[110] The small size of this codex militates against four gospels and Acts, for about 325 leaves would be required; H. A. Sanders judges this not impossible, but thinks Matthew plus Acts would be a reasonably sized codex, though no such combination of books exists elsewhere: "A Third Century Papyrus of Matthew and Acts," *Quantulacumque: Studies Presented to Kirsopp Lake* (ed. R. P. Casey, Silva Lake, and Agnes K. Lake; London: Christophers, 1937) 153.

[111] P44 and P84 also have two gospels each, but they date in the sixth century or later.

[112] P72, with 1–2 Peter separated from Jude, cannot be considered a codex of the Catholic Epistles, nor can its predecessor codex (see above). P74 contains Acts and the Catholic Epistles, though this is seventh century. P6 does have John and James, but the latter is preserved in Coptic only.

[113] Gamble, *Books and Readers in the Early Church*, 62–63.

gence of the fourfold Gospel must be connected with the "Christian adoption of the codex, for no roll could contain four gospels,"[114] and J. K. Elliott adds the interesting point that no extant codices up to the third century exceed three hundred pages, indicating that this early codex format "helped to limit the number of Gospels to these four and no more!" He notes also that we have no manuscripts in which "apocryphal" gospels were bound with any one or more of the "canonical" four, and that the codex possessed an automatic limiting or "canon" factor, for (unlike a roll) it demands advance planning, especially if it consists of a single quire.[115]

Something more can be said about the general sizes of early "New
Testament" papyri, a relevant factor in the use and collection of
Christian writings and therefore in canon issues. Any who have studied the codex format will be aware of E. G. Turner's classification
of codices. Though highly complex, it can be stated that eighteen
of our earliest "New Testament" papyri appear in his lists; that, with 512
one exception (P45), all fall into the various "modest" size categories
(Groups 5, 6, 7, 8, and 9: no more than about seven inches wide
and either narrow and tall or narrow and "squarish"); and, most
important, that eleven of these codices fall into the two categories
(Groups 8 and 9) judged by Turner most likely to represent the earliest codex form.[116]

This suggests that the media commonly used by and most appealing to early Christians were codices in the earliest attested form and sizes, which, in turn, rated high in portability, a feature not only valuable to early Christian travelers in their mission, but also convenient and practical in the dissemination of the writings they carried and used. Complete clarity on these matters remains to be

[114] Stanton, "Fourfold Gospel," 337; see 338–39, and Skeat, "Origin of the Christian Codex," 263–68. For more detailed discussion, see Epp, "Codex and Literacy in Early Christianity and at Oxyrhynchus," 19–26.

[115] J. Keith Elliott, "Manuscripts, the Codex and the Canon," *JSNT* 63 (1996) 110 and 107. As to size, codices developed so that by the mid-fourth century B consisted of some 1600 pages and ℵ of about 1460; both have lost portions at the end (ibid., 110). On the evolution of the codex, see Gamble, *Books and Readers in the Early Church*, 63–66; Bogaert, "Ordres anciens des évangiles et tétraévangile," 313.

[116] This analysis and interpretation of Turner's data may be found in Epp, "Codex and Literacy in Early Christianity and at Oxyrhynchus," 19–20; see E. G. Turner, *The Typology of the Early Codex* (Haney Foundation Series, 18; Philadelphia: University of Pennsylvania Press, 1977) 13–25.

achieved. Our earliest papyrus manuscripts offer tantalizing clues, but their fragmentary nature is a continuing frustration.

III. Textual Variants and Canonicity

The manuscripts that carried and preserved the texts destined to be part of the "New" or Second Testament are relevant for canon through their groupings, their contents, and the apparatuses accompanying them, as well as their very format. Yet, the texts themselves offer the most creative and vibrant interrelationship with matters canonical. A simple question will introduce the issue: When two meaningful variants occur in an authoritative writing, which reading is canonical, or are both canonical? Though the factors in achieving "canonical" status for either an entire writing or for a single reading are elusive, the phenomenon is essentially the same for both: acceptance as authoritative by an individual or a group. To be sure, community acceptance is the more common path for writings, and perhaps a more secure one, though it may be easier for a variant reading to become authoritative as an individual scribe creates it and/or incorporates it into a community's scripture.

A fascinating issue raised occasionally in the past and more intensely by several current scholars, might be described by invoking an old phrase in a new way: "A canon within the canon." Traditionally this refers to defining one's beliefs and practice by reliance mainly on certain selected books from an authoritative canon (e.g., Luther's reliance upon Romans and Galatians while virtually dismissing James, or Zwingli's rejection of Revelation), though it may refer also to dependence on selected ideas. When it is applied to the textual variants within a New Testament variation unit and to the selection of one variant over the others, suddenly numerous disquieting questions arise, as a few examples will show. Actually, almost any variation unit where there are at least two meaningful textual readings would be illustrative,[117] though some of the issues raised may be cleaner and simpler than others. For example, it may appear to be easy to decide whether any of the endings of Mark beyond γάρ in 16:8 are

[117] For further examples, see Epp, "Textual Criticism in the Exegesis of the New Testament, with an Excursus on Canon," 81–82.

canonical, or whether the pericope of the adulteress woman (John 7:53–8:11) is canonical. In the Marcan instance, neither appended
ending is likely to have been part of the early Gospel of Mark, yet 513
one or another of the so-called "shorter" and "longer" endings, and the latter's further expansions, surely was part of the canonical Mark as far as some early churches were concerned, and widely so where the Byzantine text prevailed. Even the "shorter" ending, with its grandiose, obviously non-Marcan language, was used in Greek-speaking churches, as well as in churches using Latin, Syriac, Coptic, Armenian, and Ethiopian, judging from manuscripts containing it).[118] It is quite possible that the "longer" ending of Mark, with its post-resurrection appearances, "could have functioned to bring Mark's gospel into harmony with the fourfold collection," and in this fashion influenced the canonical process.[119]

On the other hand, resolution of some seemingly less significant variants actually may be quite difficult, such as the two small, similar readings in two letters of the Pauline collection: "in Rome" in Rom 1:7 (and 1:15) and "in Ephesus" in Eph 1:1. Both are lacking in a small number of manuscripts, though the latter is absent from the very old P46, ℵ, and B. So, are these geographical designations canonical or not? In addition, a doxology appears in several different locations in various manuscripts of Romans, is absent in some, and occurs twice in others.[120] So, is the doxology in Romans canonical after 14:23, after 15:33, or after 16:23, or after both 14:23 and 16:23, where several manuscripts place it, or was it never part of Romans, as other manuscripts and patristic witnesses testify? The further issue is whether Romans originally had fourteen chapters, or fifteen, or sixteen, as demarcated by the various positions of the concluding doxology, and, more importantly, what does this placement of the doxology tell us about the textual history of Romans and therefore its canonical form?[121] These three examples might appear to involve

---

118 Metzger, *Canon of the New Testament*, 270.

119 Brevard S. Childs, *The New Testament as Canon: An Introduction* (Philadelphia: Fortress, 1984) 51–52.

120 See Metzger, *Textual Commentary*, 470–73.

121 Tracing out the evolution and interrelation of these three forms of Romans is highly complex, to say the least, but, according to Gamble, *The Textual History of the Letter to the Romans: A Study in Textual and Literary History* (SD 42; Grand Rapids, MI: Eerdmans, 1977) 15–35; 96–129, it leads to the conclusion that a fourteen-chapter version of Romans, secondary to the sixteen-chapter original, was pre-

somewhat insignificant variations, yet all are significant in themselves and important for understanding the history of the Roman and Ephesian letters and of the Pauline collection process, which in turn are critical for explaining some major factors in canon formation.

We may expand upon our question: when there are competing variant readings is only the "original" reading canonical? And when decisions between variants are difficult or impossible, are two or more of the plausible readings canonical? Or, in what sense are readings canonical that are suspected of being theologically motivated—for example, when a variant with an "orthodox" bias can be shown to be secondary to one that might be described as "heterodox"? Undoubtedly the scribes introducing such secondary readings considered their replacements to be canonical, as did those who unwittingly used the resultant text in worship and practice. The reverse
514 situation is no different, when an "orthodox" reading has been replaced by a "heretical" one. In all such cases, to what extent are variants canonical that now have been judged secondary by textual critics but once were authoritative scripture? Finally, to raise the question to its highest level and broadest range, what can "canonical" mean when each of our 5,300 Greek New Testament manuscripts and perhaps 9,000 versional manuscripts, as well as every one now lost, was considered authoritative—and therefore canonical—in worship and instruction in one or more of the thousands upon thousands of individual churches *when no two manuscripts are exactly alike*? A corollary heightens the force of the question: If no two manuscripts are alike, then no two collections of Gospels or Epistles are alike, and no two canons—no two "New Testaments"—are alike; therefore, are all canonical, or some, or only one? And if some or one, which?

If, as we have affirmed, a scribe effecting a theologically motivated textual alteration was making a canonical decision, the process of canon formation was operating at two quite different levels: first, at the level of church leaders of major Christian localities or regions, who were seeking broad consensus on which *books* were to be accepted as authoritative for the larger church, and, second, also at the level

Marcionite and came into existence prior to the collection of a Pauline corpus. Cf. idem, *Books and Readers*, 58–65; Schmid, *Marcion und sein Apostolos*, 284–94. For a very brief summary, see Epp, "Multivalence of the Term 'Original Text,'" 262–63. [See now Harry Y. Gamble, "New Testament Canon: Recent Research," 282–87.]

of individual scribes, perhaps representing a monastic or some other small community, concerned about *individual variants* that properly express their theological or other understanding of the sentences and paragraphs within their already authoritative books.

But there are other dimensions of these issues as well, for it is necessary to ask when the term “canonical” might or should be applied to a writing that ended up in the New Testament canon: at the completion of the writing (unlikely), upon its delivery to or receipt by a church or church representative (somewhat more likely); upon the writing's first use in worship in some local congregation (quite likely, but “canonical” in a local or limited sense); upon a consensus acceptance as authoritative in wider circles (very likely); at the time of incorporation into a collection, as the fourfold Gospel, or the Pauline collection (almost certainly); or when a writing is one of the final twenty-seven books at the time when that corpus, or a major portion thereof, achieved wide acceptance (certainly)? Recognition of individual readings as “canonical” might coincide with the “more likely” of such moments, but also at points much farther along in the process of transmission, extending the possibilities not only forward in time (up to the invention of printing), but also increasing their quantity and breadth as the manuscript stream widened.

To cite one instructive instance, David C. Parker in 1997 analyzed the twenty variations in the marriage-divorce passages in the Synoptic Gospels that arose over an extended period. Some reflect, for example, mores of the Roman Empire rather than a Jewish setting; some define adultery as divorcing one's spouse and remarrying, another sees divorce itself as adultery for a man, while others understand the divorce of one's wife to be treating her as though she were an adulteress (even if it is not so), etc. Parker's conclusion is that the recovery of a single original reading here is “impossible,” for we are presented with “a collection of interpretive rewritings of a tradition,” which means that “the recovery of a definitive ‘original’ text that is consequently ‘authoritative’ cannot be presumed to be an attainable target.”[122] Rather, Parker asserts, rightly in my judgment, that we are compelled to recognize, not one form of a text,
but all (meaningful) forms as “living” interpretations stemming from 515

[122] David C. Parker, *The Living Text of the Gospels* (Cambridge/New York: Cambridge University Press, 1997) 78–93.

actual church situations, and "there is no authoritative text beyond the manuscripts which we may follow without further thought."[123] Though Parker is not explicit about the relationship of this manifold gospel tradition to canon, it is this multiplicity of competing variants with which we are left, along with the questions raised earlier: which variant or (more realistically) which variants are canonical?

The compelling answer is that most if not all such competing variants were held to be canonical, wittingly or not, at various times and places in real-life Christian contexts, requiring the perhaps disquieting conclusion that canonicity of readings has virtually the same degree of multiformity as do the meaningful competing variants in a variation unit. That is, in many, many instances the term "canonical" can no longer be applied only to one variant reading; hence, no longer only to a single form of a New Testament writing; hence, no longer only to a single form of the fourfold Gospels or the Pauline Letters; and, hence, no longer only to any single text of the New Testament as a whole. Indeed, when viewed in the context of textual variation, the terms "canon" and "canonical," perhaps quite unexpectedly for most, have exploded into notions that are now both polyvalent and multileveled.[124]

IV. Conclusion

Textual criticism and canon have long been placed in juxtaposition in introductions to the New Testament and elsewhere, but not always with good reason. A clearer rationale for analyzing their interrelation has appeared in recent times, and the primary difference stems from the ever-increasing number and importance of the "New Testament" papyri over the past century. Should this be doubted, one need only witness their prominence in the essay just concluded During the period when the great parchment codices of the mid-fourth century and later constituted the bulk of raw material for both text-critical and canon investigations, scholars were limited to documents from the period when consensus already had been reached in major sectors of Christianity on the dominant canonical issues:

[123] Ibid., 212; cf. 209–211.

[124] For additional discussion, see Epp, "Multivalence of the Term 'Original Text,'" 271–75, and the references to earlier views.

the fourfold Gospel, the Pauline Collection, and Acts. Lacking was second- and third-century evidence on the early codex, especially its Christian use, and on the contents and order of writings in these Christian books up to the turn of the third/fourth century. That lack has been remedied, providing previously unknown opportunities to explore both text and canon in that early period, even though definitive answers are far fewer than we would like, as our summaries show. Indeed, it has been the overriding purpose of our explorations to identify relevant raw materials for canon issues and then, wherever necessary, to analyze and to clarify the nature of those data, as we have attempted to do for such manuscripts as P72 and P46. And the implicit hope throughout this exercise is that others will employ these data, and perhaps also the interpretations offered, to lead us to new insights on the development of the New Testament canon in its early and significant formative period.

Added Notes, 2004

This essay first appeared in a large volume on *The Canon Debate* (ed. Lee Martin McDonald and James A. Sanders; Peabody, MA: Henrickson, 2002), which contains other essays related to the interconnections between New Testament textual criticism and canon:

Robert A. Kraft, "The Codex and Canon Consciousness," 229–33.

Harry Y. Gamble, "The New Testament Canon: Recent Research and the Status Quaestionis," 267–94, esp. 273–78, 290–91.

Daryl D. Schmidt, "The Greek New Testament as a Codex," 469–84.

CHAPTER TWENTY-TWO

ISSUES IN NEW TESTAMENT TEXTUAL CRITICISM: MOVING FROM THE NINETEENTH CENTURY TO THE TWENTY-FIRST CENTURY[1]

Introduction

I begin with a textual variant, though not from the New Testament. 17
For many years I kept on a note card—and in my mind—a couplet that has guided my own work, for it describes a common weakness of interpreters that I was determined to avoid. It read:

> Exegetes who major issues shun
> And hold their farthing candles to the sun.

My scribbled note said that this was from Alexander Pope (1688–1744), and when I decided to quote it here, I consulted a complete concordance of Pope's poetry. I was unable, however, to confirm the 18
reference, so I put a footnote in the preliminary version of the paper saying I had been unsuccessful in locating its source. Almost immediately, J. K. Elliott sent an e-mail message, kindly informing me that my quotation obviously was a textual variant (probably by way of oral tradition) of the following couplet by Edward Young (1683–1765), whose life overlapped that of Pope for fifty-seven years; it reads:

> How commentators each dark passage shun
> And hold their farthing candle to the sun.

[1] This essay originated as the Keynote Address at the Textual Criticism section of a "Symposium on New Testament Studies" held in April 2000 at Southeastern Baptist Theological Seminary. It was published in *Rethinking New Testament Textual Criticism*, edited by David Alan Black, the Symposium organizer, along with the papers of the other participants: Michael W. Holmes, J. Keith Elliott, and Maurice A. Robinson, with Moisés Silva as respondent.

The essay, by its nature, covers vast aspects of the New Testament text-critical discipline. To avoid even more extensive footnotes, the reader often is pointed to my earlier writings for detailed discussions with full references. Apologies are due, therefore, to researchers whose works are bypassed here, though fully acknowledged in those earlier publications.

The former reading had considerable influence on me, yet it now appears to be a variant of the latter that has been altered in the process of transmission. Therefore, in the face of these two variant readings, I decided to follow a line of interpretation that I shall describe near the end of this essay, namely, adopt both readings and pronounce that textual critics will do well (a) if they do not try to avoid dark, difficult passages and (b) if they stick to major issues. Both actions will prevent the light they cast on the New Testament text from being obliterated by the sunshine of the great textual critics that have gone before.

In what follows, I hope to sketch several major issues facing the discipline at this fascinating point in its history. Some may be rather familiar, traditional issues, while others will offer new challenges well beyond the familiar. If we are to move further toward resolution, some issues will require continued labors on long-standing and well-defined tasks, while others not only will demand accommodation to radical new ideas but also are likely to generate resistance among those who may view them as paths too risky to follow.

As an instructive framework for our considerations, I shall identify several issues facing New Testament textual criticism at the outset of the twenty-first century and then compare them with the same or similar issues in the nineteenth century. More specifically, I shall describe, first, the status of each issue at the end or perhaps in the latter half of the nineteenth century, a period of significant progress in discovering and analyzing manuscripts, in addressing principles for approving or disapproving variant readings, and in creating widely-
19 accepted critical editions of the Greek New Testament text. Second, after tracing progress during the twentieth century, each issue's present status will be assessed, followed by suggestions about where the discipline might be headed in the year 2000 and beyond. Incidentally, merely postulating this particular framework implies at the outset that the issues in textual criticism have not changed markedly during the past century, and, indeed, to a large extent this is the case, since some issues remain largely or partially unresolved and we have learned to live with compromises. At the same time, however, with the entire twentieth century now in view, we can see the prodigious labors expended in analyzing the numerous and notably early manuscripts that came to light during that period and in the development of theories, tools, and methods for studying the transmission, history, and nature of the New Testament text—including some rad-

ical new approaches and attitudes.[2] So, the trick is to determine how our successes or failures during the twentieth century position us now to move forward decisively in this new century.

I propose to identify five issues currently requiring attention, though some will have to be treated in cursory fashion due to space limitations. I begin with a truism: Since New Testament textual criticism is both an art and a science, as a discipline it is all about *choice* and *decision*. I therefore would characterize the major issues as follows:

1. *Choosing among* ***variants****—and deciding on* ***priority***. This is the issue
of the so-called "canons of criticism"—what are the arguments
we employ to decide between the variant readings in a given variation unit and, as a consequence, how do we put it all together 20
to reconstruct readings that make up a text most like that of the
early Christian community?
2. *Choosing among* ***manuscripts****—and deciding on* ***groups***. Here the concern is text types—can we isolate clusters of manuscripts that constitute distinguishable kinds of texts as evidenced by shared textual characteristics? And can we marshal these to sketch the history of the New Testament text?
3. *Choosing among* ***critical editions****—and deciding for* ***compromise***. Do our current critical editions of the Greek New Testament reflect a reasonable approximation to the text (or a text) that was extant in very early Christianity? The difficulties inherent in reconstructing such a text suggest that compromise may be the order of the day.
4. *Choosing to address* ***context****—and deciding on* ***influence***. This engages the issue of placing manuscripts and variant readings in their church-historical, cultural, and intellectual contexts—how did they influence the church and its theology and how, in turn, did the

[2] This optimism may appear contradictory to my Hatch Memorial Lecture delivered at the 1973 Annual Meeting of the Society of Biblical Literature in Chicago ("The Twentieth Century Interlude in New Testament Textual Criticism," *JBL* 93 [1974] 386–414), but a quarter century has passed and, as the following discussions show, progress has been made in numerous respects. I now find myself in agreement, therefore, with the more optimistic outlook in L. W. Hurtado's "Beyond the Interlude? Developments and Directions in New Testament Textual Criticism," in *Studies in the Early Text of the Gospels and Acts: The Papers of the First Birmingham Colloquium on the Textual Criticism of the New Testament* (ed. D. G. K. Taylor; TS 3/1; Birmingham, England: University of Birmingham Press, 1999) 26–49.

church and the surrounding culture influence the manuscripts and their variant readings?

Finally,

5. *Choosing to address* ***goals and directions***—*and deciding on* ***meanings and approaches***. What is the goal or what are the goals of New Testament textual criticism? More specifically, what *do* we mean by "original" text and what *can* we mean by it? And how will our decisions inform our future directions and our methods?

Obviously, this is a tall order for a single essay, and at point after point we shall have to be content with broad strokes on a very large canvas (and tolerate numerous footnotes).

I. Choosing among Variants—and Deciding on Priority: The Issue of the Canons of Criticism

Utilizing canons of criticism, that is, rules or principles to judge the quality and priority of competing variant readings in New Testament
21 manuscripts goes back at least as far as Irenaeus (second century), Origen (third century), and Jerome (fourth and early fifth centuries), who on occasion discuss the age or nature of manuscripts or explain why they prefer one reading over another. As examples, Irenaeus prefers a reading in the Apocalypse 13:18 "found in all the good [or weighty] and ancient copies," and Origen rejects the reading *Jesus* prefixed to *Barabbas* in Matthew 27:16–17 both because "in many copies" it is not present and because the name *Jesus* would not be used of evil-doers.[3]

[3] B. M. Metzger, "The Practice of Textual Criticism among the Church Fathers," *StPatr* XII (1975) 1:340–41 (on Irenaeus, *Against Heresies* 5.30.1) and 1:342 (on Origen, *Commentary on Matthew*, 121 [GCS 38 = Origenes Werke 11:255, 24–31 Klostermann]). See also K. K. Hulley, "Principles of Textual Criticism Known to St. Jerome," *HSCP* 55 (1944) 87–109; B. M. Metzger, "Explicit References in the Works of Origen to Variant Readings in New Testament Manuscripts," in *Biblical and Patristic Studies in Memory of Robert Pierce Casey* (ed. J. N. Birdsall and R. W. Thomson; Freiburg: Herder, 1963) 78–95 (repr. in Metzger's *Historical and Literary Studies: Pagan, Jewish, and Christian* [NTTS 8; Leiden: Brill, 1968] 88–103); idem, "St Jerome's Explicit References to Variant Readings in Manuscripts of the New Testament," in *Text and Interpretation: Studies in the New Testament Presented to Matthew Black* (ed. E. Best and R. McL. Wilson; Cambridge: Cambridge University Press, 1979) 179–90 (repr. in Metzger's *New Testament Studies: Philological, Versional, and Patristic* [NTTS 10; Leiden: Brill, 1980] 199–210).

The modern formulation and discussion of criteria for judging variants accelerated from the list of forty-three drawn up by Gerhard von Mastricht in 1711 to Richard Bentley's *Proposals for Printing a New Edition* [of a Greek and Latin New Testament] in 1720, to the increasingly influential canons of J. A. Bengel (1725), J. J. Wettstein (1730 and 1751–52), J. J. Griesbach (1796–1806), and Karl Lachmann (1831 to 1850).[4] Noteworthy from this period is Bentley's insistence on using "the most ancient and venerable MSS. in Greek and Roman capital letters," whose readings are to be confirmed by the old versions and Fathers "within the first five centuries," because "what has crept into any copies since is of no value or authority."[5] Noteworthy
also are Bengel's celebrated principle that "the harder reading is to 22
be preferred,"[6] as well as his reliance on the oldest Greek manuscripts and the geographical distribution of witnesses. In addition, Bengel was the first to enunciate the influential affirmation that textual witnesses must be *weighed and not merely counted.*[7] Wettstein reaffirmed most of these criteria in 1730, stating also his preference for the shorter reading and for the reading in conformity with the author's style, though not necessarily preferring the more orthodox reading. Wettstein, however, had abandoned this general approach by the time his 1751–52 edition appeared, having convinced himself that the oldest Greek manuscripts had been corrupted by those in Latin—not a defensible view. Then, Griesbach reinforced and refined Bengel's criterion on preferring the harder reading, and, like Wettstein, he also favored the shorter reading (the first criterion in his list, though stated with numerous qualifications); however, again like Wettstein, Griesbach was suspicious of readings that supported piety or that suited orthodox theology. In addition, Griesbach clearly favored the

[4] These scholars are discussed in considerable detail in E. J. Epp, "The Eclectic Method in New Testament Textual Criticism: Solution or Symptom?" *HTR* 69 (1976) 217–29 (repr. in Epp and Fee, *Studies*, 144–55 [see "Added Notes," below]). (The dates refer to these editors' critical editions of the Greek New Testament.)

[5] Proposals I and IV. For Bentley's text, see Arthur Ayres Ellis, ed., *Bentleii critica sacra: Notes on the Greek and Latin Text of the New Testament, Extracted from the Bentley MSS. in Trinity College Library, with the Abbé Rulotta's Collation of the Vatican Codex B, a Specimen of Bentley's Intended Edition, and an Account of His Collations* (Cambridge: Deighton, Bell, 1862), xvii–xix.

[6] Bengel phrased it as *proclivi scriptioni praestat ardua*, though it is more commonly expressed as *difficilior lectio potior* (see Epp, "Eclectic Method," 220 [repr. in Epp and Fee, *Studies*, 146–47]).

[7] Ibid., 220–22 (repr. in Epp and Fee, *Studies*, 247–48).

ancient witnesses, as did Lachmann after him. Indeed, it was the latter who afforded the "received text" of the sixteenth century no authority, thus effecting a decisive break with the *textus receptus*, until then the standard critical text of the New Testament.[8]

In the mid- to late nineteenth century, however, these canons of criticism came into their own in the hands of Constantin von Tischendorf (1849), S. P. Tregelles (1854), and B. F. Westcott and F. J. A. Hort (1881–82). Tischendorf and Tregelles provided straightforward principles, while those employed by Westcott and Hort must be extracted and systematized from Hort's detailed discussions. Over
23 all, the result was extensive agreement among the three approaches.[9] Tischendorf, for example, stressed that "the text should be sought solely from ancient witnesses" and, echoing Lachmann, that the resulting authority of the oldest Greek codices is not "surmounted by the disagreement of most or even of all the recent codices."[10] He also gave preference to "the reading that appears to have occasioned the other readings," which he describes as the basic rule.[11] Tregelles, in turn, emphasized "the authority of ancient copies without allowing the 'received text' any prescriptive rights" and preferred the harder reading and the shorter reading.[12] Finally, as we near the end of the nineteenth century, the edition of Westcott-Hort exemplified all of the principles highlighted above, particularly their preference for the older readings, manuscripts, or groups; for the reading that most aptly explains the existence of the others; the harder (rather than the smoother) reading; and "quality" readings rather than those with numerous supporting witnesses. In addition, Westcott-Hort preferred the single elements in a conflated reading; the reading best conforming to the author's style and grammar; and readings that are found in a manuscript that habitually contains superior readings, especially if such a manuscript is also an older one. As for the *tex-*

[8] For detail on Griesbach and Lachmann, ibid., 225–31 (repr. in Epp and Fee, *Studies*, 150–55).

[9] For discussion, see ibid., 231–42 (repr. in Epp and Fee, *Studies*, 155–63)

[10] This formulation was published in the second edition of Tischendorf's Greek New Testament (1849) and also quoted in the seventh edition (1859; pp. xxvii–xviii) and by C. R. Gregory in his *Prolegomena* to Tischendorf's eighth edition (1896; 3.47–48).

[11] See discussion in Epp, "Eclectic Method," 231–32 (repr. in Epp and Fee, *Studies*, 155–56).

[12] Ibid., 232–34 (repr. in Epp and Fee, *Studies*, 156–57).

tus receptus, which they called the Syrian text, it is the farthest removed chronologically and qualitatively from the "original" text. Also, Westcott-Hort established a clear division between *external* and *internal* criteria,[13] an approach that will characterize all subsequent discussion of the canons of criticism. At the end of the nineteenth century, then, there was widespread agreement in the use of two differing sets of criteria, external and internal.

Before summarizing these categories, the term *criteria* deserves some 24
thought. The Alands use the word *rules* ("Twelve Basic Rules [Grundregeln] for Textual Criticism") in their manual,[14] but they and all theorists and practitioners in the field know that these are not really rules that are or can be applied mechanically to decide priority among variants. On occasion, however, the criteria are misunderstood as functioning in that fashion,[15] for all the terms employed—"rules," "criteria," "principles," and the like—lend themselves to that kind of rigid interpretation. For a brief moment I considered a return to the old, perhaps obsolete term, *canons* for these criteria, because *canon* refers to a measure; we might then call the criteria "measures" or "yardsticks" of priority, which we hold up to each variant to "take its measure" (as we say), even if that measure is not scientifically exact. Yet, the term *canon* more commonly implies a fixed and final measure, as in a limited collection of writings or a canonized saint. The criteria for priority, however, really are measures of *probability* or various complementary or even competing *arguments* for priority.

[13] B. F. Westcott and F. J. A. Hort, *The New Testament in the Original Greek* (2 vols.; London: Macmillan, 1881–1882; vol. 2, 2d ed., 1896) 2.19–39 on "Internal Evidence"; 2.39–66 on external evidence, which Hort calls "Genealogical Evidence." See discussion in Epp, "Eclectic Method," 234–42 (repr. in Epp and Fee, *Studies*, 157–63). (In my abstracted list on 234–35 [= repr. 157–58] of principles used by Westcott-Hort, I neglected to separate the external from the internal, though they are clearly distinguished by these editors.)

[14] K. Aland and B. Aland, *The Text of the New Testament: An Introduction to the Critical Editions and to the Theory and Practice of Modern Textual Criticism* (trans. E. F. Rhodes; 2d ed.; Grand Rapids, MI: Eerdmans; Leiden: Brill, 1989) 280–81; German ed., 282–83. They specifically reject a mechanical function for the rules on the harder reading, the shorter reading, and harmonization, as well as a mechanical following of a single manuscript or group of manuscripts (281).

[15] For example, E. Tov thinks that such criteria are used mechanically by some in his field; he himself uses the term *rules* but rejects not only any mechanical application, but largely rejects the criteria themselves as too subjective to be practical: *Textual Criticism of the Hebrew Bible* (2d ed.; Minneapolis, MN: Fortress; Assen/Maastricht: Van Gorcum, 2001) 302–10; see also the discussion below and notes 25 and 38.

Hence, we might use *probabilities*, a term drawn from Hort's phrases, *transcriptional probabilities* and *intrinsic probabilities*,[16] which Bruce Metzger employed along with the term *criteria*.[17] Better, perhaps, is the simple term *arguments*, for arguments, after all, are of varying force, some more compelling and some less compelling, some more relevant, some less relevant, to a given situation or context, and arguments also can be used singly or in multiple, complementary fashion. All of this fits very well the external and internal canons as they have developed historically and have been applied practically—and as they have been weakened or strengthened in efficacy during their utilization by textual criticism.

External arguments involve documentary factors—information about manuscripts and the history of their transmission—that is, the more clearly empirical data, such as the age and provenance of a manuscript in which a given reading is found; the age of a reading as ascertained by patristic support; the geographical range of a reading; and the identification of a manuscript's text type and its place in the history of the New Testament text.[18] On the other hand, *internal arguments* relate to factors or characteristics *within* the text itself (over against the external data) and usually comprise a much longer list. Examples can be described in question form: Can this variant account for the rise of all the others in a variation unit? Does this variant conform to the writer's literary style and vocabulary, or theology? Is this variant harder than others, that is, rougher, less elegant, or less clear (though still making sense)? If the answer in these cases is "yes," the variant more probably should be accorded priority. Does a variant conform to/harmonize with a parallel passage (e.g., in another gospel), or an Old Testament passage, or liturgical forms or usage, or some extraneous item in the context? Does a

[16] Westcott and Hort, *New Testament in the Original Greek*, 2.20–22.

[17] B. M. Metzger, *The Text of the New Testament: Its Transmission, Corruption, and Restoration* (3d ed.; New York: Oxford University Press, 1992) 209–10; idem, *A Textual Commentary on the Greek New Testament: A Companion Volume to the United Bible Societies' Greek New Testament (Fourth Revised Edition)* (2d ed.; New York/Stuttgart: United Bible Societies, 1994) 12*–13*.

[18] My latest formulation of external and internal considerations is "Textual Criticism in the Exegesis of the New Testament, with an Excursus on Canon," in *Handbook to Exegesis of the New Testament* (NTTS 25; ed. S. E. Porter; Leiden: Brill, 1997) 62–63 (internal) and 71–72 (external). Earlier formulations appeared in my "Eclectic Method," 243 (repr. in Epp and Fee, *Studies*, 163–64); idem, "Textual Criticism (NT)," *ABD* 6.431.

variant show the influence of ideas from the later history or theology of the church? In these instances, if the answer is affirmative, the variant is more likely to be considered secondary or derivative. Also, can a variant be readily or plausibly explained as one of the usual, unintentional scribal errors? If so, we reverse the process and restore the probable reading of the scribe's exemplar.

Two internal arguments found in most lists are absent from the
preceding summary: the Atticized reading and the shorter reading
arguments; they require discussion, for they were seriously challenged 26
during the twentieth century. In 1963 George D. Kilpatrick suggested that scribes in the second century tended to alter Koine Greek toward Attic Greek style, indicating that a reading should be discredited if it showed Atticist tendencies.[19] Subsequently, however, questions were raised about the efficacy of this argument on the grounds, among others, (a) that scribes in these cases may have had other intentions—other than moving toward Attic style—such as harmonization, and so on, and that Atticism, if it is assumed to have operated, had not functioned very well statistically;[20] (b) that some of the examples offered are not true Atticisms and that it is difficult in any case to assess Atticism before 400 C.E.;[21] or (c) that the scribal

[19] G. D. Kilpatrick, "Atticism and the Text of the Greek New Testament," in *Neutestamentliche Aufsätze: Festschrift für Prof. Josef Schmid zum 70. Geburtstag* (ed. J. Blinzler, O. Kuss, and F. Mussner; Regensburg: Pustet, 1963) 125–37 (repr. in Kilpatrick's *The Principles and Practice of New Testament Textual Criticism: Collected Essays of G. D. Kilpatrick* [ed. J. K. Elliott; BETL 96; Leuven: Leuven University Press/Peeters, 1990] 15–32. See also J. K. Elliott, "The United Bible Societies Greek New Testament: An Evaluation," *NovT* 15 (1973) 298–99; idem, "The Atticist Grammarians" [Phrynichus and Moeris], in Elliott's *Essays and Studies in New Testament Textual Criticism* (Estudios Filología Neotestamentaria, 3; Cordoba: El Almendro, 1992) 65–77; this chapter is adapted from two earlier works, yet it does not take into account the critiques of Colwell, Martini, or Fee, referred to in the following discussion and notes (but see n. 23, below). M. W. Holmes, "Reasoned Eclecticism in New Testament Textual Criticism" in *The Text of the New Testament in Contemporary Research: Essays on the* Status Quaestionis (ed. B. D. Ehrman and M. W. Holmes; SD 46; Grand Rapids, MI: Eerdmans, 1995) 339 n. 11, points out that Günther Zuntz already in 1946 included Atticist tendencies among his criteria.

[20] E. C. Colwell, "Hort Redivivus: A Plea and a Program," in *Transitions in Biblical Scholarship* (ed. J. C. Rylaarsdam; Essays in Divinity, 6; Chicago: University of Chicago Press, 1968) 137–38 (repr. in Colwell's *Studies in Methodology in Textual Criticism of the New Testament* [NTTS 9; Leiden: Brill, 1969] 154–55).

[21] C. M. Martini, "Eclecticism and Atticism in the Textual Criticism of the Greek New Testament" in *On Language, Culture, and Religion: In Honor of Eugene A. Nida* (ed. M. Black and W. A. Smalley; The Hague/Paris: Mouton, 1974) 151–55 (repr. in

tendency may well have been to alter Attic Greek style to biblical
(i.e., Septuagint) Greek rather than the other way around.[22] Kilpatrick
27 and his pupil, Keith Elliott, defended the Atticizing principle against
its detractors,[23] but some textual critics currently are reluctant to
employ it.

But it is the shorter reading argument that has received the most vigorous reassessment in the past three decades or so. This argument says that the shorter/shortest reading in a variation unit has priority because—as most of us have repeated time and again—scribes tend to expand the text rather than to shorten it (to quote one of my own statements). It was Ernest Colwell, in 1965, who provided the impetus for a critique of this principle in his analysis of variants in the singular readings (i.e., unique readings—found nowhere else) of three early, extensive New Testament papyri, P45, P66, and P75; his aim was to discern individual scribal habits. His result regarding omissions and additions—that each scribe more frequently omitted than added material[24]—caught the interest of James Royse, whose investigation doubled the number of early manuscripts by using P45, P46, P47, P66, P72, and P75; tightened the methodology in this meticulous exercise; and reached the same result: "The general tendency during the early period of textual transmission was

Martini's *La parola di Dio alle origini della Chiesa* [AnBib 93; Rome: Biblical Institute Press, 1980] 147–55).

[22] G. D. Fee, "Rigorous or Reasoned Eclecticism—Which?" in *Studies in New Testament Language and Text: Essays in Honour of George D. Kilpatrick on the Occasion of his Sixty-fifth Birthday* (ed. J. K. Elliott; NovTSup 44; Leiden: Brill, 1976) 184–91 (repr. in Epp and Fee, *Studies*, 131–36).

[23] G. D. Kilpatrick, "Eclecticism and Atticism," *ETL* 53 (1977) 107–12 (repr. in Kilpatrick's *Principles and Practice*, 73–79) (response to Martini); J. K. Elliott, "Thoroughgoing Eclecticism in New Testament Textual Criticism," in *The Text of the New Testament in Contemporary Research: Essays on the* Status Quaestionis (ed. B. D. Ehrman and M. W. Holmes; SD 46; Grand Rapids, MI: Eerdmans, 1995) 326–27 (response to Fee).

[24] Ernest C. Colwell, "Scribal Habits in Early Papyri: A Study in the Corruption of the Text," in *The Bible in Modern Scholarship: Papers Read at the 100th Meeting of the Society of Biblical Literature, December 28–30, 1964* (ed. J. Philip Hyatt; Nashville: Abingdon, 1965) 370–89 (repr. as "Method in Evaluating Scribal Habits: A Study of P^{45}, P^{66}, P^{75}," in Colwell's *Studies in Methodology in Textual Criticism of the New Testament* [NTTS 9; Leiden: Brill, 1969] 106–24). His analysis is discussed by Klaus Junack, "Abschreibpraktiken und Schreibergewohnheiten in ihrer Auswirkung auf die Textüberlieferung," in *New Testament Textual Criticism, Its Significance for Exegesis: Essays in Honour of Bruce M. Metzger* (ed. E. J. Epp and G. D. Fee; Oxford: Clarendon Press, 1981) 288–92.

to omit" and, therefore, "other things being equal, one should prefer the longer reading."[25] Thoroughgoing eclectics, of whom Elliott is currently the foremost advocate and practitioner, follow this reversal of the shorter reading principle. Elliott, in one of his two most
recent formulations of his eclectic method, argues that, "in general, 28
the longer text is more likely to be original providing that that text is consistent with the language, style, and theology of the context" because "in general, manuscripts tended to be accidentally shortened rather than deliberately lengthened in the process of copying."[26]

However, as Royse readily acknowledges—and as others point out—the matter is not quite that simple, and, indeed, he offers some caveats of his own. For example, Royse rightly states that his evidence relates to and questions the validity of the shorter reading criterion only for the "earliest period of the transmission of the New Testament text,"[27] leading him to a further conclusion that "as a rule early scribes did not exercise the care evidenced in later transcriptions."[28] Royse also recognizes that "normal" scribal behavior (such as his detailed analysis uncovers) does not explain, for example, the 7%–8% greater length of the D-text of Acts over against

[25] J. R. Royse, "Scribal Tendencies in the Transmission of the Text of the New Testament," in *The Text of the New Testament in Contemporary Research: Essays on the Status Quaestionis* (ed. B. D. Ehrman and M. W. Holmes; SD 46; Grand Rapids, MI: Eerdmans, 1995) 239–52, esp. 242–47, quotation from 246. See also Royse's "Scribal Habits in the Transmission of New Testament Texts," in *The Critical Study of Sacred Texts* (ed. Wendy Doniger O'Flaherty; Berkeley Religious Studies Series, 2; Berkeley, Cal.: Graduate Theological Union, 1979) 139–61; idem, "The Treatment of Scribal Leaps in Metzger's *Textual Commentary*," *NTS* 29 (1983) 539–51. The impracticality of the criterion is argued by E. Tov, *The Text-Critical Use of the Septuagint in Biblical Research* (2d ed.; Jerusalem: Simor, 1997) 228–30; idem, "Criteria for Evaluating Textual Readings: The Limitation of Textual Rules," *HTR* 75 (1982) 440–41; idem, *Textual Criticism of the Hebrew Bible*, 305–7. For a response to Royse and Tov, see M. Silva, "Internal Evidence in the Text-Critical Use of the LXX," in *La Septuaginta en la investigación contemporánea (V Congresso de la IOSCS)* (ed. N. Fernández Marcos; Madrid: Instituto Arias Montano, 1985) 154–64; idem, "The Text of Galatians: Evidence from the Earliest Greek Manuscripts," in *Scribes and Scripture: New Testament Essays in Honor of J. Harold Greenlee* (ed. D. A. Black; Winona Lake, IN: Eisenbrauns, 1992) 23–24 (who counts all omissions/additions, not just those in singular readings).

[26] J. K. Elliott, "Can We Recover the Original Text of the New Testament? An Examination of the Rôle of Thoroughgoing Eclecticism," in Elliott's *Essays and Studies*, 40; see also idem, "Thoroughgoing Eclecticism," 327.

[27] Royse, "Scribal Habits," 155.

[28] Royse, "Scribal Tendencies," 248.

the B-text,[29] nor, one might add, does it explain items such as the
29 additional endings of Mark or the Pericope Adulterae, or numerous smaller phrases (unless homoeoteleuton and homoeoarcton—scribal leaps from the same to the same—can be identified confidently). One reason for this is that Royse's methodology of analyzing scribal habits only from the singular readings of a manuscript yields omissions that, perhaps more than half the time, consist of a single word.[30] Yet, he has certainly chosen the best research model if one wants to ascertain in the most accurate fashion a particular scribe's own foibles, for his procedure avoids the inclusion in the study of previous scribal errors—those already present in the manuscript the scribe is copying—and thereby assures the least contaminated data. Moisés Silva has pointed this out but has also reminded Royse and us that a fuller profile of a particular scribe's habits and of the manuscript being produced requires that all variants need to be taken into account and that we need to know what kinds of omissions are involved (whether very brief omissions, including single words; or homoeoteleuton; or intentional alterations; etc.) and how many affect the sense of the passage.[31] In other words, judgments must be made as to whether omissions were accidental or intentional, followed by a count of each type. So, when Royse's full and fully updated study appears in the near future,[32] we will have a rich database on early scribal habits based on singular readings, but also one from which further studies can be launched.

This assessment is meant to imply that we should not give up entirely on the shorter reading criterion, though it may well turn out that Michael Holmes is correct when he states that, "in the light of Royse's study the venerable canon of *lectio brevior potior* is now seen as relatively useless, at least for the early papyri."[33]

---

[29] Royse, "Scribal Habits," 156. On the differing length of the B-text and D-text of Acts, see the recent study of J. Read-Heimerdinger, "The 'Long' and 'Short' Texts of Acts: A Closer Look at the Quantity and Types of Variation," *RCT* 22 (1997) 245–61. She concludes (247) that the D-text is 6.6% longer than the B-Text.

[30] Silva, "Internal Evidence," 159 n. 24.

[31] Silva, "The Text of Galatians," 23; idem, "Internal Evidence," 158, see 157–61. See Hurtado, "Beyond the Interlude?" 37, for a similar qualification: "Head and Royse agree in showing that omission is much more common than addition, *at least in unintentional scribal tendencies*" [emphasis added].

[32] J. R. Royse, *Scribal Habits in Early Greek New Testament Manuscripts* (SD 47; Grand Rapids, MI: Eerdmans, 2005).

[33] Holmes, "Reasoned Eclecticism," 343.

It may still be worthwhile, however, to ponder the usefulness of 30
the shorter reading criterion in view of some relatively recent studies that would appear to support one side of the issue or the other. For example, Silva offers a ministudy of Galatians variants in P46 and the three major Pauline parchment manuscripts of the fourth and fifth centuries, Sinaiticus, Vaticanus, and Alexandrinus. In the process, he sorts the variants into categories, such as (mere) function words, phrases, etc., and watches for omissions likely due to homoeoteleuton; his results show, for example, five additions in P46 against thirty-three omissions, though most of these variants are function words or explicable by homoeoteleuton.[34] Peter Head studies the singular readings of fourteen fragmentary New Testament papyri and finds twelve different omissions against seven additions. He admits that the sample is small, precluding firm conclusions, though he claims that his results "fully support" Royse's finding that "omission is more common than addition."[35] Finally, Jenny Read-Heimerdinger has presented a quantitative analysis of types of variation between Codex Vaticanus (B) and Codex Bezae (D), including additions and omissions. While not prejudging the relationship between the two manuscripts (i.e., referring to an "omission" in D is not meant to imply that B was original and D was secondary), the statistical result shows that (over against B) Codex D "adds" 1,448 words while it "omits" 579 words.[36] Though this is a very different kind of study from those considered above, it may nonetheless be relevant to the shorter reading discussion and one that invites discrimination among unintentional and intentional alterations.

Two other criteria or arguments were challenged in recent decades,
including the well-established "author's style" argument, namely, that
the reading has priority that best conforms to the author's style. The 31
basis for objection was that "it cannot be expected or presupposed

[34] Silva, "The Text of Galatians," 23–24.

[35] Peter M. Head, "Observations on Early Papyri of the Synoptic Gospels, Especially on the 'Scribal Habits,'" *Bib* 71 (1990) 240–47, esp. 246–47.

[36] Read-Heimerdinger, "The 'Long' and 'Short' Texts of Acts," 245–61, esp. 250–51. The issue is complex, of course, because, if one were to assume that the D-text (or, more precisely, the primitive text behind it) was earlier than B, the result would be that B omits 1,448 words, while adding only 579 over against D. Cf. also M. Black, "Notes on the Longer and the Shorter Text of Acts," *On Language, Culture, and Religion: In Honor of Eugene A. Nida* (ed. M. Black and W. A. Smalley; Approaches to Semiotics, 56; The Hague/Paris: Mouton, 1974) 119–31.

that the language employed in the New Testament documents will of necessity be consistent."[37] This criterion should be tested further; yet, employed in a contextual manner along with other arguments, it appears to function about as well as many—all of which require appropriate qualification. Second, the very old argument that the harder reading is preferable is characterized as too subjective to be practical by Emanuel Tov, among the leading textual critics of the Hebrew Bible and the LXX. Once, however, obvious scribal errors are ignored and other reasonable qualifications are employed, as Silva, again, points out, the principle functions well enough; after all, these internal arguments are not "rules" that operate automatically, but require adaptation to the various specific contexts of textual variation.[38]

Finally, as we have intimated all along, it is important to understand how these arguments for priority of readings function—both the external and the internal—and, above all, to recognize that they do not operate in a mechanical fashion as if they were tests to be applied *seriatim* to a variation unit, which—if a variant passes all of them—accredit that reading. On the contrary, many will not be relevant to a given variation unit or, what is more troublesome, in a single case one or more criteria may accredit one reading, while other arguments support a competing reading. For example, in
32 Matthew 6:33 a reading that explains the others competes with another reading that better conforms to Matthew's style. At other times, a reading may be the harder reading, while a competing variant may be strongly supported by old and geographically diverse manuscripts.[39] At this point the felicitous phrase, "the balance of

[37] J. H. Petzer, "Author's Style and the Textual Criticism of the New Testament," *Neot* 24 (1990) 186 185–97, esp. 192–96, quotation from 186. See Petzer's later "Eclecticism and the Text of the New Testament," in *Text and Interpretation: New Approaches in the Criticism of the New Testament* (ed. P. J. Hartin and J. H. Petzer; NTTS 15; Leiden: Brill, 1991) 58–59.

[38] Tov, *Text-Critical Use of the Septuagint*, 228–30; idem, "Criteria for Evaluating Textual Readings," 439–40; idem, with more examples, *Textual Criticism of the Hebrew Bible*, 302–5; B. Albrektson, "Difficilior Lectio Probabilior—A Rule of Textual Criticism and Its Use in Old Testament Studies," *OTS* 21 (1981) 5–18. For the response to Tov and a positive evaluation of the criterion in New Testament use, see M. Silva, "Internal Evidence," 154–57. Further in defense of the criterion, see E. A. Nida, "The 'Harder Reading' in Textual Criticism: An Application of the Second Law of Thermodynamics," *BT* 32 (1981) 101–7.

[39] The use of internal evidence is illustrated profusely in the works of G. D.

probabilities" comes into play: a process by which we measure each variant against both the external and the internal arguments for relevance; compare the results by weighing any competing arguments against one another; and form a reasonable judgment—that is, choose the most probable reading. This, I hasten to add, is not for the reason suggested in these lines from *The Painter Who Pleased Nobody* by John Gay in the early eighteenth century:

> Lest men suspect your tale untrue,
> Keep probability in view.

Moreover, in the course of measuring two or more readings in a variation unit, we soon discover that even the more clearly empirical data we have (as found in the external canons) must be applied with art and skill, just as required for the internal arguments. Yet, even if the various arguments conflict with one another, that does not mean that they should be discarded; it only means that they are more sophisticated than simple "rules." Taking another example, if the history of the text is incomplete, that does not mean that it cannot be written or that what has been constructed has no merit; it means only that we must work harder to interpret and to integrate the data we have.

Though this issue is far more complex than our brief treatment suggests, as the end of the nineteenth century approached, New Testament textual criticism had arrived at two sets of guidelines or arguments for measuring the priority of variant readings, external and internal. Now, a century later, we have the same two sets, with one or two items added and one or two deleted from the internal side. We also find, unlike a century ago, that thoroughgoing or rigorous eclectics, such as Kilpatrick and Elliott, give relatively less 33
weight to the external list and rely rather on the internal considerations—a subject beyond this presentation.

In what precedes, however, I have almost totally neglected the external arguments, where my own major interest lies and my work has been concentrated. In the 1980s I spoke of the "crisis of criteria," expressing the hope that both the external and internal

---

Kilpatrick (see his *The Principles and Practice of New Testament Textual Criticism*) and J. K. Elliott (see his *Essays and Studies*). A perusal of Metzger, *Textual Commentary*, quickly illumines the balance and also the alternation of external and internal arguments.

considerations could be made more effective, but expecting that more progress could be made on the external side—the historical-documentary approach that would enable us to write the history of the New Testament text and thereby largely obviate or at least significantly reduce the need for the internal arguments.[40] After all, Westcott and Hort had written, to their satisfaction, a rather clear history of the text that isolated for them the "best" documentary witnesses, and why couldn't we do much better since they had virtually no early papyri to aid them. Of course, I knew very well that they had employed internal arguments to accredit their so-called "best" manuscripts,[41] but we had the Chester Beatty and Bodmer papyri and more to assist in our reconstruction of the history of transmission. Indeed, we now have 116 New Testament papyri, representing perhaps 112 different manuscripts, of which sixty-one or 54% date prior to around the turn of the third/fourth centuries. Should we not be able to write the very early history of our text—something that the vast majority of textual critics are convinced would improve our external arguments?

Have we made progress on the internal side? Wherever discussion and debate have raised questions, generated hypotheses, devised tests and evaluative methods, and even weakened the efficacy of existing principles, progress is evident, but it is far from adequate. And if present means for testing and refinement are lacking or insufficient, we need to develop new procedures, better methods. Michael Holmes, at the conclusion of a similar discussion, affirmed that "the primary effect of recent discussions of the various [inter-
34 nal] criteria . . . has been to increase our skepticism. We are less sure than ever that their use . . . will produce any certainty with respect to the results obtained."[42] I do not disagree, because skepticism can be a productive reaction, instigating renewed investigation and fresh

[40] E. J. Epp, "Textual Criticism," in *The New Testament and Its Modern Interpreters* (ed. E. J. Epp and †G. W. MacRae; Philadelphia: Fortress/Atlanta: Scholars Press, 1989) 100–103 (repr. as "Decision Points in Past, Present, and Future New Testament Textual Criticism," in Epp and Fee, *Studies*, 39–42).

[41] Extended discussion may be found in my "Eclectic Method," 236–42 (repr. in Epp and Fee, *Studies*, 158–63).

[42] Michael W. Holmes, "Reasoned Eclecticism," 343. J. H. Petzer draws a more extreme conclusion: "There is still no more certainty with regard to our choices of readings than a century ago"; see "A Survey of the Developments in the Textual Criticism of the Greek New Testament since UBS^{3}," *Neot* 24 (1990) 82.

insights. I would not, therefore, interpret recent work as lacking in progress or the future as devoid of hope. In the twenty-first century we can and will refine *both* the external and internal arguments.

II. Choosing among Manuscripts—and Deciding on Groups: The Issue of Text-Types

The relative emphasis placed upon external and internal considerations in the evaluation of variants divides textual critics into two classes (though theoretically into three).[43] On the one hand are thoroughgoing or rigorous eclectics, who utilize the internal arguments largely to the exclusion of the external. (Theoretically, there should be an opposite class, historical-documentary eclectics, or the like, who emphasize the external considerations to the virtual exclusion of the internal, but I know of no one currently who would fit into such a group.) So, in reality, on the other hand are the reasoned eclectics, as they are named, who employ a combination of the external and internal arguments, applied evenly and without prejudice (though, admittedly, many lean toward the external whenever appropriate or even as often as they dare), with the goal of reaching a reasonable decision based on the relative probabilities among all applicable arguments for priority.

When we now turn to the issue of New Testament text-types—that is, the attempt to isolate clusters of manuscripts that constitute distinguishable kinds of texts as evidenced by similar textual characteristics, with the further goal of utilizing them to sketch the history of the New Testament text—it will be obvious that reasoned 35
eclectics take a great interest in the enterprise while thoroughgoing or rigorous eclectics tend not to do so. This is because text types are established largely (though not exclusively) on the basis of external evidence—and they themselves then become an element of external evidence as part of the argument that priority may be granted to a variant supported by "one or more established groups of manuscripts of recognized antiquity, character, and perhaps location."[44]

---

[43] For detailed descriptions, see Epp, "Eclectic Method," 244–57 (repr. in Epp and Fee, *Studies*, 164–73); idem, "Textual Criticism in the Exegesis of the New Testament," 61–64; 70–73.

[44] External criterion 4 in my list in "Eclectic Method," 243 (repr. in Epp and

After all, text-types can be characterized as to age and quality—though internal evidence is employed in judging the latter.

The establishment of text-types (though I prefer the term, *textual clusters*)[45] is an integral part of the textual critic's attempt to reconstruct the history of the New Testament text by tracing the lines of transmission back through the extant manuscripts to the earliest stages and then selecting the readings that seem best to represent the earliest attainable level of the textual tradition. In theory, at least, we should be able to organize our extant manuscripts into groups or clusters, each of which has a similar kind or character of text. Next, as a result of this process, we should be able to isolate the earliest known group or groups. Then we should be able to identify other groups that can be arranged in chronological succession—that is, later groups. If only one very early group or cluster were to emerge, that would simplify matters a great deal, for it could be claimed with a high measure of legitimacy that this earliest type of text is closest to the text (or a text) of the early Christian community. Or, to view the matter at the level of readings, within each variation unit the reading would be selected that comes from that earliest cluster (other things being equal, as we say—i.e., after applying also the internal arguments), again with a plausible claim that it represents the or a text of the early or earliest period.

36 This—though much oversimplified—is the traditional method of historical-documentary textual criticism (as I call it),[46] so named because it places the greater emphasis on external criteria, including the age of documents, their provenance (if known), their place in the history of the text, as well as the general quality of their scribes and their texts as a whole.

As it turns out, however, this process of grouping (according to most scholars) isolates not one earliest New Testament group or text-

Fee, *Studies*, 163); idem, "Textual Criticism in the Exegesis of the New Testament," 72.

[45] See my "The Significance of the Papyri for Determining the Nature of the New Testament Text in the Second Century: A Dynamic View of Textual Transmission," *Gospel Traditions in the Second Century: Origins, Recensions, Text, and Transmission* (ed. W. L. Petersen; Christianity and Judaism in Antiquity 3; Notre Dame, IN: University of Notre Dame Press, 1989) 84–101 (repr in Epp and Fee, *Studies*, 283–95); idem, "Textual Criticism (NT)," *ABD* (1992) 6.430–31.

[46] For discussion, see Epp, "Textual Criticism," 92–94 (repr. in Epp and Fee, *Studies*, 32–34); idem, "Textual Criticism (NT)," *ABD* (1992) 6.432.

type, but two early clusters: the B-text and the D-text, though the latter is a matter of some debate. How is the general age or antiquity of a text type established? Primarily by the age of the oldest manuscripts that are found to be in the resulting groups; to be more exact, however, it is not the age of a manuscript that counts but the age of the text it contains, thereby complicating the matter considerably. A second and significant factor in determining the antiquity of a text-type is to identify any early church writers who support readings characteristic of each group. Indeed, the latter is of great importance because coincidence of readings between a given manuscript and church writings provides a reasonably objective verification of the age of the readings in question—dependent, of course, on the degree to which our critical editions of patristic sources are reliable.

Naturally, if we have two early text-types, followed by one or more later text-types, a rather simplistic kind of historical-documentary approach will not work It is at this point that those otherwise naturally inclined toward a historical-documentary approach will embrace reasoned eclecticism and will utilize with vigor both the external and internal arguments for the priority of readings.

New Testament textual critics began to place manuscripts into classes or groups at least as far back as Bengel (1740), whose Asiatic (i.e., later) and African (ancient) families were expanded by J. S. Semler in 1767 to three groups comparable to our own three main text types, Alexandrian (≈B-text), Western (≈D-text), and Oriental (≈A text or Byzantine).[47] By the end of the nineteenth century a clear-cut proposal by Westcott and Hort was widely accepted: two early text-
types, inappropriately named "Neutral" for the B-text and "Western" 37
for the D-text, and one later Syrian text-type, commonly designated the *textus receptus*. Equally broadly accepted, at least for the moment, was Westcott-Hort's conclusion that the original text is generally to be identified with the Neutral or B-text. This made the Western or D-text an equally early but corrupt text parallel to the Neutral, with the Syrian or Byzantine text-type a later, conflated version built largely upon the other two. This nuanced form of Hort's view soon faced criticism and redevelopment, but this is where the issue of text-types stood as the nineteenth century moved toward its conclusion.

---

[47] Marvin R. Vincent, "*A History of the Textual Criticism of the New Testament*" (New York: Macmillan, 1903) 89–93.

Before the century ended, however, the discovery of early New Testament papyri at Oxyrhynchus, beginning in 1898, cast bright rays of sunshine down through the entire twentieth century and became the harbinger of many more discoveries of early and extensive New Testament papyri—culminating (for the moment, at least) in a third/fourth century Oxyrhynchus papyrus containing some three hundred lines from twelve chapters of the Apocalypse of John (P115), published in 1999–in which, incidentally, the "number of the Beast" is 616 (as in Codex C) instead of 666 (Revelation 13:18). Such manuscripts, but more so the Chester Beatty (P45, P46, P47) and Bodmer papyri (P66, P72, and P75), published in the 1930s and 1950s respectively, provided rich and fresh material for the construction of text-types, though by no means was it always clear just where the contribution of these new papyri lay, especially with the highly fragmentary ones.

Modifications to the Westcott-Hort scheme of text-types appeared
as the twentieth century proceeded, though not at first because of
the papyri. A major development was the identification of a Caesarean
text of the gospels, first by Kirsopp Lake and Robert Blake, then
elaborated by B. H. Streeter and further by Lake, Blake, and Silva
New, as well as others.[48] In addition, the D-text became a matter
of discussion and debate, involving questions such as whether it was
closer to the original than the B-text; whether it was rough and
38 early, or corrupt and later; whether the author of Luke-Acts wrote
one edition or two; whether the D-text represents an early text-type
or only a later one; and so on—issues, by the way, that remain
largely unresolved or at least debated even today.[49]

Where do we stand at the outset of the twenty-first century? The scheme I advocate identifies (1) an early cluster designated the B-text, with roots in the second century and represented chiefly by

[48] K. Lake and R. P. Blake, "The Text of the Gospels and the Koridethi Codex," *HTR* 16 (1923) 267–86; B. H. Streeter, *The Four Gospels: A Study of Origins, Treating of the Manuscript Tradition, Sources, Authorship, & Dates* (London: Macmillan, 1924) 77–108; K. Lake, R. P. Blake, and S. New, "The Caesarean Text of the Gospel of Mark," *HTR* 21 (1928) 207–404.

[49] Recent arguments for and against the priority of the D-text are summarized in Jacobus H. Petzer, "The History of the New Testament Text—Its Reconstruction, Significance and Use in New Testament Textual Criticism," in *New Testament Textual Criticism, Exegesis, and Early Church History: A Discussion of Methods* (ed. B. Aland and J. Delobel; CBET, 7; Kampen: Kok Pharos, 1994) 18–25.

P75 and Codex B; (2) a perhaps equally early D-text (represented chiefly by some fragmentary papyri, Codex D, the Old Latin, the Old Syriac [in part], and a Middle Egyptian manuscript, cop^{G67}); (3) an abortive C-text (in Mark, represented by P45 and Codex W but continuing no farther);[50] and (4) a later cluster, the A-text (represented by Codex A and most later majuscules and minuscules).[51] Kurt Aland and Barbara Aland, however, do not assign to the D-text a date earlier than the fourth century, nor to any others; for them, "not until the fourth century . . . did the formation of text types begin."[52] They do, however, speak of Codex D's "very few precursors" and list in their Category IV (= D-text) two third century papyri (P48, P69) and two third/fourth century manuscripts (P38, 0171) prior to the fifth (or possibly late fourth) century Codex D.[53] 39
The difference is that many textual critics, contrary to the Alands, consider that to be evidence of a textual cluster—existing at least by the third century. As noted, however, the Alands are willing to identify three text types, but only from 300 C.E. and after: "the Alexandrian text, the Koine text, and the D text"—that is, our B-text, A-text (or Byzantine), and D-text, respectively, but not a Caesarean text.[54]

---

[50] Note that the Caesarean text is no longer listed in Metzger, *Textual Commentary*: it appears on pp. xxix–xxx of the first edition (1972) but its representatives are nowhere to be found on p. 15* of the second edition, though their text is described (6*) as "a mixture of Western [D-text] and Alexandrian [B-text] readings." Indeed, I had earlier designated this the C-text because in textual character (just as Metzger says) it stands midway between the B-text and the D-text; see Epp, "Twentieth Century Interlude," 393–96 (repr. in Epp and Fee, *Studies*, 89–92); idem, "Significance of the Papyri," 88 (repr. in Epp and Fee, *Studies*, 285); idem, "Textual Criticism (NT)," *ABD* (1992) 6.431. The major work resulting in the demise of the "Caesarean" text is Larry W. Hurtado, *Text-Critical Methodology and the Pre-Caesarean Text: Codex W in the Gospel of Mark* (SD 43; Grand Rapids, MI: Eerdmans, 1981); see the conclusions, 85–89. Though family 13 (f^{13}) is often associated with this text, Hurtado argues that it is a secondary and not a primary witness.

[51] For discussion of this structure, see Epp, "Twentieth Century Interlude," 392–400 (repr. in Epp and Fee, *Studies*, 88–95); idem, "Significance of the Papyri," 84–88 (repr. in Epp and Fee, *Studies*, 283–86); idem, "Textual Criticism," 97–100 (repr. in Epp and Fee, *Studies*, 37–39); idem, "Textual Criticism (NT)," *ABD* 6.430–31.

[52] Aland and Aland, *Text of the New Testament*, 64.

[53] Ibid., 65, 159; see 64 (which speaks of some forms of the text before 300 that "anticipated or were more closely akin to the D text") and 93 (where P38, P48, and P69 "may be regarded as precursors or branches of the D text.") [At the April 2000 symposium at Southeastern Seminary, J. Keith Elliott alerted me to an Oxyrhynchus papyrus of Acts, not yet numbered or published, that appears to be of the D-text-type (I am unaware of the date assigned to the manuscript).]

[54] Ibid., 66–67.

There is also difference of opinion among textual critics as to which fragmentary papyri can be placed in these groups with confidence, due to the small number of variant readings in many of them. What is clear and significant, however, is that no pre-sixth century papyri support the A-text.[55]

The status of the text-type issue at the outset of the twenty-first century, then, is that virtually all textual critics accept the existence, at least by 300 C.E., of three text types (B, D, and A). Though many believe that a C-text (but no longer to be called Caesarean) existed in the early fourth century, it is not essential to the basic documentary history of the New Testament text generally postulated—that is, the three text types around 300. As for the crucial period preceding the fourth century, two views are dominant. The first view is that of Kurt Aland and Barbara Aland, who evaluate and categorize the witnesses in this early period according to their manner of transmission (rather than by similarity of readings), and they suggest four degrees of fidelity in the copying of exemplars:

1. Some manuscripts were transmitted with *normal* care (i.e., relatively faithfully, with a limited amount of variation, and keeping "significantly closer to the original text").
2. Some manuscripts were copied from their exemplars with *strict* (i.e., meticulous) care.
3. Some manuscripts were passed along in a relatively *free* manner (i.e., with greater variation than the *normal*).
4. Some manuscripts were transmitted in a *paraphrastic* fashion (i.e., in the manner of the D-text), with the last two categories showing the "most diverse variants."[56]

Then the Alands employ two overlapping groups of manuscripts to reconstruct the "text of the early period," which for all practical pur-

[55] Papyri that represent or were influenced by the Byzantine text are P63 (ca. 500), P84 (sixth century), P68, perhaps P73 and P74 (seventh century), and P42 (seventh/eighth century).

[56] Aland and Aland, *Text of the New Testament*, 64, 93, 95. The classification system is more complex than the summary above, for there are in-between or qualified classifications as well, such as "at least normal" (P15, P22, P30, P32, P49, P53, P77), "strict text, somewhat carelessly written" (P70), "very free text" (P69), and "free text, carelessly written" (P40). Also, not all manuscripts are assigned a classification.

poses means, for them, the original text.[57] While (first) they rely on manuscripts transmitted in a strict manner, they depend more heavily on those passed along in a normal fashion, combined (secondly) with all papyri and majuscules that date prior to or around the turn of the third/fourth centuries, for these latter witnesses (now totaling sixty-one) have "inherent significance" by virtue of predating the text-type era.[58] In addition, they state that the text circulated in this period in the four specified Textforms (not text-types) without any ecclesiastical control.[59]

I have no strong objection to this general view that in the early 41
period the New Testament text was transmitted in varying textforms and without controls, except that the Alands' fourfold categorization seems patently to be based on a circular argument, for the witnesses claimed to preserve most faithfully the original text are at the same time the manuscripts employed to construct the (now identical) Greek text of the Nestle/Aland and UBS editions, which, in turn, is claimed to be the virtual "original text." If, for the sake of argument, an editor thought that the precursors of the Alands' D-text best represented the original text (on the grounds, e.g., that it is rough and therefore primitive), would not these precursors of D (P38, P48, P69, and 0171) then likely be labeled normal and/or strict Textforms, with the presently designated strict and normal manuscripts called something else?[60]

---

[57] K. Aland, "The Twentieth-Century Interlude in New Testament Textual Criticism," in *Text and Interpretation: Studies in the New Testament Presented to Matthew Black* (ed. E. Best and R. McL. Wilson; Cambridge/New York: Cambridge University Press, 1979) 11; idem, "Der neue 'Standard Text' in seinem Verhältnis zu den frühen Papyri und Majuskeln," in *New Testament Textual Criticism: Its Significance for Exegesis: Essays in Honour of Bruce M. Metzger* (ed. E. J. Epp and G. D. Fee; Oxford: Clarendon Press, 1981) 274–75 (note that the term, *standard text* has been replaced by *new text* in subsequent publications); Aland and Aland, *Text of the New Testament*, 333, cf. 335.

[58] Aland and Aland, *Text of the New Testament*, 93, 95; see the list of forty-seven pre-third-/fourth-century manuscripts on 56–57. With the publication of P98 and of thirteen early Oxyrhynchus papyri, the total is now sixty-one early New Testament manuscripts.

[59] Ibid., 59, 64; see the categories assigned to papyri through P96 on pp. 96–101. For a careful description of this "Münster theory," see Petzer, "History of the New Testament Text," 30–35.

[60] Epp, "New Testament Textual Criticism Past, Present, and Future: Reflections on the Alands' *Text of the New Testament*," *HTR* 82 (1989) 223–26. See also, B. D. Ehrman, "A Problem of Textual Circularity: The Alands on the Classification of New Testament Manuscripts," *Bib* 70 (1989) 381 n. 19. Like my discussion, Ehrman's

The second view of the text in the pre-300 period is held, it is fair to say, by most textual critics[61]—and it is my own position as well. It argues that two early textual clusters or text-types (B and D) were functioning from perhaps as early as the second century, with a third text-type (A or Byzantine) developing later. Even in the early, uncontrolled period, many papyri share enough similarities in readings to be identified as clusters in conjunction with later manuscripts, although—as noted earlier—the fragmentary papyri often are difficult to place. Doing the best we can, however, we draw lines of connectedness between the earliest witnesses and any later manu-
42 scripts that share similar textual characteristics, and we conclude that the resulting clusters form the various text-types. The resulting schema—given the proper cautions—permits both the larger clusters and individual readings to be placed in a temporal continuum, with a good probability of tracing the textual footprints back to the earliest possible levels. This is not the place to review various attempts to match manuscripts with others of similar textual complexion,[62] but it is of current interest to note that the rather extensive third/fourth century P115, published only in 1999, enters the picture as "the earliest witness" to the A/C type of text of the Apocalypse of John, a text that, says David Parker, now—in the light of P115–may be "more carefully reconstructed."[63] In this connection, it is worth noting also that, while excluding text-types before approximately 300,

essay is devoted not primarily to the four categories we have discussed above, but to the Alands' classification of manuscripts under five headings (I–V) that indicate the degree of relevance for establishing the original text; Ehrman, however finds the same circularity there. Cf. Petzer, "History of the New Testament Text," who, in his description of the Alands' general approach, is not explicit about a circular argument, but points out that, for them, the Alexandrian text is "the vehicle by means of which the original text was most faithfully transmitted" (32) and is "*de facto* equal to the original text," and that "the Alexandrian text in N^{26} is explicitly acknowledged and used as a point of departure and decisive norm for the study of variant readings" (34).

[61] Petzer, "History of the New Testament Text," 15: "Beyond dispute today seems to be the fact of the existence of these three main text-types."

[62] See Epp, "Significance of the Papyri," 84–101 (repr. in Epp and Fee, *Studies*, 283–95).

[63] D, C. Parker, "The Newly Published Oxyrhynchus Papyrus of Revelation," a paper read at the 1999 Annual Meeting of the Society of Biblical Literature in Boston; see the abstract in *AAR-SBL Abstracts 1999* ([Atlanta: AAR & SBL], 1999) 266. (Note that text-types for the Apocalypse of John are different from those in the rest of the New Testament.) [Parker's full study has now appeared: "A New Oxyrhynchus Papyrus of Revelation: P^{115} (P.Oxy. 4499)," *NTS* 46 (2000) 159–74.]

nonetheless the Alands, for all practical purposes, trace out for us the lines not only of the pre-300 D-text, but also of the pre-300 B-text by their categorization of the earliest papyri (even though they do not group manuscripts by textual consanguinity but by degrees of faithfulness to their exemplars).[64]

On either approach, then, we will have sketched out a history of 43
the New Testament text, though the Alands' approach, it seems to me, is less clear and less objectively based than the second procedure. What remains to be determined is whether this understanding of the history of the text is merely a rough sketch or one that already has numerous elements of refinement. Although that is unclear, the main point is that there is sufficient agreement to conclude that the vast majority of textual critics worldwide are convinced that the development of the New Testament text can be traced from very early times to the period of the great majuscules, with some textual scholars taking one path of explanation and others another for the earliest portion of that period. Our task now is to move toward a greater measure of refinement, either by clarifying the Alands' categories and/or by firming up the constituent membership of early textual clusters.

Jacobus Petzer's excellent assessment of the history of the New Testament text and its reconstruction—exactly what we have been discussing here—has a compact summary of what New Testament textual criticism has accomplished, in broad strokes, in the last two centuries. The nineteenth century, he says, "managed to solve the

[64] To arrive at this conclusion, I compared my lists of papyri up to and around the turn of the third/fourth centuries that appear to fit into the various text-types, namely, the A, B, C, and D ("Significance of the Papyri," 100 [repr. in Epp and Fee, *Studies*, 294]) and the Alands' list of category I papyri of the same period (Aland and Aland, *Text of the New Testament*, 159). Of their thirty-seven papyri in category I, twenty-five were somewhere in my lists, but fully twenty of those twenty-five were in my roster of B-text representatives. Since, according to the Alands, category I consists of "manuscripts with a very high proportion of the early text . . ., presumably the original text" (335) and since "most of the manuscripts of this category belong to the 'Alexandrian' text type" [= B-text] (335 n. 13), I interpret this striking overlap of the papyri in my B-text list with those in the Alands' category I as significant evidence that a pre-third-/fourth century-text-type can be traced through their category I and connected with the mid-fourth-century Codex B and other witnesses to that text-type. I take this position in spite of Petzer, "History of the New Testament Text," 36, who, in describing the "Münster theory," asserts that "although one is tempted to associate these 'text-types' [i.e., the Alands' 'strict,' 'normal,' 'free' texts] with the traditional text-types, they are in fact very different, because their constituent parts are not necessarily genealogically related."

textual riddles of the fourth century and settled the question of the Byzantine text"; the twentieth century solved the mysteries of the third century (though I am not as sure as he is that we have finished the task), and, he concludes, it remains now for the twenty-first century "to solve the two remaining riddles, that of (a) . . . the nature of the earliest transmission of the text, or the second century, and (b) the nature of the original text and its relation to the 'autographs', or the first century."[65] I agree completely that our next task is to clarify textual transmission in the second century, though I am less confident that any simple solutions—or any solutions at all—will come quickly with respect to the first century. One small reason for renewed optimism about the second century is that, whereas P52, containing a fragment of John's Gospel, used to be the only second-century papyrus of the New Testament, now there are two or three
44 more: P90 (John), P104 (Matthew), and perhaps P98 (the Apocalypse of John).[66] Further analysis of the use by second century church writers of books that were in the process of becoming canon in that period will also assist us. So, let us press the second century for the answers we want and need.

III. Choosing among Critical Editions—and Deciding for Compromise: The Issue of Current Critical Editions of the Greek New Testament

Critical editions of the Greek New Testament—from the first one *printed* in 1514 as volume five of the Complutensian Polyglot and

[65] Petzer, "History of the New Testament Text," 36. Hurtado, "Beyond the Interlude?" 38–43, also stresses the cruciality of the second century—with which I wholeheartedly agree.

[66] Three other papyri date around 200: P46, P64+P67, and P66, while two others (both containing portions of Matthew) stem from the late second/early third century: P103 (P.Oxy. LXIV.4403) and P77 (P.Oxy. XXXIV.2683+LXIV.4405). Y. K. Kim proposed a first century date (ca. 80) for P46 ("Palaeographical Dating of P^{46} to the Later First Century," *Bib* 69 [1988] 248–57). D. B. Wallace (review of Kim's *Biblica* article in *BSac* [1989] 451–52) suggests that this proposal will attract as much attention as J. O'Callaghan's identification of 7Q5 as Mark 6:52–53 (mid-first century!), but obviously it has not; Wallace himself says "wait and see." Hurtado, "Beyond the Interlude?" 40 n. 38, reminds us that the editors of P75 (V. Martin and R. Kasser, *Papyrus Bodmer XIV–XV* [Geneva: Bibliotheca Bodmeriana, 1961] 1.13) posed a date between 175–200 as most probable, but the beginning of the third century is the current view.

from the first one *published* in 1516 by Erasmus to those of the present day—all contain texts that never existed in any actual, exact manuscript form, for (as everyone knows) they have been reconstructed by incorporating individual readings from a vast array of Greek manuscripts, using in the process the arguments for priority discussed above, comparisons with supporting versions and church writers, and insights from recognized text-types. If one wished a critical edition closely resembling an actual manuscript over extended portions, Tischendorf's eighth edition (giving great weight to his greatest discovery, Codex Sinaiticus) or Westcott-Hort's text (with its close reliance on Codex Vaticanus) might be chosen. At the other extreme, the unfinished *Greek-English Diglot for the Use of Translators* by George D. Kilpatrick, in which he employed his form of eclecticism in selecting readings, would, I presume, resemble any actual manu- 45
script even less than other current editions.[67] Yet, the artificiality of our critical editions is a nonissue, for a critical edition of any ancient writing is by nature a reconstruction. The only way it could be identical to a particular manuscript is if the editor rejected every variant in every other manuscript; moreover, even a writing extant in only one manuscript inevitably requires a critical edition, for emendations invariably are requisite to explain nonsense or otherwise difficult readings when no basis of comparison is available.

When we ask about critical editions of the New Testament in the second half of the nineteenth century, we must remember that Codex Vaticanus (B) came to prominence and that Codex Sinaiticus (א) was discovered in this period, along with many more manuscripts. Tischendorf utilized these and other celebrated fourth- and fifth-century codices to produce his various critical editions of the New Testament, culminating in the eighth major edition of 1869–72, with

[67] Elliott, *Essays and Studies*, 28, says that the *Diglot* fascicles "represent to some extent the conclusions of Kilpatrick's text-critical method, though [they] do not give the results of a completely thoroughgoing eclecticism." Fascicles of the *Diglot* appeared as follows, issued for private circulation by the British and Foreign Bible Society: *Mark* (1958), *Matthew* (1959), *John* (1960), *The General Letters* (1961), *Luke* (1962), *The Pastoral Letters and Hebrews* (1963), *Romans and 1 and 2 Corinthians* (1964). See Metzger, *Text of the New Testament*, 177–78, 257; Aland and Aland, *Text of the New Testament*, 25, 32. The Alands report that the cessation of Kilpatrick's project was due to the shift of the British Bible Society's support to the newly launched UBS project, an action, they claim, that "simply expressed a basic recognition that the text of the *GNT*, as far as it had been completed, was superior to that of the diglot edition" (32).

an extensive apparatus still useful today. But the most influential critical *text* [there was no apparatus] was that of Westcott and Hort in 1881, and both Tischendorf and Westcott-Hort, as noted earlier, gave the greatest authority to the most ancient manuscripts, carrying through the principles exemplified in Irenaeus and Jerome of old and emphasized from the time of Bentley (1720) through Bengel (1742), supported by Griesbach (1775), but triumphant in Lachmann (1831, 1850). So, as the twentieth century approached, the Westcott-Hort critical text—similar in nature to that of Tischendorf—
46 stood as the monument of nineteenth century New Testament textual criticism.[68]

Yet, before the nineteenth century was out, several major works of Dean John William Burgon appeared, some posthumously, that reverted to the pre-Lachmannian view of preference for the *textus receptus*.[69] To be sure, Westcott-Hort pushed their case too far in the audacious title of their edition, *The New Testament in the Original Greek*, but the textual edifice they constructed so carefully by a synergism of external and internal evidence on a modern foundation laid some 160 years earlier was not likely to fall, though it was to be modified in various ways during the twentieth century and to give way to the now almost universal Nestle-Aland and United Bible Societies text. Modifications to the Westcott-Hort text arose primarily from the issues reviewed in the first two sections of this paper.

First, text-types figured largely in Westcott-Hort's theory, and that they continue to play a role in establishing the text, at least for the vast majority of textual critics, is obvious enough from our earlier treatment, but also from the descriptions in manuals and handbooks and, pointedly, in the *Textual Commentary* accompanying the UBS edition, where the components of the currently accepted text types are

---

[68] Although the older Nestle editions are championed in Aland and Aland, *Text of the New Testament*, 19–22; 26–30, and their text—with that of the Nestle-Aland editions—is called "the dominant text for eighty . . . years," the Nestle text of 1898 and following did not attract the vigorous debate that the Westcott-Hort edition did, for there was no grand theory that lay behind the Nestle edition. On the principles for establishing the early Nestle text, see the discussion below.

[69] E.g., J. W. Burgon, *The Last Twelve Verses of the Gospel according to S. Mark* (Oxford: Parker, 1871); idem, *The Revision Revised* (London: John Murray, 1883); idem, *The Causes of the Corruption of the Traditional Text of the Holy Gospels* (ed. E. Miller; London: Bell, 1896); idem, *The Traditional Text of the Holy Gospels Vindicated and Established* (ed. E. Miller; London: Bell, 1896).

listed.[70] The differing viewpoints about pre-fourth-century text-types discussed earlier suggest that there might be correspondingly different opinions about the time frame assigned to the reconstructed text of
a critical edition such as the UBS/Nestle-Aland. On the one hand, 47
most of us who are convinced that at least two text-types existed in the second century would claim that such a critical text quite probably takes us back to that early period, though many of that persuasion might be reluctant to make claims about having reached the original text. On the other hand—surprisingly, I think—Kurt Aland, who does not acknowledge any pre-fourth-century text-types, nonetheless claims that the recent Nestle-Aland editions do represent the original text.[71] At first blush, would we not have expected a less absolutist view? The explanation, of course, lies in the Alands' use of their classifications (free, normal, strict, and paraphrastic texts) and their five categories of manuscripts, of which category I designates "manuscripts with a very high proportion of the early text . . ., presumably the original text,"[72] though, as noted earlier (see n. 60 above), a circular argument operates here.

Second, the discussion, refinement, and alteration of the arguments for priority of readings led to reassessment of numerous points in Westcott-Hort, especially by testing their use of both external evidence and internal evidence—though the two can never quite be separated.

On the one hand, testing the internal arguments employed by Westcott-Hort took various avenues, resulting in the questioning of

[70] I speak of the continuing role of text-types in establishing the text as something affirmed "pointedly" in the *Textual Commentary* because the Alands, who served on the UBS editorial committee, do not accept pre-fourth-century text-types; yet, the *Commentary* lists the traditional text types and their manuscript members, *including pre-fourth-century papyri*. Note that the Caesarean text is diminished in the *Textual Commentary* (second edition), 6*–7*, and is absent from the "Lists of Witnesses according to Type of Text," 15* (see n. 50 above).

[71] On Kurt Aland's equation of the Nestle-Aland text with the original, see note 57 above. Cf. Petzer, "History of the New Testament Text," 32–34, who notes: "Recently B. Aland has explicitly stated that the original text, i.e. the text reflected in the manuscript tradition, is something quite different from the autographs." Petzer refers to B. Aland's "Die Münsteraner Arbeit am Text des Neuen Testaments und ihr Beitrag für die frühe Überlieferung des 2. Jahrhunderts: Eine methodologische Betrachtung," *Gospel Traditions in the Second Century: Origins, Recensions, Text, and Transmission* (ed. W. L. Petersen; Christianity and Judaism in Antiquity, 3; Notre Dame, Ind.: University of Notre Dame Press, 1989) 68–69.

[72] Aland and Aland, *Text of the New Testament*, 335.

some, the addition of a couple, and the refinement of others (as considered earlier), leading, about halfway between the time of Westcott-Hort and our own time, to thoroughgoing eclecticism in distinction from reasoned eclecticism. On the other hand, Westcott-Hort's reliance on Codex B, along with ℵ, was tested (to use Elliott's emotionally charged but not incorrect phrase) to see whether their "cult of the
48 best manuscripts" was justified.[73] The resultant general conclusion was that a single or merely a few manuscripts should not—could not—be the basis for a critical edition. Nonetheless, and ironically, even those editors who embraced this latter principle still came up with a critical text of the New Testament that was similar in large measure to the Westcott-Hort edition, including the various editions by Eberhard Nestle and Erwin Nestle (beginning in 1898, with Erwin taking over from his father in 1927), the Nestle-Aland editions (from 1956 with the twenty-second ed.), the UBS text (beginning in 1966 with the first edition), and finally the unified text adopted in 1975 for UBS^{3} (1975) and Nestle-Aland^{26} (1979) and their successors (UBS^{4} and Nestle-Aland^{27}, issued in 1993). That these various post-Westcott-Hort texts remain close in textual character to Westcott-Hort is demonstrated by the Alands themselves, who report that, while Nestle-Aland^{25} shows, e.g., 2,047 differences from von Soden, 1,996 from Vogels, 1,161 from Bover, and 770 from Merk, it contains only 558 differences from Westcott-Hort.[74] This "relatively close relationship between Nestle and Westcott-Hort"[75] may appear to be an almost inevitable result of the methods employed by Eberhard Nestle for his editions, namely, comparing the texts of Tischendorf and Westcott-

[73] See Elliott, "Rational Criticism and the Text of the New Testament," *Theology* 75 (1972) 339–40; idem, "Can We Recover the Original Text," *Theology* 77 (1974) 345; idem, *Essays and Studies*, 27, among many examples. One may compare a statement of A. E. Housman: "Providence played the editors of Ovid a cruel trick; it put into their hands a 'best MS,' and this was giving gunpowder to a child." The reviewer quoting this adds, ". . . but Housman admits . . . that some MSS are better than others" (in Georg Luck, "Textual Criticism Today," *AJP* 102 [1981] 169). Luck also cites the *Encyclopaedia Britanica* article on Housman: "He led the attack on superstitious fidelity to the 'best manuscript' and 'paleographical probability'" (167). Can Housman be invoked on the former point and not also the latter?

[74] Aland and Aland, *Text of the New Testament*, 26–30. Other comparisons showing similar results are reported in my "Twentieth Century Interlude," 387–90 (repr. in Epp and Fee, *Studies*, 84–86). Incidentally, the Alands make a further claim (24), that the Nestle-Aland^{27} "comes closer to the original text of the New Testament than did Tischendorf or Westcott and Hort, not to mention von Soden."

[75] Aland and Aland, *Text of the New Testament*, 26.

Hort, consulting a third edition when the two disagreed, and then printing as his text the reading of two agreeing editions, with the reading of the third put into the apparatus. Beginning in 1901 Nestle used Bernhard Weiss's edition for the third, which tended to rely 49
on Codex Vaticanus (as did Westcott-Hort).[76] This purely mechanical procedure was maintained when Erwin Nestle became editor; his more distinctive contribution was the substantial expansion of the apparatus, albeit by drawing the readings from published editions rather than from manuscripts—and he did so with an extremely high degree of accuracy.[77] After Kurt Aland succeeded to the editorship of Nestle-Aland, readings increasingly were verified from primary sources—the manuscripts themselves.

It may surprise many to learn that, over a period of eighty years, these Nestle and Nestle-Aland texts (through the twenty-fifth edition) "remained the same (apart from a few minor changes adopted by Erwin Nestle—no more than a dozen at most),"[78] and therefore also maintained their same closeness to Westcott-Hort. Yet, as noted above, Nestle-Aland^{26} and now Nestle-Aland^{27} (with the UBS equivalent texts) still remained closer to Westcott-Hort than to other editions, in spite of the striking fact that in the deliberations over UBS^{2} (1968) "the editorial committee (or more precisely its majority) decided to abandon the theories of Westcott-Hort and the 'Western non-interpolations.'"[79] Moreover, we are informed by the preface of UBS^{3} (1975) that "more than five hundred changes" were made over against the second edition,[80] and still the closeness to Westcott-Hort remained.

Is there a reasonable explanation for this anomaly? One possible answer may be worthy of suggestion—though no proof is possible—namely, that our modern solidarity in supporting an almost universally adopted critical text may represent a kind of unintentioned and almost unconscious consensus in what we, during the last century and now, are able to reconstruct as our earliest and preferable text of the New Testament. It is almost as if a generally Westcott-Hort kind of text is a "default position," a dormant text that rises to the

[76] Ibid.

[77] Ibid., 20–22.

[78] Ibid., 26.

[79] Ibid., 33. The editorial committees for the Nestle-Aland^{26} and UBS^{3}, and for the Nestle-Aland^{27} and UBS^{4} were each composed of the same scholars.

[80] UBS^{3} viii; also quoted in Aland and Aland, *Text of the New Testament*, 33.

surface time and again no matter what textual scholars do. The late
50 classical textual critic at Johns Hopkins University, Georg Luck, said a couple decades ago that "our critical texts are no better than our textual critics."[81] Earlier I had taken this statement as an indictment of the discipline, but I now prefer to interpret it as a compliment to us in the field of New Testament—because we are doing the very best we can given our complex situation, even though the result is a compromise. That recognition, however, is neither to invalidate my career-long appeal for refining our arguments for the priority of readings and for clarifying our history of the text, nor is it to renounce an urgent plea that refined methods be utilized in the improvement of our critical editions—whatever that might mean. The Alands in their 1989 manual assert that "any further development of the text must begin with Nestle-Aland[26]. It remains to be seen what the next developments will be." I can readily accept this statement, but we cannot, I think, accede to what follows: "Rash decisions should always be avoided. Many will undoubtedly feel strongly inclined to improve it [the Nestle-Aland text] here and there. This temptation should be resisted. . . ."[82]

Certainly part of the reason for this reluctance to change the current text is that recently the Münster Institute for New Testament Textual Research, founded by Kurt Aland and now under the competent leadership of Barbara Aland, has published the first fascicles of its long awaited *Editio critica maior*—a new critical text and extensive apparatus that has received critical acclaim for its clear presentation and meticulous care.[83] Although this first installment of text,

---

[81] Luck, "Textual Criticism Today," 166.

[82] Aland and Aland, *Text of the New Testament*, 35–36. Nestle-Aland[27] has the same text as Nestle-Aland[26], though the apparatus is different. The introduction to Nestle-Aland[26] carries a similar statement, though not with the same thrust: "It should naturally be understood that this text is a working text (in the sense of the century-long Nestle tradition): it is not to be considered as definitive, but as a stimulus to further efforts toward defining and verifying the text of the New Testament. For many reasons, however, the present edition has not been deemed an appropriate occasion for introducing textual changes" (45*). By contrast, the preface to UBS[4] (vi) invites readers to submit proposals and suggestions.

[83] The Institute for New Testament Textual Research (ed.), *Novum Testamentum Graecum, Editio Critica Maior: IV, Catholic Epistles, Installment 1: James* (ed. B. Aland, †K. Aland, G. Mink, and K. Wachtel; 2 parts; Stuttgart: Deutsche Bibelgesellschaft, 1997), which contains two changes from the text of Nestle-Aland[27]/UBS[4]. Vol. IV.2: *Catholic Epistles: The Letters of Peter*, appeared in 2000 [and IV.3: *The First Letter of John* in 2003].

containing James, diverges from the Nestle-Aland[27]/UBS[4] text twice,
there is an understandable interest in retaining a measure of stabil- 51
ity in our commonly used text. At the same time, however, scholars cannot—and will not—be deterred in their calling, and textual critics may be fully expected to continue publishing their proposals for revisions of readings in the Nestle-Aland/UBS text.

Also rather recently, the so-called International Greek New Testament Project has published the papyri of the Gospel of John and continues to work on a full apparatus of that Gospel.[84] A recent and fortunate breakthrough has brought about close cooperation between the Münster Institute and the International Greek New Testament Project after a half-century as separate projects,[85] and the future is much brighter because of these efforts—though achievements in creating critical editions and apparatuses are slow even in the best of circumstances.

So, we ask, finally, whether our current critical text of the Greek New Testament—and there is really only one—reflects a reasonable approximation to the text (or, better, a text) extant in very early Christianity? Unfortunately, we hear two or three answers, which sound quite different: "Yes, we have the original text," and "No, but we have the earliest attainable text." What is anomalous and yet fortunate is that both of these viewpoints, by compromise, can embrace the same general text and continue their labors for progressive improvement as we continue our work in the twenty-first century. A third answer may be, "No, but we have the internal criteria to create it out of the commonly used text"—again a text that appears to be accepted, by compromise, as a working basis. In all of this, however, I still have a lingering question: In view of the numerous, rich discoveries since Westcott-Hort, shouldn't we have been able to produce something better and perhaps very different? The response appears to be the proverbial saying, "The more

The Münster Institut für Neutestamentliche Textforschung was founded by Kurt Aland (1915–1994) in 1959 and directed by him until his retirement; Barbara Aland became director in 1983 and served in that position until her retirement in 2002.

[84] The American and British Committees of the International Greek New Testament Project, *The New Testament in Greek IV: The Gospel according to St. John, Volume One: The Papyri* (ed. W. J. Elliott and D. C. Parker; NTTS 20; Leiden: Brill, 1995).

[85] E. J. Epp, "The International Greek New Testament Project: Motivation and History," *NovT* 39 (1997) 1–20.

things change, the more they stay the same"—but that is no answer after all.

52 IV. Choosing to Address Context—and Deciding on Influence: The Issue of Manuscripts and Variant Readings in Their Church-Historical, Cultural, and Intellectual Contexts

New Testament textual criticism is far broader and richer than mere arguments for priority of readings, proposals about text types, and the construction of critical texts and apparatuses. The contexts in which manuscripts and variant readings are found and used, as well as the contexts in which we choose to examine them, illumine for us the history and thought of the church, both in the early period and later. In approaching these contexts, it is relevant to note that each of the issues treated earlier has a lengthy history: critical editions reach back to the early sixteenth century, and canons of criticism and text-types to the early eighteenth century, though all three received major attention in the twentieth century. Much less attention, however, was afforded the present issue in the late nineteenth and early twentieth centuries—the influence of the church and its theology on the manuscripts and variants of the New Testament text, and the reverse, the influence of the text on the church. In addition, we extend this issue to include the cultural and intellectual context of our New Testament manuscripts.

A. *Textual Criticism and Early Church History*

With a few notable exceptions, the relationship of textual criticism and the theology of the church was much neglected in the second half of the twentieth century—until very recently. Already in 1904, however, Kirsopp Lake was urging textual critics to examine variants as a window on exegesis in the church: "We need to know," he said, "what the early Church thought [a passage] meant and how it altered its wording in order to emphasize its meaning."[86] Two decades earlier Hort had alerted textual critics to the issue, though

[86] Kirsopp Lake, *The Influence of Textual Criticism on the Exegesis of the New Testament* (An Inaugural Lecture Delivered before the University of Leiden, on January 27, 1904; Oxford: Parker, 1904) 12.

in a negative fashion, by his frequently-quoted statement of 1882
that in the New Testament "there are no signs of deliberate falsification
of the text for dogmatic purposes."[87] In his continuing discussion, he 53
allows one exception, the "wilful tampering with the text" by Marcion, the first declared heretic in the church. Curiously, Hort's view was first "refuted" by Dean Burgon and Edward Miller by their accusations of intentional corruption in the old uncial manuscripts—part of their defense of the *textus receptus*.[88] Other scholars, more enlightened in their criticism of Hort, pointed to anti-Jewish intrusions into the text or suggested textual variants showing the influence of additional heretics, such as Montanus, particularly in the D-text.[89] J. Rendel Harris argued the latter and, more generally along the lines of Lake, urged that the history of the text be read side by side with second-century church history and in view of various parties in it.[90] Indeed, in 1914, Harris, recalling the famous dictum of Hort that "knowledge of documents should precede final judgment upon readings,"[91] sharpened the issue succinctly by adding that "knowledge . . . of Church History should precede final judgment as to readings."[92] By 1926, however, James Hardy Ropes, who edited the D-text of Acts, drew a conclusion clear to him: "Of any special point of view, theological or other, on the part of the 'Western' reviser it is difficult to find any trace."[93] Actually, it was this sentence in Ropes that provided the challenge for my 1966 investigation of anti-Judaic tendencies in the D-text of Acts, which attempted on a large scale to place the variant readings of that early textual tradition in an ideological/theological context.[94] Previously, little had been done to identify theologically motivated textual variants in a systematic fashion

[87] Westcott and Hort, *New Testament in the Original Greek*, 2.282–83; cf. "Notes on Select Readings," 64–69 in the same volume.

[88] See n. 69, above.

[89] Summary in E. J. Epp, *The Theological Tendency of Codex Bezae Cantabrigiensis in Acts* (SNTSMS 3; Cambridge: Cambridge University Press, 1966) 2–4; 15.

[90] J. R. Harris, untitled introduction in *Bulletin of the Bezan Club* 6 (1929) 2; idem, "New Points of View in Textual Criticism," *Expositor* VIII:7 (1914) 322.

[91] Westcott and Hort, *New Testament in the Original Greek*, 2.31.

[92] Harris, "New Points of View," 322.

[93] J. H. Ropes, *The Text of Acts* (vol. 3 of *The Beginnings of Christianity, Part I: The Acts of the Apostles*; 5 vols.; ed. F. J. Foakes Jackson and K. Lake; London: Macmillan, 1926) ccxxxiii.

[94] See Epp, *Theological Tendency of Codex Bezae*. [See now "Anti-Judaic Tendencies in the D-Text of Acts: Forty Years of Conversation," in *The Book of Acts as Church History: Text, Textual Traditions and Ancient Interpretations/Apostelgeschichte als Kirchengeschichte:*

54 throughout a text-type in a lengthy New Testament book, and the Book of Acts was an eminently appropriate place to attempt it because of its dual-stream textual tradition. I found that challenge heightened by a view of New Testament textual criticism that emerged from the University of Chicago in the years just before and after World War II, a view that is well summarized by a single paragraph from Donald W. Riddle:

> The legitimate task of textual criticism is not limited to the recovery of approximately the original form of the documents, to the establishment of the "best" text, nor to the "elimination of spurious readings." It must be recognized that every significant variant records a religious experience which brought it into being. This means that there are no "spurious readings": the various forms of the text are sources for the study of the history of Christianity.[95]

Later, his colleague, Merrill M. Parvis, picked up on the words, "spurious readings":

> All are part of the tradition; all contribute to our knowledge of the history of Christian thought. And they are significant contributions because they are interpretations which were highly enough thought of in some place and at some time to be incorporated into the Scripture itself.[96]

In the same year, Ernest C. Colwell, soon to be recognized as a brilliant text-critical methodologist, wrote, "Most variations, I believe, were made deliberately" and "The majority of the variant readings in the New Testament were created for theological or dogmatic reasons." In the same context, Colwell added: "It was because they [the books of the New Testament] were the religious treasure of the church that they were changed" and:

> The paradox is that the variations came into existence because they
> were religious books, sacred books, canonical books. The devout scribe
> 55 felt compelled to correct misstatements which he found in the manu-
> scripts he was copying.[97]

Text, Texttraditionen und antike Auslegungen (ed. T. Nicklas and M. Tilly; BZNW 120; Berlin: de Gruyter, 2003) 111–46.]

[95] D. W. Riddle, "Textual Criticism as a Historical Discipline," *AThR* 18 (1936) 221.

[96] M. M. Parvis, "The Nature and Tasks of New Testament Textual Criticism: An Appraisal," *JR* 32 (1952) 172.

[97] E. C. Colwell, *What Is the Best New Testament?* (Chicago: University of Chicago

(Of course, neither Colwell nor his colleagues were speaking of obvious scribal errors.)

In 1966 I described this Chicago view as "Present-Day Textual Criticism,"[98] but, as I wrote elsewhere recently,[99] I was overly optimistic by a quarter of a century and more, for only the recent works of Bart Ehrman and David Parker have brought that general approach into currency.

Ehrman, in his *Orthodox Corruption of Scripture*, for example, demonstrated more than adequately that numerous textual variations were fostered by those supporting orthodox theological views (in surprising contrast to the view at the turn of the last century that only heretics could be accused of such behavior).[100] Though it is trite to say it, obviously not all of Ehrman's examples are persuasive, but clearly he has made his point that, in various ways in the second and third centuries, proto-orthodox scribes (as he calls them) "modified their texts of scripture in light of the polemical contexts within which they worked, altering the manuscripts they reproduced to make them more orthodox on the one hand and less susceptible to heretics on the other."[101] To what church-historical context does he refer? He points to the christological controversies in the first centuries of Christianity and specifically to three groups that resisted the emerging orthodoxy: adoptionists, docetists, and separationists.

Ehrman enlightens us further about scribal mentality in such a 56
setting. As scribes introduced intentional changes into the writings that were to become the New Testament, they would "make them *say* what they were already known to *mean*,"[102] thus "corrupting" their

---

Press, 1952) 52–53. He also states: "The importance of the Book in their religious life led them to 'correct' the mistakes. Unfortunately, they thought they knew more than they actually did, and thus, with the best intentions in the world, they corrupted the text of the New Testament" (53). Cf. this with the view of Ehrman, discussed below.

[98] Epp, *Theological Tendency of Codex Bezae*, 12–21.

[99] E. J. Epp, "The Multivalence of the Term 'Original Text' in New Testament Textual Criticism," *HTR* 92 (1999) 271–72.

[100] B. D. Ehrman, *The Orthodox Corruption of Scripture: The Effect of Early Christological Controversies on the Text of the New Testament* (New York: Oxford University Press, 1993); cf. his "The Text as Window: New Testament Manuscripts and the Social History of Early Christianity," *The Text of the New Testament in Contemporary Research: Essays on the* Status Quaestionis (ed. B. D. Ehrman and M. W. Holmes; SD 46; Grand Rapids, MI: Eerdmans, 1995) 361–79.

[101] Ehrman, *Orthodox Corruption of Scripture*, 15; cf. 275.

[102] Ibid., xii (emphasis in original).

texts for theological reasons in support of the emerging main-stream theology of the time, that is, orthodoxy (which accounts for the title of his book). Clearly scribes such as these acted with noble motivation and were compelled by conviction. Ehrman's own summary at the very end of his book describes his view concisely:

> Understanding a text . . . involves putting it "in other words." Anyone who explains a text "in other words," however, has altered the words.
>
> This is exactly what the scribes did: they occasionally altered the words of the text by putting them "in other words." To this extent, they were textual interpreters. At the same time, by *physically* altering the words, they did something quite different from other exegetes, and this difference is by no means to be minimized. Whereas all readers change a text when they construe it in their minds, the scribes actually changed the text on the page. As a result, they created a new text . . . over which future interpreters would dispute, no longer having access to the words of the original text, the words produced by the author.[103]

In a subsequent article, Ehrman has directed his analysis to textual variants that reveal broader sociocultural issues in the early church, such as Jewish-Christian relations, attitudes toward women, and even the use of New Testament manuscripts to foretell the future.[104] So, Ehrman, in several ways, spells out in detail what Kirsopp Lake sought from textual critics nearly ninety years ago: to know what the early church thought a passage meant and how it altered its wording to emphasize its meaning, and also what Rendel Harris recommended, namely, reading textual criticism side by side with church history. As William Petersen put it, Ehrman's book "demonstrates
57 once again that the most reliable guide to the development of Christian theology is the ever-changing text of the New Testament."[105] By way of summary, textual variants that disclose theological thought, doctrinal controversy, and other sociocultural attitudes and practices become a window[106] that enlarges our vista on early Christianity, enriching, confirming, and correcting our conception of that crucial period of church history.

---

[103] Ibid., 280 (emphasis in original).

[104] Ehrman, "The Text as Window." Note the references to recent work by others in these and additional areas.

[105] W. L. Petersen, review of B. D. Ehrman's *Orthodox Corruption of Scripture*, *JR* 74 (1994) 563–64.

[106] Reflecting his title "The Text as Window"; see n. 100, above.

Four years after Ehrman's work, a disarmingly small volume appeared, *The Living Text of the Gospels* by David Parker.[107] His views arose primarily from consideration of important cases in the manuscript tradition where the readings in a variation-unit are multiple and do not yield an easily-determined original reading, or any plausible original at all. Confronted with numerous such bundles of textual variants, Parker describes the text of the four gospels as one that from the beginning grew freely,[108] for "sayings and stories continued to be developed by copyists and readers."[109] He reaffirms what textual critics generally hold, that the most dramatic changes in the text occurred in the first 150 years, leading him to describe the Gospel text "as a free, or perhaps, as a living, text,"[110] which accounts for the title of his book. The Gospels are "not archives of traditions but living texts,"[111] and, therefore, he says bluntly, "The concept of a Gospel that is fixed in shape, authoritative, and final as a piece of literature has to be abandoned."[112] When we ask what church-historical context Parker is invoking here, it is this: "The [free] text indicates that to at least some early Christians, it was more important to hand on the spirit of Jesus' teaching than to remember the letter: . . . The material about Jesus was preserved in an interpretive rather than an exact fashion."[113]

I can refer only to one of Parker's extended examples, with brief 58
reference to one or two others. When Parker, an accomplished textual critic, surveys the array of variant readings that accompany the Gospel sayings on marriage and divorce, he is compelled to conclude that, in this case, "the recovery of a single original saying of Jesus is impossible"; rather, "what we have here is a collection of interpretive rewritings of a tradition":[114] "The early church rewrote the sayings in their attempt to make sense of them."[115] So, when Parker says that "the Gospel texts exist only as a manuscript tradi-

[107] David C. Parker, *The Living Text of the Gospels* (Cambridge: Cambridge University Press, 1997).
[108] Ibid., 203.
[109] Ibid., 45–46.
[110] Ibid., 200.
[111] Ibid., 119.
[112] Ibid., 93.
[113] David C. Parker, "Scripture is Tradition," *Theology* 94 (1991) 15.
[114] Parker, *The Living Text of the Gospels*, 92–93.
[115] Ibid., 183.

tion"[116] and not in an early, fixed form, he meant that to apply both to the past and to the present, allowing the richness of the manuscripts, with all of their variants and with the interpretations and insights that they offer, to illuminate not only the culture of the early church but of today as well. In other words, the full manuscript tradition in a given variation unit provides us today vastly more than if we were limited to a single original reading or text. Yet, this does not mean that all variants on divorce, for example, now have the authority traditionally ascribed only to one of those readings. "The tradition is manifold. . . . There is no authoritative text beyond the manuscripts which we may follow without further thought"; hence, says Parker, "The people of God have to make up their own minds. There is no authoritative text to provide a short-cut."[117]

This is the intriguing new direction in which Parker pulls New Testament textual criticism—making a virtue out of complex and often insoluble text-critical cruxes by showing, first, how they cast light on both routine and controversial issues in the early church and, second, how they still have practical relevance for the church today. Some surely will see his view as a negative move, but I join Parker in claiming the positive side. He remarks that "the church came into being . . . as the community of the Spirit," but the tradition of this community is manifold, including both oral and written
59 forms. Yet, that tradition has come down to us only in manuscripts with multiple texts and readings:

> Rather than looking for right and wrong readings, and with them for right or wrong beliefs and practices, the way is open for the possibility that the church is the community of the Spirit even in its multiplicities of texts. . . . Indeed, we may suggest that it is not in spite of the variety but because of them that the church is that community.[118]

Hence, as Parker views it, we actually find ourselves in a favorable situation: "Who before in the history of theological thought has had access to the text of dozens of early manuscripts? More than at any other time, we are able to see how the tradition developed"[119]—that is, the multiple variants permit us to be part of the discussions and

[116] Ibid., 203.
[117] Ibid., 212.
[118] Ibid.
[119] Ibid., 93.

controversies—indeed, the very life—of the early church as they agonized over certain difficult issues, allowing us to understand, for example, that there was not only one interpretation, prescription, or practice of marriage and divorce, nor was there a unitary view of other crucial matters. From this, Parker draws a far-reaching conclusion about the task of textual criticism, which, he says, has "long accepted the role that has been demanded of it as provider of authoritative text."[120] While the discipline need not give up its more traditional goals,[121] this new perspective broadens and enriches the tasks of textual criticism by showing how variants both were influenced by situations in the church and, in turn, influenced church thought and practice—and (a major point for Parker) they retain the power to do so today. In the marriage/divorce case, for example, "we find that the saying(s) of Jesus on this subject had, as we might say, a life of their own,"[122] and this rich multitextual tradition is still available for our instruction. Lest it be thought that such a view had no precedent, notice that Origen (died 254) was "able to make both
readings [in Hebrews 2:9] yield edifying truths" and, in another 60
instance (Matthew 18:1), after mentioning two variant readings "it makes no difference which reading is original, and he expresses no opinion on the matter."[123]

When Parker examines another case where myriad variant readings occur, the (so-called) Lord's prayer, he finds (as textual critics well know) six main forms in the tangled manuscript tradition:

> All six forms contribute to our understanding. Once we have discovered their existence, they will be part of the way in which we read and interpret the Lord's Prayer. We shall not be able to erase them from our minds, and to read a single original text as though the others had never existed.[124]

Again, the church has been in the past and continues to be instructed by all meaningful multiple variants since they disclose how the early church dealt with or thought about theological or ethical issues and

---

[120] Ibid., 94.

[121] See Parker's views on seeking the original text (ibid., 132–37; 211; also 182, 209), but see the discussion below on goals and directions in relation to meanings and approaches.

[122] Ibid., 94.

[123] For details, see Metzger, "Practice of Textual Criticism among the Church Fathers," 342–43.

[124] Parker, *The Living Text of the Gospels*, 102.

about worship. Indeed, permit me to add a paradoxical statement of my own: *the greater the ambiguity in the variant readings in a given variation unit, the more clearly we are able to grasp the concerns of the early church.* If that is a fair paraphrase of Parker's viewpoint (and I think it is), we have fascinating, profound, and enlarged parameters for text-critical studies in the present century.

Parker later treats the last three chapters of Luke as a whole and finds that variants in some forty of the last 167 verses in that gospel provide, as he says, "incontrovertible evidence that the text of these chapters was not fixed, and indeed continued to grow for centuries after its composition,"[125] including "a significant number of passages which were added to the Gospel in order to emphasize its orthodoxy."[126] "We might say," he concludes (in a memorable statement), "that Luke is not, in these early centuries, a closed book. It is open, and successive generations write on its pages."[127]

61 We see now how Parker's analysis and his bold statements and Ehrman's creative position reconnect us with the views of Lake, Harris, and the Chicago school, and—it should be noted—meet the complaint of the Alands that "New Testament textual criticism has traditionally neglected the findings of early Church history, but only to its own injury."[128] Now we have new possibilities in this important arena, with the goals of textual criticism properly expanded as well.

B. *New Testament Manuscripts in Their Cultural, Intellectual Context*

A very different approach to context in New Testament textual criticism involves placing manuscripts in their contemporary setting. Regrettably, this is a subject in which there are many questions and few answers; any answers, however, that can be found will assist in the writing of the history of the New Testament text. Hence, the effort is well worthwhile. The most obviously relevant area is the provenance of manuscripts, which, in its simplest form, provides known places of origin of individual manuscripts that can be used to explain and illumine the distinctive or characteristic readings of

[125] Ibid., 172.
[126] Ibid., 183.
[127] Ibid., 174.
[128] Aland and Aland, *Text of the New Testament*, 49; cf. 52.

each manuscript and, more broadly, to place each manuscript within the history of the text. Thus, a manuscript from Egypt or Caesarea or Constantinople may be expected to reflect its context—its brand of Christianity in its period. Of course, the difficulties and complexities are great: for instance, a manuscript from a known locality may reflect, rather, the context of its exemplar, whose provenance is unknown, or a manuscript may have been found in one locality, such as Egypt, but may have been written elsewhere and brought to Egypt.

The greatest obstacle, however, is that the provenance of most of our important New Testament manuscripts is debated or simply unknown, undoubtedly depriving us of much useful information.[129]
For example, among the notable fourth- and fifth-century parchment 62
codices, it has long been suggested that the two most famous ones, Vaticanus (B) and Sinaiticus (א) were among the fifty parchment manuscripts that Eusebius says were ordered by Constantine (around 331) for new churches in Constantinople;[130] others, however, think Vaticanus could have originated in Egypt (Lake), or specifically Alexandria (Birdsall), or Caesarea (Milne and Skeat).[131] As for Codex Alexandrinus (A), its origin is usually assumed to have been Alexandria, but it might have come from Constantinople, Caesarea, or Beirut.[132] David Parker, in his meticulous monograph on Codex Bezae (D), dismisses nine (!) proposals for its place of origin and opts for Beirut, though more recently Allen Callahan argues, once again, for an Egyptian origin.[133] And, H. A. Sanders furnishes evidence that Codex

[129] For a summary, see E. J. Epp, "The New Testament Papyri at Oxyrhynchus in Their Social and Intellectual Context," in *Sayings of Jesus: Canonical and Non-Canonical: Essays in Honour of Tjitze Baarda* (ed. W. L. Petersen, J. S. Vos, and H. J. de Jonge; NovTSup 89; Leiden: Brill, 1997) 50–51.

[130] Based on Eusebius's reference (*Life of Constantine*, 4.36) to "volumes of three-fold and fourfold forms," a tenuous but perhaps plausible way of describing the three- and four-column formats, respectively, of these two grand codices; see Metzger, *Text of the New Testament*, 7–8.

[131] See now T. C. Skeat, "The Codex Sinaiticus, the Codex Vaticanus and Constantine," *JTS* 50 (1999) 583–625, esp. 598–604; see also J. N. Birdsall, "The New Testament Text," in *The Cambridge History of the Bible, Volume 1: From the Beginnings to Jerome* (ed. P. R. Ackroyd and C. F. Evans; Cambridge: Cambridge University Press, 1970) 359–60; Metzger, *Text of the New Testament*, 7–8.

[132] Streeter, *The Four Gospels*, 120 n. 1.

[133] D. C. Parker, *Codex Bezae: An Early Christian Manuscript and Its Text* (Cambridge: Cambridge University Press, 1992), 261–78. A. D. Callahan ("Again: The Origin of Codex Bezae," in *Codex Bezae: Studies from the Lunel Colloquium June 1994* [ed. D. C.

Washingtonianus (W) was found near a ruined Monastery near Gizeh.[134] Yet, virtually all of these designations fall short of demonstration.

When we ask about the New Testament papyri, the Chester Beatty manuscripts (P45, P46, P47), at the time of their purchase about
63 1930, were reported to have been discovered near Atfih (Aphroditopolis) in the Fayûm,[135] while P52, usually considered the earliest New Testament manuscript, was assumed to have come from the Fayum or Oxyrhynchus.[136] Again, certainty of provenance is elusive. More recently James M. Robinson identifies the Bodmer Papyri with the Dishna Papers, discovered near Dishnā in Upper Egypt, east of Nag Hammadi; the collection included P66, P72, and P75 (though not P74), which were part of the nearby Pachomian monastic library until they were buried in a large earthen jar, probably in the seventh century. Robinson concludes, however, that these three early New Testament papyri, which antedate the founding of that monastic Order (in the early fourth century), came from elsewhere.[137] Thus, the ultimate origin of P66, P72, and P75 still eludes us.

We have more precise information on about two dozen other papyri: P4 (third century) containing Luke was found *in situ* in Coptos (= Qift, about 250 miles up the Nile from Oxyrhynchus) in a jar walled up in a house; the papyrus had been utilized in the binding of a (presumably Christian) codex of Philo, though the house showed no evident connection to a church. P92 (third/fourth century) turned

Parker and C.-B. Amphoux; NTTS 22; Leiden: Brill, 1996] 56–64) proposes as the scribe of Codex Bezae a native Egyptian whose mother tongue was Subachmimic Coptic and who "neither spoke nor wrote either Greek or Latin with scholarly proficiency" (63–64).

[134] H. A. Sanders, *The New Testament Manuscripts in the Freer Collection: Part I: The Washington Manuscript of the Four Gospels* (University of Michigan Studies: Humanistic Series, 9; New York: Macmillan, 1912) 1–4. He refers to the Monastery of the Vinedresser.

[135] C. H. Roberts, *Manuscript, Society and Belief in Early Christian Egypt* (Schweich Lectures, 1977; London: Oxford University Press for the British Academy, 1979) 7.

[136] C. H. Roberts, *An Unpublished Fragment of the Fourth Gospel in the John Rylands Library* (Manchester: Manchester University Press, 1935) 24–25; H. I. Bell and T. C. Skeat, *Fragments of an Unknown Gospel and Other Early Christian Papyri* (London: British Museum, 1935) 7.

[137] J. M. Robinson, *The Pachomian Monastic Library at the Chester Beatty Library and the Bibliothèque Bodmer* (Occasional Papers, 19; Claremont, CA: Institute for Antiquity and Christianity, 1990), esp. 4–6; 22–26. A shorter version appeared as "The First Christian Monastic Library," in *Coptic Studies: Acts of the Third International Congress of Coptic Studies, Warsaw, 20–25 August, 1984* (ed. W. Godlewski; Centre d'archéololo-gie méditerranéenne de l'Académie Polonaise des Sciences; Warsaw: Éditions scientifiques de Pologne, 1990) 371–78.

up at Madînat Mâdî (modern Narmouthis, in the Fayum) in a rubble-filled structure near a race course. P40 (third century) was discovered at Qarara in Middle Egypt, only about ten miles down the Nile from Oxyrhynchus, while P43 (sixth/seventh century) turned up in a sixth/seventh century monastic settlement at Wadi Sarga (fifteen
miles south of Asyut). Nine other papyri were found at various sites 64
in the Fayum (P3, P12, P33+P58, P34, P53, P55, P56, P57, P79) and one at Thebes (P44). Outside Egypt, several were discovered in the Negeb (P59, P60, and P61 at 'Auja-el-Hafir [ancient Nessana] in a collapsed room annexed to a small church, and P11, P14, and P68 at Sinai), and two more at Khirbet Mird in a ruined Christian monastery on the site of the earlier fortress, Hyrcania, near the Dead Sea in Judaea (P83, P84).[138]

All such information is to be valued, though it is not yet clear exactly how this sort of discrete information might assist us. About all we can say at this juncture is that something is known of the provenance of these thirty-five New Testament papyri but almost nothing of some thirty-six others. There remains, however, one large group of manuscripts whose provenance is certain, or at least their place of use and discovery is indisputable (thus allowing for the possibility that some among them may have originated elsewhere). That group consists of the papyri (and majuscule fragments) discovered in the rubbish heaps and deserted houses at Oxyrhynchus in Egypt, some two hundred miles up the Nile from Alexandria. At this site, to date, forty-seven (or 42%) of our 112 different New Testament papyri were discovered (116 is the numbered total to date),[139] and collectively they contain portions of fifteen New Testament books. More striking is the fact that among the sixty-one earliest New Testament manuscripts (those dating up to and around the turn of

[138] On P4, see Roberts, *Manuscript, Society and Belief*, 8, 13; on P92, see Claudio Gallazzi, "Frammenti di un codice con le Epistole di Paoli," *ZPE* 46 (1982) 117; on P43, see W. E. Crum and H. I. Bell (eds.), *Wadi Sarga: Coptic and Greek Texts from the Excavations undertaken by the Byzantine Research Account* (Hauniae: Gyldenalske Boghandel, 1922) 43–45; cf. 29–45; on P59, P60, P61, see Jack Finegan, *Encountering New Testament Manuscripts* (Grand Rapids, MI: Eerdmans, 1974) 94–100. For the place of discovery—whenever known—of New Testament papyri through P88, see K. Aland, *Repertorium der griechischen christlichen Papyri, I: Biblische Papyri* (PTS 18; Berlin: de Gruyter, 1976) 215–322.

[139] For P116 (sixth or seventh century), containing portions of Hebrews 2:9–11 and 3:3–6, see A. Papathomas, "A new Testimony to the Letter of Hebrews," *Journal of Greco-Roman Christianity and Judaism* 1 (2000) 18–24.

the third/fourth centuries), thirty-five (or 57%) come from Oxyrhynchus.

65 Such data thrust these forty-seven Oxyrhynchus papyri of known provenance into a unique position, offering an unparalleled opportunity for New Testament textual criticism to assess a large number of copies of Christianity's earliest writings within the literary and intellectual environment of a single location. Many thousands of other papyrus documents have been recovered from the same site, including business and official documents, private letters, and literary works, of which more than 4,600 have been published to date in the sixty-seven volumes of *The Oxyrhynchus Papyri*,[140] as well as hundreds elsewhere. These papyri furnish for us the immediate and larger context for the New Testament manuscripts from Oxyrhynchus, for they range across the entire gamut of life and livelihood in Oxyrhynchus, covering education and learning; commerce, agriculture, and transportation; legal transactions and proceedings; politics, government, and the military; cultural, religious, and social life; work and leisure, as well as everyday events such as marriage and divorce, child rearing, family joys and sorrows, health and sickness, and natural disasters. I cannot review here either this wealth of material or my own research on it, though I would like to present five private letters from everyday life in Oxyrhynchus and then offer a brief description of the city.

In the third century, a boy away at school writes his father at Oxyrhynchus:

> Now do not be uneasy, father, about my studies; I am working hard and taking relaxation; I shall do well. (Third century C.E.; P.Oxy X.1296; Loeb Classical Library, *Select Papyri*. 1.137)

About the same time, another son throws a tantrum in a letter to his father, but changes his tone near the end of the letter:

> Theon to . . . his father, greeting. You did a fine thing; you didn't take me with you to the city. If you do not wish to take me with you to Alexandria, I'll not write you a letter or talk to you or wish you good health. What's more, if you do go to Alexandria, I won't shake your hand or greet you again. So if you do not wish to take me with you, that's that! . . . But you did a fine thing; you sent me presents, big ones,
> 66 [bean] pods! . . . But send for me, I beg you. If you do not send, I

[140] *The Oxyrhynchus Papyri* (67 vols. to date; Graeco-Roman Memoirs; London: Egypt Exploration Society for the British Academy, 1898–2001).

> won't eat, won't drink! There! I pray for your good health. (Second or third century C.E.; P.Oxy I.119)[141]

Just about the time of Jesus' birth, a husband writes this disturbing letter to his wife:

> Know that I am still in Alexandria. . . . I ask and beg you to take good care of our baby son, and as soon as I receive payment I will send it up to you. If you are delivered of child [before I get home], if it is a boy keep it, if a girl discard [expose] it. You have sent me word, "Don't forget me." How can I forget you? I beg you not to worry. (17 June 1 B.C.E.; P.Oxy IV.744)[142]

A man in some unknown distress in the fourth century sends this impassioned plea for help, which is surprisingly philosophical:

> Hermias to his sister, greeting. What remains to write to you about I do not know, for I have told you of everything till I am tired, and yet you pay no attention. When a man finds himself in adversity he ought to give way and not fight stubbornly against fate. We fail to realize the inferiority and wretchedness to which we are born. Well, so far nothing at all has been done; make it your business to send some one to me . . . to stay with me until I know the position of my affairs. Am I to be . . . oppressed until Heaven takes pity on me? . . . See that matters are properly conducted on your own part or our disasters will be complete. We are resolved not to continue in misfortune. Farewell; I wish you all prosperity.

On the reverse side, he pleads again:

> Whatever you do, do not fail me in my trouble. . . . Can time accomplish everything after all? (Fourth century C.E.; P.Oxy I.120; Loeb Classical Library, *Select Papyri*, 1.162)

Finally, another unknown calamity prompts a defiant threat even to 67
the gods:

> To Stephanus from Hephaestion. On the receipt of the letter . . . put off everything and come at once to the homestead because of what has happened to me. If you take no heed, as the gods have not spared

[141] Translation from J. G. Winter, *Life and Letters in the Papyri* (Jerome Lectures; Ann Arbor, MI: University of Michigan Press, 1933) 60.

[142] Translation from N. Lewis, *Life in Egypt under Roman Rule* (Oxford: Clarendon Press, 1983) 54; cf. Loeb Classical Library, *Select Papyri*, 1.105. Fortunately, Egyptian religion forbade exposure of children, and they were often rescued from the dung heaps, as we learn from other Oxyrhynchus papyri.

me, so will I not spare the gods. Goodbye. (Third century C.E.; P.Oxy VII.1065; Loeb Classical Library, *Select Papyri*, 1.138)

Apart from these reflections of everyday events and emotions, what was Oxyrhynchus like? The papyri from the period 30 B.C.E.—96 C.E. alone provide us with some fifty-seven hundred names of residents in this district capital, which had a population of perhaps twenty-five thousand in Roman times, a figure based on the ruins of a theater that seated between eight to twelve thousand.[143] Oxyrhynchus also had some twenty temples,[144] at least two churches (P.Oxy I.43 verso; after 295 C.E.), and a Jewish synagogue (P.Oxy IX.1205; 291 C.E.) around the turn of the third/fourth centuries. It is of interest that the synagogue paid fourteen talents of silver (a large sum) to free a woman and her two small children, one of whom was named Jacob.[145] Of course, religion in Oxyrhynchus was dominated by Greek and Roman practices and by the continuance of traditional Egyptian rites, as attested by innumerable references in the papyri to temples, deities, officiants, festivals, and sacrifices, in addition to the inevitable prayers and invocations of the gods in private letters,[146] yet Christianity obviously flourished there as well, for in the early sixth century a bishop, some forty churches, and a
68 calendar of church services are attested by the papyri (P.Oxy XI.1357; 535–536 C.E.). We even have an early fourth century letter showing that Christians exchanged books: "To my dearest lady sister, greetings in the Lord. Lend [me] the Ezra, since I lent you the little Genesis. Farewell in God from us" (P.Oxy LXIII.4365).

---

[143] On names, see B. W. Jones and J. E. G. Whitehorne, *Register of Oxyrhynchites 30 B.C.–A.D. 96* (ASP 25; Chico, CA: Scholars Press, 1983). On population and the theater, see E. G. Turner, *Greek Papyri: An Introduction* (Oxford: Clarendon Press, 1968), 81–82; Petrie, the excavator in 1922, estimated that the theater held 11,200 spectators (see E. G. Turner, "Roman Oxyrhynchus," *JEA* 38 [1952] 81; J. Krüger, *Oxyrhynchos in der Kaiserzeit: Studien zur Topographie und Literaturrezeption* (European University Studies, III.441; Frankfurt am Main/New York, 1990) 8. On population, see also I. F. Fichman, "Die Bevölkerungszahl von Oxyrhynchos in byzantinischer Zeit," *APF* 21 (1971) 111–20, who, citing extensive evidence, suggests 15,000 to 25,000. [Recently D. Obbink, *Egyptian Archaeology* 22 (Spring, 2003) 3, speaks of "perhaps 20,000 inhabitants of the Greek-speaking settler class, Egyptian Greeks, and their later Roman counterparts."]

[144] Turner, "Roman Oxyrhynchus," 82–83, provides a list of temples.

[145] See P.Oxy. IX.1205, pp. 239–42, and *Corpus Papyrorum Judaicarum* (ed. V. Tcherikover and A. Fuks; 3 vols.; Cambridge, MA: Harvard University Press, 1957–64) 1.94.

[146] See, e.g., Turner, "Roman Oxyrhynchus," 82–83.

What are more relevant—and more intriguing—for the issue at hand are some seventeen hundred published literary papyri found at Oxyrhynchus, containing fragments as well as substantial portions of classical literature and dating over a seven-hundred-year period (ca. second/first century B.C.E. to sixth/seventh centuries C.E.). If we count up the manuscripts from the same general period as the early group of New Testament papyri (i.e., to about 325), we encounter, to give a very short list, forty-two copies of Euripides, fifty-eight of Plato, sixty-two of Demosthenes, seventy-two of Thucydides, eighty-four of Hesiod, and two hundred thirty-four of Homer. But there is more than classical literature; Jewish and Christian writings (other than the New Testament papyri) are found in some abundance from the period selected. For example, about ten manuscripts with Jewish scripture (plus ten more from later in the fourth century) have been published, many of which doubtless were made for Christian use; about twenty-five Christian writings, including ten apocryphal gospels, six apocryphal apocalypses, and various others books (plus nearly twenty more later in the fourth century).[147] Remember, all these writings, as well as the New Testament papyri, represent what the Oxyrhynchites discarded—threw out in their rubbish heaps—perhaps because the volumes were worn out, and we have no way of knowing how many books were in use at a given time or what happened to those that were.

The *Oxford Classical Dictionary* reports that "over 70 percent of surviving literary papyri come from Oxyrhynchus,"[148] suggesting that
this city was exceptional in its possession and use of literature, just 69
as it appears to be exceptional in the number of New Testament writings found there. To count literary works available is not necessarily to say much about literary activity and particularly literary criticism in Oxyrhynchus, but there is abundant evidence in the papyri of a lively literary scene, of the study of literature in the schools, of the procural and exchange of books, of the active critique of literature, and of intellectual interchange with Alexandria.[149]

---

[147] For more detail, see Epp, "The New Testament Papyri at Oxyrhynchus in Their Social and Intellectual Context," 59–62; idem, "The New Testament Papyri at Oxyrhynchus: Their Significance for Understanding the Transmission of the Early New Testament Text," *Oxyrhynchus: A City and Its Texts* [centennial volume of *The Oxyrhynchus Papyri*] (London: Egypt Exploration Society for the British Academy, forthcoming).

[148] W. E. H. Cockle, "Oxyrhynchus," in *OCD* (3d ed.) 1088.

[149] For examples and discussion, see Epp, "New Testament Papyri at Oxyrhynchus

Now come the questions. The location within this cultural-intellectual milieu of so high a percentage of our extant New Testament papyri prompts us to ask what impact this kind of community might have had upon Christianity up to the early fourth century—and what Christianity's impact upon Oxyrhynchus might have been. More specifically, what might be the significance for understanding the use, study, and transmission of the New Testament text when 42% of all known New Testament papyri and 57% of the oldest group of manuscripts have spent their useful life in a city with a vibrant intellectual climate, including literary activity in the form of scholarly analysis, criticism, and editing? Does this suggest, for example, that Christians might have engaged in similar scholarly editing of their own literature, including their copies of the Gospels, of Paul, etc? (I tried to answer this question by testing for some phenomena, namely, whether the Oxyrhynchus New Testament papyri reveal the same kinds of scholar's notations and editor's critical marks that are found with considerable frequency in manuscripts of Homer and the numerous other authors represented at Oxyrhynchus; my preliminary investigations led to a negative answer.)[150] And, somewhat farther afield, what does this intellectual climate in Oxyrhynchus say about liter-
70 acy among Oxyrhynchites in general and the Christians there in particular,[151] and what might this all tell us about the size, character, vitality, and influence of the Christian community at Oxyrhynchus[152] and about the nature of early Christianity in Egypt as a whole? Exact answers, of course, are unlikely, but this unique situation must be exploited for anything and everything it can offer. I suggest elsewhere that Oxyrhynchus is a microcosm of the textual spectrum of our New Testament manuscripts,[153] and my fond hope is that in the

in . . . Context," 56–59; 63–66; idem, "The Codex and Literacy in Early Christianity and at Oxyrhynchus: Issues Raised by Harry Y. Gamble's *Books and Readers in the Early Church*," *Critical Review of Books in Religion* 10 (1997) 32–34.

[150] See Epp, "Codex and Literacy," 30–32; idem, "New Testament Papyri at Oxyrhynchus in . . . Context," 63–68.

[151] For full (and overlapping) discussions, see Epp, "The New Testament Papyri at Oxyrhynchus in . . . Context," 63–67; idem, "The Codex and Literacy in Early Christianity and at Oxyrhynchus," 32–34.

[152] [See now E. J. Epp, "The Oxyrhynchus New Testament Papyri: 'Not without honor except in their hometown'?" *JBL* 123 (2004) 5–55 (Presidential Address, Society of Biblical Literature, 2003).]

[153] See Epp, "The New Testament Papyri at Oxyrhynchus: Their Significance for Understanding the Transmission of the Early New Testament Text" (forthcoming).

present century we may find ways in which the Oxyrhynchus New Testament papyri can help us clarify our sketch of the history of the Greek New Testament text.

V. Choosing to Address Goals and Directions—and Deciding on Meanings and Approaches: The Issue of Original Text

The final current issue actually brings us back, logically, to the beginning of the text-critical enterprise, for it concerns both the goals of textual criticism and also the methods and attitudes we bring to the process. The issue of "original text" is very old, but one that has emerged during the past dozen years in a fresh, challenging, and perhaps disturbing fashion. In pursuing it, we will encounter very directly the interaction of traditional approaches and newly emerging postures toward New Testament text-critical theory and practice. Indeed, I would begin by asserting that textual criticism is diminished to the extent that its purpose is limited to the "quest for the original text," for we have just seen how addressing the contexts of our New Testament text and manuscripts can enlighten us and expand our horizons. Examining the very foundation of the discipline might do the same.

It will surprise no one that virtually all textual critics from the outset of the discipline have assumed that their goal is to discover
and to restore the original text of the New Testament, or, taking a 71
narrower view, to isolate the original reading at each given point of textual variation between or among our New Testament manuscripts. One may look at both early and current manuals of textual criticism and find typical statements, such as this one by Alexander Souter in 1913: "Textual criticism seeks, by the exercise of knowledge and trained judgment, to restore the very words of some original document which has perished."[154] Jumping ahead fifty years, J. Harold Greenlee's 1964 manual states, "Textual criticism is the study of copies of any written work of which the autograph (the original) is unknown, with the purpose of ascertaining the original text."[155] In both cases, *original* means *autograph*. A somewhat different

[154] Alexander Souter, *The Text and Canon of the New Testament* (London: Duckworth, 1913) [2d ed. in 1954]) 3.

[155] J. H. Greenlee, *Introduction to New Testament Textual Criticism* (Grand Rapids, MI: Eerdmans, 1964) 11; (rev. ed.: Peabody, MA: Hendrickson, 1995) 1.

formulation comes from Kurt Aland and Barbara Aland, who assert very directly, "Only one reading can be original."[156]

The obvious assumptions that underlies such statements are that a *single* original reading can be discovered and that, in a larger sense, a *single* original text can be reconstructed. And that seems self-evident, does it not? Yet, this has become an open question.

As a parallel development beginning already in the nineteenth century, many—perhaps most—textual critics used the term *original text* more cautiously, for they realized increasingly that any certainty about the text that New Testament authors wrote was more and more elusive, especially as new manuscript discoveries brought into view more and more variant readings and as increasing complexity accompanied the application of the critical canons that were supposed to facilitate the identification of the original readings. Hence, textual critics, at least since Samuel Tregelles in 1854, began to speak of their goal as the restoration or reconstruction of the New Testament text "as nearly as can be done on existing evidence."[157] Hort uses
72 similar language,[158] and even B. B. Warfield expresses some reserve.[159] More recently—and more typically—Bruce Metzger's widely used handbook states that the purpose is "to ascertain from the divergent copies which form of the text should be regarded as most nearly conforming to the original."[160] Then, beginning perhaps during the last third of the twentieth century, "original text" was frequently placed within quotation marks, thereby cautioning against undue optimism.

[156] Aland and Aland, *Text of the New Testament*, 280.

[157] S. P. Tregelles, *An Account of the Printed Text of the Greek New Testament; With Remarks on Its Revision upon Critical Principles* (London: Bagster, 1854) 174. For more detail on Tregelles, see Epp, "The Multivalence of the Term 'Original Text' in New Testament Textual Criticism," *HTR* 92 (1999) 252 n. 25.

[158] Westcott and Hort, *New Testament in the Original Greek*, 2.1: "To present exactly the original words of the New Testament, *so far as they can now be determined from surviving documents*" [emphasis added].

[159] B. B. Warfield, *An Introduction to the Textual Criticism of the New Testament* (London: Hodder & Stoughton, 1886 [7th ed. in 1907]) 15: "The autographic text of the New Testament is distinctly within the reach of criticism *in so immensely the greater part of the volume*, that we cannot despair of restoring . . . His Book, word for word, as He gave it by inspiration to men" [emphasis added to show the portion of his quotation often omitted].

[160] Metzger, *Text of the New Testament*, v.

When we ask how *original text* was viewed at the end of the nineteenth century, it is clear that both of the notions just reviewed were prominent, the straightforward view that textual criticism seeks to reach *the* original text of the New Testament—that is, what its authors actually wrote—but also, and more commonly, a cautious, qualified goal of recovering "the most likely original text," "the earliest attainable text," or something similar. At the outset of the twenty-first century, it is obvious that both kinds of statements are likely to remain in manuals and handbooks, but there is also the compelling conviction that matters are not quite that simple and that we need to face the complex and perhaps unsettling notion of *multivalence* in the term *original text.* In other words, the issue is more difficult, has wider implications, and is also richer and potentially more rewarding than we might have imagined.

During the past ten years or so, notably in North America and the United Kingdom, a small number of New Testament textual critics have begun to probe the phrase *original text,* have looked afresh at it, and have insisted that we ask ourselves both what we thought we meant by it and also what we now think we can mean by it. This is an issue, it should be noted at the outset, that is not for the timid or tender minded, but for those willing to face some of the most challenging questions that the discipline has to offer. Indeed, 73
for some it may be a wedge that drives them back to more traditional views and away from what is appearing on the horizon. Yet, advances in knowledge seldom materialize apart from bold testings of the status quo or without toleration of the adventuresome spirit of the scholar willing and able to take a risk. Not all such ventures, of course, advance knowledge and many are distinct failures, but a few do succeed and lead us forward by directing us to their insightful though sometimes unsettling presentations.

This is not the place to rehearse fully the development of this new understanding of original text.[161] Essentially, this emerging stance was prompted by several observations, none of them especially new or startling. First, for example, impetus came from views that our present gospels utilized preexisting sources or existed in earlier (e.g., precanonical) forms or versions. Second, prompting came from the recognition that Acts, for instance, has come down to us in two

[161] See my essay, "The Multivalence of the Term 'Original Text.'"

differing textual streams, with the distinct probability that numerous readings in one stream represent intentional scribal alterations (or even reflecting the possibility that the author wrote two versions of Luke-Acts). Third, as a more specific example, these new views were stimulated by observing that the doxology occurs after 14:23 in some manuscripts of Romans rather than in its usual place in 16:25–27, suggesting that Romans earlier existed in a short, fourteen chapter version. Also of interest is the lack of *in Rome* in Romans 1:7, 15 in a small number of witnesses, and the similar lack of *in Ephesus* in Ephesians 1:1 in some manuscripts.[162] Data such as these (and much more could be offered) led to penetrating questions as to which is the original Acts of the Apostles, or which is the original Romans, or Ephesians, and so on. Are the originals the texts that we have in our canonical New Testament or some earlier, predecessor forms that are evidenced by literary or text-critical analyses? To press the point through another example, if it is plausible that the Gospel of Mark used by Matthew differed from the Mark used by Luke, then
which is the original Mark? And if it is plausible that our present
74 Mark differed from both Matthew's Mark and Luke's Mark, then
do we not have three possible originals? William L. Petersen puts it this way:

> Is the "original" Mark the Mark found in our fourth-century and later manuscripts? Or is it the Mark recovered from the so-called "minor agreements" between Matthew and Luke?
>
> And which—if any—of the four extant endings of "Mark" is "original"?[163]

Suddenly, textual criticism becomes more complex than we might wish, and similar questions arise at the level of variant readings. Here is where we may refer again to the works of Ehrman and Parker. If (*à la* Ehrman) textual variants reveal the alteration of a text in support, for example, of a more orthodox theological viewpoint, which text is original—the text that was altered by the scribe, or the scribe's own newly altered text? If the text or manuscript in which the alteration was made becomes current in the church, as

[162] For details, see ibid., 262–63.

[163] W. L. Petersen, "What Text Can New Testament Textual Criticism Ultimately Reach?" in *New Testament Textual Criticism, Exegesis, and Early Church History: A Discussion of Methods* (ed. B. Aland and J. Delobel; CBET; Kampen: Kok Pharos, 1994) 136–37.

many did, do we not suddenly have two originals, one virtually lost
to sight—except for the variant that was changed—and another that
gained currency and recognition, eventually being accredited as canonical? The first kind of text might be called an *autographic Textform*,
assuming there is no reason to think that it had itself been altered
from an earlier form; and the second I would designate an *interpretive Textform* because it represents an interpretation through alteration
of the earlier text. If this interpretive Textform persisted until the
fourfold Gospel was formed or, in the case of an epistle, until the
letters of Paul were collected and more formally became canon, then
the interpretive Textform is at the same time also a *canonical Textform.*
I also employ the phrase *predecessor Textform*, to indicate a level of
text discoverable behind a New Testament writing that played a role
in the latter's composition, such as the Q source, various forms of
Mark, earlier forms of John or Romans, and so on. In less careful
language, one might speak of an *autographic original*, a *canonical original*, or an *interpretive original*, but regardless of the terminology, there
is a real sense in which every intentional, meaningful scribal alteration to a text—whether motivated by theological, historical, stylis- 75
tic, or other factors—creates a new Textform, a new original. This
description of differing functions or dimensions of originality, then,
is what is covered by the phrase *multivalence of the term original text.*[164]

And if (*à la* Parker) the Gospels and other early Christian literature circulated as a free and "living text," in the early centuries, is there an original text, or specifically a "single original text," to be recovered?[165] Parker's response, in part, is "The question is not whether we *can* recover it, but why we want to."[166] When he asks "whether the task of textual criticism is to recover the original text," he replies, "It may be, but does not have to be,"[167] and, as we have seen, he chooses rather to emphasize the insights we gain from multiple variants. When he gets down to such cases, he concludes that, on occasion, identifying a single original reading is not possible and that, in many cases, we are instructed much more by considering the meanings of all the variants, both as they illumine the early church and

[164] For details, clarifications, and cautions, see Epp, "The Multivalence of the Term 'Original Text,'" esp. 276–77.

[165] Parker, *The Living Text of the Gospels*, 3–4; 208.

[166] Ibid., 209.

[167] Ibid., 182.

as they enrich our own exegesis. And when Parker describes how variants reveal the ways in which "successive generations write on [Luke's] pages,"[168] for example, he is moving in the sphere of multiple originals or, better, of multivalence in the term, *original*.

It is therefore indisputable, in my view, that the often simplistically understood term, *original text*, has been fragmented by the realities of how our New Testament writings were formed and transmitted, and *original* henceforth must be understood as a term designating several layers, levels, or meanings, though I prefer to call them *dimensions* of originality.

Conclusion

Since its beginnings in the Renaissance with Erasmus, during its
youth throughout the Enlightenment (with Mill, Bentley, Bengel,
76 Wettstein, Semler, and Griesbach), and during its young adulthood
(with Lachmann, von Tischendorf, and Tregelles) and its early maturity (with Westcott and Hort and the host of scholars since then) in the nineteenth and twentieth centuries,[169] New Testament textual criticism actually has remained much the same in terms of its goals, its arguments for priority of readings, its grouping of manuscripts, and its motivation and general procedures for producing critical editions. The only sea change occurred almost precisely two-thirds of the way through this five century period, when Lachmann's Greek New Testament of 1831 first made a clean break with the *textus receptus*, clearing the way for our prevailing critical editions, with their rather remarkable similarity ever since Tischendorf and Westcott-Hort. Work in these areas will go on, though skill and imagination will be required if progress is to be made.

Yet, the question of real interest, at least for me, now is this: Are we seeing the first waves (latent for a good while) of a second sea change in the new approaches described above, namely, (a) the disclosure through textual variants of scribal changes for theological reasons that have overwritten earlier readings and created new "orig-

---

[168] Ibid., 174 (quoted earlier).

[169] For discussion of these various scholars and their achievements, see Epp, "Eclectic Method," 217–44 (repr. in Epp and Fee, *Studies*, 144–64); idem, "Textual Criticism," 75–84 (repr. in Epp and Fee, *Studies*, 17–25); idem, "Textual Criticism (NT)," *ABD* (1992) 427–30.

inal" readings; (b) the diminution or even the abandonment of the traditional search for the original text in favor of seeing in the living text and its multiplicity of variants the vibrant interactions in the early Christian community; and (c) the recognition that (as I wrote elsewhere) "the term 'original' has exploded into a complex and highly unmanageable multivalent entity,"[170] exposing for us various dimensions of originality in and beneath our New Testament manuscripts and readings? My answer is affirmative, but, if so, what will this "brave new world" bring, and will we be able to face the demanding but intriguing challenges that it assuredly holds?

Added Notes, 2004

"Epp and Fee, *Studies*," refers to: Eldon Jay and Gordon D. Fee, *Studies in the Theory and Method of New Testament Textual Criticism* (SD 45; Grand Rapids, MI: Eerdmans, 1993), a collection of essays by the two authors.

On "Choosing among variants." A recent formulation of the arguments or criteria for determining the priority of readings may be found above in "Textual Criticism in the Exegesis of the New Testament," original pp. 62–63 on Internal Criteria, and pp. 71–72 on External Criteria.

Iterated material. The nature of this essay (see note 1, above) invited the review of themes that I have emphasized earlier, resulting in the reuse of material from previous publications. Actually, I welcome the opportunity to reemphasize salient points that I find crucial to current text-critical discipline.

---

[170] "The Multivalence of the Term 'Original Text,'" 280.

CHAPTER TWENTY-THREE

ANTI-JUDAIC TENDENCIES IN THE D-TEXT OF ACTS: FORTY YEARS OF CONVERSATION*

The text of Acts is legendary for its problems, and this is nowhere 111
more evident than in the proportion of space allocated to its variants in *A Textual Commentary on the Greek New Testament*, where Acts occupies 32% of the *Commentary* while it constitutes only 13% of the Greek New Testament.[1] In this present essay only the question of ideological bias in the so-called "Western" text of Acts will be surveyed, and then only to a limited extent.

I. New Emphasis on Textual Variants as Ideological Vehicles in the 1950s: The Conversation Evolves

Recognition of alterations in the New Testament text for theological or ideological reasons was not a new topic in 1962 when the *Harvard Theological Review* published my very first article, "The 'Ignorance Motif' in Acts and Anti-Judaic Tendencies in Codex Bezae,"[2] though much of the earlier scholarship attributed such activity only to "heretics" with "ignoble" motives and not to mainstream Christian interpreters, annotators, or scribes who might be shown to have introduced intentional changes for various ideological reasons. Indeed, two summary judgments by prominent nineteenth- and early twentieth-century scholars inspired my further investigation of theological

* The author is grateful to Dr. Tobias Nicklas for encouragement to address this topic, something I was at first reluctant to do so long after my initial efforts in 1962 and 1966. I wish also to thank ElDoris B. Epp, Ph.D., for her critical evaluations and helpful contributions.

[1] B. M. Metzger (ed.), A Textual Commentary on the Greek New Testament: A Companion Volume to the United Bible Societies' Greek New Testament, Stuttgart ^{2}1994: Acts occupies pp. 222–445 out of the 691 pages. Westcott-Hort's Greek New Testament, which has no apparatus, was used to compare Acts to the rest of the New Testament.

[2] E. J. Epp, The "Ignorance Motif" in Acts and Anti-Judaic Tendencies in Codex Bezae, in: HThR 55 (1962), 51–62.

112 tendencies in the so-called "Western" text of Acts (which I prefer to call the D-text).[3]

The first pronouncement, very frequently quoted, came from F. J. A. Hort of Cambridge University in 1882:

> ... Even among the numerous unquestionably spurious readings of the New Testament there are no signs of deliberate falsification of the text for dogmatic purposes.... It is true that dogmatic preferences to a great extent determined theologians, and probably scribes, in their choice between rival readings already in existence:... the temptation was strong to believe and assert that a reading used by theological opponents had also been invented by them. Accusations of wilful tampering with the text are accordingly not unfrequent in Christian antiquity: but, with a single exception [Marcion], wherever they can be verified they prove to be groundless, being in fact hasty and unjust inferences from mere diversities of inherited text.[4]

Hort concluded this brief discussion with reassuring words about the preservation of the New Testament text—sentiments utilized at times over the past century among conservatives to comfort themselves and their constituencies:

> The books of the New Testament as preserved in extant documents assuredly speak to us in every important respect in language identical with that in which they spoke to those for whom they were originally written.[5]

This is not the place to pursue this latter issue except to say that textual critics have learned much in the past 120 years about the treacherous pitfalls in any path toward the original text of the New

---

[3] My preference: D = Codex Bezae and its text, while D-text = the so-called "Western" text, whose most prominent representative is Codex D. Ideally, the term "Western" text should be dropped entirely, since it is no longer regarded as Western geographically, but was known in the East as well. Some, however, may understand "D-text" to mean the text of Codex D, whereas text-critical specialists will understand "D-text" to designate the broader "Western" text, especially those who adopt the A-text, B-text, C-text, D-text scheme (delineated in E. J. Epp/G. D. Fee, Studies in the Theory and Method of New Testament Textual Criticism (SD 45), Grand Rapids 1993, 283–295). Because of the potential ambiguity, in the present paper "Western' text" is used frequently instead of "D-text" to avoid confusion between the terms D (the text only of Codex D) and D-text (the "Western" text).

[4] B. F. Westcott/F. J. A. Hort, The New Testament in the Original Greek. Vol. II. Introduction, Appendix, London 1882, ^{2}1896, 282–283; cf. "Notes on Select Readings," 64–68.

[5] Ibid., 284.

Testament writings and, accordingly, that we exercise considerable caution in making claims either that such a goal has been reached or even that it can be achieved.[6]

The other pronouncement, this time specifically referring to the "Western" text of Acts, was issued by James Hardy Ropes of Harvard
University in 1926: "Of any special point of view, theological or 113
other, on the part of the 'Western' reviser it is difficult to find any trace," followed by the tantalizing challenge, "In *one or two* passages . . . the hostile attitude of the Jews receives special stress."[7]

This challenge of Ropes was taken up, explicitly or implicitly, in three small works published or presented in 1951, though only by way of pointing out several largely independent theological themes of the D-text that are revealed by comparison with the B-text (i.e., the Alexandrian or Egyptian text). First, C. S. C. Williams, in his succinct and perceptive *Alterations to the Text of the Synoptic Gospels and Acts*,[8] had a chapter on "The Text of Acts" that, to be sure, was dependent on four pages from M.-J. Lagrange's masterful *Critique textuelle, II: La critique rationnelle* of 1935.[9] Williams, following but supplementing Lagrange, noted that the D-text presented a clearer figure of Christ, emphasized the Holy Spirit, heightened the piety and activity of the apostles, singled out Peter, heightened the influence of Christian preaching, and underlined "the hostility of the Jews towards Christianity."[10] Second, P.-H. Menoud published a fourteen-page article on "The Western Text and the Theology of Acts," half of which he employed to demonstrate that the D-text version of the Apostolic Decree in Acts 15:19–29 carries an "anti-Jewish tendency."[11] Menoud then described in a single page further instances of this

---

[6] See, e.g., E. J. Epp, The Multivalence of the Term "Original Text" in New Testament Textual Criticism, in: HThR 92 (1999), 245–281.

[7] J. H. Ropes, The Text of Acts, Vol. 3 of The Beginnings of Christianity, Part I: The Acts of the Apostles, 5 vols., London 1926, ccxxxiii [italics added].

[8] C. S. C. Williams, Alterations to the Text of the Synoptic Gospels and Acts, Oxford 1951.

[9] M.-J. Lagrange, Critique textuelle, II: La critique rationnelle (ÉtB), Paris 1935, 390–393.

[10] Williams, Alterations (see n. 8), 55–58.

[11] P.-H. Menoud, The Western Text and the Theology of Acts, Studiorum Novi Testamenti Societas, Bulletin II, Oxford, 1951, 19–32 (here: 27–28). [Repr. in Bulletin of the Studiorum Novi Testamenti Societas, Nos. I–III, Cambridge, 1963, II.19–32 (here: 27–28), and in: Id., Jesus Christ and Faith: A Collection of Essays, Pittsburgh 1978, 61–83 (here: 73)].

anti-Judaic tendency, followed by a few pages on other theological emphases over against the B-text tradition, such as greater universalism, more frequent references to the Holy Spirit, and a possible anti-feminist tendency, though the latter, he affirms, "is not one of the major trends" in the D-text.[12] Lagrange, again, was invoked in Menoud's discussion.

Third, Erich Fascher, writing in East Germany and employing only six post-World War II references in his barely twenty bibliographic footnotes, presented a rather startling thesis for his day in a 1951 lecture in Eisenach and published two years later as *Textgeschichte als hermeneutisches Problem*[13] He was not so much interested in recov-
114 ering the original text as he was anxious to show how various theological and hermeneutical predispositions gave rise to textual additions, alterations, and other variants:

> These manuscripts proceed from persons who not only have copied a *Vorlage* mechanically, but who, on the basis of their own reflection, improved, elucidated, or made the text more understandable, as they thought . . .: *the interpreting copyist moves between text and copy and forces his interpretation upon his later readers, since as yet he has no knowledge of an authoritative text.*[14]

For Fascher, then, New Testament interpretation did not begin with the patristic writers, or the great fourth- and fifth-century codices, or even with the second century papyri, but already with scribes or copyists "as unknown agents in the generation between 50 and 125 A.D."[15] His treatment of D-text variants in Acts, however, was not as radical as these programmatic statements suggest, for he viewed them for the most part as alterations offering different psychological explanations or local narratives of historical scenes made more vivid to the reader, and not as theologically significant readings.[16] Yet, this

---

[12] Ibid., 28–31. [Repr. 73–77]. "Anti-feminist" is his term: 30. [Repr. 76.]

[13] E. Fascher, Textgeschichte als hermeneutisches Problem, Halle/Salle 1953.

[14] Ibid., 12 [emphasis in original].

[15] Ibid.

[16] Ibid., 26 f. W. A. Strange, The Problem of the Text of Acts (SNTSMS 71), Cambridge 1992, 19, describes Fascher's view of D-text variants thus: "the Western reviser [but Fascher does not use such a term, but only "D says," or "D has," etc.] . . . was the interpreter of Luke the historian, rather than of Luke the theologian," though he indicates that Fascher also identified theologically motivated D-readings (209 n. 89).

in no way diminishes the importance of his insights into the conscious interpretative function of very early copyists.

Coincidentally or not, another radical thrust (at least for its time) blossomed in the United States in the 1950s within the "Chicago School of New Testament textual criticism," a viewpoint, I regret to say, that was neither widely discussed nor much acknowledged at the time—or later, for that matter.[17] This neglect, I suspect, was more a resistence to unsettling ideas than to the lack of availability of the publications presenting them. After all, this "school" included faculty members of the University of Chicago and some of their students, a particularly prominent and learned group, especially Edgar J. Goodspeed, H. R. Willoughby, Donald W. Riddle, Ernest C. Colwell, Allen P. Wikgren, Kenneth W. Clark, Merrill M. Parvis, Eric L. Titus, and Ernest W. Saunders. Although Goodspeed and Willoughby appear not to have published on the theme under discussion, all the others emphasized or supported the strong influence of doctrinal and church-historical factors upon the text of what became the New 115
Testament.[18] Naturally, there were predecessors for this view, notably Kirsopp Lake, who already in 1904 stated that "we need to know what the early church thought [a passage] meant and how it altered its wording in order to emphasize its meaning,"[19] and Günther Zuntz, who in 1940 affirmed that "this [New Testament] text has not been propagated—as seems to be assumed with regard to that of most classical authors—in the sterilized atmosphere of the laboratory; *the very variety of this text reflects the pulsating life of early Christianity*."[20] Although the viewpoint of the Chicago group flourished mainly in the 1950s, D. W. Riddle boldly proclaimed it already in 1936 in this programmatic pronouncement:

> The legitimate task of textual criticism is not limited to the recovery of approximately the original form of the documents, to the establishment

---

[17] For this reason I have reviewed the Chicago viewpoint recently in Multivalence (see n. 6) 272–274, and in E. J. Epp, Issues in New Testament Textual Criticism, in: D. A. Black (ed.), Rethinking New Testament Textual Criticism, Grand Rapids 2002, 17–76 (here: 38 f.)

[18] For a summary, including predecessors, see E. J. Epp, The Theological Tendency of Codex Bezae Cantabrigiensis in Acts (SNTSMS 3), Cambridge 1966, 12–21. [Unchanged reprint: Eugene/Oregon 2001].

[19] K. Lake, The Influence of Textual Criticism on the Exegesis of the New Testament (Inaugural Lecture, University of Leiden), Oxford 1904, 12.

[20] G. Zuntz, A Textual Criticism of Some Passages of the Acts of the Apostles, in: Classica et Mediaevalia 3 (1940), 20–46 (here: 23) [italics added].

> of the "best" text, nor to the "elimination of spurious readings." It must be recognized that every significant variant records a religious experience which brought it into being. This means that there are no "spurious readings": the various forms of the text are sources for the study of the history of Christianity.[21]

Sixteen years later, in 1952, two other Chicago scholars built upon Riddle's work. M. M. Parvis commented more pointedly on the contention that there are no spurious readings:

> All [readings] are part of the tradition; all contribute to our knowledge of the history of Christian thought. And they are significant contributions because they are interpretations which were highly enough thought of in some place and at some time to be incorporated into the Scripture itself.[22]

Parvis explained that the invention of the printing press diminished the nature of "the Scripture [as] a living body of literature, which was constantly being enriched as it was interpreted and reinterpreted by each succeeding generation."[23] In the same year Ernest C. Colwell
116 moved against the common view, represented above in Fascher's citation, that scribal changes in the early period were frequent because the text of what would become the New Testament had not yet achieved an authoritative status. Colwell turned this 180 degrees:

> The paradox is that the variations came into existence because these were religious books, sacred books, canonical books. The devout scribe felt compelled to correct misstatements which he found in the manuscript he was copying.... The majority of the variant readings in the New Testament were created for theological or dogmatic reasons.... Most of the manuals and handbooks ... will tell you that these variations were the fruit of careless treatment which was possible because the books of the New Testament had not yet attained a strong position as "Bible." The reverse is the case. It was because they were the religious treasure of the church that they were changed.[24]

Finally, in the following year, K. W. Clark asserted regarding the New Testament that "the freedom men [sic!] assumed in altering its

[21] D. W. Riddle, Textual Criticism as a Historical Discipline, in: AthR 18 (1936), 220–233 (here: 221; cf. 231 and examples, 221–224).

[22] M. M. Parvis, The Nature and Tasks of New Testament Textual Criticism, in: JR 32 (1952), 165–174 (here: 172). Naturally, neither Riddle nor Parvis is speaking of scribal errors, but of meaningful alterations.

[23] Ibid., 173.

[24] E. C. Colwell, What Is the Best New Testament? Chicago 1952, 52 f.

text was inspired by their understanding of Christian doctrine, and by their purpose to make it plain to others";[25] thus, "the ultimate objective of textual criticism is theological" [and] . . . textual criticism pursues its research at the very centre of Christian faith and life."[26]

These early 1950s examples of scholarly attention to theological/ideological alterations in the "Western" text of Acts and in the New Testament text generally, while not comprehensive for that period or for the times preceding and following,[27] more than adequately characterize the mood in a few quarters of textual criticism as the 1960s approached. Together, these scholars wittingly or unwittingly were distancing themselves from the traditional text-critical task of establishing the "original" text[28] and, at the same time, embracing with enthusiasm the forward-looking goal of discerning the life and thought of the church through textual variants.

II. New D-Text Manuscripts in the 1960s: 117
The Conversation Augmented

In the late 1950s I began to work on what would be published in 1966 by Cambridge University Press as the third SNTS Monograph: *The Theological Tendency of Codex Bezae Cantabrigiensis in Acts*, whose main thesis was that the D-text of Acts, represented most prominently in Codex Bezae, embodies an anti-Judaic bias. The timely publication in 1963–1964 of three new manuscripts substantively aided the last stages of research. First, the Latin manuscript *l* (Beuron

[25] K. W. Clark, Textual Criticism and Doctrine, in: Studia Paulina. FS Johannis De Zwaan, Haarlem 1953, 52–65 (here: 54 f.).

[26] K. W. Clark, The Textual Criticism of the New Testament, in: PCB (1962), 669.

[27] See additional references in Epp, Theological Tendency (see n. 18), 12–23. Note also the 1952 volume by L. E. Wright, Alterations of the Words of Jesus as Quoted in the Literature of the Second Century, Cambridge/MA 1952, which follows the Chicago approach, though it originated as a 1945 Harvard dissertation (see 1–9).

[28] Riddle, Textual Criticism (see n. 21), 230, e.g., stated: "Of course the New Testament writers wrote something. But what is the use of picturing this original copy? It had no status as a sacred document." Parvis, Nature and Tasks (see n. 22), 172, supports the attainment of "as close an approximation of the autographs as possible." Why? To "know the form of the tradition of that time," to which he adds: "But even then we have but one form of the tradition."

67) was edited by Bonifatius Fischer,[29] presenting about a quarter of Acts with a text divided between the Old Latin and the Vulgate and dating in the 7th century—actually relatively early since, among Old Latin manuscripts of Acts, only *d*, *e*, *h*, and s predate it. Second was the Palestinian Syriac fragment of Acts from Khirbet Mird (sy^{msK}), dating around 600 and preserving Acts 10:28–29 and 32–41. It was edited in 1963 by Charles Perrot, who noted that its agreements with Codex Bezae are "numerous and very important."[30] It is, according to A. F. J. Klijn, "the first discovery to demonstrate that a Western text of Acts was known in the Palestinian-Syriac language also."[31] The most significant new manuscript, however, was certainly the Pierpont Morgan Middle Egyptian Coptic codex G67, which deserves more detailed attention.

A. *Coptic G67 and Petersen's Work*

The contents of parchment Coptic Codex G67 first appeared in humble dress and with little notice in 1964 when Theodore C. Petersen published a selection of its readings, mostly those that paralleled recognized D-text variants, but he presented them only in an English translation.[32] His plan, of course, was to provide a critical edition, but unfortunately he died in 1966. Petersen's successor,
118 Paulinus Bellet, apparently completed an edition, though he died in 1987, and his work, which was to have emphasized textual criticism, will have to be published posthumously.[33] In the meantime, a criti-

[29] B. Fischer, Ein neuer Zeuge zum westlichen Text der Apostelgeschichte, in: J. N. Birdsall/R. W. Thomson (Hg.), Biblical and Patristic Studies in Memory of Robert Pierce Casey, Freiburg 1963, 33–63.

[30] Ch. Perrot, Un fragment christo-palestinien découvert à Khirbet Mird (Actes des Apôtres, x, 28–29; 32–41), in: RB 70 (1963), 506–555 (here: 535). The symbol sy^{msK} was my designation, picked up by H.-M. Schenke (ed.), Apostelgeschichte 1,1–15,3 im mittelägyptischen Dialekt des Koptischen (Codex Glazier) (TU 137), Berlin 1991, xvi, and, e.g., A. F. J. Klijn, A Survey of the Researches into the Western Text of the Gospels and Acts, Part II: 1949–1969 (NT.S 21), Leiden 1969, 56 and n. 5.

[31] A. F. J. Klijn, Survey (see n. 30), 57: "it shows some agreement with D" (56). See his discussion of the readings, 58 f.; cf. E. J. Epp, Coptic Manuscript G67 and the Rôle of Codex Bezae as a Western Witness in Acts, in: JBL 85 (1966), 197–212 (here: 211f.)

[32] T. C. Petersen, An Early Coptic Manuscript of Acts: An Unrevised Version of the Ancient So-called Western Text, in: CBQ 26 (1964), 225–241.

[33] See Schenke, Apostelgeschichte (see n. 30), 249.

cal edition with an emphasis on linguistics, finally was published in 1991 by the late Hans-Martin Schenke.[34]

This extensive manuscript in the so-called Middle-Egyptian (or Oxyrhynchite) dialect contains the whole of Acts 1:1–15:3 in an extraordinarily well-preserved state. Petersen's published list of variant readings was lengthy, comprised of nearly 140 passages containing some 250 variation-units. In his enthusiasm, he designated the new manuscript in his subtitle as "An Unrevised Version of the Ancient So-Called Western Text." In 1966, using Petersen's article—since it was the only material available—I published a further analysis of the relation of G67 to the D-text, echoing Petersen's exuberance about its strong D-text character, and, on the basis of Petersen's late 4th or early 5th century date for the manuscript, extolling its importance as "the earliest nonfragmentary Western ms of the text of Acts."[35] Granting Petersen's dating, this was a reasonable judgment in 1966, since Codex Bezae at that time was dated almost universally to the late 5th century.[36] Naturally, I carried the views expressed in my article into the *Theological Tendency* volume, which again placed a very high value upon G67 as one of the relatively few "pure" D-text witnesses,[37] though I did not make a claim similar to Petersen's, that G67 was an "unrevised version" of the ancient D-text.

Within a year or so, Petersen's study—and my *JBL* article and the use of G67 in *Theological Tendency*—became part of the conversation about the "Western" text in a frequently-quoted article in *New Testament Studies* by Ernst Haenchen and Peter Weigandt.[38] It appeared to me that they were rather hard on Petersen, and a close reading of both Petersen and his two critics suggested to me that Haenchen

[34] Ibid. Schenke died in 2002.

[35] Epp, Coptic Manuscript G67 (see n. 31), 197.

[36] In 1964, however (as noted in Ibid. 197 n. 4), H. J. Frede argued for a fourth-century date: Id., Altlateinische Paulus-Handschriften (Vetus Latina: AGLB 4), Freiburg, 1964, 18 n. 4.

[37] Epp, Theological Tendency (see n. 18), 29 f.

[38] E. Haenchen/P. Weigandt, The Original Text of Acts? in: NTS 14 (1967/68), 469–481. They mistakenly called the manuscript G68, an error repeated by Gerd Mink, Die koptischen Versionen des Neuen Testaments, in: K. Aland, Die Alten Übersetzungen des Neuen Testaments, die Kirchenväterzitate und Lektionare (ANTF 5), Berlin-New York, 1972, 160–299 (here: 171 n. 68), who placed an "!" after G67 when he cited the title of my Coptic Manuscript G67 article (see n. 31) to point out my error. But in n. 2 of that article I reported that a curator at the Pierpont Morgan Library had provided to me the correct designation: G67.

and Weigandt at times focused on marginal issues, such as Petersen's comments on "recensions" in his sketch of the context of his new
119 manuscript.[39] In my judgment, however, the recension issue was neither central nor essential to his article, for he obviously intended his contribution to lie elsewhere, namely, the demonstration that numerous readings of G67 evinced a content similar to that of other established witnesses to the D-text.

Primarily, however, Haenchen and Weigandt focused on what appeared to be Petersen's claim, that "the new Coptic text of Acts might be 'the earliest completely preserved and entirely unadulterated' witness to the 'western' recension."[40] They were correct in using the word "might" here, for Petersen (who was referring also to a similar Middle Egyptian Matthew manuscript that had come to light at the same time[41]) said that only when these new Coptic texts are published will scholars "be able to learn whether or not these two texts can be accepted as the earliest completely preserved and entirely unadulterated witnesses" to the D-text.[42] Yet, Haenchen and Weigandt pressed their case, first, by offering three examples of a "mixed text" [they meant "conflated"] in the Acts manuscript to show that it could not be an "entirely unadulterated witness."[43] They had a point and clearly Petersen was unwise to have used such strong adjectives as "unadulterated" and "unrevised" when describing the potential nature of his new manuscript, for textual critics recognize that mixture, especially among New Testament manuscripts, is everywhere to be found. More than half of Haenchen and Weigandt's critique was

---

[39] Haenchen/Weigandt, Original Text of Acts? (see n. 38), 469. Klijn, Survey (see n. 30), 60 n. 5, states that Petersen has some "strange ideas" about the "Western" recension, though he does not explain. See the recent, judicious analysis of "recension" by M. W. Holmes, Codex Bezae as a Recension of the Gospels, in: D. C. Parker/C.-B. Amphoux (eds.), Codex Bezae: Studies from the Lunel Colloquium June 1994 (NTTS 22), Leiden 1996, 123–160 (here: 142–150).

[40] Haenchen/Weigandt, Original Text of Acts? (see n. 38), 469. E. Grässer, Acta-Forschung seit 1960, in: ThR 41 (1976), 141–194 (here: 167–169); [Repr. in: Id., Forschungen zur Apostelgeschichte (WUNT 137), Tübingen 2001, 134–179 (here: 160–162)], generally sides with Haenchen and Weigandt and indicates incorrectly that I supported Petersen's views on recension and especially his subtitle ("unrevised"), 167–169; [Repr. 160–163].

[41] Petersen, Early Coptic Manuscript (see n. 32), 225. The Matthew manuscript is the Scheide Codex, published by H.-M. Schenke, Das Matthäus-Evangelium im mittelägyptischen Dialekt des Koptischen (Codex Scheide) (TU 127), Berlin 1981.

[42] Petersen, Early Coptic Manuscript (see n. 32), 226.

[43] Haenchen/Weigandt, Original Text of Acts? (see n. 38), 470 f.

devoted to showing that "the longer variant readings of the Coptic text are secondary,"[44] thereby to undermine further any claim that the Coptic manuscript is "an unadulterated witness to the original 'western' text."[45] This, to be sure, was a valuable discussion, though the effort to distinguish between original and secondary readings was 120
vitiated, it seemed to me, by the two critics' obvious *certainty* and precise *knowledge* as to what text, what intertext, what idiom, what interpretation, and what motivation lay behind each variant in G67—revealing an audacity that few textual critics will be comfortable with today.

Petersen, of course, was working with a late 4th century date for G67 and a late 5th century for Codex D, which would place G67 at a significant advantage, especially if the two manuscripts were textually very similar. But G67 does not contain the same high percentage of readings similar to Codex D or to the broader D-text that exists, for example, with respect to P^{75} and Codex B. This lack of a close identity between G67 and Codex D is evident from Petersen's list of G67 readings,[46] which are supported by D 68 times, with 22 additional G67 readings attested by other recognized D-text witnesses, though they do not have the support of D. Together these readings total 90. But then Petersen listed 46 more readings that he also explicitly referred to as "Western variants," but these are readings with no support from any D-text witnesses or anywhere else—that is, they are unique readings. The conclusion to be drawn is two-fold: first, no tight relationship—i.e., a statistically significant one—is likely to be demonstrated between G67 and any established D-text witness, and, second, the large number of unique readings in G67 obviates against it being an "unadulterated" example of any textual tradition. Altogether then, G67, like every other D-text witness known to us, is mixed in its textual character, and any implication to the contrary in Petersen's phraseology is an overstatement. And when the current dates for G67 and D are considered, namely, Codex D somewhat earlier than G67 (see below), it will be clear that he overrated G67 also with respect to its temporal position in the history of the D-text. Yet, this does not detract from the

[44] Ibid., 471–477.
[45] Ibid., 473.
[46] Petersen, Early Coptic Manuscript (see n. 32), 230–241.

contribution made by Petersen's impressive compilation and publication of the G67 material, especially in view of the 27 year delay that was to follow before the appearance of a critical edition.

Haenchen and Weigandt's final consideration was the date of the manuscript, which they judged to be "probably" 5th or 6th century,[47] rather than Petersen's "4th or early 5th century." The latter, incidentally, was based on the judgment of a sterling group of palaeographers, including C. H. Roberts, T. C. Skeat, E. Husselman, and
121 W. Till, all of whom dated it in the late fourth or in the fifth century.[48] However, when Petersen presented his list of G67's variants, he opted for the earlier date and used the heading, "passages in the 4th century Coptic codex,"[49] thereby opening himself again to the charge of overestimating the manuscript's significance.

Incidentally, Haenchen and Weigandt had access, through the Münster Institut für neutestamentliche Textforschung, to microfilms and photographs of G67,[50] and the numerous readings they discussed became valuable data for further work. Yet, in the end—remembering that G67 consists of 107 leaves (213 pages)—they were able to fault Petersen's work by pointing only to some eight errors in his reading of the text![51]

---

[47] Haenchen/Weigandt, Original Text of Acts? (see n. 38), 480; M.-É. Boismard/A. Lamouille, Le texte occidental des Actes des Apôtres: Reconstitution et Réhabilitation ("Synthèse" 17), 2 vols., Paris, 1984, 1.76.231 n. 65. E. Grässer, Acta-Forschung seit 1960 (see n. 40), 168 f.; [repr. 161 f.], accepts their date rather than Petersen's, adding that the significance of G67 would be overrated if it is seen as anything more than a means of clarifying the role of D as a "Western" witness, 169; repr. 162; contrast this with Schenke's statement below: "G67 as a witness to the western text can hardly be overrated. . . ."

[48] Petersen, Early Coptic Manuscript (see n. 32), 225 and n. 3. On date, see below. Also B. M. Metzger, The Early Versions of the New Testament: Their Origin, Transmission, and Limitations, Oxford, 1977, 117; and H.-M. Schenke, Matthäus-Evangelium (see n. 41), 3 f. and n. 12.

[49] Petersen, Early Coptic Manuscript (see n. 32), 230. Petersen was reported to hold a 4th century date by J. S. Kebabian in a 1967 study of the codex's binding: *apud* Schenke, Apostelgeschichte (see n. 30), 5.

[50] Haenchen/Weigandt, Original Text of Acts? (see n. 38), 469.

[51] Ibid., 481 n. 2. They head this list by saying, "Here we would like to draw attention to some faults in Petersen's report, before they find their way into learned literature on the subject, as has already happened twice, in Epp's two essays . . .," pointing to a pair of Petersen's readings I had taken over.

B. *Schenke's Critical Edition of G67*

In his 1991 critical edition, Schenke appears to have settled at least two of these issues. First, he dated Coptic G67 in the 5th century, essentially on palaeographic and codicological grounds and in accordance with a growing consensus.[52] At about the same time, David C. Parker dated Codex Bezae about 400, after an extensive and thorough analysis of its origin and history.[53] Hence, my 1966 statements that G67 is "the earliest nonfragmentary Western ms of the text of Acts . . . since it antedates Codex Bezae by a century"[54] require modification, but this does not obviate my analysis of G67 readings in relation to those of the D-text, or the assignment of G67
to the category of primary or relatively "pure" D-text witnesses,[55] or 122
the high value placed on G67 in ascertaining the readings of the D-text. The readings of G67, by the way, have been incorporated into the apparatus of Nestle-Aland[26] and following with the symbol mae (*mittelägyptisch*) and in the UBS Greek New Testament, 3rd ed. and after, using cop^{meg}.

Second, Schenke evaluated what he called the "oppositional tendencies between American and German textual critics" that we have just reviewed, and offered his conclusion:

> While the Americans (Petersen, Epp) were inclined to stress—perhaps to exaggerate—the importance of the new witness, German scholarship (Haenchen, Weigandt, K. Aland, B. Aland) tends to minimize its relevance, for fear that this witness might be overestimated. No doubt there is some prepossession at work. And truth does not, in this case, lie in the middle, but very near to the American position. It is the conviction of the present editor . . . that the value of G 67 as a witness to the western text can hardly be overrated and that its publication will change the textual basis considerably, thereby enabling a completely new approach of the whole issue of the western text of Acts.[56]

---

[52] Schenke, Apostelgeschichte (see n. 30), 5 f.249. He notes the difficulties involved in Coptic palaeography, 5

[53] D. C. Parker, Codex Bezae: An Early Christian Manuscript and Its Text, Cambridge 1992, 261–286; on the date, 30.280 f., and below.

[54] Epp, Coptic Manuscript G67 (see n. 31), 197, and the similar statement in Theological Tendency (see n. 18), 10–11; cf. 29. The dating of D and G67 in both works also requires correction.

[55] Epp, Theological Tendency (see n. 18), 29 f.

[56] Schenke, Apostelgeschichte (see n. 30), 250 f. [from his "English Summary," 249–251].

Schenke's confident assessment supplanted the colorful summation given by Haenchen and Weigandt:

> Thus only one conclusion seems possible to us: our manuscript is . . . a late and exotic flower in the tree of our text tradition, which soon withered and fell to the ground without bearing fruit.[57]

But this, of course, was not to be the final word on G67, and Schenke's vindication is both welcome and encouraging. Yet, vastly more important is the fact that his edition of G67 facilitates a precise analysis of this manuscript's position among the D-text witnesses and thereby a fresh assessment of the nature of the D-text—something long overdue a quarter century and more after G67 was brought to light.

123 III. Publication of Theological Tendency in 1966: Conversation about Methods

The Theological Tendency of Codex Bezae Cantabrigiensis in Acts, published in 1966, was labeled an "epoch-making thesis" recently by Joël Delobel in that it signaled, along with two 1979 articles by Carlo M. [Cardinal] Martini and Max Wilcox, "a new interest and a new approach" to the "Western" text in the 1960s and 1970s. "The question of a possible particular tendency and the Lucan characteristics of the 'Western' text of Acts became the centre of a larger debate," he adds, and "may have inspired new attempts to produce comprehensive theories" that have appeared since the mid-1980s.[58] A few years earlier, Bart Ehrman related that "only since the 1960s have scholars begun to recognize the full extent to which early ideological conflicts affected the NT text," and then adds, "By all accounts, the impetus was provided by Eldon Jay Epp's groundbreaking study, *The Theological Tendency* . . ."[59] So the period of rela-

---

[57] Haenchen/Weigandt, Original Text of Acts? (see n. 38), 481. Grässer, Acta-Forschung (see n. 40), 168f.; [repr. 161 f.], also uses this quotation, along with Haenchen and Weigandt's late dating, to close his discussion of G67.

[58] J. Delobel, Focus on the "Western" Text in Recent Studies, in: EThL 73 (1997), 401–410, here: 401. The essay provides an excellent summary of work since the 1960s and 1970s.

[59] B. D. Ehrman, The Text as Window: New Testament Manuscripts and the Social History of Early Christianity, in: B. D. Ehrman/M. W. Holmes (eds.), The

tive calm from the end of the 1930s to the mid-1960s, mentioned by Delobel, was broken, and conversations on the "Western" text began again and have continued very much into the present.

A. *The Title: Conversation Misunderstood*

Two misconceptions of *Theological Tendency* rather quickly surfaced among some of its readers and reviewers: (1) a misunderstanding that the tendency being described was that of Codex Bezae only and not that of the so-called "Western" text in its broader (and earlier) form, and (2) an expectation that the book sought to resolve the long-standing question as to which was prior, the B-text or the D-text.

As to the first, it soon became clear to me that the title of the monograph had invited some needless misunderstanding and that it should have been *The Theological Tendency of the So-Called "Western" Text of Acts*, for the actual title suggested an investigation of ideological alterations in a single manuscript. Of course, the methodological first chapter carefully defined the inquiry as one directed to the early "Western" text of Acts, and not merely to its most famous
representative, Codex Bezae (D).[60] After all, the "Western" text 124
evolved over time, and the final text of Codex D evidences strong contamination from the B-text,[61] requiring careful efforts to reach behind its more recent strata.[62]

A second misunderstanding was the perception, or perhaps more often the assumption that *Theological Tendency* was implicitly affirming

Text of the New Testament in Contemporary Research: Essays on the *Status Quaestionis* (StD 46), Grand Rapids 1995, 361–379 (here: 364; cf. 367).

[60] Epp, Theological Tendency (see n. 18), 21–34; cf. 165. It seemed appropriate for the title to emphasize this famous and recognizable manuscript, and also to use its full designation, including "in Cambridge [University]," for a work to be published by the Cambridge University Press.

[61] See M.-É. Boismard, Le Codex de Bèze et le texte Occidental des Actes, in: D. C. Parker/C.-B. Amphoux, (eds.), Codex Bezae: Studies from the Lunel Colloquium June 1994 (NTTS 22), Leiden 1996, 257–270 (here: 269), for a recent opinion; cf. M. W. Holmes, Codex Bezae as a Recension of the Gospels, in the same Lunel volume, 123–160 (here: 125–142, see 126–128.141 f.)

[62] B. Aland, Entstehung, Charakter und Herkunft des sog. Westlichen Textes untersucht an der Apostelgeschichte, in: EThL 62 (1986), 5–65 (here: 65), isolated three stages: (1) 2nd century: readings tending toward the "Western" text; (2) first half of the 3rd century: "Western main redaction" with the well-known "Western" characteristics; (3) "free" copies made with individual variations, including D.

that the D-text was secondary to and derivative from the B-text. This misapprehension could arise easily enough from the comparative method employed, namely, placing the two text-forms in parallel columns, the B-text on the left and the D-text on the right (as many other researchers have done). These two issues, along with other methodological matters, will be treated in the following section.

B. *Assessing Theological/Ideological Bias: Animated Dialog*

How might tendentious textual variants be persuaded to disclose their bias? Quite simply if a particular variant or an entire textual tradition is known—or can be determined—to have been derived from another, earlier text. But that is not often the case, which leaves the researcher two paths: (1) decide which variation-unit or tradition is prior and then make a judgment as to the differing ideology expressed by the latter text-formulation, or (2) ascertain the "story" likely being told by the text of a passage, a manuscript, or a larger textual tradition. Alternatively, when a literary work has been transmitted in two rather different textual streams, determine the story each one is telling by comparing their variation-units point by point, without prejudice as to the derivation of one from the other. The latter, comparative approach is far more convenient and efficient, and this was the procedure employed in the search for tendentious aspects of the "Western" text of Acts.

125 1. *Codex Bezae or the "Western" Text?*

I was confident that any who read the 40-page introduction to *Theological Tendency* would realize that consideration would be accorded only to those textual variants, whether found in Codex Bezae or not, that arguably were distinctive readings of the early "Western" text and that idiosyncratic variations of the late 4th/early 5th century Codex Bezae itself would command no serious attention, except when no other "Western" witnesses were available or to note them for information or curiosity.[63] To accomplish this goal was no easy task,

[63] Naturally, the symbols D and/or *d* appeared as the sole attestation for some words and phrases in a longer variation-unit, where the additional evidence supports the larger unit as "Western"; also, sole D*d* readings were noted to give a more complete picture of what is in Codex D and how it relates to the broader D-text. On occasion, D*d* stand as sole support with the note, "No other leading

and to assess the variants only of Codex D itself would have been far easier, but—to my mind—much less a contribution. The procedure devised was to identify witnesses in Acts (Greek manuscripts, patristic writers, versional manuscripts, and versions as a whole) that regularly contain what have been recognized or could be construed as "Western" readings. These witnesses were divided into two categories: the "best" or "pure" D-text witnesses, and the "mixed" witnesses. [It would have been better, in retrospect, to have designated them "primary" and "secondary."] Then, since Codex Bezae is a continuous and almost complete text of Acts, and since it evinces an enormous number of readings that diverge from the "rival" B-text, I chose to give the most weight in the ensuing investigation, first, to readings in Codex Bezae (both the Greek and Latin sides[64]) that share the support of one or more primary witnesses, and second, to readings, while not in Codex Bezae, that find support among other members of the primary group. The secondary witnesses were employed in a supporting role, and variants attested only in that group were unlikely to accredit themselves as early D-text readings, except in special circumstances.

Briefly stated, the most prominent primary D-text witnesses in Acts, besides D (and *d*), are P^{38}, P^{48}, and Irenaeus; the Old Latin codex *h*, Cyprian, Augustine (where he uses a Cyprianic text), and Tertullian; the Coptic manuscript G67; and (for Syriac) Ephrem,
sy^{hmg} and sy^{h*}, and sy^{msK}. Along with Greek minuscules 614 and 383, 126
secondary witnesses include more than a dozen Old Latin manuscripts and some seven Latin patristic writings; the Sahidic Coptic version; the Syriac Peshitta and Harclean; and the Ethiopic, Armenian, and Georgian versions.[65]

'Western' witnesses are available;" at times this might be a case where G67 has the reading, but Petersen did not include it, though now Schenke's edition of G67 may have the text (if it is in Acts 1:1–15:3); see, e.g., Acts 2:47 (Theological Tendency [see n. 18], 74), though in this case G67 does not support D (Schenke, Apostelgeschichte (see n. 30), 108–110)—perhaps a cause for reconsideration.

[64] Parker, Codex Bezae (see n. 53), 191, offers the criticism that ". . . those who find theological tendencies seem to ignore the Latin text altogether." In *Theological Tendency*, however, this is certainly not the case. The Latin column of Codex Bezae was always and everywhere considered, and places where the Greek and Latin differ were assiduously noted in each instance (cf. Epp, Theological Tendency (see n. 18), 8–10).

[65] Epp, Theological Tendency (see n. 18), 28–34. For M.-É. Boismard, Codex de Bèze (see n. 61) 257 f. 269, the three main witnesses, beside D, are *h*, Harclean

Though without specific reference to my work, I respect the recent warnings of Joël Delobel, that "the transition from "Western" readings to "Western" text is made a little too quickly" and that "the so-called 'broad distribution' of the 'Western' text is not confirmed by the Greek manuscripts,"[66] but these problems were avoided in *Theological Tendency*, I think, both by use of the method just described and by the invariable practice of considering all available primary and secondary "Western" witnesses at each variation-unit.

Hence, variant readings in Acts that appeared to convey a theological/ideological viewpoint differing from the presentation in the parallel B-text [which provided a convenient basis of comparison] were treated only if a case could be made that an early "Western" reading was evident. Again, this is seldom a simple matter. My working assumption—based on the long-standing views of Westcott-Hort and
127 Ropes, and much subsequent work[67]—was that the D-text had its roots in the 2nd century, and the goal, ideally, was to seek readings

Syriac, and G67; see his full discussion in Id., Le texte occidental des Actes des Apôtres: Édition nouvelle entièrement refondue (EtB n.s. 40), Paris 2000, 13–46; cf. Boismard/Lamouille, Le texte occidental (see n. 47), 1–76. On the important early D-text witnesses for the gospels, see C.-B. Amphoux, Le Texte, in: D.C. Parker/C.-B. Amphoux (eds.), Codex Bezae: Studies from the Lunel Colloquium June 1994 (NTTS 22), Leiden 1996, 337–354 (here: 339–343).

[66] J. Delobel, The Achilles' Heel of New Testament Textual Criticism, in: Bijdr. 63 (2002), 3–21 (here: 18 f.).

[67] B. F. Westcott/F. J. A. Hort, The New Testament in the Original Greek, 2 vols., Cambridge 1881–1882; ²1896, 2.120.148 f.; and J. H. Ropes, Text of Acts (see n. 7), ccxxi–ccxxvi. See now, Parker, Codex Bezae (see n. 53), 280: "the *kind* of text it represents is as old as the beginnings of the Gospel traditions" [italics in original]; cf. 277 f. and his preceding discussion; Parker, The Living Text of the Gospels, Cambridge 1997, 201 f.; Ehrman, The Text of the Gospels at the End of the Second Century, in: D. C. Parker/C.-B. Amphoux (eds.), Codex Bezae: Studies from the Lunel Colloquium June 1994 (NTTS 22), Leiden 1996, 95–122 (here: 100–102). After a discerning discussion, which does not embrace an early D *text-type*, Ehrman concluded: "Codex Bezae must be like manuscripts that were available in the second century" (102). See also J. N. Birdsall, The Western Text in the Second Century, in: W. L. Petersen (ed.), Gospel Traditions in the Second Century: Origins, Recensions, Text, and Transmission (Christianity and Judaism in Antiquity, 3), Notre Dame/IN 1989, 3–17 (here: 16 f.); J. Delobel, The Text of Luke-Acts: A Confrontation of Recent Theories, in: J. Verheyden (ed.), The Unity of Luke-Acts (BEThL 142), Leuven 1999, 83–107 (here: 104); and E. J. Epp, The Significance of the Papyri for Determining the Nature of the New Testament in the Second Century: A Dynamic View of Textual Transmission, in: Petersen, Gospel Traditions (see earlier in this note), 71–103 (here: 101–103); [repr. in: Epp/Fee, Studies in the Theory (see n. 3), 274–297 (here: 295–297). Against such views, B. Aland, with reference to *Theological Tendency*, affirms that to seek a tendency in the early, second century D-„text-type" would already basically falsify the results: Id., Neutestamentliche

that might reasonably be presumed to stem from that period or from a time close to it. Of course, there is no direct 2nd century manuscript evidence for the D-text of Acts or for Acts at all (though now four 2nd century papyri are extant for other parts of the New Testament).[68] And New Testament citations in 2nd century patristic writers, of course, must be drawn from critical editions based on generally later manuscripts than those available for the New Testament text. At the risk of oversimplification, the usual rationale (in my work and others) for any claim that a reading existed in the 2nd century or in near proximity to it involves support by 2nd century or other early patristic writings, support by early Greek manuscripts, and by versional manuscripts or versions that plausibly have originated in the 2nd or 3rd centuries (e.g., Old Syriac, Old Latin, Sahidic and Bohairic Coptic), even though there are virtually no manuscripts from so early a time that contain these versions.[69] Yet a vast array of scholars since Westcott-Hort have affirmed or presumed the 2nd century existence of some entity that might be called a D-text, just as they have assumed that there was a competing B-text in that period, with the latter usually considered to be the mainstream and the D-text a tributary. Although Kurt and Barbara Aland were unwilling to recognize any "text types" prior to the 4th century, to my way of thinking they had already traced the outlines of the D-type-of-text in their "Category IV" of New Testament manuscripts, where P^{48} and P^{69} of the 3rd century and P^{38} and 0171 of the 3rd/4th century were presented as "precursors" of Codex Bezae.[70] This, however, is not the place to reopen the controversial conversation about text-types.[71]

Textkritik heute, in: Verkündigung und Forschung: Neues Testament (BEvTh 2), 1976, 3–22 (here: 21). Naturally, she and I have diverse views on the possibility of an early D *text type*.

[68] P^{52} (John), P^{90} (John), P^{98} (Revelation), and P^{104} (Matthew). Dated as second/third century are P^{32} (Titus), P^{46} (Pauline Epistles), P^{64+67} (Matthew), P^{66} (John), P^{77} (Matthew), and P^{103} (Matthew); also the majuscule fragment, 0189, which contains Acts 5:3–21.

[69] For a summary see E. J. Epp, Art. Textual Criticism (NT), in: AncBD 6 (1992), 412–435 (here: 425–427). This is not the venue for further discussion of this complex area.

[70] K. Aland/B. Aland, The Text of the New Testament: An Introduction to the Critical Editions and to the Theory and Practice of Modern Textual Criticism, rev.ed., Grand Rapids-Leiden 1989, 159 f.; cf. 64f.93. Cf. E. J. Epp, Issues (see n. 17), 38 f.

[71] All these issues have been covered, presenting my point of view, in various

128 Once *Theological Tendency* appeared, a few reviewers and other readers[72] concluded that the tendency or bias only of Codex Bezae was in view. For example, in his otherwise careful, meticulous, and altogether superb book on *Codex Bezae: An Early Christian Manuscript and Its Text*,[73] David Parker offered a succinct assessment of *Theological Tendency*, compressed into four brief paragraphs, where he spoke of methodological faults that raised "considerable doubts about the validity" of its results. For instance, alluding to the manner in which variants were selected to support the case, he suggested: "Given the enormous number of places where Bezae's text is unique, the isolation of certain 'theological' tendencies in a number of them is likely to be arbitrary."[74] What he apparently envisioned here was that tendencies were derived from a number of unique readings of Bezae's text.[75] As noted earlier, however, in *Theological Tendency* it was not Codex Bezae's readings in isolation that were considered for assessment as to theological bias, but variants, whether attested in Codex Bezae or not, that had some reasonable and broader claim to represent the "Western" text, whereas unique readings of Codex Bezae

essays: see Epp/Fee, Studies (see n. 3), e.g., 31–44.87–96.283–297; Epp, Issues (see n. 17) 34–44.

[72] See A. F. J. Klijn, Survey (see n. 30) 62 f. C. K. Barrett, both in *LQHR* 192 (1967), 345f., and in his review article: Id., Is There a Theological Tendency in Codex Bezae? in: E. Best/R. McL. Wilson (eds.), Text and Interpretation. FS Matthew Black, Cambridge 1979, 15–27, spoke almost exclusively of D and Codex D, except at the end, when he used the clarifying phrase, "the Western text" (26). Others who think of D alone might include J. Coppens, in: EThL 43 (1967) 274 f.; Z. C. Hodges, in: BSac 125 (1968), 79f.; and J. C. Truro, in: TS 29 (1968), 161 f., though these reviews are brief and succinct. J. Read-Heimerdinger, Where is Emmaus? Clues in the Text of Luke 24 in Codex Bezae, in D. G. K. Taylor (ed.), Studies in the Early Text of the Gospels and Acts: The Papers of the First Birmingham Colloquium on the Textual Criticism of the New Testament (SBL Text-Critical Studies 1), Atlanta 1999, 229–244 (here: 232 n. 7), certainly misunderstands my *Theological Tendency*, when she says, ". . . his discussion is flawed in so far as it draws on other mss when Codex Bezae does not support his claims." On the contrary, that is precisely the proper approach in my case—for I was seeking the viewpoint of the pre-Codex Bezae "Western" text, not the ideology of Codex Bezae only.

[73] Parker, Codex Bezae (see n. 53).

[74] Ibid., 190. Cf. Parker, JThS n.s. 45 (1994), 704–708 (here: 704), where the reference is to my study of "an entire manuscript."

[75] Parker, Codex Bezae (see n. 53), 190 f., employed the terms "Bezae's text," and "Bezan reading" or "Bezan text," which, I assume, he used to refer to the text or readings of Codex D (including the Latin side, *d*). Note the comment of Ropes, The Text of Acts (see n. 7), lxxxiv. n. 2: "The term 'Bezan text,' by which it was sought to avoid the fallacy . . . implied in the name 'Western text,' has done more positive harm than the latter."

were granted little if any status as witnesses to the presumably earlier "Western" text or as candidates for revealing that text-type's bias. Thus, the aim was to isolate readings distinctive of the "Western" text and quite specifically to avoid readings unique to Codex D (or to any other individual D-text witness) except in special circumstances. This is not to obviate an assessment of unique readings, for meaningful ideological variants might well disclose distinct viewpoints of Codex Bezae itself, a worthy project but not one that I pursued.[76]

Incidentally, Coptic G67 already had nullified some five or six 129
previously "unique" readings of D (and *d*) by providing the only other known textual support for them: see Acts 4:24; 5:8 (D, not *d*); 5:18; the last part of the long variant in 11:2; Acts 13:44; and perhaps 7:54.[77] These are all meaningful variants of some length, but they would not have been taken seriously without the support of G67.

2. *The Comparative Method and Issues of Priority: B-text or D-text?*

In its pursuit of bias in the "Western" text, *Theological Tendency* adopted the procedure used by Ropes and most others since, namely, placing the two textual streams over against one another for purposes of comparison. It is easy to see, therefore, how the implication could arise, in accordance with the dominant view, that the D-text was dependent upon and derived from the B-text. It was not the task of *Theological Tendency*, however, to determine or even to discuss the priority of either the B-text or the D-text (though occasional judgments were offered in passing). This intractable issue of priority had clouded most of the assessments of the D-text over several generations, and it seemed that the time had come to view the D-text independently of that question. Hence, the sole aim was to display formulations of thought and portrayals of scenes resident in readings of the "Western" text over against those in the parallel B-text without concern as to

[76] See Epp, Theological Tendency (see n. 18), 27–28. Curiously, C. K. Barrett, in: LQHR (1967), 345, thinks "it might have been better to focus attention on D [= Codex D] as a single delimited witness." See also below on the recent studies of J. Read-Heimerdinger.

[77] For these, see Nestle-Aland[27]—8th printing ad loc., except for 7:54; Epp, Coptic Manuscript G67 (see n. 31), 199 f., for details on all; Schenke, Apostelgeschichte (see n. 30), 144 f. on 7:54, and ad loc. for the others; Epp, Theological Tendency (see n. 18), 10 f.

whether one text-form was prior to another or whether there was any intertextual relationship between them; rather, I wished to permit the "Western" or D-text to reveal its "inner consistency and meaning" and to have "a chance to speak for itself" without prejudice as to priority, influence, or dependence.[78] In each discussion, therefore, a judgment was offered as to how the B-text saw the scene in its way and how the D-text viewed it in another way—descriptions of each narrative on its own.

Quite naturally, some readers, probably influenced by the well-known convictions of Westcott-Hort and Ropes—and most others ever since—may have read into the parallel displays and discussions their own preference for the priority of the B-text and ascribing a
130 secondary status to the D-text.[79] W. A. Strange, for instance, reported that "Epp assumed the existence of a Western reviser when he should have set himself to demonstrate it."[80] but this was not my assumption, nor does it follow from the comparative process used, where the aim was merely to see how one variation-unit differed from another in its presentation. Of course this distinction between the B- and D-texts was compromised, I admit, when phrases were used such as "Peter is enhanced in the D-text," or "christology is heightened," etc., but one could as well have reversed the descriptions of the comparable elements and have stated that the B-text, in the comparison, "diminishes Peter," or "places less emphasis on the Spirit," etc. In many cases such comparatives were not required to describe the differing scenes, but at other times they were essential for a meaningful comparison of the evidence. In short, the point was not to prejudge the relationship of the two rival texts, but to point out, as objectively and conveniently as possible, their *differences in conception and portrayal.*

---

[78] Epp, Theological Tendency (see n. 18), 21. Cf. 165: The goal was "simply to *understand* the D-text of Acts on its own terms without reference to the questions of origin or originality" (italics in original).

[79] E.g., J. Heimerdinger, Unintentional Sins in Peter's Speech: Acts 3:12–26, in: RCatT 20 (1995), 269–276, esp. 269 f., where, in addition, she describes her own method exactly as I described mine: an approach to the D-version "not as a modification of any prior text but as a coherent text which stands in its own right" (270); Smit Sibinga, in: VigChr 24 (1970) 75–77 (here: 76); Strange, Problem of the Text (see n. 16), 20. Note that G. D. Kilpatrick, Language and Text in the Gospels and Acts, in: VigChr 24 (1970), 161–171 (here: 168), who did not misunderstand my goal, yet wished that I had made more observations on variants preserving the original text.

[80] Strange, Problem of the Text (see n. 16), 20.

In the meantime, perhaps the clearest example of my comparative method was a 1981 article on the ascension in Luke-Acts, where no extraneous theological tendency was urged, but each of the two quite different portrayals of the ascension in the B-text and D-text traditions was permitted to speak for itself—to tell its own story.[81]

Is the method credible as described? David Parker has a way of raising issues by succinct, challenging formulations, as in this statement with reference to the general method in *Theological Tendency*:

> But the only possible way to establish theological tendency is by comparison with the Fathers' understanding of the text: given *their* interpretations of Luke and Acts, the critic would then have to ask whether the Bezan reading can credibly be regarded as representative of one or more of them.[82]

If taken at face value, the procedure proposed here for revealing 131
tendency in the "Western" text would generate, it seems to me, extraordinarily sparse results when an early form of the "Western" text is being sought and assessed. In a given instance—actually a best-case scenario—we would have Irenaeus, Cyprian, Tertullian, some manuscripts of Augustine, and Ephrem as primary patristic witnesses for our selected text, plus several other patristic writers as secondary support. The next step, then, would be to compare the relevant *Bezan* readings [again, only Codex Bezae appears to be in Parker's view] with the Fathers' understanding of the text of Acts. Without going farther, does not an immediate difficulty arise when it is realized that these early patristic writers are part and parcel of the evidence for the relevant "*Western*" readings [since not merely the Bezan text is in view]; hence, they cannot by nature be the basis of comparison—i.e., the standard against which we place our selected

[81] E. J. Epp, The Ascension in the Textual Tradition of Luke-Acts, in: E. J. Epp/G. D. Fee (eds.), New Testament Textual Criticism: Its Significance for Exegesis. FS Bruce M. Metzger, Oxford 1981, 131–145. Here the D-text formulation can be seen as a virtually consistent narrative—lacking the literal transfer from earth to heaven—without considering or knowing the B-text version. But that would be pointless since the latter portrayal is ubiquitous in standard Greek and versional New Testament texts. For an evaluation, see B. D. Ehrman, The Orthodox Corruption of Scripture: The Effect of Early Christological Controversies on the Text of the New Testament, New York-Oxford 1993, 230–232. Cf. M. C. Parsons, The Departure of Jesus in Luke-Acts: The Ascension Narratives in Context (JSNT.S 21), Sheffield 1987, 128 f. 134.

[82] Parker, Codex Bezae (see n. 53), 190 [italics in original].

variants. To be sure, if only Codex Bezae as a separate manuscript were being investigated, it might well be compared to early patristic sources and to other "Western" witnesses to discover its own bias, but in *Theological Tendency* the relevant patristic evidence is as much the "Western" textual material itself as are the Greek and other manuscripts.

What was required for comparison then, it seemed to me, was a standard that creates *polarity*, one that brings into relief the scenes and formulations where the "Western" text is distinctive. And would it not be appropriate in such a situation to select some form of the B-text as an effective and efficient basis of comparison, especially in view of the two sharply differing textual streams in Acts? In this respect, again following the example of several past scholars, including Ropes, I opted to use Codex Vaticanus (B) for comparison, though never blindly, but always consulting other B-text witnesses when the evidence was seriously divided or where otherwise there was a question whether B best represents that textual tradition. These difficulties in selecting a basis for comparison were anticipated in my introductory discussion of the project.[83]

3. *Tendency or Merely Enhancement?*

The line between a tendency in a text and simple enhancement or heightening of a figure or an event may be thin, and several reviewers and readers of *Theological Tendency* were not convinced that an anti-Judaic bias had been clearly or fully established, but thought, rather, that Codex D and the "Western" text "exaggerate existing tendencies," as C. K. Barrett argued in a substantial review article.[84] While agreeing that "there are places where the D text shows a
132 greater animosity against Jews, a greater readiness to blame them rather than the Gentiles for the attack on Jesus and subsequent

[83] Epp, Theological Tendency (see n. 18), 35–37.

[84] Barrett, Is There a Theological Tendency? (see n. 72), 26. Cf. Barrett, in: LQHR 192 (1967), 345 f. Others who saw heightening rather than or in addition to an anti-Judaic tendency include F. W. Danker, in: CTM 39 (1968) 413 f.; B. M. Metzger, in: Gn 40 (1968), 831–833 (here: 833); J. C. O'Neill, in: New Blackfriars 48 (1967), 498 f.; M. Wilcox, Luke and the Bezan Text of Acts, in: J. Kremer (ed.), Les Actes des Apôtres: Traditions, rédaction, théologie (BEThL 48), Gembloux-Leuven, 1979, 447–455 (here: 448), and R. Maddox, The Purpose of Luke-Acts (Studies of the New Testament and its World), Edinburgh 1982, 61 n. 87.

attacks on the apostles," he asserted that "the tendency . . . is not a specially anti-Jewish tendency but a tendency to emphasize whatever is to be found in the underlying text."[85] Then he concluded:

> It is erroneous to charge the Western Text with a special tendency to anti-Judaism. This interest, along with other characteristics, was found in the original text of Acts, and all were developed and exaggerated by the Western editor.[86]

Barrett's view, of course, clearly placed the D-text in a secondary and derivative position to the B-text, which, for him, was the "original" text. The result is that the D-text's voice is considerably muffled when its intertextual "source" is thought to be known and its *modus operandi* already preestablished, namely (to use Barrett's words), "to increase interest, to heighten tension, to make descriptions more vivid, in a word, to brighten the colours of Luke's narrative, where no theological, ecclesiastical, racial, or any other such interest is involved."[87] *Theological Tendency*, as already noted, sought as much as possible to give the D-text its own voice, and if comparison, for instance, showed heightened tension or urgency, the question was, what might that high tension or great urgency mean, and how might such characterizations have been motivated? Moreover, such questions should be asked, to the extent feasible, by looking at the D-text formulation separately and apart from any theory of derivation (even though another form of text is utilized for convenient comparison). Space does not permit either a further report here of Barrett's always learned discussions (eight pages!) or a detailed response to them, but his main points were clear: a tendency to anti-Judaism is not to be doubted in some D-passages, but this cannot be claimed as either a special or a general tendency throughout the D-text; rather, for Barrett, the D-text's "real tendency" was simply to exaggerate.[88] His forward-looking suggestion was that the apocryphal Acts excel in such exaggeration and scholars ought to seek from their setting clues to the explanation of the "Western" text of the canonical Acts.[89]

---

[85] Barrett, Is There a Theological Tendency? (see n. 72), 22. Cf. Barrett, The Acts of the Apostles (ICC), 2 vols., Edinburgh, 1994–1998, 1:28.
[86] Ibid., 26 f.
[87] Ibid., 22.
[88] Ibid., 27.
[89] Ibid.

133 Barrett was not alone in preferring enhancement over a full-blown tendency, for recently David Parker raised the very issue of whether one text's enhancement of an emphasis or character found in another text constitutes a tendency, as, for example, a heightened interest in the Holy Spirit or in Peter. His view, like Barrett's, was that such a phenomenon "just indicates that what the text sets out to do is give us Luke, only more of him . . . . That is, once one is expanding a story about the apostles, then it is tautology to say that the apostles' role will be expanded."[90] But identifying enhancement is not inevitably tautologous, for enhancement by its very nature is registered in degrees, and each degree or stage of heightening represents a separate entity—expressing, for example, a different portrayal of an event or person for one purpose or another. When J. H. Crehan[91] and Carlo M. Martini[92] argued that the "Western" text in Acts enhances Peter and/or Paul, that, I think, was not tautology, but the report of a different, more lofty conception of those apostles. A more saintly, a more resolute, a more authoritative apostle is different from a less resolute or less authoritative apostle. So it is with other aspects of heightening: a different image, scene, portrayal, or characterization emerges. Naturally, not all will have a specific tendentious motivation, or an identifiable one, yet that is something to look for in the event that patterns emerge that enlighten us as to the viewpoint resident in a text.

A very recent assessment of the "enhancement" factor, with specific reference to Barrett's viewpoint on *Theological Tendency*, issued

---

[90] Parker, Codex Bezae (see n. 53), 190. He suggests (Ibid.) another tautology in *Theological Tendency*: "As a matter of fact any alteration to a theological text will by nature be a theological alteration . . .," but there are hundreds of intentional variants in manuscripts of our theological texts involving orthography and grammar, use of preferable synonyms, conflation of readings from two or more manuscripts, and adjudicating perceived historical, geographical, chronological, and other difficulties that are not likely, *prima facie*, to involve theological or even broader ideological matters (though each case should be examined for any possible bias). I now notice that the same response to Parker's affirmation has been made by Ehrman, Text of the Gospels (see n. 67), 110.

[91] J. H. Crehan, Peter according to the D-text of Acts, in: TS 18 (1957), 596–603.

[92] C. M. Martini, La figura di Pietro secondo le varianti del codice D negli Atti degli Apostoli, in: San Pietro: Atti della XIX Settimana Biblica, Brescia, 1967) 279–289; [Repr. in: Id., La parola di Dio alle origini della Chiesa (AnBib 93), Rome 1980, 103–113; Id., Pierre et Paul dans l'Église ancienne: Considérations sur la tradition textuelle des Actes des Apôtres, in: L. De Lorenzi (ed.), Paul de Tarse: Apôtre du nôtre temps [memorial to Pope Paul VI], Rome 1979, 261–268 (here: 267 f.); repr. in Id., La parola, 181–188, (here: 187 f.)].

from Bart Ehrman, who treated it within the second-century social context:

> . . . any heightening of Luke's own emphases is significant—especially when it comes to important social issues like the relationship of Jews and Christians. For indeed, the social context at the end of the second century was far more serious in this regard than at the end of the first; and the scribes who obviously stood within Luke's tradi-
> tion . . . had an additional century's worth of turmoil. . . . No wonder 134
> they found many of Luke's statements palatable, and worked to make them even more stringent. But to argue on these grounds that the changes of Codex Bezae are somehow not "anti-Judaic" or "theological" is really to miss the point, and to engage in special pleading on behalf of these anti-Jewish scribes.[93]

Ehrman's ensuing discussion and his pointed examples[94] of anti-Jewish scribal alterations from the gospel texts in Codex D constitute a significant corrective to the "mere enhancement" view, especially in terms of methodology, though he makes no pretense that an anti-Jewish tendency could be documented throughout the gospels in D.

Similar in nature and usually in support of a cumulative argument in *Theological Tendency* was the use of christological expansions to support the anti-Judaic thesis, namely, variants that filled out the phrase "the Lord Jesus Christ" when one or two elements were lacking. To George Kilpatrick, for example, "it seems unlikely that they represent degrees of anti-Jewish feeling,"[95] and this expansion of christological titles was explained by others as simply a habit of "common Christian piety"[96] or due to liturgical influence.[97] Recently Ehrman, again, demonstrated in case after case that such filling out was not a haphazard habit of scribes, but that it:

---

[93] Ehrman, Text of the Gospels (see n. 67), 109–114, here: 111. Ian Moir, in: JThS n.s. 19 (1968), 277–281 (here: 278), wished in another way to exonerate doctrine-altering scribes when he suggested that *Theological Tendency* should have described the tendency as "a sociological or ecclesiastical-political bias," for "theological" "would imply a deliberate falsification of basic dogmatics."

[94] Ehrman, Text of the Gospels (see n. 67), 111–114: Luke 23:34; Matt 27:26; Mark 15:8 and 15:12; Luke 23:37.

[95] G. D. Kilpatrick, Language and Text (see n. 79), 166–168. Cf. Parker, Codex Bezae (see n. 53), 191: "The discovery of shades of Christological emphasis by Epp and Rice is likely to be spurious." See also R. H. Fuller, in: CBQ 30 (1968), 447 f.; Metzger, in: Gn 40 (1968), 833; C. H. Pinnock, in: ChrTo 11 (1966/1967), 34 f. For treatment in *Theological Tendency*, see "Jesus as Christos" in the Index of Subjects.

[96] Metzger, in: Gn 40 (1968), 833.

[97] J. H. Crehan, in: HeyJ 8 (1967), 412 f.; Fuller, in: CBQ 30 (1968), 447.

> . . . ultimately stems from theological disputes of the second century in which proto-orthodox Christians emphasized the unity of Jesus Christ in the face of separationist Christologies that claimed that each of Jesus' names and titles referred to distinct divine entities.[98]

Ehrman, though, did not view this scribal phenomenon as worthy of being "a polemical stratagem," but rather a "by-product of the debates"—resulting in readings incorporated to show how the texts
135 should properly be read against those who view them differently[99]—nor did he accept them in any way as an anti-Judaic polemic.[100] What he did, however, was clearly to vindicate their interpretation as theologically motivated, thereby supporting the *method* though certainly not the *conclusion* drawn from them in *Theological Tendency*.

4. *A Socio-Ecclesiastical Context for Anti-Judaic Bias?*

The question of identifying a social-polemical setting for the anti-Jewish sentiment in the D-text arose, and quite understandably, because *Theological Tendency* did not attempt to connect it with a contemporary historical situation or social context. R. P. C. Hanson and others[101] made this point, and more recently Bart Ehrman called this lack of connection the "major drawback" of the book.[102] Indeed, the strongest point of his own pivotal work on *Orthodox Corruption* was the adroit placement of nearly 180 variation units into contexts of christological debate in the 2nd and 3rd centuries. Now in a recent study, drawing upon this previous, extensive interaction with the early Christian politico-theological scene, he offered several examples of anti-Jewish textual formulations in the gospel texts of Codex D (noted above)[103] and once again judiciously placed them in the

---

[98] Ehrman, Orthodox Corruption (see n. 81), 161–165, here: 163. See his numerous examples, 150–165.

[99] Ibid., 164.

[100] Ibid., 161 and 179 f. n. 192.

[101] R. P. C. Hanson, The Ideology of Codex Bezae in Acts, in: NTS 14 (1967/68), 282–286 (here: 283). Others include J. N. Birdsall, The Recent History of New Testament Textual Criticism (from Westcott and Hort, 1881, to the Present), in: ANRW II.26.1 (1992), 99–197 (here: 161); G. B. Caird, in: ET 78 (1966/67), 287; A. F. J. Klijn, Survey (see n. 30), 62; C. M. Martini, in: VD 46 (1968), 62 f.; Id., in: Bib. 51 (1970), 115–117; E. Rasco, in: Gregorianum 48 (1968), 365–368 (here: 368); Smit Sibinga, in: VigChr 24 (1970), 76; and Ehrman (see next note).

[102] Ehrman, Text of the Gospels (see n. 67), 110. Cf. Ehrman, The Text as Window (see n. 59), 367; and Id., Orthodox Corruption (see n. 81), 161.231.

[103] See n. 94.

2nd century Jewish-Christian context. He pointed to 2nd century writings such as the Epistle of Barnabas and those of Justin Martyr and Melito, and recalled the anti-Jewish climate as one that could easily accommodate scribal alterations conveying similar sentiments.[104] In the same 1996 publication, Michael W. Holmes in his extensive examination of the text of D, particularly in Matthew, also pointed to seven "early Bezan readings" that "represent the closest thing there is to any 'anti-Judaic' tendency (or any 'theological' tendency, for that matter) in Bezan Matthew."[105]

The lack of connection to church history arose in another way, 136
though not as a direct challenge to *Theological Tendency*: Kurt and Barbara Aland in their text-critical manual, so indispensable for the study of New Testament manuscripts, affirmed years ago in discussing the improbability of "a special 'Western' type of text" in the early period that:

> no important personality can be identified at any time or place in the early Western church who would have been capable of the singular theological achievement represented by the text of the Gospels and Acts in the ancestor of Codex Bezae. . . .[106]

They added, in the same context, that the text of the 5th century Codex D "represents (in its exemplar) the achievement of an outstanding early theologian of the third/fourth century,"[107] though they do not offer a name! Elsewhere, they posit that "it is quite inconceivable that the text of Codex Bezae . . . could have existed as early as the second century."[108]

First, of course, no one would claim an exclusive Western venue for the D-text, so if a major early figure were to be sought, it more probably should be sought in the East, particularly if David Parker's closely-argued historical sketch of Codex D is followed, which envisions independent Latin versions in Berytus (Beirut) early in the 3rd century, made from Greek texts already in use there; then in the

[104] Ehrman, Text of the Gospels (see n. 67), 109–114; Id., The Text as Window (see n. 59), 366 f.

[105] Holmes, Codex Bezae as a Recension (see n. 39), 132 n. 42. He is treating an "early layer of variants" in D, 140 f.

[106] Aland/Aland, Text of the New Testament (see n. 70), 69; cf. 54 f.

[107] Ibid.

[108] Ibid., 55.

early 3rd century the formation of these texts into a series of bilingual codices, culminating in Codex Bezae around 400.[109] In 1986 Barbara Aland herself had opted for Syria as the origin of the "Western main redaction."[110] These considerations, in my judgment, speak both to the East-West issue and also to the earlier history and date of the "Western" text (i.e., of certain of its layers).

Second, on the need for a powerful personality to account for the kind of text behind the "Western" text and Codex D, Michael Holmes recently proposed an intriguing new approach. He argued first, referring to Origen and Jerome, that "ancient textual critics had a *much smaller effect* upon the wording of the texts they studied, commented upon, and transmitted than we generally assume."[111] Next, he cited James Zetzel on Latin classical manuscripts to the effect that they belonged to "amateur and wealthy book-lovers" who commented in
137 the margins, corrected errors, and made the books serviceable for themselves; hence, Zetzel asserted:

> . . . it is pure wishful thinking to believe that our manuscripts descend only from those in which a scrupulous or cautious reader had made corrections. In general, there is no escaping the disturbing fact that, in antiquity, the preservation and the quality of a text were the result of the interests of its successive owners or readers, not of a scholarly editor.[112]

Zetzel added that readers and scribes, as intelligent people, "read and copied books because they had an interest in them," and therefore "because they understood what they read and wrote, they inevitably affected the texts in accordance with their own ideas. . . ."[113] Holmes carried this over to New Testament manuscripts in the second and early third centuries, recognizing, of course, that many New Testament manuscripts belonged to churches, but he points out that

---

[109] Parker, Codex Bezae (see n. 53), 280 f.; cf. 30. The Nestle-Aland[27] and the UBS[4] Greek New Testaments date it as 5th century, and at the Lunel Colloquium on Codex Bezae in 1994, on palaeograophic grounds, especially of the Latin side, J. Irigoin dated D in the second quarter of the 5th century and L. Holtz from 380 to 400: D. C. Parker/C.-B. Amphoux (eds.), Codex Bezae: Studies from the Lunel Colloquium June 1994 (NTTS 22), Leiden 1996, 9.30; cf. 332 (Parker).

[110] B. Aland, Entstehung (see n. 62), 63.65.

[111] Holmes, Codex Bezae as a Recension (see n. 39), 147 [italics in original].

[112] J. E. G. Zetzel, Latin Textual Criticism in Antiquity, New York 1981, 238 f.; see Holmes, Codex Bezae as a Recension (see n. 39), 147 f.

[113] Zetzel, Latin Textual Criticism (see n. 112), 254.

they still would be copied and read by individuals "with widely varying levels of skill, taste, ability, and scruples."[114]

This scenario finds support in Harry Y. Gamble's judgment that the earliest Christian books represent the "intermediate phase" of the evolution of the codex—they were neither notebooks nor fine literature, but "practical books for everyday use,"[115] and is supported also by my preliminary search for specific editor's or scholar's critical marks in New Testament papyri, particularly from Oxyrhynchus, that might identify them as scholar's copies—but that cursory search disclosed no such signs.[116] Moreover, as C. H. Roberts pointed out long ago, books produced for use in the earliest Christian communities utilized copying practices from the documentary papyri (rather than the literary), including a consistent use of the codex form, the lack of a calligraphic hand, the use of contractions (notably the *nomina sacra*), among others—all indications of utilitarian books.[117] Holmes's point then—which I have attempted to buttress with some additional evidence—is that an outstanding individual would not be
essential in the production of a text like the "Western"; rather "a 138
well-educated, well-informed, conscientious but unscholarly anonymous *reader* is much more likely to have been responsible than any 'important personality.'"[118] This delineation also fits well with our sense of the D-text as a collection of scribal or readers' alterations with many interests: correction of grammar or of perceived historical, geographical, or chronological errors; improvement of sense or style; expansion or enhancement for vividness of narrative; stressing or minimizing social conventions; and doctrinal defense or persuasion; among others. Of course, all manuscripts show various such phenomena, though by no means to the extent found in the "Western" text of Acts, and—most significantly—many of the D-text

[114] Holmes, Codex Bezae as a Recension (see n. 39), 148 f.

[115] H. Y. Gamble, Books and Readers in the Early Church: A History of Early Christian Texts, New Haven 1995, 66; cf. 77 f.

[116] E. J. Epp, The New Testament Papyri at Oxyrhynchus in Their Social and Intellectual Context, in: W. L. Petersen et al. (eds.), The Sayings of Jesus: Canonical and Non-canonical. FS Tjitze Baarda (NT.S 89), Leiden 1997, 63–68; Id., The Codex and Literacy in Early Christianity and at Oxyrhynchus: Issues Raised by Harry Y. Gamble's *Books and Readers in the Early Church*, in: Critical Review of Books in Religion 10 (1997), 33 f. To be sure, more manuscripts need to be surveyed.

[117] C. H. Roberts, Manuscript, Society and Belief in Early Christian Egypt (SchwL 1977), London 1979, 12–22.29.

[118] Holmes, Codex Bezae as a Recension (see n. 39), 149 [italics in original].

variations are "of a kind," possessing a similar nature or character unlike any other New Testament manuscript tradition.

5. *Alternatives to Anti-Judaic Bias?*

Over the years a number of scholars who interacted with *Theological Tendency* preferred modifications or alternatives to the anti-Judaic hypothesis. For example, within a year or so R. P. C. Hanson released a full-length (and frequently quoted) review article in New Testament Studies which began with assertions that *Theological Tendency* "will for long be valuable as a new and very competent review of the whole interesting question of the 'Western' tradition of readings,"[119] and with the concession that "nobody could deny" the presence of passages in the D-text that "betray a sharpened animus against the Jews."[120] Beyond that, however, he felt that "in his zeal to prove his thesis Dr Epp often presses the evidence too hard. He detects an 'anti-Judaic' tendency in all sorts of unlikely and unconvincing contexts."[121] Hanson, of course, had his own agenda, that an "interpolator... of some wealth and education with no strong connexions with Judaism" was at work on the text of Acts in Rome between 120–150, and that his alterations found their way into the D-text.[122] Describing his preferences for other explanations in an array of passages afforded valuable insights into the D-text. Yet, perhaps partly out of enthusiasm for his own formulations, he concluded: "The final impression left on the reader by Dr Epp's determination to see theological tendencies... may well be that he suffers from an obses-
139 sion with a King Charles' head."[123] Yet, in the end, Hanson provided a quite balanced view: "It is as unwise to try to fit all the alterations... into a single theological pattern as it is to refuse to see theological tendency in any of them."[124]

[119] Hanson, Ideology of Codex Bezae (see n. 101) 282.
[120] Ibid., 283.
[121] Ibid., 284.
[122] Ibid., 285, but esp. his earlier study, published when *Theological Tendency* was in the press: The Provenance of the Interpolator in the 'Western' Text of Acts and of Acts Itself, in: NTS 12 (1965/66), 211–230 (here: 223). Hanson's two studies on the "Western" text, arguing for an "interpolator" in Rome, are evaluated by Klijn, Survey (see n. 30), 64: "Thus we see that finally Hanson's idea only rests on one reading."
[123] Hanson, Ideology (see n. 101), 286—à la Dickens, David Copperfield, XIV.
[124] Hanson, Ideology (see n. 101), 286.

About a decade later, Carlo M. Martini agreed that the D-text enhanced Peter and Paul, but did not find congenial any connection with an anti-Judaic theme. His rationale, echoing Barrett's interpretation, essentially was that, with the exception of the Apostolic Decree, there was only "minimal" opposition between the B- and D-text readings that *Theological Tendency* presented, neutralizing any theory of doctrinal tendency in the "Western" text.[125] More precisely, he argued that the D-text paralleled Peter and Paul, placing them on about the same level, but that the D-text did not thereby modify the emphasis on the two apostles already given by the author of Acts, but enriched the narrative and provided paraenetic expansions.[126]

Then Matthew Black, on at least the issue of the Holy Spirit in the "Western" text, reversed the thrust of *Theological Tendency*, by arguing that the B-text, e.g., at Acts 18:4–6, reveals "a pro-Jewish bias which has led to the shortening and altering of the text of D."[127] His procedure, unlike that of *Theological Tendency*, was to defend the Lucan originality of the variants in one text-form, in this case the D-text, and to interpret the variants in the light of that decision—a method, incidentally, that Bart Ehrman would employ later in *The Orthodox Corruption of Scripture*.[128]

Finally, in a spate of articles during the past decade, with frequent reference to *Theological Tendency*, Jenny Read-Heimerdinger has proposed, first, that the readings of Codex Bezae "derive from a context of traditional Jewish teaching and scriptures," and, second, that 140
though the variants are critical of the Jews and their actions, for example, in Acts 3:12–26, yet:

---

[125] C. M. Martini, La tradition textuelle des Actes des Apôtres et les tendances de l'Église ancienne, in: J. Kremer (ed.), Les Actes des Apôtres: Traditions, rédaction, théologie (BEThL 48), Gembloux-Leuven 1979, 23–35 (here: 26–28); [Repr. in: Id., La parola (see n. 92), 165–179 (here: 170 f.)].

[126] Martini, Pierre et Paul (see n. 92), 267–268; [Repr. in Id., La parola (see n. 92), 187 f.]. See his earlier La figura di Pietro (see n. 92), 279–289; [Repr. in Id., La parola (see n. 92), 103–113].

[127] M. Black, The Holy Spirit in the Western Text of Acts, in: E. J. Epp/G. D. Fee (eds.), New Testament Textual Criticism: Its Significance for Exegesis. FS Bruce M. Metzger, Oxford 1981, 159–179 (here 169).

[128] Of interest is D. C. Parker's suggestion (JTS 45 [1994] 706): Could not Ehrman, rather than try to establish the "original" text in each case, simply point out "that one set of readings supports an orthodox interpretation and another set favours a heretical one, and leave aside the question of priority?" This, he added, would "describe the function of the variant forms as they were received and circulated. This is one possible future avenue for the discipline" (ibid.). *Theological Tendency*, of course, employed this very procedure in the past—thirty-five years ago.

> the Bezan text is not hostile to the Jewish people so much as admonitory and hortatory in line with the prophetic writings of the Jewish scriptures. Peter's speech in Codex Bezae is no more anti-Judaic than is the book of Isaiah on which he draws.[129]

Hence, ". . . the perspective of the Bezan writer is Jewish and not Gentile."[130] Indeed:

> the preoccupation with things Jewish, rightly detected by Epp and J.T. Sanders . . . is so detailed and exact that it can only occur from an insider Jewish point of view . . .; even more specifically, it reflects Judaism in the Diaspora rather than in Jerusalem. Christianity is seen as the continuation, and not the abrogation, of the faith of Israel. . . .[131]

And in a later study on Barnabas in Acts, she stated:

> Many of the assumptions about Codex Bezae have been influenced by the analysis of its text of Acts offered by E.J. Epp in 1966, which concluded that the Bezan text displayed an accentuated hostility towards the Jews . . ., the work of second-century Christians who viewed Christianity as superior to Judaism and who wished, from an outsider viewpoint, to emphasize their distance from the Jews. The present analysis . . . suggests, on the contrary, that the critical attitude towards Jewish ways of thinking which is apparent in the text of Acts in Codex Bezae reflects an *insider's* point of view, that is, it is expressed from within, from the standpoint of the Jewish people.[132]

In both of these studies and elsewhere Read-Heimerdinger concluded that Codex Bezae represents the original text of Acts,[133] and a perusal of her several articles discloses how she arrived at this view. First,
141 the argument went, Codex Bezae (apart from scribal errors) is a

[129] J. Heimerdinger, Unintentional Sins (see n. 79), 275 f.

[130] Ibid., 276.

[131] J. Heimerdinger, International Colloque: Le Codex de Bèze 27–30 June 1994, in Lunel, France, in: RCatT 20 (1995), 401–409 (here: 406).

[132] J. Read-Heimerdinger, Barnabas in Acts: A Study of His Role in the Text of Codex Bezae, in: JSNT 72 (1998), 23–66 (here: 65) [italics in original].

[133] Heimerdinger, Unintentional Sins (see n. 79), 276; Ead., International (see n. 131), 406; Ead., La tradition targumique et le Codex de Bèze: Actes 1:15–26, in: A. Borrell et al. (eds.), La Bíblia I el mediterrani: Actes del Congrés de Barcelona 18–22 de setembre de 1995, vol. 2 (Scripta Biblica 2), Montserrat 1997, 171–180 (here: 180); Ead., Word Order in Koine Greek: Using a Text-Critical Approach to Study Word Order Patterns in the Greek Text of Acts, in: FilolNT IX:18 (1996), 139–180, (here: 177); Ead., Barnabas (see n. 132), 65 f.; cf. 26. Puzzling is the opposite view in J. Heimerdinger/S. Levinsohn, The Use of the Definite Article before Names of People in the Greek Text of Acts with Particular Reference to Codex Bezae, FilolNT V:10 (1992), 15–44 (here: 17 f.).

highly consistent, coherent, homogeneous writing, "both linguistically and theologically."[134] "The editor . . . has not only an intimate knowledge of Jewish traditions . . . but also a keen awareness of how the church fits into the scheme of Jewish history."[135] This coherence can be demonstrated, she avers, through discourse analysis,[136] and—to take the next step in the argument—this systematic homogeneity "is also evidence that it [the Bezan text] has been well preserved in what is probably close to its original form."[137] Next, then, this inner textual consistency, along with its insider Jewish viewpoint, "persuades me personally," she affirmed, "that Codex Bezae represents the original text, in at least the book of Acts."[138] And if D is original, then, finally, it is the Vaticanus/Sinaiticus text, as illustrated for example in the variants involving Barnabas, that "was modified in order to attenuate the Jewish perspective and to remove the embarrassment of apostolic fallibility."[139]

Naturally, a number of questions arise in the face of this proposal. First, for instance, if we were to grant both that D's coherence can be validated through detailed discourse analysis, and then also that D as it stands—i.e., the text produced about 400—is homogeneous (a long-debated issue), on what grounds is it legitimate to jump from 400 back to the late first-century "original author of Acts"? Read-Heimerdinger's answer was that the original text has been "well preserved" down to 400. But is D's "high degree of consistency" an adequate demonstration of such careful preservation? And does it have any necessary bearing on the fidelity of transmission, for is not such coherence rather the fruit of the final rewriting and refinement of a long-standing textual tradition?

Second, she stated that the text transmitted in D "shows clear signs of dating from an earlier period,"[140] but the evidence given, as noted, is D's homogeneity, rather than the customary appeal to early patristic writers, relevant papyri, and extant witnesses to presumably earlier versions. Indeed, looking at some eight of her essays that

---

[134] Read-Heimerdinger, Barnabas (see n. 132), 26.
[135] Ibid., 65.
[136] Ibid., 27–34.
[137] Ibid., 26.
[138] Heimerdinger, International (see n. 131), 406.
[139] Read-Heimerdinger, Barnabas (see n. 132), 66.
[140] See Ibid., 25 f.

discuss readings of D discloses that other "Western" witnesses are
only invoked in one of them and then minimally.[141] The avoidance
of this evidence would appear both inappropriate and rash to most
of us, but she has two reasons for doing so: (1) she did not wish to
142 "assimilate" D with the "Western" text, for the latter "does not share
a large collection of distinctive readings," and D itself, of course,
offers numerous singular readings;[142] and (2) she wished to treat, not
the "Western" text, but only Codex Bezae[143]—a valid task to be
sure—and she wanted to investigate it apart from the "Western"
text, so that D can be assessed "as a homogeneous whole standing
in its own right."[144]

Yet questions persist: Can the claim that Codex Bezae has been transmitted as a text "probably close to its original form" be sustained without appeal to the array of other "Western" witnesses and to its complex transmission history? More specifically, what about the early patristic writers? Theoretically, of course, a text copied around 400 could preserve its three-century old "original" even if no 2nd and 3rd century witnesses attested it, but is it not reasonable to ask to what extent these earliest datable sources support or do not support the distinctive and idiosyncratic readings of D? And should not the same question be answered with respect to the early papyri and uncials, and the early versional witnesses? Nonetheless, Read-Heimerdinger's reversal from seeing the D-text as anti-Judaic to viewing D as thoroughly Jewish and pro-Jewish is an interesting road to traverse, though our two approaches proceed down very different paths: my interest was to isolate the bias of the early "Western" text, whereas she focused on the viewpoint of the extant form of Codex Bezae alone.

---

[141] Ibid., 25.41. "Western" witnesses are provided also in the treatment of Acts 8:7, but here D is not extant: Heimerdinger, La foi de l'eunuque éthiopien: Le problème textuel d'Actes 8/37, in: EThR 63 (1988), 521–528.

[142] Heimerdinger, International (see n. 131), 403.

[143] And apparently only the Greek column of D: cf. Heimerdinger, Barnabas (see n. 132), 24–26; Ead., Unintentional Sins (see n. 79), 276.

[144] Heimerdinger, International (see n. 131), 405; cf. Ead., The "Long" and the "Short" Texts of Acts: A Closer Look at the Quantity and Types of Variation, in: RCatT 22 (1997), 245–261 (here: 260).

C. *Overview: The Conversation Summarized*

Often the first reviews of a book set out the parameters of the discussion likely to ensue, and, if so, *Theological Tendency* was no exception. J. Neville Birdsall, a distinguished textual critic, spoke for the affirmative:

> This is a magnificent piece of work, fascinating to read and highly instructive, one of the most significant treatises even amongst the brilliant galaxy of works devoted to the "Western" text.[145]

And Leon Morris, after an appreciative nod to the affirmative, spoke 143
for the negative:

> It is a learned and valuable study, and I think it could scarcely be denied that Professor Epp has demonstrated that the tendency of which he speaks exists. But . . . if the tendency were as clear as Epp suggests one wonders why generations of highly competent textual critics have missed it.[146]

Where might this swinging pendulum come to rest? Among the earliest reviews was that of Henry J. Cadbury, taking the middle ground: "At least sufficient material is collected and explained to produce persuasive evidence that much of the variation can be attributed to what is called 'theological tendency.'"[147] He added, however, that not every one of the textual aberrations adduced in support of an anti-Judaic viewpoint necessarily requires that explanation, and ". . . one is left with the feeling that the complexity of the problem remains not completely solved. But perhaps we have here a partial solution."[148]

---

145 J. N. Birdsall, in: ThLZ 93 (1968), 663: "Epp has been able to use much material, minute to be sure in many cases, but almost everywhere convincing. He is able to show a clear and consistent tendency in the text of Codex Bezae and its allies." Similar, though sometimes with the usual qualification that not all the evidence carries the same weight, etc. were reviews by R. P. Martin, in: EvQ 39 (1967), 175; F. Balchin, South East Asia Journal of Theology 9 (1968), 78 f.; M. É. Boismard, in: RB 74 (1967), 293; G. B. Caird, in: ET 78 (1966/67), 287; J. Coppens, in: EThL 43 (1967), 274 f.; M. Ward Redus, in: Perkins School of Theology Journal (Fall, 1967), 52–54; J. Schmid, in: BZ 11 (1967), 301 f.; A. Segovia, in: ATG 30 (1967), 375 f.; J. C. Truro, in: TS 29 (1968), 161 f.

146 L. Morris, in: ABR 15 (1967), 48. Negative reviews were by J. C. O'Neill, in: New Blackfriars 48 (1967), 499; C. H. Pinnock, in: ChrTo 11 (1966/1967), 34 f.; R. P. Markham, in: BT 19 (1968), 189–191; Z. C. Hodges, in: BSac 125 (1968), 80.

147 H. J. Cadbury, in: JBL 86 (1967), 112.

148 Ibid., 114. Cf. Similar language in Metzger, in: Gn 40 (1968), 833.

By way of summary, numerous reviewers and readers since then have followed a similar line in acknowledging that the anti-Judaic thesis had been justified, or at least that various single variation-units revealed such a bias in the "Western" text, while at the same time professing that the evidence had been overly pressed, the argument overly subtle, or that factors other than an anti-Judaic bias could have given rise to certain textual alterations—factors such as liturgical or stylistic influences, or a wish to enhance the apostles or to produce a vivid narrative, etc.[149] This reticence toward the more subtle supporting evidence was to be expected, but it had been pur-
144 sued in *Theological Tendency* as part of a sustained *cumulative argument*.[150] That the work has been and continues to be part of a lively conversation about the D-text of Acts suggests that it was either sufficiently convincing or sufficiently provocative—or both—to engage the interest and at times to evoke the consternation of scholars in the field, and that is perhaps legacy enough.

IV. Narrative Textual Criticism: Future Paths for Conversation

David Parker, in his review of Bart Ehrman's landmark work on *The Orthodox Corruption of Scripture*, referred to studies such as *Theological Tendency* and that 1993 book by Ehrman as "narrative textual criticism,"[151] a new term, I believe, and one very well worth embracing, for it indicates that these studies and others like them demonstrate

[149] Reviews along this line came from R. H. Fuller, in: CBQ 30 (1968), 447 f.; A. R. C. Leaney, in: Theol. 70 (1967), 461–463; B.M. Metzger, in: Gn 40 (1968), 831–833; I. A. Moir, in: JTS n.s. 19 (1968), 277–281; J. Smit Sibinga, in: VigChr 24 (1970), 76 f.; and, e.g., I. Alfaro, in: DRev 280 (1967), 356–358; F. W. Danker, in: CTM 39 (1968), 413 f.; E. Rasco, in: Gregorianum 48 (1967), 365–368; F. Stagg, in: RevExp 65 (1968), 101 f.; cf. J. H. Crehan, in: HeyJ 8 (1967), 412 f.; C. K. Barrett, in: LQHR 192 (1967), 345.

[150] The cumulative effect was acknowledged, e.g., by Birdsall (see n. 145); R. H. Fuller, in: CBQ 30 (1968), 447; J. Gill, in: OCP 34 (1968), 172 f.; J. C. Truro, in: TS 29 (1968), 162; cf. Markham, in: BT 19 (1968), 190; C. K. Barrett, Is There a Theological Tendency? (see n. 72), 19. It was dismissed by others: several, e.g., thought unconvincing the linking to the anti-Judaic tendency of a heightened universalism in the D-text, expressed in a greater interest in Gentiles and the Gentile mission: Grässer, Acta-Forschung (see n. 40), 179; [Repr.: 172]; Metzger, Gn 40 (1968), 833; Leaney, Theol. 70 (1967), 462; Stagg, RevExp 65 (1968), 102. For treatment in *Theological Tendency*, see "Universalism" in the Index of Subjects.

[151] D. C. Parker, JTS 45 (1994), 704.

that textual variants have a story to tell. Parker's subsequent book, *The Living Text of the Gospels*, itself eminently qualifies for the same designation, in my judgment, for many of his pointed examples reveal to us problems that the church was facing and invite inquiry as to the stories behind them, which Parker tells so effectively,[152] while at the same time informing us quite passionately of their poignant—if sometimes unsettling—significance for textual criticism and for theology.[153] The fresh, expansive landscape embraced by text-critical scholarship of this kind is convincing evidence that a new, vibrant phase—if not a new epoch—has dawned for the discipline of New Testament textual criticism, a field frequently characterized as dull and mechanical. If it deserved such epithets in the past, they are distinctly out of place now. Whether or not we adopt the name "narrative textual criticism," *The Orthodox Corruption of Scripture* and *The Living Text of the Gospels*, and other books and articles akin to them, have opened (or at least reopened after a lengthy interlude) a newly creative period of New Testament textual criticism that permits textual variants, often in their very multiplicity and quite apart from
any search for the "original" text, to tell their own stories. Through 145
the narratives they conceal, textual variations alert us to a variety of vital concerns in the faith and practice of the church and bring us into touch (1) with the serious and very real struggles for proper beliefs by leaders in the early church, (2) with real people and their everyday life-experiences and worship in the church community, and (3) with broader socio-cultural involvements and sometimes the formidable socio-political encounters of early Christianity. In Ehrman, for example, we discover the ever-vigilant concern for faith and its defense even if the proto-Orthodox must "corrupt" the text to do so. In Parker we glimpse differing liturgical emphases in the Lord's Prayer and relevant ethical considerations in the numerous divorce and remarriage variants, as well as in the large single variant of the Adulterous Women. And in *Theological Tendency* and elsewhere,[154] including portions of Ehrman's work, we uncover evidence of sometimes unsettling Jewish-Christian relations.

---

[152] Parker, Living Text (see n. 67), e.g., 49–74 on the Lord's prayer; 75–94 on marriage and divorce sayings.

[153] E.g., Ibid., 45f.92–94.172–174.203–213.

[154] E.g., two of my students, H. Eshbaugh, Textual Variants and Theology: A Study of the Galatians Text of Papyrus 46, in: JSNT 1 (1979), 60–72 [Repr. in:

Though many of these textual variations arise as points of doctrinal debate or reflection (à la Ehrman), many, many others flow subtly from conceptions, sentiments, and imageries embedded in the Christian group-culture of various times and locations. They emerge as clarifying expressions of the belief system or the socio-political mind set of early Christianity, Some textual alterations are overt with clear purpose, while others arise through a vaguely unconscious process, yet in both cases they disclose differing convictions, or rival ethical norms and practices endemic in church life, or they mirror conflict between "us" and the "other." Traditionally we call all of them intentional changes, but there is, after all, a fine line between openly conscious changes and subtle, almost unconscious reformulations that find their way at times into the textual fabric of the New Testament.

Does this diminish or obviate the traditional procedures and the customary goal of textual criticism—establishing the most likely "original" text? Not necessarily, though David Parker raises some poignant
146 questions about the search for a single "original" text.[155] In the end, though, I am convinced that the "Chicago School" fifty years ago showed us the path that New Testament textual criticism must take. On the one hand, they formulated and practiced an exploration of textual variation oriented to and revelatory of the developing church and designed to illuminate aspects of the doctrine and life of the church in its successive periods. This approach freely embraced the notion of the New Testament as a living text, breathing and growing and changing as it was reinterpreted in each generation. Sometimes, as in the "Chicago School" and among the new practitioners today,

S. E. Porter/C. A. Evans (eds.),New Testament Text and Language: A Sheffield Reader, Sheffield, 1997, 81–91]; and G. E. Rice, Luke 3:22–38 in Codex Bezae: The Messianic King, in: AUSS 17 (1979), 203–208; Id., The Anti-Judaic Bias of the Western Text in the Gospel of Luke, in: AUSS 18 (1980), 51–57; Id., Some Further Examples, in: AUSS 18 (1980), 149–156; Id., Western Non-Interpolations: A Defense of the Apostolate, in: C. H. Talbert (ed.), Luke-Acts: New Perspectives from the Society of Biblical Literature Seminar, New York 1985, 1–16; Id., Is Bezae a Homogeneous Codex? in: C. H. Talbert (ed.), Perspectives on the New Testament. FS Frank Stagg, Macon 1985, 39–54. On Rice, see Parsons, Departure (see n. 81), 41 f.; for a critique, see J. Delobel, The Sayings of Jesus in the Textual Tradition, in: Id. (ed.), Logia: Les paroles de Jésus—The Sayings of Jesus: Mémorial Joseph Coppens (BEThL 59), Leuven 1982, 431–457, here: 443 f. n. 41.

[155] Parker, Living Text (see n. 67), 208–212. For a recent analysis, see P. Ellingworth, Text, Translation, and Theology: The New Testament in the Original Greek?, in: FilolNT XIII: 25–26 (2000), 61–73. See also Ehrman, Text as Window (see n. 59), 361–362 and n. 1; Epp, Multivalence (see n. 6), passim.

this emphasis disparaged the search for the "original" text by shifting the focus elsewhere or by raising all meaningful variants to a high, if not equal level. On the other hand, however, all of these "Chicago" scholars were active participants in the International Greek New Testament Project (IGNTP), whose goal was a new, critical apparatus for the Greek New Testament that would lead us closer to the "original" or early text. In fact, E. C. Colwell was Chair of the American Executive Committee from 1948 to 1971, and the three current scholars mentioned are now active as that Project moves forward.[156]

Some readers will be familiar with the enigmatic American baseball figure, Yogi Berra, and his malaprops, one of which is, "If you come to a fork in the road, take it!"[157] New Testament textual criticism may be doing just that: (1) following on the right the traditional path in search of the "original" or earliest form of the text—though acutely aware of the obstacles; and (2) at the same time taking the avenue on the left that affords a clearer and sharper—and often a very distinctly human—view of the church in both its internal relationships and its external contexts. The discipline will be richer and its contributions more relevant if we do both.

Added Notes, 2004

The preceding article is too recent to have elicited comment, at least as far as I know. That the Codex Bezae, its related manuscripts, and its abiding mysteries continue to attract interest and to fascinate is well attested, for example, by the publication of the more than twenty papers from the Lunel Colloquium on that famous manuscript: *Codex Bezae: Studies from the Lunel Colloquium, June 1994* (eds. D. C. Parker and C.-B. Amphoux; NTTS 22; Leiden: Brill, 1996).

[156] See E. J. Epp, The International Greek New Testament Project: Motivation and History, in: NT 39 (1997), 1–20 (here: 8.2.17). See n. 28, above, for their views of the "original" text. David Parker follows the same two-fold pattern: alongside his research as expressed in *The Living Text of the Gospels*, he serves on the British Committee of the IGNTP and is Director of the ambitious Principio Project for completing two tasks for the IGNTP edition of John: see Parker, The Principio Project: A Reconstruction of the Johannine tradition, in: FilolNT XIII: 25–26 (2000), 111–118. Likewise, B. D. Ehrman and I are members of the North American Committee of the IGNTP.

[157] Yogi Berra, The Yogi Book: "I Really Didn't Say Everything I Said!", New York 1998, 48.

PRESIDENTIAL ADDRESS

by
Eldon Jay Epp

President of the Society of Biblical Literature 2003 3
Annual Meeting of the Society of Biblical literature
November 22, 2003
Atlanta, Georgia

Introduction given by David L. Petersen,
Vice President, Society of Biblical Literature

Eldon Jay Epp received his Ph.D. degree from Harvard University and held faculty appointments at the University of Southern California and at Case Western Reserve University. In 1998, Epp retired from Case Western Reserve, where he is Harkness Professor of Biblical Literature *emeritus* and Dean of Humanities and Social Sciences *emeritus*. Most recently he was a visiting professor of New Testament at Harvard Divinity School. Epp has authored or edited four books and over forty articles. A volume of his collected essays is forthcoming. He currently sits on a number of editorial boards, including Hermeneia, the North American executive committee of the International Greek New Testament Project, the New Testament Language Project, and the Electronic New Testament Manuscript Project. In this and related ways, Epp has distinguished himself as a textual critic. His books and articles have done much to summarize and synthesize an enormous body of scholarship in a clear and cogent way. Moreover, he has recently, particularly in an article published in 1999, identified and described a subtle shift in recent textual studies. He has offered a proposal for a more honest and more self-conscious use of the term "original text," one that opens up the field of New Testament text-critical studies in new ways. As one scholar recently put it, Eldon has the ability not only to contribute to the field; he is in the process of helping redefine and reinvent the field of New Testament text critical studies.

Beyond his roles as teacher, author, editor, and administrator, Epp has contributed in vital ways to the life of this Society. For twenty years, he was New Testament book review editor of the *Journal of Biblical Literature* and for four years he served as editor of the *Critical Review of Books in Religion*. He chaired the textual criticism section of the annual meeting for fourteen years and served for twelve years as a member of the editorial board for the Society of Biblical Literature Centennial Publications Series. And he is not yet finished with us, since he currently serves as chair of the Council's Programs and Initiatives Committee. Here, as in so many other ways, Eldon has been the consummate colleague and scholar.

Last, I cannot resist one brief biographic note. Early in his career, Eldon Epp was involved in consequential ways with the beginnings of the American Academy of Religion. John Priest and Eldon had
4 been nominated to serve as president and vice-president of the American Academy of Religion in 1966. There were, at that time, a number of complicated dynamics within the leadership of that young society. Recognizing the precarious state of the new organization, both Eldon and John withdrew their nominations, attempting to do their share to permit the American Academy of Religion to develop. So, Eldon, we look back at your work over the past decades and thank you not only for what you did for the Society of Biblical Literature, but also for your contributions to the American Academy of Religion.

CHAPTER TWENTY-FOUR

THE OXYRHYNCHUS NEW TESTAMENT PAPYRI: "NOT WITHOUT HONOR EXCEPT IN THEIR HOMETOWN"?

> The papyri offer us the most direct access we have 5
> to the experience of ordinary people in antiquity.
>
> —E. A. Judge[1]

A year and a half ago I presented to a distinguished New Testament
scholar an offprint of an article I had just published on the Junia/Junias
variation in Rom 16:7.[2] A few weeks later, in his presence, I handed
a copy also to another New Testament scholar. At that point, the
first colleague said to the second, "You must read this article. Can
you imagine—something interesting written by a textual critic!" This
was meant to be a genuine compliment, yet it echoed a common 6
and almost unconscious impression that biblical textual critics are
dull creatures who spend their careers tediously adjudicating textual
minutiae that only impede the exegete's work. Of course, critical
editions are considered essential and therefore welcome, but must

Presidential Address delivered on November 22, 2003, at the annual meeting of the Society of Biblical Literature in Atlanta, Georgia. This is an expanded version of the oral presentation. The text in the title is Mark 6:4 NRSV.

Note: References to Oxyrhynchus papyri will be given as P.Oxy. + papyrus no.; discussions of a papyrus will be indicated by P.Oxy. + vol. no. + pp. All such references relate to *The Oxyrhynchus Papyri* (Greco-Roman Memoirs; London: British Academy for the Egypt Exploration Society) 1898– [67 vols. to date]. Oxyrhynchus papyri published elsewhere use the appropriate abbreviations, e.g., PSI + vol. + papyrus no. Basic data on papyri (contents, names, date, etc.) are taken from these sources without further acknowledgment.

References to the papyri in Joseph van Haelst, *Catalogue des papyrus littéraires juifs et chrétiens* (Université de Paris IV, Papyrologie 1; Paris: Sorbonne, 1976), will be reported as van Haelst + no.

[1] E. A. Judge, *Rank and Status in the World of the Caesars and St Paul* (Broadhead Memorial Lecture 1981; University of Canterbury Publications 29; Christchurch, NZ: University of Canterbury, 1982), 7.

[2] Eldon Jay Epp, "Text-Critical, Exegetical, and Socio-Cultural Factors Affecting the Junia/Junias Variation in Romans 16,7," in *New Testament Textual Criticism and Exegesis: Festschrift J. Delobel* (ed. A. Denaux; BETL 161; Leuven: Leuven University Press/Peeters, 2002), 227–91.

we really be bothered by that complex apparatus at the foot of the page?

I. Introduction: Traditional and New Goals of Textual Criticism

Naturally, textual critics will continue their tradition of establishing the earliest or most likely "original" text, though now we use such a term, if we use it at all, with caution and even with reluctance, recognizing that "original text" carries several dimensions of meaning.[3] Indeed, ever since Westcott-Hort entitled their famous edition *The New Testament in the Original Greek*,[4] we have learned that many a pitfall awaits those who, whether arrogantly or naively, rush headlong into that search for the Holy Grail. Yet the aim to produce better critical editions by refining the criteria for the priority of readings and by elucidating the history of the text will remain; at the same time, however, textual criticism's other goals will be pursued in accord with significant changes that recent decades have brought to the discipline. For example, emphasis has fallen on scribal activity, especially the purposeful alteration of texts that reflect the theology and culture of their times. One dramatic presentation was Bart Ehrman's *Orthodox Corruption of Scripture*, a work so well known that I need only summarize his main point: During the christological controversies of the first three centuries, "proto-orthodox scribes," as he calls them, "sometimes changed their scriptural texts to make them *say* what they were already known to *mean*."[5] Hence, they "corrupted" their texts to maintain "correct" doctrine. Much earlier, textual critics had been willing to attribute such arrogance only to heretics, but Ehrman boldly and correctly turned this on its head. Though startling and unexpected, his thesis, as he recognized, issued quite naturally from text-critical developments of the preceding four decades.[6]

---

[3] See Eldon Jay Epp, "The Multivalence of the Term 'Original Text' in New Testament Textual Criticism," *HTR* 92 (1999): 245–81.

[4] Brooke Foss Westcott and Fenton John Anthony Hort, *The New Testament in the Original Greek* (2 vols.; Cambridge/London: Macmillan, 1881–82; 2nd ed., 1896).

[5] Bart D. Ehrman, *The Orthodox Corruption of Scripture: The Effect of Early Christological Controversies on the Text of the New Testament* (New York/Oxford: Oxford University Press, 1993), xii (his italics); see also 24–31.

[6] Ibid., 42 n. 94, but esp. his "The Text as Window: New Testament Manuscripts

A second phenomenon, long troubling to textual critics, concerns 7
multiple readings in one variation-unit that defy resolution, and attention has turned to what these multiple—often competing—variants might tell us about crucial issues faced by the churches and how they dealt with them. David Parker, whose small volume is at risk of being overlooked owing to its simple yet significant title, *The Living Text of the Gospels*,[7] confronted the problem head-on, with fascinating results.

For instance, the six main variant forms of the so-called Lord's Prayer in Matthew and Luke show the evolution of this pericope under liturgical influence. This is well known, but my description of it is much too detached. What obviously happened, of course, was that the fervent, dynamic worship environment in early churches at various times and places evoked appropriate expansions of the shorter and certainly earlier forms that we print in our Greek texts of Matthew and Luke, including additional clauses such as "Your Holy Spirit come upon us and cleanse us," but especially the lofty praise of the Almighty and Eternal God offered with grandeur and dignity and beauty in the famous doxology, "For the kingdom and the power and the glory are yours forever and ever. Amen" [additions to Matt 6:13]. Once hearing the variants of these six forms and reciting them again and again, ". . . they will be a part of the way in which we read and interpret the Lord's Prayer," says Parker, and "we shall not be able to erase them from our minds, and to read a single original text as though the others had never existed."[8]

A second, more poignant example in its relevance to anguishing life situations concerns the twenty-some variants in the four passages on divorce/remarriage in the Synoptic Gospels. Parker's analysis of this complex array shows that some variants concern Jewish, others Roman provisions for divorce; some condemn divorce but not remarriage, while others prohibit remarriage but not divorce; some variants describe adultery as remarriage, others as divorce and remarriage, and others as marrying a divorced man; and some variants portray

---

and the Social History of Early Christianity," in *The Text of the New Testament in Contemporary Research: Essays on the* Status Quaestionis (ed. Bart D. Ehrman and Michael W. Holmes; SD 46; Grand Rapids: Eerdmans, 1995), 363–65.

[7] David C. Parker, *The Living Text of the Gospels* (Cambridge: Cambridge University Press, 1997).

[8] Ibid., 102.

Jesus as pointing to the cruelty of divorcing one's wife—thereby treating her as if she were an adulteress, though she was not—perhaps with the outcome of establishing her right to remain single, yet without affirming that the divorcing man commits adultery. Some variants, therefore, are concerned with the man, others with the woman, and still others with both. Sometimes the divorcing man commits adultery, sometimes not; sometimes the divorced or divorcing woman
8 commits adultery, sometimes she is made an adulteress, sometimes she commits adultery if she remarries, and, finally, sometimes a man marrying a divorced woman commits adultery.[9] "The main result of this survey," says Parker, "is to show that the recovery of a single original saying of Jesus is impossible." Nor can we say that one variant is more original than the others, he adds, for "what we have is a collection of interpretative rewritings of a tradition."[10] Indeed, in the early centuries of Christianity, the collection of writings that was to become or had become the New Testament was not a closed book, but—through textual variation—to quote Parker again, "it is open, and successive generations write on its pages."[11]

What do multiple variants without resolution about originality mean for textual criticism and for us today? On the one hand, we are permitted to glimpse something of the creative dynamism and eloquent expansiveness of early Christian liturgy as new expressions evolved within the Lord's Prayer, and, in the divorce/remarriage morass, a window is opened for us to observe and to experience with early Christians over wide areas and lengthy periods the pathos and the agonizing, intractable ethical dilemmas that they faced. On the other hand, multiple variants, with no single original or simple

---

[9] Ibid., 77–89. For a graphic display of Parker's analysis of these variants, see S. R. Pickering, "A Classified Survey of Some Recent Researches Relevant for New Testament Textual Studies," *New Testament Textual Research Update* 8 (2000): 66–69.

[10] Parker, *Living Text of the Gospels*, 92–93.

[11] Ibid., 174. He was speaking of Luke, but it is clear from the larger context that he views the Gospels and, by extension, the entire New Testament in this fashion. Cf. the recent statement of Traianos Gagos, "The University of Michigan Papyrus Collection: Current Trends and Future Perspectives," in *Atti del XXII Congresso Internazionale di Papirologia, Firenze, 23–29 agosto 1998* (ed. Isabella Andorlini *et al.*; 2 vols. + 1 vol. of plates; Florence: Istituto Papirologico "G. Vitelli," 2001), 1:515: "An edited text is no more a static, isolated object, but a growing and changeable amalgam: the image [a reference to electronic images of papyri] allows the user to look critically at the 'established' text and to challenge continuously the authoritative readings and interpretations of its first or subsequent editors."

resolution within grasp, can show us the way for our own times: there is no one right path or answer, no single directive, but the multiple variants reveal an array of differing situations, leaving open multiple options for us as well. In such cases, to quote Parker a final time, "the People of God have to make up their own minds. There is no authoritative text to provide a short-cut."[12]

Suddenly textual criticism comes alive and becomes relevant in ways that no one might have imagined. Why didn't we see this sooner and how could we have missed it? One of the earliest reviews of my 1966 book on theological tendency in the so-called Western
text of Acts[13] contained this line: ". . . if the tendency were as clear 9
as Epp suggests one wonders why generations of highly competent textual critics have missed it."[14] Well, the time was right forty years ago—though not a hundred years ago[15]—to observe that the New Testament text suffered alteration for ideological and theological purposes. And the time was right during the past decade to see the positive aspects of multiple variants. At last New Testament textual criticism has lost its innocence and has learned to tolerate ambiguity—one of the sure signs of maturity.

And why was an earlier time not propitious? Perhaps because textual critics, often working in isolation, focusing resolutely on their

[12] Parker, *Living Text of the Gospels*, 212.

[13] E. J. Epp, *The Theological Tendency of Codex Bezae Cantabrigiensis in Acts* (SNTSMS 3; Cambridge/New York: Cambridge University Press, 1966; unchanged repr. Eugene, OR: Wipf and Stock, 2001). By request, I presented an update of the issues in "Anti-Judaic Tendencies in the D-Text of Acts: Forty Years of Conversation," in *The Book of Acts as Church History: Text, Textual Traditions and Ancient Interpretations/Apostelgeschichte als Kirchengeschichte: Text, Texttraditionen und antike Auslegungen* (ed. Tobias Nicklas and Michael Tilly; BZNW 120; Berlin/New York: de Gruyter, 2003), 111–46.

[14] Leon Morris, *ABR* 15 (1967): 48. He introduces this comment by saying, "It is a learned and valuable study, and I think it could scarcely be denied that Professor Epp has demonstrated that the tendency of which he speaks exists."

[15] Except with respect to "heretics": see, e.g., the often quoted statement of Hort (1882) in Westcott and Hort, *New Testament in the Original Greek*, 2:282–83: "Even among the numerous unquestionably spurious readings of the New Testament there are no signs of deliberate falsification of the text for dogmatic purposes. . . . It is true that dogmatic preferences to a great extent determined theologians, and probably scribes, in their choice between rival readings already in existence: . . . the temptation was strong to believe and assert that a reading used by theological opponents had also been invented by them. Accusations of wilful tampering with the text are accordingly not unfrequent in Christian antiquity: but, with a single exception [Marcion], wherever they can be verified they prove to be groundless, being in fact hasty and unjust inferences from mere diversities of inherited text."

traditional tasks and employing overly mechanical methods, could not see through to real-life situations. Recently David Parker, again, has called some of the newer approaches "narrative textual criticism,"[16] which I understand to mean, simply and at a minimum, that textual variants have a story to tell—and that they allow new voices to be heard beyond the traditional call for "the original" text. This, for me, has energized textual criticism. Establishing the earliest text-forms provides one dimension; grasping the real-life contexts of variant readings adds richness by showing how Christians made meaning out of the *living* text as they nurtured and shaped it in worship and in life.

Our discipline, to be sure, has its technical aspects, but it remains primarily an art, and therefore it is for neither the perfunctory, nor the inflexible, nor the unimaginative, nor the tender-minded; and above all it is not the safe harbor that for so long and by so many it has been perceived to be. And "this"—as the saying goes—"is not your father's" textual criticism, but an entrance into a brave new world, with provocative challenges and captivating promises!

10 II. New Testament Papyri in their Cultural and Intellectual Context

During the past half-dozen years my research has emphasized the provenance of manuscripts, a factor much neglected in discussing fragmentary papyri. Provenance translates into *context*—the sociocultural and intellectual character of the communities where manuscripts resided and which left its mark on those manuscripts. But the manuscripts, as shaped by that context, in turn illuminate their own community contexts—not unlike the hermeneutical circle.

Previously, manuscripts—when viewed as impersonal and perfunctory sources of data—were not seen as living and dynamic, with individual "personalities" that emerged out of the everyday life and exigencies of the churches, reflecting their faith and practice and the controversies of the time. Today, by placing New Testament manuscripts in their immediate contexts, we can more clearly understand

---

[16] D. C. Parker, review of Bart Ehrman, *Orthodox Corruption of Scripture*, *JTS* 45 (1994): 704. He was referring to my *Theological Tendency* and to Ehrman's book; I would include Parker's *Living Text* in this category as well.

their role as witnesses to the New Testament text. It is these issues, confined to the environment of the New Testament papyri at Oxyrhynchus and to the first three and a half centuries of Christianity in that locality, that I wish to explore on this occasion. After all, it is well known that the New Testament papyri found at Oxyrhynchus constitute the most numerous, the most geographically concentrated, and as a whole the oldest at any single location. It is natural then to ask, first, about the Christian environment of the city with this remarkable corpus of manuscripts and, second, whether their reception, use, and influence in their own time and place were proportionate to these superlatives—and whether they enjoyed a special place of honor there.

At Oxyrhynchus, the context of its New Testament papyri must be recovered almost entirely from other papyri, and we face two frustrating barriers: the fragmentary nature of most evidence and the randomness of its survival, for at Oxyrhynchus the vast majority of papyri were recovered from rubbish heaps. Yet there is no scarcity of data, for the literary and documentary remains to date exceed five thousand published manuscripts—enormous riches compared to other sites. And there are more to come.[17]

A. *The Provenance of New Testament Manuscripts*

1. *The relevance of provenance*

Those who consult the *editio princeps* of a manuscript inevitably will find a statement of its ascertained date and provenance (or often the confession that these are uncertain or unknown). Hence, lengthy discussions of a manuscript's place of origin and/or discovery and its 11
travels and utilization as it made its way to its present location will be found for such grand codices as Sinaiticus (א), Vaticanus (B), and Bezae (D), though their places of origin—discussed for centuries—may have reached resolution just in the last several years.[18] Only

[17] I recall the 1998 Oxford University centenary of the publication of Oxyrhynchus papyri, when the research team publicly thanked the British Academy for one hundred years of support—and promptly requested funding for the next hundred years!

[18] On Sinaiticus and Vaticanus and their origin in Caesarea, see T. C. Skeat, "The Codex Sinaiticus, the Codex Vaticanus and Constantine," *JTS* 50 (1999): 583–625, esp. 603–4; on Bezae's origin in Berytus (Beirut), see David C. Parker,

occasionally, however, is more than a minimal treatment offered for lesser manuscripts, particularly the fragmentary papyri. This was understandable over the long history of textual criticism, when manuscripts were viewed largely in isolation—as objective, detached repositories of readings useful in establishing the text, but all the while remaining impersonal and lifeless. To be sure, their dates and sometimes their geographical diversity were factors in assessing their value for establishing the text, but manuscripts and the texts they carried were not often seen as influences upon the liturgy, thought, and ethics of early Christian congregations, nor as reliquaries for past theological expressions or controversies—preserving for us the artifacts of both discarded and prevailing Christian faith and practice.

Beyond Oxyrhynchus, a number of papyri of known provenance might be investigated in this fashion. For example, P4, consisting of six fragments of a double-column codex containing Luke and dated in the late second century, was actually found *in situ* at Coptos (just north of Thebes) in a jar walled up in a house. More precisely, it was used in the binding of a (presumably Christian) codex of Philo, but the house showed no evident connection to a church.[19] Yet there is likely more to this story, for books are known to have been hidden in private homes during periods of persecution, and Diocletion sacked Coptos in 292. Hence, it might be surmised that the owner of this codex concealed it then or perhaps later during a further severe persecution, with the intention of retrieving it after the danger was past.[20] Beyond this, though, we would move only deeper into speculation. One might also consider P92, found in 1969 at Medînet Mâdi in the Fayum in a rubble-filled structure near a racing course.[21] Surely there is more to this story also, but no one knows what it might be.

Codex Bezae: An Early Christian Manuscript and Its Text (Cambridge: Cambridge University Press, 1992), 261–78, esp. 266–78.

[19] Colin H. Roberts, *Manuscript, Society, and Belief in Early Christian Egypt* (Schweich Lectures 1977; London: British Academy by Oxford University Press, 1979), 8, 13. Roberts dates P4 in the later second century, as does T. C. Skeat in an extensive discussion: "The Oldest Manuscript of the Four Gospels?" *NTS* 43 (1997): 26–31. There is debate as to whether P4 was part of the same codex as P64 + P67; see Skeat, above. The definitive edition of P4 was by Jean Merell, "Nouveaux fragments du papyrus 4," *RB* 47 (1938): 5–22 + 7 pls.

[20] Roberts, *Manuscript, Society, and Belief*, 8.

[21] Claudio Gallazzi, "Frammenti di un codice con le Epistole di Paoli," *ZPE* 46 (1982): 117.

2. *The New Testament papyri at Oxyrhynchus* 12

The most obvious candidates for study, however, are the New Testament papyri from Oxyrhynchus, for they number an astounding forty-seven, or 42 percent of the currently known 116 (but perhaps 112 different) papyri. More striking is their proportion among all *early* New Testament manuscripts (including four majuscules, one from Oxyrhynchus), for out of the sixty-one that date up to or around the turn of the third/fourth centuries,[22] thirty-five or 57 percent were found at Oxyrhynchus.[23] As a whole, New Testament papyri date from the second century to ca. 600, but we should include also eleven additional majuscules found at Oxyrhynchus, for they all date within the same range—from the third/fourth through the fifth/sixth centuries.[24] All together, these papyri and majuscules, though mostly highly fragmentary, preserve portions of seventeen of the twenty-seven books that eventually formed the New Testament canon,[25] and,

---

[22] Or sixty-two if P4 is treated as a separate manuscript rather than part of P64 + 67 (see n. 19 above). K. Aland and B. Aland (*The Text of the New Testament: An Introduction to the Critical Editions and to the Theory and Practice of Modern Textual Criticism* [rev. ed.; Grand Rapids: Eerdmans; Leiden: Brill, 1989], 96, 159) treat it separately, though others speak of P64 + 67 + 4: T. C. Skeat, "The Oldest Manuscript of the Four Gospels?" *NTS* 43 (1997): 1–34, esp. 1–9; Graham N. Stanton, "The Fourfold Gospel," *NTS* 43 (1997): 327–28.

The figure sixty-one (or sixty-two) includes majuscules 0162 (P.Oxy. 847, 3rd/4th c.), as well as 0189 (2nd/3rd c.), 0220 (3rd c.), 0171 (3rd/4th c.) from other locations; 0212 (3rd c.) is usually omitted because it is a Diatessaron manuscript, and not strictly of the New Testament: see Aland and Aland, *Text of the New Testament*, 56, 95, 125.

[23] This includes majuscule 0162 (see preceding note).

[24] The twelve Oxyrhynchus majuscules, by century, are third/fourth: 0162 (P.Oxy. 847); fourth: 0169 (P.Oxy. 1080), 0206 (P.Oxy. 1353), 0308 (P.Oxy. 4500); fifth: 069 (P.Oxy. 3), 0163 (P.Oxy. 848), 0172 (PSI 1.4), 0173 (PSI 1.5), 0174 (PSI II.118), 0176 (PSI 3.251); fifth/sixth: 071 (P.Oxy. 401), 0170 (P.Oxy. 1169). On the possibility that P52 (P.Ryl. 457, 2nd c.) came from Oxyrhynchus, see C. H. Roberts, ed., *Catalogue of the Greek and Latin Papyri in the John Rylands Library, Manchester, III: Theological and Literary Texts* (Manchester: Manchester University Press, 1938), 2. Roberts is more cautious in *An Unpublished Fragment of the Fourth Gospel in the John Rylands Library* (Manchester: Manchester University Press, 1935), 24–25.

According to its editor, Oxyrhynchus is the likely provenance of the highly important fifth-century Coptic manuscript G67, containing Acts 1:1–15:3 in the Middle Egyptian (or Oxyrhynchite) dialect: Hans-Martin Schenke, ed., *Apostelgeschichte 1,1–15,3 im mittelägyptischen Dialekt des Koptischen (Codex Glazier)* (TU 137; Berlin: Akademie Verlag, 1991), 88, 249.

[25] Oxyrhynchus papyri contain portions of fifteen books of the New Testament: Matthew, Luke, John, Acts, Romans, 1 Corinthians, Galatians, Philippians, 1–2 Thessalonians, Hebrews, James, 1 John, Jude, Apocalypse of John. Hence, those

as I have argued elsewhere, they may be viewed as a microcosm of the various textual clusters (text-types) that present themselves across the entire New Testament manuscript tradition.[26]

13 So, if provenance is central, no other group of papyri begins to match Oxyrhynchus, for no more than three or four New Testament papyri are known with certainty to have been found at any other single location, and even if one considers a region, such as all the cities of the Fayum (the Arsinoite nome), where thousands of papyri were recovered, only a dozen of the New Testament survived there.[27] Noting that about thirty-eight New Testament papyri stem from unknown localities means that Oxyrhynchus has furnished 64 percent of all New Testament papyri of known provenance.

Naturally, because of their early dating and extensive coverage of the text, the prominent Chester Beatty and Bodmer papyri are of greater importance for the various tasks of textual criticism than those of Oxyrhynchus, but the Egyptian provenance of the Beatty group (P45, P46, P47) cannot be more narrowly identified than the supposition that they came from the Fayum. As for the Bodmer papyri (P66, P72, P75), James M. Robinson has clearly located their place of *discovery* among the Dishna Papers (at Dishnā, some 220 miles upstream from Oxyrhynchus), which were part of the nearby

---

missing are Mark, 2 Corinthians, Ephesians, Colossians, Pastoral Epistles, Philemon, 1–2 Peter, 2–3 John. However, Mark (069 = P.Oxy. 847, 5th c.) and 1 Peter (0206 = P.Oxy.1353, 4th c.) are represented among the Oxyrhynchus majuscules, for a total of seventeen.

[26] See E. J. Epp, "The New Testament Papyri at Oxyrhynchus: Their Significance for Understanding the Transmission of the Early New Testament Text," in *Oxyrhynchus: A City and Its Texts* (ed. Peter Parsons et al.; London: Egypt Exploration Society, [forthcoming]); see section on "Oxyrhynchus as a microcosm for New Testament text-types"; see also idem, "The Significance of the Papyri for Determining the Nature of the New Testament Text in the Second Century: A Dynamic View of Textual Transmission," in *Gospel Traditions in the Second Century: Origins, Recensions, Text, and Transmission* (ed. William L. Petersen; Christianity and Judaism in Antiquity 3; Notre Dame, IN: University of Notre Dame Press, 1989), 89–90 [reprinted in E. J. Epp and Gordon D. Fee, *Studies in the Theory and Method of New Testament Textual Criticism* (SD 45; Grand Rapids: Eerdmans, 1993), 286–87]; idem, "Textual Criticism in the Exegesis of the New Testament, with an Excursus on Canon," in *Handbook to Exegesis of the New Testament* (ed. Stanley E. Porter; NTTS 25; Leiden: Brill, 1997), 58.

[27] Papyri known or thought to come from the Fayum (ca. forty miles east to west and ca. thirty miles north to south in area) are P3, P12, P33 + 58, P34, P45 (?), P46 (?), P53, P55, P56, P57, P79, and P92 (Medînet Mâdi). Sinai provided three: P11, P14, P68, as did Auja el-Hafir (Nessana): P59, P60, P61; the Dishna Papers, found near Dishnā, include P66, P72, P75, and P90 (see next note).

Pachomian monastic library until they were buried in a large earthen jar in (probably) the seventh century. Yet the Bodmer *New Testament* papyri clearly originated at another uncertain place or places, for they all antedate the founding of the monastic order.[28] Thus, we do not know their earlier or original provenance.

By way of contrast, the forty-seven papyri and twelve majuscules 14
discovered and presumably utilized at Oxyrhynchus—with many of them, though not necessarily all, likely to have originated there[29]—provide a statistically significant sample for examining their specific local Christian context.[30]

B. *"Canonical" and "Extracanonical" New Testament Manuscripts at Oxyrhynchus: An Environmental Scan*

Our first step is to provide an environmental scan of Christian literature in Oxyrhynchus to discover the extent to which the New

---

[28] James M. Robinson, *The Pacomian Monastic Library at the Chester Beatty Library and the Bibliothèque Bodmer* (Occasional Papers 19; Claremont, CA: Institute for Antiquity and Christianity, 1990), esp. 4–6, 22–27. A shorter version: "The First Christian Monastic Library," in *Coptic Studies: Acts of the Third International Congress of Coptic Studies, Warsaw, 20–25 August, 1984* (ed. W. Godlewski; Centre d'archéologie méditerranéenne de l'Académie Polonaise des Sciences; Warsaw: Éditions scientifiques de Pologne, 1990), 371–78. See also idem, "Introduction," in *The Chester Beatty Codex AC. 1390: Mathematical School Exercises in Greek and John 10:7–13:38 in Subachmimic* (ed. W. Brashear, W.-P. Funk, J. M. Robinson, and R. Smith; CBM 13; Leuven: Peeters, 1990), 3–29, esp. 3–7, 15–23.

P99 is included in the Dishna Papers: see Alfons Wouters, *The Chester Beatty Codex AC 1499: A Graeco-Latin Lexicon on the Pauline Epistles and a Greek Grammar* (CBM 12; Leuven: Peeters, 1988), esp. xi–xii.

In the *editio princeps* of P72, Michel Testuz argued that P72 was copied in Thebes by a Coptic scribe (*Papyrus Bodmer VII–IX: VII: L'Epître de Jude, VIII: Les deux Epîtres de Pierre, IX: Les Psaumes 33 et 34* [Cologny-Geneva: Bibliothèque Bodmer, 1959], 10, 32–33); this is based on "the presence of a Coptic word in the margin of 2 Peter 2:22 . . . and the frequent confusion of its K and G, characteristic of Copts of Thebes" (p. 10). Cf. Kurt Aland, ed., *Repertorium der griechischen christlichen Papyri, I: Biblische Papyri* (PTS 18; Berlin/New York: de Gruyter, 1975), 303.

[29] See E. J. Epp, "New Testament Papyrus Manuscripts and Letter Carrying in Greco- Roman Times," in *The Future of Early Christianity: Essays in Honor of Helmut Koester* (ed. B. A. Pearson *et al.*; Minneapolis: Fortress, 1991), 35–56, esp. 52–56.

[30] In earlier studies, I treated the New Testament papyri in their literary/intellectual context in Oxyrhynchus: "The New Testament Papyri at Oxyrhynchus in Their Social and Intellectual Context," in *Sayings of Jesus: Canonical and Non-Canonical: Essays in Honour of Tjitze Baarda* (ed. W. L. Petersen *et al.*; NovTSup 89; Leiden: Brill, 1997), 47–68; "The Codex and Literacy in Early Christianity and at Oxyrhynchus: Issues Raised by Harry Y. Gamble's *Books and Readers in the Early Church*," *CRBR* 10 (1997): 15–37; and "New Testament Papyri at Oxyrhynchus: Their Significance for Understanding the Transmission of the Early New Testament Text."

Testament manuscripts there shared space with additional Christian writings, keeping the issue of canon formation in mind. Of course, any notion of "New Testament papyri" as a formed and isolated body of literature is anachronistic: I know of nothing at Oxyrhynchus informing us of the canonical process there during the first three centuries or so of Christianity, except the very telling presence of numerous and often early manuscripts of what we—again often anachronistically—call the "apocryphal New Testament." Hence, for a clearer picture of "New Testament papyri" at Oxyrhynchus into the late fourth century, the following writings discovered there—or at least most of them—should be included. Many are fragmentary, yet each is a remnant of a more extensive copy that was present in the ancient city. Naturally, one copy is significant, though two or more copies of a writing portray a more expansive and richer context. There are:

- Seven copies of the *Shepherd of Hermas* (P.Oxy. 404 [late 3rd/early 4th c.]; 1172 + 3526 [Greek and Coptic, 4th c.]; 1599 [4th c.]; 1783 [vellum palimpsest, early 4th c.]; 1828 [vellum codex, 3rd c.];[31] 3527 [early 3rd c.]; and 3528 [late 2nd/early 3rd c.]—note the exceptionally early date of the last one)
- Three copies of the *Gospel of Thomas* (P.Oxy. 1; 654; and 655, all 3rd c.)—the only ones extant in Greek[32]
- Two copies of the *Gospel of Mary* (P.Oxy. 3525, 3rd c.; P.Ryl. III.463, early 3rd c.)[33]
- One copy of the *Acts of Peter* (P.Oxy. 849, parchment, early 4th c.)
- One copy of the *Acts of John* (P.Oxy. 850, 4th c.)
- One copy of the *Acts of Paul* (P.Oxy. 1602, parchment, 4th/5th c.)[34]

[31] See van Haelst, no. 665, who noted that Silvio Giuseppe Mercati ("Passo del Pastore di Erma riconosciuto nel pap. Oxy. 1828," *Bib* 6 [1925]: 336–38) identified the fragment as *Hermas* (*Sim.* 6.5.3 and 6.5.5); cf. Ulrich H. J. Körtner and Martin Leutzsch, *Papiasfragmente, Hirt des Hermas* (Schriften des Urchristentums 3; Darmstadt: Wissenschaftliche Buchgesellschaft, 1998) 117 and 360 n. 9.

[32] For the latest critical edition, see Harold W. Attridge, "The Greek Fragments," in *Nag Hammadi Codex II.2–7, together with XIII.2*, Brit. Lib. Or.4926, and P.Oxy. 1, 654, 655: Volume One* (Coptic Gnostic Library; NHS 20; ed. Bentley Layton; Leiden: Brill, 1989), 95–128.

[33] These two fragments are not from the same manuscript: P.Oxy. L, p. 12.

[34] A portion of "From Corinth to Italy": see Wilhelm Schneemelcher, ed., *New Testament Apocrypha* (rev. ed.; Eng. trans. ed. by R. McL. Wilson; Cambridge: James Clarke; Louisville: Westminster John Knox, 1991–92), 2:259. In P.Oxy. XIII, pp.

- One copy of the *Didache* (P.Oxy. 1782, late 4th c.)[35]
- One copy of the *Sophia Jesu Christi* (P.Oxy. 1081, 3rd/4th c.)[36]
- Two copies doubtless of the *Gospel of Peter* (P.Oxy. 2949 [not a codex], late 2nd/early 3rd c.; P.Oxy. 4009, 2nd c.)—again, extraordinarily early[37]
- *Possibly* a copy of the *Apocalypse of Peter* (P.Vind. G, 3rd/4th c.)[38] 16
- Single copies of three unknown Gospels/sayings of Jesus:[39]
  - A narrative in which Jesus discusses the "good," including the parable of the good and bad fruit, and makes direct claims to be in the image/form of God (P.Oxy. 210, 3rd c.)[40]
  - A "Dispute between the Savior and a Priest in Jerusalem"[41] (P.Oxy. 840, parchment, 4th c.)
  - Some sayings of Jesus (P.Oxy. 1224, 3rd/4th c.)[42]

23–25, 1602 was unidentified, but see van Haelst, no. 606, and, for a revised text, Henry A. Sanders, "A Fragment of the Acta Pauli in the Michigan Collection," *HTR* 31 (1938): 79 n. 2.

[35] For the importance of P.Oxy. 1782 for the *Didache* text, see Kurt Niederwimmer, *The Didache* (Hermeneia; Minneapolis: Fortress, 1998), 21–23.

[36] For a restoration of the Greek text of P.Oxy. 1081, see Harold W. Attridge, "P. Oxy. 1081 and the Sophia Jesu Christi," *Enchoria* 5 (1975): 1–8. Aland (*Repertorium*, 1:373) dates it 3rd/4th c.; P.Oxy. VIII, p. 16, early 4th c.

[37] See P.Oxy. 2949 and pl. II; P.Oxy. 4009 (by D. Lührmann and P. Parsons) and plates I–II. They report that 2949 and 4009 are not from the same manuscript; for the view that both are likely copies of the *Gospel of Peter*, see D. Lührmann, "POx 2949: EvPt 3–5 in einer Handschrift des 2./3. Jahrhunderts," *ZNW* 72 (1981): 216–26; "P.Oxy. 4009: Ein neues Fragment des Petrusevangeliums?" *NovT* 35 (1993): 390–410. Lührmann's identification of P.Oxy. 2949 is accepted, e.g., by Schneemelcher (*New Testament Apocrypha*, 1:217–18 [though, curiously, the identification is dismissed on p. 93]); and by Helmut Koester (*Introduction to the New Testament* [2 vols.; 2nd ed.; New York/Berlin: de Gruyter, 1995, 2000], 1:167).

[38] P.Vindob. G.[no number], from the Rainer collection, Vienna [no further identification appears to be available], a vellum leaf, 3rd/4th c. Provenance is described by van Haelst, no. 619, as "Oxyrhynchos (?)." Provenance is not discussed by any of the authors referred to by van Haelst, nor by Schneemelcher (*New Testament Apocrypha*, 2:620–21).

[39] See also P.Oxy. 1384 (but 5th c.). Perhaps P.Egerton 2 (P.Lond. Christ. 1), with four gospel-like pericopes, is from Oxyrhynchus (van Haelst, no. 586).

[40] I adopt the case for an apocryphal Gospel made by Stanley E. Porter, "P.Oxy. II 210 as an Apocryphal Gospel and the Development of Egyptian Christianity," in *Atti del XXII Congresso internazionale di papirologia, Firenze, 23–29 agosto 1998*, ed. Andorlini et al., 2:1095–1108, esp. 1101–8. Cf. P.Oxy. II, pp. 9–10.

[41] I use François Bovon's description: see "Fragment Oxyrhynchus 840, Fragment of a Lost Gospel, Witness of an Early Christian Controversy over Purity," *JBL* 119 (2000): 705–28. Bovon marshals voluminous evidence to show that it reflects an intra-Christian dispute: cf. 728. Although this writing is sometimes thought to be an amulet, Michael J. Kruger opted for a miniature codex: "P.Oxy. 840: Amulet or Miniature Codex?" *JTS* 53 (2002): 81–94.

[42] Aland, *Repertorium*, 1:374.

Three more copies of well-known "apocryphal" writings were found, though in manuscripts later than our period: the *Acts of Paul and Thecla* (P.Oxy. 6, 5th c.), the *Protevangelium of James* (P.Oxy. 3524, 6th c.), and the *Letter of Abgar to Jesus* (P.Oxy. 4469, 5th c., amulet), as well as a tiny, unidentified fragment of "the Acts of some apostle or saint" (P.Oxy. 851, 5th/6th c.). What is not known is whether these were late imports or copies of earlier exemplars that were used in the city during the period of our concern.

Some of these well-known writings were contenders for canonicity at various Christian localities—indeed, possibly most of them,
since all except the *Letter of Abgar* certainly or plausibly stem from
17 the second century.[43] Or, if we adopt the principle that canon contenders can be identified by their inclusion in a canon list or by discussion in a canon context—even if only as rejected books—or by
being cited as authoritative by early Christian writers, nearly all
would qualify under these criteria as potentially canonical.[44]

The collocation with our so-called "New Testament" papyri of such recognized or possible candidates for canonicity raises serious issues, such as the propriety of designating *two* categories of writings

[43] Dates generally accepted: end of first or first half of second century: *Shepherd of Hermas*; early to mid-second century: *Gospel of Thomas*, *Didache*, *Gospel of Peter*, *Sophia Jesu Christi*; second century: *Gospel of Mary*, *Acts of Paul* (*and Thecla*); second half of second century: *Acts of Peter*, *Protevangelium of James*, *Acts of John* [or first half of third century]. For most, see Schneemelcher, *New Testament Apocrypha*, ad loc.; Bruce M. Metzger, *The Canon of the New Testament: Its Origin, Development, and Significance* [Oxford: Clarendon, 1987], ad loc. (see index); Helmut Koester, *Introduction to the New Testament*, vol. 1, ad loc. (see index). On the date of the *Shepherd*, see esp. Carolyn Osiek, *Shepherd of Hermas: A Commentary* (Hermeneia; Minneapolis: Fortress, 1999), 19–20. The *Letter of Abgar* stems from the end of the third century (Schneemelcher, 1:496).

[44] The exceptions appear to be the *Gospel of Mary*, *Sophia Jesu Christi*, and the *Letter of Abgar*. On *Sophia*, see "Eugnostos the Blessed and the Sophia of Jesus Christ," in *Coptic Encyclopedia* (New York: Macmillan, 1991), 4:1069. For notice of the others in canon lists or discussions, see Metzger, *Canon*, esp. Appendix IV, 305–11, and ad loc.; Schneemelcher, *New Testament Apocrypha*, ad loc. For example, *Hermas* was included in Codex Sinaiticus (א, mid-4th c.) following the twenty-seven New Testament books; in the Muratorian Canon, though only to be read but not "publicly to the people in church"; and in the Latin canon inserted in Codex Claromontanus (D^p) of the sixth century, though the list is older. In the latter, *Hermas*, *Barnabas*, the *Acts of Paul*, and the *Apocalypse of Peter* are marked with a horizontal line in the left margin, doubtless to indicate less authority or the like (see Metzger, *Canon*, 230; for the D^p text and that of the Muratorian Canon, 310–11, 305–7). For patristic references to the *Gospel of Thomas*, see Schneemelcher, *New Testament Apocrypha*, 1:110–11; Marvin Meyer, *The Gospel of Thomas: The Hidden Sayings of Jesus* (San Francisco: HarperSan Francisco, 1992), 6–7.

in this early period: "New Testament" and "apocryphal," and whether we have given sufficient weight to the provenance of these "extra-canonical" books and to their juxtaposition and utilization alongside our "New Testament" manuscripts. And where better might these canonical issues be investigated than at Oxyrhynchus—in a local, real-life context?

For example, the seven surviving copies of the *Shepherd of Hermas* are spread evenly from the late second through the fourth centuries, which is striking evidence of an early and continuous textual tradition of a single writing in one locality—especially in a situation of random preservation. The extended rivalry, well documented elsewhere, among the Apocalypse of John, the *Apocalypse of Peter*, and the *Shepherd of Hermas*, for a place in the canon draws our attention also to the substantial textual tradition of the Apocalypse of John at Oxyrhynchus: six manuscripts from the turn of the third/fourth century (P18, P115) to the fourth (P24, 0308), then to the fifth century (0163), and to ca. 600 C.E. (P26). Too much must not be drawn from such comparative data, but it is clear by any measure available to us that the *Shepherd of Hermas* was very much a part of Christian literature in Oxyrhynchus at an early period.[45]

Furthermore, if—as is likely—the *Gospel of Peter* is represented in
two fragments that date from the second or early third centuries 18
(P.Oxy. 2949 and 4009), and if the *Apocalypse of Peter* is extant from Oxyrhynchus (see above), we would have manuscripts of three unsuccessful canon contenders—the *Shepherd of Hermas,* and both the *Gospel* and the *Apocalypse of Peter,* with the first two dating in the range of our earliest ten New Testament papyri.[46] If one were to play comparative statistical games—not well advised in this situation—it could be said that up to around 200 C.E. Oxyrhynchus yielded one copy of the *Shepherd* and two of the *Gospel of Peter* alongside three of

[45] G. H. R. Horsley, *NewDocs* 2 (1977): 159–61, lists seventeen manuscripts of the *Shepherd* to that date, though this includes P.Oxy. 5—a citation not a text—but not P.Oxy. 3526 (same codex as 1172), 3527, or 3528.

[46] Dates are from Aland and Aland, *Text of the New Testament,* 96–102, supplemented by Nestle-Aland, *Novum Testamentum Graece* (27th rev. ed, 8th cor. and exp. printing [with Papyri 99–116]; Stuttgart: Deutsche Bibelgesellschaft, 2001) [card insert].

New Testament papyri dated to the second century are P52 (ca. 125), P90 (P.Oxy. 3523), P98, P104 (P.Oxy. 4404; ca. 200), dated to the second/third century are P32, P46, P64 + 67 + 4[?], P66, P77 (P.Oxy. 2683), P103 (P.Oxy. 4403).

Matthew, and one of John[47] If we were to extend this playful approach to around 400 C.E., it could be claimed that, while Oxyrhynchus had forty "New Testament" papyri (plus four parchments) containing portions of sixteen[48] of our New Testament books, there were present also twenty copies of nine known "apocrypha," plus three unidentified Gospel-like writings, in the city. Moreover, the presumption—though not provable—would be that at least some of these writings that had originated in the second century, but are now preserved only in third- and fourth-century manuscripts, had earlier exemplars in Oxyrhynchus.

When this broader definition of "New Testament papyri" is applied—bringing early so-called "apocrypha" under the same umbrella—it will be clear that any position of exclusive honor in ancient Oxyrhynchus that we might have assumed for the forty-seven papyri of our New Testament has been compromised, for that honor had to be shared with numerous other early Christian writings, of which some twenty-three manuscripts have survived, and there is no basis, therefore, to claim that the "New Testament" manuscripts stand out as a separate or separable group.

C. *The Jewish Bible in Oxyrhynchus*

A fragment of a third-century roll (P.Oxy. 1075) holds the final thirteen verses of Exodus, and later in the third or early in the fourth century someone else copied on the verso the Apocalypse of John (P18 = P.Oxy. 1079), though only 1:1–7 survive. Naturally, there is no context for a New Testament papyrus more intimate than having been written on the back of another document. This manuscript,
19 then, is an opisthograph, but with the writing of the Apocalypse (on the verso) running in the opposite direction of Exodus (on the recto), so that—when the end of the roll was reached and the roll was turned over—the conclusion of Exodus led directly to the beginning of the Apocalypse. Whether this was deliberate and, if so, what the motivation might have been are not obvious, though there are ready parallels between the end of Exodus and the opening of Revelation. Exodus, for example, concludes with the anointing and consecration

[47] *Shepherd of Hermas*: P.Oxy. 3528; *Gospel of Peter*: P.Oxy. 2949 and 4009; Matthew: P77, P103, P104; and John: P90.

[48] Seventeen if majuscule 0206 (P.Oxy. 1353, 4th c.) of 1 Peter is added.

of the tabernacle and of Aaron and his sons as *priests* (esp. Exod 39:32–40:33), followed by:

> . . . the *cloud* of the Lord was on the tabernacle by day, and fire was in the *cloud* by night, before the eyes of all the house of Israel at each stage of their journey. (Exod 40:38)

And the opening doxology of the Apocalypse of John (1:6) refers to Christ who "made us to be a kingdom, *priests* serving his God and Father," and then, reminiscent of Dan 7:13, it says, "Look! He is coming with the *clouds*. . . ." Whether this or another form of intertextuality was operative is a matter of speculation, but not without interest, for the collocation—on a single papyrus roll—of Jewish Scripture and an authoritative Christian writing[49] opens an inquiry about the use of Jewish writings by Christians at Oxyrhynchus, and of the relation between Jews and Christians there.

The discovery at Oxyrhynchus of some twenty-three Greek manuscripts of the Septuagint and one in the Old Latin dating up to the end of the fourth century further enlarge the body of "biblical" material with which our New Testament papyri had to share their space. The following copies, largely fragmentary, survive: Genesis (P.Oxy. 656, papyrus codex, early 3rd c.; 1007, vellum leaf, late 3rd c.; 1166, papyrus roll, 3rd c.; 1167, papyrus codex, 4th c.; 1073, Old Latin, vellum codex, 4th c.); Exodus (P.Oxy. 1074, papyrus codex, 3rd c.; 1075, papyrus roll, 3rd c.; 4442, papyrus codex, early 3rd c.;[50] P.Mil.R.Univ. I.22 [van Haelst, no. 39], vellum codex, 4th c.); Leviticus (P.Oxy. 1225, papyrus roll, 1st half of 4th c.; 1351, vellum codex, 4th c.); Joshua (P.Oxy. 1168, vellum codex, 4th c.); Esther (P.Oxy. 4443, papyrus roll, late 1st/early 2nd c.); Job (P.Oxy.

---

[49] Another papyrus with Jewish Scripture/New Testament contents is P.Amh. 1.3b, with Gen 1:1–5 on the verso, and Heb 1:1 on the recto (= P12), suggesting that Hebrews was copied earlier! However, only Heb 1:1 is present, though the recto also contains a Christian letter written from Rome by someone important in the church, dating between 250 and 285: B. P. Grenfell and A. S. Hunt, *The Amherst Papyri* (2 vols.; London: H. Frowde, Oxford University Press, 1900–1901), 1:28–31. See Tobias Nicklas, "Zur historischen und theologischen Bedeutung der Erforschung neutestamentlicher Textgeschichte," *NTS* 48 (2002): 154–55. Aland and Aland view the Heb 1:1 text as "occasional notes," and not as a proper New Testament papyrus (*Text of the New Testament,* 85).

[50] See Daniela Colomo, "Osservazioni intorno ad un nuovo papiro dell'Esodo (P.Oxy. 4442)," in *Atti del XXII Congresso internazionale di papirologia, Firenze, 23–29 agosto 1998,* ed. Andorlini *et al.*, 1:269–77.

20 3522, papyrus roll, 1st c.; PSI X.1163, papyrus codex, 3rd/4th c.); Psalms (P.Oxy. 845, papyrus codex, late 4th/5th c.; 1226, papyrus codex, late 3rd/early 4th c.; 1352, vellum codex, early 4th c.; 1779, papyrus codex, 4th c. [van Haelst, no. 90 = 3rd c.]; P.Harr. 31, papyrus roll, 4th [Haelst no. 148, Oxyrhynchus?]; P.Oxy. 2386, papyrus roll, 4th/5th c.); Wisdom of Solomon (P.Oxy. 4444, vellum codex, 4th c.); Tobit (P.Oxy. 1594, vellum codex, late 3rd c.); and *Apocalypse of Baruch* (P.Oxy. 403, papyrus codex, 4th/5th c.). There are in addition fragments of a papyrus codex of *1 Enoch* (P.Oxy. 2069, late 4th c.).[51] Five other LXX manuscripts and one Old Latin date in the fifth and sixth centuries.[52]

Incidentally, criteria for determining whether these texts were copied for Jewish or for Christian use have not been clearly defined, and certainly not agreed upon by all. Commonly, however, two principles are employed: (1) writings on rolls, especially if from the first or early second centuries, presumably are Jewish, with the likelihood that codices from the third century and later are Christian, though each case must be decided on its own merits; and (2) the employment of *nomina sacra* (contracted divine names and terms, but in this context "Lord" [κύριος, κ̅ω̅] and "God" [θεός, θ̅ω̅]) has been taken as a sign of Christian origin and use[53] (see further below). Though this is not the occasion to explore these issues, sorting out LXX manuscripts of Jewish origin from those copied by Christians would provide useful information both about the Jewish community at Oxyrhynchus and the Christian community there.

Without belaboring the point, did our "New Testament" papyri hold a special, separable place of honor among all the related Christian

---

[51] See van Haelst, nos. 576 and 577: it was identified as *1 Enoch* and republished by J. T. Milik, "Fragments grecs du livre d'Hénoch (P.Oxy. XVII 2069)," *ChrEg* 46 (1971): 321–43.

[52] Genesis (in Old Latin): P.Oxy. 1007 (vellum leaf, 6th c.); Judges: PSI 2.127 (papyrus codex, early 3rd c.); Ecclesiastes: P.Oxy. 2066 (papyrus codex, 5th or 6th c.); Amos: P.Oxy. 846 (papyrus codex, 6th c.); Ecclesiasticus: P.Oxy. 1595 (papyrus codex, 6th c.); Tobit: P.Oxy. 1076 (vellum codex, 6th c.). There are also two amulets with LXX Ps 90 (P.Oxy. 1928, roll, Christian, with 1–16; and P.Ryl. 3, with 5–16, both 5th/6th c.). On P.Oxy. 846, see Robert A. Kraft, "*P.Oxy.* VI 846 (Amos 2, Old Greek) Reconsidered," *BASP* 16 (1979): 201–4.

[53] See, e.g., Roberts, *Manuscript, Society, and Belief*, 28–34, 74–78; E. A. Judge and S. R. Pickering, "Biblical Papyri prior to Constantine: Some Cultural Implications of Their Physical Form," *Prudentia* 10 (1978): 2–3. See also n. 58 below.

and Jewish literature at Oxyrhynchus? Criteria for establishing such a position are not apparent.

The second step in assessing our New Testament papyri in their local context is to take several "core samples" of the sociocultural soil of Oxyrhynchus, probing Christian letters, hymns, prayers, treatises, and petitions, and our first probe reveals a private letter already famous though published only in 1996.

D. *A Letter about Lending Books: Jewish-Christian Issues and Women's* 21
Literacy and Leadership in Christianity at Oxyrhynchus

An early-fourth-century private letter at Oxyrhynchus (P.Oxy. 4365) reads simply:

> To my dearest lady sister, greetings in the Lord. Lend the Ezra, since I lent you the little Genesis. Farewell in God from us.

This is the complete letter, twenty-one words written in six short lines on the back of a piece of papyrus cut from a roll that contained a petition written in the late third century—hence, the presumed early-fourth-century date for the letter. Its six lines elicit at least six significant questions:

1. Are the writer and recipient Jews or Christians, and how can we tell?
2. Why aren't they named?
3. Is the writer a man or, like the recipient, a woman?
4. What books are being loaned?
5. Why would they be read? And
6. What might a woman's voice tell us about female literacy, and does her interest in these books inform us about women's leadership in the implied community?

1. *Are the writer and recipient Christians?* On the face of it, everything in our tiny letter could be Jewish, and the terms "Ezra" and "Genesis" confirm a biblical context. "Lord" and "God," by themselves as singular terms, do not aid the decision between Jewish and Christian. It is of methodological interest, moreover, that, if "Ezra" and "Genesis" were *not* present, a context in Greco-Roman religions would be possible, for "god" in the singular occurs often in phrases such as "I pray to god" or "to the lord god" or "before the lord god"; "I thank

god"; "god willing"; "god knows"; or "until god takes pity";[54] and
22 *nomina sacra*[55]—contracted divine names, to which we turn in a
moment—do not occur in several dozen examples from Oxyrhynchus.
The singular is common also in the frequent formula, "I make obeisance every day before god," or "the lord god," often specifically

[54] Oxyrhynchus occurrences through the fourth century: "I pray to the god": P.Oxy. 1680, line 3 (3rd/4th c.); 1773, line 4 (3rd c.); 3065, line 3 (3rd c.); 3816, line 3 (3rd/4th c.); "to the lord god": P.Oxy. 1298, line 4 (4th c.); 1299, lines 3–4 (4th c.); 1677, line 3 (3rd c.); 1678, line 3 (3rd c.); 1683, line 5 (late 4th c.); 2728, line 5 (3rd/4th c.); 3860, line 3 (later 4th c.); " before the lord god": P.Oxy. 3999, line 3 (4th c.); "in god": P.Vindob.Sijp. XI.26, line 23 (3rd c.); "in the lord god": P.Oxy. 2276, lines 29–30 (end 3rd c.); "I/we thank the god": P.Oxy. 1299, lines 5–6 (4th c.); 3816, line 11 (3rd/4th c.); "god willing/with god's help/by god's grace": σὺν θεῷ as in P.Oxy. 1220, line 24 (3rd c.); 1763, line 11 (3rd c.); 3814, line 25 (3rd/4th c.), or τάχα σὺν θεῷ in P.Oxy. 4624, lines 3–4 (1st c.); "god knows": P.Oxy. 3997, lines 8–9 (3rd/4th c.); 4628, line 3 (4th c.); "until the god takes pity": P.Oxy. 120, line 16 (4th c.); "barring an act of god": P.Oxy. 2721, line 24 (234 C.E.) [cf. 411, line 11].

Other occurrences of "god"or "lord" in singular: "(the) god": P.Oxy. 112, line 4 (3rd/4th c.); cf. 2474, line 6 (3rd c.) [lacuna preceding]; 1680, line 3 (3rd/4th c.); 1682, line 6 (4th c.); 3356, lines 16–17 (76 C.E.); 3859, line 10 (4th c.); 3997, lines 4, 12; "the lord god": P.Oxy. 3819, line 10 (early 4th c.); 3998, line 2 (4th c.); 4493, lines 3–5 (1st half of 4th c.); ὁ δεσπότης θεός: 939, line 4 (4th c.) [cf. Christian use with *nomen sacrum* in P.Oxy. 2729, line 3]; "the great/est god, Sarapis": P.Oxy. 1070, line 8 (3rd c.); 1453, line 5 (30–29 B.C.); "the great/est god, Apollo": P.Oxy. 1449, line 4 (213–217 C.E.); 1435, lines 2–3 (147 C.E.); "Sarapis, the great god": 2837, line 12 (50 C.E.); "the lord Sarapis": P.Oxy. 110, lines 2–3 (2nd c.); 523, lines 2–3 (2nd c.); 1484, lines 3–4 (2nd/3rd c.); 1755, line 4 (2nd/3rd c.); 3693, lines 3–4 (2nd c.); 4339, lines 2–3 (2nd/3rd c.); "O lord Sarapis Helios": P.Oxy. 1148, line 1 (1st c.); "the greatest god, Ammon": P.Oxy. 3275, lines 5–6 (early 1st c). "Goddess," as in P.Oxy. 254, lines 2–3 (20 C.E.); 2722, lines 2, 6 (154 C.E.); 1449, line 11 (213–217 C.E.), is not relevant.

Nomina sacra do not occur in the cases above. On "God knows," see A. M. Nobbs, "Formulas of Belief in Greek Papyrus Letters of the Third and Fourth Centuries," in *Ancient History in a Modern University*, volume 2, *Early Christianity, Late Antiquity, and Beyond* (ed. T. W. Hillard *et al.*; Grand Rapids: Eerdmans, 1998), 235–36; on "I pray to god" as both Christian and non-Christian, 237. On "god willing," etc., see B. R. Rees, "Popular Religion in Graeco-Roman Egypt, II: The Transition to Christianity," *JEA* 36 (1950): 94–95; he provides fifty fifth- to seventh-century Oxyrhynchus examples (Christian and non-Christian) of σὺν θεῷ on 94 nn. 14–16; 95 nn. 1–6 (though, curiously, only P.Oxy. vols. through XVI [1924] are used).

Though disputed and often doubtful, a number of the expressions above have been taken as Christian (of course, not those with Sarapis), including P.Oxy. 120; 939; 1298; 1299; 1678; 1680; 1682; 1683; 1773; 2276; 2474; 3816; 3819; 3997; 3998; 3999. See Horsley, *NewDocs* 4 (1979): 57–63; cf. P.Oxy. XIV, p. 138.

[55] See Aland, *Repertorium*, 1:420–28, for an index of *nomina sacra* in biblical and apocryphal manuscripts, showing their numerous formations.

"before god, the . . . lord Sarapis."[56] *Nomina sacra* do not occur in these cases either.

Nomina sacra, however, do occur with virtual consistency through
the fourth century in letters otherwise clearly Christian, and the
instances are numerous.[57] As is well known, this is a complex matter, though a criterion commonly taken as virtually decisive is that 23

---

[56] Obeisance before "the god": P.Oxy. 2682, lines 3–5 (3rd/4th c.); 3997, lines 9–11 (3rd/4th c.); "the lord god": P.Oxy. 3998, lines 4–5 (4th c.); 4493, lines 3–5 (1st half of 4th c.); P.Alex. 30 (4th c.) from Oxyrhynchus; "the master god": 1775, line 4 (4th c.); specifically "before the god, the . . . lord Sarapis": P.Oxy. 3992, lines 13–16 (2nd c.); cf. 1670, lines 3–6 (3rd c.); 1769, lines 4–5 (3rd c.); 1677, line 3 (3rd c.); 2984, lines 4–7 (2nd/3rd c.). For an obeisance passage (non-Christian) without mention of a deity, see P.Oxy. 1482, lines 22–23 (2nd c.). "The obeisance formula is typically pagan" (P.Oxy. LIX, p. 148); cf. Horsley, *NewDocs* 4 (1987): 61–62. Some instances have been taken as Christian, e.g., P.Oxy. 1775; 3997; 3998. *Nomina sacra* do not occur in the preceding instances. See n. 59 below.

[57] Oxyrhynchus evidence through the fourth century: letters clearly, likely, possibly, or alleged to be Christian; those clearly Christian are marked with an asterisk (*); those possibly Christian have a question mark (?):

(1) *Nomina sacra* in clearly or likely Christian letters: 1161, line 7 (4th c.)*; 1162, lines 4, 12, 14, and ϙ̅θ̅ in 15 (4th c.)*; 2601, line 5 (early 4th c.) [complex case, see P.Oxy. XXXI, pp. 167–71; it contains a bungled *nomen sacrum* and ϙ̅θ̅ (line 34)]; 2729, line 3 (4th c.) [*nomen sacrum*: one of two]; 2785, lines. 1, 13 (4th c.)*; 3857, line 15, plus ϙ̅θ̅ (4th c.)*; 3858, lines 3, 25 (4th c.)*; 3862, lines 4, 39, plus χμγ bis, ϙθ (4th/5th c.)*; PSI 3.208, lines 1, 12 (vellum, 4th c.); PSI 9.1041, lines 1, 16 (vellum, 3rd/4th c.)*.

P.Oxy. 1592, lines 3, 5 (3rd/4th c.) is a special case, with *nomina sacra*, κ̅ε̅ μου π̅ρ̅ and π̅η̅ρ̅, though all refer, not to deity, but to a high church official, and the *nomina sacra* obviously were used to show the greatest possible respect, further enhanced by the use of "exalted " and "rejoiced" from the Magnificat (Luke 1:46–47): ". . . greetings. I received your letter, my *lord father*, and I was very much *exalted* and I *rejoiced*, that such a *father* of mine remembers me. For when I received it, I [worshiped?] your holy [face?]"—trans. and interpretation by AnneMarie Luijendijk, Harvard doctoral student, in a paper "What's in a *nomen*?" at the SBL annual meeting, Atlanta, 2003 [italics added]. The Magnificat verbs are without context and doubtless came from liturgy. On the allusions, see B. F. Harris, "Biblical Echoes and Reminiscences in Christian Papyri," in *Proceedings of the XIV International Congress of Papyrologists, Oxford, 24–31 July 1974* (Graeco-Roman Memoirs, 61; London: British Academy, 1975), 156.

On ϙ̅θ̅ = 99, isopsephism of ἀμήν, see P.Oxy LVI, pp. 116 n. 13; 135–36 n. 1; P.Oxy. XXXI, p. 171; as "exclusive to Christians," see E. A. Judge and S. R. Pickering, "Papyrus Documentation of Church and Community in Egypt to the Mid-Fourth Century," *JAC* 20 (1977): 69; cf. 54: "the cryptogram for Amen . . . was coming into fashion at the beginning of the fourth century"; cf. S. R. Llewelyn, *NewDocs* 8 (1984–85): 171–72. On the enigmatic χμγ, see Horsley, *NewDocs* 2 (1977): 177–80; esp. Llewelyn, *NewDocs* 8 (1984–85): 156–68; P.Oxy. LVI, pp. 135–36. It occurs also in a prayer: P.Oxy. 1058 (4th or 5th c.).

(2) *Nomina sacra* in letters with virtually no other Christian identifiers: P.Oxy. 1493, lines 4–5 (3rd/4th c.): mixed: κ̅ω̅ θεῷ; 1495, lines 4–5 (4th c.); 1774, line 3 (early

"god" and "lord" in the singular (when the latter refers to deity) are non-Christian when *nomina sacra* are absent and Christian when present.[58] However, there are a fair number of ambiguous cases,[59] and
24 the principle, I think, has been applied too loosely.

But we can be more precise because our letter on exchanging books has more specific and evidentiary phrases, namely, "Greetings *in* the Lord" and "Farewell *in* God," where both "Lord" (κυρίῳ) and "God" (θεῷ) are in contracted forms (κ̅ω̅ and θ̅ω̅). Moreover, these two phrases, when written as *nomina sacra,* appear to be virtually

4th c.); 2156, (4th/5th c.): mixed: line 6, "divine providence of God (no *nomen sacrum*), line 25, ἐν κυρί[ω̣] θ̅ω̅; 2609, line 2 (4th c.) [may also contain a chi-rho monogram]; 2731, line 2 (4th/5th c.); 3858, lines 3, 25 (4th c.); 4127, line 4 (1st half 4th c.). PSI 8.972, line 3, probably from Oxyrhynchus (4th c.): line 4 refers to "the evil eye"; on the evidence that the letter is Christian, see Horsley, *NewDocs* 1 (1976): 134–36.

(3) *Nomina sacra* lacking in letters clearly, likely, or alleged to be Christian: P.Oxy. 939, line 4 (4th c.)?: P.Oxy. VI, p. 307 assumes it is Christian due to its phraseology and sentiments in lines 3–10, 28–30; 1492, line 19 (3rd/4th c.)*; 1494, line 3 (early 4th c.); 1593, line 12[?] (4th c.)?; 3421, line 4 (4th c.): "I pray to the all-merciful god"; 3819, line 10 (early 4th c.): "the lord god"—basis for Christian origin is a rare word (δυνατέω) found only in Philodemus, Epicurean philosopher of the first century B.C.E., and in the Pauline epistles; 4003, line 4 (4th/5th c.)*: Christian letter, but shaky grammar and vulgar spelling could account for lack of *nomen sacrum.*

[58] On the basis of the discussion and evidence in Roberts (*Manuscript, Society, and Belief,* 26–34, 74–78), *nomina sacra* do not occur in clearly Jewish manuscripts; his one exception (van Haelst, no. 74, fragments of 1–2 Kings, 5th/6th c.) has four instances (κ̅υ̅ once and ι̅σ̅λ̅ ['Ισραήλ] three times), but all at the ends of lines, perhaps to save space, because no other divine terms are contracted (pp. 32–33). More recently Robert A. Kraft has noted two instances where κ̅υ̅ has been inserted in an apparently blank space (by a later hand in P.Oxy. 656 of Genesis, ca. 200 C.E.; likely by a later hand in P.Oxy. 1075 of Exodus 40, 3rd c.): http://ccat.sas.upenn.edu/rs/rak/lxxjewpap/kyrios.jpg; see his cautions on the identification of Christian manuscripts: http://ccat.sas.upenn.edu/rs/rak/jewishpap.html, "The Debated Features," §4.

[59] Ambiguous cases would include those listed in (2) and (3) in n. 57 above. Another criterion would be that the "obeisance" formula indicates a Greco-Roman religions context and not a Christian one. There is, however, an occurrence of this formula in a certainly Christian letter, though from Arsinoë (P.Mich.Inv. 346, 4th c.). Its identity as Christian is based on "characteristically Christian titles," and the formula reads, "I make obeisance for you daily"; here, though, there is no deity specified, so we cannot test the *nomen sacrum* criterion: see Herbert C. Youtie, "P.Mich.Inv. 346: A Christian ΠΡΟΣΚΥΝΗΜΑ," *ZPE* 28 (1978): 265–68. Youtie dismisses other alleged Christian examples—where "god" in the singular occurs—as "inference which cannot be proved" (p. 265). See the earlier discussion in G. Geraci, "Ricerche sul Proskynema," *Aeg* 51 (1971): 197–200, 207, which includes P.Oxy. 1775 (4th c.); 2682 (3rd/4th c.); and P.Alex. 30 (4th c.), found at Oxyrhynchus; and Horsley, *NewDocs* 4 (1979): 62, who accepts Youtie's view.

exclusive to Christian letters,[60] although—as in the present instance—there is an occasional ambiguous case.[61] To be sure, at least one clearly Christian letter, probably from Oxyrhynchus,[62] employs "in God" without the contracted *nomen sacrum*: the letter, from a young man to his mother (P.Harr. 107, beginning of 3rd c.), opens as follows:

> To my most precious mother Mary, from Besas, many greetings in God. Before all things I pray to the Father, the God of truth, and to the Spirit, the Comforter, that they may preserve you in both soul and body and spirit, and [give] to your body health, and to your spirit gladness, and to your soul eternal life.[63]

---

[60] For instances without *nomina sacra* and with no evidence of Christian or non-Christian religion, see (4) in the next note.

[61] Ambiguous cases would be (2) and (4) below. Oxyrhynchus evidence through the fourth century for greetings/rejoice, etc. "in the Lord/God/Lord God":

(1) With *nomina sacra* and other Christian evidence: (a) "in the Lord": P.Oxy. 1162, ter lines 4, 12, 14 (4th c.); 1774, line 3 (early 4th c.); 2609, line 2 (4th c.) + a defaced Christian monogram; 2785, bis lines 1, 13 (4th c.); 3857, line 15 (4th c.); 3858, bis lines 3, 25 (4th c.); PSI 3.208, bis lines 1, 12 (4th c.); 9.1041, bis lines 1, 16 (3rd/4th c.). (b) "in the Lord God": P.Oxy. 1162, bis lines 4, 14 (4th c.); 3862, bis lines 4, 39, but not ἐν Χριστῷ in line 7 (4th/5th c.). P.Oxy. 2156 (4th/5th c.) is mixed: line 6, θεός (no *nomen sacrum*); line 25, ἐν κυρί[ῳ] $\overline{\theta\omega}$. P.Oxy. 2729 (4th c.) is complex: ἐν κυρίῳ in line 2 is not contracted (though the first two and last letters are obscure) but in the next line $\overline{\theta\omega}$ is.

(2) With *nomina sacra* but no (or virtually no) other Christian evidence: "in the Lord": P.Oxy. 4127, line 4 (1st half 4th c.); "in the Lord God": 2731, line 2 (4th/5th c.).

(3) Without *nomina sacra* but with evidence of non-Christian religion: (a) "in the lord god": P.Oxy. 2276, lines 29–30 (late 3rd/4th c.); cf. lines 28–29: "I greet your children, those secure from enchantment (τὰ ἀβάσκαντα)," trans. "whom the evil eye shall not harm."

(4) Without *nomina sacra* and with no evidence of non-Christian religion: P.Vind.Sijp. 26, line 23 (3rd c.): "I pray for your good health . . . in god"; P.Oxy. 3998, lines 2–3 (4th c.): "very many greetings in the lord god," followed (lines 4–5) by a statement of obeisance "before the lord god," again without *nomina sacra*. Nothing else in these letters suggests they are Christian, and I would not view them as such; cf. P.Oxy. LIX, p. 148. Similar is P.Oxy. 182 (mid 4th c.), published by Dominic Montserrat, Georgina Fantoni, and Patrick Robinson, "Varia Descripta Oxyrhynchita," *BASP* 31 (1994): 48–50: greetings "in the lord god" (lines 2–3), with reference in line 5 to "divine providence"; possibly connected with the archive of Papnuthis and Dorotheus (P.Oxy. 3384–3429).

[62] Van Haelst, no. 1194.

[63] Trans. slightly modified from J. Enoch Powell, ed., *The Rendel Harris Papyri* [I] (Cambridge: Cambridge University Press, 1936), 89–90. Later the letter refers to Easter (lines 20–21). Powell (p. 90, followed by Stanley K. Stowers, *Letter Writing in Greco-Roman Antiquity* [LEC; Philadelphia: Westminster, 1986], 74) asserted that the trichotomy (soul, body, spirit) was "based on" 1 Thess 5:23, but then added

Nomina sacra do not appear in this clearly Christian letter, but the letter itself undoubtedly contains the explanation: in spite of a smooth translation into English (and the lofty sentiments expressed), the editor describes it as "an illiterate letter written . . . in a boyish hand."[64]—which may explain the failure to execute the *nomina sacra*.

Hence, the preceding evidence, here almost entirely from Oxyrhynchus—though similar throughout the papyri—permits us to claim with great assurance that a letter, dating through the fourth century, may be deemed Christian if it employs the phrase "in the Lord" or "in God" with *nomina sacra* present.[65] Moreover, these two particular *nomina sacra* are frequent in Christian letters, while other forms are rare.[66] Exceptions would be *nomina sacra* due not to the "writer" but to a scribe who had picked up the practice.[67] In our letter about books, however, a scribe is unlikely to have been engaged for so
26 brief a note—six very short lines—or to have omitted the writer's and recipient's names (see below).

So our letter about exchanging books, which might at first blush seem Jewish, must be taken as Christian because the expressions "in the Lord," and "in God" exhibit *nomina sacra* (κυρίῳ > κ̅ω̅ and θεῷ > θ̅ω̅), thus conforming to a pattern established elsewhere.

We should pause here for a further methodological moment. Beginning about thirty years ago, identifying papyrus letters as

that this order is "characteristic of Egyptian liturgies" rather than in the body, soul, spirit order in 1 Thessalonians. Hence, the boy's phraseology undoubtedly stems from liturgy rather than directly from a text of 1 Thess 5:23, especially since the verbs are different: διαφυλάξωσιν . . . σέ in the letter and ὁλόκληρον . . . τηρηθείη in 1 Thessalonians. Stowers allows for this: "Besas has either studied the letters of Paul or picked up a local Christian tradition" (p. 74). On the theological orientation of the letter, see B. F. Harris, "Biblical Echoes and Reminiscences in Christian Papyri," in *Proceedings of the XIV International Congress of Papyrologists*, 157. P.Oxy. 1161 (4th c.), a fragment of a clearly Christian letter, refers to "body, soul, and spirit" (lines 6–7).

[64] Powell, *Rendel Harris Papyri* [I], 89.

[65] This argument may border on being circular, for letters otherwise clearly Christian that contain one of these phrases are used, at times, as a basis for calling "Christian" letters that contain no other Christian evidence, whereas, if letters with one or both phrases, but without other Christian evidence, were designated "non-Christian," then the phrases would have to be said to occur in both Christian and non-Christian letters. Hence, each case must be considered on its own merits. For an expanded list of criteria, see Nobbs, "Formulas of Belief," 235.

[66] J. R. Rea in P.Oxy LXIII, p. 45; cf. Judge and Pickering, "Papyrus Documentation of Church and Community in Egypt," 69.

[67] See Horsley, *NewDocs* 3 (1978): 143; idem, *NewDocs* 2 (1977): 70, though I find no relevant examples in his discussion.

Christian, unless unambiguous Christian references occurred, has been made with much more caution than earlier had been the practice.[68] Yet two tendencies of the past have clouded our picture of early Christian documents, especially letters. First, too many have been called Christian that in reality reflect a context of Greco-Roman religions or may be of Jewish or even secular origin. Second, and more specifically, editors—at the mere sight of a word, phrase, or idea reminiscent of our New Testament—too often have exclaimed "citation" or "source," seizing myopically on the "New Testament" as the virtually exclusive resource for tenuously related expressions. Such hyper-parallelism—such a rush to judgment—about the source for a document's vocabulary, phraseology, or stream of consciousness, however, runs counter to our current views of intertextuality, for it ignores the wider range of available Christian literature or tradition—as well as Jewish and secular material. What we need is a microscope with less power of magnification so that our field of vision is broader. Hence, one or several similar words or partial parallelism in thought do not a citation make. Various editors' notes in *The Oxyrhynchus Papyri* and elsewhere illustrate such faults, as do occasional recent articles.[69] This is not to say that pointing out similar-

[68] Criteria for identifying Christian letters have been much discussed over time and especially recently; see Horsley, *NewDocs* 4 (1979): 58–63, for a critical assessment and comparison of significant earlier works by G. Ghedini (1923) and Mario Naldini (1968), and the more recent critiques by G. Tibiletti (1979), and by Ewa Wipszycka, "Remarques sur les lettres privées chrétiennes des siècles (a propos d'un livre de M. Naldini)," *JJP* 18 (1974): 203–21; cf. Naldini's response, containing additional Christian letters, "In margine alle 'lettere cristiane' nei papiri," *CClCr* 2 (1981): 167–76; "Nuove testimonianze cristiane nelle lettere dei papiri greco-egizi (sec. II–IV)," *Aug* 35 (1995): 831–46. See also *NewDocs* 2 (1977): 156–58; Nobbs, "Formulas of Belief," 233–37.

Commendable caution is displayed by Judge, *Rank and Status*, 20–31, where, correctly in my judgment, he declines to identify as Christian P.Oxy. 3057 (thought by some to be the earliest Christian letter extant), or P.Oxy. 3313, or 3069, or even 3314 (the letter of Judas, who, he says, "may be safely left a Jew" [p. 31]—a view with which I concur; cf. G. H. R. Horsley, "Name Change as an Indication of Religious Conversion in Antiquity," *Numen* 34 [1987]: 8–12: "our Judas could perhaps be . . . a Jewish convert to Christianity" [p. 12]).

[69] E.g., the very helpful article of B. F. Harris ("The Use of Scripture in Some Unidentified Theological Papyri," in *Ancient History in a Modern University*, volume 2, *Early Christianity, Late Antiquity, and Beyond*, ed. Hillard et al., 228–32) refers, I think incautiously at times, to New Testament "citations," "expressions," "echoes," "reflections," etc., and states, in summary, that the Old Testament and New Testament writings "were employed, often with some liberty of citation and adaptation, in a great variety of contexts" (p. 232). Actually, options abound for "sources":

27 ities to the New Testament is inappropriate or unhelpful, but only to plead for caution in identifying material as Christian and for a more enlightened view of intertextuality.

2. *Why do the writer and recipient lack names?* Even in brief letters lack of names is uncommon. Our letter's editor, John Rea, noting the possibility of an early-fourth-century date (that is, prior to 325, "when Constantine's acquisition of Egypt finally made it safe to profess Christianity there") speculated that this lack of names "denotes a degree of discretion" on the part of its author.[70] I think it is easier, however, to account for the absence of names by reference to a well-known and partially parallel phenomenon: papyrus invitations, for example, to a wedding or dinner, which were very brief, small in size, and written in short lines. The following example from

---

other Christian writings (including "apocryphal" and patristic), liturgy, oral tradition, etc.; cf. his discussion of P.Oxy. 2072, "echoing Acts 2 and 4" (p. 231), and our discussion below, questioning the connection with Acts; a connection with Heb 10:34 (ibid.) seems tenuous indeed.

I would grant, however, that two verbs in P.Oxy. 1592, lines 3, 5 (3rd/4th c.) may well be an "echo" of Luke 1:46–47, even though there is no further context, because (a) their collocation in the Magnificat and (b) the context of the papyrus letter makes an allusion likely (see n. 57 above).

Harris, in an earlier article ("Biblical Echoes and Reminiscences in Christian Papyri"), uses the classifications "citations, verbal echoes, and lesser verbal reminiscences" (p. 156). For him, e.g., in P.Oxy. 1161, lines 3–4 (4th c.) there is an "echo" of Mark 1:11 in "beloved son," but so common a Christian expression cannot easily be linked to a specific text without fuller parallel contexts. Similarly tenuous is his link (p. 157) of "body, soul, and spirit" in lines 6–7 with 1 Thess 5:23—where the order is spirit, soul, and body (see n. 63 above). His possible "reminiscence" of Titus 2:11 and/or Titus 3:4 in lines 3–4 of P.Oxy. 939 (4th c.) points to one option (pp. 157–58), though I am not entirely convinced that this is a Christian letter (no *nomen sacrum*, though several Christian-sounding phrases).

P.Oxy. 1494 (early 4th c.) is similar: no *nomina sacra* (lines 3, 7), some common expressions, e.g., "god willing" (line 3), some less common, e.g., "sweetest brothers" (but this occurs also, in singular, e.g., in P.Oxy. 935, lines 22–23 [3rd c.], a non-Christian letter [note "ancestral gods," line 10]); hence Harris's "reminiscence" of Matt 3:3 or Acts 13:10 in "straight path" (ὁδὸς εὐθεῖα, lines 8–9) is unlikely: it is a biblical phrase to be sure (e.g., LXX Hos 14:10), but found elsewhere, as in Diod. S. 14.116.9; *2 Clem.* 7.3. A. L. Connolly agrees, though he provides further evidence for his claim that "the letter is almost certainly Christian" ("Miscellaneous NT Quotations," *NewDocs* 4 [1979]: 193).

Finally, Harris mentions a "general similarity" of the mirror passage that introduces P.Oxy. 2603, lines 3–19 (4th c.) to Jas 1:23, but mirror has the opposite effect in each passage: in the papyrus, it fully displays a person who can then "speak about his own likeness" (lines 8–9), while in James a person "observes himself and goes away and at once forgets what he was like" (pp. 158–59).

[70] J. R. Rea in P.Oxy LXIII, p. 44; cf. 43.

Oxyrhynchus (where two-thirds of all extant invitations have been found)[71] is typical:

> Eros invites you to a wedding tomorrow the 29th at the 9th hour. 28
> (P.Oxy. 927, 3rd c.)

The inviter was always mentioned, though almost never were the invited guests named, presumably because weddings, birthdays, and dinners were largely local events and the invitations were from known friends, delivered by the host's servant or slave, who in turn would report back whether the invitation had been accepted or not.[72]

Similarly, the letter about lending "the Ezra" and "the little Genesis," though not an invitation, was obviously a quick communication between close acquaintances, doubtless delivered locally by a personally connected messenger, rendering names superfluous.

3. *The recipient of the letter was a woman, but was the writer male or female?* Normally the reused side of a piece of papyrus would not be closely related in content to the side first written upon, but here again the most immediate context of the letter should not be ignored. The petition on the recto survives in only nine lines, which disclose

---

[71] P.Oxy. 110–112, 181, 523, 524, 747, 926, 927, 1214, 1484–1487, 1579, 1580, 1755, 2147, 2592, 2678, 2791, 2792, 3202, 3501, 3693, 3694, 4339, 4539–4543; SB X.10496; P.Lond.Inv. 3078; P. Köln VI.280 [probably Oxyrhynchus]; no. 7 in O. Giannini, *Annali della Scuolo Normale di Pisa* ser. 2, 35 (1966): 18–19. Most of these consist of four or five short lines. Other invitations found to date include BGU I.333, II.596; P.Apoll. 72; P.Fay. 132; P. Fouad III.76, VIII.7; P.Oslo III.157; P. Yale 85; P.Coll.Youtie I.51, 52; SB V. 7745, VIII. 11652, 12511, 12596, 13875. On the thirty invitations known in the mid-1970s, see Chan-Hie Kim, "The Papyrus Invitation," *JBL* 94 (1975): 391–402; on Sarapis banquets, see *Yale Papyri in the Beinecke Rare Book and Manuscript Library, I* (ed. J. F. Oates, A. E. Samuel, and C. B. Welles; ASP 2; New Haven/Toronto: American Society of Papyrologists, 1967), 260–64; Horsley in *NewDocs* 1 (1976): 5–9; on wedding invitations, see Llewelyn, *NewDocs* 9 (1986–87): 62–65.

[72] Of thirty-six Oxyrhynchus invitations to date (out of a total of about fifty-two), four have "today" with the date (P.Oxy. 1485, 1486, 4542, 4543); four say "tomorrow" (P.Oxy. 111, 1580, SB X.10496; Köln VI.280—probably Oxyrhynchus); ten have "tomorrow"plus the date (P.Oxy. 110, 524, 926, 927, 1487, 1579, 2791, 3202, 3693, 4540; thirteen give the date only (P.Oxy. 112, 523, 747, 1214, 1755, 2147, 2592, 2678, 2792, 3501, 3694, 4339, 4539); one provides no day or date (P.Oxy. 4541); and three have lacunae (P.Oxy. 181, 1484, P.Lond.Inv. 3078). The vast majority are from the second and third centuries, with a few earlier or later. The latest, 1214 (dated 5th c.), provides the name of the invited guest, as does 112 (late 3rd or early 4th c.), but the latter invitation went to someone who must travel, either by donkey or boat, and the invitation would have gone in the usual mail fashion rather than by local messenger.

little of its nature, but two subscriptions remain, the first in the petitioner's own hand, stating her name, Aurelia Soteira, and certifying her submission of the request. The second, written now by the third hand, was the response to the petition—"the reply of a high Roman
29 official."[73] John Rea concluded that, although different in size and using different pens, the writing of the petitioner's own hand and that of the Christian letter on its reverse are "rather similar" in the formation of letters and "it is quite possible that the same person wrote both."[74] In view of Rea's earlier explanation for the lack of names, this conclusion caused him to wonder why, if this were a pre-Constantinian environment, she would not make sure "that there was nothing on the sheet to identify her as the writer of the letter."[75] However, rather than invoking a persecution context, for which there is no other evidence in the letter, it is easier to say that the woman named Aurelia also wrote the letter about books and to explain, then, the absence of names by its nature as a very personal, local correspondence. So writer and recipient doubtless were both women.[76]

4. *What books were these Christians exchanging?* At first glance, both books might be taken not only as Jewish but as Jewish canonical writings. "Ezra" (῎Εσρας) doubtless referred, however, not to the book of Ezra of the Jewish Bible but to one of several other works written under that name, most likely *4 Ezra* (*2 Esdras* of the English Apocrypha).[77] It so happens that a fourth-century miniature codex

---

T. C. Skeat speculated that the very small size of invitations "might have formed a kind of 'status symbol' in the upper classes at Oxyrhynchus" and conjectured that "some means were found for displaying them to visitors in the house of the recipient, in much the same way as the bowl of visiting-cards in the hall of a Victorian residence" ("Another Dinner-Invitation from Oxyrhynchus [P.Lond.Inv. 3078]," *JEA* 61 [1975]: 251–54, here 254).

[73] P.Oxy LXIII, pp. 42–43.

[74] Ibid., 44; cf. 43. Cf. Rosa Otranto, *Antiche liste di libri su papiro* (Sussidi eruditi 49; Rome: Edizioni di Storia e Letteratura, 2000), 128.

[75] P.Oxy LXIII, p. 44.

[76] Simon Franklin takes the same position ("A Note on a Pseudepigraphical Allusion in Oxyrhynchus Papyrus No. 4365," *VT* 48 [1998]: 95).

[77] On the identification with *4 Ezra*, see the reference in P.Oxy. LXIII, p. 44, to a seventh/eighth century papyrus "Inventory of Church Property" that refers to Ezra: P.Leid.Inst. 13, line 36 = F. A. J. Hoogendijk and P. van Minnen, eds., *Papyri, Ostraca, Parchments and Waxed Tablets in the Leiden Papyrological Institute* (Pap.Lugd.Bat. XXV; Leiden: Brill, 1991), 51, 54, 70. See also Dieter Hagedorn, "Die 'Kleine Genesis' in P.Oxy. LXIII 4365," *ZPE* 116 (1997): 147–48; Thomas J. Kraus, "Bücherleihe im 4. Jh. N. Chr.: P.Oxy. LXIII 4365—ein Brief auf Papyrus und

of *6 Ezra*[78]—an early Christian apocalypse added to and now constituting chs. 15–16 of *4 Ezra*—was found at Oxyrhynchus (P.Oxy. 1010), though only the wildest speculation would identify that with the "Ezra" of our letter. As for "the little Genesis," this, again, was not the Genesis of the Jewish Bible but the book of *Jubilees*,[79] designated "the little Genesis," e.g., by Epiphanius[80] (ca. 315–403) in 30
the very time frame of our letter (and, by the way, of the *6 Ezra* codex). Incidentally, P.Oxy. 4365 provides the oldest witness for the existence of the Greek version of *Jubilees*.[81]

5. *Why these two Jewish deuterocanonical books?* Certainly the two Christians were exchanging books to read them, and not merely for leisure but for knowledge through study. Why, then, in the early fourth century, were they engaging a second-century B.C.E. Jewish account of revelations to Moses on Mt. Sinai and a late-first-century C.E. Jewish apocalypse, especially when two or three prominent Christian apocalypses—in multiple copies—presumably were available in Oxyrhynchus at this time? And why were these Christians not reading one of the fourteen writings from what we call the "New Testament" that are extant from the period preceding the date of their letter? These papyri survive in thirty-four copies (plus one majuscule) from that period and include, for example, nine of the popular Gospel of John and seven of Matthew.

Were our "New Testament" papyri without relevance, or, to offer an opposite—and more likely—spin on the situation, had the study

die gegenseitige Leihe von apokryph gewordener Literatur," *Biblos* 50 (2001): 287 and n. 14.

[78] *6 Ezra* was written in the third century, probably by a Christian. The small Oxyrhynchus fragment "suggests that the sixth book of Ezra was originally current independently of the fourth" (P.Oxy. VII, p. 13); that *6 Ezra* was not an integral part of *4 Ezra* and is Christian is affirmed by Michael Stone, *ABD* 2:612.

[79] Hagedorn, "Die 'Kleine Genesis,'" 148; supported by Franklin in 1998 ("Note on a Pseudepigraphical Allusion," 95–96), who states that λεπτή here means not "little" but "detailed," and there is no reference to the canonical Genesis. Then A. Hilhorst ("Erwähnt P.Oxy. LXIII 4365 das Jubiläenbuch?" *ZPE* 130 [2000]: 192) argued convincingly against the view of Rosa Otranto (*Aeg* 77 [1997]: 107–8; reprinted in her *Antiche liste di libri su papiro*, 128–29) that "little Genesis" referred to a miniature codex; cf. Kraus, "Bücherleihe," 288 and n. 22.

[80] *Panarion* 39.6.1 (GCS 31, p. 76, 16–17); Hagedorn refers to additional uses of "the little Genesis" (λεπτὴ Γένεσις) for *Jubilees* ("Die 'Kleine Genesis,'" 148); see also O. S. Wintermute, "Jubilees," *OTP* 2:41. On "little books" in Coptic lists, see Otranto, *Antiche liste di libri su papiro*, 129; cf. 141.

[81] Hagedorn, "Die 'Kleine Genesis,'" 148; Franklin, "Note on a Pseudepigraphical Allusion," 96; Kraus, "Bücherleihe," 289.

of the "New Testament" and related Christian books advanced so far in the Oxyrhynchus churches of the third and fourth centuries that some of their inquisitive members had moved beyond—or behind—them to related interests in the Jewish Scriptures? For example, is a special interest in apocalyptic signaled by the dozen or more copies of the Revelation of John and the *Shepherd of Hermas*[82] found there, along with an otherwise unknown Christian prophetic work that quotes the *Shepherd* (P.Oxy. 5),[83] as well as copies of *6 Ezra* and
31 the *Apocalypse of Peter*?[84] And were they drawn also to Jewish apocalypses, not only *4 Ezra*, but also the *Apocalypse of Baruch* (P.Oxy. 403), and *1 Enoch* (P.Oxy. 2069)—copies of which were discovered at Oxyrhynchus?[85]

To be sure, statistics of surviving papyri may prove little, yet the abundance of apocalyptic material at this site, Jewish and Christian, is striking and may well suggest that this early Christian community ascribed canonical authority to these Jewish apocalyptic writings. Again, though, nothing at Oxyrhynchus provides any confirmation except the very presence of these many books and the stated or implied use of them—apparently an extensive use.

6. *What might a woman's voice—or better, two women's voices—tell us about female literacy and about women's likely leadership in Oxyrhynchus churches?* Literacy is a vast topic that cannot be explored here, and discerning the existence and nature of leadership not only would be speculative but also is hampered by the scarcity of relevant material. It is worth noting, however, that while papyri in Roman Egypt reveal

[82] On the *Shepherd* as an apocalypse, see Osiek, *Shepherd of Hermas*, 10–12; Helmut Koester, *Introduction*, 1:262–66. On its popularity, see Osiek: "No other noncanonical writing was as popular before the fourth century as the *Shepherd of Hermas*. It is the most frequently attested postcanonical text in the surviving Christian manuscripts of Egypt well into the fifth century" (p. 1). On its reception and canonicity, see pp. 5–8. Her list of manuscripts includes those with extensive text but also a fragment possibly of the early second century (P.Iand. 1.4), though not any Oxyrhynchus papyri (pp. 1–2).

[83] The quotation is *Mandate* 11.9–10. The fragment dates in the third/fourth century (P.Oxy. I, p. 8) or fourth/fifth; see Körtner and Leutzsch, *Papiasfragmente, Hirt des Hermas*, 118 and 361 n. 15, which refers to E. G. Turner, *The Typology of the Early Codex* (Philadelphia: University of Pennsylvania Press, 1977), 131, no. 528.

[84] See n. 38 above.

[85] This supposition, however, would require that earlier copies of the *Apocalypse of Baruch* (P.Oxy. 403, 4th/5th c.) and *1 Enoch* (P.Oxy. 2069, late 4th c.) had been present in Oxyrhynchus, for the surviving copies are later than the letter about lending books.

that families with literate men commonly had illiterate women, an Oxyrhynchus papyrus of the year 215 provides a striking exception: a literate Oxyrhynchite woman whose Alexandrian (!) husband and his brother were illiterate (P.Oxy. 1463).[86] In addition, in 263 a woman petitions a prefect of Egypt for the right to carry out business transactions without a guardian, and she supports her argument by her ability to write (P.Oxy. 1467, see below). A further example is an application dated 201 for remarriage to her former husband by a woman who states, "I know how to write" (P.Oxy. 1473). Such pride in writing, however, ran counter to another source of pride: upper-class women—whether literate or not—may have felt it below their dignity to write when they had slaves or secretaries to do it for them.[87]

Further insight may be gained from a copy of a lease for prop- 32
erty (P.Oxy. 1690, dated about 287) owned by a literate woman, Aurelia Ptolemais, that was found with fragments of two papyri containing the *Iliad* (P.Oxy. 1386, 1392) and portions of a much rarer *History of Sikyon* (P.Oxy. 1365), literary works that she owned and presumably read.[88] Roger Bagnall argued that her father was Aurelius Hermogenes, a councillor at Oxyrhynchus, whose will named as heirs a daughter, Aurelia Ptolemais, along with another daughter, three

[86] See William V. Harris, *Ancient Literacy* (Cambridge, MA: Harvard University Press, 1989), 279–80. On cautions in generalizing from papyri data, see T. J. Kraus, "(Il)literacy in Non- Literary Papyri from Graeco-Roman Egypt: Further Aspects of the Educational Ideal in Ancient Literary Sources and Modern Times," *Mnemosyne* 53 (2000): 333, 338–41.

[87] On the larger subject, see Catherine Hezser, *Jewish Literacy in Roman Palestine* (TSAJ 81; Tübingen: Mohr-Siebeck, 2001), 474–75, 484–85; E. Randolph Richards, *The Secretary in the Letters of Paul* (WUNT 42; Tübingen: Mohr-Siebeck, 1991), 18–23, esp. 22; Roger S. Bagnall, *Egypt in Late Antiquity* (Princeton: Princeton University Press, 1993), 230–60, esp. 246–47, 255–56, 258–59; idem, *Reading Papyri, Writing Ancient History* (Approaching the Ancient World; London/New York: Routledge, 1995), 24–25; Kim Haines-Eitzen, *Guardians of Letters: Literacy, Power, and the Transmission of Early Christian Literature* (Oxford/New York: Oxford University Press, 2000), 7, 21. For speakers and writers in Egyptian, "illiteracy in Greek, the language of the alien and worldly bureaucracy, may have become a point of pride" (Herbert C. Youtie, "'Because they do not know letters,'" *ZPE* 19 [1975]: 108).

[88] Roger Bagnall, "An Owner of Literary Papyri," *CP* 87 (1992): 137–40; reprinted in his *Later Roman Egypt: Society, Religion, Economy, and Administration* (Aldershot, UK: Ashgate; Burlington, VT: Variorum, 2003), no. VII. Her literacy is confirmed by her "fairly rapid cursive" signature, "Not the hand of someone who could barely sign, certainly" (p. 140 and n. 18), and by her presumed ownership of the literary papyri found with the lease.

sons, and his wife, Isidora (P.Oxy. 907, dated 276). Curiously the will was written on the verso of a papyrus that contained the *Kestoi* of the Christian writer Sextus Julius Africanus (P.Oxy. 412, mid-3rd c.), though this particular work is not specifically Christian in nature.[89] E. A. Judge and S. R. Pickering, appealing to Julius Africanus's Christian identity and to a phrase in Hermogenes' will that conveys "an idea familiar to [New Testament] readers," suggested that Hermogenes—and therefore perhaps his family, including Aurelia—were also Christians.[90] If this plausible though tenuous thread of evidence is accepted, another literate woman of a prominent Oxyrhynchus family will have been identified as Christian. It remains unclear, however, whether these papyri are evidence that literate women in Oxyrhynchus were more numerous than elsewhere, or that literate women, like those in our short letter, were the exception, as has been the common view.[91]

33 Equally difficult to determine is whether the letter about lending books implies that women held positions of leadership in the early churches at Oxyrhynchus, and if so, exactly what they might have been. One approach—though it might not apply directly or necessarily to churches—would be to assess the extent to which women in Oxyrhynchus acted without guardians, that is, were entitled to act independently of a male, for whom the standard term was κύριος, or to ask what proportion of women (especially around the mid-third

---

[89] Ibid., 138–39 and n. 16.

[90] Judge and Pickering, "Papyrus Documentation," 65; cf. Bagnall, "Owner of Literary Papyri," 139 n. 16. The phrase in question (line 17) is πρεπόντως περὶ τὴν συμβίωσιν ἀναστραφείσῃ ("who has conducted herself becomingly in our married life"), which Judge and Pickering correctly characterize as "not a direct New Testament echo," but nonetheless refer to it as "an idea familiar to its readers" (p. 65); Bagnall appropriately labels this argument for designating Hermogenes as Christian "less compelling" (p. 139 n. 16). Hermogenes' wife, Isidora, was also called Prisca (lines 16, 21), though Judge and Pickering's comment, "the name of a prominent collaborator of St Paul" (p. 65) is doubtless gratuitous. Current intertextuality views would broaden the search for "sources."

[91] Harris adopts the latter view—evidence that literacy was the exception even among affluent women (*Ancient Literacy*, 280). On literacy of women in Roman Egypt, see Susan G. Cole, "Could Greek Women Read and Write?" in *Reflections of Women in Antiquity* (ed. H. P. Foley; New York: Gordon & Breach, 1981), 233–38 and notes. Bagnall notes that "men of the bouleutic class were expected to be able to read and write," as an edict seems to suggest (PSI 6.716, from Oxyrhynchus, ca. 306), and that most women of this class "could do little but sign their names" (*Egypt in Late Antiquity*, 246–47; see also 230–60 on literacy in urban and rural areas, and in the church, esp. from the fourth century on).

century and later) claimed the *ius liberorum*, that is, an exemption from guardianship "by the right of children."[92] An instructive instance is P.Oxy. 1467, dated 263, in which Aurelia Thaïsous petitions for this status by appealing to laws:

> . . . which enable women who are honoured with the right of three children to be independent and act without a guardian in all business which they transact, especially those women who know how to write. Accordingly I too, fortunately possessing the honour of being blessed with children, and a writer who am able to write with the greatest ease, in the fulness of my security appeal to your highness by this my application with the object of being enabled to carry out without hindrance all business which I henceforth transact. . . .

Indeed, one of her subsequent, independent transactions survives, a sale of land (P.Oxy. 1475, dated 267).

As Sarah Pomeroy points out, however, "illiteracy was not burdensome, since unless a woman enjoyed the *ius* iii *liberorum* . . . she was always accompanied by a *kyrios*,"[93] so that "literacy had no effect upon legal capacity."[94] Yet, for those granted the *ius liberorum*, "only
literacy enables women to make legally binding commitments with- 34
out the assistance of men."[95] Hence, independence empowered women in Roman Egypt, and the more so for *literate* independent women.

Jennifer Sheridan has brought up to date previous compilations of women functioning independently, showing that during the first

[92] See Antti Arjava, "The Guardianship of Women in Roman Egypt," in *Akten des 21. internationalen Papyrologenkongresses, Berlin, 13.–19.8.1995* (ed. B. Kramer et al.; 2 vols.; *APF* Beiheft 3; Stuttgart/Leipzig: Teubner, 1997), 1:25–30, esp. 25–27. Under the *ius liberorum*, decreed by Augustus, "all freeborn women who had borne three living children should be free from guardianship (freed-women needed four births after their manumission)" (p. 27). Many helpful details of Arjava's discussion cannot be treated here. For a detailed treatment in the papyri, see Joëlle Beaucamp, *Le statut de la femme à Byzance (4e–7e siècle)* (2 vols.; Travaux et mémoires 5–6; Paris: de Boccard, 1990, 1992), 193–267; on the formula, 198–202 [though P.Oxy. 1467 is not mentioned]; see also R. S. Bagnall's affirmative review: "Women, Law, and Social Realities in Late Antiquity: A Review Article," *BASP* 32 (1995): 75–77; reprinted in his *Later Roman Egypt*, no. II; also Herbert C. Youtie, "AGRAMMATOS: An Aspect of Greek Society in Egypt," *HSCP* 75 (1971): 166–68.

See also Sarah B. Pomeroy, "Women in Roman Egypt: A Preliminary Study Based on Papyri," in *Reflections of Women in Antiquity*, ed. Foley, 308–9, 313, 315–17. See P.Oxy. 2777, lines 10–11 (A.D. 212).

[93] Pomeroy, "Women in Roman Egypt," 313.

[94] Ibid., 315.

[95] Ibid., 316; see Herbert C. Youtie, "ΥΠΟΓΡΑΦΕΥΣ: The Social Impact of Illiteracy in Graeco-Roman Egypt," *ZPE* 17 (1975): 221 n. 62.

six centuries (in data on papyri from at least fifteen cities) 123 women acted without guardians, and thirty-six of these (or 29 percent) were in Oxyrhynchus.[96] If one restricts the data to our period of interest—through the fourth century—thirty-five out of 110 (or 32 percent) were in Oxyrhynchus. Sheridan's main point, however, was that one-third of the third- and fourth-century women in the list (wherever status can be determined) were of the bouleutic class or otherwise wealthy and therefore more likely to act without a guardian.[97] Using her data, out of twenty-two Oxyrhynchite women whose socioeconomic status can be determined, ten (or 46 percent) were of the wealthy class.

Naturally, such statistics can be only suggestive at best owing to randomness in the survival of papyri; and of course the numbers are *extremely small*, yet the resultant broad strokes are of interest, pointing, for example, to the plausibility that Oxyrhynchus contained a fair number of literate women and women who could act independently, thereby raising the possibility that *Christian* women in these classes might have assumed leadership positions in the churches. To spin a slightly larger web of speculation, perhaps the literate Christian women identified earlier, whether with guardians or without, might have become leaders in their churches—but most likely the two who exchanged "biblical" books—though there is no direct evidence.[98]

---

[96] Jennifer A. Sheridan, "Women without Guardians: An Updated List," *BASP* 33 (1996): 117–25. She noted (p. 118 n. 4) that only seven women listed are definitely literate, and—perhaps surprisingly—only one was from Oxyrhynchus, Aurelia Thaïsous, mentioned above. Extensive lists of women with or without guardians are provided by Edgar Kutzner, *Untersuchungen zur Stellung der Frau im römischen Oxyrhynchos* (Europäische Hochschulschriften III/392; Frankfurt am Main: Peter Lang, 1989), 79–99; for women without guardians, see 90–97. See further Tina Saavedra, "Women as Property-Owners in Roman Spain and Roman Egypt: Some Points of Comparison," in *Le rôle et le statut de la femme en Égypte hellénistique, romaine et byzantine: Acts de colloque international, Bruxelles-Leuven 27–29 novembre 1997* (ed. H. Melaerts and L. Mooren; Leuven: Peeters, 2002), 302–3, 310–11. In the first to third centuries in papyri from Socnopaiou Nesos, women were "principals in about half of the 32 documents recording house ownership"; and owners of about one-third of the village real estate attested, almost two-thirds of the slaves, and one-fifth of the camels (pp. 309–10).

[97] Sheridan, "Women without Guardians," 126–31. The percentages are based on her data.

[98] The evidence for women in leadership positions who were not literate must also be recognized: e.g., even in 600, Maura, the (presumably Christian) female steward of an Oxyrhynchus hospital, was illiterate (P.Oxy. 4131).

We have elicited from our six-line letter much information about 35
identifying Christian letters, the use of Jewish writings, the issue of canon, and women's literacy and leadership—all significant facets of the Oxyrhynchus environment for our New Testament papyri there. The likely identity of authorship between this Christian letter and the secular petition on the other side begs for discussion of how Christians interacted with their economic and political context of Roman Egypt, but this would carry us beyond the scope of the present paper.

When we pause again to ask what position our group of "New Testament" papyri held in the situations described, silence reigns. We have no information about any role they might have played or any honor they enjoyed, but their impact is likely to be more evident in documents relevant to church and piety, and perhaps also in personal letters.

E. *The Role of "New Testament" Papyri in Christian Worship in Oxyrhynchus*

The extent to which our New Testament (and other Christian) texts were utilized by or had direct influence on worship and theology might best be discerned, at least to our way of thinking, by examining the remnants of hymns, prayers, sermons, and theological treatises in Oxyrhynchus into the late fourth century. Our core sample turns up no early examples—which appear not to exist—but several items stem from the third and fourth centuries, and naturally they increase as one moves beyond our period into the fifth and sixth centuries. That progression of church-related materials parallels the increase in known churches from two sometime after the year 295 (P.Oxy. 43),[99] to fifteen in the fifth century (P.Oxy. 4617, 5th c.),[100]

[99] P.Oxy. 43 is a list of Oxyrhynchite watchmen on the verso of an account dated 295 C.E., recording streets and public buildings, including a north church (col. 1, line 10) and a south church (col. 3, line 19), with streets named after each ἐκκλησία. Bagnall reminds us that the date of the watchmen's list could be closely after 295 or much later (*Egypt in Late Antiquity*, 53, 280 n. 118).

[100] See G. Schmelz, P.Oxy. LXVII, pp. 241–45; P.Oxy. 4618 (6th c.) lists fifteen also, but not all are the same as in 4617; 4619 (early 6th c.), a fragment, names six: see N. Gonis, P.Oxy. LXVII, pp. 245–50. Rufinus reported twelve early in the fifth century: see P.Oxy. XI, p. 26.

to forty or more by 535,[101] in a city that by Roman times had perhaps 20,000 residents, more or less.[102]

36 1. *A Hymn to the Trinity*

A hymn with musical notation (P.Oxy. 1786) was found on the verso of a corn account dated in the first half of the third century, placing the hymn later in that century. Undoubtedly it remains "the most ancient piece of Church music extant."[103] Portions of the last five lines survive, written on a narrow strip of papyrus about two by twelve inches, with corresponding vocal notes above each line.[104] What remains of the text calls upon the light-giving stars to be silent and the rushing rivers to sing praises with all power to Father, Son, and Holy Spirit, Amen, Amen, and for dominion and praise to the giver of all good things, Amen, Amen.[105]

To be sure, the whole hymn is not extant, though nothing here could come from our New Testament papyri, except the reference to the Trinity. This, however, is not likely to be a direct citation of Matt 28:19, for there is no similarity of context in the two passages.

---

[101] P.Oxy. XI, p. 26.

[102] Estimates are difficult; Itzhak F. Fichman [elsewhere Fikhman] suggests, on extensive relevant evidence, 15,000 to 25,000 ("Die Bevölkerungszahl von Oxyrhynchos in byzantinischer Zeit," *APF* 21 [1971]: 111–20, esp. 120); cf. Julian Krüger, *Oxyrhynchos in der Kaiserzeit: Studien zur Topographie und Literaturrezeption* (Europäische Hochschulschriften III/441; Frankfurt am Main/New York: Peter Lang, 1990), 8 (about 30,000). Very recently Dirk Obbink speaks of "perhaps 20,000 inhabitants of the Greek-speaking settler class, Egyptian Greeks, and their later Roman counterparts" ("Imaging Oxyrhynchus," *Egyptian Archaeology* 22 [Spring 2003]: 3).

[103] P.Oxy. XV, p. 21.

[104] P.Oxy. XV, pp. 21–25 + pl. I; see Charles Wessely, ed., *Les plus anciens monuments du Christianisme écrits sur papyrus* (PO IV.2; Paris: Firmin-Didot, 1907), 506–7. For a critique of earlier reconstructions of the musical structure and other technical issues, see E. J. Wellesz, "The Earliest Example of Christian Hymnody," *CQ* 39 (1945): 34–45, esp. 41–43; and A. W. J. Holleman, "The Oxyrhynchus Papyrus 1786 and the Relationship between Ancient Greek and Early Christian Music," *VC* 26 (1972): 1–17. The music, with choral rendition, is available on a CD: *Musique de la grèce antique* (Atrium musicae de Madrid, Gregorio Paniaqua; Germany: Harmonia mundi [HMA 1951015, HM 31], 1979, 2000); it contains also P.Oxy. 2436 (1st/2nd c.) and other music from papyri.

[105] Cf. P.Oxy. XV, p. 22. Apparently the only other hymn from Oxyrhynchus is 4011 (6th c.), mostly derived from Ps 75; see pl. IV in P.Oxy. LX. On other papyri with musical notation, see William A. Johnson, "Musical Evenings in the Early Empire: New Evidence from a Greek Papyrus with Musical Notation," *JHS* 120 (2000): 57–85, esp. 57–59.

Rather, the hymn's Trinity undoubtedly was drawn from church liturgy.

2. Prayers

Our core sample next contains P.Oxy. 4010, a single sheet from the fourth century containing the *Pater Noster* with a preliminary prayer. The ends of all lines are missing, but a few readable phrases remain from the prefatory prayer: "Have mercy . . . Master of all [something] . . . and God of all consolation, . . . and have mercy and lead. . . . Make us worthy [of something] . . . ."[106] "Consolation" and "to console" occur a remarkable ten times in 2 Cor 1:3–7, including the uncommon phrase, "God of *all* consolation," so—with all our caveats in mind—perhaps we have our first match with the New Testament,[107] especially in view of God's "mercy" in both immediate contexts and the fact that, as the editors of the papyrus propose, 37
"father of mercies" would fit in the lacuna before "and God of all consolation"—as in 2 Cor 1:3, though our prayer has no further citation of that passage.

The Lord's Prayer follows immediately in the Matthean form (6:9–13) rather than the Lucan (11:2–4), and there is no added doxology present.[108] However, after ". . . but rescue us from the evil one," a second "rescue us" occurs just as the text breaks off. K. Treu, the editor, attributed this to the carelessness of the scribe, but Alan H. Cadwallader proposed that the repetition was deliberate–in the pattern of "numerous liturgies" that follow "rescue us" with various expansions or embolisms, such as that in St. Mark's Liturgy: "Rescue us from all his works."[109] Embolism is most frequently used for such additional requests for deliverance, and they are inserted just at this point—before the doxology. The further implications for Cadwallader,

[106] Alan H. Cadwallader restores line 11, just before the Lord's Prayer, to read: καταξίωσον ἡμᾶς ε[ὔχεσθαι], "Make us worthy to pray" ("An Embolism in the Lord's Prayer?" *New Testament Textual Research Update* 4 [1996]: 86).

[107] P.Oxy. LX, p. 6; so also Stuart R. Pickering, "A New Papyrus Text of the Lord's Prayer," *New Testament Textual Research Update* 2 (1994): 111.

[108] Unless its text carried over into another column, something not ruled out by the editor, K. Treu (see P.Oxy. LX, pp. 5, 7, and pl. III). Hence, Cadwallader proposed that this papyrus was part of a roll, noting the possibility that remains of a letter of a prior column are visible, and also that extant Christian liturgical texts were often on rolls ("An Embolism in the Lord's Prayer?" 83–84).

[109] Ibid., 85.

therefore, are, first, that a doxology followed on a next page of P.Oxy. 4010, which for him is a roll rather than a single sheet—though this cannot be demonstrated from the surviving portion—and, second, that 4010 is a liturgical text, for which he makes a substantial case.[110]

Whether or not we concede that a doxology was present in 4010, it is well known that the doxology is a later accretion in the text of Matt 6:13, owing to liturgical influence.[111] Oxyrhynchus has yielded fifteen manuscripts containing Matthew, but only one has the Lord's Prayer, and it stems from around 500 C.E. (P.Oxy. 1169, 5th/6th c.),[112] yet, even at that late date, no doxology is present. Initially this might favor a claim that our independent *Pater Noster* (4010)—which shows little if any direct evidence of a doxology—was derived from a Matthean manuscript, but the availability of the passage in only one out of fifteen manuscripts is insufficient evidence that the doxology was absent generally from Matthean manuscripts at Oxyrhynchus.

More instructive, our text is one of some thirteen instances of the Lord's Prayer circulating independent of any Matthean or Lucan
38 context, either as an independent unit or as one member of a compilation of separate biblical citations, using, for example, the first verse of one or more Gospels, or a verse or more of a Psalm, and so on. Of the five earliest survivors of these out-of-context Lord's Prayers (up to around 400),[113] only the three from Oxyrhynchus have sufficient text to decide whether or not they contained doxologies. Two of

---

[110] See his further evidence, ibid., 83–86. "Designed for public recitation" (Pickering, "New Papyrus Text of the Lord's Prayer," 112).

[111] On the text and liturgical influence, see Bruce M. Metzger [for the Editorial Committee], *A Textual Commentary on the Greek New Testament* (2nd ed.; Stuttgart: Deutsche Bibelgesellschaft/United Bible Societies, 1994), 13–14; Hans Dieter Betz, *The Sermon on the Mount* (Hermeneia; Minneapolis: Fortress, 1995), 414–15.

[112] New Testament majuscule 0170; the others are P1, P19, P21, P35, P70, P71, P77, P101, P102, P103, P104, P105, P110, 071. Papyri of Luke from Oxyrhynchus (P69, P111) do not have 11:2–4.

[113] They are P.Ant. II.54 (miniature codex, 3rd c.); P.Princ. 2.107 (4th/5th c.); P.Oslo inv. 1644 (late 4th c., Oxyrhynchus); PSI 6.719 (4th/5th c., probably Oxyrhynchus); and P.Oxy. 4010. A clay tablet, inscribed with the Lord's Prayer and then fired (O.Athens inv. 12227 = van Haelst 348, 4th c.), has no doxology, nor is it a true ostracon: see A. Deissmann, *Light from the Ancient East: The New Testament Illustrated by Recently Discovered Texts of the Graeco-Roman World* (New York: Harper, 1927), 56 n. 3. See the helpful survey of these texts by G. H. R. Horsley, *NewDocs* 3 (1978): 103–5 (where he also discusses an inscription containing a line from the Prayer). His inclusion of P.Oxy. 407, which has only a doxology and no (other) remnant of the Lord's Prayer, is probably unwarranted.

them do, while our subject, 4010, appears not to have contained one, though four of the seven later examples have the doxology.[114] Normally, the presence of doxologies would indicate, I think, that these Lord's Prayers were drawn from church liturgy rather than from Gospel texts, and more so in view of their independent circulation. In addition, virtually all of the manuscripts of this type were written on one side only and were either amulets or were used for magical purposes, indicating that these independent Lord's Prayers had developed into a separate tradition of their own as charms or for magical use. This is confirmed by the repeated use of several accompanying texts, especially Matt 1:1; Mark 1:1; Luke 1:1; John 1:1 (along with Ps 91:1 [LXX Ps. 90:1]). Of course, these New Testament texts ultimately derive from New Testament manuscripts, but soon they, like the Lord's Prayer, became standard elements in a fixed genre.[115]

Yet P.Oxy. 4010 is likely too large to have been an amulet and evidences no folding; nonetheless, the verso is blank, and the double prayer appears either to have occupied all of a single sheet with wide margins[116] or possibly to have been part of a scroll. In either event, it most likely is a liturgical text, and, especially in view of its fourth-century date, was likely drawn from liturgical tradition, with the numerous papyri of Matthew at Oxyrhynchus playing no direct role.

Incidentally, Christian amulets and other manuscripts that contain
short passages of our New Testament present a peculiar problem:
those, for example, that quote the first verse of each Gospel, such 39
as PSI 6.719 (4th/5th c.), or the many that circulated the Lord's
Prayer separately are said to pick up their citations from church
liturgy (and rightly so), although P.Oxy. 209 (early 4th c.), with Rom
1:1–7 in a similar continuous text form, is placed among the New

[114] See G. H. R. Horsley, *NewDocs* 3 (1978): 104–5.

[115] On the use of the Lord's Prayer in magic, with additional examples, see Leiv Amundsen, "Christian Papyri from the Oslo Collection," *SO* 24 (1945): 143–44. I was pleased to discover that he had already espoused the view I formulated on the use of the Prayer "for magical purposes, alone or with other texts" (p. 142), followed by a reference to "a strong tradition that manifests itself also in the fixed group of texts with which the Lord's Prayer is coupled" (p. 143). Cf. his comments on the similar but even more popular use of Ps 91 (90 LXX), with thirty examples (pp. 144–47).

[116] P.Oxy. LX, p. 5 and pl. III.

Testament papyri as P10.[117] This papyrus was at first taken to be a school exercise, though Adolf Deissmann later argued that it was an amulet, because of its obvious folds.[118] Placing it among the official New Testament papyri seemed justified, of course, for, as a school exercise it undoubtedly would have been copied from a manuscript containing Romans. Yet, if it had not been placed among our forty-seven Oxyrhynchus New Testament papyri, it would have been treated as an amulet made for religious or magical purposes or as a product of education at Oxyrhynchus that—in either case—showed the utilization of our [other] New Testament texts present in the city. So, we get caught in a circular argument when attempting to find cases where our New Testament text was employed in Christian practice.

Other prayers within our period are not common. A short, intriguing one reads simply, "O God ($\overline{\theta\varsigma}$) of the crosses that are laid upon us, help your servant Apphouas. Amen" (P.Oxy. 1058, 4th or 5th c.): God, who is responsible for the burdens, is asked to relieve them. Another, an amulet (P.Oxy. 407, 3rd/4th c.), quotes a phrase from LXX Ps 145:6, followed by a prayer for mercy and salvation "through our Lord and Savior Jesus Christ," with a concluding doxology,[119] and one of the few pre-fifth-century Christian charms that survive (P.Oxy. 924, 4th c.) aims to ward off fever for a woman named Apia. There is no close reflection of New Testament texts in these or in later extant Oxyrhynchus prayers.[120]

---

[117] See P.Oxy. II, p. 8 and pl. II. Aland and Aland doubt the validity of placing these among the New Testament papyri (*Text of the New Testament*, 85).

[118] Deissmann, *Light from the Ancient East*, 239–40 and n. 1+ fig. 46. The folds are more visible here than in P.Oxy. II, pl. II.

[119] There are no *nomina sacra*. The doxology contains only "the glory and the power," a form appropriate to Egypt (Giuseppe Ghedini, "Frammenti liturgici in un papiro milanese," *Aeg* 13 [1933]: 672–73).

[120] Later prayers, oracular prayers, charms, often amulets, from Oxyrhynchus, with no citations of New Testament texts, but with *nomina sacra* include P.Oxy. 1059 (5th c.); 925 (5th or 6th c.); or without *nomina sacra*, 1060 (6th c.); 1150 (6th c.; van Haelst, no. 957, says 4th c.) to ward off reptiles; 1152 (5th or 6th c.); 1926 (6th c.); P.Amst. Inv. 173 (probably Oxyrhynchus, 4th/5th c.) (see P. J. Sijpesteijn, "Ein christliches Amulett aus der Amsterdamer Papyrussammlung," *ZPE* 5 [1970]: 57–59 + pl.); with mixed *nomina sacra*, P.Harr. I.54 (Oxyrhynchus, 6th c.); or without divine names, P.Oxy. 2063 (6th c., van Haelst, no. 965).

Amulets or charms that contain a freestanding, continuous-text, out-of-context portion of the New Testament are a separate issue: some are treated as New Testament papyri: P.Oxy. 209 (early 4th c.) = P10, with Rom 1:1–7; 2684 (3rd/4th

3. *Local homilies and theological treatises* 40

Oxyrhynchus has yielded copies of well-known theological writings made in the second, third, and fourth centuries, including the *Apology* of Aristides (P.Oxy. 1778, 4th c.), the *Didache* (P.Oxy. 1782, late 4th c.), *Against Heresies*, by Irenaeus (P.Oxy. 405, 2nd/3rd c.),[121] the *Passion of Dioscurus* (P.Oxy. 3529, 4th c.), a homily perhaps by Origen (P.Oxy. 1601, late 4th or 5th c.),[122] and possibly *On Prophecy* by Melito of Sardis (P.Oxy. 5, 3rd/4th c.).[123] These, however, are not relevant, for we wish to assess *local* treatises that might inform us of the use of our New Testament texts or their influence on worship and faith in Oxyrhynchus. Relevant materials are scarce indeed, though our probe brings forth one highly certain candidate, and possibly two others through the fourth century.[124]

---

c.) = P78, preserving portions of Jude; and P50 (4th or 5th c., provenance unknown) containing portions of Acts 8–10.

Others with portions of New Testament text are P.Oxy. 1151 (5th c.), with John 1:1–3 (*nomina sacra*); P.Osl. Inv. 1644 (perhaps Oxyrhynchus, end 4th c.) (van Haelst, no. 345), with the Lord's Prayer (*nomina sacra*) (edition by Amundsen, "Christian Papyri from the Oslo Collection, 141–47); PSI 6.719 (perhaps Oxyrhynchus, 4th/5th c.) [van Haelst, no. 423], with the first verse of John, Matthew, Mark, Luke, and LXX Ps 90, plus John 1:23 and Matt 6:9 with doxology. P.Oxy. 1928 (5th/6th c.), a Christian amulet, contains LXX Ps 90 replete with *nomina sacra* and concluding with mention of John, Luke, Mark, and Matthew.

121 Initially unidentified in P.Oxy. III, p. 10, but soon shown to be from Irenaeus by J. Armitage Robinson (see P.Oxy. IV, pp. 264–65, with revised text). See Andreas Schmidt, "Der mögliche Text von P. Oxy. III 405, Z. 39–45," *NTS* 37 (1991): 160.

122 Unidentified in P.Oxy. XIII, pp. 21–23; see van Haelst, no. 692, p. 249, who stated that R. Reitzenstein attributed it to Origen. P.Oxy. 406 has also been attributed to Origen according to Roberts (*Manuscript, Society, and Belief*, 24 and n. 8), crediting Giovanni Ausenda, "Contributo allo studio dell'omiletica cristiana nei papiri greci dell'Egitto," *Aeg* 20 (1940): 46, for the identification, though Ausenda's evidence is not apparent to me.

123 Unidentified in P.Oxy. I, pp. 8–9; see van Haelst, no. 682, who reported that A. Harnack suggested that the fragment was from Melito. Two later fragments are possibly from works by Melito: P.Oxy. 1600 (end of 4th or 5th c.), unidentified there, but see van Haelst, no. 679, who reports that C. Bonner identified it as *Homily on the Passion*; and P.Oxy. 2074 (5th c.), again unidentified; see van Haelst, no. 680: possibly Melito's *On Truth*.

124 As to other possible "local" treatises, P.Oxy. 4 (early 4th c., *nomen sacrum*) may be "from the school of Valentinus" (van Haelst, no. 1070, pp. 332–33); P.Oxy. 406 (3rd c.) is a Christian text (as indicated by *nomina sacra*, including Xς and a contraction for the preceding "crucified") that quotes LXX Isa 6:10, though in a form found in Matt 13:15 and Acts 28:27 that differs from the LXX. Beyond this, there is insufficient text to speculate on its nature. P.Oxy. 210 is a narrative and very likely from an apocryphal Gospel: see n. 40 above.

First, P.Oxy 2070 from the late third century meets and exceeds our primary criterion—it is virtually without doubt a local document, and, in addition, is the autograph itself:

> This is suggested by the frequent alterations which have been made in the text, apparently by the original hand, and are difficult to explain except on the hypothesis that we here have a fragment of the author's own manuscript.[125]

41 That it is a Christian document is clear from the name "Jesus" (line 10), written in the usual abbreviated fashion ($\overline{\text{I}\eta}$). Portions of eighty-eight lines survive of this seriously deteriorated papyrus roll, though only some fifty lines contain one or more complete words, permitting almost nothing beyond its general character to be discerned. Even that is possible only because citations from two Psalms and Isaiah can be restored.[126] Their identification, in turn, clinches the nature of this treatise, for these very passages from the Jewish Scripture occur, for instance, in Justin's *Dialogue with Trypho the Jew*, in either anti-Jewish contexts or as proof-texts for the messiahship of Jesus.[127]

In col. 1 of our document, for example, Ps 18:43–44 (LXX Ps 17:44–45) is cited: "People whom I had not known served me; as soon as they heard of me they obeyed me" (lines 5–7). We may reasonably surmise that this is used somewhat as it was in Justin, *Dial.* 28, where explicitly Gentiles were shown to be receptive to Christ when (in Justin's view) Israel should have been. Following this citation, our document speaks "concerning Jesus" and that "many more . . . believed his word" (lines 10–12). Shortly thereafter—continuing the argument—Isa 29:13 is cited, stating that the people of Israel "honor me with their lips, while their hearts are far from me" (lines 24–27), again undoubtedly utilized as it was in *Dial.* 27 and

[125] P.Oxy. XVII, p. 9. Roberts ventures that the presence of this dialogue in autograph form suggests that "Oxyrhynchus in the third century may have been something of a Christian intellectual centre" (*Manuscript, Society, and Belief*, 24 n. 5).

[126] Lines 5–7, 19–22 = Ps 18:43–45 (LXX Ps 17:44–46) = 2 Sam 22:44–46; lines 46–59 = Ps 22:15–22 (LXX Ps 21:16–23); lines 24–27 = Isa 29:13.

[127] P.Oxy. XVII, p. 9: the Oxyrhynchus treatise is not from Justin, since it does not match and is an autograph. Isaiah 29:13–14 occurs in Justin, *Dial.* 27 and 78, in the context of prophecies being fulfilled in Christ and of the unfaithfulness of Israel; Ps 18:43–44 (LXX Ps 17:44–45) = 2 Sam 22:44–45 occurs in *Dial.* 28 in contexts of the rejection of Israel and their replacement by Gentiles; and Ps 22:15–22 (LXX Ps 21:16–23) is found in *Dial.* 98 not only as a prophecy of Christ's suffering, but showing his opponents.

78, that is, specifically to stress that Gentiles are the recipients of God's grace instead of a hardhearted Israel. Later, col. 2 of our document quotes Ps 22:15–22 (LXX Ps 21:16–23), though no context has been preserved, but once again we may presume that it was employed as in *Dial.* 98, in which Justin quoted the entire Psalm not only as predictive of Jesus' sufferings but (as Justin explicitly affirmed) as a disclosure of "who they are that rise up against him." This makes for some nasty assertions when we get to the Psalm portion that survived in the Oxyrhynchus fragment: "You lay me in the dust of death. For dogs are all around me: a company of evildoers encircles me. . . . They divide my clothes among themselves. . . . Deliver
my soul from the sword, [my life from the power of the dog]!" (lines 42
46–59).

Minor details in our document confirm that it is both a dialogue and anti-Jewish: twice it reports, "then he said" (line 4) and "he said to him" (line 18), undoubtedly the Christian interlocutor, and once, using an abbreviation for a personal name or descriptive term, καὶ ὁ φ̄ εἶπε occurs, with a horizontal superscript line over φ (line 30), plausibly standing for "and the Pharisee said," an interpretation the more likely because this character speaks just after the anti-Jewish use of Isa 29:13,[128] though we cannot tell what he said. So, we have the unpleasant presence in Oxyrhynchus of an anti-Jewish dialogue, clearly in the polemical tradition of Justin.[129]

On the basis of this papyrus, it would be rash, of course, to assert that Christian polemic in Oxyrhynchus relied only on Jewish Scripture and not on New Testament texts, for only a small portion of the dialogue has survived. Yet, as we shall see, Jewish Scripture (i.e., the LXX) appears to take the lead time and again.

Two other possibly local treatises are still less forthcoming about their exact nature. The first, P.Oxy. 2073 (late fourth century), however, may yield its secret in the same manner as P.Oxy. 2070 above, that is, by the reconstruction of two clear citations from the Wisdom of Solomon and the Wisdom of Jesus Son of Sirach.[130] Though only a sentence of each was taken over, Wis 11:19, whose immediate context spoke of wild beasts, including specifically "bold lions," is quoted:

[128] P.Oxy, XVII, p. 9.
[129] Ibid.
[130] P.Oxy. XVII, pp. 16–17.

"Not only could the harm they did destroy people, but the mere sight of them could kill by fright" (lines 11–12). Then our document immediately cites Sir 25:16, "I would rather live with a lion and a dragon than live with an evil woman" (lines 14–15). This contextual sequence, the first citation introducing the second, is strong confirmation that our papyrus—surely in part and perhaps in whole—was a diatribe or homily against women. Little else left can be pieced together meaningfully, though the sentence following the two citations includes ". . . the righteous and mighty God . . ."—with θεός written as θ̅ς̅), the usual *nomen sacrum* and a strong signal for a Christian document.

Is it more than coincidence that this "evil woman" quotation (Sir 25:16) occurs also at the outset of a brief Ps.-Chrysostom treatise (*PG* 59:486–87)[131] and that a portion of it—beginning just two dozen lines farther down—turned up at Oxyrhynchus (P.Oxy. 1603, roll, 5th or 6th c.), namely, a twenty-one line catalogue of evil deeds by women in Hebrew Scripture and in the John the Baptist episode, concluding with "A wicked woman is the worst of all [ills] . . . and if she also has wealth as her ally in wickedness, the evil is double" (lines 17–20)?[132]

43 Once again, our fourth-century diatribe (P.Oxy. 2073) made its case on the basis of Septuagint writings and not using the New Testament—although, of course, this must remain partly (and perhaps largely) an argument from silence, since the entire document has not survived.

Though beyond our period, it is striking that four other theological treatises or homilies from Oxyrhynchus employ, in their fairly extensive surviving portions, themes from the Jewish Bible and—even in the fifth and sixth centuries—with only an occasional reminiscence of New Testament events or language.[133]

---

[131] *In decollationem præcursoris et Baptistæ Joannis*. In *PG* 59:487, Sir 25:16 is quoted in lines 38–40; the P.Oxy. 1603 portion on p. 487, lines 56–70. P.Oxy. 1603 was unidentified by the editors, but soon was shown to be from Ps.-Chrysostom (cf. van Haelst, no. 634). It is reminiscent in form of the litany of faith heroes in Heb 11, though the papyrus refers to evil women.

[132] P.Oxy. XIII, pp. 25–26.

[133] P.Oxy. 1600 (5th c., 58 lines) refers to Abel, Joseph, Moses, and cites Ps 2:1, etc. 1601 (late 4th/5th c., 34 lines) cites and interprets Joel 1:6, speaks of "our battle/wrestling is spiritual" (a possible but not necessary allusion to Eph 6:12), and quite clearly alludes to 1 Pet 5:8: the devil as a lion seeking to devour. In 1602

So, our early local treatises have revealed an anti-Jewish dialogue and a diatribe against women. Was there anything positive in Christian exhortation at Oxyrhynchus? P.Oxy. 2072 (late third century) in its sparse remains (thirty-two lines, all broken off on both sides, with indeterminate line lengths) appears to have dealt with two issues, a community matter and one more theological, though what the preceding fifty or more pages held is unknown.[134]

The recto uses words such as "opinion," "truth," and "brother," but no reconstruction seems possible; then follows a statement about having "both good things and bad things in common" (lines 11–13). The editor's notes refer to Acts 2:44 and 4:32, and he avers that "the recto apparently commends the communistic society of [Christ's] followers,"[135] but the only significant word the papyrus shares with the Acts passages is κοινά (line 13), precluding, I think, any clear decision about a communal life, and perhaps speaking only of "sharing both the good and bad," in some fashion. The verso in lines 21–26 refers to something that happened "absolutely," though it was "not he himself but . . . Jesus Christ, who was appointed" to do something "to/for Israel and to/for all . . . those who believe," accomplishing something through/of "him to/with God." This was reconstructed by the editor, accommodating the likely length of lines, as "[God saved us] absolutely . . . not he himself, but [his son] Jesus Christ, who was set apart [in glory and who became a savior] to Israel and to all [the Gentiles] who believe [and who have been reconciled] through? him to God,"[136] though the reconstructed portion exceeds the surviving text and the result must be considered tentative, since there is no obvious intertext. Finally, there is a second
reference to "Christ" (line 28).[137] Two points stand out: the nature 44
of this treatise is likely beyond reach, and nothing here reflects direct influence from New Testament texts.[138]

(late 4th/5th c., 40 lines) events of Israelite history lead to Christ Jesus; 1603 (5th or 6th c., 21 lines), as noted above, lists evil deeds by women in the Bible, including the beheading of John the Baptist.

[134] P.Oxy. XVII, p. 15. Pagination indicates the presence of lost preceding pages. Van Haelst's characterization of P.Oxy. 2072 (no. 1156, p. 351) as "a question of the parousia" is puzzling.

[135] Ibid.

[136] P.Oxy. XVII, p. 16, where the proposed Greek text is provided.

[137] "Christ" (lines 23, 28), "God" (line 26), and "Israel" (line 24) occur as *nomina sacra*.

[138] Even less can be said about the nature of P.Oxy. 2068 (4th c.), which has

F. *The Role of "New Testament" Papyri in Everyday Christian Life in Oxyrhynchus*

Our penultimate core sample runs through the rich stratum of private letters to explore everyday Christian life in Oxyrhynchus, yielding some two dozen clearly or likely Christian letters from the late third century and the fourth that are relevant to our assessment. First, a New Testament papyrus, P10 (P.Oxy. 209, mentioned above), containing Rom 1:1–7 and written in the early fourth century, was "found tied up with a contract dated 316 A.D. and other documents of the same period."[139] Written "in a large rude uncial," the Romans papyrus was likely a school pupil's exercise,[140] or, recognizing its folds, an amulet.[141] Either way, this manuscript's juxtaposition with a business document and others of an ordinary nature opens the issue of how our "New Testament" papyri were related to the everyday life of Christians in Oxyrhynchus. The most obvious path of exploration is to examine private letters and official records.

1. *Private letters*

Private letters are numerous from Oxyrhynchus, and those that may be Christian include family correspondence, business matters, letters of recommendation and condolence, and others, such as the one about lending books. Letters from the early third century are rare, so we must be content with those dating in the later third and in the fourth centuries.

A number of Christian letters, such as P.Oxy. 4127 (1st half of 4th c.), after a quick Christian greeting and the customary wish for good health (though here "in soul and body"), move directly to business: "Ptolemaeus to Thonius, his beloved brother, greetings in the Lord (κ̅ω̣̅). Before all things I pray that you be in good health in soul and body" (lines 1–10), but then speaks immediately of linen yarn, "a pair of girl's full-sized shoes made of hair," and (perhaps) a garment. That is the full burden of the letter.[142]

---

common *nomina sacra* (lines 18, 33, 43), but also β̅ς̅ (lines 7, 14), possibly for βας-ιλεύς. Whether a liturgical piece or homily, it has "several allusions to, or reminiscences of, the Greek of the Old Testament" (P.Oxy. XVII, pp. 5–6).

[139] P.Oxy. II, p. 8.

[140] Ibid. See pl. II.

[141] See n. 118, above.

[142] Similar, e.g., are P.Oxy. 1774 (early 4th c.); 2729 (4th c.); 2731 (4th/5th c.); cf. 2156 (late 4th/5th c.).

a. *Letters of introduction or recommendation* 45

Letters of introduction or recommendation might be expected to show more extensive use of our New Testament papyri, though quickly we discover that they follow regular patterns[143] that largely exclude the use of alternate or creative phraseology. Among several surviving Christian examples, P.Oxy. 3857 (4th c.) is typical: the opening, which is lacking, would have given the sender's name and doubtless, "Greetings in the Lord,"[144] as in the majority of such Christian letters:

> ... to my beloved brothers and fellow ministers in every locality. Receive in peace our daughter Germania, who is coming to you, because she needs your help. Through her I and those with me greet you and those with you. Emmanuel. Amen. I pray for your health in the Lord, beloved brothers.[145]

Other Christian letters from Oxyrhynchus request that the one introduced be received "according to custom" (PSI 3.208, 4th c.), or "as is proper" (PSI 9.1041, 3rd/4th c.),[146] and two refer to catechumens, one being instructed "in the beginning of the gospel" (PSI 9.1401, line 11) and another "in Genesis" (P.Oxy. 2785, line 8, 4th c.). New Testament language may be reflected in P.Oxy. 2603 (4th c.), where the writer, Paul, when referring to the "acquaintances" he intro-

[143] M. G. Sirivianou, P.Oxy. LVI, p.111; cf. Chan-Hie Kim, *Form and Structure of the Familiar Greek Letter of Recommendation* (SBLDS 4; Missoula, MT: Society of Biblical Literature, 1972), passim, though Kim argues that the Christian letters available to him followed the general pattern only in the opening and closing, and not in the body (p. 117).

[144] It is said that χαίρειν is omitted in contrast to all other letters of recommendation (P.Oxy. LVI, p. 114; cf. 112–15; see S. R. Llewelyn, *NewDocs* 8 [1984–85]: 170–71), but the first line has only remote traces.

[145] *Nomina sacra* in line 15: κ̅ω̅, and line 13: ε̅μ̅λ̅ ('Εμμανουήλ), followed by ϙ̅θ̅ [see n. 57 above].

[146] "Receive in peace": P.Oxy. 1162 (4th c.), 2785 (4th c.), P.Alex. 29 (3rd c.); P.Berol. 8508 (*APF* 28, p. 54; 3rd/4th c.); "Receive in accordance with custom": SB III.7269 (4th/5th c.); SB X.10255 (3rd/4th c.), phrases, along with "Receive as is proper," that are found only in Christian letters of recommendation (Kim, *Form and Structure*, 108–13). P.NagHamm. 78 (4th c.), a Christian letter, has "Receive our brother Herakleios . . .," but the text following cannot be reconstructed. For the distinction between letters of peace and of recommendation, see the enlightening discussion by Timothy M. Teeter, "Letters of Recommendation or Letters of Peace?" in *Akten des 21. Internationale Papyrologenkongresses, Berlin, 13.–19. 8 1995*, 2:954–60, esp. 956–58. Stowers calls them letters of mediation (*Letter Writing in Greco-Roman Antiquity*, 153–65). For general analysis, see Sirivianou, P.Oxy. LVI, pp. 111–16; cf. Llewelyn, *NewDocs* 8 (1984–85): 171–72, and the older study by Clinton W. Keyes, "The Greek Letter of Introduction," *AJP* 56 (1935): 28–44.

duces, says, "if you do anything for them, you have done it for me" (lines 28–29), reminiscent of Matt 25:40: "... just as you did it to one of the least of these ..., you did it to me," though the allusion, while possible, lies "more in the realms of conjecture,"[147] because
46 some earlier non-Christian Oxyrhynchus letters of commendation read, "Look upon him as if he were myself," followed at the conclusion by "When you read this letter, imagine that I am speaking to you" (P.Oxy 32 [Latin], lines 6–9, 31–33, 2nd c.)[148] and "... receive him as if he were I" (P.Osl. 55, lines 8–9, 2nd/3rd c.),[149] but especially P.Oxy 3646 (3rd/4th c.), "And whatever you do for the *prophetes*, you do for me" (lines 21–22), where προφήτης refers to a priest at an Egyptian oracle or the like.[150]

b. *Letters of condolence*

A second sample turns up letters of condolence to the bereaved, which—we might suppose—would be an even more natural locale for New Testament quotations and allusions or at least for Christian sentiments, and the latter do occur in the sixth/seventh-century P.Oxy. 1874, though even then explicit New Testament passages are not evident (see below). Actually, among some two thousand private papyrus letters, only about a dozen qualify as letters of sympathy and comfort following a death.[151] They range from the first/second to the sixth/seventh centuries, with ten written during the first four centuries. Five indicate no religious context; three give clear or implied reference to Roman religions; two are clearly Christian (P.Princ. II,102, 4th c.; P.Oxy. 1874, 6th/7th c.);[152] two others are probably or possibly Christian (P.Oxy. 4004, 5th c., and 3819, early 4th c.)—

[147] Harris, "Biblical Echoes and Reminiscences in Christian Papyri," 157; the link to Matt 25:40 is suggested, e.g., by J. H. Harrop ("A Christian Letter of Recommendation," *JEA* 48 [1962]: 136), but then he proceeds to point out several examples of "a favour to the bearer is a favour to the sender."

[148] For lines 22–34, see P.Oxy. II, pp. 318–19; see also Stowers, *Letter Writing in Greco-Roman Antiquity*, 157.

[149] From Oxyrhynchus: see S. Eitrem and Leiv Amundsen, *Papyri Osloenses, Fasc. II* (Oslo: Norske Videnskaps-Akademi I Oslo, 1931), xi, 132–35.

[150] See John Rea, P.Oxy. LI, p. 129, who suggests further that there may be a "connection with the worship of Hermes Trismegistus."

[151] See the superb analysis by Juan Chapa, *Letters of Condolence in Greek Papyri* (Pap. Flor. 29; Florence: Gonnelli, 1998). He mentions four others, but excludes them because "condolence is included in the body of the letter, as one among other topics, treated with what seems to us heartless speed" (p. 16).

[152] On P.Princ. II. 102, see n. 166 below.

and these four are the latest among the twelve. Altogether five are from Oxyrhynchus (those just noted plus P.Oxy. 115, 2nd c.; PSI 12.1248, ca. 235 C.E.). Finally, eight are complete, while four are lacunose at the beginning and/or the end.[153]

In all these letters, Christian or not, condolence is expressed with 47
close consistency through one or more common elements, including (1) nothing can be done about mortality, it is the human condition, (2) death is common to all, and (3) bear it bravely and/or comfort yourselves.[154] The second-century example from Oxyrhynchus (P.Oxy. 115) is brusque:

> Eirene to Taonnophris and Philo, take heart. I grieved and wept over the departed as much as I wept over Didymas. I and all mine, Epaphroditus, Thermuthion, Philion, Apollonius and Plantas, did all that was due. However, one can do nothing against such things. So comfort yourselves. Farewell.[155]

Another Oxyrhynchus letter (P.Oxy. 3819, early 4th c.) has been thought by some to be Christian,[156] based first of all on the following portion:

> For when I heard about my mother Sarapias, I was greatly grieved. Well, the lord god has the power for the future to give us good health.

---

[153] Chapa, *Letters of Condolence*, 15–18, 23–24. No religious content: P.Oxy. I.115 (2nd c., complete); BGU III.801 (2nd c., complete); P.Wisc. II.84 (2nd/3rd c., complete); P.Rainer Cent. 70 (2nd/3rd c., incomplete); SB XVIII.13946 (3rd/4th c., complete); Roman religions: SB XIV.11646 (1st/2nd c., complete); PSI 12.1248 (from Oxyrhynchus; 235 or later; complete); P.Ross.Georg. III.2 (3rd c., complete); clearly Christian: P.Princ. II.102 (4th c., incomplete: lacking end); P.Oxy. XVI.1874 (6th/7th c., incomplete: lacking beginning and end); and probably/possibly Christian: P.Oxy. LV.3819 (1st half 4th c., incomplete: lacking end); P.Oxy. LIX.4004 (5th c., complete).

[154] SB XVIII. 13946 (3rd/4th c.) claims that those who die escape the sufferings of this life: see Chapa, *Letters of Condolence*, 115–18.

[155] The same day, whether earlier or later, Eirene, a business woman of some kind, wrote a matter-of-fact business letter to the same addressees (P.Oxy. 116), with no mention of the bereavement: on the dates, see Chapa, *Letters of Condolence*, 64. On self-consolation, see ibid., 62, 64, 144; cf. Deissmann (*Light from the Ancient East*, 176–78) and John L. White (*Light from Ancient Letters* [FF; Philadelphia: Fortress, 1986] 184–85), who translate "comfort one another"; Chapa (p. 64) to the contrary and against a Pauline parallel in 1 Thess 4:18.

PSI 12.1248 (ca. 235), from Oxyrhynchus, says, in part, "But bear it bravely! For this is something which lies in store even for the gods." See Chapa, *Letters of Condolence*, 96–97.

[156] John Rea, its editor in P.Oxy. LV, pp. 219–20; cf. Chapa, *Letters of Condolence*, 128–29.

> So do not be grieved. For these things are (part of being) human. Indeed, for all of us this is laid down.

The phrase, "lord god," as noted earlier, is hardly a Christian indicator by itself (especially uncontracted, as here), and the Christian origin of this letter comes to rest, then, on the rare word, δυνατέω, found only in the first-century B.C.E. Epicurean philosopher Philodemus and in Paul.[157] The editor focuses on this "Pauline" word, indicating that "the reminiscence suggests that [the author of the letter] is Christian."[158] To be sure, Oxyrhynchus preserves five Pauline letters dating prior to the condolence letter, but Philodemus also had a presence in the city, for a first-century list of epigrams found there
48 is totally dominated by those of Philodemus (P.Oxy. 3724),[159] and there is no compelling reason to link the verb usage in our letter to Paul rather than Philodemus—or to either one for that matter.

More probably Christian is a fifth-century Oxyrhynchus letter (P.Oxy. LIX. 4004), though the thoughts expressed reveal no such origin, for the customary pattern of condolence appears:

> We were very much grieved when we heard about your blessed wife [*or* about your wife, Macaria].... But what can we do against mortality? So please console yourself and brave the journey and come to me....[160]

Though this letter is beyond our period,[161] it is instructive if it is Christian, for its identity is based on names later in the text, especially Neson, a location in the Heracleopolite nome, probably on the west bank of the Nile across from Oxyrhynchite territory, where an archive attests to a monastery, and two personal names: a biblical name, Nathanael (also a Coptic saint), and an unusual name,

---

[157] See the references in BDAG ad loc., and P.Oxy. LV, p. 220. See the latter for other speculative evidence of Christian origin; cf. Chapa, *Letters of Condolence*, 128–29.

[158] See P.Oxy. LV, p. 219. The five Pauline papyri dating to the turn of the third/fourth centuries are P.Oxy. 1355 = P27 and 4497 = P113 of Romans; 1008 = P 15 of 1 Corinthians; 1009 = P16 of Philippians; and 1598 = P30 of 1–2 Thessalonians. δυνατέω occurs in Rom 14:4; 2 Cor 13:3; 9:8, but none of these passages is preserved in the Oxyrhynchus papyri, nor in the later P.Oxy. 209 = P10 of Romans; or 2157 = P51 of Galatians.

[159] See P.Oxy. LIV, pp. 65–67.

[160] Chapa, *Letters of Condolence*, 141, cf. 139–47.

[161] Though its hand most resembles those of two papyri from about the first third of the fifth century (ibid., 140).

Syncletice, the name of an Egyptian nun who became a saint.[162]

Yet if this letter is Christian, there is nothing of Christian sentiment, let alone any reflection of New Testament texts; rather, traditional formulaic statements of condolence reign. An Oxyrhynchus letter from around 600 C.E. (P.Oxy. 1874) shows us, however, language that we might have expected much earlier:

> But let us glorify God, because he gave and he took away; and pray that the Lord may give them rest and may He allow you to see them in paradise, when the souls of people are judged; for they have gone to the bosom of Abraham, and of Isaac and of Jacob,[163]

and

> . . . pray that the Lord may send upon you his blessing, for the Lord has many good things and gives courage to those in sorrow who seek a blessing from him, and we hope to God that through this sorrow the Lord sends you joy. . . .[164]

But this is two centuries (!) beyond the period we are exploring, 49
though even then nothing reminds us specifically of New Testament texts.[165] If we move beyond Oxyrhynchus, one fourth-century letter (P.Princ. II.102) reads "nobody among humans is immortal, but only God, and remember the promise of the blessed Paul, as . . .," where, regrettably, the text breaks off.[166] Undoubtedly an appropriate Pauline text followed, though we cannot know what it was. But Oxyrhynchus, where the majority of condolence letters were found, has no such explicit reference to our New Testament, regardless of date.

---

[162] For details, see P.Oxy. LIX, pp. 171–75; Chapa, *Letters of Condolence*, 139–47, who remarks that Neson and these names, in relation to Theodorus, the writer, "might tempt one to identify them as monks or as otherwise connected with the monastery of Hathor . . ., perhaps a Meletian monastery during the schism" (pp. 139–40, cf. 145).

[163] See Horsley, "The Bosom of Abraham," *NewDocs* 3 (1978): 106.

[164] Chapa, *Letters of Condolence*, 152, cf. 149–59. P.Oxy. 1874, like other fifth- to seventh-century Christian letters, prayers, and other documents, has no *nomina sacra* (e.g., P.Oxy. 1830; 1832; 1926; 3864–3865; 3870; 3872–3873; 3932; 3936–3943; 3945; 3946–3959; 3961; 4535–4536; P.Wisc. I.11. To the contrary, e.g., P.Oxy. 1927–1928; 2067 [Nicene Creed]; 2071; 2074; 3863; 4394, line 11; 4397, lines 226, 239.

[165] See Horsley, "Bosom of Abraham," 106, for evidence that the formula "derives from liturgy rather than directly from the NT."

[166] The provenance of P.Princ. II.102 is unknown; I accept Chapa's argument that, in line 17, "blessed Paul" is to be restored, assuring its Christian origin (*Letters of Condolence*, 136–37, cf. 132–33).

Although conclusions on the basis of a dozen or fewer letters are risky, within the first four centuries of Christianity there was very little difference between letters of condolence written by Christians and those written by non-Christians, for they all consist mainly in an array of the shared formulaic phrases, with the exception of the one non-Oxyrhynchus letter just noted. The surprises are not only that so few letters of condolence are extant, but that they are so terse and blunt, almost lacking in feeling (except for the latest Christian example, P.Oxy. 1874). Two, in fact, after a brief expression of grief, a statement that death is common to all, and advice to console oneself, proceed immediately to matter-of-fact discussions of business or other events. For example, P.Oxy. 1248, partly quoted above, has seven lines of condolence and thirty-nine additional lines describing someone acting inhumanly and causing trouble, and so on.[167]

2. *Official records*

Our exploration necessarily encompasses but a small portion of what might be explored of the Christian environment at Oxyrhynchus through the fourth century, but we must be content with a final core sample from official documents relevant to the city's Christian terrain. As we place the samples on our laboratory table, we find, first, an order from February 256 to arrest a certain "Petosorapis, son of Horus, Christian" (P.Oxy. 3035). Parentage is a common identifier in official records, as is a professional designation, such as "weavers" (P.Oxy. 2575) or "wine-merchant" (P.Oxy. 2576), but "Christian" is unusual, leading to the notion that religion was the critical factor in his summons, but this order was issued "more than a year before legal measures were taken against the Christians" in the Valerian persecution.[168]

[167] Ibid., 96–98. P.Oxy. 3819 has eighteen lines of consolation (quoted above), but then begins to discuss a dalmatic—a wide-sleeved overgarment, though the text breaks off at this point (ibid., 127, 130).

[168] P. J. Parsons in P.Oxy. XLII, p. 100: the text reads χρησιανὸν (see pl. X), but no alternative to "Christian" is apparent. A similar spelling occurs in PSI 14.1412, also from Oxyrhynchus (2nd/3rd c.): see P.Oxy. XXXVI, p. 84 n. 2; cf. Horsley, *NewDocs* 2 (1977): 173.

"Arrest orders" are more properly summonses, though often a guard was involved: see Traianos Gagos in P.Oxy. LXI, pp. 90–91; T. Gagos and P. J. Sijpesteijn, "Towards an Explanation of the Typology of the So-Called 'Orders to Arrest,'" *BASP* 33 (1996): 77–97, esp. 78–79. For a list up to 1986, including some twenty-seven involving Oxyrhynchus, see Adam Bülow-Jacobsen, "Orders to Arrest," *ZPE* 66 (1986): 95–98.

Hence, "Christian" is likely just an identifier,[169] and we have no clue to the occasion for the summons.

Further items, however, do take us into the context of persecution. P.Oxy. 3119 (259/260 in reign of Valerian),[170] in what can be deciphered, reads "concerning an investigation," followed in the next line by Χρηστιανοί (line 14), "Christians," allowing for the possibility of an inquiry in time of persecution, though this cannot be confirmed.

About forty years later, in February 303, an edict from Diocletian required all litigants to sacrifice,[171] and Copres, a Christian,[172] who was preparing a lawsuit in another town, confirms such a requirement when he writes back to Oxyrhynchus (P.Oxy. 2601, early 4th c.): "It became known to us that those who present themselves in court are being made to sacrifice." And how does he handle this? "I made a power-of-attorney in favor of my brother" (lines 8–13). Such casual treatment may suggest either that this requirement was routinely circumvented by assigning it to someone else (perhaps—by Christians—to a non-Christian?) or that the procedure was new enough that Copres and others had not yet realized that "a serious crisis of conscience was posed."[173]

Then in 304, Ammonius, an illiterate lector,[174] declares to the authorities "concerning the surrender of all the goods" in his "for- 51

[169] Parsons in P.Oxy. XLII, p. 100. At the time (1974), Parsons considered this "by far the earliest use of the word 'Christian' in the papyrus documents."

[170] Dating is complex; the reference is to a "seventh year," including (among seven possibilities in the third century) "7 Valerian and Gallienus," i.e. 259/260, viewed by John Rae as a standout, but still doubtful (P.Oxy. XLIII, pp. 77–78 + pl. VI); J. E. G. Whitehorne confirms the 259/260 date by careful argumentation ("P.Oxy. XLIII 3119: A Document of Valerian's Persecution," *ZPE* 24 [1977]: 187–96, esp. 196).

[171] Judge and Pickering, "Papyrus Documentation," 53.

[172] This is clear enough from the attempted *nomina sacra* in line 5 and from ϙ̅θ̅, the isopsephism of ἀμήν in the address (line 34): see P.Oxy. XXXI, pp. 170–71; cf. n. 57 above.

[173] Judge and Pickering, "Papyrus Documentation," 53, based on P.Oxy. XXXI, pp. 167–68. The person given the power of attorney "was certainly pagan" (Ewa Wipszycka, "Un lecteur qui ne sait pas ecrire ou un chrétien qui ne veut pas se souiller? [P.Oxy. XXXIII 2673]," *ZPE* 50 [1983]: 121).

[174] See P.Oxy. XXXIII, pp. 105, 108, where it is suggested that the lector read in Coptic services but was illiterate in Greek; Wipszycka ("Un lecteur," esp. 121) sees his illiteracy as a "subterfuge": reluctant to be a hero and defy the authorities, yet unwilling to sign a document handing over the church's goods to persecutors of the faithful, thereby defiling himself, he took an ambiguous action "consistent

mer church"—apparently in accord with Diocletian's edict—that nothing remains except "the bronze objects"[175] which had been handed over for shipment to Alexandria (P.Oxy. 2673, 5 February 304, lines 14–24).

The very next year, 305, an official report affirms that a certain "Paul from the Oxyrhynchite nome" had been sentenced and that no property was currently registered in his name (P.Oxy. 2665, lines 16–20)—presumably because it was confiscated. Though there is no direct evidence, the presumption is that he was a Christian who suffered under persecution—the more likely because the document states that the sentencing agent (lines 14–15) was "Satrius Arrianus, the governor of the Thebaid, who appears so frequently in the martyrologies."[176]

Though details are lacking, these papyri disclose Oxyrhynchus Christians who were objects of persecution under Valerian and Diocletian.

A further probe reveals trouble in two Christian homes. In P.Oxy. 903 (4th c.), a woman files a thirty-seven line accusation, narrating the abusive behavior of her husband toward her, her foster daughters, and her slaves, as well as toward his foster son and his own

with declaring himself illiterate" and did not sign the declaration himself. In response, G. W. Clarke presents cases, including five-year-old (!) lectors and others who allegedly did not "know letters," to suggest that the possibility of illiterate lectors "cannot be rejected outright" ("An Illiterate Lector?" *ZPE* 57 [1984]: 103–4, esp. 104). See also Bagnall, *Egypt in Late Antiquity*, 256 n. 142; Kraus, "(Il)literacy in Non-Literary Papyri," 330–31 and n. 27. Haines-Eitzen (*Guardians of Letters*, 27–29) and Kraus ([Il]literacy in Non-Literary Papyri," 329, 334–38), at greater length, discuss the striking case of two village scribes in the Fayum near Karanis who could neither read nor write, except for writing their own signatures (P.Petaus, an archive of 127 items); see also Robert A. Kaster, *Guardians of Language: The Grammarian and Society in Late Antiquity* (Transformation of the Classical Heritage 11; Berkeley/Los Angeles: University of California Press, 1988; repr. 1997), 42–43, esp. nn. 41, 44; Harris, *Ancient Literacy*, 278–79; 320 and n. 169.

[175] John Rea, the editor, corrected πύλη in line 22 to read ὕλη; hence "bronze material" rather than "bronze gate" ("P.Oxy. XXXIII 2673: πύλην to ὕλην" *ZPE* 35 [1979]: 128); cf. P.Oxy. XLVIII, p. xvii; Horsley, *NewDocs* 2 (1977): 169; Bagnall, *Egypt in Late Antiquity*, 289–90.

[176] P.Oxy. XXXIII, p. 89; see E. A. Judge, "Fourth-Century Monasticism in the Papyri," in *Proceedings of the Sixteenth International Congress of Papyrology, New York, 24–31 July 1980* (ed. Roger S. Bagnall et al.; Chico, CA: Scholars Press, 1981), 614–15; Bagnall, *Egypt in Late Antiquity*, 280 n. 117. I see no reason to think, as some have, that P.Oxy. 1464 (250 C.E.), a *libellus* or certificate of sacrifice in the Decian persecution, is that of a Christian. On the subject, see P.Oxy. LVIII, p. 39. Other *libelli* at Oxyrhynchus are P.Oxy. 658, 2990, and 3929.

slaves over an extended period. We know the couple were Christians
because on one occasion he took an oath before the bishops, affirming,
"I will stop and not insult her" (lines 15–17)—though he abused her
again—and because of references to "the church" (lines 19–21),
including her statement, "I departed and went into the church on 52
the Sabbath" [*sic!*] (line 19).[177]

In P.Oxy. 3581 (the dating is complex: late fourth or fifth century), another woman submits a detailed petition seeking charges against Paul, her husband, who left her and her infant daughter to live with another woman, but then, she says, "Again he beguiled [me] through presbyters" (line 8) to return, presumably ecclesiastical elders; this time she was wiser and secured an agreement for two ounces of gold, with written surety from his father, if he were to "indulge in the same vile behavior" (lines 10–). Well, matters were worse than before and, she says, "I endured insults and punishments to within an inch of my life" (lines 14–15). So she asks the tribune to exact the gold and to punish Paul "for his outrages against me" (lines 21–23). The results, of course, are unknown.

Two additional samples reveal troubling situations in the churches. In P.Oxy. 2344 (ca. 336) Dionysius, bishop of the [local] "catholic church" in Oxyrhynchus, petitions the strategus apparently to be relieved of the administration of an estate and the guardianship of some children, though the matter is not further clarified.[178] In another (P.Wash.Univ. I.20, 4th c., found at Oxyrhynchus), two brothers, upon returning to Oxyrhynchus, file a complaint against "the presbyter of the catholic church" of a nearby village because he had taken possession of their houses and lands and refuses to turn them

[177] The *editio princeps* read Σαμβαθώ (as if a location), but was revised to σαββάτῳ: see M. David, B. A. Van Groningen, and E. Kiessling, *Berichtigungsliste der Griechischen Papyrusurkunden aus Ägypten*, vol. 3 (Leiden: Brill, 1958), 133. There is also an apparent attempt at a *nomen sacrum* at the very end (line 37): θ(εός) in "God knows these things." On both P.Oxy. 903 and 3581 (treated below), see Roger S. Bagnall, "Church, State, and Divorce in Late Roman Egypt," in *Florilegium Columbianum: Essays in Honor of Paul Oskar Kristeller* (ed. Karl-Ludwig Selig; New York: Italica, 1987) 41–42, 58–59 [reprinted in Bagnall, *Later Roman Egypt*, no. IV]; and idem, *Egypt in Late Antiquity*, 194–95.

[178] This may be in the context of seeking relief or exemption from a mandatory liturgical appointment—public service: see Royce L. B. Morris, "Reflections of Citizen Attitudes in Petitions from Late Roman and Byzantine Oxyrhynchus," in *Akten des 21. Internationale Papyrologenkongresses, Berlin, 13.–19. 8 1995*, ed. Kramer *et al.*, 2:746–47.

back. Again, we do not know the other sides of these stories or their outcomes.[179]

Finally, Christians were doing some good—or at least interesting—things in Oxyrhynchus. An athlete, presumably a professional,
53 sent money to his mother "via Sotas the Christian" (PSI XIV.1412,
line 10, 2nd/3rd c.).[180] A certain Barus requests a fellow Christian, Diogenes, to grant Horus a four-month leave or an extension of time—it is hard to tell which—"because he is of moderate means" and will be obligated for public service (P.Oxy. 3858, 4th c.).[181] We assume that he granted the favor. And two anchorite nuns agree to rent rooms to "Aurelius Jose son of Judas, Jew" (P.Oxy. 3203, 400 C.E., line 7).[182] Besides these random acts of kindness, there is little else, and our New Testament texts—though perhaps not to be expected in these contexts—make no appearance.

III. Conclusion

As we look back, much was happening in Christian circles in Oxyrhynchus, giving us a glimpse of the good, the bad, and even the ugly. Of course, these events did not take place in the course of a decade or even a lifetime, but over several lifetimes. Yet what we witness is instructive.

First,

- We find individual Christians, including women specifically, reading and studying biblical books and exploring Jewish and doubt-

[179] See also the reprimand of a Christian for some unknown action in P. Laur. 42 recto (4th/5th, Oxyrhynchite nome): "I was very pained and we are exceedingly pained that you dared to do such a thing to Atheas, since you are a Christian, because she also is a laywoman, and she has never been discovered (doing) worldly business" (text and tr. in Horsley, *NewDocs* 2 [1977]: 172– 73; cf. Bagnall, *Egypt in Late Antiquity*, 282 and n. 126). P.Oxy. 3311 (373–374 C.E.) is a petition from two sisters to recover property that had been used/controlled (?) by a monk, Ammonius; upon his death, Ammon—perhaps a fellow monk—refuses to turn back the property (see Judge, "Fourth-Century Monasticism," 618–19).

[180] The text preserves only χρησια [. . .] (line 10), restored to χρηστιανοῦ in P.Oxy. XXXVI, p. 84 n. 2, by analogy with the restoration in P.Oxy. 3035 (see n. 168 above).

[181] See P.Oxy. LVI, pp. 117–20; *nomina sacra* occur in lines 3 and 25.

[182] P.Oxy. XLIV, pp. 182–84; cf. Horsley, *NewDocs* 1 (1976): 126–30.

less Christian apocalyptic, and likely teaching or exercising leadership in other ways.
- We discover catechumens at various stages of instruction, and individuals who pray for help or carry amulets for protection.

And
- We hear of Christians writing letters of comfort—such as they are—in times of grief.

Second,
- We observe churches, with their majestic hymns, lofty prayers, and liturgical texts.
- We witness ministers asking other Christians to help a woman in need, and bishops trying to assist a battered woman, who later sought refuge in the church.

And
- We hear of churches dismantled and of Christians whose property had been confiscated under persecution, though with no
details, but also of one Christian who casually assigns someone 54
else to fulfill his obligation to sacrifice.

Third,
- At the same time, we uncover an anti-Jewish dialogue and a diatribe against women, both theologically motivated, indicating—to put them in the best possible light—that the churches were wrestling with ideas that we find uncongenial.

And
- We hear of a bishop recusing himself from a legal responsibility for children, and of church presbyters who, allegedly, convince a woman to take back her husband only to be further abused, and of another presbyter who, allegedly, took houses and land illicitly and declined to make amends.

Our goal from the outset has been to disclose the local context of our fifty-nine New Testament manuscripts from Oxyrhynchus, and, indeed, the Christian community there has come alive for us, if only in a partial and random fashion—but alive nonetheless. Yet the anomaly is that any overt influence from our New Testament texts remains largely undocumented.[183] Would a different picture have

[183] See Horsley, *NewDocs* 2 (1977): 157–58, who refers to "less than two dozen Biblical citations and verbal echoes" among some one hundred (alleged) Christian

emerged if Christian letters and documents from the second and early third centuries were as abundant as those from the late third and early fourth? Probably not, because forty-one of the fifty-nine Oxyrhynchus New Testament manuscripts issued from the third and fourth centuries, and apparently they were imported or copied and available[184] in the very same time frame as most of our letters and documents, supporting the reliability of our findings.

The churches at Oxyrhynchus by this later period, therefore, appear to have moved well beyond the direct use of New Testament texts to a reliance on the liturgical forms that had developed and on the abiding Septuagint texts for much of their worship and polemic. Liturgy, of course, was drawn mainly from Jewish Scripture and from texts that were becoming the New Testament, but by our period the liturgical formulations have overshadowed their Christian sources. Yet the Greek Jewish Bible—as understood and used by Christians—shows considerable direct influence on the Christian hymns, prayers, and theological treatises. All of this could be the uneven result of randomness in the survival of papyrus documents, yet sometimes silence is itself a loud voice that demands our attention.

Moreover, as we assess this abundance of early Christian writings
55 at Oxyrhynchus through the fourth century, including those we call "New Testament" and those we designate "apocrypha," there is no basis for assigning preference to one group over the other, or even for claiming that they were separable groups, nor—with available evidence—can we discern varying degrees of canonical authority among the writings. Because these books as a whole show precious little direct impact on worship or teaching in the Oxyrhynchus churches or on the daily lives of Christians in Oxyrhynchus, one is tempted to remark, "Why should the third and fourth centuries be any different from the twentieth and the twenty-first? After all, in any modern liturgical service, are not the hymnals and prayer books used more heavily than the Bibles in the pews?" Beyond the lessons latent in these remarks, however, what is significant for us is that we have been able to expose something of the sociocultural and

letters through the fourth century, though only half that many would remain if "reminiscences of Biblical wording which are less than certain" were excluded.

[184] On speed of transfer of letters—and books—in the Mediterranean area, see Epp, "New Testament Papyrus Manuscripts and Letter Carrying," 35–56, esp. 52–56.

intellectual context of one locality—one real-life situation in which more than 40 percent of our New Testament papyri lived and were shaped in the company of numerous other Jewish and early Christian writings. To disclose and to illuminate that context, after all, was the main point—though now it remains for textual critics and others to fill out the picture and to find ways to exploit the results.

Added Notes, 2004

Follow-up research. A continuation of the preceding essay arose from an invited paper, presented at a joint session of the Early Jewish Christian Relations Section, the New Testament Textual Criticism Section, and the Papyrology and Early Christian Backgrounds Group at the 2004 Annual Meeting of the Society of Biblical Literature at San Antonio, Texas. It will be published in a much expanded form as "The Jews and the Jewish Community in Oxyrhynchus: Socio-Religious Context for the New Testament Papyri," *New Testament Manuscripts: Their Texts and Their World.* Ed. Thomas J. Kraus and Tobias Nicklas. Leiden: Brill, 2005.

BIBLIOGRAPHY AND TEXT-CRITICAL RESPONSIBILITIES OF THE AUTHOR, 1962–2004

Books and Articles

The Theological Tendency of Codex Bezae Cantabrigiensis in Acts. Society for New Testament Studies Monograph Series, 3. Cambridge: Cambridge University Press, 1966. Pp. xvi+210. [Unchanged reprint: Eugene, OR: Wipf and Stock, 2001.]

New Testament Textual Criticism: Its Significance for Exegesis: Essays in Honour of Bruce M. Metzger, ed. by Eldon Jay Epp and Gordon D. Fee. Oxford: Clarendon Press, 1981. Pp. xxviii+410.

The New Testament and Its Modern Interpreters, ed. by Eldon Jay Epp and †George W. MacRae, S.J. Society of Biblical Literature Centennial Publication Series. The Bible and Its Modern Interpreters, 3. Philadelphia: Fortress Press/Atlanta, GA: Scholars Press, 1989. Pp. xxxii+601.

Studies in the Theory and Method of New Testament Textual Criticism, by Eldon Jay Epp and Gordon D. Fee. Studies and Documents, 45. Grand Rapids, MI: Eerdmans, 1993. Pp. xiv+414.

"The 'Ignorance Motif' in Acts and Anti-Judaic Tendencies in Codex Bezae," *Harvard Theological Review* 55 (1962) 51–62.

"Coptic Manuscript G67 and the Rôle of Codex Bezae as a Western Witness in Acts," *Journal of Biblical Literature* 85 (1966) 197–212.

"The Claremont Profile Method for Grouping New Testament Minuscule Manuscripts," *Studies in the History and Text of the New Testament in Honor of Kenneth Willis Clark, Ph.D.* Eds. Boyd L. Daniels and M. Jack Suggs. Studies and Documents, 29. Salt Lake City, UT: University of Utah Press, 1967. Pp. 27–38.

"Norman Perrin on the Kingdom of God," *Christology and a Modern Pilgrimage: A Discussion with Norman Perrin.* Ed. Hans Dieter Betz. Claremont, CA: New Testament Colloquium, 1971. Pp. 113–22. Revised edition: Missoula, MT: Society of Biblical Literature and Scholars Press, 1974. Pp. 75–80.

"The Twentieth Century Interlude in New Testament Textual Criticism," *Journal of Biblical Literature* 93 (1974) 386–414.
Japanese serial translation in *Studia Textus Novi Testamenti* 103–109 (1975) 856–60; 866–68; 875–76; 890–92; 898–90; 907–8.

"Wisdom, Torah, Word: The Johannine Prologue and the Purpose of the Fourth Gospel," *Current Issues in Biblical and Patristic Interpretation: Studies in Honor of Merrill C. Tenney*. Ed. Gerald F. Hawthorne. Grand Rapids, MI: Eerdmans, 1975. Pp. 128–46.

"Anti-Semitism and the Popularity of the Fourth Gospel in Christianity," *CCAR Journal: A Reform Judaism Journal* (Central Conference of American Rabbis) 22 (1975) 35–57. [Now *Journal of Reform Judaism*]

"Toward the Clarification of the Term 'Textual Variant,'" *Studies in New Testament Language and Text: Essays in Honour of George D. Kilpatrick on the Occasion of his Sixty-Fifth Birthday*. Ed. J. K. Elliott. Supplements to Novum Testamentum, 44. Leiden: Brill, 1976. Pp. 153–73.

"Textual Criticism, New Testament," *The Interpreter's Dictionary of the Bible, Supplementary Volume*. Ed. Keith Crim. Nashville, TN: Abingdon Press, 1976. Pp. 891–95.

"The Eclectic Method in New Testament Textual Criticism: Solution or Symptom?" *Harvard Theological Review* 69 (1976) 211–57.

"Jews and Judaism in The Living New Testament," *Biblical and Near Eastern Studies:*

Essays in Honor of William Sanford LaSor. Ed. Gary Tuttle. Grand Rapids, MI: Eerdmans, 1978. Pp. 80–96.
Summary in *Bible Translator* 31 (1980) 141–42; excerpts in *The Atlantic Monthly* 255 (No. 2, February, 1985) 55–56.

"Paul's Diverse Imageries of the Human Situation and His Unifying Theme of Freedom," *Unity and Diversity in New Testament Theology.* Ed. R. A. Guelich. Grand Rapids, MI: Eerdmans, 1978. Pp. 100–116.

"A Continuing Interlude in New Testament Textual Criticism?" *Harvard Theological Review,* 73 (1980) 131–51.

"The Ascension in the Textual Tradition of Luke-Acts," *New Testament Textual Criticism: Its Significance for Exegesis: Essays in Honour of Bruce M. Metzger.* Ed. E. J. Epp and G. D. Fee. Oxford: Clarendon Press, 1981. Pp. 131–45.

"Should 'The Book' Be Panned?" *Bible Review* 2 (No. 2, Summer 1986) 36–41, 52.

"Jewish-Gentile Continuity in Paul: Torah and/or Faith? (Romans 9:1–5)," *Harvard Theological Review* 79 (1986) 80–90.
Also published as a chapter in *Christians among Jews and Gentiles: Essays in Honor of Krister Stendahl.* Ed. G. W. E. Nickelsburg with G. W. MacRae, S.J. Philadelphia: Fortress Press, 1986. Pp. 80–90.

"Mediating Approaches to the Kingdom: Werner Georg Kümmel and George Eldon Ladd," *The Kingdom of God in 20th-Century Interpretation.* Ed. Wendell Willis. Peabody, MA: Hendrickson Publishers, 1987. Pp. 35–52.

"Biblical Literature in Its Historical Context: The Apocrypha and the New Testament," *Harper's Bible Commentary.* 1st ed. Ed. James L. Mays. San Francisco: Harper & Row, 1988. Pp. 27–32.

"Textual Criticism," *The New Testament and Its Modern Interpreters.* Ed. E. J. Epp and †G. W. MacRae, S.J. Philadelphia: Fortress Press; Atlanta, GA: Scholars Press, 1989. Pp. 75–126.
Reprinted later as "Decision Points in New Testament Textual Criticism."

"New Testament Textual Criticism Past, Present, and Future: Reflections on the Alands' *Text of the New Testament,*" *Harvard Theological Review* 82 (1989) 213–29.

"The New Testament Papyrus Manuscripts in Historical Perspective," *To Touch the Text: Studies in Honor of Joseph A. Fitzmyer, S.J.* Ed. M. P. Horgan and P. J. Kobelski. New York: Crossroad, 1989. Pp. 261–88.

"The Significance of the Papyri for Determining the Nature of the New Testament Text in the Second Century: A Dynamic View of Textual Transmission," *Gospel Traditions in the Second Century.* Ed. William L. Petersen. Studies in Christianity and Judaism in Antiquity, 3. Notre Dame, IN: University of Notre Dame Press, 1989. Pp. 71–103.

"New Testament Papyrus Manuscripts and Letter Carrying in Greco-Roman Times," *The Future of Early Christianity: Essays in Honor of Helmut Koester.* Ed. B. A. Pearson, in collaboration with A. T. Kraabel, G. W. E. Nickelsburg, and N. R. Petersen. Minneapolis, MN: Fortress, 1991. Pp. 35–56.

"Textual Criticism (New Testament)," *Anchor Bible Dictionary.* 6 vols. Garden City: Doubleday, 1992. 6.412–35.

"Western Text of the New Testament," *Anchor Bible Dictionary.* 6 vols. Garden City: Doubleday, 1992. 6.909–12.

"The Papyrus Manuscripts of the New Testament," *The Text of the New Testament in Contemporary Research: Essays on the* Status Quaestionis. Ed. B. D. Ehrman and M. W. Holmes. Studies and Documents, 46; Grand Rapids, MI: Eerdmans, 1995. Pp. 3–21.

"Ancient Texts and Versions of the New Testament," *The New Interpreter's Bible.* 12 vols. Nashville, TN: Abingdon Press, 1994–1998. 8.1–11 (1995).

"*Humanitas* in the Greco-Roman Papyri," *Biblical and Humane: A Festschrift for John F. Priest.* Ed. Linda Bennett Elder, David L. Barr, and Elizabeth Struthers Malbon.

Scholars Press Homage Series. Atlanta, GA: Scholars Press, 1996. Pp. 189–213.
"The International Greek New Testament Project: Motivation and History," *Novum Testamentum* 39 (1997) 1–20.
"Textual Criticism in the Exegesis of the New Testament, with an Excursus on Canon," *Handbook to Exegesis of the New Testament*. Ed. Stanley E. Porter. New Testament Tools and Studies, 25. Leiden: Brill, 1997. Pp. 45–97.
"The New Testament Papyri at Oxyrhynchus in Their Social and Intellectual Context," *Sayings of Jesus: Canonical and Non-Canonical. Essays in Honour of Tjitze Baarda*. Ed. W. L. Petersen, J. S. Vos, and H. J. de Jonge. Supplements to Novum Testamentum, 89. Leiden: Brill, 1997. Pp. 47–68.
"The Codex and Literacy in Early Christianity and at Oxyrhynchus: Issues Raised by Harry Y. Gamble's *Books and Readers in the Early Church*," *Critical Review of Books in Religion* 11 (1998) 15–37.
"The Multivalence of the Term 'Original Text' in New Testament Textual Criticism," *Harvard Theological Review* 92 (1999) 245–81.
"Text-Critical, Exegetical, and Socio-Cultural Factors Affecting the Junia/Junias Variation in Romans 16,7," *Textual Criticism and Exegesis: Festschrift J. Delobel*. Bibliotheca Ephemeridum Theologicarum Lovaniensium, 161. Ed. A. Denaux. Leuven: Leuven University Press/Peeters, 2002. Pp. 227–91.
"Issues in the Interrelation of New Testament Textual Criticism and Canon," *The Canon Debate: On the Origins and Formation of the Bible*. Ed. Lee M. McDonald and James A. Sanders. Peabody, MA: Hendrickson, 2002. Pp. 485–515.
"Issues in New Testament Textual Criticism: Moving from the Nineteenth Century to the Twenty-First Century," *Rethinking New Testament Textual Criticism*. Ed. David Alan Black. Grand Rapids, MI: Baker Academic, 2002. Pp. 17–76.
"Anti-Judaic Tendencies in the D-Text of Acts: Forty Years of Conversation," *The Book of Acts as Church History: Text, Textual Traditions and Ancient Interpretations/ Apostelgeschichte als Kirchengeschichte: Text, Texttraditionen und antike Auslegungen*. Ed. Tobias Nicklas and Michael Tilly. BZNW 120. Berlin/New York: de Gruyter, 2003. Pp. 111–46.
"The Oxyrhynchus New Testament Papyri: 'Not without honor except in their hometown'?" *Journal of Biblical Literature* 123 (2004) 5–55.
[Presidential Address, Society of Biblical Literature, 2003.]
"The New Testament Papyri at Oxyrhynchus: Their Significance for Understanding the Transmission of the Early New Testament Text," *Oxyrhynchus: A City and Its Texts*. Ed. Peter Parsons, et al. London: Egypt Exploration Society [forthcoming].
"The Jews and the Jewish Community in Oxyrhynchus: Socio-Religious Context for the New Testament Papyri," *New Testament Manuscipts: Their Texts and Their World*. Ed. Thomas J. Kraus and Tobias Nicklas. Leiden: Brill, 2005.

Critical Notes

"Some Important Biblical Studies," *Journal of Biblical Literature* 84 (1965) 172–75.
"A Textus Receptus Continuus?" *Protocol of the Thirty-Second Colloquy, The Center for Hermeneutical Studies in Hellenistic and Modern Culture*. Ed. E. C. Hobbs. Berkeley, CA, 1978. Pp. 18–23. [A discussion with George D. Kilpatrick.]
"New Testament Textual Criticism in America: Requiem for a Discipline," *Journal of Biblical Literature* 98 (1979) 94–98.
"Preface" to the reprint of Fenton John Anthony Hort and Brooke Foss Westcott, *The New Testament in the Original Greek*. Peabody, Mass.: Hendrickson [forthcoming].

Book Reviews (Textual Criticism—selected)

P72 and the Codex Vaticanus, by Sakae Kubo. (Studies and Documents, 27; Salt Lake City: University of Utah Press, 1965): *JBL* 85 (1966) 512–13.

Der Text des Neuen Testaments: Eine Einführung in die neutestamentliche Textkritik (Stuttgart: Kohlhammer, 1966) and *The Text of the New Testament* (New York: Oxford University Press, 1964), by Bruce M. Metzger: *JBL* 86 (1967) 339–41.

Nine Uncial Palimpsests of the Greek New Testament, by J. Harold Greenlee (Studies and Documents, 39; Salt Lake City: University of Utah Press, 1968): *JBL* 89 (1970) 123–24.

Studies in Methodology in Textual Criticism of the New Testament, by Ernest C. Colwell (New Testament Tools and Studies, 9; Leiden: Brill, 1969): *Perspective* [Pittsburgh Theological Seminary] 13 (1972) 82–83.

A Textual Commentary on the Greek New Testament: A Companion Volume to the United Bible Societies' Greek New Testament (Third Edition), by Bruce M. Metzger (London/New York: United Bible Societies, 1971): *CBQ* 37 (1975) 134–36.

Vollständige Konkordanz zum griechischen Neuen Testament: Unter Zugrundelegung aller modernen kritischen Textausgaben und das Textus Receptus, ed. by K. Aland (2 vols.; Berlin: de Gruyter, 1975–83): *CBQ* 41 (1979) 148–51; 42 (1980) 258–61; 46 (1984) 778–80.

Manuscripts of the Greek Bible: An Introduction to Greek Palaeography, by Bruce M. Metzger (New York: Oxford University Press, 1981): *ThTo* 39 (1982) 234–37.

Synopse der drei ersten Evangelien mit Beigabe der johanneischen Parallelstellen (Synopsis of the First Three Gospels with the Addition of the Johannine Parallels), by Heinrich Greeven (Tübingen: Mohr-Siebeck, 1981): *Emmanuel* 37 (1983) 208–12.

I.MA.G.E.S.: Index in manuscriptorum graecorum edita specimina, by Sever J. Voicu and Serenella D'Alisera (Rome: Borla, 1981): *JBL* 103 (1984) 133–34.

Kirchenschriftsteller Verzeichnis und Sigel, by Hermann Josef Frede (Vetus Latina, 1/1; 3d ed.; Freiburg: Herder, 1981): *JBL* 103 (1984) 308–9.

The Birth of the Codex, by Colin H. Roberts and T. C. Skeat (Oxford/New York: Oxford University Press [for the British Academy], 1983): *JBL* 105 (1986) 359–61.

Specimina Sinaitica: Die datierten griechischen Handschriften des Katharinen-Klosters auf dem Berge Sinai 9. bis 12. Jahrhundert, by Dieter Harlfinger, Diether Roderich Reinisch, and Joseph A. M. Sonderkamp, in collaboration with Giancarlo Prato (Berlin: Reimer, 1983): *JBL* 105 (1986) 361–62.

Humanists and Holy Writ: New Testament Scholarship in the Renaissance, by Jerry H. Bentley (Princeton: Princeton University Press, 1983): *JBL* 105 (1986) 552–54.

F. J. A. Hort: Eminent Victorian, by Graham A. Patrick. (Historical Texts and Interpreters in Biblical Scholarship, 6. Sheffield, UK: Almond, 1988): *CRBR* 2 (1989) 235–37.

The Text of the New Testament: An Introduction to the Critical Editions and to the Theory and Practice of Modern Textual Criticism, by Kurt Aland and Barbara Aland (Grand Rapids, MI: Eerdmans, 1987): *Int* 44 (1990) 71–75.

Text-Critical Responsibilities

TEXTUAL CRITICISM SECTION, Society of Biblical Literature, Chair, 1971–1984; Member, Steering Committee, 1985–2000.

INTERNATIONAL GREEK NEW TESTAMENT PROJECT, Member of the American Executive Committee, 1968–1988. Reorganized as the North American Committee, 1989–.

STUDIES AND DOCUMENTS (Eerdmans), Editor, 1993–2005; Member of the Editorial Board, 1971–.
[Founded by Kirsopp and Silva Lake in England in the 1930s].

ENDOWED LECTURESHIPS: The Kenneth Willis Clark Lectures, Duke University, April, 1986: "Papyrus Manuscripts of the New Testament: Treasure from the Past—Challenge for the Future." The Ratner Lecture in Religion, Case Western Reserve University, October 1998: "The Cultural Context of the New Testament Text: One Hundred Years of Symbiosis with the Oxyrhynchus Papyri of Egypt."

INDEX OF AUTHORS (ANCIENT AND MODERN)

Note: Editors of volumes of collected essays are not indexed

I. Ancient Authors and Persons

II. Modern Authors

INDEX OF PASSAGES

I. Biblical Citations

A. Hebrew Bible (Old Testament)

B. New Testament

II. Papyri (excluding New Testament)

[For New Testament papyri, see Index of New Testament Manuscripts. . . .]

III. Classical, Extra-Canonical and Patristic Citations

INDEX OF GREEK AND LATIN WORDS

I. Greek Words

II. Latin Words

INDEX OF NEW TESTAMENT MANUSCRIPTS, VERSIONS, EDITIONS, AND MODERN TRANSLATIONS

I. Greek Manuscripts

Greek majuscules

Greek minuscules

Greek lectionaries

II. Versions

III. Editions

[Dates below usually indicate the first edition]

IV. Modern Translations

INDEX OF SUBJECTS

SUPPLEMENTS TO NOVUM TESTAMENTUM

ISSN 0167-9732

2. Strobel, A. *Untersuchungen zum eschatologischen Verzögerungsproblem auf Grund der spätjüdische-urchristlichen Geschichte von Habakuk 2,2 ff.* 1961. ISBN 90 04 01582 5
16. Pfitzner, V.C. *Paul and the Agon Motif.* 1967. ISBN 90 04 01596 5
27. Mussies, G. *The Morphology of Koine Greek As Used in the Apocalypse of St. John.* A Study in Bilingualism. 1971. ISBN 90 04 02656 8
28. Aune, D.E. *The Cultic Setting of Realized Eschatology in Early Christianity.* 1972. ISBN 90 04 03341 6
29. Unnik, W.C. van. *Sparsa Collecta.* The Collected Essays of W.C. van Unnik Part 1. Evangelia, Paulina, Acta. 1973. ISBN 90 04 03660 1
31. Unnik, W.C. van. *Sparsa Collecta.* The Collected Essays of W.C. van Unnik Part 3. Patristica, Gnostica, Liturgica. 1983. ISBN 90 04 06262 9
34. Hagner, D.A. *The Use of the Old and New Testaments in Clement of Rome.* 1973. ISBN 90 04 03636 9
37. Reiling, J. *Hermas and Christian Prophecy.* A Study of The Eleventh Mandate. 1973. ISBN 90 04 03771 3
43. Clavier, H. *Les variétés de la pensée biblique et le problème de son unité.* Esquisse d'une théologie de la Bible sur les textes originaux et dans leur contexte historique. 1976. ISBN 90 04 04465 5
47. Baarda, T., A.F.J. Klijn & W.C. van Unnik (eds.) *Miscellanea Neotestamentica.* I. Studia ad Novum Testamentum Praesertim Pertinentia a Sociis Sodalicii Batavi c.n. Studiosorum Novi Testamenti Conventus Anno MCMLXXVI Quintum Lustrum Feliciter Complentis Suscepta. 1978. ISBN 90 04 05685 8
48. Baarda, T., A.F.J. Klijn & W.C. van Unnik (eds.) *Miscellanea Neotestamentica.* II. 1978. ISBN 90 04 05686 6
50. Bousset, D.W. *Religionsgeschichtliche Studien.* Aufsätze zur Religionsgeschichte des hellenistischen Zeitalters. Hrsg. von A.F. Verheule. 1979. ISBN 90 04 05845 1
52. Garland, D.E. *The Intention of Matthew 23.* 1979. ISBN 90 04 05912 1
53. Moxnes, H. *Theology in Conflict.* Studies in Paul's Understanding of God in Romans. 1980. ISBN 90 04 06140 1
56. Skarsaune, O. *The Proof From Prophecy.* A Study in Justin Martyr's Proof-Text Tradition: Text-type, Provenance, Theological Profile. 1987. ISBN 90 04 07468 6
59. Wilkins, M.J. *The Concept of Disciple in Matthew's Gospel, as Reflected in the Use of the Term 'Mathetes'.* 1988. ISBN 90 04 08689 7
64. Sterling, G.E. *Historiography and Self-Definition.* Josephos, Luke-Acts and Apologetic Historiography. 1992. ISBN 90 04 09501 2
65. Botha, J.E. *Jesus and the Samaritan Woman.* A Speech Act Reading of John 4:1-42. 1991. ISBN 90 04 09505 5
66. Kuck, D.W. *Judgment and Community Conflict.* Paul's Use of Apologetic Judgment Language in 1 Corinthians 3:5-4:5. 1992. ISBN 90 04 09510 1
67. Schneider, G. *Jesusüberlieferung und Christologie.* Neutestamentliche Aufsätze 1970-1990. 1992. ISBN 90 04 09555 1
68. Seifrid, M.A. *Justification by Faith.* The Origin and Development of a Central Pauline Theme. 1992. ISBN 90 04 09521 7

69. Newman, C.C. *Paul's Glory-Christology*. Tradition and Rhetoric. 1992. ISBN 90 04 09463 6
70. Ireland, D.J. *Stewardship and the Kingdom of God*. An Historical, Exegetical, and Contextual Study of the Parable of the Unjust Steward in Luke 16: 1-13. 1992. ISBN 90 04 09600 0
71. Elliott, J.K. *The Language and Style of the Gospel of Mark*. An Edition of C.H. Turner's "Notes on Marcan Usage" together with other comparable studies. 1993. ISBN 90 04 09767 8
72. Chilton, B. *A Feast of Meanings*. Eucharistic Theologies from Jesus through Johannine Circles. 1994. ISBN 90 04 09949 2
73. Guthrie, G.H. *The Structure of Hebrews*. A Text-Linguistic Analysis. 1994. ISBN 90 04 09866 6
74. Bormann, L., K. Del Tredici & A. Standhartinger (eds.) *Religious Propaganda and Missionary Competition in the New Testament World*. Essays Honoring Dieter Georgi. 1994. ISBN 90 04 10049 0
75. Piper, R.A. (ed.) *The Gospel Behind the Gospels*. Current Studies on Q. 1995. ISBN 90 04 09737 6
76. Pedersen, S. (ed.) *New Directions in Biblical Theology*. Papers of the Aarhus Conference, 16-19 September 1992. 1994. ISBN 90 04 10120 9
77. Jefford, C.N. (ed.) *The* Didache *in Context*. Essays on Its Text, History and Transmission. 1995. ISBN 90 04 10045 8
78. Bormann, L. *Philippi – Stadt und Christengemeinde zur Zeit des Paulus*. 1995. ISBN 90 04 10232 9
79. Peterlin, D. *Paul's Letter to the Philippians in the Light of Disunity in the Church*. 1995. ISBN 90 04 10305 8
80. Jones, I.H. *The Matthean Parables*. A Literary and Historical Commentary. 1995. ISBN 90 04 10181 0
81. Glad, C.E. *Paul and Philodemus*. Adaptability in Epicurean and Early Christian Psychagogy. 1995. ISBN 90 04 10067 9
82. Fitzgerald, J.T. (ed.) *Friendship, Flattery, and Frankness of Speech*. Studies on Friend-ship in the New Testament World. 1996. ISBN 90 04 10454 2
83. Tilborg, S. van. *Reading John in Ephesus*. 1996. 90 04 10530 1
84. Holleman, J. *Resurrection and Parousia*. A Traditio-Historical Study of Paul's Eschatology in 1 Corinthians 15. 1996. ISBN 90 04 10597 2
85. Moritz, T. *A Profound Mystery*. The Use of the Old Testament in Ephesians. 1996. ISBN 90 04 10556 5
86. Borgen, P. *Philo of Alexandria - An Exegete for His Time*. 1997. ISBN 90 04 10388 0
87. Zwiep, A.W. *The Ascension of the Messiah in Lukan Christology*. 1997. ISBN 90 04 10897 1
88. Wilson, W.T. *The Hope of Glory*. Education and Exhortation in the Epistle to the Colossians. 1997. ISBN 90 04 10937 4
89. Peterson, W.L., J.S. Vos & H.J. de Jonge (eds.) *Sayings of Jesus: Canonical and Non-Canonical*. Essays in Honour of Tjitze Baarda. 1997. ISBN 90 04 10380 5
90. Malherbe, A.J., F.W. Norris & J.W. Thompson (eds.) *The Early Church in Its Context*. Essays in Honor of Everett Ferguson. 1998. ISBN 90 04 10832 7
91. Kirk, A. *The Composition of the Sayings Source*. Genre, Synchrony, and Wisdom Redaction in Q. 1998. ISBN 90 04 11085 2
92. Vorster, W.S. *Speaking of Jesus*. Essays on Biblical Language, Gospel Narrative and the Historical Jesus. Edited by J. E. Botha. 1999. ISBN 90 04 10779 7
93. Bauckham, R. *The Fate of Dead*. Studies on the Jewish and Christian Apocalypses. 1998. ISBN 90 04 11203 0

94. Standhartinger, A. *Studien zur Entstehungsgeschichte und Intention des Kolosserbriefs.* 1998. ISBN 90 04 11286 3
95. Oegema, G.S. *Für Israel und die Völker.* Studien zum alttestamentlich-jüdischen Hintergrund der paulinischen Theologie. 1999. ISBN 90 04 11297 9
96. Albl, M.C. *"And Scripture Cannot Be Broken".* The Form and Function of the Early Christian *Testimonia* Collections. 1999. ISBN 90 04 11417 3
97. Ellis, E.E. *Christ and the Future in New Testament History.* 1999. ISBN 90 04 11533 1
98. Chilton, B. & C.A. Evans, (eds.) *James the Just and Christian Origins.* 1999. ISBN 90 04 11550 1
99. Horrell, D.G. & C.M. Tuckett (eds.) *Christology, Controversy and Community.* New Testament Essays in Honour of David R. Catchpole. 2000. ISBN 90 04 11679 6
100. Jackson-McCabe, M.A. *Logos and Law in the Letter of James.* The Law of Nature, the Law of Moses and the Law of Freedom. 2001. ISBN 90 04 11994 9
101. Wagner, J.R. *Heralds of the Good News.* Isaiah and Paul "In Concert" in the Letter to the Romans. 2002. ISBN 90 04 11691 5
102. Cousland, J.R.C. *The Crowds in the Gospel of Matthew.* 2002. ISBN 90 04 12177 3
103. Dunderberg, I., C. Tuckett and K. Syreeni. *Fair Play: Diversity and Conflicts in Early Christianity.* Essays in Honour of Heikki Räisänen. 2002. ISBN 90 04 12359 8
104. Mount, C. *Pauline Christianity.* Luke-Acts and the Legacy of Paul. 2002. ISBN 90 04 12472 1
105. Matthews, C.R. *Philip: Apostle and Evangelist.* Configurations of a Tradition. 2002. ISBN 90 04 12054 8
106. Aune, D.E., T. Seland, J.H. Ulrichsen (eds.) *Neotestamentica et Philonica.* Studies in Honor of Peder Borgen. 2002. ISBN 90 04 126104
107. Talbert, C.H. *Reading Luke-Acts in its Mediterranean Milieu.* 2003. ISBN 90 04 12964 2
108. Klijn, A.F.J. *The Acts of Thomas.* Introduction, Text, and Commentary. Second Revised Edition. 2003. ISBN 90 04 12937 5
109. Burke, T.J. & J.K. Elliott (eds.) *Paul and the Corinthians.* Studies on a Community in Conflict. Essays in Honour of Margaret Thrall. 2003. ISBN 90 04 12920 0
110. Fitzgerald, J.T., T.H. Olbricht & L.M. White (eds.) *Early Christianity and Classical Culture.* Comparative Studies in Honor of Abraham J. Malherbe. 2003. ISBN 90 04 13022 5
111. Fitzgerald, J.T., D. Obbink & G.S. Holland (eds.) *Philodemus and the New Testament World.* 2004. ISBN 90 04 11460 2
112. Lührmann, D. *Die Apokryph gewordenen Evangelien.* Studien zu neuen Texten und zu neuen Fragen. 2004. ISBN 90 04 12867 0
113. Elliott, J.K. (ed.) *The Collected Biblical Writings of T.C. Skeat.* 2004. ISBN 90 04 13920 6
114. Roskam, H.N. *The Purpose of the Gospel of Mark in its Historical and Social Context.* 2004. ISBN 90 04 14052 2
115. Chilton, B.D. & C.A. Evans (eds.) *The Missions of James, Peter, and Paul.* Tensions in Early Christianity. 2005. ISBN 90 04 14161 8
116. Epp, E.J. *Perspectives on New Testament Textual Criticism.* Collected Essays, 1962-2004. 2005. ISBN 90 04 14246 0
117. Parsenios, G.L. *Departure and Consolation.* The Johannine Farewell Discourses in Light of Greco-Roman Literature. 2005. ISBN 90 04 14278 9
118. Hakola, R. *Identity Matters.* John, the Jews and Jewishness. 2005. ISBN 90 04 14224 6
119. Fuglseth, K.S. *Johannine Sectarianism in Perspective.* A Sociological, Historical, and Comparative Analysis of Temple and Social Relationships in the Gospel of John, Philo, and Qumran. 2005. ISBN 90 04 14411 0 (in preparation)

120. Ware, J. *The Mission of the Church.* in Paul's Letter to the Philippians in the Context of Ancient Judaism. 2005. ISBN 90 04 14641 5 (in preparation)
121. Watt, J.G van der (ed.) *Salvation in the New Testament.* Perspectives on Soteriology. ISBN 90 04 14297 5 (in preparation)